The Thomas Guide

PACIFIC NORTHWEST
ROAD ATLAS & DRIVER'S GUIDE

Table of Contents

Thomas Bros. Maps
A RAND McNALLY COMPANY

Call Toll Free:
1-800-899-MAPS
1-800-899-6277

Corporate Office & Showroom
17731 Cowan, Irvine, CA 92614 (949) 863-1984 or 1-888-826-6277

Thomas Bros. Maps & Books
550 Jackson St., San Francisco, CA 94133 (415) 981-7520 or 1-800-969-3072
521 W. 6th St., Los Angeles, CA 90014 (213) 627-4018 or 1-888-277-6277
Customer Service: 1-800-899-6277
World Wide Web: www.thomas.com
e-mail: comments@thomas.com
For more information regarding licensing and copyright permission, please contact us at:
licensing@thomas.com

How To Use this Road Atlas & Driver's Guide

To Find a City or Community:

If you know the general area in which the city or community is located, start with the *Key Map* on page "D", then turn to the *Highway Map* indicated.

You can also look up major cities in the *City Listings* on page "E".

— OR —

Look up the city or community name in the *Cities and Communities Index* on pages "G - M". Turn to the page number indicated.

Community	STATE	PAGE	GRID
❖ BEAVERTON	OR	199	B2
❖ BELLEVUE	WA	175	C2
❖ BONNEY LAKE	WA	182	C4
Cabell City	OR	129	C3
❖ CAMAS	WA	193	B7
Cornelius Pass	OR	192	A6
❖ EVERETT	WA	267	G3
❖ GIG HARBOR	WA	181	C1
❖ GRESHAM	OR	200	B1
❖ HOOD RIVER	OR	195	D5
❖ ISLAND CITY	OR	130	A2
Kenton	OR	308	D4
Kingston	WA	170	D5
❖ KOOTENAI	ID	244	A1
❖ MERIDIAN	ID	253	A3
Murphy	ID	147	C2
❖ PORTLAND	OR	316	C3
❖ SEATAC	WA	288	C3
❖ SEATTLE	WA	273	G3
Starlake	WA	175	B7
❖ TACOMA	WA	292	D5
❖ TROY	ID	123	A1
❖ WALLA WALLA	WA	344	E6

Map Pages and Indexes

This Road Atlas & Driver's Guide is divided into three types of map pages: Highway, Metro, and Detail. The Highway map pages cover the entire Pacific Northwest area in this guide. These map pages can be used for trip planning. Highway Map pages can be found on pages 92-155 in this guide.

The Metro Map pages cover major cities and points of interest areas with more map detail. The Metro Map pages provide greater detail and many points of interest within the area shown. Metro Maps pages can be found on pages 156-253.

The Detail Map pages provide full street detail and points of interest in areas covered. Detail Maps can be found on pages 254-355. Some Detail Map pages have two sets of page numbers. The large number represents the page number in this Road Atlas. The smaller number labeled with a "TBM" (Thomas Bros. Maps) corresponds to a map page in a full county Thomas Guide.

You will find major streets and points of interest in the single Street and Points of Interest indexes in the back of this guide. The Street Index can be found on pages 357-418 and the Points of Interest Index can be found on pages 419-445.

For full street detail beyond the areas shown in this Road Atlas & Driver's Guide, Thomas Bros. publishes County Street Guides of the major counties in Oregon and Washington.

To Find a Location:

① Look up the street name in the *Street Index*. If there are multiple listings, choose the proper city.

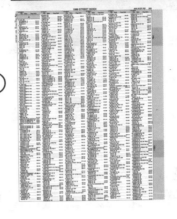

Also, major points of interest can be located by category and are listed alphabetically in the *Points of Interest Index* in the back of this guide.

②
S MAIN ST SEATTLE, WA	278-A7

The index entry will include a *Thomas Bros. Maps® Page and Grid* where the street or point of interest is located.

③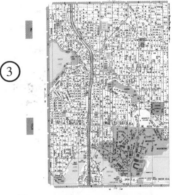

Turn to the page indicated.

④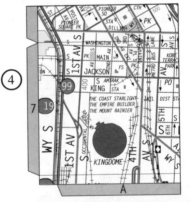

Locate the street or point of interest by following the indicated *Letter Column and Number Row* until the two intersect. The street name or point of interest is in this grid.

We Welcome Your Suggestions

Thomas Bros. Maps is proud to provide you with superior mapping products to meet your special needs.

Since 1915, Thomas Bros. Maps has been publishing mapping products, and is recognized as an industry leader. We believe that our best products and enhancements come from your suggestions. We also appreciate your corrections to the map or index. We welcome your suggestions and look forward to providing you with many fine mapping products in the future.

How to Use the Map Pages

Key to Map Pages: 1 inch = 62 Miles

The ***Key Map*** page shows the entire Pacific Northwest area covered in this guide. If you know the general area in which the city, community, or your destination is located, start with the ***Key Map*** located on page "D". Find the general area, then turn to the ***Highway Map*** indicated.

Highway Map: 1 inch = 7.5 Miles

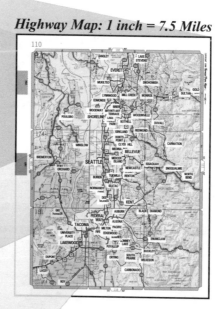

The ***Highway Map*** can be used as a guide for long distance driving. Once on the ***Highway Map***, find the area in which the city, community, or your destination is located, then turn to the ***Metro Map*** indicated.

Metro Map: 1 inch = 2.5 Miles

The ***Metro Map*** covers major cities, recreation areas, and areas of special interest. The ***Metro Maps*** provide greater detail and many Points of Interest within the area shown. Once on the ***Metro Map***, find the area in which the city, community, or your destination is located, then turn to the ***Detail Map*** indicated.

Detail Map: 1 inch = 1900 Feet / 1 inch = 3800 Feet

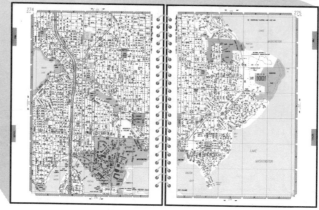

The ***Detail Map*** provides street detail and extensive Points of Interest information for selected areas. Over 100 pages of ***Detail Maps*** are included in this atlas.

D

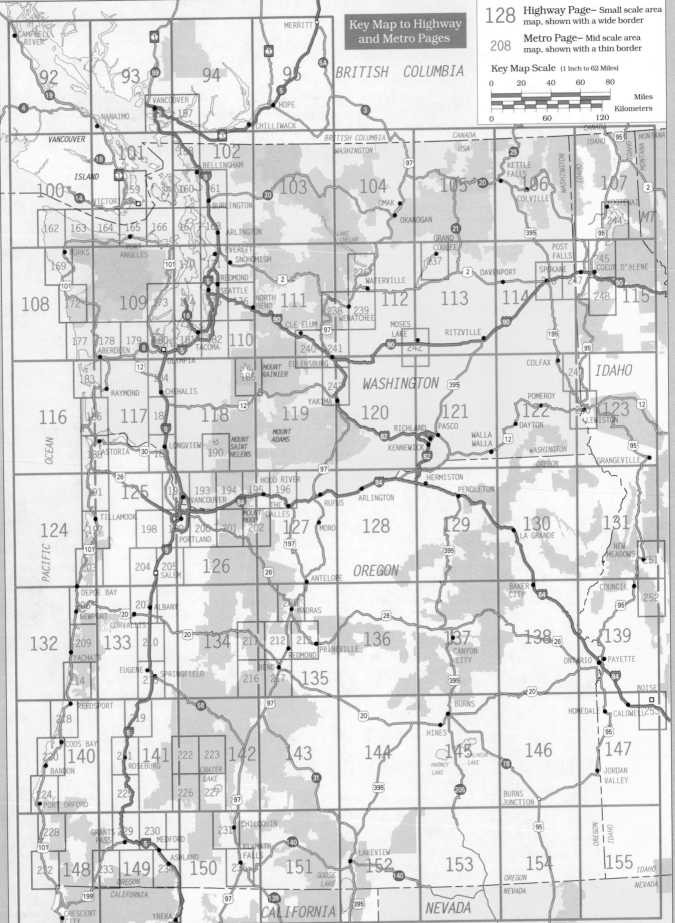

Key Map to Highway and Metro Pages

| 128 | Highway Page– Small scale area map, shown with a wide border |
| 208 | Metro Page– Mid scale area map, shown with a thin border |

Key Map Scale (1 Inch to 62 Miles)

Miles
Kilometers

PNW

INTRO

Listing of Cities and Map Pages

British Columbia

CITY NAME	DETAIL PAGE	METRO PAGE	HIGHWAY PAGE
City of North Vancouver	254	156	93
City of Victoria	256	159	101
District of Burnaby	255	156	93
District of North Vancouver	254	156	93
District of Oak Bay	257	159	101
District of Saanich	256	159	101
District of West Vancouver	254	156	93
Town of Esquimalt	256	159	101
Town of View Royal	256	159	101
Vancouver	254	156	93

Washington

CITY NAME	DETAIL PAGE	METRO PAGE	HIGHWAY PAGE
Anacortes	259	160	102
Bellingham	258	161	102
Bremerton	270	174	110
Burien	285	175	110
Burlington	260	161	102
Centralia	299	184	117
College Place	344	–	121
Des Moines	290	175	110
Everett	264	171	110
Fircrest	294	181	110
Kelso	303	189	117
Kennewick	342	–	121
Kent	291	175	110
Lakewood	294	181	110
Longview	303	189	117
Mercer Island	283	175	110
Millwood	350	246	114
Mount Vernon	260	161	102
Mukilteo	266	171	110
Ocean Shores	298	177	108
Olympia	296	180	109
Pasco	343	–	121
Port Angeles	261	165	101
Port Orchard	270	174	110
Port Townsend	263	167	102
Renton	289	175	110
Richland	341	–	121
Seatac	288	175	110
Seattle	278	175	110
Sequim	262	166	101
Spokane	348	246	114
Tacoma	295	181	110

Washington cont...

CITY NAME	DETAIL PAGE	METRO PAGE	HIGHWAY PAGE
Tukwilla	289	175	110
Tumwater	296	180	109
University Place	294	181	110
Vancouver	305	192	126
Veradale (community)	351	247	114
Walla Walla	345	–	121
West Richland	340	–	121
Westport	298	183	116

Oregon

CITY NAME	DETAIL PAGE	METRO PAGE	HIGHWAY PAGE
Albany	326	207	133
Ashland	337	234	149
Astoria	300	188	116
Bend	332	217	135
Central Point	336	230	149
Coos Bay	333	218	140
Corvallis	327	207	133
Eugene	330	215	133
Gearhart	301	188	116
Grant Pass	335	229	149
Klamath Falls	338	235	150
Lake Oswego	320	199	126
Maywood Park	315	199	126
Medford	336	234	149
Millersburg	326	207	133
Milwaukie	321	199	126
North Bend	333	218	140
Portland	309	199	126
Roseburg	334	221	141
Salem	323	204	125
Seaside	301	188	116
Springfield	331	215	133
Turner	325	205	125
Waldport	328	209	132

Idaho

CITY NAME	DETAIL PAGE	METRO PAGE	HIGHWAY PAGE
Coeur D'Alene	355	245	115
Dalton Gardens	355	245	115
Hauser	353	247	115
Hayden	355	245	115
Huetter	354	247	115
Post Falls	353	247	115

F

LEGEND OF MAP SYMBOLS

N
NORTH

Freeway
Interchange/Ramp
Highway
Scenic Route
Primary Road
Secondary Road
Minor Road
Restricted Road
Alley
Unclassified Road
Tunnel
Toll Road
High Occupancy Veh. Lane
Stacked Multiple Roadways
Proposed Road
Proposed Freeway
Freeway Under Construction
One-Way Road
Two-Way Road
Trail, Walkway
Stairs
Railroad
Rapid Transit
Rapid Transit, Underground
City Boundary
County Boundary
State Boundary
International Boundary
Military Base, Indian Resv.
River, Creek, Shoreline
Ferry

PNW

INTRO

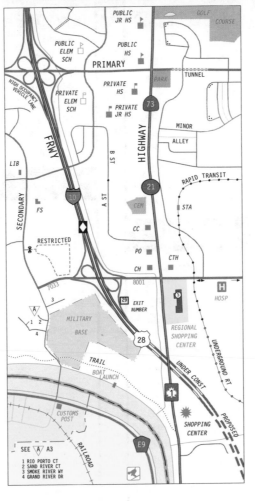

Interstate
Interstate (Business)
U.S. Highway
Trans Canada Highway
State, Provincial Highway
State Highway
County Highway
Carpool Lane
Street List Marker
Street Continuation
Exit Number
Airport
Winery
Campground
Hospital
Mountain
Ski Area
Hotel/Motel
Scenic Viewpoint
Rest Area
Building (See List of Abbr. Page)
Lighthouse
Government Seat
Incorporated City
Community

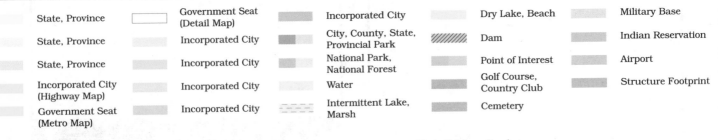

State, Province
State, Province
State, Province
Incorporated City (Highway Map)
Government Seat (Metro Map)

Government Seat (Detail Map)
Incorporated City
Incorporated City
Incorporated City
Incorporated City

Incorporated City
City, County, State, Provincial Park
National Park, National Forest
Water
Intermittent Lake, Marsh

Dry Lake, Beach
Dam
Point of Interest
Golf Course, Country Club
Cemetery

Military Base
Indian Reservation
Airport
Structure Footprint

Highway Map Scale
Pages 92-155
1 Inch to 7.5 Miles

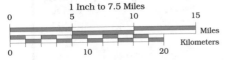

0   5   10   15
Miles
0   10   20
Kilometers

Highway Grid Equivalents
18 x 24.5 Miles
1 Grid Equals:
1 Metro Page

Detail Map Scale
Pages 264-269, 272-295, 304-321
1 Inch to 1900 Feet

0   .25   .5   .75
Miles
0   .5   1.0
Kilometers

Detail Grid Equivalents
2640 x 2640 Feet
1 Grid Equals:
.5 x .5 Miles

Metro Map Scale
Pages 156-253
1 Inch to 2.5 Miles

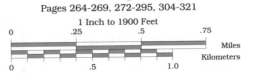

0   1   2   3   4
Miles
0   2.5   5
Kilometers

Metro Grid Equivalents
4.5 x 3.5 Miles

Detail Map Scale
Pages 254-263, 270-271, 296-303, 322-355
1 Inch to 3800 Feet

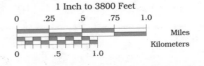

0   .25   .5   .75   1.0
Miles
0   .5   1.0
Kilometers

Detail Grid Equivalents
2640 x 2640 Feet
1 Grid Equals:
.5 x .5 Miles

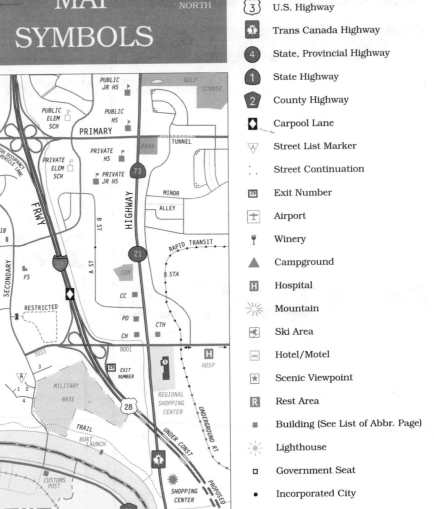

COPYRIGHT 1999 Thomas Bros. Maps®

Cities & Communities Index

COMMUNITY	ST.	PG.	GD.
A			
❖ ABBOTSFORD	BC	102	B1
Aberdeen	BC	102	B1
❖ ABERDEEN	WA	178	A7
Aberdeen Gardens	WA	178	B5
Abernethy	OR	317	H1
Abrams	OR	141	C1
Acme	WA	161	C2
Acton	WA	120	C2
Ada	OR	214	B5
❖ ADAIR VILLAGE	OR	207	B4
❖ ADAMS	OR	129	C1
Addy	WA	106	A3
Adel	WA	152	B2
Adelaide	WA	175	D1
Adelaide	WA	182	A1
Adna	WA	184	A7
Advance	OR	199	C5
Agassiz	BC	94	C3
Agate Beach	OR	206	B3
Agness	OR	148	B1
Agnew	WA	165	D6
Ahsahka	ID	123	C2
Ahtanum	WA	243	A7
Ainsworth Corner	CA	150	C3
Ainsworth Corner	OR	151	A2
Airlie	OR	207	A2
❖ AIRWAY HEIGHTS	WA	246	A4
Ajlune	OR	118	A2
Alameda	OR	314	A1
❖ ALBANY	OR	326	A12
Albee	OR	129	B2
❖ ALBION	WA	249	A4
Alder	OR	130	C2
Alder	OR	133	A1
Alder	WA	118	B1
Alder Creek	OR	201	A4
Aldergate	WA	128	B1
Alderton	WA	182	C4
Alderwood Manor	WA	171	B5
Alexander Beach	WA	259	D6
Alfalfa	OR	135	B3
Alger	WA	161	B3
Algoma	OR	235	C1
❖ ALGONA	WA	182	B2
Alicel	OR	130	A2
Alkali Lake	OR	144	B3
Alki	WA	280	B3
Allegany	OR	218	D7
Allentown	WA	286	D7
Allison	WA	182	A4
Allyn	WA	173	D6
Allyn-Grapeview	WA	173	D7
❖ ALMIRA	WA	237	D7
Almota	WA	122	B1
Aloha	OR	199	A2
Aloha	WA	177	B2
Alpha	WA	118	A2
Alpine	OR	128	C1
Alpine	OR	133	B2
Alsea	OR	133	A2
Alston	OR	189	A4
Altamont	OR	338	H11
Alta Vista	WA	118	B2
Alto	WA	122	A2
Altoona	WA	117	A2
Alvadore	OR	133	B2
Amanda Park	WA	109	A2
Amber	WA	114	B2
Amboy	WA	193	B1
American	OR	210	A3
American	WA	181	C4
❖ AMITY	OR	204	B2
❖ ANACORTES	WA	259	D4
Anatone	WA	122	C3
Anderson	OR	200	B3
Andrews	OR	153	C1
Angle Lake	WA	290	D2
Anlauf	OR	219	B2
❖ ANMORE	BC	157	A3
Annapolis	WA	271	A13
Annex	OR	139	A2
Annieville	BC	156	D6
❖ ANTELOPE	OR	127	C3
Antone	OR	136	B2
Apex	OR	129	B1
Apiary	OR	189	B5
Applegate	OR	149	B2
Appleton	WA	196	B3
Appleyard	WA	239	A5
Arago	OR	220	D6
Arbor Heights	WA	284	D4
Arbor Lodge	OR	308	D5
Arbutus	BC	254	D14
Arcadia	WA	180	C3
Archabal	ID	251	C6
Arch Cape	OR	191	A2
Arden	WA	171	A6
Ardenvoir	WA	112	A1
Ardenwald	OR	318	A6
Argay	OR	193	A7
Ariel	OR	118	A3
Arletta	WA	181	B1
❖ ARLINGTON	OR	128	A1
❖ ARLINGTON	WA	168	D5
Arlington Heights	OR	312	B7
Arlington Heights	WA	102	C3
Arnold Creek	OR	320	C2
Arock	OR	146	C3
Arrow Head Beach	WA	167	D3
Artondale	WA	181	B1
Asert	OR	200	B1
Ashdale	OR	199	D4
Ashford	WA	118	B1
❖ ASHLAND	OR	337	D9
Ashwood	OR	135	C1
❖ ASOTIN	WA	250	B6
Aspen Grove	BC	95	C1
❖ ASTORIA	OR	300	F5
❖ ATHENA	OR	129	C1
❖ ATHOL	ID	245	B2
Atkinson	WA	176	A6
❖ AUBURN	WA	182	C2
❖ AUMSVILLE	OR	205	B7
❖ AURORA	OR	199	B7
Aurora Village	WA	171	A6
Austa	OR	133	A2
Austin	OR	137	C1
Austin	WA	170	D2
Austin Junction	OR	137	C1
Avon	WA	161	A7
Avondale	WA	171	D7
Ayer	WA	121	C2
Azalea	OR	225	C6
Azwell	WA	112	B1
B			
Baby Island Heights	WA	167	D7
Bade	OR	129	C1
Badger Corner	OR	323	E12
Bagdad Junction	WA	237	D4
Bagley Junction	WA	176	C6
Bainbridge Island	WA	174	D2
❖ BAKER CITY	OR	138	B1
Baker-Langdon	WA	345	E13
Balch	WA	117	B1
Balder	WA	114	C3
Ballard	WA	272	D4
Ballston	OR	204	A3
Bamberton	BC	159	B3
Bamfield	BC	100	A1
Bancroft	OR	140	C3
❖ BANDON	OR	220	B6
Bangor	WA	170	A7
Barber	ID	253	B3
Barberton	WA	192	D5
Baring	WA	111	A1
Barnesdale	OR	191	B5
Barneston	WA	176	B7
Barnett	OR	128	A2
Barnhart	OR	129	B1
Barton	OR	200	B4
Barton Heights	OR	131	B2
Barview	OR	191	A7
Barview	OR	220	C1
Basin City	WA	121	A2
Basque	OR	154	B1
Bassett Junction	WA	113	A3
Bates	OR	137	C1
Batterson	OR	191	D4
Battin	OR	319	G7
❖ BATTLE GROUND	WA	192	D3
Bay Center	WA	183	C7
❖ BAY CITY	OR	191	B7
Bay City	WA	183	B2
Bayne	WA	110	C3
Bayocean	OR	191	A7
Bay Park	OR	333	J13
Bayshore	WA	180	B2
Bayside Gardens	OR	191	B4
Bayview	ID	245	C1
Bayview	OR	328	C2
Bay View	WA	160	D6
Bayview	WA	170	D1
Bay View	WA	181	C2
Bazan Bay	BC	159	B3
Beach Grove	BC	101	C1
Beach Haven	BC	101	C2
Beacon Hill	WA	282	C2
Beacon Hill	WA	303	C3
Bear	ID	131	B3
Beatty	OR	151	A1
Beaumont Wilshire	OR	314	B1
Beaver	OR	197	C5
Beaver	WA	163	A6
Beavercreek	OR	200	A6
Beaver Homes	OR	189	C6
Beaver Marsh	OR	142	C2
Beaver Springs	OR	189	B5
❖ BEAVERTON	OR	199	B2
Bedford	OR	117	B1
Beebe	WA	236	D3
Beech Creek	OR	137	A1
Bel Air	OR	199	B2
❖ BELCARRA	BC	157	A3
Belfair	WA	173	D5
Belknap Springs	OR	134	B2
Bellevue	OR	204	A2
❖ BELLEVUE	WA	175	C2
Bellfountain	OR	133	B2
❖ BELLINGHAM	WA	258	G4
Bells Beach	WA	167	D7
❖ BEND	OR	332	E7
Bendemeer	OR	192	A7
Benewah	ID	115	A3
Benge	WA	122	A1
❖ BENTON CITY	WA	120	C3
Berkeley	WA	182	A6
Berne	WA	111	B1
Berrydale	WA	182	D1
Berteleda	CA	148	B3
Bertsche Terrace	CA	148	B3
Bethany	OR	192	A7
Bethel	OR	329	F4
Bethel	WA	174	B4
Bethel Gospel Park	OR	205	A3
Beulah	OR	138	A3
Beverly	WA	120	B1
Beverly Beach	OR	206	B2
Beverly Beach	WA	167	D7
Beverly Park	WA	268	D4
Bickleton	WA	120	A3
Biggam	WA	120	C3
Biggs	OR	127	C1
Biggs Junction	OR	127	C1
Biloxi	WA	174	D4
❖ BINGEN	WA	195	D5
Bingham Springs	OR	130	A1
Birch	WA	110	C3
Birch Bay	WA	158	B4
Birkenfeld	OR	117	B3
Bissell	OR	200	D6
Bitter Lake	WA	171	A7
Blachly	OR	133	A2
Black Butte Ranch	OR	211	C3
Black Creek	BC	92	A1
❖ BLACK DIAMOND	WA	110	C3
Black River Junction	WA	289	H2
Blaine	OR	197	D6
❖ BLAINE	WA	158	A3
Blakeley	OR	129	C1
Blalock	OR	128	A1
Blanchard	ID	107	A3
Blanchard	WA	161	A4
Blewett	WA	238	A5
Bliss Landing	BC	92	B1
Blitzen	OR	153	B1
Blockhouse	WA	127	B1
Blodgett	OR	133	A1
Blooming	OR	198	C2
Blubber Bay	BC	92	B1
Bluecreek	WA	106	A3
Blue Mountain	OR	129	C1
Blue Ridge	WA	171	A7
Blue River	OR	134	A2
Bluestem	WA	114	A2
Bly	OR	151	B1
Blyn	WA	109	C1
❖ BOARDMAN	OR	128	C1
Boardman Junction	OR	128	C1
Bodie	OR	129	C2
Bogachiel	WA	169	D3
Boise	OR	313	F1
Boise	WA	110	C3
❖ BOISE	ID	253	D3
Boise Hills Village	ID	253	D2
Boistfort	WA	187	A2
Bolton	OR	199	D4
❖ BONANZA	OR	151	A2
Bonifer	OR	129	C1
Bonita	OR	199	B3
Bonlow	WA	243	A4
❖ BONNERS FERRY	ID	107	B2
Bonnerville	OR	194	B7
❖ BONNEY LAKE	WA	182	C4
Bonny Slope	OR	199	B1
Bordeaux	WA	184	A2
Boring	OR	200	B3
Boston Bar	BC	95	A1
Boston Harbor	WA	180	C4
❖ BOTHELL	WA	171	C6
Boulevard Park	WA	285	J6
Boundary	WA	106	B1
Bourne	OR	138	A1
❖ BOVILL	ID	123	B1
Bow	WA	161	A4
Bowen Island	BC	93	B3
Bowers Junction	OR	192	A7
Bowmont	OR	147	C1
Bowser	BC	92	B2
Boyd	OR	127	B2
Brackendale	BC	93	C1
Bradwood	OR	117	B3
Brady	WA	179	A7
Brandstrom	WA	168	B3
Braymill	OR	150	C2
Breakers	WA	186	A5
Breidablick	WA	170	B5
Breitenbush Hot Spgs	OR	134	B1
❖ BREMERTON	WA	270	G10
Bremerton Junction	WA	174	A4
Brentwood Bay	BC	159	C4
Brentwood-Darlington	OR	318	D6
❖ BREWSTER	WA	104	B3
Briarwood	OR	321	G4
Brickerville	OR	214	D1
Bridal Veil	OR	201	A1
Bridesville	BC	105	A1
Bridge	OR	140	C3
Bridgeport	OR	138	B1
❖ BRIDGEPORT	WA	112	C1
Bridgeton	OR	309	G2
Bridgeview	OR	233	B5
Bridlemile	OR	316	A2
❖ BRIER	WA	171	B6
Brighouse	BC	156	B6
Brighton	OR	191	B5
Brightwood	OR	201	B4
Bristol	WA	196	A4
Britannia Beach	BC	93	C2
Broadacres	OR	205	B1
Broadbent	OR	140	B3
Broadmoor	BC	156	B7
Brogan	OR	138	C2
Bromart	WA	171	D3
Brookdale	WA	182	A5
Brookfield	WA	117	A2
❖ BROOKINGS	OR	232	C6
Brooklyn	OR	317	H2
Brooks	OR	205	A3
Brookwild	OR	318	D7
Brothers	OR	135	C3
Brownsboro	OR	149	C1
Brownsmead	OR	117	A3
Browns Point	WA	181	D1
Brownstown	WA	119	C2
❖ BROWNSVILLE	OR	210	C2
Brush Prairie	WA	193	A4
Bryant	WA	168	D4
Bryn Mawr	WA	175	D4
Buchanan	OR	145	C1
Buck Fork	OR	141	B2
❖ BUCKLEY	WA	182	D4
Buckman	OR	313	H6
Bucks Corners	OR	129	A1
❖ BUCODA	WA	184	D4
Buell	OR	125	B3
Buena	WA	120	A2
Buena Vista	OR	207	C2
Buenna	WA	175	A7
Bull Run	OR	200	D3
Bunker Hill	OR	333	J11
Burbank	WA	121	B3
Burbank Heights	WA	121	A3
❖ BURIEN	WA	285	F7
Burley	WA	174	B6
Burlington	OR	192	A6
❖ BURLINGTON	WA	260	D7
❖ BURNABY	BC	255	H10
Burnett	WA	182	D5
❖ BURNS	OR	145	A1
Burns Junction	OR	146	B3
Burnt Woods	OR	133	A1
Buroker	WA	122	A3
Burop	WA	111	A3
Burr Canyon	WA	121	B2
Burrows	WA	177	C5
Burton	WA	174	D6
Busby	WA	249	B6
❖ BUTTE FALLS	OR	150	A1
Butter Creek Junction	OR	128	C1
Butterfield	OR	301	H1
Butteville	OR	199	A6
Buxton	OR	125	B1
B Z Corner	WA	195	D2
C			
Cabell City	OR	129	C3
Cadboro Bay	BC	257	E4
Calder	ID	115	C2
❖ CALDWELL	ID	147	B1
Calhounville	WA	121	C3
Callahan	OR	141	A2
Cama Beach	WA	167	D6
Camano	WA	167	D5
❖ CAMAS	WA	193	B7
Camas Valley	OR	141	A3
❖ CAMBRIDGE	ID	139	B1
Cameron	ID	123	B1
❖ CAMPBELL RIVER	BC	92	A1
Camp Discover	WA	170	A5
Camp Elkanah	OR	129	C2
Camp Grande	WA	167	D4
Camp Lagoon	WA	167	D4
Camp Sealth	WA	174	C7
Camp Sherman	OR	211	C1
Camp Twelve	OR	206	C3
Camp Union	WA	173	D2
Canaan	OR	189	C7
Canary	OR	214	B4
❖ CANBY	OR	199	C6
Canby	WA	114	A2
Canemah	OR	199	D5
❖ CANNON BEACH	OR	188	A7
Cannon Beach Jct	OR	188	B6
❖ CANYON CITY	OR	137	B2
Canyon Park	WA	171	C6
❖ CANYONVILLE	OR	225	C3
Cape Meares	OR	197	A1
Capitol Hill	WA	278	C3
❖ CARBONADO	WA	182	D6
Carders	WA	351	B6
Carlsborg	WA	166	A6
Carlson	WA	118	B1
❖ CARLTON	OR	198	B5
Carlton	WA	104	A3
Carnahan	OR	188	B3
Carnation	OR	198	B1
❖ CARNATION	WA	176	B1
Carpenterville	OR	232	C2
Carrolls	WA	189	C4
Carson	OR	131	A3
❖ CARSON	WA	194	D4
Carson River Valley	WA	194	D4
Carus	OR	199	D6
Carver	OR	200	A4
Cascade	BC	105	C1
❖ CASCADE	ID	252	D6
Cascade Gorge	OR	150	A1
Cascade Heights	BC	156	C5
❖ CASCADE LOCKS	OR	194	D5
Cascade Summit	OR	142	B1
Cascade Valley	WA	242	C3
Cascadia	OR	134	A2
❖ CASHMERE	WA	238	C2
Casino	BC	106	B1
Casino Corner	WA	268	B5
Casland	WA	111	C3
❖ CASTLE ROCK	WA	187	C7
Cataldo	ID	115	B2
Cathcart	WA	171	D5
Cathedral Park	OR	192	B6
❖ CATHLAMET	WA	117	B3
Caufield	BC	156	A3
Cavalero Corner	WA	171	D1
❖ CAVE JUNCTION	OR	233	A5
Cavelero Beach	WA	167	D5
Caycuse	BC	100	C1
Cayuse	OR	129	C1
Cecil	OR	128	B1
Cecil	WA	106	C2
Cedar	BC	93	A3
Cedardale	BC	254	G4
Cedardale	OR	126	A3
Cedar Falls	WA	176	C6
Cedar Hills	OR	199	B1
Cedarhome	WA	168	B3
Cedarhurst	WA	174	D5
Cedar Mill	OR	199	B1
Cedar Mountain	WA	175	D6
Cedar Point	OR	220	D4
Cedar Valley	WA	171	B5
Cedarville	WA	117	B1
Celilo Village	OR	127	B1
Centennial	OR	200	A1
Center	OR	314	D5
Center	WA	170	A2
Centerville	WA	127	B1
Central Area	WA	278	C5
Central Ferry	WA	122	B1
❖ CENTRALIA	WA	299	E4
Central Park	WA	178	C7
Central Point	OR	199	C6
❖ CENTRAL POINT	OR	336	A6
Central Valley	WA	174	B1
Ceres	WA	117	B2
Chaffee	WA	120	C3
Chain Hill	WA	184	D2
Chamber	WA	249	B7
Chapman	OR	125	C1
Chard	WA	122	B2
Charleston	OR	220	C1
Charleston	WA	270	G11
Charlestown	OR	129	A1
Chattaroy	WA	114	C1
❖ CHATCOLET	ID	248	A6
❖ CHEHALIS	WA	299	C10
Chehalis Junction	WA	299	B14
Chehalis Village	WA	117	B1
❖ CHELAN	WA	236	D3
Chelan Falls	WA	236	D4
Chelatchie	WA	118	A3
Chemainus	BC	101	A1
Chemawa	OR	323	D5
Chemult	OR	142	C2
❖ CHENEY	WA	246	A7
Chenois Creek	WA	177	D6
Chenoweth	OR	196	C6
Cherry Grove	OR	198	A2
Cherry Heights	OR	196	C7
Cherry Valley	WA	110	C1
Cherryville	OR	201	A4
Chesaw	WA	105	A1
Cheshire	OR	133	B2
Chester	WA	350	H14
❖ CHEWELAH	WA	106	B3
Chico	WA	270	B4
Chilco	ID	245	A3
❖ CHILLIWACK	BC	102	C1
❖ CHILOQUIN	OR	231	D4
Chimacum	WA	170	A1
Chinook	WA	186	B7
Chiwaukum	WA	111	C2
❖ CHRISTINA LAKE	BC	105	C1
Christmas Valley	OR	143	C2
Christopher	WA	182	C1
Chrome	OR	220	D4
Chuckanut Village	WA	258	B13
Chumstick	WA	111	C2
Cicero	WA	102	C3
Cinebar	WA	118	A2
❖ CITY OF COLWOOD	BC	159	B7
❖ CTY OF N VANCVR	BC	254	J4
❖ CITY OF VICTORIA	BC	256	H7
❖ CITY OF WHT ROCK	BC	158	A2
Clackamas	OR	199	D3
Clackamas Heights	OR	199	D4
Clallam Bay	WA	163	B3
Claquato	WA	184	B6
Clarkes	OR	200	A7
❖ CLARK FORK	ID	107	C3
Clarkia	ID	115	C3
❖ CLARKSTON	WA	250	B4
Clarkston Heights	WA	250	B4
Clarksville	ID	245	B5
Clarno	OR	128	A3
❖ CLATSKANIE	OR	117	B3
Clatsop Station	OR	188	B3
Clay City	WA	118	B1
Clayton	WA	114	B1
Clearbrook	BC	102	B1
Clear Creek	CA	149	A3
Clear Creek	OR	125	B1
Clear Lake	OR	204	D4
Clear Lake	WA	161	C6
Clearview	WA	171	D5
Clearwater	OR	222	D4
❖ CLE ELUM	WA	240	B2
Clem[illegible]	OR	128	A2
Cleo	OR	220	D2
Cleveland	OR	221	A3
Clevland	WA	120	A3
Clifton	OR	117	B3
Clifton	OR	195	C5
Clinton	WA	171	A2
Clo-oose	BC	100	B2
Cloquallum	WA	179	C4
Cloverdale	BC	158	B1
Cloverdale	ID	253	B3
Cloverdale	OR	197	B7
Cloverdale	OR	212	D4
Cloverdale	WA	189	D6
Cloverland	WA	122	C2
Clow Corner	OR	204	B6
Clyde	WA	161	C2
❖ CLYDE HILL	WA	175	C2
Coal Canyon	WA	118	B2
Coal Creek	WA	175	D4
Coal Creek	WA	189	B2
Coaledo	OR	220	D3
Coalfield	WA	175	D4
Coalmont	BC	95	C2
Cobble Hill	BC	159	A1
❖ COBURG	OR	210	B7
Cocolalla	ID	107	A3
❖ COEUR D'ALENE	ID	355	E11
Cohassett	WA	183	B2
Cokedale	WA	161	D5
Colbert	WA	114	C1
Colburn	ID	107	B2
Colby	WA	271	H13

❖ -Indicates City, District or Township

Cities & Communities Index

COMMUNITY	ST.	PG.	GD.
Colchester	WA	271	H14
Cold Springs	OR	129	A1
Cold Springs Junction	OR	129	A1
Coles Corner	WA	111	C1
Colestin	OR	234	D7
❖ COLFAX	WA	122	C1
College Hill	OR	329	J9
❖ COLLEGE PLACE	WA	344	G11
Collins	WA	195	A5
Collins View	OR	320	D2
Colton	OR	126	A3
❖ COLTON	WA	250	A1
Columbia	WA	283	E5
Columbia Beach	WA	171	A2
❖ COLUMBIA CITY	OR	192	B1
Columbia Gardens	BC	106	B1
Columbia Heights	WA	302l	G2
Columbia Vly Gardens	WA	302	G6
❖ COLVILLE	WA	106	A2
Colvos	WA	174	D5
❖ COMOX	BC	92	A2
Comstock	OR	219	C1
Concomly	OR	205	A2
❖ CONCONULLY	WA	104	B2
Concord	OR	321	J7
Concordia	OR	310	A6
❖ CONCRETE	WA	102	C2
❖ CONDON	OR	128	A2
Conkling Park	ID	248	A5
Conley	OR	130	A2
❖ CONNELL	WA	121	B1
Conway	WA	168	B2
Cook	WA	195	B5
Coolin	ID	107	A2
Coombs	BC	92	C3
❖ COOS BAY	OR	333	D10
Cooston	OR	218	B7
Copalis Beach	WA	177	B4
Copalis Crossing	WA	177	C4
Copco	CA	150	A3
Copeland	ID	107	B1
Coppei	WA	122	A3
Copperfield	OR	131	A3
Copperville	ID	131	C1
❖ COQUILLE	OR	220	D4
❖ COQUITLAM	BC	157	A3
Corbett	OR	200	C1
Corbtt-Terwillgr-Lair Hill	OR	317	F4
Cordova Bay	BC	159	C5
❖ CORNELIUS	OR	198	C1
Cornelius Pass	OR	192	A6
Cornell	WA	168	A6
Cornell Place	OR	129	A1
Corner	WA	168	B3
Cornucopia	OR	130	C3
Coronado Shores	OR	203	A6
Cortes Bay	BC	92	B1
❖ CORVALLIS	OR	327	F7
❖ COSMOPOLIS	WA	178	B7
❖ COTTAGE GROVE	OR	215	B7
❖ COTTONWOOD	ID	123	C3
Cottonwood Bay	WA	158	B4
Cottrell	OR	200	C3
Cougar	WA	190	A5
❖ COULEE CITY	WA	113	A2
❖ COULEE DAM	WA	237	C2
❖ COUNCIL	ID	139	C1
Country Homes	WA	347	B11
County Line	BC	158	D1
❖ COUPEVILLE	WA	167	B4
❖ COURTENAY	BC	92	A2
Courtrock	OR	137	A1
❖ COVE	OR	130	B2
Cove	WA	174	D5
Covello	WA	122	B2
Cove Orchard	OR	198	B4
❖ COVINGTON	WA	175	D7
Cowichan Bay	BC	101	B1
Cowiche	WA	119	C1
Cowlitz	WA	118	A2
Crabtree	OR	133	C1
Crab Tree	WA	114	C3
❖ CRAIGMONT	ID	123	B2
Crane	OR	145	C2
Crates	WA	196	C6
Crawfordville	OR	133	C2
Creosote	WA	174	D2
Crescent	OR	142	C1
Crescent Beach	BC	158	A1
❖ CRESCENT CITY	CA	148	B3
Crescent Lake	OR	142	B1
Crescent Lake Junction	OR	142	B1
❖ CRESTON	WA	113	C1
Creston Kenilworth	OR	318	B2
Crestwood	OR	316	A7
❖ CRESWELL	OR	215	C5
Creswell Heights	WA	193	C5
Criterion	OR	127	B3
Crocker	WA	182	C5
Crofton	BC	101	B1
Cromwell	WA	181	B2
Crosby	WA	173	D3
Cross	WA	174	C6
Crossing	WA	168	C6
Crow	OR	133	B3
Crowfoot	OR	133	C1
Crown Hill	WA	273	E1
Crown Point	OR	220	C2
Cruzatt	WA	194	A7
Crystal Springs	WA	271	D5
❖ CULDESAC	ID	123	B2
Cully	OR	310	D7
Culp Creek	OR	141	C1
Cultus Lake	BC	102	C1
❖ CULVER	OR	208	B7
Cumberland	BC	92	A2
Cumberland	WA	110	C3
Cunningham	WA	121	B1
Cuprum	ID	131	B3
Curlew	WA	105	B1
Currinsville	OR	200	C5
Curtin	OR	219	B1
Curtis	WA	187	A1
Cushman	OR	214	B3
❖ CUSICK	WA	106	C3
Custer	WA	158	C4
Cutler City	OR	203	A5

D

COMMUNITY	ST.	PG.	GD.
Dabob	WA	170	A4
Dahl Pine	OR	127	A3
Dahua	WA	117	A2
Dairy	OR	151	A2
Dale	OR	129	B3
❖ DALLAS	OR	204	A6
Dallesport	WA	196	C7
❖ DALTON GARDENS	ID	355	E3
Damascus	OR	200	A3
Danner	OR	146	C3
Dant	OR	127	B3
Danville	WA	105	C1
Danville	WA	175	D7
Darknell	WA	114	C2
Darlington	WA	267	J1
Darlingtonia	CA	148	C3
❖ DARRINGTON	WA	103	A3
Dartford	WA	346	H5
Dash Point	WA	181	D1
Dash Point	WA	182	A1
❖ DAVENPORT	WA	114	A2
Davidson	ID	131	B1
Davis	WA	117	B1
Davis Creek	CA	152	A3
Davis Terrace	WA	303	F10
Dawson	OR	133	B2
Day Island	WA	181	C2
Days Creek	OR	225	D2
❖ DAYTON	OR	198	C7
❖ DAYTON	WA	122	A2
Dayton	WA	179	D2
❖ DAYVILLE	OR	136	C2
Deadwood	OR	132	C3
Deady	OR	221	C2
❖ DEARY	ID	123	B1
Deckerville	WA	179	A2
Deep Cove	BC	156	D3
Deep Cove	BC	159	B2
Deep Creek	ID	107	B2
Deep Creek	WA	114	B2
Deep Harbor	WA	101	C2
Deerhorn	OR	133	C3
Deer Island	OR	189	C7
❖ DEER PARK	WA	114	B1
Dehlinger	OR	235	D6
Delake	OR	203	A5
Delaney	WA	122	A2
Delano Heights	WA	237	C3
Delena	OR	189	A4
Delkena	WA	106	C3
Dellwood	OR	140	C2
Dellwood	OR	198	B3
Delphi	WA	184	B1
Delta	ID	115	C2
Deming	WA	102	B1
Denio	NV	153	C3
Denison	WA	114	B1
Denman Island	BC	92	B2
Denmark	OR	224	B3
Denneux	OR	199	B2
❖ DEPOE BAY	OR	203	A7
Deroche	BC	94	C3
De Smet	ID	115	A3
❖ DES MOINES	WA	290	B5
Deschutes Rivr Woods	OR	217	B4
Detour	OR	198	B1
❖ DETROIT	OR	134	B1
Dewatto	WA	173	B5
Dewdney	BC	94	B3
Dewey	OR	198	C4
Dewey	WA	259	J14
Dexter	OR	133	C3
Dexter By The Sea	WA	183	B5
Diablo	WA	103	B2
Diamond	OR	145	C3
Diamond	WA	122	B1
Diamond Lake	OR	223	C6
Diamond Lake	WA	106	C3
Diamond Lake Junction	OR	142	C3
Dickey Prairie	OR	126	A3
Dieringer	WA	182	C2
Dillard	OR	221	B7
Dilley	OR	198	B2
Dilworth	WA	174	D5
Disautel	WA	105	A3
Dishman	WA	350	A9
Disque	WA	164	C5
Disston	OR	141	C1
❖ DIST OF CNTL SNICH	BC	159	C3
❖ DIST OF CHILLIWACK	BC	94	C3
❖ DIS OF DELTA	BC	101	C1
❖ DIST OF KENT	BC	94	C3
❖ DIST OF LANGFORD	BC	159	B6
❖ DIST OF MATSQUI	BC	94	B3
❖ DIST OF METCHOSIN	BC	159	A7
❖ DIST OF MISSION	BC	94	B3
❖ DIST OF N SAANICH	BC	159	C2
❖ DIST OF N VANCVR	BC	254	H2
❖ DIST OF OAK BAY	BC	257	C7
❖ DIST OF SAANICH	BC	256	B1
❖ DIST OF SURREY	BC	157	B7
❖ DIST OF W VANCVR	BC	254	C1
Divide	OR	219	C1
Divide	WA	118	B1
Dixie	WA	122	A3
Dixonville	OR	221	D5
Dockton	WA	174	D7
Dodge	WA	122	B2
Dodson	OR	194	B7
Dole	WA	193	C3
Dollarton	BC	156	D3
Dollers Corner	WA	192	D3
Dolomite	WA	106	A1
❖ DONALD	OR	199	A7
Donald	WA	120	A2
❖ DONNELLY	ID	252	D1
Dora	OR	140	C2
Dorena	OR	141	C1
Dorris	CA	150	B3
Dot	WA	128	A1
Doty	WA	117	B1
Douglas	WA	236	D7
Douglas Ridge	OR	200	C5
❖ DOVER	ID	244	A1
Dover	OR	200	D5
Downing	OR	189	A3
Downs	OR	205	C4
Downtown	OR	313	F6
❖ DRAIN	OR	219	A3
Drakes Crossing	OR	205	D6
Draperville	OR	207	D4
Drew	OR	141	C3
Drewsey	OR	137	C3
Drift Creek	OR	209	B1
Dryad	WA	117	B1
Dry Creek	WA	121	C3
Dryden	OR	233	C2
Dryden	WA	238	B2
Dryland	OR	205	D1
Duckabush	WA	173	C1
Dudley	ID	115	B2
Dudley	WA	240	D3
❖ DUFUR	OR	127	B2
Dukes Valley	OR	195	C7
❖ DUNCAN	BC	101	A1
Duncan	WA	246	C7
Duncan Bay	BC	92	A1
Dundarave	BC	254	B2
❖ DUNDEE	OR	198	C6
Dune	OR	127	B1
❖ DUNES CITY	OR	214	B4
Dungeness	WA	262	D2
Dunnean	OR	146	A2
Dunthorpe	OR	321	G4
❖ DUPONT	WA	181	B5
Durham	WA	110	C3
Durkee	OR	138	C1
Duroc	OR	129	C1
Dusty	WA	122	B1
❖ DUVALL	WA	110	C1
Dynamite	WA	246	B7

E

COMMUNITY	ST.	PG.	GD.
Eagle	ID	115	C1
❖ EAGLE	ID	253	B1
Eagle Creek	OR	200	B4
Eagledale	WA	174	D2
Eagle Harbour	BC	156	A2
❖ EAGLE POINT	OR	230	D5
Eakin	OR	127	C2
Earlington	WA	289	H3
Earlmont	WA	175	C1
Earls Cove	BC	93	A2
East Aberdeen	WA	17	B7
East Bremerton	WA	270	H6
East Columbia	OR	309	H3
East Farms	WA	352	G7
East Gardener	OR	218	D1
Eastgate	WA	175	D3
❖ EAST HOPE	ID	244	D2
East Hoquiam	WA	178	A7
East Kamiah	ID	123	C2
East Kittitas	WA	241	D6
East Lind	WA	121	C1
Eastman	WA	122	A3
East Maupin	OR	127	B3
Eastmoreland	OR	318	A5
East Olympia	WA	184	D1
Easton	WA	111	B3
Eastport	ID	107	B1
East Port Orchard	WA	174	C4
Eastside	OR	220	D1
East Sooke	BC	164	D1
Eastsound	WA	101	C2
East Spokane	WA	350	A9
❖ EAST WENATCHEE	WA	239	A4
East Wenatchee Bench	WA	239	A4
❖ EATONVILLE	WA	118	B1
Eby	OR	126	A3
❖ ECHO	OR	129	A1
Echo Beach	ID	115	A1
Echo Dell	OR	200	A5
Eckman Lake	OR	328	G7
Eddyville	ID	248	B1
Eddyville	OR	133	A1
Edgecomb	WA	168	D6
Edgewater	WA	171	B2
Edgewick	WA	176	C6
❖ EDGEWOOD	WA	182	B3
Edison	WA	161	A4
Edison Station	WA	161	A4
❖ EDMONDS	WA	171	A5
Edwall	WA	114	A2
Eglon	WA	170	D4
Eightmile	OR	128	B2
Elbe	WA	118	B1
Elberton	WA	114	C3
Eldon	WA	173	B3
❖ ELECTRIC CITY	WA	237	C3
Elgarose	OR	221	A3
❖ ELGIN	OR	130	A1
Elgin	WA	174	B7
Eliot	OR	313	G2
Elk	WA	114	C1
Elk City	OR	206	D4
Elkhead	OR	219	C5
Elkhorn	OR	134	A1
Elk Lake	OR	216	A4
❖ ELK RIVER	ID	123	C1
❖ ELKTON	OR	141	A1
Elk Valley	CA	233	A7
Ella	OR	128	B1
Ellendale	OR	125	B3
❖ ELLENSBURG	WA	241	B6
Elliott Avenue	WA	243	A6
Ellisford	WA	104	C1
Ellisport	WA	174	D6
Ellsworth	WA	311	G2
❖ ELMA	WA	179	B7
❖ ELMER CITY	WA	237	C2
Elmira	ID	107	B2
Elmira	OR	133	B2
Elmonica	OR	199	A1
Elsie	OR	125	A1
Eltopia	WA	121	A2
Elwood	OR	200	B7
Embro	WA	111	B1
Emerson	OR	127	B2
Emida	ID	115	B3
❖ EMMETT	ID	139	C3
Empire	OR	333	C6
Enaville	ID	115	C2
❖ ENDICOTT	WA	122	B1
Enetai	WA	271	C9
Englewood	OR	333	F12
❖ ENTERPRISE	OR	130	C2
❖ ENTIAT	WA	236	A6
❖ ENUMCLAW	WA	110	C3
Eola Village	OR	204	C1
❖ EPHRATA	WA	112	C3
Erlands Point	WA	270	D6
Ernies Grove	WA	176	D4
Espanola	WA	114	B2
❖ ESTACADA	OR	200	C6
Eufaula	WA	189	A2
❖ EUGENE	OR	330	B6
Eureka	WA	121	C3
Evaline	WA	187	C2
❖ EVERETT	WA	267	G3
Evergreen	ID	131	C3
Evergreen	OR	321	F6
❖ EVERSON	WA	102	B1
Ewan	WA	114	B3
Excelsior Beach	ID	115	A1

F

COMMUNITY	ST.	PG.	GD.
Factoria	WA	175	C3
Fairbanks	OR	127	B1
Fairchild	WA	114	B2
Fairfax	WA	110	C3
Fairfield	OR	204	D2
❖ FAIRFIELD	WA	114	C2
Fairholm	WA	164	A6
Fairmont	WA	109	C1
Fairmount	WA	171	A2
Fairoaks	OR	221	D1
Fair Oaks	OR	321	H5
Fairview	OR	128	B2
Fairview	OR	140	B2
Fairview	OR	197	C2
❖ FAIRVIEW	OR	200	B1
Fairview	WA	270	E3
Fairview Sumach	WA	243	C7
Fairwood	WA	175	D5
Fairwood	WA	346	H7
Falcon Heights	OR	235	C5
Fall City	WA	176	B3
Fall Creek	OR	133	C3
❖ FALLS CITY	OR	125	A3
Falls View	OR	200	A7
Fanny Bay	BC	92	B2
Fargher Lake	WA	193	A1
Farmington	OR	198	D3
❖ FARMINGTON	WA	115	A3
Farron	WA	119	C2
Faubion	OR	201	C5
Fauntleroy	WA	284	D3
Fawn	OR	134	A1
Fayetteville	OR	210	A1
❖ FEDERAL WAY	WA	182	A1
Felida	WA	192	C5
Fenn	ID	123	C3
❖ FERDINAND	ID	123	B3
❖ FERNAN LK VILLAGE	ID	355	J11
Ferncliff	WA	174	D1
Ferndale	WA	121	C3
❖ FERNDALE	WA	158	C6
Fern Heath	WA	175	A6
Fern Hill	OR	188	D2
Fernwood	ID	115	B3
Fernwood	WA	173	A7
Fernwood	WA	174	B4
Fields	OR	153	C2
❖ FIFE	WA	182	A3
Finley	WA	121	A3
Finn Rock	OR	134	A3
❖ FIRCREST	WA	294	A1
Firdale	WA	117	A1
Firdale	WA	171	A6
Fir Grove	OR	200	A5
Fir Grove	OR	215	A1
First Hill	WA	278	C5
Fir Villa	OR	204	A6
Firwood	OR	200	D4
Fischers Mill	OR	200	B5
Fisher	OR	209	D4
Fisher	WA	193	A7
Fishers Corner	OR	199	D6
Five Corners	OR	152	A2
Five Corners	WA	192	D5
Fletcher Bay	WA	174	C1
Flett	WA	181	C3
Flora	OR	122	C3
❖ FLORENCE	OR	214	B3
Florence	WA	168	B4
Flynn	OR	133	B1
Foley Springs	OR	134	B2
Folkenberg	OR	192	A6
Foothills	WA	247	A2
Fordair	WA	113	A2
Fords Prairie	WA	299	A2
Forest	ID	123	B3
Forest	WA	187	D1
Forest Beach	WA	173	C6
Forest Beach	WA	181	B1
Forest Glade	WA	110	C1
❖ FOREST GROVE	OR	198	B1
Forest Knolls	BC	157	D7
Forest Park	OR	192	B7
Forfar	OR	206	B6
❖ FORKS	WA	169	D1
Fort Bidwell	CA	152	B3
Fort Dick	CA	148	B3
Fort Hill	OR	125	A3
Fort Klamath	OR	231	C1
Fort Klamath Junction	OR	231	C1
Fort Langley	BC	157	D6
Fort Nisqually	WA	181	C1
Fort Rains	WA	194	C6
Fort Rock	OR	143	B2
Fort Steilacoom	WA	181	C4
Fort Stevens	OR	188	B2
Fortune Branch	OR	225	C6
Foss	OR	191	C4
❖ FOSSIL	OR	128	A3
Foster	OR	134	A2
Foster	WA	289	E2
Foster-Powell	OR	319	E3
Four Corners	OR	200	B6
Four Corners	OR	234	C7
Four Corners	OR	323	F14
Four Corners	OR	336	E4
Four Corners	WA	110	C1
Four Corners	WA	118	A1
Four Corners	WA	170	B5
Four Corners	WA	263	B13
Four Lakes	WA	176	A5
Four Lakes	WA	246	A6
Fourmile	OR	224	B1
Fox	OR	137	A1
Fox Valley	OR	134	A1
Fragaria	WA	174	C5
Frances	WA	117	B2
Franklin	OR	133	B2
Franklin Camp	BC	100	B1
Fraser	BC	156	B5
Fraserview	BC	156	C5
Fredrickson	WA	182	A5
Freedom	WA	114	C2
Freeland	WA	170	D1
Freeman	WA	247	A6
Fremont	WA	273	J7
Frenchglen	OR	145	B3
❖ FRIDAY HARBOR	WA	101	C2
Friend	OR	127	A2
Frisken Wye	WA	179	A2
❖ FRUITLAND	ID	139	A3
Fruitland	OR	205	A6
Fruitvale	ID	131	C3
Fruitvale	WA	243	B6
Fryelands	WA	110	C1
Fulford Harbour	BC	101	B1
Fulton	OR	129	B1

G

COMMUNITY	ST.	PG.	GD.
Gabriola	BC	93	A3
Galena	OR	137	B1
Galena	WA	111	A1
Gales Creek	OR	125	B1
Galiano	BC	101	B1
Galice	OR	149	A1
Galvin	WA	184	B5
Ganges	BC	101	B1
Gap	OR	219	D1
❖ GARDEN CITY	ID	253	B2
Garden City	WA	179	C6
Garden Home	OR	199	B2
Garden Village	BC	156	C5
Gardiner	OR	218	C1
Gardiner	WA	166	D7
Garfield	OR	200	C6
❖ GARFIELD	WA	114	C3
Garibaldi	BC	93	C1
❖ GARIBALDI	OR	191	B7
Garibaldi Highlands	BC	93	C2
Garrett	WA	344	E8
Gasquet	CA	148	C3
❖ GASTON	OR	198	B3
Gas Works	OR	234	B2
Gate	WA	184	A3
❖ GATES	OR	134	A1
Gateway	OR	208	C2
Gaylord	OR	140	B3
Gazley	OR	225	D3
❖ GEARHART	OR	301	G4
Geiger Heights	WA	246	B5
Gem	OR	235	D5
❖ GENESEE	ID	250	C1
Geneva	WA	161	A1
George	OR	200	D6
❖ GEORGE	WA	112	B3
Georgetown	WA	176	A7
Georgetown	WA	282	A7
❖ GERVAIS	OR	205	B2
Getchell	WA	168	D7
Getchell Hill	WA	168	D7
Gibbon	OR	129	C1

❖ -Indicates City, District or Township

Cities & Communities Index

❖ -Indicates City, District or Township

Cities & Communities Index

COMMUNITY	ST.	PG.	GD.
Littell	WA	184	B7
Little Albany	OR	209	C2
Little Falls	WA	114	A1
Little Hoquiam	WA	180	C1
Little Oklahoma	WA	165	D7
Little River	BC	92	A2
Littlerock	WA	184	B2
Little Shasta	CA	150	A3
Little Valley	OR	138	C3
Lobert Junction	OR	231	D4
Lochdale	BC	156	D4
Lochsloy	WA	102	C3
Locoda	OR	117	B3
Lofall	WA	170	B5
Logan	OR	200	B5
Logan Hill	WA	184	D7
Logsden	OR	133	A1
London	OR	219	D3
Lone Cemetery	ID	248	D3
Lone Elder	OR	199	C7
Lone Pine	OR	150	C1
Lone Pine	WA	237	C2
❖ LONEROCK	OR	128	B3
Lone Tree	OR	130	A2
❖ LONG BEACH	WA	186	A5
Longbranch	WA	181	A3
❖ LONG CREEK	OR	137	A1
Long Lake	WA	114	A1
Longmire	WA	185	B5
Long Tom Station	OR	133	A2
❖ LONGVIEW	WA	302	F8
Looking Glass	OR	130	B1
Lookingglass	OR	221	A5
Lookout	OR	142	A1
Loomis	WA	104	C1
Loon Lake	WA	106	B3
Lopez	WA	101	C2
Lorane	OR	133	B3
Lorella	OR	151	A2
❖ LOSTINE	OR	130	C2
Loveland	WA	182	A6
Lowden	WA	121	C3
❖ LOWELL	OR	133	C3
Lowell	WA	265	F7
Lower Highland	OR	200	B7
Lower Nicola	BC	95	C1
Loyal Heights	WA	272	D2
Lucerne	WA	103	C3
Lucile	ID	131	C1
Lummi Island	WA	160	B1
Lund	BC	92	B1
Lunnville	OR	198	B4
Lyle	WA	196	B5
❖ LYMAN	WA	102	C2
❖ LYNDEN	WA	158	D4
Lynn Creek	BC	255	F1
Lynn Valley	BC	255	C1
❖ LYNNWOOD	WA	171	B5
Lynwood Center	WA	271	F6
❖ LYONS	OR	134	A1
M			
Mabel	OR	133	C2
❖ MABTON	WA	120	B3
Macdoel	CA	150	B3
Machias	WA	110	C1
Mack	WA	122	A1
Macksburg	OR	199	C7
Macleay	OR	205	B6
Madison Park	WA	279	F2
Madison South	OR	315	G3
❖ MADRAS	OR	208	C5
Madras Station	OR	208	C5
Madrona Beach	WA	167	D4
Madrona Park	WA	278	D4
Magnolia Beach	WA	174	D7
Magnolia Bluff	WA	276	D1
Mahan	OR	198	D1
Malahat	BC	159	A4
Malaya	WA	239	B5
❖ MALDEN	WA	114	B3
❖ MALIN	OR	151	A3
Malone	WA	179	C7
Malott	WA	104	C3
Maltby	WA	171	D5
Manchester	WA	271	H12
Manette	WA	271	B10
Manhattan	WA	290	A1
Manhattan Beach	OR	191	B5
Manitou Beach	WA	174	D1
Manning	OR	125	B1
Manning	WA	122	C1
❖ MANSFIELD	WA	112	C1
Manson	WA	236	B2
Manson Landing	BC	92	A1
❖ MANZANITA	OR	191	B4
Manzanita	WA	174	C1
Manzanita	WA	174	D7
Maple Bay	BC	101	B1
Maple Grove	WA	164	D6
❖ MAPLE RIDGE	BC	157	D6
Mapleton	OR	214	D2
❖ MAPLE VALLEY	WA	176	A6
Maplewood	WA	174	C6
Maplewood	WA	175	C5
Marble Creek	ID	115	C3
Marblemount	WA	103	A2
Marcellus	WA	113	C3
Marcola	OR	210	D7
Marcus	WA	106	A2
Marengo	WA	122	B2
Marial	OR	140	C3
Marietta	WA	158	C7
Marine Drive	WA	270	D8
Marion	OR	133	C1
Marion Forks	OR	134	C1
Markham	OR	320	B1
❖ MARLIN	WA	113	A2

COMMUNITY	ST.	PG.	GD.
Marmot	OR	201	A4
Marquam	OR	205	D3
Marshall	WA	246	B6
Marshall Park	OR	320	C1
Marshland	OR	117	B3
❖ MARSING	ID	147	B1
Martin	WA	111	A3
Martindale	WA	121	B3
Maryhill	WA	127	C1
Marylhurst	OR	199	C4
Marys Corner	WA	187	D2
❖ MARYSVILLE	WA	168	C7
Mason	WA	114	B2
Massinger Corner	OR	200	A7
Matlock	WA	179	B2
Matsqui	BC	102	B1
❖ MATTAWA	WA	120	B1
❖ MAUPIN	OR	127	B3
Maury	WA	175	A6
May Creek	WA	175	C4
Mayfield	WA	118	A2
Mayger	OR	189	A2
Maynard	WA	109	C1
Mayne	BC	101	B1
Maytown	WA	184	C2
Mayview	WA	122	C1
Mayville	OR	128	A3
Maywood	OR	133	B3
❖ MAYWOOD PARK	OR	315	J2
Mazame	OR	142	C3
McBee	OR	129	B1
❖ MCCALL	ID	251	D5
❖ MCCLEARY	WA	179	D6
McCormac	OR	333	J14
McCormick	WA	117	B2
McCormmach	OR	129	B1
McCoy	OR	204	B3
McCoy	WA	114	C3
McCredie Springs	OR	142	B1
McDermitt	NV	154	B2
McDermitt	OR	154	B2
McDonald	WA	242	D4
McEwan	OR	138	A1
McGuire	ID	353	D7
McKay	OR	129	C2
McKee Bridge	OR	149	B2
McKenna	WA	118	A1
McKenzie Bridge	OR	134	B2
McKinley	OR	140	C2
McLeod	OR	149	C1
McLoughlin Heights	WA	306	D6
McMicken Heights	WA	288	D6
McMillin	WA	182	C5
❖ MCMINNVILLE	OR	198	A7
McMurray	WA	168	C2
McNab	OR	128	B2
McNary	OR	129	A1
Meacham	OR	129	C2
Meacham Corner	OR	125	C1
Mead	WA	347	F7
Meadow Creek	WA	111	A3
Meadowdale	WA	171	B4
Meadowdale	WA	270	H2
Meadows	ID	251	B4
Meadows	WA	184	B4
Meaghersville	WA	238	A7
❖ MEDFORD	OR	336	D11
❖ MEDICAL LAKE	WA	114	B2
Medical Springs	OR	130	B3
Medimont	ID	248	C4
❖ MEDINA	WA	279	J4
Mehama	OR	134	A1
❖ MELBA	ID	147	C1
Melbourne	WA	117	A1
Melmont	ID	147	C1
Melrose	OR	221	A4
Melville	OR	188	C4
Mendota	WA	184	D5
Menlo	WA	117	A1
Menlo Park	WA	181	C3
❖ MERCER ISLAND	WA	283	J2
Merideth	WA	175	B7
❖ MERIDIAN	ID	253	A3
Merlin	OR	229	A4
❖ MERRILL	OR	150	C2
Merritt	BC	95	C1
Merritt	WA	111	C1
Merville	BC	92	A1
Mesa	ID	139	C1
❖ MESA	WA	121	A2
Meskill	WA	117	B1
❖ METALINE	WA	106	B1
❖ METALINE FALLS	WA	106	C1
Metchosin	BC	165	A1
Methow	WA	104	B3
❖ METOLIUS	OR	208	C5
Metzger	OR	199	B3
Mica	ID	247	D4
Mica	WA	247	A5
Michigan Hill	WA	184	A4
Middle Grove	OR	323	F9
❖ MIDDLETON	ID	147	B1
Middleton	OR	199	A5
Midland	OR	235	B5
Midland	WA	182	A4
❖ MIDVALE	ID	139	B1
Midway	BC	105	B1
Midway	ID	147	B1
Midway	OR	125	A3
Midway	OR	129	B1
Midway	OR	198	D3
Midway	OR	336	A3
Midway	WA	181	C1
Midway	WA	290	D7
Mikkalo	OR	128	A2
Milan	WA	114	C1
Milburn	WA	184	A7
Miles	WA	113	C1
Miles Crossing	OR	300	C10

COMMUNITY	ST.	PG.	GD.
Mileta Raeco	WA	175	A7
Mill A	WA	195	B4
Mill Bay	BC	159	A2
❖ MILL CITY	OR	134	A1
❖ MILL CREEK	WA	171	C4
Miller	OR	192	B6
Miller River	WA	111	A1
❖ MILLERSBURG	OR	326	G2
Millican	OR	135	B3
Millington	OR	220	D2
Mill Park	OR	200	A1
Mill Plain	WA	193	A6
Millwood	OR	141	A2
❖ MILLWOOD	WA	350	D5
Milner	BC	157	C7
Milnes Landing	BC	101	A2
Milo	OR	141	B3
❖ MILTON	WA	182	B2
❖ MILTON-FREEWATER	WA	121	C3
❖ MILWAUKIE	OR	318	A7
Milwaukie Heights	OR	321	J4
Mima	WA	184	B3
Minam	OR	130	B1
Mineral	ID	139	A1
Mineral	WA	118	B1
Minerva	OR	214	C1
Minnehaha	WA	305	J1
Minnick	WA	122	A3
Mirrormont	WA	176	A5
Mission	OR	129	B1
Mist	OR	117	B3
Mitchell	OR	136	A1
Moclips	WA	177	B2
Modoc Point	OR	231	D6
Mohler	OR	191	B4
Mohrweis	WA	179	D1
❖ MOLALLA	OR	126	A3
Monitor	OR	205	C2
Monitor	WA	238	C3
Monkland	OR	127	C2
❖ MONMOUTH	OR	204	B7
Monohon	WA	175	D3
❖ MONROE	OR	133	B2
❖ MONROE	WA	110	C1
Monson Corner	WA	168	B3
❖ MONTAGUE	CA	150	A3
Montavilla	OR	315	G6
Montborne	WA	168	C1
Monte Cristo	WA	111	A1
❖ MONTESANO	WA	178	D6
Monte Vista	WA	181	D4
Montlake	WA	278	C1
Montour	ID	139	C3
❖ MONTROSE	BC	106	B1
❖ MONUMENT	OR	136	C1
Moody	OR	127	B1
Moores Corner	WA	186	A5
Moreland	OR	317	H6
Morgan	OR	128	B2
Morgan Acres	WA	347	D11
❖ MORO	OR	127	C2
❖ MORTON	WA	118	B2
❖ MOSCOW	ID	249	C5
❖ MOSES LAKE	WA	242	C3
❖ MOSIER	OR	196	A5
❖ MOSSYROCK	WA	118	A2
Mountaindale	OR	125	C1
Mountain Home	OR	198	D4
Mountain Home	WA	238	A6
Mountain Home Park	WA	122	A3
Mountain View	WA	158	C6
Mountain View Beach	WA	168	A6
❖ MOUNT ANGEL	OR	205	C3
Mount Baker	WA	282	E2
Mount Hebron	CA	150	B3
Mount Hood	OR	200	B1
Mount Hood	OR	202	C1
Mount Hope	OR	126	A3
Mount Hope	WA	114	C2
Mount Idaho	ID	123	C3
❖ MOUNTLAKE TER	WA	171	B6
Mount Pleasant	WA	193	D7
Mount Scott-Arleta	OR	318	D3
Mount Tabor	OR	314	D6
❖ MOUNT VERNON	OR	137	A2
❖ MOUNT VERNON	WA	260	H12
Mount View	OR	150	A2
Mowich	OR	142	C2
❖ MOXEE CITY	WA	243	D7
❖ MOYIE SPRINGS	ID	107	B1
Mud Springs	WA	112	B1
❖ MUKILTEO	WA	266	D5
Mulino	OR	199	D7
Mulloy	OR	199	B5
Multnomah	OR	316	B6
Mumby	WA	184	B2
Munra	OR	129	B1
Murdock	WA	196	C6
Murnen	WA	117	B1
Murphy	ID	147	C2
Murphy	OR	229	B7
Murrayhill	OR	199	A3
Murrayville	BC	158	C1
Myrick	OR	129	B1
❖ MYRTLE CREEK	OR	225	C1
❖ MYRTLE POINT	OR	140	B2
N			
❖ NACHES	WA	243	A4
Naef	OR	199	D4
Nahcotta	WA	186	A2
❖ NAMPA	ID	147	B1
❖ NANAIMO	BC	93	A3
Nanoose Bay	BC	92	C3
❖ NAPAVINE	WA	187	C1
Naples	ID	107	B2
Napton	OR	147	A1
Narrows	OR	133	C2

COMMUNITY	ST.	PG.	GD.
Narrows	OR	145	B2
Naselle	WA	186	C5
Nashville	OR	133	A1
Nason Creek	WA	111	C1
Natal	OR	117	B3
National	WA	118	B1
Navy Heights	OR	300	H4
Navy Yard City	WA	270	E11
Naylor	WA	112	C3
Neah Bay	BC	100	B2
Neahkahnie Beach	OR	191	B3
Neawanna Station	OR	301	J6
Necanicum Junction	OR	188	D7
Nedonna Beach	OR	191	B5
Needy	OR	205	D1
❖ NEHALEM	OR	191	B4
Neilton	WA	109	A2
Nelscott	OR	203	A5
Nelson	WA	240	A2
Nelway	BC	106	C1
Nena	OR	127	B3
Neotsu	OR	203	B4
Neptune Beach	WA	158	B6
Nesika Beach	OR	228	A4
Neskowin	OR	203	B2
❖ NESPELEM	WA	105	A3
Netarts	OR	197	A2
Newaukum	WA	184	B7
❖ NEWBERG	OR	198	D5
New Bridge	OR	139	A1
New Brighton	BC	93	B2
❖ NEWCASTLE	WA	175	C4
New Era	OR	199	C5
Newell	CA	151	A3
Newhalem	WA	103	B2
New Hope	OR	229	B7
New Idaho	OR	152	A2
New Idanha	OR	134	B1
New Kamilche	WA	180	A5
New London	WA	178	A5
Newman Lake	WA	352	F6
❖ NEW MEADOWS	ID	251	A4
New Pine Creek	CA	152	A3
New Pine Creek	OR	152	A3
❖ NEW PLYMOUTH	ID	139	B3
❖ NEWPORT	OR	206	B4
❖ NEWPORT	WA	106	C3
Newport Heights	OR	206	B4
Newport Hills	WA	175	C3
New Princeton	OR	145	C2
Newton	BC	157	A7
Newton	OR	198	D1
Newton	WA	177	B5
❖ NEW WESTMINSTER	BC	156	D5
❖ NEZ PERCE	ID	123	C2
Niagara	OR	134	A1
Nicola	BC	95	C1
Nighthawk	WA	104	C1
Nile	WA	119	B1
Nimrod	OR	134	A3
Ninety One	OR	205	C1
Nippon	WA	111	B1
Nisqually	WA	181	A6
Nisson	WA	178	B4
Nitinat	BC	100	B1
Nolin	OR	129	A1
Nonpareil	OR	141	B2
❖ NOOKSACK	WA	102	B1
Nooksack Slmn Htchry	WA	102	B1
Noon	OR	133	B1
Norgate	BC	254	H5
Norma Beach	WA	171	B4
Norman	WA	168	B4
❖ NORMANDY PARK	WA	175	A6
North Albany	OR	326	B5
North Beach	OR	214	B5
North Beach	WA	171	A7
North Bend	BC	95	A1
❖ NORTH BEND	OR	333	F6
❖ NORTH BEND	WA	176	C4
❖ NORTH BONNEVILLE	WA	194	C6
North Central	OR	200	B1
North City	WA	171	B6
North Cowichan	BC	101	A1
Northeast	OR	200	B1
Northfork	OR	151	B1
North Fork	OR	214	C7
North Gate	WA	171	B7
North Gresham	OR	200	A1
North Howell	OR	205	B4
Northilla	WA	174	D7
North Jctn (Davidson)	OR	127	B3
North Lewiston	ID	250	C4
North Olympia	WA	180	D5
❖ NORTH PLAINS	OR	125	C1
❖ NORTHPORT	WA	106	A1
❖ NORTH POWDER	OR	130	B2
North Prosser	WA	120	C3
North Puyallup	WA	182	A3
North Santiam	OR	133	C1
North Scholls	OR	198	D3
North Springfield	OR	330	G2
Northwest	OR	312	C4
Northwest Industrial	OR	312	B2
Norway	OR	220	D6
Norwood	ID	251	C7
Norwood	OR	199	B4
Noti	OR	133	A2
❖ NOTUS	ID	147	B1
Novelty	WA	110	C1
Nulls Crossing	WA	184	D6
Nye	OR	129	B2
Nyland	WA	110	C1
❖ NYSSA	OR	139	A3
O			
❖ OAKESDALE	WA	114	C3
Oak Grove	OR	195	C6

COMMUNITY	ST.	PG.	GD.
Oak Grove	OR	195	C6
Oak Grove	OR	321	J6
❖ OAK HARBOR	WA	167	B2
Oak Hills	OR	199	A1
❖ OAKLAND	OR	219	A7
Oakland	WA	180	B2
Oak Park	OR	323	E9
Oak Park	WA	193	B7
Oak Point	WA	117	B3
❖ OAKRIDGE	OR	142	A1
Oaks	OR	334	E11
Oak Springs	OR	127	B3
❖ OAKVILLE	WA	117	B1
OBrien	OR	233	A6
OBrien	WA	291	J5
Ocasta	WA	183	B2
Ocean City	WA	177	B5
Oceanlake	OR	203	A4
Ocean Park	BC	158	D1
Ocean Park	WA	186	A2
❖ OCEAN SHORES	WA	298	C2
Oceanside	OR	197	A2
Oceanside	WA	186	A4
Odell	OR	195	C7
Odell Lake	OR	142	B1
Odessa	OR	231	B6
❖ ODESSA	WA	113	B3
Ohop	WA	118	B1
❖ OKANOGAN	WA	104	C3
Oklahoma Hill	OR	117	B3
Olalla	OR	141	A2
Olalla	WA	174	C6
Old Colton	OR	126	A3
Old Town	OR	219	A7
Oldtown	WA	106	C3
Oldtown-Chinatown	OR	313	F5
Olene	OR	150	C2
Olex	OR	128	A2
Olga	WA	160	A3
Olney	OR	188	D3
❖ OLYMPIA	WA	297	C7
Olympic View	WA	170	A7
❖ OMAK	WA	104	C2
Ona	OR	206	B7
Onalaska	WA	118	A2
❖ ONAWAY	ID	249	D1
ONeil	OR	213	A4
ONeil Corners	OR	199	C6
❖ ONTARIO	OR	139	A3
Ontario Heights	OR	139	A3
Opal City	OR	212	D2
Ophir	OR	228	A3
Opportunity	WA	350	H12
Orcas	WA	101	C2
Orchard	WA	193	A6
Orchard Avenue	WA	350	B5
Orchard Heights	WA	271	B14
Orchard Park	WA	349	J6
Orchard View	OR	198	A6
Ordnance	OR	128	C1
Oreana	ID	147	C2
❖ OREGON CITY	OR	199	D5
Oregon Trunk Junction	OR	127	B1
Orenco	OR	199	A1
Oretown	OR	203	B1
Orient	OR	200	C1
Orient	WA	105	C1
Orilla	WA	289	J7
❖ OROFINO	ID	123	C2
Orondo	WA	236	A1
❖ OROVILLE	WA	104	C1
Orrs Corner	OR	204	B6
❖ ORTING	WA	182	C5
Osborn Corner	WA	171	C4
❖ OSBURN	ID	115	C2
Osceola	WA	182	D3
Oso	WA	102	C3
❖ OSOYOOS	BC	104	C1
Ostrander	WA	303	F1
❖ OTHELLO	WA	121	A1
Otis	OR	203	B3
Otis Junction	OR	203	B3
Otis Orchards	WA	352	B9
Otter Bay	BC	101	
Otter Point	BC	101	A2
Otter Rock	OR	206	B2
Outlet Bay	ID	107	A2
Outlook	OR	200	A4
Outlook	WA	120	B2
Overland	OR	220	D3
Overlook	OR	308	C6
Owyhee	ID	253	D6
Owyhee	OR	139	A3
Oxman	OR	138	C1
Oxyoke	OR	229	B3
Oyhut	WA	177	B6
Oyster River	BC	92	A1
Oysterville	OR	206	B5
Oysterville	WA	186	A1
P			
❖ PACIFIC	WA	182	B2
Pacific Beach	WA	177	B2
Pacific Beach	WA	186	A4
Pacific City	OR	197	A7
Packard	WA	113	C3
Packwood	WA	118	C2
Page	ID	115	C2
❖ PAISLEY	OR	151	C1
Palmer Junction	OR	130	B1
❖ PALOUSE	WA	249	B1
Panakanic	WA	196	B1
Pandora	WA	114	C3
Park	WA	161	C2
Parkdale	OR	202	C2
Parker	WA	120	A2
Parkersburg	OR	220	B5
Parkers Mill	OR	128	C3

❖ -Indicates City, District or Township

PNW

INTRO

Cities & Communities Index

❖ -Indicates City, District or Township

M

PNW

INTRO

Cities & Communities Index

COMMUNITY	ST.	PG.	GD.
Starvation Heights	OR	229	D5
State Line Village	ID	352	H9
Stave Falls	BC	94	B3
❖ STAYTON	OR	133	C1
Steelhead	BC	94	B3
Stehekin	WA	103	C3
❖ STEILACOOM	WA	181	B4
Stephens	OR	221	B1
Steptoe	WA	114	C3
Stevens	ID	131	C3
❖ STEVENSON	WA	194	C5
Steveston	BC	156	B7
Stillwater	BC	92	C2
Stillwater	WA	176	B1
Stimson Mill	OR	198	B2
Stoddard	ID	147	C2
Stratford	WA	113	A2
Strawberry	OR	128	C2
Striebels Corner	WA	170	C5
Stronghold	CA	151	A3
Stuck	WA	182	C2
Sturdies Bay	BC	101	B1
Sturgeon	ID	115	A1
❖ SUBLIMITY	OR	133	C1
Sudden Valley	WA	161	B1
Sullivans Gulch	OR	313	J4
Sulphur Springs	OR	214	D7
❖ SULTAN	WA	110	C1
❖ SUMAS	WA	102	B1
Summer Lake	OR	143	C3
❖ SUMMERVILLE	OR	130	A2
Summit	OR	195	C6
Summit	WA	176	A7
Summit	WA	182	A4
Summits	OR	133	A1
Sumner	OR	140	B2
❖ SUMNER	WA	182	B3
❖ SUMPTER	OR	138	A1
Suncrest	BC	156	C5
Sundale	WA	128	A1
Sunderland	OR	310	B4
Sunlight Beach	WA	170	D2
Sunnycrest	OR	198	C5
Sunnydale	WA	175	A5
Sunnydale	WA	184	C3
Sunny Shores	WA	168	B6
Sunny Shores Acres	WA	168	A6
Sunnyside	OR	200	A2
Sunnyside	OR	314	A7
Sunnyside	OR	324	J12
❖ SUNNYSIDE	WA	120	B2
Sunnyside	WA	121	C3
Sunnyslope	WA	174	A4
Sunnyslope	WA	238	D3
Sunny Valley	OR	229	B2
Sunriver	OR	217	A6
Sunset	BC	156	B5
Sunset	OR	131	A3
Sunset	OR	199	D4
Sunset	WA	114	B3
Sunset Beach	OR	188	B3
Sunset Beach	WA	167	D4
Sunset Beach	WA	173	D6
Sunset Beach	WA	174	D6
Sunset Beach	WA	177	B2
Sunset Beach	WA	181	C3
Suplee	OR	136	C3
Suquamish	WA	170	C7
Surrey Centre	BC	157	B7
Susanville	OR	137	B1
❖ SUTHERLIN	OR	221	C1
Sutico	WA	117	B1
Sutton	WA	122	A1
Suver Junction	OR	207	B2
Svensen	OR	117	A3
Svensen Junction	OR	117	A3
Swansonville	WA	170	B3
Swedetown	OR	189	A5
Sweeney	ID	115	C2
Sweet	ID	139	C3
❖ SWEET HOME	OR	134	A2
Sweetwater	ID	123	A2
Swem	WA	117	B1
Swift	WA	122	B1
Swinomish Village	WA	160	D7
Swisshome	OR	132	C3
Sylvan	WA	181	B2
Sylvan Beach	WA	174	D5
Sylvan Highlands	OR	312	A7
Sylvanite	MT	107	C1
T			
Table Rock	OR	230	C6
❖ TACOMA	WA	292	D5
Taft	OR	203	A5
Tahlequah	WA	181	D1
Taholah	WA	172	B6
Tahuya	WA	173	B7
Takilma	OR	233	B6
Talache	ID	244	B5
Talbot	OR	207	C2
❖ TALENT	OR	234	B3
Tamarack	ID	131	C3
Tampico	WA	119	C2
❖ TANGENT	OR	207	C6
Tanner	WA	176	C5
Tasker	WA	119	C1
Taylorville	OR	117	B3
Teanaway	WA	240	C2
❖ TEKOA	WA	114	C3
Telford	WA	113	C1
Telma	WA	111	C1
Telocaset	OR	130	B3
Templeton	OR	218	C4
❖ TENINO	WA	184	D3
Tenino Junction	WA	184	D3
Tenmile	OR	141	A2
Tenmile	OR	218	B4
❖ TENSED	ID	115	A3
Terrace Heights	WA	243	C6
Terrebone	OR	212	D4
Terrys Corner	WA	167	D4
❖ THE DALLES	OR	196	C7
Thomas	WA	175	B7
Thompson	BC	156	A6
Thompson Place	WA	181	A6
Thorndyke	WA	289	E4
Thorn Hollow	OR	129	C1
Thornton	WA	114	C3
Thorp	WA	241	A4
Thrall	WA	241	B7
Thrashers Corner	WA	171	C5
Three Lakes	WA	110	C1
Three Lynx	OR	126	B3
Three Pines	OR	229	B3
Three Rivers	OR	217	A7
Three Rocks	OR	203	A3
Three Tree Point	WA	175	A5
Thrift	WA	182	B6
Thurston	OR	331	J6
Tide	OR	132	C3
Tidewater	OR	209	C1
Tiernan	OR	214	C2
Tierra Del Mar	OR	197	A6
❖ TIETON	WA	119	C1
Tietonview Grange	WA	119	C2
❖ TIGARD	OR	199	B3
❖ TILLAMOOK	OR	197	B2
Tillamook Junction	OR	125	C1
Tiller	OR	141	C3
Tillicum	BC	256	E5
Tillicum	WA	181	C5
Timber Grove	OR	126	A3
Timberlane	WA	175	D7
Tokeland	WA	183	C5
Toketee Falls	OR	222	D4
Tokio	WA	113	C3
Tokul	WA	176	C4
❖ TOLEDO	OR	206	C4
❖ TOLEDO	WA	187	D4
Tolovana Park	OR	191	B1
❖ TONASKET	WA	104	C2
Tongue Point Village	OR	188	D1
Tono	WA	184	D4
Top Hat	WA	285	J5
❖ TOPPENISH	WA	120	A2
Torga	WA	111	A2
Touchet	WA	121	B3
Toutle	WA	118	A2
Town & Country	WA	346	J14
❖ TOWN OF ESQUIMLT	BC	256	C8
❖ TOWN OF SIDNEY	BC	159	C2
❖ TOWN OF VW ROYAL	BC	256	A4
❖ TWNSHIP OF LANGLY	BC	157	D7
Tracy	OR	200	C6
Tracyton	WA	270	G4
Trail	OR	230	D2
Treharne	OR	125	B1
Trenholm	OR	125	C1
Trent	OR	215	D4
Trentwood	WA	351	A3
Trestle Creek	ID	244	C2
Tri-City	OR	225	C2
Trinity	WA	103	C3
❖ TROUTDALE	OR	200	B1
Trout Lake	WA	119	A3
❖ TROY	ID	123	A1
❖ TROY	MT	107	C2
Troy	OR	122	C3
Trude	WA	176	B7
Tsawwassen	BC	101	C1
❖ TUALATIN	OR	199	B4
Tucannon	WA	122	A2
❖ TUKWILA	WA	289	F3
Tulalip	WA	168	B7
Tulalip Shores	WA	168	B7
Tulameen	BC	95	C2
Tulare Beach	WA	168	B6
Tulelake	CA	151	A3
Tulips	WA	177	C5
Tumalo	OR	217	B1
❖ TUMWATER	WA	296	F9
Tumtum	WA	114	B1
Turkey	WA	166	D7
❖ TURNER	OR	325	G12
Turner	WA	122	B2
Turner Corner	WA	171	C5
Twickenham	OR	136	A1
Twin Beaches	ID	248	A1
Twin Lakes	WA	182	A1
Twinlow	ID	115	A1
Twin Rocks	OR	191	A6
❖ TWISP	WA	104	A3
Twomile	OR	220	B7
Tye	WA	111	B1
Tyee	OR	141	A1
Tyee Beach	WA	168	A7
Tygh Valley	OR	127	B2
Tyler	WA	114	B2
Tynehead	BC	157	B6
U			
❖ UKIAH	OR	129	B3
Umapine	WA	121	C3
❖ UMATILLA	OR	129	A1
Umli	OR	142	B1
Umpqua	OR	221	A1
Umtanum	WA	243	C1
Uncas	WA	109	C1
Underwood	WA	195	C4
Underwood Heights	WA	195	C4
❖ UNION	OR	130	B2
Union	WA	173	A7
Union Bay	BC	92	B2
Union Creek	OR	141	C3
Union Creek	OR	226	D4
Union Gap	OR	221	C1
❖ UNION GAP	WA	243	C7
Union Junction	OR	130	B2
Union Mills	OR	126	A3
Union Mills	WA	181	A6
❖ UNIONTOWN	WA	250	B2
Unionville	OR	204	C2
United Junction	OR	192	B6
❖ UNITY	OR	138	A2
University	WA	274	C5
❖ UNV ENDWMNT LNDS	BC	156	A4
University Park	OR	308	A5
❖ UNIVERSITY PLACE	WA	294	A4
Upper Farm	OR	206	D2
Upper Highland	OR	200	B7
Upper Mill	WA	110	C3
Upper Preston	WA	176	B4
Upper Soda	OR	134	B2
Usk	WA	106	C3
Ustick	ID	253	B2
Utsalady	WA	167	D3
V			
❖ VADER	WA	187	C4
Vadis	OR	125	C1
Vail	WA	118	A1
Valby	OR	128	B2
❖ VALE	OR	138	C3
Valle Vista	OR	192	A7
Valley	WA	106	B3
Valleycliffe	BC	93	C2
Valley Falls	OR	152	A1
Valleyford	WA	246	D6
Valley Junction	OR	125	A3
Van	OR	137	B3
Vananda	BC	92	B2
Van Asselt	WA	286	D1
❖ VANCOUVER	BC	254	G13
❖ VANCOUVER	WA	305	F3
Vancouver Junction	WA	192	C5
Van Horn	OR	195	D6
Vantage	WA	120	B1
Van Zandt	WA	102	B1
Vasa Park	WA	175	D3
Vashon	WA	174	D5
Vashon Center	WA	174	D6
Vashon Heights	WA	174	D4
Vaughn	OR	133	A2
Vaughn	WA	174	A7
Vega	WA	181	A4
Venator	OR	146	A2
Venersborg	WA	193	B3
❖ VENETA	OR	133	B3
Venice	WA	174	C1
Veradale	WA	351	C8
Verboort	OR	125	B1
Vernon	OR	309	J6
❖ VERNONIA	OR	125	B1
Vesuvius	BC	101	B1
Victoria	BC	156	C5
Vida	OR	134	A2
View Ridge	WA	275	G3
Village Bay	BC	101	B1
Vineland	WA	250	B4
Vinemaple	OR	125	A1
Vinland	WA	170	B6
Vinson	OR	129	A2
Viola	ID	249	C3
Viola	OR	200	B6
Virden	WA	240	D1
Virginia	WA	170	B7
Vision Acres	WA	189	C4
Voltage	OR	145	B2
Voorhies	OR	234	B2
W			
Wabash	WA	182	D2
Waconda	OR	205	A3
Wagner	WA	110	C1
Wagnersburg	WA	239	A1
Wagontire	OR	144	B2
Wahkiacus	WA	196	D3
❖ WAITSBURG	WA	122	A2
Waitsburg Junction	WA	122	A2
Wakonda Beach	OR	328	B10
Waldale	WA	241	B5
❖ WALDPORT	OR	328	C7
Walker	OR	215	B6
❖ WALLACE	ID	115	C2
Wallace	OR	199	B6
❖ WALLA WALLA	WA	344	E6
Walla Walla East	WA	345	E9
Wallingford	WA	274	A5
❖ WALLOWA	OR	130	B1
Wallula	WA	121	B3
Walnut Grove	BC	157	C6
Walnut Grove	WA	192	D5
Walters	WA	114	C3
Walters Ferry	ID	147	B2
Walterville	OR	133	C3
Walton	OR	133	A2
Walville	WA	117	B2
Wamic	OR	127	A2
Wanapum Village	WA	120	B1
Waneta	BC	106	B1
Wankers Corner	OR	199	C4
Wapato	OR	198	B3
❖ WAPATO	WA	120	A2
Wapinitia	OR	127	A3
❖ WARDEN	WA	121	A1
❖ WARDNER	ID	115	C2
Warm Beach	WA	168	A5
Warm Springs	OR	208	A3
Warner	OR	140	B3
Warren	OR	192	A2
Warren	WA	181	B1
❖ WARRENTON	OR	188	B2
Warwick	WA	127	B1
❖ WASCO	OR	127	C1
Washington Harbor	WA	166	B7
❖ WASHOUGAL	WA	193	B7
❖ WASHTUCNA	WA	121	C1
❖ WATERLOO	OR	133	C1
Waterman	OR	129	C1
Waterman	OR	136	B1
Waterman	WA	271	E9
Waterman Point	WA	271	F8
❖ WATERVILLE	WA	236	C7
Watseco	OR	191	A6
Wauna	OR	117	B3
Wauna	WA	174	B6
Wautauga Beach	WA	271	G8
❖ WAVERLY	WA	114	C2
Wawawai	WA	122	C1
Wayland	OR	129	C1
Wayside	WA	114	B1
Weaver	OR	225	C1
Webster Corners	BC	157	D5
Wecoma Beach	OR	203	A4
Wedderburn	OR	228	A5
Weikel	WA	243	A6
❖ WEISER	ID	139	A2
Welches	OR	201	C5
Wellington	BC	93	A3
Wellpinit	WA	114	A1
Wells	WA	114	A3
Wemme	OR	201	C5
❖ WENATCHEE	WA	238	D4
Wenatchee Heights	WA	239	A6
Wendling	OR	133	C2
Wendson	OR	214	C3
West Beach	WA	101	C2
West Blakely	WA	271	H7
West Fairfield	WA	114	C2
❖ WESTFIR	OR	142	A1
West Fork	WA	105	B2
West Haven	OR	199	B1
Westhaven	WA	298	F11
West Highlands	WA	342	H10
West Kelso	WA	303	B7
West Klamath	OR	235	B4
West Lake	OR	188	B4
Westlake	OR	214	A5
Westlake	WA	242	C3
Westland	OR	129	A1
❖ WEST LINN	OR	199	C4
Westma	ID	147	C1
Westmond	ID	244	A5
❖ WESTON	OR	129	C1
Weston	WA	111	A3
West Park	WA	270	D11
West Pastco	WA	342	E5
Westport	OR	117	B3
❖ WESTPORT	WA	298	G13
West Portland Park	OR	320	A2
❖ WEST RICHLAND	WA	341	A3
West Salem	OR	322	F12
West Seattle	WA	280	D4
West Side	OR	152	A2
West Slope	OR	199	B2
Westsound	WA	101	C2
West Spokane	WA	348	F8
West Stayton	OR	133	C1
West Union	OR	192	A7
West Valley	WA	243	A6
West Wenatchee	WA	238	D4
Westwood	WA	285	G2
West Woodbury	OR	205	B1
Wetico	WA	118	A1
Wetmore	OR	128	B3
Wetzels Corner	OR	200	B3
Wheatland	OR	204	D3
❖ WHEELER	OR	191	B4
Wheeler Heights	OR	191	B4
Whelan	WA	249	B4
Whetstone	OR	122	A2
Whiskey Hill	OR	205	C1
❖ WHISTLER	BC	93	C1
Whitstran	WA	120	C3
White	WA	171	D7
❖ WHITE BIRD	ID	131	C1
White Center	WA	285	G4
White City	OR	230	D6
Whites	WA	179	C6
❖ WHITE SALMON	WA	195	D4
Whiteson	OR	204	B1
White Swan	WA	119	C2
Whitewater	OR	126	B3
Whitlow	WA	249	B5
Whitman	WA	121	A3
Whitney	OR	138	A1
Whitney	WA	344	J12
Whittier	WA	111	A3
Whonnock	BC	94	B3
Wickersham	WA	161	C3
Wilbur	OR	221	C2
❖ WILBUR	WA	113	B1
Wilburton	WA	175	C2
Wilcox	OR	127	C3
Wildcat Lake	WA	174	A2
❖ WILDER	ID	147	A1
Wilderness	WA	176	A7
Wilderville	OR	229	A7
Wildwood	WA	187	A4
Wildwood Heights	BC	92	B1
Wiley City	WA	243	A7
Wilhoit Springs	OR	126	A3
Wilkes	OR	200	A1
Wilkes East	OR	200	A1
❖ WILKESON	WA	182	D5
Wilkins	OR	210	B6
Willada	WA	114	B3
Willamette	OR	199	C5
Willamette City	OR	142	A1
❖ WILLAMINA	OR	125	A3
Willapa	WA	117	A1
Willard	WA	195	B3
Williams	OR	149	B2
Willow Creek	OR	138	C2
Willow Ranch	CA	152	A3
Willows	WA	263	A8
Wilson	OR	316	D5
Wilson	WA	118	A2
Wilson Corner	OR	200	B3
❖ WILSON CREEK	WA	113	A2
❖ WILSONVILLE	OR	199	B5
Wimer	OR	229	D4
Winant	OR	206	B5
Winberry	OR	133	C3
Winchester	ID	123	B2
Winchester	OR	221	C3
Winchester	WA	112	C3
Winchester Bay	OR	218	C2
Windermere	WA	275	F5
Windmaster Corner	OR	195	C5
Winema Beach	OR	203	B1
Wingville	OR	130	B3
Winlock	OR	128	B3
❖ WINLOCK	WA	187	C3
Winona	OR	229	C3
Winona	OR	322	E13
Winona	WA	122	B1
Winslow	WA	271	H2
❖ WINSTON	OR	221	B6
Winston	WA	118	A2
Winterville	OR	220	B6
❖ WINTHROP	WA	104	A2
Winton	WA	111	C1
Wishkah	WA	178	B6
Wishram	WA	127	B1
Wishram Heights	WA	127	B1
Witch Hazel	OR	198	D2
Withrow	WA	112	B2
Wocus	OR	338	B1
Wolf Creek	OR	229	B1
Wolf Lodge	ID	248	C1
Wollochet	WA	181	C2
Wonder	OR	149	A1
❖ WOODBURN	OR	205	B1
Woodfibre	BC	93	C2
❖ WOODINVILLE	WA	171	D6
Woodland	ID	131	C3
❖ WOODLAND	WA	189	D7
Woodland Beach	WA	167	D4
Woodland Park	OR	200	A1
Woodland Park	OR	315	J4
Woodland Park	WA	118	A3
Woodlawn	OR	309	H5
Woodmans	WA	170	A1
Woodmont	WA	175	B7
Woodruff	WA	110	C1
Woodruff Mill	WA	196	D2
Woods	OR	197	A7
Woodson	OR	117	B3
Woodstock	OR	318	B4
❖ WOOD VILLAGE	OR	200	B1
❖ WOODWAY	WA	171	A6
Worden	OR	235	B7
❖ WORLEY	ID	115	A2
Wren	OR	133	A1
Wrentham	OR	127	B2
Wye	BC	256	F4
Wyeth	OR	195	A5
Wymer	WA	243	C2
Wynaco	WA	182	C1
Y			
❖ YACHATS	OR	209	A3
❖ YACOLT	WA	193	B1
Yaculta	BC	92	A1
❖ YAKIMA	WA	243	B6
Yale	BC	95	A2
Yale	WA	118	A3
❖ YAMHILL	OR	198	B5
Yamsay	OR	142	C3
Yankton	OR	192	A1
Yaquina	OR	206	B5
❖ YARROW POINT	WA	175	C1
❖ YELM	WA	118	A1
Yennadon	BC	157	D5
Yeomalt	WA	174	D2
Yoakum	OR	129	A1
Yoder	OR	205	D2
Yokeko Point	WA	160	C7
Yoman	WA	181	A3
Yoman Dock	WA	181	B4
❖ YONCALLA	OR	219	A4
Youbou	BC	100	C1
Young	OR	133	C1
❖ YREKA	CA	149	C3
Z			
Zena	OR	204	C4
Zenith	WA	290	A7
Zigzag	OR	201	C5
❖ ZILLAH	WA	120	A2
Zumwalt	OR	131	A1
Zumwalt	WA	122	B2

❖ -Indicates City, District or Township

HIGHWAY PATROL

British Columbia
Washington State   In case of emergency,
Oregon State   call 911
Idaho State

Road Conditions

British Columbia   British Columbia Ministry of Transportation and Highways: (205) 387-7788
            www.th.gov.bc.ca/bchighways/
Washington State   Washington State Department of Transportation: (888) 766-4636
         http://traffic.wsdot.wa.gov/
Oregon State   Salem Online: (503) 976-7277
            www.oregonlink.com/weather/index.html
Idaho State   Weather Net: (208) 336-6600
            www.state.id.us/itd/rdreport.htm

Department of Transportation

British Columbia   BC Ministry of Transportation & Highways: (250) 387-7788
            www.th.gov.bc.ca/bchighways/
Washington State   Washington State Department of Transportation: (360) 709-5520
         www.wsdot.wa.gov/
Oregon State   Oregon Department of Transportation: (888) ASK-ODOT
            www.odot.state.or.us
Idaho State   Idaho State Department of Transportation: (208) 334-8000
            www.state.id.us/itd/itdhmpg.htm

Ferry Crossing

British Columbia   BC Ferries' Corporate Marketing Group: (250) 381-1401
            www.bcferries.bc.ca/ferries
Washington State   Washington State Department of Transportation: (360) 709-5520
            www.wsdot.wa.gov/ferries

Crossing the Border

British Columbia   Revenue Canada: (604) 666-0545
            http://www.rc.gc.ca/
Washington State   U.S. Customs: (206) 553-0770
            www.customs.ustreas.gov/

Weather Conditions

British Columbia   www.weather.com/weather/int/regions/north_america.html#Canada
Washington State   www.weather.com/weather/us/states/Washington.html
Oregon State   www.weather.com/weather/us/states/Oregon.html
Idaho State   www.weather.com/weather/us/states/Idaho.html

Visitor's Information

British Columbia   British Columbia Visitor's Information: (888) 475-3396
            www.th.gov.bc.ca/tourismhome.html
Washington State   Washington State Tourism Division Info Package: (800) 544-1800
         www.tourism.wa.gov/011.htm
Oregon State   Oregon Association of Convention & Visitors Bureau: (541) 994-2164
            www.oregonlink.com/scva/staff.html
Idaho State   Idaho Department of Commerce: (208) 334-2631
            www.idoc.state.id.us/

PNW

INTRO

[handwritten in margin: Wanapum State Park $20 for RV Site no tent sites]

Z

CAMPING & LODGING INFORMATION

British Columbia
Travel Canada
www.Travelcanada.ca/index-0.html

Washington State
Washington State Online Travel Information
→ www.tourism.wa.gov

Oregon State
Oregon Economic Developement Dept. Tourism Commission: (503) 986-0000
www.state.or.us/quality-.htm

Idaho State
Discover Idaho
www.visitid.org/

NATIONAL & STATE PARK INFORMATION

British Columbia
British Columbia Ministry of Environment Lands & Parks: (800) 689-9025
www.env.gov.bc.ca/bcparks/reserv/campers.htm

Washington State
Washington State Parks & Recreation Commission
→ www.parks.wa.gov

Oregon State
Oregon Online Highways
www.ohwy.com/or/oloprd.htm

Idaho State
Idaho State Parks
http://www.idoc.state.id.us/Lasso/InfoNet/questframe.html

Selected National & State Parks Including Recreation Areas, Forests, and National Monuments

Prov	Park	Page & Grid	Camping	Trailer / RV	Picnicking	Swimming	Fishing	Hiking	Boating	Beach
BC	**National Parks**									
	Pacific Rim National Park	100, A1	●	◐	●	●	◐	●	◐	●
	Provincial Parks									
	Carmanah Pacific Provincial Park	92, B2	●		●			●		
	Cathedral Provincial Park	104, A1	●	◐	●		◐	●		
	Cultus Lake Provincial Park	102, C1	●	◐	●	●	◐	●	◐	●
	Desolation Sound Provincial Marine Park	92, B1	●			●	◐	●		
	Garibaldi Provincial Park	94, A1	●		●		◐	●		
	Golden Ears Provincial Park	94, B2	●	◐	●	●	◐	●	●	●
	Manning Provincial Park	95, C3	●	◐	●	●	◐	●	●	●
	Skagit Valley Provincial Park	103, B1	●	◐	●	●	◐	●	●	●
	Strathcona Provincial Park	92, A2	●	◐	●	●	◐	●	◐	●
State	**Park**									
WA	**National Parks**									
	Mount Rainier National Park	118, C1	●	◐	●		◐	●	◐	
	North Cascades National Park	103, A1	●	◐	●		◐	●	◐	
	Olympic National Park	109, B1	●	◐	●		◐	●	◐	
	National / State Forests									
	Colville National Forest	105, C2	●	◐	●	●	●	●	●	●
	Gifford Pinchot National Forest	118, C2	●	◐	●	●	●	●	●	●
	Kaniksu National Forest	106, C2	●	◐	●	●	●	●	●	●
	Mount Baker National Forest	103, A2	●	◐	●	●	●	●	●	●
	Mount Baker-Snoqualmie National Forest	111, A2	●	◐	●	●	●	●	●	●
	Okanogan National Forest	104, B2	●	◐	●	●	●	●	●	●
	Olympic National Forest	109, B2	●	◐	●	●	●	●	●	●
	Wenatchee National Forest	112, A1	●	◐	●	●	●	●	●	●
	Parks / Recreation Areas / Monuments									
	Beacon Rock State Park	194, B6	●	◐	●		◐		◐	
	Birch Bay State Park	158, B5	●	◐	●		◐			●
	Bogachiel State Park	169, D3	●	◐	●		◐			
	Brooks Memorial State Park	119, C3	●	◐	●		◐			
	Columbia River Gorge National Scenic Area	200, C1	●	◐	●		◐		●	◐
	Coulee Dam National Recreation Area	237, D3	●	◐	●	◐	●	●	●	●
	Fort Canby State Park	186, A6	●	◐	●		◐		●	●
	Fort Flagler State Park	167, B6	●	◐	●		◐		●	●
	Fort Worden State Park	167, A6	●	◐	●		◐		●	●
	Kanaskat-Palmer State Park	110, C3	●	◐	●		◐		●	
	Lake Chelan National Recreation Area	103, C3	●	◐	●	●	◐	●	●	●
	Larrabee State Park	160, D2	●	◐	●		◐		●	●
	Millersylvania State Park	184, C2	●	◐	●	●	◐			
	Mount Saint Helens National Volcanic Monument	190, B1			●			●		
	Mount Spokane State Park	114, C1	●		●			●		
	Ocean City State Park	177, B6	●	◐	●		◐			●
	Pacific Beach State Park	177, B2	●	◐	●		◐			●
	Potholes State Park	242, C6	●	◐	●		◐		◐	◐
	Ross Lake National Recreation Area	103, B1	●	◐	●		◐	●	●	
	Schafer State Park	179, A5	●	◐	●		◐			●
	Seaquest State Park	187, D7	●	◐	●		◐			
	Sequim Bay State Park	166, C7	●	◐	●		◐		◐	●

Selected National & State Parks Including Recreation Areas, Forests, and National Monuments

Q

State	Park	Page & Grid	Camping	Trailer / RV	Picnicking	Swimming	Fishing	Hiking	Boating	Beach
WA	**Parks/Recreation Areas/Monuments cont...**									
	Sun Lakes State Park	112, C2	●	○	●	●	○		●	
	Twanoh State Park	173, C7	●	○	●	●	○		●	●
	Wenberg State Park	168, B6	●	○	●		○		●	●
	Yakima Sportsman State Park	243, C7	●	○	●		○			●
OR	**National Parks**									
	Crater Lake National Park	227, C3	●	○	●			●		
	National/State Forests									
	Clatsop State Forest	191, D2	●	○	●	●	●	●	●	●
	Deschutes National Forest	143, A1	●	○	●	●	●	●	●	●
	Elliott State Forest	140, C1	●	○	●	●	●	●	●	●
	Fremont National Forest	151, C2	●	○	●	●	●	●	●	●
	Malheur National Forest	137, B1	●	○	●	●	●	●	●	●
	McDonald State Forest	207, A5	●	○	●	●	●	●	●	●
	Mount Hood National Forest	202, B2	●	○	●	●	●	●	●	●
	Ochoco National Forest	136, B2	●	○	●	●	●	●	●	●
	Rogue River National Forest	149, B3	●	○	●	●	●	●	●	●
	Santiam State Forest	134, A1	●	○	●	●	●	●	●	●
	Siskiyou National Forest	148, B2	●	○	●	●	●	●	●	●
	Siuslaw National Forest	132, C2	●	○	●	●	●	●	●	●
	Tillamook State Forest	125, A1	●	○	●	●	●	●	●	●
	Umatilla National Forest	129, B3	●	○	●	●	●	●	●	●
	Umpqua National Forest	142, A2	●	○	●	●	●	●	●	●
	Wallowa-Whitman National Forest	138, A1	●	○	●	●	●	●	●	●
	Willamette National Forest	134, B1	●	○	●	●	●	●	●	●
	Winema National Forest	142, C2	●	○	●	●	●	●	●	●
	Parks/Recreation Areas/Monuments									
	Beachside State Park	328, A11	●	○	●		●			
	Beverly Beach State Park	206, B2	●	○	●		●	●		
	Bullards Beach State Park	220, B5	●	○	●		●	●	●	
	Cape Blanco State Park	224, A4	●	○	●		●	●		●
	Cape Lookout State Park	197, A3	●	○	●		●	●		●
	Champoeg State Park	199, A6	●	○	●		●	●	●	
	Collier Memorial State Park	231, D2	●	○	●		●	●		
	Columbia River Gorge National Scenic Area	200, C1	●	○	●		●	●	●	
	Detroit Lake State Park	134, B1	●	○	●	●	●		●	●
	Emigrant Lake County Recreation Area	243, D4								
	Fort Stevens State Park	188, B1	●	○	●	●	●	●	●	●
	Harris Beach State Park	232, C6	●	○	●		●	●		●
	Hells Canyon National Recreation Area	131, B1	●	○	●		●	●	●	●
	Humbug Mountain State Park	224, B7	●	○	●		●	●		●
	Jessie M Honeyman Memorial State Park	214, B4	●	○	●	●	●	●	●	●
	John Day Fossil Beds National Monument	136, C1						●		
	Joseph Stewart State Park	149, C1	●	○	●		●	●	●	
	Lake Owyhee State Park	147, A1	●	○	●		●		●	
	Memaloose State Park	196, A5	●	○						
	Milo McIver State Park	200, B6	●	○	●		●	●	●	
	Nehalem Bay State Park	191, B5	●	○	●		●		●	●
	Newberry National Volcanic Monument	143, B1						●		
	Oregon Cascades Recreation Area	142, B1	●	○	●	●	●	●	●	●
	Oregon Caves National Monument	149, D5			●			●		
	Oregon Dunes National Recreation Area	214, A5	●		●		●	●		●
	Silver Falls State Park	205, D7	●	○	●	●		●		
	South Beach State Park	206, B5	●	○	●		●	●		●
	Sunset Bay State Park	220, B1	●	○	●	●	●	●		●
	The Cove Palisades State Park	208, A6	●	○	●	●	●	●	●	
	Umpqua Lighthouse State Park	218, B2	●	○	●		●	●	●	●
	Valley of the Rogue State Park	229, D6	●	○	●		●	●	●	
	Viento State Park	195, B5	●	○	●					
	Wallowa Lake State Park	130, C2	●	○	●		●	●	●	●
	William M Tugman State Park	218, C3	●	○	●	●	●		●	●
ID	**National/State Forest**									
	Coeur d'Alene National Forest	115, B1	●	○	●	●	●	●	●	●
	Kaniksu National Forest	106, C2	●	○	●	●	●	●	●	●
	Nez Perce	131, C1	●	○	●	●	●	●	●	●
	Payette National Forest	131, B3	●	○	●	●	●	●	●	●
	Saint Joe National Forest	115, B3	●	○	●	●	●	●	●	●
	Parks/Recreation Areas/Monuments									
	Farragut State Park	245, C1	●	○	●	●	●	●	●	
	Heyburn State Park	248, A6	●	○	●	●	●	●	●	
CA	**National Parks**									
	Redwood National Park	148, B3	●	○	●		●	●		●
	National/State Forests									
	Klamath National Forest	149, B3	●	○	●	●	●	●	●	●
	Modoc National Forest	151, B3	●	○	●	●	●	●	●	●
	Siskiyou National Forest	148, B2	●	○	●	●	●	●	●	●
	Six River National Forest	148, C3	●	○	●	●	●	●	●	●
	Parks/Recreation Areas/Monuments									
	Del Norte Coast Redwoods State Park	148, B3	●	○	●		●	●		●
	Lava Beds National Monument	151, A3	●		●			●		
	Smith River National Recreation Area	148, C3	●		●		●	●	●	
NV	**National/State Forests**									
	Humboldt National Forest	154, C3	●				●	●	●	
MT	**National/State Forests**									
	Kootenai National Forest	107, C1	●	○	●		●	●	●	

COPYRIGHT 1999

Thomas Bros. Maps®

PNW

INTRO

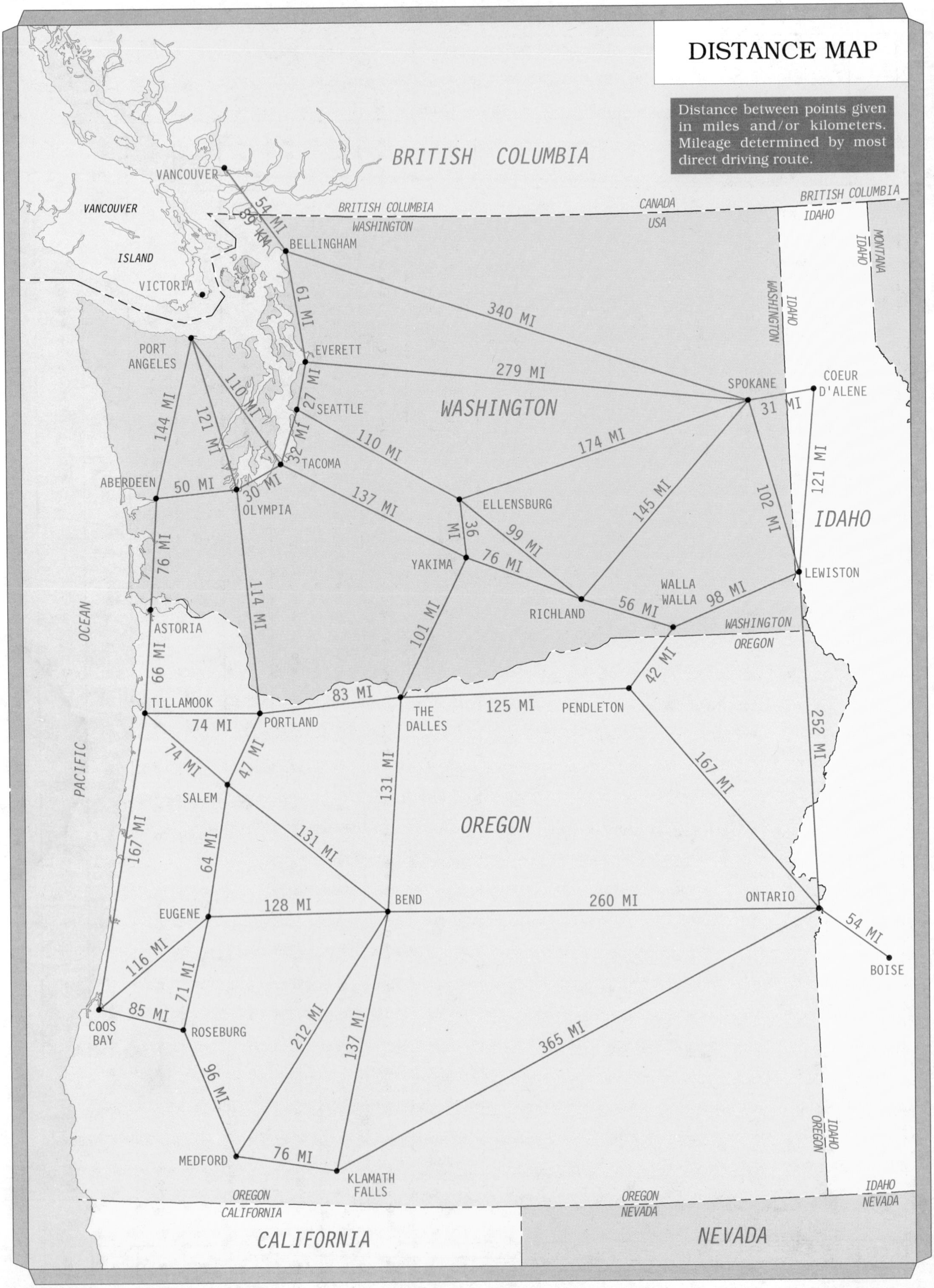

R

DISTANCE MAP

Distance between points given in miles and/or kilometers. Mileage determined by most direct driving route.

BRITISH COLUMBIA

VANCOUVER ISLAND

VANCOUVER

VICTORIA

BRITISH COLUMBIA
WASHINGTON

CANADA
USA

BRITISH COLUMBIA
IDAHO

MONTANA
IDAHO

54 MI

89 KM

BELLINGHAM

61 MI

340 MI

EVERETT

279 MI

SPOKANE

COEUR D'ALENE

31 MI

27 MI

PORT ANGELES

144 MI

121 MI

110 MI

32 MI

SEATTLE

110 MI

WASHINGTON

174 MI

145 MI

102 MI

121 MI

IDAHO

ABERDEEN

50 MI

30 MI

TACOMA

137 MI

ELLENSBURG

99 MI

OLYMPIA

36 MI

YAKIMA

76 MI

RICHLAND

WALLA WALLA

56 MI

98 MI

LEWISTON

76 MI

114 MI

OCEAN

101 MI

WASHINGTON
OREGON

ASTORIA

66 MI

83 MI

THE DALLES

125 MI

PENDLETON

42 MI

252 MI

TILLAMOOK

74 MI

PORTLAND

131 MI

167 MI

PACIFIC

74 MI

47 MI

SALEM

131 MI

OREGON

167 MI

64 MI

EUGENE

128 MI

BEND

260 MI

ONTARIO

54 MI

116 MI

71 MI

212 MI

137 MI

365 MI

BOISE

85 MI

COOS BAY

ROSEBURG

96 MI

MEDFORD

76 MI

KLAMATH FALLS

IDAHO
OREGON

OREGON
CALIFORNIA

OREGON
NEVADA

IDAHO
NEVADA

CALIFORNIA

NEVADA

COPYRIGHT 1999 Thomas Bros. Maps ®

Pacific Northwest Mileage Chart

	Astoria, Or	Bellingham, Wa	Bend, Or	Boise, Id	Coos Bay, Or	Corvallis, Or	Ellensburg, Wa	Eugene, Or	Grants Pass, Or	Hood River, Or	Medford, Or	Moses Lake, Wa	Newport, Or	Oak Harbor, Wa	Olympia, Wa	Pasco, Wa	Port Angeles, Wa	Portland, Or	Prosser, Wa	Salem, Or	Sea-Tac Airport, Wa	Seattle, Wa	Spokane, Wa	The Dalles, Or	Vancouver, BC	Victoria, BC	Yakima, Wa
Aberdeen, Wa	76	198	303	573	309	224	198	253	388	205	416	266	211	142	50	290	144	143	253	190	94	107	368	226	248	146	203
Albany, Or	158	330	123	437	147	11	293	44	179	131	207	349	65	330	183	287	300	69	268	24	227	241	420	152	382	302	257
Anacortes, Wa	251	39	410	559	462	331	179	360	495	312	523	239	364	21	137	286	87	250	261	297	90	78	329	333	92	25	211
Ashland, Or	374	546	200	483	182	222	468	178	41	346	12	534	252	546	399	461	516	285	447	240	443	457	597	331	598	518	432
Astoria, Or		262	255	518	233	151	266	199	334	154	362	338	135	220	114	305	212	95	267	136	163	176	413	175	319	214	217
Baker City, Or	396	451	247	126	466	356	270	356	488	242	459	230	393	469	408	159	454	304	197	350	383	389	296	221	521	456	247
Bellingham, Wa	262		421	570	473	342	189	371	506	323	534	249	375	50	148	297	116	261	272	308	101	89	340	344	54	64	222
Bend, Or	255	421		314	237	127	281	128	241	152	212	323	183	421	274	252	391	160	276	131	318	332	423	131	473	393	245
Boise, Id	518	570	314		552	442	384	442	524	366	496	350	478	570	521	279	643	430	313	446	492	491	379	347	623	645	361
Bremerton, Wa	150	116	329	533	381	250	110	279	414	231	442	179	283	73	59	218	79	169	193	216	13	1	280	252	142	81	143
Burns, Or	385	547	130	184	367	257	370	259	339	282	311	330	310	551	404	259	554	290	297	261	448	462	395	260	603	556	347
Chehalis, Wa	102	175	247	507	299	168	176	197	332	149	360	245	201	171	29	234	145	87	197	154	73	87	343	170	228	147	147
Cheney, Wa	396	341	406	370	541	415	161	447	647	279	618	92	448	341	307	123	342	338	158	381	268	267	17	249	395	269	183
Coeur d'Alene, Id	444	371	454	427	589	463	205	495	695	327	667	136	496	371	351	167	385	382	202	429	312	311	31	297	423	313	227
Coos Bay, Or	233	473	237	552		135	431	116	142	273	170	488	98	473	326	444	443	212	407	177	370	384	558	294	558	445	396
Corvallis, Or	151	342	127	442	135		305	40	182	142	210	361	54	342	195	299	312	81	280	35	239	254	432	163	394	314	269
Crater Lake, Or	332	504	98	412	177	173	379	133	86	250	71	421	225	504	357	350	474	243	374	197	401	415	521	229	556	476	343
Ellensburg, Wa	266	189	281	384	431	305		330	522	153	493	72	338	188	149	111	187	224	86	271	111	110	174	137	242	112	36
Eugene, Or	199	371	128	442	116	40	330		138	172	166	387	92	371	224	328	341	110	306	64	268	282	464	193	423	343	295
Everett, Wa	204	61	360	509	412	281	128	310	445	262	473	188	314	61	87	236	80	200	211	247	40	27	279	283	114	29	161
Florence, Or	184	425	190	504	48	83	391	61	162	224	190	448	50	432	285	389	402	164	367	118	329	343	525	245	484	404	356
Forks, Wa	185	93	411	681	418	332	241	361	496	313	524	310	320	122	158	406	56	251	368	298	144	132	408	334	226	58	319
Gold Beach, Or	311	551	316	630	78	213	597	194	134	468	162	639	179	551	404	568	521	290	592	555	448	462	739	373	603	523	561
Grand Coulee, Wa	366	262	384	424	547	416	123	446	580	274	596	75	449	265	269	145	286	340	166	382	230	226	87	253	315	228	153
Grants Pass, Or	334	506	241	524	142	182	522	138		307	29	564	212	506	359	493	476	245	517	199	403	417	664	327	558	478	486
Hillsboro, Or	87	278	176	445	206	78	241	117	252	79	280	297	106	278	131	235	248	17	216	50	175	189	368	101	330	250	205
Hood River, Or	154	323	152	366	273	142	153	172	307		335	209	174	323	176	165	293	62	128	108	220	234	296	21	375	295	117
Kennewick, Wa	301	295	248	275	440	295	109	324	489	161	460	77	328	293	246	4	293	212	36	261	217	216	142	141	348	295	86
Klamath Falls, Or	364	540	137	419	245	213	418	173	104	289	76	460	265	540	393	389	510	279	413	234	437	451	560	268	592	512	382
La Grande, Or	352	401	271	169	471	340	226	369	504	198	484	186	372	412	363	115	410	259	153	306	334	333	252	177	465	412	203
Lake Oswego, Or	102	269	169	435	216	78	232	108	239	70	271	288	110	269	122	226	239	8	207	41	166	180	359	89	321	241	196
Lewiston, Id	437	391	379	277	557	425	202	455	590	289	591	159	226	390	377	128	389	362	176	492	313	312	102	263	444	314	216
Long Beach, Wa	17	260	272	534	250	168	260	216	351	171	379	329	152	214	112	323	206	126	294	153	157	170	431	192	313	208	244
Long View, Wa	50	214	210	478	260	131	200	160	295	112	323	265	162	214	67	246	184	48	217	97	112	126	362	133	267	186	167
McMinnville, Or	105	299	158	465	174	46	262	86	224	99	252	318	76	299	152	256	269	38	237	26	196	210	389	120	351	271	226
Medford, Or	362	534	212	496	170	210	493	166	29	335		535	240	534	387	464	504	273	488	227	431	445	635	343	586	506	457
Milton-Freewater, Or	329	350	271	242	449	317	164	347	482	181	483	123	118	350	301	55	350	237	90	284	271	270	166	155	402	352	140
Moses Lake, Wa	338	249	323	350	488	361	72	387	564	209	535		394	250	218	71	255	280	106	327	179	178	105	194	302	180	102
Mt. Rainier, Wa	142	156	302	431	352	188	106	252	38	187	415	172	254	156	66	158	164	140	120	189	55	68	266	171	209	166	70
Mount St. Helens, Wa	107	235	267	535	317	188	222	217	352	169	380	288	219	231	89	274	205	105	236	154	133	147	382	190	288	207	186
Mount Vernon, Wa	237	28	392	542	44	313	161	342	477	294	505	221	346	29	120	269	94	232	243	279	73	60	311	315	81	46	193
Newport, Or	135	375	183	478	98	54	338	92	212	174	240	394		375	228	332	345	114	313	83	272	286	465	196	427	347	302
Newport, Wa	482	387	435	436	627	482	221	511	676	348	647	153	515	387	367	183	401	439	218	448	328	327	47	313	439	329	243
Oak Harbor, Wa	220	50	421	570	473	342	188	371	506	323	534	250	375		148	297	66	261	272	308	101	89	340	324	104	46	222
Okanogan, Wa	386	204	445	461	596	469	158	495	686	317	657	112	502	207	271	182	272	377	203	435	231	221	145	301	256	221	190
Olympia, Wa	114	148	274	521	326	195	149	224	359	176	387	218	228	148		248	121	114	211	161	46	60	320	195	201	123	161
Ontario, Or	464	508	260	54	498	388	322	388	470	312	442	288	424	508	459	217	581	374	251	392	430	429	317	293	561	583	299
Pasco, Wa	305	297	252	279	444	299	111	328	493	165	464	71	332	297	248		295	218	38	265	219	218	136	130	350	297	88
Pendleton, Or	300	349	241	221	419	288	174	318	452	146	454	134	321	360	311	63	358	208	101	254	282	281	200	125	413	360	151
Port Angeles, Wa	212	116	391	643	443	312	187	341	476	293	504	255	345	66	121	295		231	257	278	90	77	354	311	168	2	282
Portland, Or	95	261	160	430	212	81	224	110	245	62	273	280	114	261	114	218	231		199	47	158	172	351	83	313	233	188
Portland Airport, Or	98	261	160	430	223	92	213	121	256	51	284	269	125	261	114	207	220	11	188	58	158	172	340	72	313	222	177
Prosser, Wa	267	272	276	313	407	280	86	306	517	128	488	106	313	272	211	38	257	199		246	186	182	171	116	324	259	50
Richland, Wa	323	285	255	285	447	302	99	331	496	168	467	80	335	285	236	9	286	219	28	268	207	206	145	136	338	288	76
Roseburg, Or	266	438	192	507	85	111	473	71	68	239	96	515	144	438	291	444	408	177	468	132	335	349	615	260	490	410	437
St. Helens, Or	66	236	189	453	240	109	222	139	274	91	302	287	143	236	89	268	206	29	239	76	134	148	384	108	289	208	189
Salem, Or	136	308	131	446	177	35	271	64	199	108	227	327	83	308	161	265	278	47	246		205	219	398	129	360	280	235
Sea-Tac Airport, Wa	163	101	318	492	370	239	111	268	403	220	431	179	272	101	46	219	90	158	186	205		13	281	238	154	15	136
Seattle, Wa	176	89	332	491	384	254	110	282	417	234	445	178	286	89	60	218	77	172	192	219	13		280	244	141	2	142
Shelton, Wa	112	167	292	543	344	113	174	242	377	194	405	240	246	170	22	269	98	132	232	179	68	82	342	215	223	100	182
Spokane, Wa	413	340	423	379	558	432	174	464	664	296	635	105	465	340	320	136	354	351	171	398	281	280		266	392	282	196
Tacoma, Wa	145	121	303	422	355	224	122	253	388	205	416	190	257	121	30	224	110	143	187	190	18	32	292	226	173	112	137
The Dalles, Or	175	344	131	347	294	163	137	193	327	21	343	194	196	324	195	130	311	83	116	129	238	244	266		376	313	101
Tillamook, Or	66	335	206	502	167	90	502	130	269	136	297	354	69	235	188	292	305	74	273	74	232	246	425	157	387	307	262
Vancouver, BC	319	54	473	623	558	394	242	423	558	375	586	302	427	104	210	350	168	313	324	360	154	141	392	376		69	274
Vancouver, Wa	90	253	168	438	220	89	216	118	253	70	281	272	122	253	106	210	222	8	191	55	150	164	343	91	305	224	180
Victoria, BC	214	64	393	645	445	314	112	343	478	295	506	180	347	46	123	297	2	233	259	280	15	2	282	313	43		290
Walla Walla, Wa	337	342	279	250	457	325	156	355	490	189	491	115	126	342	293	47	342	262	82	392	263	262	158	163	394	344	132
Wenatchee, Wa	304	184	353	407	504	377	75	403	594	225	565	66	410	184	188	134	198	296	126	343	148	138	164	209	236	140	108
Yakima, Wa	217	222	245	361	396	269	36	295	486	117	457	102	302	222	161	88	282	188	50	235	136	142	196	101	180	290	

Mileage requires Ferry use and does not include Ferry miles

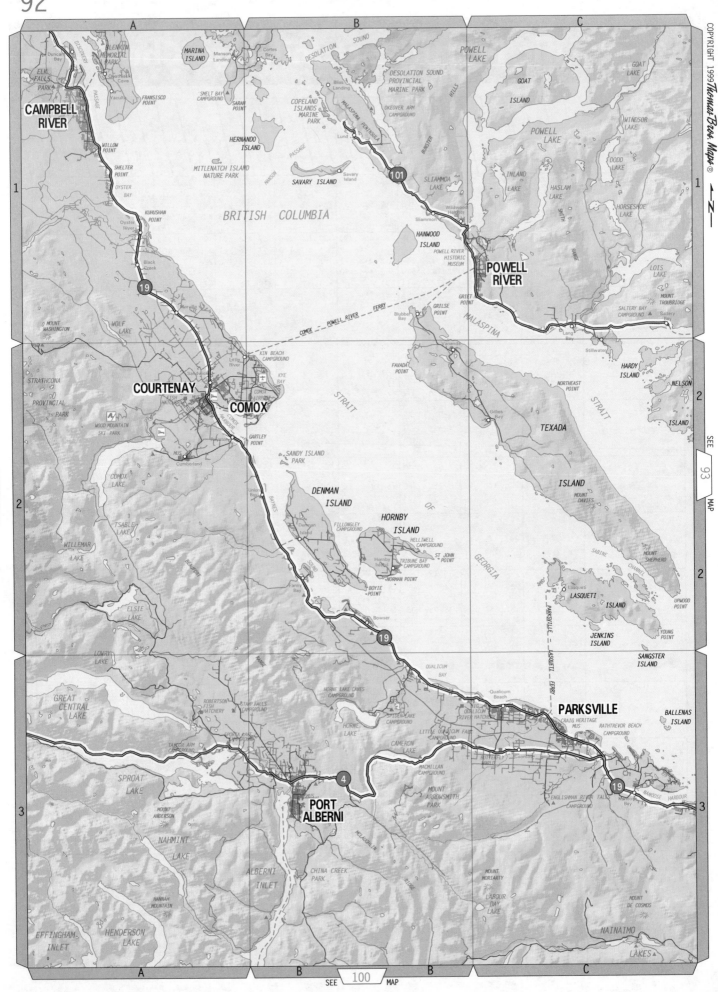

—N—

PNW

HWY

SEE 93 MAP

SEE 100 MAP

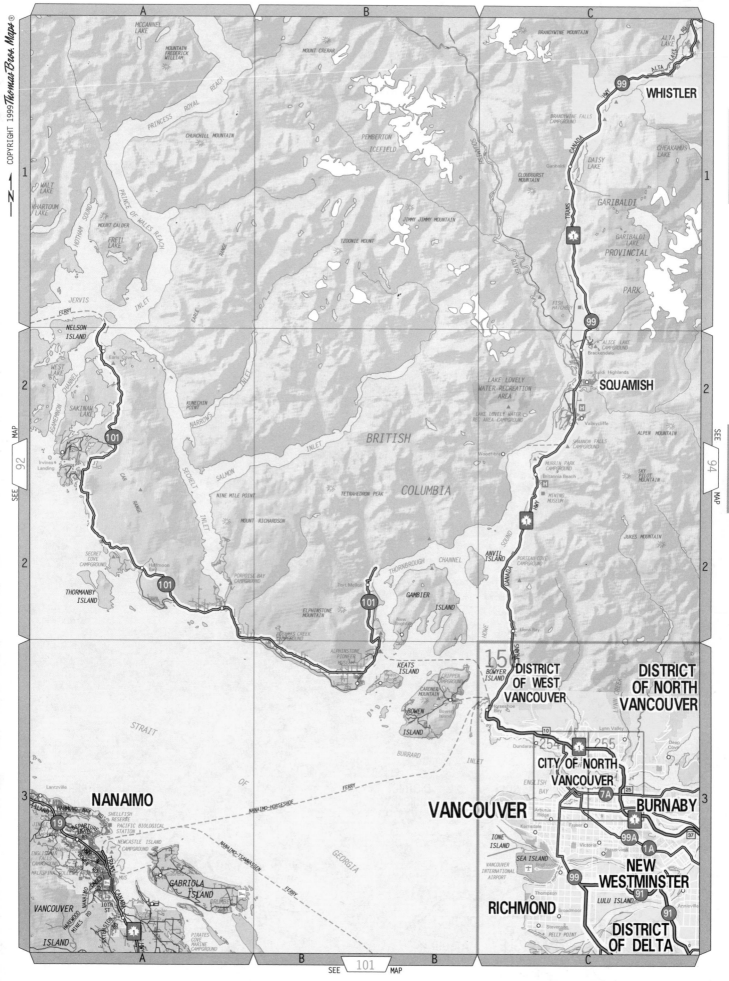

COPYRIGHT 1999 *Thomas Bros. Maps* ®

—N→

SEE 92 MAP

SEE 94 MAP

PNW

HWY

WHISTLER

SQUAMISH

BRITISH

COLUMBIA

GARIBALDI

GARIBALDI
LAKE
PROVINCIAL

PARK

PEMBERTON
ICEFIELD

MCCANNEL
LAKE

MOUNTAIN
FREDERICK
WILLIAM

MOUNT CRERAR

BRANDYWINE MOUNTAIN

ALTA
LAKE

BRANDYWINE FALLS
CAMPGROUND

CHEAKAMUS
LAKE

DAISY
LAKE

CLOUDBURST
MOUNTAIN

CHURCHILL MOUNTAIN

JIMMY JIMMY MOUNTAIN

FISH
HATCHERY

ALICE LAKE
CAMPGROUND

Brackendale

TZOONIE MOUNT

Garibaldi Highlands

ALPEN MOUNTAIN

Valleycliffe

SHANNON FALLS
CAMPGROUND

SKY
PILOT
MOUNTAIN

LAKE LOVELY
WATER RECREATION
AREA

LAKE LOVELY WATER
REC AREA CAMPGROUND

MURRIN PARK
CAMPGROUND

Woodfibre

Britannia Beach

MINING
MUSEUM

JUKES MOUNTAIN

NINE MILE POINT

TETRAHEDRON PEAK

MOUNT RICHARDSON

PRINCESS ROYAL REACH

PRINCE OF WALES REACH

HOTHAM SOUND

JERVIS

INLET

WALT
LAKE

KHARTOUM
LAKE

MOUNT CALDER

FREIL
LAKE

NELSON
ISLAND

FERRY

Earls Cove

WEST
LAKE

AGAMEMNON CHANNEL

SAKINAW
LAKE

KUNECHIN
POINT

NARROWS

EARLE

SECHELT

SALMON

INLET

INLET

101

Irvines
Landing

CARR
RANGE

Halfmoon
Bay

PORPOISE BAY
CAMPGROUND

SECRET
COVE
CAMPGROUND

THORMANBY
ISLAND

101

Sechelt

ANVIL
ISLAND

PORTEAU COVE
CAMPGROUND

HOWE

SOUND

TRANS CANADA HWY

THORNBROUGH CHANNEL

GAMBIER
ISLAND

Port Mellon

New
Brighton

Lions Bay

ELPHINSTONE
MOUNTAIN

ROBERTS CREEK
CAMPGROUND

101

Gibsons

ALPHINSTONE
PIONEER
MUSEUM

KEATS
ISLAND

GARDNER
MOUNTAIN

CRIPPEN
CAMPGROUND

BOWER
ISLAND

BOWEN
ISLAND

BOWYER
ISLAND

Horseshoe
Bay

DISTRICT
OF WEST
VANCOUVER

DISTRICT
OF NORTH
VANCOUVER

LYNN CREEK

Lynn Valley

Deep
Cove

Dundarave

CITY OF NORTH
VANCOUVER

BURNABY

ENGLISH
BAY

VANCOUVER

Arbutus
Ridge

Kitsilano

Fraser

NEW
WESTMINSTER

IONE
ISLAND

Victoria

Champlain

SEA ISLAND

Burkeville

VANCOUVER
INTERNATIONAL
AIRPORT

RICHMOND

Gabriola

Thompson

LULU ISLAND

Annieville

Broadmoor

DISTRICT
OF DELTA

Stevenson

PELLY POINT

STRAIT

OF

GEORGIA

NANAIMO

NANAIMO BAY

Lantzville

SHELLFISH
RESERVE

PACIFIC BIOLOGICAL
STATION

NEWCASTLE ISLAND
CAMPGROUND

FERRY

NANAIMO–HORSESHOE

FERRY

NANAIMO–TSAWWASSEN

BURRARD

INLET

19

DEPARTURE BAY RD

ENGLISH
FALLS
CAMPGROUND

MALASPINA
COLLEGE

TRANS CANADA HWY

GABRIOLA
ISLAND

Cedar

PIRATES
COVE MARINE
CAMPGROUND

VANCOUVER

ISLAND

10TH
ST

HAREWOOD

MINES RD

EXTENSION RD

1

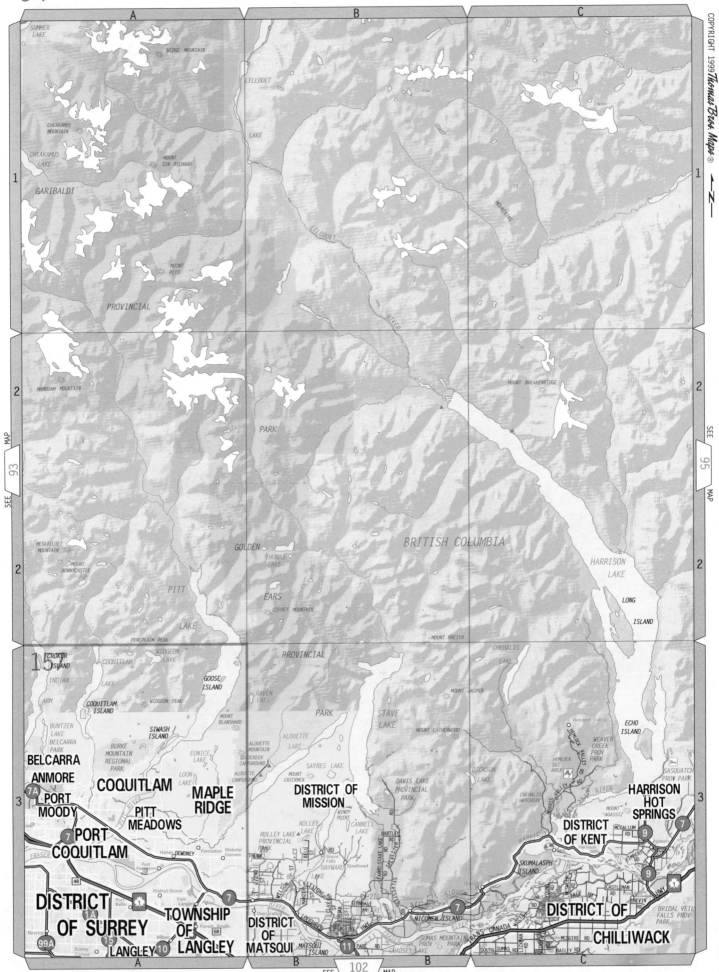

94

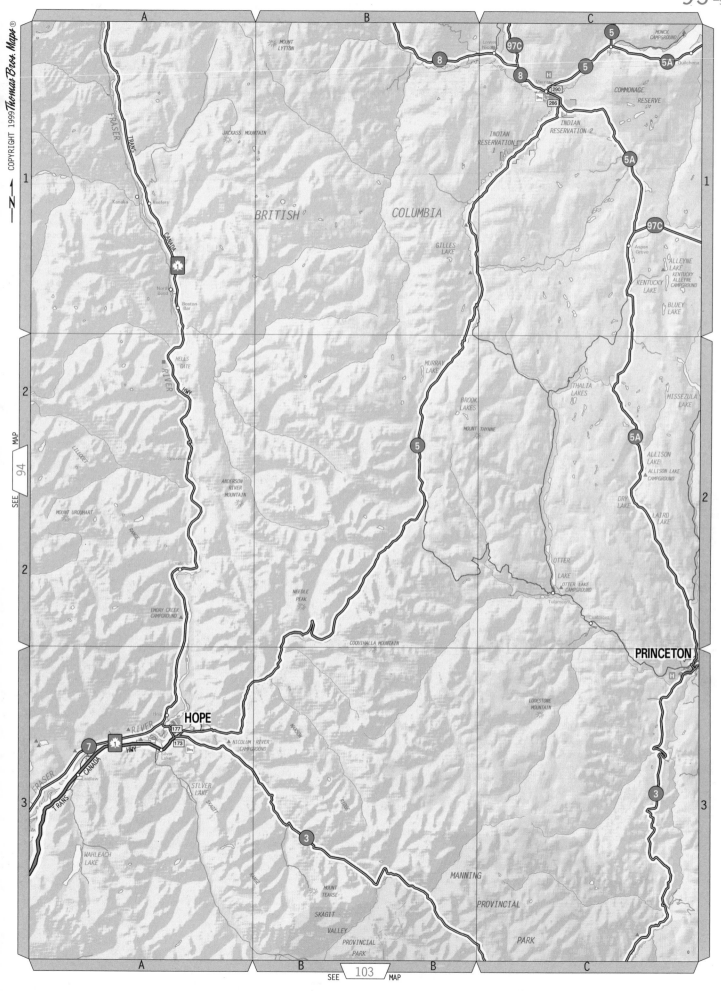

PNW

HWY

SEE 94 MAP

A   B   C

1

2

2

3

BRITISH   COLUMBIA

FRASER

TRANS

CANADA

Kanaka

Keefers

JACKASS MOUNTAIN

MOUNT LYTTON

8

8

97C

5

5

5A

Nicola

MONCK CAMPGROUND

5A Quilchena

H

290

286

COMMONAGE RESERVE

INDIAN RESERVATION 2

INDIAN RESERVATION 1

5A

97C

Aspen Grove

ALLEYNE LAKE

KENTUCKY ALLEYNE CAMPGROUND

KENTUCKY LAKE

BLUEY LAKE

North Bend

Boston Bar

HELLS GATE

RIVER

HWY

GILLES LAKE

MURRAY LAKE

BROOK LAKES

MOUNT THYNNE

5

THALIA LAKES

MISSEZULA LAKE

5A

ALLISON LAKE

ALLISON LAKE CAMPGROUND

DRY LAKE

LAIRD LAKE

LILLOOET

Spuzzum

ANDERSON RIVER MOUNTAIN

MOUNT URQUHART

RANGE

Yale

EMORY CREEK CAMPGROUND

NEEDLE PEAK

COQUIHALLA MOUNTAIN

OTTER LAKE

OTTER LAKE CAMPGROUND

Tulameen

Coalmont

PRINCETON

H

RIVER

TRANS

CANADA

7

1

HWY

Laidlaw

Hope

HOPE

177

173

Silver Lake

NICOLUM RIVER CAMPGROUND

WAHLEACH LAKE

SILVER LAKE

SKAGIT

RIVER

RANGE

MOUNT TEARSE

SKAGIT VALLEY PROVINCIAL PARK

3

MANSON

RIDGE

LODESTONE MOUNTAIN

MANNING

PROVINCIAL

PARK

3

3

A   B   B   C

SEE 103 MAP

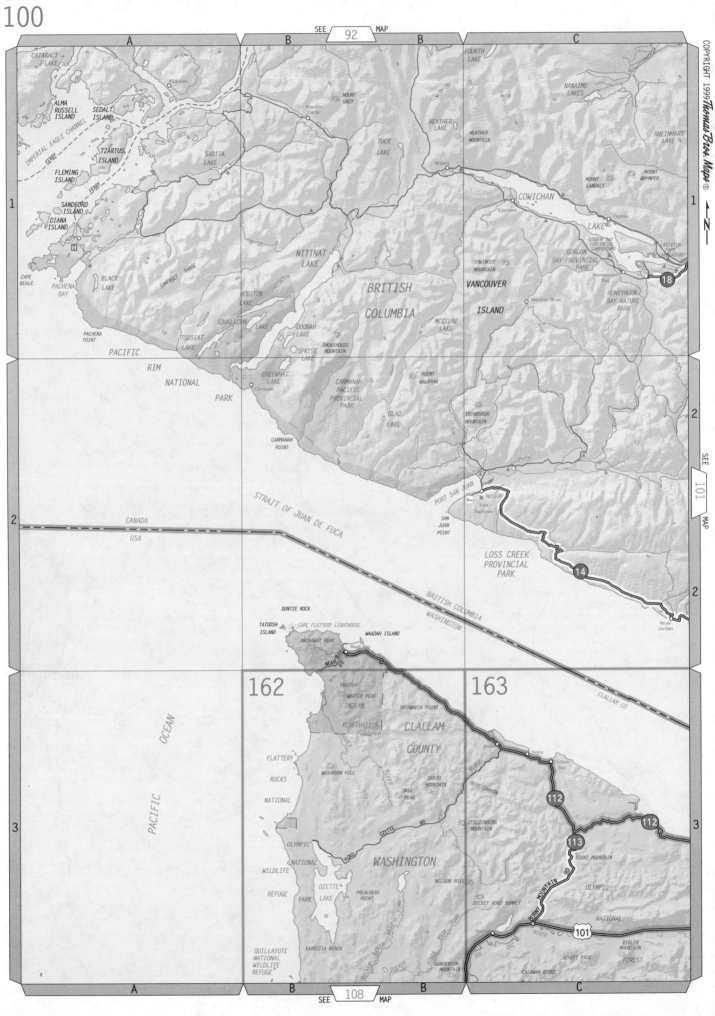

PNW

HWY

SEE 92 MAP

A · B · B · C

CATARACT
LAKE
Kildonan
MOUNT GREY
Franklin Camp
FOURTH LAKE
NANAIMO LAKES
RHEINHART LAKE

ALMA RUSSELL ISLAND
SEDALT ISLAND
IMPERIAL EAGLE CHANNEL
FERRY
TZARTUS ISLAND
FLEMING ISLAND
FERRY
SANDFORD ISLAND
DIANA ISLAND
Bamfield
H

SARITA LAKE
SOMERSET RANGE

TUCK LAKE
HEATHER LAKE
HEATHER MOUNTAIN
Nitinat

MOUNT LANDALT
MOUNT WHYMPER

COWICHAN
Caycuse
Youbou
LAKE
GORDON BAY PROVINCIAL CAMPGROUND
LAKEVIEW PARK CAMPGROUND

1

CAPE BEALE
PACHENA BAY
BLACK LAKE
PACHENA POINT

NITINAT LAKE
HOBITON LAKE
SQUALICUM LAKE
TSUSIAT LAKE
DOOBAH LAKE
SPRISE LAKE
SMOKEHOUSE MOUNTAIN

BRITISH
COLUMBIA

TONINCUT MOUNTAIN

VANCOUVER
ISLAND
MCCLURE LAKE
Gordon River

GORDON BAY PROVINCIAL PARK
Honeymoon Bay
HONEYMOON BAY NATURE PARK

18

PACIFIC
RIM
NATIONAL
PARK

CHEEWHAT LAKE
Clo-oose
CARMANAH POINT

CARMANAH PACIFIC PROVINCIAL PARK
GLAD LAKE

MOUNT WALBRAN

EDINBURGH MOUNTAIN

2

PORT SAN JUAN
Port Renfrew
MUSEUM
SAN JUAN POINT

LOSS CREEK PROVINCIAL PARK

14

SEE 101 MAP

CANADA
USA

STRAIT OF JUAN DE FUCA

BRITISH COLUMBIA
WASHINGTON

River Jordan

2

DUNTZE ROCK
TATOOSH ISLAND
CAPE FLATTERY LIGHTHOUSE
ARCHAWAT PEAK
WAADAH ISLAND
Neah Bay
NEAH BAY RD

CLALLAM CO

162

163

PACIFIC
OCEAN

FLATTERY
ROCKS
NATIONAL

MAKAH WAATCH PEAK
INDIAN
RESERVATION

WASHBURN HILL

SHIPWRECK POINT

CLALLAM
COUNTY

Hoko
Sekiu
Clallam Bay

SEKIU RIVER
SNAG PEAK
SEKIU MOUNTAIN
BLUE CANYON

112

112

3

OZETTE RD
HOKO
OLYMPIC
NATIONAL
WILDLIFE
REFUGE
PARK
OZETTE LAKE
PREACHERS POINT

WASHINGTON
HOKO RIVER
OZETTE RD

STOLZENBERG MOUNTAIN
NELSON HILLS
DICKEY HORD SUMMIT

113

BURNT MOUNTAIN

BURNT MOUNTAIN RD

OLYMPIC
NATIONAL

3

QUILLAYUTE NATIONAL WILDLIFE REFUGE
KAYOSTLA BEACH

BLOCK BAKER RD
DICKEY RIVER WEST FORK
EAST FORK DICKEY RIVER
GUNDERSON MOUNTAIN
CALAWAH RIDGE
Beaver
Sappho
SOL DUC RIVER
101
SCHITZ PASS
BIGLER MOUNTAIN
FOREST

A · B · B · C

SEE 108 MAP

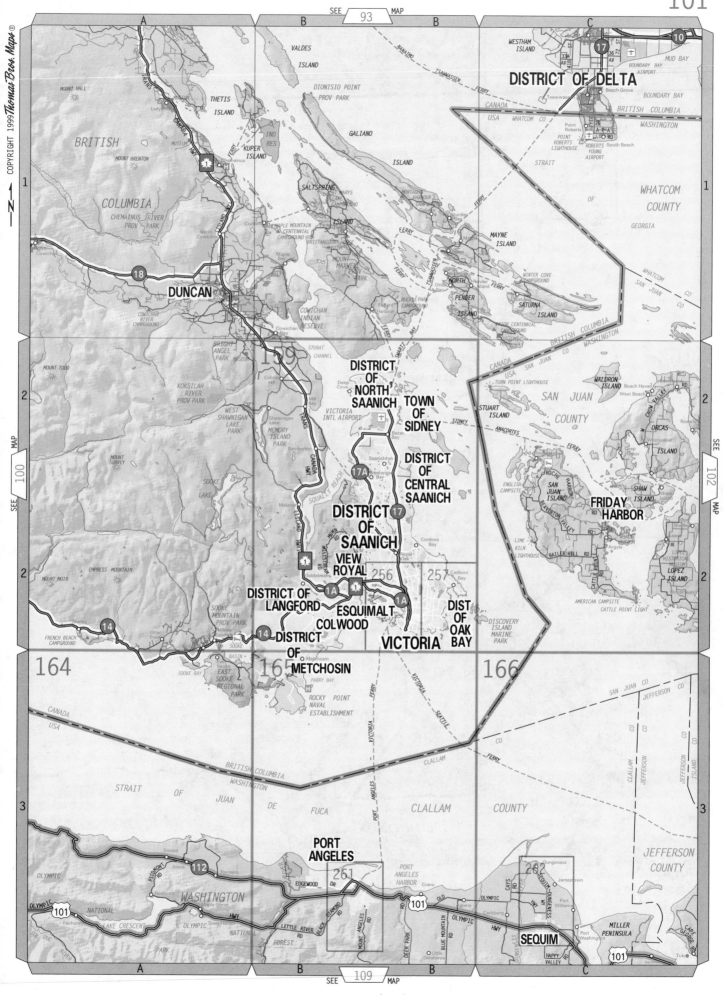

PNW

HWY

SEE 93 MAP

SEE 100 MAP

SEE 102 MAP

DISTRICT OF DELTA

WESTHAM ISLAND

BOUNDARY BAY AIRPORT

BRITISH COLUMBIA
WASHINGTON

WHATCOM COUNTY

BRITISH
COLUMBIA

MOUNT HALL

THETIS ISLAND

KUPER ISLAND

MOUNT BRENTON

CHEMAINUS RIVER PROV PARK

DUNCAN

VALDES ISLAND

DIONISIO POINT PROV PARK

GALIANO

ISLAND

SALTSPRING

ISLAND

MAYNE ISLAND

NORTH PENDER ISLAND

SATURNA ISLAND

STRAIT

OF

GEORGIA

SAN JUAN COUNTY

WALDRON ISLAND

ORCAS ISLAND

SAN JUAN ISLAND

FRIDAY HARBOR

SHAW ISLAND

LOPEZ ISLAND

DISTRICT OF NORTH SAANICH

TOWN OF SIDNEY

DISTRICT OF CENTRAL SAANICH

DISTRICT OF SAANICH

VIEW ROYAL

DISTRICT OF LANGFORD

ESQUIMALT

COLWOOD

DISTRICT OF METCHOSIN

VICTORIA

DIST OF OAK BAY

DISCOVERY ISLAND MARINE PARK

256

257

164

165

166

SOOKE LAKE

EMPRESS MOUNTAIN

MOUNT MUIR

FRENCH BEACH CAMPGROUND

EAST SOOKE REGIONAL PARK

ROCKY POINT NAVAL ESTABLISHMENT

STRAIT   OF   JUAN   DE   FUCA

CLALLAM   COUNTY

JEFFERSON COUNTY

3

PORT ANGELES

261

PORT ANGELES HARBOR

262

SEQUIM

MILLER PENINSULA

OLYMPIC NATIONAL PARK

WASHINGTON

101

101

101

SEE 109 MAP

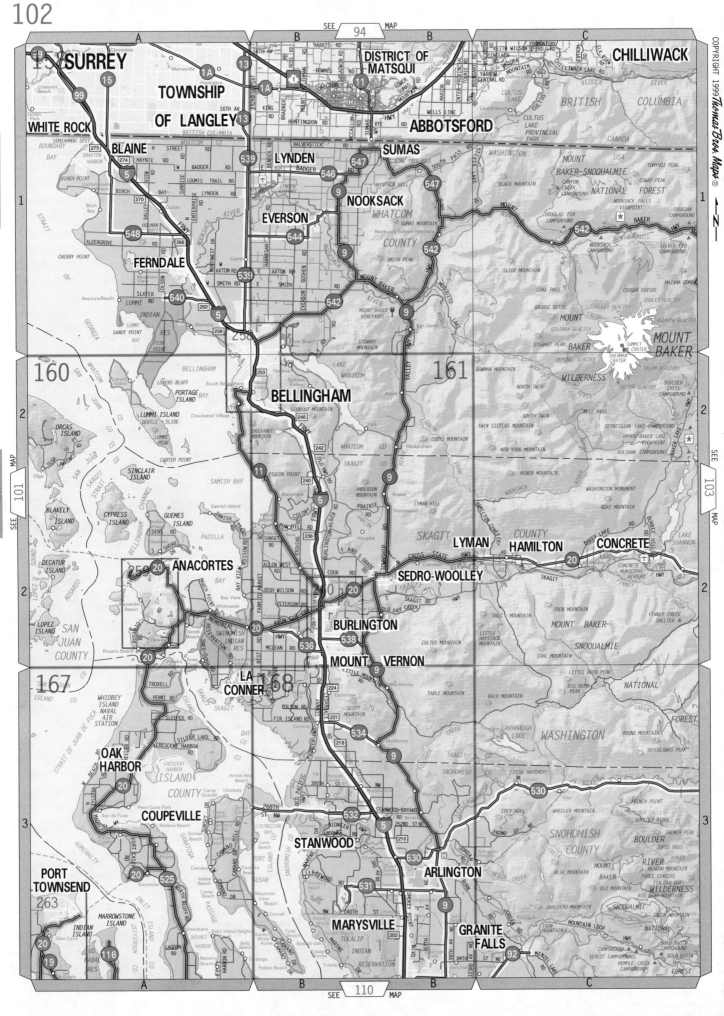

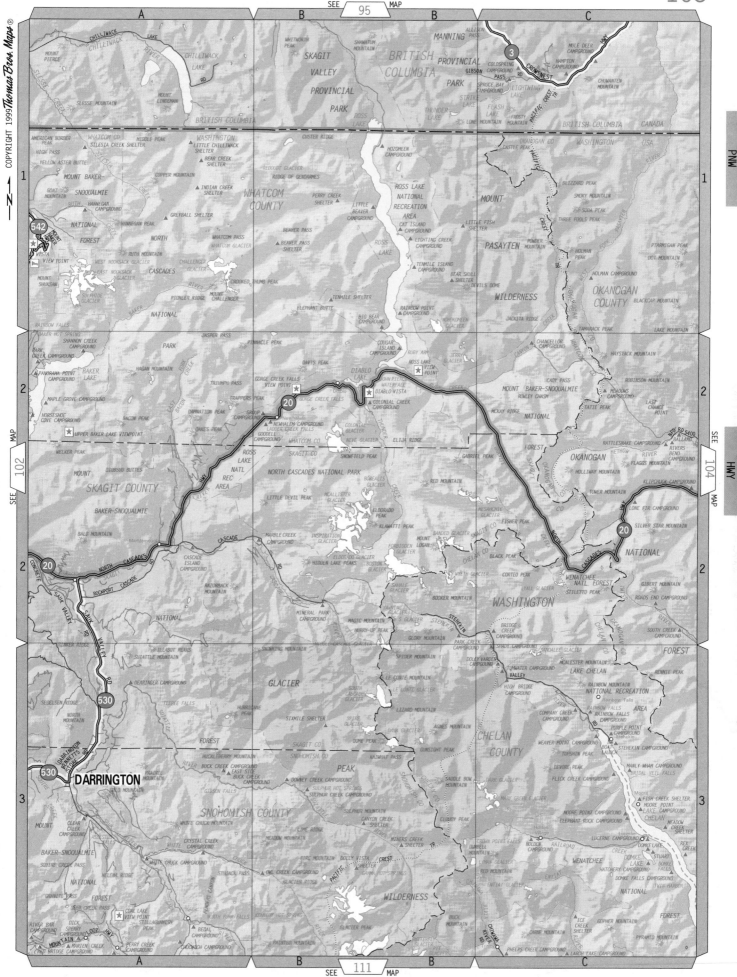

104

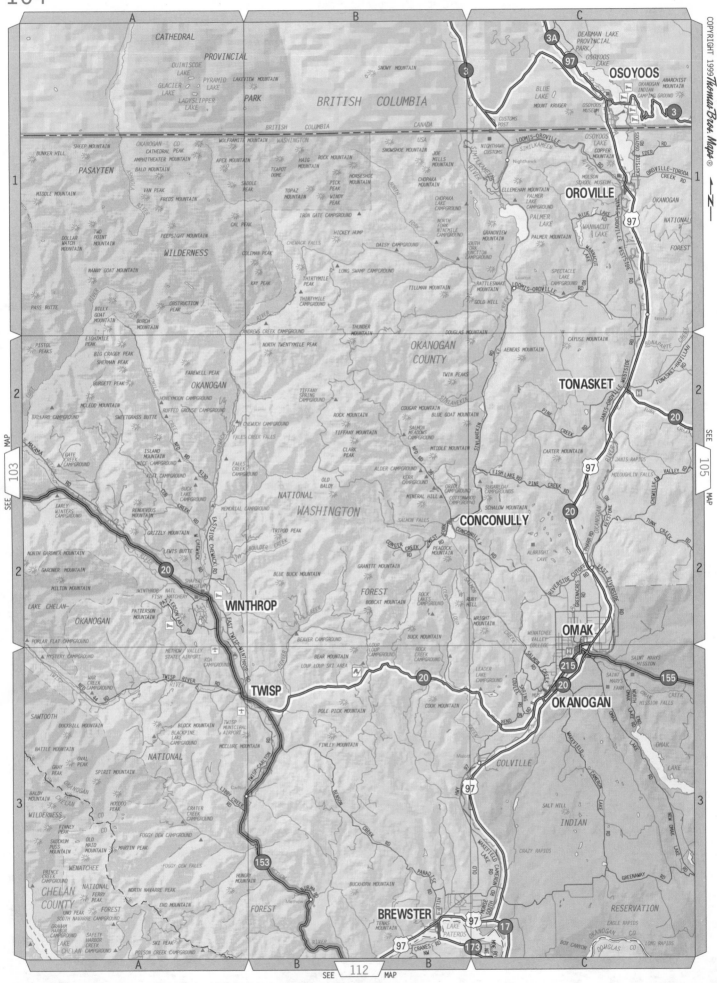

—N—

PNW

HWY

SEE 103 MAP

SEE 105 MAP

SEE 112 MAP

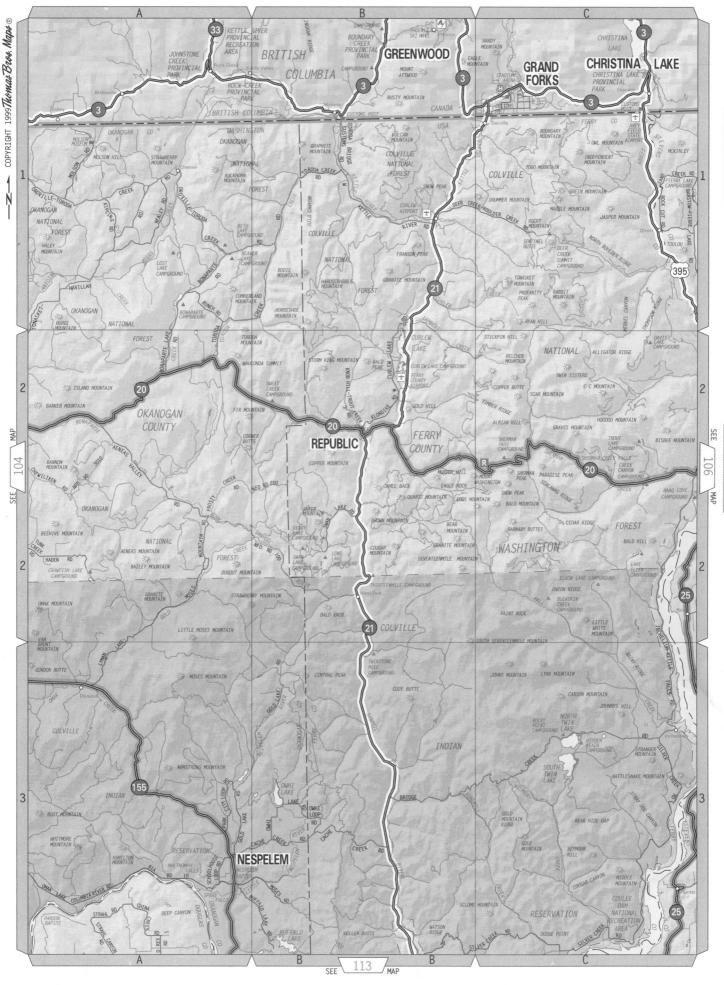

PNW

HWY

PNW

HWY

A   B   C

—N—

ROSSLAND   MONTROSE   BRITISH COLUMBIA

22   22A   6   3

NANCY GREENE RECREATIONAL AREA
RED MOUNTAIN SKI AREA
MOUNT JELDNESS

LOST MOUNTAIN
RIPPLE MOUNTAIN
STAGLEAP PROVINCIAL PARK

BALDY MOUNTAIN
GROUSE RIDGE
VIOLIN LAKE
LAKE MOUNTAIN
SILICA

Casino
BEAVER CREEK PROV PARK
Columbia Gardens
Remac

COLUMBIA RIVER
PEND OREILLE RIVER
BRITISH COLUMBIA
CANADA   USA

Peterson   Waneta   Boundary
MITCHELL MOUNTAIN
FRISCO MOUNTAIN
PEWEE FALLS

Nelway
PEND OREILLE CRESCENT LAKE CAMPGROUND
SLUMBER PEAK

BOUNDARY CO
SNOWY TOP
WASHINGTON   SALMO-PRIEST   IDAHO

25   251

STEVENS CO
HOPE MOUNTAIN
COLVILLE   NATIONAL   FOREST
CHURCHILL MOUNTAIN
LEAD PENCIL MOUNTAIN
BELSHAZZAR MOUNTAIN
SHEEP CREEK FALLS
SHEEP CREEK RD

NORTHPORT

LAEL FLAT
BILLY GOAT MOUNTAIN
JUMBO MOUNTAIN
COUGAR MOUNTAIN
NORTHPORT-FLAT
LITTLE DALLES
BLACK HAWK MOUNTAIN
Dolomite

NORTH FORK
BOUNDARY
COLVILLE-ALADDIN-NORTHPORT RD

STONE MOUNTAIN
ELECTRIC POINT
ABERCROMBIE MOUNTAIN
BEAVER MOUNTAIN

BLUE BIRD RIDGE
GYPSY PEAK
WILDERNESS
CROWELL MOUNTAIN
GREEN MOUNTAIN

31   METALINE FALLS

COLVILLE
THUNDER MOUNTAIN
HELMER MOUNTAIN

HUGHES RIDGE VIEW POINT ★

25

HILL LOOP RD
NORTH GORGE CAMPGROUND
WILLIAMS LAKE RD
COULEE DAM NATIONAL RECREATION AREA
LOOKOUT MOUNTAIN
FREDERICKSON HILL

METALINE
Pend Oreille Village
MILL POND CAMPGROUND
SULLIVAN CREEK RD
SULLIVAN LAKE CAMPGROUND
SULLIVAN LAKE
NOISY CREEK CAMPGROUND

ROUND TOP MOUNTAIN
GOLD PEAK
NORTH

NATIONAL
LASOTA FALLS
GRANITE FALLS
STAGGER INN CAMPGROUND
KANIKSU
HIGH ROCK MOUNTAIN

395

SPION KOP
BOSSBURG
BONANZA HILL
EVANS HILL CUTOFF RD
EVANS CAMPGROUND
SNAG COVE CAMPGROUND
KETTLE RIVER CAMPGROUND
NAPOLEON-MARBLE RD

DEER MOUNTAIN
NATIONAL
BOX CANYON DAM VIEW POINT ★
HUCKLEBERRY MOUNTAIN
BALDY MOUNTAIN

IONE

IONE MUNI AIRPORT

EDGEWATER CAMPGROUND
MAITLEN
PEND OREILLE COUNTY
MOLYBDENITE MOUNTAIN
PETIT LAKE CAMPGROUND
KANIKSU

TILLICUM PEAK
DUSTY PEAK
IDAHO

2

COLVILLE
STEVENS COUNTY
NATIONAL   FOREST

FRANKLIN D ROOSEVELT LAKE
SAINT PAULS MISSION
ECHO MOUNTAIN
DOUGLAS FALLS
DOUGLASS FALLS
CLUGSTON
COLVILLE MOUNTAIN
FORK MILL CREEK RD
MIDDLE FORK MILL CREEK RD
SOUTH FORK MILL CREEK RD

RABBIT MOUNTAIN
GREEN MOUNTAIN
LAKE THOMAS CAMPGROUND
JOLIFF RD
CMEADOW CREEK RD
MEADOW CREEK
ALADDIN MOUNTAIN
SELDOM SEEN MOUNTAIN
HANKS BUTTE
LAKE LEO CAMPGROUND
GRANITE PEAK

KANIKSU
FOREST
HANLON MOUNTAIN
KALISPELL FALLS
DIAMOND PEAK
HUNGRY MOUNTAIN
FOURTH OF JULY PEAK
GLEASON MOUNTAIN
NORTH BALDY

WASHINGTON   NATIONAL   FOREST

KETTLE FALLS
OLD KETTLE
LIONS ISLAND
BONANZA LEAD MILL
MINGO MOUNTAIN
BRADBURY CAMPGROUND
CARTER CANYON
NORTH BASIN
DAY MOUNTAIN
RICE-ORIN RD
FREEMAN HILL

COLVILLE
H H
COLVILLE MUNI AIRPORT
COLVILLE-TIGER RD
20

LITTLE CRYSTAL FALLS
PEND OREILLE
SCRABBLER MOUNTAIN
MILL BUTTE
BEAR CANYON RD
LITTLE PEND OREILLE NATIONAL WILDLIFE REFUGE

KANIKSU
BOULDER MOUNTAIN
PANHANDLE CAMPGROUND
GROUSE KNOB
TOLA POINT

RUBY MOUNTAIN
20
RIVER BEND AIRPORT
PELKE RIVER

NATIONAL   FOREST

25

DOUGLAS FALLS
MARBLE SOUTH
TOWNSEND-SACKMAN RD

WASHINGTON

TACOMA PEAK
ROCKY BUTTE
BREWER MOUNTAIN
FOURTH OF JULY MOUNTAIN
LITTLE CALISPELL PEAK
KINGS MOUNTAIN

PEND OREILLE RIVER
SULLIVAN POINT
BROWNS LAKE CAMPGROUND
NORTH SKOOKUM CAMPGROUND
SOUTH SKOOKUM LAKE CAMPGROUND

57

MCKERN-SCOTT RD
GOLD HILL
NILES RD
DEADMAN HILL
QUARTZ MOUNTAIN
CLOVERLEAF BEACH CAMPGROUND
COULEE DAM NATIONAL RECREATION AREA

DUNN MOUNTAIN
SUMMIT VALLEY
ADDY-GIFFORD RD
ZIMMER RD
Bluecreek
Addy
DEER

COLVILLE
WILSON MOUNTAIN
FORTY NINE DEGREES NORTH SKI AREA
WINCHESTER PEAK
EAGLE MOUNTAIN
GOLD HILL
FLOWERY TRAIL RD

CUSICK

KALISPEL INDIAN RESERVATION
COOKS MOUNTAIN
FOREST
NO NAME PEAK
SKOOKUM PEAK
NO NAME LAKE CAMPGROUND

395

CHEWELAH
H
QUARTZITE MOUNTAIN
NATIONAL
PARKER MOUNTAIN
MCNALL CANYON
HEINE RD

ROUNDTOP MOUNTAIN
NELSON PEAK
BARTLETTE RD
POWER PEAK
BOYER MOUNTAIN
CALISPELL LAKE
Delkena
NEWPORT GEOPHYSICAL OBSERVATORY
CUBAN HILL
STONE JOHNNY

FOREST
GRANITE MOUNTAIN
LITTLE ROUNDTOP
SACHEEN LAKE
DAVIS LAKE
ROCKY MOUNTAIN

20
COOKS MOUNTAIN
SADDLE MOUNTAIN
NEWPORT   H
Priest
2

3

HUCKLEBERRY MOUNTAIN
CEDONIA-ADDY
LESSIG
SOUTH FORK RD
STENSGAR MOUNTAIN
LANE MOUNTAIN
WAITTS LAKE
NEWTON
HAFER RD
RED MARBLE RD
BLUE CREEK WEST RD
BODY-GIFFORD RD

232

231

292

395

FARM TO MARKET RD
LITTLE COYOTE MOUNTAIN
BOUDES HILL
LONG PRAIRIE RD
HESSELTINE RD
JUMPOFF JOE MOUNTAIN
LIMEKILN HILL
GLASER CREEK RD
GROUSE CREEK RD
BALD MOUNTAIN
DEER LAKE
BENSON PEAK
BLUE GROUSE MOUNTAIN

SPRINGDALE
SPRINGDALE-HUNTERS RD
EMPEY MOUNTAIN
CAMAS VALLEY
DEER CREEK RD
DEER LAKE MOUNTAIN
LOON LAKE
LOON LAKE LOOP

BENSON VALLEY
SHADOW VALLEY
FERTILE VALLEY
BRUSA MOUNTAIN
LITTLE BLUE GROUSE MOUNTAIN
SACHEEN LAKE

211

LITTLE BLUE GROUSE MOUNTAIN
DEER VALLEY
SAND BUTTE
SCOTIA VALLEY
SCOTIA
LONE BARE MOUNTAIN
DIAMOND LAKE
LITTLE BLUE LAKE

Oldtown
20
Diamond
41

SPRING VALLEY
PEND OREILLE CO
SPOKANE CO
Poocanota Bay

A   B   B   C

SEE 105 MAP
SEE 107 MAP
SEE 114 MAP

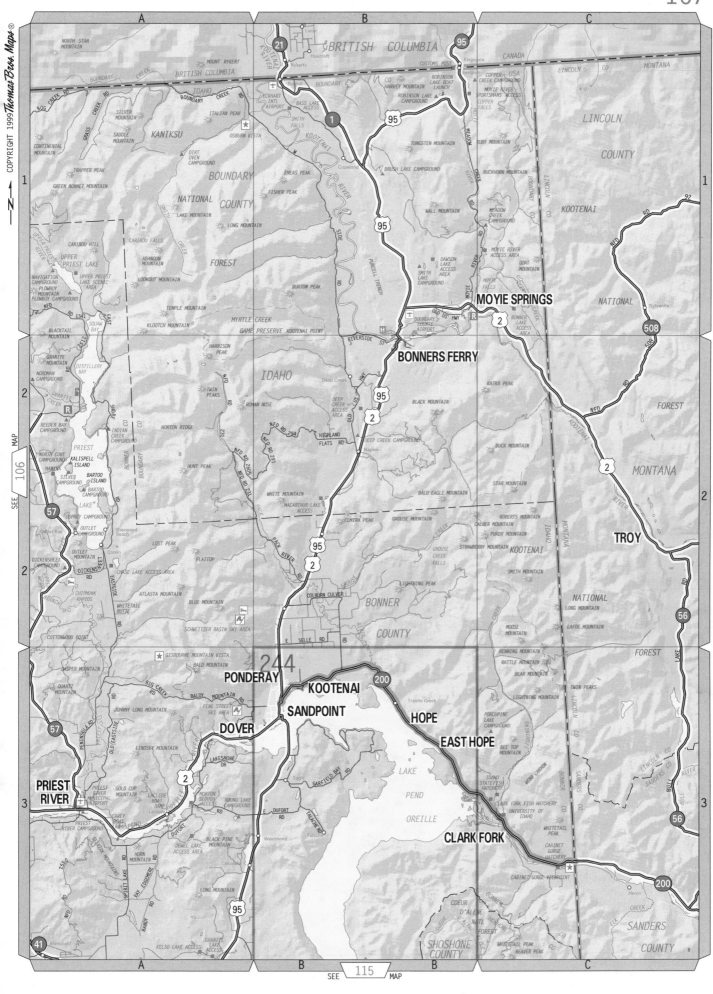

108

PNW

HWY

169

B   B   C

101

FORKS

OLYMPIC   NATIONAL   HUNGER MOUNTAIN

SITKUM
SHELTER

ELK RIDGE   CLALLAM   RUGGED RIDGE

QUILLAYUTE RD   COUNTY

110   DICKEY RIVER   CALAWAH SHELTER   OLYMPIC   FIFTEENMILE
SHELTER

MORA RD   BOGACHIEL   NATIONAL   FLAPJACK
SHELTER

LA PUSH RD   SHELTER   PARK

La Push   CLALLAM   CO   Bogachiel

JEFFERSON   CO

OLYMPIC   BOGACHIEL   RIVER

SPRUCE MOUNTAIN   GEODETIC HILL

NATIONAL   UPPER
HOH
OX   MINNIE
PETERSON
CAMPGROUND   1

BOW   HOH   HUELSDONK
CAMPGROUND   RD   SOUTH
FORK
HOH

PARK   HOH WILLOUGHBY
CREEK
CAMPGROUND   RIVER

HUELSDONK RIDGE

CITY   JEFFERSON

OIL   COUNTY   CLEARWATER   CREEK   OWL   RIVER

HOH INDIAN
RESERVATION   101   WASHINGTON

COPPER MINE
BOTTOM
CAMPGROUND   UPPER
CLEARWATER
CAMPGROUND   YAHOO
LAKE
CAMPGROUND

DESTRUCTION
ISLAND   BROWNS POINT

PACIFIC   172   CLEARWATER   OLYMPIC
NATIONAL
FOREST

OLYMPIC   NATIONAL   2

QUEETS   RIVER   OLYMPIC
NATIONAL   RD

Queets   QUEETS   RIVER   JEFFERSON   PARK   CO   FOREST

GRAYS HARBOR   SEE 109 MAP

GRAYS HARBOR   101

COUNTY

QUINAULT   THIMBLE MOUNTAIN

OCEAN   WILLOUGHBY
ROCK   LONE MOUNTAIN

SPLIT
ROCK   INDIAN   2

QUINAULT   RIVER

Taholah   RESERVATION   OLYMPIC
NATIONAL
FOREST

109

177

Moclips

Sunset Beach   Humptulips

Highland Heights

Pacific Beach

Aloha

YELLOW
BLUFF   RIVER

Iron Springs

COPALIS ROCK   COPALIS HEAD

Copalis Beach   Copalis
Crossing   3

Newton

Ocean City   COPALIS   Tulips

Burrows   RD

109

115   BURROWS   Chenois Creek
RD

Illahee   Oyhut   Gray Gables

OCEAN   Grays
Harbor
SHORES   City

298   BRECKENRIDGE
BLUFF

A   B   B   C

SEE 116 MAP

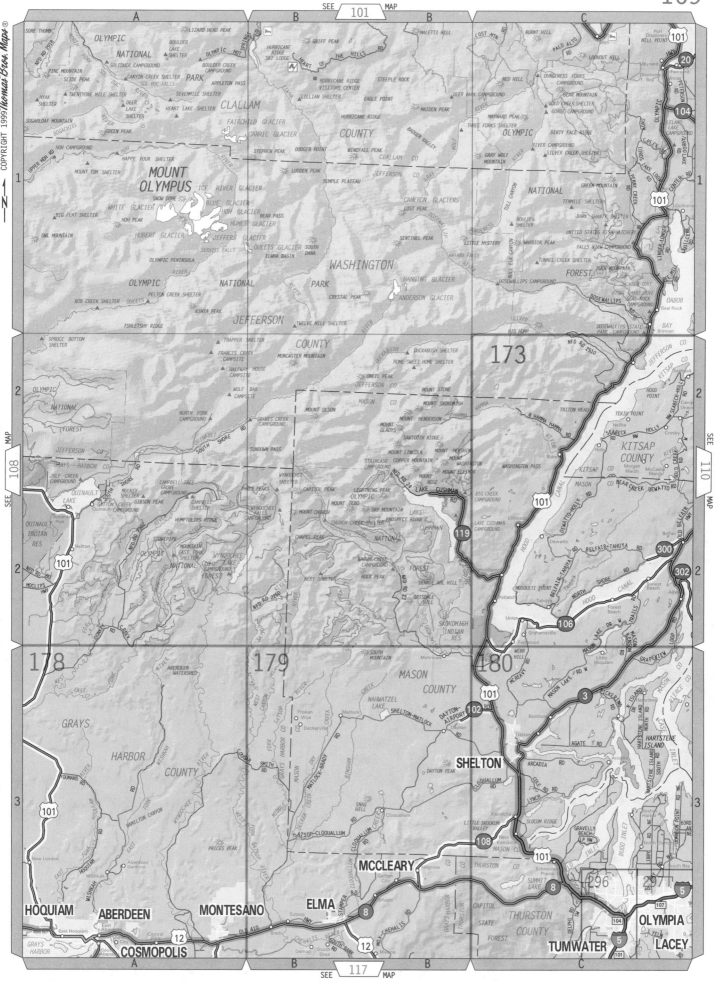

PNW

HWY

—N—

A

B

B

C

SEE 101 MAP

20

104

101

1

OLYMPIC

NATIONAL

PARK

CLALLAM

COUNTY

OLYMPIC

NATIONAL

FOREST

MOUNT OLYMPUS

WASHINGTON

NATIONAL   PARK

JEFFERSON   COUNTY

1

SEE 108 MAP

173

SEE 110 MAP

2

OLYMPIC

NATIONAL

FOREST

JEFFERSON CO

MASON CO

KITSAP COUNTY

KITSAP CO

2

QUINAULT INDIAN RES

OLYMPIC NATIONAL FOREST

101

119

101

106

300

302

2

2

178

179

180

MASON COUNTY

GRAYS HARBOR COUNTY

SKOKOMISH INDIAN RES

102

3

SHELTON

3

3

101

108

HOQUIAM

ABERDEEN

MONTESANO

ELMA

MCCLEARY

THURSTON COUNTY

THURSTON STATE FOREST

296

297

8

8

5

107

104

5

101

COSMOPOLIS

12

12

8

TUMWATER

OLYMPIA

LACEY

GRAYS HARBOR

A

A

B

B

C

SEE 117 MAP

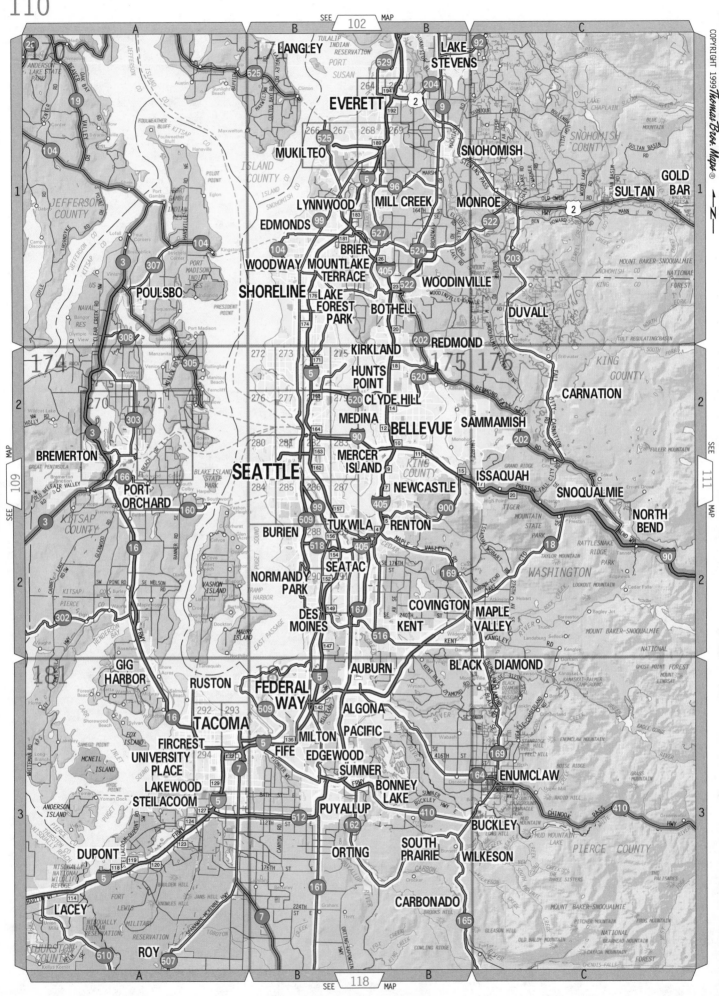

PNW

HWY

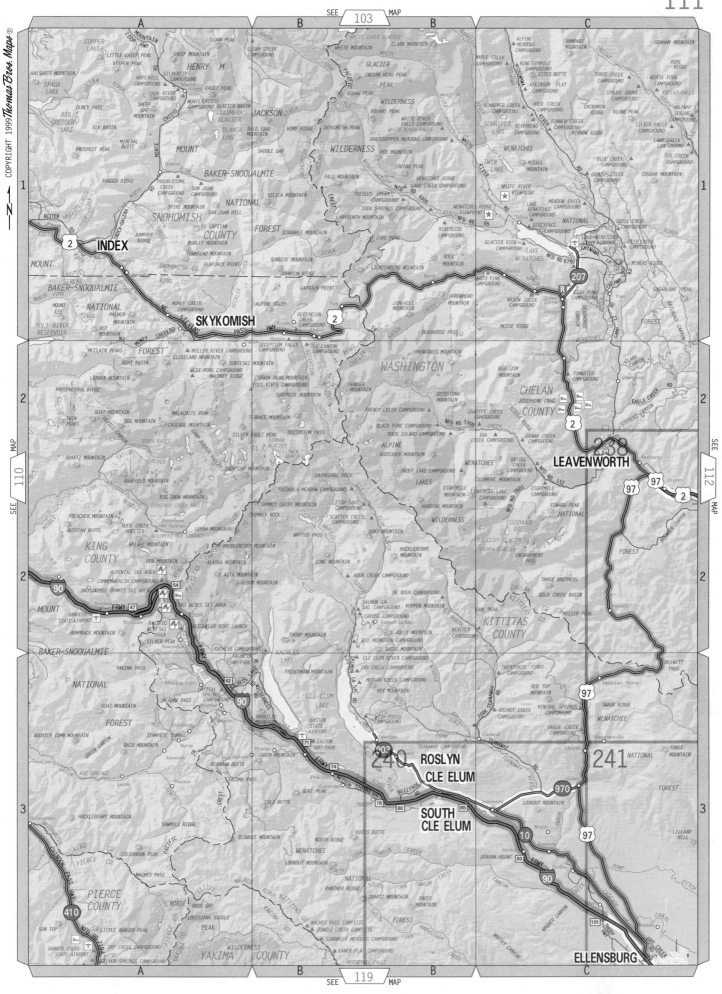

PNW

HWY

SEE 104 MAP

SEE 111 MAP

SEE 113 MAP

SEE 120 MAP

COPYRIGHT 1999 *Thomas Bros. Maps* ® —N—

A | B | C

PATEROS

BRIDGEPORT

COLVILLE INDIAN RESERVATION

OKANOGAN NATIONAL FOREST

OKANOGAN COUNTY

WENATCHEE NATIONAL FOREST

CHELAN

LAKE CHELAN

MANSFIELD

ENTIAT

WATERVILLE

DOUGLAS COUNTY

CHELAN COUNTY

WASHINGTON

CASHMERE

WENATCHEE

EAST WENATCHEE

ROCK ISLAND

GRANT COUNTY

SOAP LAKE

EPHRATA

SUN LAKES STATE PARK

LENORE LAKE NATIONAL WILDLIFE REFUGE

KITTITAS COUNTY

QUINCY

GEORGE

THE POTHOLES RESERVOIR

236 150 971 ALT 97 97 172 174 173 17 153 238 239 2 282 283 281 28 90 143 169 164 151 154 349 241 242

1 | 2 | 3

237

114

PNW

A B B B 1

ELMER CITY

COULEE DAM

GRAND COULEE
ELECTRIC CITY

OKANOGAN COUNTY

COLVILLE

FERRY COUNTY INDIAN

NINEMILE FALLS
WHITESTONE MOUNTAIN

SPOKANE INDIAN RESERVATION

WHITESTONE RIDGE

RESERVATION

174

DOUGLAS COUNTY

STEAMBOAT ROCK STATE PARK
STEAMBOAT ROCK

BANKS LAKE

155

174

COULEE DAM NATIONAL RECREATION AREA

FRANKLIN D ROOSEVELT LAKE

COULEE DAM NATIONAL RECREATION AREA

SPOKANE

FORT SPOKANE

PORCUPINE BAY CAMPGROUND

25

MEEKER MOUNTAIN

STERLING VALLEY
STERLING POINT

KIRBY DRAW

LINCOLN

HAWK CREEK FALLS

21

R

R

ALMIRA

HARTLINE

2

WILBUR

CRESTON

MILES

CRESTON BUTTE

R

Telford

2

TRACY ROCK

LINCOLN COUNTY

2

SEE 112 MAP

COULEE CITY

SUN LAKES STATE PARK

GRANT COUNTY

21

WASHINGTON

COFFEEPOT

COFFEEPOT BUTTE

HARRINGTON

23

SEE 114 HWY MAP

SUMMER FALLS STATE PARK

BILLY CLAPP LAKE

WILSON CREEK

MARLIN

REISER FALLS

DELZER FALLS

ODESSA MUNICIPAL AIRPORT

DUCK LAKE

28

28

2 2

ODESSA

SYLVAN LAKE

242

21

SCHOONOVER

TOKIO

ADAMS COUNTY

TOKIO

LINCOLN CO
ADAMS CO

231

395

90

RITZVILLE

RITZVILLE MUNICIPAL AIRPORT

226

220

221

17

MOSES LAKE

171

175

179

182

184

90

188

90

196

261

THE POTHOLES RESERVOIR

17

395

A A B B C

A B B C

—N—

STEVENS
COUNTY

SPOKANE

BLUE MOUNTAIN
BOUNDARY BUTTE
SPRINGDALE HUNTERS RD
LYONS HILL
DEER MOUNTAIN
ROUND MOUNTAIN RD
BEAR MOUNTAIN
COTTONWOOD
SPOKANE MOUNTAIN
MCCOY LAKE
WELLPINIT
ELLJAY
INDIAN
RESERVATION
COULEE DAM NATIONAL RECREATION AREA
WELLPINIT MOUNTAIN
FORD-WELLPINIT RD
LOOP RD
SHERWOOD MOUNTAIN
WALHALLA
BROADWAY
PITNEY BUTTE
PORCUPINE BAY
CAYUSE MOUNTAIN
LINCOLN
SPOKANE

DEER PARK

ELOIKA LAKE
ELK
BLANCH
E
MILAN-ELK
MILAN
MOUNT SPOKANE STATE PARK
BAY MOUNTAIN
MOUNT SPOKANE
SELKIRK MOUNTAIN
TRIPPS KNOB
BALD KNOB
ROUND TOP MOUNTAIN
SPOKANE CO
KOOTENAI CO
WASHINGTON
GREEN MOUNTAIN
SPOKANE COUNTY
NEWMAN LAKE
352
290

2

395

STALEY RD
CRAWFORD ST
DEER PARK MUNICIPAL AIRPORT
MILAN HILL
ELK-CHATTAROY
CHATTAROY
CLAYTON
COLBERT
MEAD
BIGELOW GULCH
206
247
346
347
216
348 349

MILLWOOD
SPOKANE
TRENT
90
OTIS ORCHARDS
GREENACRES
SPOKANE BRIDGE
LIBERTY LAKE

AIRWAY HEIGHTS

DAVENPORT
LINCOLN COUNTY HISTORICAL MUSEUM
28
2
REARDAN
231
LINCOLN COUNTY
HANNING BUTTE
MAGNISON BUTTE
CLOVERDALE RD
25
231
TEEL HILL
GETTYS BUTTE
GRAYS BUTTE
MCDOWELL HILL
ESPANOLA
291
LITTLE FALLS
LONG LAKE
W SOUTH BANK
SOUTH BANK
EAGLE ROCK
CORKSCREW CANYON
CORKSCREW CANYON RD
MCMILLAN MOUNTAIN
HAPPY HILL
BECKS HILL
STONY PEAK
SADDLE MOUNTAIN
MOUNT GODFREY RD
BALD MOUNTAIN
SCOOP MOUNTAIN
LITTLE MOUNTAIN
DUNNS MOUNTAIN
TURNBULL
RIVERSIDE STATE PARK
INDIAN TRAIL RD
TOWN & COUNTRY
COUNTRY HOMES
MORGAN ACRES
HILLYARD
DARTFORD
FAIRWOOD
WAYSIDE
PEASE HILL
MCKAY HILL
MONROE
DENISON
SPOKANE STATE GAME FARM
W PREWETT RD
W PINE
W BLUFF RD
FOUR MOUND RD
W CHARLES
W DENO RD
FAIRCHILD
SUNSET HWY
RAMBO RD
DEEP CREEK RD
DEEP CREEK
MCFARLANE
W THORPE RD
W SPOTTED
S BROOKS RD
FITCH
RIDDLE HILL
OLSON
902
272
270
FOUR LAKES
MARSHALL
SCRIBNER
GEIGER HEIGHTS
S HALLETT
276
FAIRCHILD AIR FORCE BASE
HAYFORD
S CHENEY SPOKANE RD
S SPOTTED RD
S SHORT
S SHERMAN RD
TINLAND
EMPIRE
PALOUSE HWY
S PALOUSE HWY
DUNCAN
S SANDS RD
S MADISON RD
S JACKSON RD
MICA
VALLEYFORD
FREEMAN
SAXBY
ROCK
VALLEY CHAPEL
HANGMAN

MEDICAL LAKE
TOOTH HILL
LAKELAND VILLAGE
SALNAVE FRWY
W SALNAVE
CHENEY
SALNAVE
904
264
395
90
257
DEEP CREEK
SOUTH CHENEY
BUNKER HILL
PINE SPRINGS RD
S DOVER RD
PINE SPRING RD
TYLER
MILL RD
MILL CREEK RD
CHENEY-PLAZA
BADGER LAKES
MASON
APABOR
TURNBULL NATIONAL WILDLIFE REFUGE
WILLIAMS LAKE
W WILLIAMS LAKE RD
S WILLIAMS LAKE RD
MARTIN
DOWNS LAKE
WILLIAMS LAKE RD
WATERMELON HILL
WELLS
DANEKAS RD
245
23
LINCOLN CO
WHITMAN CO
ADAMS CO

MOHLER RD
23
231
SPRAGUE
395
90
231
SPRAGUE LAKE
HARPER ISLAND
LAMONT
LAMONT RD
POTTS RD
IMBLER RD
WAGNER RD
CARLCO HILLS
WELLSMONT RD
COW LAKE
COW CREEK
ADAMS COUNTY
COTTONWOOD CREEK
GEORGE KNOTT RD
TEXAS LAKE
TOWELL FALLS
MASON DRAW
TEXAS DRAW
CHERRY CREEK
WILLADA
LANCASTER
JONES RD
END COTT-SAINT JOHN
MULKEY RD
KAHLOTUS
PALOUSE
ROCK CREEK FALLS
PIERSON RD
EWAN
WILLADA

WASHINGTON
WHITMAN COUNTY
WHITMAN CO
27
ROCKFORD
278
SPANGLE
E STRINGHAM RD
MOUNT HOPE
E KEEVEY RD
FAIRFIELD
195
MOREFIELD BUTTE
BRADSHAW RD
HANSEN BUTTE
TRUAX
STARR BUTTE
S PRAIRIE VIEW RD
WAVERLY
FREEDOM
SPANGLE WAVERLY RD
S CAHILL RD
S MARSH RD
GELBERT MOUNTAIN
PLAZA
JEFFERSON
SR 195
LATAH
SPRING VALLEY RD
TEKOA MOUNTAIN
WHEELER RD
TEKOA
OAKSDALE
ROSALIA
ROSALIA MUNICIPAL AIRPORT
271
PANDORA
SAINT JOHN
FAIRBANKS
MCCOY RD
MALDEN
MALDEN RD
SPOKANE CO
WHITMAN CO
ROLLINS
PRAIRIE NIEM
SPRING VALLEY
SQUAW CANYON
BELDER
ROCK LAKE
CASTLE ROCK
JOHNSONS BEACH
THE AMY SLAUGHTER PEN BAY
PINE CITY
PINE CREEK
THORN
JIM DAVIS RD
SUNSET
THORNTON
FINCH
OLD THORNTON
NAFF RIDGE
GRANITE BUTTE
STEAM SHOVEL HILL
SAKU
27
OAKESDALE
195
SAINT JOHN
JUNO
HUNTIS
PLEASANT
SUNSET RD
PLEASANT VALLEY
OLD STATE
STEPTOE BUTTE
CRAB TREE
WAITERS
DRY CREEK
23
GARFIELD
ELBERTON
STEPTOE
OLD STATE RD
MCGRADY RD
PINE HOLLOW

2
2
1
1

3
3

A B B C

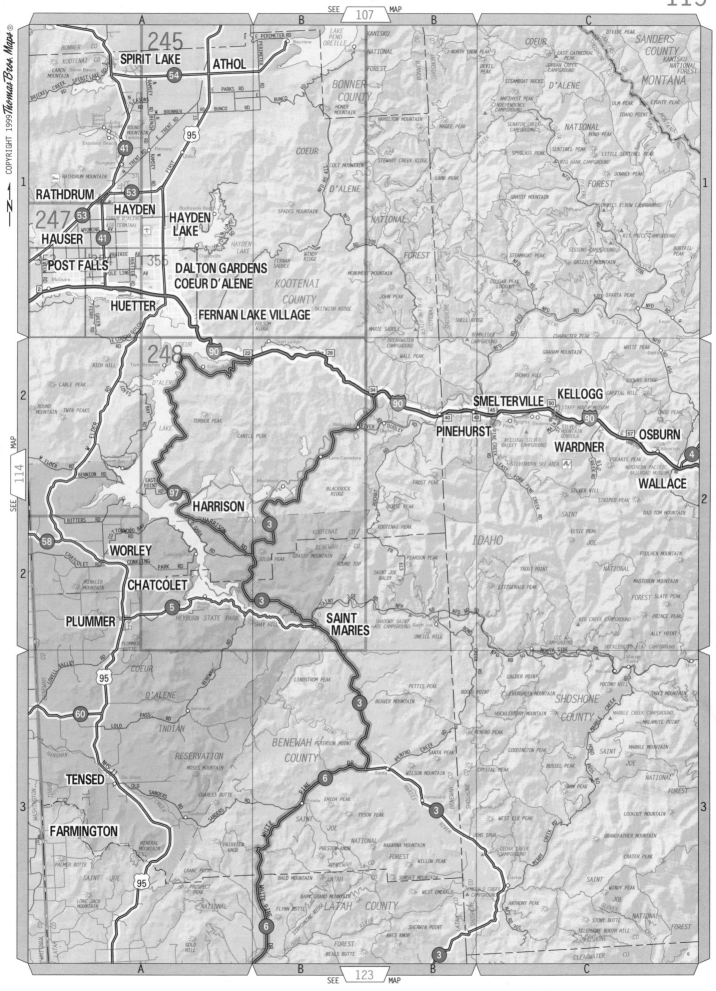

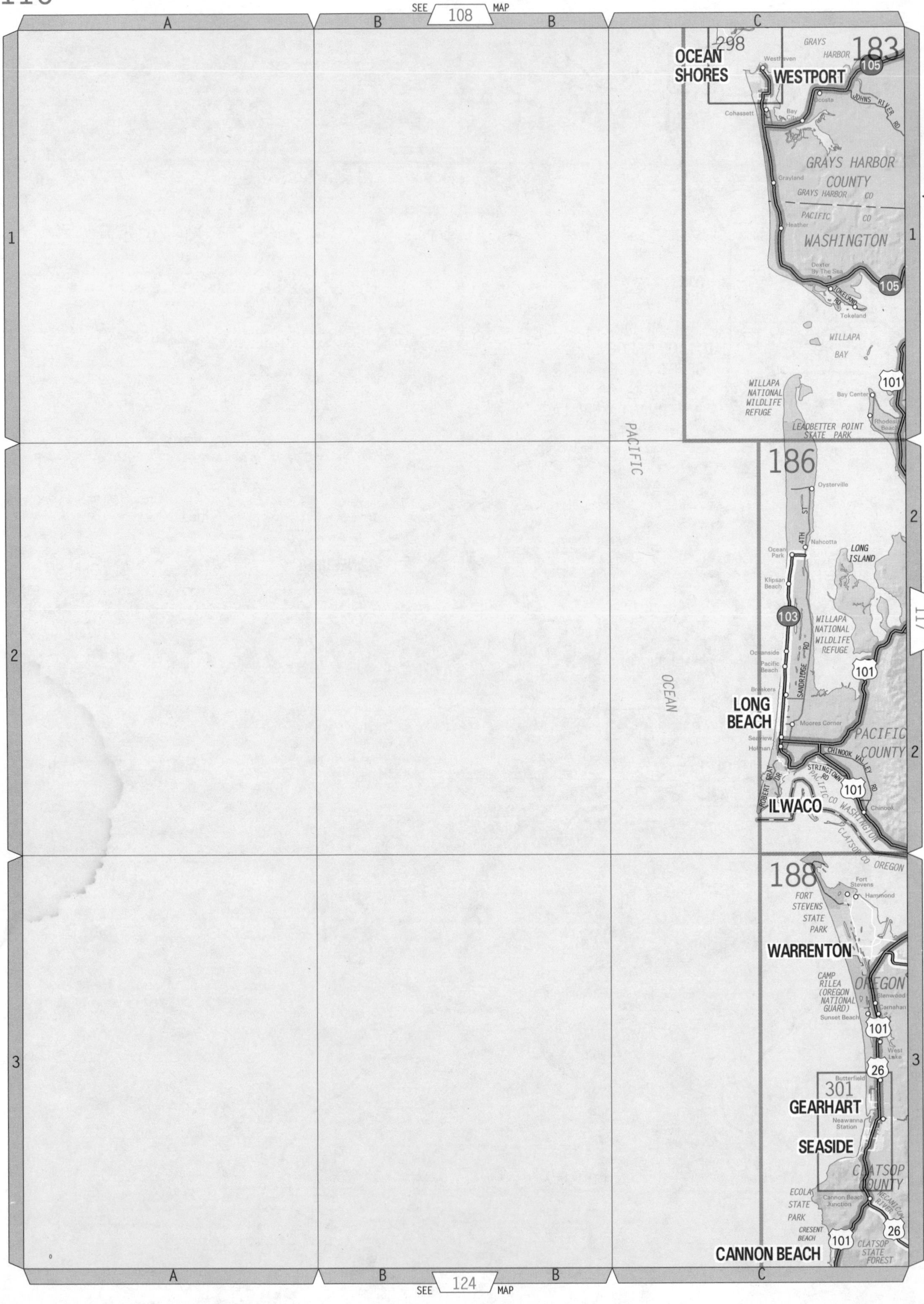

PNW

HWY

SEE 108 MAP

A B B C

COPYRIGHT 1999 *Thomas Bros. Maps* ® —N—

298

OCEAN SHORES

WESTPORT

183

105

Westhaven

GRAYS HARBOR

Cohassett

Bay City

Costa

JOHNS RIVER RD

GRAYS HARBOR COUNTY

GRAYS HARBOR CO

Grayland

PACIFIC CO

Heather

WASHINGTON

Dexter By The Sea

105

TOKELAND RD

Tokeland

WILLAPA BAY

101

Bay Center

WILLAPA NATIONAL WILDLIFE REFUGE

LEADBETTER POINT STATE PARK

Rhodesia Beach

1

186

Oysterville

4TH ST

Nahcotta

LONG ISLAND

Ocean Park

Klipsan Beach

103

WILLAPA NATIONAL WILDLIFE REFUGE

SANDRIDGE RD

101

Oceanside

Pacific Beach

Breakers

LONG BEACH

Moores Corner

PACIFIC COUNTY

Seaview

Holman

CHINOOK VALLEY

ROBERT GRAY DR

STRINGTOWN RD

PACIFIC CO

101

Chinook

WASHINGTON

ILWACO

2

SEE 117 MAP

CLATSOP CO   OREGON

188

Fort Stevens

Hammond

FORT STEVENS STATE PARK

WARRENTON

OREGON

CAMP RILEA (OREGON NATIONAL GUARD)

Glenwood

Carnahan

Sunset Beach

101

West Lake

26

Butterfield

301

GEARHART

Neawanna Station

SEASIDE

CLATSOP COUNTY

ECOLA STATE PARK

Cannon Beach Junction

NECANICUM RIVER

CRESENT BEACH

101

CANNON BEACH

26

CLATSOP STATE FOREST

PACIFIC OCEAN

3

2

1

SEE 124 MAP

A B B C

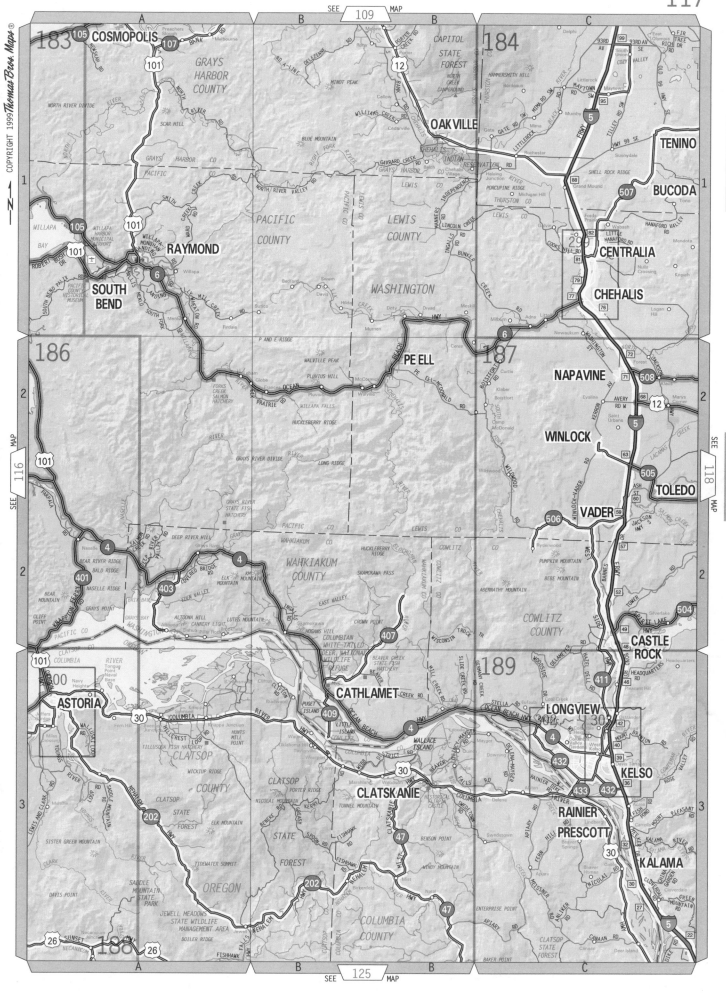

PNW

HWY

PNW

HWY

COPYRIGHT 1999 *Thomas Bros. Maps* ® —N—

SEE 110 MAP

A B B **C**

510 507
YELM 507 702
MCKENNA TANWAX
RAINIER
507

FORT LEWIS MILITARY RESERVATION
RAINIER
304TH ST E 320TH
KAPOWSIN LAKE KAPOWSIN PUYALLUP
352ND ST E Ohop
EATONVILLE CUT OFF RD
7 161 Clay City TWENTY FIVE MILE CREEK
EATONVILLE
PIERCE COUNTY
185 165 MEADOWS RD INDEPENDENCE RIDGE AUGUST PEAK SLUISKIN MOUNTAIN
MOUNT BAKER SNOQUALMIE EAGLE CLIFF OLD DESOLATE
MASHELL AV
HUGO PEAK MASHELL BEAVER DOBBS MOUNTAIN PTARMIGAN RIDGE
MOUNT RAINIER
POINT SUCCESS
DESCHUTES FALLS LAKE ALDER 7 MOUNTAIN
MOUNT RAINIER NATIONAL PARK
PIERCE CO LEWIS CO
SATULICK MOUNTAIN

1 1 1 **1**

WASHINGTON
THURSTON COUNTY
SKOOKUMCHUCK RESERVOIR CLAM MOUNTAIN THURSTON CO LEWIS CO
706 Ashford NATIONAL Longmire NISQUALLY RIVER
MINERAL LAKE SKATE CREEK BIG CREEK CAMPGROUND
GIFFORD
MOUNT BAKER-SNOQUALMIE Carlson
LEWIS COUNTY
NATIONAL Divide PINCHOT
FOREST 7

CENTRALIA ALPHA 508 INDIAN HOLE CAMPGROUND Packwood
MIDDLE FORK RD Alpha HARMONY HOPKINS HILL VIEW POINT Randle NATIONAL
122 KOSMOS CAMPGROUND MORTON 12 131 SILVER CREEK CAMPGROUND MAPLE LEAF CAMPGROUND FOREST 12

2 2 2 **2**

12 **MOSSYROCK** 12 Glenoma 12
MAYFIELD LAKE WINSTON CREEK CAMPGROUND RIFFE LAKE GIFFORD PINCHOT NATIONAL FOREST
TOWER ROCK CAMPGROUND
505 LEWIS CO
504 GREEN RIVER SALMON HATCHERY QUARTZ CREEK BIG TREES CAMPGROUND IRON CREEK CAMPGROUND BLUE LAKE CREEK CAMPGROUND
COWLITZ CO IRON CREEK INFORMATION CENTER SKAMANIA CO BLUE LAKE RIDGE
BEIGLE MOUNTAIN RD STRAWBERRY MOUNTAIN GREENHORN BUTTES
BLACK MOUNTAIN GOAT MOUNTAIN RYAN LAKE VIEW POINT POLE PATCH CAMPGROUND SPUD HILL
TOUTLE MOUNTAIN **MOUNT SAINT HELENS NATIONAL VOLCANIC MONUMENT** FRENCH BUTTE PINTO ROCK ADAMS FORK CAMPGROUND
DEBRIS DAM VIEW POINT BEAR PASS JUMBO PEAK DARK MOUNTAIN
SIGNAL PEAK 504 ELK ROCK FOREST LEARNING CENTER COLDWATER LAKE SPIRIT LAKE MOUNT SAINT HELENS VIEW POINT BEAR MEADOW VIEW POINT
INDEPENDENCE PASS VIEW POINT KIRK ROCK

2 2 2 **2**

COWLITZ COUNTY **190** SPUD MOUNTAIN SNAGTOOTH MOUNTAIN **SKAMANIA COUNTY**
SPOTTED BUCK MOUNTAIN CASTLE PEAK CLEARWATER OVERLOOK QUARTZ CREEK RIDGE
HEMLOCK PASS SHEEP CANYON **MOUNT SAINT HELENS** SMITH CREEK BUTTE MOUNT ADAMS VIEW POINT QUARTZ CREEK BUTTE
LOGGING WOLF POINT MERIDIAN MOUNTAIN PUMICE BUTTE TWIN FALLS CAMPGROUND
LITTLE COW ONEIL PEAK BIG BULL GIFFORD PINCHOT NATIONAL FOREST PIPE ISLAND SHELTER
BAIRD MOUNTAIN WASHBOARD FALLS LEWIS RIVER CAMPGROUND STEAMBOAT MOUNTAIN
SMITH MOUNTAIN ELK MOUNTAIN SWIFT CREEK FLOW BREEZY POINT STEAMBOAT LAKE CAMPGROUND
NINETEEN MOUNTAIN BUTLER BUTTE SPENCERS PEAK LOWER FALLS CAMPGROUND TILLICUM CAMPGROUND
GOBLE MOUNTAIN GEORGES PEAK CINNAMON PEAK BIG CREEK FALLS VIEW POINT SADDLE CAMPGROUND
WILD HORSE PEAK BOLT SHELTER SOUTH CAMPGROUND

3 3 3 **3**

MONUMENT PEAK SHELLEY MOUNTAIN BEAR PASS PIGEON SPRINGS MERRILL LAKE HOUSE ROCK KUM BACK SHELTER COLD SPRING CAMPGROUND
BALDY MOUNTAIN LONE BUTTE INDIAN VIEW POINT
WOOLFORD MOUNTAIN LAKEVIEW PEAK NFD RD 90 CURLY CREEK SAWTOOTH MOUNTAIN
Cougar CURLY CREEK CAMPGROUND OUTLAW RIDGE VOLCANIC VIEWPOINT CULTUS CREEK CAMPGROUND
LOWER KALAMA RIVER FALLS WILKINSON SADDLE SWIFT CREEK RESERVOIR SMOKY CREEK CAMPGROUND
KALAMA FALLS SALMON HATCHERY CLARK CO SKAMANIA CO TERMINATION POINT EAST CRATER
DEVILS PEAK REID MOUNTAIN DAVIS PEAK YALE LAKE McCLELLAN MOUNTAIN GIFFORD PEAK ICE CAVES
ROSS PEAK 503 ROCK POINT LAVA CAVES PETERSON BUTTE
BUTTE HILL CLOVER VALLEY SCHUMAKER MOUNTAIN 503 LAKE MERWIN PARADISE CREEK CAMPGROUND PETERSON PRAIRIE CAMPGROUND GOOSE LAKE CAMPGROUND
CLARK COUNTY INDIAN VIEW POINT NORTH BUTTE
LYONS RD TUMTUM MOUNTAIN

A B B **C**

SEE 126 MAP

SEE 117 MAP

SEE 119 MAP

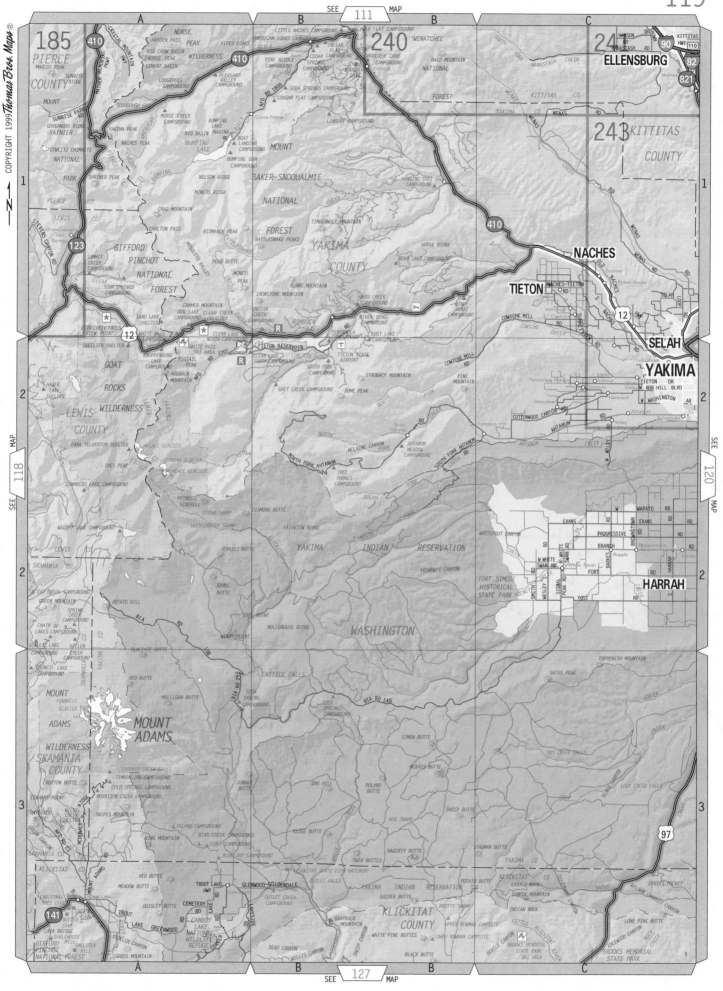

SEE 111 MAP

SEE 127 MAP

SEE 118 MAP

SEE 120 HWY MAP

PNW

HWY

SEE 112 MAP

COPYRIGHT 1999 Thomas Bros. Maps ®

—N—

SEE 242 MAP

KITTITAS

24 KITTITAS HWY 115

VANTAGE HWY

HULT BUTTE ROCKY COULEE

90

FRWY I-90

137

FRWY

26

243

ROYAL CITY

FRENCHMAN HILL RD

LOW GAP PASS

RD 11-SW

SAND HOLLOW

ROYAL SLOPE

11-SW

RD 13-SW

13-SE

COLUMBIA NATIONAL WILDLIFE REFUGE

262

7-SW DODSON

B-SE

C-SW

KITTITAS COUNTY

JOHNSON CANYON

CASCADE CANAL

THRALL CLEMAN RD

COLEMAN RD

East Kittitas

3

BADGER POCKET

VANDERBILT GAP

BADGER GAP

82

821

97

YAKIMA RIVER

BALDY PEAK

Roza

Wymer

Umtanum

KITTITAS CO

YAKIMA CO

U S MILITARY RESERVATION

YAKIMA FIRING CENTER

ALKALI CANYON

CORRAL CANYON

SOURDOUGH CANYON

UMTANUM RIDGE

GINKO PETRIFIED FOREST STATE PARK

KOA VANTAGE

Vantage

RYEGRASS MOUNTAIN

WANAPUM LAKE WANAPUM DAM

WANAPUM DAM AND HERITAGE CENTER

BEVERLY BURKE RD

Wanapum Village

Beverly

Schwana

PRIEST RAPIDS LAKE

SENTINEL GAP

SENTINEL MOUNTAIN

LOWER CRAB CREEK RD

MATTAWA

RD 23 SW

WAHLUKE SLOPE

SADDLE MOUNTAIN

24-SW

RD

27-SW

GOOSE ISLAND

RD 13-SE

GRANT COUNTY

NATURAL CORRAL

RED ROCK COULEE

CRAB

WAHATIS PEAK

CRAB CREEK

26

U S DEPARTMENT OF ENERGY HANFORD SITE

SADDLE MOUNTAIN NATIONAL WILDLIFE REFUGE

COLUMBIA RIVER

GABLE BUTTE

LOCKE ISLAND

WHITE BLUFFS

GRANT CO

BENTON CO

FRANKLIN CO

24

YAKIMA

33

Terrace Heights

34

MIERAS RD

36

E BELL

Birchfield

Yiew-Sun-ach

FIRING CENTER RD

SELAH RD

26

PRIEST RAPIDS DAM

Priest Rapids

CAIRN HOPE PEAK

COLD CREEK RD

R

PRIEST RAPIDS RD

24

24

GABLE MOUNTAIN

MOXEE CITY

UNION GAP

YAKIMA COUNTY

BLACK ROCK VALLEY

24

U S DEPARTMENT OF ENERGY HANFORD SITE

GOOSE EGG HILL

240

BENTON COUNTY

82

12

44

YAKIMA VALLEY FRWY

MAPENISH

SPRING CANYON

DEEP CANYON

241

SNIVELY BASIN

LOOKOUT

RATTLESNAKE MOUNTAIN

WAPATO

97

Ashue

BRANCH

Vonna

YAKIMA INDIAN RESERVATION

FORT

CAMPBELL RD

50

52

54

HIGHLAND DR

E ZILLAH DR

ZILLAH

YAKIMA CANAL

WASHINGTON

CROSBY

SAGEBRUSH RIDGE

MISSIMER

BLACK CANYON

CORRAL CANYON

HORN RAPIDS

US RESERVATION RD

22

YAKIMA INDIAN RESERVATION HEADQUARTERS

TOPPENISH MUSEUM

AMERICAN HOP MUSEUM

TOPPENISH

YOST

DRAIN

MARION

58

223

COOK

82

N OUTLOOK

PRICE

INDEPENDENCE

VAN BELLE

FORCE RD

MONTREAL

SUNNYSIDE

BETHANY

ALLEN RD

ALEXANDER RD

FINN

SHELLER RD

FACTORY

12

67

69

GRANGER

SUNNYSIDE

EMERALD

W SATUS RD

PLANK

MIDVALE RD

MANETA

73

75

HANKS RD

KING RD

TULL

SNIPES RD

ROTHROCK RD

INLAND EMPIRE HWY

Chaffee

DISTRICT LINE RD

WEST RICHLAND

225

RUPPERT RD

224

BENTON CITY

12

82

96

Kiona

GOOSE HILL

97

SATUS CREEK

SATUS

22

MABTON

E EUCLID RD

MABTON-BICKLETON RD

GRANDVIEW

80

BENTON CO HISTORICAL MUSEUM

82

Bickleton

R

MIEHL LIBRARY AND POWELL MUSEUM

Grandview

Gibbon

CHANDLER BUTTE

MCBEE RD

WEBBER CANYON RD

BADGER CANYON RD

DENNIS

221

COUNTY WELL RD

PROSSER

LINCOLN RD

BERT JAMES RD

WAHL GAP RD

SELLARDS RD

221

McKINLEY SPRINGS RD

HORRIGAN RD

HORRIGAN

GWINN RD

TRAVIS

TYRELL RD

SELLARDS RD

CARTER CANYON

BADGER CANYON

YAKIMA INDIAN RESERVATION

MULE BUTTE

GLADE CREEK

MABTON-BICKLETON RD

YAKIMA CO KLICKITAT CO

DEAD CANYON

TULE

MATSEN RD

FERGUSON RD

STEGEMAN RD

Cleveland

GOLDENDALE BICKLETON RD

DOT RD

KLICKITAT COUNTY

SAND RIDGE

PETERSON RD

SMITH RD

ALDERDALE RD

BENTON CO KLICKITAT CO

EAST CANYON

JOHN DAY WILDLIFE MANAGEMENT AREA

Paterson

14

BING CANYON

CHRISTIE RD

SEE 128 MAP

PNW

HWY

SEE 119 MAP

SEE 121 MAP

A B C

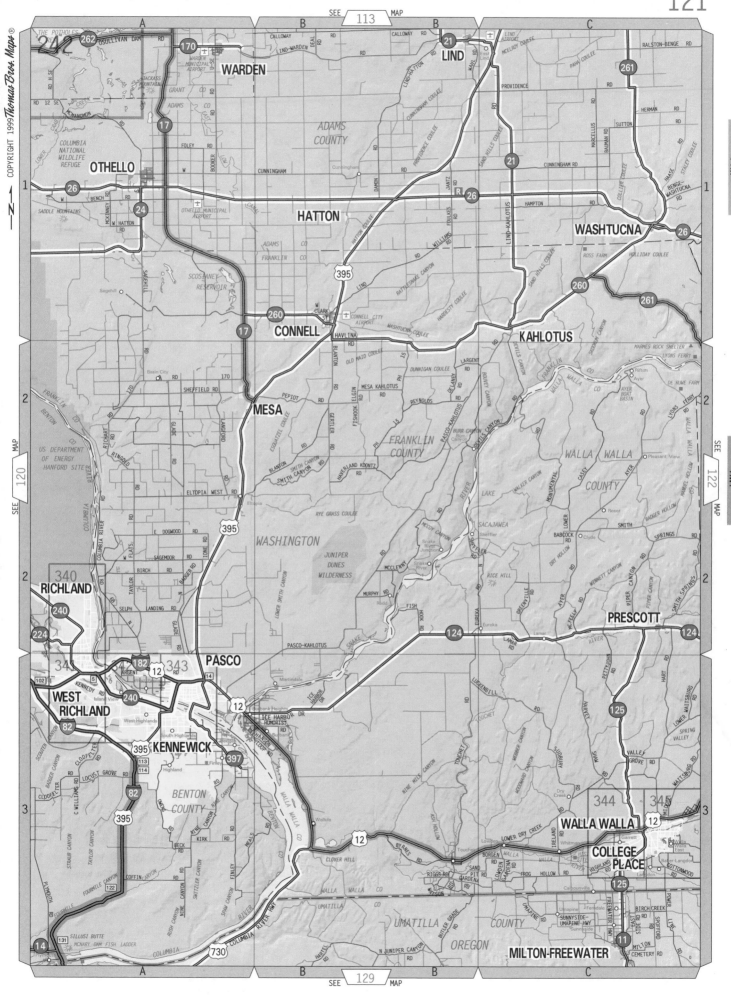

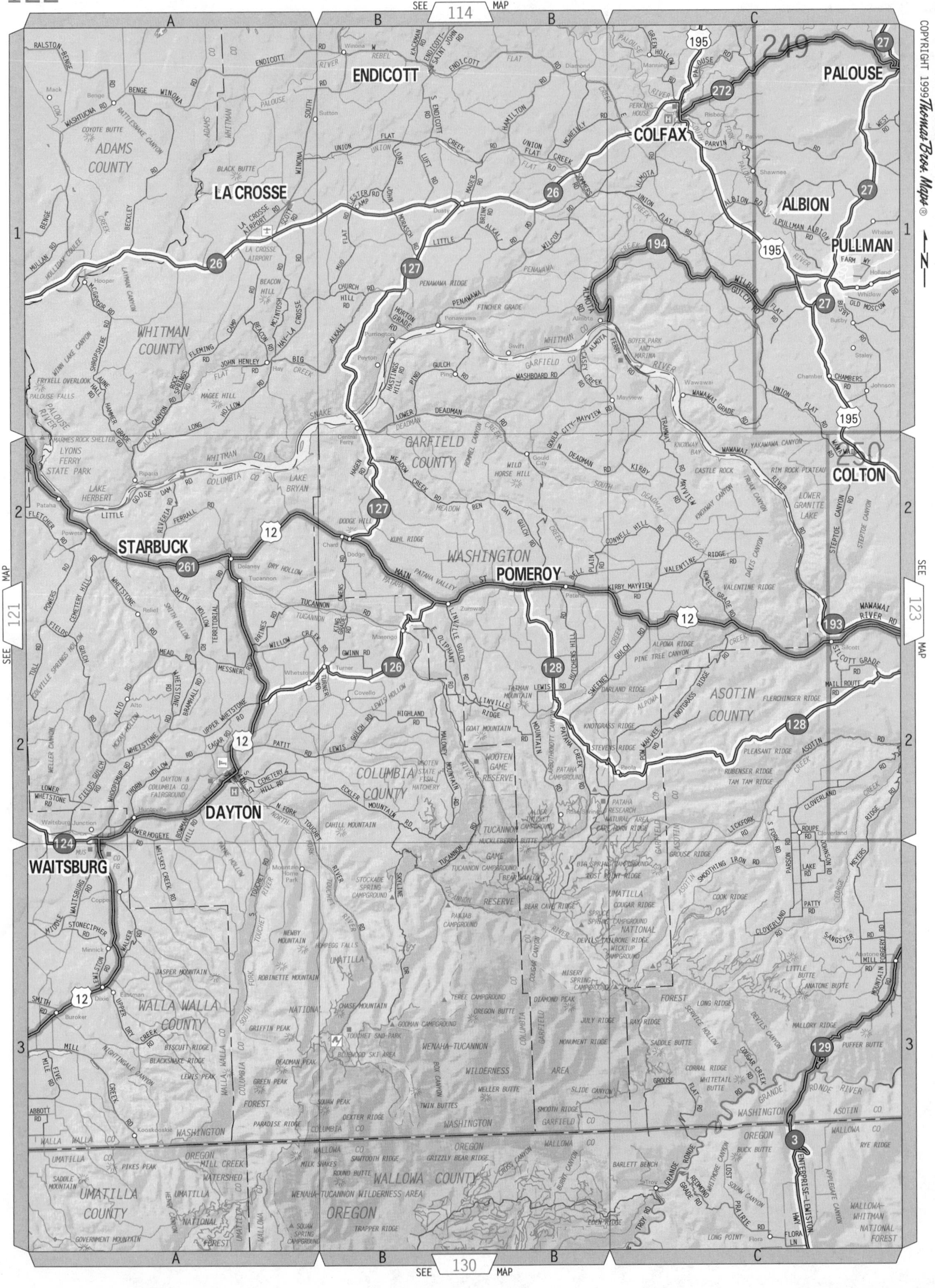

SEE 114 MAP

COPYRIGHT 1999 *Thomas Bros. Maps* ®

PNW

HWY

249

ENDICOTT

PALOUSE

COLFAX

ALBION

PULLMAN

LA CROSSE

ADAMS COUNTY

WHITMAN COUNTY

WHITMAN CO

GARFIELD CO

250

COLTON

STARBUCK

POMEROY

WASHINGTON

GARFIELD COUNTY

ASOTIN COUNTY

SEE 121 MAP

SEE 123 MAP

DAYTON

COLUMBIA COUNTY

WAITSBURG

WALLA WALLA COUNTY

UMATILLA NATIONAL FOREST

WENAHA-TUCANNON WILDERNESS AREA

OREGON

WALLOWA COUNTY

UMATILLA COUNTY

WALLOWA-WHITMAN NATIONAL FOREST

WASHINGTON

OREGON

ENTERPRISE-LEWISTON

SEE 130 MAP

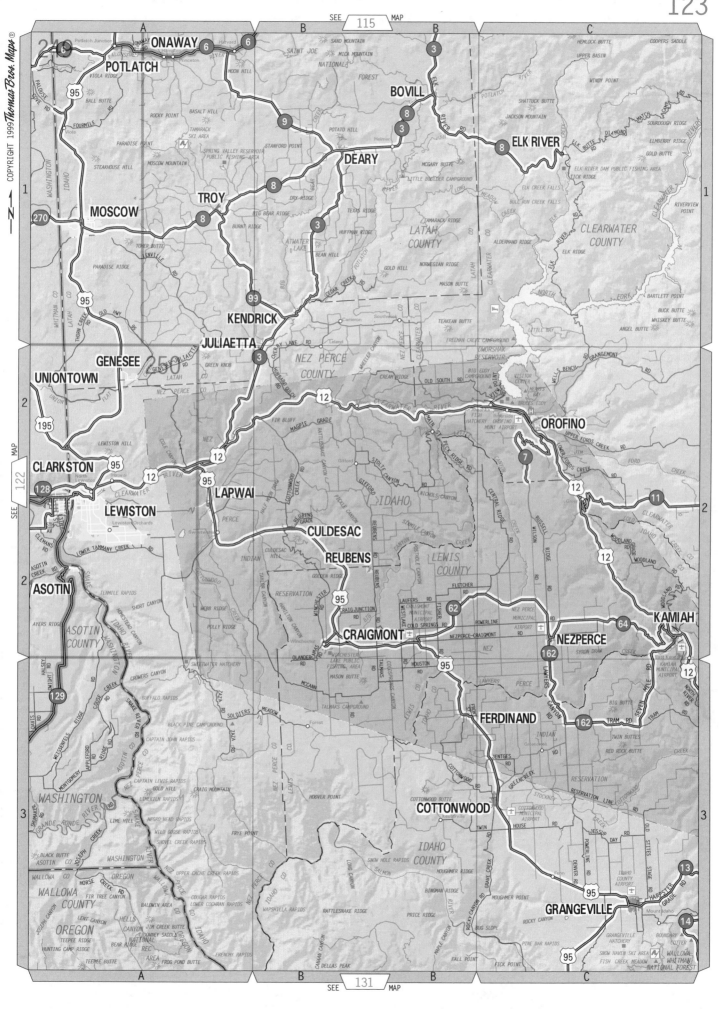

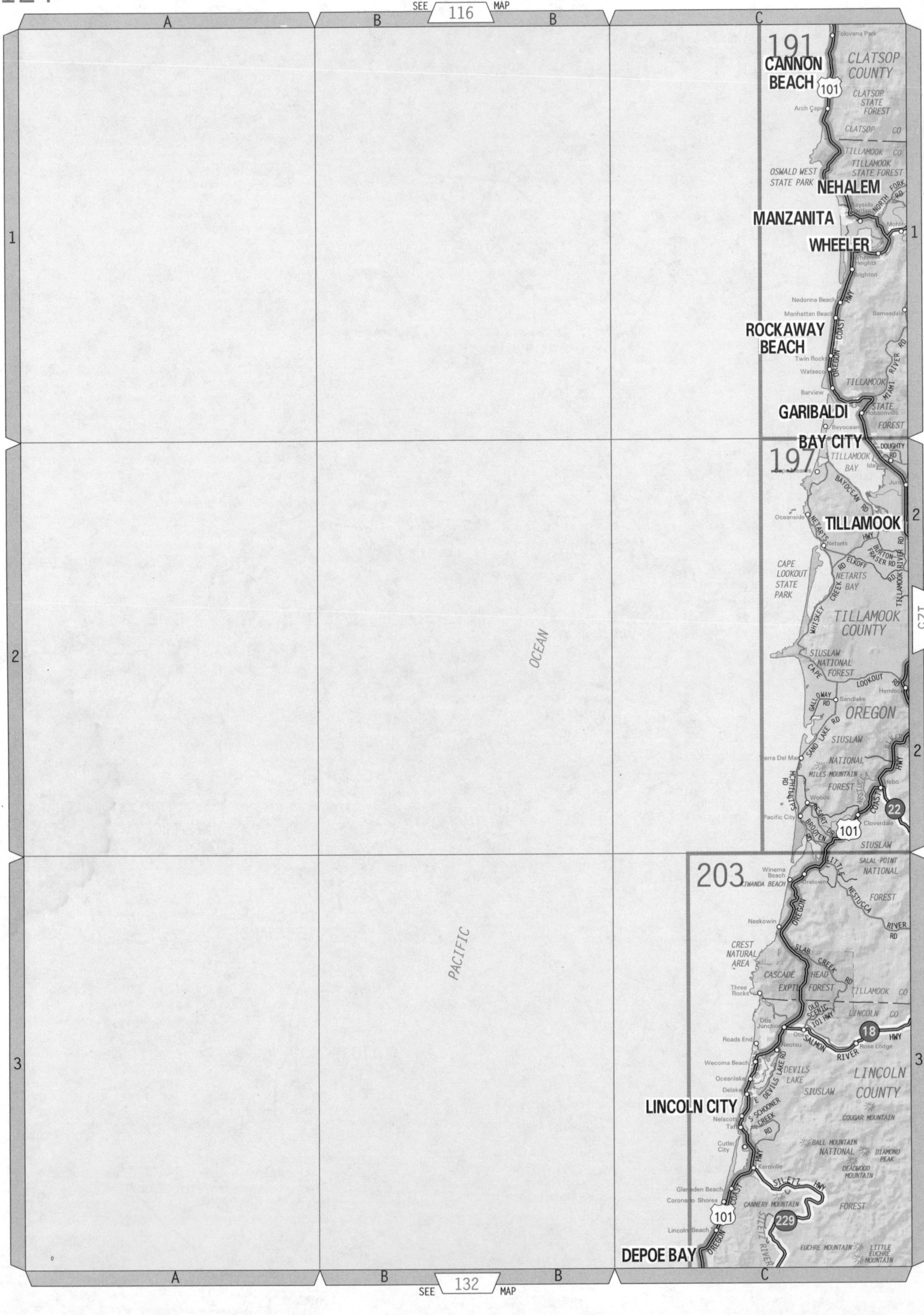

PNW

HWY

SEE 116 MAP

A   B   B   C

—N—

191

Tolovana Park

CANNON BEACH

101

CLATSOP COUNTY

CLATSOP STATE FOREST

Arch Cape

CLATSOP CO

TILLAMOOK CO

TILLAMOOK STATE FOREST

OSWALD WEST STATE PARK

NEHALEM

NORTH FORK RD

Wayside

MANZANITA

Mohler

WHEELER

1

Nehalem Heights

Brighton

Nedonna Beach

Manhattan Beach

Barneedale

ROCKAWAY BEACH

OREGON COAST HWY

Twin Rocks

MIAMI RIVER RD

Watseco

TILLAMOOK

Barview

STATE

GARIBALDI

Bayocean

Hobsonville

FOREST

BAY CITY

Doughty

197

TILLAMOOK BAY

Idaville

BAYOCEAN RD

Jun

2

Oceanside

Netarts

TILLAMOOK

HWY

BEWLEY CREEK RD

CAPE LOOKOUT STATE PARK

NETARTS BAY

ELKOFF RD

BURTON-FRASER RD

NESTUCCA RD

MEADOW LN

Netarts

WHISKEY CREEK RD

TILLAMOOK COUNTY

SIUSLAW NATIONAL FOREST

LOOKOUT RD

Hemlock

GALLOWAY RD

Sandlake

SAND LAKE RD

OREGON

Tierra Del Mar

SIUSLAW NATIONAL FOREST

MILES MOUNTAIN

Hebo

MCPHILLIPS RD

Woods

COAST HWY

RESORT DR

Pacific City

2

22

BROOTEN RD

101

203

Winema Beach

Cloverdale

LITTLE NESTUCCA

SALAL POINT NATIONAL FOREST

Kiwanda Beach

Beaver

OREGON

RIVER RD

Neskowin

CREST NATURAL AREA

SLAB CREEK RD

CASCADE HEAD EXPTL FOREST

TILLAMOOK CO

Three Rocks

OLD SCENIC 101 HWY

LINCOLN CO

Otis Junction

Otis

18 HWY

Rose Lodge

Roads End

Neotsu

SALMON RIVER

LINCOLN COUNTY

3

Wecoma Beach

DEVILS LAKE

E DEVILS LAKE RD

Oceanlake

Delake

SIUSLAW

COUGAR MOUNTAIN

LINCOLN CITY

Nelscott

S SCHOONER CREEK RD

Taft

Cutler City

Kernville

BALL MOUNTAIN NATIONAL

DIAMOND PEAK

DEADWOOD MOUNTAIN

Gleneden Beach

STILETZ HWY

Coronado Shores

CANNERY MOUNTAIN

FOREST

101

SILETZ RIVER

229

Lincoln Beach

EUCHRE MOUNTAIN

LITTLE EUCHRE MOUNTAIN

OREGON COAST HWY

DEPOE BAY

OCEAN

PACIFIC

1

2

3

A   B   B   C

SEE 132 MAP

SEE 125 MAP

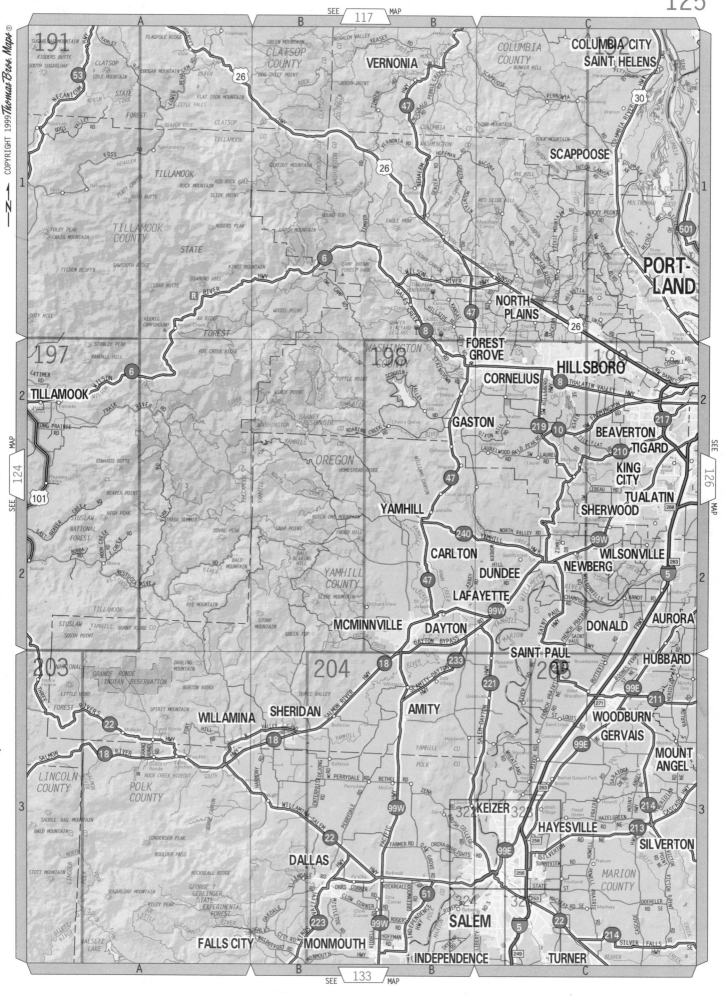

PNW

—N→

SEE 117 MAP

SEE 133 MAP

SEE 124 MAP

SEE 126 MAP

HWY

191

197

203

204

205

198

199

COLUMBIA CITY
SAINT HELENS

PORT-
LAND

VERNONIA

SCAPPOOSE

CLATSOP
COUNTY

COLUMBIA
COUNTY

TILLAMOOK
COUNTY

TILLAMOOK

NORTH
PLAINS

FOREST
GROVE

HILLSBORO

CORNELIUS

BEAVERTON

TIGARD

KING
CITY

TUALATIN

SHERWOOD

WILSONVILLE

NEWBERG

AURORA

DONALD

HUBBARD

GASTON

YAMHILL

CARLTON

DUNDEE

LAFAYETTE

MCMINNVILLE

DAYTON

SAINT PAUL

WOODBURN

GERVAIS

MOUNT
ANGEL

SILVERTON

HAYESVILLE

WILLAMINA

SHERIDAN

AMITY

KEIZER

DALLAS

SALEM

INDEPENDENCE

TURNER

FALLS CITY

MONMOUTH

LINCOLN
COUNTY

POLK
COUNTY

MARION
COUNTY

YAMHILL
COUNTY

WASHINGTON
COUNTY

OREGON

TILLAMOOK
STATE

FOREST

SIUSLAW
NATIONAL
FOREST

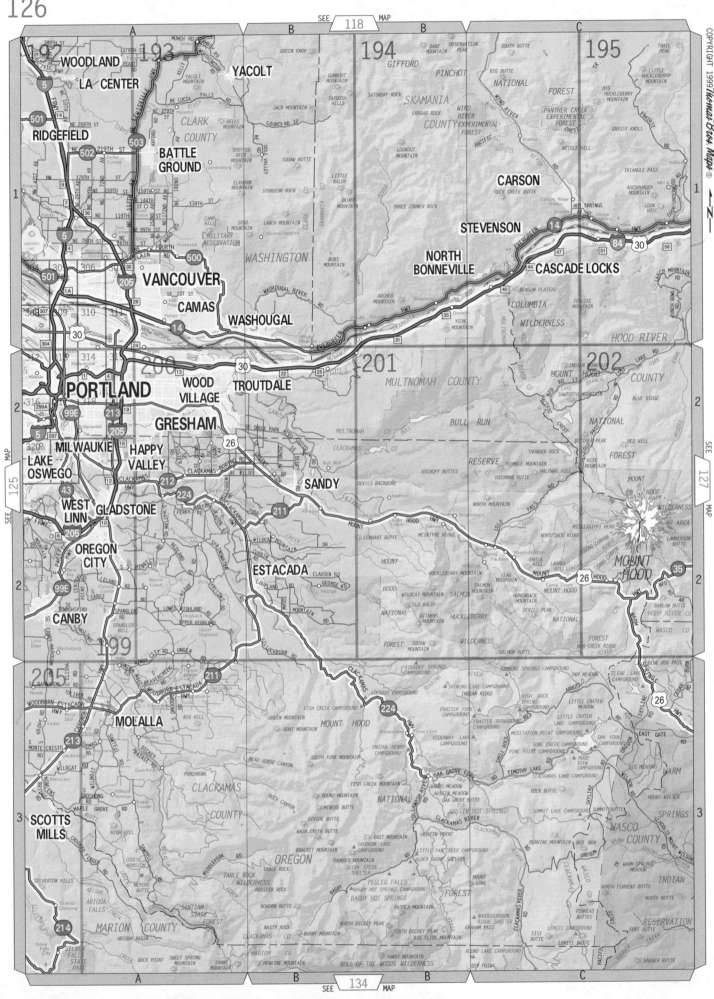

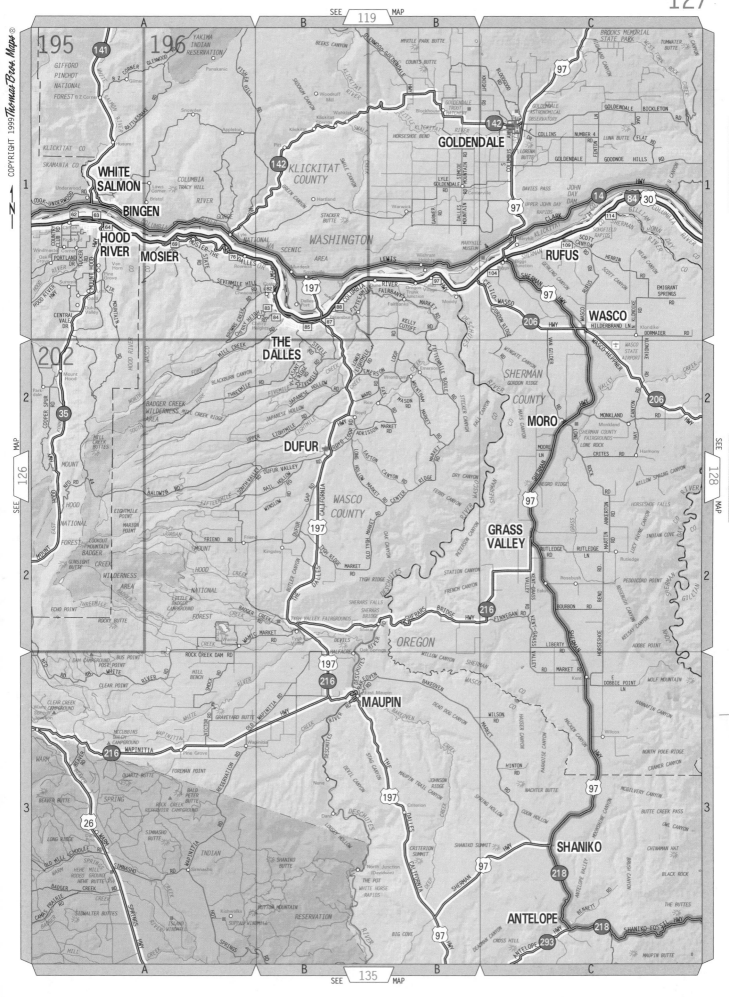

PNW

HWY

SEE 119 MAP

195   196

YAKIMA INDIAN RESERVATION

GIFFORD PINCHOT NATIONAL FOREST

KLICKITAT CO

SKAMANIA CO

WHITE SALMON

BINGEN

HOOD RIVER

MOSIER

GOLDENDALE

KLICKITAT COUNTY

WASHINGTON

COLUMBIA RIVER

COLUMBIA RIVER GORGE NATIONAL SCENIC AREA

BROOK'S MEMORIAL STATE PARK

RUFUS

WASCO

202

MOUNT HOOD

MOUNT HOOD NATIONAL FOREST

THE DALLES

DUFUR

SHERMAN COUNTY

MORO

WASCO COUNTY

GRASS VALLEY

SEE 126 MAP

SEE 128 MAP

OREGON

MAUPIN

WAPINITIA

WARM SPRINGS INDIAN RESERVATION

SHANIKO

ANTELOPE

SEE 135 MAP

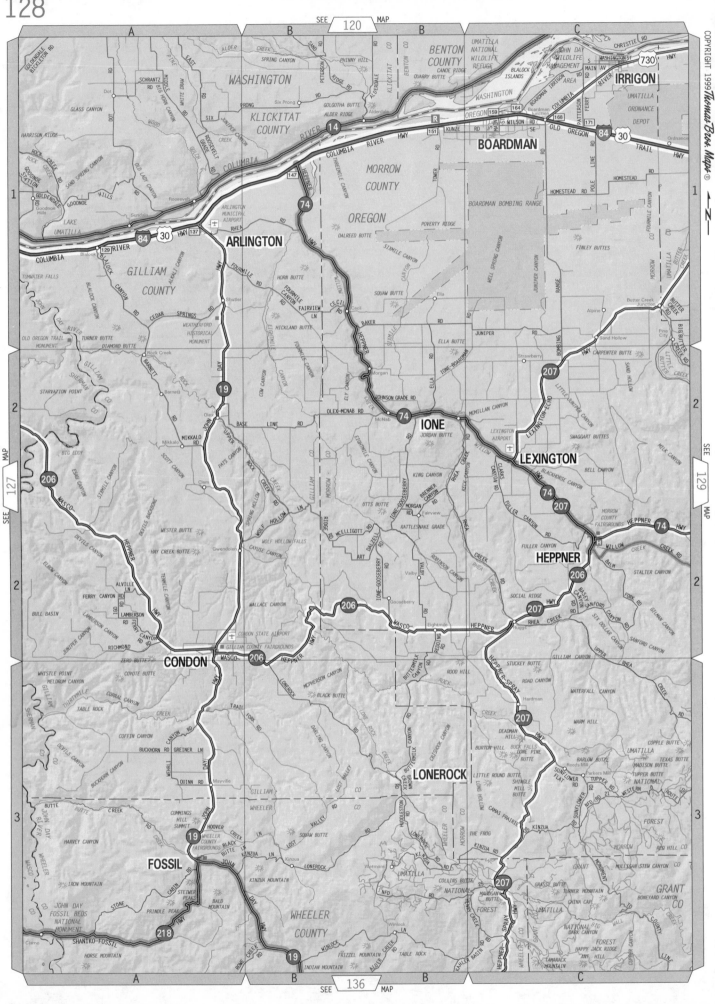

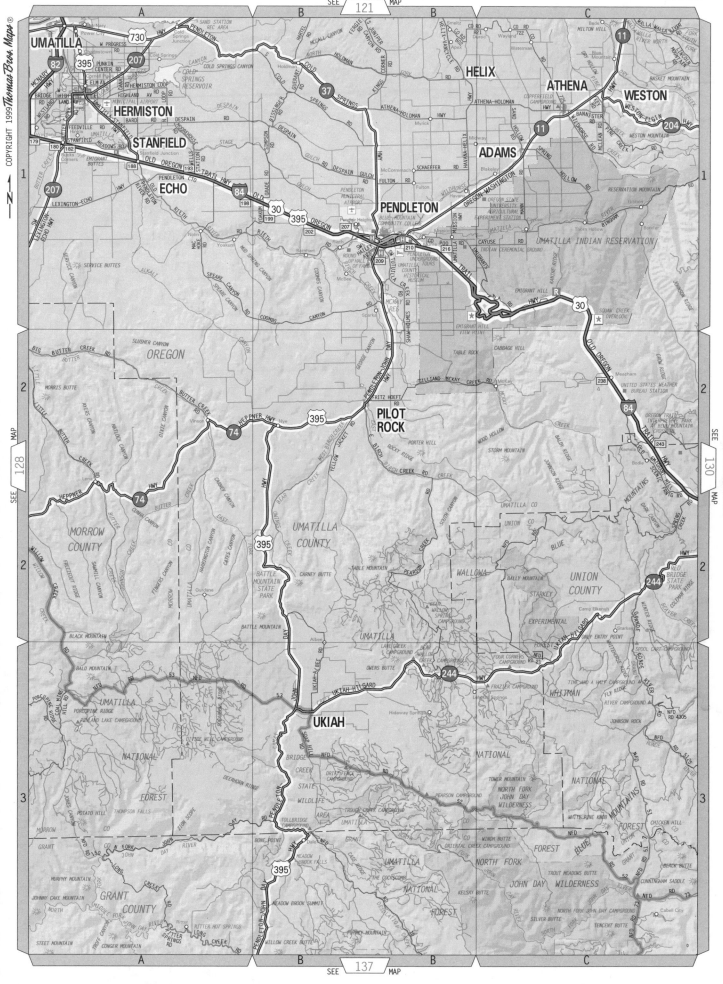

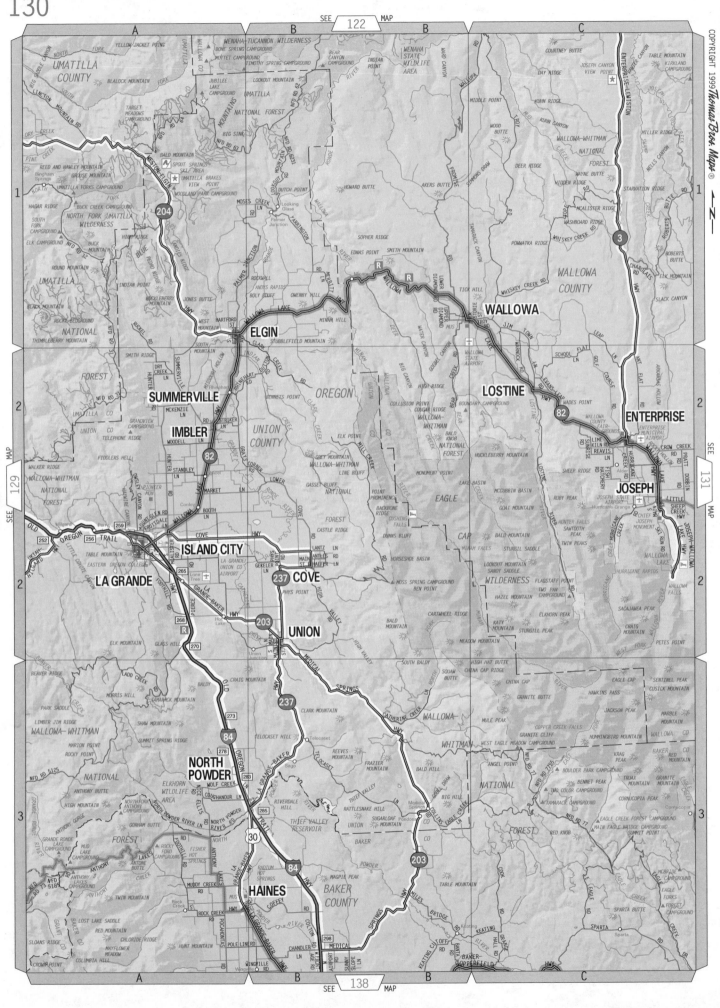

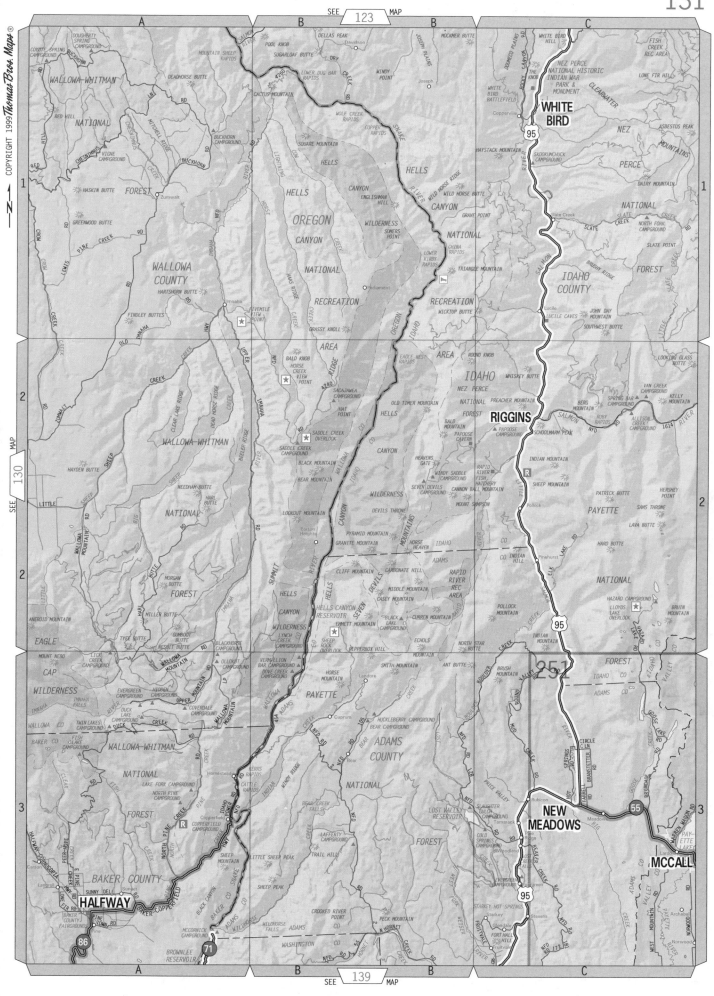

COPYRIGHT 1999 *Thomas Bros. Maps®*

PNW

HWY

SEE 130 MAP

A B B C

1

2

2

3

WALLOWA-WHITMAN

NATIONAL

FOREST

WALLOWA COUNTY

HELLS CANYON

OREGON

NATIONAL

RECREATION

AREA

IDAHO

NEZ PERCE

NATIONAL

FOREST

WHITE BIRD

NEZ PERCE NATIONAL HISTORIC INDIAN WAR PARK & MONUMENT

CLEARWATER

NEZ PERCE MOUNTAINS

IDAHO COUNTY

FOREST

RIGGINS

PAYETTE

NATIONAL

FOREST

251

HELLS CANYON WILDERNESS

SEVEN DEVILS MOUNTAINS

RAPID RIVER REC AREA

PAYETTE

ADAMS COUNTY

NATIONAL

FOREST

NEW MEADOWS

55

MCCALL

95

EAGLE CAP WILDERNESS

WALLOWA-WHITMAN

NATIONAL FOREST

BAKER COUNTY

HALFWAY

86

71

BROWNLEE RESERVOIR

WASHINGTON

ADAMS CO

BAKER CO

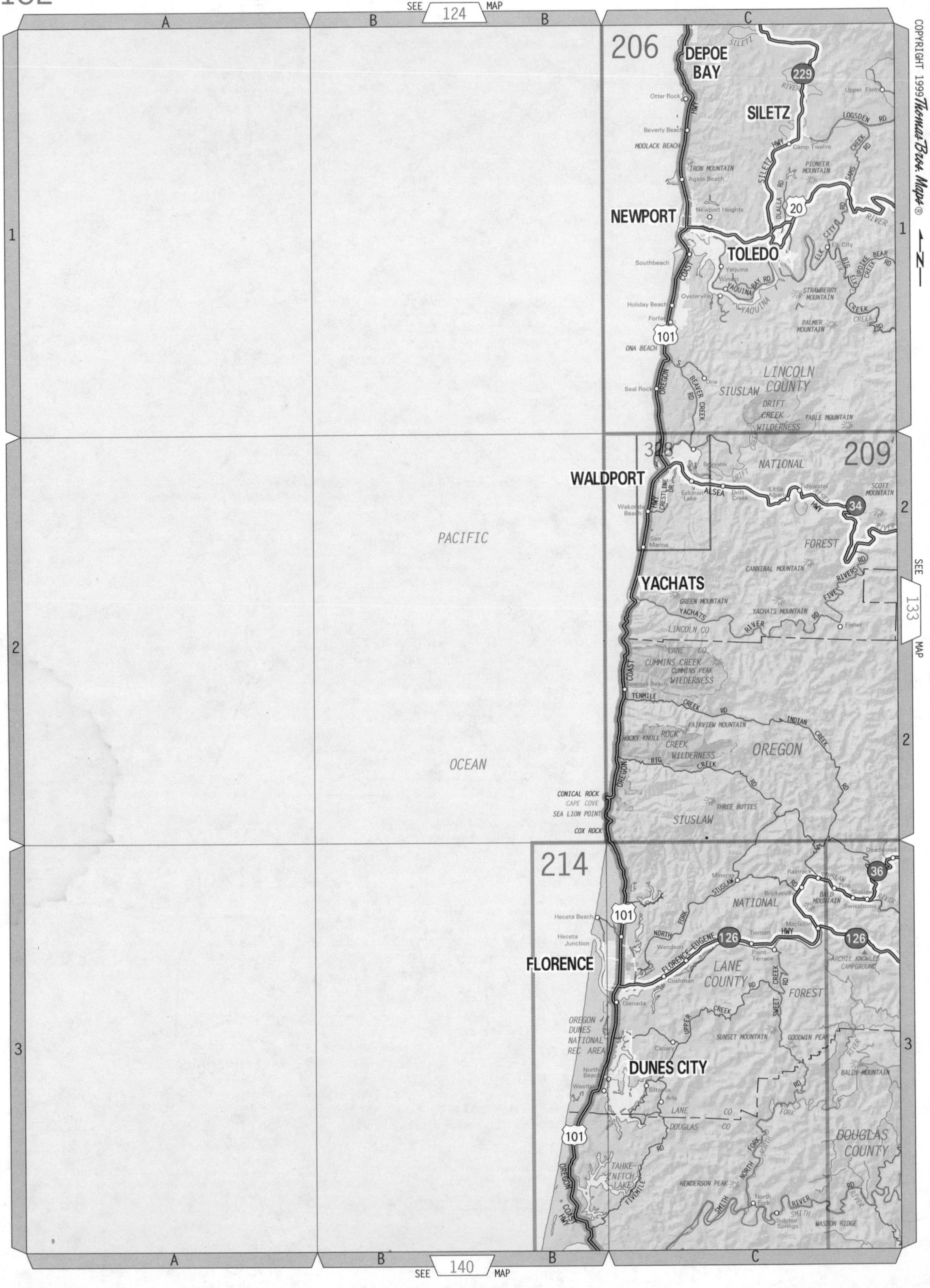

PNW

HMY

SEE 124 MAP

A | B | B | C

206

DEPOE BAY

SILETZ

229

Upper Farm

Otter Rock

Beverly Beach

MOOLACK BEACH

Camp Twelve

LOGSDEN RD

IRON MOUNTAIN

Agate Beach

PIONEER MOUNTAIN

NEWPORT

20

ELK CITY

BIG ELK CREEK RD

UPRIVER RD

BEAR CREEK RD

TOLEDO

Southbeach

Newport Heights

Yaquina

Winant

YAQUINA BAY RD

Oysterville

STRAWBERRY MOUNTAIN

Holiday Beach

YAQUINA

PALMER MOUNTAIN

Forlas

101

ONA BEACH

LINCOLN COUNTY

Ona

BEAVER CREEK RD

SIUSLAW

DRIFT CREEK WILDERNESS

TABLE MOUNTAIN

Seal Rock

OREGON

1

328

209

Bayview

NATIONAL

WALDPORT

CRESTLINE DR

Eckman Lake

ALSEA

Little Albany

Tidewater

DRIFT CREEK

SCOTT MOUNTAIN

34

Wakonda Beach

San Marine

HWY

FOREST

RIVER

FIVE RIVERS RD

SEE 133 MAP

PACIFIC

YACHATS

CANNIBAL MOUNTAIN

GREEN MOUNTAIN

YACHATS

YACHATS MOUNTAIN

RD

LINCOLN CO

RIVER

Fisher

LANE CO

CUMMINS CREEK

CUMMINS PEAK

WILDERNESS

Seadrae Beach

COAST

TENMILE

CREEK

RD

FAIRVIEW MOUNTAIN

INDIAN CREEK

RD

OCEAN

ROCKY KNOLL

ROCK CREEK WILDERNESS

OREGON

BIG CREEK

CONICAL ROCK

CAPE COVE

SEA LION POINT

THREE BUTTES

OREGON

RD

SIUSLAW

COX ROCK

2

214

Deadwood

Minerva

Rainrock

SIUSLAW

36

101

Brickerville

BALD MOUNTAIN

NATIONAL

RIVER

Swisshome

Heceta Beach

NORTH FORK

Wendson

126

Tiernan

Mapleton

HWY

126

Heceta Junction

FLORENCE-EUGENE

Point Terrace

ARCHIE KNOWLES CAMPGROUND

FLORENCE

Cushman

LANE COUNTY

SWEET CREEK RD

FOREST

Glenada

UPPER

CREEK

SUNSET MOUNTAIN

GOODWIN PEAK

OREGON DUNES NATIONAL REC AREA

Canary

BALDY MOUNTAIN

North Beach

DUNES CITY

Siltcoos

FIVE RIVERS RD

Westlake

Ada

LANE CO

NORTH FORK

3

101

DOUGLAS CO

DOUGLAS COUNTY

TAHKENITCH LAKE

FIVEMILE

HENDERSON PEAK

NORTH FORK

SMITH RIVER RD

North Fork

Sulphur Springs

SMITH RIVER

MASON RIDGE

A | B | B | C

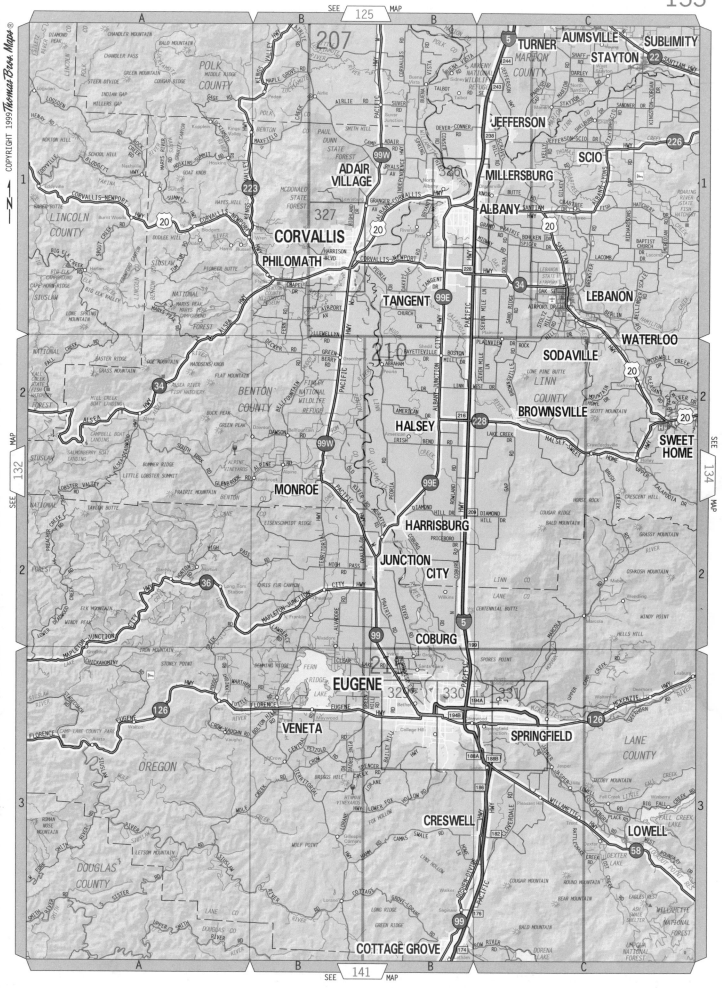

PNW

HWY

SEE 125 MAP

SEE 132 MAP

SEE 134 MAP

SEE 141 MAP

207

327

210

223

A   B   B   C

1

2

2

3

TURNER
AUMSVILLE
STAYTON
SUBLIMITY
JEFFERSON
SCIO
MILLERSBURG
ALBANY
CORVALLIS
PHILOMATH
ADAIR VILLAGE
TANGENT
LEBANON
WATERLOO
SODAVILLE
BROWNSVILLE
HALSEY
SWEET HOME
MONROE
HARRISBURG
JUNCTION CITY
COBURG
EUGENE
SPRINGFIELD
VENETA
CRESWELL
LOWELL
COTTAGE GROVE

POLK COUNTY
LINCOLN COUNTY
BENTON COUNTY
LINN COUNTY
MARION COUNTY
LANE COUNTY
DOUGLAS COUNTY

OREGON

PNW

HWY

SEE 126 MAP

SEE 133 MAP

SEE 135 MAP

SEE 142 MAP

—N—

A B B C

LYONS
MILL CITY GATES
226

DETROIT
IDANHA

SWEET HOME

McKENZIE

58

126

372

211

216

22

20

126

242

SILVER FALLS STATE PARK

SANTIAM STATE FOREST

WILLAMETTE NATIONAL FOREST

LINN COUNTY

MARION COUNTY

JEFFERSON COUNTY

WARM SPRINGS INDIAN RESERVATION

WASCO CO

MOUNT HOOD NATIONAL FOREST

MOUNT JEFFERSON WILDERNESS AREA

BULL OF THE WOODS WILDERNESS

DETROIT LAKE STATE PARK

DETROIT LAKE

MIDDLE SANTIAM WILDERNESS AREA

MENAGERIE WILDERNESS AREA

FOSTER LAKE

GREEN PETER LAKE

CASCADIA STATE PARK

MOUNT WASHINGTON WILDERNESS AREA

DESCHUTES NATIONAL FOREST

DESCHUTES COUNTY

LANE COUNTY

THREE SISTERS WILDERNESS AREA

BLUE RIVER LAKE

COUGAR RESERVOIR

WALDO LAKE WILDERNESS AREA

LOOKOUT POINT RESERVOIR

WILLAMETTE NATIONAL FOREST

PRINGLE FALLS EXPERIMENTAL FOREST ADDITION

WHITEWATER GLACIER

WALDO GLACIER

MILK CREEK GLACIER

1 1 1

2 2 2

3 3 3

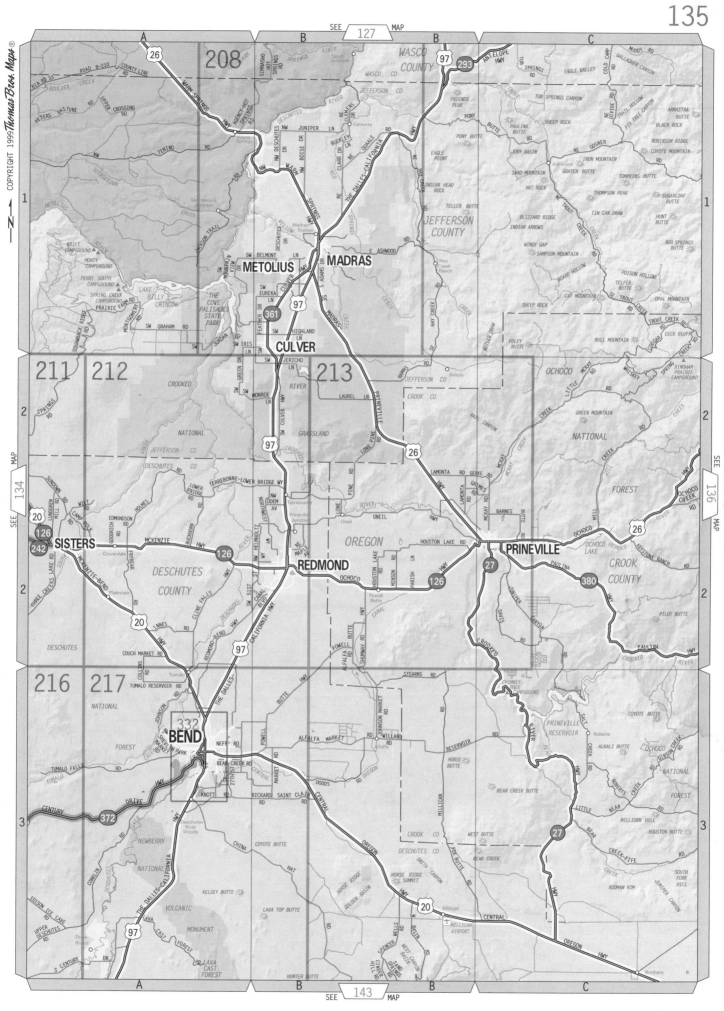

—N→

208

WASCO
COUNTY

WASCO
CO

JEFFERSON CO

JEFFERSON
COUNTY

PNW

METOLIUS

MADRAS

CULVER

211 | 212

213

OCHOCO

NATIONAL

JEFFERSON CO

CROOK CO

GRASSLAND

HWY

SISTERS

OREGON

PRINEVILLE

DESCHUTES
COUNTY

REDMOND

FOREST

CROOK
COUNTY

DESCHUTES

216 | 217

NATIONAL

FOREST

BEND

PRINEVILLE
RESERVOIR

OCHOCO

NATIONAL

FOREST

NEWBERRY

NATIONAL

VOLCANIC

MONUMENT

CROOK CO

DESCHUTES CO

SEE 128 MAP

SEE 144 MAP

SEE 135 MAP

SEE 137 MAP

COPYRIGHT 1999 Thomas Bros. Maps ®

—N—

PNW

HWY

SPRAY

MONUMENT

DAYVILLE

A   B   B   C

1

2

2

3

19   207   19   207   19

380   26   26

JEFFERSON COUNTY

WHEELER COUNTY

GRANT COUNTY

CROOK COUNTY

OREGON

HARNEY COUNTY

WHEELER CO

CROOK CO

JOHN DAY FOSSIL BEDS NATIONAL MONUMENT PAINTED HILLS UNIT

JOHN DAY FOSSIL BEDS NATIONAL MONUMENT

OCHOCO NATIONAL FOREST

MALHEUR NATIONAL FOREST

OCHOCO NATIONAL FOREST

MALHEUR NATIONAL FOREST

UMATILLA NATIONAL FOREST

BLACK CANYON WILDERNESS

MAURY MOUNTAINS

OCHOCO MOUNTAINS

Currant Peak · Sheep Mountain · Jennies Peak · Corral Mountain · Harper Mountain · Masiker Mountain · Little Tamarack Mountain · Franklin Mountain · Rains Creek · Thorn Spring Butte · Johnson · Portuguese Canyon · Jack O Clubs · China Peak · Grant County · China Hat Peak · Kimberly · Franks · Sentinel Peak · Mount Misery · Steamboat Mountain · Iron Mountain · Butler Mountain · Sisnoter · Keys Mountain · Camel Hump · Richmond · Baldy · Toney Butte · Scott Butte · Sutton Mountain · Marshall Butte · Peggy Butte · Flock Mountain · Keyes Mountain · Waterman · Picture Gorge · Table Rock · Cottonwood Basin · Monulty Basin · Vanata Basin · Dead Pine · Aldrich Mountain · Battle Creek Mountain · Spanish Peak · Cottonwood Campground · Windy Point · Black Canyon · Bear Mountain · Bear Skull · Groundhog Knoll · Wolf Mountain · Jackass Mountain · Timber Basin · Middle Mountain · Big Basin · Sugarloaf · Rudio Mountain · Hog Ridge · Juniper Butte · Table Mountain · Mitchell Parrish Mountain · Dollarhide · Bailey Butte · Black Butte · Gilchrist Butte · Dove Mountain · White Butte · Lewis Butte · Richard Butte · Ochoco Divide Campground · Old Kelly Mill · Wildcat Campground · Carrol Campground · Bridge Creek · Peterson Point · Badger Camp · Mount Pisgah · Walton Lake Campground · Scotts Campground · Lonesome Spring Campground · Jones Lava · Allen Creek Campground · Big Summit Prairie · Deep Creek Campground · Paulina · Buck Butte · Twin Springs Campground · Roba Butte · Timothy Meadow · Little Summit Campground · Bear Butte · Mud Spring Campground · Tamarack Butte · Frazier Campground · Cougar Mountain · Pine Tree Campground · Kelly Gap · Prairie Hill · Lutsey Point · Pine Mountain · Ruby Butte · Minifie Ridge · Wolf Creek Campground · Big Rattlesnake Butte · Sugar Creek Campground · Rattlesnake Butte · Powell Valley Butte · Powell Mountain · Dahlgren Rim · Spur Butte · Ellingson Hill · Frenchy Butte · Isadore Butte · Mills Butte · Faulkner Butte · Juniper Butte · Cabin Butte · Rough Canyon · Rabbit Valley · Birdsong Butte · Salem Ridge · Dorschied Butte · Allyn Draw · Suplee Butte · Little Baldy · Sugarloaf Mountain · Morgan Mountain · Harrison Mountain · Green Mountain · Forbes Butte · Soda Table · Smith Basin · Suplee · Pitt Ridge · Windy Ridge · Sheep Creek Butte · Joe Butte · Milk Butte · Maupin Butte · Ryegrass Table · Angel Butte · Colpitts Butte · Weberg Butte · Iron Mountain · Little Mowich Mountain · Mule Deer Ridge · Pine Creek Campground · Tower Point · Hawk Rim · Wiley Flat Campground · Arrowwood Point · Homestead Butte · Twelvemile Table · Yreka Rim · Wade Butte · Great Sandy Desert · Coffee Butte · Orr Point · Duck Ridge · Turpin Canyon · Big Mowich Mountain · Utley Butte · Steens Ridge · Logan Butte · Smoky Butte · Moon Mountain · Gerry Mountain · Sand Hollow · Twelvemile · Price-Twelvemile · Magpie Butte · Sherman Rim · Saddle Butte · Speckle Butte · Walker Ridge · Three Buttes · Whistle Creek · Delintment Lake · Donelly Butte · Howard Valley · Emigrant Creek · Bear Canyon Butte · Ann Butte · Willow Butte · Kid Peak · Ibex Butte · Freezeout Ridge · Bradford Ridge · Howard Ridge · Grassy Butte · Merrill · Pringle Flat · Montgomery Rd

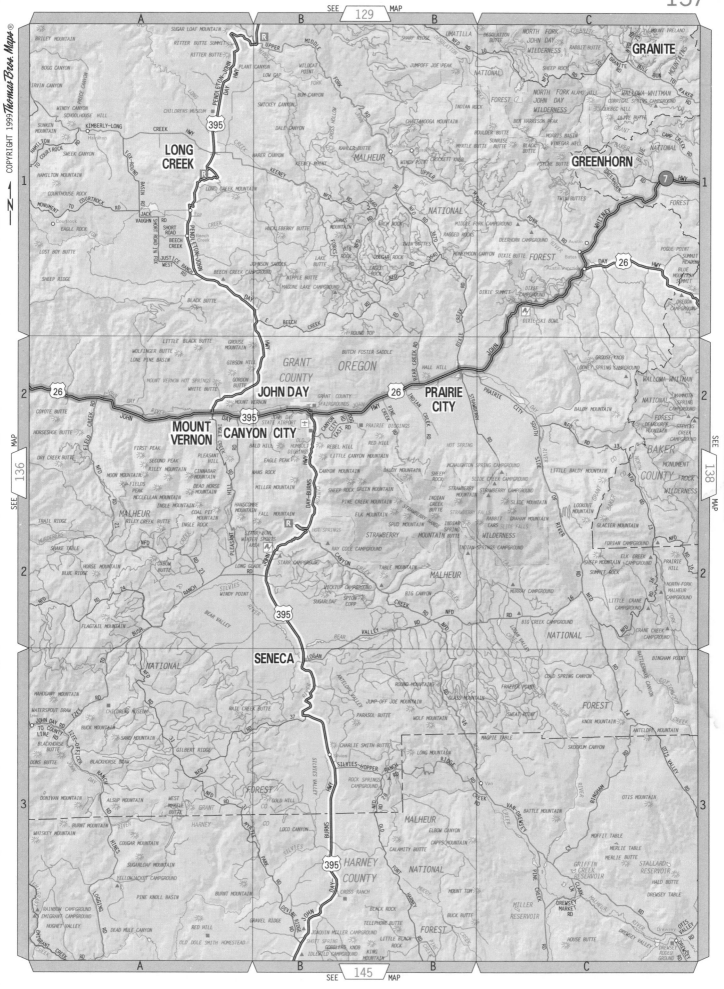

SEE 130 MAP

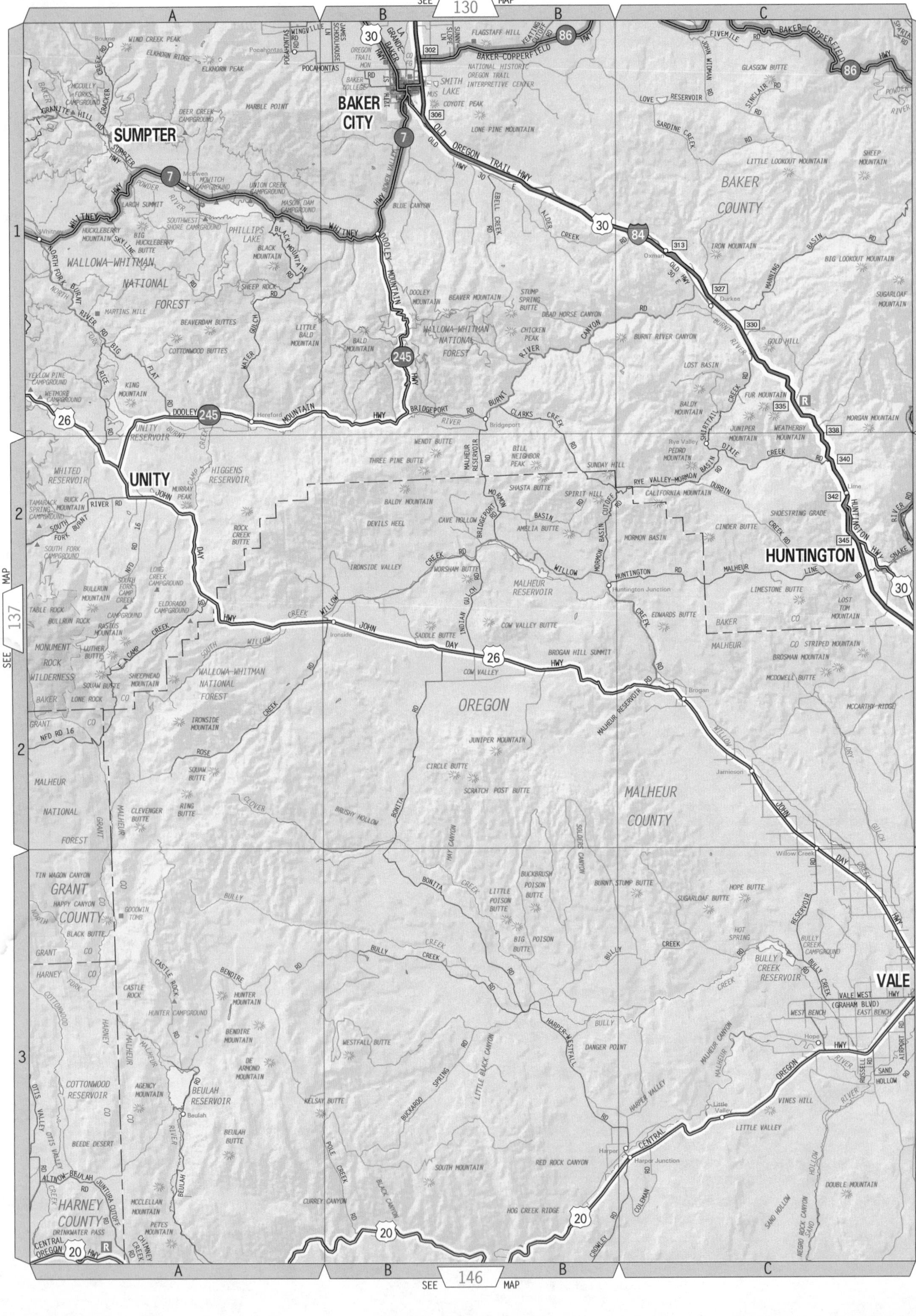

PNW

HWY

SEE 137 MAP

SEE 139 MAP

—N—

A   B   B   C

BAKER CITY

SUMPTER

UNITY

HUNTINGTON

VALE

WALLOWA-WHITMAN NATIONAL FOREST

BAKER COUNTY

MALHEUR COUNTY

GRANT COUNTY

HARNEY COUNTY

MALHEUR NATIONAL FOREST

MONUMENT ROCK WILDERNESS

OREGON

Baker-Copperfield National Historic Oregon Trail Interpretive Center

Phillips Lake

Unity Reservoir

Malheur Reservoir

Beulah Reservoir

Bully Creek Reservoir

Cottonwood Reservoir

Higgens Reservoir

Whited Reservoir

Old Oregon Trail Hwy

7

26

20

30

84

86

245

313

327

330

335

338

340

342

345

302

306

R

1   2   2   3

SEE 146 MAP

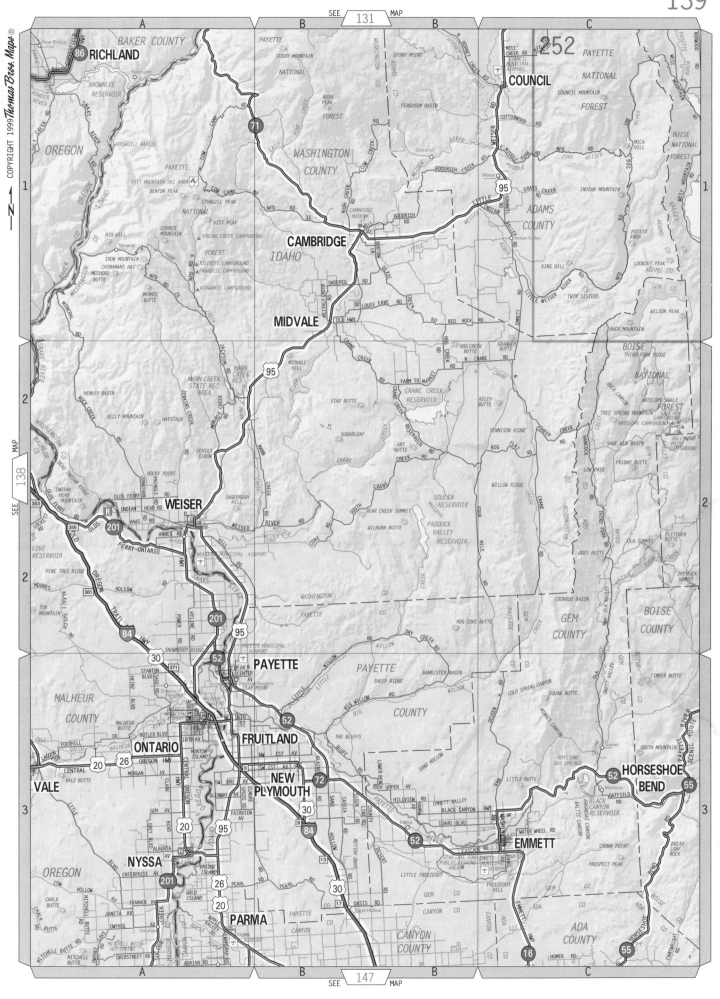

SEE 131 MAP

SEE 147 MAP

SEE 138 MAP

PNW

HWY

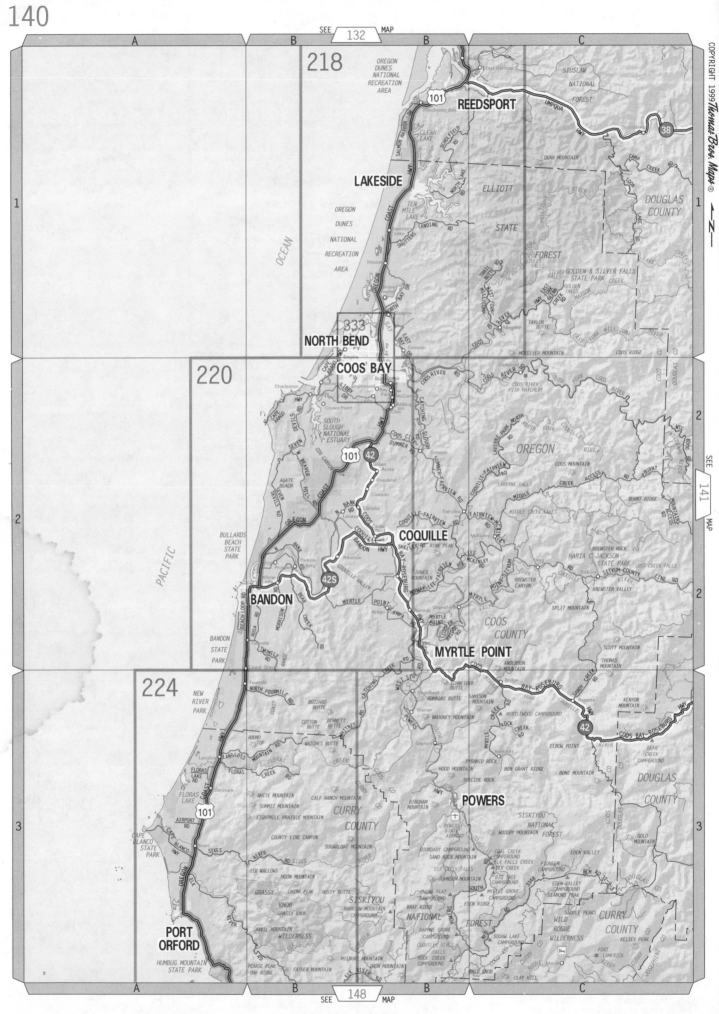

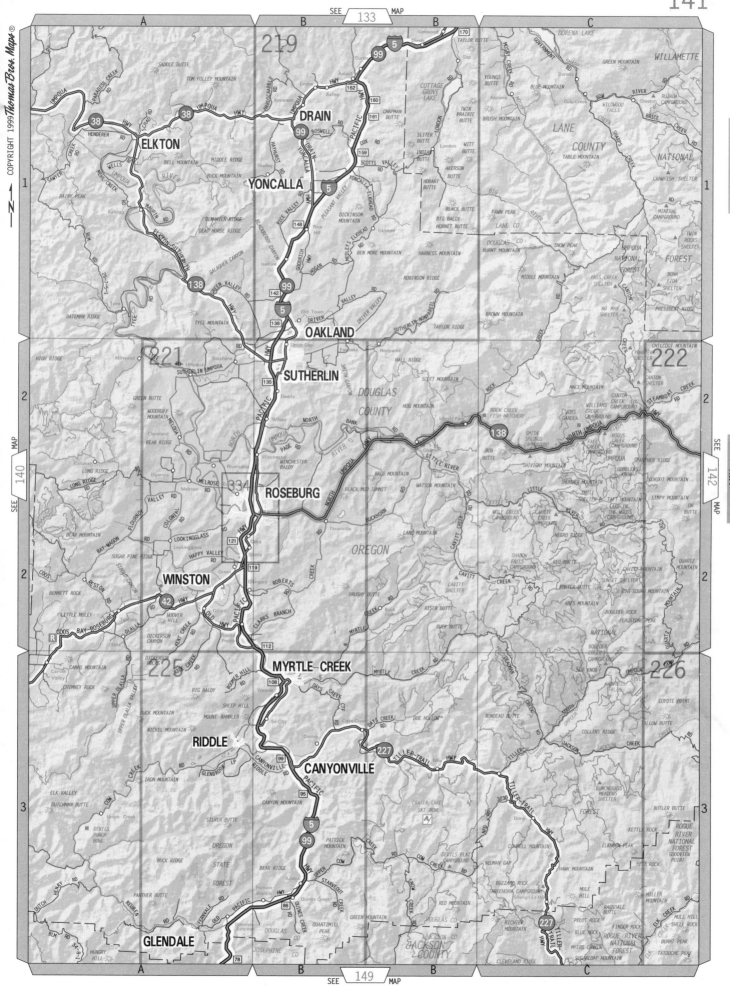

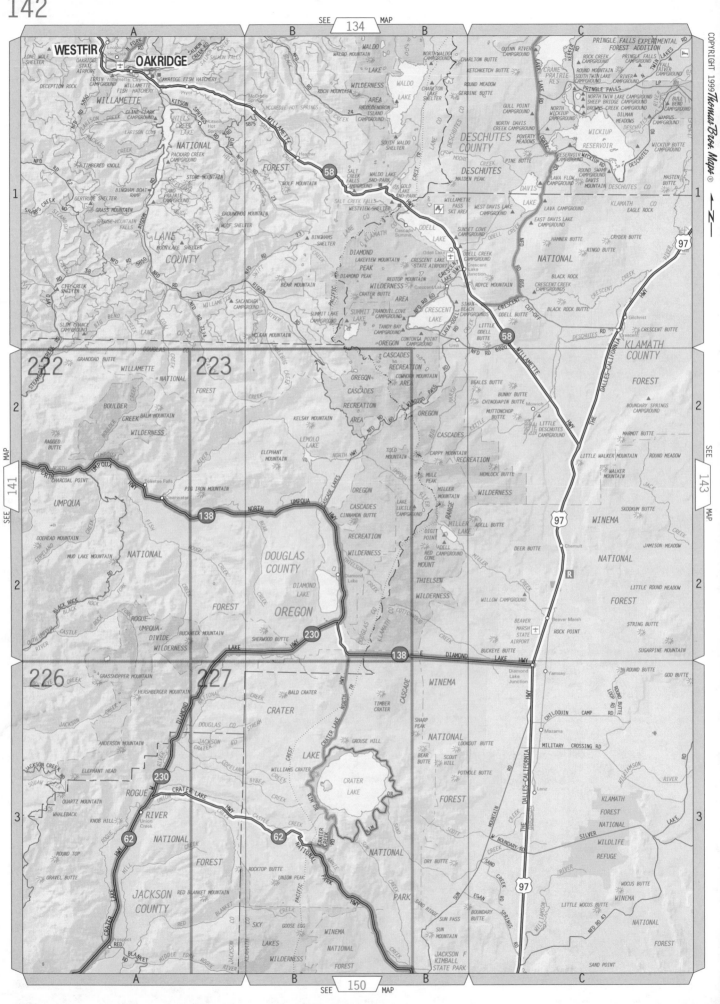

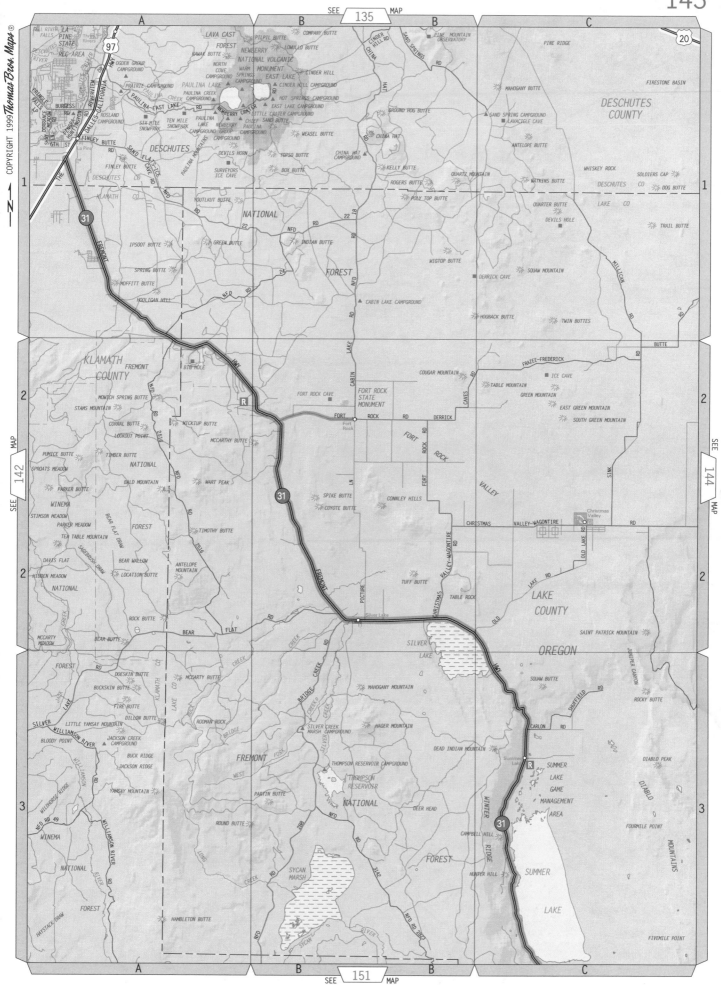

SEE 142 MAP

SEE 144 MAP

PNW

HWY

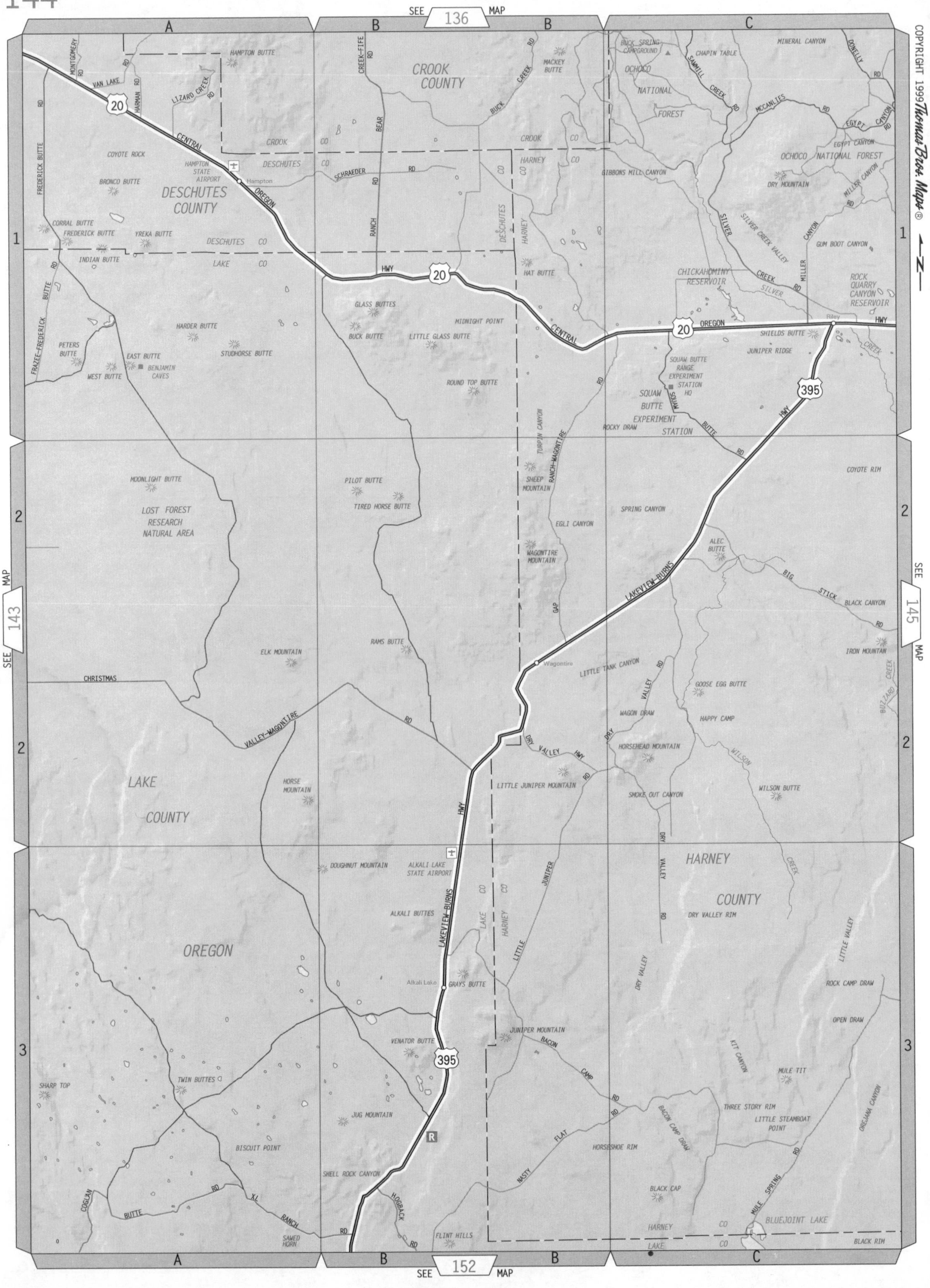

PNW

HWY

—N—

SEE MAP 136

A   B   B   C

MONTGOMERY RD
VAN LAKE
HARMAN RD
LIZARD CREEK RD
HAMPTON BUTTE
CREEK-FIFE
CROOK COUNTY
BUCK CREEK
MACKEY BUTTE
RD
BUCK SPRING CAMPGROUND
OCHOCO
NATIONAL
FOREST
MINERAL CANYON
CHAPIN TABLE
SAWMILL CREEK
DONELLY RD
EGYPT CANYON
MCCANLIES
20
CENTRAL
COYOTE ROCK
CROOK
CO
DESCHUTES
CO
HAMPTON STATE AIRPORT
Hampton
OREGON
SCHRAEDER RD
BEAR
RANCH RD
RD
CROOK CO
HARNEY CO
GIBBONS MILL CANYON
OCHOCO NATIONAL FOREST
DRY MOUNTAIN
SILVER
SILVER CREEK VALLEY
MILLER CANYON
EGYPT CANYON
MILLER RD
FREDERICK BUTTE
BRONCO BUTTE
DESCHUTES COUNTY
DESCHUTES CO
GUM BOOT CANYON

1   1

CORRAL BUTTE
FREDERICK BUTTE
YREKA BUTTE
INDIAN BUTTE
FRAZEE-FREDERICK BUTTE
RD
DESCHUTES CO
LAKE CO
HWY
20
HAT BUTTE
CHICKAHOMINY RESERVOIR
CREEK
SILVER
MILLER RD
Riley
HWY
ROCK QUARRY CANYON RESERVOIR

PETERS BUTTE
HARDER BUTTE
GLASS BUTTES
BUCK BUTTE
MIDNIGHT POINT
LITTLE GLASS BUTTE
CENTRAL
20
OREGON
SHIELDS BUTTE
JUNIPER RIDGE
EAST BUTTE
BENJAMIN CAVES
WEST BUTTE
STUDHORSE BUTTE
ROUND TOP BUTTE
SQUAW BUTTE RANGE EXPERIMENT STATION HQ
SQUAW BUTTE EXPERIMENT STATION
RD
SQUAW BUTTE
ROCKY DRAW
HWY
395

SEE MAP 143

MOONLIGHT BUTTE
LOST FOREST RESEARCH NATURAL AREA
PILOT BUTTE
TIRED HORSE BUTTE
TURPIN CANYON
RANCH-WAGONTIRE
SHEEP MOUNTAIN
EGLI CANYON
WAGONTIRE MOUNTAIN
SPRING CANYON
COYOTE RIM
ALEC BUTTE
LAKEVIEW-BURNS
BIG STICK
BLACK CANYON
RD
IRON MOUNTAIN

2   2

ELK MOUNTAIN
RAMS BUTTE
RD
GAP
Wagontire
LITTLE TANK CANYON
VALLEY RD
GOOSE EGG BUTTE
CHRISTMAS
VALLEY-WAGONTIRE
WAGON DRAW
HAPPY CAMP
WILSON
BUZZARD CREEK

LAKE
COUNTY
HORSE MOUNTAIN
DRY VALLEY HWY
LITTLE JUNIPER MOUNTAIN
HORSEHEAD MOUNTAIN
DRY
SMOKES OUT CANYON
WILSON BUTTE

2   2

DOUGHNUT MOUNTAIN
ALKALI LAKE STATE AIRPORT
LAKE CO
HARNEY CO
JUNIPER
HARNEY COUNTY
DRY VALLEY
DRY VALLEY RIM
CREEK

ALKALI BUTTES
LAKEVIEW-BURNS
LITTLE
OREGON
Alkali Lake
GRAYS BUTTE
JUNIPER MOUNTAIN
BACON
KIT CANYON
LITTLE VALLEY
ROCK CAMP DRAW
OPEN DRAW
MULE TIT
ONSANA CANYON

3   3

SHARP TOP
TWIN BUTTES
VENATOR BUTTE
395
JUG MOUNTAIN
BACON CAMP RD
NASTY FLAT
THREE STORY RIM
LITTLE STEAMBOAT POINT
R
BISCUIT POINT
HORSESHOE RIM
BLACK CAP
COGLAN BUTTE
XL RANCH RD
SHELL ROCK CANYON
HOBACK RD
FLINT HILLS
HARNEY LAKE
MULE SPRING
BLUEJOINT LAKE
HARNEY CO
BLACK RIM
SAWED HORN

A   B   B   C

SEE MAP 152

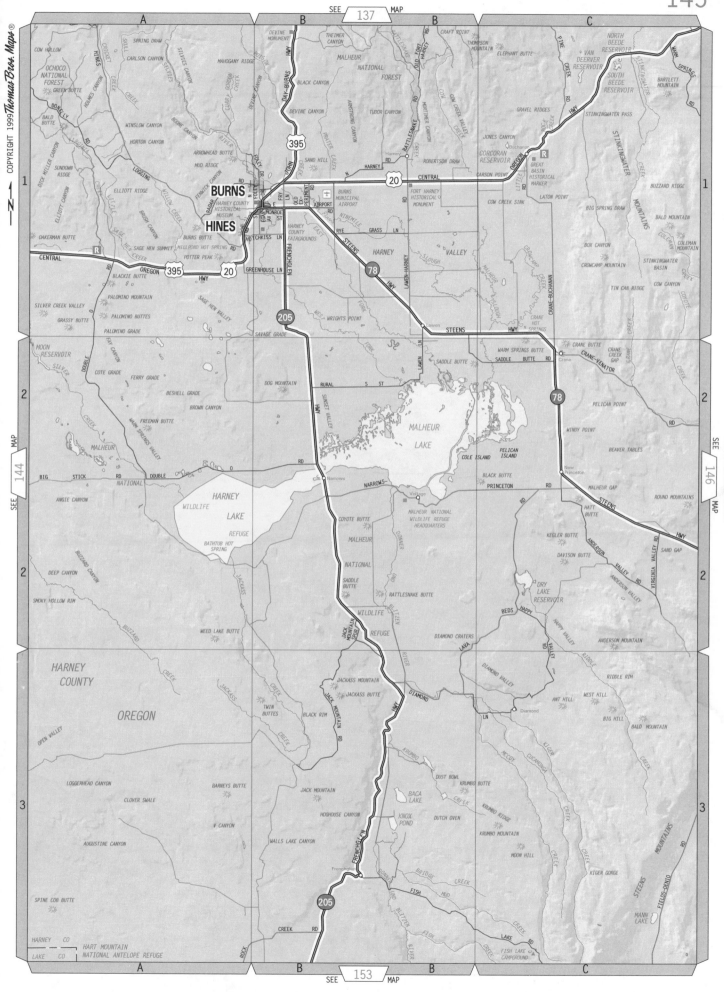

COPYRIGHT 1999 *Thomas Bros. Maps* ®

BURNS

HINES

PNW

HWY

—N—

SEE 138 MAP

SEE 145 MAP

SEE 147 MAP

SEE 154 MAP

A | B | B | C

20

20

95

95

78

78

MALHEUR CREEK CENTRAL OREGON HWY

BEULAH

ALTNOW GAP
BLACK BUTTE
CAT ROCK
UPTON MOUNTAIN
WARM SPRINGS
RILEY BUTTE
WARM SPRINGS RESERVOIR
TEXACO BASIN

HARNEY COUNTY

MALHEUR RIVER
RIVERSIDE
HUNTER CREEK
SHUMWAY
MEEKER MOUNTAIN
TABLE TOP
TWIN KNOLLS
MOSQUITO MOUNTAIN

JUNTURA
CHIMNEY CREEK
RESERVOIR RD
GRANITE CREEK
COLEMAN CREEK
COYOTE CREEK
CRANE CREEK
BUCK MOUNTAIN
LUCE HOT SPRINGS
MCEWEN BUTTE
SWAMP CREEK
WHISKEY CREEK
DUNNEAN
SOUTH FORK
CROWLEY-RIVERSIDE

HARNEY CO.
MALHEUR CO.

VENATOR
CRANE
SADDLE DRAW
CHINA HILL
CAVE
SOUTH FORK
MALHEUR RIVER
BARREN VALLEY
RED MOUNTAIN
MALHEUR CAVE
BIG GULCH
STEENS
REEDS BASIN
INDIAN CREEK BUTTE
CROWLEY-RIVERSIDE

OREGON

HAT BUTTE
STOCKADE BUTTES
WHITEHORSE MOUNTAIN
INDIAN CREEK BUTTES
DOWELL BUTTE
DUCK CREEK BUTTE
MUSTANG BUTTE
WRANGLE BUTTE
SADDLE BUTTE

SWAMP CREEK BUTTES
STAR MOUNTAIN
STOCKADE MOUNTAIN
PIUTE LAKE BED
CROWLEY
RINEHART
DRY LAKE
SACRAMENTO BUTTE
IRON POINT

CLARK CANYON
HUNTER PEAK
TIMS PEAK
JONES BUTTE
PRAVA PEAK
MONUMENT PEAK
HAT TOP
RUFINO BUTTE
RED BUTTE
CUTOFF
SKULL SPRING
MONUMENTAL ROCK
COPELAND BUTTE

SHUMWAY RANCH
CAMP CREEK
SQUAW CREEK
COTTONWOOD CREEK
NEW CREEK
CROWLEY CREEK
DRY CREEK
DRY CREEK
BUTTE CREEK
ANTELOPE FLAT
PAGE
JUNIPER
MUD
RINEHART
OWYHEE

MALHEUR COUNTY

TURNBULL MOUNTAIN
CEDAR MOUNTAIN
OWYHEE BREAKS
MORCOM
RIVER
BIRCH CREEK
BLOWOUT RESERVOIR
COFFEEPOT CRATER
DEER BUTTE
CRATER LAKE RD
JORDAN CRATERS
BISCUIT BUTTE
BISCUIT BUTTE
CLARKS BUTTE

HARPER BASIN
HOLLOW
HOODOO RIDGE
SAND
NEGRO ROCK
SOURDOUGH MOUNTAIN
NEGRO
FREEZEOUT MOUNTAIN
CTO
DEER BUTTE
HAMMOND HILL
SAND HILLS
QUARTZ MOUNTAIN
KNOTTINGHAM BUTTE
BLACK BUTTE
RED BUTTE
OWYHEE BUTTE
DIAMOND BUTTE

SHELL ROCK BUTTE
MITCHELL
HAYSTACK
SPRINGS
GRASSY MOUNTAIN
BURNT MOUNTAIN
NANNYS NIPPLE
BURNT MOUNTAIN
IRON MOUNTAIN
DRY CREEK BUTTES
OWYHEE LAKE
SADDLE BUTTE
DEADMAN GULCH
OWYHEE RESERVOIR STATE AIRPORT
NORTH TABLE MOUNTAIN
SOUTH TABLE MOUNTAIN
ROOSTER COMB
LESLIE GULCH
HOT SPRING
THE TONGUE

UPPER COW LAKE
LOWER COW LAKE
LOWER COW CREEK RD
W COW CREEK RD

TENCENT LAKE
FIFTEENCENT LAKE
SQUAW FLAT
FIELDS-DENIO
TUDOR LAKE
STONEHOUSE CANYON
COFFIN BUTTE
TABLE MOUNTAIN
MICKEY BASIN

FOLLY FARM RD
IRON
RYEGRASS BUTTE
SMALL BUTTE
N FORK
SHEEPSHEAD MOUNTAINS
RESERVOIR RD
RYEGRASS RD
PALOMINO RD
THREE
WILDCAT
WILDCAT CREEK

TURNBULL PEAK
STEENS HWY
KIGER
IRON MOUNTAIN
PALOMINO HILLS
SCOTT BUTTE
CREEK
FLAT TOP MOUNTAIN
GILBERT RANCH

MOUNTAIN
TIRE TUBE CAVE
FORTYMILE CAVE
COYOTE TRAP CAVE
BURNS CAVE
OWYHEE RIVER CAVE
TUB SPRINGS
OWYHEE RIVER

BOGUS CREEK CAVE
WEST CRATER
SADDLE BUTTE
LAVA BUTTE
THREEMILE HILL
BOGUS RANCH
OWYHEE BUTTE
TUCKNESS RD
LITTLE OWYHEE BUTTE
AIRSTRIP
STITZEL RD
AROCK
OREGON-NEVADA
GRAHAMS HILL
JORDAN CREEK
NEVADA HWY
DANNER
RATTLESNAKE CAVE
THREE FORKS RD

CROOKED CREEK
IDAHO-OREGON
BURNS JUNCTION
OLD OREGON-NEVADA HWY
ROME
CREEK STATE HISTORIC MONUMENT
ROME STATE AIRPORT
OLD IDAHO-OREGON HWY
DRY CREEK
CROOKED CREEK
OLD CREEK RD
ROCK CREEK
GRASS
OWYHEE CANYON
ROUND MOUNTAIN
SKULL
MOUNTAIN
ARRITOLA
LITTLE GRASSY MOUNTAIN
LITTLE GRASSY PLACE
GRASSY RESERVOIR
DEAD HORSE BUTTE
INDIAN FORT
FORT CREEK
MUSTANG RESERVOIR
INDIAN CREEK
FORT CREEK
RIVER

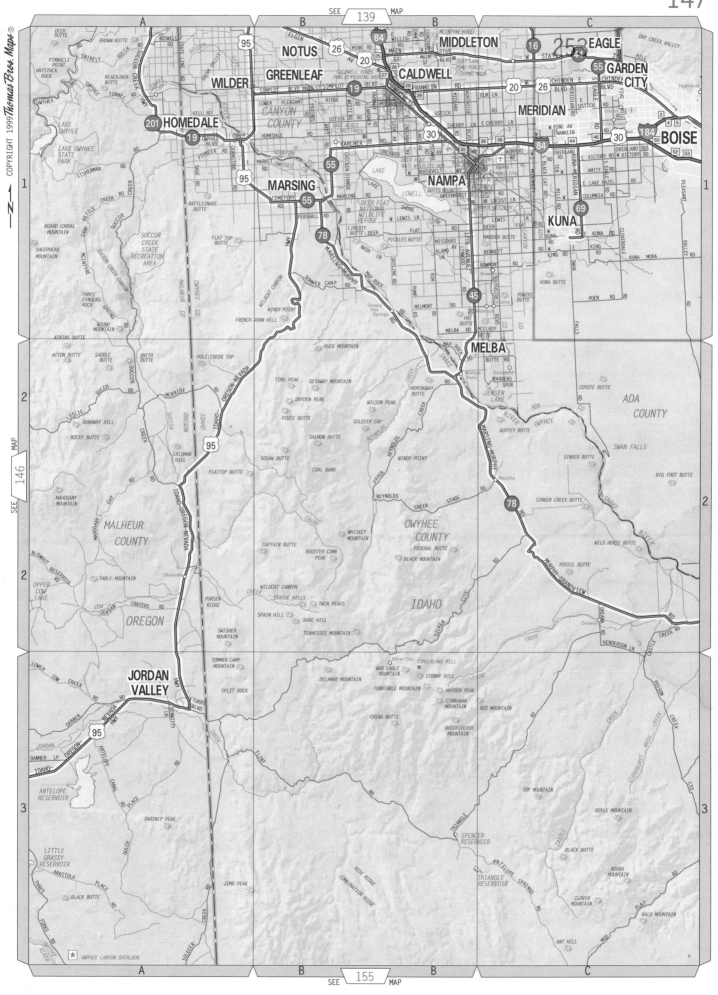

SEE 139 MAP

SEE 146 MAP

SEE 155 MAP

PNW

HWY

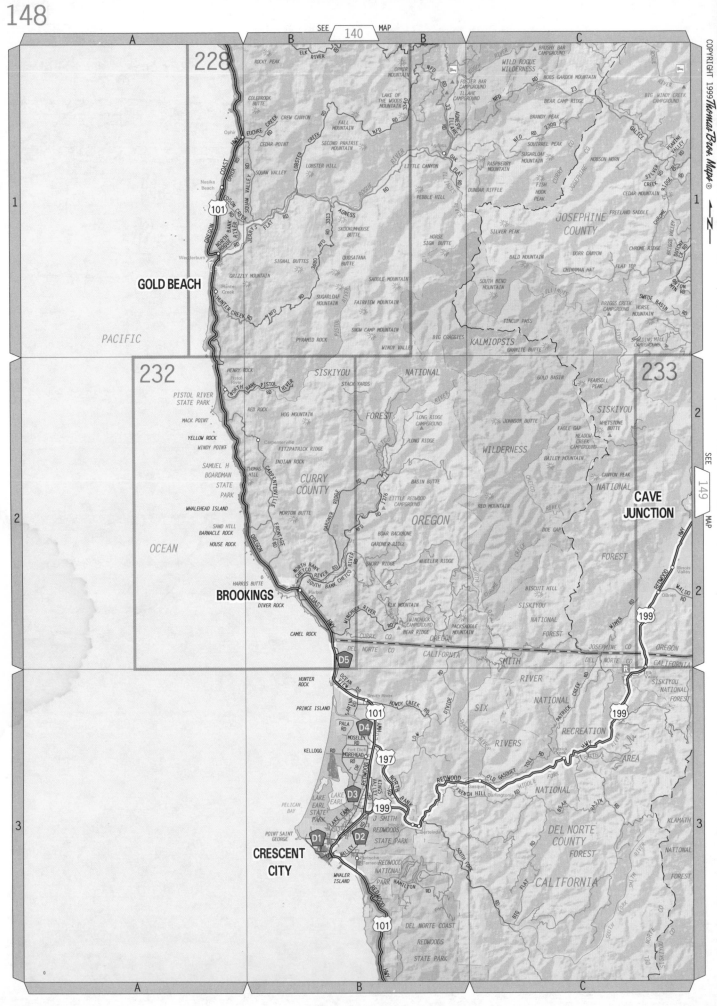

PNW

HWY

SEE MAP 140

228

GOLD BEACH

232

BROOKINGS

233

CAVE JUNCTION

SEE MAP 149

CRESCENT CITY

PACIFIC

OCEAN

JOSEPHINE COUNTY

SISKIYOU NATIONAL FOREST

CURRY COUNTY

OREGON

WILDERNESS

KALMIOPSIS

SIX RIVERS NATIONAL RECREATION AREA

SMITH RIVER NATIONAL FOREST

DEL NORTE COUNTY FOREST

CALIFORNIA

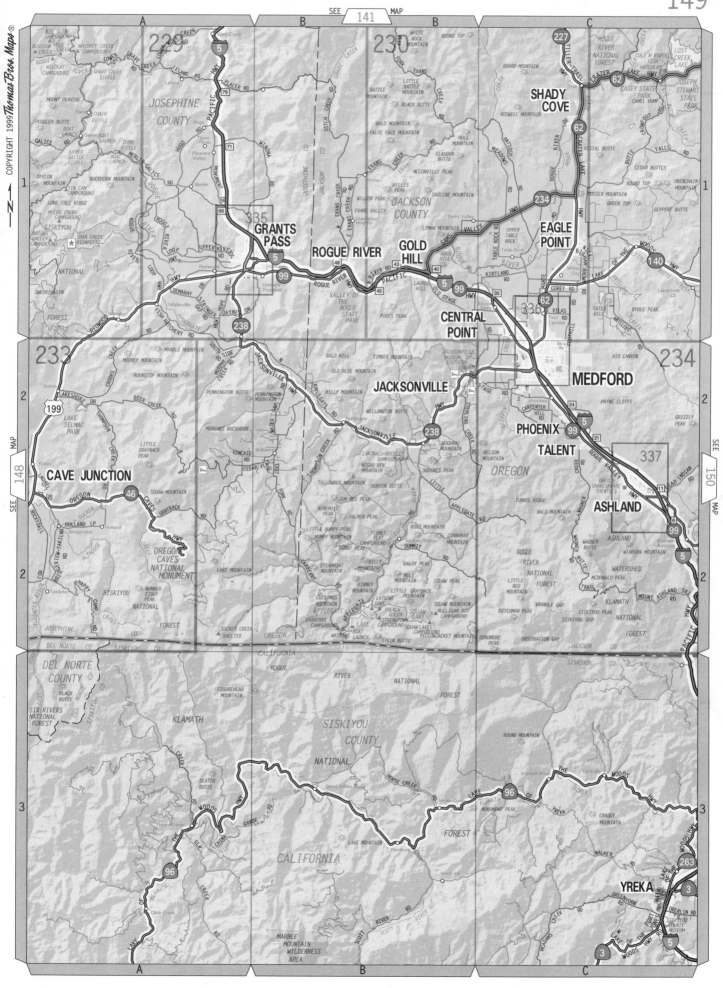

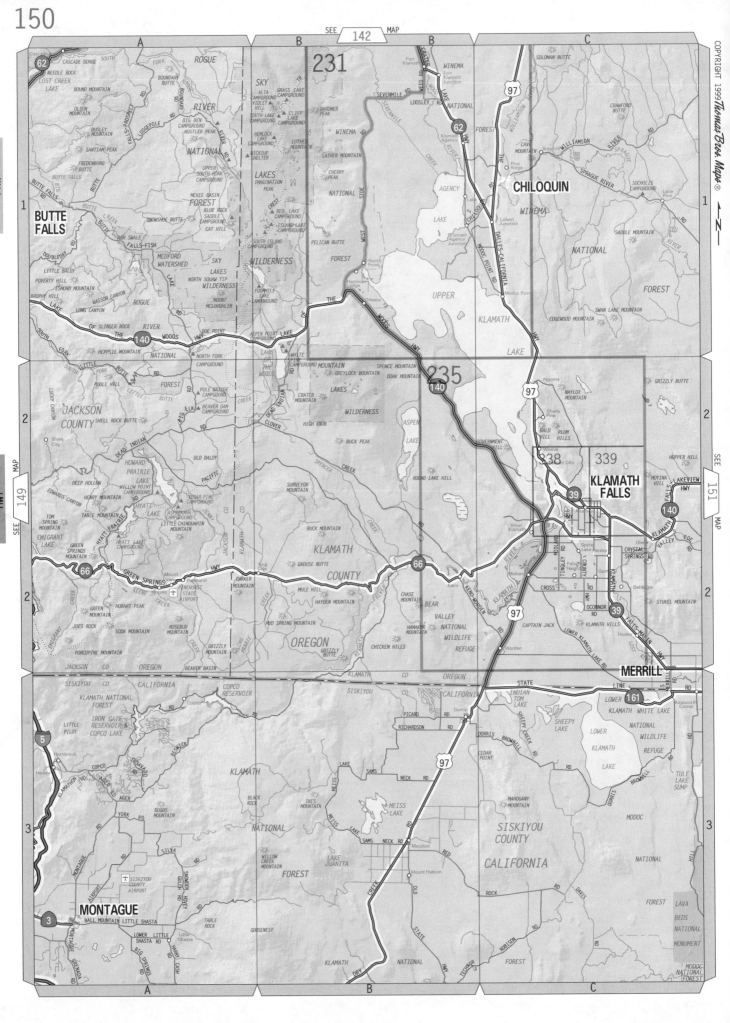

SEE 142 MAP

231

SEE 149 MAP

SEE 151 MAP

235

338 339

CHILOQUIN

KLAMATH FALLS

BUTTE FALLS

MERRILL

MONTAGUE

PNW

HWY

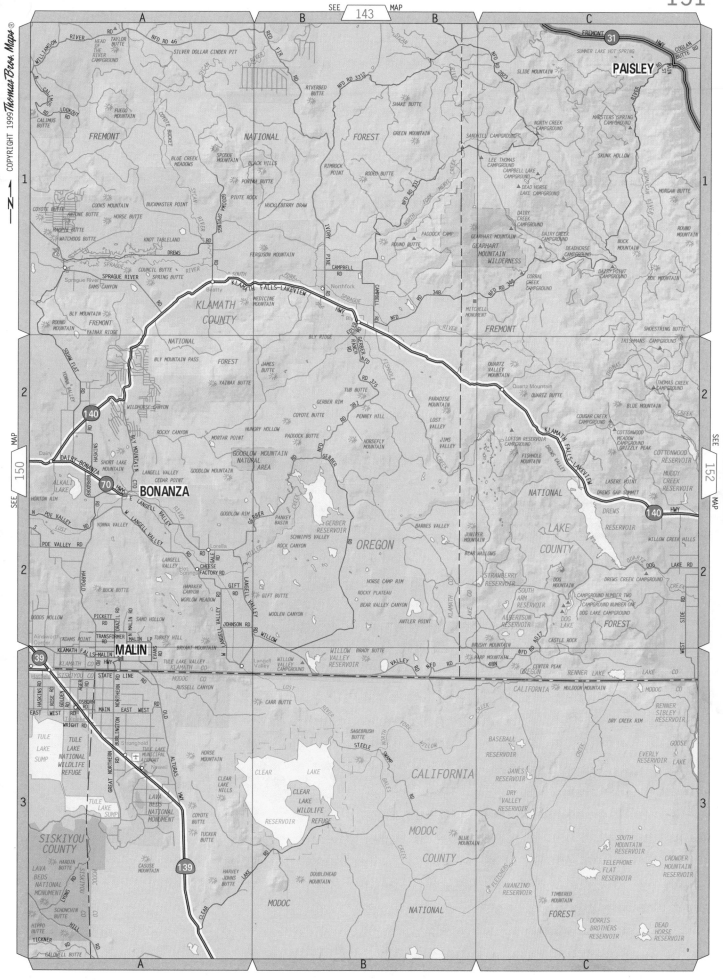

PNW
HWY

SEE 143 MAP
SEE 150 MAP
SEE 152 MAP

—N→

A B B C

PAISLEY

FREMONT

NATIONAL

FOREST

KLAMATH
COUNTY

FREMONT

BONANZA

MALIN

OREGON

LAKE
COUNTY

NATIONAL

FOREST

SISKIYOU
COUNTY

TULE
LAKE
NATIONAL
WILDLIFE
REFUGE

LAVA
BEDS
NATIONAL
MONUMENT

CLEAR
LAKE
WILDLIFE
REFUGE

CALIFORNIA

MODOC

COUNTY

MODOC

NATIONAL

FOREST

A B C

152

A B B C

COPYRIGHT 1999 *Thomas Bros. Maps* ® —N—

PNW

HWY

SEE 151 MAP

SEE 153 MAP

1

COGLAN BUTTE
RED HOUSE RD
COGLAN BUTTES
LAKE ABERT
CHEWAUCAN RIVER
FREMONT HWY
TUCKER HILL
31
395
ABERT RIM HISTORICAL MARKER
LAKEVIEW-BURNS
Valley Falls
ABERT RIM VIEW POINT
FREMONT NATIONAL
CAMPBELL MILL
FOREST
LAKE COUNTY OREGON
RABBIT
HORSBACK RD
CREEK
COYOTE HILLS
RABBIT HILLS
FLAGSTAFF
MUGWUMP LAKE
SWAMP LAKE
ANDERSON LAKE
FLAGSTAFF LAKE
HART MOUNTAIN NATIONAL ANTELOPE REFUGE STATION
HART MOUNTAIN RD
HOT SPRINGS
HOT SPRINGS CAMPGROUND
SOUTH FORK DEGARMO CANYON
WARNER PEAK
BLUEJOINT LAKE
SNYDER CANYON
TURPIN LAKE
STONE CORRAL LAKE
CAMPBELL LAKE
FRENCHGLEN
ROCK CREEK
HART MOUNTAIN NATIONAL ANTELOPE REFUGE
BLM RD

2

THOMAS GILMORE PEAK
New Idaho
Five Corners
KLAMATH FALLS-LAKEVIEW
140
WEST SIDE RD
TUNNEL HILL RD
DOG LAKE RD
West Side
WARNER
FREMONT HWY
395
NORTH WARNER VIEW POINT
FISK HILL
CROOK PEAK
MCDOWELL PEAK
TWELVEMILE PEAK
LIGHT PEAK
DRAKE PEAK
WARNER CANYON SKI AREA
MUD CREEK CAMPGROUND
SQUAW BUTTE
OLD PERPETUAL GEYSER
BLACK CAP
SCHMINCK MEMORIAL MUSEUM
LAKEVIEW
LAKE COUNTY AIRPORT
STOCK DRIVE RD
OAK
9TH ST
ROBERTA AV
HWY
FREMONT
TWELVEMILE CUTOFF
PLUSH
CAMAS CREEK
FREMONT NATIONAL FOREST
SAGE HEN BUTTE
CRUMP RESERVOIR
DEEP CREEK FALLS
140
WARNER
COLEMAN
IRISH HILL
PRIDAY RESERVOIR
CRUMP LAKE
CRUMP GEYSER
PELICAN LAKE
FISHER LAKE
CALDERWOOD RESERVOIR
MUD LAKE RESERVOIR
HOT SPRINGS
BIG FLAT
CAT BUTTE
HART LAKE
Plush
HART MOUNTAIN
HORSBACK RD
COLEMAN VALLEY RD
GREASER RESERVOIR
GREASER CANYON
GREASER BASIN
LITTLE JUNIPER MOUNTAIN
SHIRK LAKE
BARRY RESERVOIR
PLUTE RESERVOIR
LANGSLET MONUMENT
GUANO VALLEY
BEATYS BUTTE
HWY
R
R

3

GOOSE LAKE
MODOC CO
WEST
FREMONT HWY
395
2015
Davis Creek
RD
GOOSE LAKE REC AREA
NEW PINE RD
New Pine Creek
RED PEAK
WILLOW CREEK CAMPGROUND
WILLOW POINT
CRANE MOUNTAIN
DEEP CREEK CAMPGROUND
SUGAR PEAK
BALD HILLS
ROUND MOUNTAIN
BIG VALLEY
DEEP CREEK
TWENTYMILE CREEK
COUNTY RD 139
HIGHGRADE
MOUNT VIDA
BIDWELL MOUNTAIN
MODOC
LAKE ANNIE
FORT BIDWELL INDIAN RESERVATION
Fort Bidwell
FANDANGO PASS
FANDANGO PASS RD
MODOC COUNTY CALIFORNIA
UPPER LAKE
SURPRISE CREEK
NORTH FORK PIT RIVER
OREGON
CALIFORNIA
SURPRISE VALLEY
TWIN LAKES
BIG MUD LAKE
FEE RESERVOIR
LITTLE MUD LAKE
LAKE CO
WASHOE CO
HORSE CREEK
MOSQUITO LAKE
CROOKS LAKE
STATE LINE CANYON
OREGON
NEVADA
WASHOE COUNTY
COLEMAN VALLEY
RACETRACK RESERVOIR
CHARLES SHELDON ANTELOPE REFUGE
CHARLES SHELDON WILDLIFE REFUGE
CALCUTTA LAKE
CON LAKE
HORSE LAKE
LONG LAKE
MIDDLE LAKE
BALD MOUNTAIN
SWAN LAKE RESERVOIR
NEVADA
CATNIP RES
CATNIP CANYON
FISH CREEK
BADGER CREEK

A B B C

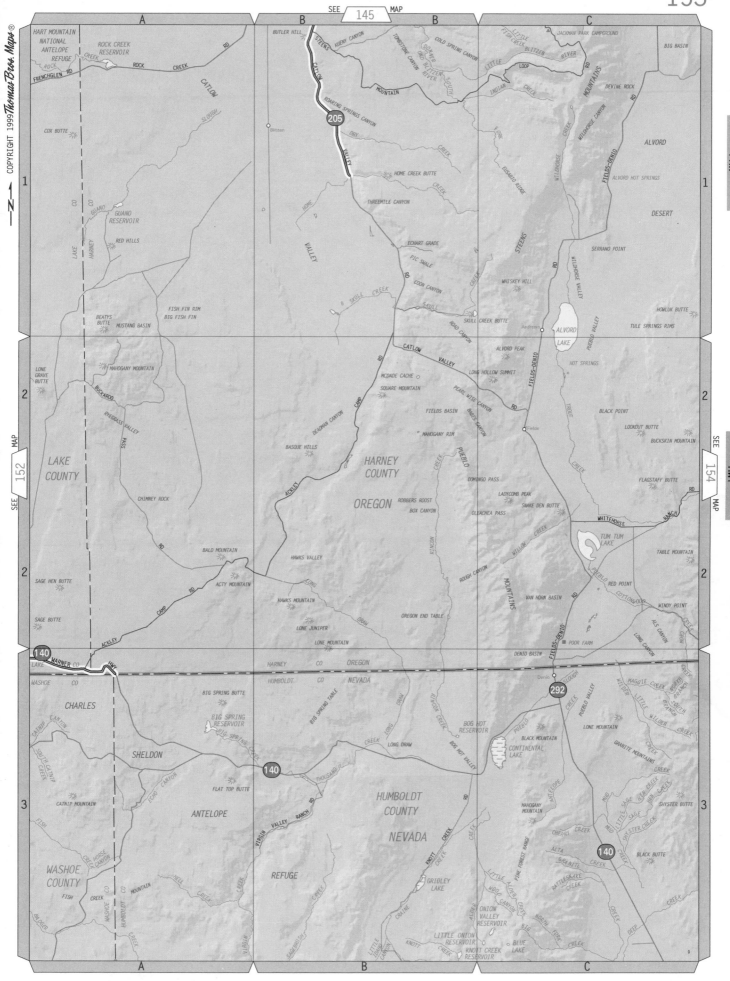

SEE 146 MAP

SEE 153 MAP

SEE 155 MAP

A B B C

—N→

Harney County

MICKEY BUTTE
MICKEY HOT SPRINGS
HARNEY COUNTY
BIG SAND GAP
LITTLE SAND GAP
WHITEHORSE VALLEY
TWIN BUTTES
TWELVEMILE CREEK
WHITEHORSE CREEK
HARNEY CO MALHEUR CO
RANGE
CROOKED
WHITEHORSE
THREE MAN BUTTE
OREGON
RED LOOKOUT BUTTE
OLD PONY EXPRESS STATION (RUINS)
RED MOUNTAIN RANCH
HOT SPRING
WHITEHORSE BUTTE
WILLOW BUTTE
ANTELOPE
MUD SPRING CREEK
FLAGSTAFF BUTTE
WHITEHORSE
FIFTEENMILE
TWIN PEAKS
TROUT CREEK
WHITEHORSE CREEK
LITTLE WHITEHORSE CREEK
RESERVOIR
CHALK CANYON
POLE CANYON
TROUT
TROUT CREEK MOUNTAINS
FIFTEENMILE
RED MOUNTAIN
WINDY PASS
CATLOW PEAK
GRASSY BASIN
EAST BASIN
SHERMAN FIELD
MCDERMITT CREEK RD
TURNER RANCH RD
ZIMMERMAN RANCH
DISASTER PEAK
COTTONWOOD CK HARNEY CO
CHEROKEE CREEK RD
ARCHIE MYERS RANCH RD
COTTONWOOD CREEK
BRETZ MINE RD
MENDI SURI

Malheur County

N FORK RYEGRASS CREEK RD
WILDCAT CREEK RD
BLACK HILLS
RATTLESNAKE
HWY
BATTLESNAKE CREEK
IDAHO-OREGON-NEVADA
RED HILLS
BOWDEN
RANCH
OLD
BOWDEN HILLS
MALHEUR COUNTY
BEBER RANCH
CROOKED CREEK RD
Basque
BLUE MOUNTAIN
SCHOOLHOUSE HILL
OREGON CANYON
ECHAVE RANCH RD
OREGON CANYON
POLE CREEK RD
TROUT CREEK
CLETO
HWY
BATTLE CREEK
JACKSON CREEK
ALBERT
JACKSON
OREGON JACKSON CANYON RD
HOT SPRINGS RD
MCDERMITT
HOT SPRING
TENMILE RD
TENMILE RD
MALHEUR CO
HUMBOLDT CO
MCDERMITT STATE AIRPORT
OREGON
NEVADA
McDermitt
US 95

Corbin / Mustang area

CORBIN CREEK
MUSTANG BUTTE
MUSTANG RESERVOIR RD
GRASSY MOUNTAIN
JACKIES BUTTE
WATER HOLE BUTTE
GARLOW BUTTE
UPPER HORSE CAMP RESERVOIR RD
COYOTE BUTTE
DEADMAN BUTTE
RATTLESNAKE
BATTLE
PO
LITTLE GRASSY MOUNTAIN
POTOMAC RANCH RD
BATTLE CREEK
POLE CREEK
BATTLE MOUNTAIN
ANTELOPE
FIELD CREEK RD
ROCKY SEVEN COM. CAMP RD
POLE CREEK RD
HIGH PEAK
NOQUIE
SUGARLOAF
RANCH RD
HORSE HILL
WEST LITTLE OWYHEE RIVER
CORRAL
WILKINSON
FRENCHMAN CREEK
AIRPLANE RESERVOIR RD
FORT MCDERMITT INDIAN RESERVATION
QUINN RIVER

Humboldt County, Nevada

HUMBOLDT CO
HUMBOLDT
SOUTH FORK KINGS RIVER CO
HALLOWAY MOUNTAIN
LINE CANYON
CORRAL CANYON
SAGE CK
DISASTER PEAK
LONG RIDGE
WASHBURN CREEK
KINGS RIVER
WEST FORK KINGS CREEK
GRANITE CREEK
CHIMA CREEK
FRANCES CREEK
LITTLE
RODEO CREEK
HOUSE CREEK
KINGS RIVER
HORSE CREEK
WILDCAT CREEK
WASHBURN CREEK
JORDAN CREEK
CROWLEY CREEK
HUMBOLDT COUNTY NEVADA
BILK CREEK
DRY CREEK
BILK CREEK MOUNTAINS
KINGS RIVER VALLEY
MONTANA MOUNTAINS
POLE CREEK
ROCK CREEK
NINEMILE RD
JOHN CTO
KINGS RIVER
SENTINEL ROCK
MCDERMITT CREEK
GOOSE CREEK
QUINN RIVER
CANYON CREEK
THREEMILE CREEK
INDIAN CREEK-CANYON CREEK
SKULL CREEK
FLAT CREEK
WILLOW CREEK
EAGLE CREEK
SANTA ROSA RANGE
HUMBOLDT NATIONAL FOREST
MCCONNELL PEAK
EAST FORK QUINN RIVER
SOUTH FORK QUINN RIVER
NFD RD
BUCKSKIN MOUNTAIN
NORTH FORK LITTLE HUMBOLDT RIVER
STOCKS RD
CABIN CREEK
NFD RD 96
NFD RD 84
NFD RD B7
NFD RD 471
GRANITE PEAK
DEEP CREEK
SINGLE TREE TR
SANTA ROSA
MARTIN CREEK
GROUNDHOG
529
531
83
US 95
IDAHO-OREGON-NEVADA HWY

1 2 2 2 3

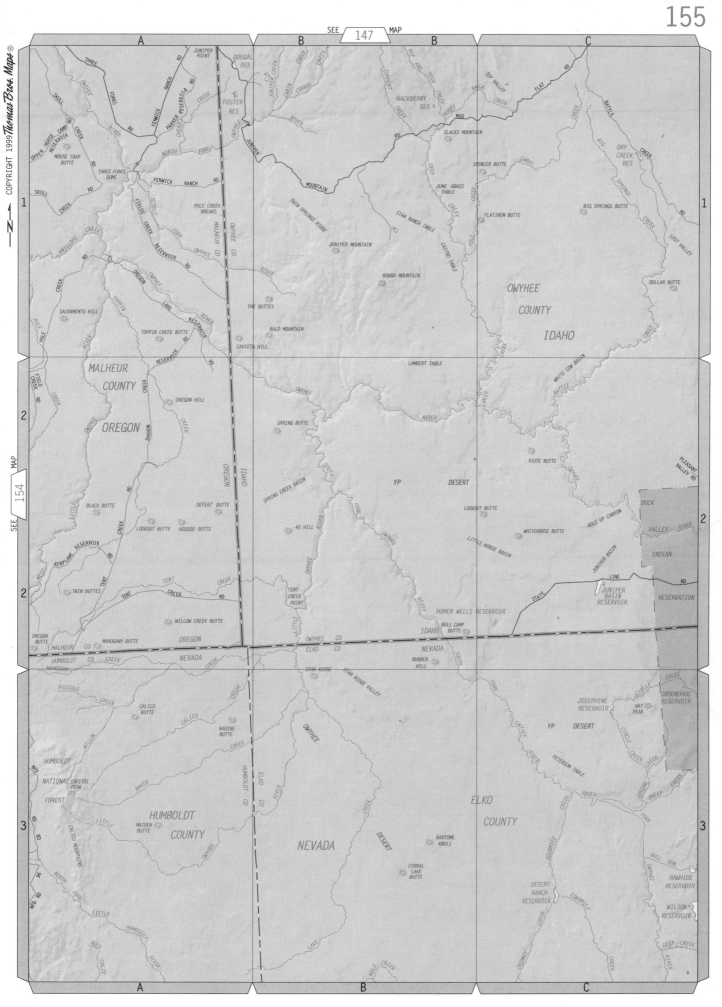

SEE 147 MAP

SEE 154 MAP

PNW

HWY

A B B C

THREE FORKS RD
JUNIPER POINT
DOUGAL RES
SKULL
OWYHEE
PARKER RESERVOIR RD
FENWICK RD
FOSTER RES
JUNIPER CREEK
CABIN CREEK
JUNIPER CREEK
CORRAL CREEK
NIP AND TUCK CREEK
CURRENT CREEK
TOY VALLEY
FLAT
BATTLE CREEK
UPPER HORSE CAMP RESERVOIR
CREEK RD
RIVER RD
NORTH FORK
HACKBERRY RES
CURRENT CREEK
RANGE
MUD
DRY CREEK RES
BIG SPRINGS
MOUSE TRAP BUTTE
FIELDS
MIDDLE FORK
OWYHEE CO
MALHEUR CO
SLACKS MOUNTAIN
DEEP CREEK
SPENCER BUTTE
CAMAS
1
SKULL RD
THREE FORKS DOME
FENWICK RANCH
RD
POLE CREEK BREAKS
JUNIPER
OWYHEE
MOUNTAIN
TWIN SPRINGS RIDGE
JUNIPER MOUNTAIN
STAR RANCH TABLE
JUNE GRASS TABLE
FLATIRON BUTTE
POLE CREEK
BIG SPRINGS BUTTE
SPRINGS RD
1
LOST VALLEY
ANTELOPE RD
OREGON
OWYHEE RESERVOIR
RIVER
ROUGH MOUNTAIN
CASTRO TABLE
CREEK
SACRAMENTO HILL
TOPPIN CREEK
LAKE RESERVOIR
THE BUTTES
OWYHEE COUNTY
IDAHO
DOLLAR BUTTE
POLE CREEK RIVER
TOPPIN CREEK BUTTE
RESERVOIR
BALD MOUNTAIN
CAVIETA HILL
LAMBERT TABLE
WHITE COW BASIN
MALHEUR COUNTY
FIELD CREEK RD
OREGON HILL
CREEK
OWYHEE
RIVER
BATTLE CREEK
2
OREGON
OWYHEE RD
SHARON CREEK
SPRING BUTTE
DEEP CREEK
PIUTE BUTTE
PLEASANT VALLEY RD
2
LITTLE CREEK
BLACK BUTTE
DEFEAT BUTTE
SPRING CREEK BASIN
YP DESERT
LOOKOUT BUTTE
OWYHEE
DUCK
IDAHO
OREGON
AIRPLANE RESERVOIR RD
LOOKOUT BUTTE
HOODOO BUTTE
45 HILL
SOUTH FORK RIVER
WHITEHORSE BUTTE
HOLE UP CANYON
VALLEY RIVER
NSS RD
TENT RD
TENT CREEK
CREEK RD
OWYHEE RIVER
LITTLE HORSE BASIN
JUNIPER BASIN
INDIAN
2
TWIN BUTTES
TENT
TENT CREEK POINT
JUNIPER BASIN RESERVOIR
LINE
STATE
RD
RESERVATION
WILLOW CREEK BUTTE
LITTLE
HOMER WELLS RESERVOIR
JUNIPER BASIN RESERVOIR
OREGON BUTTE
MALHEUR
MAHOGANY BUTTE
OREGON
OWYHEE CO
RIVER
BULL CAMP BUTTE
IDAHO
NEVADA
HUMBOLDT CO
CREEK
NEVADA
ELKO CO
SOUTH
MAHOGANY
RUBBER HILL
PICCOLO
CREEK
CALICO BUTTE
CREEK
STAR RIDGE
STAR RIDGE VALLEY
OWYHEE RIVER
CIRCLE CREEK
GROUNDHOG RESERVOIR
WILLOW
CALICO
NADINE BUTTE
CREEK
OWYHEE
JOSEPHINE RESERVOIR
HAT PEAK
HUMBOLDT
RAVEN
OWYHEE
ELKO CO
HUMBOLDT CO
YP DESERT
CIRCLE CREEK
NATIONAL CAPITOL PEAK
PETERSON TABLE
3
FOREST
LITTLE
HUMBOLDT
MAIDEN BUTTE
HUMBOLDT COUNTY
NEVADA
DESERT
BARTOME KNOLL
ELKO COUNTY
SOUTH FORK
FOURMILE CREEK
SHEEP CREEK
BULL RUN
OWYHEE
3
RD 83
CALICO MOUNTAINS
LITTLE
CORRAL LAKE BUTTE
SPRINGS CREEK
RAWHIDE RESERVOIR
96
NORTH FORK
DESERT RANCH RESERVOIR
WILSON RESERVOIR
NFD RD
LITTLE
HUMBOLDT RIVER
FOURMILE CREEK
CHIMNEY CREEK
ROCK CREEK
LAKE CREEK
WOLF CREEK
DEEP CREEK RIVER

A B B C

PNW

METRO

SEE MAP 93

SEE MAP 157

DISTRICT OF WEST VANCOUVER

DISTRICT OF NORTH VANCOUVER

CITY OF NORTH VANCOUVER

DISTRICT OF BURNABY

UNIVERSITY ENDOWMENT LANDS

VANCOUVER

NEW WESTMINSTER

RICHMOND

DISTRICT OF DELTA

BELCARRA

PORT MOODY

CYPRESS PROVINCIAL PARK

CYPRESS BOWL

CYPRESS FALLS PARK

NELSON CANYON PARK

LIGHTHOUSE PARK

LARSEN BAY

EAGLE LAKE

BALLANTREE PARK

CAPILANO LAKE

LYNN HEADWATERS

REGIONAL PARK

SEYMOUR RIVER

MOUNT SEYMOUR PROVINCIAL PARK

FISH HATCHERY

INDIAN ARM

Deep Cove

ADMIRALTY PARK

CATES PARK

Dollarton

BURRARD INLET

SIMON FRASER UNIV

BURNABY LAKE PARK

DEER LAKE PARK

MUSEUM OF ANTHROPOLOGY

UNIV OF BRITISH COLUMBIA

GOLF COURSE

PACIFIC SPIRIT REGIONAL PARK

WRECK BEACH

SHAUGHNESSY GOLF COURSE

Point Grey

Wreck Beach

IONE ISLAND

SEA ISLAND

VANCOUVER INTERNATIONAL AIRPORT

GRANT McCONACHIE WY

SWISHWASH ISLAND

STURGEON BANK

STRAIT OF GEORGIA

Gary Point

REIFEL WILDLIFE SANCTUARY

WOODWARD ISLAND

KIRKLAND ISLAND

GULF OF GEORGIA CANNERY NATIONAL HISTORIC SITE

DEAS ISLAND REGIONAL PARK

TILBURY ISLAND

GRAVESEND REACH

Steveston

LULU ISLAND

FRASER RIVER

FRASER RIVER PARK

DOUGLAS COLLEGE

Queen Borough

South Westminster

Annieville

ANNACIS ISLAND

Horseshoe Bay

Point Atkinson

BEACON LN

Caulfield

Dundarave

Norgate

Hollyburn

Cedardale

Lower Lonsdale

Central Park

Trout Lake

Cedar Cottage

Cascade Heights

Killarney

Fraserview

Sunset

Marpole

Karrisdale

Brighouse

Thompson

Broadmoor

Ferguson Point

English Bay

Burnaby Village Museum

Garden Village

TRANS CANADA HWY

MARINE DR

99

1A

7

7A

7A

7

91

91A

91

1

1A

99A

99

10

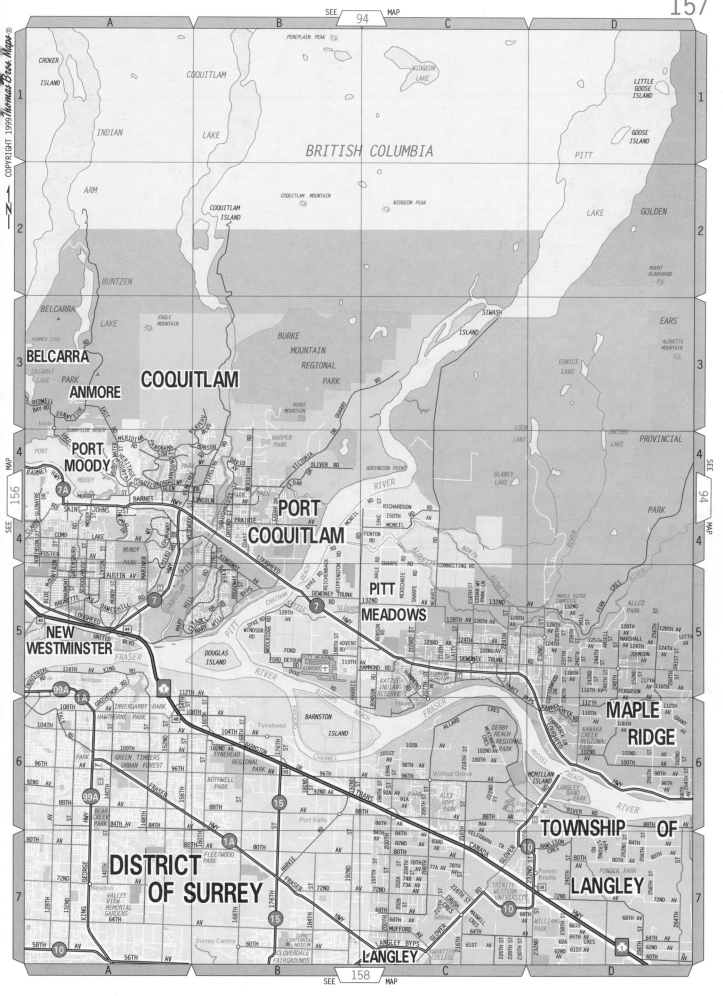

PNW

METRO

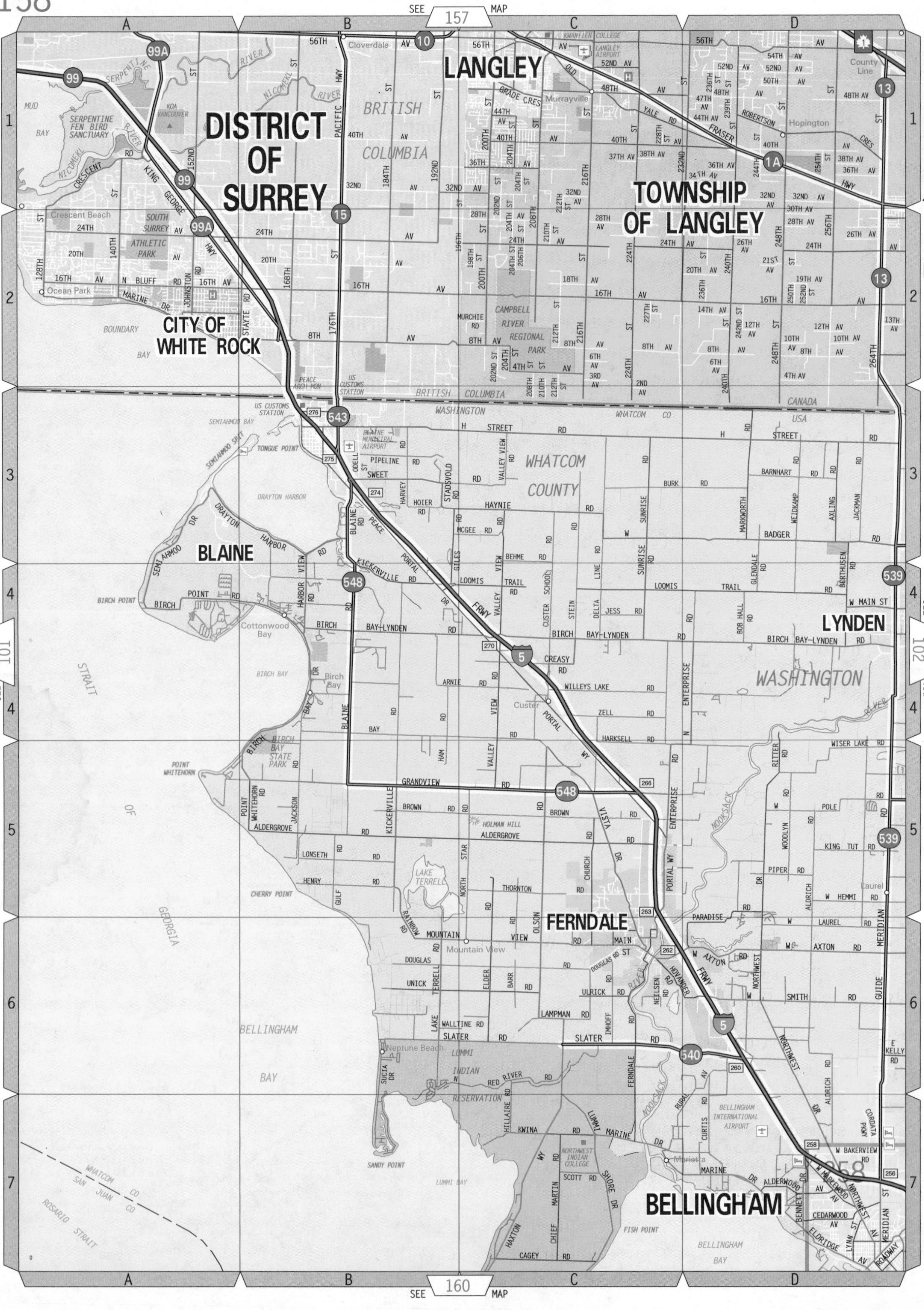

PNW

METRO

SEE MAP 157

SEE MAP 101

SEE MAP 102

SEE MAP 160

LANGLEY

DISTRICT OF SURREY

BRITISH COLUMBIA

TOWNSHIP OF LANGLEY

CITY OF WHITE ROCK

Murrayville

Kwantlen College

Langley Airport

Hopington

County Line

SERPENTINE FEN BIRD SANCTUARY

MUD BAY

KOA Vancouver

Crescent Beach

South Surrey

ATHLETIC PARK

Ocean Park

BOUNDARY BAY

Cloverdale

Campbell River Regional Park

BRITISH COLUMBIA

WASHINGTON

WHATCOM CO

CANADA

USA

US CUSTOMS STATION

US CUSTOMS STATION

PEACE ARCH MON

WHATCOM COUNTY

Semiahmoo Bay

Tongue Point

DRAYTON HARBOR

BLAINE

Blaine Municipal Airport

Birch Point

Cottonwood Bay

BIRCH BAY

Birch Bay

STRAIT OF GEORGIA

LYNDEN

WASHINGTON

Custer

BIRCH BAY STATE PARK

Point Whitehorn

Aldergrove

Aldergrove

Holman Hill

FERNDALE

Mountain View

LAKE TERRELL

CHERRY POINT

POINT WHITEHORN

Laurel

BELLINGHAM BAY

Neptune Beach

LUMMI INDIAN RESERVATION

Sandy Point

LUMMI BAY

Fish Point

Bellingham International Airport

Marietta

Northwest Indian College

BELLINGHAM

ROSARIO STRAIT

WHATCOM CO

SAN JUAN CO

BELLINGHAM BAY

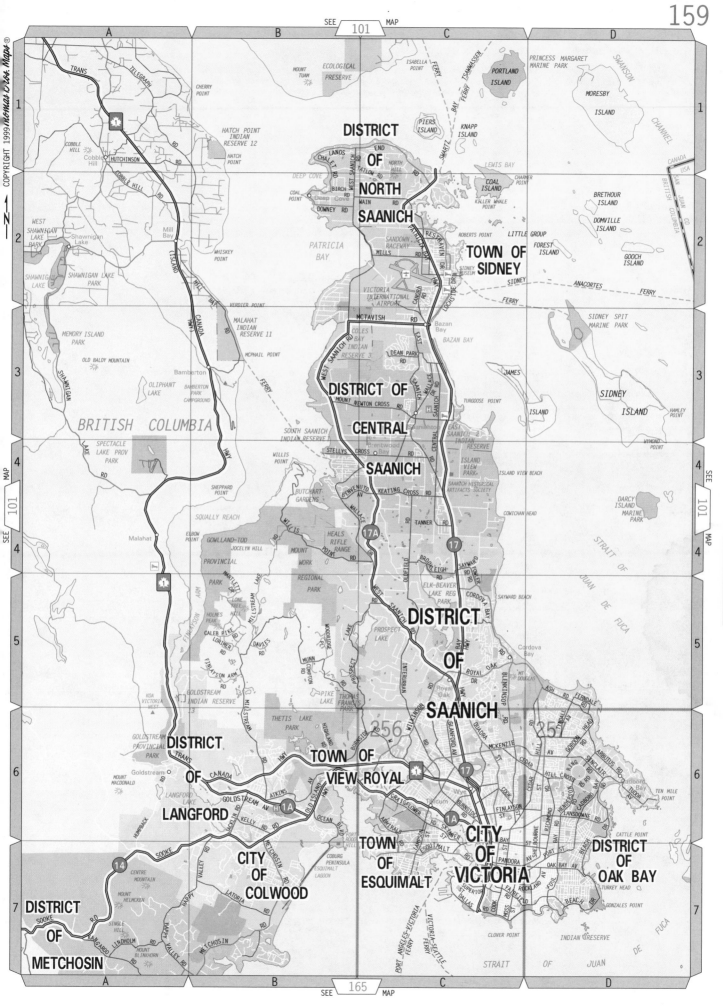

COPYRIGHT 1999 Thomas Bros. Maps ®

PNW

METRO

SEE 101 MAP

A   B   C   D

1

2

3

4

SEE 101 MAP

4

5

6

7

DISTRICT OF NORTH SAANICH

TOWN OF SIDNEY

DISTRICT OF CENTRAL SAANICH

DISTRICT OF SAANICH

DISTRICT OF LANGFORD

TOWN OF VIEW ROYAL

CITY OF COLWOOD

TOWN OF ESQUIMALT

CITY OF VICTORIA

DISTRICT OF OAK BAY

DISTRICT OF METCHOSIN

BRITISH COLUMBIA

PORTLAND ISLAND

PRINCESS MARGARET MARINE PARK

SWANSON CHANNEL

MORESBY ISLAND

SIDNEY ISLAND

256   257

SEE 165 MAP

A   B   C   D

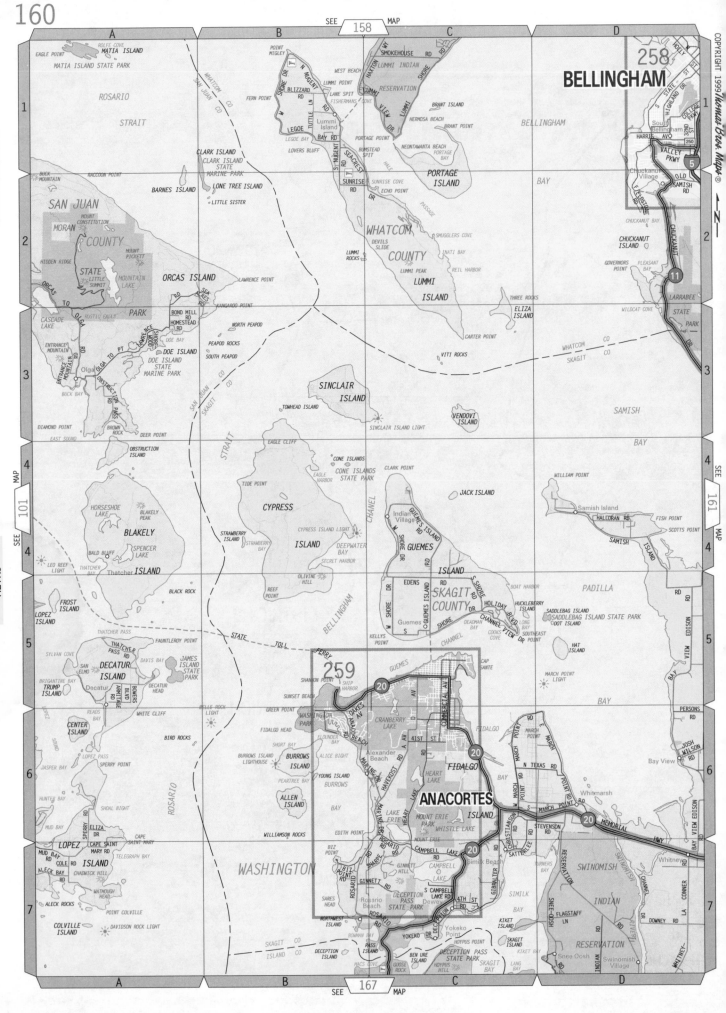

PNW

METRO

258
BELLINGHAM

—N—

A   **B**   **C**   **D**

ROLFE COVE
EAGLE POINT
MATIA ISLAND
MATIA ISLAND STATE PARK

POINT MIGLEY
N NUGENT
WEST BEACH
LANE SPIT
FISHERMANS COVE
SMOKEHOUSE RD
LUMMI INDIAN
RESERVATION
LUMMI VIEW
BRANT ISLAND

HIGHLAND DR
STATE ST
HOLLY ST
COLLEGE DR
32ND ST

1

ROSARIO
STRAIT

FERN POINT
SHORE DR
BLIZZARD RD
TUTTLE LN
LEGOE
LEGOE BAY
LOVERS BLUFF
BAY RD
LUMMI
ISLAND
LUMMI POINT
SEACREST
PORTAGE POINT
BUMSTEAD SPIT
HALF
PASSAGE
NEONTAWANTA BEACH
PORTAGE BAY
HERMOSA BEACH
BRANT POINT

PORTAGE
ISLAND

BELLINGHAM

HARRIS AVE
VALLEY PKWY
250
5

WHATCOM CO
SAN JUAN CO

CLARK ISLAND
CLARK ISLAND STATE MARINE PARK
LONE TREE ISLAND
BARNES ISLAND
LITTLE SISTER

SUNRISE RD
SUNRISE COVE
ECHO POINT
DR
DEVILS SLIDE
LUMMI ROCKS

WHATCOM
COUNTY

SMUGGLERS COVE
INATI BAY

BAY

South Bellingham
Chuckanut Village
OLD SAMISH RD

2

SAN JUAN
COUNTY
MORAN
MOUNT CONSTITUTION
MOUNT PICKETT
STATE
LITTLE SUMMIT
MOUNTAIN LAKE
HIDDEN RIDGE
PARK

ORCAS ISLAND
LAWRENCE POINT
SEA ACRES
KANGAROO POINT

LUMMI PEAK
REIL HARBOR
LUMMI
ISLAND
THREE ROCKS

ELIZA ISLAND

GOVERNORS POINT
PLEASANT BAY
CHUCKANUT BAY
CHUCKANUT ISLAND
CHUCKANUT DR
11
LARRABEE

2

ORCAS TO
OLGA
CASCADE LAKE
ENTRANCE MOUNTAIN
BUCK MOUNTAIN
RACCOON POINT
BUCK BAY
OLGA TO PT
Olga
ORCAS TO OLGA
LAWRENCE ROAD
SHORE ROAD
OBSTRUCTION PASS
BOND MILL RD
HOMESTEAD RD
DOE BAY
DOE ISLAND
DOE ISLAND STATE MARINE PARK
NORTH PEAPOD
PEAPOD ROCKS
SOUTH PEAPOD

SAN JUAN CO
SKAGIT CO

SINCLAIR
ISLAND
TOWHEAD ISLAND
SINCLAIR ISLAND LIGHT

CARTER POINT

VITI ROCKS

WHATCOM CO
SKAGIT CO

VENDOVI ISLAND

SAMISH

WILDCAT COVE
STATE
PARK

3

DIAMOND POINT
BROWN ROCK
DEER POINT
EAST SOUND

OBSTRUCTION ISLAND

SAN JUAN CO
SKAGIT CO

EAGLE CLIFF
CONE ISLANDS
CONE ISLANDS STATE PARK
EAGLE HARBOR
CLARK POINT

JACK ISLAND

WILLIAM POINT
Samish Island
HALCORAN RD
FISH POINT

BAY

4

HORSESHOE LAKE
BLAKELY PEAK
BLAKELY
BALD BLUFF
THATCHER BAY
SPENCER LAKE
Thatcher ISLAND
LEO REEF LIGHT

TIDE POINT
CYPRESS
ISLAND
STRAWBERRY ISLAND
STRAWBERRY BAY
CYPRESS ISLAND LIGHT
DEEPWATER BAY
SECRET HARBOR

CHANNEL
INDIAN VILLAGE
W SHORE DR
GUEMES ISLAND RD
GUEMES
ISLAND

SCOTTS POINT
SAMISH
SAMISH ISLAND

PADILLA

RD
VIEW EDISON
RD
RD

4

FROST ISLAND
LOPEZ ISLAND
THATCHER PASS

BLACK ROCK

OLIVINE HILL
REEF POINT

EDENS RD
W SHORE DR
O GUEMES SHORE DR
Guemes
GUEMES ISLAND RD
S

SKAGIT
COUNTY
S SHORE RD
HOLIDAY BLVD
DEADMAN BAY
CHANNEL VIEW DR
COOKS POINT
HUCKLEBERRY ISLAND
SADDLEBAG ISLAND
SADDLEBAG ISLAND STATE PARK
DOT ISLAND
LONG BAY
SOUTHEAST POINT

5

SYLVAN COVE
DECATUR
THATCHER PASS
DAVIS BAY
SAN ELMO
DECATUR ISLAND
JAMES ISLAND STATE PARK
FAUNTLEROY POINT

STATE
TOLL
BELLINGHAM
KELLYS POINT
CHANNEL
FERRY
259
SHANNON POINT
SHIP HARBOR
20
GUEMES

CAP SANTE

MARCH POINT LIGHT

HAT ISLAND

BAY

PERSONS

5

BRIGANTINE BAY
TRUMP ISLAND
Decatur
DECATUR HEAD
BOKERS BLVD
ARMITAGE RD
READS BAY
WHITE CLIFF
BELLE ROCK LIGHT
BIRD ROCKS

GREEN POINT
WASHINGTON PARK
FIDALGO HEAD
SUNSET BEACH
OAKES AV
ANACORTES
CRANBERRY LAKE
41ST ST
COMMERCIAL AV
ID
T ST
FIDALGO

MARCH POINT RD
N TEXAS RD
Bay View
JOSH WILSON RD

6

CENTER ISLAND
LOPEZ PASS
SPERRY POINT
JASPER BAY
HUNTER BAY

SHORT BAY
BURROWS ISLAND LIGHTHOUSE
BURROWS ISLAND
FLOUNDER BAY
ALICE BIGHT
YOUNG ISLAND
BURROWS BAY
ALLEN ISLAND
PEARTREE BAY
MARINE DR
HAVEKOST RD
LAKE ERIE
HEART LAKE
HEART LAKE RD
ANACORTES
FIDALGO
ISLAND
MOUNT ERIE PARK
WHISTLE LAKE
MOUNT ERIE

MARCH POINT RD
Whitmarsh
CHRISTIANSON RD
STEVENSON RD
20

6

MUD BAY
SPERRY RD
ELIZA DR
CAPE SAINT MARY RD
LOPEZ
ISLAND
SHOAL BIGHT
CAPE SAINT MARY
TELEGRAPH BAY

WILLIAMSON ROCKS

EDITH POINT
BIZ POINT
BIZ POINT RD
ROSARIO RD
SHARPE RD
GINNETT
CAMPBELL LAKE RD
GINNETT HILL
CAMPBELL LAKE
S CAMPBELL LAKE RD
GIBRALTER RD
SATTERLEE RD
TURNERS BAY
SIMILK BAY
SIMILK BEACH
RESERVATION
SNEE OOSH
FLAGSTAFF LN
SWINOMISH
INDIAN
Whitney
20
MEMORIAL HWY
BAY VIEW EDISON

7

COLVILLE ISLAND
ALECK BAY
COLE RD
CHADWICK HILL
WATMOUGH HEAD
ALECK ROCKS
POINT COLVILLE
DAVIDSON ROCK LIGHT

SKAGIT CO
ISLAND CO
DECEPTION ISLAND
NORTHWEST ISLAND
BOWMAN BAY
MACS COVE
GOOSE ROCK
BEN URE ISLAND
HOYPUS HILL
Rosario Beach
DECEPTION PASS STATE PARK
SARES HEAD
ROSARIO RD
DECEPTION RD
4TH ST
Dewey
20
YOKEKO
Yokeko Point
HOYPUS POINT
DECEPTION PASS STATE PARK
SKAGIT ISLAND
KIKET ISLAND
KIKET BAY
LANG BAY
SKAGIT BAY
Snee Oosh
Swinomish Village
WASHINGTON
RESERVATION
LA CONNER
DOWNEY
SWINOMISH CHANNEL
SNOHOMISH RIVER

7

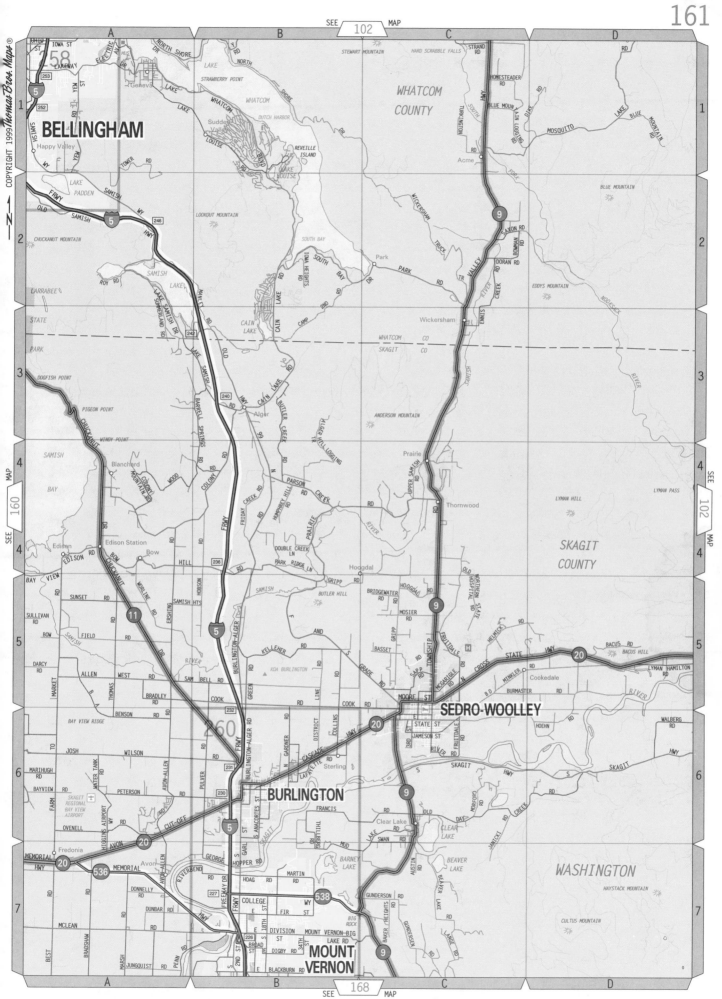

PNW

METRO

—N→

A   B   C   D

BELLINGHAM

WHATCOM
COUNTY

1

2

SEE 160 MAP

SEE 102 MAP

WHATCOM CO
SKAGIT CO

3

SKAGIT
COUNTY

4

SEDRO-WOOLLEY

5

BURLINGTON

6

WASHINGTON

**MOUNT
VERNON**

7

SEE 258 MAP

SEE 260 MAP

A   B   C   D

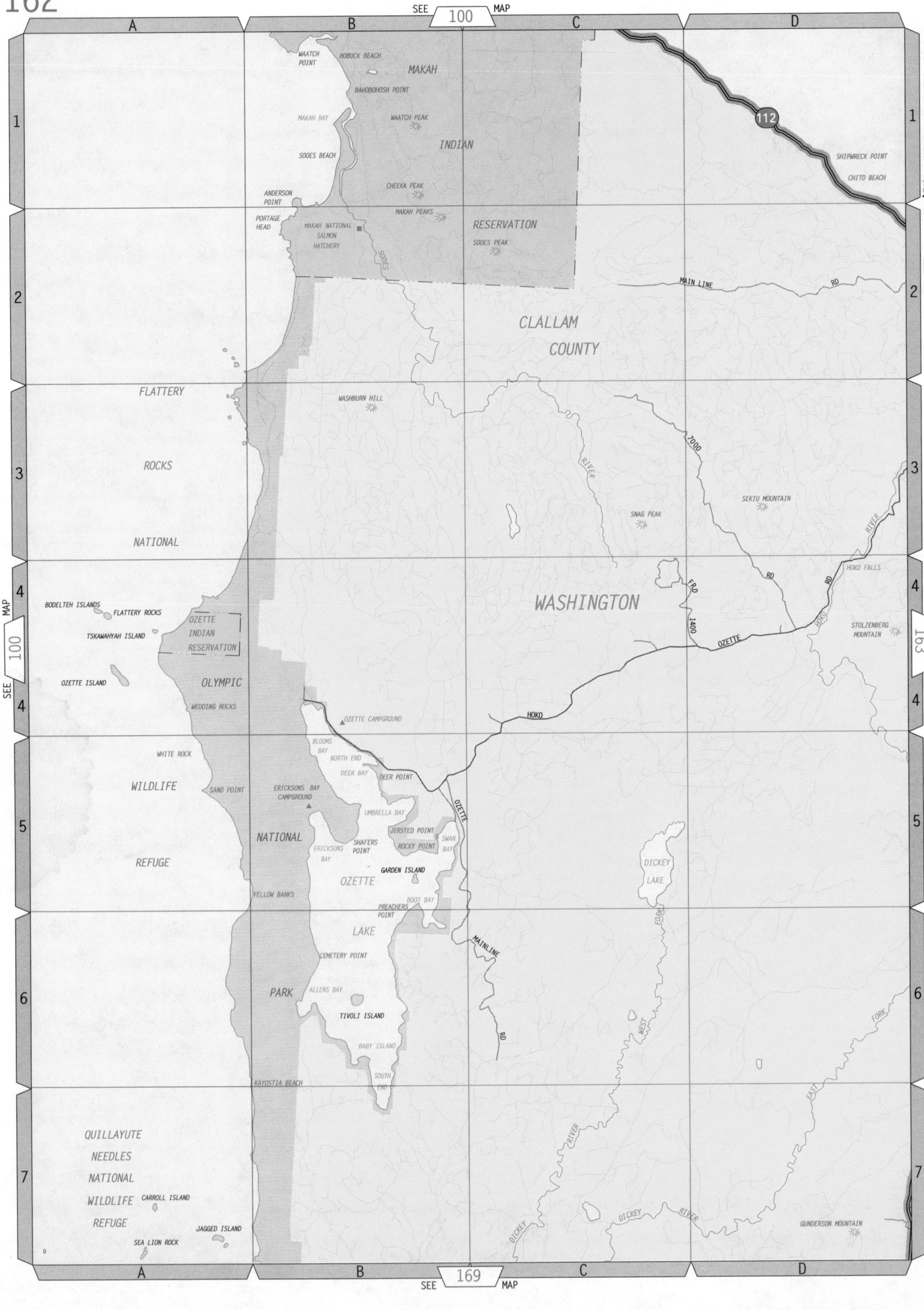

PNW

METRO

—N—

SEE 100 MAP

A   B   C   D

1

WAATCH POINT
HOBUCK BEACH
MAKAH
BAHOBOHOSH POINT
MAKAH BAY
WAATCH PEAK
SOOES BEACH
INDIAN
SHIPWRECK POINT
CHITO BEACH
112

ANDERSON POINT
CHEEKA PEAK
PORTAGE HEAD
MAKAH PEAKS
RESERVATION
MAKAH NATIONAL SALMON HATCHERY
SOOES PEAK
SOOES

2

MAIN LINE   RD

CLALLAM
COUNTY

FLATTERY
WASHBURN HILL

3

ROCKS
RIVER
7000
SEKIU MOUNTAIN
SNAG PEAK

NATIONAL
RIVER
HOKO FALLS

4

BODELTEH ISLANDS   FLATTERY ROCKS
OZETTE INDIAN RESERVATION
WASHINGTON
F.R.D.
RD
HOKO
TSKAWAHYAH ISLAND
1400
RD
STOLZENBERG MOUNTAIN
OZETTE ISLAND
OLYMPIC
OZETTE
WEDDING ROCKS
OZETTE CAMPGROUND
HOKO

SEE 100 MAP
SEE 163 MAP

WHITE ROCK
BLOOMS BAY
NORTH END
DEER BAY   DEER POINT
WILDLIFE
SAND POINT
ERICKSONS BAY CAMPGROUND
UMBRELLA BAY
OZETTE

5

NATIONAL
JERSTED POINT
SWAN BAY
ERICKSONS BAY
SHAFERS POINT
ROCKY POINT
REFUGE
GARDEN ISLAND
DICKEY LAKE
OZETTE
BOOT BAY
YELLOW BANKS
PREACHERS POINT
LAKE
MAINLINE

CEMETERY POINT

6

PARK
ALLENS BAY
TIVOLI ISLAND
RD
WEST FORK

BABY ISLAND
KAYOSTLA BEACH
SOUTH END
DICKEY RIVER
FORK

7

QUILLAYUTE
NEEDLES
NATIONAL
WILDLIFE   CARROLL ISLAND
REFUGE
JAGGED ISLAND
DICKEY RIVER
GUNDERSON MOUNTAIN
SEA LION ROCK
EAST FORK

A   B   C   D

SEE 169 MAP

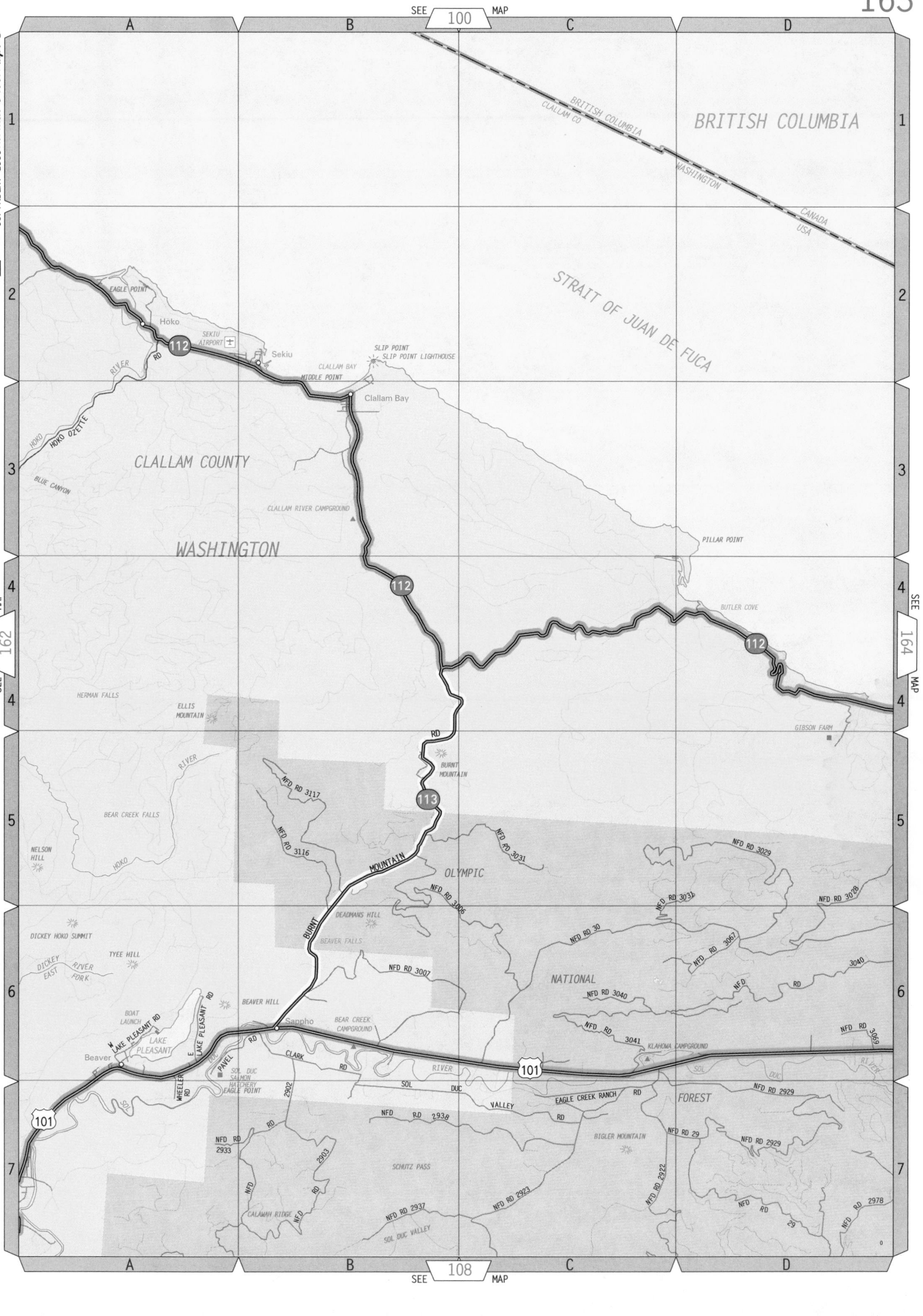

A   B   SEE 100 MAP   C   D

COPYRIGHT 1999 *Thomas Bros. Maps*®

←N→

PNW

METRO

SEE 162 MAP

SEE 164 MAP

BRITISH COLUMBIA

BRITISH COLUMBIA
CLALLAM CO
WASHINGTON
CANADA
USA

STRAIT OF JUAN DE FUCA

EAGLE POINT

Hoko

HOKO RIVER RD

SEKIU AIRPORT

Sekiu

112

MIDDLE POINT

CLALLAM BAY

SLIP POINT
SLIP POINT LIGHTHOUSE

Clallam Bay

PILLAR POINT

BUTLER COVE

112

GIBSON FARM

HOKO OZETTE

BLUE CANYON

CLALLAM COUNTY

WASHINGTON

CLALLAM RIVER CAMPGROUND

112

RD

HERMAN FALLS

ELLIS MOUNTAIN

BURNT MOUNTAIN

113

NFD RD 3117

NFD RD 3116

BEAR CREEK FALLS

NELSON HILL

HOKO

RIVER

MOUNTAIN

BURNT

OLYMPIC

DEADMANS HILL

BEAVER FALLS

NFD RD 3006

NFD RD 3031

NFD RD 3029

NFD RD 3033

NFD RD 3078

NFD BD 30

NFD RD 3067

NFD RD 3040

NFD RD 3040

3040

RD

NFD RD 3069

DICKEY HOKO SUMMIT

TYEE HILL

DICKEY EAST RIVER FORK

BOAT LAUNCH

BEAVER HILL

LAKE PLEASANT RD

E LAKE PLEASANT RD

Beaver

LAKE PLEASANT

Sappho

BEAR CREEK CAMPGROUND

NFD RD 3007

NATIONAL

NFD RD 3041

KLAHOWYA CAMPGROUND

101

CLARK RD

SOL DUC SALMON HATCHERY
EAGLE POINT

PAVEL

WHEELER RD

SOL

101

2902

SOL DUC

RIVER

VALLEY

EAGLE CREEK RANCH

RD

SOL DUC

FOREST

NFD RD 2929

NFD RD 2938

BIGLER MOUNTAIN

NFD RD 29

NFD RD 2929

SCHUTZ PASS

NFD RD 2933

2903

NFD RD 2923

NFD RD 2922

CALAWAH RIDGE

NFD

NFD RD 2937

SOL DUC VALLEY

NFD RD 2978

29

A   B   SEE 108 MAP   C   D

PNW

METRO

—N—

SEE 101 MAP

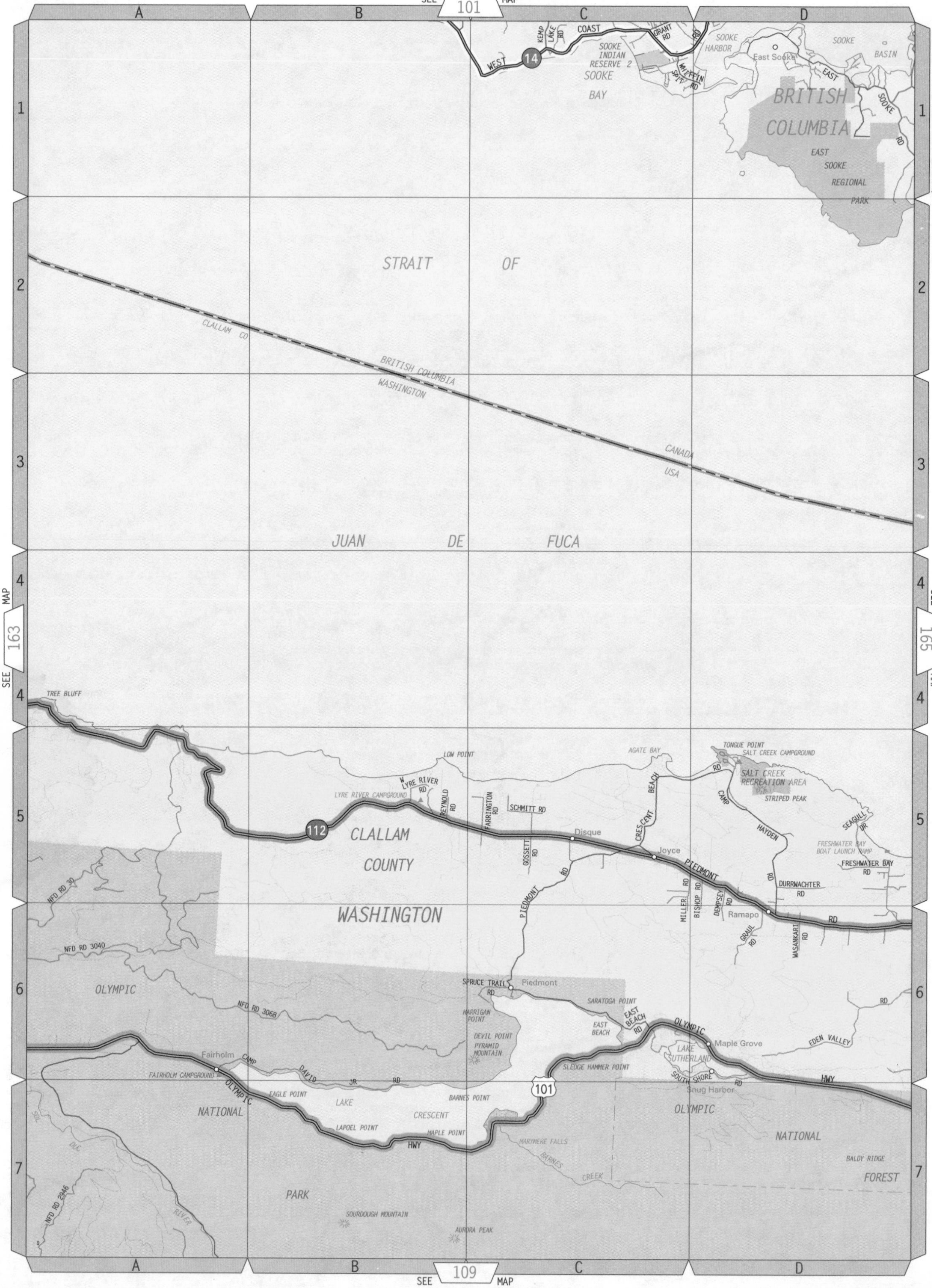

A   B   C   D

1

SOOKE
COAST
KEMP LAKE RD
GRANT RD
WEST
14
SOOKE INDIAN RESERVE 2
SOOKE BAY
SOOKE HARBOR
MUFFIN SPIT RD
East Sooke
SOOKE EAST RD
SOOKE BASIN
SOOKE
BRITISH COLUMBIA
EAST SOOKE REGIONAL PARK

STRAIT   OF

2

CLALLAM CO
BRITISH COLUMBIA
WASHINGTON

CANADA
USA

3

JUAN   DE   FUCA

SEE 163 MAP

SEE 165 MAP

4

TREE BLUFF

LOW POINT
AGATE BAY
TONGUE POINT
SALT CREEK CAMPGROUND
SALT CREEK RECREATION AREA
STRIPED PEAK

5

W LYRE RIVER RD
LYRE RIVER CAMPGROUND
REYNOLD RD
FARRINGTON RD
SCHMITT RD
112
CLALLAM
COUNTY
GOSSETT RD
RD
Disque
CRESCENT BEACH
Joyce
PIEDMONT
CAMP HAYDEN RD
DURRWACHTER RD
SEAGULL DR
FRESHWATER BAY BOAT LAUNCH RAMP
FRESHWATER BAY RD

6

WASHINGTON
PIEDMONT RD
MILLER RD
BISHOP RD
DEMPSEY RD
Ramapo
WASANKARI RD
GRAUL RD
RD
NFD RD 30
NFD RD 3040
OLYMPIC
NFD RD 3068
SPRUCE TRAIL RD
Piedmont
HARRIGAN POINT
DEVIL POINT
PYRAMID MOUNTAIN
SARATOGA POINT
EAST BEACH
EAST BEACH RD
OLYMPIC
Maple Grove
LAKE SUTHERLAND
EDEN VALLEY
RD

7

Fairholm
FAIRHOLM CAMPGROUND
CAMP
RAPID
JR
RD
OLYMPIC
EAGLE POINT
LAPOEL POINT
LAKE
CRESCENT
BARNES POINT
MAPLE POINT
HWY
SLEDGE HAMMER POINT
101
SOUTH SHORE RD
Snug Harbor
OLYMPIC
HWY
NATIONAL
NATIONAL
BALDY RIDGE
FOREST

NFD RD 30
SOL
DUC
RIVER
NFD RD 2946
PARK
SOURDOUGH MOUNTAIN
MARYMERE FALLS
BARNES CREEK
AURORA PEAK

A   B   C   D

SEE 109 MAP

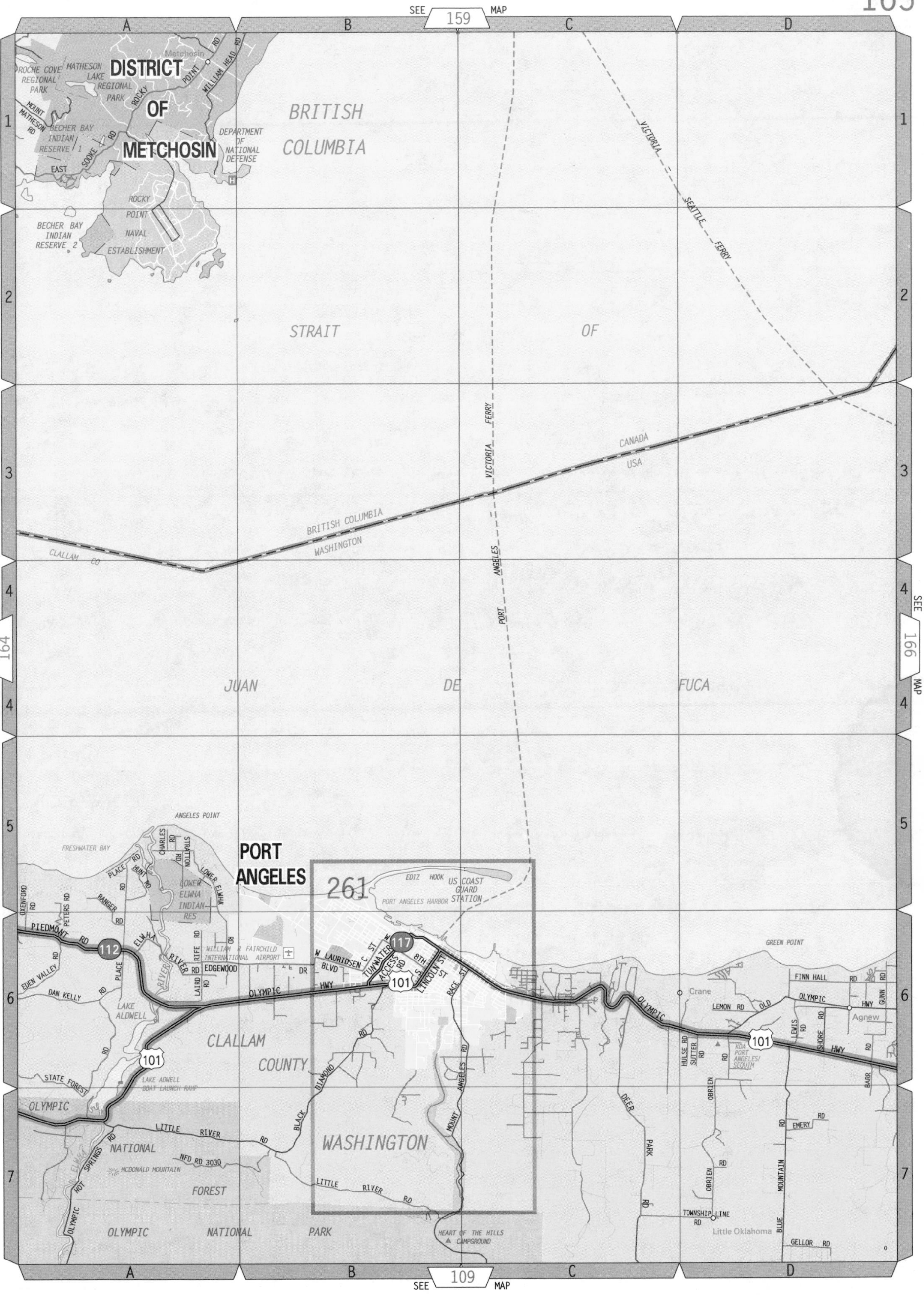

PNW

METRO

A B C D

SEE MAP 159

DISTRICT OF METCHOSIN

ROCHE COVE REGIONAL PARK
MATHESON LAKE REGIONAL PARK
MOUNT MATHESON RD
BECHER BAY INDIAN RESERVE 1
EAST
SOOKE RD
ROCKY POINT
WILLIAM HEAD RD
Metchosin
DEPARTMENT OF NATIONAL DEFENSE

BECHER BAY INDIAN RESERVE 2
ROCKY POINT NAVAL ESTABLISHMENT

BRITISH COLUMBIA

STRAIT OF

VICTORIA SEATTLE FERRY

VICTORIA FERRY
PORT ANGELES

BRITISH COLUMBIA
WASHINGTON

CLALLAM CO

CANADA
USA

JUAN DE FUCA

SEE MAP 164

SEE MAP 166

ANGELES POINT
FRESHWATER BAY
PORT ANGELES
261
EDIZ HOOK
US COAST GUARD STATION
PORT ANGELES HARBOR
GREEN POINT

CHARLES
STRATTON
PLACE
BUNN RD
LOWER ELWHA
LOWER ELWHA INDIAN RES
OXENFORD
PETERS RD
RANGER RD
PIEDMONT RD
112
ELWHA RIVER RD
RIFFE RD
LAIRD RD
EDGEWOOD
WILLIAM R FAIRCHILD INTERNATIONAL AIRPORT
DR
W LAURIDSEN BLVD
TUMWATER
C ST
8TH
ACCESS RD
117
101
LINCOLN ST
RACE ST
OLYMPIC HWY
Crane
FINN HALL RD
OLYMPIC
HWY GINN
LEMON RD
OLD
Agnew
EDEN VALLEY RD
DAN KELLY RD
LAKE ALDWELL
OLYMPIC
HWY
DIAMOND
BLACK
MOUNT ANGELES RD
DEER PARK RD
HULSE RD
SUTTER RD
101
KOA PORT ANGELES/ SEQUIM
LEWIS RD
SHORE RD
HWY
BARR
OBRIEN RD
MOUNTAIN RD
101
CLALLAM COUNTY
STATE FOREST
OLYMPIC
LAKE ALDWELL BOAT LAUNCH RAMP
LITTLE RIVER RD
WASHINGTON
LITTLE RIVER RD
OBRIEN RD
EMERY RD
ELWHA HOT SPRINGS RD
NFD RD 3030
McDONALD MOUNTAIN
NATIONAL FOREST
TOWNSHIP LINE RD
BLUE MOUNTAIN RD
Little Oklahoma
GELLOR RD
OLYMPIC NATIONAL PARK
HEART OF THE HILLS CAMPGROUND

SEE MAP 109

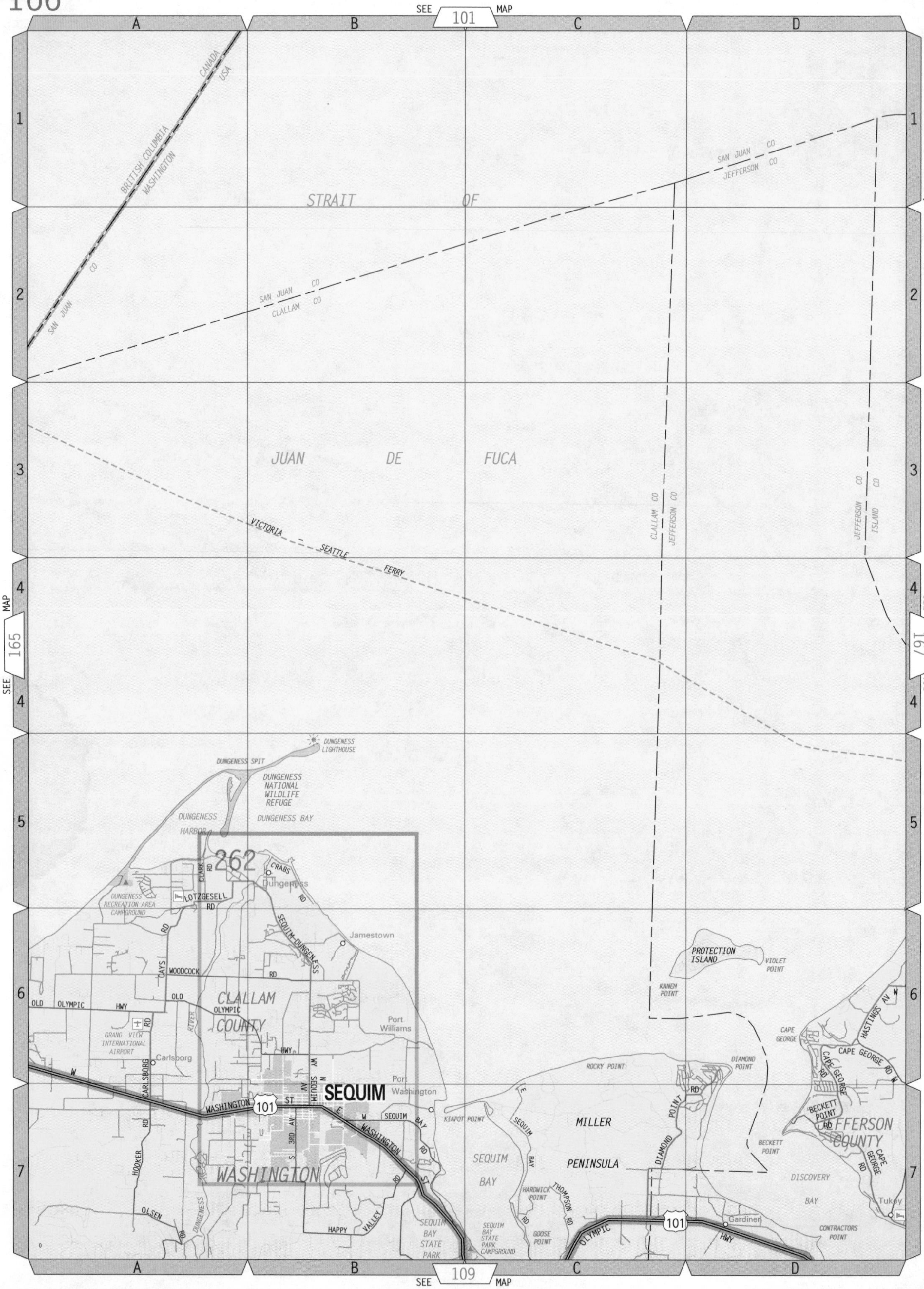

PNW

METRO

—N—

SEE 101 MAP

A   B   C   D

1

BRITISH COLUMBIA
CANADA
USA
WASHINGTON

SAN JUAN CO
JEFFERSON CO

1

STRAIT   OF

SAN JUAN

CO

2

SAN JUAN CO
CLALLAM CO

CLALLAM CO
JEFFERSON CO

JEFFERSON CO

ISLAND CO

2

JUAN   DE   FUCA

3

VICTORIA — SEATTLE — FERRY

3

SEE 165 MAP

4

SEE 167 MAP

4

DUNGENESS LIGHTHOUSE

DUNGENESS SPIT

DUNGENESS NATIONAL WILDLIFE REFUGE

DUNGENESS BAY

5

DUNGENESS HARBOR

262

CRABS

Dungeness

DUNGENESS RECREATION AREA CAMPGROUND

LOTZGESELL RD

CLARK RD

SEQUIM-DUNGENESS

Jamestown

PROTECTION ISLAND

VIOLET POINT

5

CAYS

WOODCOCK

RD

CLALLAM COUNTY

OLYMPIC

Port Williams

KANEM POINT

CAPE GEORGE

HASTINGS AV W

6

OLD OLYMPIC HWY

RIVER RD

OLD

HWY

GRAND VIEW INTERNATIONAL AIRPORT

Carlsborg

Port Washington

ROCKY POINT

DIAMOND POINT

CAPE GEORGE

CAPE GEORGE RD

6

CARLSBORG RD

WASHINGTON

101

SEQUIM

ST

3RD AV

W WASHINGTON

SEQUIM BAY RD

SEQUIM BAY

Kiapot Point

MILLER PENINSULA

DIAMOND POINT

BECKETT POINT

JEFFERSON COUNTY

7

HOOKER RD

DUNGENESS

S 3RD AV S

WASHINGTON

HAPPY VALLEY

SEQUIM BAY STATE PARK

SEQUIM BAY STATE PARK CAMPGROUND

HARDWICK POINT

THOMPSON RD

GOOSE POINT

OLYMPIC

101

HWY

Gardiner

DISCOVERY BAY

CONTRACTORS POINT

Tukey

BECKETT POINT

7

OLSEN

A   B   C   D

SEE 109 MAP

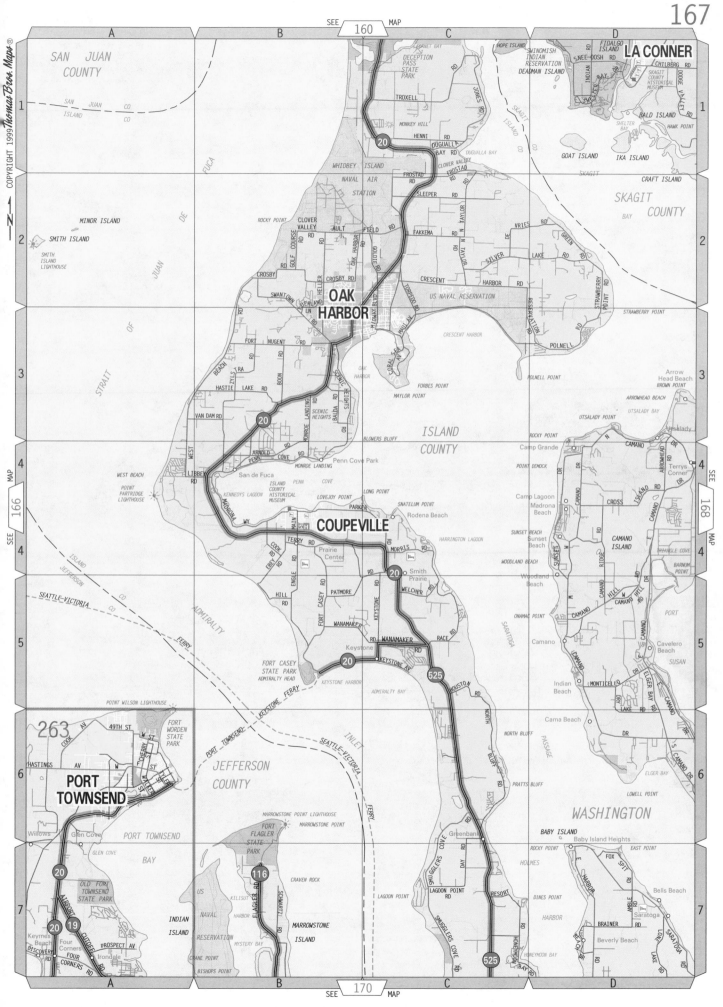

A   B   C   D

PNW

METRO

MOUNT VERNON

STANWOOD

ARLINGTON

MARYSVILLE

SKAGIT COUNTY

ISLAND COUNTY

SNOHOMISH COUNTY

WASHINGTON

CAMANO ISLAND

FIR ISLAND

SKAGIT BAY

SKAGIT RIVER

Big Lake
Montborne
Lake McMurray
McMurray
Pilchuck
Bryant
Stanwood-Bryant Rd
Armstrong Lake
Split Rock
Table Mountain
Devils Mountain
Scott Mountain
Little Mountain
Pilchuck Bridge Campground
Stimson Hill

Cedardale
Conway
Milltown
Starbird
Monson Corner
Cedarhome
Brandstrom
Florence
Silvana
Norman
Lakewood
Lake Goodwin
Lake Martha
Lake Natha
Warm Beach
Kayak Point County Park
Kayak Point
Tulare Beach
Sunny Shores
Tulalip
Tulalip Shores
Hermosa Point
Possession Sound
Saratoga Passage
Camano Head
Pebble Beach
Mabana
Dallman
Tyee Beach
Spee-bi-dah
Cornell
Mountain View Beach
Lona Beach
Iverson
Utsalady
Juniper Beach
Livingston Bay
Port Susan
Snohomish
Stillaguamish
Island School Crossing
Smokey Point
Arlington Airport
Edgecomb
Sisco
Sisco Heights
Crossing
Getchell Hill
Getchell
Tulalip Storage Depot
Tulalip Marina
Skiou Point
Indian Reservation

Highways: 5, 9, 530, 531, 532, 534, 161, 171, 167, 102, 218, 221, 224, 212, 215, 206, 208, 210, 202, 200

—N—

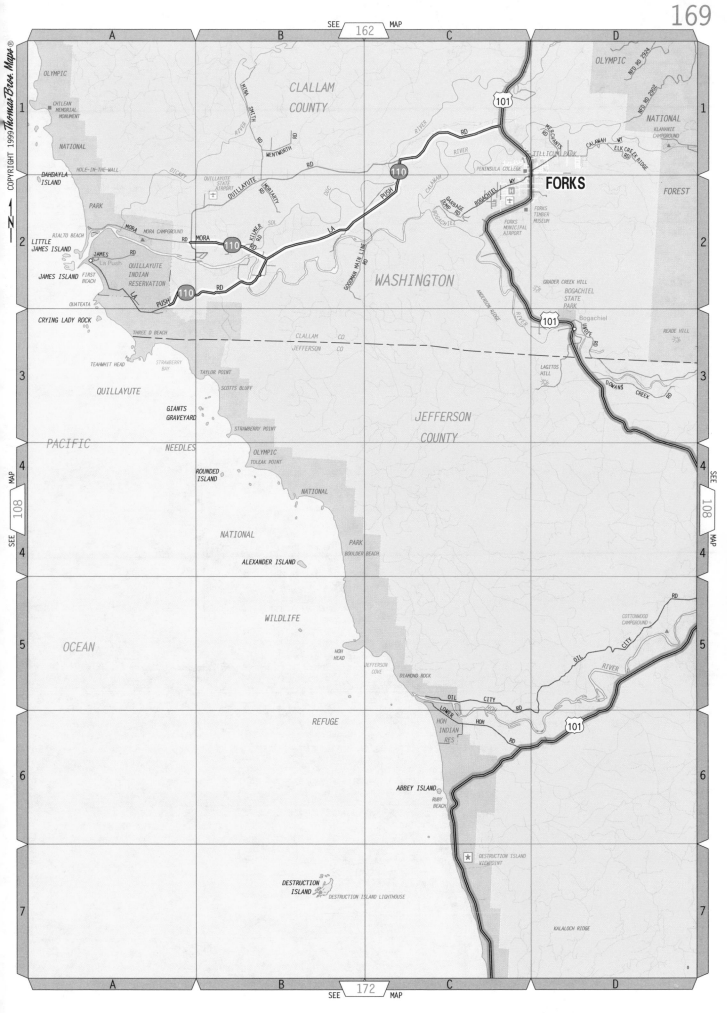

PNW

METRO

SEE 108 MAP

SEE 108 MAP

—N→

A　　B　　C　　D

OLYMPIC

CLALLAM
COUNTY

CHILEAN
MEMORIAL
MONUMENT

NATIONAL

HOLE-IN-THE-WALL

DAHDAYLA
ISLAND

PARK

RIALTO BEACH
LITTLE
JAMES ISLAND

JAMES

MORA CAMPGROUND

MORA

La Push

JAMES ISLAND

FIRST
BEACH

QUILLAYUTE
INDIAN
RESERVATION

QUATEATA

CRYING LADY ROCK

THREE O BEACH

TEAHWHIT HEAD

STRAWBERRY
BAY

QUILLAYUTE

PACIFIC

GIANTS
GRAVEYARD

NEEDLES

ROUNDED
ISLAND

TAYLOR POINT

SCOTTS BLUFF

STRAWBERRY POINT

OLYMPIC
TOLEAK POINT

NATIONAL

NATIONAL

ALEXANDER ISLAND

PARK
BOULDER BEACH

WILDLIFE

OCEAN

HOH
HEAD

JEFFERSON
COVE

DIAMOND ROCK

REFUGE

OIL
LOWER
HOH
INDIAN
RES

CITY
HOH

ABBEY ISLAND

RUBY
BEACH

DESTRUCTION
ISLAND

DESTRUCTION ISLAND LIGHTHOUSE

DESTRUCTION ISLAND
VIEWPOINT

KALALOCH RIDGE

OLYMPIC

NFD RD 2924

NFD RD 2902

NATIONAL

KLAHANIE
CAMPGROUND

MERCHANTS
RD

CALAWAH
WY

ELK CREEK RIDGE

TILLICUM PARK

PENINSULA COLLEGE

FORKS

FOREST

GARBAGE
DUMP RD

FORKS
TIMBER
MUSEUM

FORKS
MUNICIPAL
AIRPORT

GRADER CREEK HILL

BOGACHIEL
STATE
PARK

ANDERSON RIDGE

Bogachiel

READE HILL

LAGITOS
HILL

WHITE
RD

DOWANS
CREEK
RD

WASHINGTON

JEFFERSON
COUNTY

CLALLAM CO
JEFFERSON CO

COTTONWOOD
CAMPGROUND

OIL
CITY

RIVER

HOH
RD

RD

COTTONWOOD

MINA
SMITH
RD

WENTWORTH
RD

RD

DICKEY

QUILLAYUTE
STATE
AIRPORT

QUILLAYUTE

MORIARTY
RD

MORA
RD

KILMER
RD

SOL

DUC

LA
PUSH

GOODMAN MAIN LINE

RD

RIVER

CALAWAH

BOGACHIEL
WY

BOGACHIEL

RIVER

101

110

110

110

101

101

101

RD

LA
PUSH
RD

PNW

METRO

—N—

SEE 167 MAP

SEE 109 MAP

SEE 171 MAP

SEE 174 MAP

A   B   C   D

1   2   3   4   5   6   7

QUIMPER PENINSULA

ANDERSON LAKE STATE PARK

Woodmans

ANDERSON LAKE

20
19

IRONDALE
HESS CORNER
Hadlock
Chimacum

INDIAN ISLAND
US NAVAL RESERVATION

JORGENSON HILL

FLAGLER

SCOW BAY

MARROWSTONE ISLAND

116

Nodule Point

OAK BAY

KINNEY POINT

LIPLIP POINT

PUGET

ADMIRALTY

INLET

BUSH POINT LIGHT

WHIDBEY ISLAND

SMUGGLERS COVE

HONEYMOON BAY

HOLMES HARBOR

GOSS LAKE

LONE LAKE

ISLAND COUNTY

525

Freeland

SCENIC DR

MILLMAN RD

Bayview

MUTINY BAY

LANCASTER RD

Austin

DOUBLE BLUFF

DOUBLE BLUFF LIGHT

DEER LAGOON

Sunlight Beach

USELESS BAY

EWING ST

GIBBS LAKE

WEST VALLEY

CENTER

VAN TROJAN

EGG AND I RD

CHIMACUM VALLEY

19

BEAVER VALLEY RD

SWANSONVILLE

OLYMPUS BLVD

OLELE POINT

MATS MATS BAY

BASALT POINT

BURNER POINT

COLVOS ROCKS LIGHT

SOUND

SEATTLE-VICTORIA

FERRY

FOULWEATHER BLUFF

Foulweather Bluff

SKUNK BAY LIGHT

Hansville

SPITS

NORWEGIAN POINT

POINT NO POINT LIGHT

CENTER RD

EAGLEMOUNT RD

Center

JEFFERSON COUNTY

LARSON LAKE

Port Ludlow

Swansonville

BULLS HEAD

LUDLOW RD

PARADISE BAY RD

WATSON RD

E LUDLOW RIDGE RD

TALA SHORE DR

TALA POINT

TWIN

NE MADRONA BLVD

HOOD CANAL DR

104

104

SANDY SHORE LAKE

THORNDIKE

POINT NO POINT RD

WHITE ROCK

POINT HANNON LIGHT

HOOD HEAD

TERMINATION POINT

BYWATER BAY

Shine

SQUAMISH HARBOR

NE 360TH ST

PILOT POINT

NE EGLON RD

Eglon

COYLE RD

DABOB POST OFFICE

DABOB RIVER

Dabob

COYLE

CREEK

Camp Discovery

CAMP DISCOVERY RD

THORNDYKE BAY

TARBOO BAY

TOANDOS

PORT GAMBLE HISTORIC MUSEUM

OF SEA AND SHORE MUSEUM

Port Gamble

NE BABCOCK ST

PORT GAMBLE

LITTLE BOSTON

Hansville

HOFFMAN RD

PORT GAMBLE INDIAN RESERVATION

SANDY BEACH LN NE

APPLE COVE

POINT LIGHT

APPLE COVE POINT

3

KITSAP COUNTY

WASHINGTON

Four Corners

104

GAMBLE PL NE

NE 288TH ST

GAMBLE BAY RD NE

PARCELL RD

104

NE SHORTY CAMPBELL RD

Kingston

Edmonds-Kingston Ferry

W KINGSTON RD NE

APPLETREE COVE

LEMONDS DR

Lofall

Breidablick

Striebels Corner

HIGHLAND RD

NE CRAWFORD DR

307

PIONEER

PIONEER HILL RD

WAGHORN RD NW

BIG VALLEY RD

NE SAWDUST HILL RD

NE ROVA RD

GAMBLE

HANSVILLE RD NE

S KINGSTON RD NE

PRESIDENT POINT

Vinland

LUMBERJACK AV

RHODODENDRON LN NW

FINN HILL RD

BIG VALLEY RD

BOND RD

NE IVERSON RD

NE GUNDERSON RD

INDIANOLA RD NE

PORT MADISON INDIAN RESERVATION

MILLER BAY RD

TULIN RD NE

DARTER RD NW

SEABOLD

RUDE RD NW

STOTTLEMEYER RD

PUGH RD

LINCOLN RD

NOLL RD NE

MILLER BAY

MILLER BAY

NW FINN HILL

305

ARCHER FISH

SEAHORSE

BULLHEAD

FRONT ST

NE MESFORD RD

NE HOSTMARK ST

MARINE SCIENCE CENTER

Suquamish

NE COLUMBIA RD

AUGUSTA AV NE

3

POULSBO

US NAVAL RESERVATION

Bangor

SEALION

STURGEON ST

TRIGGER AV

LIBERTY INLET

Lemolo

FRONT ST

LEMOLO SHORE DR

NAVAL UNDERSEA MUSEUM

Keyport

Virginia

SUQUAMISH WY NE

DIVISION AV NE

TOTTEN RD

WIDME RD

Port Madison

AGATE POINT

SUQUAMISH MUSEUM

PORT MADISON

POINT MONROE LIGHT

SOUND

ZELATCHED POINT RD

HAZEL POINT

FT SHERMAN HARBOR

OLYMPIC VIEW

CLEAR CREEK

THREE SHER AV

LUOTO

NW

SILVERDALE

VIKING WY NW

308

AGATE POINT RD

BLOEDEL RESERVE

PORT MADISON

POINT BOLIN

Seabold

305

KITSAP CO

KING CO

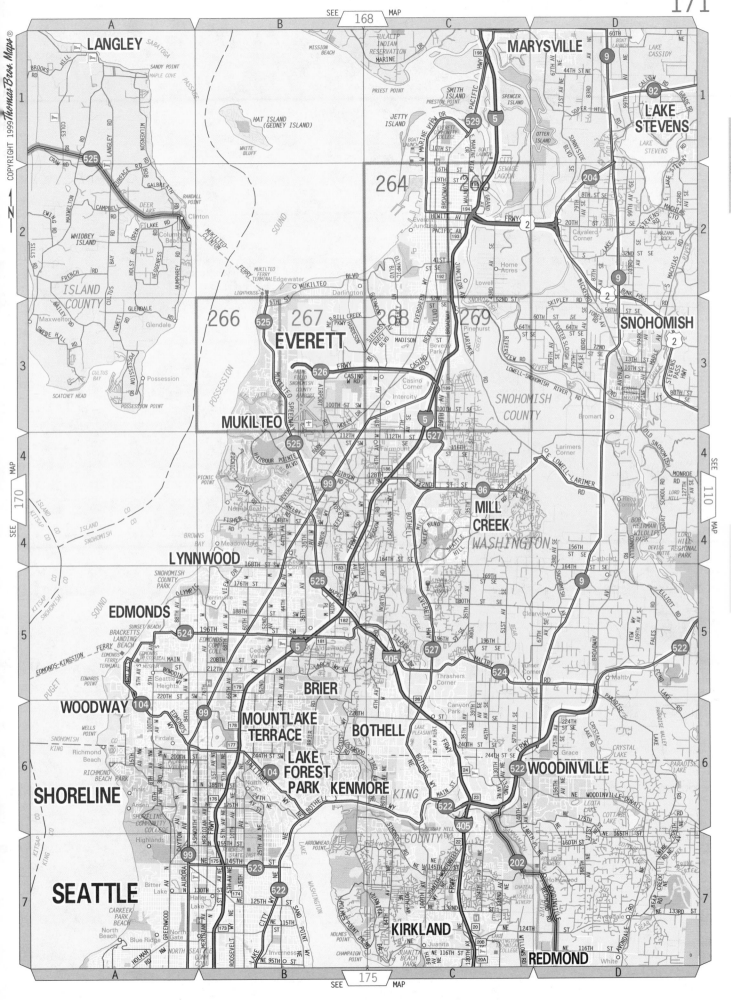

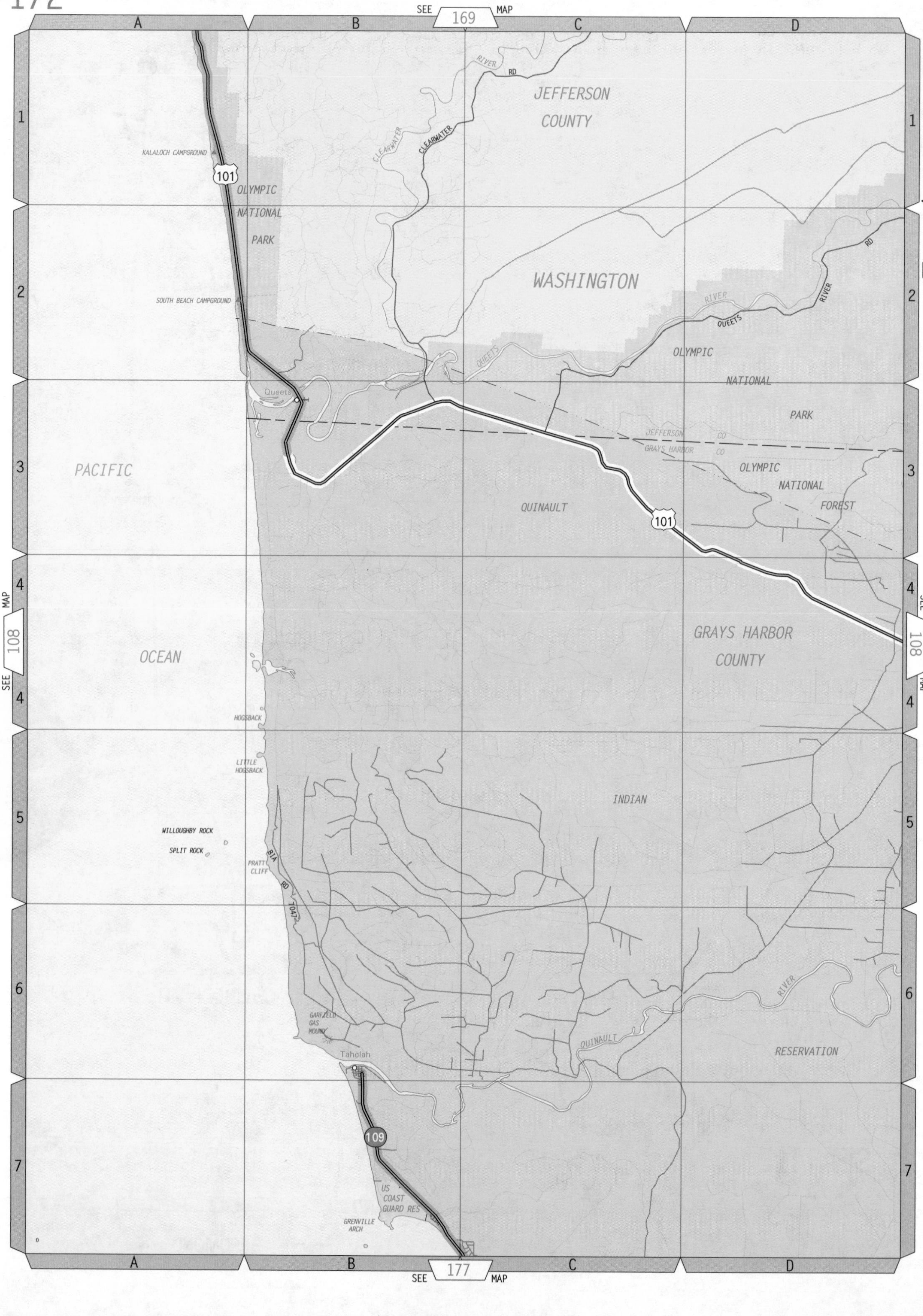

PNW

METRO

—N—

SEE 169 MAP

A B C D

1

JEFFERSON
COUNTY

CLEARWATER RIVER RD
CLEARWATER

KALALOCH CAMPGROUND

101

OLYMPIC

WASHINGTON

NATIONAL

2

SOUTH BEACH CAMPGROUND

PARK

RIVER RD

QUEETS RIVER

OLYMPIC

NATIONAL

PARK

Queets

QUEETS

JEFFERSON CO
GRAYS HARBOR CO

3

PACIFIC

QUINAULT

OLYMPIC

NATIONAL

101

FOREST

SEE 108 MAP

4

OCEAN

GRAYS HARBOR

COUNTY

HOGSBACK

LITTLE
HOGSBACK

INDIAN

5

WILLOUGHBY ROCK

SPLIT ROCK

PRATT
CLIFF

BIA 80 7047

6

GARFIELD
GAS
MOUND

RIVER

QUINAULT

RESERVATION

Taholah

7

109

US
COAST
GUARD RES

GRENVILLE
ARCH

SEE 177 MAP

A B C D

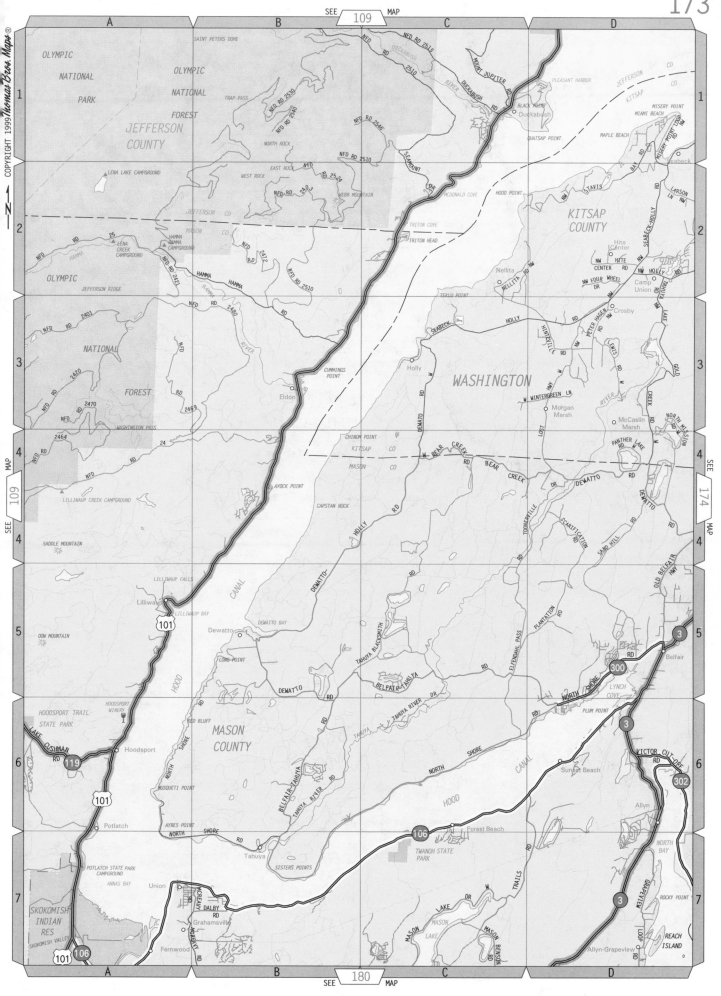

PNW

METRO

SEE 109 MAP

SEE MAP 109

SEE 174 MAP

SEE 180 MAP

A   B   C   D

1 2 3 4 5 6 7

OLYMPIC NATIONAL PARK

OLYMPIC NATIONAL FOREST

JEFFERSON COUNTY

SAINT PETERS DOME

TRAP PASS

NORTH ROCK

EAST ROCK

WEST ROCK

WEBB MOUNTAIN

LENA LAKE CAMPGROUND

JEFFERSON CO

MASON CO

LENA CREEK CAMPGROUND

HAMMA HAMMA CAMPGROUND

JEFFERSON RIDGE

OLYMPIC

NATIONAL FOREST

WASHINGTON PASS

LILLIWAUP CREEK CAMPGROUND

SADDLE MOUNTAIN

DOW MOUNTAIN

LILLIWAUP FALLS

LILLIWAUP

LILLIWAUP BAY

HOODSPORT TRAIL STATE PARK

LAKE CUSHMAN

HOODSPORT WINERY

Hoodsport

MUSQUETI POINT

AYRES POINT

POTLATCH

POTLATCH STATE PARK CAMPGROUND

ANNAS BAY

Union

SKOKOMISH INDIAN RES

SKOKOMISH VALLEY

Fernwood

Grahamsville

DALBY RD

McCREAVY RD

MARGIN RD

Tahuya

SISTERS POINTS

MASON COUNTY

RED BLUFF

NORTH SHORE RD

DEWATTO

DEWATTO BAY

FLONS POINT

Dewatto

AYOCK POINT

CAPSTAN ROCK

Eldon

CUMMINGS POINT

HOOD CANAL

BELFAIR-TAHUYA

TAHUYA RIVER

TAHUYA

TAHUYA BLACKSMITH

BELFAIR-TAHUYA

TAHUYA RIVER DR

NORTH SHORE RD

HOOD CANAL

TWANOH STATE PARK

Forest Beach

MASON LAKE DR W

MASON LAKE

MASON BENSON RD

TRAILS

ELFENDAHL PASS

PLANTATION RD

TOONERVILLE

SCARIFICATION

SAND HILL

BEAR CREEK RD

BEAR CREEK DR

DEWATTO RD

DEWATTO

NORTH SHORE RD

Sunset Beach

Allyn

NORTH BAY

ROCKY POINT

REACH ISLAND

GRAPEVIEW LOOP RD

Allyn-Grapeview

VICTOR CUT-OFF RD

Belfair

LYNCH COVE

PLUM POINT

OLD BELFAIR HWY

WASHINGTON

KITSAP CO

MASON CO

CHINOM POINT

HOLLY RD

DEWATTO RD

Holly

W WINTERGREEN LN

Morgan Marsh

McCaslin Marsh

PANTHER LAKE RD W

NORTH MISSION RD

LOST RD

RIVER

TAHUYA LAKE

SEABECK

TEKIU POINT

SEABECK HWY

HINTZVILLE RD NW

PETER HAGEN RD NW

LEWIS RD NW

NW HOLLY RD

HOLLY

SEABECK-HOLLY RD

NW FOUR WHEEL DR

NW CENTER RD

Nellita

NELLITA RD NW

Crosby

Camp Union

KITSAP COUNTY

Hite Center

NW HITE CENTER RD

STAVIS BAY RD NW

LARSON LN NW

MISERY POINT LOOP NW

Seabeck

MIAMI BEACH

MISERY POINT

MAPLE BEACH

HOOD POINT

QUATSAP POINT

McDONALD COVE

TRITON COVE

TRITON HEAD

SEAMOUNT DR

Black Point

Duckabush

PLEASANT HARBOR

DUCKABUSH RIVER

DUCKABUSH RD

MOUNT JUPITER

JEFFERSON CO

KITSAP CO

NFD RD 2515

NFD RD 2510

NFD RD 2530

NFD RD 2540

NFD RD 2546

NFD RD 2510

NFD RD 2524

NFD RD 2403

NFD RD 2472

NFD RD 2421

NFD RD 2510

HAMMA HAMMA RD

HAMMA RIVER

NFD RD 2480

NFD RD 2401

NFD RD 2420

NFD RD 2470

NFD RD 2464

NFD RD 2469

NFD RD 24

NFD RD 25

101

119

101

106

101

106

3

300

3

3

302

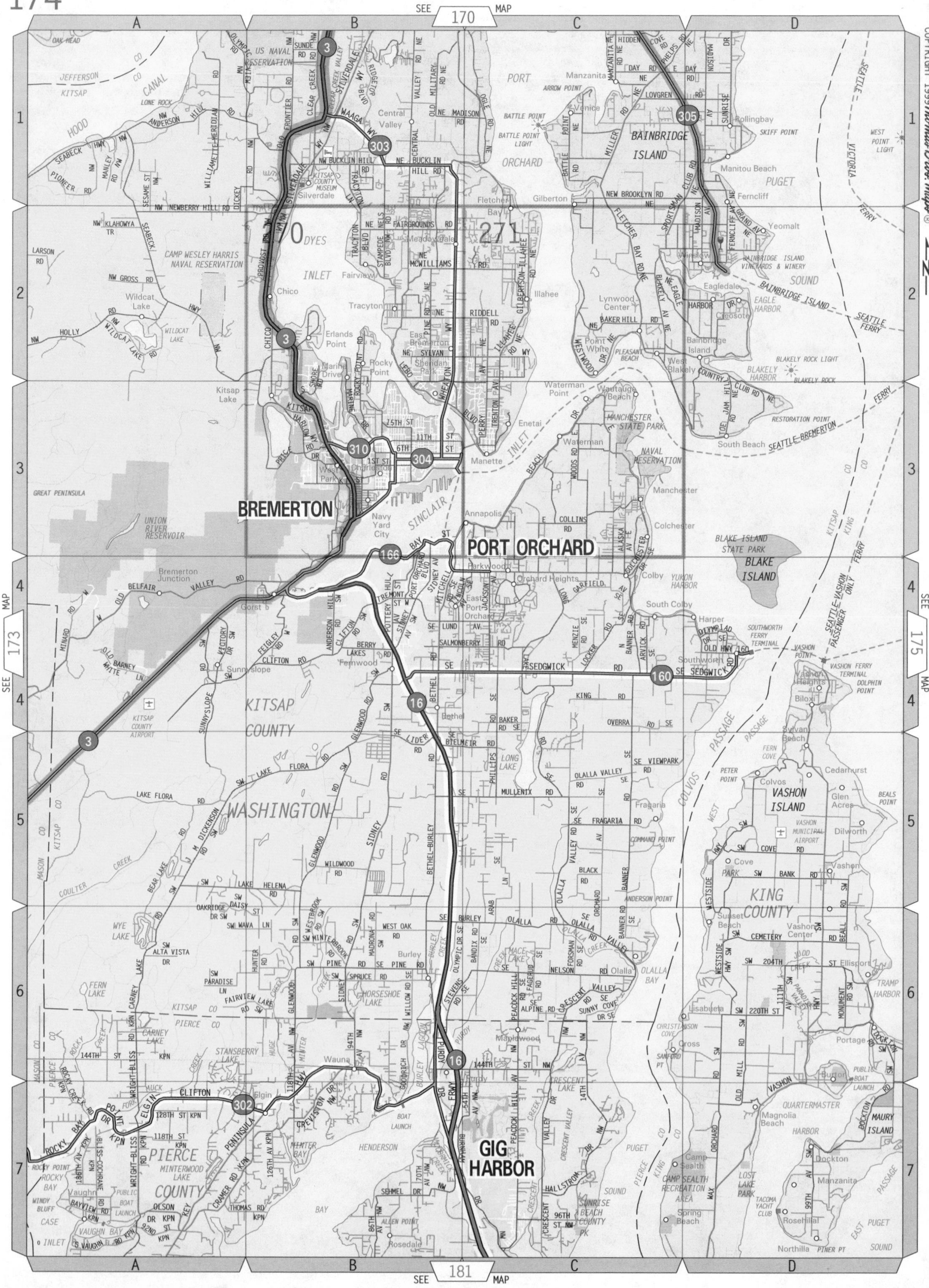

SEE 170 MAP

SEE 181 MAP

SEE 173 MAP

SEE 175 MAP

COPYRIGHT 1999 Thomas Bros. Maps®

—N—

PNW

METRO

BREMERTON

PORT ORCHARD

GIG HARBOR

BAINBRIDGE ISLAND

VASHON ISLAND

KING COUNTY

KITSAP COUNTY

PIERCE COUNTY

MASON CO

WASHINGTON

PUGET SOUND

HOOD CANAL

DYES INLET

SINCLAIR INLET

PORT ORCHARD

BLAKE ISLAND STATE PARK

MAURY ISLAND

COLVOS PASSAGE

GREAT PENINSULA

UNION RIVER RESERVOIR

270   271

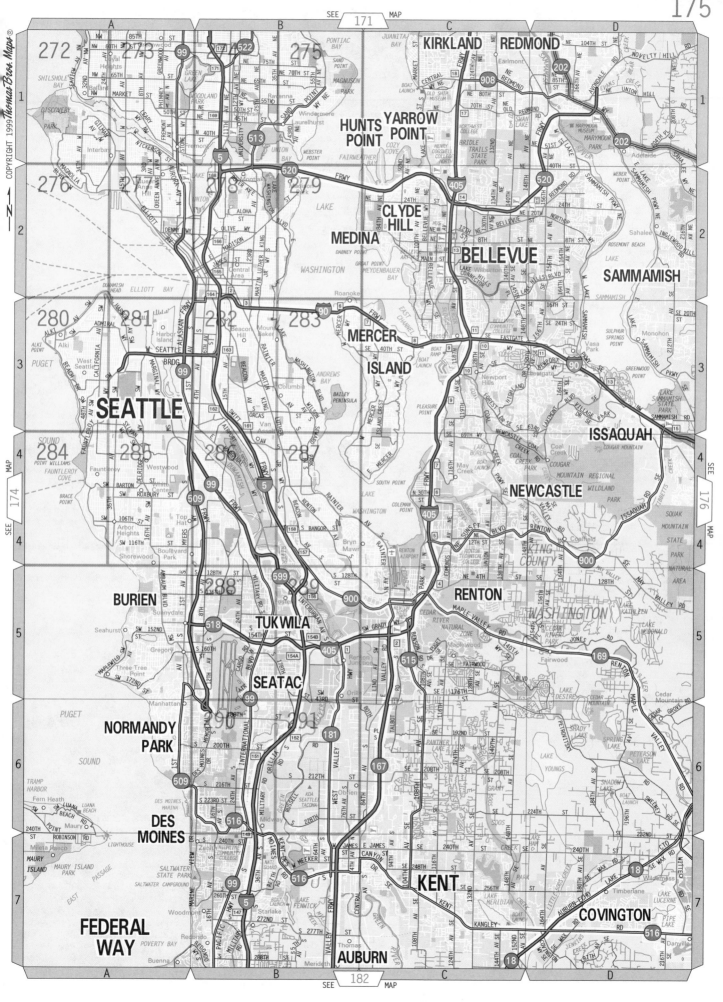

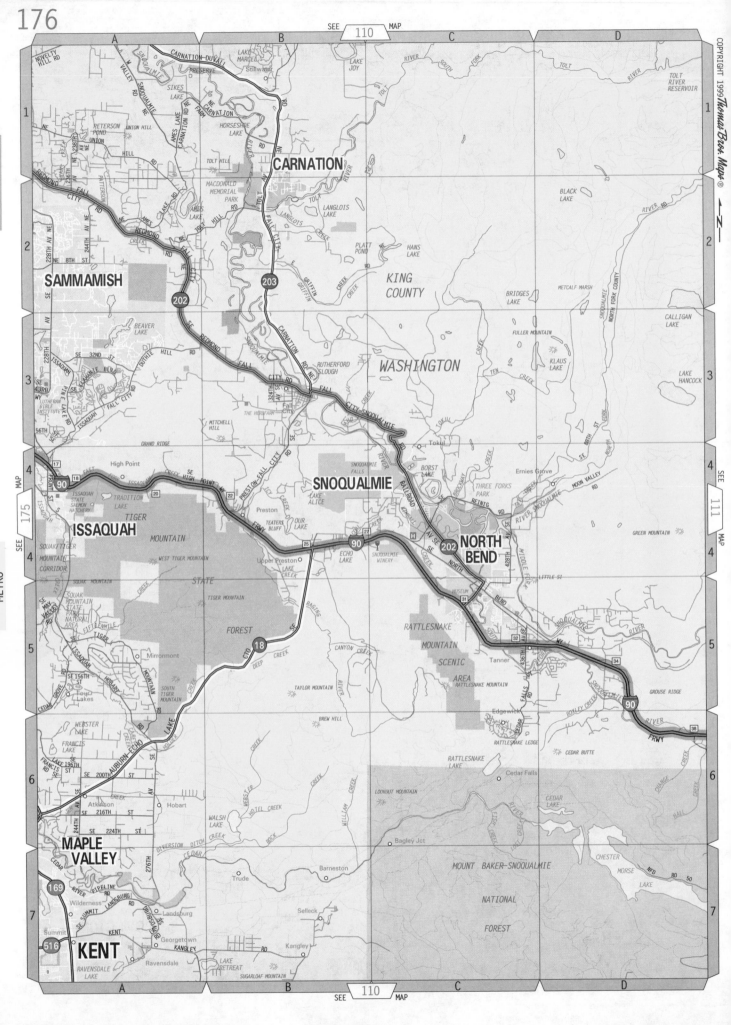

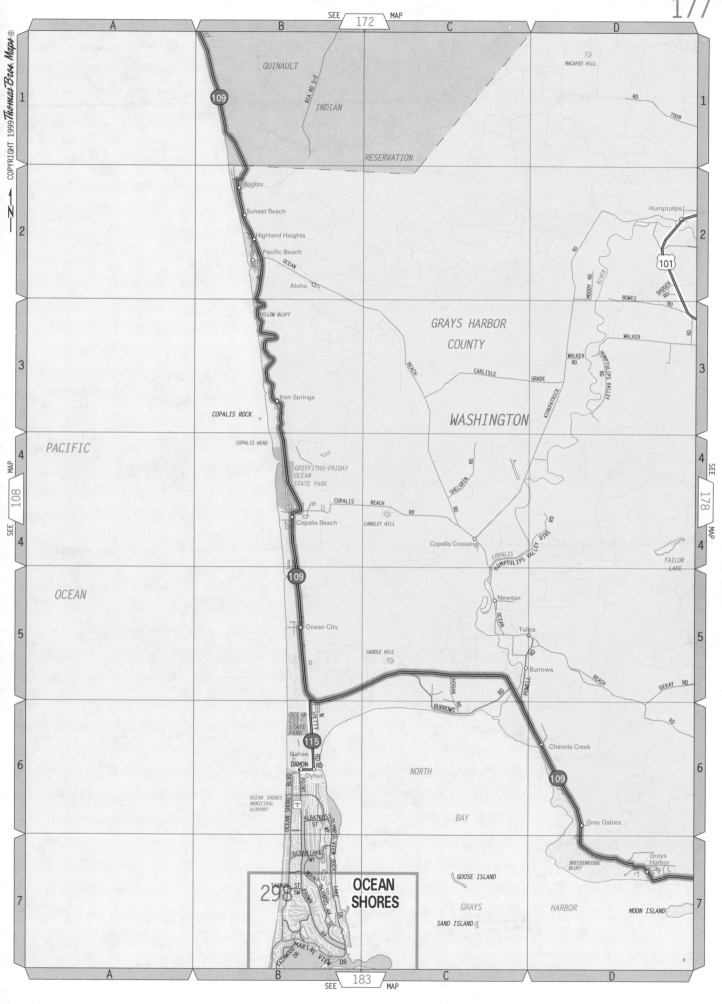

COPYRIGHT 1999 Thomas Bros. Maps®

—N→

SEE 172 MAP

QUINAULT

B1A RD S-2

INDIAN

RESERVATION

MACAFEE HILL

RD

7009

Moclips

Sunset Beach

Highland Heights

Pacific Beach

OCEAN

Humptulips

HUMPTULIPS RIVER

MOODY RD

RD

BADGER RD

US 101

Aloha

BOWES RD

WALKER

YELLOW BLUFF

GRAYS HARBOR

COUNTY

WALKER RD

HUMPTULIPS VALLEY

Iron Springs

BEACH

CARLISLE

GRADE

KIRKPATRICK

RD

WASHINGTON

COPALIS ROCK

PACIFIC

COPALIS HEAD

GRIFFITHS–PRIDAY OCEAN STATE PARK

COPALIS

BEACH

RD

SHELGRTN RD

RD

Copalis Beach

LANGLEY HILL

Copalis Crossing

COPALIS

HUMPTULIPS

VALLEY DIKE RD

SEE 108 MAP

SEE 178 MAP

FAILOR LAKE

OCEAN

109

Newton

OCEAN

Ocean City

Tulips

SADDLE HILL

RD

Burrows

BEACH

DEKAY RD

OCEAN CITY STATE PARK

N JETTY

115

Illahee

DAMON RD

Oyhut

BURROWS

HOGAN RD

RD

POWELL

Chenois Creek

RD

109

NORTH

OCEAN SHORES MUNICIPAL AIRPORT

OCEAN SHORES BLVD

POINT BROWN

ALBATROSS ST

OLYMPIC VIEW

DUCK

WY

BAY

Gray Gables

OCEAN LAKE WY

MOUNT OLYMPUS DR

BRECKENRIDGE BLUFF

Grays Harbor City

298

TAURUS ST SW

BROWN

SAND ISLAND

GOOSE ISLAND

OCEAN SHORES

GRAYS

HARBOR

MOON ISLAND

FIRWOOD DR

MARINE VIEW DR

SEE 183 MAP

PNW

METRO

COPYRIGHT 1999 Thomas Bros. Maps® —N—

SEE 109 MAP

A B C D

1

RD 8802

DONKEY CREEK

OLYMPIC NATIONAL FOREST

COUGAR MOUNTAIN

REED HILL

ABERDEEN WATERSHED

RIVER

WEST FORK HUMPTULIPS RIVER

HUMPTULIPS RIVER

EAST FORK

101

MCNUTT RD

NEWBURY RD

TUFFRE RD

HUMPTULIPS RD

E

2

HUMPTULIPS

WISHKAH RIVER

WYNDOCHEE

GRAYS HARBOR COUNTY

3

HENSEL RD

YOUMANS RD

RIVER

E HOQUIAM RD

GREENWOOD RD

WISHKAH RD

WISHKAH RD

RIVER

WYNDOCHEE RIVER

COUGAR SMITH RD

VALLEY RD

A7200

SATSOP RIVER

WEST FORK

SEE 177 MAP

SEE 179 MAP

4

101

Nisson

HOQUIAM WISHKAH RD

Greenwood

W WISHKAH FORK

HAMILTON CANYON

WASHINGTON

WYNDOCHEE

ROAD A-LINE

A6000 RD

A5000

A3030

ROAD D-LINE

CANYON RD

5

New London

LYTLE LANDING

HOQUIAM RD

E FORK

EAST FORK

WYNDOCHEE WISHKAH

OLD WYNDOCHEE RD

WYNDOCHEE

WYNDOCHEE VALLEY

PRICES PEAK

Wishkah

ABERDEEN GARDENS RD

Aberdeen Gardens

WISHKAH RD

GEISSLER VALLEY RD

6

OCEAN BEACH RD

WEST FORK

EAST

HOQUIAM

HOQUIAM RIVER

BLACK CREEK

WYNDOCHEE VALLEY RD

MONTESANO

7

HOQUIAM

ABERDEEN

PERRY AV

ANDERSEN RD

BROADWAY

N 11TH ST

EMERSON

ADAMS ST

PAULSON

AIRPORT WY

109

Hoquiam Castle

POLSON PARK & MUSEUM

SUMNER AV

BAY AV

INDUSTRIAL

COW POINT

OLYMPIC STADIUM

East Hoquiam

WISHKAH ST

B ST

East Aberdeen

GRAYS HARBOR HISTORICAL

101

LAKE ABERDEEN HATCHERY

Lake Aberdeen

CHEHALIS RIVER

WEST BEND

SOUTH RD

Junction City

Central Park

12

W GEISSLER

W GEISSLER

WYNDOCHEE RD

PIONEER AV W

KATON RD

MONTESANO ABERDEEN RD

LAKE SYLVIA

LAKE SYLVIA STATE PARK

CAMP CREEK RD

SYLVIA LAKE RD

MCBRYDE AV E

BEACON

33RD STN

1ST ST

OLD 410 HWY

107

12

GRAYS HARBOR

RENNIE ISLAND

HARDING RD

BOONE ST

W CURTIS ST

South Aberdeen

GRAYS HARBOR COLLEGE

HUNTLEY ST

105

101

COSMOPOLIS

Higgins Island

CHEHALIS RIVER

SOUTH BANK

CHEHALIS RIVER

SEE 117 MAP

A B C D

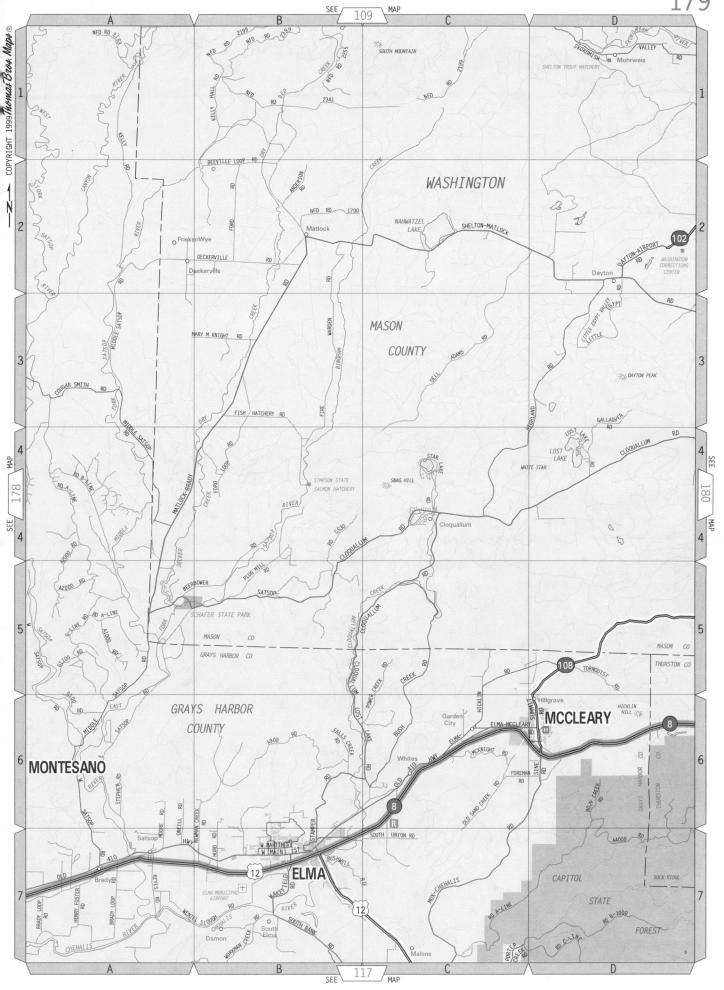

PNW

METRO

PNW

METRO

SEE MAP 173

—N—

A   B   C   D

MASON COUNTY

WEBB HILL

SKOKOMISH INDIAN RES

106

MASON LAKE

Little Hoquiam

MASON BENSON RD

GRAPEVIEW LOOP RD

STRETCH ISLAND

PIERCE COUNTY

MCLANE COVE

DOUGALL POINT

PURDY CUTOFF

McREAVY RD

MASON LAKE DR W

MASON LAKE RD W

INDIAN COVE

HERRON BAY

1

GEORGE ADAMS SALMON HATCHERY

101

LAKE LIMERICK

MASON LAKE RD

3

SPENCER LAKE

SUN POINT

PICKERING

JARRELL COVE

HERRON ISLAND

Herron

PURDY CANYON

BROCKDALE RD

CRANBERRY LAKE

McEWAN RD

PRAIRIE RD

MASON LAKE RD W

SPENCER LAKE RD

Graham Point

NORTH ISLAND

YATES RD

MASON CO

STEDMAN

205TH AV

KPS

102

DAYTON AIRPORT RD

JOHNS PRAIRIE RD

Bayshore

PHILLIPS LAKE

PICKERING PASSAGE

HARTSTENE ISLAND

MCMICKEN ISLAND

2

SANDERSON FIELD AIRPORT

SHELTON

Oakland

DANIELS RD

AGATE RD

BALLOW RD

FUDGE POINT

JOEMMA BEACH CAMPGROUND

WHITMAN COVE

MASON COUNTY MUSEUM

RAILROAD

N NORTHCLIFF PINE ST

CAPITOL HILL RD

CHAPMAN COVE

OAKLAND BAY

CRESTVIEW DR

AGATE RD

CHURCH POINT

HUNGERFORD POINT

SQUAXIN ISLAND INDIAN RES

HARTSTENE

ISLAND SHORE DR

POINT WILSON

WILSON POINT

CASE

INLET

3

SHELTON-MATLOCK RD

EAGLE POINT

MILLER POINT

HAMMERSLEY

ARCADIA

INLET

CAPE COD

Arcadia

ARCADIA POINT

PITLATCH POINT

LANSKY DR

JARED RD

SLIVA LN

THURSTON CO

PIERCE CO

SHELTON VALLEY RD

OLD OLYMPIC HWY

3

LOST LAKE

ISABELLA LAKE

DEEGAN RD

COLE RD

WASHINGTON

LYNCH RD

HOPE ISLAND

BELSPECK POINT

JOHNSON POINT

SEE MAP 179

CLOQUALLUM RD

MAINLINE

ISABELLA VALLEY RD

2900

101

LYNCH RD

DEER HARBOR

MUD-CAT POINT

229

TOTTEN

INLET

WINDY POINT

MASON CO

THURSTON CO

HUNTER POINT

SALTY POINT

85TH AV NW

90TH AV NW

81ST AV NW

Sanderson Harbor

DANA PASSAGE

TUCKSEL POINT

BRISCO POINT

DOVER POINT

HENDERSON INLET

PONCIN COVE

BAIRD COVE

BAIRD RD NE

78TH AV NE

SEE MAP 181

4

KAMILCHE VALLEY

LITTLE SKOOKUM VALLEY

108

HURLEY-WALDRIP RD

Kamilche

New Kamilche

OLD OLYMPIC HWY

LITTLE SKOOKUM INLET

KAMILCHE POINT

QUARTERS POINT

SLOCUM RIDGE

BLOOMFIELD RD

DEEPWATER POINT

KAMILCHE POINT

78TH AV NW

79TH AV NW

GALLAGHER COVE

COUGAR POINT

HUDSON COVE

69TH AV NW

61ST AV NW

64TH AV NW

66TH AV NW

ELD INLET

57TH WY NW

JEAL POINT

LIGHTHOUSE Boston Harbor

73RD AV NE

77TH AV NE

Chapman Bay

WOODARD BAY

WOODARD RD

WHITHAM RD

LIBBY RD

63RD AV NE

61ST AV NE

5

KAMILCHE VALLEY

BURNS POINT

BURNS COVE

OYSTER BAY

SHELLRIDGE RD NW

SCOTT RD NW

HOLIDAY VALLEY RD NW

STEAMBOAT ISLAND RD NW

42ND AV NW

GRAVELLY BEACH

KEATING RD NW

YOUNG COVE

GREEN COVE

COOPER POINT

SNYDER COVE

BISCAY ST NW

46TH AV NW

43RD AV NW

LITTLE TYKLE COVE

BIG TYKLE COVE

GULL HARBOR

North Olympia

F BOSTON HARBOR RD

GULL HARBOR RD NE

46TH AV NE

36TH AV NE

BIG FISHTRAP

LP COTTRAP

CLIFF POINT

ZANGLE RD NE

BUDD INLET

LIBBY RD

LEMON RD

SHINCKE RD NE

KINNEY RD NE

JOHNSON RD NE

PUGET

61ST AV NE

46TH AV NE

41ST AV NE

HAWKS PRAIRIE RD NE

MASON CO THURSTON CO

SUMMIT LAKE SHORE RD NW

SUMMIT LAKE

WILSON RD NW

SUMMIT LAKE RD NW

Schneiders Prairie

WHITTAKER RD NW

ROCKY POINT

SIMMONS RD NW

ASPINWALL RD NW

BREWER RD NW

SUNRISE BEACH RD NW

HOFFMAN RD NW

SIMPSON AV NW

54TH AV NW

36TH AV NW

THE EVERGREEN STATE COLLEGE

DRIFTWOOD RD NW

BUTLER COVE

DIVISION ST NW

ELLIS COVE

26TH AV NE

South Bay

SOUTH BAY RD NE

26TH AV NE

15TH AV NE

6

FIVE FORKS RD SW

PORTER PASS RD SW

POWERLINE RD SW

ROCK CANDY MOUNTAIN RD SW

THURSTON COUNTY

CEDAR FLATS RD SW

BAKER RD SW

MUNSON DR SW

TEMPLE VALLEY DR SW

8

OLD HWY

OLYMPIC HWY SW

RANDALL RD SW

McKENZIE RD SW

MUD BAY

THE EVERGREEN PKWY

KAISER RD NW

11TH AV NW

14TH AV NW

MUD BAY RD SW

96

COLLEGE ST SW

HARRISON AV

COOPER POINT RD SW

28TH AV NW

WEST BAY DR

STATE AV E

4TH AV E

UNION AV SE

N BETHEL ST

PINE AV NE

12TH AV NE

MARTIN WY

PACIFIC AV

297

108

107

5

109

LACEY

6

CAPITOL STATE FOREST

LARCH MOUNTAIN

ROCK CANDY MOUNTAIN

DELPHI RD SW

BLACK LAKE BLVD SW

PERCIVAL CREEK

HUDSON RD SW

49TH AV SW

54TH AV SW

SAPP RD SW

RURAL AV SW

LINWOOD AV SW

103

CLEVELAND AV

NORTH ST SE

TUMWATER

CAPITOL BLVD

104

105

22ND AV

FONES RD SE

HOFFMAN RD SE

BOULEVARD RD SE

COLLEGE ST SE

37TH AV SE

OLYMPIA

YELM HWY SE

RUDDELL RD SE

7

SAXON HARBOR LAKE

CAPITOL PEAK

THURSTON CO GRAYS HARBOR CO

BORDEAUX CAMPGROUND

BROWN RD SW

ALPINE DR SW

62ND AV SW

66TH AV SW

BLACK LAKE

70TH AV SW

ISRAEL RD SW

LITTLEROCK RD SW

5

102

CAPITOL BLVD

HENDERSON BLVD SE

RIVER RD SE

RAINIER RD SE

YELM HWY SE

101

SEE MAP 184

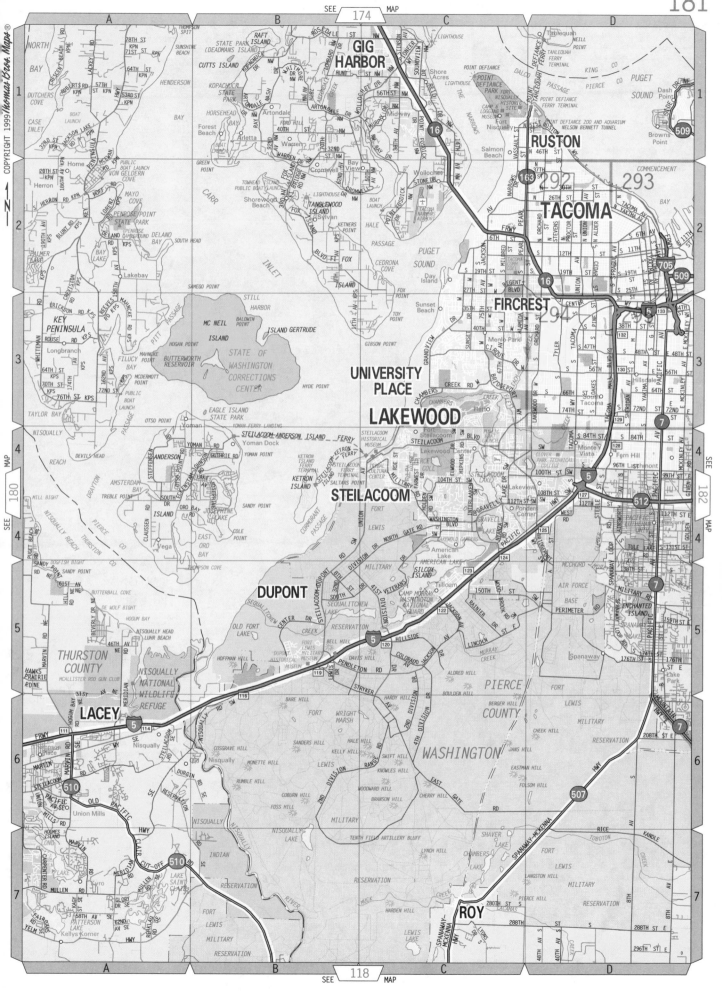

PNW

METRO

SEE MAP 180

SEE MAP 182

PNW

METRO

SEE 175 MAP

SEE 181 MAP

SEE 110 MAP

SEE 118 MAP

A   B   C   D

FEDERAL WAY

KENT

ALGONA

AUBURN

PACIFIC

MILTON

FIFE

TACOMA

EDGEWOOD

SUMNER

BONNEY LAKE

PUYALLUP

BUCKLEY

SOUTH PRAIRIE

ORTING

WILKESON

CARBONADO

KING COUNTY

PIERCE COUNTY WASHINGTON

MUCKLESHOOT INDIAN RES

FORT LEWIS MILITARY RESERVATION

509   99   5   18   167   164   165   161   162   410   512   7   135   136   137   142   143

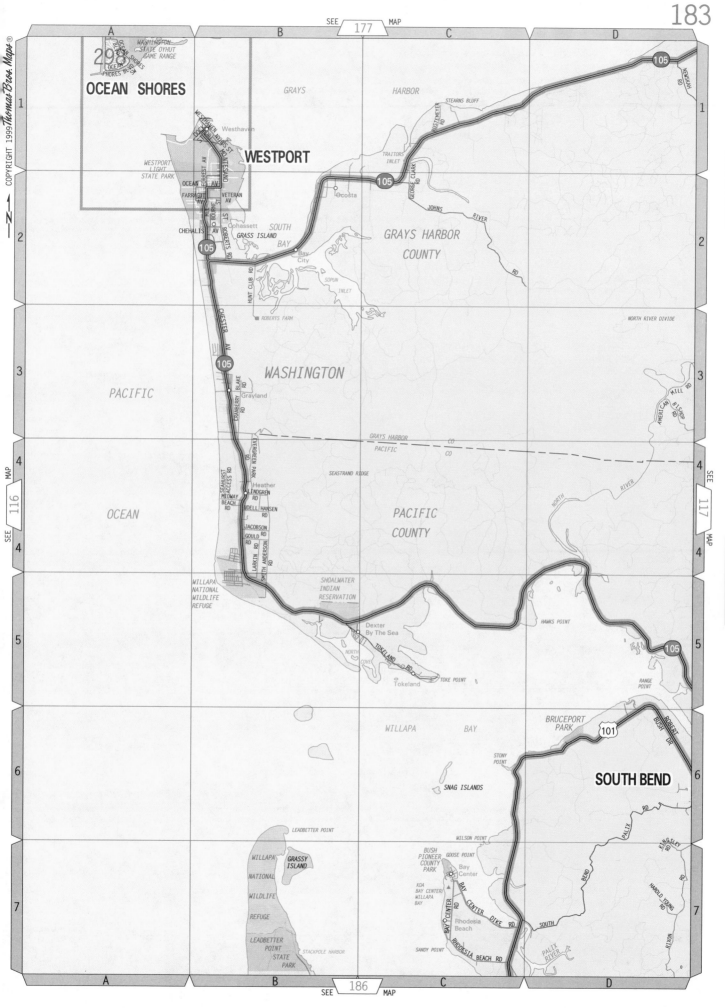

A B C D

1 1

2 2

3 3

4 4

5 5

6 6

7 7

OCEAN SHORES

298

WASHINGTON STATE OYHUT GAME RANGE

GRAYS HARBOR

STEARNS BLUFF

105

NEKASKI RD

OCEAN SHORES BLVD

OCEAN SHORES BLVD SW

Westhaven

NEWHAVEN AV

FORREST

WESTPORT

WESTPORT LIGHT STATE PARK

Cohassett

OCEAN AV

EVEREST AV

MONTESANO

FARRAGUT AV

VETERAN AV

PIER ST

BOURNE ST

CHEHALIS AV

ROBERTS RD

GRASS ISLAND

SOUTH GRASS BAY

BAY CITY

105

TRAITORS INLET

GEORGE CLARK RD

RUSTEMEYER RD

Ocosta

JOHNS RIVER

GRAYS HARBOR COUNTY

RD

HUNT CLUB RD

SOPUN INLET

ROBERTS FARM

NORTH RIVER DIVIDE

CHESTER AV

105

WASHINGTON

CRANBERRY RD

BLAKE RD

Grayland

PACIFIC

OCEAN

AMERICAN MILL RD

BISHOP RD

GRAYS HARBOR CO
PACIFIC CO

EVERGREEN PARK RD

SEASTRAND RIDGE

SEABHURST ACCESS RD

MIDWAY BEACH RD

Heather

LINDGREN RD

UDELL RD

HANSEN RD

JACOBSON RD

GOULD RD

LARKIN RD

SMITH RD

ANDERSON RD

PACIFIC COUNTY

NORTH RIVER

SEE 116 MAP

SEE 117 MAP

PNW

METRO

WILLAPA NATIONAL WILDLIFE REFUGE

SHOALWATER INDIAN RESERVATION

HAWKS POINT

105

NORTH COVE

Dexter By The Sea

TOKELAND RD

Tokeland

TOKE POINT

RANGE POINT

WILLAPA BAY

SNAG ISLANDS

BRUCEPORT PARK

101

BUSH DR

ROBERT DR

SOUTH BEND

STONY POINT

LEADBETTER POINT

WILSON POINT

PALIX RD

WILLAPA

NATIONAL

WILDLIFE

REFUGE

LEADBETTER POINT STATE PARK

GRASSY ISLAND

STACKPOLE HARBOR

BUSH PIONEER COUNTY PARK

GOOSE POINT

Bay Center

KOA BAY CENTER WILLAPA BAY

BAY CENTER RD

Rhodesia Beach

RHODESIA BEACH RD

SANDY POINT

BAY CENTER DIKE RD

SOUTH BEND

PALIX RIVER

KINGSLEY RD

HAROLD YOUNG RD

RIXON RD

PNW

METRO

A B C D

1

CAPITOL

Little Larch Mountain
Fall Creek Campground
Fuzzy Top
Mount Molly Campground
Yew Tree Campground
Middle Waddell Campground

STATE

Margaret McKenny Campground

2

FOREST

Sherman Valley Campground
Mina Falls Trailhead Campground

Bordeaux
Bordeaux

Mumby

Mima

3

Gate
Hunter Rd SW
175TH AV SW
176TH AV SW
173RD AV SW
Littlerock
Albany
Pendleton
173RD AV SW

Rochester

CHEHALIS INDIAN RESERVATION

4

Manners
Helsing Junction
James St SW
Jordan St SW
Michigan Hill Rd SW
Lundeen Rd SW
Van Dyke Rd SW

Michigan Hill
Prather
Langworthy Rd SW
MICHIGAN HILL
Meadows

THURSTON COUNTY

BUCODA

507

Delphi

Maytown
Littlerock
Maytown
Maytown

MILLER-SYLVANIA STATE PARK

South Union

OLYMPIA MUNICIPAL AIRPORT

East Olympia
FIR TREE DR

FORT LEWIS MILITARY RESERVATION

Sunnydale
Tenino Junction
TENINO DEPOT MUSEUM

TENINO

Chain Hill
Lemon Hill
Oregon Trail Monument
STRAWN
507

Offutt Lake
BLUMER HILL
NORTHCRAFT MOUNTAIN

Tono
Tono

5

LINCOLN CREEK RD
Galvin
Galvin AV
299

Downing RD
Wabash

Reynolds ST
W Sixth ST
E Sixth ST
Halliday

CENTRALIA

LEWIS COUNTY

Mendota

Nulls Crossing
Kopiah

6

5

12

CHEHALIS

Claquato

7

Milburn
Adna
6
Littell
Chehalis Junction
Newaukum

STAN HEDWALL PARK

Logan Hill
Rogerson
Pollman

WASHINGTON

Alpha

A B C D

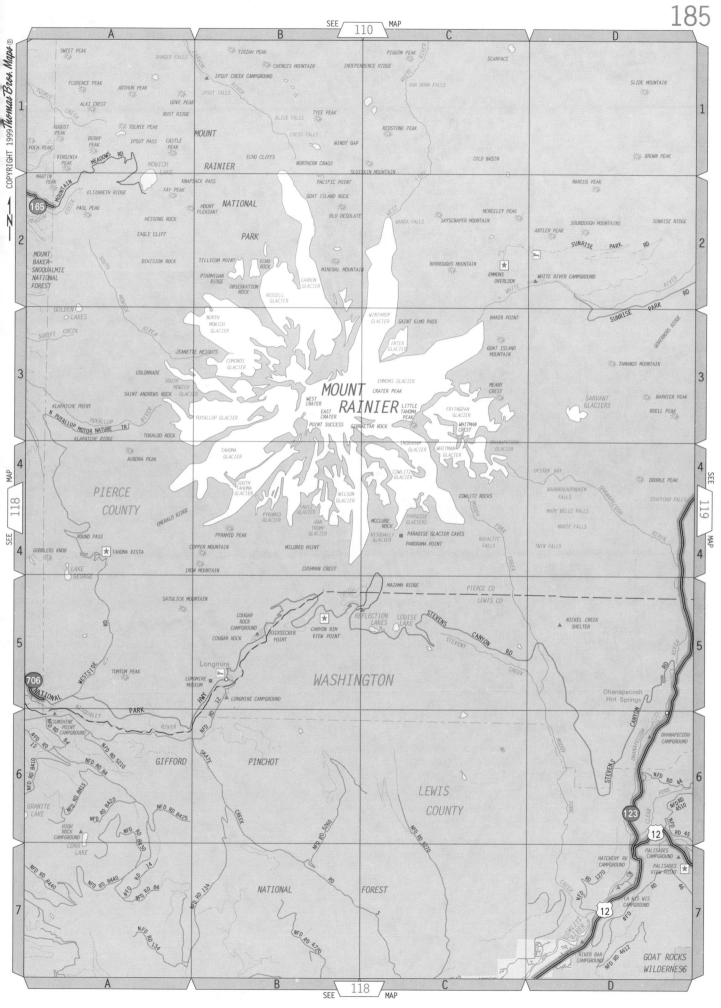

PNW

METRO

COPYRIGHT 1999 *Thomas Bros. Maps* ®

SEE 110 MAP

A   B   C   D

SWEET PEAK

RANGER FALLS

TIRZAH PEAK

CHENUIS MOUNTAIN

PIGEON PEAK

SCARFACE

FLORENCE PEAK   ARTHUR PEAK

IPSUT CREEK CAMPGROUND

INDEPENDENCE RIDGE

WHITE RIVER

SLIDE MOUNTAIN

VAN HORN FALLS

1   1

ALKI CREST

GOVE PEAK

IPSUT FALLS

IPSUT RIVER

ALICE FALLS

TYEE PEAK

CARBON

RUST RIDGE

AUGUST PEAK

TOLMIE PEAK

BERRY PEAK

CASTLE PEAK

CRESS FALLS

REDSTONE PEAK

COLD BASIN

BROWN PEAK

POCH PEAK

VIRGINIA PEAK

MEADOWS RD

IPSUT PASS

MOUNT

RAINIER

ECHO CLIFFS

WINDY GAP

NORTHERN CRAGS

SLUISKIN MOUNTAIN

MARCUS PEAK

165

MARTIN PEAK

ELIZABETH RIDGE

FAY PEAK

MOWICH LAKE

MOUNTAIN

KNAPSACK PASS

NATIONAL

MOUNT PLEASANT

GOAT ISLAND ROCK

PACIFIC POINT

WEST FORK

OLD DESOLATE

GARDA FALLS

SKYSCRAPER MOUNTAIN

MCNEELEY PEAK

SOURDOUGH MOUNTAINS

SUNRISE RIDGE

2   2

PAUL PEAK

HESSONG ROCK

PARK

ANTLER PEAK

SUNRISE PARK RD

MOUNT BAKER-SNOQUALMIE NATIONAL FOREST

EAGLE CLIFF

BURROUGHS MOUNTAIN

EMMONS OVERLOOK

WHITE RIVER CAMPGROUND

DIVISION ROCK

TILLICUM POINT

ECHO ROCK

MINERAL MOUNTAIN

WHITE RIVER RD

PTARMIGAN RIDGE

CARBON GLACIER

OBSERVATION ROCK

RUSSELL GLACIER

GOLDEN LAKES

SOUTH MOWICH RIVER

NORTH MOWICH GLACIER

WINTHROP GLACIER

SAINT ELMO PASS

BAKER POINT

SUNRISE PARK RD

SURIFF CREEK

INTER GLACIER

GOAT ISLAND MOUNTAIN

GOVERNORS RIDGE

JEANETTE HEIGHTS

EDMONDS GLACIER

TAMANOS MOUNTAIN

3   3

COLONNADE

SOUTH MOWICH GLACIER

EMMONS GLACIER

MEANY CREST

SARVANT GLACIERS

BARRIER PEAK

SAINT ANDREWS ROCK

CRATER PEAK

MOUNT RAINIER

LITTLE TAHOMA PEAK

FRYINGPAN GLACIER

BUELL PEAK

KLAPATCHE POINT

N PUYALLUP MOTOR NATURE TR

WEST CRATER

EAST CRATER

PUYALLUP GLACIER

PUYALLUP RIVER

POINT SUCCESS

GIBRALTAR ROCK

WHITMAN CREST

KLAPATCHE RIDGE

TOKALOO ROCK

THORADAY GLACIER

WHITMAN GLACIER

OHANAPECOSH GLACIER

AURORA PEAK

TAHOMA GLACIER

COWLITZ GLACIER

OYSTER BAY

DOUBLE PEAK

4   4

PIERCE COUNTY

SOUTH TAHOMA GLACIER

WILSON GLACIER

WAUHAUKAUPAUKEN FALLS

OHANAPECOSH RIVER

STAFFORD FALLS

EMERALD RIDGE

PYRAMID GLACIER

KAUTZ GLACIER

COWLITZ ROCKS

MARY BELLE FALLS

MARIE FALLS

ROUND PASS

PYRAMID PEAK

VAN TRUMP GLACIER

MCCLURE ROCK

PARADISE GLACIERS

MUDDY FORK

GOBBLERS KNOB

TAHOMA VISTA

COPPER MOUNTAIN

MILDRED POINT

NISQUALLY GLACIER

PARADISE GLACIER CAVES

BASALTIC FALLS

TWIN FALLS

4   4

LAKE GEORGE

IRON MOUNTAIN

CUSHMAN CREST

PANORAMA POINT

SATULICK MOUNTAIN

MAZAMA RIDGE

PIERCE CO

LEWIS CO

WESTSIDE RD

COUGAR ROCK CAMPGROUND

CANYON RIM VIEW POINT

REFLECTION LAKES

LOUISE LAKE

STEVENS

NICKEL CREEK SHELTER

5   5

COUGAR ROCK

RICKSECKER POINT

STEVENS CANYON RD

Longmire

WASHINGTON

STEVENS CREEK

706

TUMTUM PEAK

LONGMIRE MUSEUM

HWY 12

Ohanapecosh Hot Springs

NATIONAL

LONGMIRE CAMPGROUND

NISQUALLY PARK

NFD RD

RIVER

OHANAPECOSH CAMPGROUND

SUNSHINE POINT CAMPGROUND

NFD RD 84

MUDDY FORK

NFD RD 12

NFD RD 84

NFD RD 5210

GIFFORD

SKATE

PINCHOT

STEVENS

NFD RD 44

6   6

NFD RD 8410

LEWIS COUNTY

NFD RD 451.0

NFD RD 8415

NFD RD 842.0

NFD RD 8425

CLEAR FORK

123

GRANITE LAKE

NFD RD 8420

CREEK

NFD RD 5260

OHANAPECOSH RIVER

NFD RD 45

HIGH ROCK CAMPGROUND

NFD RD 5270

12

CORA LAKE

NFD RD 8420

HATCHERY RV CAMPGROUND

NFD RD 1270

PALISADES CAMPGROUND

NFD RD 8440

NFD RD 84

NFD RD 74

NFD RD 134

PALISADES VIEW POINT

A6

7   7

LA WIS WIS CAMPGROUND

12

NFD RD 134

NFD RD 4780

NFD

COWLITZ RIVER

RIVER BAR CAMPGROUND

NFD RD 4612

GOAT ROCKS WILDERNESS6

A   B   C   D

SEE 118 MAP

PNW

METRO

—N—

SEE 183 MAP

A   B   C   D

1

NORTH

STACKPOLE RD

WILLAPA

RAMSEY POINT

101

BEACH

Oysterville
OYSTERVILLE RD
ESPY
PL
DR

BAY

DOUGLAS RD

LYNN POINT

2

PENINSULA

MUSEUM

JOE JOHNS RD

NEEDLE POINT

Nahcotta

BAY AV
Ocean
Park

245 ST

SEE 116 MAP

PACIFIC

DIAMOND POINT

3

Klipsan
Beach
227

JENSEN
POINT

WILLAPA

PARADISE
POINT

SUNSHINE POINT

CHETLO

101

208
PL

198
PL

LONG ISLAND

NATIONAL

STANLEY
PENINSULA

HARBOR

OCEAN

4

377TH
ST

WILDLIFE

SMOKY HOLLOW

REFUGE

PARPALA

SEE 117 MAP

Oceanside
Pacific
Beach
CRANBERRY RD

BIRCH

HIGH POINT

SHOALWATER BAY

OMEARA POINT

4

SANDRIDGE

113
ST

ROUND ISLAND

101

NASELLE STATE
SALMON HATCHERY

LONGFELLOW HILL

103

101
PL
SPRUCE
ST

PORTER
POINT

PACIFIC

COUNTY

RD

5

PIONEER RD

LONG
BEACH

WILLAPA

NATIONAL

Naselle

4

WASHINGTON AV S

PL

JELDNESS RD

SALMON
CREEK RD

WORLD KITE
MUSEUM AND
HALL OF FAME

WOODGATE
RD

67TH

WILDLIFE

BEAR
RIVER
RIDGE

TARLATT RD
55
ST

Moores Corner

REFUGE

Seaview

JIM
ST

101

WASHINGTON

BALD
RIDGE

6

41 PL

101

Holman

CHINOOK

BEAR RIVER RD

SHOALWATER
BAY

FERRY

NASELLE
RIDGE

PACIFIC CO

WAHKIAKUM CO

101

WILLOWS

NORTH

KOM
TILWACO

STRINGTOWN RD

BEAR RIVER RIDGE

401

BRIX RD

NORTH
HEAD
RD

HEAD

ILWACO

VALLEY

NORTH
HEAD
LIGHTHOUSE
RD

ROBERT GRAY DR

2ND ST

Ilwaco Heritage
Museum

BAKER BAY

101

ROD

BEAR MOUNTAIN

ROCKY
POINT
LIGHT

MCKENZIE
HEAD

US
NAVAL
RESER-
VATION

LINGENFELTER
RD

GRAYS
POINT

GRAYS BAY
LIGHT

FORT
CANBY
STATE
PARK

CAPE
DISAPPOINTMENT
LIGHTHOUSE

SAND
ISLAND

PACIFIC
CO

CLATSOP
CO

COLUMBIA

Chinook

HOUTCHEN ST

FORT COLUMBIA
STATE PARK

CLIFF
POINT

KNAPPTON

GRAYS POINT LIGHT

GRAYS BAY

7

WASHINGTON

OREGON

BEAR ENTRANCE
RANGE LIGHTHOUSE

RIVER

SCARBORO HILL

HUNGRY HARBOR

COLUMBIA

RIVER

PACIFIC CO

CLATSOP CO

SAND ISLAND DIKE
MIDDLE LIGHT

SAND ISLAND
DIKE LIGHT

CHINOOK POINT

CLATSOP COUNTY

CHINOOK
DIKE
LIGHT

FORT STEVENS
STATE PARK

SEE 188 MAP

A   B   C   D

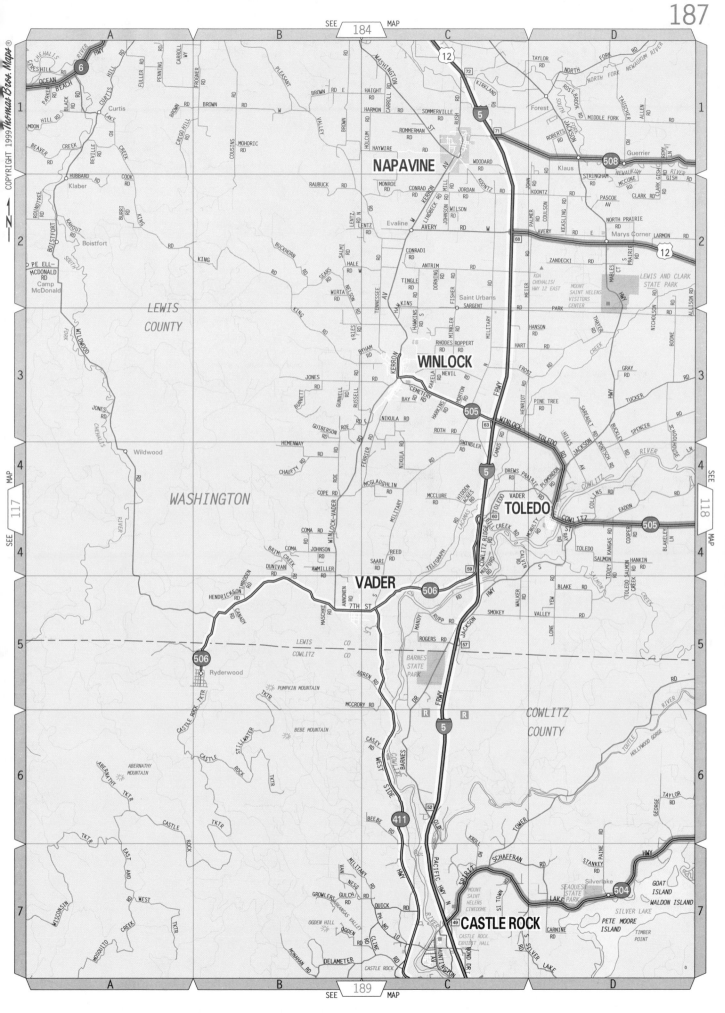

PNW

METRO

SEE MAP 186

SEE MAP 191

SEE 116 MAP

SEE 117 MAP

A B C D

1 2 3 4 5 6 7

—N—

300

301

WARRENTON

ASTORIA

GEARHART

SEASIDE

CANNON BEACH

COLUMBIA RIVER

PACIFIC OCEAN

CLATSOP COUNTY

CLATSOP STATE FOREST

OREGON

FORT STEVENS STATE PARK

ECOLA STATE PARK

SADDLE MOUNTAIN STATE PARK

CLATSOP SPIT

JETTY RD

POINT ADAMS
Fort Stevens
POINT ADAMS COAST GUARD STATION

PACIFIC
Hammond
KOA ASTORIA/SEASIDE

LAKE DR

NW WARRENTON DR

E HARBOR ST

WARRENTON DUMP

SCHOOL RD

COLUMBIA BEACH

CAMP RILEA

OCEANVIEW CEMETERY RD

MAIN

SE 7TH

SE 9TH

COAST HWY

STEVENS

OREGON

BUS 101

WARRENTON

YOUNGS BAY ENTRANCE LIGHT

SKIPANON WATERWAY LIGHTHOUSE

PORT OF ASTORIA AIRPORT

YOUNGS BAY

Jeffers Garden

Miles Crossing

LEXINGTON
IRVING
NIAGARA AV
VISTA DR
7TH ST
8TH ST

30 AV

202

Navy Heights

NEHALEM HWY

YOUNGS

CLATSOP STATE FOREST

WALLUSKI LOOP RD

Fern Hill

GENERAL ANCHORAGE

TONGUE POINT
NAVAL BASE (HISTORICAL)
Tongue Point Village

MOTT ISLAND

WEST LIGHT

LOIS ISLAND

REAR RANGE LIGHT

FRONT RANGE LIGHT

TONGUE POINT LIGHTHOUSE

COLUMBIA HWY

FORT CLATSOP NATIONAL MEMORIAL

Clatsop Station

PERKINS RD

CLARK AND LEWIS

FORT CLATSOP RD

CLATSOP RIDGE

TUCKER CREEK

LOGAN RD

YOUNGS RIVER

PETER JOHNSON LOOP

NEHALEM HWY

LABISKE RD

PALMER RD

Olney

LILLENAS RD

GREEN MOUNTAIN RD

KLASKANINE FISH HATCHERY

SADDLE MOUNTAIN

Glenwood

Carnahan

CULLABY LAKE

CULLABY LAKE COUNTY PARK

West Lake

CULLABY LAKE

Sunset Beach

SUNSET BEACH

LEWIS AV

MANION

OCEAN

DELLMOOR LP

SURF PINES RD

Butterfield

GEARHART LOOP RD

MARION AV

PACIFIC WY

G ST

Neawanna Station

BEACH DR

PROM

WAHANNA RD

N HOLLADAY DR

BROADWAY

AVE S

TILLAMOOK HEAD RD

SUNSET BEACH

WEST POINT

RIPPET RD

RIPPET MOUNTAIN

101

26

Cannon Beach Junction

TWIN PEAKS

DAVIS POINT

KLOOTCHIE CREEK CAMPGROUND

SUNSET HWY

NECANICUM

Necanicum Junction

Hamlet

53

26

SADDLE MOUNTAIN RD

CLATSOP STATE FOREST GREEN MOUNTAIN

SISTER GREEN MOUNTAIN

EELS RIDGE

LONE RIDGE

Melville

MADSWORTH RD

WADSWORTH RD

CLARK AND LEWIS RD

Youngs River Falls

HUMBUG MOUNTAIN

SADDLE MOUNTAIN

RIVER

SUNSET HWY

OREGON COAST HWY

TILLAMOOK HEAD

TILLAMOOK ROCK

BIRD POINT

BALD MOUNTAIN

INDIAN BEACH

SUBMARINE ROCK

SEA LION ROCK ARCH

CRESCENT BEACH

BIRD ROCKS

CHAPMAN BEACH

HAYSTACK ROCK

N HEMLOCK ST

SUNSET BLVD

CLATSOP STATE FOREST

BAILEY POINT

NECANICUM

CAMP CLATSOP MILITARY RESERVATION

SOUTH POST

(OREGON) NATIONAL GUARD

HAVEN ISLAND

GRANT ISLAND

FRY ISLAND

101 26 30 202

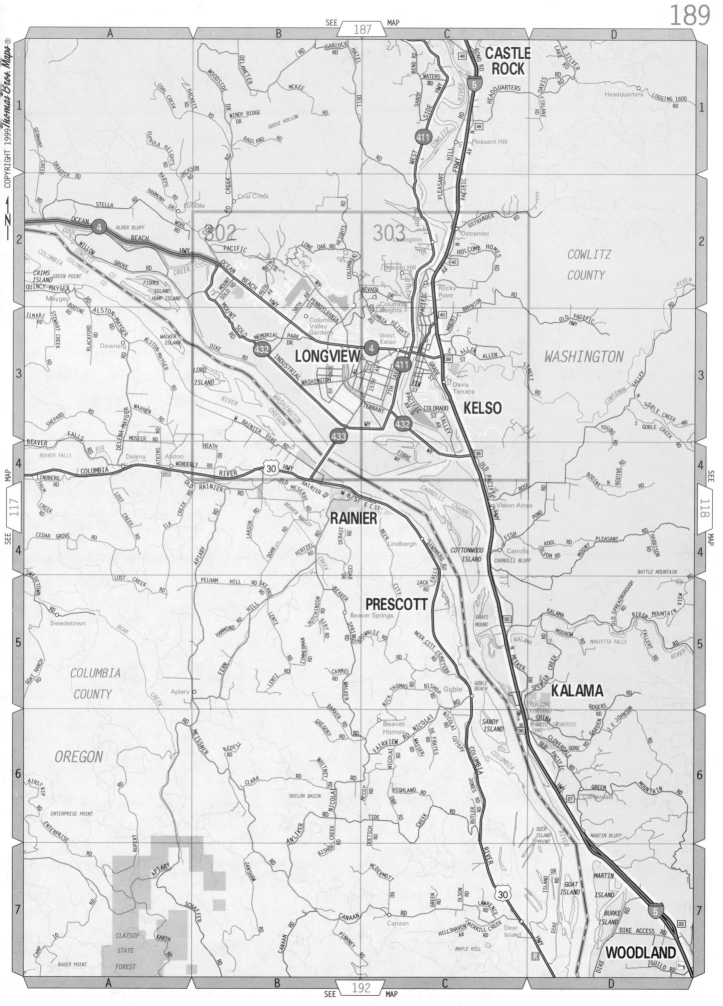

PNW

METRO

SEE 187 MAP

SEE 192 MAP

SEE 117 MAP

SEE 118 MAP

CASTLE ROCK

LONGVIEW

KELSO

RAINIER

PRESCOTT

KALAMA

WOODLAND

COWLITZ COUNTY

WASHINGTON

COLUMBIA COUNTY

OREGON

CLATSOP STATE FOREST

SEE 118 MAP

PNW

METRO

A | B | C | D

COPYRIGHT 1999 *Thomas Bros. Maps* ® —N—

504

JOHNSTON RIDGE

HARRYS RIDGE

SPIRIT LAKE

NORTH FORK TOUTLE RIVER

DUCK BAY

HARMONY VIEW POINT

CEDAR CREEK VIEW POINT

DENNY BROOK VIEW POINT

SMITH CREEK VIEW POINT

NFD RD 2560

NFD RD 2560

NFD RD 94

NFD RD 9403

SPOTTED BUCK MOUNTAIN

SPUD MOUNTAIN

CASTLE PEAK

CASTLE CREEK MARSH

MOUNT

MOUNT SAINT HELENS

NATIONAL VOLCANIC

MONUMENT

STUDEBAKER RIDGE

WINDY RIDGE VIEW POINT

NFD RD 99

COWLITZ COUNTY

SOUTH FORK TOUTLE

SAINT

RIVER

HELENS

NATIONAL

VOLCANIC

MONUMENT

MOUNT SAINT HELENS

TIMBERLINE CAMPGROUND

WISHBONE GLACIER

ALPINE BUTTE

RIVER

NFD RD 270

SHEEP CANYON VIEW POINT

SHEEP CANYON

TALUS GLACIER

TOUTLE GLACIER

NELSON GLACIER

APE CANYON

CRESCENT RIDGE

APE GLACIER

PUMICE BUTTE

1980 CRATER

SHOESTRING GLACIER

NFD RD 83

NFD RD 380

GIFFORD

PINCHOT

NATIONAL

FOREST

GOAT MOUNTAIN

RD 81

NFD RD 30

RD 8123

NFD

RIVER

DRYER GLACIER

BUTTE CAMP DOME

SWIFT GLACIER

MONITOR RIDGE

WORM FLOWS

PINE

MUDDY RIVER GORGE

LAVA CANYON

JACKPINE SHELTER

LAHAR VIEW POINT

NFD RD 810

NFD RD 8320

NFD RD 700

RD 2.5

SWIFT CREEK FLOW

BEDROCK PASS

NFD RD 81

NFD RD 83

GIFFORD

NFD RD 8320

NFD RD 2588

NFD RD 2586

KALAMA

KALAMA FALLS

NFD RD 81

CINNAMON PEAK

NFD RD 8303

APE CAVE MUSEUM

PINCHOT

NATIONAL

FOREST

MARBLE MOUNTAIN

MUDDY RIVER VIEW POINT

MERRILL LAKE CAMPGROUND

MERRILL LAKE

GREEN MOUNTAIN

NFD

RD

9015

NFD RD

SEE 118 MAP

SWIFT DAM OVERLOOK

RD

NFD RD

NFD RD 90

SWIFT FOREST CAMPGROUND

WASHINGTON

503

Cougar

BEAVER BAY CAMPGROUND

CHRISTMAS CANYON

LEWIS

RIVER

91013

SWIFT

CREEK

RESERVOIR

COONEY POINT

SKAMANIA COUNTY

McCLELLAN MOUNTAIN

SPEELYAI STATE HATCHERY

SPEELYAI HILL VIEW POINT

LEWIS

503

WILLIAMS RD

YALE LAKE

CLARK COUNTY

CLARK CO

SKAMANIA CO

GIFFORD

PARADISE VALLEY

NFD RD 3105

NFD RD 6403

NFD RD 507

NFD RD 64

HAM RD

FRAZIER RD

SADDLE DAM CAMPGROUND

COWLITZ CO

CLARK CO

PRIVATE

503

PINCHOT

NFD RD 6401

NFD RD 64

TIMBERED PEAK

RD

HEALY

TUMTUM MOUNTAIN

NATIONAL

FOREST

NFD RD 6405

NFD RD 203

SISTER ROCKS

NFD RD 5701

NFD RD 320

HORSESHOE RIDGE

NFD RD 317

OBSERVATION BERRYFIELD CAMPGROUND

NFD RD 54

CALAMITY PEAK

RD

0

A | B | C | D

SEE 193 MAP

SEE 118 MAP

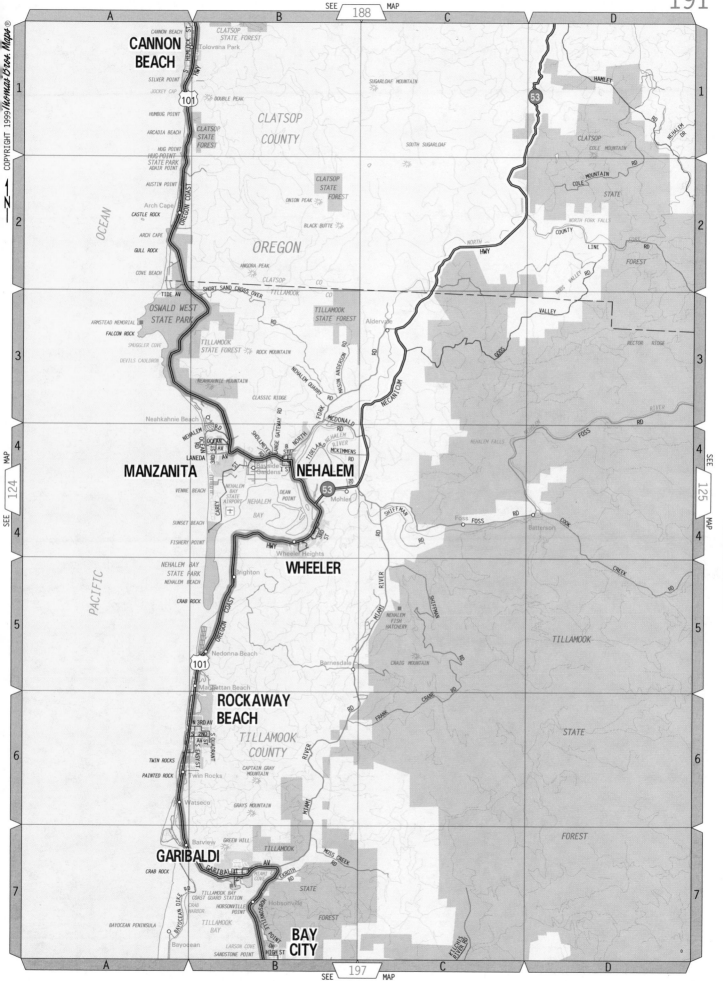

PNW

METRO

SEE MAP 188

SEE MAP 124

SEE MAP 125

SEE MAP 197

A   B   C   D

1   2   3   4   5   6   7

CANNON BEACH

CANNON BEACH
Tolovana Park
SILVER POINT
JOCKEY CAP
DOUBLE PEAK
HUMBUG POINT
ARCADIA BEACH
CLATSOP STATE FOREST
HUG POINT
HUG POINT STATE PARK
ADAIR POINT
AUSTIN POINT
Arch Cape
CASTLE ROCK
ARCH CAPE
GULL ROCK
COVE BEACH

CLATSOP COUNTY

CLATSOP STATE FOREST

OREGON

SUGARLOAF MOUNTAIN
SOUTH SUGARLOAF
ONION PEAK
CLATSOP STATE FOREST
BLACK BUTTE
ANGORA PEAK
CLATSOP CO
TILLAMOOK CO

HAMLET RD
53
CLATSOP
COLE MOUNTAIN
COLE MOUNTAIN RD
STATE
NORTH FORK FALLS
NORTH HWY
COUNTY LINE
FORK RD
FOREST
RECTOR RIDGE
GODS VALLEY RD
VALLEY
RIVER
FOSS RD

OCEAN

OREGON COAST HWY
101

SHORT SAND CROSS OVER

TIDE AV
OSWALD WEST STATE PARK
ARMSTEAD MEMORIAL
FALCON ROCK
SMUGGLER COVE
DEVILS CAULDRON
TILLAMOOK STATE FOREST
ROCK MOUNTAIN
NEAHKAHNIE MOUNTAIN
CLASSIC RIDGE
Neahkahnie Beach

TILLAMOOK STATE FOREST
Aldervale
MASON ANDERSON RD
NEHALEM QUARRY RD
NEHALEM FORK RD
GATEWAY RD
NECANICUM

MANZANITA
NEHALEM RD
OCEAN RD
3RD ST
OCEAN AV
LANEDA
CAREY
Bayside Gardens
SHOLMEYER RD
ORANGE AV
NEHALEM BAY STATE AIRPORT
VENNE BEACH
NEHALEM BAY
DEAN POINT
SUNSET BEACH
FISHERY POINT

NEHALEM
MCDONALD RD
NORTH FORK
TIDELAND
NEHALEM RIVER
MCKIMMENS RD
53
Mohler
SHIFFMAN RD

NEHALEM FALLS
FOSS RD
Foss FOSS RD
Batterson
COOK RD
NEHALEM FALLS

WHEELER
3RD ST
HWY
Wheeler Heights
CREEK

MIAMI RIVER
SHIFFMAN RD
Nehalem Fish Hatchery

TILLAMOOK

PACIFIC

OREGON COAST
NEHALEM BAY STATE PARK
NEHALEM BEACH
CRAB ROCK
Brighton
Nedonna Beach
101
Manhattan Beach

Barnesdale
CRAIG MOUNTAIN
RD
CRANE RD

ROCKAWAY BEACH
N 3RD AV
S 2ND AV
N 1ST
S 1ST ST
AV
S QUADRANT
TWIN ROCKS
PAINTED ROCK
Twin Rocks
Watseco

TILLAMOOK COUNTY
CAPTAIN GRAY MOUNTAIN
GRAYS MOUNTAIN
MIAMI RIVER
FRANK RD
RD

STATE

Barview
GREEN HILL
GARIBALDI
CRAB ROCK
BAYOCEAN DIKE RD
GARIBALDI
AV
MIAMI COVE
EKROTH RD
TILLAMOOK
MOSS CREEK
STATE
FOREST

TILLAMOOK BAY COAST GUARD STATION
CRAB HARBOR
BAYOCEAN PENINSULA
Bayocean
TILLAMOOK BAY
LARSON COVE
SANDSTONE POINT
Hobsonville
HOBSONVILLE POINT
LINDSON
HIGH ST
HOBSONVILLE POINT DR

BAY CITY

KILCHIS RIVER RD
FOREST

SEE 189 MAP

WOODLAND

COLUMBIA CITY

SAINT HELENS

COWLITZ COUNTY

LA CENTER

PETER JOHNSON RD

CARDAI HILL
GOOSE HILL
LYONS ST
389TH ST
WOODLAND STATE AIRPORT
LYONS RD

MARTIN
VIEW-AIR AIRPORT
379TH ST

WHALEN
COLUMBIA CITY
US 30
PEKIN
PACIFIC HWY
HWY

CLARK CO

COLUMBIA COUNTY
CHURCH
COLUMBIA CHURCH COUNTY

Warren

BRINN PITTSBURG
YANKTON

PITTSBURG
GENSMAN
DART CREEK
SMITH
PERRY CREEK
JACKASS CANYON
COLUMBIA
CITY

BACHELOR FLAT RD
MILLARD
BLAHA
BENNETT
STONE
SAUTER
CATER
HAZEN
MORSE
MORSE
OLD PORTLAND
GABLE RD
RAILROAD
McCORMICK PARK

SCAPPOOSE LAKE
BRYCE LAKE

BACHELOR ISLAND

MUD LAKE
LANCASTER LAKE
NARROWS DAM

NW LA CENTER RD
NE LANDERHOLM RD

NE 299TH

NE 314TH

CLARK COUNTY

NW 299TH
NE 289TH
NE 279TH AV
NE MOORE RD

RIDGEFIELD

RIDGEFIELD NATIONAL WILDLIFE REFUGE

BACHELOR POINT

CAMPBELL LAKE

WASHINGTON

BATTLE GROUND

Dollers Corner

SCAPPOOSE

SCAPPOOSE VERNONIA
SCAPPOOSE RESERVOIR
HOGEN RANCH
FREEMAN RD
HONEYMAN
WIKSTROM
SHERMAN
DAHLGREN
LEXTON
AIRPORT PARK
MULTNOMAH

OREGON

SAUVIE ISLAND

McNARY LAKE
REEDER RD
WILLOW POINT
RENTENAAR POINT
GUILES LAKE

COLUMBIA RIVER

WILLAMETTE RIVER

LEWIS

NE 259TH
NE 239TH
NE 219TH

NW 209TH
199TH ST
NW 194TH
NW 189TH
NW 184TH
NW 179TH
NW 169TH
NW 164TH
149TH

502

5

9

NE 199TH
NE 179TH
NE 159TH

SEE 125 MAP

DUTCH CANYON
RAYMOND CREEK
CALLAHAN
SATTLER DR
KANNEYER
GILKINSON
JONES CREEK

SW JP WEST
MOUNTAIN VIEW DR
JACKSON
DIKE RD
STEELMAN RD
COLUMBIA
CO
MULTNOMAH CO

MUD LAKE
STURGEON LAKE
GAY LAKE

OAK ISLAND
HORSESHOE ISLAND

Knapp

WHIPPLE CREEK PARK

CURTIS LAKE

NW 139TH
NW 134TH
NW 127TH
NW 119TH

7
36
7
6

NE 139TH
NE 134TH

DIXIE MOUNTAIN
ROCKY POINT
ROCKY POINT RD
CRABAPPLE CREEK
WILDWOOD GOLF COURSE
PATTERSON CREEK
SKYLINE
LOGIE TRAIL

US 30
LUCY REEDER RD
SAUVIE
MOAR LAKE
SAND LAKE
BELLE VUE POINT
SCHOOL SECTION LAKE
OAK RIDGE
KELLEY POINT

MULTNOMAH COUNTY

SAUVIE ISLAND

LOWER RIVER RD

CATERPILLAR ISLAND RECREATION AREA

Vancouver Lake

Vancouver Junction

NW 78TH ST
NE 78TH ST
NE 68TH ST
NW FRUIT VALLEY

205

Barberton
NE 109TH

Five Corners
NE 88TH ST
NE 78TH
NE 63RD
NE 76TH

503

JOHNSON RD
ELLIOT
CORNELIUS
ROCK
ROCK CREEK
HOLCOMB
YUNGEN RD
MEIER RD
VALLEY VISTA

Burlington
Rafton
Folkenberg
United Junction
Harborton
Cornelius Pass

HOWELL TERRITORIAL PARK
BYBEE-HOWELL
River Junction
Miller

KELLEY POINT PARK
SMITH & BYBEE LAKES PARK
Saint Johns
LOMBARD

501
504
NW LOWER RIVER RD
FOURTH
PLAIN BLVD

500
306
307

VANCOUVER

Minnehaha
ANDRESEN RD
BURTON

Meadow Glen
MINNEHAHA
ST JOHNS RD
N WALNUT GROVE

FOURTH
PLAIN BLVD
E MILL PLAIN BLVD
MACARTHUR BLVD
McLoughlin Heights
E 18TH ST

Helvetia
PHILLIPS
Bowers Junction
Bendemeer

WEST UNION
CORNELIUS PASS
KAISER
GERMANTOWN
SKYLINE
SKYLINE BLVD

LINNTON PARK
Linnton

FOREST PARK

HAYDEN ISLAND
Hayden Island

Cathedral Park
PIER PARK
Portland Astronomy Center
N LOMBARD
N MARINE DR

SMITH LAKE

PORTLAND INTERNATIONAL AIRPORT

LEWIS AND CLARK HWY
14
EVERGREEN BLVD
LIESER RD
Russell Landing
Ellsworth

28
27

HILLSBORO

West Union
Bethany
BROWER CREEK
TUALATIN MOUNTAINS
DOANE CREEK
Doane Point

26
4

PORTLAND

Portsmouth
University Park
Portland
Arbor Lodge
Piedmont
Woodlawn
Kenton
Vernon
Overlook
Humboldt
King ST
Cully ST
Sunderland

308
306B
306A
1C
1A
307
310
311
5
99E
304
305
KILLINGSWORTH
KILLINGSWORTH NE
23B
213
205
24
30

Bridgeton
East Columbia
Portland Meadows
N MARINE DR
COLUMBIA BLVD
MARTIN LUTHER KING JR
LEMON ISLAND
SAND ISLAND
OREGON SLOUGH
COLUMBIA RIVER

SEE 199 MAP

SEE 193 MAP

COPYRIGHT 1999 Thomas Bros. Maps®

—N—

PNW

METRO

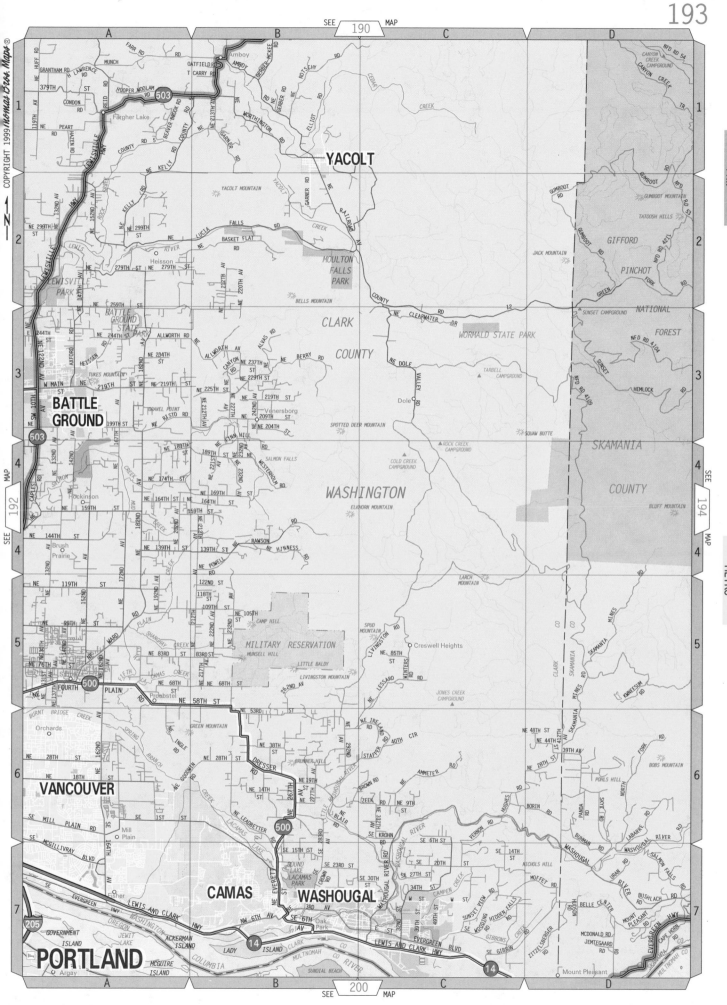

194

PNW

METRO

SEE 190 MAP

COPYRIGHT 1999 Thomas Bros. Maps® —N—

A **B** **C** **D**

1

CALAMITY PEAK
CALAMITY PEAK
NFD RD 5.8
PEAK
NFD RD 58
CANYON
NFD RD 54
CREEK
NFD RD 527
OBSERVATION PEAK
BARE MOUNTAIN
RIDGE
GIFFORD
HOWE RIDGE
MIDDLE BUTTE
NFD RD 64
CREEK
SOUTH BUTTE
NFD RD 65
NFD RD 6053
SOG2
NATIONAL
CARSON
GILER
MEADOW
NFD
RD

2

SATURDAY ROCK
TWIN ROCKS
TR
WEST CRATER
SODA PEAKS
SODA PEAK
GREEN LOOKOUT MOUNTAIN
NFD RD 42
RIDGE
NFD RD 42
COUGAR ROCK
GREEN
FORK
RD
SODA PEAK
NFD RD 4306
NFD RD 413
TROUT CREEK HILL
WIND RIVER
EXPERIMENTAL
FOREST
MINERAL SPRINGS RD
CARSON NATIONAL FISH HATCHERY
LITTLE SODA SPRINGS CAMPGROUND
NFD RD 3090
BEAVER CAMPGROUND
LITTLE SODA SPRINGS
NFD RD 417
CARSON
RD
WARREN GAP
NFD RD 6517
PINCHOT
FOREST
PANTHER CREEK
GOBBLERS KNOB
EXPERIMENTAL FOREST
PANTHER CREEK CAMPGROUND
PANTHER CREEK

3

LITTLE LOOKOUT MOUNTAIN
HEMLOCK
SUNSET
MCKINLEY RIDGE
RD
SKAMANIA COUNTY
SNAG
CREEK
PACIFIC
CREST
SUNSET
RD
HEMLOCK
EXPERIMENTAL
FOREST
GREEN KNOB
STEVENSON
HEMLOCK RD
FOSTER RD
BLACKLEDGE RD
STABLER
WIND
WIND RIVER
PILOT KNOB
WEIGLE HILL

4

RIVER
WASHOUGAL
WASHINGTON
CREEK
TR
SNAG
ROCK CREEK BUTTE
CREEK
RIDGE
TR
SKAAR RD
STEVENSON RIDGE
BEAR CREEK
RD
CARSON
CARSON RIVER VALLEY
HOT SPRINGS AV

SEE 193 MAP

SEE 195 MAP

5

WASHOUGAL
RIVER
RD
DOUGAN CREEK CAMPGROUND
HOT SPRINGS
GREENLEAF PEAK
GREENLEAF BASIN
TABLE MOUNTAIN
AALVIK RD
TR
RYAN-ALLEN RD
KANAKA CREEK
LOOP
COLUMBIA RIVER
ANDERSON POINT
GOVERNMENT COVE
HERMAN RD
CREEK
HWY 14
47
BOW FISH HATCHERY

6

WASHOUGAL STATE SALMON HATCHERY
WASHOUGAL MINES
MCCLOSKEY
CREEK
CEDAR RD
SCOTT RD
SWAMP
MABEE CREEK
RD
BEACON ROCK STATE PARK
HAMILTON MOUNTAIN
HARDY FALLS
KUEFFLER RD
COUNTRY QUARRY
EAGLE CREEK CAMPGROUND
NORTH BONNEVILLE
EVERGREEN
FORT RAINS
COLUMBIA
STEVENSON
ROCK COVE
ASH LAKE
SKAMANIA CO
HOOD RIVER CO
CASCADE LOCKS HWY
IGA LAKE RD
RIVER
CASCADE LOCKS
MARINE PARK AND CAMPGROUND
CASCADE LOCKS-STEVENSON STATE AIRPORT
44
CASCADE SALMON HATCHERY
HOOD RIVER COUNTY
PACIFIC

7

MCCLOSKEY
RYAN-TAVELLI RD
ELLIOTT
SNEIDER-BARKS
DIMRILL RD
DALE RD
DUNCAN CREEK
DEVILLE RD
WOODWARD CREEK
FRANZ RD
ARCHER MOUNTAIN
SKAMANIA
HWY
CRUZATT
EVERGREEN
SKAMANIA ISLAND
WASHINGTON
OREGON 35
SUMMIT
RD
COLUMBIA RIVER
DODSON
HWY 37
HWY 14
BEACON ROCK
PIERCE ISLAND
MOFFETT FALLS
WAHKEENA POINT
ELOWAH FALLS
WAUNA POINT
MUNRA POINT
30
84
40
ROCK TUNNEL RD
SOUTH
BONNEVILLE
WETLAND FALLS
HOOD RIVER RD
EAGLE CREEK
TANNER CREEK
MULTNOMAH CO
COLUMBIA
MULTNOMAH COUNTY
MOUNT HOOD
NESMITH POINT
NATIONAL FOREST
YEON MOUNTAIN
NE SMITH RD
PALMER PEAK
TALAPUS RIDGE RD
OREGON
PUNCH BOWL FALLS
LOOWIT FALLS
CREST
WILDERNESS
BENSON PLATEAU
WY'EAST CAMPSITE
BLUE GROUSE CAMPSITE
TUNNEL FALLS
SEVEN-AND-A-HALF MILE CAMPSITE
TR

CROWN POINT
MIST FALLS
DALTON POINT
WAHKEENA FALLS
SKAMANIA CO
MULTNOMAH CO
31
MULTNOMAH FALLS
HORSETAIL FALLS
ONEONTA FALLS
WAHSPIE POINT

SEE 201 MAP

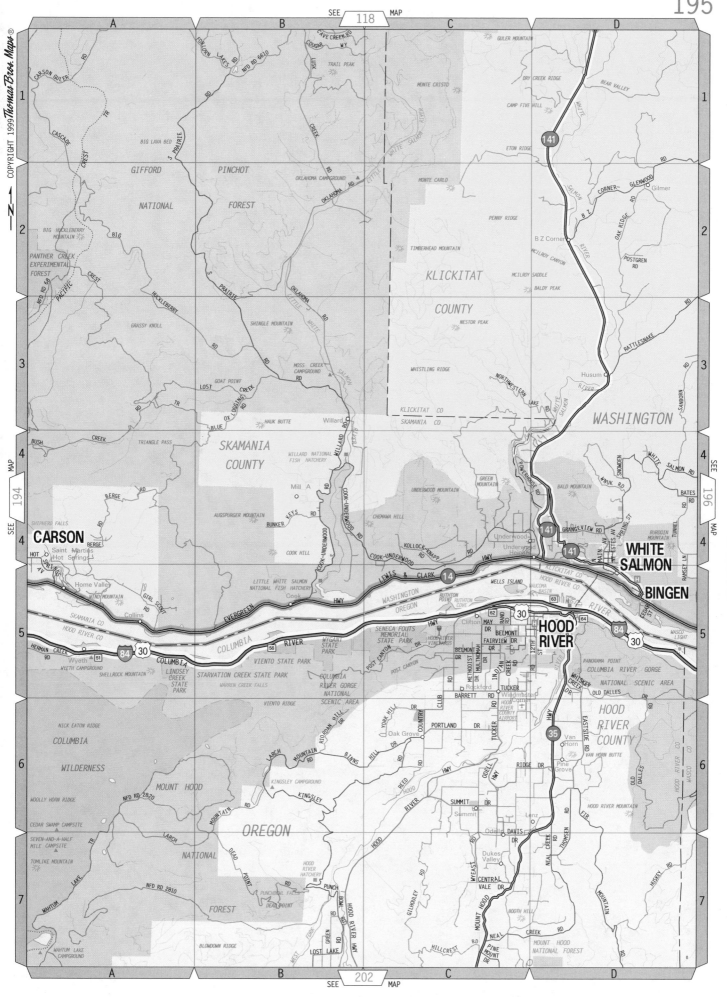

COPYRIGHT 1999 *Thomas Bros. Maps* ®

PNW

METRO

SEE MAP 194

SEE MAP 196

GIFFORD   PINCHOT

NATIONAL   FOREST

KLICKITAT

COUNTY

WASHINGTON

SKAMANIA
COUNTY

KLICKITAT CO
SKAMANIA CO

CARSON

WHITE
SALMON

BINGEN

HOOD
RIVER

COLUMBIA RIVER GORGE
NATIONAL   SCENIC   AREA

HOOD
RIVER
COUNTY

COLUMBIA

WILDERNESS

MOUNT HOOD

NATIONAL

OREGON

FOREST

MOUNT HOOD
NATIONAL   FOREST

1 41

14

84 30

35

PNW

METRO

—N—

A B SEE 119 MAP C D

1

CORNER-GLENWOOD RD

YAKIMA INDIAN RESERVATION

WAHKIACUS HEIGHTS RD

WILLIS CANYON

WILLIS CANYON

GLENWOOD-GOLDENDALE HWY

Panakanic

PANAKANIC RD

LOG RD

CORRAL FENCE RD

DIVISION RD

SKOOKUM CANYON RD

BEEKS CANYON RD

BEEKS CANYON RD

SODA SPRINGS RD

SODA SPRINGS CAMPGROUND

BATTLESNAKE RD

B L Z

FISHER RD

DUNKARD RD

LEGALL RD

RATHERT RD

PARADISE RD

WAHKIACUS RD

HOME ACRES RANCH RD

BREWER RD

MILL DR

KLICKITAT HEIGHTS RD

2

STAUCH RD

BILL MOORE RD

ONEAL RD

LAYALL RD

BREWER RD

PARADISE RD

SKOOKUM CANYON RD

BREWER

Woodruff Mill

LONG RD

LONG BUTTE

WAHKIACUS CANYON

KLICKITAT RIVER

SALMON RD

SLEEPY HOLLOW RD

SNOWDEN RD

LYLE RD

SLEEPY HOLLOW RD

Snowden

PYLE RD

SNYDER SWALE

KLICKITAT COUNTY

SKOOKUM CANYON RD

Wahkiacus

HORSESHOE BEND RD

3

WHITE RD

ACME RD

DORSEY RD

BAKER RD

SNOWDEN RD

APPLETON CANYON RD

CYMIOTTI RD

Appleton

FISHER HILL RD

OLD APPLETON GRADE RD

SNYDER CANYON RD

KLICKITAT APPLETON RD

Klickitat Springs

142

Klickitat

Pitt

WASHINGTON

PRAIRIE RD

SWALE RD

PEARCE RD

PLATT RD

COLUMBIA RIVER GORGE NATIONAL SCENIC AREA

JOHNSON RD

MCGOWEN RD

LYLE RD

CANYON RD

SHADY LN

JOHNSON RD

LOGGING CAMP CANYON

KLICKITAT RIVER

WHEELER CANYON

JOHNSON CANYON

MORRIS RD

SCHILLING RD

KLICKITAT CREEK

SEE 127 MAP

4

SEE 195 MAP

Laws Corner

JOHNSON RD

LAZY RD

ALLEN OAKS RD

TRACY HILL

BRISTOL RD

Bristol

COOKE RD

MAJOR CREEK RD

MCCLAIN RD

TUTHILL RD

SNOWDEN RD

BALCH RD

FISHER HILL RD

FISHER HILL RD

HIGH PRAIRIE

PAT MARK RD

HARTLAND RD

Hartland

CLARK RD

KNIGHT RD

GREEN CANYON RD

ST RUCK RD

DILLACORT CANYON

CENTERVILLE HWY

STACKER CANYON

STACKER BUTTE

5

ATWOOD RD

MANSFIELD RD

BARKER RD

RICH VIEW RD

BINGEN GAP RD

ROWLAND LAKE

OLD HWY

14

CHAMBERLAIN LAKE

R

142

R

KLICKITAT RIVER

Lyle

INDIAN POINT

CENTERVILLE RD

HUB SPRING CANYON

WIDE SKY CANYON

KNIGHT CANYON

COLUMBIA RIVER GORGE NATIONAL

6

Hood River

84

30

MOSIER-THE DALLES HWY

3RD AV

69

MOSIER

MOSIER CREEK RD

DELNIN RD

CATRON RD

CAROL RD

MORGANSON RD

STATE RD

MARSH CTO

MEMALOOSE STATE PARK

DELL RD

MAYER STATE PARK

CANYON RD

COLUMBIA RIVER

MAYER STATE PARK

HWY

76

Rowena

MCCALL POINT

BINGEN BELL

DOUGS BEACH

COLD SPRING FLAT

LEWIS AND CLARK RD

30

WINDY POINT

STOKELY CANYON

COLUMBIA RIVER GORGE NATIONAL

SCENIC AREA

DALLES MOUNTAIN RD

TWIN OAK RD

Murdock

HORSETHIEF BUTTE

14

HORSETHIEF LAKE STATE PARK

WASHINGTON

OREGON

COLUMBIA RIVER HWY

SIGNAL HILL

7

HUSKEY RD

WILSON RD

DIGGER RD

CAROL CREEK RD

OSBURN CUTOFF RD

SEVENMILE HILL RD

SEVENMILE HILL

HIDDEN VALLEY

CRATES POINT

WASCO COUNTY

OREGON

SNYDER CANYON RD

BAKER CANYON RD

BADS BACKBONE RD

WYSE RD

WASCO BUTTE

CHENOWETH CREEK RD

MAHTONKA RD W

SANDLIN RD

CHENOWETH CREEK

Chenoweth

Crates

82

RIVER RD

HILL ST

Dallesport

DALLESPORT

TYADMAN

THE DALLES MUNICIPAL AIRPORT

PARALLEL AV

RANDOCK RD

THE DALLES DAM

88

CUSHING FALLS

Petersburg

FIFTEENMILE FAIRBANKS MARKET RD

SUGARLOAF

GORBERTSON RD

LUCKY CANYON RD

KETCHUM RD

BROWNS RD

LUTZ LN

CHERRY HEIGHTS RD

MILL CREEK

MILL CREEK RD

Cherry Heights

CHERRY HEIGHTS RD

SCENIC DR

SKYLINE RD

83

84

85

87

84

197

13TH ST

OLD DUFUR RD

FIVEMILE CREEK

LOWER EIGHTMILE CREEK

LOWER EIGHTMILE CREEK

COLUMBIA VIEW DR

LOWER EIGHTMILE RD

THE DALLES

A B SEE 127 MAP C D

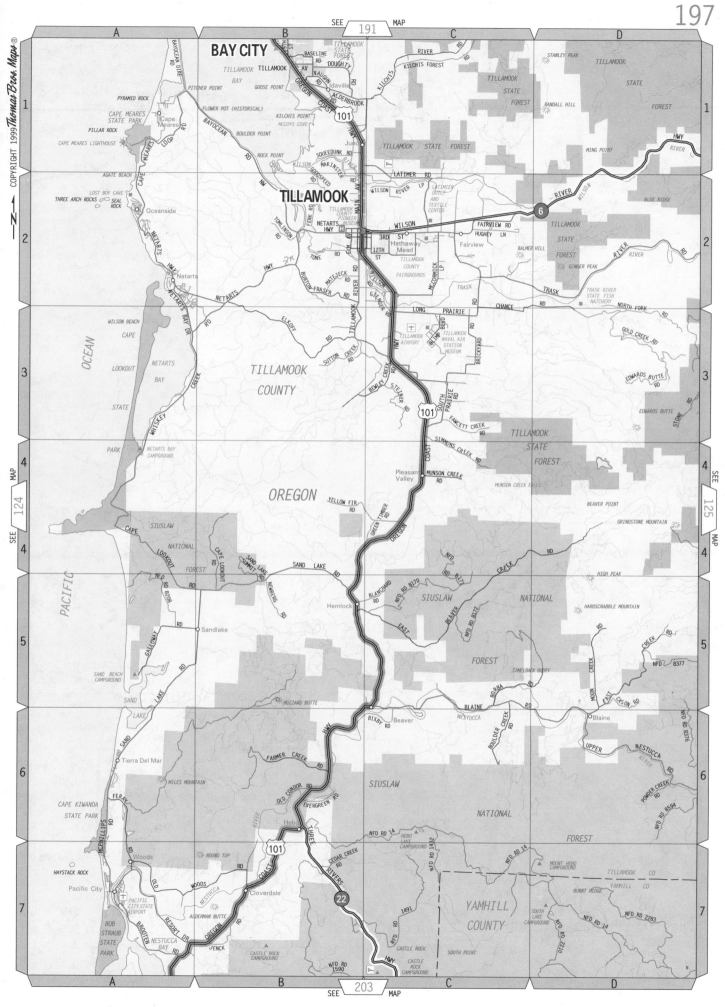

197

PNW

METRO

SEE 191 MAP

A   B   C   D

BAY CITY

TILLAMOOK BAY

TILLAMOOK

PACIFIC OCEAN

TILLAMOOK STATE FOREST

TILLAMOOK COUNTY

OREGON

SIUSLAW NATIONAL FOREST

SIUSLAW NATIONAL FOREST

YAMHILL COUNTY

CAPE MEARES STATE PARK
CAPE MEARES LIGHTHOUSE
PYRAMID ROCK
PILLAR ROCK
THREE ARCH ROCKS
SEAL ROCK
LOST BOY CAVE
AGATE BEACH
Oceanside
Netarts
NETARTS BAY
CAPE LOOKOUT STATE PARK
WILSON BEACH
NETARTS BAY CAMPGROUND
SAND BEACH CAMPGROUND
Sandlake
Tierra Del Mar
CAPE KIWANDA STATE PARK
HAYSTACK ROCK
Pacific City
PACIFIC CITY STATE AIRPORT
BOB STRAUB STATE PARK
Woods
Cloverdale
Hebo
Beaver
Blaine
Hemlock
STANLEY PEAK
RANDALL HILL
MING POINT
BLUE RIDGE
GINGER PEAK
BALMER HILL
Fairview
TRASK RIVER STATE FISH HATCHERY
GOLD CREEK RD
EDWARDS BUTTE
EDWARDS BUTTE RD
BEAVER POINT
GRINDSTONE MOUNTAIN
HIGH PEAK
HARDSCRABBLE MOUNTAIN
CAMELBACK BLUFF
BURNT RIDGE
MOUNT HEBO CAMPGROUND
SOUTH LAKE CAMPGROUND
CASTLE ROCK
CASTLE ROCK CAMPGROUND

101

6

22

SEE 124 MAP

SEE 125 MAP

SEE 203 MAP

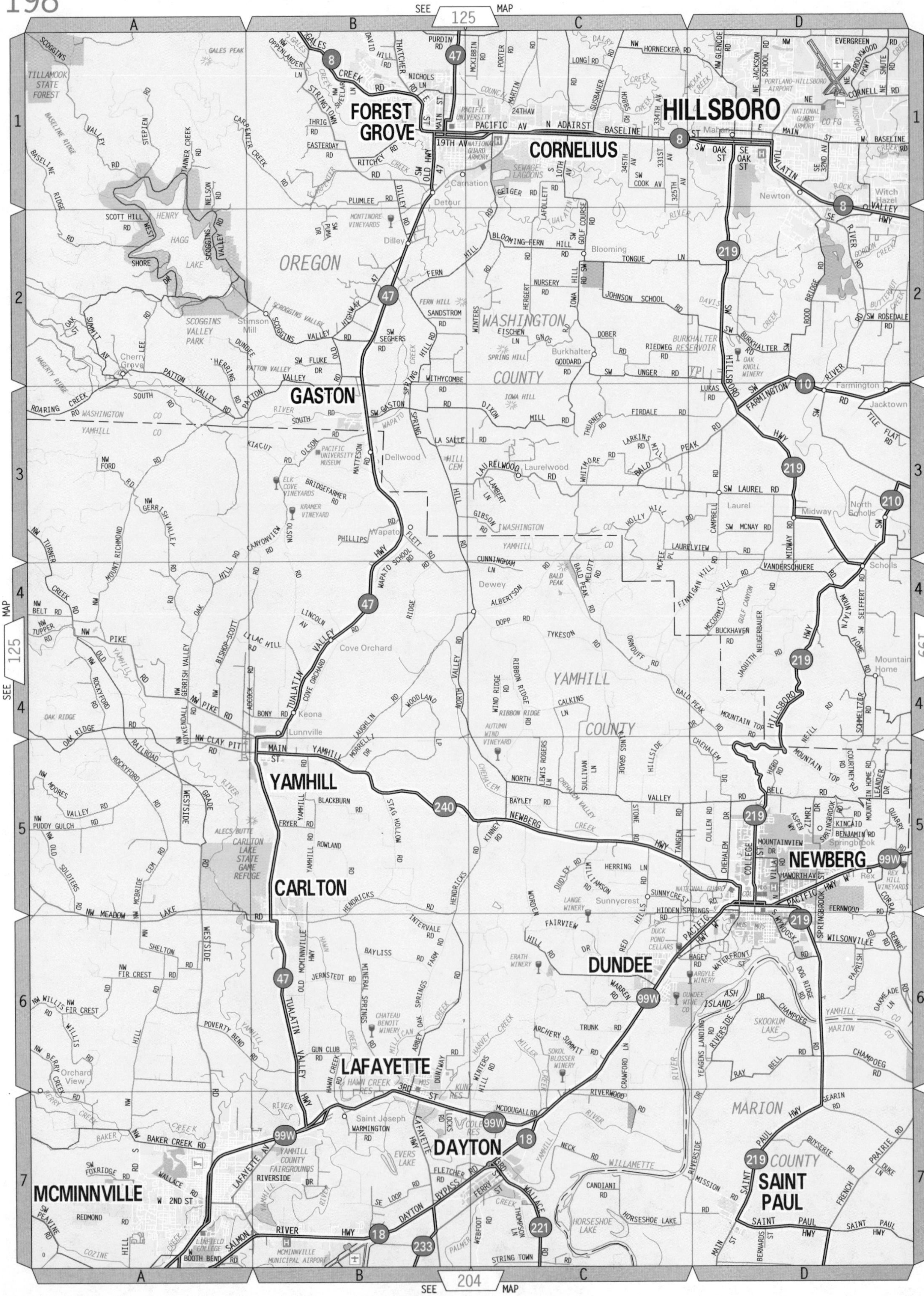

PNW

METRO

SEE MAP 125

SEE 125 MAP

SEE 199 MAP

SEE MAP 204

COPYRIGHT 1999 *Thomas Bros. Maps* ® —N—

HILLSBORO

FOREST GROVE

CORNELIUS

GASTON

YAMHILL

CARLTON

NEWBERG

DUNDEE

LAFAYETTE

DAYTON

MCMINNVILLE

SAINT PAUL

OREGON

WASHINGTON COUNTY

YAMHILL COUNTY

MARION COUNTY

TILLAMOOK STATE FOREST

CARLTON LAKE STATE GAME REFUGE

SCOGGINS VALLEY PARK

HAGG LAKE

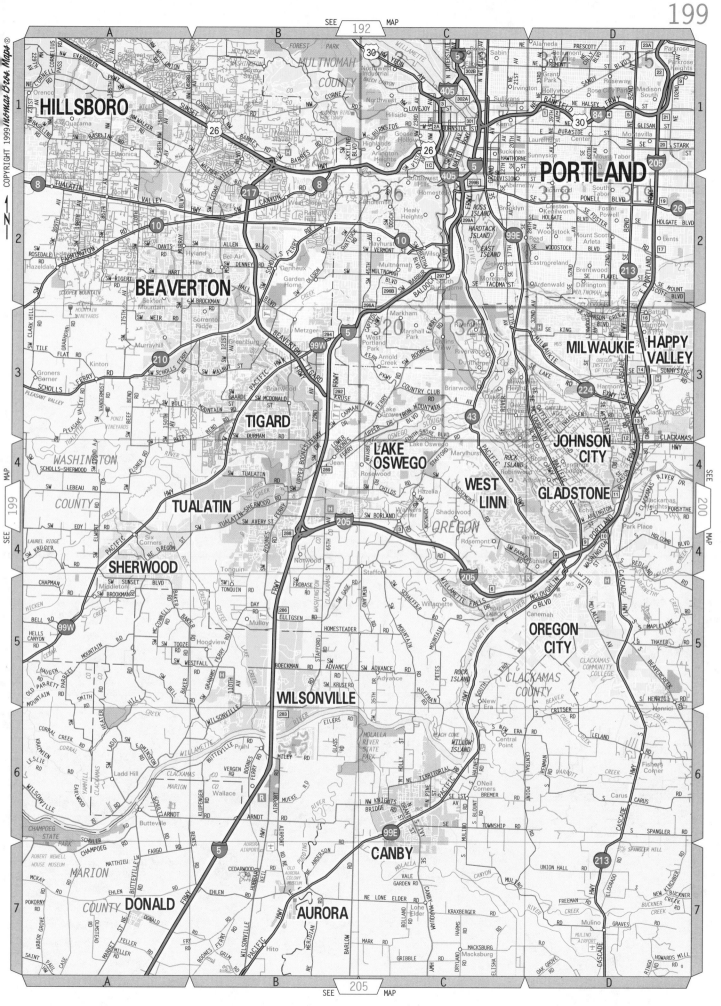

PNW

METRO

SEE 193 MAP

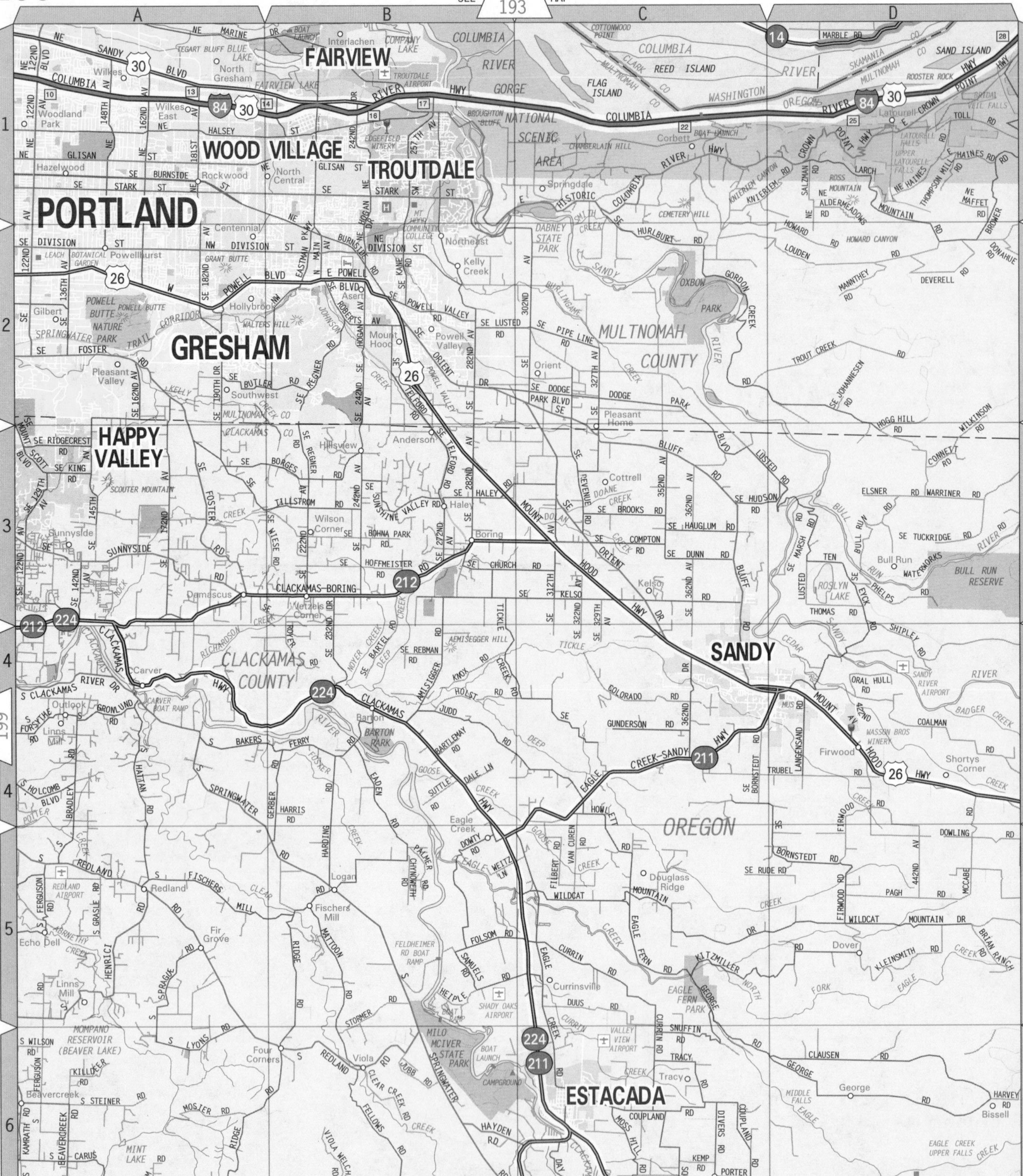

SEE 199 MAP
SEE 201 MAP
SEE 126 MAP

PNW
METRO

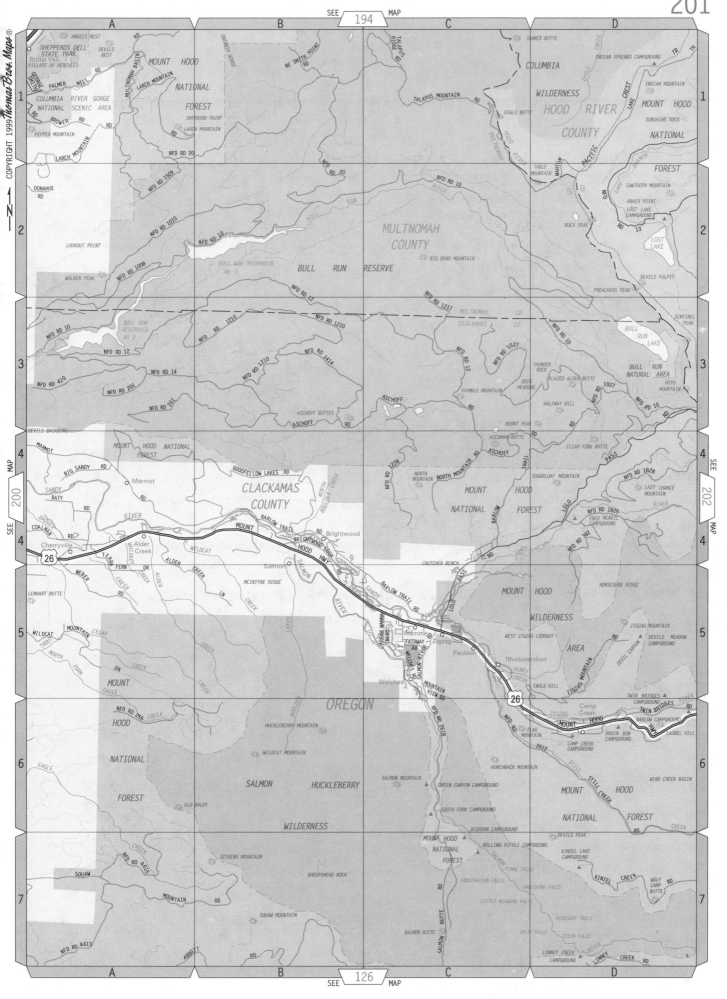

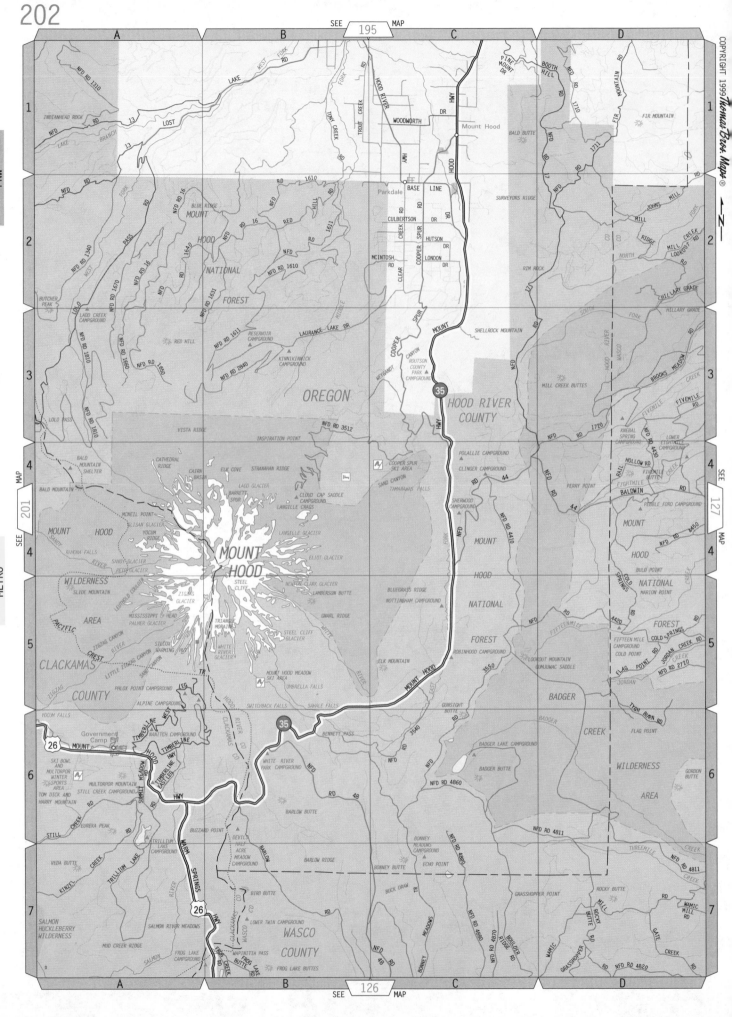

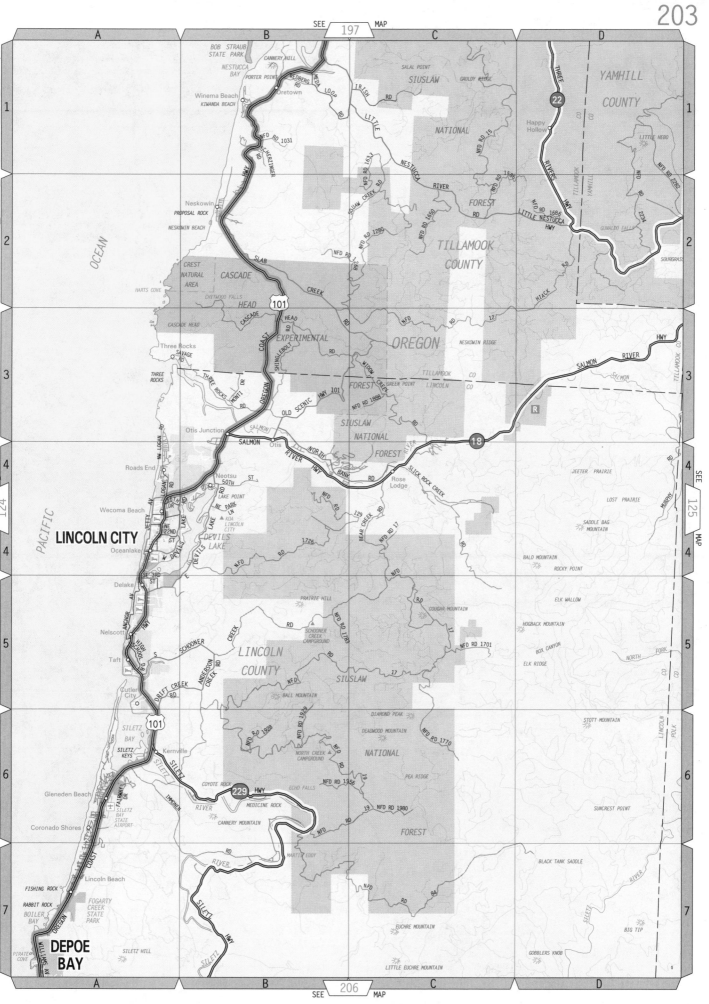

PNW

METRO

A B C D

1

2

3

4

5

6

7

OCEAN

PACIFIC

LINCOLN CITY

DEPOE BAY

BOB STRAUB
STATE PARK
NESTUCCA
BAY
Porter Point
CANNERY HILL
Winema Beach
KIWANDA BEACH
Oretown
REDBERG RD
MEDA LOOP RD
IRISH RD
SIUSLAW
SALAL POINT
GAULDY RIDGE
THREE

NESTUCCA RIVER

NATIONAL

HWY NFD RD 1031
SCHERZINGER RD

Neskowin
PROPOSAL ROCK
NESKOWIN BEACH
SOLIAW CREEK RD
NFD RD 163.3
NFD RD 1280
NFD RD 1.268
NFD RD 1650

YAMHILL COUNTY

22

Happy Hollow

LITTLE HEBO

NFD RD 15
NFD RD 1586
NFD RD 1686
LITTLE NESTUCCA HWY
GUNALDO FALLS

NFD RD 2292
NFD RD 2234

RIVERS HWY
TILLAMOOK CO
YAMHILL CO

SOURGRASS

FOREST RD

TILLAMOOK
COUNTY

HARTS COVE
CREST
NATURAL
AREA
CASCADE
HEAD
CHITWOOD FALLS

SLAB
CREEK
101
CASCADE HEAD
De

CASCADE HEAD
EXPERIMENTAL
COAST
SHINGLEBOLT

RD
NFD
RD

HIACK RD

12
OREGON
NESKOWIN RIDGE

TILLAMOOK CO
LINCOLN CO

SALMON RIVER
SALMON
HWY
TILLAMOOK CO

Three Rocks
SAVAGE
THREE ROCKS
THREE ROCKS RD
MONTI DR
OREGON
COAST
OLD SCENIC HWY 101
Otis Junction
SALMON
Otis
NFD RD 1888
WIDOW CREEK RD
GREEN POINT
SIUSLAW
NATIONAL
FOREST
RIVER
R
18

SALMON RIVER HWY
NORTH BANK RD
Rose Lodge
SLICK ROCK CREEK

JEETER PRAIRIE

LOST PRAIRIE

Roads End
Neotsu
50TH ST
LAKE POINT
NE PARK LN
KOA LINCOLN CITY
NFD RD
129
BEAR CREEK RD
NFD RD 17

SADDLE BAG MOUNTAIN

Wecoma Beach
NORTH DR
JETTY AV
LAKE RD
NE 22ND ST
LAKE RD
DEVILS LAKE
1726
NFD RD

BALD MOUNTAIN
ROCKY POINT

Oceanlake
SE 3RD ST
DEVILS

Delake
ANCHOR AV
HWY
HIGH SCHOOL DR
PRAIRIE HILL
SCHOONER CREEK CAMPGROUND
NFD RD 1783
17
ELK WALLOW
HOGBACK MOUNTAIN

Nelscott
SCHOONER CREEK RD
RD
LINCOLN COUNTY
COUGAR MOUNTAIN
NFD RD 1701
BOX CANYON
ELK RIDGE
NORTH FORK

Taft
S
ANDERSON CREEK RD
SIUSLAW
17

Cutler City
DRIFT CREEK RD
BALL MOUNTAIN
NFD RD 1928
NFD RD 1929
DIAMOND PEAK
DEADWOOD MOUNTAIN
NFD RD 1770
STOTT MOUNTAIN
LINCOLN CO
POLK CO

101
SILETZ BAY
SILETZ KEYS
Kernville
SILETZ RIVER
COYOTE ROCK
229 HWY
MEDICINE ROCK
ECHO FALLS
NORTH CREEK CAMPGROUND
NFD RD 1556
NFD RD
19
NFD RD 1980
NATIONAL
PEA RIDGE
SUNCREST POINT

Gleneden Beach
FAIRWAY DR
SILETZ BAY STATE AIRPORT
IMMONEN
CANNERY MOUNTAIN
MARTIN EDDY
19
FOREST

Coronado Shores
RIVER
RD
NFD RD
BLACK TANK SADDLE
SILETZ RIVER

Lincoln Beach
FOGARTY CREEK STATE PARK
SILETZ HWY
NFD RD
RD
BA

FISHING ROCK
RABBIT ROCK
BOILER BAY
COAST
OREGON
SILETZ HILL
EUCHRE MOUNTAIN
GOBBLERS KNOB
BIG TIP

PIRATE COVE
WILLIAMS AV
LITTLE EUCHRE MOUNTAIN

A B C D

PNW

METRO

SEE 198 MAP

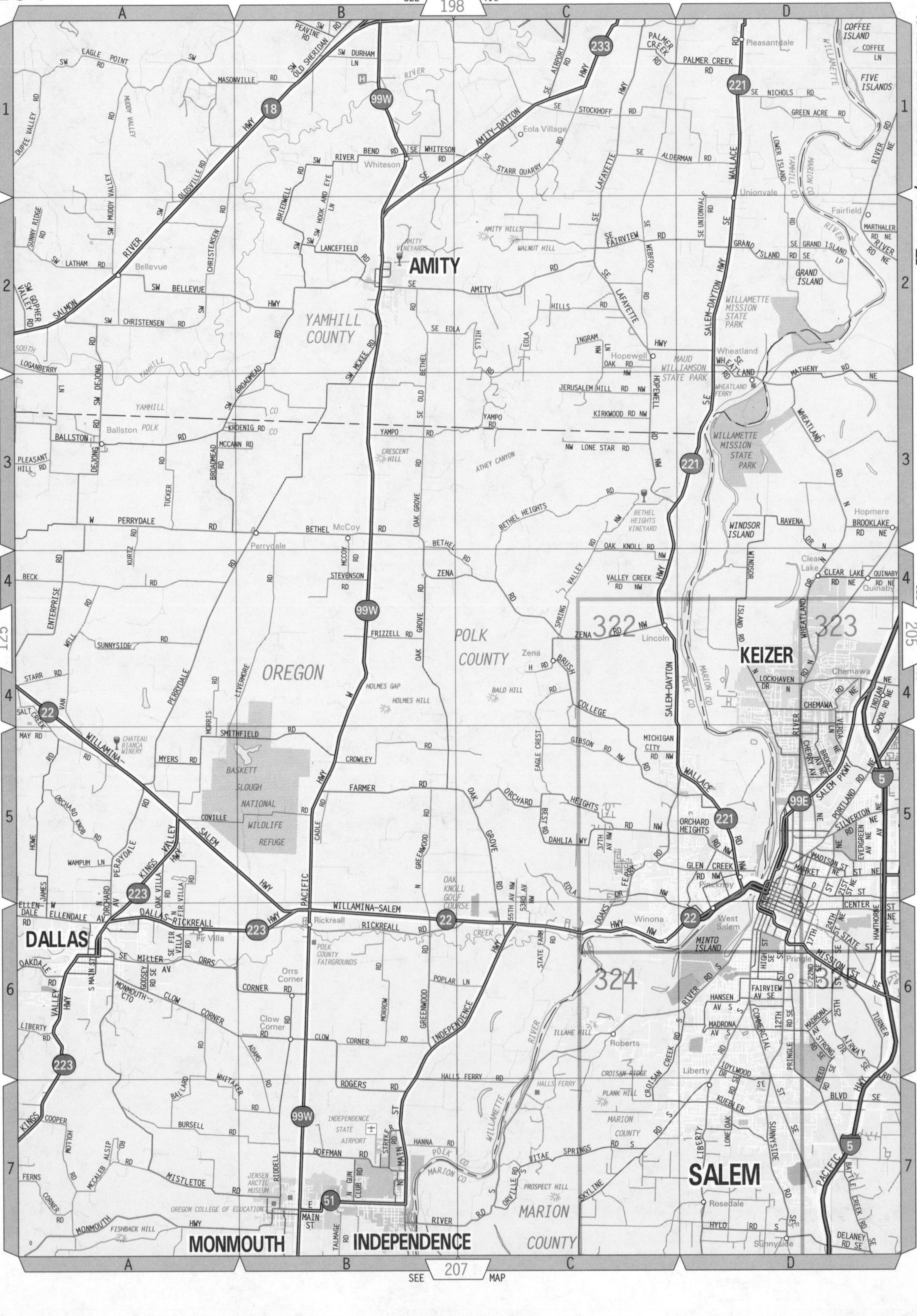

A   B   C   D

SEE MAP 125

SEE MAP 205

AMITY

KEIZER

DALLAS

SALEM

MONMOUTH   **INDEPENDENCE**

YAMHILL COUNTY

POLK COUNTY

MARION COUNTY

OREGON

322   323   324

Willamette Mission State Park

Maud Williamson State Park

Baskett Slough National Wildlife Refuge

Chateau Bianca Winery

Amity Vineyards

Bethel Heights Vineyard

Oak Knoll Golf Course

Polk County Fairgrounds

Independence State Airport

Jensen Arctic Museum

Oregon College of Education

Hwy 18, 99W, 22, 221, 223, 233, 51, 99E, 5, 205

Bellevue, Ballston, Pleasant Hill, Perrydale, McCoy, Whiteson, Eola Village, Hopewell, Wheatland, Lincoln, Zena, Chemawa, Lockhaven, Clear Lake, Quinaby, Brooklake, Hopmere, Fairfield, Unionvale, Marthaler, Pleasantdale, Coffee Island, Five Islands, Grand Island, Windsor Island, Minto Island, West Salem, Rickreall, Orrs Corner, Clow Corner, Fir Villa, Winona, Roberts, Rosedale, Sunnyside, Smithfield

PNW

METRO

SEE MAP 199

N

SEE MAP 204

SEE MAP 126

SEE MAP 133

HUBBARD

WOODBURN

GERVAIS

MOUNT ANGEL

SCOTTS MILLS

SILVERTON

SALEM

TURNER

AUMSVILLE

CLACKAMAS COUNTY

MARION COUNTY

OREGON

SILVER FALLS STATE PARK

Oregon State Fish Hatchery

Feasters Rocks

Saint Louis

Concomly

Waconda

Brooks

Hazelgreen

Hayesville

Badger Corner

Swegle

Fruitland

Pratum

Waldo Hills

Silverton Hills

Drakes Crossing

Silver Falls City

Whiskey Hill

Ninety One

Barnards

Needy

Dryland

Rural Dell

Hamricks Corner

Yoder

Monitor

Gladtidings

Marquam

S Hartman Rd

99E

214

211

213

213

213

214

214

214

214

219

271

5

263

22

22

99E

99E

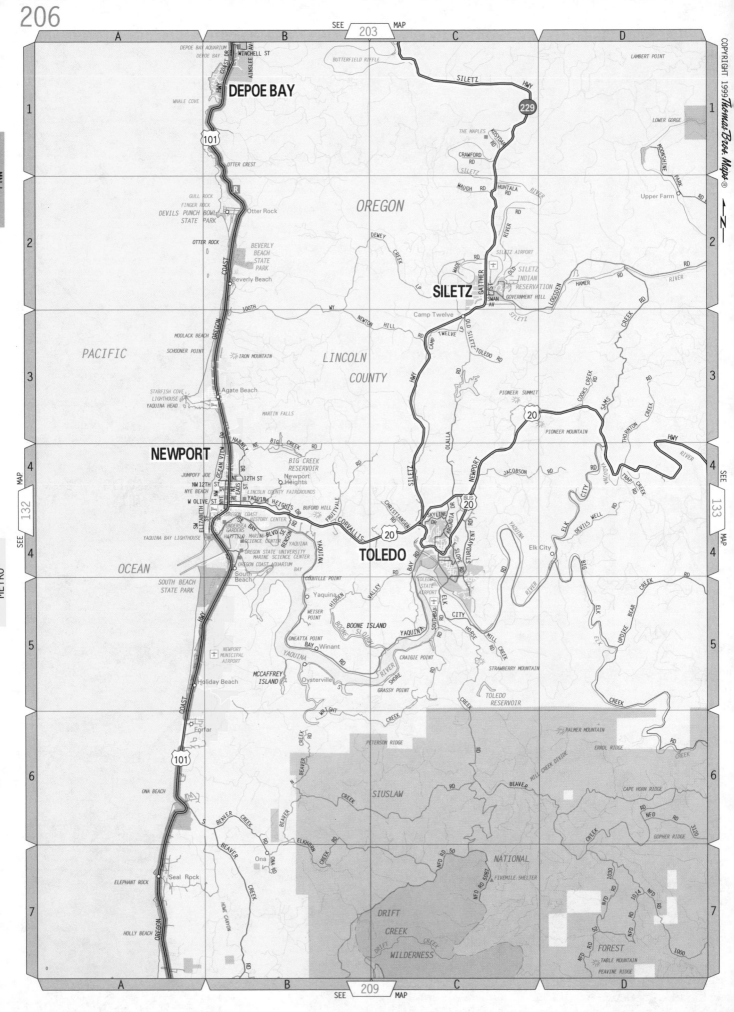

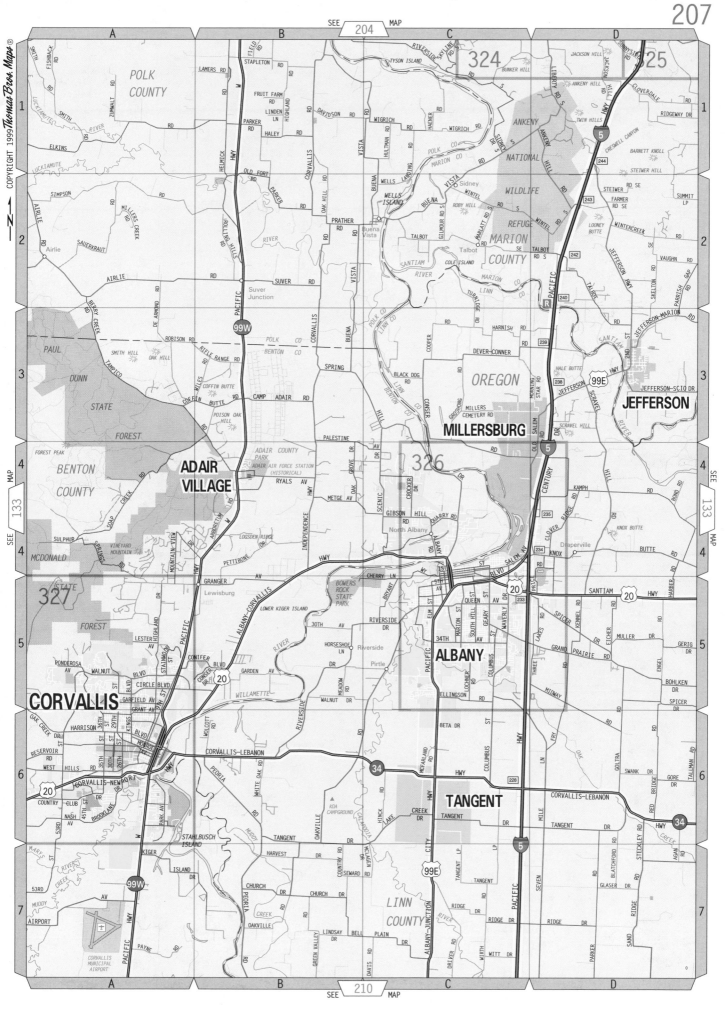

PNW

METRO

SEE 133 MAP

SEE 133 MAP

SEE 204 MAP

SEE 210 MAP

POLK COUNTY

PAUL DUNN STATE FOREST

BENTON COUNTY

ADAIR VILLAGE

CORVALLIS

MCDONALD STATE FOREST

MILLERSBURG

JEFFERSON

ALBANY

TANGENT

MARION COUNTY

LINN COUNTY

OREGON

ANKENY NATIONAL WILDLIFE REFUGE

North Albany

Lewisburg

Draperville

Riverside

Pirtle

Airlie

Sidney

Talbot

Buena Vista

Suver Junction

324

325

326

327

99W

99E

5

20

34

244

243

242

240

239

238

235

234

233

228

PNW

METRO

—N—

SEE 127 MAP

A   B   C   D

WASCO
COUNTY

KLAMHOP BUTTE

RIVER

WARM
SPRINGS

HELLGATE   Kahneeta Hot Springs

WARM   SPRINGS

3RD   RD

South
Junction   SOUTH JUNCTION   RD

1

WARM   SPRINGS

INDIAN

EAGLE BUTTE

SIMNASHO HOT SPRINGS RD

WEBSTER   FLAT   RD

WASCO CO
JEFFERSON CO

GATE SPRING CANYON

NE   COLEMAN

COLEMAN POINT

BAKER CANYON

DRY CREEK   TRAIL

UPPER DRY CREEK RD

AGENCY-HOT

SPRINGS

DRY   CREEK   RD

RESERVATION

TEE WEES BUTTE

DRY CREEK
CAMPGROUND

DESCHUTES

FIRS SPRINGS CANYON

NE   COOK   LN

OREGON

COLEMAN   RD

TROUT

CREEK

2

WARM   SPRINGS

26

WOLFORD CANYON RD

THE MUSEUM
AT WARM
SPRINGS

MILLER
HEIGHTS

MECCA GRADE

NE
GATEWAY
GRADE

NE
MARKET
ST

CLEMENS DR

Gateway
NE McFARLAND

NE EMERSON DR

IVY LN

97

OLD   HWY

HWY   97

NW TENINO   RD

WEST HILLS

Warm
Springs

ELLIOT HEIGHTS

NW   JUNIPER   LN   NE JUNIPER LN

NEFF

BUCKLEY
LN

DALLES-CALIFORNIA

3

DRY HOLLOW RD

TRAIL   RD

DESCHUTES   DR

COLUMBIA DR

NW   IVY   LN

HICKORY   LN

NW   BOISE   DR

NW   GUMWOOD   DR

ADAMS   DR

NE BARNES   DR

MUD   SPRINGS   DR

CLARK   RD

NE FERN   LN

NE

NE

THE

EMERSON DR

HEREFORD   LN

OLD MUTIS CANYON

HAY   CREEK   RD

4

DRY HOLLOW RD

RD P-210

JACKSON

SEEKSEEQUA   RD

LUNA BUTTE

JACKSON BUTTES

NEGRO BROWN CANYON

JEFFERSON
COUNTY

SPRINGS   RD

NW FIR   LN

ELM   LN

DESCHUTES DR

ELBE   DR

NW DOGWOOD   LN

WILLOW CREEK RD

HARBERS CANYON

ADAMS   DR

NE DOGWOOD   LN

NE   ELM   LN

MUD SPRINGS VALLEY   RD

CROOKED

COLEMAN CANYON   RD

DEVILS CANYON

4

METOLIUS BENCH RD

BOX CANYON   TRAIL

JACKSON   RD

SEEKSEEQUA CREEK RD   OLD

Seekseequa
Junction

SEEKSEEQUA   CREEK

CLACKAMAS

MADRAS
CITY-COUNTY
AIRPORT

NE   CHERRY   LN

RIVER

NATIONAL

RED SHED CANYON

5

RD M-110

ELK   DR   NW

ELK   DR

SW ALMA LN   ALMA   LN

DESCHUTES   DR

WILLOW CREEK CANYON

BIRCH

Madras Station

SW   CANYON RD

SW ASHWOOD

NE LOUCKS RD

HENDERSON RD

NE

LOUCKS   RD

ASHWOOD   RD

BUCK BUTTE

BALDWIN HILLS

5

LOWER BEND RD

MOUNTAIN VIEW   DR

SW   BELMONT

DRY CANYON

ROUND BUTTE

ELBE   DR

MADRAS

NE B ST ASHWOOD

SE
BUFF
ST

J   ST   J ST

GRIZZLY   RD

DOVER   RD

WAGONBLAST CANYON

6

THE COVE PALISADES

CANADIAN BENCH

RIVERVIEW
RD
OBSERVATORY

STATE   PARK

CROOKED
RIVER
NATIONAL
GRASSLAND

ROUND BUTTE DR

EUREKA   LN

METOLIUS

SW DOVER

CULVER

BEAR

JEFFERSON AV

9TH ST

COLUMBIA BUTTE AV

SW   EUREKA   LN

MADRAS-PRINEVILLE HWY

SE

ADAMS   DR

SE   DIXON   DR

MID SPRINGS RD

NATIONAL

6

Crooked

CROOKED

RIVER

NATIONAL

JUNIPER DR

DAM

FEATHER DR

GALLOWAY

FRANKLIN   DR

361

CULVER   HWY

ELBE   DR

FALCON   LN

CROOKED
RIVER
GORGE

97

BEAR   DR

FORD   RD

26

FRANKLIN   LN

FOSTER   LN

MADRAS-PRINEVILLE   HWY

BALDWIN DR

GRASSLAND

FRANK FOREST RD

7

SW GLOVER RD

GRASSLAND

SW   SW   GEM   LN

SW PECK
RD

SW   FRAZIER   RD

SW HIGHLAND

DALLES-CALIFORNIA

BEAR   RD

ADAMS   DR

SE JASPER

HOLLY   LN

GRIZZLY   RD

LAKE BILLY
CHINOOK STATE
AIRPORT

SW
JORDAN

CULVER

HUBER AV C

SW IRIS LN

6TH ST

1ST AV

H   ST

D ST

VIEWPOINT

SW IRIS

THE

COLUMBIA

SW IRVING   LN

IMBLER   LN

A   B   C   D

SEE 212 MAP

SEE 135 MAP

SEE 135 MAP

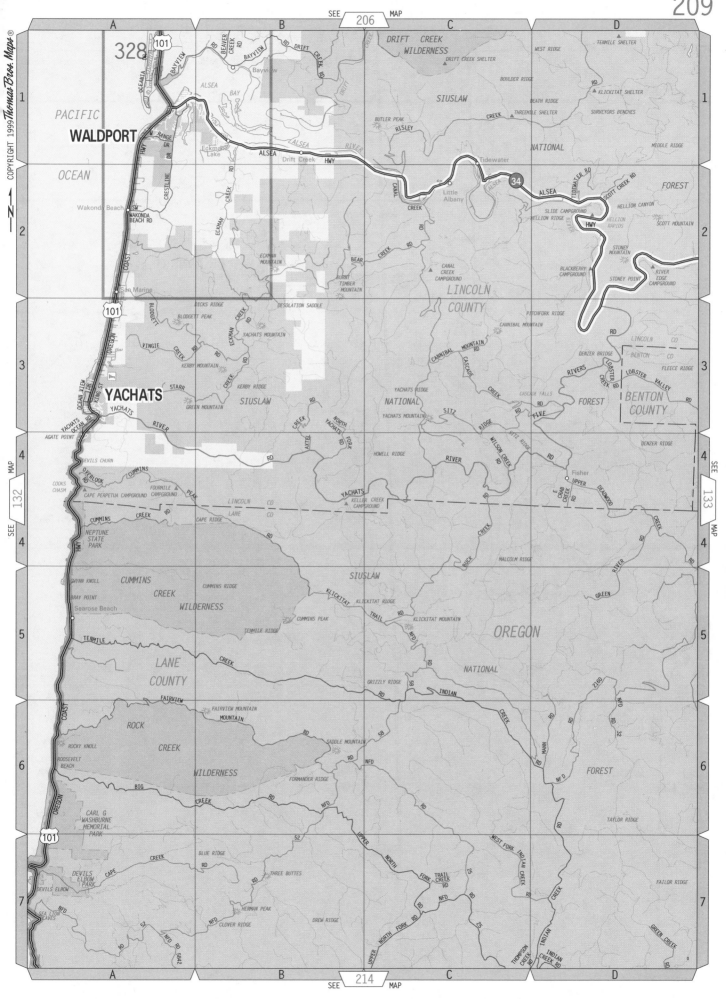

PNW

METRO

328

A   B   C   D

PACIFIC

OCEAN

WALDPORT

BEAVER CREEK RD

BAYVIEW RD

DRIFT CREEK RD

Bayview

ALSEA

BAY

ALSEA

VIEW DR

RANGE DR

CRESTLINE

Eckman Lake

ALSEA

Drift Creek

ALSEA RIVER HWY

DRIFT CREEK WILDERNESS

Drift Creek Shelter

WEST RIDGE

TENMILE SHELTER

BOULDER RIDGE

KLICKITAT SHELTER

DEATH RIDGE

SIUSLAW

THREEMILE SHELTER

SURVEYORS BENCHES

Butler Peak

Risley

MIDDLE RIDGE

NATIONAL

Tidewater

CANAL

CREEK

Little Albany

ALSEA

34

ALSEA

TIDEWATER RD

SCOTT CREEK RD

FOREST

HELLION CANYON

Wakonda Beach

SW WAKONDA BEACH RD

ECKMAN

CREEK

ECKMAN MOUNTAIN

BEAR

BURNT TIMBER MOUNTAIN

CREEK RD

CANAL CREEK CAMPGROUND

SLIDE CAMPGROUND

HELLION RIDGE

HELLION RAPIDS

HWY

SCOTT MOUNTAIN

STONEY MOUNTAIN

BLACKBERRY CAMPGROUND

STONEY POINT

RIVER EDGE CAMPGROUND

San Marine

DESOLATION SADDLE

LINCOLN COUNTY

PITCHFORK RIDGE

CANNIBAL MOUNTAIN

RD

DENZER BRIDGE

LINCOLN CO

BENTON CO

FLEECE RIDGE

DICKS RIDGE

BLODGETT PEAK

BLODGETT

ECKMAN CREEK RD

YACHATS MOUNTAIN

KERBY MOUNTAIN

VINGIE

CREEK RD

KERBY RIDGE

SIUSLAW

YACHATS

OREGON

YACHATS

STARR

GREEN MOUNTAIN

OCEAN VIEW DR

KING ST

YACHATS

YACHATS RIVER

Agate Point

OCEAN RD

CREEK

AXTEL

NORTH YACHATS FORK RD

YACHATS RIDGE

YACHATS MOUNTAIN

SITZ

RIDGE

NATIONAL

CANNIBAL MOUNTAIN RD

CASCADE

CREEK

CASCADE FALLS

RIVERS

LOBSTER CREEK

LOBSTER VALLEY

BENTON COUNTY

RD

FOREST

DENZER RIDGE

Devils Churn

COOKS CHASM

Overlook

CUMMINS RD

FOURMILE CAMPGROUND

CAPE PERPETUA CAMPGROUND

PEAK

CUMMINS CREEK

CAPE RIDGE

HOWELL RIDGE

RIVER

WILSON CREEK

SITZ RIDGE

RD

FIVE

Fisher

UPPER

E CRAB CREEK RD

DEADMOND

LINCOLN CO LANE CO

YACHATS KELLER CREEK CAMPGROUND

SEE 132 MAP

SEE 133 MAP

NEPTUNE STATE PARK

HWY

BUCK

CREEK

MALCOLM RIDGE

RIVER

GREEN

GWYNN KNOLL

BRAY POINT

Searose Beach

CUMMINS CREEK WILDERNESS

CUMMINS RIDGE

TENMILE RIDGE

CUMMINS PEAK

KLICKITAT

KLICKITAT RIDGE

KLICKITAT TRAIL

KLICKITAT MOUNTAIN

RD

NFD

OREGON

TENMILE

LANE COUNTY

CREEK

NATIONAL

RD

2160 RD

NFD 32

FAIRVIEW

ROCK

FAIRVIEW MOUNTAIN

MOUNTAIN

GRIZZLY RIDGE

58 RD

INDIAN

CREEK

MANN RD

COAST

ROCKY KNOLL

ROOSEVELT BEACH

CREEK

BIG

WILDERNESS

FORMANDER RIDGE

SADDLE MOUNTAIN

58

NFD

RD

NFD

FOREST

TAYLOR RIDGE

OREGON

CARL G WASHBURNE MEMORIAL PARK

CREEK

52

RD

BLUE RIDGE

RD

THREE BUTTES

UPPER NORTH FORK

WEST FORK INDIAN CREEK

101

DEVILS ELBOW

DEVILS ELBOW PARK

CAPE

CREEK

RD

NORTH FORK RD

TRAIL CREEK RD

25

THOMPSON CREEK

INDIAN CREEK RD

FAILOR RIDGE

SEA LION CAVES

NFD

52 RD

NFD RD

NFD 5942 RD

HERMAN PEAK

CLOVER RIDGE

DREW RIDGE

UPPER NORTH FORK RD

NFD RD

25

GREEN CREEK

INDIAN

A   B   C   D

PNW

METRO

SEE 207 MAP

A B C D

1

BRATTAIN DR
GREEN VALLEY RD
GREENBACK RD
FAYETTEVILLE DR
PECKENPAUGH DR
Shedd
Fayetteville
BOSTON MILL DR
SHEDD CEMETERY RD
Peoria
Abraham
MUDDY
CALAPOOIA
SODOM
ROBERTS RD
PLAINVIEW
Plainview DR
MORGAN DR
WARD BUTTE
ROCK HILL RD
ROCK HILL RD
TY VALLEY RD
SAND RIDGE RD
MANN LN
BROWNSVILLE
OAK RIDGE

HOACUM ISLAND
PETERON RD
POTTER
OAK
PLAIN DR
DANNEN RD
99E
LINN
WEST
DITCH
DR
SEVEN MILE LN
HARRISON
HARRISON
LONE PINE BUTTE
WASHBURN BUTTE
COCHRAN CREEK
CEDAR BUTTE

2

BENTON CO
LINN CO
PEORIA RD
HARMONY
CREEK BEND
CREEK
AMERICAN DR
LINN COUNTY
5 HWY
OREGON
SEVEN MILE LN
POWELL HILLS
OAKVIEW
ROBE HILL
SNAKE HILL
KIRK DR
HOME

NICEWOOD DR
IRISH BEND LP
NICEWOOD LN
CROOK DR
CROOK DR
HALSEY-SWEET
228
216
THE LIVING ROCK MUSEUM
HOME RD
LINN COUNTY HISTORICAL MUSEUM
BROWNSVILLE
KIRK AV
NORTHERN
MOUNTAIN

3

IRISH BEND LP
CREEK
LAKE
American Lake
POWERLINE RD
CITY
HALSEY
SEEFELD DR
LAKE CREEK
FALK
SEEFELD DR
WEBER RD
CREEK DR
SCHOOL
COURTNEY CREEK RD
228
RIVER
TIMBER RD
COURTNEY CREEK

NIXON DR
OREGON
CREEK DR
BRANDON RD
TWIN BUTTES W DR
WAGENER RD
CENTER
TWIN BUTTES
DIMIDDLE VALLEY
DR

4

WILLAMETTE
RICKARD RD
CARTNEY DR
MALPASS
CARTNEY
ISOM LN
ALBANY-JUNCTION
BOND
BUTTE DR
MUDDY
INDIAN HEAD
GAP
NORTHERNWOOD DR
LITTLE VALLEY LN
HORSE ROCK

SUBSTATION
TANDY LN
POWERLINE RD
HARRIS DR
ROMLAND
BELTS
DIAMOND HILL

SEE 133 MAP

99E
BENTON CO
LANE CO
TALBOTT LN
DIAMOND HWY
HILL RD
209
DR
COUGAR RIDGE

5

JAGER LN
MCMULLEN LN
NORBLEN
9TH ST
TERRITORIAL ST
WEATHERFORD DR
BALD MOUNTAIN
CROOKED CREEK RD
LINGO LN
HOWARD RD
HARRISBURG
PRICEBORO
GAP
RD 15-2-25
RD 15-1-31
Lancaster
ALBANY-JUNCTION CITY
RIVER
PRICEBORO DR
COBURG RD
GAP
15-1-31
15-2-25-1
PACIFIC HWY
99W
OAKLEA
LINK LN
DALE DR
5
R
ROUND MOUNTAIN
RD 16-2-10-2

6

W 18TH AV
LANE LAKE RD
WILLAMETTE
CURTIS RD
BOWERS DR
BUSH GARDEN DR
MOUNT TOM DR
TOM MOUNT
RD 16-2-10
DANE LN
W 6TH AV
JUNCTION CITY
WYATT DR
EL RIO DR
CURTIS RD
SLOUGH
LINN CO
LANE CO
MARSHALL ISLAND
HERMAN RD
Wilkins
WEST POINT HILL
16-2-18-1

36
PITNEY LN
PRAIRIE RD
CULVER RD
HAYES LN
MORGAN LN
COBURG LN
POWERLINE RD
PACIFIC
BUCK MOUNTAIN
RD 16-2-18-1
MOUNT TOM RD
RD 16-2-10
16-2-7-1
16-2-17-1
PARSONS RD

99
MILLIRON RD
HARPER RD
VIEW LN
COMPTON LN
RIVER DR
LANES TURN
MAPLE DR
COUNTRY LN
CENTENNIAL BUTTE
LANE COUNTY
ROCK HILL
MOUNT TOM RD
16-2-7-1
16-2-18
JONES ACRES
PITCH CREEK LN
ROSE RD
Marcola
SOVERN RD

7

MEADOWVIEW RD
PRAIRIE RD
HEATHER OAK DR
MONTMORENCE DR
LONE PINE DR
BISHOP LN
VICTORY RD
LASSEN LN
GREEN ISLAND RD
COBURG
WILKINS RD
LENON HILL
TRIPLE OAK RD
HERFERD RD
16-2-29
16-2-27
16-3-13
MCGOWAN CREEK RD
MOHAWK HILL RD
SUNDERMAN RD
MARCOLA RD
MOHAWK VALLEY RD
CALONE RD
RIVER

GREEN
PACIFIC
R
COBURG BOTTOM LOOP RD
PEARL ST
FLINKE RD
VAN DUYN RD
OAK CREST RD
16-2-28
MOHAWK RIVER
W BEACON DR
BEACON DR
COBURG
199

A B C D

SEE 215 MAP

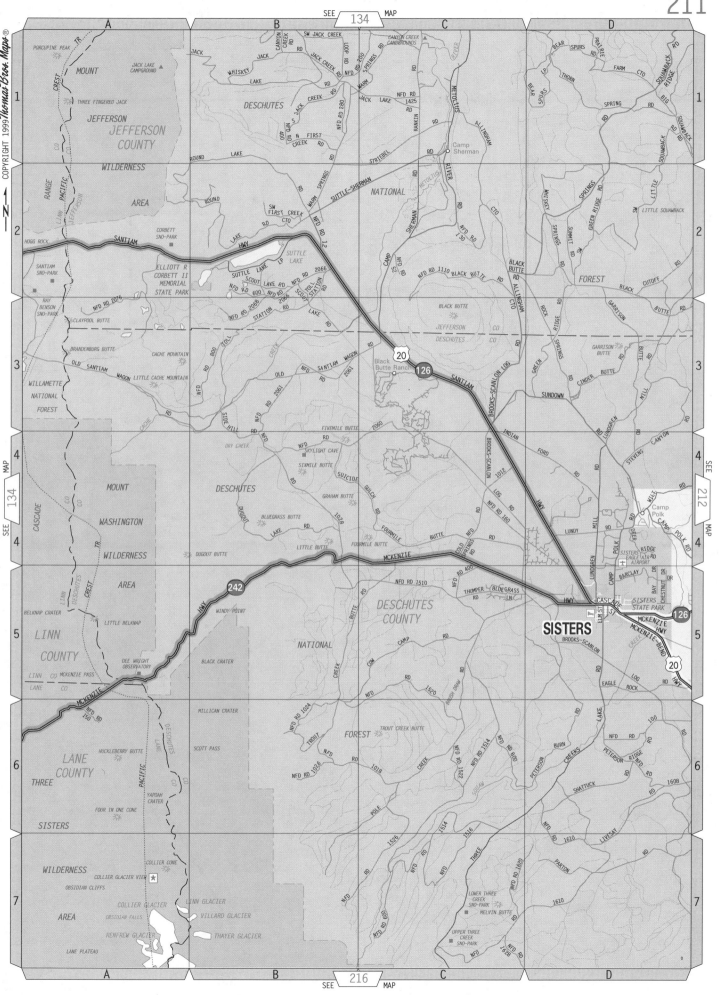

PNW

METRO

SEE MAP 134

SEE MAP 216

SEE MAP 134

SEE MAP 212

A **B** **C** **D**

MOUNT

JEFFERSON COUNTY

JEFFERSON

WILDERNESS

AREA

PORCUPINE PEAK TR.

THREE FINGERED JACK

JACK LAKE CAMPGROUND

DESCHUTES

NATIONAL

FOREST

CANYON CREEK CAMPGROUNDS

Camp Sherman

RANGE

PACIFIC CREST

SANTIAM HWY

HOGG ROCK

SANTIAM SNO-PARK

ELLIOTT R CORBETT II MEMORIAL STATE PARK

SUTTLE LAKE

CORBETT SNO-PARK

RAY BENSON SNO-PARK

CLAYPOOL BUTTE

BRANDENBURG BUTTE

OLD SANTIAM WAGON

WILLAMETTE NATIONAL FOREST

CACHE MOUNTAIN

LITTLE CACHE MOUNTAIN

CACHE RD

SIDE HILL RD

DRY CREEK

FIVEMILE BUTTE

SKYLIGHT CAVE

SIXMILE BUTTE

BLUEGRASS BUTTE

DUGOUT LAKE

DUGOUT BUTTE

GRAHAM BUTTE

SUICIDE GULCH

LITTLE BUTTE

FOURMILE BUTTE

Black Butte Ranch

BLACK BUTTE

JEFFERSON CO
DESCHUTES CO

GARRISON BUTTE

SUNDOWN

INDIAN FORD

BROOKS-SCANLON LOG

MCKENZIE

SISTERS EAGLE AIR AIRPORT

Camp Polk

SISTERS STATE PARK

SISTERS

BROOKS-SCANLON

CASCADE ST

ELM ST

CASCADE

126

20

MCKENZIE HWY

MCKENZIE BEND

MOUNT

WASHINGTON

WILDERNESS

AREA

242 HWY

WINDY POINT

BELKNAP CRATER

LITTLE BELKNAP

LINN COUNTY

CASCADE CO

LINN DESCHUTES

CREST TR.

DEE WRIGHT OBSERVATORY

LINN CO MCKENZIE PASS
LANE CO

MCKENZIE

BLACK CRATER

DESCHUTES COUNTY

NATIONAL

FOREST

THUMPER

BLUEGRASS LN

COLD SPRINGS

LUNDGREN

CAMP POLK RD

DEER RD

WILT RD

BARCLAY

CAMP

BAY

CHESTNUT DR

RIDGE RD

EAGLE ROCK RD

LANE COUNTY

THREE

SISTERS

WILDERNESS

AREA

MCKENZIE

NFD 150 RD

HUCKLEBERRY BUTTE

YAPOAH CRATER

FOUR IN ONE CONE

COLLIER CONE

COLLIER GLACIER VIEW ★

OBSIDIAN CLIFFS

COLLIER GLACIER

OBSIDIAN FALLS

LANE PLATEAU

RENFREW GLACIER

LINN GLACIER

VILLARD GLACIER

THAYER GLACIER

MILLICAN CRATER

SCOTT PASS

PACIFIC CREST TR.

DESCHUTES CO
LANE CO

TROUT CREEK BUTTE

TROUT CREEK

SQUAW CREEK

BASIN DRAW

THREE CREEK RD

POLE CREEK RD

LOWER THREE CREEK SNO-PARK

MELVIN BUTTE

UPPER THREE CREEK SNO-PARK

PETERSON RIDGE

BURN

PARTON

LIVESAY

SHATTUCK

1 2 3 4 4 5 5 6 7

212

PNW

METRO

A B C D

DESCHUTES NATIONAL FOREST

Squawback Ridge

CROOKED RIVER NATIONAL GRASSLAND

JEFFERSON COUNTY

SW SQUAW FLAT RD

Green Mountain

Geneva Overlook

NFD RD 1399

Trahan Canyon

Squaw Creek Canyon

Potter Canyon

PENINSULA DR

CRATER LP

SW KENT DR

SW KING

SW LA SALLE

SW NORMAN RD

GREEN

SMITH

JERICHO

CULVER HWY

HAYSTACK RESERVOIR

KOA MADRAS/CULVER

Juniper Butte

KING LN

Haystack Butte

MONROE LN

NORRIS

OPAL LN

Opal City

SHERWOOD

THE DALLES-CALIFORNIA

CULVER PARK

OSBORNE CANYON

CHIPMUNK

GOLDEN MANTEL

HORNY HOLLOW TR

SHAD

SWALLOW

RIM RD

CHICKADEE

ROBIN

STEELHEAD RD

PERCH RD

MEADOWLARK DR

SPARROW DR

RAINBOW DR

Steelhead Falls

ERMINE DR

DINGO

COUGAR RD

BLACKTAIL DR

JEFFERSON CO

DESCHUTES CO

Deschutes River

GALENA

PARKEY DR

RAINBOW DR

FLUME

WIMP

DONEY LN

Coyote Butte

SMITH ROCK STATE PARK

DESCHUTES COUNTY

Stevens Canyon

Fremont Canyon

WILT VIEW

SQUAW MOUNTAIN DR

Big Falls

Falls River

P S OGDEN RD

NW 43RD ST

NW 27TH ST

NE EBY

NE 9TH AV

NE 13TH AV

W LAMBERT

LaFollette Butte

TERREBONNE-LOWER BRIDGE WY

NE WILCOX

NE 17TH WY

BRIDGE RD

Bessie Butte

THEATER AV

NW SEDGEWICK

NW 31ST ST

NW 19TH ST

SMITH ROCK

Terrebonne

HOLMES RD

HUNT RD

JAEGER

McKENZIE CANYON

BUCKHORN CANYON

GRUBSTAKE WY

NW 660TH

NW 650TH

NW KNICKERBOCKER

NW ODEM

NE 1ST ST

NE 11TH

NE 5TH

HOMESTEAD ST

NW 83RD ST

ODIN FALLS

NW COYER AV

NW COYNER AV

NE O'NEIL

NE YUCCA

CANYON CREST DR

HENKLE BUTTE

Buffalo

NIMSHIA LN

GREEN RIDGE LP

SQUAW CREEK LN

HENKLE BUTTE DR

EDMUNDSON RD

HOLMES RD

FADJUR LN

DEER CANYON

HUNT

NW 91ST ST

YUCCA AV

NW 74TH ST

NW ATKINSON AV

ATKINSON AV

TETHEROW

PERSHALL

NE 117TH

Prineville Junction

CAMP POLK RD

HURTLEY RANCH RD

GOODRICH RD

HOLMES

McKENZIE

Cloverdale

126 HWY

BARR RD

NW KACHINA

NW SPRUCE AV

QUINCE AV

CASHMUR CT

REASON CT

OAK RD

LARCH AV

POPLAR DR

TULLAR

TULLAR

POLK

NW SPRUCE

UPAS AV

NE KING

NE MAPLE

NE 35TH ST

NW MAPLE AV

HEMLOCK

REDMOND-POWELL BUTTE RD

UPAS AV

NE 11TH

JORDAN

GEO CYPRUS RD

EAGLE DR

CLINE FALLS

FRANK

LS HL65

LS HL65

LAVA PL

ANTLER

NW 58TH

NW 5TH ST

NW 6TH ST

NE 9TH ST

NE LAKE RD

OCHOCO HWY

126 HWY

McKENZIE

DESCHUTES CO FAIR GROUNDS

SISTERS AV

A J WARRIN

FRYREAR BUTTE

FORKED HORN

KENT RD

IVY LN

DRY CANYON

FRYREAR RD

CLINE FALLS STATE PARK

Cline Butte

OBSIDIAN AV

NW 35TH ST

SW 23RD ST

SE AIRPORT WY

REDMOND MUNICIPAL AIRPORT

KOA SISTERS/BEND

20

HARRINGTON LP

TROUT RD

CASCADE ESTATES DR

Plainview

WEST ST

CENTRAL

THIRD

2ND AV

1ST ST

OREGON

SALMON

WICKIUP AV

SW YEW AV

SW ZENITH

SW COYOTE

51ST

REDMOND CAVE

97

REDMOND

VARCO RD

BARBARA WY

SISEMORE ST

DELICIOUS ST

BRANDYWINE

McKENZIE-BEND HWY

DUSTY LP

INNES

OLSON RD

NEWCOMB RD

WHITE ROCK LOOP RD

HARPER RD

MARSH RD

KRIEGER RD

WHITTEMORE RD

DESCHUTES HWY

PLEASANT RIDGE

PETERSON MARKET RD

AMBERY FALLS

SW BROWN RD

WHITE ROCK LOOP

REDMOND-BEND

93RD ST

ARID AV

GIFT AV

THE DALLES-CALIFORNIA

SWALLEY

CONNARN RD

94TH

85TH

LIMESTONE AV

DESCHUTES NATIONAL FOREST

BROOKS-SCANLON LG RD

KONFIELD RD

SNOW CREEK RD

COLLINS RD

ALLEN RD

COUCH RD

SMOKY BUTTE

RUDI

DAYTON RD

GERKING MARKET RD

CLINE

TWEED

MARKET RD

STURGEON RD

TUMALO-DESCHUTES HWY

DESCHUTES-PLEASANT RIDGE MARKET RD

HORNER RD

MORRILL

1 2 3 4 5 6 7

SEE 211 MAP

SEE 213 MAP

—N—

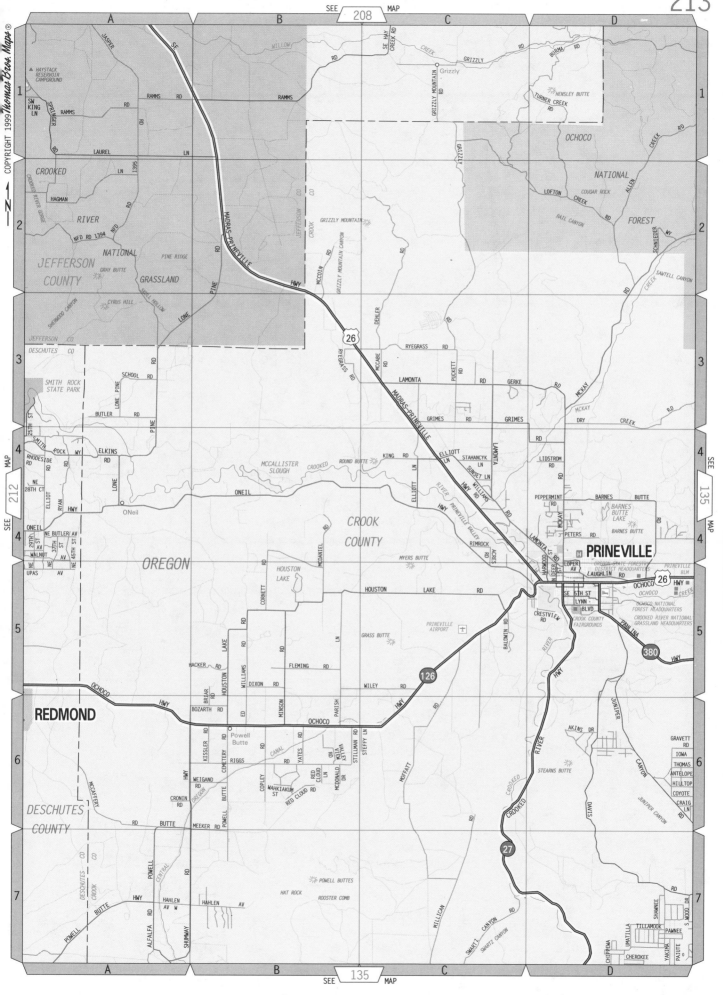

PNW

METRO

SEE 212 MAP

SEE 135 MAP

SEE 208 MAP

SEE 135 MAP

A B C D

1

2

3

4

5

6

7

JASPER

SW KING LN

SPRINGER RD

HAYSTACK RESERVOIR CAMPGROUND

RAMMS RD

RAMMS RD

LAUREL LN

CROOKED

CROOKED RIVER GORGE

HAGMAN

LN 1395

RIVER

NFD RD 1394

NFD RD

NATIONAL

PINE RIDGE

GRAY BUTTE

JEFFERSON
COUNTY

GRASSLAND

SKULL HOLLOW

SHERWOOD CANYON

CYRUS HILL

JEFFERSON CO

DESCHUTES CO

SMITH ROCK STATE PARK

LONE PINE

SCHOOL RD

BUTLER RD

PINE RD

25TH ST

SMITH ROCK WY

RHODESIDE RD

ELKINS RD

LONE RD

ELLIOT RYAN HWY

ONEIL

ONEIL

29TH ST AV

NE 28TH CT

NE BUTLER AV

37TH ST AV

NE 45TH ST

WALNUT

UPAS AV

OREGON

MADRAS-PRINEVILLE RD

MADRAS-PRINEVILLE HWY

PINE

LONE

MCCOIN RD

GRIZZLY MOUNTAIN CANYON

JEFFERSON CO

CROOK CO

GRIZZLY MOUNTAIN

DEHLER

RYEGRASS RD

MCCABE RD

RYEGRASS RD

26

RYEGRASS RD

LAMONTA

PUCKETT RD

GRIMES RD

GRIMES RD

GERKE RD

MCCALLISTER SLOUGH

CROOKED

ROUND BUTTE

KING RD

ELLIOTT LN

ELLIOTT LN

STAHANCYK LN

SUNSET LN

WILLIAMS RD

LAMONTA RD

ONEIL

CROOK
COUNTY

MCDANIEL

HOUSTON LAKE

CORNETT

MYERS BUTTE

RIMROCK

ACRES

PRINEVILLE VALLEY

LAKE RD

WILLIAMS RD

HOUSTON RD

DIXON RD

FLEMING RD

LN

HOUSTON LAKE RD

GRASS BUTTE

PRINEVILLE AIRPORT

WILEY RD

126

HWY

RD

BALDWIN RD

CRESTVIEW RD

PRINEVILLE

OCHOCO

ST FORESTRY

GRIZZLY

OCHOCO

NATIONAL

FOREST

LOFTON CREEK

COUGAR ROCK RD

RAIL CANYON

SAWTELL CANYON

CREEK

MCKAY RD

MCKAY DRY CREEK

LIDSTROM RD

PEPPERMINT RD

BARNES RD

BARNES BUTTE

BARNES BUTTE LAKE

PETERS

MCKAY

LAMONTA ST

HARWOOD ST

N DEER ST

LOPER AV

LAUGHLIN RD

PRINEVILLE BLM

OCHOCO

26

HWY

SE 5TH ST

LYNN BLVD

OCHOCO NATIONAL FOREST HEADQUARTERS

CROOKED RIVER NATIONAL GRASSLAND HEADQUARTERS

CROOK COUNTY FAIRGROUNDS

PAULINA

380

HWY

CROOKED RIVER

JUNIPER

AKINS DR

STEARNS BUTTE

JUNIPER CANYON

GRAVETT RD

IOWA

THOMAS

ANTELOPE

HILLTOP

COYOTE

CRAIG LN

DAVIS

JUNIPER CANYON RD

27

REDMOND

OCHOCO HWY

HACKER RD

BRIAR RD

BOZARTH RD

KISSLER RD

CEMETERY RD

RIGGS RD

WEIGAND RD

CRONIN RD

POWELL BUTTE

MEEKER RD

ED RD

MINSON RD

YATES RD

OCHOCO

POWELL BUTTE

CANAL

COPLEY

WAHKIAKUM ST

RED CLOUD

RED CLOUD LN

MCDONALD DR

OLD VALLEY YATES

STILLMAN LN

STEFFA LN

MOFFATT RD

PARISH RD

DESCHUTES
COUNTY

MCCAFFERY RD

POWELL BUTTE HWY

CENTRAL RD

ALFALFA RD

SHUMWAY

HAHLEN AV W

HAHLEN AV

HAT ROCK

POWELL BUTTES

ROOSTER COMB

MILLICAN RD

SMARTZ CANYON

SMARTZ CANYON RD

S WOOD DR

SHAWNEE

TILLAMOOK

UMATILLA

CHIPEWA

YAKIMA

PAIUTE

PAWNEE

CHEROKEE

DESCHUTES CO

CROOK CO

POWELL BUTTE

CRESTVIEW RD

N

PNW

METRO

A B C D

COPYRIGHT 1999 Thomas Bros. Maps ® —N—

FLORENCE

DUNES CITY

SIUSLAW NATIONAL FOREST

CAPE MOUNTAIN

5842

Minerva

NORTH FORK SIUSLAW CAMPGROUND

UPPER NORTH FORK RD

THOMPSON CREEK RD

36

Rainrock
ROCK CANYON
Brickerville

DAVIS RAPIDS

STOUT CANYON

DAVID RIDGE 719

NFD

2610 NFD RD 719

HANSON RIDGE

BELLSTROM CANYON

NEELY MOUNTAIN

BALD MOUNTAIN

MISERY RIDGE

MAPLETON JUNCTION CITY

E MAPLETON

Mapleton

HWY

2610

SIUSLAW

FLORENCE-EUGENE

Tiernan

CREEK

Point Terrace

RD

NATIONAL

LANE COUNTY

FOREST

BERNHARDT

KADHONSKY CREEK

MOUNT PETER

HENDERSON CREEK RD

SWEET CREEK FALLS

BEAVER CREEK FALLS

SWEET CREEK

ROCKY POINT

GOODWIN PEAK

SUNSET MOUNTAIN

2480

4830

FIDDLE CREEK RIDGE

NFD

958

MOUNT GRAYBACK

OREGON

ROBINSON RIDGE

Heceta Beach

HECETA BEACH RD

RHODODENDRON RD

101

Heceta Junction

MERCER LAKE

BEN BUNCH LAKE

MERCER LAKE

SUTTON LAKE

SUTTON BEACH RD

SUTTON LAKE CAMPGROUND

SUTTON CREEK CAMPGROUND

ENCHANTED VALLEY

COLLARD LAKE

CLEAR LAKE

THE PORTAGE

MERCER

SIUSLAW

COAST HWY

MUNSEL LAKE RD

DOLLY WARES DOLL MUS

NORTH FORK

BENDER LANDING

RICHARDSON CANYON

Wendson

126

Cushman

BULL ISLAND

SKUNK HOLLOW

COX ISLAND

35TH ST

LANE COMMUNITY COLLEGE

9TH ST

FLORENCE MUNICIPAL AIRPORT

OREGON

SIUSLAW VISTA

DUNES

SIUSLAW RIVER

Glenada

SIUSLAW PIONEER MUSEUM

SOUTH INLET

SOUTH SLOUGH

NATIONAL

953

NFD RD

CANARY RD

JESSIE M HONEYMAN MEMORIAL STATE PARK

RECREATION

WOAHINK LAKE

Canary

UPPER

CANARY RD

MAPLE CREEK RD

AREA

CLEAR LAKE

North Beach

NORTH BEACH BAY

DRIFTWOOD CAMPGROUND

DRIFTWOOD II CAMPGROUND

LAGOON CAMPGROUND

WAXMYRTLE CAMPGROUND

LODGEPOLE CAMPGROUND

Westlake

TYEE CAMPGROUND

SILTCOOS LAKE

BOOTH ISLAND

Siltcoos

SILTCOOS STATION

Ada

CANARY RD S

FIDDLE CREEK

MILES CANYON

HENDERSON CANYON

LANE DOUGLAS CO

NORTH FORK

CARTER LAKE CAMPGROUND

EAST CARTER CAMPGROUND

EAST CARTER BOAT RAMP

COUNTY LINE

REED ISLAND

ADA RD

HARMONY BAY

5.9

BOOTH RIDGE

SULPHUR RIDGE

BLM RD 2-3

CROWN ZELLERBACK CAMPGROUND

OREGON DUNES OVERLOOK

LOST LAKE CAMPGROUND

BOOTH RD

CATFISH HOLE

4811

23

NORTH

HENDERSON PEAK

BLM RD 33-0

101

COAST HWY

CLAY POINT

TAHKENITCH LAKE

HALFWAY POINT

SNARE POINT

5.9

FIVEMILE

BUZZARDS BUTTE

North Fork

SMITH RIVER RD

SMITH RIVER

BLM RD 36-0

Sulphur Springs

LITTLE BUCK

SPENCER CREEK

BLM 24-1

TAHKENITCH LANDING

TAHKENITCH CAMPGROUND

ELBOW LAKE CAMPGROUND

OREGON DUNES NATIONAL RECREATION AREA

MIDDLE POINT

GARDINER LANDING

HOME POINT

CLEAR LAKE

SMITH RIVER

WASSON RIDGE

SPARROW

FOURMILE LIGHT

THREEMILE LIGHT

UMPQUA RIVER

LOWER

DOUGLAS COUNTY

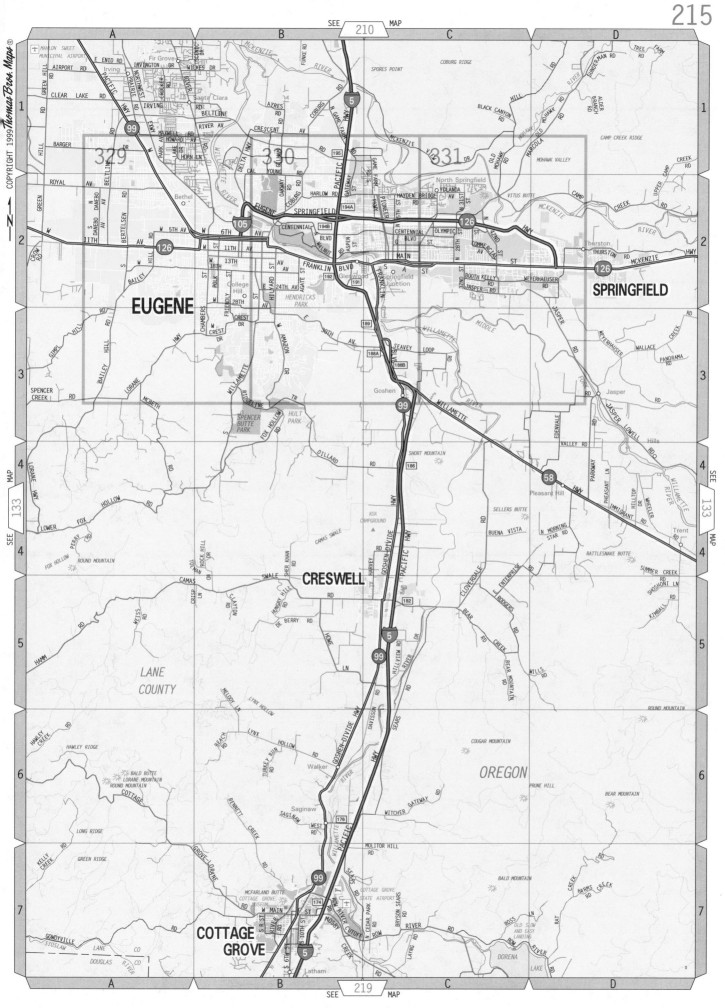

PNW

METRO

SEE MAP 210

SEE MAP 219

SEE MAP 133

SEE MAP 133

329

330

331

EUGENE

SPRINGFIELD

CRESWELL

COTTAGE GROVE

LANE COUNTY

OREGON

SEE 211 MAP

PNW

—N—

METRO

SEE 134 MAP

SEE 217 MAP

SEE 142 MAP

LANE COUNTY

HAYDEN GLACIER
DILLER GLACIER
IRVING GLACIER
THREE SISTERS
CARVER GLACIER
SKINNER GLACIER
EUGENE GLACIER
PROUTY GLACIER
LOST CREEK GLACIER
SOUTH SISTER
HODGE CREST
LEWIS GLACIER
JAMES CREEK SHELTER
CLARK GLACIER

THREE SISTERS WILDERNESS AREA

BROKEN TOP
BEND GLACIER
BROKEN HAND
CROOK GLACIER
BALL BUTTE
CAYUSE CRATER

ROCK MESA
LE CONTE CRATER

SQUAW CREEK FALLS
SQUAW CREEK

THREE CREEK BUTTE
SNOW CREEK RD
NFD RD 1628
THREE CREEKS LAKE RD
THREE CREEK MEADOW CAMPGROUND
NFD RD 370
DRIFTWOOD CAMPGROUND
TAM McARTHUR RIM
THREE CREEK LAKE CAMPGROUND
TRIANGLE HILL
BEAR WALLOW BUTTE
BEARWALLOW BUTTE
BEARWALLOWS
HAPPY VALLEY
TUMALO LOOP RD
370

PACIFIC CREST TR

RANGE

KALEETAN BUTTE
DEVILS HILL
KOKOSTICK BUTTE
CASCADE LAKES
TALAPUS BUTTE
TODD LAKE CAMPGROUND
KOOSAH MOUNTAIN
KATSUK BUTTE
RED HILL
RED RILL
SPARKS LAKE

NFD RD 4601
TUMALO FALLS
TUMALO FALLS CREEK
TUMALO FALLS SHELTER
SWEDE RIDGE SHELTER
SWEDE RIDGE RD
TUMALO
NFD RD 4615
NFD RD 4612
BIG SPRING BURN

HWY
NFD RD
TUMALO MOUNTAIN
SWAMPY LAKES SHELTER
CENTURY
SWAMPY LAKES SNOWPARK
DRIVE
372 HWY
WANOGA SNOWMOBILE SNOWPARK
VIRGINIA MEISSNER SNOWPARK
KAPKA BUTTE
BIG SPRING RD

NFD RD 450
MOOLACK BUTTE
ELK LAKE
ELK LAKE
HOSMER LAKE
DESCHUTES
ELK LAKE CAMPGROUND
LITTLE FAWN CAMPGROUND
ELK MOUNTAIN
SOUTH CAMPGROUND
POINT CAMPGROUND
MALLARD MARSH CAMPGROUND
BEACH CAMPGROUND
MUD LAKE RD
RED CRATER
TOT MOUNTAIN
NATIONAL
OREGON
KWOLH BUTTE
KATALO BUTTE
NFD RD 4613
KIWA BUTTE

POMA SKI TOW
BACHELOR SKI LIFT

CASCADE

FOREST
WILLIAMSON MOUNTAIN
LAVA LAKE
LAVA LAKE CAMPGROUND
LITTLE LAVA LAKE
LAVA RD
LAVA LAKE
LITTLE LAVA LAKE CAMPGROUND
SHERIDAN MOUNTAIN
UPPER CAMPGROUND
MILE CAMPGROUND

DESCHUTES COUNTY
EDISON BUTTE
EDISON SNO-PARK
EDISON ICE CAVE
KAPKA BUTTE RD
EDISON ICE CAVE
WANOGA LOOKOUT RD
KUAMAKSI BUTTE
NFD RD 400
NFD RD 4180
PITSUA BUTTE
TELEPHONE
PITSUA BUTTE RD
NFD RD 160

WILLIAMSON MOUNTAIN RD
LAKES HWY
BUTTE RD
SIAH BUTTE
LOLO BUTTE
KLAK BUTTE
K'LAK
LOLO BUTTE
PRATER RD
EDISON ICE CAVE RD
DESCHUTES
ANNS BUTTE
NFD RD 4220

MARK BUTTE
BENCH MARK BUTTE
SIAH BUTTE
LOLAH BUTTE
LLIHRUM BUTTE
LOLAH BUTTE
WAKE BUTTE
UPPER RD
SITKUM BUTTE
LLOYD
LLOYD RD

CULTUS LAKE
CULTUS LAKE CAMPGROUND
NFD RD 4630
BENCH LAKE RD
LOOKOUT MOUNTAIN
CENTURY DR
LOLAH BUTTE RD
THREE TRAPPER RD
LOOKOUT MOUNTAIN RD
DRY BUTTE
UPPER DESCHUTES RD
INDIAN CREEK RD
PISTOL BUTTE RD
PISTOL BUTTE
CENTURY DR
BATES BUTTE
BIG RIVER CAMPGROUND

NFD RD 4635
LAVA
COW CAMP CAMPGROUND
CRANE PRAIRIE RESERVOIR
CRANE PRAIRIE CAMPGROUND
LOOKOUT MOUNTAIN
PRINGLE FALLS EXPERIMENTAL FOREST ADDITION

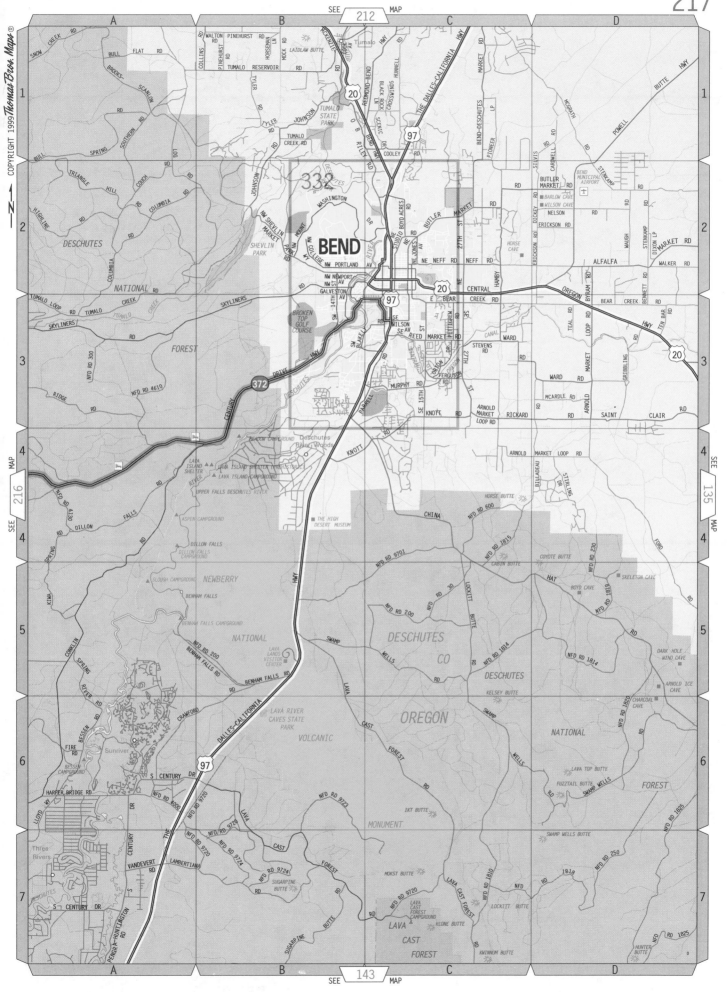

PNW

METRO

SEE 212 MAP

SEE 216 MAP

SEE 135 MAP

SEE 143 MAP

PNW

METRO

—N—

SEE 214 MAP

SEE 220 MAP

SEE 140 MAP

SEE 140 MAP

A | B | C | D

STEAMBOAT ISLAND

BARRETTS LANDING

BRUSHY HILL

OREGON DUNES NATIONAL RECREATION AREA

HENDERSON COVE

DOUBLE COVE POINT

LEEDS ISLAND

BOLON ISLAND STATE PARK

Gardiner

East Gardiner

SMITH RIVER RD

SOUTH SIDE RD

OTTER SLOUGH

SIUSLAW NATIONAL FOREST

HUNT COVE

MACEY COVE

ARMY HILL

JERDEN COVE

RIDGEWAY DR

SMITH RIVER LIGHT

LOWER SMITH RD

BUTLER RD

DISCOVER CENTER

UMPQUA

38 HWY

CORNWALL POINT

Winchester Bay

BOWMAN RD

REEDSPORT

DOUGLAS COUNTY

SCHOLFIELD RD

SCHOLFIELD RIDGE RD

DEAN MOUNTAIN RD

UMPQUA LIGHTHOUSE

UMPQUA LIGHTHOUSE STATE PARK

101

Lake Marie Campground

CLEAR LAKE

SALMON HARBOR DR

OREGON

LAKE EDNA

WILLIAM M TUGMAN STATE PARK

EEL LAKE

ELLIOTT

TWIN SISTERS

OCEAN

OREGON DUNES NATIONAL RECREATION AREA

DOUGLAS CO COOS CO

BLACKS ARM

CARSON ARM

BIG CREEK RD

NOBLE CREEK RD

NORTH TENMILE LAKE

NORTH EEL CAMPGROUND

MIDDLE EEL CAMPGROUND

EEL CREEK CAMPGROUND

SOUTH EEL CREEK CAMPGROUND

SPINREEL CAMPGROUND

BIG CREEK ARM

LINDROS ARM

BIG CREEK ARM

LAKESIDE

NORTH EEL LAKE RD

STATE

Tenmile

SCHOOL LAND BAY

DEVORE ARM

WILLOW POINT

COLEMAN ARM

TENMILE LAKE

BENSON CREEK RD

CREEK RD

ROBERT

FOREST

COAST HWY

STAGE RD

SHUTTER ARM

SHUTTERS LANDING RD

TEMPLETON ARM

TEMPLETON RD

Templeton

OREGON DUNES NATIONAL RECREATION AREA

Saunders Lake

WILDWOOD DR

COOS COUNTY

OREGON

TENMILE BUTTE

TRAIL BUTTE

OREGON DUNES NATIONAL RECREATION AREA

PACIFIC

Hauser

NORTH LAKE RD

ZARA DR

HAYNES WY

WY

WILLICOMA TRAIL WEST

BUTTE RD

HENRYS FALLS

101

KDA OREGON DUNES

RIDGE DR

MEADOW LN

LARSON WY

BALDY BUTTE

DEAN MOUNTAIN

WEST FORK-MILLICOMA

ESTELL FALLS

PIDGEON FALLS

HORSEFALL BEACH

BLUEBILL LAKE CAMPGROUND

Shorewood

HAYNES INLET

NORTH BAY RD

LARSON RD

WY

METTMAN CREEK RD

WY

WILLANCH CREEK WY

WEST FORK-MILLICOMA RD

DEVILS ELBOW

ELK MOUNTAIN RD

EAST

TRANS PACIFIC PKWY

Glasgow

333

COOS BAY

JORDAN COVE

COAST EAST BAY DR

KENTUCK

Allegany

COLORADO AV

NORTH BEND

KENTUCK INLET

Cooston

NOAH BUTTE

MILLICOMA RIVER

EAST FORK MILLICOMA RIVER

COOS BAY

FENWICK ST

VIRGINIA AV

Empire

CAPE ARAGO HWY

EMPIRE COOS BAY HWY

NEWMARK ST

TREMONT ST

AYRSHIRE ST

COOS BAY

MCKEEVER MOUNTAIN

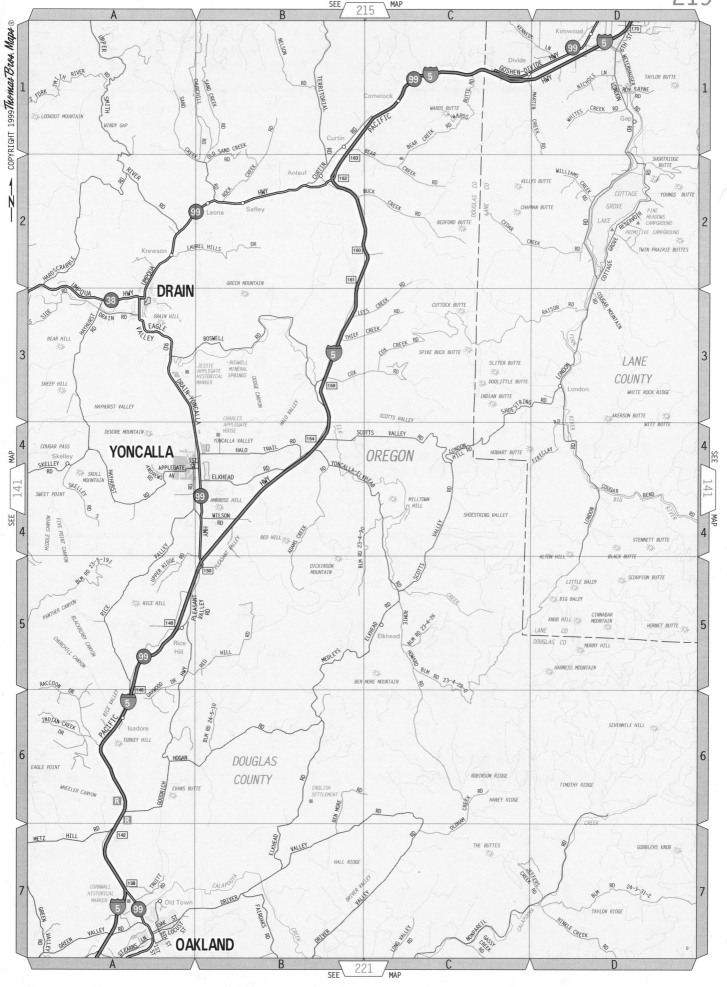

A B C D

—N—

PNW

METRO

SEE 140 MAP

SEE 140 MAP

COOS BAY

COQUILLE

BANDON

333

101

42

42S

42S

42

101

COOS COUNTY

OREGON

COOS FOREST

COOS COUNTY

OCEAN

PACIFIC

UPPER PONY CREEK RES

EMPIRE-COOS BAY

Eastside

COOS RIVER

Bunker Hill

Englewood

Bay Park

McCormac

Millington

Cleo

EASTSIDE-SUMNER RD

CITY-SUMNER RD

BOONE CREEK RD

Green Acres

Overland

BEAVER CREEK

Coaledo

Chrome

Leneve

BANK RD

OLD BEAVER HILL RD

BEAVER HILL RD

BEAVER HILL RD

COQUILLE

COQUILLE RIVER

Cedar Point

W CENTRAL BLVD

2ND ST

E 1ST ST

SHELLEY RD

DUTCH JOHN RAVINE

BUDD MOUNTAIN

COQUILLE-FAIRVIEW RD

Riverton

COQUILLE-FAT ELK RD

COQUILLE-FAT ELK

BAKER

GATEWAY RD

HATCHET SLOUGH RD

BANK RD

N

LANDING

COQUILLE VALLEY

LAMPA MOUNTAIN

POINT-LAMPA

MYRTLE RD

LAMPA VALLEY

Arago

MYRTLE

ARAGO LN

Norway

LOWER NORWAY RD

POINT-LAMPA

PLEASANT VALLEY

PLEASANT VALLEY RD

WEST SIDE RD

MATHENY CREEK RD

CATCHING CREEK RD

HALL CREEK RD

WARD CREEK RD

HORSE HOLLOW RD

GRIGSBY ROCK

Johnson

GLEN AIKEN RD

COOS CREEK RD

TRUNK CREEK RD

FISHTRAP RD

BAY-ROSEBURG HWY

GARDEN VALLEY RD

COOS BAY-ROSEBURG HWY

DELMAR RD

OVERLAND RD

UPPER LOOP RD

TIMBER WY

GREEN ACRES RD

COOS COAST RD

COOS-ARAGO HWY

COOS BAY

BARVIEW

Charleston

Crown Point

CROWN POINT RD

JOE NEY-DAVIS SL

CULVER POINT

YOUNKER POINT

SEVEN DEVILS RD

SALAL LN

HINCH RD

SOUTH SLOUGH NATIONAL ESTUARY

LONG ISLAND POINT

THE BUTTES

YOAKAM HILL

COS CANYON

BEAVER HILL RD

AGATE BEACH

FIVEMILE POINT

WHISKEY RUN RD

W HUMPHREYS RD

E HUMPHREYS RD

SEVEN DEVILS RD

SEVEN MILE RD

ROCKY POINT

BULLARDS BEACH STATE PARK

BANK RD

PARKERSBURG-PROSPER JUNCTION

Parkersburg

Prosper

SPRUCE HOLLOW

TOM SMITH RD

PARK RD

RIVERSIDE DR

1ST ST

2ND ST

BATES

RANDALL

Winterville

BEAR CREEK

COQUILLE-BANDON

N

BANDON-MYRTLE POINT

8TH ST SW

BEACH LOOP DR SW

FIVE FOOT ROCK

COQUILLE POINT

BANDON BEACH

CAT AND KITTENS ROCK

SEA BIRD DR

HAYSTACK ROCK

BANDON STATE AIRPORT

WINDHURST RD

MORRISON RD

BARKLOW RD

BARNEKOFF RD

ROSA RD

BEACH LOOP

BOAT RD

Twomile

TWOMILE RD

DEW VALLEY RD

DEW VALLEY RD

BANDON STATE PARK

Laurel Grove

SQUAW ISLAND

ARAGO LIGHT

SUNSET BAY

SUNSET BAY STATE PARK

BASTENDORFF BEACH

YOAKAM POINT COUNTY PARK

COOS HEAD US NAVAL FACILITY

SHELL ISLAND

NORTH COVE

CAPE ARGO STATE PARK

CAPE ARAGO

SEA LION VIEW POINT

SHORE ACRES STATE PARK

DRAKE POINT

SOUTH COVE

DEVILS RD

BEAVER HILL RD

DEW VALLEY

101

1 2 3 4 4 5 6 7

EMPIRE-COOS BAY

101 HWY

OLIVE BARBER RD

ROSS INLET RD

SOUTHWEST BLVD

ELROD AV

LOCKHART AV

LIBBY DR

Libby

COPYRIGHT 1999 Thomas Bros. Maps®

—N—

SUTHERLIN

ROSEBURG

WINSTON

DOUGLAS COUNTY

OREGON

WILDLIFE SAFARI

Umpqua Community College

Sutherlin Municipal Airport

UMPQUA RIVER

PNW

METRO

SEE 141 MAP

SEE 141 MAP

A B C D

1 2 3 4 5 6 7

Wapiti Ln, Tyee Rd, Churchill Rapids, Umpqua, Coles Valley, Hubbard Creek Rd, Umpqua Estate Winery, Iverson Rd, Joelson Rd, Woodruff Mountain, Crow Rapids, Melqua, Edenbower River, Henry Rd, Turkey Creek Ln, Millwood, Heydon Rd, Cleveland, Leatherwood Rapids, Cleveland Rapids, Ponderosa Dr, Big Bend, Bear Ridge, Elgarose, Becker Rd, Woodruff Rd, Meloua, Cleveland Hill, Donbuss St, Loop, Orchard Ln, Doerner Rd, Melrose, Flournoy Valley Rd, Champagne Creek Valley Rd, Tangelwood Ln, Kulff Ln, Colonial Rd, Mirror Ln, Lookingglass Hill, Mount Nebo, White Tail Ridge, Sunrise Ln, Bay-Wagon Rd, Lookingglass Valley, Coos, Criteser, Morgan Hill, Larson, Lookingglass Creek, Indian Nose, Happy, Valley, Strickland Canyon, Swan Hill, Brockway, Porter Creek Rd, Olalla, Hoover Hill, McNabb, Kent Creek Rd, Squam Creek Rd, Rice Creek, Rainbow Hollow, Dillard, Willis Creek Rd, South Umpqua, River Rd, Round Prairie, R. Richardson, Clarks Branch, Gobblers Knob, Glengary, Roberts Mountain, Roberts Creek, Burg Mountain, Oaks, Shady, Green, Carnes Rd, Roseburg, Brosi Orchard Rd, Darrell Av, Thompson Av, Coos-Bay Av, Brockway Rd, Dillard, Hoover Hill, Ollalla Creek, Bilger Creek, Big Lick Creek, Myrtle Creek, North Myrtle Park, Right Fork, Frozen Creek, Hoot N Holler Ln, Deer Creek, Dixonville, Buckhorn Rd, Black Mud Summit, Round Top, Sunshine Rd, Echo Butte, Oak Creek Valley Hwy, Whistlers Bend Park, South Bank Umpqua, Bank, North Rd, Rio Nes Ln, Wild Fern Dr, Winchester Baldy, Page Rd, North Umpqua River, Oakland, Klahowya Ln, Red Hill, Upper Cleveland Rapids, Wilbur-Garden Valley, Twin Rivers Campground, Coyote Hill, Riversdale Rd, Moorea Dr, Curry, Fisher, Garden Valley, Edenbower, Stewart Pkwy, Newton Creek, Diamond Lake Blvd, Douglas, Buckhorn, Harvard Blvd, Troost, Broad St, Stephens St, Pipeline Rd, Davis Hill, Halfmile Rd, Deady, Deady Caves, Deady Crossing Rd, Round Timber, Fairoaks Rd, Calapooya Creek, Fairoaks, North Side Rd, Sutherlin-Nonpareil Rd, Valley View, Camas Swale, Cooper Creek Rd, Fraser Canyon, Smith Canyon, Calapooya St, Central, South Side, NW 6th Av, NE 6th Av, Duke St, Park Mill, Comstock, Richards Butte, Fort McKay, Stephens, Cole Rd, Wilcox Rd, Cole Creek, Gross Ln, Old Hwy, Stearns Ln, Elkton-Sutherlin Hwy, Ulalpn Gap, Wilbur, Wilbur-Rogers Rd, Shady Rd, West Valley Dr, Brozio Rd, Winchester, Pacific Hwy, Clearview, Rogers Rd, Sutherlin-Umpqua Rd, Wilbur-Umpqua Rd, Calapooya, Tyee, Wapiti, Melqua Rd, Glengary Rd, Roberts Creek Rd, Valley, Mount Nebo Rd, Lookingglass, Bay-Wagon Rd

Highway markers: 5, 99, 138, 136, 135, 129, 125, 124, 123, 121, 120, 119, 113, 112, 42, 334

SEE 142 MAP

—N—

PNW

METRO

SEE 141 MAP

SEE 223 MAP

SEE 226 MAP

A B C D

1 2 3 4 5 6 7

NFD RD 3817
NFD RD 100
REYNOLDS RIDGE
BULLDOG ROCK
LOST PRAIRIE ROCK
STALEY RIDGE
COAL CREEK
WILLAMETTE
NATIONAL
FOREST
REYNOLDS CREEK
GRANDDAD BUTTE
BULLDOG RD
REYNOLDS BUTTE
REYNOLDS SHELTER
WABASH
CREEK
RD

STEAMBOAT
STEAMBOAT FALLS CAMPGROUND
STEAMBOAT
SINGLE CREEK RD
QUARTZ POINT
WILD ROSE POINT
HARDING BUTTE
DEVILS STAIRWAY
SPRING MOUNTAIN
BOULDER
CREEK
WILDERNESS
SILVER ROCK
BALM MOUNTAIN
NFD RD 34
UMPQUA
NATIONAL
LITTLE FALLS
NFD RD 500
NFD RD 200
DOG MOUNTAIN
RAGGED BUTTE
BARTRUMS ROCK
BEAR POINT
ILLAHEE ROCK
DOUGLAS
COUNTY
BOULDER CREEK
PERRY BUTTE
THORN MOUNTAIN
FOREST

JACK FALLS
UMPQUA RIVER
JACK POINT
RAGGED RIDGE
LIMPY ROCK
INDIAN CAVE
BRADLEY RIDGE
REYNOLDS RIDGE
EAGLE RIDGE
RD
RATTLESNAKE RIDGE
PINE POINT
RATTLESNAKE ROCK
EAGLE ROCK
PINE BENCH
BOULDER FLAT CAMPGROUND
OLD MAN ROCK
NORTH UMPQUA
CAMEL HUMP
OREGON
LEMOLO TWO FOREBAY CAMPGROUND
NORTH
PANTHER LEAP
WEEPING ROCK CAMPGROUND
EAGLE ROCK CAMPGROUND
CHARCOAL POINT
BIG
FLATIRON POINT
NORTH UMPQUA HWY
TOKETEE FALLS
TOKETEE LAKE CAMPGROUND
NFD RD 34
HORSESHOE BEND CAMPGROUND

CALF RIDGE
CALF CREEK
CAMAS RD
SNUFF SHELTER
RD
COPELAND CREEK
FISH CREEK
138
TOKETEE RESERVOIR
NFD RD 75
CLEARWATER
CLEARWATER RIVER
WATSON FALLS
RD
FAIRY SHELTER
BACHELOR BUTTE
LIMPY MOUNTAIN
CODWATER CAMPGROUND
YAKSO FALLS
OK BUTTE
BIG TWIN LAKES CAMPGROUND
TWIN LAKES
UMPQUA
BRINK RD
NFD RD 35
CAMAS
BIG CAMAS
FISH CREEK CAMPGROUND
NFD RD
FISH CREEK RD

LITTLE RIVER RD
LITTLE RIVER
HEMLOCK FALLS
QUARTZ MOUNTAIN
SNOWBIRD SHELTER
CALF CREEK
TWIN LAKES MOUNTAIN
DOEHEAD MOUNTAIN
COPELAND
CAMAS CREEK CAMPGROUND
RHODODENDRON RIDGE
FISH CREEK DESERT
CREEK
ROUGH CREEK
HEMLOCK LAKE CAMPGROUND
QUARTZ MOUNTAIN
RIVER
SNOWBIRD MOUNTAIN
RAVEN ROCK
NATIONAL
MUD LAKE MOUNTAIN
RD
NFD RD
HEMLOCK MEADOW CAMPGROUND
BUCKHEAD MOUNTAIN
SNOWBIRD
BEAR WALLOW
RD

BUCKHEAD MOUNTAIN CAMPGROUND
FOREST
BEAVER SHELTER
QUARTZ MOUNTAIN
BLACK ROCK FORK
BLACK ROCK
RD 950
BLACK ROCK
ROLLING GROUNDS CAMP
QUARTZ CANYON
HAPPY VALLEY
FISH CREEK

RD
BOZE SHELTER
DEER LICK FALLS
ROCK
ROCK FORK
ROGUE-UMPQUA
RATTLESNAKE MOUNTAIN
DIVIDE
FISH CREEK VALLEY
FISH CREEK SHELTER

MOUNTAIN
FLAGSTONE PEAK
QUARTZ CREEK RD
BLACK ROCK FORK
FISH RIVER LAKE
CASTLE
BEAVER SWAMP CAMPGROUND
WINDY GAP
ROCKY RIDGE
CASTLE ROCK
FISH CREEK
BUCKNECK MOUNTAIN
WILDERNESS
QUARTZ
TILLER-SOUTH UMPQUA CAMP RD
SOUTH UMPQUA
EMERSON RD
FISH CREEK RD
SKIMMERHORN CAMPGROUND
FISH LAKE CAMPGROUND
FISH LAKE
DEVILS SLIDE
WILEY CAMP
ROGUE RIVER NATIONAL FOREST
BUCK CANYON

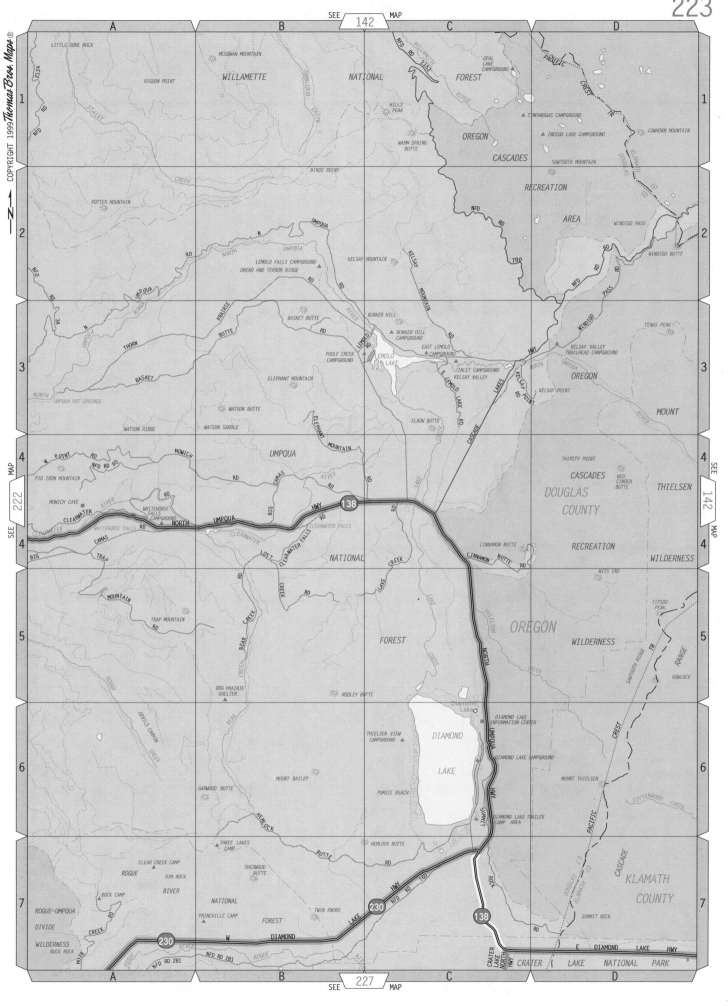

PNW

METRO

SEE 142 MAP

SEE 222 MAP

SEE 142 MAP

SEE 227 MAP

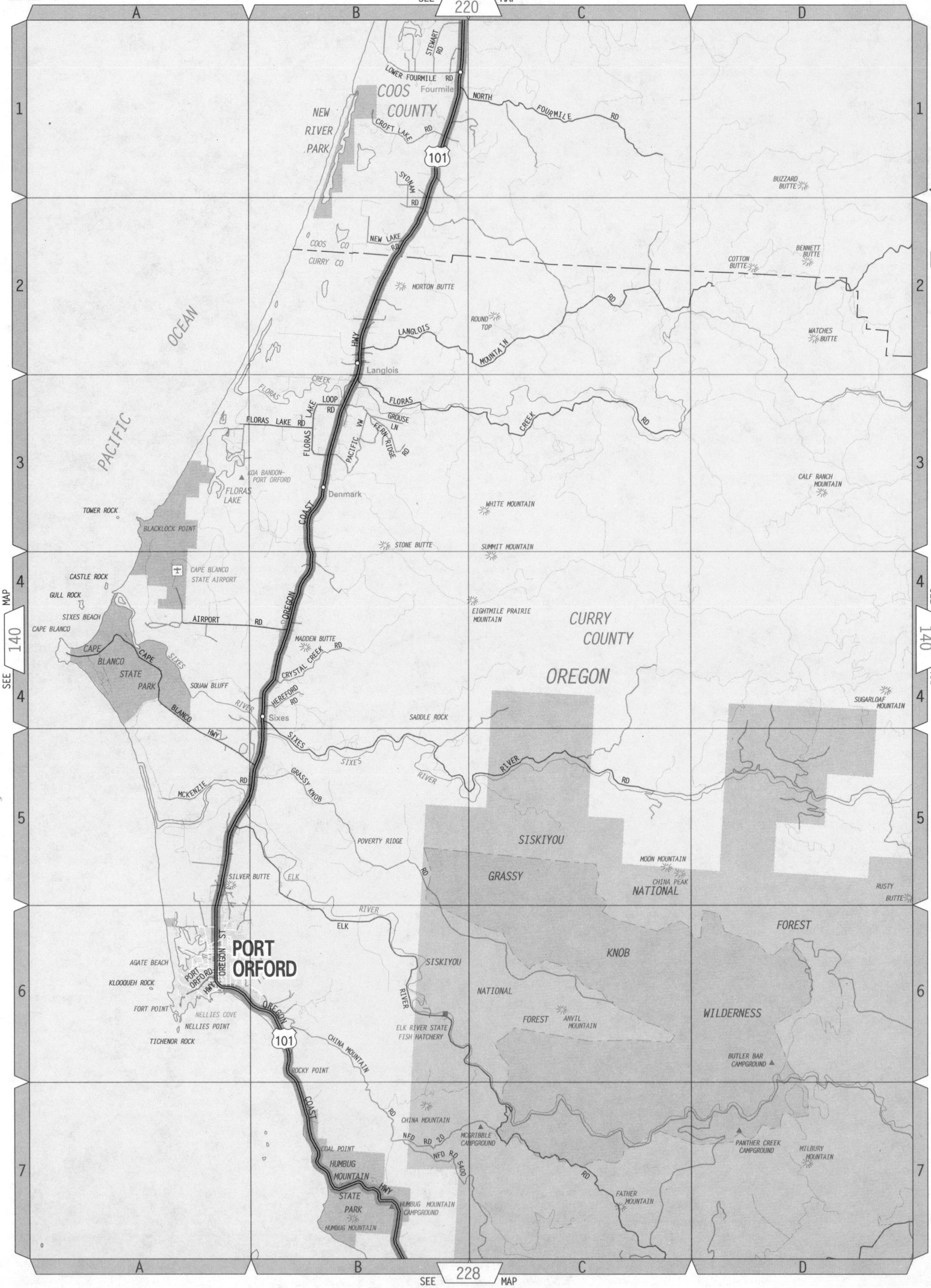

224

A | B | C | D

COPYRIGHT 1999 Thomas Bros. Maps® —N—

PNW

1

COOS COUNTY

NEW RIVER PARK

STEWART RD

LOWER FOURMILE RD

Fourmile

NORTH FOURMILE RD

CROFT LAKE RD

101

SYDNAM RD

BUZZARD BUTTE

2

NEW LAKE RD

COOS CO

CURRY CO

MORTON BUTTE

LANGLOIS

ROUND TOP MOUNTAIN

BENNETT BUTTE

COTTON BUTTE

WATCHES BUTTE

OCEAN

3

PACIFIC

FLORAS LAKE

FLORAS LAKE RD

LOOP RD

FLORAS CREEK

GROUSE LN

FERN RIDGE RD

FLORAS RD

CREEK

PACIFIC VW

COA BANDON-PORT ORFORD

FLORAS LAKE

Denmark

WHITE MOUNTAIN

CALF RANCH MOUNTAIN

TOWER ROCK

BLACKLOCK POINT

STONE BUTTE

SUMMIT MOUNTAIN

4

SEE 140 MAP

CASTLE ROCK

GULL ROCK

SIXES BEACH

CAPE BLANCO

CAPE BLANCO STATE AIRPORT

AIRPORT RD

CAPE BLANCO STATE PARK

SQUAW BLUFF

SIXES

BLANCO HWY

RIVER

HEREFORD RD

Sixes

MADDEN BUTTE RD

CRYSTAL CREEK RD

SADDLE ROCK

EIGHTMILE PRAIRIE MOUNTAIN

CURRY COUNTY

OREGON

SUGARLOAF MOUNTAIN

SEE 140 MAP

5

MCKENZIE RD

GRASSY KNOB

SIXES

SIXES RIVER

RIVER

RD

POVERTY RIDGE

SILVER BUTTE

ELK

SISKIYOU

GRASSY

NATIONAL

MOON MOUNTAIN

CHINA PEAK

RUSTY BUTTE

6

AGATE BEACH

KLOOQUEH ROCK

FORT POINT

NELLIES COVE

NELLIES POINT

TICHENOR ROCK

PORT ORFORD

PORT ORFORD HWY

OREGON ST

OREGON

101

ELK

RIVER

ELK RIVER STATE FISH HATCHERY

CHINA MOUNTAIN

SISKIYOU RIVER

NATIONAL

FOREST

ANVIL MOUNTAIN

KNOB

WILDERNESS

FOREST

BUTLER BAR CAMPGROUND

METRO

7

ROCKY POINT

COAL POINT

COAST

HUMBUG MOUNTAIN HWY

STATE PARK

HUMBUG MOUNTAIN CAMPGROUND

HUMBUG MOUNTAIN

CHINA MOUNTAIN

NFD RD 20

NFD RD 5400

MCGRIBBLE CAMPGROUND

RD

FATHER MOUNTAIN

PANTHER CREEK CAMPGROUND

MILBURY MOUNTAIN

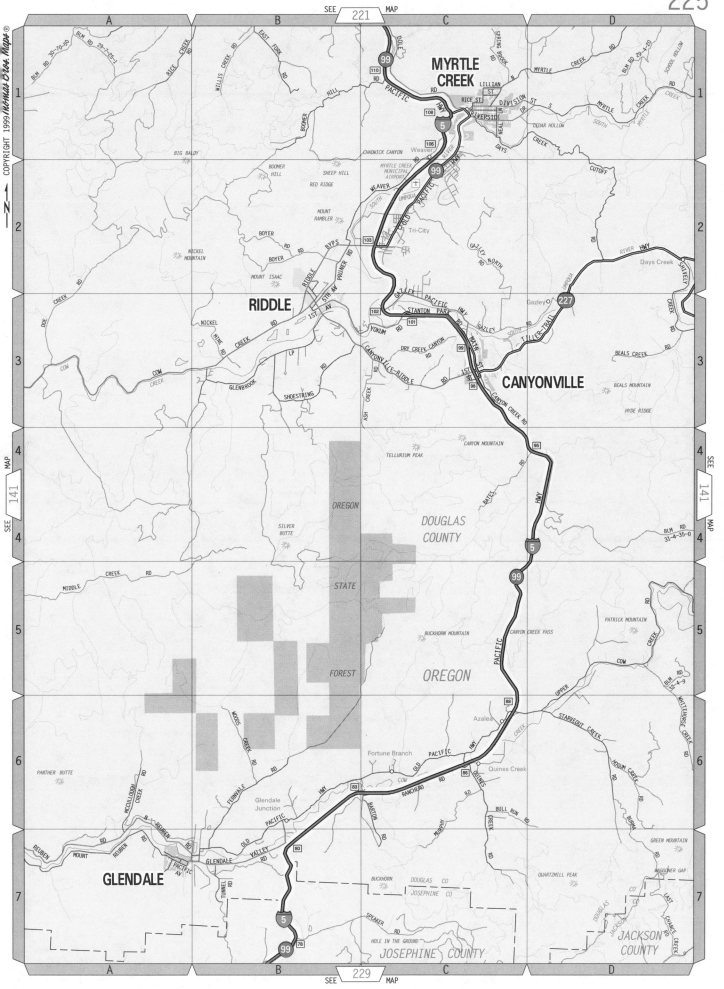

A   B   C   D

SEE MAP 221

PNW

METRO

SEE MAP 141

MYRTLE CREEK

RIDDLE

CANYONVILLE

DOUGLAS COUNTY

OREGON

STATE

FOREST

GLENDALE

JOSEPHINE COUNTY

JACKSON COUNTY

SEE MAP 229

PNW

METRO

—N—

| | A | B | C | D |

1

TILLER-SOUTH UMPQUA CAMP RD

SOUTH UMPQUA RIVER

SOUTH UMPQUA FALLS

ACKER ROCK

BUCKEYE CREEK RD

BUCKEYE CREEK

TWINBUCK SHELTER

DOUGLAS COUNTY

UMPQUA

BUCKEYE LAKE CAMPGROUND

ROGUE-UMPQUA

HIGHROCK MOUNTAIN

GRASSHOPPER MOUNTAIN

JACKASS MOUNTAIN

DIVIDE

WEAVER MOUNTAIN

HOLE IN THE GROUND

FISH MOUNTAIN

ALKALI CAMP

LEWIS CAMP

ROGUE

FOSTER CREEK RD

RIVER

2

TALLOW BUTTE

FIVESTICKS RD

JACKSON CREEK

JACKSON

NATIONAL

CLIFF LAKE CAMPGROUND

WILDERNESS

CREEK

ANDERSON MOUNTAIN

OREGON

HERSHBERGER MOUNTAIN

HERSHBERGER

RABBIT EARS

PRAIRIE CREEK RD

RD

NATIONAL

230

LAKE

COPELAND CREEK

3

COW HORN ARCH

COUGAR BUTTE

CREEK RD

SQUAW CREEK

ABBOTT BUTTE

FALCON BUTTE

ELEPHANT HEAD

ABBOTT

CREEK

NATURAL

RESEARCH

AREA

DOUGLAS CO.

JACKSON CO.

WOLF PEAK

MOUNT STELLA RD

MOUNT STELLA

DIAMOND RIVER

OLD BYBEE CREEK RD

BYBEE CREEK RD

DEER CREEK RD

CASTLE CREEK

CASTLE CREEK

WHISKEY CREEK

CRATER LAKE HWY

4

FOREST

WINDY GAP

NFD RD 950

HUCKLEBERRY GAP

NEAL SPRINGS CAMPGROUND

HUCKLEBERRY LAKE CAMPGROUND

QUARTZ MOUNTAIN

WHALEBACK

RD

RD

COLD SPRING

ROGUE

CREEK

NATURAL

RIVER

ABBOTT CREEK RD

SUNSHINE CREEK RD

KNOB HILL

NATURAL BRIDGE

RD

UNION CREEK CAMPGROUND

ROGUE GORGE VIEW POINT

★

Union Creek

62

NATURAL BRIDGE VIEW POINT

★

ROGUE

UNION CREEK

UNION CREEK RD

62

JACKSON COUNTY

HUCKLEBERRY RD

SEE 141 MAP

SEE 227 MAP

4 (lower)

BUTLER BUTTE

TUCKER GAP

SUGARPINE SHELTER

GREY ROCK

CAMP RD

TRIPOD

OLD

ABBOTT CREEK CAMPGROUND

ABBOTT CREEK RD

WOODRUFF

TAKEELMA GORGE

NATIONAL

LAKE LOOP RD

WEST HWY

MILL

5

GOODVIEW POINT

GREY

GRUB BOX GAP

BUCK BASIN

JIM CREEK SPUR

HOR CREEK

ROUND TOP

NEEDLE ROCKS

NEEDLE ROCK

NEEDLE

GRAVEL BUTTE

LICK ROCK

BUZZARD MINE RD

BUZZARD MINE RD

NEEDLE RIDGE

NEEDLE CREEK RD

ABBOTT CREEK RD

ELK CREEK

GINKGO

MILL CREEK

CREEK

UPPER TRAIL CREEK

ELK

RIDGE RD

MILL CREEK

GINKGO

6

ELKHORN RIDGE RD

TIMBER CREEK RD

MILLER MOUNTAIN

SUGAR PINE RD

MULE HILL

GREY RD

ELK CREEK RD

HIBBARD POINT

SANDOZ GAP

HALLS POINT

BALD MOUNTAIN

LARSON CREEK RD

GRAHAM CREEK RD

WHETSTONE POINT

RIVER BRIDGE CAMPGROUND

KITER CREEK

KITER CREEK SPUR

ROGUE RIVER

MILL CREEK CAMPGROUND

FOREST

RED BLANKET MOUNTAIN RD

7

ELK CREEK

ELK CREEK RD

BAILEY BUTTE

LODDES CREEK RD

BURNT PEAK

WILLITS RIDGE

ULRICH RD

CASCADE GORGE

FLOUNCE ROCK

TATOUCHE PEAK

WHITE POINT

SCHOOLMARM SPUR

CRATER

62

MILL CREEK DR

RED BLANKET RD

Prospect

MILL CREEK FALLS

BESSIE CREEK RD

RED CREEK

RED BLANKET CREEK

BLANKET RD

RED BLANKET RD

BESSIE CREEK RD

BUTTE FALLS-PROSPECT RD

MIDDLE FORK

ROGUE RIVER

PARKER MEADOWS RD

| | A | B | C | D |

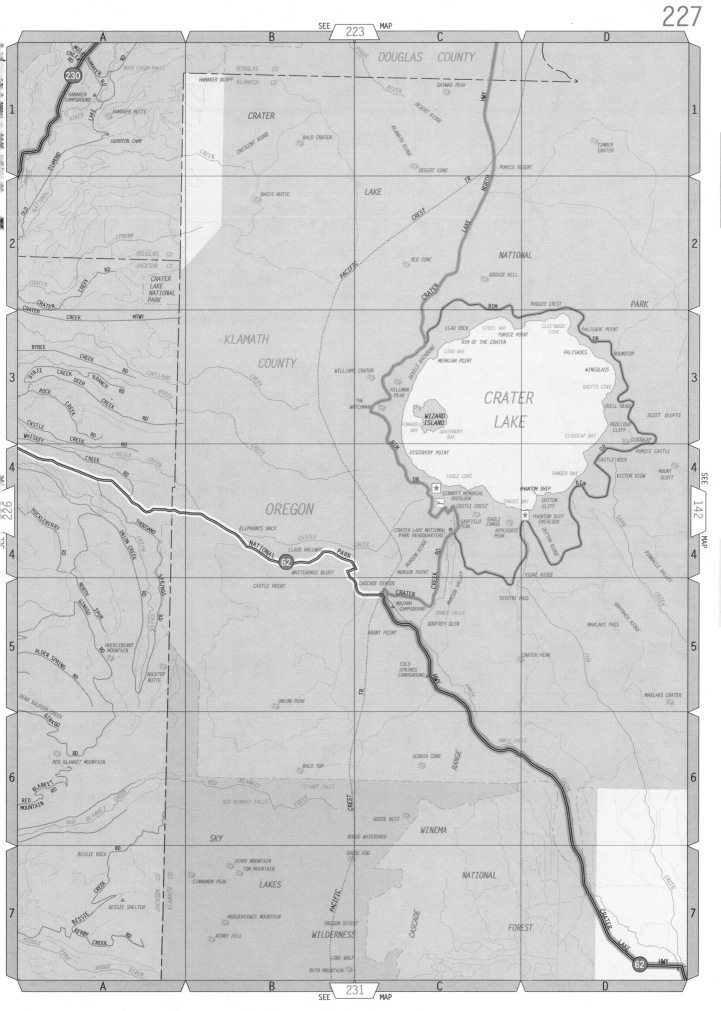

SEE 223 MAP

DOUGLAS COUNTY

A   B   C   D

PNW

METRO

SEE 226 MAP

SEE 142 MAP

HAMAKER BLUFF   DOUGLAS CO   KLAMATH CO

230

HAMAKER CAMPGROUND

HAMAKER RD   MUIR CREEK RD

MUIR CREEK FALLS

HAMAKER BUTTE

HURRYON CAMP

DIAMOND   LAKE   RIVER

OLD   NATIONAL

STREAM

DOUGLAS CO   JACKSON CO

CRATER LAKE NATIONAL PARK

CRATER CREEK RD

CRATER CREEK MTWY

BYBEE CREEK RD

BYBEE CREEK   DEER   BRANCH RD   BYBEE RD

ROCK   CREEK

COPELAND CREEK

CASTLE WHISKEY CREEK RD

CASTLE CREEK

HUCKLEBERRY RD

THOUSAND   UNION   SPRINGS   RD

NATIONAL

62

OREGON

ELEPHANTS BACK

CASTLE CREEK

LLAOS HALLWAY   PARK

WHITEHORSE BLUFF

CASTLE POINT

CASCADE DIVIDE

CRATER

MAZAMA CAMPGROUND

ARANT POINT

COLD SPRINGS CAMPGROUND

NORTH   GINKGO   SPUR

HUCKLEBERRY MOUNTAIN

ROCKTOP BUTTE

ALDER SPRING RD

DEAD SOLDIER CREEK   GINKGO

RED BLANKET MOUNTAIN

RD

BLANKET RD

RED MOUNTAIN

RED   BLANKET   CREEK

RED BLANKET FALLS

SKY

BESSIE ROCK RD

JERRY MOUNTAIN   TOM MOUNTAIN

CINNAMON PEAK

LAKES

JACKSON CO   KLAMATH CO

BESSIE CREEK

BESSIE SHELTER

BESSIE KERBY CREEK RD

MIDDLE FORK   ROGUE RIVER

MUDJEKEEWIS MOUNTAIN

KERBY HILL

WILDERNESS

CRATER

KLAMATH COUNTY

WILLIAMS CRATER

THE WATCHMAN

HILLMAN PEAK

DEVILS BACKBONE

LLAO ROCK   STEEL BAY   PUMICE POINT

RIM OF THE CRATER

LIDO BAY

MERRIAM POINT

FUMAROLE BAY

WIZARD ISLAND

GOVERNORS BAY

CLEETWOOD COVE

RIM

RUGGED CREST

PALISADE POINT

DR

PALISADES

ROUNDTOP

WINEGLASS

GROTTO COVE

SKELL HEAD

SCOTT BLUFFS

REDCLOUD CLIFF

CLOUDCAP

CLOUDCAP BAY

CRATER LAKE

DISCOVERY POINT

RIM DR

EAGLE COVE

SINNOTT MEMORIAL OVERLOOK ★

CASTLE CREST

CRATER LAKE NATIONAL PARK HEADQUARTERS

GARFIELD PEAK

EAGLE CRAGS

APPLEGATE PEAK

CHASKI BAY

DANGER BAY

PHANTOM SHIP

DUTTON CLIFF

PHANTOM SHIP OVERLOOK ★

CASTLE ROCK

PUMICE CASTLE

VICTOR VIEW

MOUNT SCOTT

RIM DR

DUTTON RIDGE

VIDAE RIDGE

MUNSON RIDGE

CREEK RD

MUNSON VALLEY

MUNSON POINT

DUMEE FALLS

GODFREY GLEN

TUTUTNI PASS

MAKLAKS PASS

GRAYBACK RIDGE

PINNACLE VALLEY

SUN CREEK

UNION PEAK

BALD TOP

STUART FALLS

SCORIA CONE

CRATER PEAK

MAKLAKS CRATER

RANGE

ANNIE FALLS

ANNIE

WINEMA

GOOSE NEST

ROGUE WATERSHED

GOOSE EGG

NATIONAL

CASCADE

FOREST

CRATER LAKE HWY

62

LONE WOLF

RUTH MOUNTAIN

GAYWAS PEAK

DESERT RIDGE

KLAMATH RIDGE

DESERT CONE

PUMICE DESERT

TIMBER CRATER

RED CONE

GROUSE HILL

PACIFIC   CREST   CRATER   LAKE   NORTH   TR   HWY

PACIFIC   CREST   TR

OASIS BUTTE

BALD CRATER

CRESCENT RIDGE

ROGUE RIVER

DOUGLAS CO   KLAMATH CO

1   2   3   4   5   6   7

SEE 231 MAP

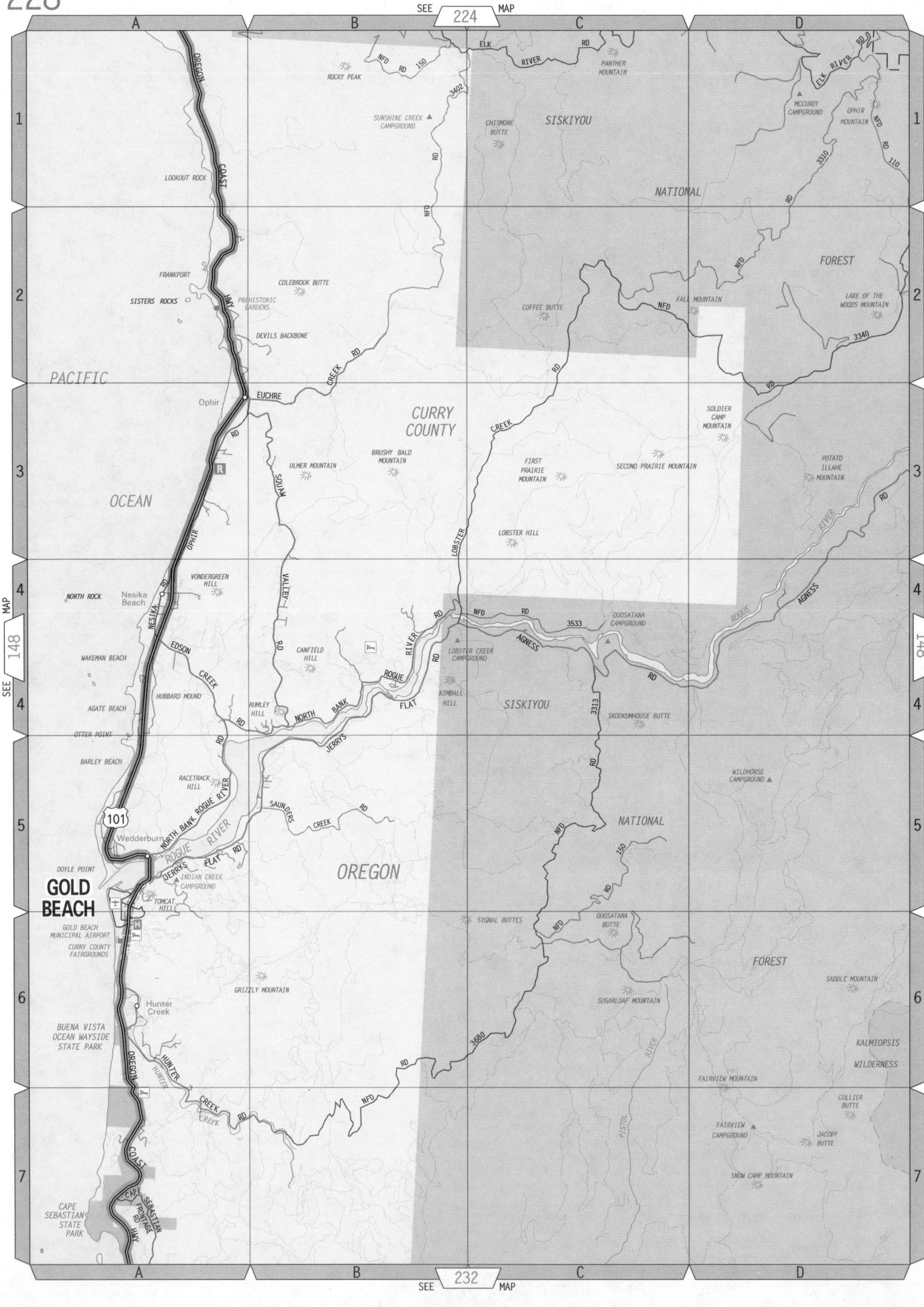

SEE 224 MAP

PNW

METRO

A B C D

ELK RIVER RD

RD

ROCKY PEAK

NFD RD 150

ELK RIVER RD

PANTHER MOUNTAIN

SISKIYOU

McCURDY CAMPGROUND

OPHIR MOUNTAIN

3402

SUNSHINE CREEK CAMPGROUND

CHISMORE BUTTE

NFD RD 110

RD 3310

LOOKOUT ROCK

COAST

OREGON

HWY

NATIONAL

FOREST

FRANKPORT

SISTERS ROCKS

COLEBROOK BUTTE

PREHISTORIC GARDENS

RD

COFFEE BUTTE

NFD

FALL MOUNTAIN

LAKE OF THE WOODS MOUNTAIN

3340

DEVILS BACKBONE

CREEK RD

PACIFIC

Ophir

EUCHRE

CURRY COUNTY

CREEK

SOLDIER CAMP MOUNTAIN

RD

RD

OCEAN

RD

SOUAM

ULMER MOUNTAIN

BRUSHY BALD MOUNTAIN

FIRST PRAIRIE MOUNTAIN

SECOND PRAIRIE MOUNTAIN

POTATO ILLAHE MOUNTAIN

OPHIR

LOBSTER

RIVER

LOBSTER HILL

RD

SEE 148 MAP

NORTH ROCK

Nesika Beach

VONDERGREEN HILL

VALLEY

RD

RD

NFD RD

3533

QUOSATANA CAMPGROUND

AGNESS

RIVER

ROGUE

NESIKA

EDSON

CREEK

CANFIELD HILL

RIVER

LOBSTER CREEK CAMPGROUND

AGNESS

RD

WAKEMAN BEACH

RD

ROGUE

FLAT

AGNESS RD

SISKIYOU

3313

148

AGATE BEACH

HUBBARD MOUND

RUMLEY HILL

NORTH BANK

KIMBALL HILL

SKOOKUMHOUSE BUTTE

OTTER POINT

RD

JERRYS

BARLEY BEACH

RACETRACK HILL

NORTH BANK ROGUE RIVER

SAUNDERS

CREEK

RD

OREGON

NFD

RD

NATIONAL

WILDHORSE CAMPGROUND

101

Wedderburn

ROGUE RIVER

FLAT RD

RD

150

DOYLE POINT

JERRYS

INDIAN CREEK CAMPGROUND

GOLD BEACH

TOMCAT HILL

SIGNAL BUTTES

NFD

QUOSATANA BUTTE

GOLD BEACH MUNICIPAL AIRPORT

CURRY COUNTY FAIRGROUNDS

GRIZZLY MOUNTAIN

SUGARLOAF MOUNTAIN

FOREST

SADDLE MOUNTAIN

BUENA VISTA OCEAN WAYSIDE STATE PARK

Hunter Creek

RIVER

KALMIOPSIS WILDERNESS

OREGON

HUNTER

3680

NFD RD

PISTOL

FAIRVIEW MOUNTAIN

COLLIER BUTTE

COAST

HUNTER

CREEK RD

CREEK

FAIRVIEW CAMPGROUND

JACOBY BUTTE

HWY

CAPE SEBASTIAN STATE PARK

CAPE SEBASTIAN FRONTAGE HWY

SNOW CAMP MOUNTAIN

SEE 232 MAP

A B C D

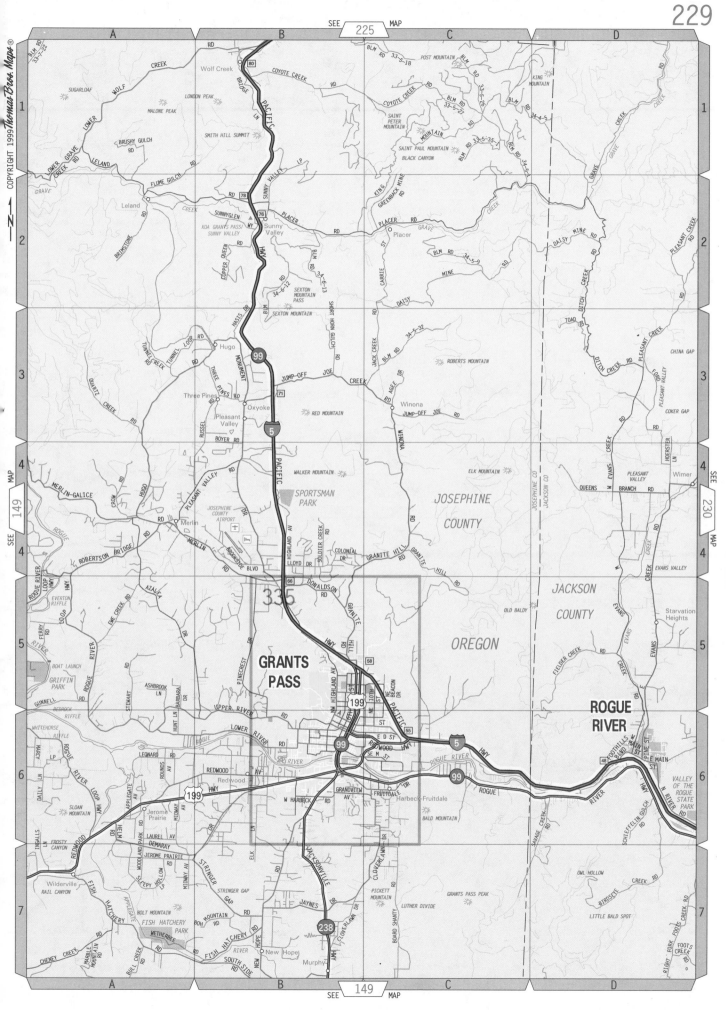

—N—

A   B   C   D

PNW

METRO

SUGARLOAF

WOLF   CREEK

LOWER   GRAVE   CREEK   RD

LELAND

GRAVE

BRIMSTONE

MALONE PEAK

LONDON PEAK

BRUSHY GULCH   RD

LELAND

FLUME GULCH

Leland

SMITH HILL SUMMIT

Wolf Creek

80

COYOTE CREEK

BRIDGE   LN

PACIFIC   HWY   99

COYOTE CREEK   RD

POST MOUNTAIN

BLM RD   33-5-18

BLM RD   33-5-26

KING MOUNTAIN

COYOTE CREEK

SAINT PETER MOUNTAIN

SAINT PAUL MOUNTAIN

BLACK CANYON

MOUNTAIN

BLM RD   33-5-35

BLM RD   34-4-1

BLM   33-7-22

GRAVE   CREEK   RD

1

SUNNY VALLEY   LP

SUNNYGLEN   76

KOA GRANTS PASS/   SUNNY VALLEY

HWY   75

Sunny Valley

PLACER

PLACER   RD

KING   ST

CARRIE   ST

GRAVE   CREEK   RD

Placer

DAISY   MINE   RD

PLEASANT CREEK   RD

2

COPPER QUEEN   RD

BLM RD   34-6-12

SEXTON MOUNTAIN PASS

SEXTON MOUNTAIN

BLM RD   34-6-13

SHORT HORN GULCH

JACK CREEK   RD

BLM RD   34-5-9

BLM RD   34-5-32

DAISY   ST

ROBERTS MOUNTAIN

MINE

DITCH CREEK   RD

TOAD   RD

CHINA GAP

3

Hugo

MONUMENT   DR

71

Oxyoke

JUMP-OFF   JOE   CREEK

RED MOUNTAIN

Winona

WINONA   RD

JUMP-OFF JOE   RD

AGEE   DR

DITCH CREEK

PLEASANT VALLEY RD

COKER GAP

TUNNEL   ROCK   TUNNEL   LOOP   RD

THREE PINES   RD

Three Pines

QUARTZ   CREEK   RD

RUSSEL   RD

PLEASANT VALLEY   RD

Pleasant Valley

BOYER   RD

99

5

PACIFIC   HWY

WALKER MOUNTAIN

ELK MOUNTAIN

HOERSTER   LN

4

SEE 149 MAP

MERLIN-GALICE   RD

CROW   RD

HUGO   RD

Merlin

MERLIN   RD

JOSEPHINE COUNTY AIRPORT

SPORTSMAN PARK

JOSEPHINE   CO   JACKSON   CO

JOSEPHINE COUNTY

Wimer

PLEASANT VALLEY

W EVANS   BRANCH   RD

QUEENS   RD

SEE 230 MAP

ROBERTSON BRIDGE   RD

ROGUE   RIVER

BROOKSIDE   BLVD

HIGHLAND   AV

LLOYD   DR

SOLDIER CREEK   RD

COLONIAL   DR

GRANITE HILL   RD

GRANITE   HILL   RD

EVANS VALLEY   RD

5

ROGUE   RIVER   LOOP   HWY

EVERTON RIFFLE

EWE CREEK   RD

AZALEA   DR

66

335

DONALDSON   RD

GRANITE   HILL   HWY

OLD BALDY

JACKSON COUNTY

OREGON

Starvation Heights

EVANS   CREEK   RD

FERRY   RD

GRIFFIN PARK

BOAT LAUNCH

RIVER

ROGUE   RIVER   RD

ASHBROOK   LN

STEWART   RD

BARBARA   DR

PINECREST   DR

GRANTS PASS

HIGHLAND   AV

NW   HIGHLAND   AV

58

NE BEACON   DR

PACIFIC   HWY

FIELDER CREEK   RD

EVANS   CREEK   RD

6

GUNNELL   RD

BEDROCK   RIFFLE

WHITEHORSE   RIFFLE

MABY   LP

ROGUE   RIVER   LOOP   HWY

LEONARD   RD

ROUNDS   AV

HUNT   LN

LOWER   RIVER   RD

UPPER   RIVER   RD

199

REDWOOD   AV

6TH   ST

5TH   ST

199

E D ST

NE M   ST

SE M   ST

REDWOOD   HWY

55

ROGUE RIVER   HWY

ROGUE   RIVER

5

99

ROGUE RIVER

W   MAIN   ST

PINE   ST

E MAIN   ST

FOOTHILLS   BLVD

48

ROGUE RIVER

DAILY   LP

SLOAN MOUNTAIN

REDWOOD   HWY

APPLEGATE   RD

Jerome Prairie

WOODLAND PARK   RD

MIDWAY   RD

LAUREL   AV

DEMARAY   DR

JEROME PRAIRIE

MIDWAY   AV

STRINGER   GAP   RD

ELK   LN

REDWOOD   AV

Redwood

W HARBECK   RD

GRANDVIEW   AV

FRUITDALE   DR

Harbeck-Fruitdale

CLOVERLAWN   DR

BALD MOUNTAIN

VALLEY OF THE ROGUE STATE PARK

SAVAGE   CREEK   RD

N RIVER   RD

SCHLEFFELIN GULCH   RD

7

INGALLS   LN

Wilderville

FROSTY CANYON

RAIL CANYON

FISH HATCHERY   RD

HELM   RD

SLEEPY HOLLOW   RD

BOLT MOUNTAIN   RD

FISH HATCHERY PARK

WETHERBEE   RD

MOUNTAIN   RD   BOH

JAYNES   DR

238

JACKSONVILLE   RD

PICKETT MOUNTAIN

BOARD SHANTY   RD

LUTHER DIVIDE

GRANTS PASS PEAK

OWL HOLLOW   CREEK   RD

BIRDSEYE   CREEK   RD

LITTLE BALD SPOT

FOOTS   CREEK   RD

RIGHT FORK   FOOTS   CREEK   RD

CHENEY CREEK   RD

MARBLE MOUNTAIN   RD

BULL   RD

APPLEGATE   RIVER   RD

FISH HATCHERY   RD

SOUTH SIDE   RD

NEW   HOPE   RD

New Hope

Murphy

HWY   AMH

7

A   B   C   D

PNW

METRO

SEE MAP 141

A   B   C   D

1

2

3

4

4

5

6

7

SEE MAP 229

SEE MAP 149

SHADY COVE

JACKSON COUNTY

OREGON

EAGLE POINT

GOLD HILL

CENTRAL POINT

MEDFORD

336

—N—

WHITE ROCK MOUNTAIN

PEAVINE RIDGE

HORSE MOUNTAIN

ROUND TOP RD

MISTY

CLEVELAND RIDGE

WILLY ROCK

WILLY MOUNTAIN

TILLER-TRAIL HWY

227

ROGUE NATIONAL RIVER FOREST

Trail

BATTLE MOUNTAIN

LITTLE BATTLE MOUNTAIN

BATTLE CREEK

BEAR WALLOW

BOARD MOUNTAIN

FRY PEAK

SPIGNET BUTTE

BOSWELL MOUNTAIN

BLACK BUTTE

MILL HOLLOW

SAWYER RD

SMASE CREEK

BALD MOUNTAIN

LUCKY HOLLOW CREEK

EVANS

FANN CREEK RD

FALSE FACE MOUNTAIN

HULL MOUNTAIN

RAMSEY CANYON

CINNABAR MOUNTAIN

MEADOWS

62

LOVER PEAK

MAPLE GULCH RD

NEATHAMMER GULCH

EVANS CREEK

BRATON HOLLOW

ELKHORN BUTTE

CHIMNEY ROCK BUTTE

JONES RD

DEBENGER GAP

IRONWOOD DR

LEAFWOOD DR

HAMMELL

MURPHY GULCH RD

McCONVILLE PEAK

TURTLE ROCK

NEIL ROCK

EAGLE DR

BEAGLE RD

MOSSER MOUNTAIN

BUTTE FALLS

HILLIS PEAK

SARDINE MOUNTAIN

RAMSEY

BALL RD

SARDINE

RIGHT FORK

DODGE RD

234

GLASS LN

WILCOX PEAK

THE OREGON VORTEX & HOUSE OF MYSTERY

PERRY RD

RATTLESNAKE RAPIDS

LONG MOUNTAIN

SAMS VALLEY

OLD SAMS VALLEY RD

UPPER TABLE ROCK

LYMAN MOUNTAIN

DILLON FALLS

VALLEY

TRESHAM LN

TABLE ROCK TRAIL RD

WHEELER RD

W LINN RD

EAGLE POINT

BOXLAN

JOHN DAY DR

HARDY RIFFLE

S SHASTA AV N

NICK

YOUNG

ALTA VISTA

99

234

GOLD HILL

4TH AV

OLD STAGE RD

KOA MEDFORD/ GOLD HILL

GOLD HILL

LOWER TABLE ROCK

Table Rock

AGATE

62

43

BLACKWELL HILL

GOLD RAY

TOU VELLE STATE PARK

White City

BROWN

BIGHAM

45

40

PACIFIC

BLACKWELL RD

KIRTLAND RD

AGATE DESERT

ANTELOPE

ANTELOPE

140

5

BEAR CREEK

NEWLAND RD

LAKE OF THE WOODS HWY

KERSHAM

ROUGH & RUGGED RD

OLD

SCENIC

STAGE

TOLO RD

CRATER ROCK MUSEUM

Seven Oaks

GIBBON RD

Midway

E GREGORY

COREY

CRATER LAKE HWY

VILAS

McLAUGHLIN

FOOTS CREEK

KANE CREEK

MILLPOND CAMPGROUND

OLD STAGE

99

CENTRAL POINT

TAYLOR

W PINE ST

Four Corners

COKER BUTTE

FOOTHILL

LEFT FORK FOOTS CREEK

MIDDLE FORK FOOTS CREEK RD

BEALL LN

BEALL

FREEMAN

TABLE ROCK RD

MEDFORD

62

DELTA WATERS RD

SEE MAP 234

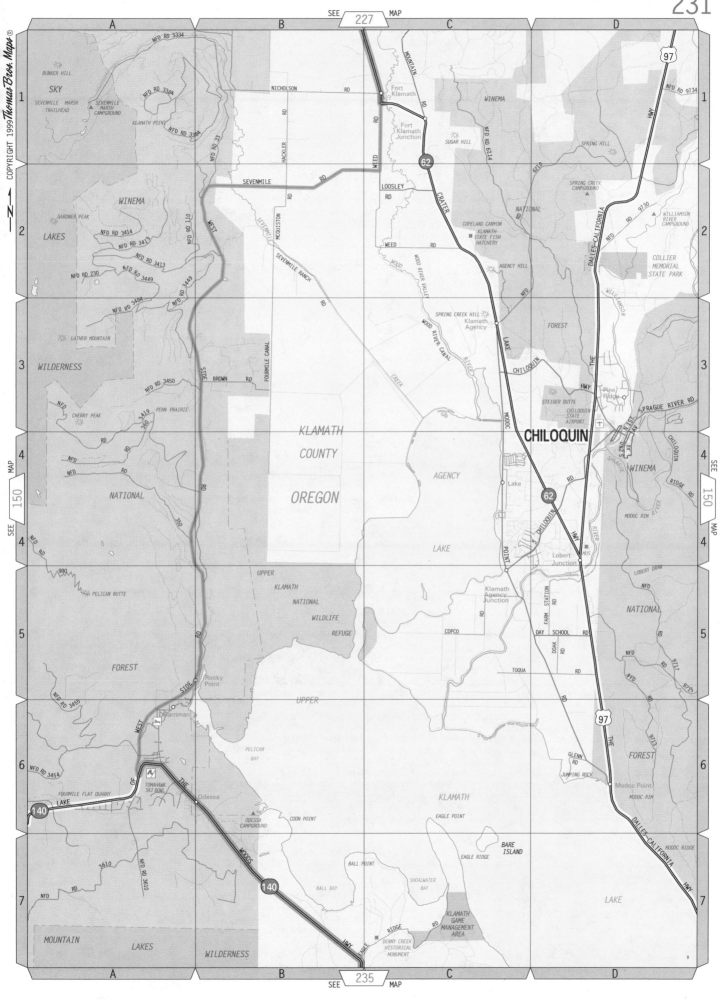

PNW

METRO

SEE 227 MAP

SEE MAP 150

SEE 150 MAP

SEE 235 MAP

CHILOQUIN

KLAMATH COUNTY

OREGON

WINEMA

LAKES

WILDERNESS

NATIONAL

FOREST

SKY

MOUNTAIN LAKES WILDERNESS

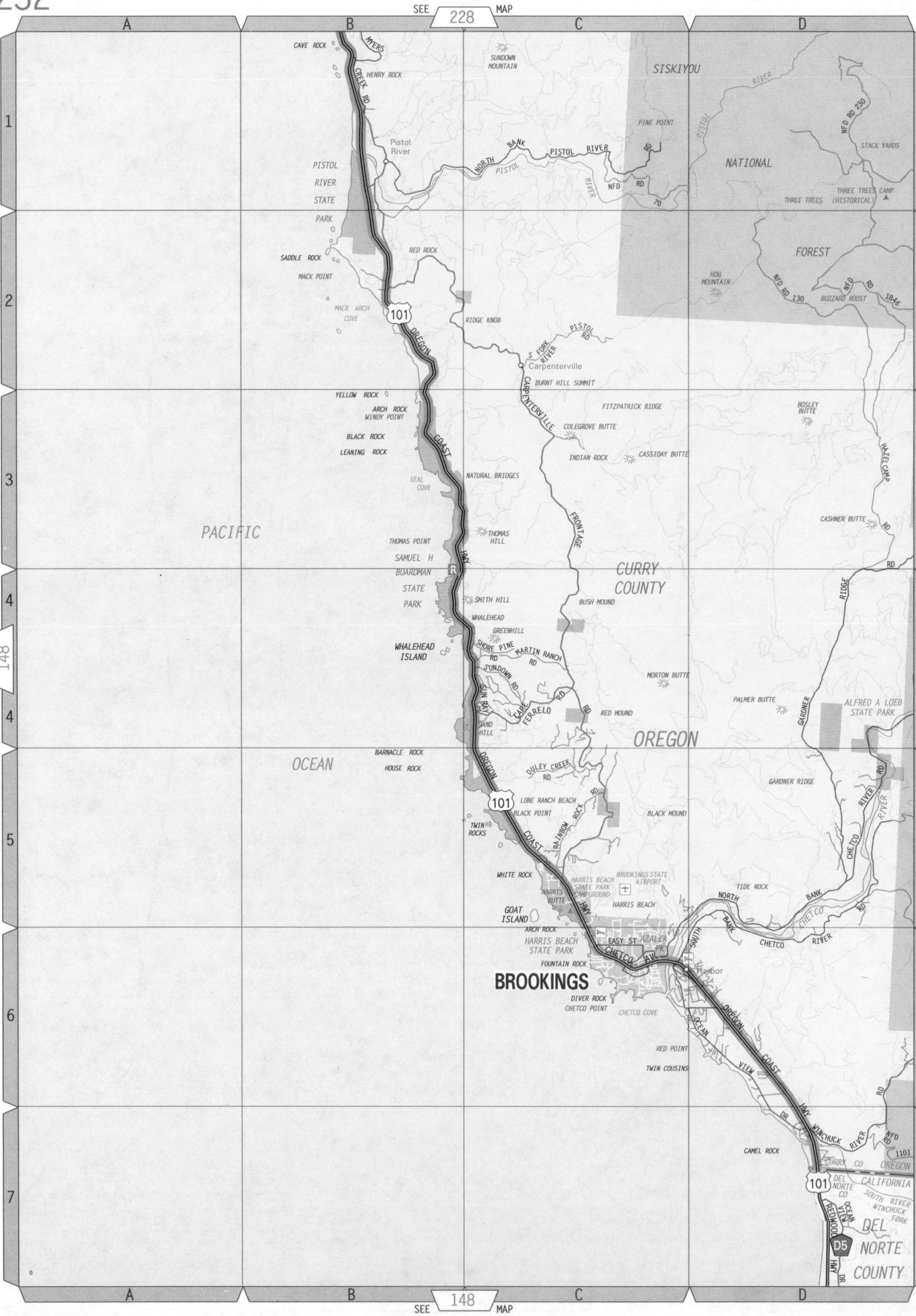

A   B   C   D

PNW

METRO

COPYRIGHT 1999 Thomas Bros. Maps ®

—N—

CAVE ROCK
MYERS
HENRY ROCK
CREEK RD

SUNDOWN MOUNTAIN

SISKIYOU

RIVER

PINE POINT

NFD RD 230

STACK YARDS

Pistol River
PISTOL RIVER STATE PARK

NORTH
PISTOL RIVER
BANK
PISTOL RIVER
NFD RD
70
RIVER
NFD

NATIONAL

THREE TREES CAMP (HISTORICAL)
THREE TREES

SADDLE ROCK
MACK POINT
RED ROCK

FOREST

HOG MOUNTAIN
NFD RD 130
BUZZARD ROOST
NFD RD 1846

MACK ARCH COVE

101

RIDGE KNOB

S FORK PISTOL RIVER
PISTOL RD
Carpenterville
BURNT HILL SUMMIT

FITZPATRICK RIDGE

BOSLEY BUTTE

YELLOW ROCK
ARCH ROCK
WINDY POINT
BLACK ROCK
LEANING ROCK

OREGON

COLEGROVE BUTTE
CASSIDAY BUTTE
INDIAN ROCK

CASHNER BUTTE
RD

SEAL COVE
NATURAL BRIDGES

CARPENTERVILLE

COAST

HAZEL CAMP

PACIFIC

THOMAS POINT
THOMAS HILL

SAMUEL H BOARDMAN STATE PARK

HWY

CURRY COUNTY

FRONTAGE

RIDGE

SMITH HILL
WHALEHEAD
GREENHILL
SHORE PINE RD
MARTIN RANCH RD
SUNDOWN RD

BUSH MOUND

MORTON BUTTE

ALFRED A LOEB STATE PARK

WHALEHEAD ISLAND

CAPE FERRELO
SAND HILL
RD

PALMER BUTTE

GARDNER

OREGON

RED MOUND

BARNACLE ROCK
HOUSE ROCK

OCEAN

OREGON

DULEY CREEK RD
LONE RANCH BEACH
BLACK POINT

RAINBOW ROCK RD

GARDNER RIDGE

CHETCO RIVER RD

RIVER

BLACK MOUND

101

TWIN ROCKS

COAST

WHITE ROCK

HARRIS BUTTE

GOAT ISLAND
ARCH ROCK
HARRIS BEACH STATE PARK
FOUNTAIN ROCK

HARRIS BEACH CAMPGROUND
HARRIS BEACH STATE PARK
AIRPORT
BROOKINGS STATE
HARRIS BEACH

EASY ST
AZALEA
CHETCO FWY

TIDE ROCK
NORTH
BANK
CHETCO
CHETCO RIVER
SOUTH BANK

BROOKINGS

DIVER ROCK
CHETCO POINT
CHETCO COVE
Harbor

OREGON

RED POINT
TWIN COUSINS

OCEAN VIEW
COAST HWY

CAMEL ROCK

OCEAN VIEW DR
WINCHUCK RIVER RD
NFD RD
1101

CURRY CO
DEL NORTE CO
OREGON
CALIFORNIA

101

SOUTH RIVER
WINCHUCK FORK

REDWOOD HWY
OCEAN VIEW DR

D5

DEL NORTE COUNTY

SEE 148 MAP

SEE 148 MAP

A   B   C   D

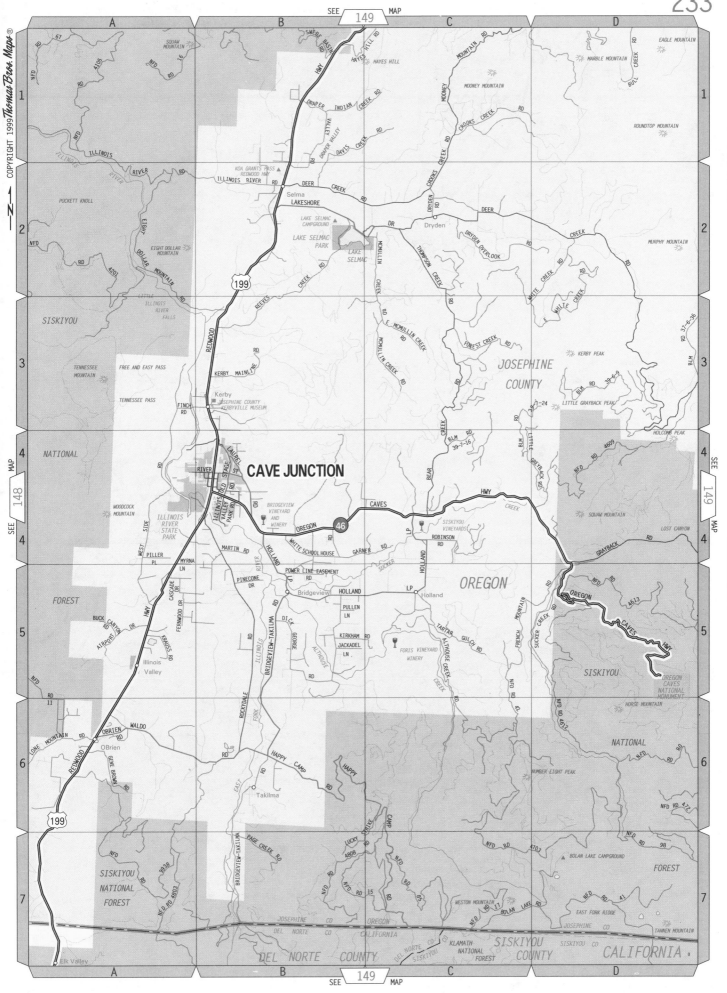

—N→

PNW

METRO

SEE 148 MAP

SEE 149 MAP

A   B   C   D

1

2

3

4

5

6

7

SISKIYOU

NATIONAL

FOREST

CAVE JUNCTION

199

JOSEPHINE
COUNTY

OREGON

SISKIYOU

NATIONAL

FOREST

Kerby
Josephine County
Kerbyville Museum

Bridgeview

Holland

Dryden

Illinois
Valley

OBRIEN
O'Brien

Takilma

199

JOSEPHINE CO
DEL NORTE CO

OREGON
CALIFORNIA

JOSEPHINE CO
SISKIYOU CO

DEL NORTE COUNTY

KLAMATH
NATIONAL
FOREST

SISKIYOU COUNTY   CALIFORNIA

A   B   C   D

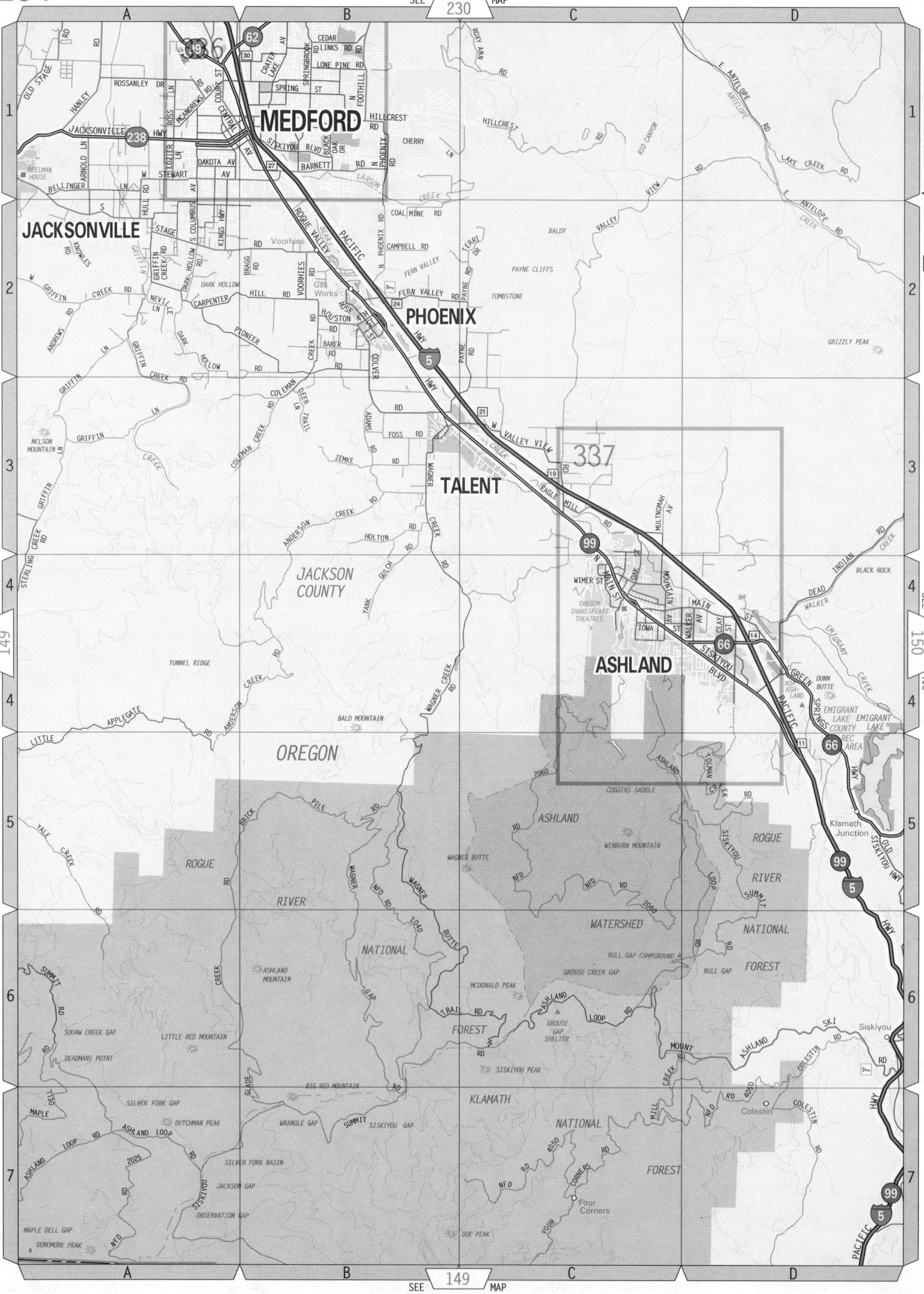

PNW

METRO

COPYRIGHT 1999 Thomas Bros. Maps®

—N—→

SEE 230 MAP

A   B   C   D

MEDFORD

JACKSONVILLE

PHOENIX

TALENT

337

ASHLAND

Oregon Shakespeare Theatres

JACKSON COUNTY

OREGON

ROGUE RIVER NATIONAL FOREST

KLAMATH NATIONAL FOREST

ASHLAND WATERSHED

ROGUE RIVER NATIONAL FOREST

SEE 149 MAP

SEE 150 MAP

Emigrant Lake

Klamath Junction

Siskiyou

Colestin

Four Corners

SEE 149 MAP

A   B   C   D

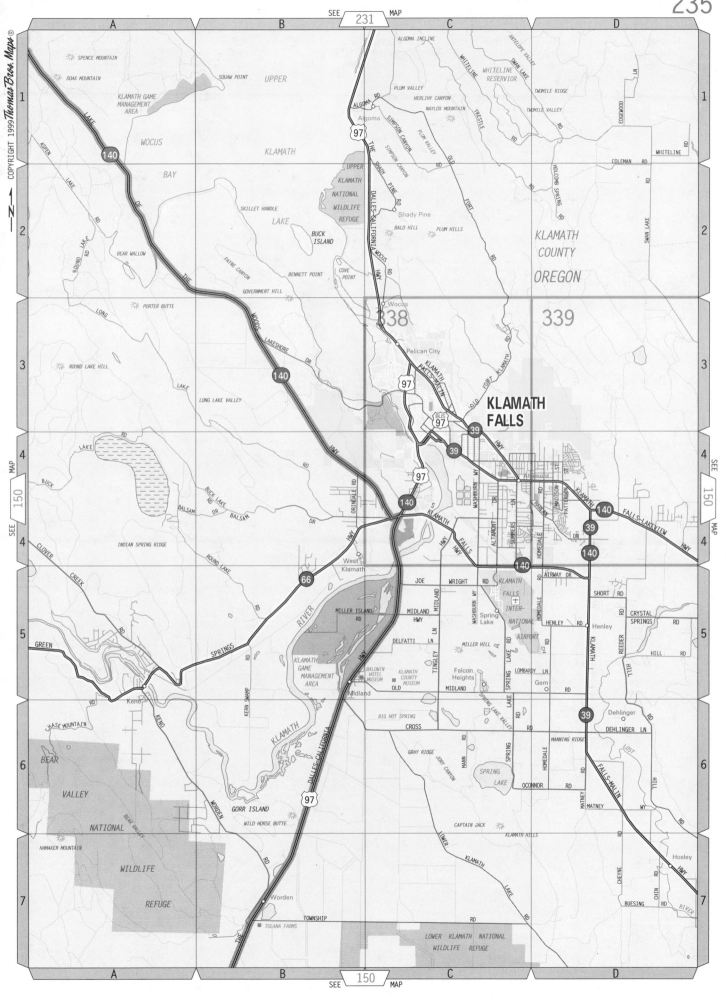

SEE MAP 231

SEE 150 MAP

SEE 150 MAP

PNW

METRO

PNW

METRO

SEE 112 MAP

COPYRIGHT 1999 *Thomas Bros. Maps* ® —N—

A **B** **C** **D**

1

RAMONA PARK CAMPGROUND

WENATCHEE

Hollywood Beach

SLIDE RIDGE
Shrine Beach

SLIDE PEAK

NATIONAL

FIRST CREEK

FOREST

WASHINGTON

FOREST MOUNTAIN

GOMAN PEAK

OKLAHOMA GULCH

PALMICH CANYON

SWITCHBACK CANYON

BYRD CANYON

RIBBON MESA

EARTHQUAKE POINT

BYERS CANYON

MCKINSTRY CANYON

DICK MESA

CRUM CANYON

HANAN CANYON

SAUNDERS CANYON

KEYSTONE POINT

WENATCHEE
NATIONAL
FOREST

MILLS CANYON

PETERS POINT

MCLEISH CANYON

MOODY CANYON

SPENCER CANYON

SPENCER LAKE

ENTIAT RIVER

ENTIAT

Orondo

ALT 97

97

2

LAKESHORE

LOWER JOE CREEK
UPPER JOE CREEK
JOE CREEK
GRADE CREEK

WAPATO LAKE

ROSES LAKE

DRY LAKE
GREEN LAKE

WASHINGTON ST

MANSON BLVD

WILLOW POINT

WAPATO WY
Manson
150

CHELAN-STEHEKIN FERRY

WAPATO POINT

IVAN MORSE RD

COOLEY RD

WINESAP AV

NORTHSHORE RD

SWANSON GULCH

COOPER MOUNTAIN

NFD RD 8020

PURTTEMAN GULCH

NFD RD 8020

ECHO VALLEY SKI AREA

WENATCHEE

NATIONAL

FOREST

CHELAN CO

HIGHLAND BENCH

ANTOINE CREEK

BROWNFIELD CANYON

BIGELOW CANYON

APPLE ACRES

HOWARD

FLAT

CHELAN MUNICIPAL AIRPORT

DEER MOUNTAIN

97

CHELAN COUNTY

UNION VALLEY LOOP

ROGERS AND RD HOBSON

BOYD RD

UNION VALLEY

CHELAN

LAKE

S LAKESHORE

BEAR MOUNTAIN

NFD RD

BEAR MOUNTAIN

MONREY RD

MINNEAPOLIS BEACH

SPADERS BAY

150

GIBSON ST

WOODIN AV

Lakeside

CHELAN

CHELAN BUTTE RD

DOWNEY GULCH

DAYBREAK CANYON

CHELAN BUTTE

CHELAN FALLS

CHELAN STATE FISH HATCHERY

WASHINGTON AV

FARNHAM CANYON

BEEBE

MCNEIL CANYON RD

DOUGLAS CO

CHELAN CO

JACKSON CANYON

HIGH RIM

ROCKY

OLMSTEAD RD NW

CHELAN HILL

10

NAVARRE COULEE RD

NAVARRE

971

FLYER CANYON

8550

KNAPP COULEE

DOWNEY GULCH RD

STAYMAN RD

ALT 97

DOUGLAS CO

HOMESTEAD CANYON

CHELAN BUTTE

GREENS CANYON

COLUMBIA RIVER

97

BIG BENCH

DOUGLAS COUNTY

BARBER RD NW

8 RD NW

7 3/4 RD NW

7 1/2

97

BRAYS RD NW

HIGGINS LOOP RD NW

BROWNS CANYON

BROWNS

BRAYS

CANYON RD

PORTER RD

NELS NELSON RD NW

JONES RD

ROCK

8 1/2 RD NW

7 1/2 RD NW

7 RD NW

5 RD NW

LAMOINE

JOHN LONG RD NW

SLUSSER

LUDEMAN

GIBSON

PIERCE

7 RD NW

PORTER

HARDIN RD

NORTH

CARLOCK

CLOSE

PINE CANYON

2

CORBALEY CANYON

2

STANDPIPE HILL

WATERVILLE

DOUGLAS COUNTY HISTORICAL MUSEUM

BARNES

BALLARD

GOLL

TOLER

2

Douglas

PLANETZ CANYON

WESTMINS CANYON

BASELINE

3 RD NW

U 1/2 RD NW

2 1/4 RD NW

1 1/2 RD NW

1

A **B** **C** **D**

SEE 239 MAP

SEE 112 MAP

150

150 WY

97

ALT 97

97

150

97

PNW

METRO

N

A   B   SEE 105 MAP   C   D

SEE 105 MAP

BALLOON ROCK
TREFRY RD
STRAHL
REY
NE
RD
MCINTOSH
Y
DEL RIO
RD E
Y 1/2 RD NE
REY
PARKS RD
LAKE RD
SMITHS
WILSON BUTTE
RD

BELVEDERE RD
RIVER
OKANOGAN
DOUGLAS
COLUMBIA RIVER
155
COLVILLE
MCGINNIS LAKE RD
BUFFALO LAKE ACCESS RD
LAKE RD
PETER
BUFFALO LAKE RD S
MCGINNIS LAKE
INDIAN
OKANOGAN COUNTY
RESERVATION
PETER DAM CREEK
DAM
RD

PENDALL
RD
BARRY
RD
BARKER

ELMER CITY
Lone Pine
REX
155

WALLACE CANYON
174
FIDDLE BUTTE
CROWN POINT VIEW POINT
174
155
COULEE DAM
GRAND COULEE DAM
MARINA WY
FRANKLIN D ROOSEVELT LAKE
OKANOGAN CO
LINCOLN CO
COLUMBIA RIVER
SAND HILL

174

STEAMBOAT BUTTE
CANYON
BARKER CANYON
DOUGLAS CO
GRANT CO
RD
F ST
GRAND COULEE
155
ALCAN RD
Delano Heights
GIBBS BAY
SPRING CANYON CAMPGROUND
COULEE DAM NATIONAL RECREATION AREA
174

DOUGLAS COUNTY
BARKER
CACHE BUTTE
BARKER BUTTE
AIRPORT RD
GRAND COULEE DAM AIRPORT
CROOKS
OSBORN BAY LAKE
ELECTRIC CITY
GRAND COULEE RD
WILBUR
OLD COULEE RD

SEE 113 MAP

BANKS
EAGLE ROCK
CASTLE ROCK
R
BOAT LAUNCH
RANGER STA
NORTHRUP CANYON
NORTHRUP
HWY
OLD COULEE RD
BAGDAD RD
Bagdad Junction
SEE 113 MAP

STEAMBOAT ROCK STATE PARK
STEAMBOAT ROCK
DEVILS
PUNCH BOWL
LAKE
MARTIN FALLS
WHITNEY CANYON
GRANT COUNTY
KLOBUSCHAR DRAW
RD W-NE
RD
GRANT CO
LINCOLN CO
LINCOLN COUNTY
JACK WOODS BUTTE
GRAND COULEE HWY

WASHINGTON
HAWKS
CLIFF RD NE
RD T-2 NE
RD 52-NE
RD
V-NE
RD 51-NE
50-NE
RD U-NE
RD
RD W-NE
RD X-NE
RD 50-NE
RD
RD 49-NE

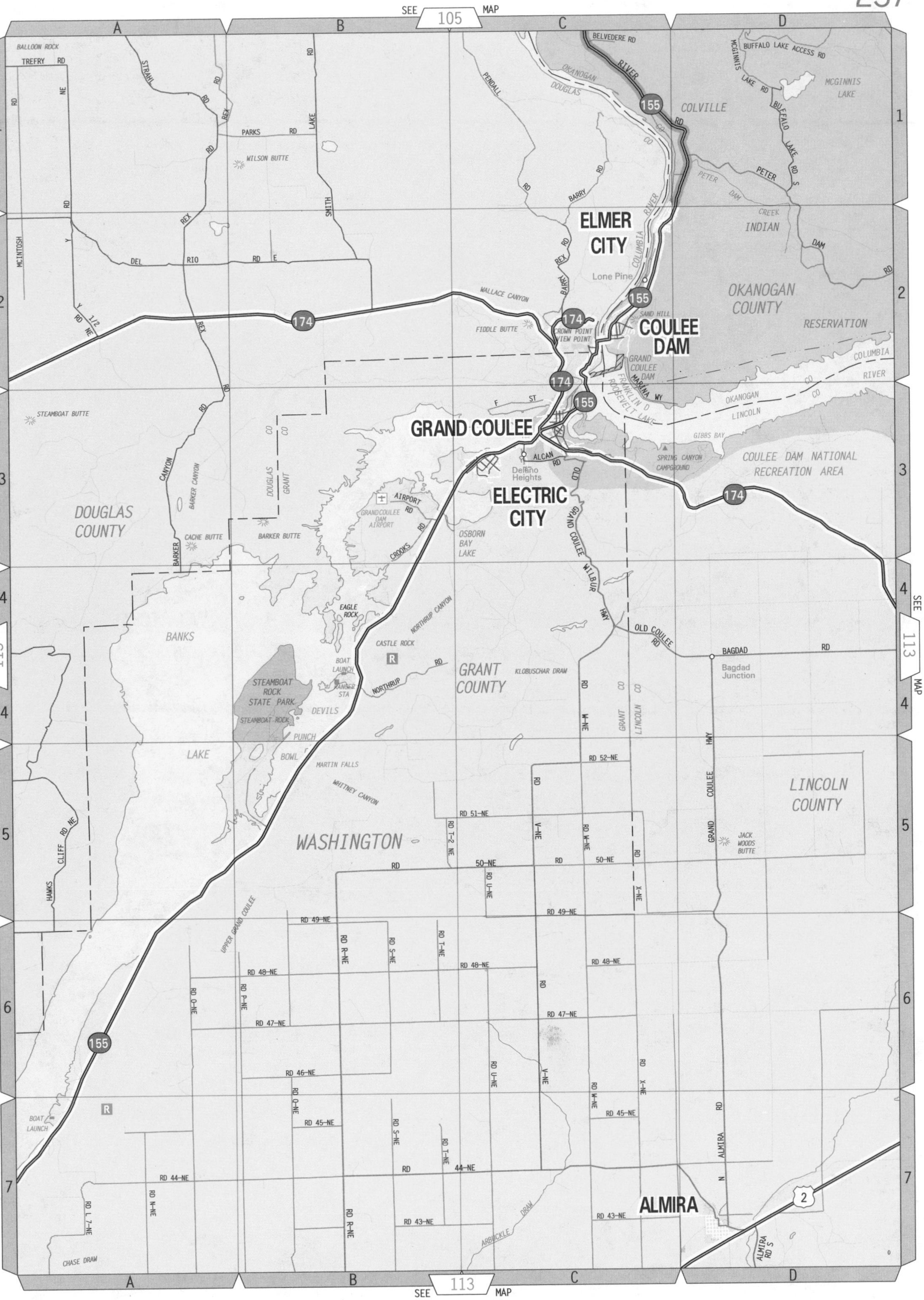

155
UPPER GRAND COULEE
RD 49-NE
RD R-NE
RD S-NE
RD T-NE
RD 48-NE
RD
RD 48-NE
RD
RD O-NE
RD P-NE
RD 48-NE
RD 47-NE
RD 47-NE
RD V-NE
RD X-NE
RD W-NE
RD 45-NE

BOAT LAUNCH
R
RD 46-NE
RD Q-NE
RD 45-NE
RD S-NE
RD T-NE
RD U-NE
RD V-NE
RD
ALMIRA RD
N
RD 44-NE
RD W-NE
RD L-7-NE
RD 44-NE
RD R-NE
RD 43-NE
RD 43-NE
ARBUCKLE DRAW
ALMIRA
2
ALMIRA RD S
CHASE DRAW

A   B   SEE 113 MAP   C   D

PNW

METRO

SEE 111 MAP

A   B   C   D

LEAVENWORTH

SKI HILL
PINE ST
KOA LEAVENWORTH WENATCHEE
E LEAVENWORTH
ANDERSON CANYON
WILLIAMS CANYON RD
JUDGE CANYON
SLAG MOUNTAIN
OLLALA CANYON
NFD
WENATCHEE
SWAKANE
BURCH MOUNTAIN
CANYON
NFD RD 7413
NFD 7412
NFD RD 5215

ICICLE RD
WILSON SHORE
PROWELL ST
MOUNTAIN HOME RD
LEAVENWORTH NATIONAL FISH HATCHERY
PETERS AV
ICICLE CREEK RD
Peshastin
BEACHER HILL
SAUNDERS RD
RIVER
TIBBETS MOUNTAIN RD
TIBBETTS MOUNTAIN
SPRING CANYON
NAHAHUM CANYON
WARNER CANYON
EAGLE ROCK
CHELAN COUNTY
NATIONAL
BURCH

MUNDUN CANYON RD
BOUNDARY BUTTE
NFD RD 7300
NFD RD 400
NFD
97 2
DEAD MAN RD
Dryden
N DRYDEN RD
STINEHILL RD
OLLALA
FRWY
WILLIS CAREY HISTORICAL MUSEUM
WARNER CANYON
HIGH SPRINGS CANYON
MOUNTAIN
FOREST

PENDLETON CANYON
NFD RD 7202
NFD RD 200
NFD RD 510
7200
CAMAS CREEK
BRENDER CANYON
TRIPP CANYON
SHY MEADOW RD
PIONEER
SUNSET HWY
DR
TIGNER RD
CASHMERE
EELS RD
HUGHES
SUNSET
KELLY RD
AM
Monitor
E MAIN ST
AMERICAN FRUIT RD
CRESTVIEW
SCHOOL ST
SUNNYSLOPE
ALT 97

WENATCHEE
WASHINGTON
TIPTOP
WINDMILL POINT
NFD RD
MISSION CREEK
SHERMAN CANYON
YAKSUM CANYON
YAKSUM CANYON
FAIRVIEW CANYON
ZAGER RD
FAIRVIEW CANYON
97 2 EASY ST
SLEEPY HOLLOW
LOWER SUNNYSLOPE RD
PETERS ST
EUCLID AV
COLUMBIA RIVER
WENATCHEE RIVER
285

CEDAR GROVE CAMPGROUND
97
NATIONAL
SHEEP MOUNTAIN
Blewett
POLSON CANYON
HORSE LAKE MOUNTAIN
West Wenatchee
WENATCHEE VALLEY JUNIOR COLLEGE
NUMBER TWO CANYON
WENATCHEE
MAPLE ST
SPRINGWATER AV
NINTH ST
FIFTH ST
ORCHARD AV
WASHINGTON ST
CASTLEROCK AV
CHERRY ST
WESTERN AV
SKYLINE DR
RED APPLE
OLD BUTTE
CRAWFORD ST
MILLER ST
ANNAPOLIS

SEE 111 MAP
SEE 239 MAP

NFD 200
7320
SCOTTY CREEK CAMPGROUND
FOREST
RED HILL
BONANZA CAMPGROUND
TRONSEN RIDGE
STUMP CAMPGROUND
PINE CAMPGROUND
7100
NFD RD
PENDLETON CANYON
SHEEP ROCK
MISSION RIDGE
PEAVINE CANYON
ROOSTER COMB
PITCHER CANYON RD
METHOW
PITCHER CANYON
SQUILCHUCK RD
WENATCHEE HEIGHTS RD
WHEELER HILL RD

NFD 7324
NFD RD 9715
NFD RD 9714
PARK CAMPGROUND
SWAUK PASS SNO-PARK
TRONSEN CAMPGROUND
ALPINE CAMPGROUND
BEEHIVE MOUNTAIN
BEEHIVE SPRING CAMPGROUND
STEMILT LOOP

BLEWETT PASS
SWAUK CAMPGROUND
Mountain Home
NFD RD 9711
NFD RD 116
NFD RD 9716
NFD RD 9712
HANEY MEADOW CAMPGROUND
MEADOW CAMPGROUND
SPRING CAMPGROUND
MISSION RIDGE WINTER SPORTS AREA

NFD RD 9705
SWAUK RIDGE
NFD RD 9718
NFD RD 9712
NFD RD 118
NFD RD 115
Meaghersville
SNOWSHOE RIDGE
NFD RD 35
NFD RD 3530
NAHSTEN
KITTITAS
NFD RD 35
NFD RD 125
CREEK
CHELAN CO
KITTITAS CO
MISSION PEAK
WENATCHEE MOUNTAIN
NANEUM POINT

COUNTY

SEE 241 MAP

1   2   3   4   5   6   7

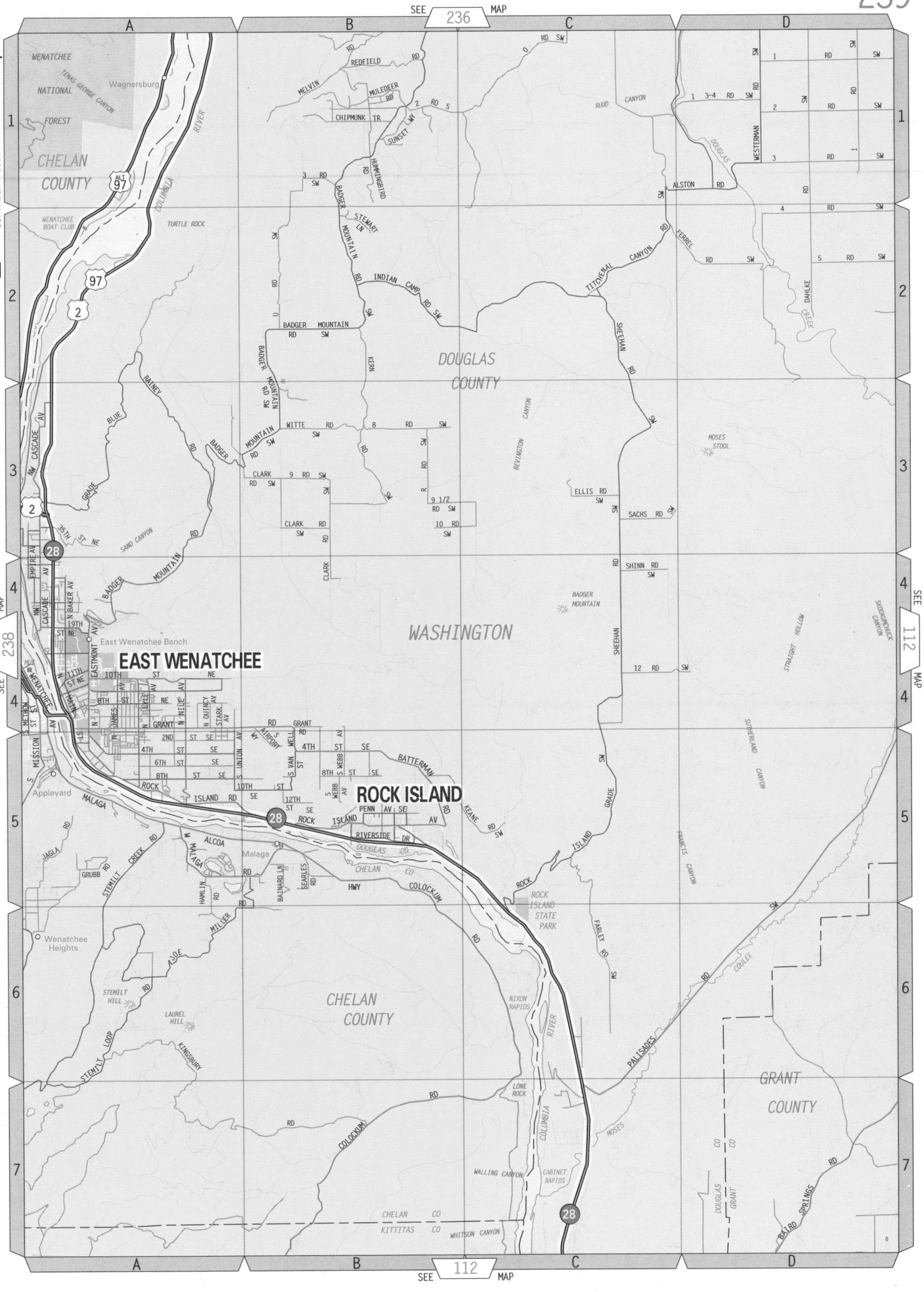

SEE 236 MAP

A   B   C   D

PNW

METRO

WENATCHEE
NATIONAL
FOREST

TEXAS GEORGE CANYON

Wagnersburg

CHELAN
COUNTY

COLUMBIA RIVER

ALT 97

WENATCHEE
BOAT CLUB

TURTLE ROCK

97

2

REDFIELD RD

MELVIN

MULEDEER RD

CHIPMUNK TR

SUNSET LN

HUMMINGBIRD RD

BADGER MOUNTAIN RD

STEWART LN

INDIAN CAMP RD SW

RD SW

RO SW

RUUD CANYON

DOUGLAS

WESTERMAN

1

3-4 RD SW

2

3

RD

RD

SW

SW

SW

RD

RD

RD

SW

SW

ALSTON RD

TITTCHENAL CANYON

FERREL RD SW

SHEEHAN RD

DAHLKE CREEK

DOUGLAS
COUNTY

BADGER MOUNTAIN RD SW

WITTE RD

KERN

8 RD SW

RD SW

RD SW

9 1/2 RD SW

10 RD SW

BEVINGTON CANYON

MOSES STOOL

ELLIS RD SW

SACHS RD SW

CLARK 9 RD SW

CLARK RD SW

CLARK RD SW

RAINEY RD

BLUE GRADE RD

BADGER

NW CASCADE AV

GRADE RD

SAND CANYON

BADGER MOUNTAIN

SHINN RD

SHEEHAN RD

BADGER
MOUNTAIN

12 RD SW

WASHINGTON

2

35TH ST NE

28

EMPIRE AV

BAKER AV

CASCADE

19TH ST NE

ST NE

East Wenatchee Bench

EAST WENATCHEE

EASTMONT

10TH ST NE

11TH ST NE

8TH ST

JAMES

GRANT

2ND ST SE

4TH ST SE

6TH ST SE

8TH ST SE

ROCK ISLAND RD

10TH ST SE

12TH ST SE

N QUINCY

STARK

AIRPORT RD

UNION ST

VAN ST

WELL ST

WEBB

8TH ST SE

GRANT AV

BATTERMAN RD

ROCK ISLAND

PENN AV SE

RIVERSIDE DR

KEANE RD SW

ISLAND GRADE RD

SUTHERLAND CANYON

STRAIGHT HOLLOW

SKOOKUMCHUCK CANYON

SEE 238 MAP

SEE 112 MAP

MISSION ST

S METRO

Appleyard

MALAGA

JAGLA RD

GRUBB RD

STEMILT CREEK RD

W MALAGA

ALCOA

Malaga

BATHARD LN

SEARLES RD

HWY

DOUGLAS CO

CHELAN CO

COLOCKUM RD

ROCK
ISLAND
STATE
PARK

FARLEY RD SW

FRANCIS CANYON

SW

Wenatchee
Heights

STEMILT HILL

LAUREL HILL

KINGSBURY

MILLER RD

JOE RD

HAMIL LN

NIXON RAPIDS

COLUMBIA RIVER

COULEE

RD SW

STEMILT LOOP

CHELAN
COUNTY

COLOCKUM RD

LONE ROCK

CABINET RAPIDS

PALISADES RD

MOSES

DOUGLAS CO

GRANT CO

TRAIL RD

SPRINGS RD

GRANT
COUNTY

CHELAN CO

KITTITAS CO

WHITSON CANYON

WALLING CANYON

28

28

A   B   C   D

SEE 112 MAP

PNW

METRO

SEE 111 MAP

A   B   C   D

1

ROSLYN

Ronald

CLE ELUM RIDGE

WENATCHEE

NATIONAL   Liberty

FOREST

ROSLYN MUSEUM

903   CLE ELUM

TEANAWAY

TEANAWAY

MASON CREEK RD

RD

RD

HARTMAN RD

LEY RD

SWAUK PRAIRIE

Virden

97

W BALLARD DR

CLE ELUM TELEPHONE MUSEUM

78

2

Nelson

80   90

SOUTH CLE ELUM

AIRPORT RD

MASTERSON

E MASTERSON

970   970

97

85

970

RIVER

Teanaway

LAMBERT RD

HIDDEN VALLEY

HIDDEN VALLEY RD

HORSE CANYON

BETTAS

RD

LOWER PEOH POINT RD   YAKIMA

HART RD

LOOKOUT MOUNTAIN

R

INDIAN JOHN HILL

UPPER PEOH POINT RD

R   THORP PRAIRIE

Bristol

CLE ELUM POINT

SOUTH CLE ELUM RIDGE

TANEUM POINT

MOONLIGHT CANYON

MORRISON CANYON

93   Horlick

RIVER   Kountze

SMAUK

HAYWARD RD

10

3

WENATCHEE

NORTH FORK TANEUM

CREEK

TANEUM RIDGE

CREEK

TANEUM CAMPGROUND

TANEUM

TANEUM CANYON

RD

HORLICK RD

BRUKETTA RD

Dudley

DUDLEY RD

QUARTZ MOUNTAIN RD

TANEUM

LEWIS AND CLARK TRAIL STATE PARK

RD

90

SEE 111 MAP   TANEUM RD   SEE 241 MAP

4

SOUTH FORK

MOLE MOUNTAIN

FROST MOUNTAIN

NATIONAL

YAHNE CANYON

CREEK

RATTLESNAKE CANYON

WATT CANYON

WATT CANYON RD

WINEGAR CANYON

TAMARACK SPRING CAMPGROUND

WAGNER CANYON

KITTITAS

COUNTY

PAGE CANYON

FOREST

SOUTH FORK

ROBINSON CANYON

SHELL ROCK RD

KLOSS RD

WHISKY CANYON

AINSLEY CANYON

5

COLEMAN CANYON

RD

NORTH RIGGS CANYON

NFD RD 1709

MANASTASH

MANASTASH RD

6

BALD MOUNTAIN

CREEK

Cliffdell

RD 1703

NFD

1720 RD

1721

NFD RD   1710 RD

HOG

NEMAS

WASHINGTON

RANCH

CREEK

SOUTH RIGGS CANYON

7

410

RD

KITTITAS CO

YAKIMA CO   WENAS RD

COTTONWOOD CAMPGROUND

RIVER

0

MOUNT BAKER-SNOQUALMIE NATIONAL FOREST   YAKIMA COUNTY

A   B   C   D

SEE 119 MAP

241

PNW

METRO

SEE 238 MAP

SEE 240 MAP

SEE 112 MAP

SEE 243 MAP

ELLENSBURG

KITTITAS

KITTITAS COUNTY

WENATCHEE NATIONAL FOREST

WASHINGTON

PNW

METRO

—N—

SEE 112 MAP

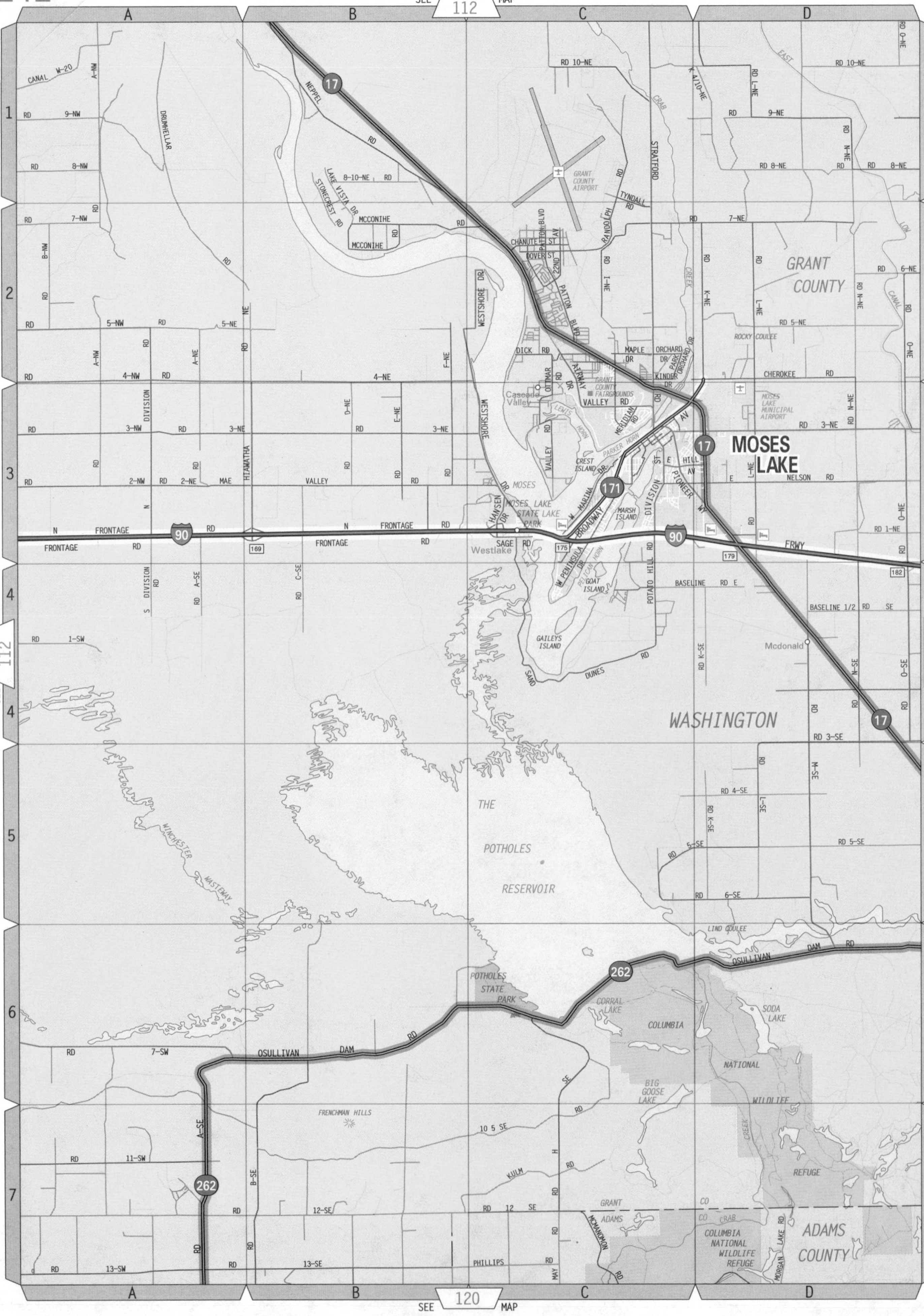

SEE 120 MAP

SEE 112 MAP

SEE 113 MAP

MOSES LAKE

GRANT COUNTY

WASHINGTON

ADAMS COUNTY

THE POTHOLES RESERVOIR

POTHOLES STATE PARK

FRENCHMAN HILLS

O'SULLIVAN DAM RD

WINCHESTER WASTEWAY

COLUMBIA NATIONAL WILDLIFE REFUGE

COLUMBIA NATIONAL WILDLIFE REFUGE

BIG GOOSE LAKE

SODA LAKE

CORRAL LAKE

LIND COULEE

CRAB CREEK

GRANT CO / ADAMS CO

GRANT COUNTY AIRPORT

MOSES LAKE MUNICIPAL AIRPORT

GRANT COUNTY FAIRGROUNDS

MOSES LAKE STATE LAKE PARK

CREST ISLAND

MARSH ISLAND

GOAT ISLAND

GAILEYS ISLAND

PELICAN HORN

PARKER HORN

ROCKY COULEE

CASCADE VALLEY

SAGE Westlake

DRUMHELLAR

STONECREST RD

LAKE VISTA DR

MCCONIHE

McDonald

SAND DUNES

N FRONTAGE RD

FRONTAGE RD

WESTSHORE DR

NEPPEL RD

STRATFORD

TYNDALL RD

CHANUTE

DOVER ST

PATTON BLVD

DICK DR

VALLEY

MAPLE DR

ORCHARD DR

KINDER

CHEROKEE

NELSON RD

PIONEER

DIVISION ST

BROADWAY

BASELINE RD E

BASELINE 1/2 RD SE

OSULLIVAN DAM RD

Routes: 17, 90, 171, 169, 175, 179, 182, 262

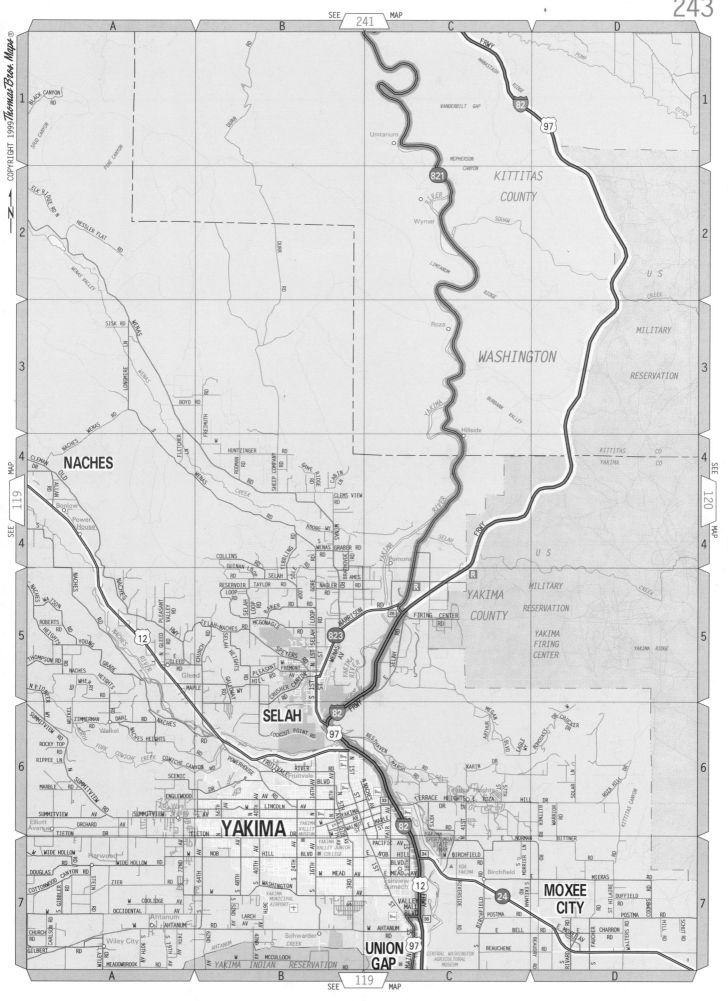

PNW

METRO

SEE MAP 241

SEE MAP 119

SEE MAP 120

COPYRIGHT 1999 *Thomas Bros. Maps*®

—N→

NACHES

KITTITAS COUNTY

WASHINGTON

YAKIMA COUNTY

US MILITARY RESERVATION

YAKIMA FIRING CENTER

Umtanum

Wymer

Roza

Hillside

KITTITAS CO
YAKIMA CO

SELAH

YAKIMA

Fruitvale

West

Elliott Avenue

Terrace Heights

Birchfield

MOXEE CITY

UNION GAP

YAKIMA INDIAN RESERVATION

CENTRAL WASHINGTON AGRICULTURAL MUSEUM

SEE MAP 119

PNW

METRO

SEE 107 MAP

A   B   C   D

—N→

HIDDEN VALLEY RD

SCHWEITZER BASIN RD

E BRONX RD

N KOOTENAI RD

W SHINGLE MILL

E SHINGLE MILL RD

HICKEY RD

COLBURN CULVER RD

LOWER PACK RIVER RD

PACK RIVER

TROUT CREEK

KANIKSU

TROUT PEAK

TRESTLE PEAK

95

2

SANDPOINT AIRPORT

MOUNTAIN VIEW DR

MOUNTAIN VIEW DR

BALDY MOUNTAIN RD

KOOTENAI

KOOTENAI CTO

1ST AV

WHISKEY JACK RD

PONDER POINT

PONDERAY

KOOTENAI BAY

KOOTENAI POINT

SUNNYSIDE

ODEN BAY

SUNNYSIDE MOUNTAIN

SUNNYSIDE RD

SUMMIT RD

Trestle Creek

GRIEF MOUNTAIN

TRESTLE CREEK

NATIONAL

COCHRAN DRAW

ROUND TOP MOUNTAIN

NFD RD 489

AUXOR BASIN

BOVER AV

N DIVISION

LARCH ST

N PINE ST

SANDPOINT

FISHERMAN ISLAND

HAWKINS POINT

PACK RIVER BOAT RAMP

TRESTLE CREEK BOAT RAMP

FOREST

COUGAR PEAK

ONTARIO ST

2

DOVER

PEND OREILLE RIVER

ROCKY POINT

LAKESHORE

SPRING POINT CAMPGROUND

SPADES DR

MURPHY BAY

OSPREY NESTS VIEWPOINT

SANDPOINT FISH HATCHERY

CONTEST POINT

SOURDOUGH POINT

BOTTLE BAY RD

GOLD HILL

GOLD HILL CTR

BOTTLE BAY RD

YUANCY LAKE

BOTTLE BAY POINT

ANDERSON POINT

SUNRISE BAY

WARREN ISLAND

GLENGARY BAY RD

MARTIN BAY

COTTAGE ISLAND

PEARL ISLAND

HOPE

EAST HOPE

PRINGLE BOAT LAUNCH

DAVID THOMPSON HISTORICAL MONUMENT

ELLISPORT BAY

RED FIR RD

HOPE PENINSULA

SPRING CREEK RD

OWENS BAY

GUN CLUB RD

LIGNITE

Sagle

GOLD MOUNTAIN RD

GOLD MOUNTAIN

GLENGARY BAY RD

BOTTLE BAY

CAMP BAY RD

PICARD POINT

ELLIOT BAY

CAMP BAY

MEMALOOSE ISLAND

SHEEPHERDER POINT

HOWE MOUNTAIN

3

95

ALGOMA SPUR

TALACHE

SAGLE RD

REED HILL

SHEPHERD LAKE ACCESS AREA

GARFIELD BAY RD

GARFIELD BAY CTO

GARFIELD BAY ACCESS AREA

GREEN BAY RD

GARFIELD BAY

GREEN BAY

MINERAL POINT

LONG POINT

LAKE

PEND

OREILLE

PETROGLYPHS

200

DERR ISLAND

4

HEATH LAKE

RD

DUFORT RD

BONNER COUNTY

GROUSE MOUNTAIN

MIRROR LAKE ACCESS

GROUSE MOUNTAIN POINT

NFD RD 2233

PONDEROSA RD

4

BEEKS RD

COCOLALLA LAKE ACCESS AREA

Westmond

WESTMOND

KANISKU

Talache

BIMETALLIC RIDGE

BUTLER MOUNTAIN

INDIAN POINT

WINDY POINT

DEADMAN POINT

JAKES MOUNTAIN

JOHNSON POINT VISTA

NFD RD 278

5

BUTLER CREEK RD

BLACKTAIL MOUNTAIN

UPPER COCOLALLA CREEK

MAIDEN ROCK

KILROY BAY

PINE COVE

ECHO ROCK

GRANITE POINT

IDAHO

GREEN MONARCH MOUNTAIN

GREEN MONARCH RIDGE

SCHAFER PEAK

SHERMAN RIDGE

WHITE QUARTZ RIDGE

JOHNSON PEAK

5

COCOLALLA CREEK

LITTLE BLACKTAIL MOUNTAIN

NATIONAL

NFD RD

NFD RD 278

TONS RIDGE

FLEMING POINT

NFD RD 1066

6

LITTLE BLACKTAIL MOUNTAIN

KANIKSU

MINERVA PEAK

MINERVA RIDGE

NFD RD 1088

PEEP A DAY RIDGE

JOHNSON SADDLE

NFD RD 332

COEUR D'ALENE

6

THREE SISTERS PEAKS

FOREST

WHISKEY ROCK BAY

WHISKEY ROCK

NFD RD

BARTON HUMP

NATIONAL

PACKSADDLE MOUNTAIN

FOREST

COEUR D'ALENE RIVER

NFD RD 306

D'ALENE

NATIONAL

FOREST

LARCH MOUNTAIN

7

SUNSET RD

NFD RD 22

NFD RD 1050

BOISE

SHOSHONE

NFD RD 332

SHOSHONE COUNTY

POWER MOUNTAIN

A   B   C   D

SEE 245 MAP

SEE 107 MAP

2

200

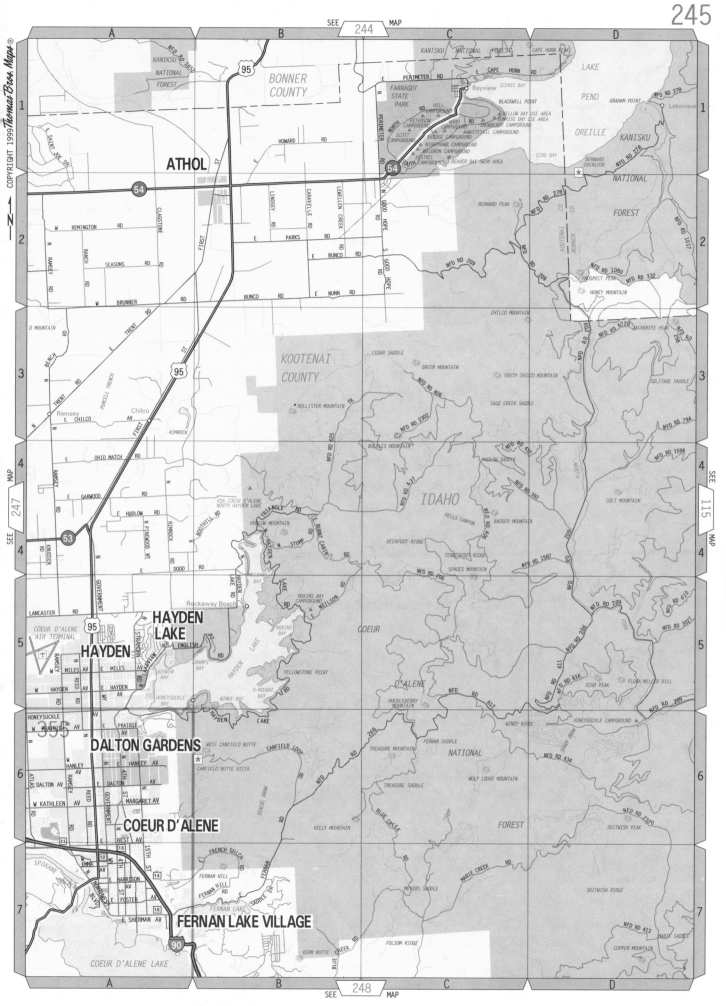

SEE MAP 244

BONNER COUNTY

KANIKSU NATIONAL FOREST

CAPE HORN PEAK

LAKE PEND OREILLE

KANISKU NATIONAL FOREST

ATHOL

54

FARRAGUT STATE PARK

Bayview

SCENIC BAY

Blackwell Point

WILLOW DAY USE AREA
SUNRISE DAY USE AREA

HILL CAMPGROUND
PETERSON CAMPGROUND
WARD CAMPGROUND
SNOWBERRY CAMPGROUND
WHITETAIL CAMPGROUND
SCOTT CAMPGROUND
BRIDGE CAMPGROUND
NIGHTHAWK CAMPGROUND
WALDRON CAMPGROUND
KESTREL CAMPGROUND
BEAVER BAY SWIM AREA

ECHO BAY

Graham Point

Lakeview

NFD RD 278

Bernard Overlook

NFD RD 278

NATIONAL

NFD RD 1017

Bernard Peak

NFD RD 278

KOOTENAI CO BONNER CO

NFD RD 209

NFD RD 1080

PROSPECT PEAK

NFD RD 332

FOREST

HONEY MOUNTAIN

CHILCO MOUNTAIN

NFD RD 6728

JACKKNIFE PEAK

NFD RD 258

NFD RD 209

KOOTENAI COUNTY

CEDAR SADDLE

GREEN MOUNTAIN

SOUTH CHILCO MOUNTAIN

SOLITAIRE SADDLE

HOLLISTER MOUNTAIN TR

SAGE CREEK SADDLE

NFD RD 794

NFD RD 406

NFD RD 625

NFD RD 2302

BUBBLES MOUNTAIN

NFD RD 1594

NFD RD 437

HUDLOW SADDLE

NFD RD 427

IDAHO

HELLS CANYON

BADGER MOUNTAIN

NFD RD 392

COLT MOUNTAIN

DEERFOOT RIDGE

NFD RD 436

TENDERFOOT RIDGE

NFD RD 1587

SPADES MOUNTAIN

NFD RD 206

NFD RD 209

NFD RD 610

NFD RD 3021

COEUR

MOKINS BAY CAMPGROUND

NEILSON

D'ALENE

HUCKLEBERRY MOUNTAIN

NFD RD 612

ECHO PEAK

FLORA MILLER HILL

NFD RD 411

NFD RD 616

NFD RD 209

HONEYSUCKLE CAMPGROUND

WINDY RIDGE

WEST CANFIELD BUTTE

CANFIELD LOOP

FERNAN SADDLE

SHADY DRAW

NFD RD 434

TREASURE MOUNTAIN

WOLF LODGE MOUNTAIN

NATIONAL

CANFIELD BUTTE VISTA

STACEL DRAW

TREASURE SADDLE

BLUE CREEK

KELLY MOUNTAIN

SKITWISH PEAK

NFD RD 2320

FOREST

FRENCH GULCH RD

FERNAN HILL

FERNAN HILL RD

MARIE CREEK

MEYERS SADDLE

SKITWISH RIDGE

FERNAN LAKE VILLAGE

FERNAN LAKE SADDLE DR

90

KERN BUTTE

FOLSOM RIDGE

NFD RD 413

MARIE SADDLE

COEUR D'ALENE LAKE

BLUE CREEK RD

COPPER MOUNTAIN

SEE MAP 248

ATHOL

95

HOWARD RD

E SAINT JOE DR

NFD RD 2659

54

W REMINGTON RD

RAMSEY RANCH RD

SEASONS

CLAYSTONE

FIRST ST

LINDSEY RD

CARAVELLE RD

LEWELLEN CREEK RD

PARKS

GOOD HOPE RD

N GOOD HOPE

S GOOD HOPE RD

E BUNCO RD

BRUNNER RD

BUNCO RD

E NUNN RD

D MOUNTAIN

BENCH RD

TRENT

PURCELL TRENCH RD

95

Ramsey

E CHILCO AV

Chilco

FIRST

RIMROCK

OHIO MATCH RD

RAMSEY RD

GARWOOD RD

E HUDLOW RD

N PINEWOOD WY

RIMROCK

BOOTHILL RD

53

KNUDSEN RD

GOVERNMENT

DODD RD

LANCASTER RD

HAYDEN LAKE

HAYDEN

95

COEUR D'ALENE AIR TERMINAL

RAMSEY RD

W MILES AV

E MILES

REED

W HAYDEN RD

E HAYDEN WY

STRAHORN RD

N 15TH

ENGLISH

HONEYSUCKLE

W PRAIRIE AV

DALTON GARDENS

HANLEY AV

E HANLEY AV

ATLAS RD

W DALTON AV

E DALTON

RAMSEY RD

REED

GOVERNMENT

MARGARET AV

W KATHLEEN AV

COEUR D'ALENE

BEST AV

11

EMMA

12

13

14

15

HARRISON ST

W FOSTER

E SHERMAN AV

NORTHWEST BLVD

SPOKANE RIVER

HAYDEN LAKE RD

Rockaway Beach

O'GARA'S BAY

CRAMP'S BAY

MOKINS BAY

BERVEN BAY

HONEYSUCKLE BAY

WINDY BAY

YELLOWSTONE POINT

O-ROURKE BAY

Harrison

HAYDEN LAKE

HUDLOW MOUNTAIN

TRIANGLE RD

E BURNT CABIN RD

HAYDEN

STUMP

NFD RD 206

KOA COEUR D'ALENE NORTH HAYDEN LAKE

PNW

METRO

STEVENS COUNTY

SPOKANE COUNTY

SPOKANE

MILLWOOD

AIRWAY HEIGHTS

WASHINGTON

CHENEY

Eastern Washington University

346 347 348 349 350

—N—

SEE 114 MAP
SEE 114 MAP 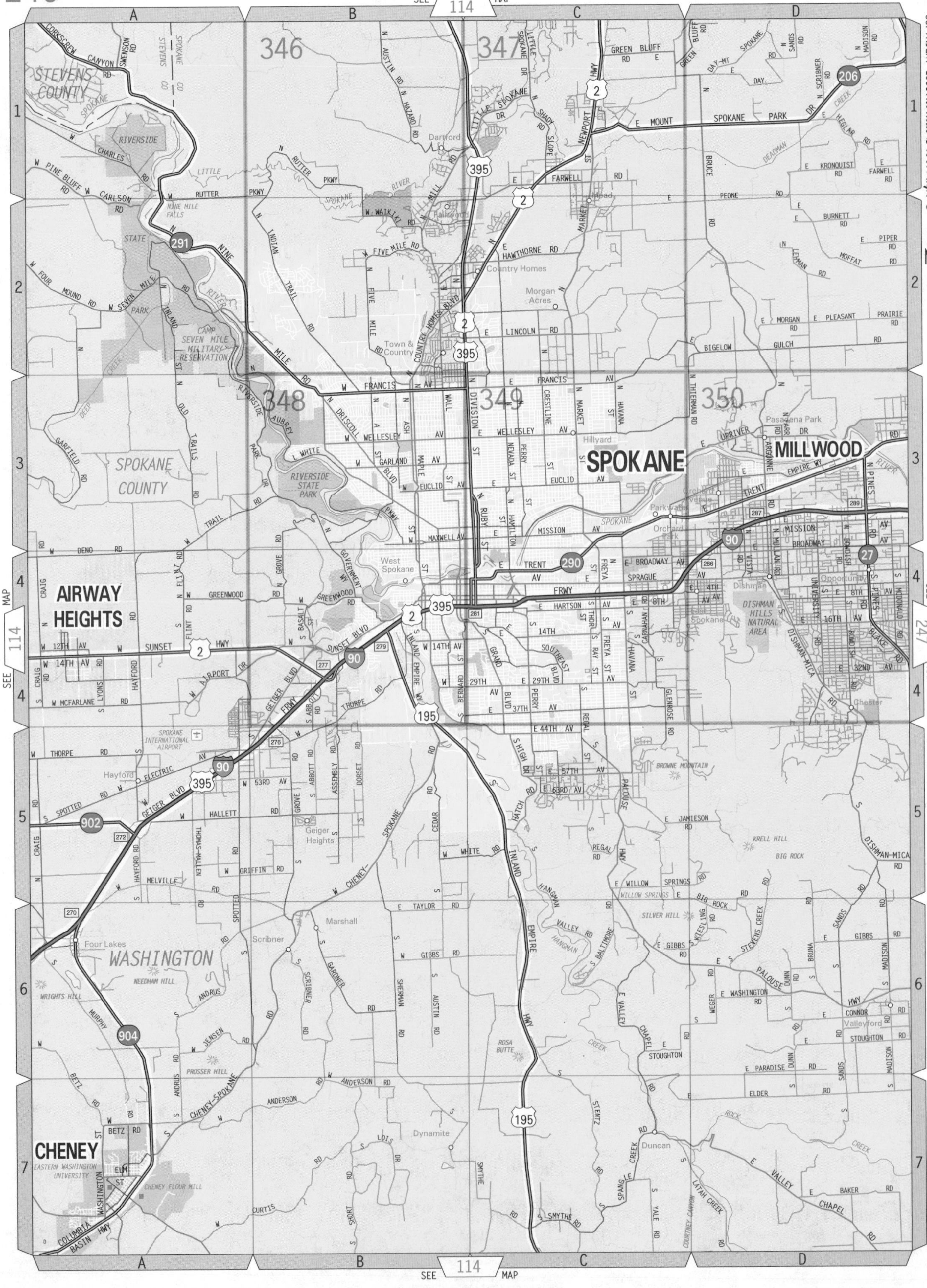
SEE 247 MAP
SEE 114 MAP

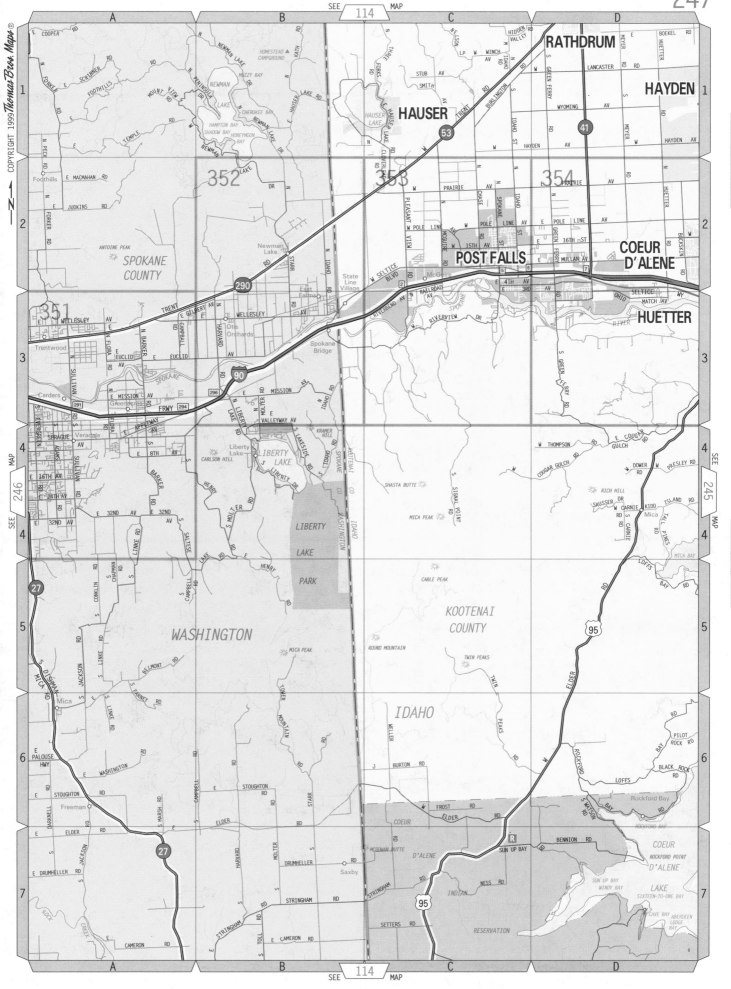

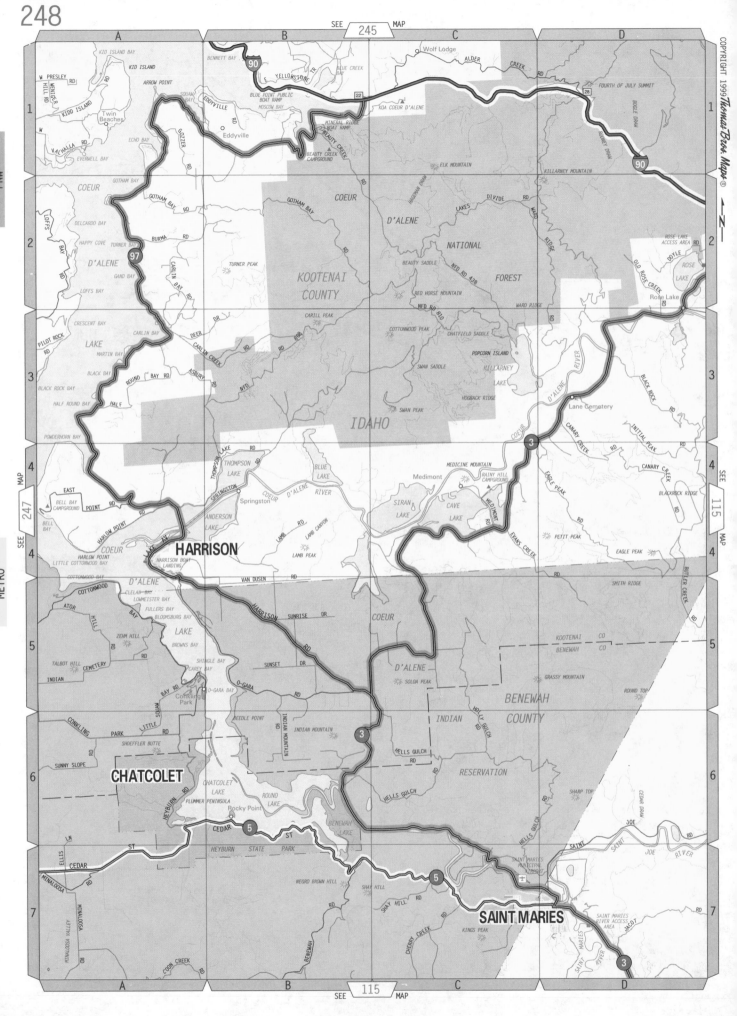

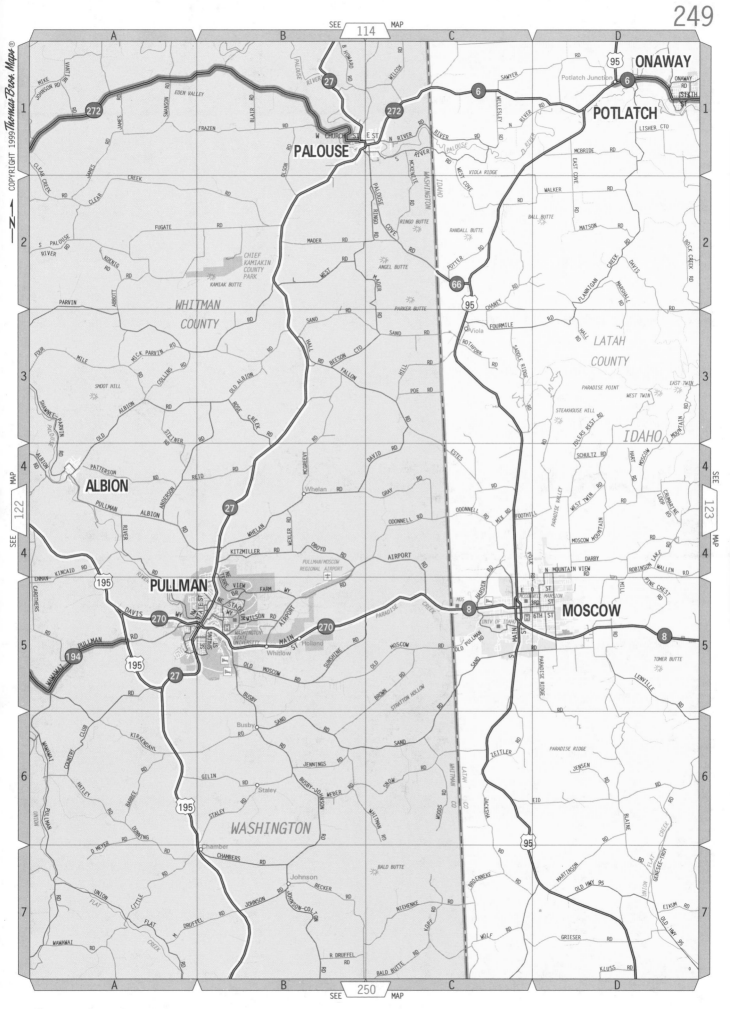

PNW

METRO

SEE 122 MAP

SEE 123 MAP

SEE 114 MAP

SEE 250 MAP

ONAWAY

POTLATCH

PALOUSE

ALBION

PULLMAN

MOSCOW

WHITMAN COUNTY

LATAH COUNTY

IDAHO

WASHINGTON

CHIEF KAMIAKIN COUNTY PARK

WASHINGTON STATE UNIVERSITY

UNIV OF IDAHO

PULLMAN/MOSCOW REGIONAL AIRPORT

PNW

METRO

A   B   C   D

COPYRIGHT 1999 Thomas Bros. Maps ®   —N—

1

COLTON

LATAH COUNTY

GENESEE

UNION FLAT CREEK RD
WAWAWAI RD
BROADWAY ST
JOHNSON-COLTON RD
BECKER RD
JOHNSON RD
BAUER RD
DENNING RD
UNIONTOWN EAST
THORN CREEK
BORGEN RD
SPRINGER RD
KLUSS RD
N JACKSON ST
OLD HWY 95
ROSENAU
STOUT
GENESEE-JULIAETTA RD
GRAY EAGLE
MAHL RD

RIMROCK RD
RIMROCK RD
STEPTOE CANYON RD
SCHLEE RD
BUSCH RD
UNIONTOWN
WARNECKE RD
LEON RD
ESSER RD
WHITMAN
LATAH CO

UNIONTOWN

2

MOERHLE RD
TAUFFEN RD
195
L SCHULTHEIS RD
KINCER RD
MOSER RD
WASHINGTON
IDAHO
COW CREEK
CARBUHN RD
MOSER RD
UNION CREEK RD
95
136
S EVANS RD
136
BECKER RD
140
CENTRAL GRADE RD
PORTER RD
CONNER RD
ARTHUR RD
DUMP RD
COYOTE
194

NEZ PERCE CO
LATAH CO NEZ PERCE CO

NEZ PERCE

3

WHITMAN COUNTY

STOUT
EVANS RD
NEZ PERCE COUNTY
LEWISTON HILL
95
OLD SPIRAL HWY
CENTRAL GRADE RD
COLE CANYON RD
12
95
RIVER

WHITMAN CO NEZ PERCE CO

INDIAN

4

SEE 122 MAP

WAWAWAI RD
12
193
RIVER
AIRPORT RD
128
Hatwai
North Lewiston
12
95
RAILROAD AV
MILL
CLEARWATER
MAGNER RD
IDAHO

SEE 123 MAP

Silcott
INLAND EMPIRE HWY
ELM ST
9TH ST
8TH ST
MILL
29TH ST
OLD LAPWAI RD
SOLDIERS CANYON RD
RESERVATION LINE

CLARKSTON

JOHNSON RD
SILCOTT
SILCOTT RD
6TH AV
SILCOTT WYE
ROUTE
MALL
EVANS RD
APPLESIDE BLVD
6TH AV
CATCHCUT RD
MAGUIRE GULCH RD
128
GRADE RD
6TH AV
24TH AV
16TH ST
11TH ST
14TH ST
17TH ST
21ST ST
AV ST
LEWIS-CLARK STATE COLLEGE
Clarkston Heights
Vineland
Lewiston Orchards
PRESTON AV
WARNER AV
BRYDEN AV
BURRELL AV
16TH AV
BURRELL AV
GRELLE AV
22ND ST
21ST ST
POWERS AV
E POWERS RD
MANN LAKE
MANN LAKE PUBLIC FISHING AREA
BEAVER RD
WEBB CANAL

LEWISTON

LINDSEY CREEK
OLD GUN CLUB RD
9TH ST
BARR
LOWER TAMMANY CREEK RD
McINTOSH HILL RD
McCANN
THIESEN RD
WAHA GRADE
CUTOFF

5

ASOTIN COUNTY

BOWMAN RD
PARSON RD
CLOVERLAND RD
CEMETERY RD
CLEMANS RD
1ST ST
ASOTIN MUSEUM
129
HELLS GATE STATE PARK
LEWISTON AIRPORT
SNAKE RIVER
KATTENBACK VOLLMER RD
ROSENGRANTZ RD
WAHA RD
POWELL RD
WAHA
WEBB RIDGE RD
SHUTTERA RD
WEBB

ASOTIN
CREEK RD
ASOTIN RD
ASOTIN CREEK

ASOTIN

6

WASHINGTON
HOSTETLER RD
SNAKE RIVER
TENMILE RAPIDS
ASOTIN RIVER
NEZ PERCE CO
WAHA PRAIRIE
POWELL RD
WAHA RD
TENMILE CANYON
MILLER RD

7

GEORGE
MEYERS
RIDGE
WEISSENFELS RIDGE RD
AYERS RIDGE
SHORT CANYON
LOCUST GROVE RD
IDAHO WASHINGTON

A   B   C   D

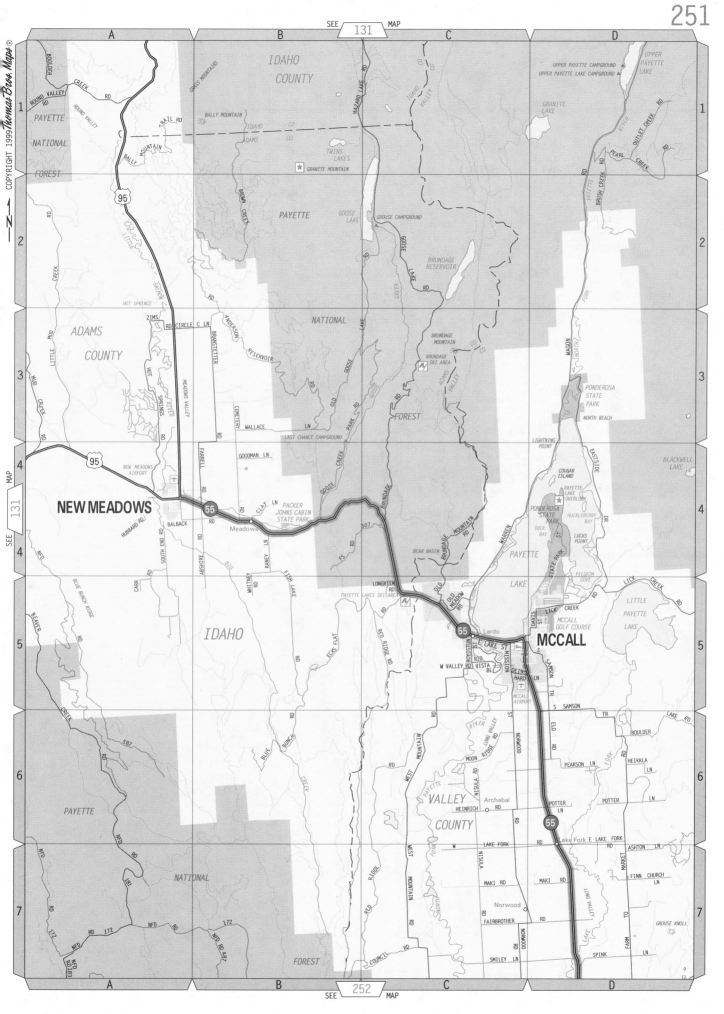

PNW

METRO

PNW

METRO

SEE 251 MAP

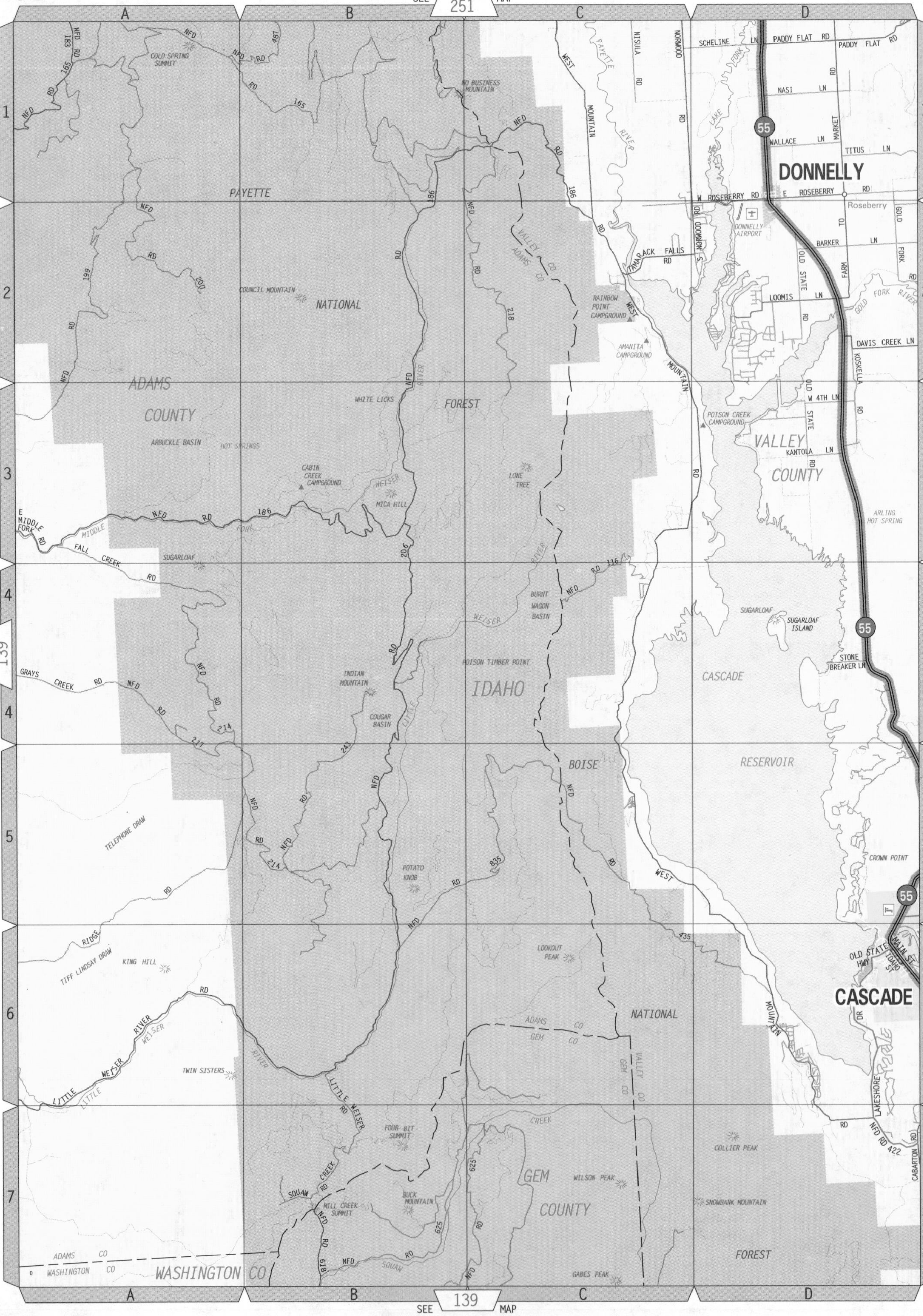

—N—

A   B   C   D

COLD SPRING SUMMIT

NFD RD 183
NFD RD 165
NFD RD 487

NO BUSINESS MOUNTAIN

NISULA RD

NORWOOD

SCHELINE LN   PADDY FLAT RD   PADDY FLAT RD

WEST   PAYETTE RIVER

LAKE FORK

NASI LN

WALLACE LN   MARKET LN   TITUS LN

55

DONNELLY

PAYETTE

NFD RD 199
NFD RD 200

COUNCIL MOUNTAIN

NATIONAL

W ROSEBERRY RD   E ROSEBERRY   Roseberry

GOLD FORK   TO FARM

DONNELLY AIRPORT

BARKER LN   OLD STATE

LOOMIS LN

GOLD FORK RIVER

DAVIS CREEK LN

KOSKELLA

ADAMS   COUNTY

VALLEY CO   ADAMS CO

218

RAINBOW POINT CAMPGROUND

WEST

AMANITA CAMPGROUND

POISON CREEK CAMPGROUND

VALLEY

COUNTY

KANTOLA LN

ARLING HOT SPRING

WHITE LICKS

FOREST

ARBUCKLE BASIN   HOT SPRINGS

CABIN CREEK CAMPGROUND

WEISER

MICA HILL

LONE TREE

MOUNTAIN

E MIDDLE FORK RD   MIDDLE FORK   NFD RD 186

FALL CREEK RD

SUGARLOAF

206

RIVER

RD 116

SUGARLOAF   SUGARLOAF ISLAND

GRAYS CREEK RD

WEISER

NFD RD 214

INDIAN MOUNTAIN

COUGAR BASIN

243

BURNT WAGON BASIN   NFD

POISON TIMBER POINT

IDAHO

CASCADE

STONE BREAKER LN

217

NFD RD 214

LITTLE

NFD RD

835

BOISE

RESERVOIR

55

TELEPHONE DRAW

POTATO KNOB

RD   NFD RD

WEST

735

CROWN POINT

55

RIDGE

TIFF LINDSAY DRAW   KING HILL

RD

LOOKOUT PEAK

OLD STATE HWY   MAIN ST   IDAHO ST

CASCADE

NATIONAL

DR

LITTLE WEISER RIVER   WEISER RIVER

TWIN SISTERS

ADAMS CO   GEM CO

GEM CO   VALLEY CO

CREEK

COLLIER PEAK

LAKESHORE RD   NFD RD 422

LITTLE   WEISER

LITTLE WEISER RD

FOUR BIT SUMMIT

625

BUCK MOUNTAIN

WILSON PEAK

GEM

SNOWBANK MOUNTAIN

CABARTON RD

MILL CREEK SUMMIT

SQUAW CREEK

NFD RD 618   NFD RD 625   SQUAW

COUNTY

GABES PEAK

FOREST

ADAMS CO   WASHINGTON CO   **WASHINGTON CO**

1   2   3   4   5   6   7

SEE 139 MAP
SEE 139 MAP

A   B   C   D

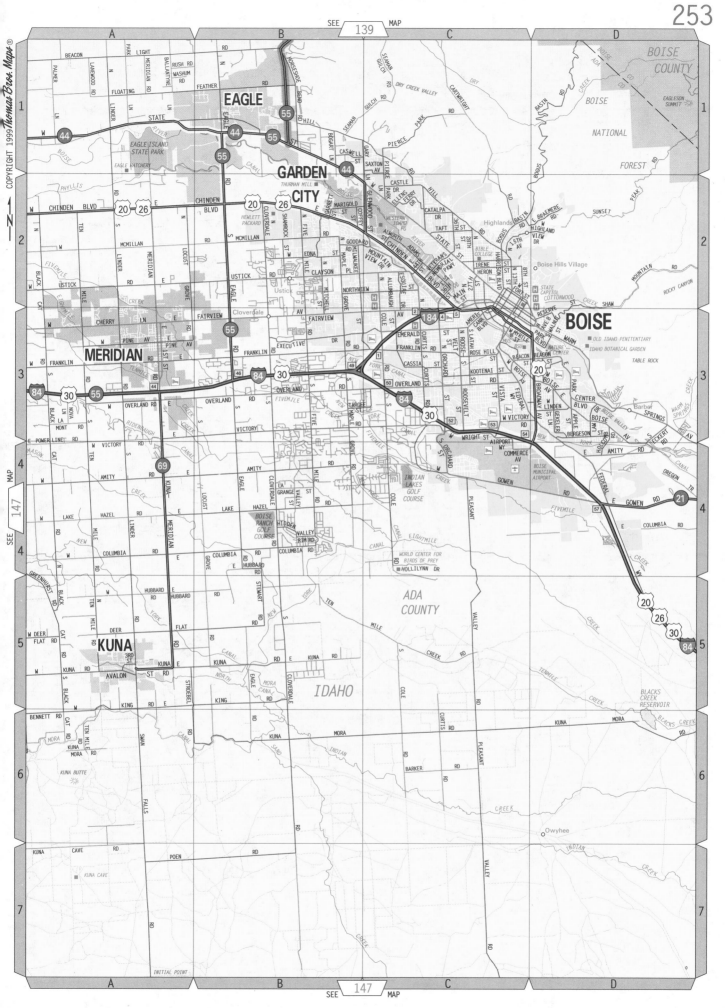

PNW

METRO

SEE MAP 147

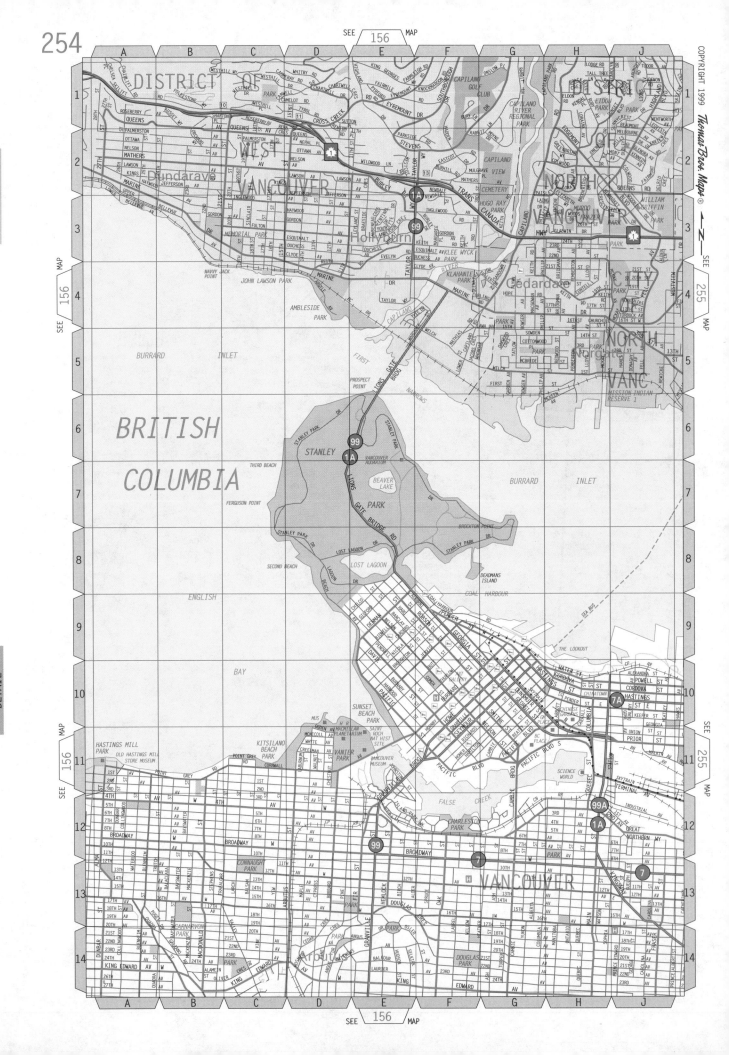

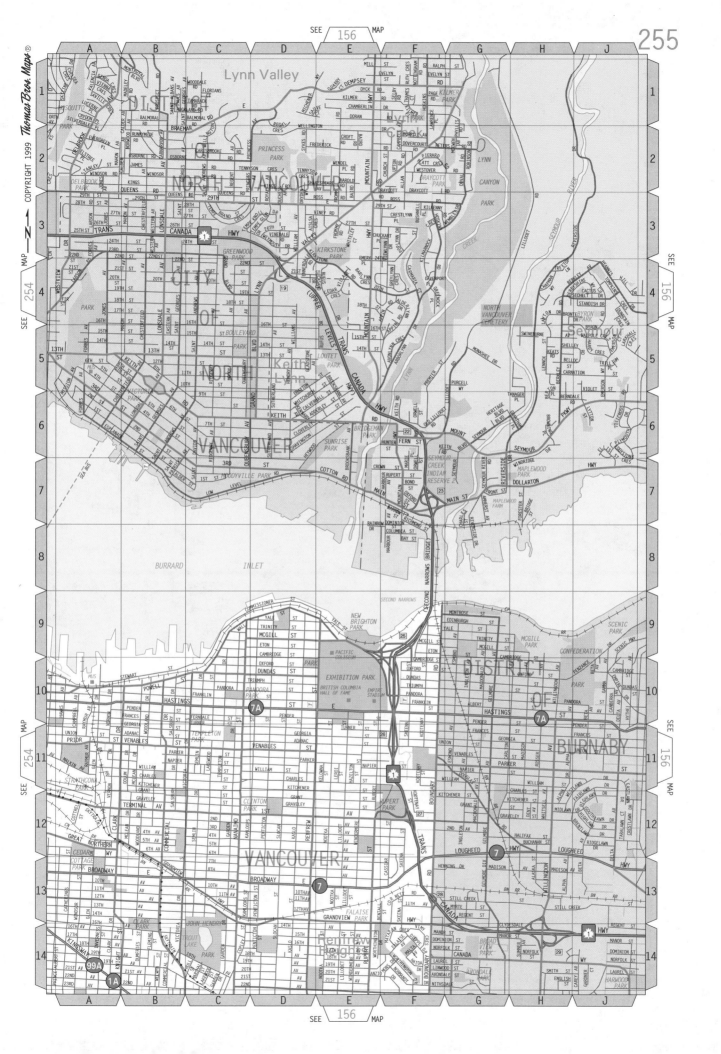

SEE 159 MAP

SEE 257 MAP

PNW

DETAIL

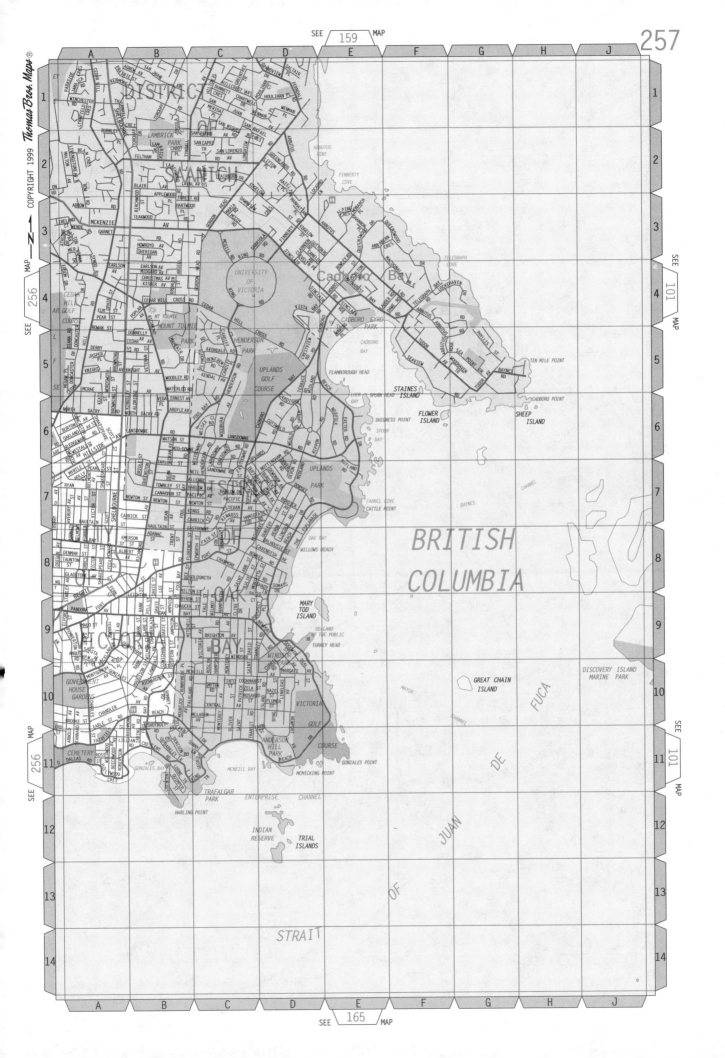

PNW

DETAIL

N
MAP

SEE 256 MAP

SEE 256 MAP

SEE 101 MAP

SEE 101 MAP

DISTRICT OF SAANICH

UNIVERSITY OF VICTORIA

Cadboro Bay

BRITISH

COLUMBIA

CITY OF OAK BAY

CITY OF VICTORIA

VICTORIA BAY

CADBORO GYRO PARK

UPLANDS GOLF COURSE

UPLANDS PARK

STAINES ISLAND

FLOWER ISLAND

SHEEP ISLAND

TEN MILE POINT

CADBORO POINT

OAK BAY

WILLOWS BEACH

MARY TOD ISLAND

SEALAND OF THE PUBLIC

TURKEY HEAD

GREAT CHAIN ISLAND

DISCOVERY ISLAND MARINE PARK

MAYOR

DE FUCA

GOVERNMENT HOUSE GARDENS

VICTORIA GOLF COURSE

ANDERSON HILL PARK

CEMETERY DALLAS

GONZALES BAY

MCNEILL BAY

GONZALES POINT

MCMICKING POINT

TRAFALGAR PARK

HARLING POINT

ENTERPRISE CHANNEL

INDIAN RESERVE

TRIAL ISLANDS

JUAN

STRAIT

OF

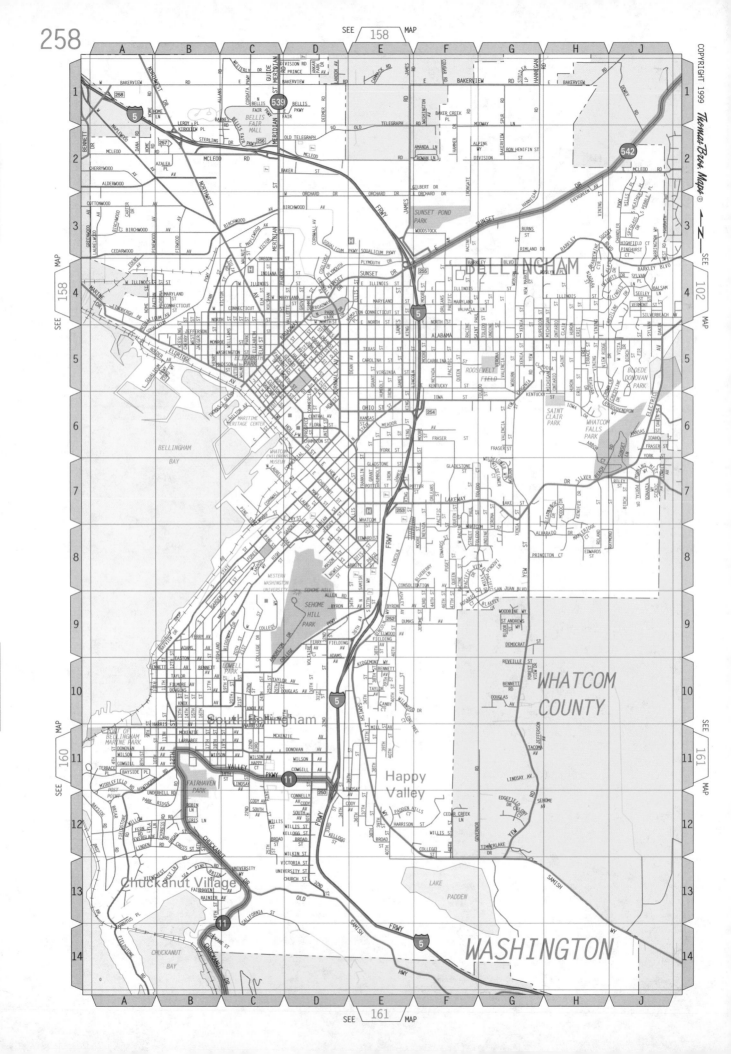

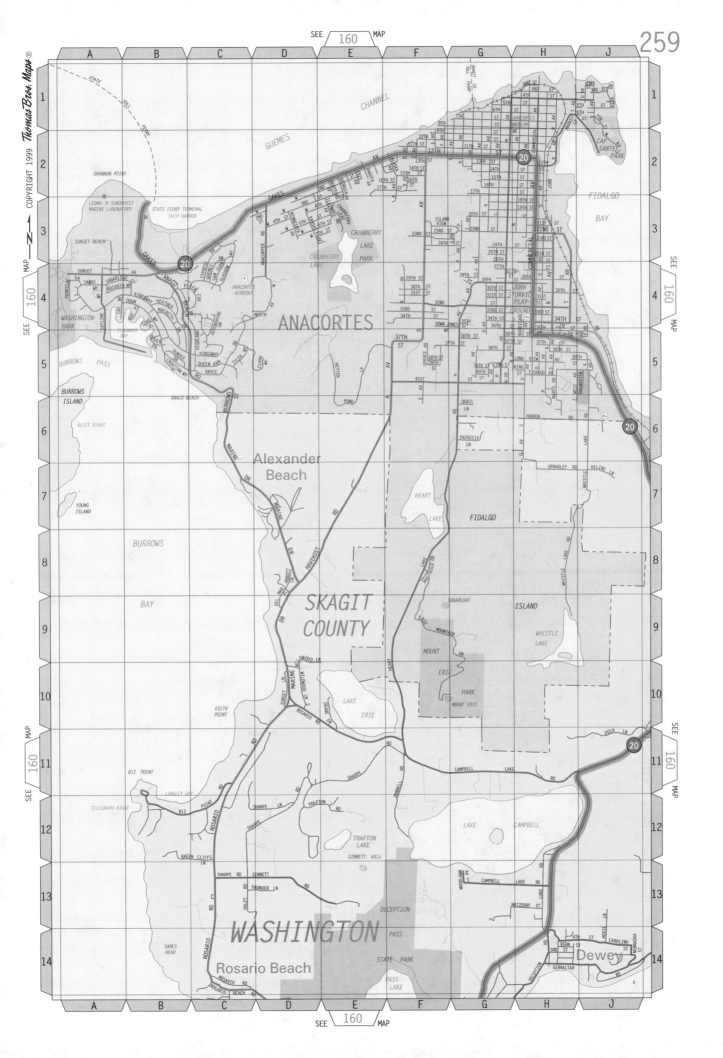

PNW

DETAIL

A B C D E F G H J

1

STATE
TOLL
FERRY

GUEMES CHANNEL

ANACORTES MUSEUM

CAP SANTE PARK

2

SHANNON POINT

GUEMES

FIDALGO BAY

20

SEE 160 MAP

3

LEONA M SUNDQUIST MARINE LABORATORY

STATE FERRY TERMINAL SHIP HARBOR

SUNSET BEACH

OAKES AV

CRANBERRY LAKE PARK

CRANBERRY LAKE

ISLAND VIEW

COMMERCIAL

4

SUNSET
SANDS
SUGARLOAF
ROSARIO WY
PARKSIDE DR
WASHINGTON PARK

ANACO BEACH

ANACORTES AIRPORT

ANACORTES

JOHN STORVIC PLAY-GROUND

SEE 160 MAP

5

BURROWS PASS

BURROWS ISLAND

FLOUNDER BAY

SKYLINE

ANACO BEACH

DOWN JONES

SPRUCE AV

37TH ST

41ST

POND

6

ALICE BIGHT

MARINE DR

QUAIL LN

PATRICIA LN

HADDON

SPRADLEY RD HILINE LN

20

7

YOUNG ISLAND

MARINE DR

HAVEKOST RD

Alexander Beach

HEART LAKE

FIDALGO

WHISTLE LAKE RD

8

BURROWS BAY

DEL MAR DR
ABBOTT
HAVEKOST DR

SKAGIT COUNTY

LAKE ERIE

SUGARLOAF

ISLAND

WHISTLE LAKE

9

ERIE MOUNTAIN

MOUNT ERIE PARK

10

EDITH POINT

SUNSET LN
MARINE
DONOHUE LN
ROSARIO RD
DEANE DR

HEART LAKE RD

MOUNT ERIE

SEE 160 MAP

11

BIZ POINT

LANGLEY BAY

ROSARIO RD

SHARPE LN

CAMPBELL LAKE RD

20

12

TELEGRAPH BIGHT

BIZ POINT

ROSARIO RD

SHARPE LN TRAFTON RD

TRAFTON LAKE

LAKE CAMPBELL

13

GREEN CLIFFS LN

SHARPE RD GINNETT

THUNDER LN

GINNETT HILL

WOODLAWN AV CAMPBELL LAKE RD

MATZDORF ST

14

SARES HEAD

ROSARIO RD

ROSARIO BEACH RD

WASHINGTON

Rosario Beach

DECEPTION PASS STATE PARK

PASS LAKE

DECEPTION

3RD VERN 4TH
GIBRALTAR
Dewey
CAROLINA ST
NEBRASKA ST

A B C D E F G H J

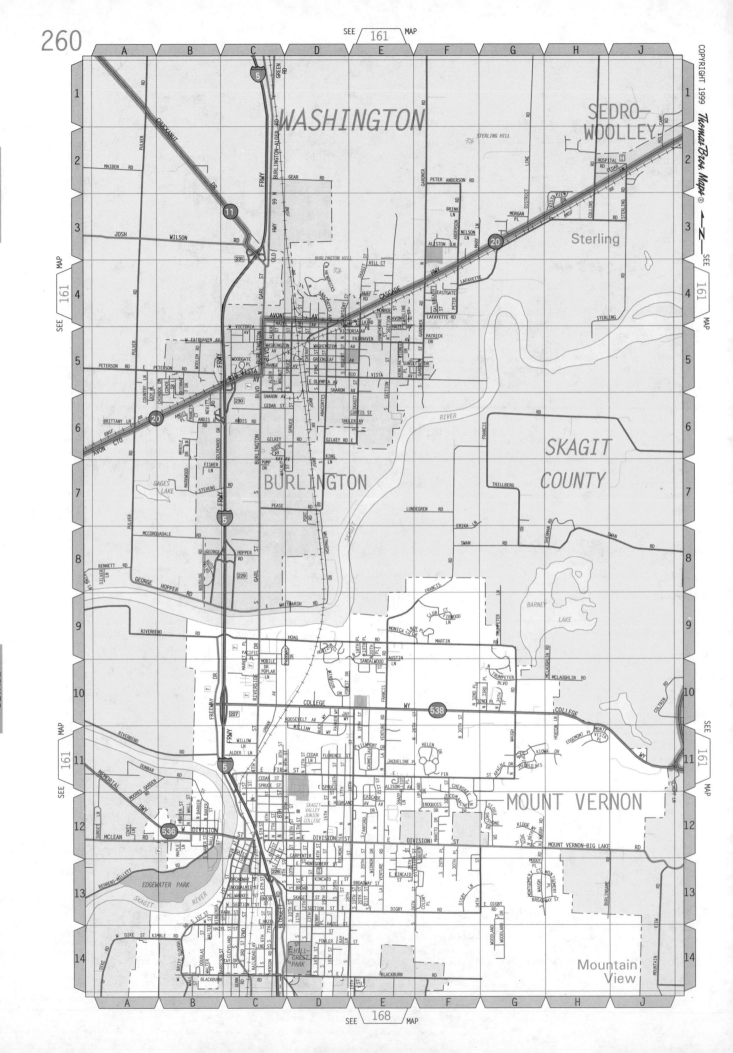

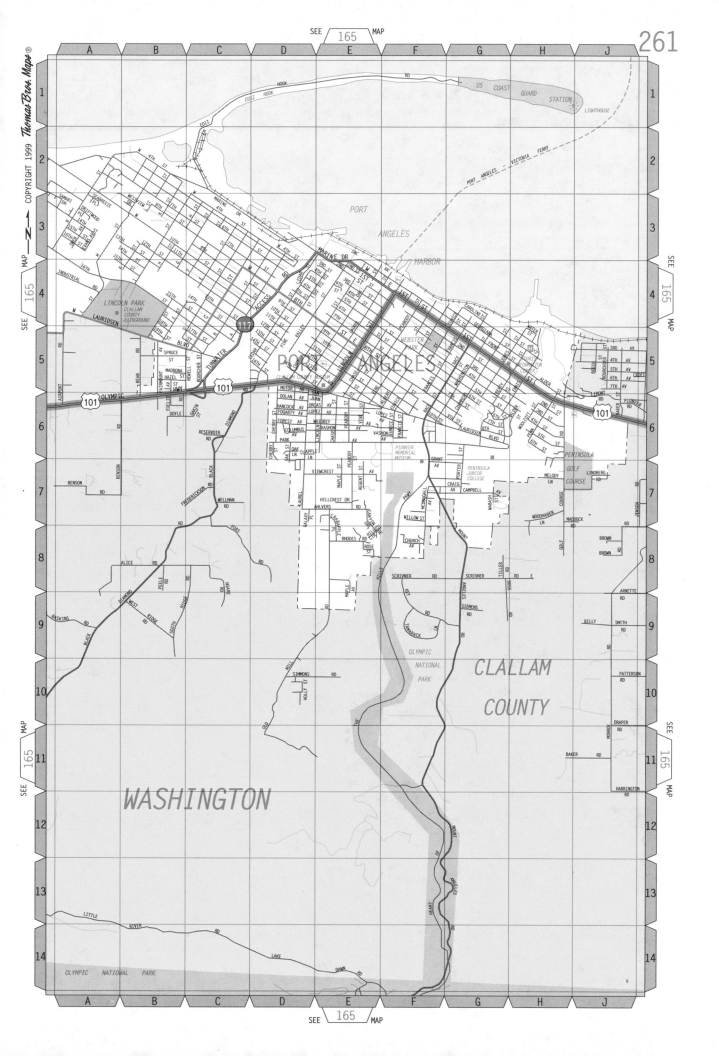

PNW

DETAIL

SEE 165 MAP

SEE 165 MAP

SEE 165 MAP

SEE 165 MAP

SEE 165 MAP

PORT ANGELES

PORT ANGELES HARBOR

US COAST GUARD STATION

LIGHTHOUSE

WASHINGTON

CLALLAM COUNTY

OLYMPIC NATIONAL PARK

LINCOLN PARK

CLALLAM COUNTY FAIRGROUND

PENINSULA GOLF COURSE

PENINSULA JUNIOR COLLEGE

PIONEER MEMORIAL MUSEUM

WEBSTER PARK

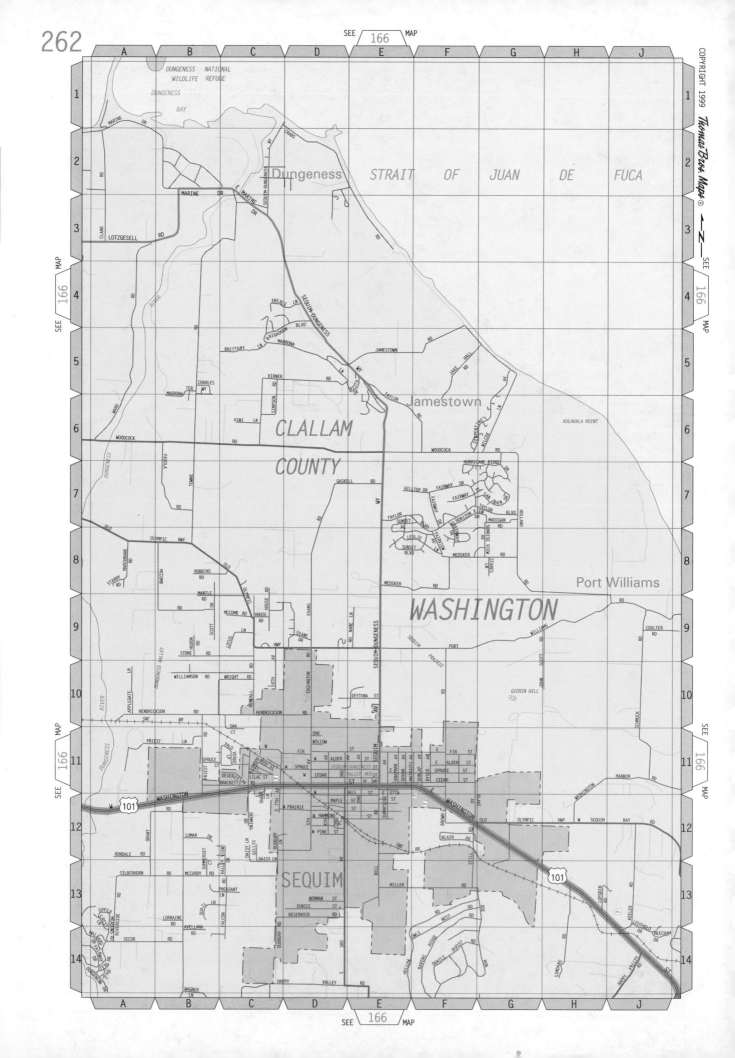

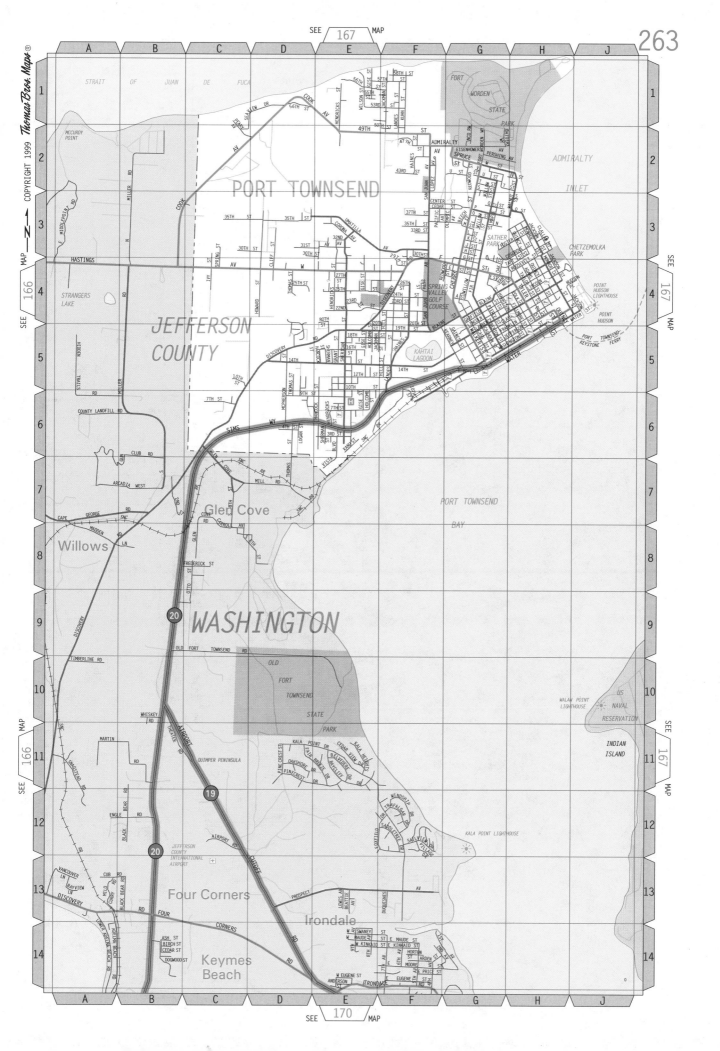

MAP N→

SEE 167 MAP

SEE 166 MAP

SEE 167 MAP

SEE 166 MAP

SEE 167 MAP

SEE 170 MAP

PNW

DETAIL

STRAIT OF JUAN DE FUCA

MCCURDY POINT

E MIDDLEPOINT RD

MILLER RD

COOK AV

SEAVIEW DR
56TH ST
PEARY AV

COOK AV

PORT TOWNSEND

HASTINGS

STRANGERS LAKE

JEFFERSON COUNTY

HIDDEN TRAILS RD

MILLER RD

COUNTY LANDFILL RD

35TH
30TH ST
7TH ST

SPRING ST
CLIFF ST

IVY ST
HOWARD ST
THOMAS ST
25TH ST

HENDRICKS ST

ROTH ST

DISCOVERY RD

14TH
10TH ST

THOMAS ST

9TH ST

MCPHERSON ST

HANCOCK ST

HENDRICKS ST

LOGAN ST
SHERMAN ST
3RD ST
4TH ST

SIMS WY

VISTA

KANT ST

GLEN COVE

GLEN COVE RD

MILL RD

RR

THOMAS

SNC

CAPE GEORGE RD
MADDEN RD
SNC

Willows

GLEN LN

2ND ST
8TH ST
S 8TH ST

CARROLL AV

FREDERICK ST

OTTO ST

GLEN ST

20

WASHINGTON

DISCOVERY RD

TIMBERLINE RD

OLD FORT TOWNSEND RD

OLD FORT TOWNSEND STATE PARK

WHISKEY RD

MARTIN

SNC

SNAGSTEAD RD

BEAR RD
BLACK BEAR RD

ENGLE RD

AIRPORT RD

THEATER RD

QUIMPER PENINSULA

19

20

JEFFERSON COUNTY INTERNATIONAL AIRPORT

VANCOUVER LN
GRAYVIEW LN
DISCOVERY

CUB RD
MILO
CORY
BLACK BEAR RD

Four Corners

FOUR CORNERS RD

CUTOFF RD

Irondale

AIRPORT RD

PROSPECT

ASH ST
BIRCH ST
CEDAR ST
DOGWOOD ST

Keymes Beach

LOWER SOUTH BEACH RD
ADELMA BEACH RD

ADMIRALTY

ADMIRALTY INLET

FORT WORDEN STATE PARK

56TH ST
WILSON ST
55TH ST
JACKMAN ST
53RD ST
50TH
49TH

47TH

43RD

LOPEZ
SAN JUAN AV

37TH
35TH
33RD ST

CENTER
CEDAR
PATTIC
OLYMPIC
BEECH
WILLOW

SATHER PARK

SPRING VALLEY GOLF COURSE

CHETZEMOKA PARK

POINT HUDSON LIGHTHOUSE

POINT HUDSON

PORT KEYSTONE

PORT TOWNSEND FERRY

KAHTAI LAGOON

WATER ST

PORT TOWNSEND BAY

WALAW POINT LIGHTHOUSE

US NAVAL RESERVATION

INDIAN ISLAND

KALA POINT DR
CEDAR VIEW DR
KALA HEIGHTS
PINE CREST ST
FAIR BREEZE DR
OAKSHORE DR
PINECREST DR
BAYCLIFF DR
BELVEDERE DR

MINOSHIP DR
TRAFALGAR DR
SABOT CIRCLE DR
S OXFORD DR
SALLY VIEW VILLAGE DR

KALA POINT LIGHTHOUSE

LEWIS AV
BEATTIE AV
DUQUESNES

AV

W SWANEY ST
W MAUDE ST
W KINKAID ST
9TH AV
8TH
7TH AV
6TH AV

E MAUDE ST
E KINKAID ST

HORTON ST
ARDEN
MOORE ST
W PRICE
W EUGENE ST
ANDERSON
Irondale
E EUGENE ST

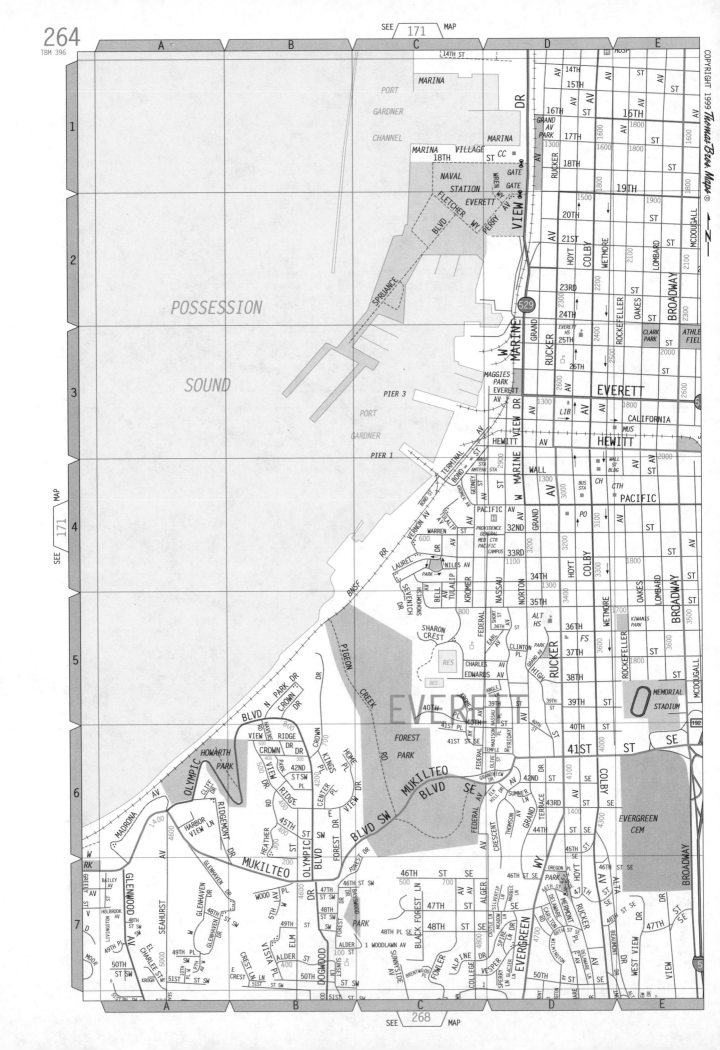

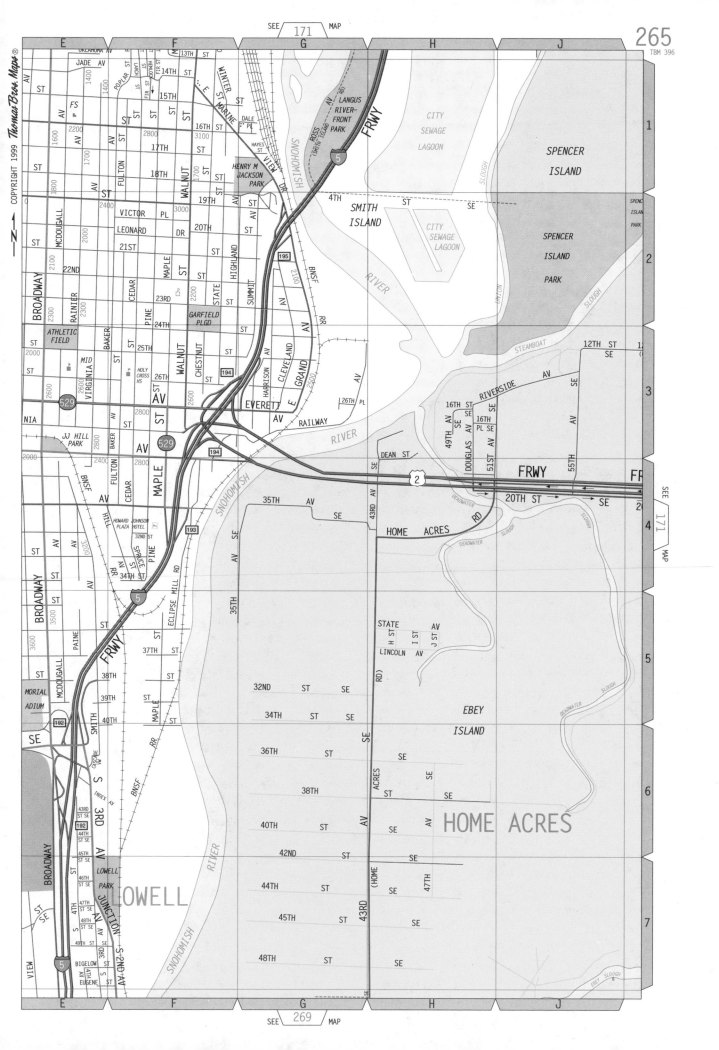

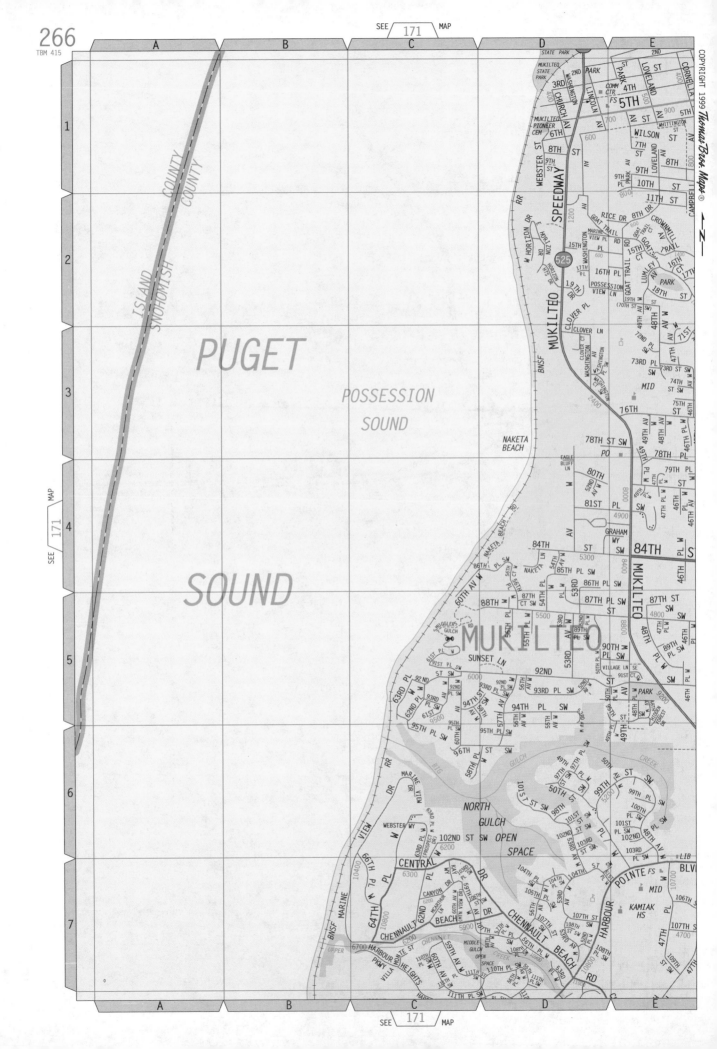

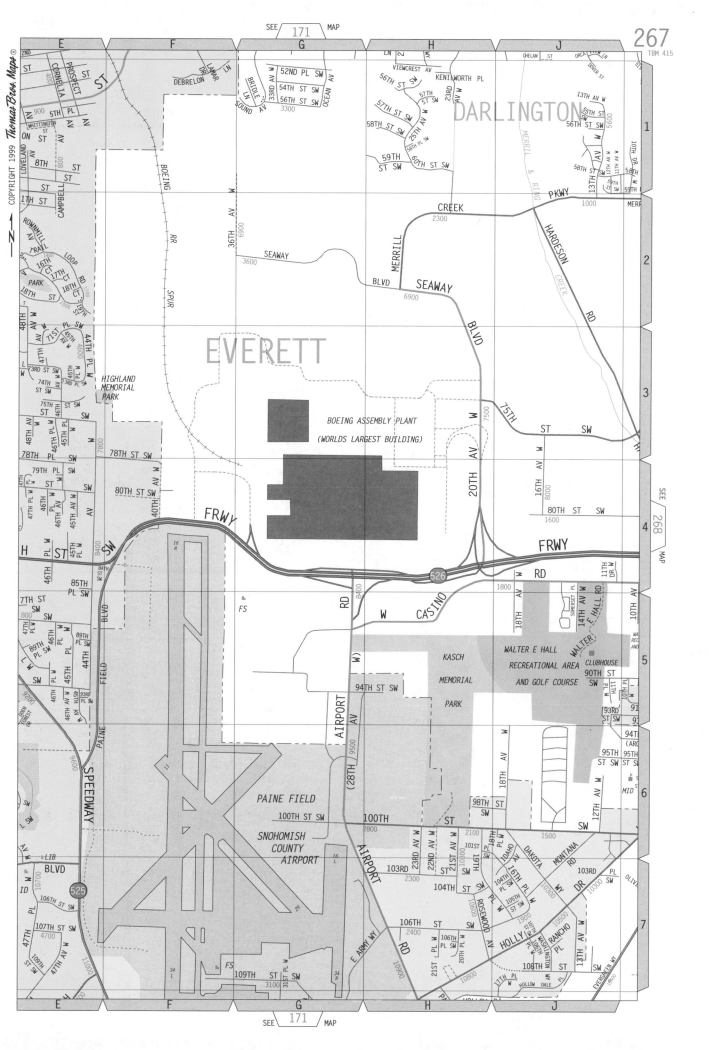

PNW

DETAIL

SEE 171 MAP

DARLINGTON

EVERETT

BOEING ASSEMBLY PLANT
(WORLDS LARGEST BUILDING)

HIGHLAND MEMORIAL PARK

FRWY

FRWY

526

CASINO

WALTER E HALL
RECREATIONAL AREA
AND GOLF COURSE

KASCH MEMORIAL PARK

CLUBHOUSE

PAINE FIELD

SPEEDWAY

SNOHOMISH COUNTY AIRPORT

525

SEE 268 MAP

SEE 171 MAP

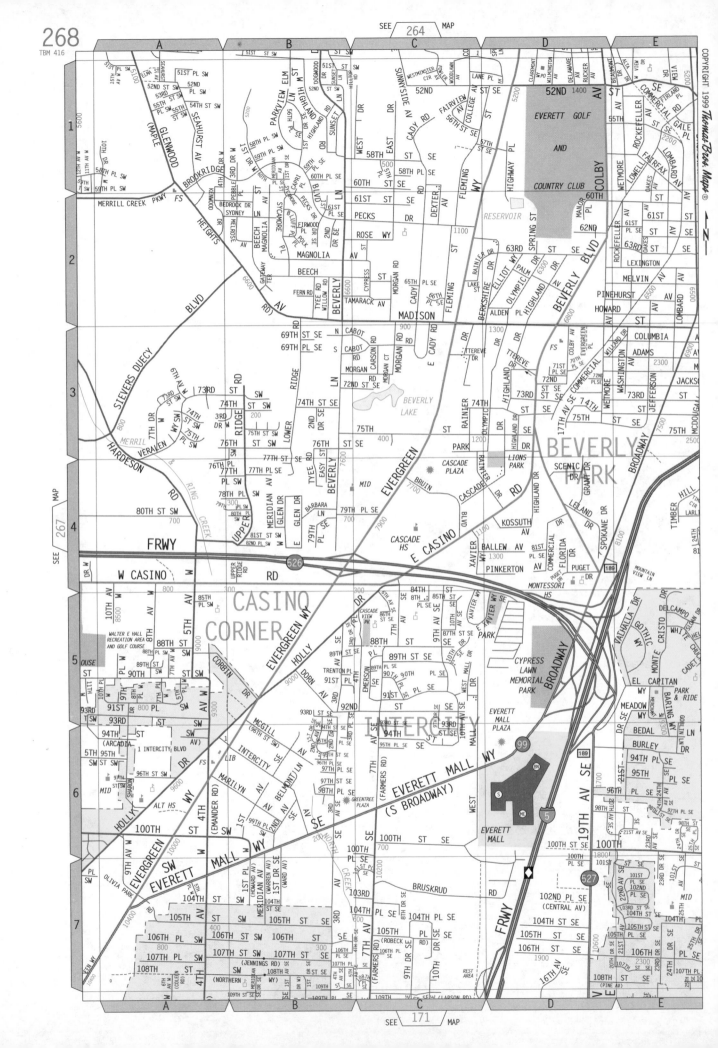

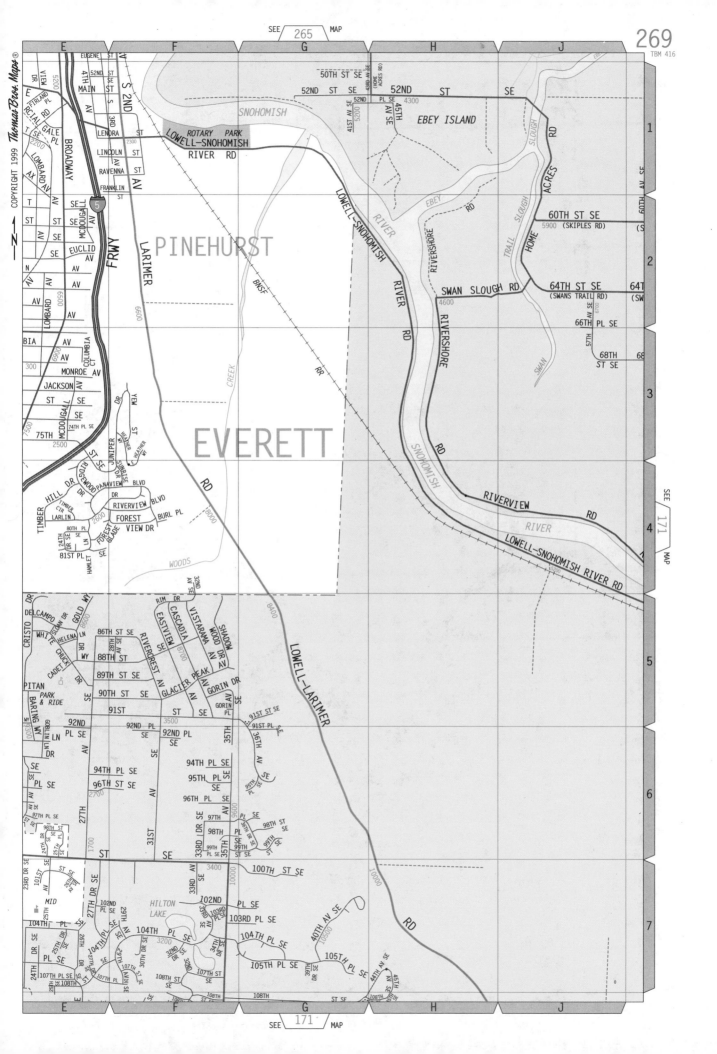

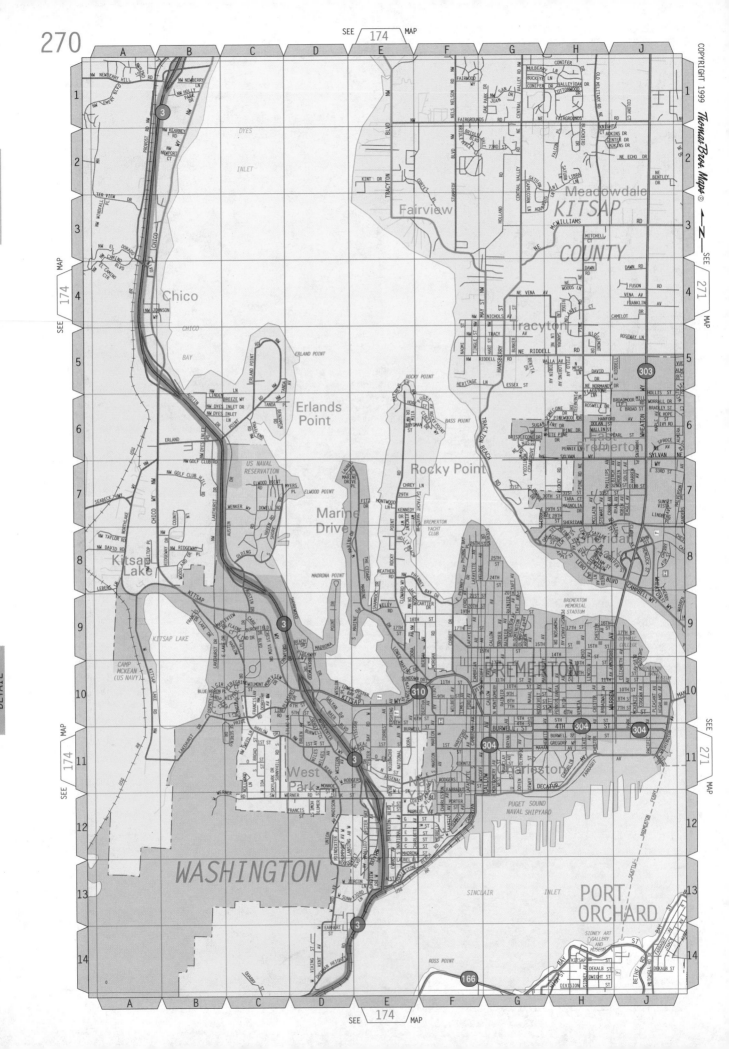

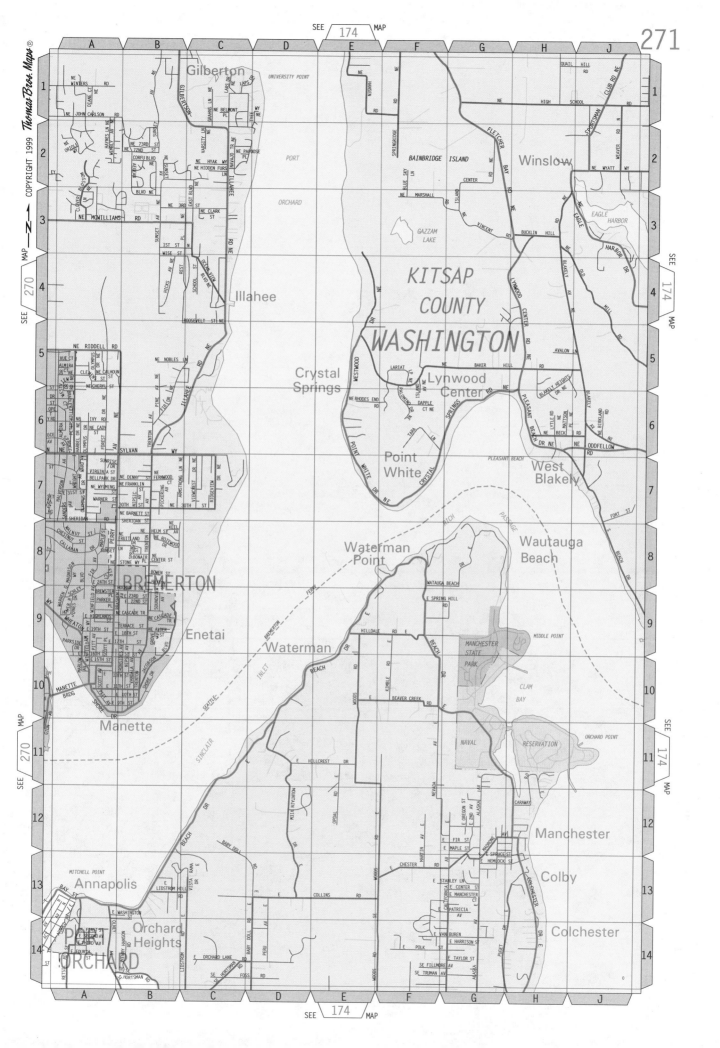

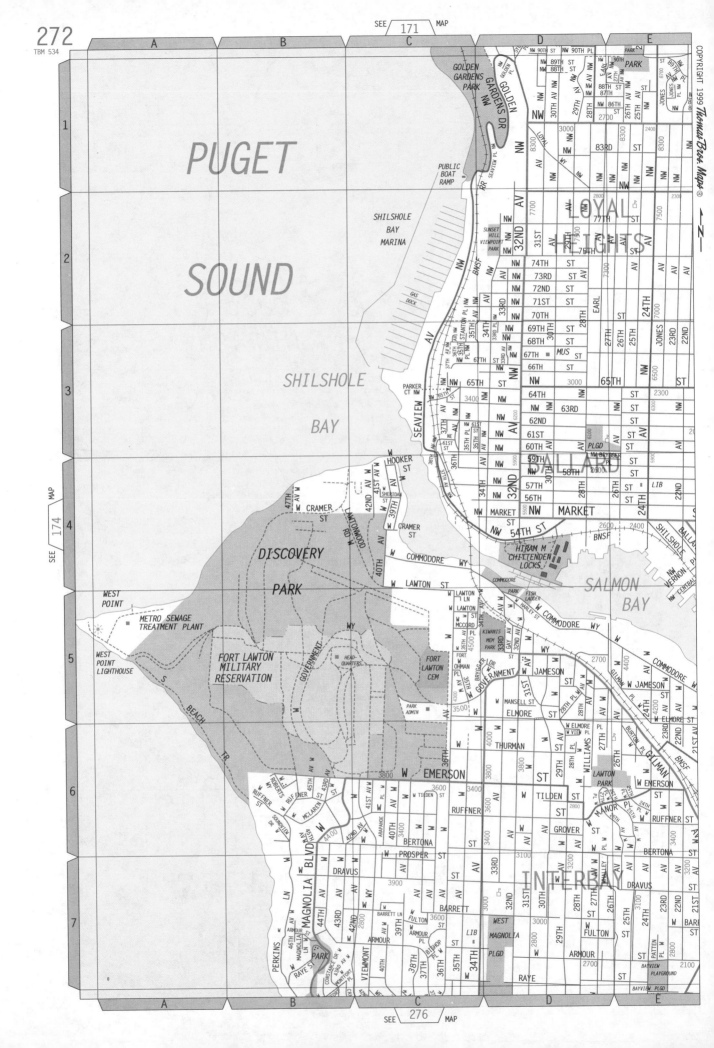

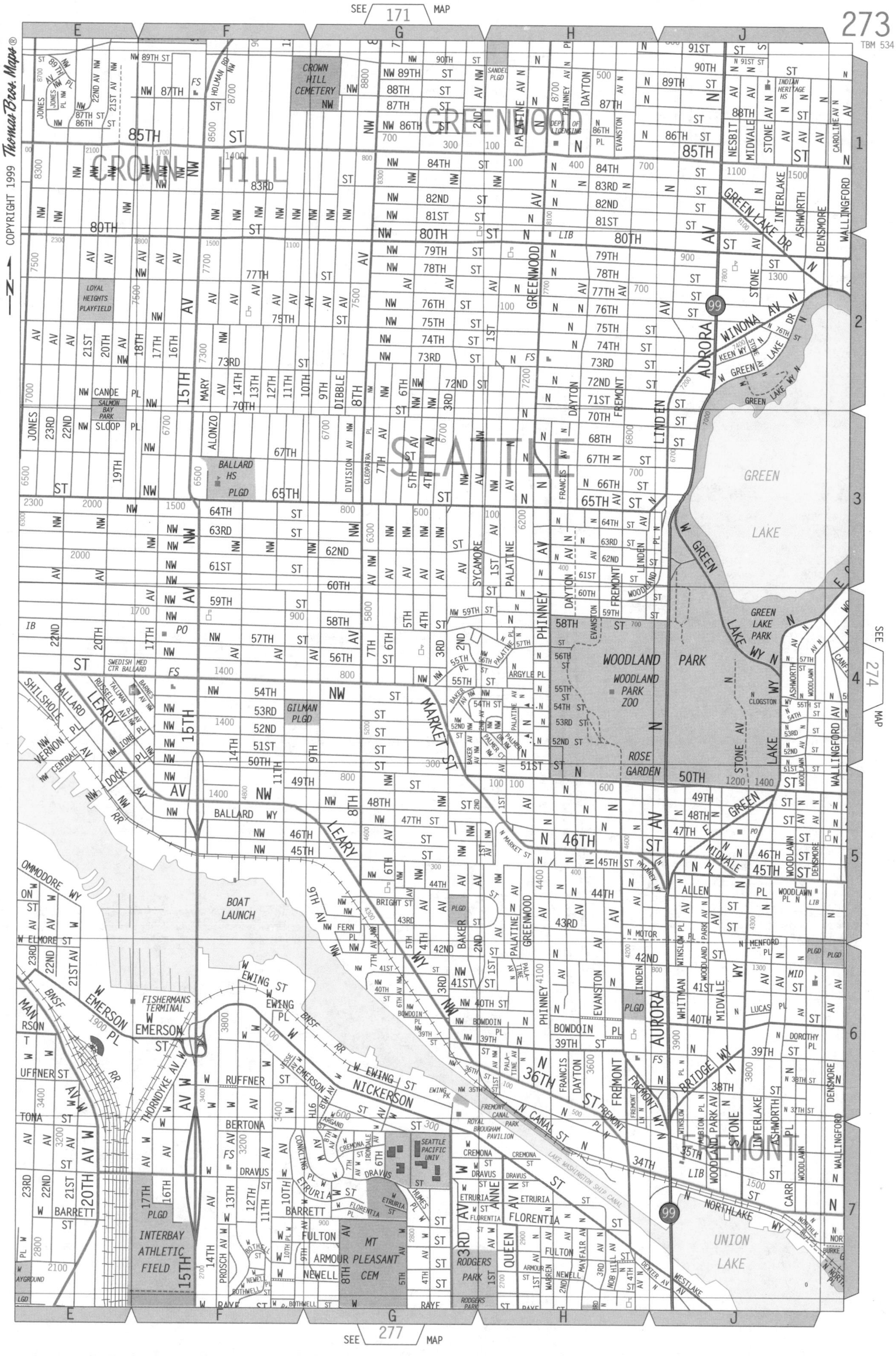
SEE 171 MAP
SEE 274 MAP
SEE 277 MAP
E
F
G
H
J
1
2
3
4
5
6
7
CROWN HILL
GREENWOOD
SEATTLE
FREMONT
CROWN HILL CEMETERY
LOYAL HEIGHTS PLAYFIELD
SALMON BAY PARK
BALLARD HS PLGD
GILMAN PLGD
SWEDISH MED CTR BALLARD
WOODLAND PARK
WOODLAND PARK ZOO
ROSE GARDEN
GREEN LAKE
GREEN LAKE PARK
BOAT LAUNCH
FISHERMANS TERMINAL
INTERBAY ATHLETIC FIELD
MT PLEASANT CEM
SEATTLE PACIFIC UNIV
RODGERS PARK
FREMONT CANAL PARK
ROYAL BROUGHAM PAVILION
LAKE WASHINGTON SHIP CANAL
UNION LAKE
INDIAN HERITAGE HS
DEPT OF LICENSING
SANDEL PLGD
85TH ST
80TH ST
65TH ST
50TH ST
46TH ST
45TH ST
AURORA AV
15TH AV NW
LEARY AV NW
MARKET ST
NW MARKET ST
BALLARD WY
SHILSHOLE AV NW
W EMERSON PL
NICKERSON ST
N 36TH ST
N 34TH ST
BRIDGE WY
GREEN LAKE DR N
WINONA AV N
W GREEN LAKE WY N
E GREEN LAKE WY N
GREENWOOD AV N
PHINNEY AV N
FREMONT AV N
STONE WY
WALLINGFORD AV
NORTHLAKE WY
WESTLAKE AV
DEXTER AV N
THORNDYKE AV W
COPYRIGHT 1999 Thomas Bros. Maps®

PNW

DETAIL

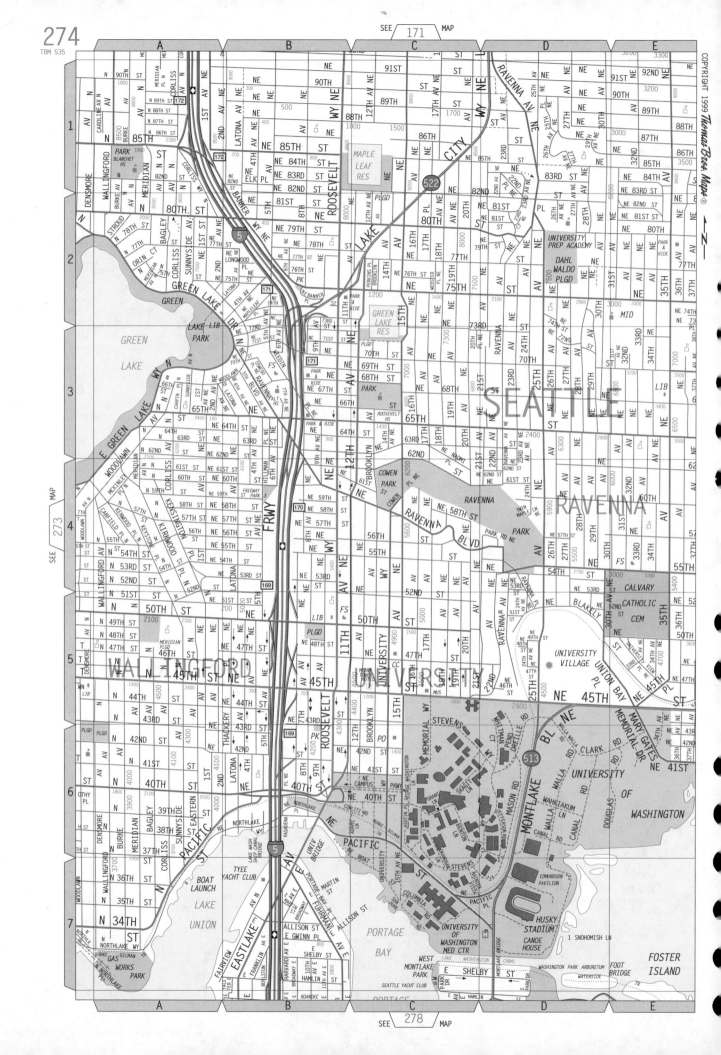

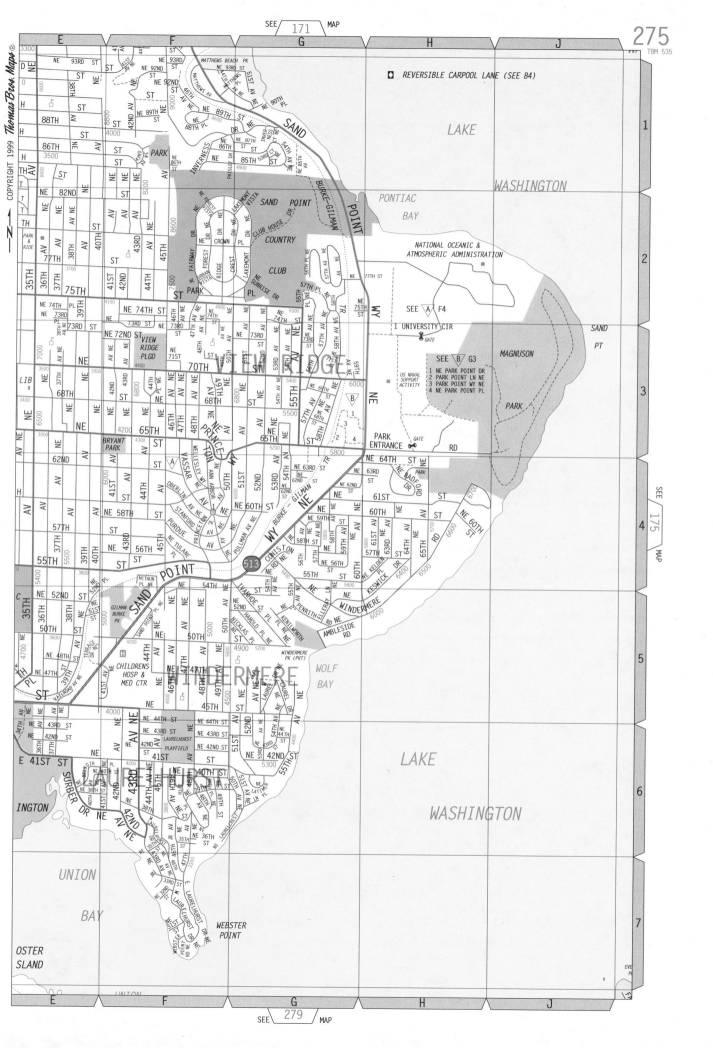

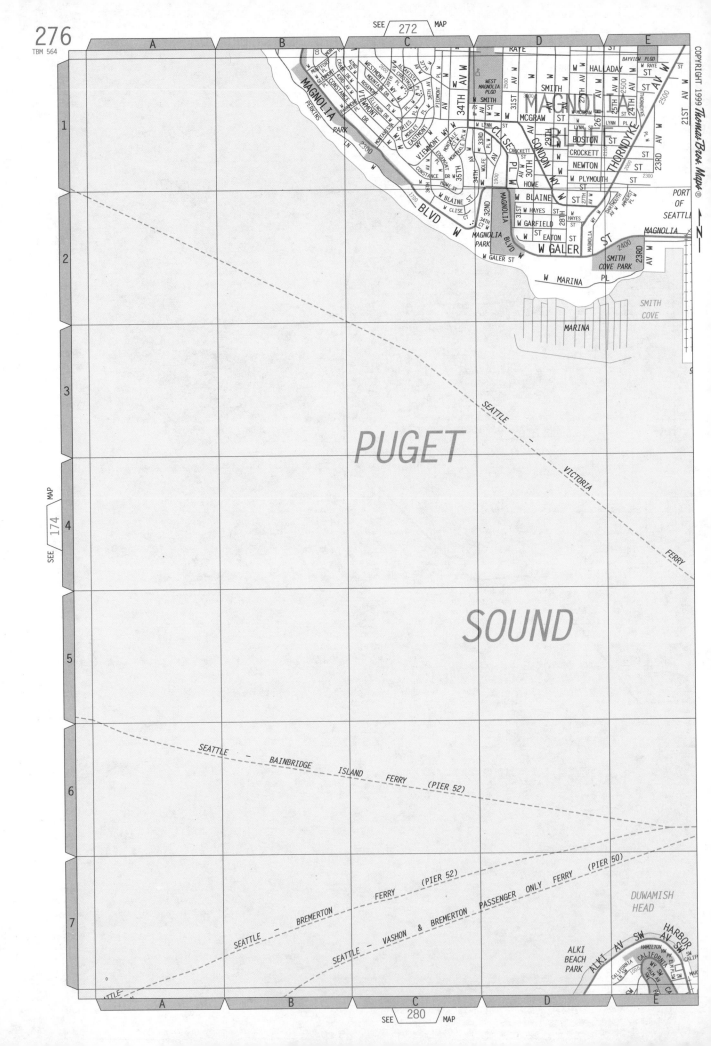

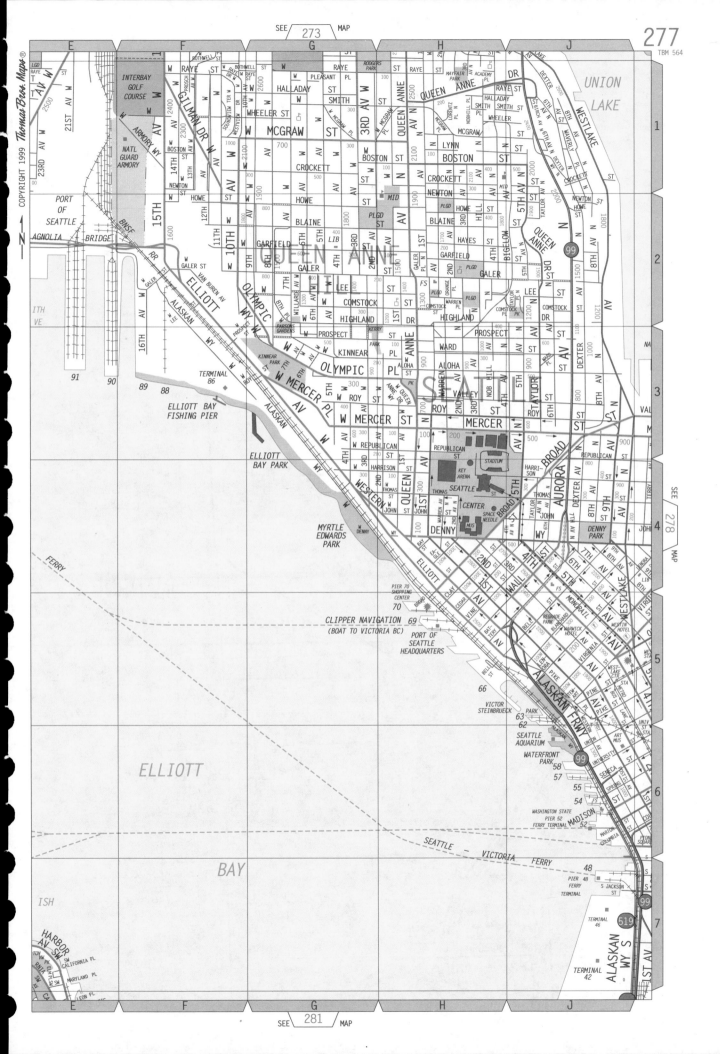

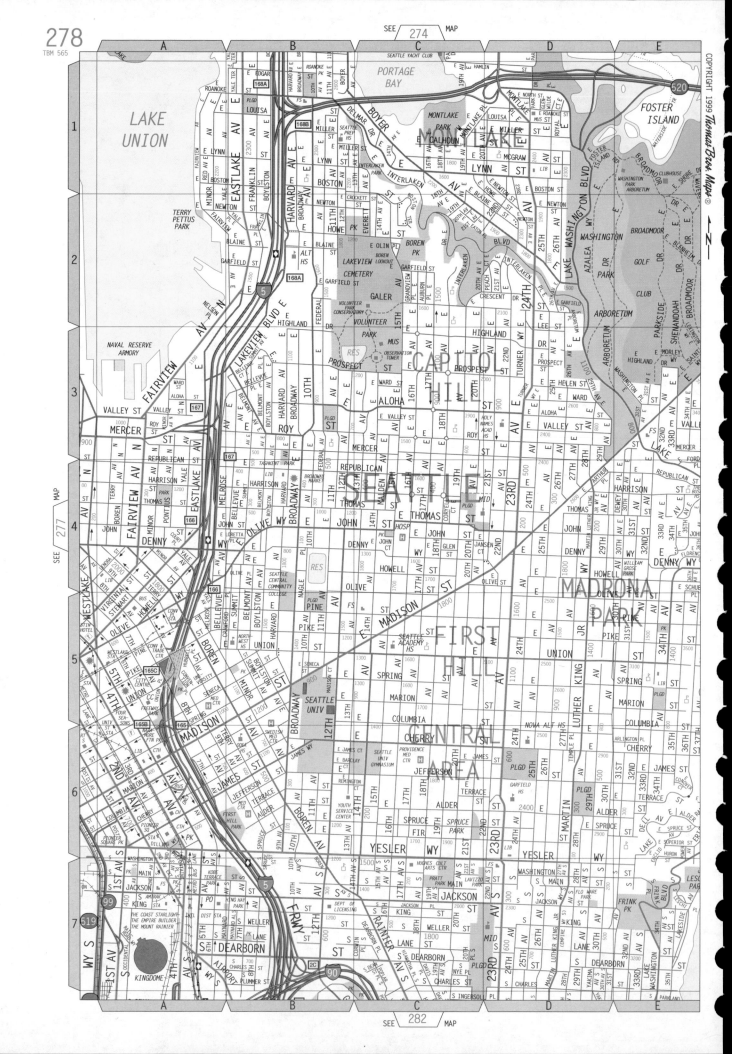

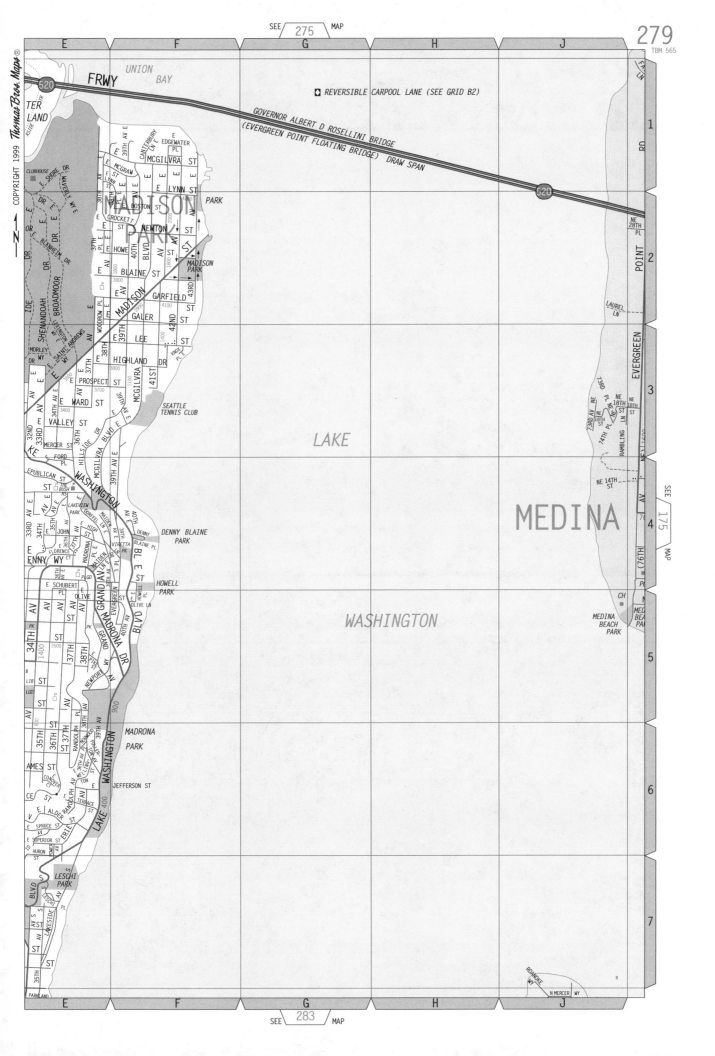

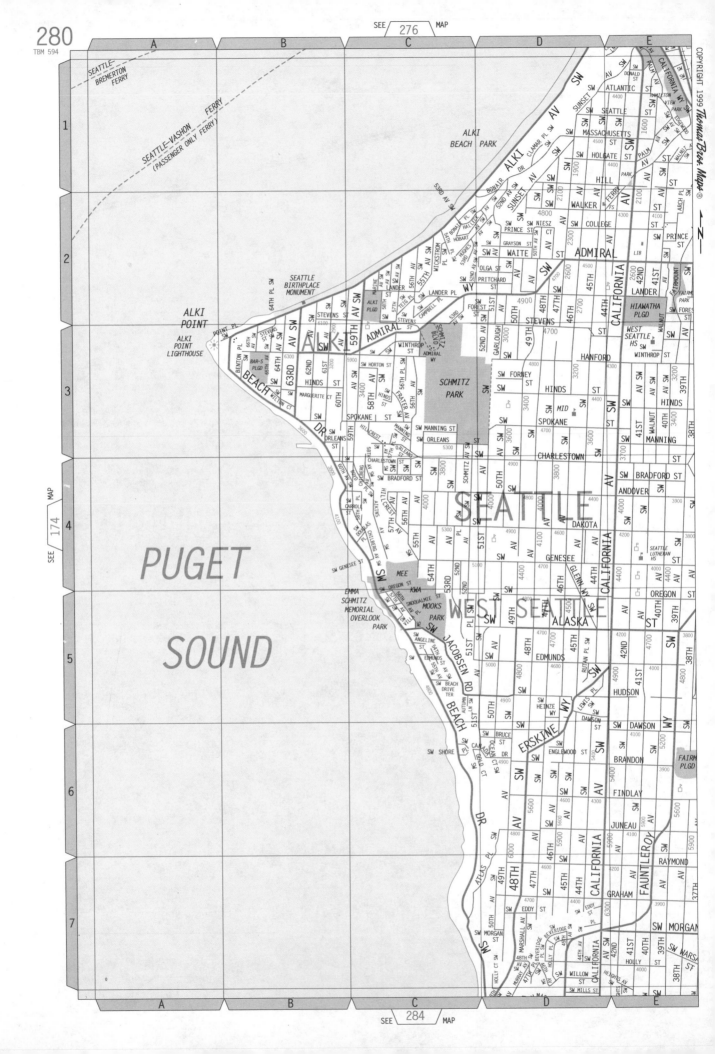

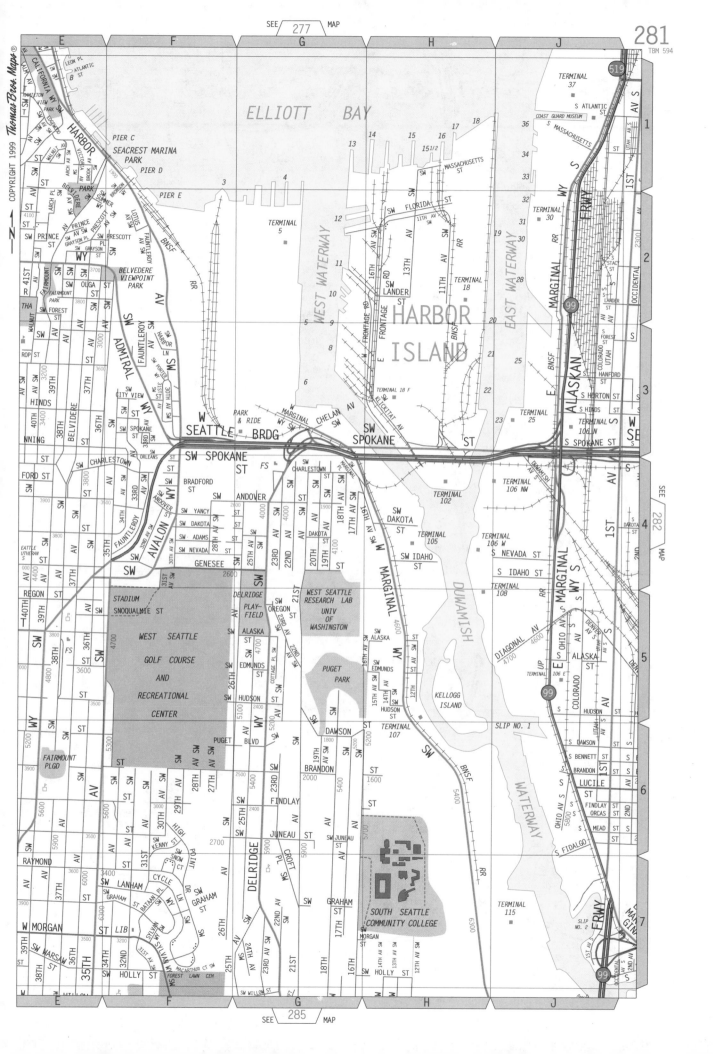

SEE 278 MAP

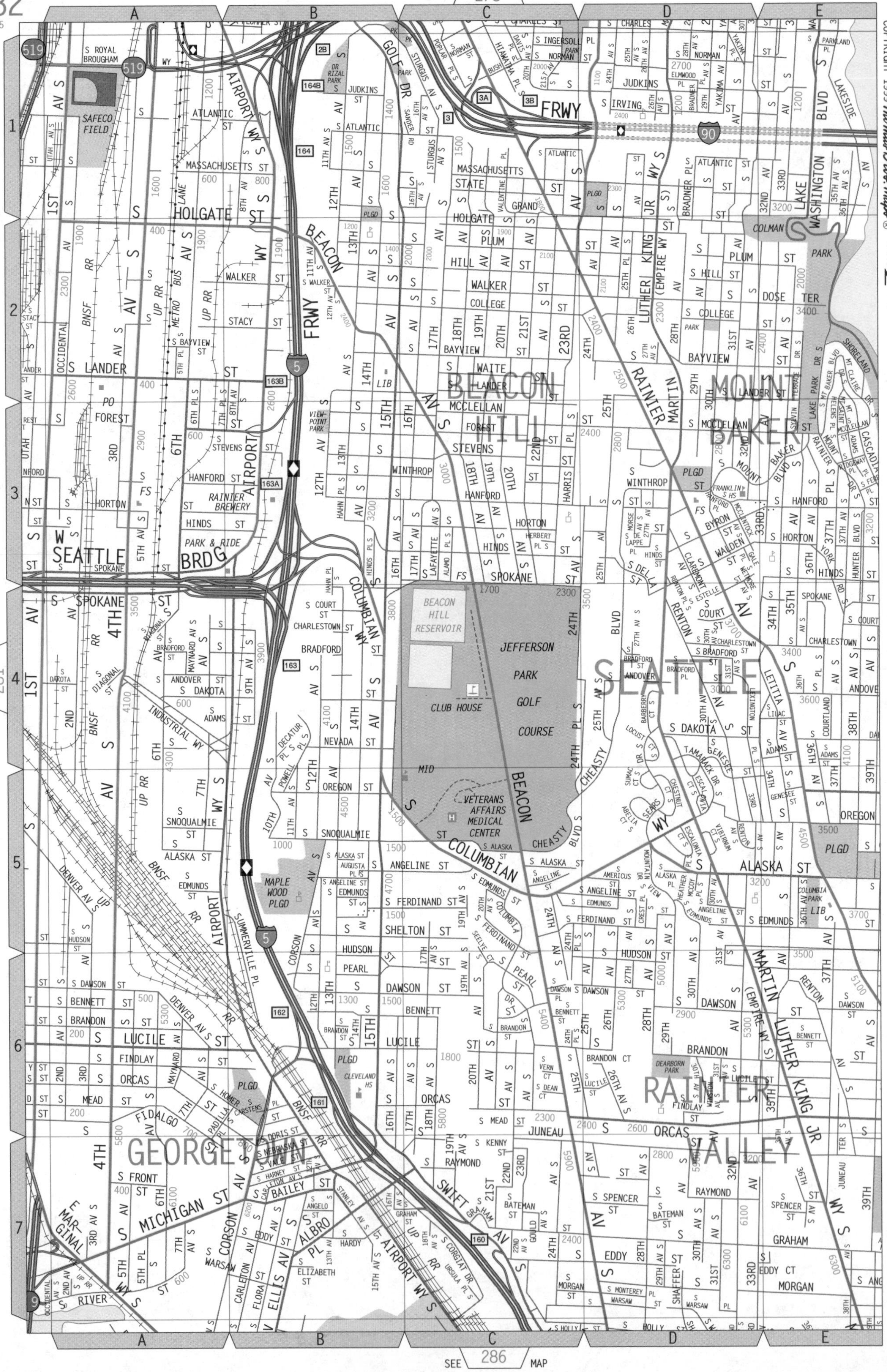

COPYRIGHT 1999 Thomas Bros. Maps®

—N—

PNW

DETAIL

SAFECO FIELD

HOLGATE ST

BEACON HILL

MOUNT BAKER

LAKE WASHINGTON

COLMAN PARK

RAINIER BREWERY

PARK & RIDE

W SEATTLE BRDG

SEATTLE

BEACON HILL RESERVOIR

JEFFERSON PARK GOLF COURSE

CLUB HOUSE

VETERANS AFFAIRS MEDICAL CENTER

MAPLE WOOD PLGD

GEORGETOWN

RAINIER VALLEY

E MARGINAL

SEE 281 MAP

SEE 286 MAP

A B C D E

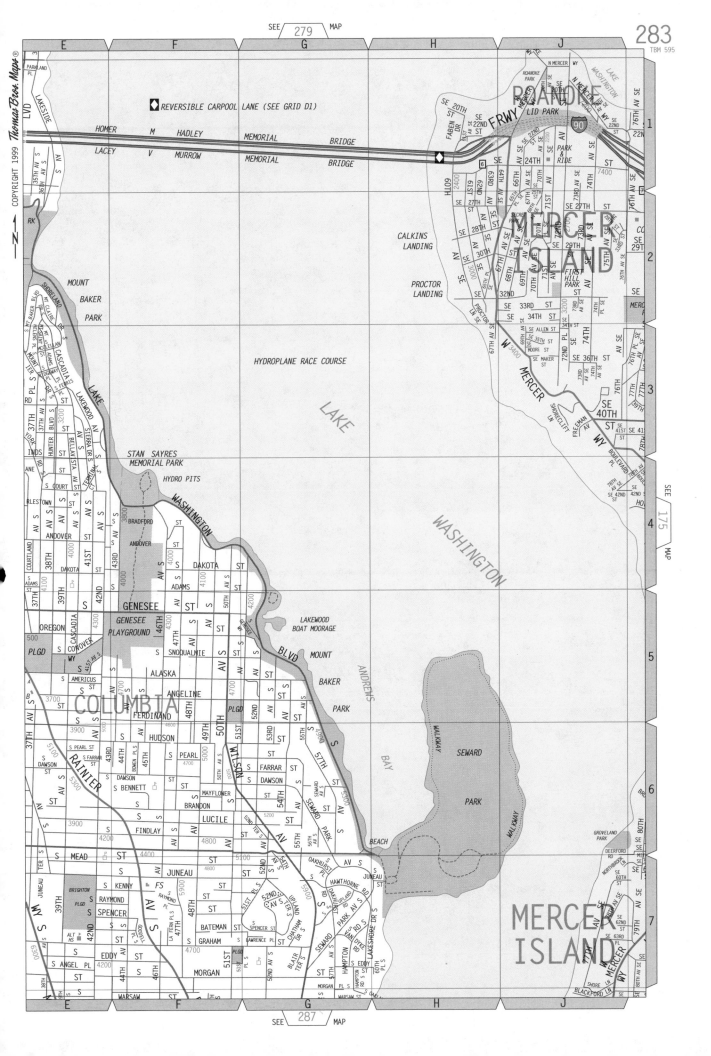

REVERSIBLE CARPOOL LANE (SEE GRID D1)

HOMER M HADLEY MEMORIAL BRIDGE

LACEY V MURROW MEMORIAL BRIDGE

ROANOKE

ROANOKE PARK

LID PARK

MERCER ISLAND

PARK & RIDE

CALKINS LANDING

PROCTOR LANDING

FIRST HILL PARK

MOUNT BAKER PARK

HYDROPLANE RACE COURSE

LAKE WASHINGTON

MERCER

SE 40TH ST

STAN SAYRES MEMORIAL PARK

HYDRO PITS

WASHINGTON

ANDOVER

DAKOTA

ADAMS

GENESEE

GENESEE PLAYGROUND

LAKEWOOD BOAT MOORAGE

MOUNT BAKER PARK

ANDREWS

SEWARD PARK

WALKWAY

OREGON

PLGD

COLUMBIA

ALASKA

ANGELINE

FERDINAND

HUDSON

PEARL

FARRAR

DAWSON

MAYFLOWER

BRANDON

LUCILE

FINDLAY

RAINIER

BAY

BEACH

MEAD ST

JUNEAU

HAWTHORNE RD

OAKHURST PL

BRIGHTON PLGD

KENNY

RAYMOND

SPENCER

BATEMAN

GRAHAM

LAWRENCE PL

EDDY

ANGEL PL

MORGAN

WARSAW

SEWARD

PARK AV S

LAKESHORE DR S

GROVELAND PARK

DEERFORD RD

MERCER ISLAND

MERCER WY

DETAIL

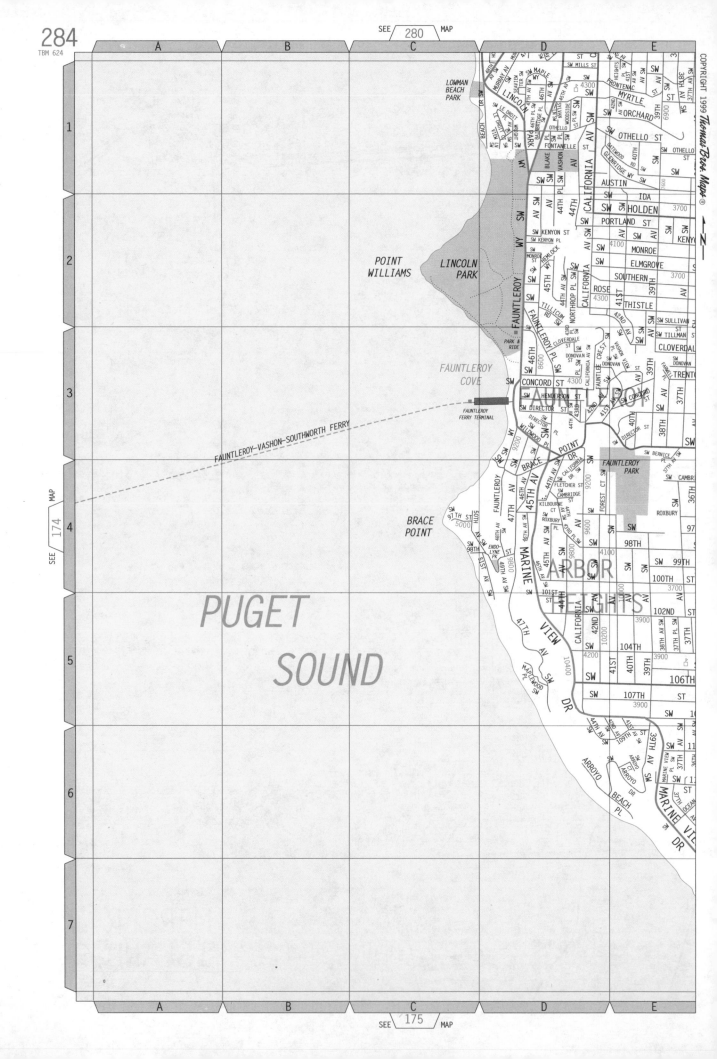

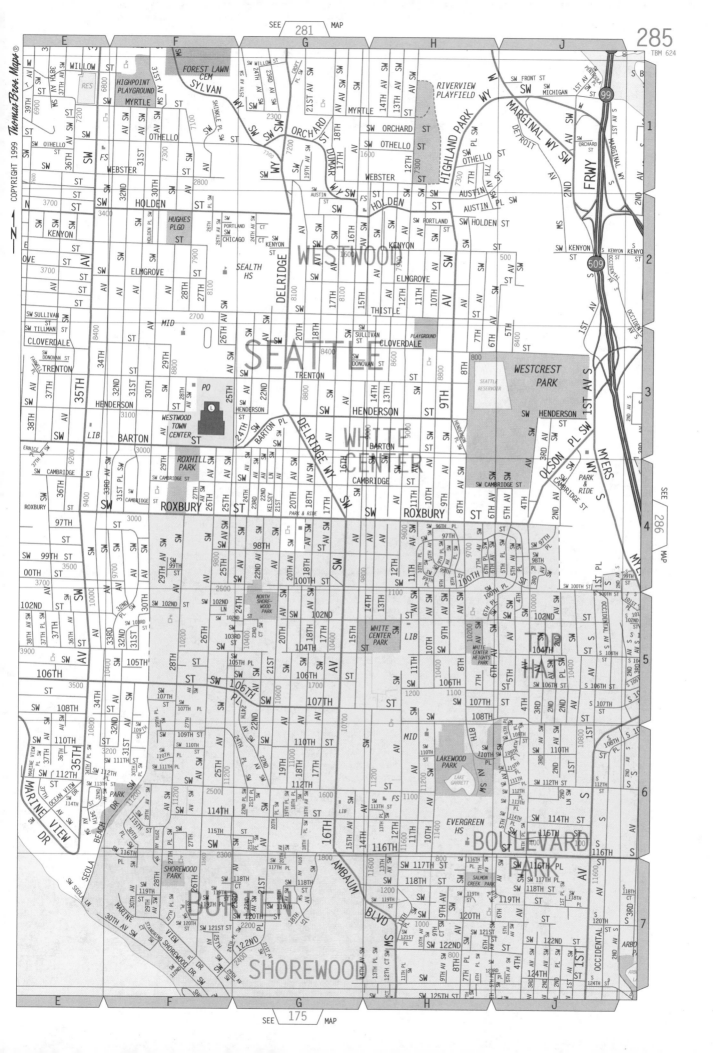

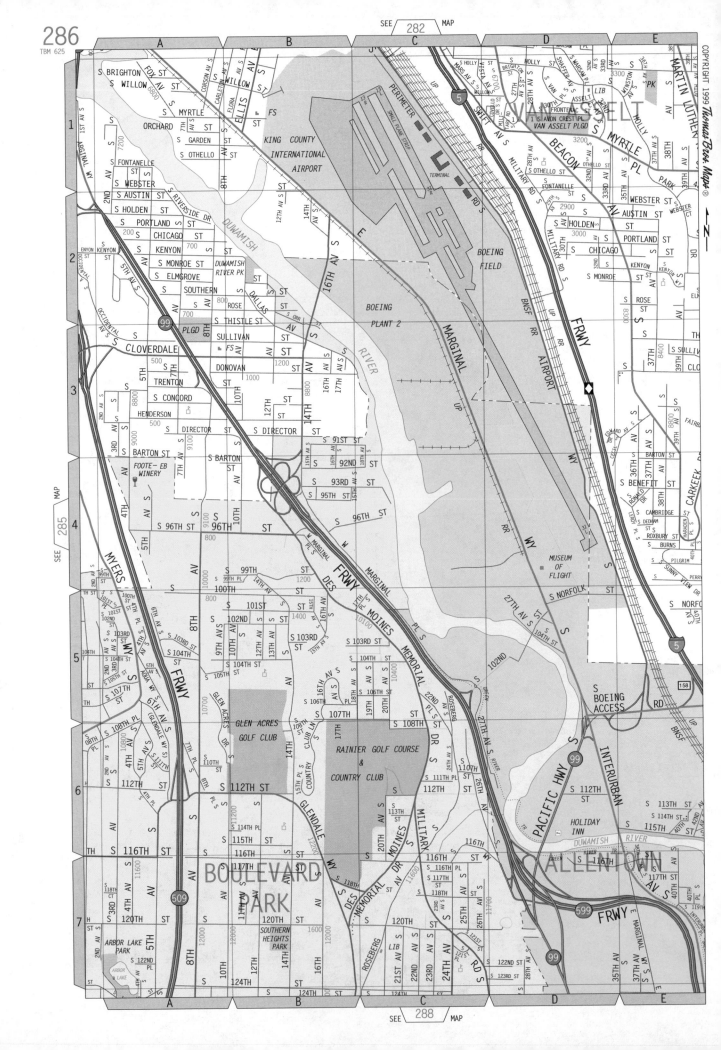

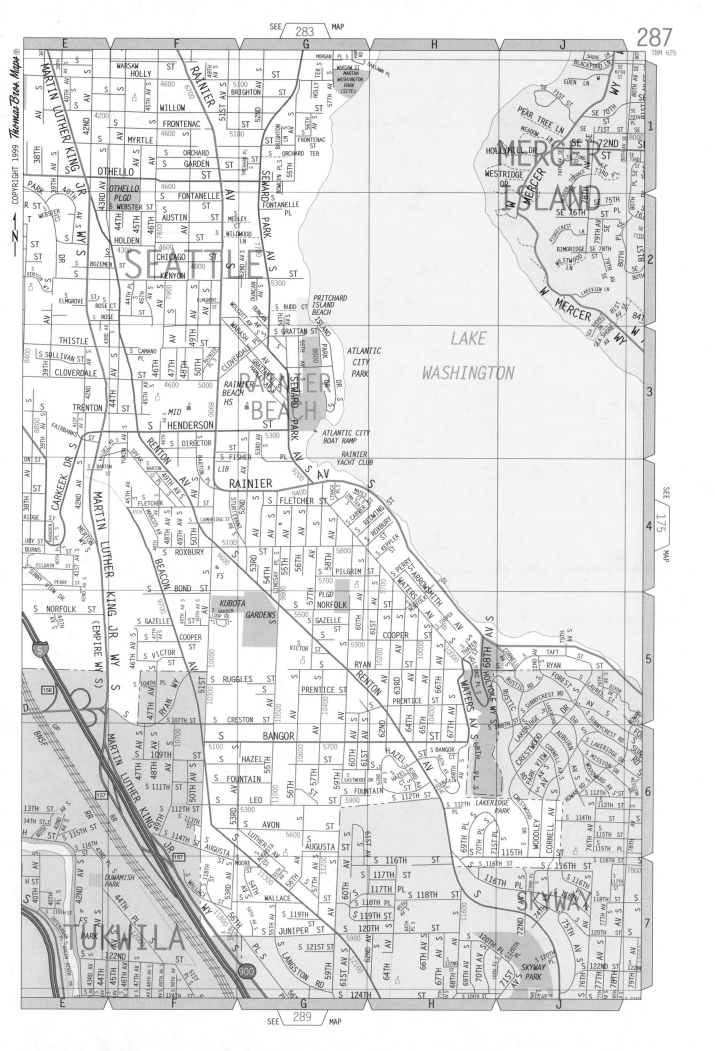

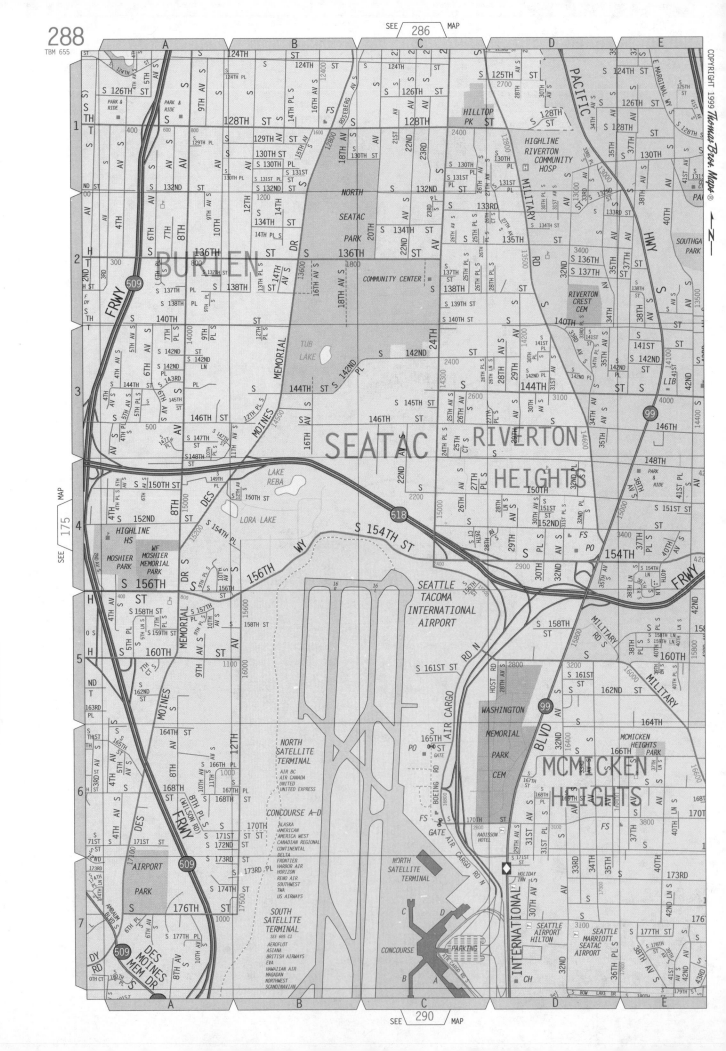

PNW

DETAIL

SEE 286 MAP

SEE 175 MAP

BURIEN

NORTH SEATAC PARK

COMMUNITY CENTER

HILLTOP PK

HIGHLINE RIVERTON COMMUNITY HOSP

RIVERTON CREST CEM

SOUTHGA PARK

TUB LAKE

SEATAC RIVERTON HEIGHTS

LAKE REBA

LORA LAKE

HIGHLINE HS

MOSHIER PARK

WF MOSHIER MEMORIAL PARK

SEATTLE TACOMA INTERNATIONAL AIRPORT

NORTH SATELLITE TERMINAL
AIR BC
AIR CANADA
UNITED
UNITED EXPRESS

CONCOURSE A-D
ALASKA
AMERICAN
AMERICA WEST
CANADIAN REGIONAL
CONTINENTAL
DELTA
FRONTIER
HARBOR AIR
HORIZON
RENO AIR
SOUTHWEST
TWA
US AIRWAYS

SOUTH SATELLITE TERMINAL
SEE 665 CI
AEROFLOT
ASIANA
BRITISH AIRWAYS
EVA
HAWAIIAN AIR
MAGADAN
NORTHWEST
SCANDINAVIAN

NORTH SATELLITE TERMINAL

CONCOURSE

PARKING

WASHINGTON MEMORIAL PARK CEM

MCMICKEN HEIGHTS PARK

MCMICKEN HEIGHTS

RADISSON HOTEL

HOLIDAY INN

SEATTLE AIRPORT HILTON

SEATTLE MARRIOTT SEATAC AIRPORT

AIRPORT PARK

DES MOINES MEM DR

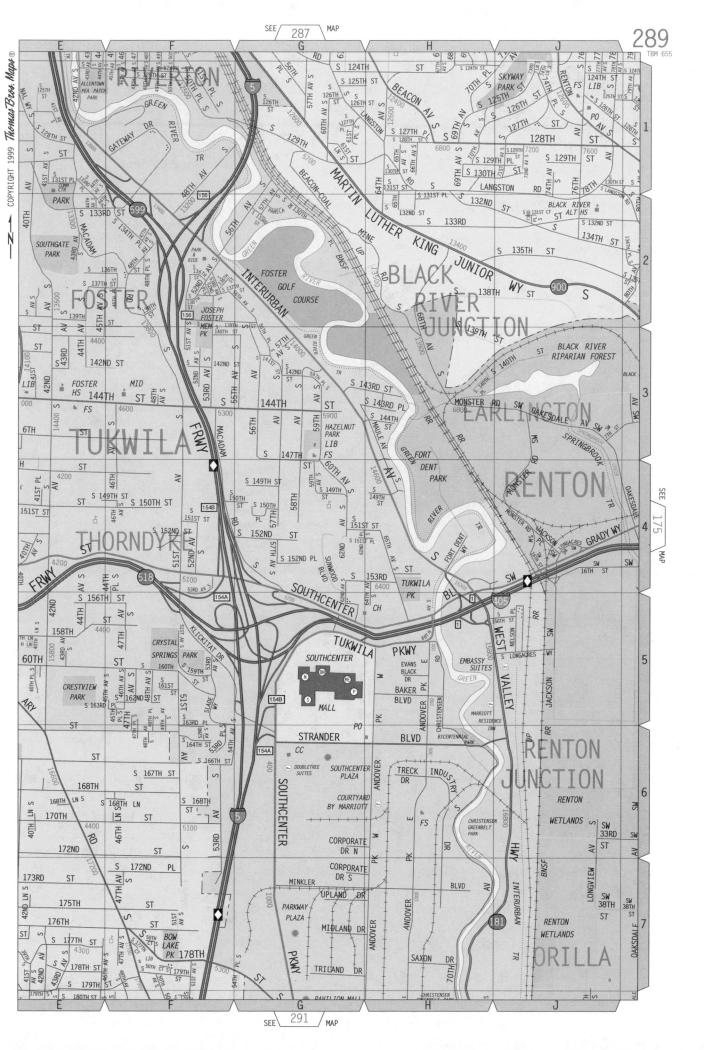

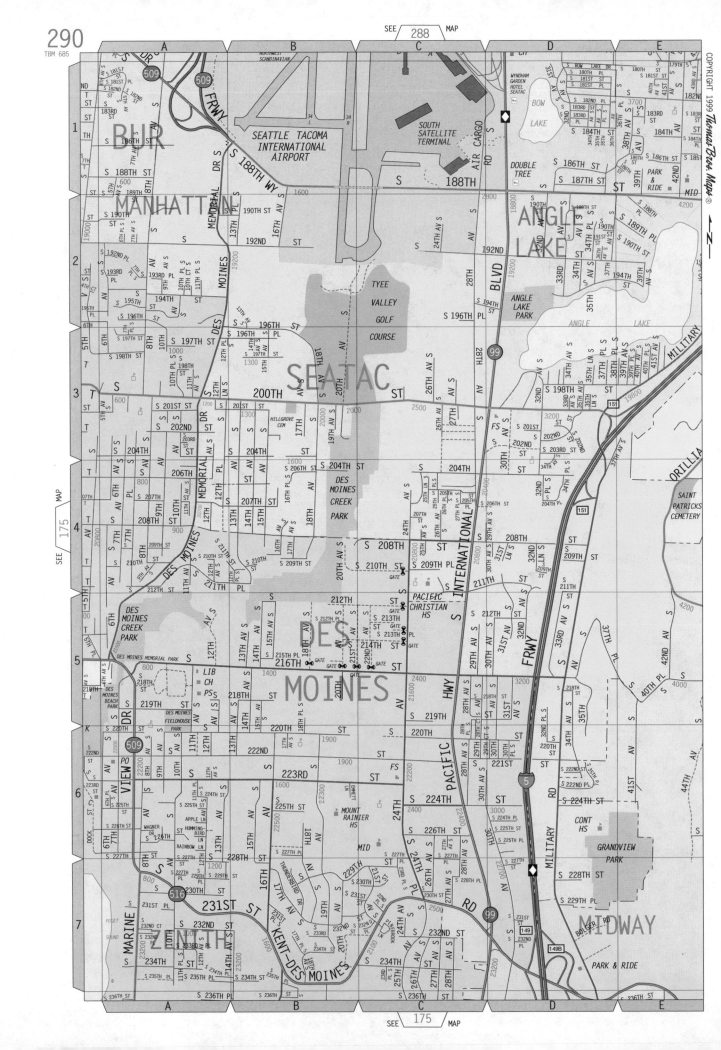

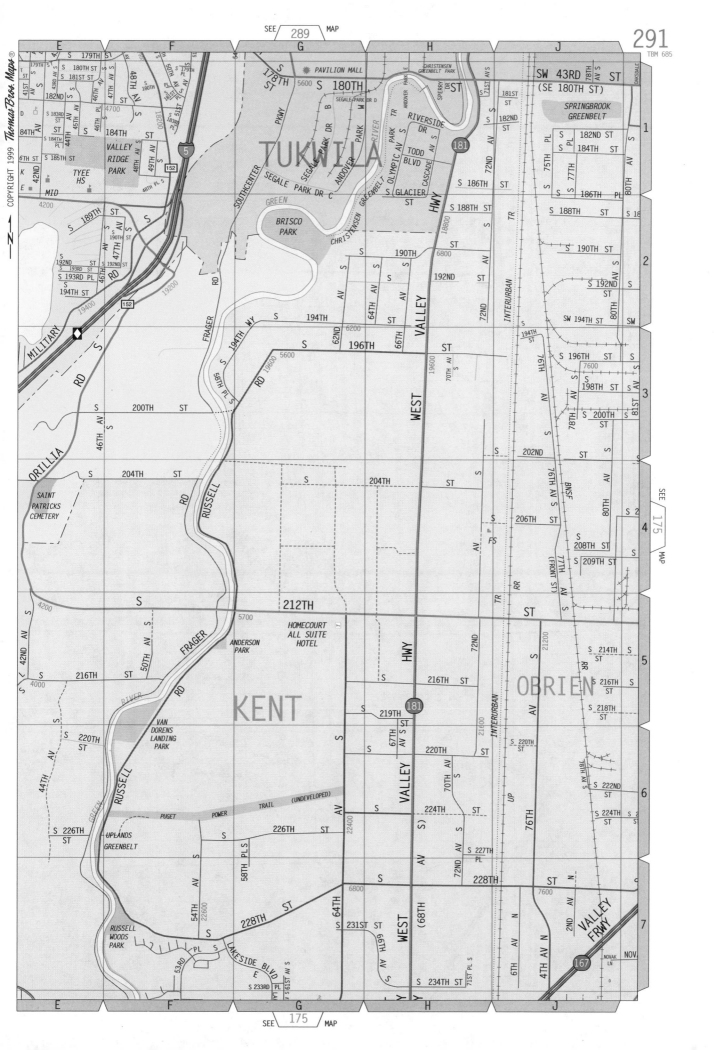

PNW

DETAIL

E   F   G   H   J

179TH ST
179TH S 180TH ST
41ST S 43RD 181ST ST
42ND AV
182ND ST
48TH AV
46TH 47TH AV
47TH AV
50TH
51ST
181ST
180TH
178TH ST
5600
S 180TH
PAVILION MALL
CHRISTENSEN GREENBELT PARK
SPERRY DR
71ST AV S
SW 43RD 78TH S ST
(SE 180TH ST)
181ST ST
182ND AV
182ND ST 184TH
SPRINGBROOK GREENBELT

S 183RD ST
84TH AV
S 184TH PL
45TH 46TH AV
4700
4200
18200
183RD PL
184TH ST
49TH AV
152
5
TUKWILA
SEGALE PARK DR B
SEGALE PARK DR C
SEGALE PARK DR D
ANDOVER PARK W
ANDOVER PARK E
OLYMPIC AV S
CHRISTENSEN GREENBELT
RIVERSIDE DR
TODD BLVD
CASCADE
GLACIER ST
181
S 186TH
S 186TH ST
75TH PL
77TH
186TH PL
80TH AV

TYEE HS
VALLEY RIDGE PARK
S 185TH ST
48TH PL S
MID
GREEN RIVER
S 188TH ST
18800
S 188TH
S 188TH ST
S 18

189TH ST
190TH AV S
192ND ST
193RD ST
192ND ST
193RD PL
194TH ST
47TH AV S
46TH RD S
19200
19400
152
MILITARY RD S
FRAGER RD
BRISCO PARK
SOUTHCENTER PKWY
SEGALE PARK DR
190TH ST
64TH AV S
66TH AV S
192ND
72ND AV
6800
INTERURBAN TR
S 190TH ST
S 192ND AV
80TH
SW 194TH ST SW

194TH WY
58TH PL S
194TH
5600
19600
62ND AV S
6200
196TH
66TH AV S
194TH ST
WEST VALLEY ST
19600
70TH AV S
76TH AV S
194TH ST
S 196TH ST
7600
S 198TH S AV
81ST AV

ORILLIA
200TH ST
46TH AV S
204TH ST
200TH
202ND
ST
81ST
87TH
S 200TH
76TH AV S
BNSF
80TH

SAINT PATRICKS CEMETERY
RUSSELL RD
204TH ST
204TH
ST
S
206TH
208TH ST
209TH ST
77TH (FRONT ST)
RR

4200
4000
212TH
5700
HOMECOURT ALL SUITE HOTEL
ST
72ND AV
21200
STA
TR
UP
214TH ST
216TH ST
218TH ST

42ND AV S
50TH AV S
FRAGER RD
ANDERSON PARK
216TH ST
216TH ST
HWY
S 219TH ST
181
OBRIEN
S 220TH ST
INTERURBAN AV
78TH AV S

KENT
VAN DORENS LANDING PARK
PUGET POWER TRAIL (UNDEVELOPED)
67TH AV S
220TH
ST
70TH AV S
76TH
S 222ND

44TH AV S
RUSSELL RD
GREEN RIVER
220TH ST
226TH ST
58TH PL S
VALLEY AV
22400
224TH ST
227TH PL
72ND AV S
S 224TH ST

S 226TH ST
UPLANDS GREENBELT
226TH ST
228TH ST
64TH AV S
6800
WEST (68TH)
S 227TH
228TH ST
7600
2ND AV N
VALLEY FRWY

RUSSELL WOODS PARK
53RD PL
54TH AV S
22600
228TH ST
231ST ST
LAKESIDE BLVD
E
S 61ST AV S
99TH
WEST VALLEY HWY
71ST PL S
6TH AV N
4TH AV N
167
NOVAK LN
NOV.

S 233RD
234TH ST

SEE 181 MAP

COPYRIGHT 1999 Thomas Bros. Maps®

PNW

DETAIL

—N—

A B C D E

PUGET SOUND

1

VISSCHER ST
HIGHLAND AV
41ST
40TH
39TH
BALTIMORE
BENNETT
JANE CLARK PLGD
41ST
MCBRIDE
38TH ST
37TH ST
36TH
35TH
N
MASON AV
MADRONA WY
DALE ST
VINE
WATERVIEW
MARINE PARK
LES DAVIS PIER
FIRE BOAT STA
RUSTON WY
HAMILTON PARK
TYLER
MADISON
39TH
38TH
37TH ST
SOUND AV
WARNER ST
PUGET GARDENS PARK

37TH ST
900
5700
3800
3700
4100
3700
3600

2

HIGHLAND DR
SHIRLEY ST
VILLARD ST
RES
BALTIMORE ST
BENNETT
WESTGATE CENTER NORTH
MANCE
33RD
31ST
30TH ST
29TH
28TH
27TH
HUSON
FERDINAND
GOVE
CHEYENNE
VERDE
MASON
TYLER
MONROE
MADISON
32ND
MID
PUGET PARK
WASHINGTON
UNION
PUGET SOUND
ADAMS ST
LAWRENCE
CEDAR
PINE
OAKES
WHITE
STEELE
OLD TOWN PARK
33RD
31ST
30TH
29TH
28TH
27TH
ROSEMOUNT WY
WEST RD
EAST RD
BRADLEY
ORCHARD
SUMMIT RD
CARR

3400
3300
3100
3000
5100
2600
4400
4000
3700
3500
3700
3400
2700
2300

3

WESTGATE CENTER SOUTH
KANDLE PLGD
23RD
HUSON
MULLEN
CHEYENNE
VERDE
25TH
24TH
22ND
21ST
19TH
18TH
MONROE
MADISON
24TH
22ND
21ST
20TH
WARNER
JUNETT
2100
1800
5700
4800
3900
3800
3700
2100

4

WOODLAWN ST
HIGHLAND
WINNIFRED
SHIRLEY
BENNETT
BALTIMORE
VILLARD
ORCHARD
FERDINAND
STEVENS
MASON
PROCTOR
16TH
15TH
14TH
13TH
12TH
11TH
10TH
9TH
WILSON HS
DAHL DR
HUNTER ST
N 13TH ST
N 12TH ST
WASHINGTON
UNION
JONES
UNIVERSITY OF PUGET SOUND
ALDER
PINE
FIFE
PROSPECT
STEELE
17TH
16TH
15TH
14TH
13TH
12TH
11TH
10TH
9TH
SEE 181 MAP
63
1500
1300
1000
4600
1300
1100

5

REMANN HALL JUVENILE COURT
HUSON
8TH
7TH
6TH AV
SHIRLEY
BENNETT
VILLARD
MULLEN
VERDE
STEVENS
ELDON
TYLER
PIERCE
8TH
9TH
10TH
11TH
12TH
7TH
8TH
9TH
10TH
11TH
JEFFERSON PARK
WARNER
LAWRENCE
UNION AV
SOUND
CEDAR
JUNETT
OAKES
ANDERSON
PO
FS
TACOMA
ALDER
STEELE
KELLOGG
8TH
7TH
8TH
9TH
10TH
11TH
12TH
600
5100
4800
800
4400
4300
4500
3900
3800
700
3800
3200
800
600
1000

6

WOODLAWN
HIGHLAND
WINNIFRED
ROUTE
BALTIMORE
ORCHARD
HUSON
MOORLANDS DR
FERDINAND DR
FIRLANDS
MULLEN
VERDE
MASON
TYLER
MONROE
MADISON
PROCTOR
ADAMS
WASHINGTON
DELONG PLGD
S 13TH ST
S 14TH
13TH
14TH
15TH
16TH
17TH
18TH
13TH ST
15TH ST
18TH
CHINA LAKE PARK
19TH ST
DURANGO
UNION AV
PUGET
LAWRENCE
FRANKLIN PARK
MELROSE
CEDAR
JUNETT
PINE
ALDER
FIFE
PROSPECT
STATE
TRAFTON
13TH
14TH
MELROSE
15TH
S 16TH ST
16TH
17TH
1200
5100
1200
1400
1500
3300
1600
3200
2900
2900
2300
1200
1400
1700
1800
3400

7

BERKELEY AV
YALE ST
DARTMOUTH
ROSE
MONTE
ELDORADO
ORLANDO DEL
FARALLONE
SUMMIT AV
PRINCETON
PARK & RIDE
GATE AV
COLUMBIA AV
STANFORD
NASSAU
GOLD
HARVARD
ORCHARD ST
16 FRWY
CHEYENNE ST
HEIDELBERG ATHLETIC FIELD
HENRY FOSS HS
S 23RD ST
NATURE CENTER AT SNAKE LAKE
SNAKE LAKE
TYLER ST
SNAKE LAKE PARK
MADISON ST
S 21ST
ADAMS
WASHINGTON
BELLARMINE PREPARATORY HS
TACOMA CENTRAL
ALLENMORE HOSP
H
LIB
ELKS LODGE
UNION AV
23RD
ELKS-ALLENMORE GOLF CLUB
STATE DEPT OF SOCIAL HEALTH SERVICES
ELKS-ALLENMORE GOLF CLUB
STEELE ST
TRAFTON ST
S 24TH ST
CHENEY STADIUM
16
REGENTS BLVD
FIRCREST
SPRING ST
100
300
200
4600
3850
3500
2020
1900
2300

A B C D E

SEE 294 MAP

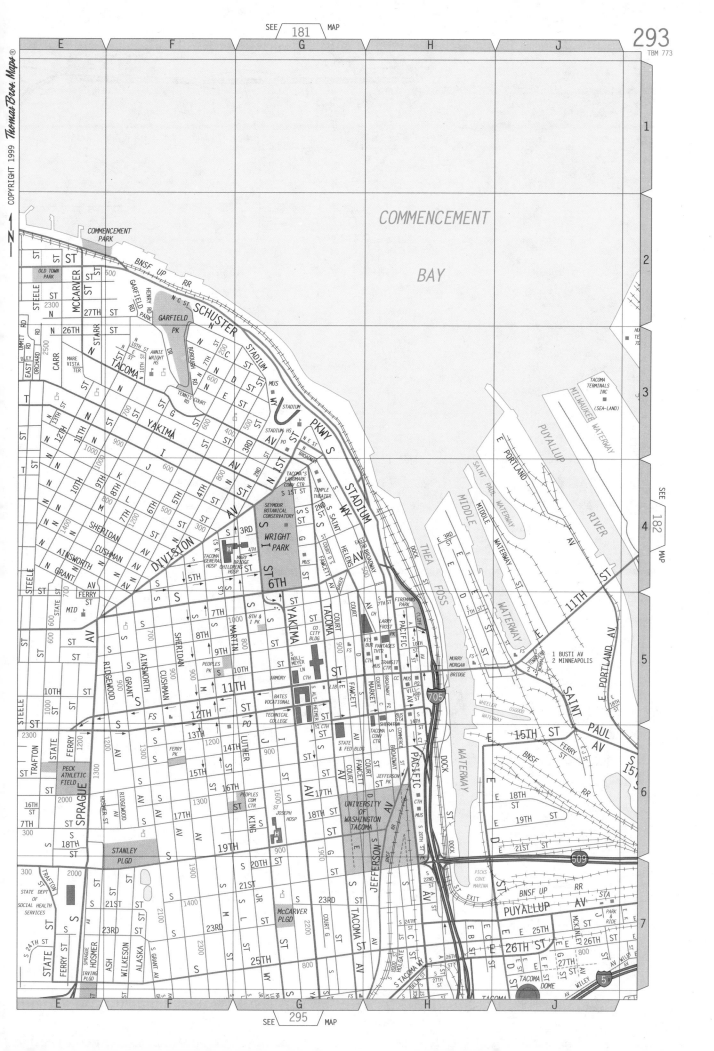

SEE 292 MAP

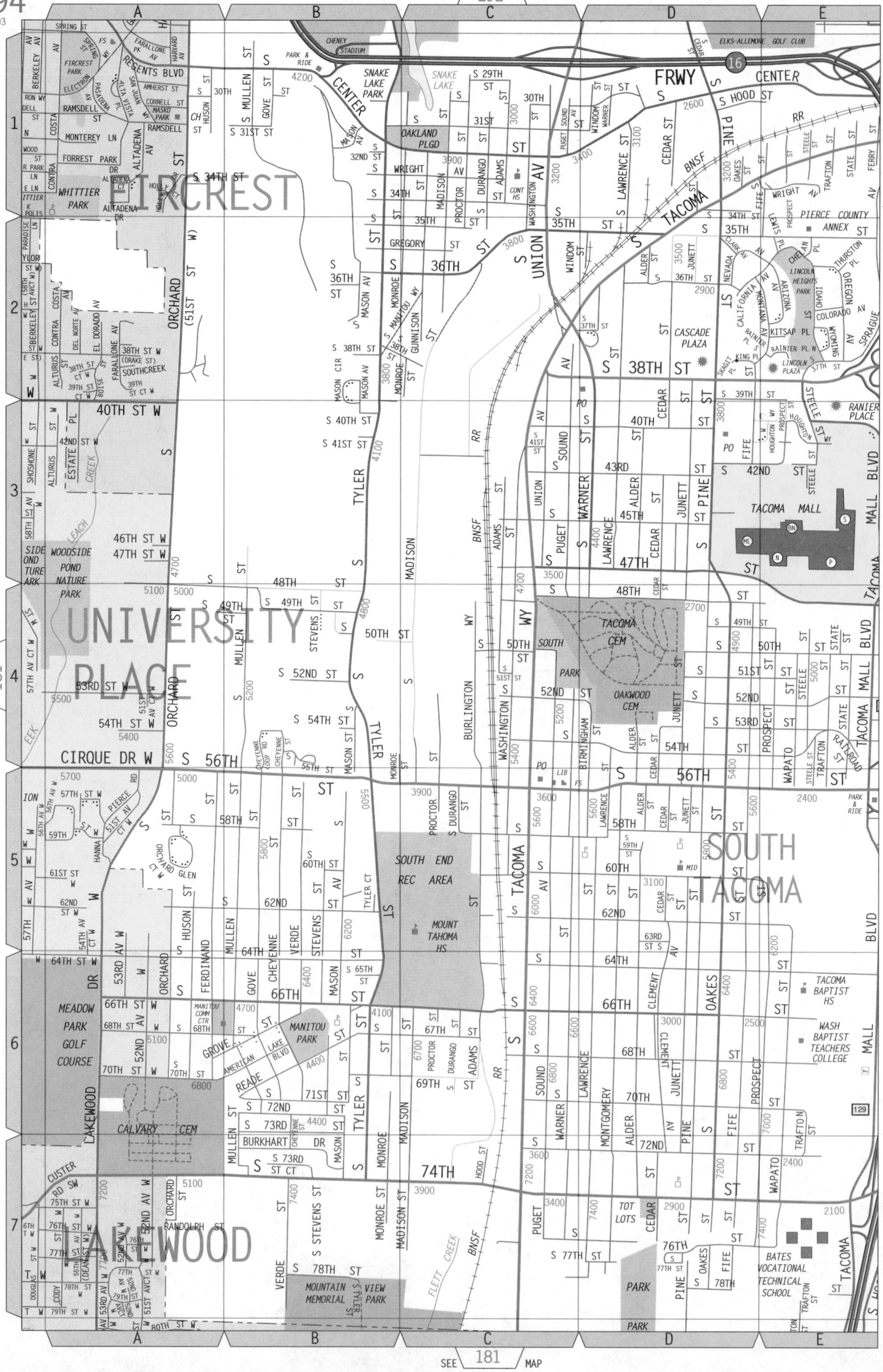

COPYRIGHT 1999 Thomas Bros. Maps® —N—

PNW

DETAIL

FIRCREST

UNIVERSITY PLACE

LAKEWOOD

SOUTH TACOMA

TACOMA MALL

TACOMA CEM

OAKWOOD CEM

CASCADE PLAZA

PIERCE COUNTY ANNEX

Lincoln Heights Park

Lincoln Plaza

RANIER PLACE

Snake Lake Park

Snake Lake

Cheney Stadium

OAKLAND PLGD

Whittier Park

Fircrest Park

Monterey Ln

Forrest Park

Woodside Pond Nature Park

Southcreek

Estate Pl

South End Rec Area

Mount Tahoma HS

Manitou Park

Manitou Comm Ctr

Meadow Park Golf Course

Calvary Cem

Mountain View Memorial Park

Bates Vocational Technical School

Tacoma Baptist HS

Wash Baptist Teachers College

Park & Ride

Elks-Allemore Golf Club

FRWY CENTER

16

129

SEE 181 MAP

SEE 181 MAP

Thomas Bros. Maps ®
COPYRIGHT 1999

PNW

DETAIL

SEE 182 MAP

TACOMA

HILLDALE

TACOMA DOME
DOME
McKINLEY PARK
Upper

LINCOLN PARK
LINCOLN HS
PUGET SOUND HOSP

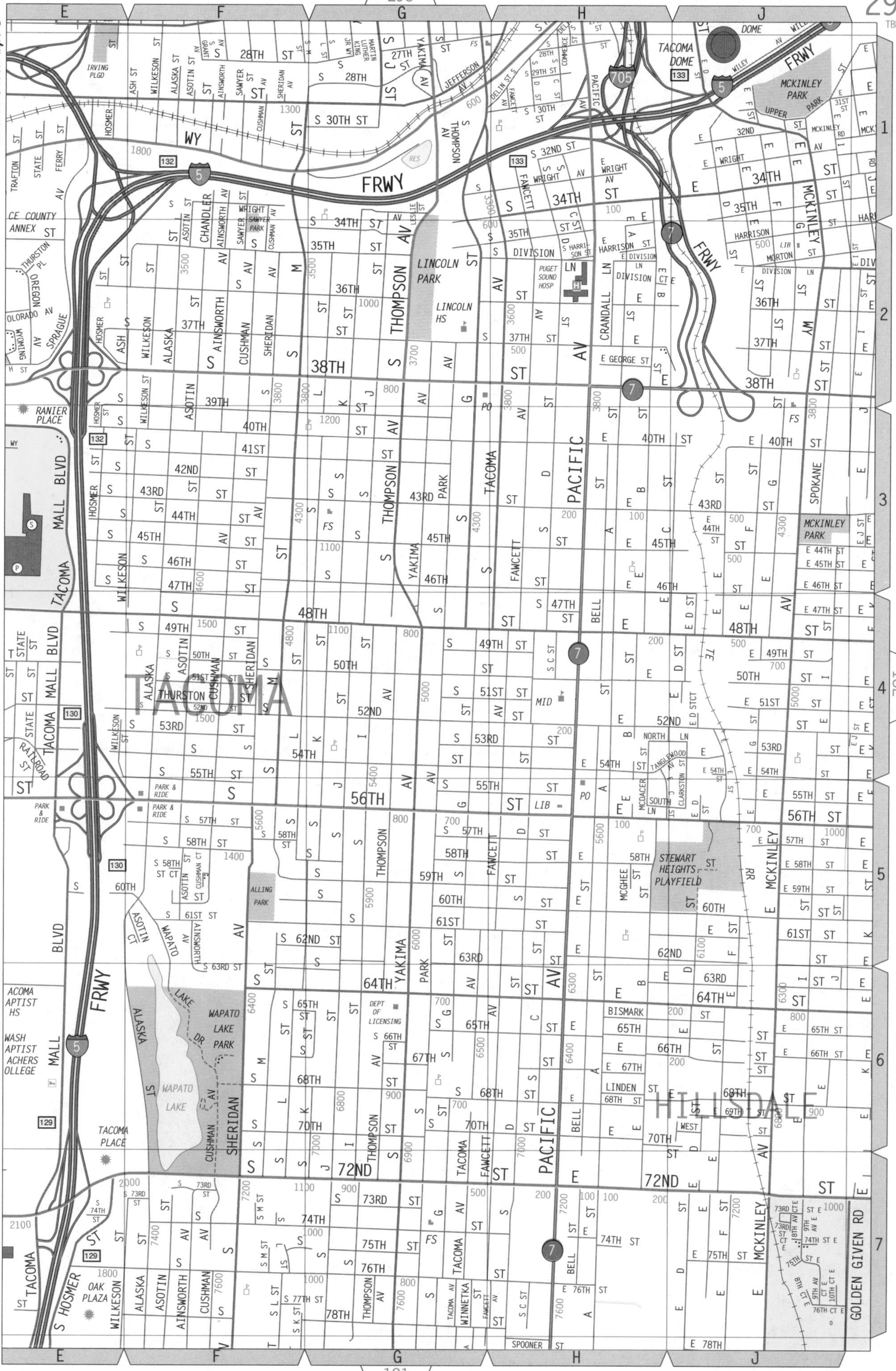

McKINLEY PARK

SPOKANE

STEWART HEIGHTS PLAYFIELD

WAPATO LAKE PARK
WAPATO LAKE
ALASKA LAKE

ALLING PARK

TACOMA PLACE

OAK PLAZA

RANIER PLACE

IRVING PLGD

CE COUNTY ANNEX

ACOMA APTIST HS
WASH APTIST ACHERS OLLEGE

TACOMA MALL BLVD

DEPT OF LICENSING

BISMARK

LINDEN

WEST

GOLDEN GIVEN RD

FRWY

Streets (partial): 27TH, 28TH, S 30TH ST, S 32ND ST, 34TH ST, 35TH ST, 36TH ST, 37TH ST, 38TH ST, 39TH, 40TH ST, 41ST, 42ND, 43RD, 44TH, 45TH, 46TH, 47TH, 48TH, 49TH, 50TH, 51ST, 52ND, 53RD, 54TH, 55TH, 56TH ST, 57TH, 58TH, 59TH, 60TH, 61ST, 62ND, 63RD, 64TH, 65TH, 66TH, 67TH, 68TH, 70TH, 72ND ST, 73RD, 74TH, 75TH, 76TH, 77TH, 78TH

THOMPSON AV, YAKIMA, PACIFIC, TACOMA, FAWCETT, BELL, McKINLEY, SHERIDAN, CUSHMAN, AINSWORTH, ASOTIN, ALASKA, WILKESON, HOSMER, ASH, STATE, SPRAGUE, OREGON, TRAFTON, FERRY

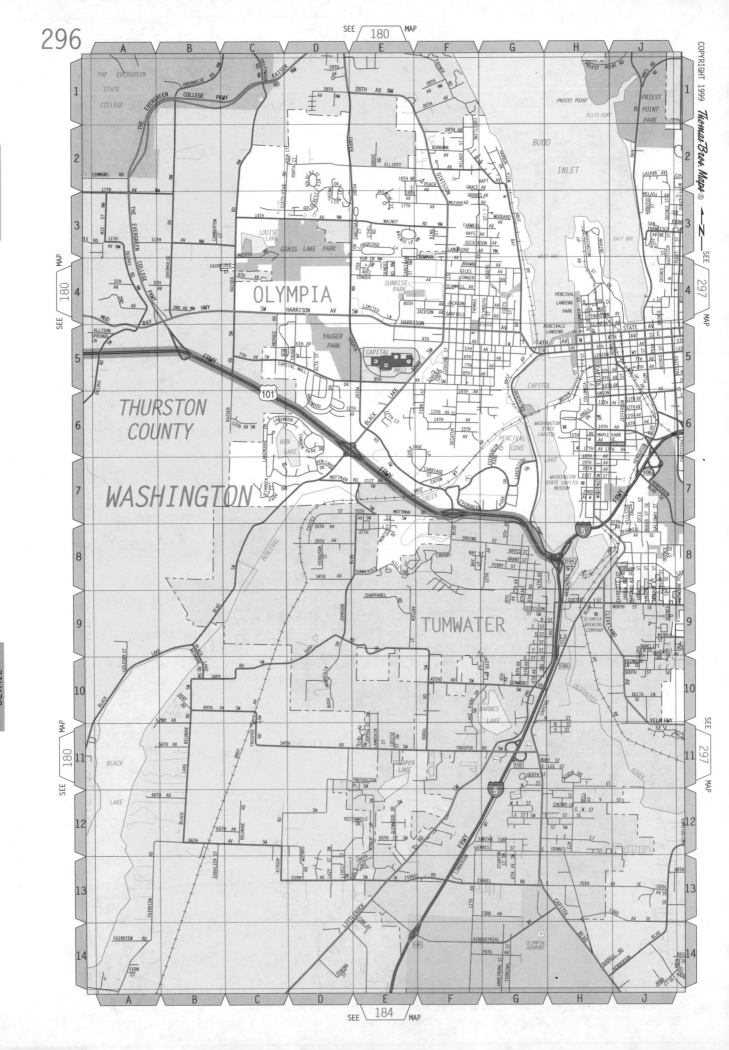

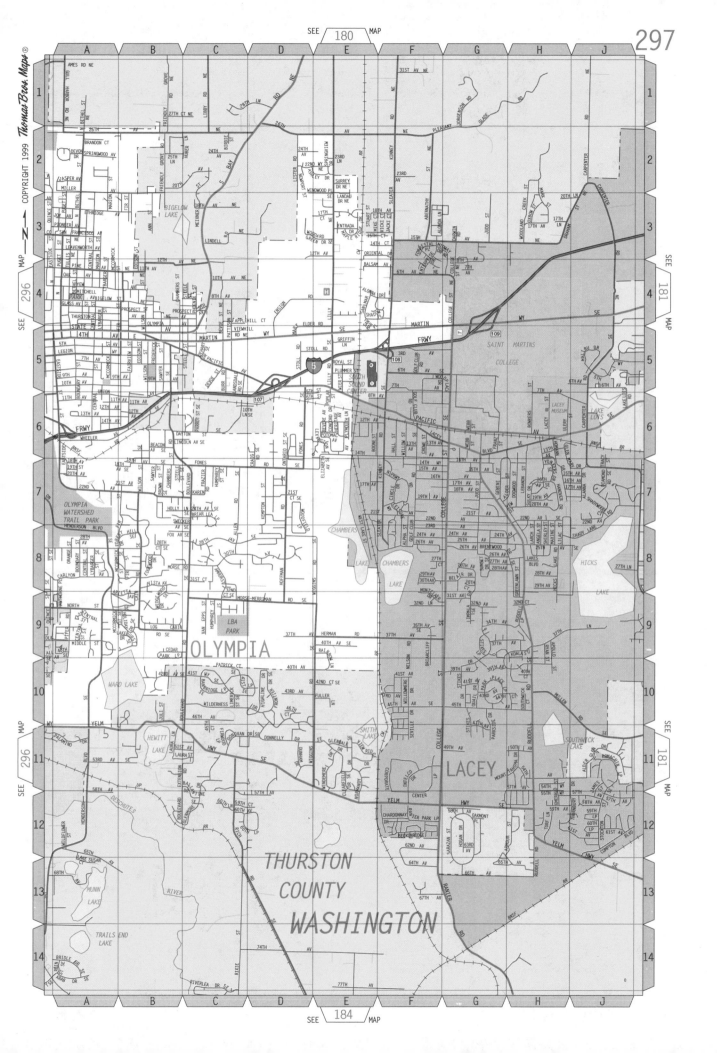

OLYMPIA

LACEY

THURSTON
COUNTY
WASHINGTON

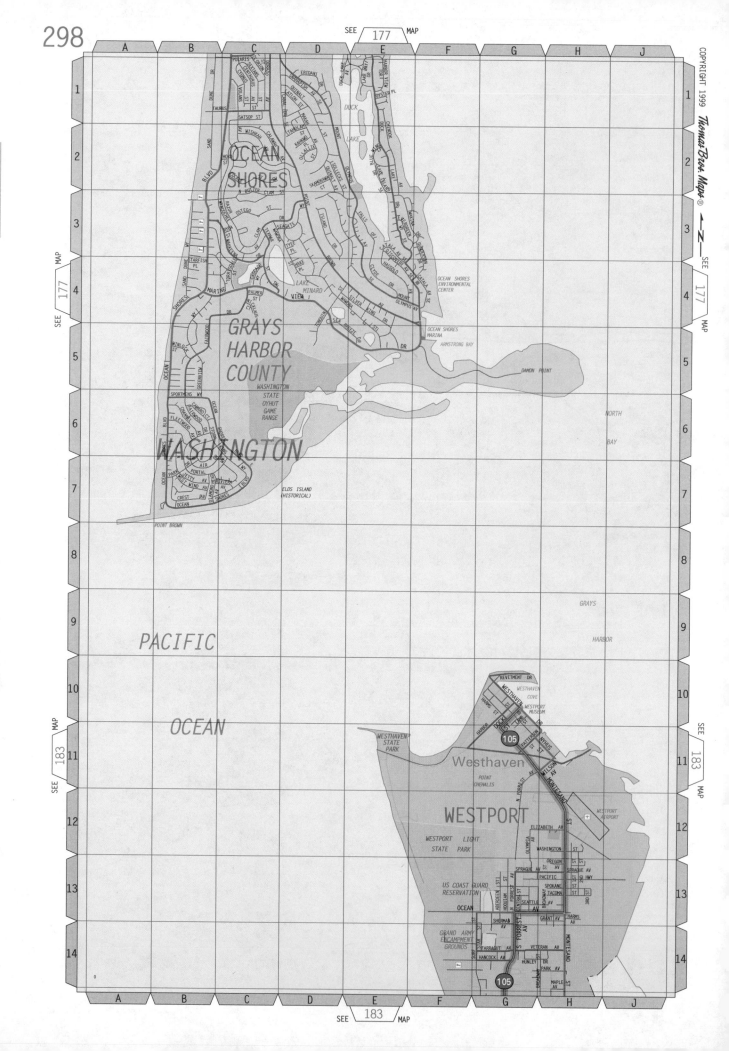

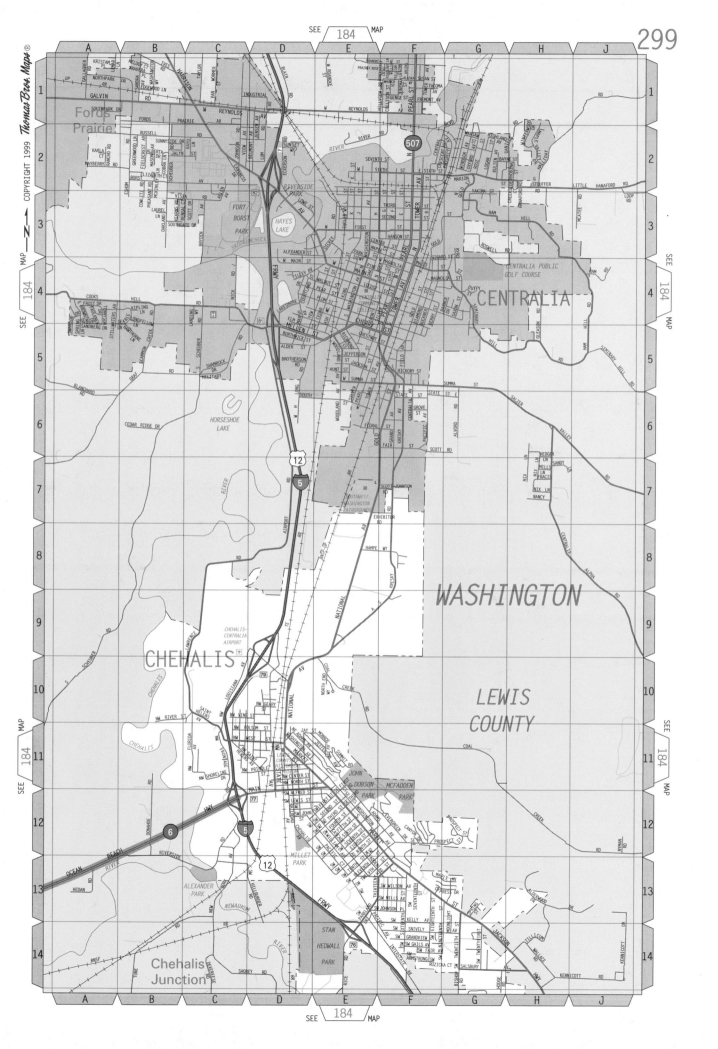

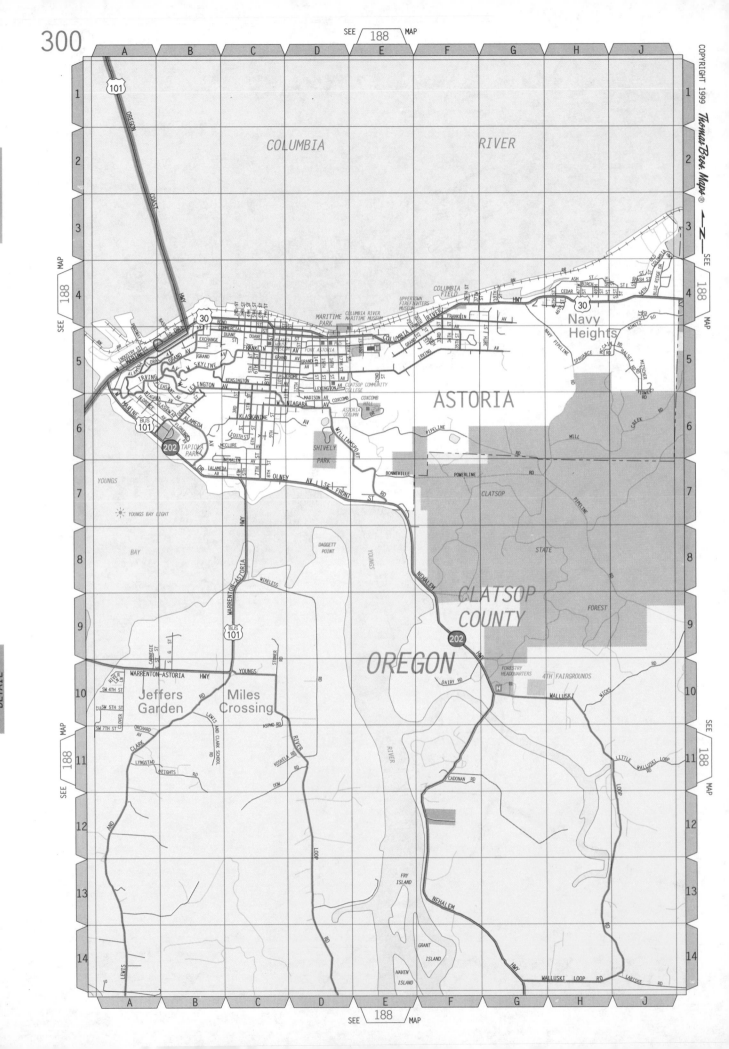

PNW

DETAIL

SEE 188 MAP

SEE 188 MAP

SEE 188 MAP

SEE 188 MAP

SEE 188 MAP

COLUMBIA   RIVER

OREGON COAST HWY

101

30

30

MARITIME PARK

COLUMBIA RIVER MARITIME MUSEUM

UPPERTOWN FIREFIGHTERS MUSEUM

COLUMBIA FIELD

Navy Heights

FORT ASTORIA

CLATSOP COMMUNITY COLLEGE

ASTORIA

CONCOMB HILL

ASTORIA COLUMN

TAPIOLA PARK

202

BUS 101

SHIVELY PARK

WILLIAMSPORT

BONNEVILLE

PIPELINE

POWERLINE RD

MILL

CLATSOP

CREEK

YOUNGS

YOUNGS BAY LIGHT

BAY

DAGGETT POINT

YOUNGS

WIRELESS

WARRENTON-ASTORIA

NEHALEM

STATE

CLATSOP COUNTY

FOREST

BUS 101

OREGON

202

DAIRY RD

FORESTRY HEADQUARTERS

4TH FAIRGROUNDS

WALLUSKI

WICKS

Jeffers Garden

Miles Crossing

WARRENTON-ASTORIA HWY

YOUNGS

STONER RD

ASPMO RD

RIVER

KOSKELA RD

LEWIS AND CLARK SCHOOL RD

DOM RD

CADONAN RD

LITTLE WALLUSKI LOOP RD

LOOP

RIVER

LOOP

ORCHARD AV

CLARK

LYNGSTAD HEIGHTS RD

FRY ISLAND

NEHALEM HWY

GRANT ISLAND

HAVEN ISLAND

WALLUSKI LOOP RD

LARISKE RD

LEWIS

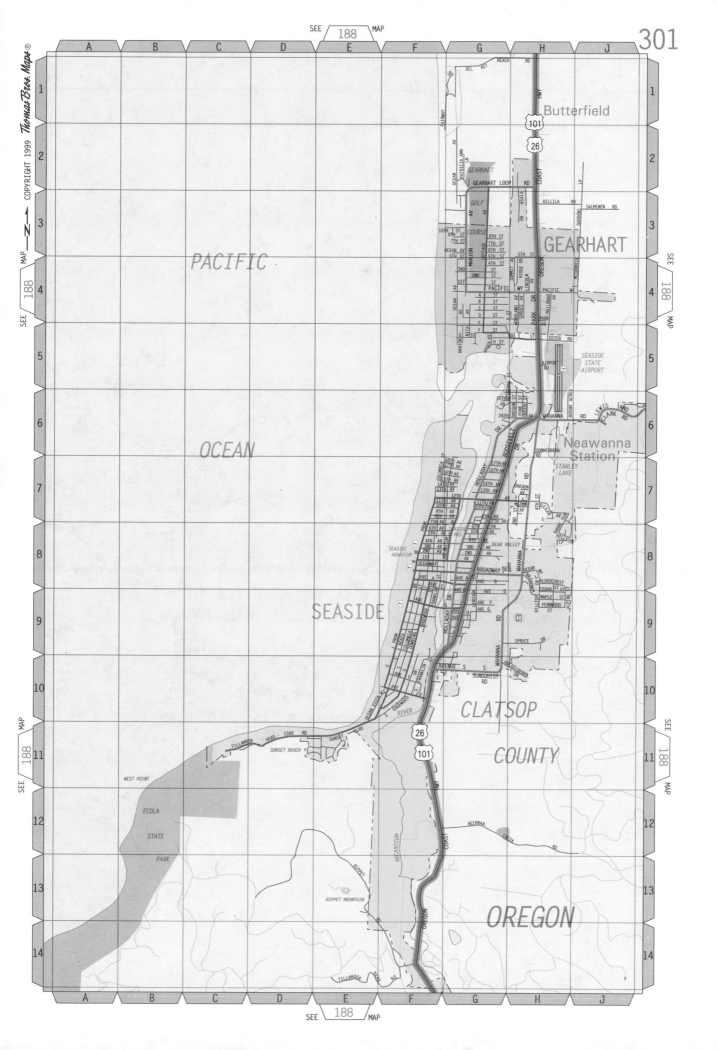

PNW

DETAIL

N ← MAP

SEE 188 MAP

A B C D E F G H J

1
2
3
4
5
6
7
8
9
10
11
12
13
14

Butterfield

101
26

Gearhart
GEARHART
Gearhart Loop RD
GOLF
COURSE

10TH ST
8TH ST
7TH ST
8TH ST
7TH ST
6TH ST
5TH ST
OCEAN AV
5TH ST
4TH ST
3RD ST
2ND ST
1ST ST
PACIFIC WY
PACIFIC WY

DEL REY
BEACH RD
FAIRWAY
PATRICIA ANN LN
OCEAN AV

HILLILA RD
SALMINEN RD
GARDENS
LP

FIFER RD
RIDGE DR
LINCOLN
SUMMIT AV
RAILROAD AV
PARK AV
PARK AV
FOSTER RD
MCCORMICK

WOODLAND AV
SPRUCE DR

SEE 188 MAP

PACIFIC

OCEAN

SEASIDE STATE AIRPORT
AIRPORT RD

WAHANNA
25TH ST
24TH ST
OREGON ST
PINE ST
ASH ST
ROOSEVELT DR

BOEIN ACRES
LEWIS AND CLARK RD

Neawanna Station
DONNERBERG RD
STANLEY LAKE

18TH AV
17TH AV
16TH AV
COLUMBIA
15TH AV
14TH AV
13TH AV
12TH
11TH AV
10TH AV
9TH AV
8TH
7TH AV
6TH AV
5TH
4TH AV
3RD AV
2ND AV
1ST AV
OCEANWAY
17TH AV
16TH AV
14TH AV
13TH AV
HOLLADAY

OREGON AV
2ND ST
3RD ST
4TH ST
OCEAN
PEPPER
HILLILA LP

SEASIDE MUS
BEAR VALLEY
WAHANNA

SEASIDE AQUARIUM

SEASIDE

Broadway
AVE A
AVE A
AVE B
AVE C
AVE D
AVE E
AVE F
AVE G.
PROM
COLUMBIA
DOWNING
FRANKLIN
HOLLADAY DR
LINCOLN
WAHANNA RD
AVE B
AVE

ALDERCREST
CEDAR ST
MAPLE
FERNWOOD ST
SPRUCE DR
H
OCEAN
BROADWAY

AVENUE
S
S
S
FRANKLIN ST
HASKELBERGER DR
SUNDQUIST RD

OCEAN VISTA DR
EDGEWOOD BLVD
NEAWANNA RIVER

CLATSOP

26
101

HEAD COVE RD
TILLAMOOK
SUNSET BLVD
SUNSET BEACH

COUNTY

WEST POINT

ECOLA
STATE
PARK

BEERMAN
CREEK RD

NEHALEM
NECANICUM

RIPPET
RIPPET MOUNTAIN

OREGON
COAST HWY

OREGON

TILLAMOOK HEAD RD

SEE 188 MAP

SEE 188 MAP

SEE 188 MAP

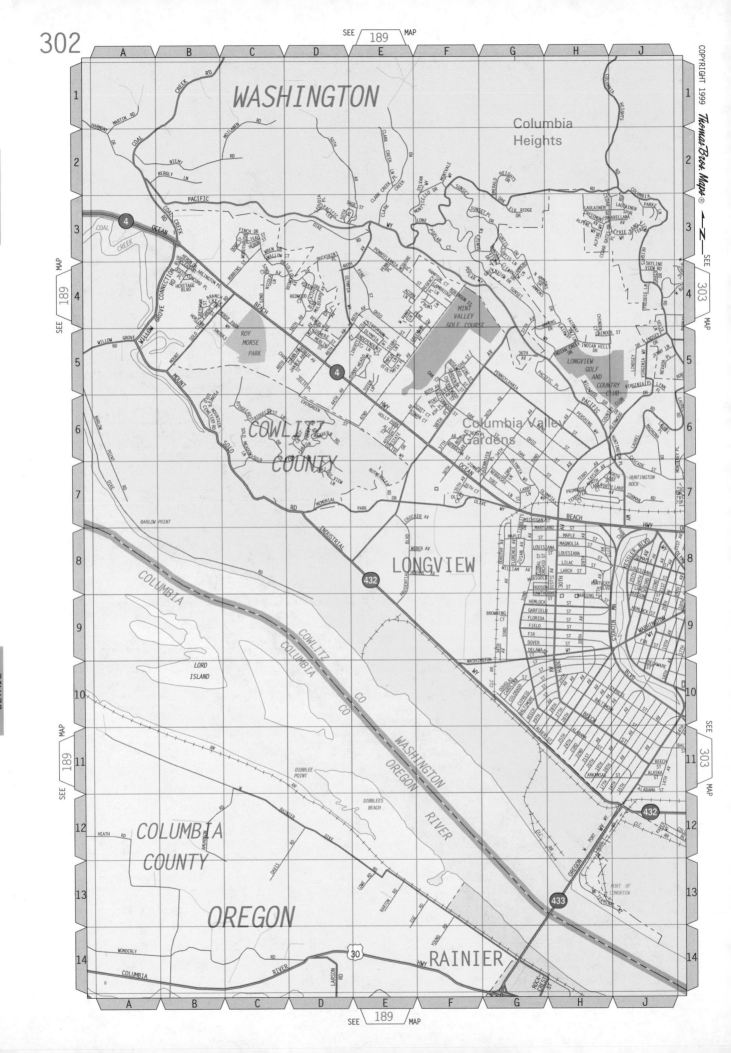

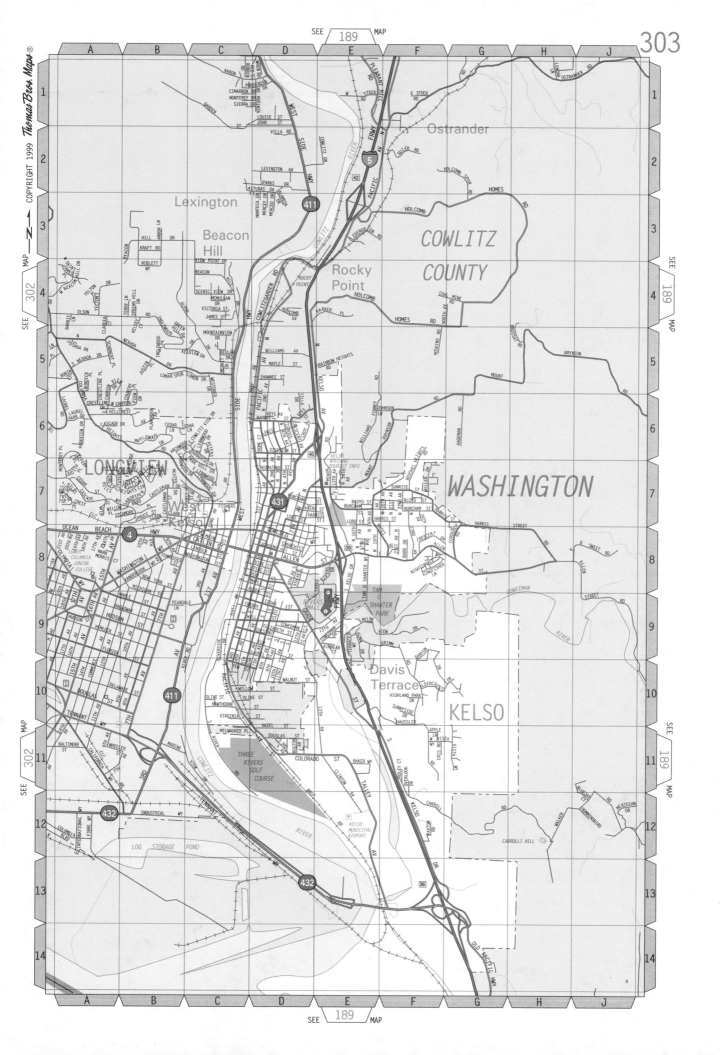

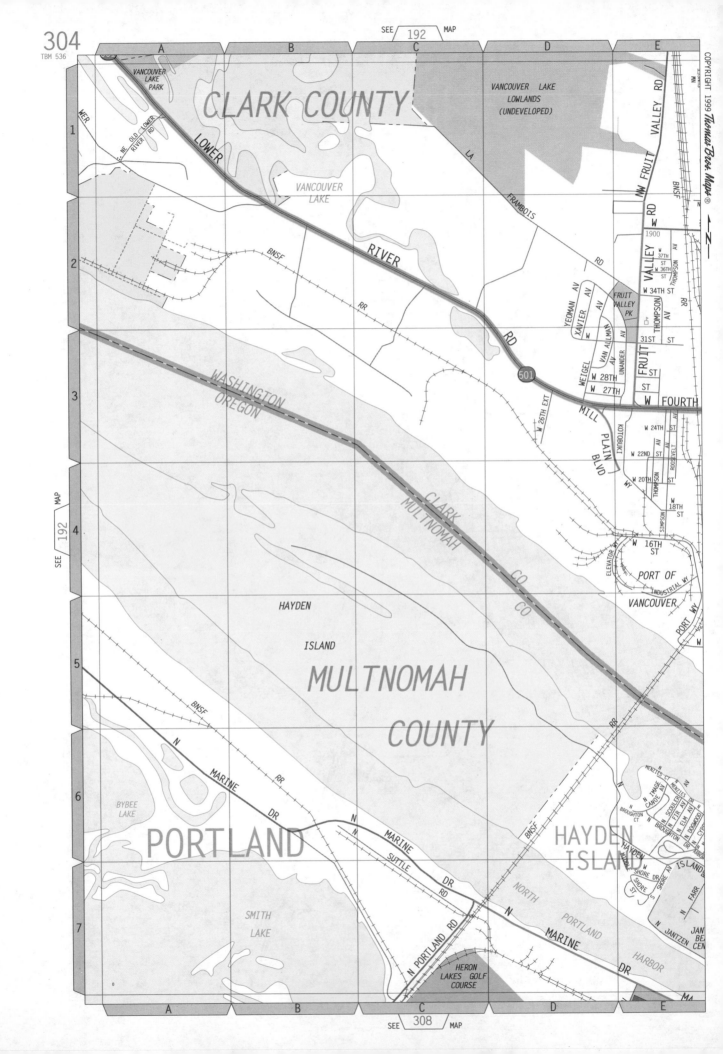

PNW

DETAIL

SEE 192 MAP

A B C D E

1

VANCOUVER
LAKE
PARK

CLARK COUNTY

VANCOUVER LAKE
LOWLANDS
(UNDEVELOPED)

NE OLD LOWER RIVER RD

WER

LOWER

VANCOUVER
LAKE

LA

FRAMBOIS

NW FRUIT VALLEY RD

BNSF

2

RIVER

BNSF

RR

RD

1900

VALLEY

RD

W

RR

W 37TH ST
W 36TH ST

THOMSON

W 34TH ST

YEOMAN AV
XAVIER AV
AV
VAN AILLMAN AV
UNANDER AV

FRUIT VALLEY PK

THOMPSON AV

31ST ST

3

WASHINGTON
OREGON

RD

501

MILL

PLAIN

BLVD

WEIGEL AV

W 28TH ST
W 27TH ST

W FOURTH

KOTOBUKI

W 24TH ST

W 22ND ST

ROOSEVELT AV

W 26TH EXT

W 20TH ST

THOMPSON AV

4

SEE 192 MAP

CLARK
MULTNOMAH
CO
CO

SIMPSON

W 18TH ST

W 16TH ST

ELEVATOR WY

PORT OF
VANCOUVER

INDUSTRIAL WY

PORT WY

WY

HAYDEN

ISLAND

5

MULTNOMAH

COUNTY

RR

N

BNSF

6

BYBEE
LAKE

MARINE

DR

RR

N

N MARINE

SUTTLE

DR

RD

N

BNSF

N

PORTLAND

HAYDEN
ISLAND

NORTH

PORTLAND

N

MARINE

MENZIES CT
N
N SCOULERIES DR
N IMAGE CANOE AV
N FTR AV
N ELM AV
N LOGWOOD
BROUGHTON CT
N BROUGHTON DR
N CYPRESS
HAYDEN ISLAND
N SHORE DR
SHORE ST
SHORE AV
N ISLAND

7

SMITH
LAKE

N PORTLAND RD

HERON
LAKES GOLF
COURSE

N

DR

HARBOR

N JANTZEN AV

N FARR

JAN
BE
CEN

A B C D E

SEE 308 MAP

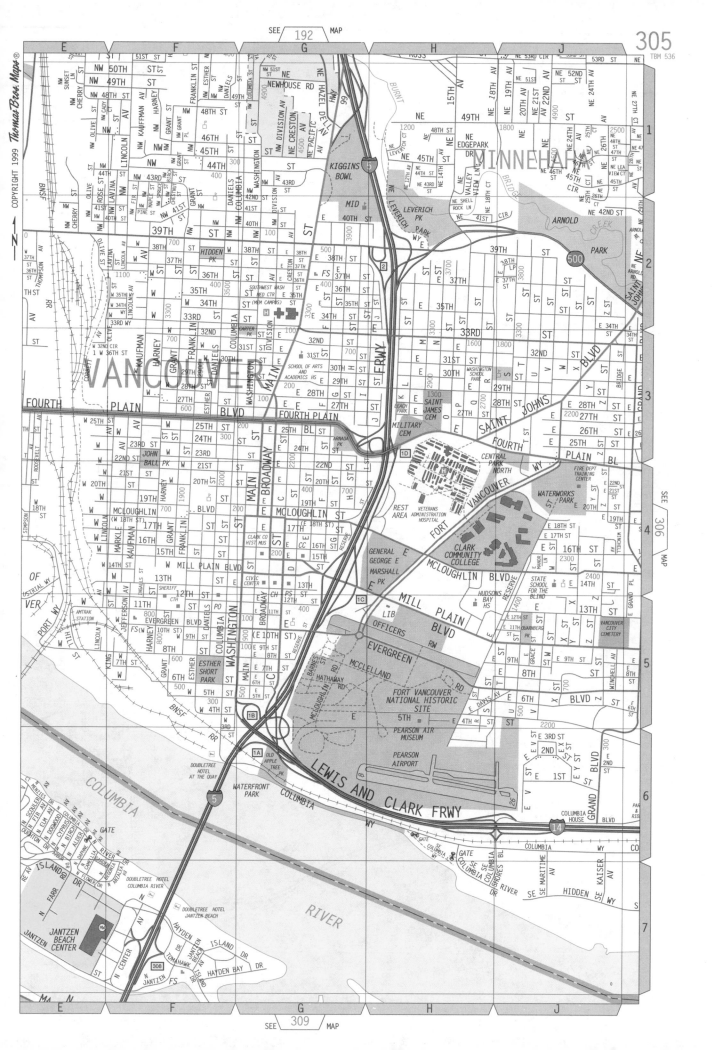

PNW

DETAIL

SEE 192 MAP

SEE 309 MAP

SEE 306 MAP

MINNEHAHA

VANCOUVER

FOURTH PLAIN BLVD

FOURTH PLAIN

COLUMBIA

RIVER

LEWIS AND CLARK FRWY

FORT VANCOUVER NATIONAL HISTORIC SITE

PEARSON AIRPORT

PEARSON AIR MUSEUM

CLARK COMMUNITY COLLEGE

JANTZEN BEACH CENTER

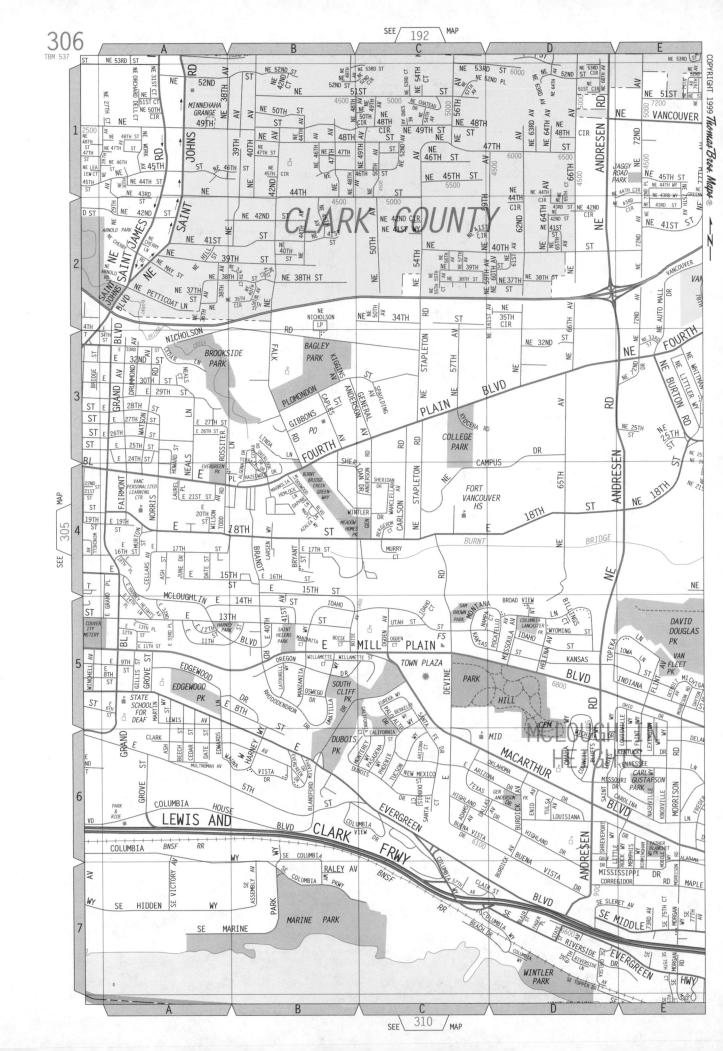

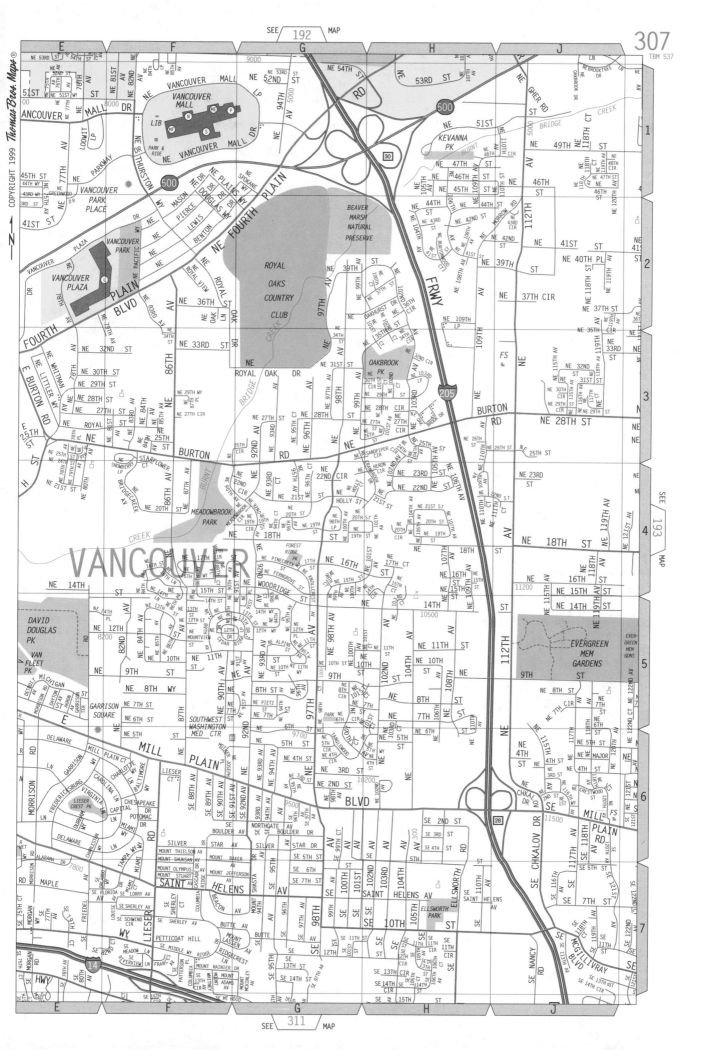

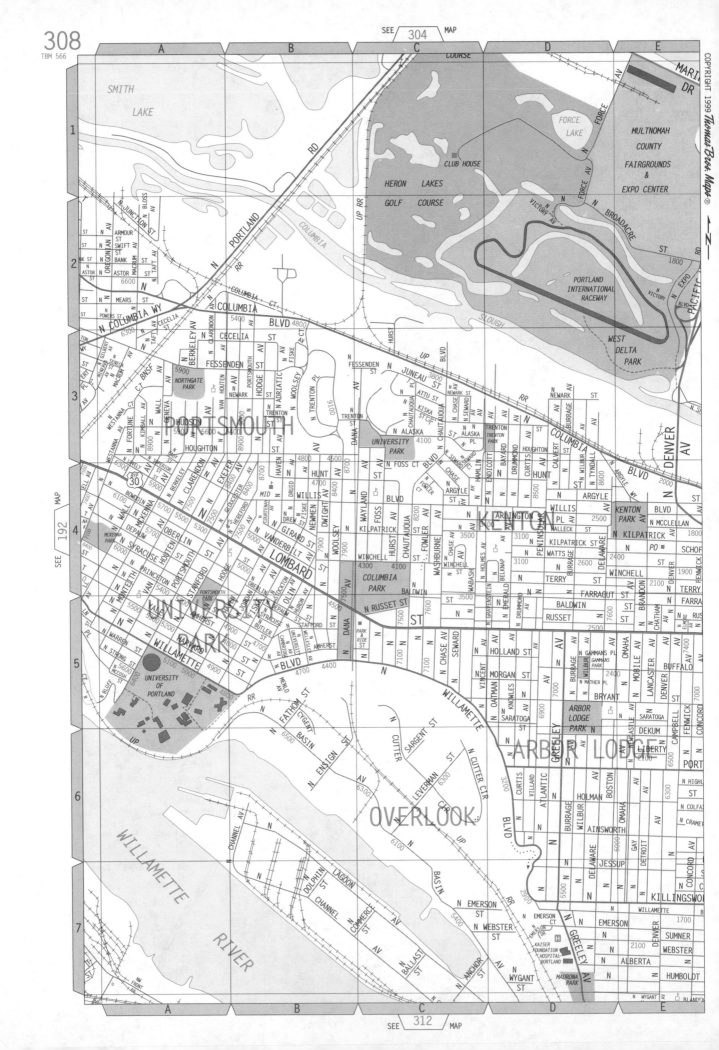

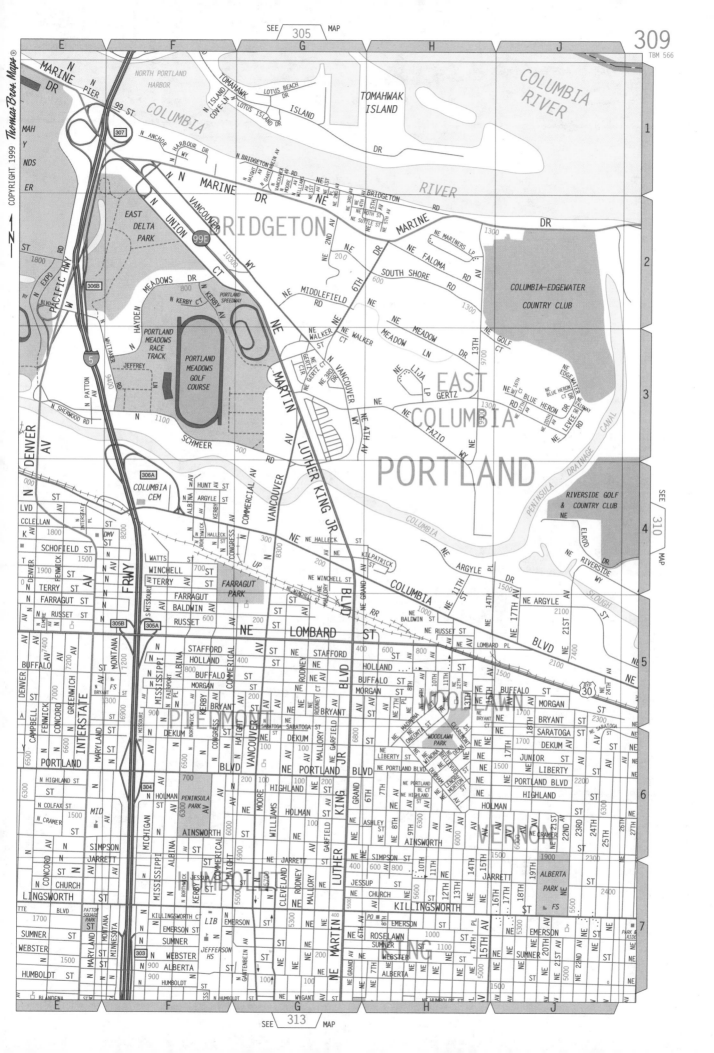

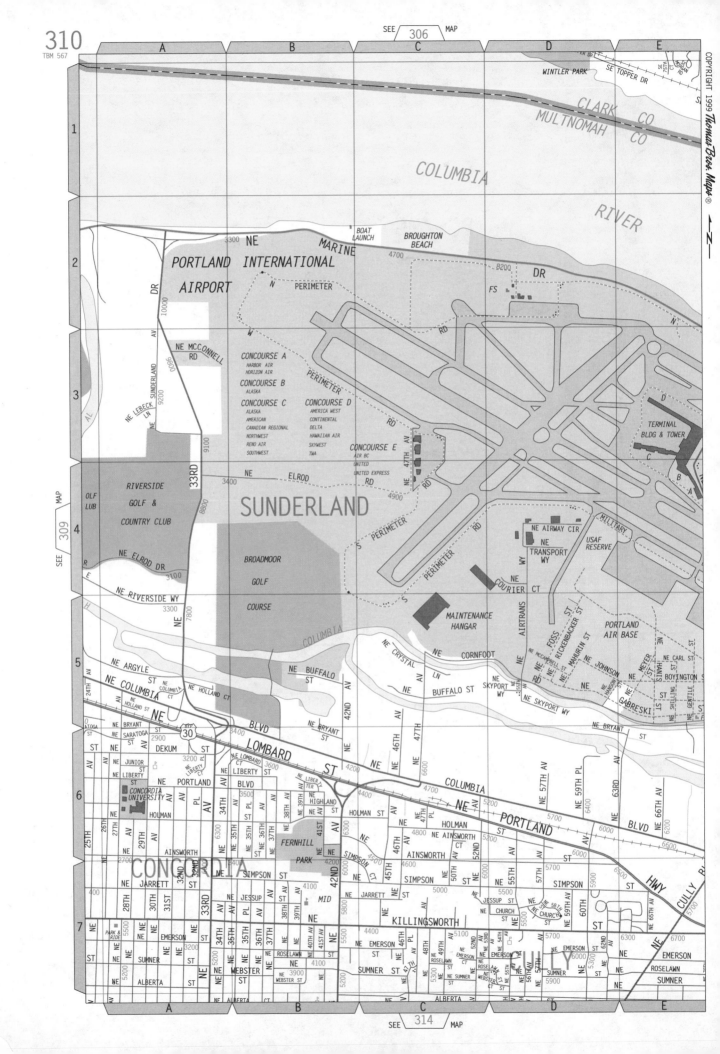

310

TBM 567

PNW

DETAIL

SEE 309 MAP

COPYRIGHT 1999 Thomas Bros. Maps® —N—

WINTLER PARK

SE TOPPER DR

CLARK CO
MULTNOMAH CO

COLUMBIA

RIVER

BOAT LAUNCH

BROUGHTON BEACH

3300 NE MARINE DR

4700

8200

FS

DR

PORTLAND INTERNATIONAL
AIRPORT

N PERIMETER

10000

NE MCCONNELL RD

W

9000

PERIMETER

CONCOURSE A
HARBOR AIR
HORIZON AIR
CONCOURSE B
ALASKA
CONCOURSE C
ALASKA
AMERICAN
CANADIAN REGIONAL
NORTHWEST
RENO AIR
SOUTHWEST

CONCOURSE D
AMERICA WEST
CONTINENTAL
DELTA
HAWAIIAN AIR
SKYWEST
TWA

CONCOURSE E
AIR BC
UNITED
UNITED EXPRESS

NE LEBECK LN SUNDERLAND
9200

9100

RD

D

TERMINAL
BLDG & TOWER

C

AL

33RD

RIVERSIDE
GOLF &
COUNTRY CLUB

3400 NE ELROD RD

4900

47TH AV

NE

B
A

OLF LUB

8600

SUNDERLAND

NE AIRWAY CIR

NE TRANSPORT WY

MILITARY

USAF RESERVE

NE ELROD DR
3100

BROADMOOR

GOLF

COURSE

S PERIMETER

PERIMETER RD

NE COURIER CT

R E H

NE RIVERSIDE WY
3300

7800

NE

COLUMBIA

AIRTRANS

FOSS ST

RICKENBACKER ST

MAHURIN ST

NE MCCAMPBELL ST

NE JOHNSON

PORTLAND
AIR BASE

MEYER ST
NE HANIS ST

NE CARL ST
BOYINGTON

NE SHILLING ST
GENTILE ST

MAINTENANCE
HANGAR

NE CRYSTAL LN

NE CORNFOOT

NE HANSON

GABRESKI

NE ARGYLE ST

NE BUFFALO ST

NE COLUMBIA CT

NE HOLLAND CT

42ND AV

NE BUFFALO ST

SKYPORT WY

155TH

NE SKYPORT WY

24TH AV

NE COLUMBIA

NE HOLLAND ST

NE

BLVD

NE BRYANT ST

47TH

NE BRYANT ST

ATOGA

NE BRYANT ST

BIE 30

8400

46TH

LOMBARD ST

COLUMBIA

NE PORTLAND BLVD

NE SARATOGA ST

2900

DEKUM ST

NE LOMBARD CT 3600

4200

4400

4700

5200

5700

6000

6400

6600

6200

6300

JUNIOR ST

3200 NE LIBERTY PL

NE LIBERTY ST

LIBERTY BLVD

NE LIBER TER

NE LIBER TER

NE HIGHLAND ST

HOLMAN ST

NE 47TH

NE

NE 57TH AV

NE 59TH PL

63RD AV

66TH AV

NE PORTLAND

CONCORDIA
UNIVERSITY

HOLMAN

34TH

PL AV

38TH AV 39TH

3500

NE

NE HOLMAN ST

46TH

NE 4800

NE AINSWORTH CT

52ND

55TH

57TH

6000

25TH

26TH

27TH

29TH

NE

AINSWORTH

33RD AV

32ND AV

8400

35TH 35TH 36TH 37TH

6300

41ST

FERNHILL
PARK

4200

42ND

6000

NE SIMPSON CT

4500

45TH

AINSWORTH

4600

NE SIMPSON

50TH

NE

55TH

57TH

SIMPSON

5700

5900

6500

CULLY

HWY

CONCORDIA

2700

NE JARRETT

28TH

30TH

31ST

SIMPSON

NE

4100

MID

NE JARRETT ST

JESSUP

NE 58TH AV

NE CHURCH

60TH

CULLY

NE JESSUP

33RD AV

NE JESSUP

38TH PL 39TH

42ND

5800

KILLINGSWORTH

5000

5500

NE CHURCH

59TH

5700

6300

6700

400

NE

34TH

35TH

36TH

37TH

40TH PL 41ST

5500

4400

NE EMERSON

46TH PL

48TH

49TH

52ND

5380

54TH

NE EMERSON

62ND

NE EMERSON

Park & Ride

5500

EMERSON ST

5200

NE ROSELAWN ST

4100

5200

5300

NE SUMNER

NE ROSELAWN

NE SUMNER ST

55TH 56TH 54TH

NE SUMNER

5900

NE ROSELAWN

SUMNER

3200 NE SUMNER ST

WEBSTER ST

3900 WEBSTER ST

5200

ALBERTA ST

NE WEBSTER

ALBERTA CT

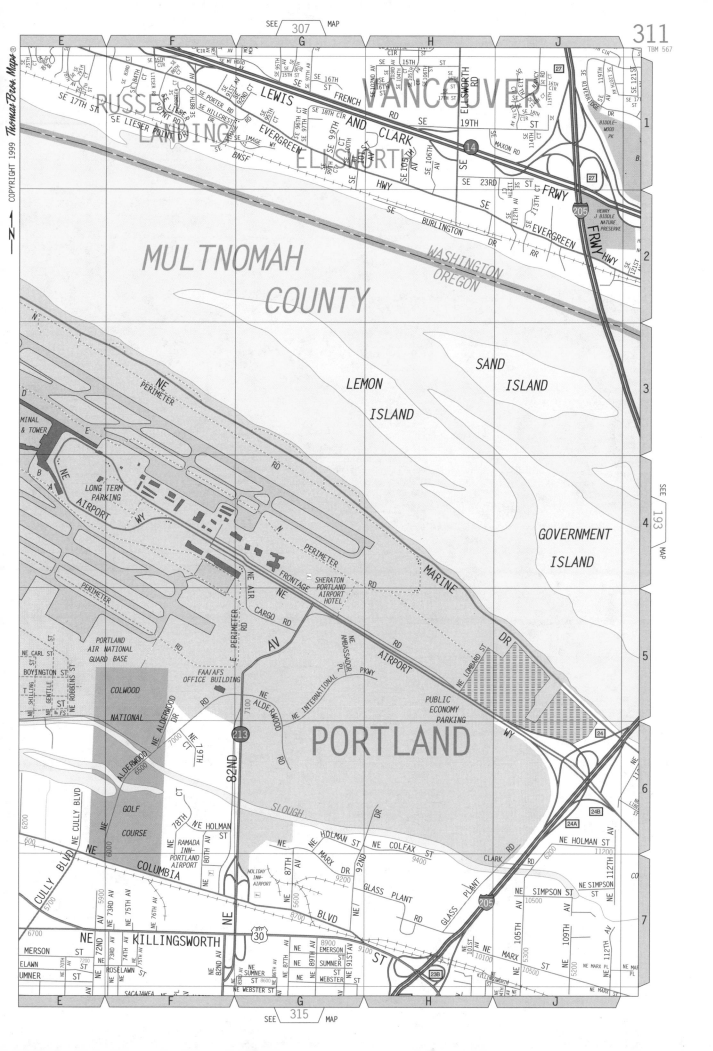

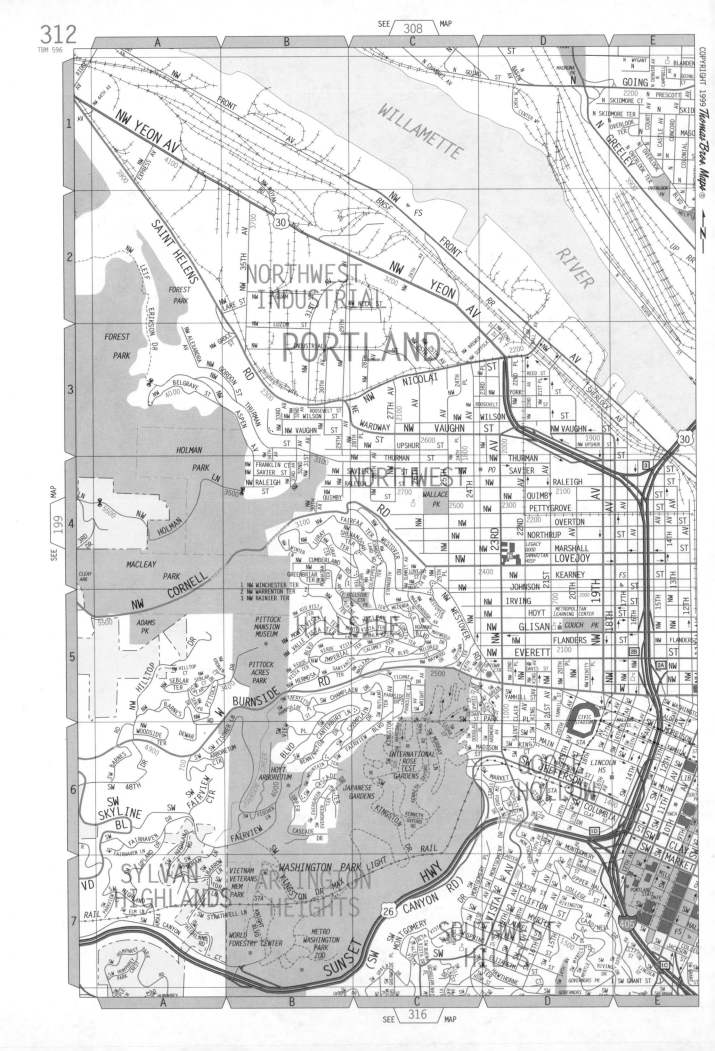

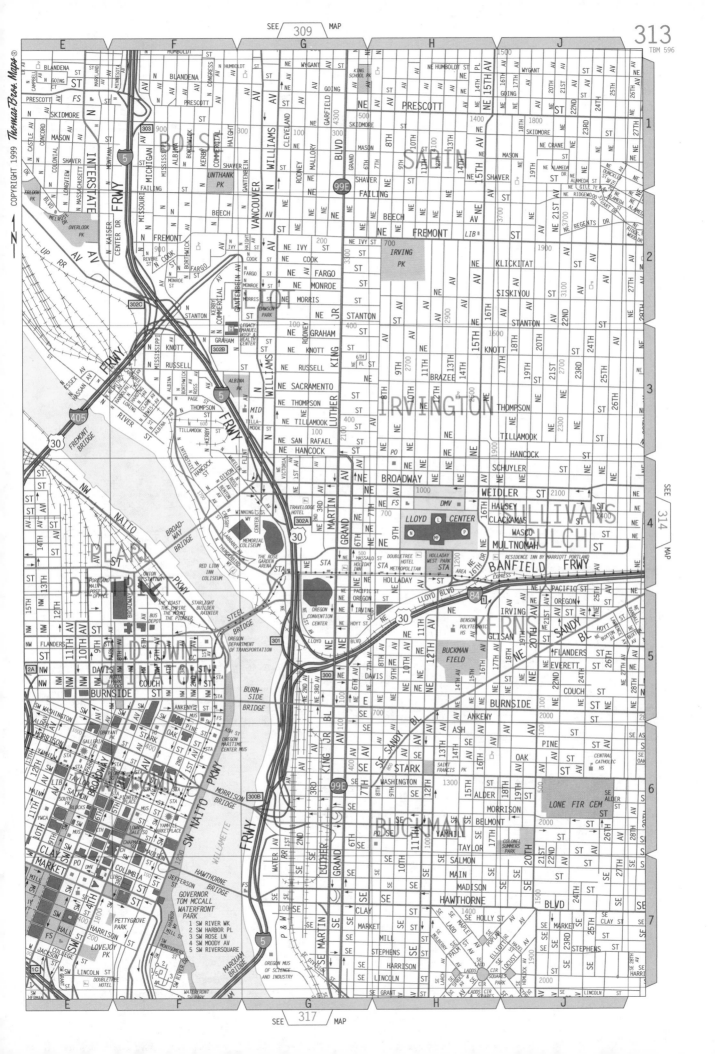

PNW

DETAIL

COPYRIGHT 1999 Thomas Bros. Maps®

—N—

ALAMEDA

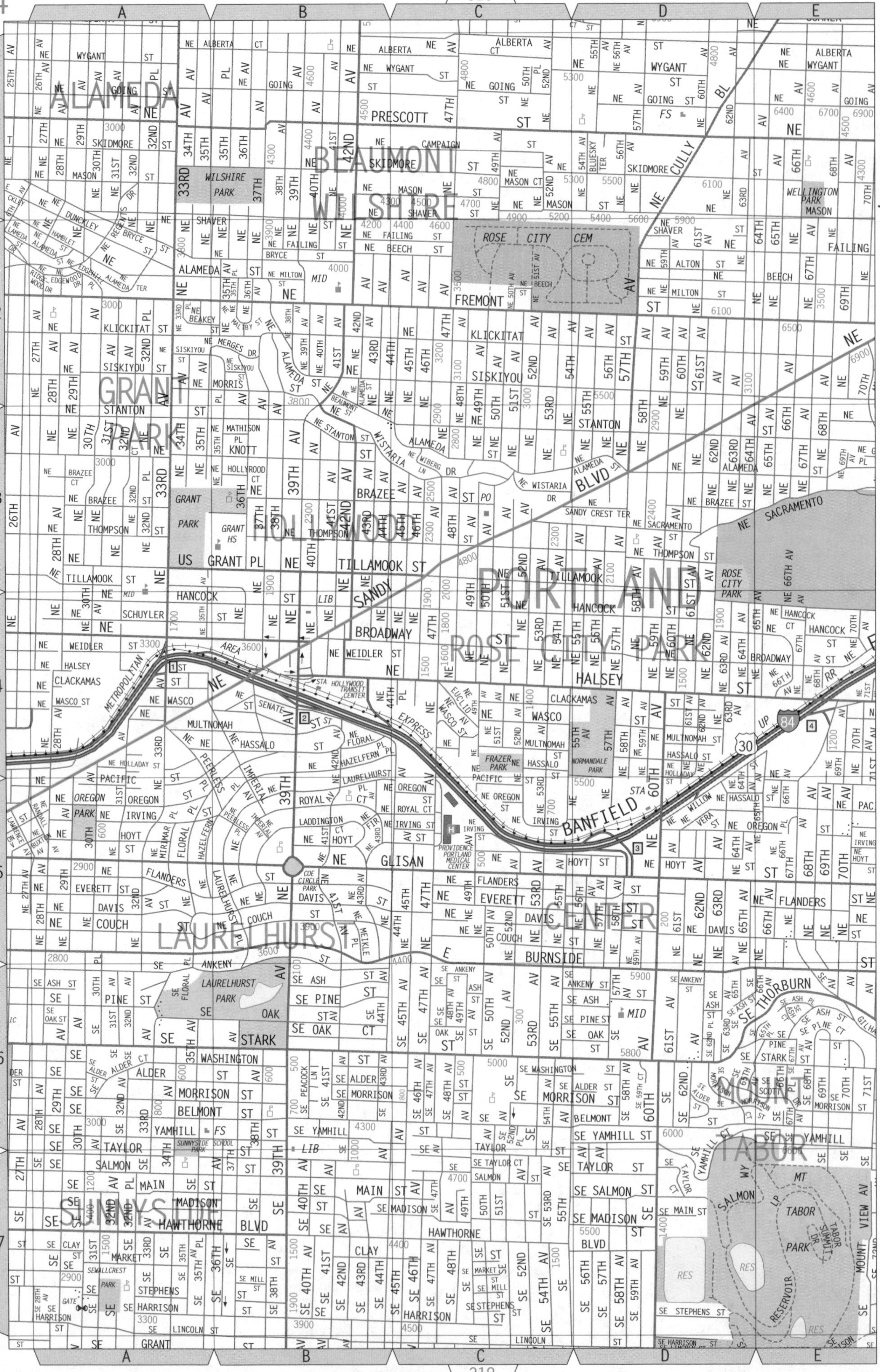

BEAUMONT WILSHIRE

GRANT PARK

HOLLYWOOD

PORTLAND

ROSE CITY PARK

ROSE CITY CEM

FREMONT

LAURELHURST

SUNNYSIDE

MT TABOR

MT TABOR PARK

WILSHIRE PARK

GRANT PARK

US GRANT PL

COE CIRCLE PARK

LAURELHURST PARK

FRAZER PARK

NORMANDALE PARK

PROVIDENCE PORTLAND MEDICAL CENTER

HOLLYWOOD TRANSIT CENTER

BANFIELD

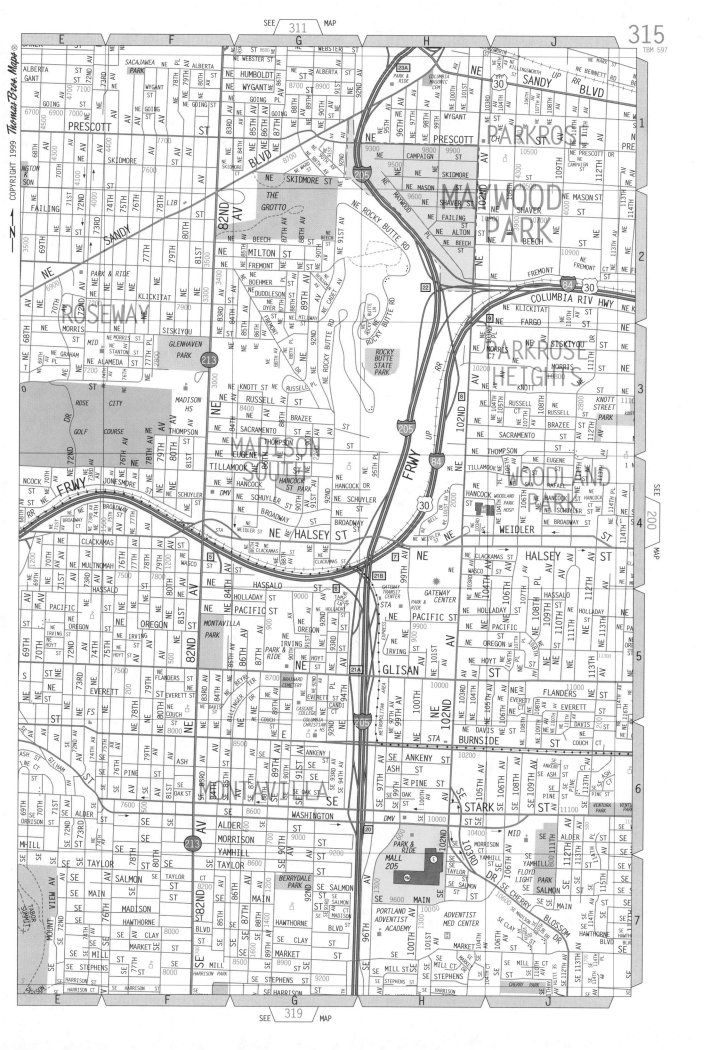

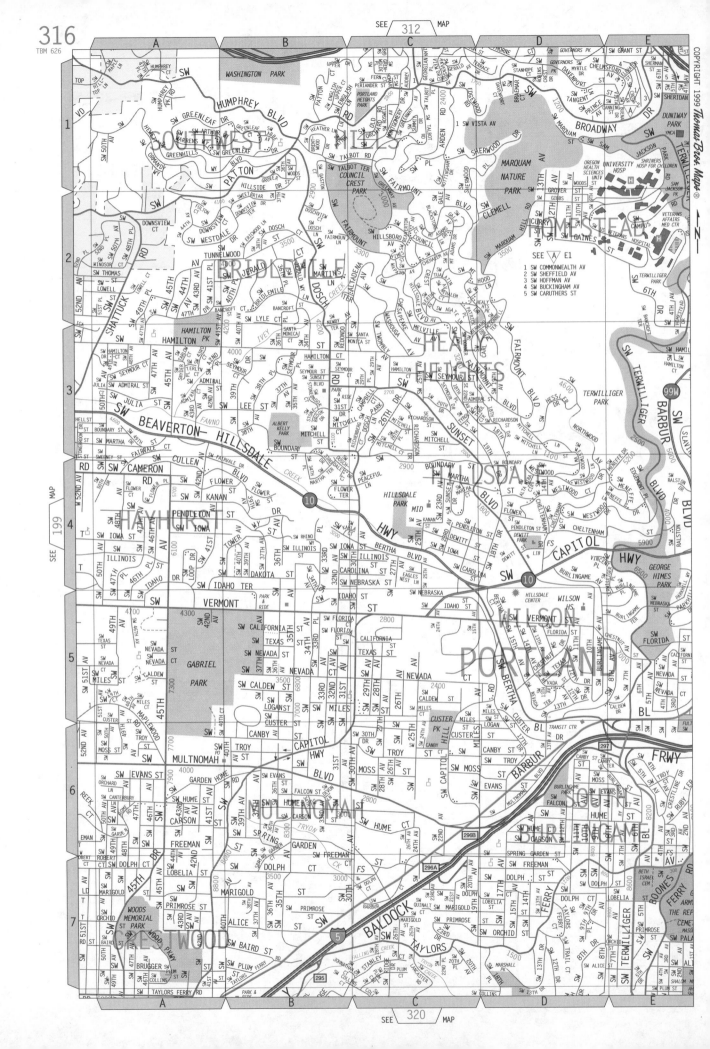

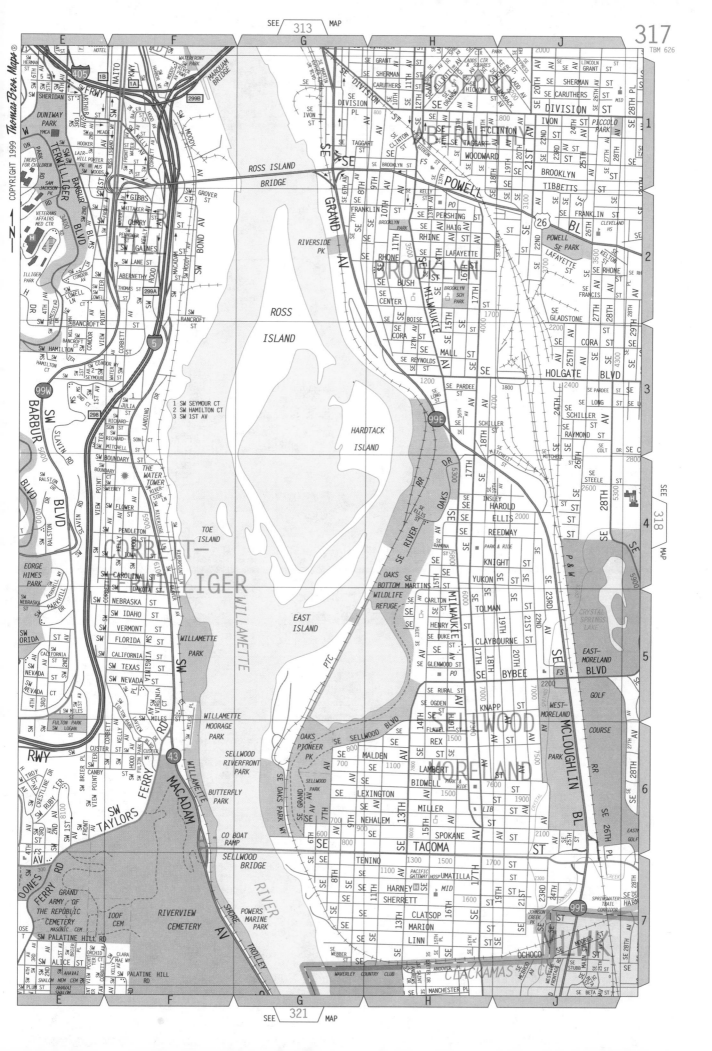

PNW

DETAIL

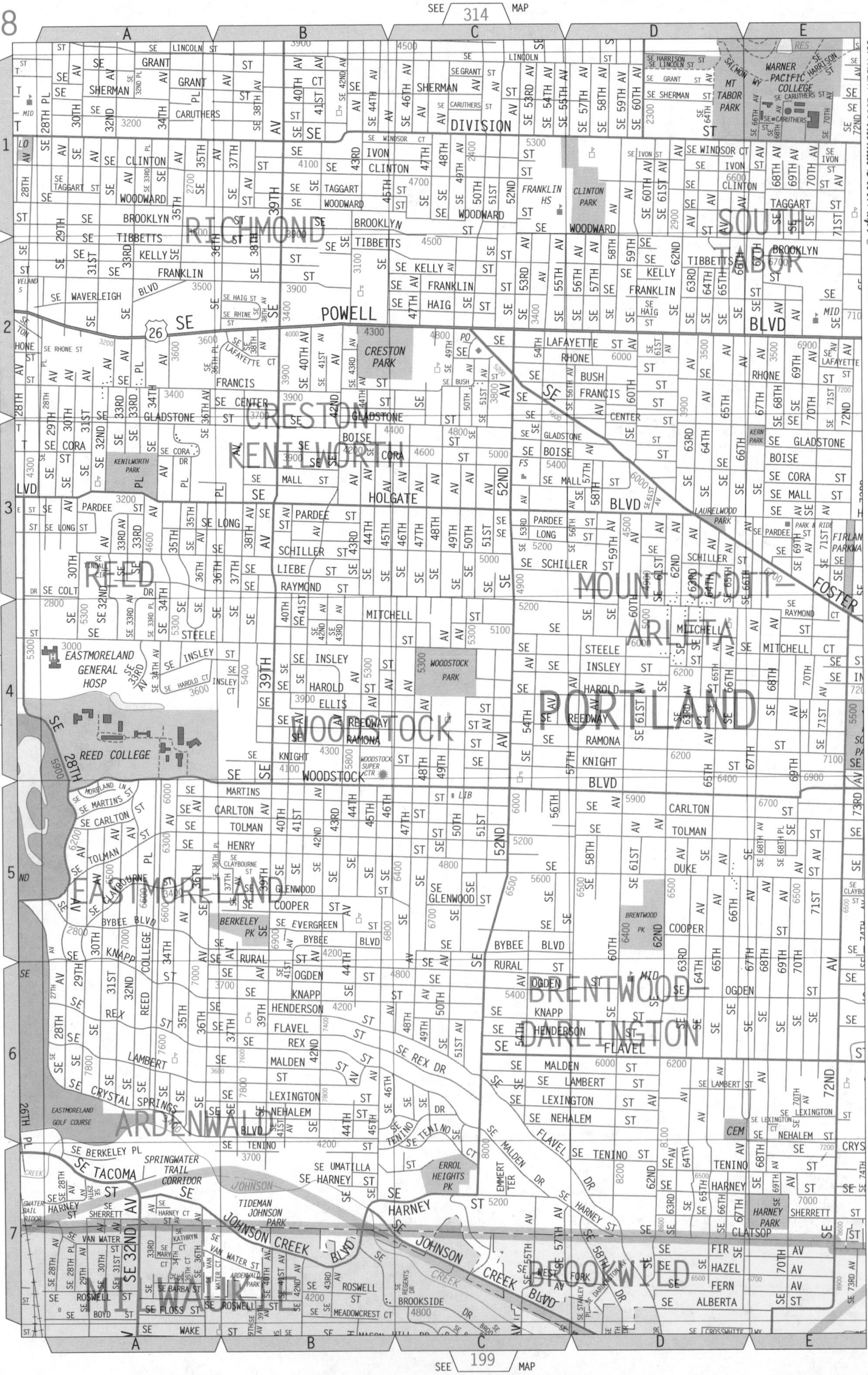

SEE 314 MAP

SEE 317 MAP

A B C D E

1
2
3
4
5
6
7

RICHMOND

SOUTH TABOR

CRESTON KENILWORTH

MOUNT SCOTT-ARLETA

PORTLAND

REED

WOODSTOCK

EASTMORELAND

BRENTWOOD-DARLINGTON

ARDENWALD

MILWAUKIE

BROOKLYN

WARNER PACIFIC COLLEGE

MT TABOR PARK

CRESTON PARK

CLINTON PARK

FRANKLIN HS

KENILWORTH PARK

WOODSTOCK PARK

EASTMORELAND GENERAL HOSP

REED COLLEGE

BERKELEY PK

BRENTWOOD PK

EASTMORELAND GOLF COURSE

CRYSTAL SPRINGS

SPRINGWATER TRAIL CORRIDOR

TIDEMAN JOHNSON PARK

ERROL HEIGHTS PK

HARNEY PARK

LAURELWOOD PARK

KERN PARK

FIRLAND PARKWAY

GRANT SHERMAN CARUTHERS DIVISION

LINCOLN

CLINTON TAGGART WOODWARD BROOKLYN TIBBETTS KELLY FRANKLIN WAVERLEIGH

POWELL BLVD

LAFAYETTE RHONE BUSH FRANCIS CENTER

GLADSTONE BOISE CORA MALL HOLGATE BLVD

PARDEE LONG SCHILLER LIEBE RAYMOND MITCHELL

STEELE INSLEY HAROLD ELLIS REEDWAY RAMONA KNIGHT WOODSTOCK BLVD

MARTINS CARLTON TOLMAN HENRY CLAYBOURNE GLENWOOD COOPER BYBEE BLVD

RURAL OGDEN KNAPP HENDERSON FLAVEL REX MALDEN LAMBERT LEXINGTON NEHALEM TENINO

UMATILLA HARNEY

TACOMA SHERRETT BERKELEY PL

JOHNSON CREEK BLVD

CLATSOP FIR HAZEL FERN ALBERTA

ROSWELL BOYD WAKE BROOKSIDE MEADOWCREST CT

PNW

DETAIL

FOSTER-POWELL

MULTNOMAH COUNTY

LENTS

SE DIVISION ST

SE POWELL BLVD

SE HOLGATE BLVD

SE FOSTER RD

SE WOODSTOCK BLVD

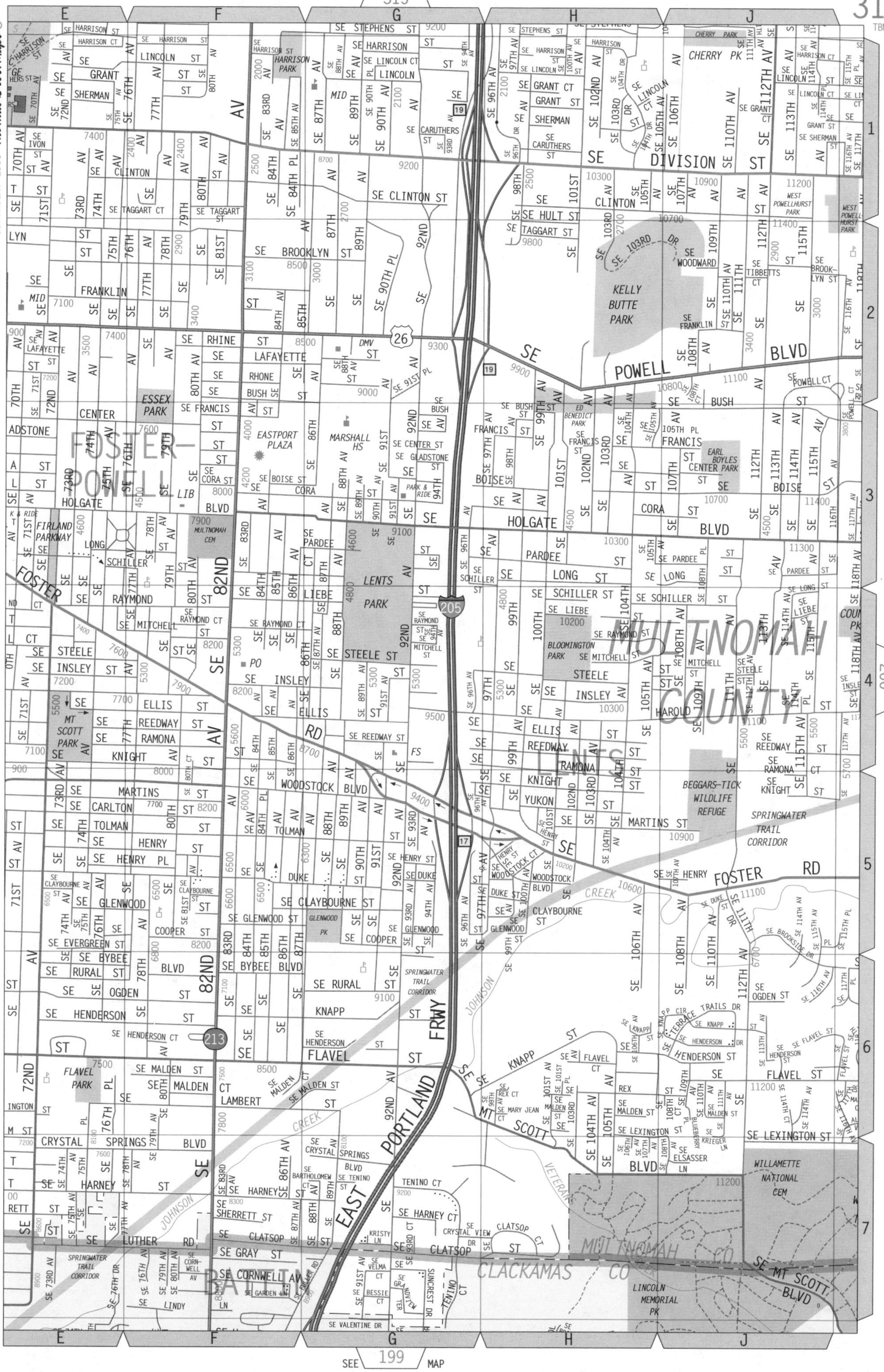

SE FLAVEL ST

SE LEXINGTON ST

EAST PORTLAND FRWY

SE MT SCOTT BLVD

CLACKAMAS CO

MULTNOMAH CO

KELLY BUTTE PARK

LENTS PARK

MT SCOTT PARK

ESSEX PARK

HARRISON PARK

CHERRY PK

WEST POWELLHURST PARK

EARL BOYLES CENTER PARK

ED BENEDICT PARK

BLOOMINGTON PARK

BEGGARS-TICK WILDLIFE REFUGE

SPRINGWATER TRAIL CORRIDOR

WILLAMETTE NATIONAL CEM

LINCOLN MEMORIAL PK

MULTNOMAH CEM

FLAVEL PARK

FIRLAND PARKWAY

EASTPORT PLAZA

MARSHALL HS

GLENWOOD PK

SEE 200 MAP

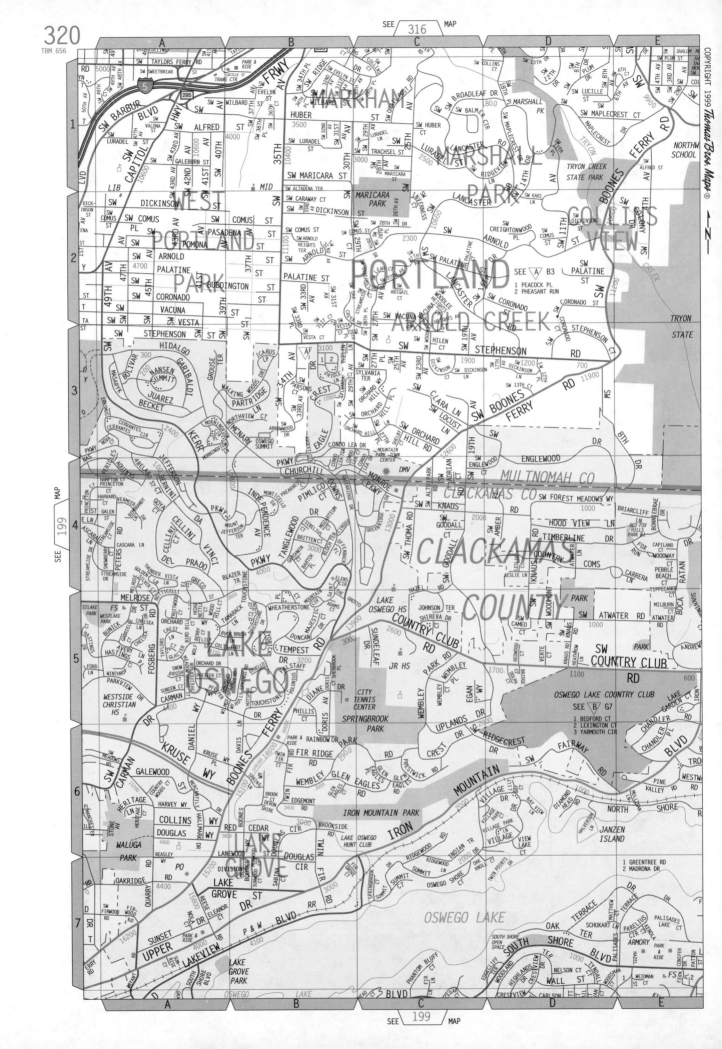

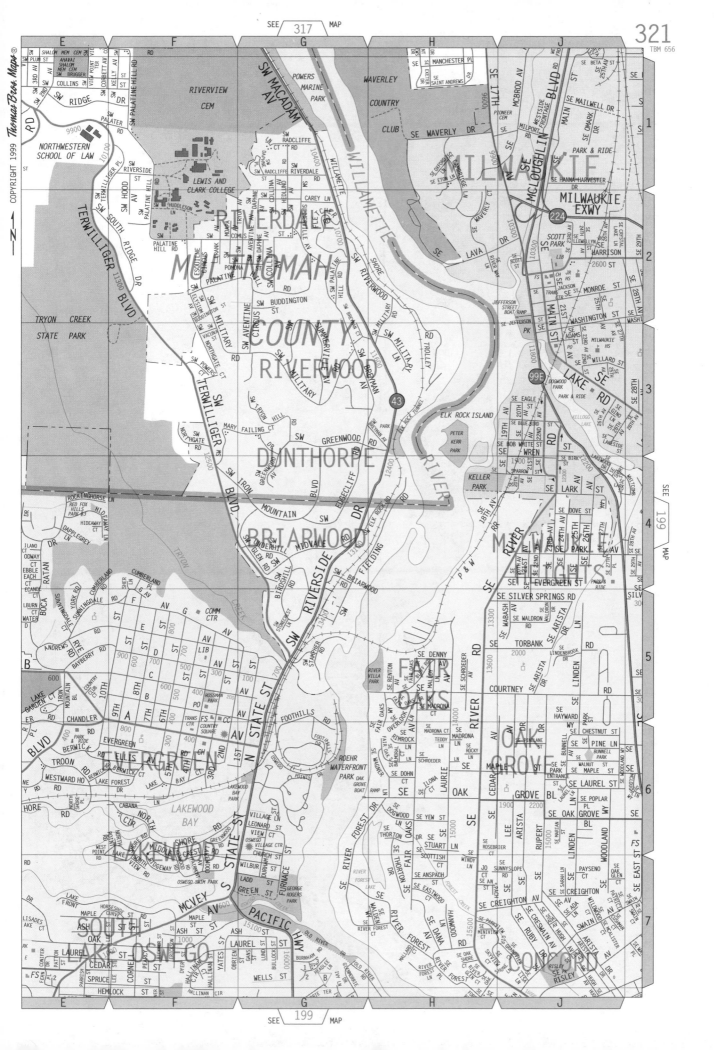

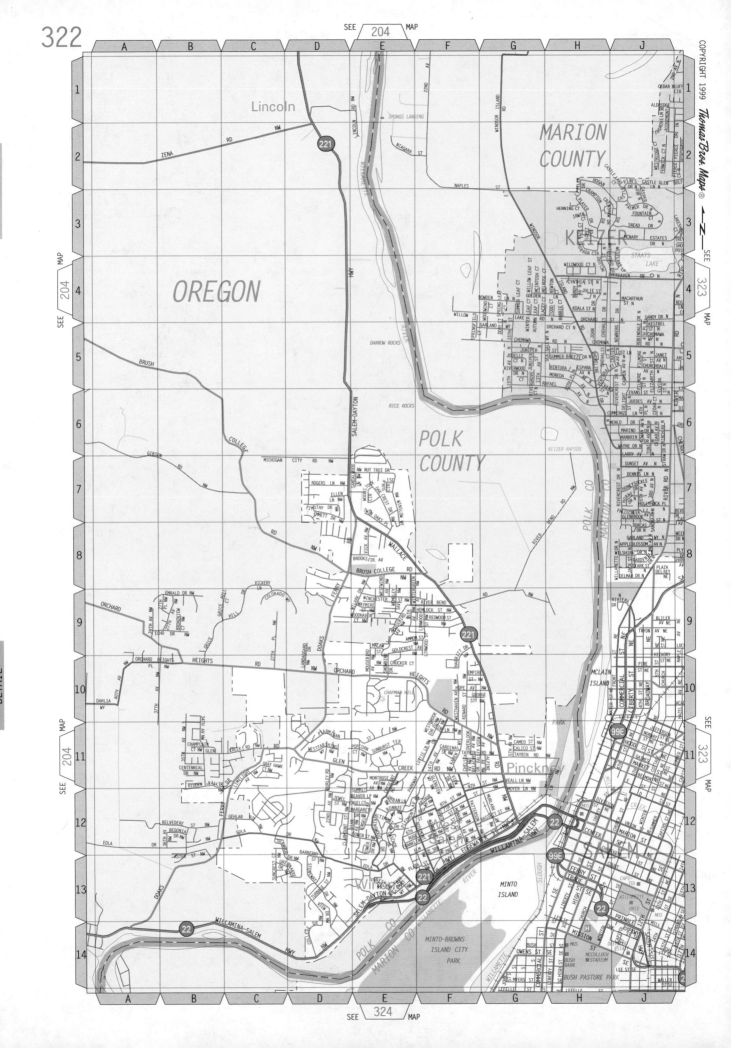

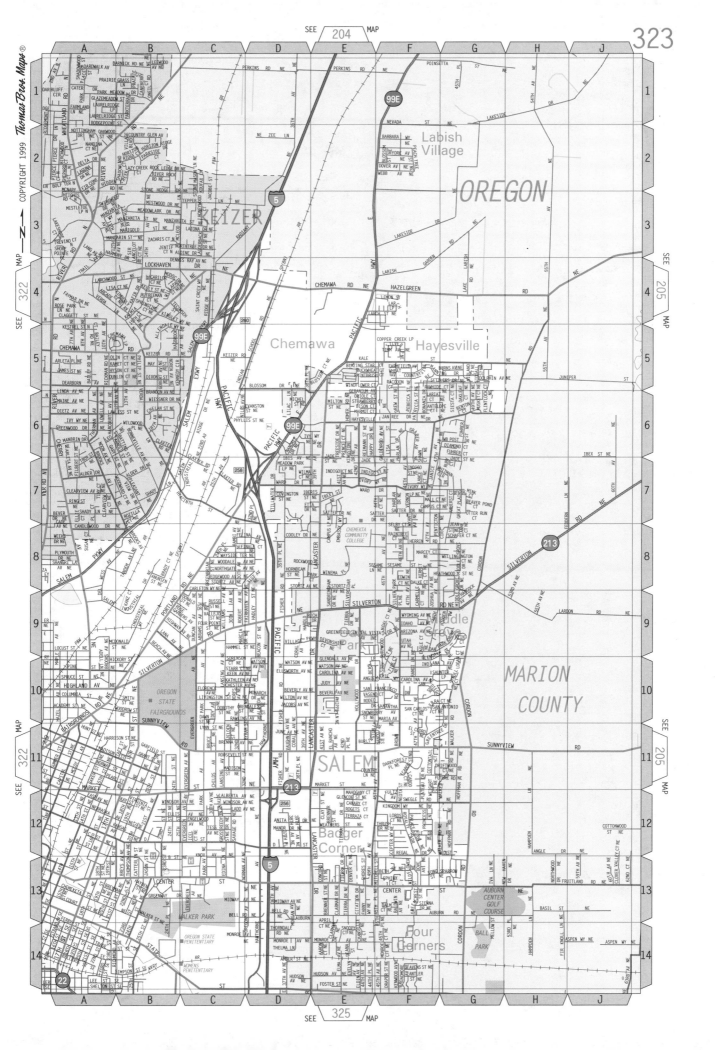

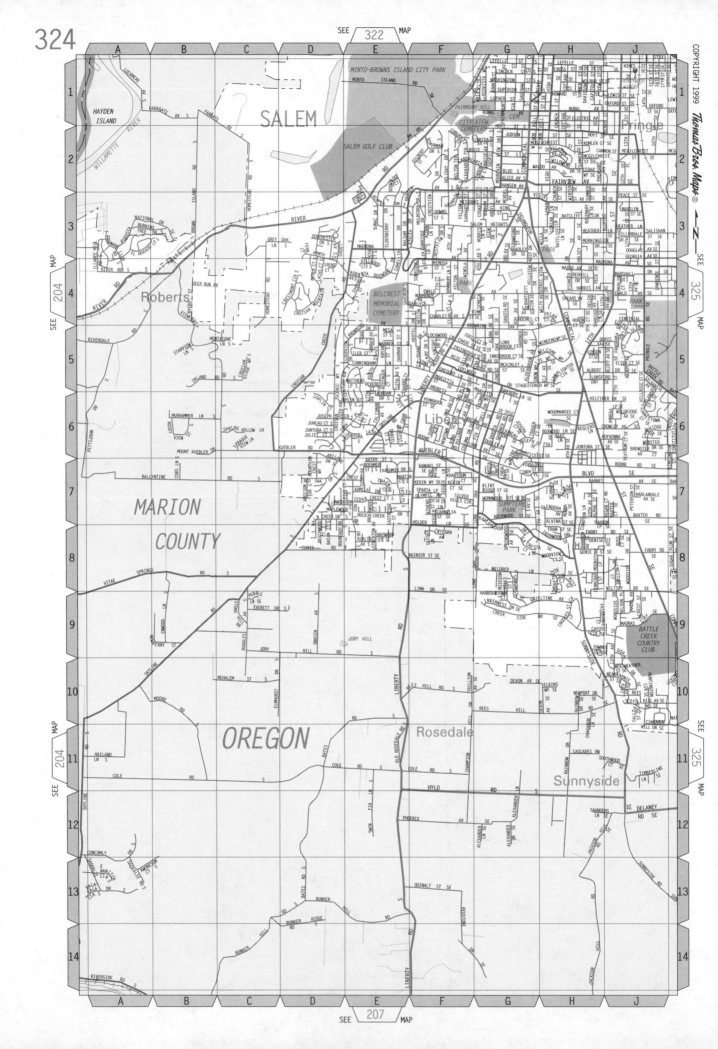

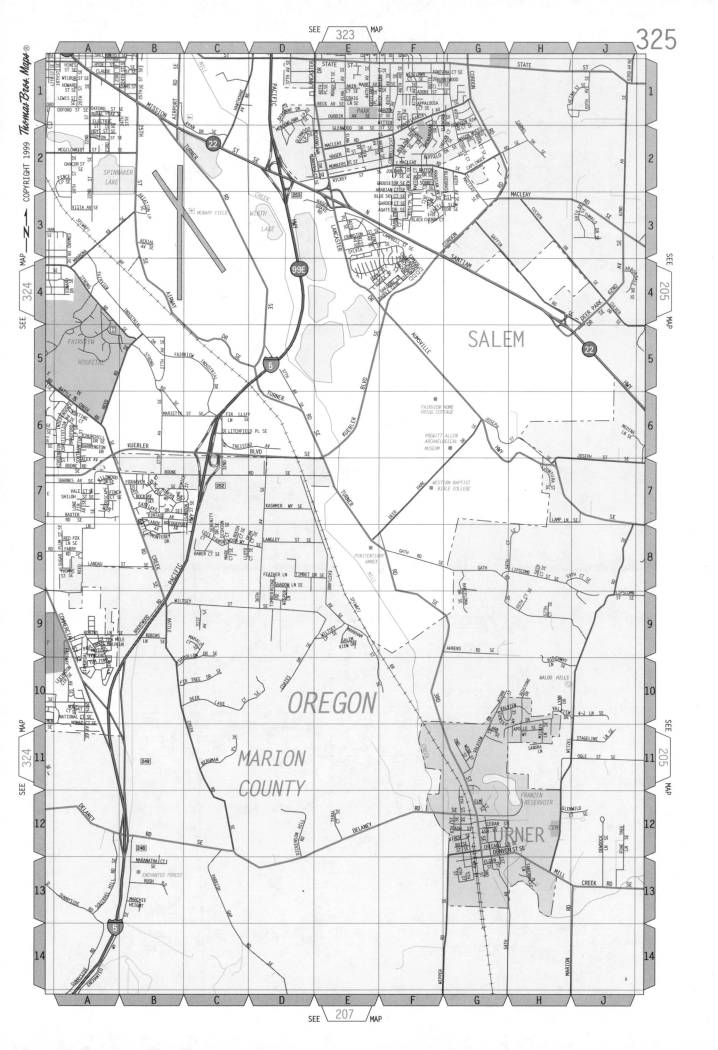

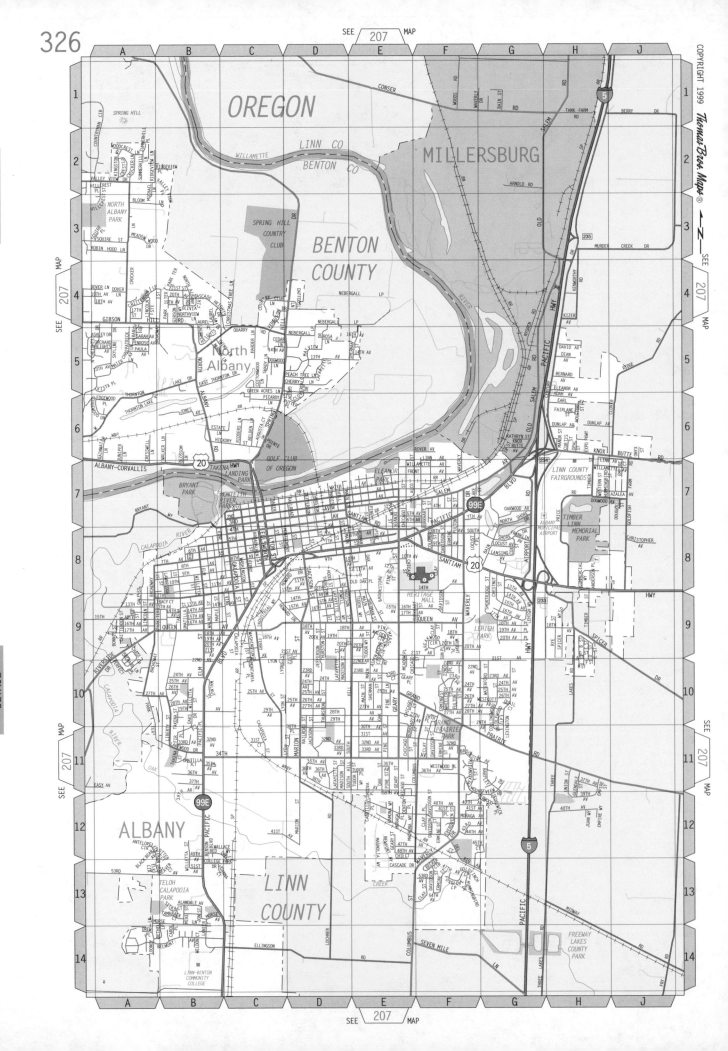

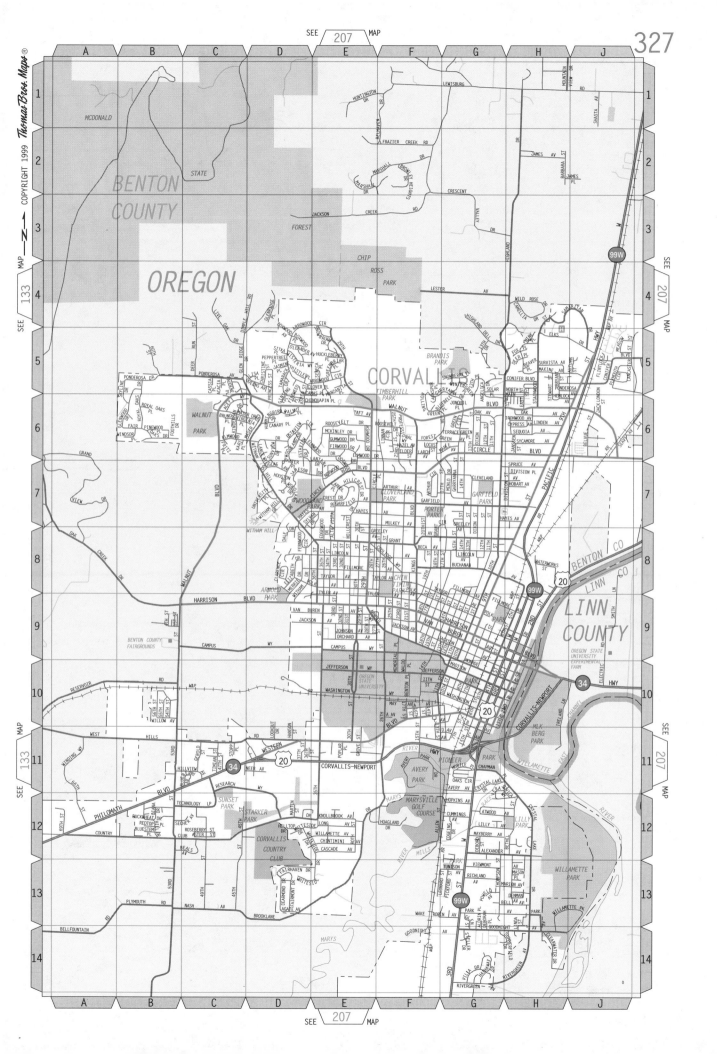

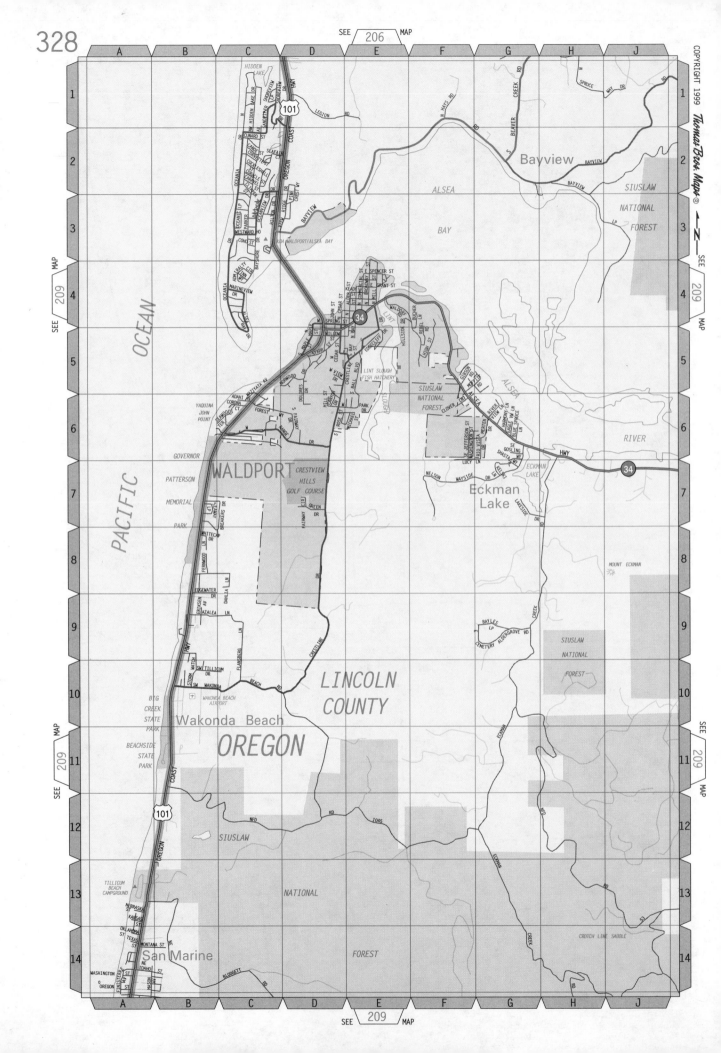

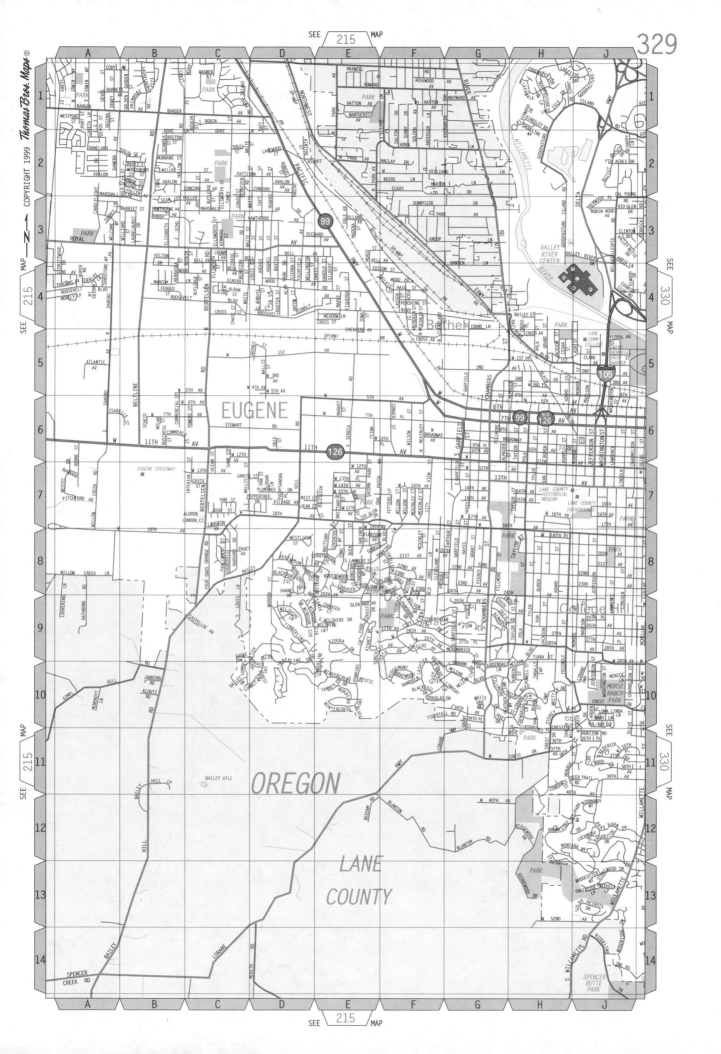

PNW

DETAIL

SEE 215 MAP

SEE 215 MAP

SEE 330 MAP

SEE 330 MAP

SEE 215 MAP

EUGENE

Bethel

College Hill

OREGON

LANE
COUNTY

VALLEY
RIVER
CENTER

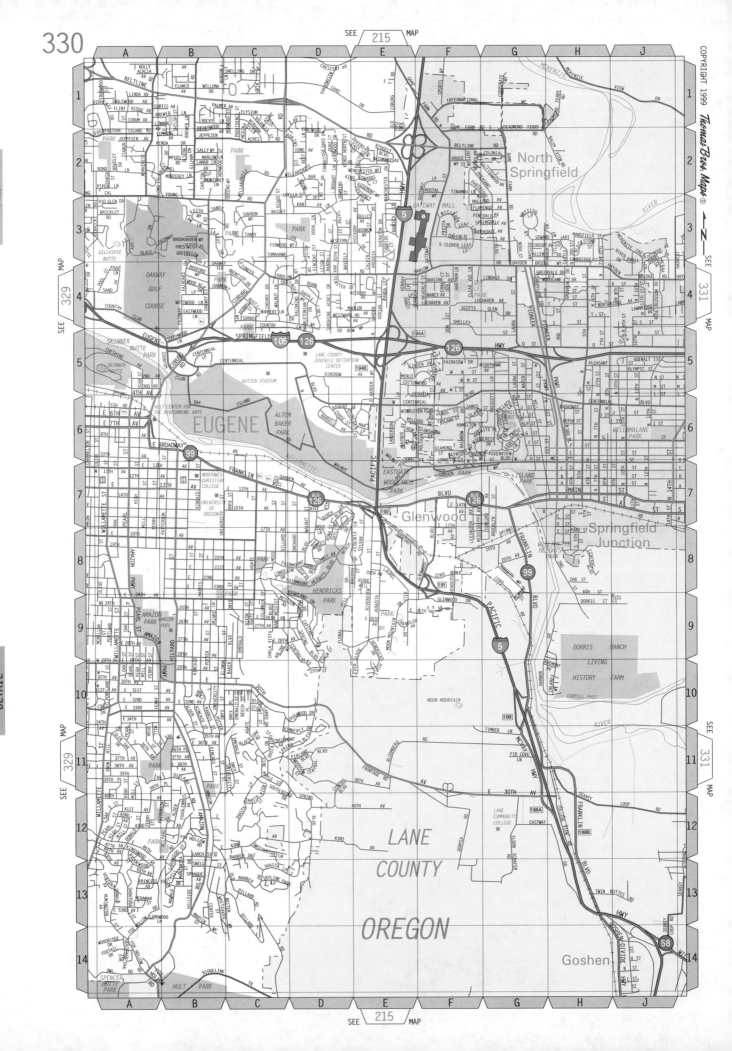

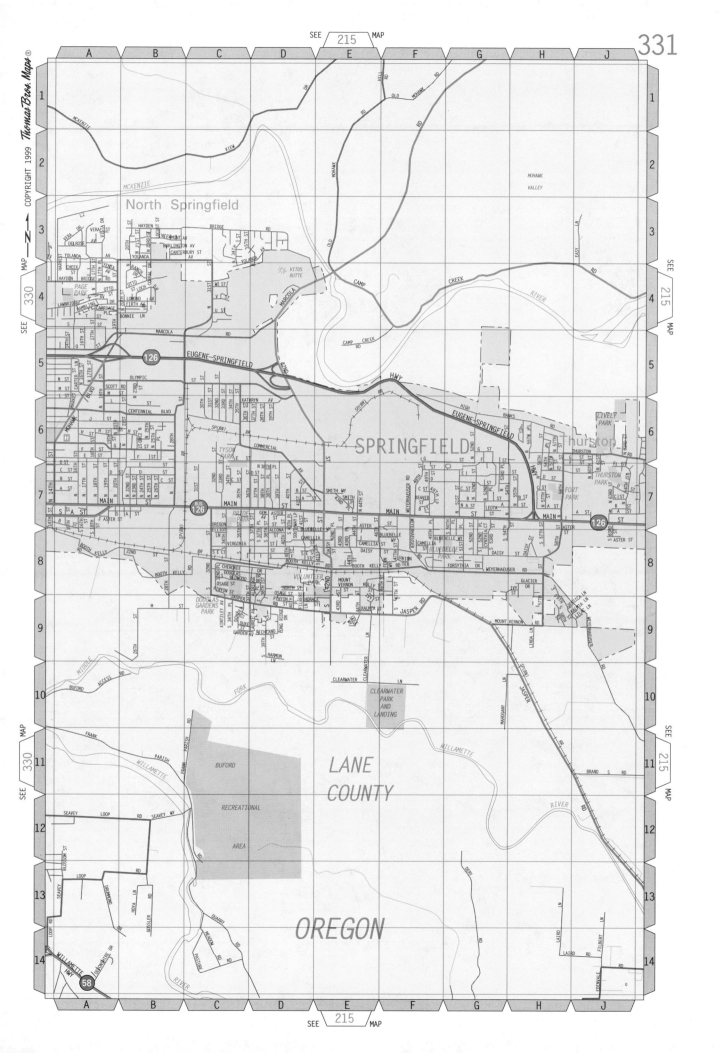

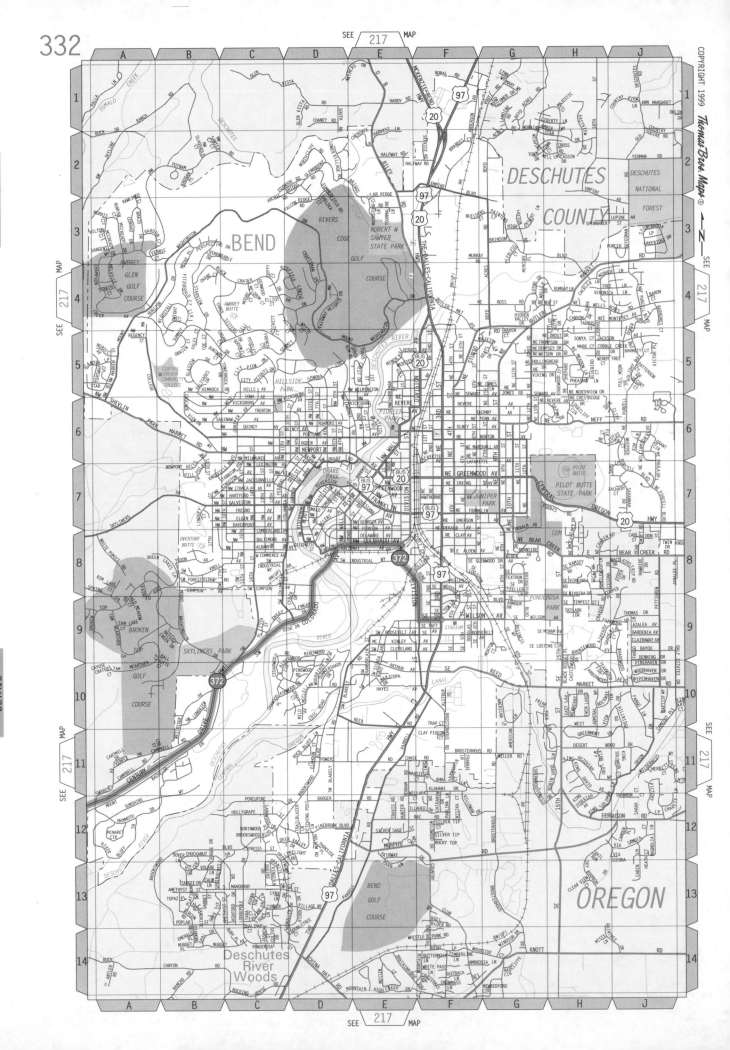

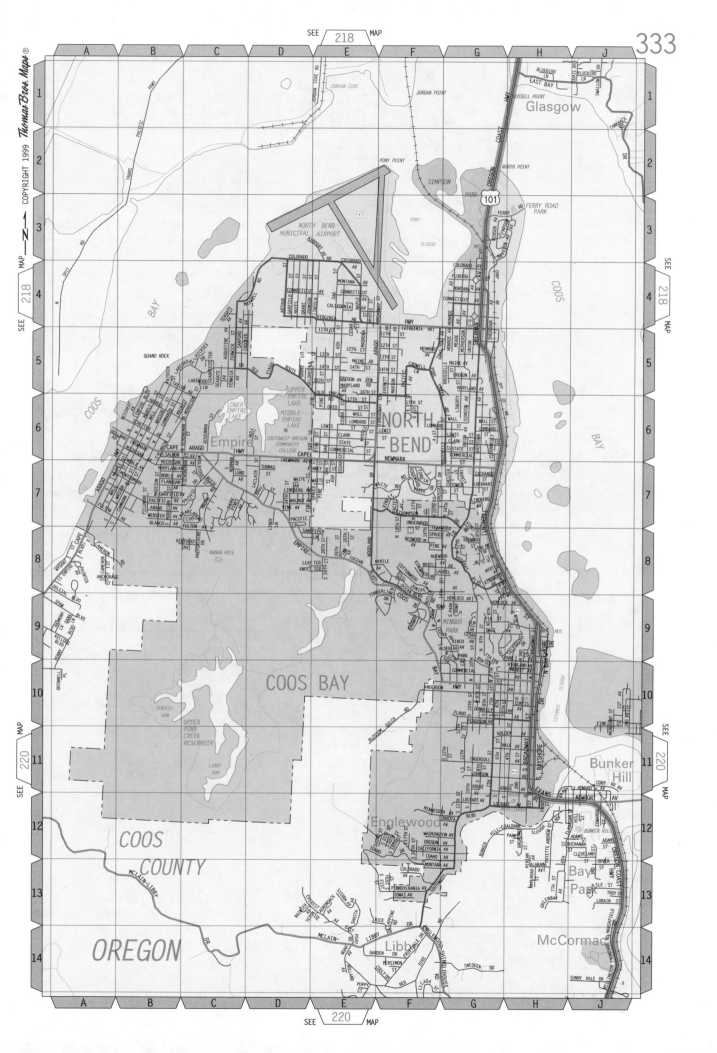

PNW

DETAIL

SEE 218 MAP

SEE 218 MAP

SEE 220 MAP

SEE 220 MAP

Glasgow

NORTH BEND

Empire

COOS BAY

COOS COUNTY

OREGON

Englewood

Libby

McCormac

Bay Park

Bunker Hill

Newport

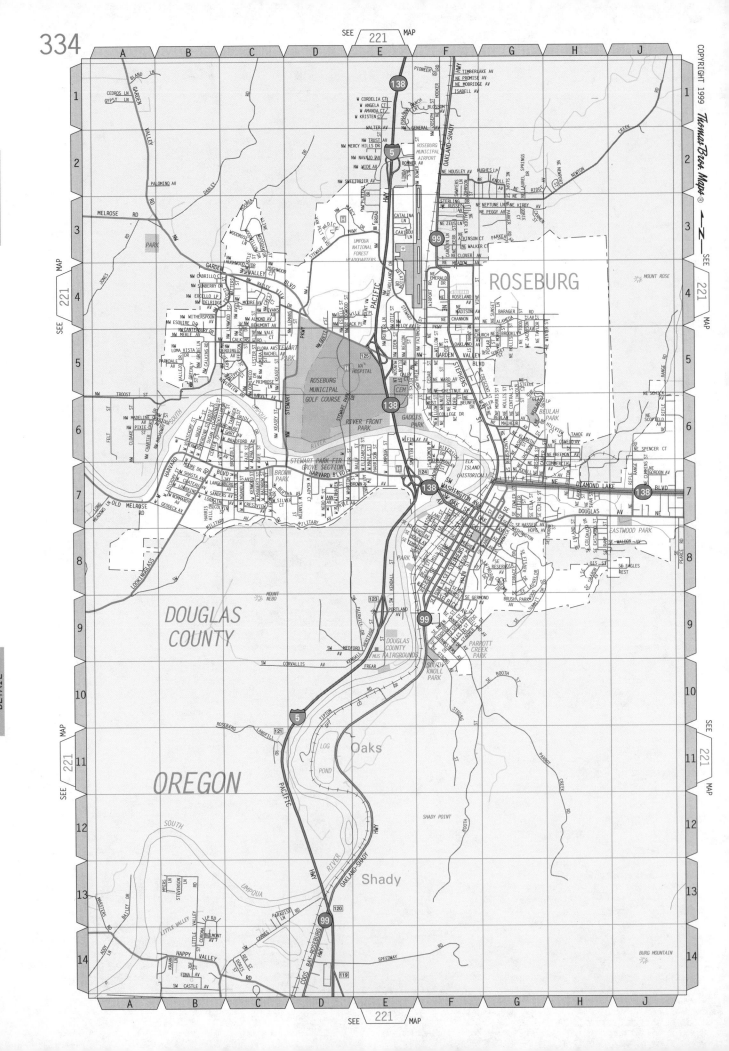

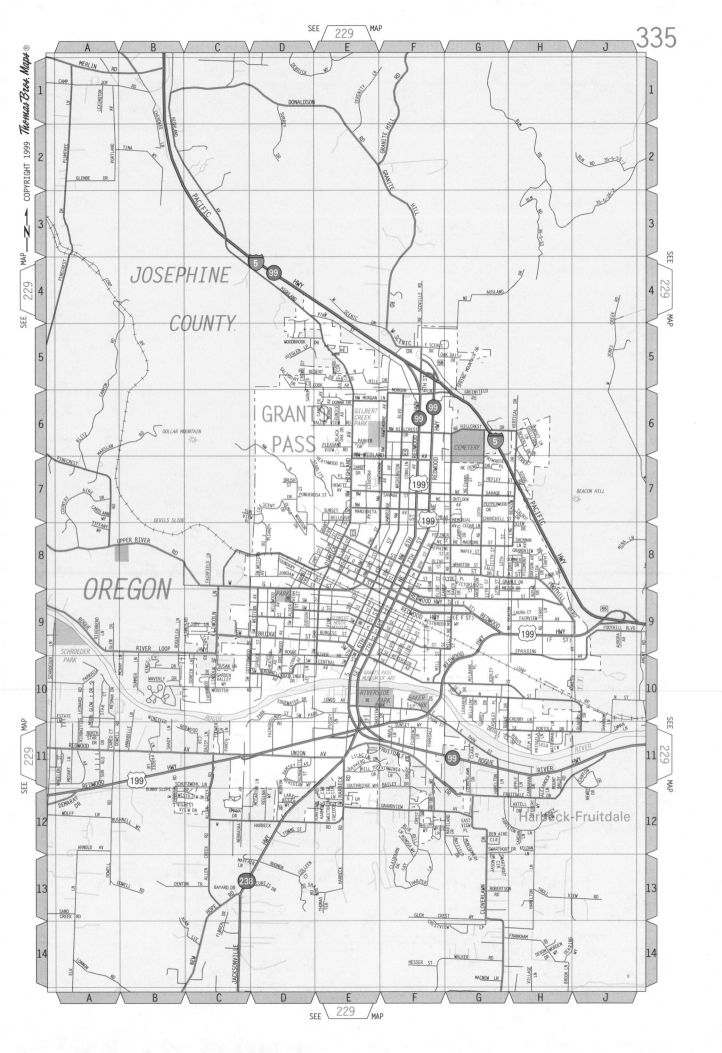

PNW

DETAIL

SEE 229 MAP

JOSEPHINE

COUNTY

GRANT
PASS

OREGON

Harbeck-Fruitdale

SEE 229 MAP

SEE 229 MAP

SEE 229 MAP

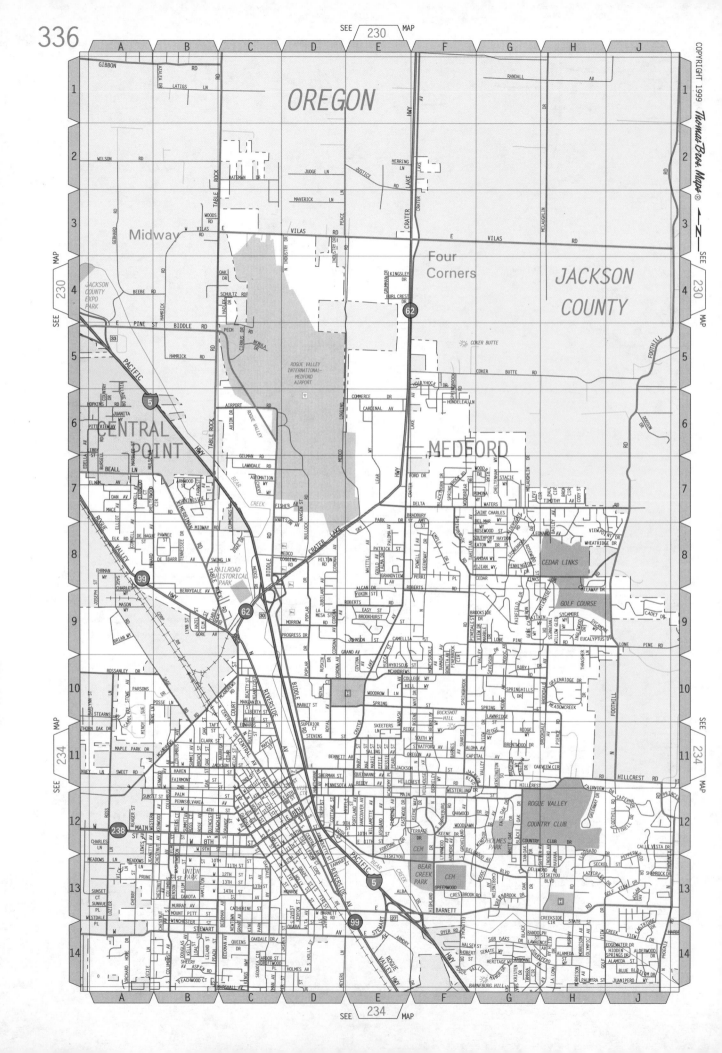

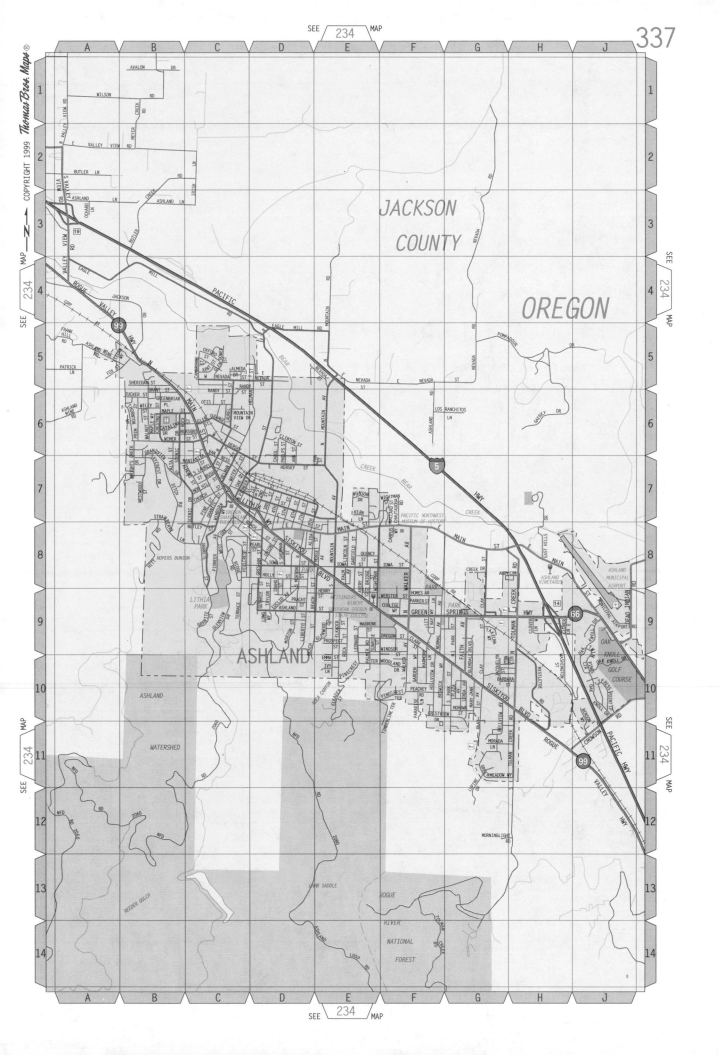

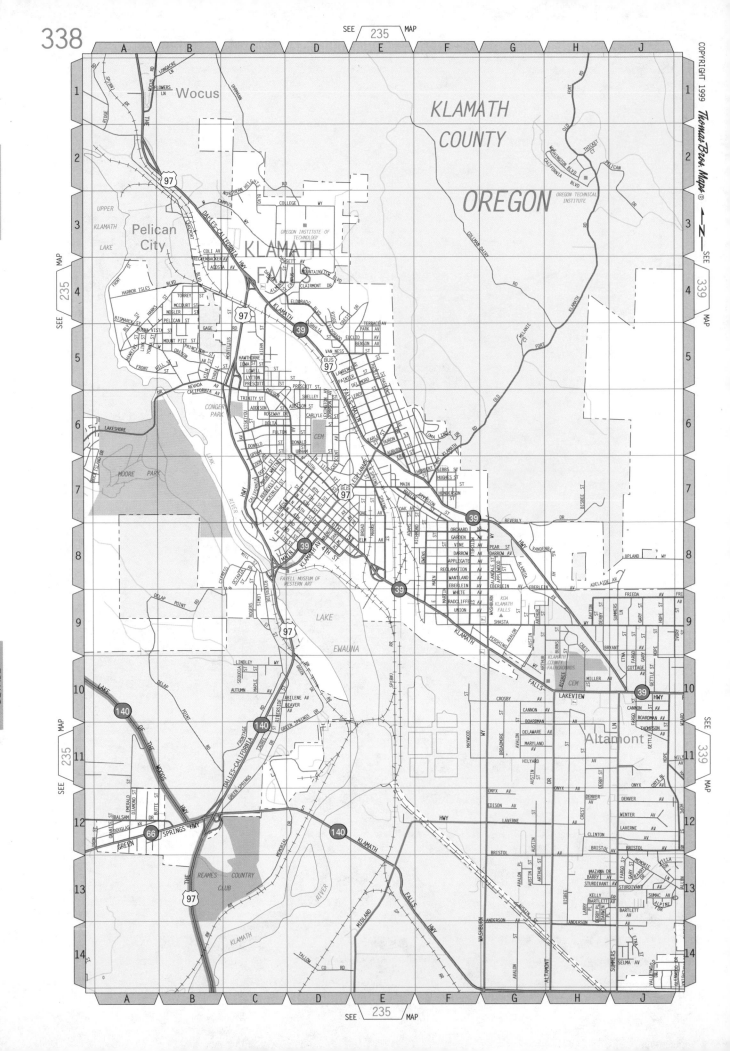

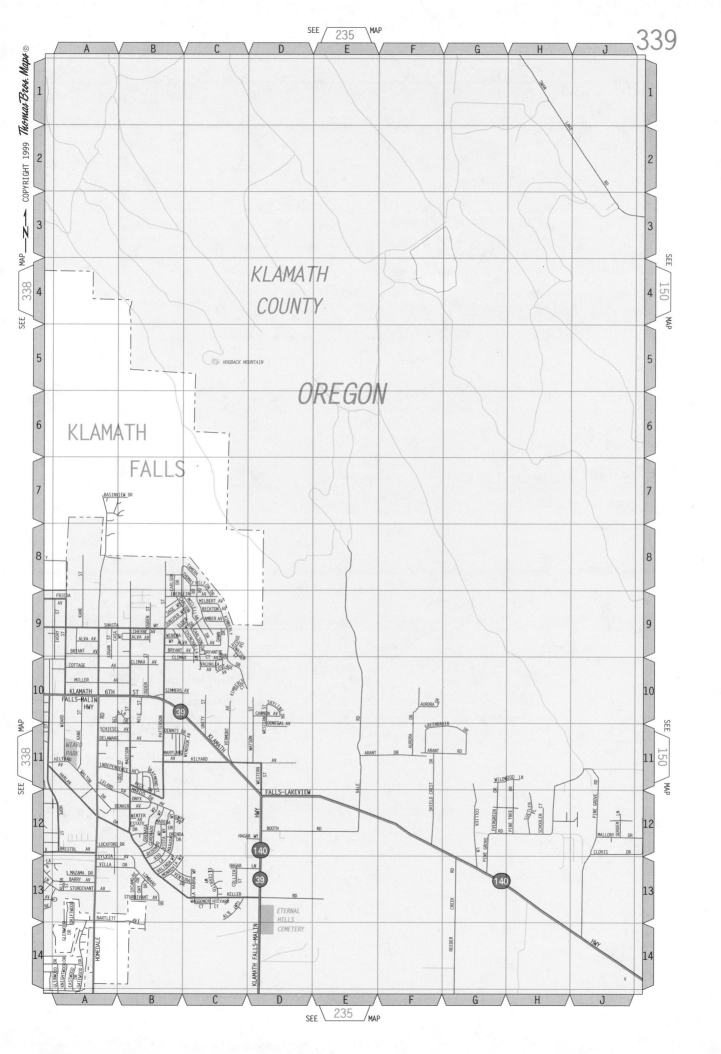

PNW

DETAIL

Thomas Bros. Maps®

COPYRIGHT 1999

N

SEE 338 MAP

SEE 150 MAP

KLAMATH COUNTY

OREGON

KLAMATH FALLS

HOGBACK MOUNTAIN

BASINVIEW DR

ETERNAL HILLS CEMETERY

KLAMATH FALLS-MALIN

FALLS-LAKEVIEW HWY

FALLS-MALIN HWY

WIARD PARK

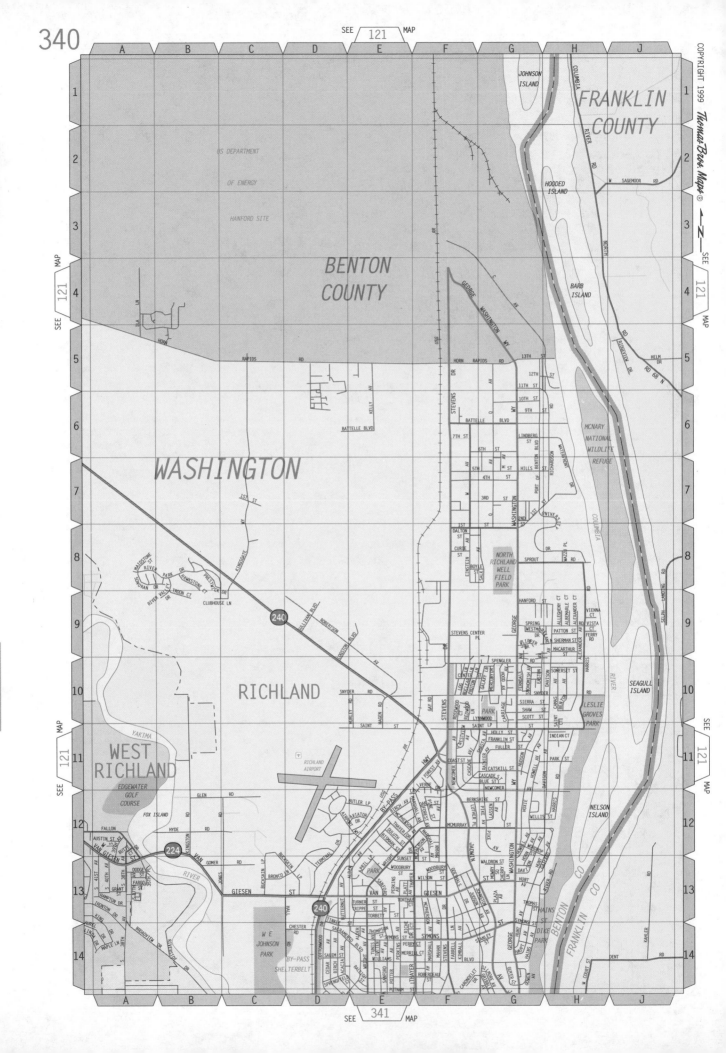

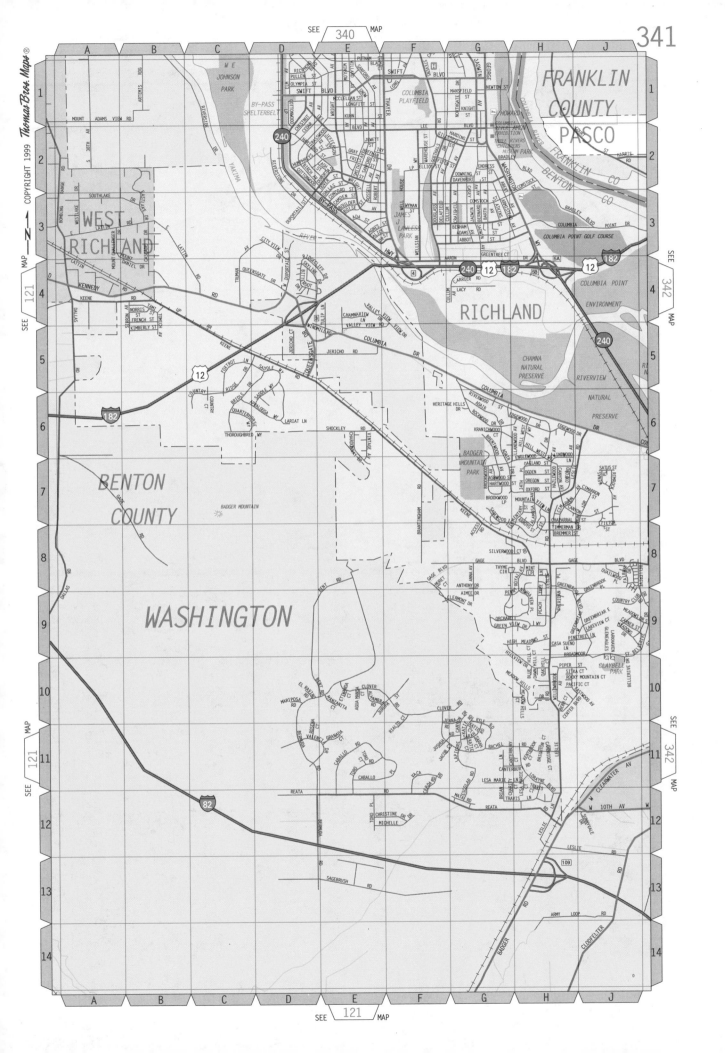

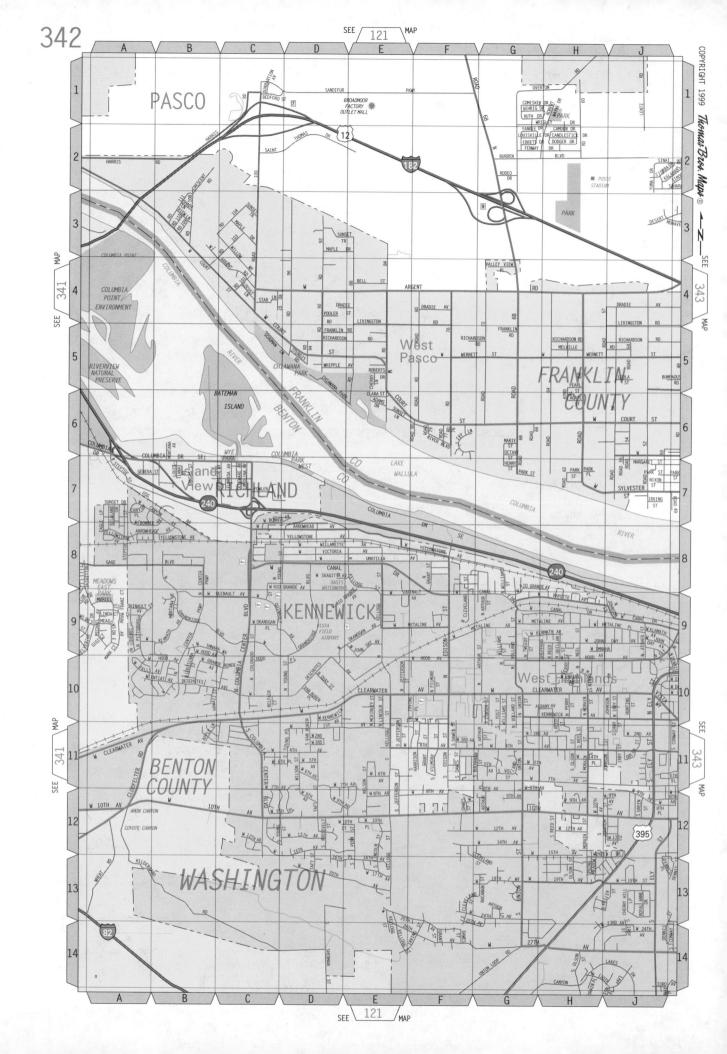

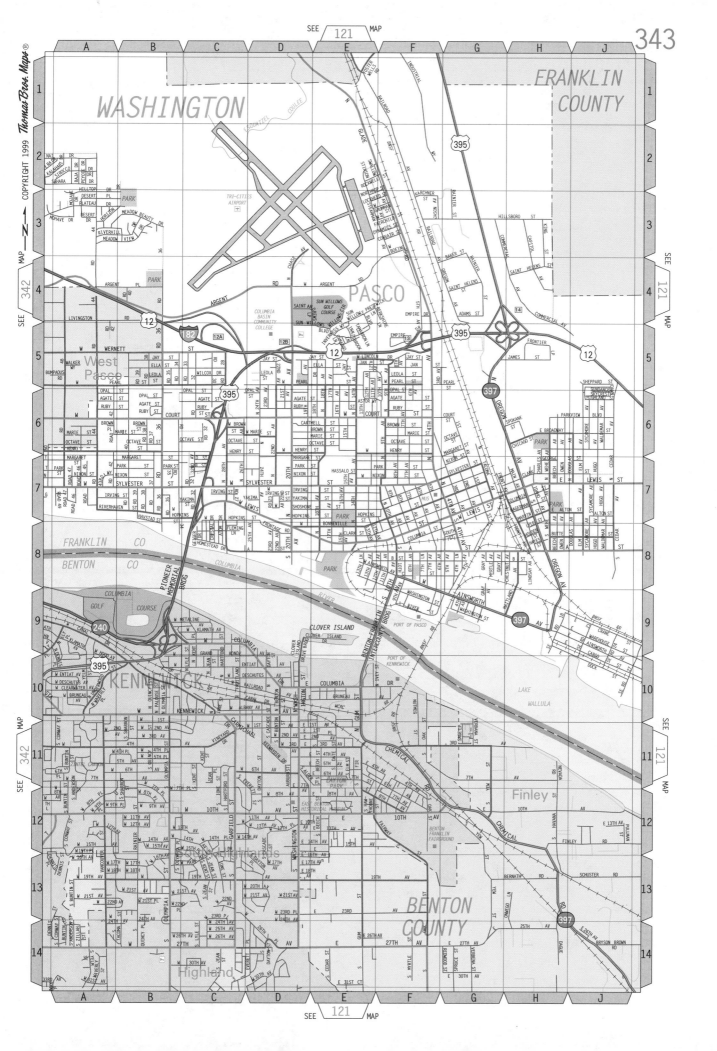

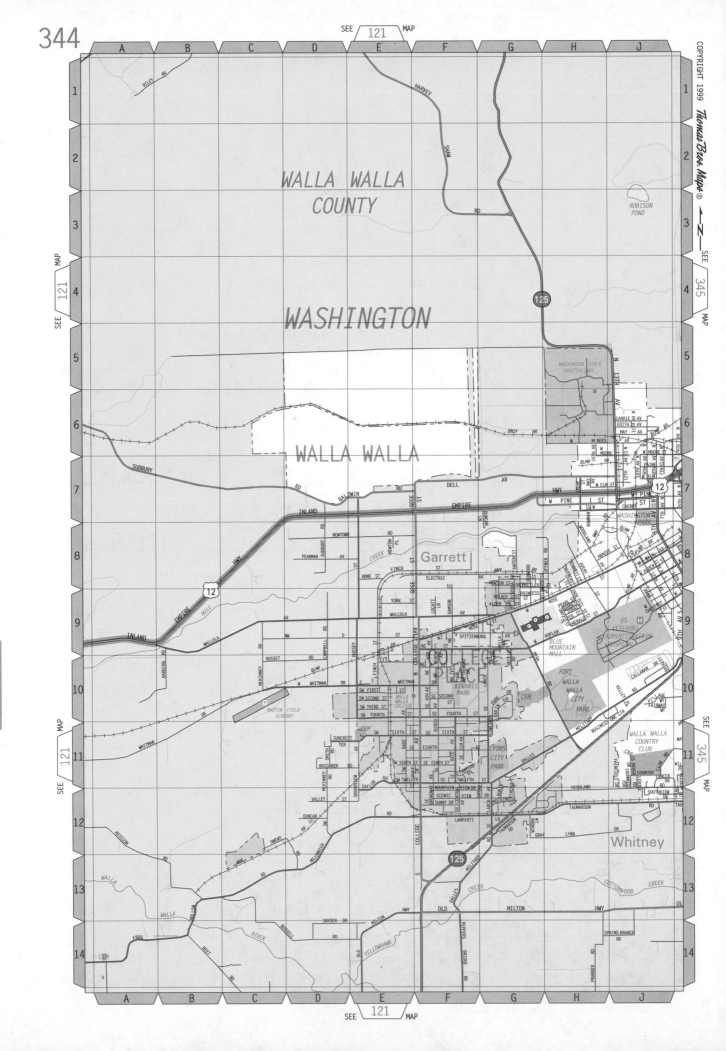

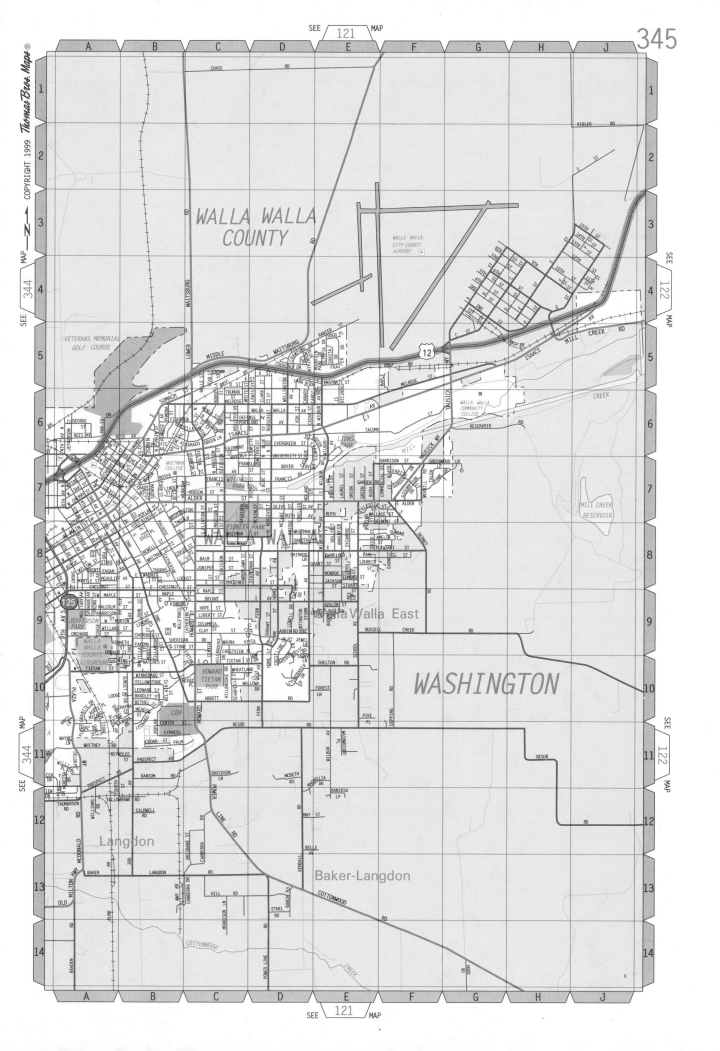

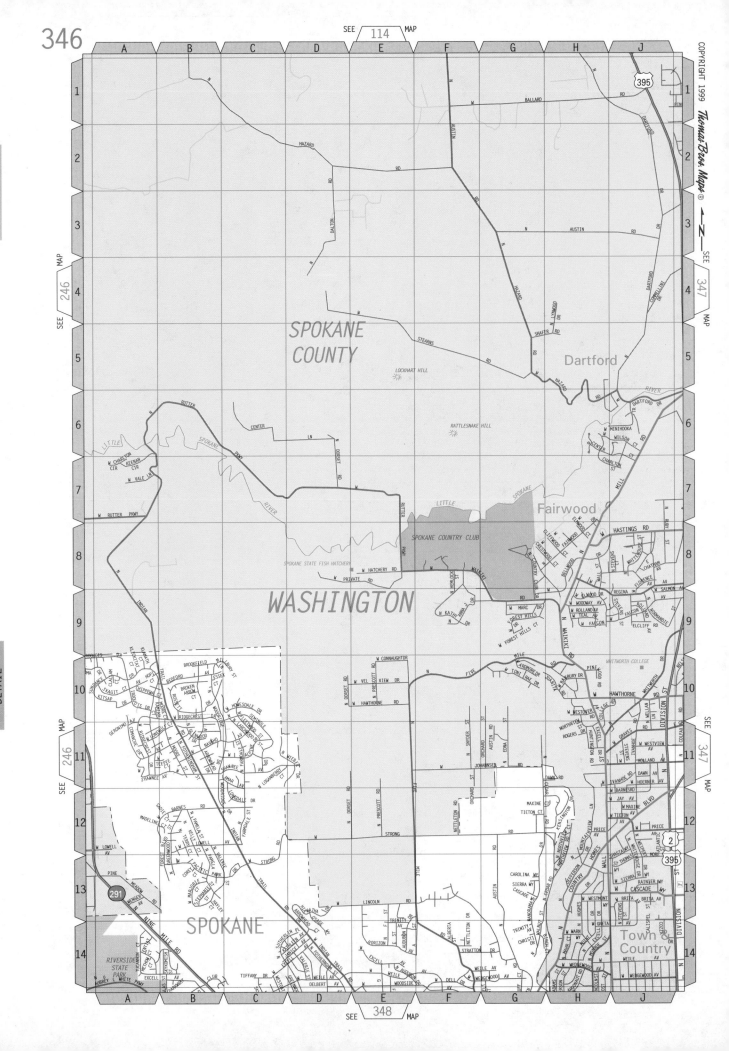

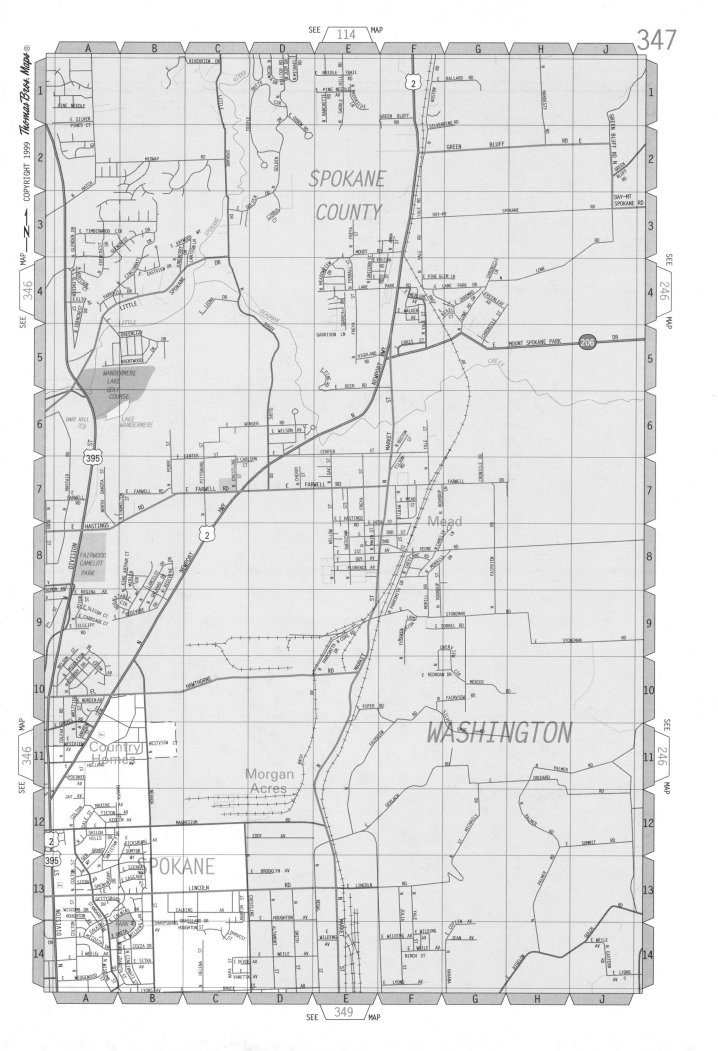

SEE 114 MAP

SEE 349 MAP

SEE 346 MAP

SEE 346 MAP

SEE 246 MAP

SEE 246 MAP

PNW

DETAIL

SPOKANE COUNTY

WASHINGTON

SPOKANE

Mead

Country Homes

Morgan Acres

WANDERMERE LAKE GOLF COURSE

LAKE WANDERMERE

DART HILL

FAIRWOOD CAMELOT PARK

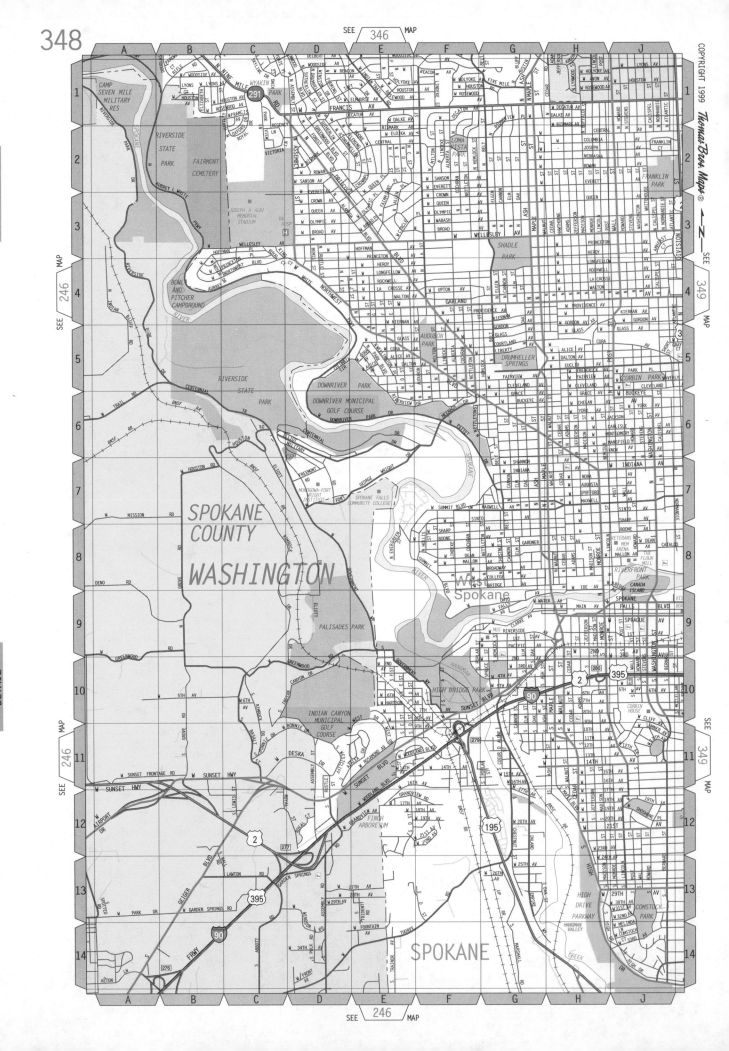

Thomas Bros. Maps® —N→

SEE 246 MAP

SEE 349 MAP

SPOKANE
COUNTY
WASHINGTON

SEE 246 MAP

SEE 349 MAP

PNW

DETAIL

SPOKANE

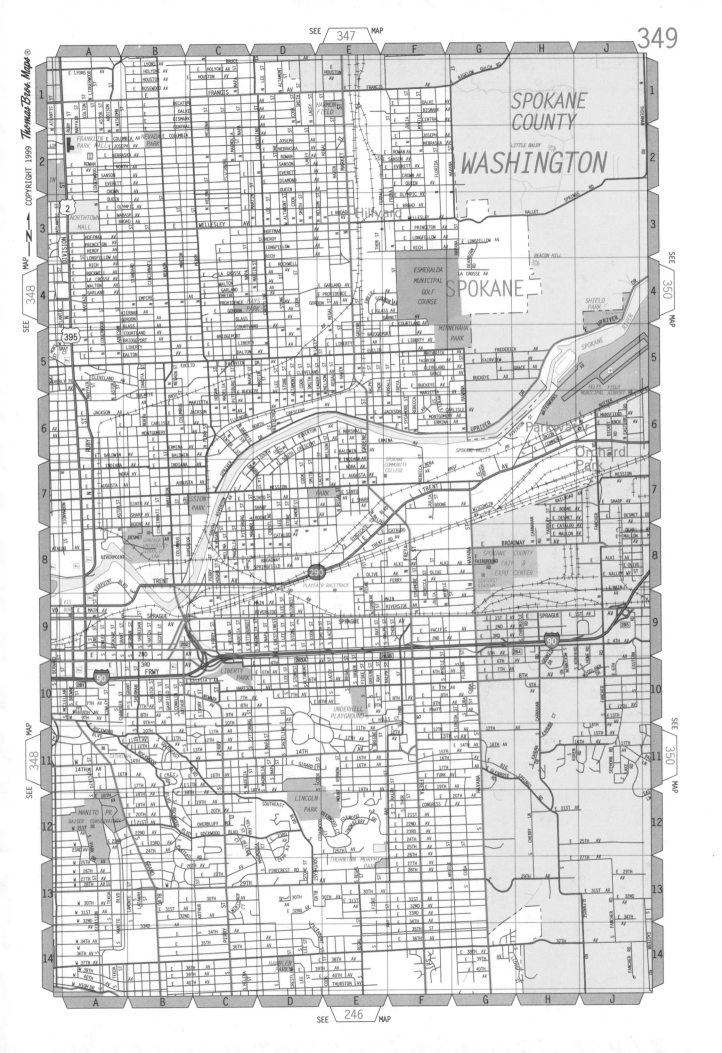

SPOKANE COUNTY

WASHINGTON

SPOKANE

PNW

DETAIL

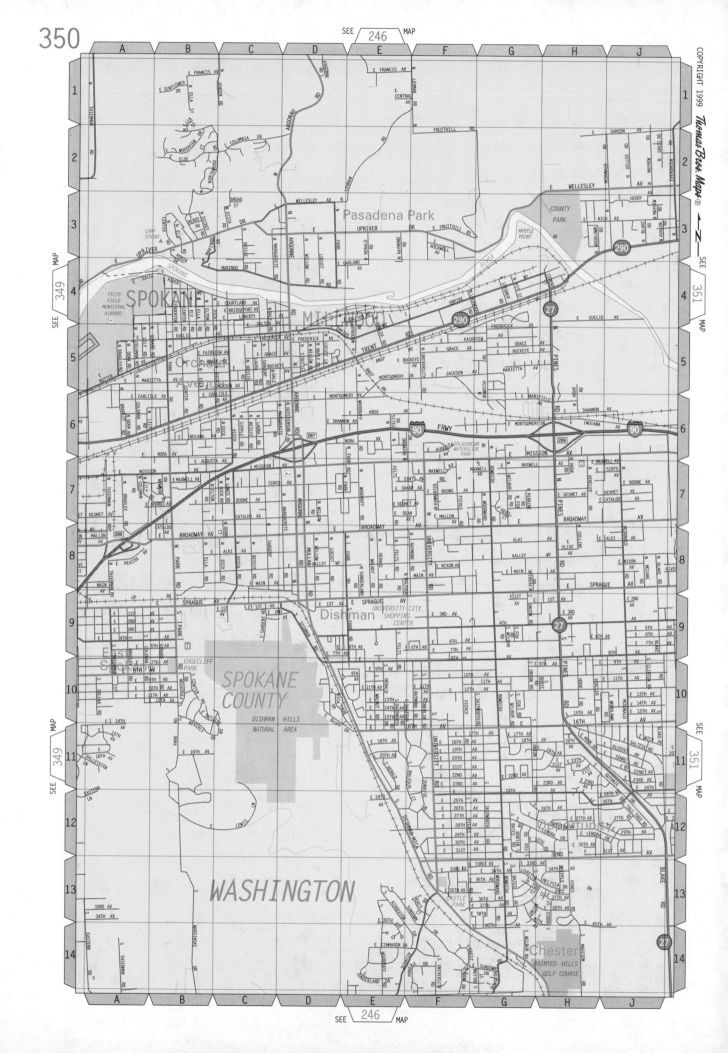

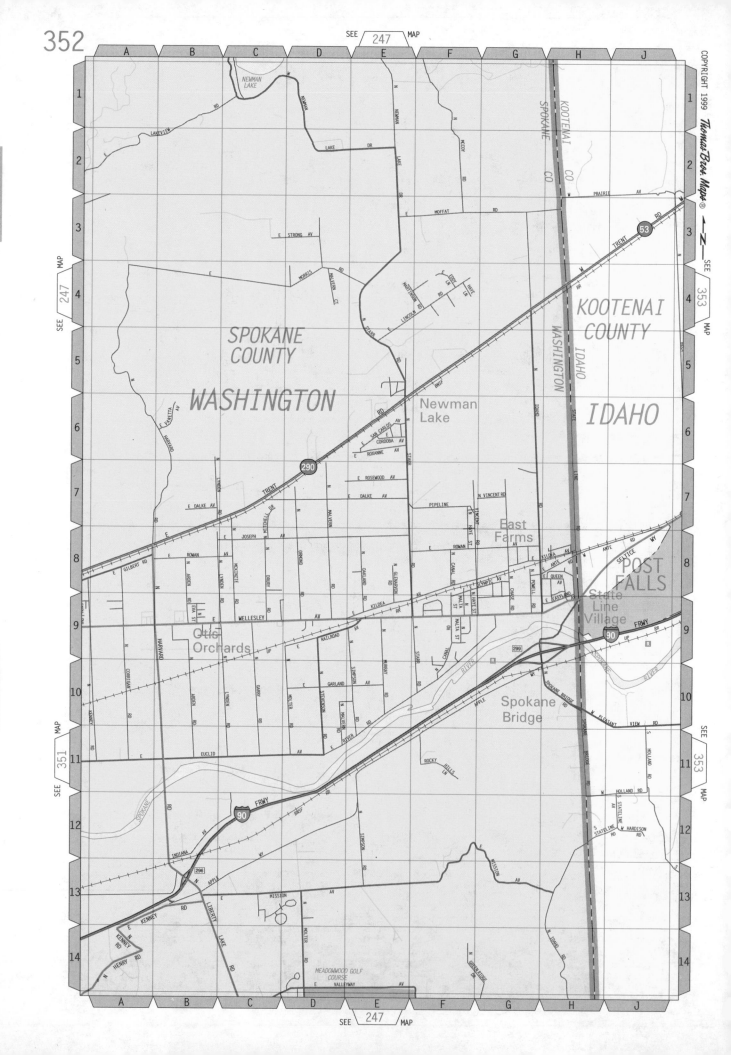

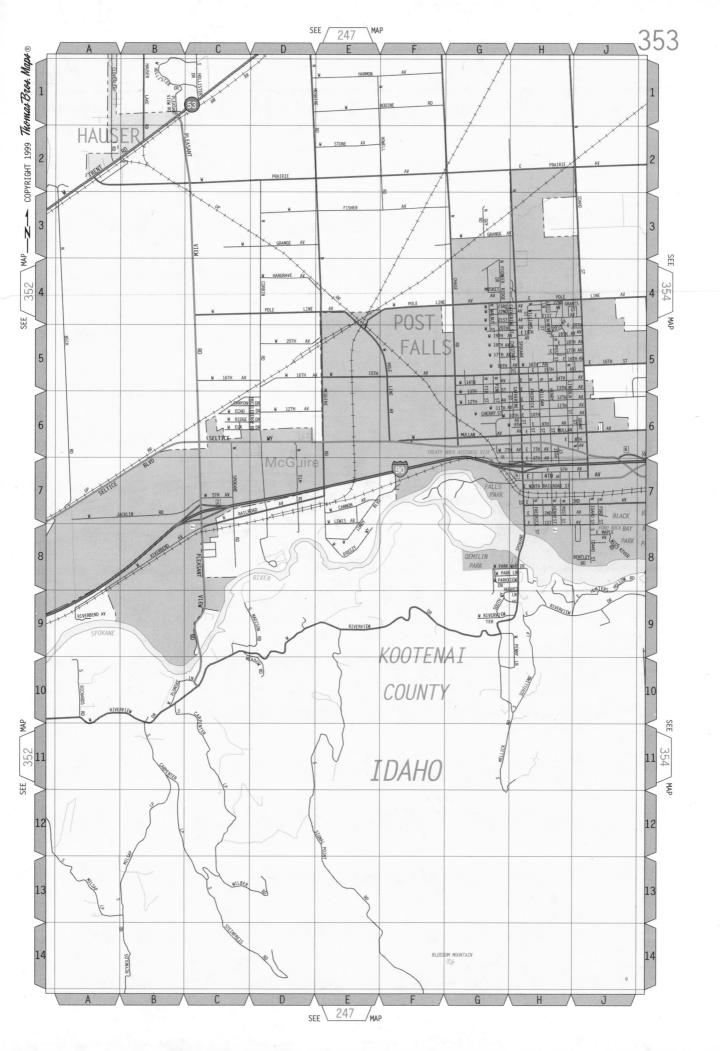

HAUSER

POST FALLS

McGuire

KOOTENAI

COUNTY

IDAHO

SPOKANE

RIVER

QEMILIN PARK

FALLS PARK

BLACK BAY PARK

TREATY ROCK HISTORIC SITE

BLOSSOM MOUNTAIN

SEE 352 MAP

SEE 352 MAP

SEE 354 MAP

SEE 354 MAP

PNW

DETAIL

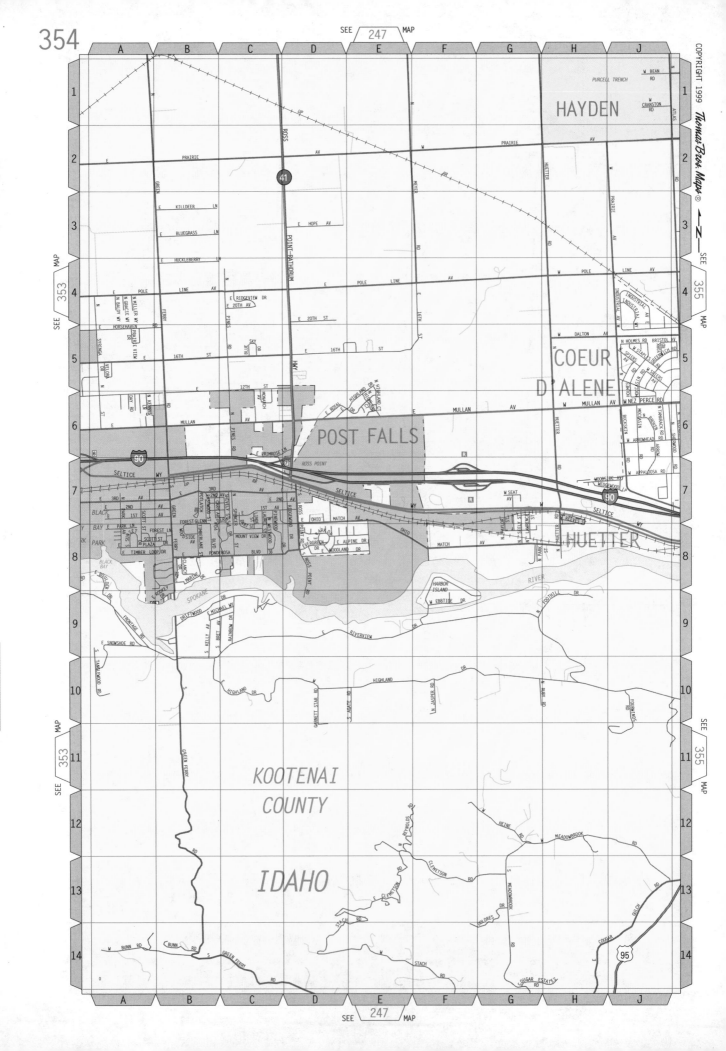

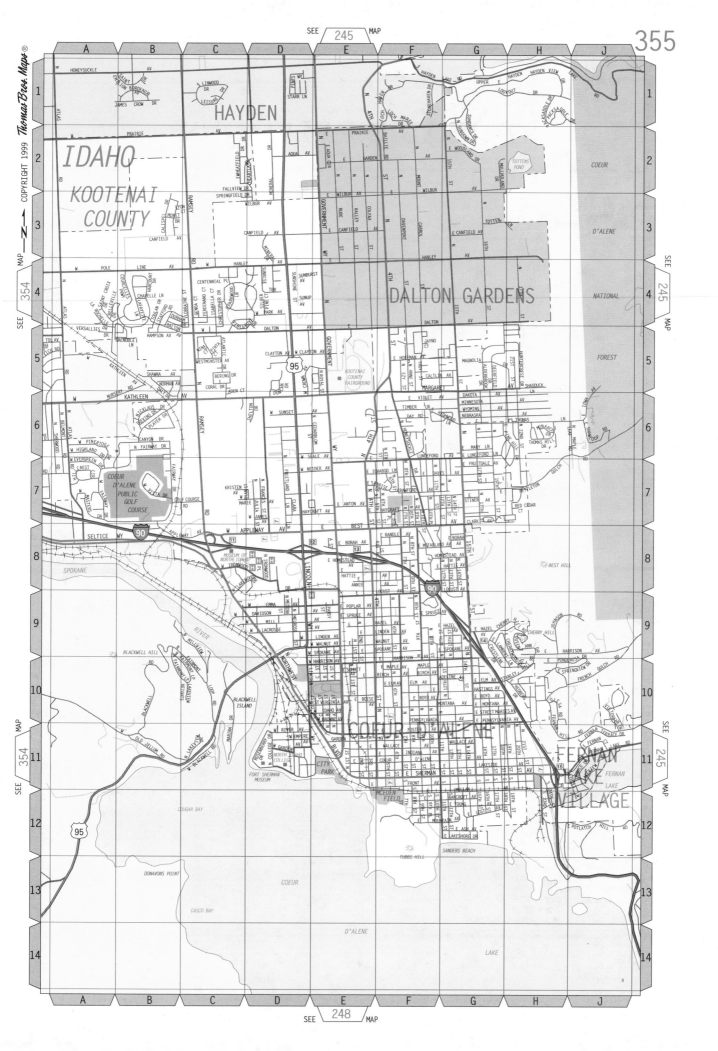

LIST OF ABBREVIATIONS

PREFIXES AND SUFFIXES

AL . . . . ALLEY
ARC . . . . ARCADE
AV, AVE . . . . AVENUE
AVCT . . . . AVENUE COURT
AVDR . . . . AVENUE DRIVE
AVEX . . . . AVENUE EXTENSION
AVPL . . . . AVENUE PLACE
BLEX . . . . BOULEVARD EXTENSION
BL, BLVD . . . . BOULEVARD
BLCT . . . . BOULEVARD COURT
BRCH . . . . BRANCH
BRDG . . . . BRIDGE
BYPS . . . . BYPASS
BYWY . . . . BYWAY
CIDR . . . . CIRCLE DRIVE
CIR . . . . CIRCLE
CLTR . . . . CLUSTER
COM . . . . COMMON
COMS . . . . COMMONS
CORR . . . . CORRIDOR
CRES . . . . CRESCENT
CRSG . . . . CROSSING
CSWY . . . . CAUSEWAY
CT . . . . COURT
CTAV . . . . COURT AVENUE
CTO . . . . CUT OFF
CTR . . . . CENTER
CTST . . . . COURT STREET
CUR . . . . CURVE
CV . . . . COVE
DIAG . . . . DIAGONAL
DR . . . . DRIVE
DRAV . . . . DRIVE AVENUE
DRCT . . . . DRIVE COURT
DRLP . . . . DRIVE LOOP
DRWY . . . . DRIVEWAY
DVDR . . . . DIVISION DRIVE
EXAV . . . . EXTENSION AVENUE
EXBL . . . . EXTENSION BOULEVARD
EXRD . . . . EXTENSION ROAD
EXST . . . . EXTENSION STREET
EXT . . . . EXTENSION
EXWY . . . . EXPRESSWAY
FRWY . . . . FREEWAY
GDNS . . . . GARDENS
GN . . . . GLEN
GRN . . . . GREEN
GRV . . . . GROVE
HTS . . . . HEIGHTS
HWY . . . . HIGHWAY
ISL . . . . ISLE
JCT . . . . JUNCTION
LN . . . . LANE
LNDG . . . . LANDING
LNLP . . . . LANE LOOP
LP . . . . LOOP
MNR . . . . MANOR
MTWY . . . . MOTORWAY
NFD . . NATIONAL FOREST DEVELOPMENT
NK . . . . NOOK
OH . . . . OUTER HIGHWAY
OVL . . . . OVAL
OVLK . . . . OVERLOOK
OVPS . . . . OVERPASS

PK . . . . PARK
PKWY . . . . PARKWAY
PL . . . . PLACE
PLZ,PZ . . . . PLAZA
PASG . . . . PASSAGE
PT . . . . POINT
PTH . . . . PATH
PZWY . . . . PLAZA WAY
RD . . . . ROAD
RDAV . . . . ROAD AVENUE
RDEX . . . . ROAD EXTENSION
RDWY . . . . ROADWAY
RDGE . . . . RIDGE
RR . . . . RAILROAD
RT . . . . ROUTE
RW . . . . ROW
RY . . . . RAILWAY
SKWY . . . . SKYWAY
SQ . . . . SQUARE
ST . . . . STREET
STAV . . . . STREET AVENUE
STCT . . . . STREET COURT
STDR . . . . STREET DRIVE
STEX . . . . STREET EXTENSION
STLN . . . . STREET LANE
STLP . . . . STREET LOOP
STOV . . . . STREET OVERPASS
STPL . . . . STREET PLACE
STPM . . . . STREET PROMENADE
STXP . . . . STREET EXPRESSWAY
TER . . . . TERRACE
TFWY . . . . TRAFFICWAY
THWY . . . . THROUGHWAY
TKTR . . . . TRUCKTRAIL
TPKE . . . . TURNPIKE
TR . . . . TRAIL
TRC . . . . TRACE
TRCT . . . . TERRACE COURT
TTSP . . . . TRUCKTRAIL SPUR
TUN . . . . TUNNEL
UNPS . . . . UNDERPASS
VW . . . . VIEW
WK . . . . WALK
WY . . . . WAY
WYPL . . . . WAY PLACE

DIRECTIONS

E . . . . EAST
KPN . . . . KEY PENINSULA NORTH
KPS . . . . KEY PENINSULA SOUTH
N . . . . NORTH
NE . . . . NORTHEAST
NW . . . . NORTHWEST
S . . . . SOUTH
SE . . . . SOUTHEAST
SW . . . . SOUTHWEST
W . . . . WEST

DEPARTMENT STORES

BN . . . . THE BON MARCHE
E . . . . EMPORIUM
L . . . . LAMONTS
ME . . . . MERVYNS

MF . . . . MEIER & FRANK
MW . . . . MONTGOMERY WARD
N . . . . NORDSTROM
P . . . . J C PENNEY
S . . . . SEARS

BUILDINGS

CC . . . . CHAMBER OF COMMERCE
CH . . . . CITY HALL
COMM CTR . . . . . . COMMUNITY CENTER
CON CTR . . . . CONVENTION CENTER
CONT HS . CONTINUATION HIGH SCHOOL
CTH . . . . COURTHOUSE
DMV . . . . DEPT OF MOTOR VEHICLES
FAA . . . . FEDERAL AVIATION ADMIN
FS . . . . FIRE STATION
HOSP . . . . HOSPITAL
HS . . . . HIGH SCHOOL
INT . . . . INTERMEDIATE SCHOOL
JR HS . . . . JUNIOR HIGH SCHOOL
LIB . . . . LIBRARY
MID . . . . MIDDLE SCHOOL
MUS . . . . MUSEUM
PO . . . . POST OFFICE
PS . . . . POLICE STATION
SR CIT CTR . . . SENIOR CITIZENS CENTER
STA . . . . STATION
THTR . . . . THEATER
VIS BUR . . . . VISITORS BUREAU

OTHER ABBREVIATIONS

BCH . . . . BEACH
BLDG . . . . BUILDING
BLM . . BUREAU OF LAND MANAGEMENT
CEM . . . . CEMETERY
CK . . . . CREEK
CO . . . . COUNTY
CTR . . . . CENTER
COMM . . . . COMMUNITY
EST, ESTS . . . . ESTATE(S)
HIST . . . . HISTORIC
HTS . . . . HEIGHTS
LK . . . . LAKE
MDW . . . . MEADOW
MED . . . . MEDICAL
MEM . . . . MEMORIAL
MHP . . . . MOBILE HOME PARK
MT . . . . MOUNT
MTN . . . . MOUNTAIN
NATL . . . . NATIONAL
PKG . . . . PARKING
PLGD . . . . PLAYGROUND
RCH . . . . RANCH
REC . . . . RECREATION
RES . . . . RESERVOIR
RIV . . . . RIVER
RT # . . . . ROUTE NUMBER
SPG . . . . SPRING
VLG . . . . VILLAGE
VLY . . . . VALLEY
VW . . . . VIEW

STREET INDEX
ANNEX RD 357

Thomas Bros. Maps ®
COPYRIGHT 1999

STREET / City State / Page-Grid

A

A U.S.-95
COTTONWOOD ID 123-C3
GRANGEVILLE ID 123-C3
IDAHO CO ID 123-B3
A AV
ANACORTES WA 259-F6
LAKE OSWEGO OR 321-F5
A RD SW
DOUGLAS CO WA 112-B2
A ST
ASHLAND OR 337-D7
CASTLE ROCK WA 187-C7
GRANTS PASS OR 335-E8
PIERCE CO WA 181-D5
WALLA WALLA CO WA 345-G4
A ST Rt#-38
DOUGLAS CO OR 141-A1
ELKTON OR 141-A1
E A ST
GRANTS PASS OR 335-G8
PASCO WA 121-A3
PASCO WA 343-H8
N A ST
ELLENSBURG WA 241-B5
SPOKANE WA 348-F2
S A ST
LANE CO OR 330-J7
SPOKANE WA 348-F10
SPRINGFIELD OR 330-J7
SPRINGFIELD OR 331-A7
W A ST
PASCO WA 343-D8
A ST E U.S.-20
VALE OR 139-A3
A ST SE
AUBURN WA 182-B1
EPHRATA WA 112-C3
GRANT CO WA 112-C3
KING CO WA 182-B1
A ST W
MALHEUR CO OR 138-C3
VALE OR 138-C3
A ST W U.S.-20
VALE OR 139-A3
A900 RD
GRAYS HARBOR CO WA 179-B6
A 1000 RD
GRAYS HARBOR CO WA 179-A5
A2000 RD
GRAYS HARBOR CO WA 179-A5
A3030 RD
GRAYS HARBOR CO WA 178-D4
A4000 RD
GRAYS HARBOR CO WA 179-D7
A5000 RD
GRAYS HARBOR CO WA 178-D4
A6000 RD
GRAYS HARBOR CO WA 178-D4
A7200 RD
GRAYS HARBOR CO WA 178-D3
AALVIK RD
SKAMANIA CO WA 194-C5
AARON DR
RICHLAND WA 341-F4
ABBEY RD
YAMHILL CO OR 198-B6
ABBOT ST
RICHLAND WA 341-G3
ABBOTSFORD-MISSION HWY Rt#-11
DISTRICT OF ABBOTSFORD BC 102-B1
DISTRICT OF MATSQUI BC 94-B3
DISTRICT OF MATSQUI BC 102-B1
ABBOTT RD
CLACKAMAS CO OR 126-C3
CLACKAMAS CO OR 201-A7
WALLA WALLA WA 345-C10
WALLA WALLA CO WA 122-A3
Walla Walla East WA 345-D10
WHITMAN CO WA 249-A2
S ABBOTT RD
SPOKANE CO WA 246-B5
SPOKANE CO WA 348-C14
ABBOTT CREEK RD
JACKSON CO OR 226-C4
ABERDEEN GARDENS RD
GRAYS HARBOR CO WA 178-B6
ABERNATHY ST NE
LACEY WA 297-F3
THURSTON CO WA 297-F3
ABERNATHY TKTR
COWLITZ CO WA 187-A6
ABIQUA RD NE
MARION CO OR 205-D4
ABRAHAM DR
LINN CO OR 210-A1
ABSHIRE RD
ADAMS CO ID 251-B4
ACADEMY ST
KELSO WA 303-D8
LEBANON OR 133-C1
ACADIA RD
UNIV ENDOWMENT LANDS BC 156-A4
ACKLEY CAMP RD
HARNEY CO OR 153-A2
ACME RD
KLICKITAT CO WA 196-A3
ADA RD
DOUGLAS CO OR 214-B5
N ADAIR ST Rt#-8
CORNELIUS OR 198-C1
FOREST GROVE OR 198-C1
ADAMS AV U.S.-30
LA GRANDE OR 130-A2
ADAMS DR
MADRAS OR 208-C5
N ADAMS DR
JEFFERSON CO OR 208-C3
S ADAMS DR
JEFFERSON CO OR 208-C6
MADRAS OR 208-C6
ADAMS RD
JACKSON CO OR 234-B3
POLK CO OR 204-B6
N ADAMS RD
Veradale WA 351-B8
S ADAMS RD
Veradale WA 351-B11
ADAMS ST
GARDEN CITY ID 253-C2
HOQUIAM WA 178-A7
OLYMPIA WA 296-J5
N ADAMS ST Rt#-42
COQUILLE OR 220-D5
NE ADAMS ST
CAMAS WA 193-B7
NW ADAMS ST Rt#-99W
MCMINNVILLE OR 198-A7
SW ADAMS ST Rt#-99W
MCMINNVILLE OR 198-A7
ADAMS CREEK RD
DOUGLAS CO OR 219-B4
ADCOCK RD
YAMHILL CO OR 198-B4
E ADDISON DR
SPOKANE WA 349-A1
N ADDISON ST
SPOKANE WA 349-A1
ADDY-GIFFORD RD
STEVENS CO WA 106-A3
ADELE AV
BREMERTON WA 270-F10
ADKISSON MARKET RD
WASCO CO OR 127-B2
ADLER RD
FRANKLIN CO WA 121-A2
SW ADMIRAL WY
SEATTLE WA 280-D2
SEATTLE WA 281-F3
ADMIRALS RD
BRITISH COLUMBIA 256-B6
DISTRICT OF SAANICH BC 256-C5
TOWN OF ESQUIMALT BC 256-B6
TOWN OF VIEW ROYAL BC 256-C5
ADMIRALTY AV
PORT TOWNSEND WA 263-F2
ADOBE WY
YAKIMA CO WA 243-B4
ADRIAN BLVD Rt#-201
NYSSA OR 139-A3
ADRIAN BLVD W Rt#-201
NYSSA OR 139-A3
SW ADVANCE RD
CLACKAMAS CO OR 199-B5
WILSONVILLE OR 199-B5
ADVENT RD
PITT MEADOWS BC 157-B5
AENEAS VALLEY RD
OKANOGAN CO WA 105-A2
AGAN RD
LINN CO OR 207-D7
AGATE RD
JACKSON CO OR 230-D6
MASON CO WA 180-B3
AGATE ST
ASTORIA OR 300-A5
EUGENE OR 330-C8
AGATE POINT RD NE
KITSAP CO WA 170-C7
AGEE DR
JOSEPHINE CO OR 229-C3
AGENCY-HOT SPRINGS RD
JEFFERSON CO OR 208-A2
Warm Springs OR 208-A2
AGER RD
SISKIYOU CO CA 150-A3
SISKIYOU CO CA 151-A3
AGER BESWICK RD
SISKIYOU CO CA 150-A3
NE AGNESS AV
GRANTS PASS OR 335-J9
AGNESS RD
CURRY CO OR 148-B1
CURRY CO OR 228-C4
AGNESS-ILLAHE RD
CURRY CO OR 148-B1
AGREN RD
COWLITZ CO WA 187-B5
AHSAHKA RD Rt#-7
OROFINO ID 123-C2
OROFINO ID 123-C2
AHTANUM RD
UNION GAP WA 243-A7
YAKIMA CO WA 119-C2
YAKIMA CO WA 243-A7
W AHTANUM RD
UNION GAP WA 243-C7
AINSLEE AV
DEPOE BAY OR 206-B1
E AINSWORTH AV Rt#-397
PASCO WA 343-G9
W AINSWORTH AV Rt#-397
PASCO WA 343-F8
AINSWORTH AV S
PIERCE CO WA 181-D4
AIR CARGO RD N
SEATAC WA 288-C4
AIRDUSTRIAL WY
TUMWATER WA 296-F14
AIRLIE RD
POLK CO OR 133-B1
POLK CO OR 207-A2
AIRPLANE RESERVOIR RD
MALHEUR CO OR 154-C2
MALHEUR CO OR 155-A2
AIRPORT AV
BENTON CO OR 133-B1
BENTON CO OR 207-A7
AIRPORT DR
BELLINGHAM WA 258-A1
JOSEPHINE CO OR 233-A5
LEBANON OR 133-C1
LINN CO OR 133-C1
WHATCOM CO WA 158-D7
WHATCOM CO WA 258-A1
W AIRPORT DR
SPOKANE CO WA 246-A4
SPOKANE CO WA 348-A12
AIRPORT RD
ALBANY OR 326-G8
BENTON CO OR 133-B1
CANYON CO ID 147-C1
CENTRALIA WA 299-D8
CLACKAMAS CO OR 199-B6
CLALLAM CO WA 261-A4
CLARKSTON WA 250-B4
AIRPORT RD
CURRY CO OR 224-A4
EUGENE OR 215-A1
EVERETT WA 171-B4
EVERETT WA 267-G6
GRANT CO WA 237-B3
HARNEY CO OR 145-B1
KITTITAS CO WA 240-C2
KITTITAS CO WA 241-B5
LEWIS CO WA 299-D8
MALHEUR CO OR 138-C3
MEDFORD OR 336-C6
OKANOGAN WA 104-C3
OKANOGAN CO WA 104-C3
PORT ANGELES WA 261-A4
PULLMAN WA 249-C4
SISKIYOU CO CA 150-A3
SNOHOMISH WA 267-G6
SNOHOMISH CO WA 171-B4
WHITMAN CO WA 249-C4
NE AIRPORT RD
ROSEBURG OR 334-F4
SE AIRPORT RD
YAMHILL CO OR 204-C1
W AIRPORT RD
BAKER CO OR 130-B3
BAKER CO OR 138-B1
AIRPORT RD NE
MARION CO OR 199-B6
AIRPORT RD SE
SALEM OR 323-B14
SALEM OR 325-B1
AIRPORT WY
BELLINGHAM WA 258-A1
BOISE ID 253-C4
GRAYS HARBOR CO WA 178-A7
LAKESIDE OR 218-B4
SNOHOMISH CO WA 171-D3
TILLAMOOK CO OR 197-A7
NE AIRPORT WY
PORTLAND OR 311-E4
S AIRPORT WY
DOUGLAS CO WA 239-B5
SE AIRPORT WY
REDMOND OR 212-D6
AIRPORT WY S
KING WA 286-D3
SEATTLE WA 278-A7
SEATTLE WA 282-B1
SEATTLE WA 286-D3
TUKWILA WA 286-D3
AIRPORT CUTOFF RD Rt#-19
Irondale WA 263-B11
JEFFERSON CO WA 263-B11
AIRSTRIP RD
COLUMBIA CO OR 189-A6
MALHEUR CO OR 146-B3
AIRWAY DR
GRANT CO WA 242-C2
KLAMATH CO OR 235-D5
MOSES LAKE WA 242-C2
AIRWAY DR SE
SALEM OR 325-B4
A J WARRIN RD
DESCHUTES CO OR 212-A5
AKINS DR
CROOK CO OR 213-D6
ALABAMA ST
BELLINGHAM WA 258-F5
LONGVIEW WA 302-G10
ALAMEDA AV
ASTORIA OR 300-A5
FIRCREST WA 181-C3
NE ALAMEDA AV
ROSEBURG OR 334-F4
ALAMEDA ST
ASTORIA OR 300-A5
ALAMO LN
CANYON CO ID 147-B1
ALASKA AV E
Colby WA 271-G14
S ALASKA ST
SEATTLE WA 282-D5
SW ALASKA ST
SEATTLE WA 280-D5
SEATTLE WA 281-E5
ALASKA ST SE
Colby WA 271-G14
ALASKAN FRWY Rt#-99
SEATTLE WA 277-J5
SEATTLE WA 278-A6
SEATTLE WA 281-J3
SEATTLE WA 282-A1
ALASKAN WY S Rt#-519
SEATTLE WA 277-J7
SEATTLE WA 278-A7
SEATTLE WA 281-J1
ALBANY RD U.S.-2
BONNER CO ID 107-A3
PRIEST RIVER ID 107-A3
ALBANY ST Rt#-82
ELGIN OR 130-A1
ALBANY ST SW
Rochester WA 184-A3
THURSTON CO WA 184-A3
ALBANY-CORVALLIS HWY U.S.-20
ALBANY OR 207-B5
ALBANY OR 326-A7
BENTON CO OR 207-B5
BENTON CO OR 326-A7
BENTON CO OR 327-J8
CORVALLIS OR 207-B5
CORVALLIS OR 327-J8
ALBANY-JCT CITY HWY U.S.-99E
ALBANY OR 207-C7
ALBANY OR 326-C14
HALSEY OR 210-A4
HARRISBURG OR 210-A5
JUNCTION CITY OR 210-A5
LANE CO OR 210-A5
LINN CO OR 207-C7
LINN CO OR 210-A4
TANGENT OR 207-C7
ALBANY-LYONS HWY Rt#-226
LINN CO OR 133-C1
LINN CO OR 134-A1
SCIO OR 133-C1
ALBATROSS ST
OCEAN SHORES WA 177-B6
ALBERT ST
NANAIMO BC 93-A3
SE ALBERTA ST
CLACKAMAS OR 318-E7
ALBERTSON RD
YAMHILL CO OR 198-C4
ALBION RD
ALBION WA 249-A4
WHITMAN CO WA 122-C1
WHITMAN CO WA 249-A4
S ALBRO PL
SEATTLE WA 282-B7
ALCAN RD
GRAND COULEE WA 237-C3
ALCORT RD
MALHEUR CO OR 154-B2
ALDER
PIERCE CO WA 182-A4
ALDER AV
SUMNER WA 182-B3
N ALDER AV
GRANITE FALLS WA 102-C3
ALDER DR NE
KEIZER OR 323-A7
ALDER ST
CATHLAMET WA 117-B3
LA GRANDE OR 130-A2
MOSES LAKE WA 242-C3
ALDER ST Rt#-507
CENTRALIA WA 299-E4
E ALDER ST
WALLA WALLA WA 345-C7
Walla Walla East WA 345-F7
N ALDER ST
TACOMA WA 292-D4
N ALDER ST U.S.-101
ABERDEEN WA 178-B7
S ALDER ST Rt#-21
ODESSA WA 113-B3
S ALDER ST U.S.-101
ABERDEEN WA 178-B7
SW ALDER ST
GRANTS PASS OR 335-D9
PORTLAND OR 313-F6
ALDER BRANCH RD
LANE CO OR 215-D1
ALDERBRIDGE WY
CITY OF RICHMOND BC 156-B6
ALDERBROOK RD
BAY CITY OR 197-B1
TILLAMOOK CO OR 197-B1
ALDER CREEK LN
CLACKAMAS CO OR 201-A4
ALDER CREEK RD
BAKER CO OR 138-B1
KOOTENAI CO ID 248-C1
WHEELER CO OR 128-B3
WHEELER CO OR 136-B1
ALDER CUTOFF RD
EATONVILLE WA 118-B1
PIERCE CO WA 118-B1
ALDERDALE RD
KLICKITAT CO WA 120-B3
KLICKITAT CO WA 128-B1
YAKIMA CO WA 120-B3
ALDERDALE WYE
YAKIMA CO WA 120-B3
ALDERGROVE RD
Birch Bay WA 158-B5
WHATCOM CO WA 158-C5
SE ALDERMAN RD
YAMHILL CO OR 204-C1
NE ALDERMEADOWS RD
MULTNOMAH CO OR 200-D1
ALDER SPRING RD
JACKSON CO OR 227-A5
ALDERWOOD AV
BELLINGHAM WA 258-A2
WHATCOM CO WA 158-D7
WHATCOM CO WA 258-A2
ALDERWOOD MALL PKWY
SNOHOMISH CO WA 171-B5
ALDRICH RD
WHATCOM CO WA 158-D5
ALECK BAY RD
SAN JUAN CO WA 160-A7
ALEXANDER AV
BENTON CO OR 327-G12
CORVALLIS OR 327-G12
ALEXANDER AV E
TACOMA WA 182-A2
ALEXANDER RD
SUNNYSIDE WA 120-B2
YAKIMA CO WA 120-B2
ALEXANDER RD Rt#-241
SUNNYSIDE WA 120-B2
YAKIMA CO WA 120-B2
ALFALFA RD
CROOK CO OR 135-B3
CROOK CO OR 213-A7
ALFALFA-GRANGER RD Rt#-223
YAKIMA CO WA 120-A2
ALFALFA MARKET RD
DESCHUTES CO OR 135-B3
DESCHUTES CO OR 217-D2
ALFRED JOHNSON RD
SKAGIT CO WA 168-B1
SKAGIT CO WA 260-C14
ALGER HILL LOGGING TR
SKAGIT CO WA 161-B3
ALGOMA RD
KLAMATH CO OR 235-B1
ALGOMA SPUR RD
BONNER CO ID 244-A4
ALICE AV S
SALEM OR 324-G2
ALKALI GULCH RD
MALHEUR CO OR 139-A2
ALKI AV SW
SEATTLE WA 276-D7
SEATTLE WA 280-D1
ALLAN RD
YAKIMA CO WA 243-A4
ALLARD CRES
TOWNSHIP OF LANGLEY BC 157-C6
SW ALLEN BLVD
BEAVERTON OR 199-B2
ALLEN RD
DESCHUTES CO OR 212-B7
LEWIS CO WA 187-D1
SUNNYSIDE WA 120-B2
YAKIMA CO WA 120-B2
ALLEN ST Rt#-4
KELSO WA 303-D8
E ALLEN ST
COWLITZ CO WA 303-F8
KELSO WA 303-F8
ALLEN CREEK RD
CROOK CO OR 213-D2
GRANTS PASS OR 335-C12
JOSEPHINE CO OR 335-C12
ALLEN WEST RD
SKAGIT CO WA 161-A5
ALLINGHAM CTO
JEFFERSON CO OR 211-C1
ALLISON RD
LEWIS CO WA 187-D3
ALLUMBAUGH ST
BOISE ID 253-C2
ALLWORTH RD
CLARK CO WA 193-A3
NE ALLWORTH RD
CLARK CO WA 193-B3
ALMA LN
JEFFERSON CO OR 208-B5
SW ALMA LN
JEFFERSON CO OR 208-A5
ALMA ST
UNIV ENDOWMENT LANDS BC 254-A13
VANCOUVER BC 254-A13
NW ALMETER WY
DESCHUTES CO OR 212-D4
N ALMIRA RD
LINCOLN CO WA 237-D7
ALMIRA RD S
LINCOLN CO WA 113-B2
LINCOLN CO WA 237-D7
ALM LANE RD
STEVENS CO WA 106-B3
ALMOTA RD
WHITMAN CO WA 122-C1
ALMOTA RD Rt#-194
WHITMAN CO WA 122-B1
ALMOTA ST Rt#-27
PALOUSE WA 249-B1
ALMOTA FERRY RD
GARFIELD CO WA 122-B1
E ALOHA ST
SEATTLE WA 278-C3
ALPINE DR SW
THURSTON CO WA 180-B7
ALPINE RD
BENTON CO OR 133-B2
SE ALPINE RD
KITSAP CO WA 174-C6
ALSEA HWY Rt#-34
BENTON CO OR 133-A1
LINCOLN CO OR 133-A2
LINCOLN CO OR 209-D2
LINCOLN CO OR 328-F6
WALDPORT OR 328-F6
ALSEA BAY DR
LINCOLN CO OR 328-C4
ALSEA-DEADWOOD HWY
BENTON CO OR 133-A2
ALSIP RD
POLK CO OR 204-A7
ALSTON RD W
DOUGLAS CO WA 239-D1
ALSTON-MAYGER RD
COLUMBIA CO OR 189-A3
ALTA LAKE RD
BRITISH COLUMBIA 93-C1
WHISTLER BC 93-C1
ALTAMONT DR
Altamont OR 235-C5
Altamont OR 338-H14
KLAMATH FALLS OR 338-H14
SW ALTA VISTA DR
KITSAP CO WA 174-A6
ALTA VISTA RD
EAGLE POINT OR 230-D6
JACKSON CO OR 230-D6
ALTHOUSE CREEK RD
JOSEPHINE CO OR 233-C5
SE ALTMAN RD
CLACKAMAS CO OR 200-C3
MULTNOMAH CO OR 200-C2
ALTNOW-BEULAH RD
HARNEY CO OR 138-A3
ALTO RD
COLUMBIA CO WA 122-A2
E ALTON ST
PASCO WA 343-H7
ALTOONA PILLAR ROCK RD
WAHKIAKUM CO WA 117-A2
ALVADORE RD
LANE CO OR 133-B2
ALVADORE RD S
LANE CO OR 133-B3
NE ALVAS RD
CLARK CO WA 193-B3
ALVILLE LN
GILLIAM CO OR 128-A2
ALWARD COUNTY RD
PIERCE CO WA 182-C5
ALWORTH ST
GARDEN CITY ID 253-C2
W AMAZON DR
EUGENE OR 330-B12
AMAZON PKWY
EUGENE OR 330-A8
AMBAUM BLVD S
BURIEN WA 175-A5
AMBAUM BLVD S Rt#-509
BURIEN WA 175-A5
BURIEN WA 288-A7
AMBAUM BLVD SW
BURIEN WA 175-A5
BURIEN WA 285-G7
KING WA 285-G7
KING CO WA 175-A5
AMBERJACK AV
KITSAP CO WA 170-B6
AMBLE RD
ISLAND CO WA 167-D7
AMBOY Rt#-503
CLARK CO WA 193-B1
AMBOY RD
CLARK CO WA 193-B1
AMERICAN DR
HALSEY OR 210-A2
LINN CO OR 210-A2
AMERICANA BLVD
BOISE ID 253-C3
AMERICAN FRUIT RD
Sunnyslope WA 238-D3
AMERICAN LAKE AV
PIERCE CO WA 181-C5
AMERICAN MILL RD
GRAYS HARBOR CO WA 183-D3
AMES RD
YAKIMA CO WA 243-B5
AMES RD NE
OLYMPIA WA 296-J1
THURSTON CO WA 296-J1
THURSTON CO WA 297-A1
NE AMES LAKE RD
KING CO WA 176-A2
AMES LAKE CARNATION RD NE
KING CO WA 176-A1
AMICK RD
SKAGIT CO WA 168-C1
AMISIGGER RD
CLACKAMAS CO OR 200-B4
E AMITY RD
ADA CO ID 253-B4
BOISE ID 253-D4
SE AMITY RD
AMITY OR 204-C2
YAMHILL CO OR 204-C2
W AMITY RD
ADA CO ID 253-A4
AMITY DAYTON HWY
DAYTON OR 198-C7
YAMHILL CO OR 198-B7
AMITY DAYTON HWY Rt#-233
YAMHILL CO OR 198-B7
YAMHILL CO OR 204-C1
SE AMITY-DAYTON HWY Rt#-233
YAMHILL CO OR 204-C1
NE AMMETER RD
CLARK CO WA 193-C6
AMNEN RD
LINCOLN CO WA 113-C3
ANACO BEACH RD
ANACORTES WA 259-B4
ANACOPPER RD
ANACORTES WA 259-D3
N ANACORTES AV
BURLINGTON WA 260-D4
S ANACORTES ST
BURLINGTON WA 260-D6
SKAGIT CO WA 260-D6
SW ANCHOR AV
LINCOLN CITY OR 203-A5
ANDERSON AV
Altamont OR 338-H14
COOS BAY OR 333-G10
ANDERSON RD
GRAYS HARBOR CO WA 184-A3
LEWIS CO WA 184-D6
MASON CO WA 179-B2
THURSTON CO WA 184-A3
WHITMAN CO WA 249-A4
S ANDERSON RD
CLACKAMAS CO OR 199-B7
W ANDERSON RD
SPOKANE CO WA 246-B7
ANDERSON RD SE
MARION CO OR 205-B7
ANDERSON RD SE Rt#-214
MARION CO OR 205-B7
ANDERSON CANYON RD
CHELAN CO WA 238-A1
ANDERSON CREEK RD
JACKSON CO OR 234-B3
LINCOLN CO OR 203-B5
NW ANDERSON HILL RD
KITSAP CO WA 174-A1
ANDERSON HILL RD SW
KITSAP CO WA 174-B4
ANDERSON LAKE RD
JEFFERSON CO WA 170-A1
ANDERSON RESERVOIR RD
ADAMS CO ID 251-B3
ANDERSON VALLEY RD
HARNEY CO OR 145-C2
ANDRAIN
PIERCE CO WA 182-A6
ANDRESEN RD
VANCOUVER WA 306-D7
NE ANDRESEN RD
CLARK WA 306-D1
CLARK CO WA 192-D5
VANCOUVER WA 306-D1
ANDREWS RD
DOUGLAS CO OR 219-A4
JACKSON CO OR 234-A2
S ANDRUS RD
SPOKANE CO WA 246-A6
ANGELINE RD
BONNEY LAKE WA 182-C4
PIERCE CO WA 182-C4
ANGUS DR
THURSTON CO WA 184-D2
ANKENY HILL RD
MARION CO OR 207-D1
ANKENY HILL RD SE
MARION CO OR 207-D2
ANKERTON RD
SHERMAN CO OR 127-C2
ANLIKER RD
COLUMBIA CO OR 189-B6
ANNACIS HWY Rt#-91
CITY OF RICHMOND BC 156-D6
NEW WESTMINSTER BC 156-D6
DISTRICT OF DELTA BC 101-C1
ANNACIS HWY Rt#-91A
CITY OF RICHMOND BC 156-D6
ANNAWALT RD
MALHEUR CO OR 146-C3
ANNEX RD
MALHEUR CO OR 139-A2

PNW
INDEX

358 ANNONEN RD — STREET INDEX — BARLOW TRAIL RD

PNW
INDEX

STREET City State Page-Grid

ANNONEN RD
LEWIS CO WA 187-B5
ANSELL ST
MAPLE RIDGE BC 157-D5
ANTELOPE
CROOK CO OR 213-D6
ANTELOPE HWY Rt#-293
JEFFERSON CO OR 135-C1
WASCO CO OR 127-C3
WASCO CO OR 135-C1
ANTELOPE RD
JACKSON CO OR 230-C6
White City OR 230-D6
E ANTELOPE RD
JACKSON CO OR 149-C1
JACKSON CO OR 234-D1
ANTELOPE CANAL RD
MALHEUR CO OR 147-A3
ANTELOPE FLAT RD
MALHEUR CO OR 146-B2
ANTELOPE SPRINGS RD
OWYHEE CO ID 147-C3
ANT FLAT RD
ENTERPRISE OR 130-C2
WALLOWA CO OR 130-C2
ANTHONY LAKES HWY
BAKER CO OR 130-A3
HAINES OR 130-A3
ANTHONY LAKES RD
BAKER CO OR 130-A3
ANTIOCH RD
JACKSON CO OR 230-C5
W ANTLER AV
DESCHUTES CO OR 212-D5
ANTLES RD
UNION CO OR 130-B2
ANTOINE CREEK RD
CHELAN CO WA 236-D1
ANTRIM RD
LEWIS CO WA 187-C2
A-P-A RD
WHATCOM CO WA 101-C1
APEL DR
PORT COQUITLAM BC 157-B4
APIARY RD
COLUMBIA CO OR 117-B3
COLUMBIA CO OR 189-B4
APPLE ST
BOISE ID 253-D3
APPLE ACRES RD
CHELAN CO WA 112-B1
CHELAN CO WA 236-D2
APPLEFORD RD
ASOTIN CO WA 123-A3
ASOTIN CO WA 123-A3
APPLEGATE AV
DOUGLAS CO OR 219-A4
JOSEPHINE CO OR 229-A6
APPLEGATE RD
JACKSON CO OR 149-B2
N APPLEGATE RD
JACKSON CO OR 149-B2
JOSEPHINE CO OR 149-B2
APPLEGATE ST
JACKSON CO OR 149-B2
JACKSONVILLE OR 149-B2
APPLESIDE BLVD Rt#-128
ASOTIN CO WA 250-B5
Vineland WA 250-B5
APPLETON RD
KLICKITAT CO WA 196-B3
APPLE VALLEY RD
CANYON CO ID 139-A3
E APPLEWAY AV
Greenacres WA 351-G8
SPOKANE CO WA 351-G8
W APPLEWAY AV
COEUR D'ALENE ID 355-C8
A P TUBBS RD
CARBONADO WA 182-D5
PIERCE CO WA 182-D5
ARAGO LN
COOS CO OR 220-D6
ARAGO-ARAGO JCT
COOS CO OR 220-D6
ARAGO CROSS RD
COOS CO OR 220-D6
ARBORETUM RD
BENTON CO OR 207-B4
ARBOR GROVE RD
MARION CO OR 199-A7
MARION CO OR 205-B1
ARBOR GROVE RD NE
MARION CO OR 205-A1
ARBORLYNN DR
DIST OF N VANCOUVER BC 255-F5
ARBUTUS RD
DISTRICT OF SAANICH BC 257-D2
ARBUTUS ST
VANCOUVER BC 156-B5
VANCOUVER BC 254-D13
E ARCADIA AV
MASON CO WA 180-A3
SHELTON WA 180-A3
ARCADIA DR NE
LINCOLN CO OR 206-C4
ARCADIA RD
MASON CO WA 180-B3
ARCHERFISH RD
KITSAP CO WA 170-B7
ARCHER MOUNTAIN RD
SKAMANIA CO WA 194-B6
ARCHIE MYERS RANCH RD
MALHEUR CO OR 154-B2
ARDENA RD
FIFE WA 182-A2
ARDMORE DR
LAKEWOOD WA 181-C4
W ARGENT RD
FRANKLIN CO WA 342-E4
FRANKLIN CO WA 343-C4
PASCO WA 342-E4
PASCO WA 343-C4
N ARGONNE RD
Dishman WA 350-D7
MILLWOOD WA 350-D3
SPOKANE CO WA 246-D2
SPOKANE CO WA 350-D2
ARGYLE DR
VANCOUVER BC 156-C5
ARGYLE DR S
SALEM OR 324-G3
ARGYLE ST
VANCOUVER BC 156-C5
ARID AV
DESCHUTES CO OR 212-C7
W ARLINGTON ST
GLADSTONE OR 199-D4
ARLINGTON HEIGHTS RD
SNOHOMISH CO WA 168-D4
ARMAR RD
ARLINGTON WA 168-C7
MARYSVILLE WA 168-C7
SNOHOMISH CO WA 168-C7
ARMITAGE RD
SAN JUAN CO WA 160-A5
ARMSTRONG RD
TOWNSHIP OF LANGLEY BC 157-D7
ARMSTRONG ST
PACIFIC CO WA 117-A1
ARMSWORTHY ST
WASCO OR 127-C1
ARMSWORTHY ST Rt#-206
WASCO OR 127-C1
ARNDT RD
CLACKAMAS CO OR 199-B6
MARION CO OR 199-A6
ARNEY RD NE
MARION CO OR 205-B1
ARNIE RD
WHATCOM CO WA 158-B4
ARNOLD LN
JACKSON CO OR 234-A1
ARNOLD RD
ISLAND CO WA 167-B4
ARNOLD WY
CORVALLIS OR 327-E9
ARNOLD MARKET LOOP RD
DESCHUTES CO OR 217-C3
ARNOT RD
SNOHOMISH CO WA 168-D4
AROCK RD
MALHEUR CO OR 146-C3
ARRAH WANNA BLVD
CLACKAMAS CO OR 201-C5
ARRITOLA PLACE RD
MALHEUR CO OR 146-C3
MALHEUR CO OR 147-A3
ARROW AV U.S.-12
NEZ PERCE CO ID 123-A2
W ARROWHEAD AV
BENTON CO WA 342-D8
KENNEWICK WA 342-D8
ARROWHEAD RD
ISLAND CO WA 167-D4
ARSENAL WY E
BREMERTON WA 270-E11
Navy Yard City WA 270-E11
ART DALZELL RD
MORROW CO OR 128-B2
ARTHUR BLVD
YAKIMA CO WA 243-C6
ARTHUR DR
DISTRICT OF DELTA BC 101-C1
ARTHUR RD
NEZ PERCE CO ID 250-D2
ARTHUR ST
NORTH BEND OR 333-D4
S ARTHUR ST
SPOKANE WA 349-B10
SW ARTHUR ST
PORTLAND OR 317-E1
ARTHUR LAING BRDG
CITY OF RICHMOND BC 156-B5
ARTHUR V GOLTZ
PIERCE CO WA 182-B5
ARTONDALE DR NW
PIERCE CO WA 181-B1
ARVICK RD SE
KITSAP CO WA 174-C4
ARVID NELSON RD
CROOK CO OR 136-A2
ASBURY RD
KOOTENAI CO ID 248-A3
ASCHOFF RD
CLACKAMAS CO OR 201-B3
N ASH AV
WARDEN WA 121-A1
S ASH AV
WARDEN WA 121-A1
ASH RD
DISTRICT OF SAANICH BC 159-D5
ASH ST
BROWNSVILLE OR 210-C2
KELSO WA 303-D8
SODAVILLE OR 133-C2
N ASH ST
SPOKANE WA 346-G14
SPOKANE WA 348-G1
NE ASH ST
PULLMAN WA 249-B5
ASH ST N
OMAK WA 104-C2
ASH ST S
OMAK WA 104-C3
ASH WY
SNOHOMISH CO WA 171-B4
ASHBROOK LN
JOSEPHINE CO OR 229-A5
ASH CREEK
SISKIYOU CO CA 150-A3
ASH CREEK RD
DOUGLAS CO OR 225-C3
ASH LAKE RD
SKAMANIA CO WA 194-C5
ASHLAND ST
ASHLAND OR 337-D9
ASHLAND LOOP RD
JACKSON CO OR 234-C6
ASHTON LN
VALLEY CO ID 251-D7
SW ASHWOOD LN
JEFFERSON CO OR 208-B5
ASHWOOD RD
JEFFERSON CO OR 208-C5
ASHWORTH AV N
SHORELINE WA 171-A7
A S KRESKY RD
CHEHALIS WA 299-E9
LEWIS CO WA 299-E9
ASOTIN RD
ASOTIN CO WA 122-C2
ASOTIN CO WA 250-A6
ASOTIN CREEK RD
ASOTIN WA 250-B6
ASOTIN CO WA 250-B6
N ASPEN ST Rt#-231
LINCOLN CO WA 114-A2
REARDAN WA 114-A2
ASPEN WY
NEWBERG OR 198-D5
YAMHILL CO OR 198-D5
ASPEN LAKE RD
KLAMATH CO OR 235-A1
ASPENWALL RD
THURSTON CO WA 180-B6
S ASSEMBLY RD
SPOKANE CO WA 246-B5
SPOKANE CO WA 348-D13
N ASSEMBLY ST
SPOKANE WA 348-D2
ATHENA-HOLDMAN HWY
ATHENA OR 129-C1
UMATILLA CO OR 129-B1
E ATHENA-HOLDMAN HWY
ATHENA OR 129-C1
ATKINS AV
DISTRICT OF LANGFORD BC 159-B6
TOWN OF VIEW ROYAL BC 159-B6
ATKINS RD
COLUMBIA CO OR 189-A4
ATKINSON AV
DESCHUTES CO OR 212-C4
NW ATKINSON AV
DESCHUTES CO OR 212-C4
N ATLAS RD
COEUR D'ALENE ID 355-A4
HAYDEN ID 355-A1
KOOTENAI CO ID 355-A6
ATOR HILL RD
KOOTENAI CO ID 248-A5
ATWOOD RD
KLICKITAT CO WA 196-A5
AUBREY L WHITE PKWY
SPOKANE WA 348-B4
SPOKANE CO WA 348-B4
N AUBREY L WHITE PKWY
SPOKANE WA 246-A2
SPOKANE WA 346-A14
SPOKANE WA 348-B2
SPOKANE CO WA 348-B2
AUBURN AV
AUBURN WA 182-B2
BAKER CITY OR 138-B1
AUBURN AV U.S.-30
BAKER CITY OR 138-B1
AUBURN AV NE
AUBURN WA 182-C1
AUBURN ST
KLAMATH FALLS OR 338-E6
AUBURN WY N
AUBURN WA 175-C7
AUBURN WA 182-C1
KING CO WA 175-C7
AUBURN WY N Rt#-164
AUBURN WA 182-C1
AUBURN WY S Rt#-164
AUBURN WA 182-C1
AUBURN BLACK DIAMOND RD
AUBURN WA 182-D1
BLACK DIAMOND WA 110-C3
KING CO WA 110-C3
KING CO WA 182-D1
SE AUBURN BLACK DIAMOND RD
KING CO WA 182-C1
AUBURN-ECHO LAKE CTO Rt#-18
KING CO WA 175-D6
KING CO WA 176-A6
KING CO WA 182-C1
AUBURN WA 182-C1
COVINGTON WA 175-D7
KENT WA 175-D7
KING CO WA 175-D7
KING CO WA 176-A6
KING CO WA 182-C1
MAPLE VALLEY WA 175-D7
AUBURN-ECHO LAKE CTO SE Rt#-18
KING CO WA 176-A6
AUBURN ENUMCLAW RD Rt#-164
AUBURN WA 182-C2
KING CO WA 182-C2
S AUDUBON ST
SPOKANE WA 348-F10
AUFDERHEIDE SCENIC BYWY
LANE CO OR 142-A1
WESTFIR OR 142-A1
LANE CO OR 134-A3
W AUGUSTA AV
SPOKANE WA 348-J7
AUGUSTA AV NE
Suquamish WA 170-C7
AULT FIELD RD
Ault Field WA 167-B2
ISLAND CO WA 167-B2
AUMSVILLE HWY SE
AUMSVILLE OR 133-C1
AUMSVILLE OR 205-B7
MARION CO OR 205-A7
MARION CO OR 325-F5
SALEM OR 325-F5
AUNE HALL RD
WHITMAN CO WA 122-A1
AURORA AV N Rt#-99
SEATTLE WA 171-A7
SEATTLE WA 273-J2
SEATTLE WA 277-J4
SHORELINE WA 171-A7
AUSTIN AV
COQUITLAM BC 157-A5
DISTRICT OF COQUITLAM BC 156-D5
AUSTIN DR
BREMERTON WA 270-C8
AUSTIN RD
DISTRICT OF BURNABY BC 156-D5
DISTRICT OF COQUITLAM BC 156-D5
SKAGIT CO WA 161-C7
N AUSTIN RD
SPOKANE CO WA 346-F2
S AUSTIN RD
SPOKANE CO WA 246-B6
AUTOCENTER WY
BREMERTON WA 270-D10
AVALON ST Rt#-69
ADA CO ID 253-A5
KUNA ID 253-A5
SW AVALON WY
SEATTLE WA 281-F4
AVENUE A
SEASIDE OR 301-F8
AVENUE B
GRANDVIEW WA 120-B3
SEASIDE OR 301-G8
N AVENUE B
BOISE ID 253-D3
GRANDVIEW WA 120-B3
AVENUE D
SNOHOMISH WA 171-D3
SNOHOMISH CO WA 171-D3
AVENUE G
SEASIDE OR 301-G9
AVENUE S
SEASIDE OR 301-G10
CLATSOP CO OR 301-F10
AVENUE U
CLATSOP CO OR 301-F10
SEASIDE OR 301-F10
AVERY RD E
LEWIS CO WA 187-D2
AVERY RD W
LEWIS CO WA 187-C2
SW AVERY ST
TUALATIN OR 199-B4
AVON AV Rt#-20
BURLINGTON WA 260-C4
AVON CTO Rt#-20
SKAGIT CO WA 161-A6
SKAGIT CO WA 260-A6
AVON-ALLEN RD
SKAGIT CO WA 161-A6
AVONDALE PL NE
KING CO WA 171-D7
AVONDALE RD NE
KING CO WA 171-D7
KING CO WA 175-D1
REDMOND WA 171-D7
REDMOND WA 175-D1
AVONDALE WY NE
REDMOND WA 175-D1
AWMILLER RD
LEWIS CO WA 187-B4
AXFORD RD
BATTLE GROUND WA 193-A3
CLARK CO WA 193-A3
AXLING RD
WHATCOM CO WA 158-D3
AXTEL CREEK RD
LINCOLN CO OR 209-B4
E AXTON RD
WHATCOM CO WA 102-B1
WHATCOM CO WA 158-D6
W AXTON RD
FERNDALE WA 158-D6
WHATCOM CO WA 158-D6
AYER RD
WALLA WALLA CO WA 121-C2
AYRES RD
EUGENE OR 215-B1
AZALEA DR
JOSEPHINE CO OR 229-A5

B

B AV
DESCHUTES CO OR 212-D4
Terrebonne OR 212-D4
W B AV Rt#-99
DRAIN OR 219-A3
B ST
ABERDEEN WA 178-B7
ASHLAND OR 337-D7
TILLAMOOK CO OR 191-B4
B ST Rt#-82
ISLAND CITY OR 130-A2
E B ST U.S.-30
RAINIER OR 189-C4
NE B ST
MADRAS OR 208-C5
S B ST
ISLAND CITY OR 130-A2
W B ST
RAINIER OR 189-B4
W B ST U.S.-30
RAINIER OR 189-C4
B ST E
PIERCE CO WA 181-D5
B 1/2-NE RD
GRANT CO WA 112-C3
B 5-NE
GRANT CO WA 112-C2
E BABB RD
SPOKANE CO WA 114-C3
BABCOCK RD
WALLA WALLA CO WA 121-C2
S BABCOCK RD
CLACKAMAS CO OR 205-D2
NE BABCOCK ST
KITSAP CO WA 170-C4
B A BENSON RD
SKAGIT CO WA 161-A5
BABY DOLL RD E
KITSAP CO WA 271-D14
BABY DOLL RD SE
KITSAP CO WA 271-D14
BACHELOR DR
LINCOLN CO WA 113-C1
BACHELOR FLAT RD
COLUMBIA CO OR 192-A2
SAINT HELENS OR 192-A2
BACONA RD
WASHINGTON CO OR 125-C1
BACON CAMP RD
HARNEY CO OR 144-B3
BACUS RD
SKAGIT CO WA 161-D5
BADGER RD
BENTON CO WA 120-C3
BADGER RD
BENTON CO WA 121-A2
BENTON CO WA 341-G14
FRANKLIN CO WA 121-A2
GRAYS HARBOR CO WA 177-D2
KENNEWICK WA 341-G14
E BADGER RD Rt#-546
WHATCOM CO WA 102-B1
WHATCOM CO WA 158-D3
E BADGER RD Rt#-547
WHATCOM CO WA 102-B1
W BADGER RD
WHATCOM CO WA 158-D3
BADGER CANYON RD
BENTON CO WA 120-C3
BADGER CREEK RD
CROOK CO OR 136-A2
WASCO CO OR 127-A3
WHEELER CO OR 136-B2
BADGER MOUNTAIN RD
DOUGLAS CO WA 239-A4
BADGER MOUNTAIN RD SW
DOUGLAS CO WA 239-B2
BADGER POCKET RD
KITTITAS WA 241-C6
KITTITAS CO WA 241-C6
BAGBY RD
CLACKAMAS CO OR 126-B3
BAGDAD RD
LINCOLN CO WA 113-B1
LINCOLN CO WA 237-D4
BAILER HILL RD
SAN JUAN CO WA 101-C2
BAILEY RD
DISTRICT OF CHILLIWACK BC 94-C3
ISLAND CO WA 171-A3
S BAILEY ST
SEATTLE WA 282-B7
BAILEY HILL RD
EUGENE OR 329-C8
LANE CO OR 329-A14
BAINARD LN
CHELAN CO WA 239-B5
BAIRD RD NE
THURSTON CO WA 180-D4
BAIRD SPRINGS RD
GRANT CO WA 112-C3
GRANT CO WA 239-D7
BAKEOVEN RD
MAUPIN OR 127-B3
WASCO CO OR 127-B3
BAKEOVEN MARKET RD
WASCO CO OR 127-B3
N BAKER AV
East Wenatchee Bench WA 239-A4
BAKER RD
CLACKAMAS CO OR 199-A5
COOS CO OR 220-C5
JACKSON CO OR 234-B2
KLICKITAT CO WA 196-B3
MORROW CO OR 128-B1
SHERWOOD OR 199-A5
YAKIMA CO WA 243-B5
E BAKER RD
SPOKANE CO WA 246-D7
SE BAKER RD
KITSAP CO WA 174-C4
BAKER RD SW
THURSTON CO WA 180-B6
NE BAKER ST
MCMINNVILLE OR 198-A7
NE BAKER ST Rt#-99W
MCMINNVILLE OR 198-A7
SE BAKER ST Rt#-99W
MCMINNVILLE OR 198-A7
BAKER-COPPERFIELD HWY Rt#-86
BAKER CO OR 130-B3
BAKER CO OR 131-A3
BAKER CO OR 138-C1
BAKER CO OR 139-A1
RICHLAND OR 139-A1
NW BAKER CREEK RD
MCMINNVILLE OR 198-A7
YAMHILL CO OR 198-A7
BAKER HEIGHTS RD
SKAGIT CO WA 161-C7
NE BAKER HILL RD
KITSAP CO WA 271-G5
BAKER LAKE HWY
WHATCOM CO WA 102-C2
BAKER LAKE RD
SKAGIT CO WA 102-C2
BAKER LANGDON RD
WALLA WALLA CO WA 345-A13
S BAKERS FERRY RD
CLACKAMAS CO OR 200-A4
E BAKERVIEW RD
BELLINGHAM WA 258-F1
WHATCOM CO WA 258-F1
BALBACK RD
ADAMS CO ID 251-A4
BALCH RD
KLICKITAT CO WA 196-B5
BALDA RD
ISLAND CO WA 167-B3
BALD BUTTE RD
WHITMAN CO WA 249-C7
BALD HILLS RD SE
THURSTON CO WA 118-A1
BALDOCK FRWY I-5
PORTLAND OR 316-C7
PORTLAND OR 317-F2
PORTLAND OR 320-B1
BALD PEAK RD
WASHINGTON CO OR 198-C3
YAMHILL CO OR 198-C4
SE BALDWIN DR
JEFFERSON CO OR 208-C6
BALDWIN RD
CROOK CO OR 213-C5
Walla Walla West WA 344-D7
HOOD RIVER CO OR 202-D4
WALLA WALLA WA 344-D7
WASCO CO OR 127-A2
WASCO CO OR 202-D4
BALDY MOUNTAIN RD
BONNER CO ID 107-A3
BONNER CO ID 244-A2
BALL RD
JACKSON CO OR 230-D4
BALL ST
MOUNT VERNON WA 260-B12
BALLANTYNE LN
ADA CO ID 253-A1
W BALLARD DR
KITTITAS CO WA 240-D2
BALLARD RD
POLK CO OR 204-A7
BALLARD RD NW
DOUGLAS CO WA 236-D7
BALLINGER DR
GRANTS PASS OR 335-D10
BALLINGER WY NE Rt#-104
LAKE FOREST PARK WA 171-B6
SHORELINE WA 171-B6
BALL MOUNTAIN LITTLE SHASTA RD
SISKIYOU CO CA 150-A3
BALLOW RD
MASON CO WA 180-D2
BALLSTON RD
POLK CO OR 204-A3
SW BALLSTON RD
YAMHILL CO OR 125-B3
YAMHILL CO OR 204-A3
BALLY MOUNTAIN TRAIL RD
ADAMS CO ID 251-A1
BALM FORK RD
MORROW CO OR 128-C2
BALSAM DR
KLAMATH CO OR 235-A4
KLAMATH CO OR 338-A12
KLAMATH FALLS OR 338-A12
BALSAM DR S
SALEM OR 324-F3
S BALTIMORE RD
SPOKANE CO WA 246-C6
BANDIX RD SE
KITSAP CO WA 174-C6
BANDY RD
BONNER CO ID 107-A3
BANFIELD FRWY I-84
PORTLAND OR 313-H4
PORTLAND OR 314-D5
PORTLAND OR 315-J2
S BANGOR ST
SEATTLE WA 287-G6
N BANK RD
COOS CO OR 220-C4
S BANK RD
GRAYS HARBOR CO WA 117-B1
S BANK RD Rt#-107
GRAYS HARBOR CO WA 117-A1
SW BANK RD
KING CO WA 174-D5
NE BANNER PL
SEATTLE WA 274-B2
N BANNER RD
KITSAP CO WA 174-C4
BANNER RD SE
KITSAP CO WA 174-C5
BANNER WY NE
SEATTLE WA 274-B2
BANNISTER RD
UMATILLA CO OR 129-C1
WESTON OR 129-C1
BANTA RD
BAKER CO OR 130-B3
BAPTIST CHURCH DR
LINN CO OR 133-C1
BAR 14 RD
KITTITAS CO WA 241-C4
BARBARA DR
JOSEPHINE CO OR 229-A5
BARBARA WY
DESCHUTES CO OR 212-A7
BARBEE RD
WHITMAN CO WA 249-A6
BARBER RD NW
DOUGLAS CO WA 236-B5
SW BARBUR BLVD
PORTLAND OR 316-D6
PORTLAND OR 317-E1
PORTLAND OR 320-A1
SW BARBUR BLVD I-99
PORTLAND OR 316-E3
PORTLAND OR 317-E2
SW BARBUR BLVD Rt#-99W
PORTLAND OR 199-B3
TIGARD OR 199-B3
BARCLAY DR
DESCHUTES CO OR 211-D5
BARD RD
UMATILLA CO OR 129-A1
BARGER AV
EUGENE OR 329-A1
BARKER LN
VALLEY CO ID 252-D2
BARKER RD
ADA CO ID 253-C6
COLUMBIA CO OR 189-B5
LANE CO OR 133-B3
N BARKER RD
Greenacres WA 351-G3
SPOKANE CO WA 351-G3
S BARKER RD
Greenacres WA 351-G8
SPOKANE CO WA 351-G10
BARKER CANYON RD
DOUGLAS CO WA 237-A3
BARKES RD
White Swan WA 119-C2
BARKLEY BLVD
BELLINGHAM WA 258-J4
E BARKLEY BLVD
BELLINGHAM WA 258-H3
BARLOW RD
BARLOW OR 199-B7
CLACKAMAS CO OR 199-B7
CLACKAMAS CO OR 205-C1
HOOD RIVER CO OR 202-B7
S BARLOW RD
CLACKAMAS CO OR 205-C1
S BARLOW MONTE CRSTO RD
CLACKAMAS CO OR 205-C2
MARION CO OR 205-C2
BARLOW TRAIL RD
CLACKAMAS CO OR 201-B4

360 N BETHEL ST
STREET INDEX
BOW RD

STREET / City State / Page-Grid

N BETHEL ST
OLYMPIA WA 297-A3
BETHEL-BURLEY RD SE
KITSAP CO WA 174-B5
BETHEL HEIGHTS RD
POLK CO OR 204-C3
BETTAS RD
KITTITAS CO WA 240-D2
W BETZ RD
CHENEY WA 246-A7
SPOKANE CO WA 246-A6
BEULAH RD
MALHEUR CO OR 138-A3
MALHEUR CO OR 146-A1
BEVERLY BLVD
EVERETT WA 268-D2
BEVERLY DR NE
THURSTON CO WA 181-A5
BEVERLY LN
EVERETT WA 268-B2
BEVERLY BURKE RD
GRANT CO WA 120-B1
BEVERLY PARK RD
MUKILTEO WA 171-B4
SNOHOMISH CO WA 171-B4
BEVERLY PARK EDMONDS RD
EVERETT WA 268-A6
SNOHOMISH WA 268-A6
BEVILLE RD
LEWIS CO WA 187-A1
BEWLEY CREEK RD
TILLAMOOK CO OR 197-C3
BEWLEYS ST
BAY CITY OR 197-B1
B HOWARD RD
WHITMAN CO WA 249-B1
BIA RD 10
OKANOGAN CO WA 105-A3
BIA RD 33
JEFFERSON CO OR 134-C1
JEFFERSON CO OR 135-A1
BIA RD 108
YAKIMA CO WA 119-A2
BIA RD 140
YAKIMA CO WA 119-B3
BIA RD 255
YAKIMA CO WA 119-A3
BIA RD 7047
GRAYS HARBOR CO WA 172-B5
BIA RD S-2
GRAYS HARBOR CO WA 177-B1
BIBLE CREEK RD
TILLAMOOK CO OR 125-A2
SW BIBLE CREEK RD
TILLAMOOK CO OR 125-A2
YAMHILL CO OR 125-A2
BICKFORD AV
SNOHOMISH WA 171-D2
SNOHOMISH CO WA 171-D2
BIDDLE RD
JACKSON CO OR 336-B5
MEDFORD OR 336-C8
BIEHN ST
KLAMATH FALLS OR 338-C5
SE BIELMEIR RD
KITSAP CO WA 174-B5
BIG ALKALI RD
WHITMAN CO WA 122-A1
BIG BENCH RD
DOUGLAS CO WA 236-D4
BIG BEND RD
DOUGLAS CO OR 221-A3
BIG BUTTER CREEK RD
MORROW CO OR 128-C1
MORROW CO OR 129-A2
BIG CAMAS RD
DOUGLAS CO OR 222-C3
DOUGLAS CO OR 223-B4
BIG CREEK RD
BONNER CO ID 107-A3
COOS CO OR 218-D3
LANE CO OR 209-A6
SHOSHONE CO ID 115-C2
NE BIG CREEK RD
LINCOLN CO OR 206-B3
BIG ELK RD
JACKSON CO OR 150-A2
BIG ELK CREEK RD
LINCOLN CO OR 133-A1
LINCOLN CO OR 206-D4
BIGELOW ST NE
OLYMPIA WA 297-B4
E BIGELOW GULCH RD
SPOKANE CO WA 246-D2
SPOKANE CO WA 347-H14
SPOKANE CO WA 349-G1
BIG FALL CREEK RD
LANE CO OR 133-C3
LANE CO OR 134-A3
BIG FLAT RD
BAKER CO OR 138-A1
DEL NORTE CO CA 148-C3
WASHINGTON CO ID 139-C2
BIGHAM BROWN RD
JACKSON CO OR 230-D6
BIG HANAFORD RD
LEWIS CO WA 184-C5
BIG HUCKLEBERRY RD
SKAMANIA CO WA 195-A2
W BIG LAKE BLVD
SKAGIT CO WA 168-C1
BIG LICK LN
DOUGLAS CO OR 221-D7
E BIG MEADOWS RD
SPOKANE CO WA 114-C1
E BIG ROCK RD
SPOKANE CO WA 246-D5
BIG SANDY RD
CLACKAMAS CO OR 201-A4
BIG SPRING RD
DESCHUTES CO OR 216-D4
BIG SPRING BURN RD
DESCHUTES CO OR 216-D3
BIG SPRINGS RD
SISKIYOU CO CA 150-A3
E BIG SPRINGS RD
SPOKANE CO WA 349-G11
BIG SQUAWBACK RD
JEFFERSON CO OR 211-D1

BIG STICK RD
HARNEY CO OR 144-C2
HARNEY CO OR 145-A2
BIG VALLEY RD NE
KITSAP CO WA 170-B6
BIG WILLOW RD
PAYETTE CO ID 139-B3
BILGER CREEK RD
DOUGLAS CO OR 221-D7
BILLADEAU RD
DESCHUTES CO OR 217-D4
BILL CREEK RD
LEWIS CO WA 187-C4
BILL MOORE RD
KLICKITAT CO WA 196-B2
BILYEU CREEK RD
LINN CO OR 134-A1
BINGHAM AV E
PIERCE CO WA 182-A5
BINGHAM RD
UMATILLA CO OR 129-C1
BINGHAMPTON ST Rt#-507
RAINIER WA 118-A1
THURSTON CO WA 118-A1
BINNS HILL DR
HOOD RIVER CO OR 195-B6
BIRCH AV
LAPWAI ID 123-A2
White Swan WA 119-C2
NW BIRCH LN
JEFFERSON CO OR 208-B5
BIRCH PL
PACIFIC CO WA 186-A3
BIRCH RD
DIST OF NORTH SAANICH BC 159-B2
FRANKLIN CO WA 121-A2
BIRCH ST
BAKER CITY OR 138-B1
JUNCTION CITY OR 210-A6
PACIFIC CO WA 186-A4
N BIRCH ST Rt#-42S
COQUILLE OR 220-D5
BIRCH BAY DR
Birch Bay WA 158-B5
BIRCH BAY-LYNDEN RD
Birch Bay WA 158-B4
LYNDEN WA 158-D4
WHATCOM CO WA 158-C4
BIRCH CREEK RD
MALHEUR CO OR 146-C2
UMATILLA CO OR 121-C3
E BIRCH CREEK RD
PILOT ROCK OR 129-B2
UMATILLA CO OR 129-B2
S BIRCHFIELD RD
YAKIMA CO WA 243-C7
W BIRCHFIELD RD
YAKIMA WA 243-C7
YAKIMA CO WA 243-C7
BIRCH POINT RD
Birch Bay WA 158-A4
BIRCHWOOD AV
BELLINGHAM WA 258-C3
S BIRD RD
CLACKAMAS CO OR 126-A3
BIRDSEYE CREEK RD
JACKSON CO OR 229-D7
BISCAY ST NW
THURSTON CO WA 180-C5
BISCUIT BUTTE RD
MALHEUR CO OR 146-C2
BISHOP LN
LANE CO OR 210-A7
BISHOP RD
CLALLAM CO WA 164-D6
COLUMBIA CO OR 189-C5
GRAYS HARBOR CO WA 183-D3
BISHOP CREEK RD
COLUMBIA CO OR 189-B7
NW BISHOP-SCOTT RD
YAMHILL CO OR 198-A4
BISSELL RD
STEVENS CO WA 105-C3
BISSINGER RD
UMATILLA CO OR 129-B1
BITTERS RD
KOOTENAI CO ID 115-A2
KOOTENAI CO ID 115-A2
BITTNER RD
YAKIMA CO WA 243-D6
E BITTNER RD
YAKIMA CO WA 243-D7
BIXBY RD
TILLAMOOK CO OR 197-C6
BIZ POINT RD
SKAGIT CO WA 259-B12
BJORN RD
SNOHOMISH CO WA 168-C5
BJORNDAHL RD
SNOHOMISH CO WA 168-C3
BLACK RD
LEWIS CO WA 187-A1
N BLACK RD
SPOKANE CO WA 347-F4
SE BLACK RD
KITSAP CO WA 174-C5
W BLACK RD
COUPEVILLE WA 167-B4
ISLAND CO WA 167-B4
BLACK BRIDGE RD
PAYETTE CO ID 139-B3
BLACKBURN RD
DISTRICT OF CHILLIWACK BC 102-C1
YAMHILL CO OR 198-B5
E BLACKBURN RD
MOUNT VERNON WA 260-E14
SKAGIT CO WA 260-E14
W BLACKBURN RD
MOUNT VERNON WA 260-B14
SKAGIT CO WA 260-B14
BLACK BUTTE LN
WHEELER CO OR 128-A3
BLACK BUTTE RD
JEFFERSON CO OR 211-C2
JEFFERSON CO OR 212-A2
E BLACK CANYON HWY Rt#-52
GEM CO ID 139-C3
W BLACK CANYON HWY
GEM CO ID 139-B3

BLACK CANYON RD
LANE CO OR 215-C1
YAKIMA CO WA 243-A1
N BLACK CAT RD
ADA CO ID 253-A2
S BLACK CAT RD
ADA CO ID 253-A5
BLACK CREEK RD
GRAYS HARBOR CO WA 178-D6
BLACK DIAMOND RD
CLALLAM CO WA 261-C7
BLACK DOG RD
LINN CO OR 207-C3
BLACKFORD RD
COLUMBIA CO OR 189-A3
BLACK LAKE BLVD SW
OLYMPIA WA 296-E6
THURSTON CO WA 296-A10
TUMWATER WA 296-E6
BLACK LK BELMORE RD SW
THURSTON CO WA 296-B9
BLACKLEDGE RD
SKAMANIA CO WA 194-C3
BLACK MOUNTAIN RD
BAKER CO OR 138-A1
BLACK OAK DR
MEDFORD OR 336-G12
BLACK ROCK LN
DESCHUTES CO OR 217-C1
BLACK ROCK RD
DOUGLAS CO OR 222-B7
KOOTENAI CO ID 247-D6
KOOTENAI CO ID 248-D3
BLACK SNAG RD
HARNEY CO OR 136-C3
BLACKTAIL DR
JEFFERSON CO OR 212-C3
BLACKWELL RD
JACKSON CO OR 230-B6
BLAHA RDEX
COLUMBIA CO OR 192-A2
BLAINE RD
LATAH CO ID 249-D6
PAYETTE CO ID 139-B3
TILLAMOOK CO OR 197-C6
WHATCOM CO WA 158-B3
BLAINE RD Rt#-548
Birch Bay WA 158-B4
BLAINE WA 158-B3
WHATCOM CO WA 158-B3
BLAINE ST
PORT TOWNSEND WA 263-G4
BLAINE ST U.S.-30
CALDWELL ID 147-B1
W BLAINE ST
SEATTLE WA 276-D2
BLAIR RD
WHITMAN CO WA 249-B1
S BLAIR RD
CLACKAMAS CO OR 205-D3
SE BLAIR RD
CLARK CO WA 193-B6
BLAIR KNOB LOOP RD
MARION CO OR 205-D4
BLAKE RD
GRAYS HARBOR CO WA 183-B3
LEWIS CO WA 187-D5
BLAKE RD Rt#-27
SPOKANE CO WA 350-H10
SPOKANE CO WA 351-A12
BLAKELEY LN
LEWIS CO WA 187-D4
BLAKELY AV NE
KITSAP CO WA 174-D2
KITSAP CO WA 271-H4
W BLAKELY AV NE
KITSAP CO WA 271-J6
SW BLAKELY RD
BEND OR 332-D10
BLALOCK CANYON RD
GILLIAM CO OR 128-A1
BLANCA ST
UNIV ENDOWMENT LANDS BC 156-A4
BLANCHARD RD
TILLAMOOK CO OR 197-C5
E BLANCHARD RD
SPOKANE CO WA 114-C1
BLANK RD
WHITMAN CO WA 114-C3
BLANSHARD ST
CITY OF VICTORIA BC 256-H9
DISTRICT OF SAANICH BC 256-F4
BLANSHARD ST Rt#-17
CITY OF VICTORIA BC 256-G6
DISTRICT OF SAANICH BC 256-G5
BLANTON RD
FRANKLIN CO WA 121-B2
BLANTON RD Rt#-260
FRANKLIN CO WA 121-B1
BLATCHFORD RD
LINN CO OR 207-D7
BLENHEIM ST
VANCOUVER BC 156-B5
VANCOUVER BC 254-A13
BLENKINSOP RD
DISTRICT OF SAANICH BC 159-C5
DISTRICT OF SAANICH BC 256-J1
BLIMP BLVD
TILLAMOOK CO OR 197-C3
NW BLISS RD
CLARK CO WA 192-C4
BLISS-COCHRANE RD KPN
PIERCE CO WA 174-A7
BLIZZARD RD
WHATCOM CO WA 160-B1
BLM ACCESS RD
MAUPIN OR 127-B3
BLM RD 2-3
DOUGLAS CO OR 214-D6
BLM RD 23-4-26
DOUGLAS CO OR 219-C5
BLM RD 23-4-28-0
DOUGLAS CO OR 219-C5
BLM RD 23-4-90
DOUGLAS CO OR 219-B5
BLM RD 23-5-191
DOUGLAS CO OR 219-A5
BLM RD 24-1
DOUGLAS CO OR 214-D6

BLM RD 24-3-31-2
DOUGLAS CO OR 219-D7
BLM RD 24-5-10
DOUGLAS CO OR 219-B6
BLM RD 25-4-13-0
DOUGLAS CO OR 221-D1
BLM RD 25-7-5-1
DOUGLAS CO OR 141-A1
BLM RD 28-4-29-0
DOUGLAS CO OR 221-D6
BLM RD 29-4-20
DOUGLAS CO OR 225-D1
BLM RD 29-7-25-1
DOUGLAS CO OR 225-A1
BLM RD 30-70-50
DOUGLAS CO OR 225-A1
BLM RD 31-4-35-0
DOUGLAS CO OR 225-D4
BLM RD 32-4-9
DOUGLAS CO OR 225-D5
BLM RD 32-9-3
COOS CO OR 140-C3
BLM RD 33-0
DOUGLAS CO OR 214-D6
BLM RD 33-5-18
JOSEPHINE CO OR 229-C1
BLM RD 33-5-26
JOSEPHINE CO OR 229-C1
BLM RD 33-5-27
JOSEPHINE CO OR 229-C1
BLM RD 33-5-35-1
JOSEPHINE CO OR 229-C1
BLM RD 33-7-22
JOSEPHINE CO OR 229-A1
BLM RD 34-4-5
JOSEPHINE CO OR 229-C1
BLM RD 34-5-1
JOSEPHINE CO OR 229-C1
BLM RD 34-5-32
JOSEPHINE CO OR 229-C3
BLM RD 34-5-9
JOSEPHINE CO OR 229-C2
BLM RD 34-6-12
JOSEPHINE CO OR 229-B3
BLM RD 34-6-13
JOSEPHINE CO OR 229-B2
BLM RD 34-8-1
JOSEPHINE CO OR 141-A3
BLM RD 36-0
DOUGLAS CO OR 214-C7
BLM RD 37-6-36
JOSEPHINE CO OR 233-D3
BLM RD 39-6-9
JOSEPHINE CO OR 233-D3
BLM RD 39-7-16
JOSEPHINE CO OR 233-C4
BLM RD 61064
LAKE CO OR 152-C2
BLODGETT RD
LINCOLN CO OR 209-A3
MOUNT VERNON WA 260-C13
SKAGIT CO WA 168-B1
BLOMBERG RD SW
THURSTON CO WA 184-C1
BLOODGOOD RD
KLICKITAT CO WA 127-C1
BLOOMFIELD RD
MASON CO WA 180-B5
BLOOMING-FERN HILL RD
WASHINGTON CO OR 198-C2
BLOSSOM DR NE
Hayesville OR 323-D5
SALEM OR 323-D5
S BLOUNT RD
CLACKAMAS CO OR 199-C6
BLOWOUT RESERVOIR RD
MALHEUR CO OR 146-C2
MALHEUR CO OR 147-A2
BLUE BUNCH RD
ADAMS CO ID 251-B6
BLUE CREEK RD
KOOTENAI CO ID 245-C6
BLUE CREEK RD W
STEVENS CO WA 106-A3
BLUE CREEK WEST RD
STEVENS CO WA 106-A3
BLUE GRADE
DOUGLAS CO WA 239-A3
BLUEGRASS LN
DESCHUTES CO OR 211-C5
BLUE LAKE RD
OKANOGAN CO WA 104-C1
BLUE MOUNTAIN RD
CLALLAM CO WA 165-D7
WHATCOM CO WA 161-D1
BLUE MOUNTAIN ST
COQUITLAM BC 157-A5
BLUE MTN LOGGING RD
WHATCOM CO WA 161-C1
BLUE OX LOGGING RD
SKAMANIA CO WA 195-B3
BLUESTEM RD
LINCOLN CO WA 114-A2
BLUFF RD
CLACKAMAS CO OR 200-C3
PAYETTE CO ID 139-B3
SANDY OR 200-C3
N BLUFF RD
CITY OF WHITE ROCK BC 158-A2
DISTRICT OF SURREY BC 158-A2
SE BLUFF RD
CLACKAMAS CO OR 200-C3
MULTNOMAH CO OR 200-C3
BLUFF ST
WINTHROP WA 104-A2
S BLUHM RD
CLACKAMAS CO OR 200-A6
BLUMAUER RD SE
THURSTON CO WA 184-D3
BLUNDELL RD
CITY OF RICHMOND BC 156-B6
BLUNT RD KPS
PIERCE CO WA 181-A2
BLY MOUNTAIN CTO
KLAMATH CO OR 151-A2
BOARDMAN-IRRIGON RD
MORROW CO OR 128-C1
BOARD SHANTY RD
JOSEPHINE CO OR 229-C7

BOAT RD
COOS CO OR 220-A7
BOB GALBREATH RD
Clinton WA 171-A2
BOB HALL RD
WHATCOM CO WA 158-D4
BODINE RD
COLUMBIA CO OR 189-A3
COWLITZ CO WA 189-D4
N BODINE RD
COWLITZ CO WA 189-D4
BOE RD
SNOHOMISH CO WA 168-A4
BOECKMAN RD
WILSONVILLE OR 199-B5
BOEHMER RD NE
MARION CO OR 205-C3
S BOEING ACCESS RD
TUKWILA WA 286-D5
TUKWILA WA 287-E5
E BOEKEL RD
KOOTENAI CO ID 247-D1
BOGACHIEL WY
CLALLAM CO WA 169-C2
BOGART LN
ADA CO ID 253-B1
BOG CREEK RD
BOUNDARY CO ID 106-C1
BOUNDARY CO ID 107-A1
BOGUS BASIN RD
ADA CO ID 253-D2
BOISE ID 253-C2
BOGUS RANCH RD
MALHEUR CO OR 146-C3
BOHLKEN DR
LINN CO OR 133-C1
LINN CO OR 207-D5
BOH MOUNTAIN RD
JOSEPHINE CO OR 229-B7
SE BOHNA PARK RD
CLACKAMAS CO OR 200-B3
BOHOSKEY DR W
YAKIMA CO WA 243-D6
BOISE AV
BENTON CO OR 133-B2
E BOISE AV
ADA CO ID 253-D3
BOISE ID 253-D3
W BOISE AV
BOISE ID 253-C3
NW BOISE DR
JEFFERSON CO OR 208-B3
BOISE ST
KOOTENAI ID 244-A1
BOISTFORT RD
LEWIS CO WA 187-A2
BOLAN LAKE RD
DEL NORTE CO CA 233-C7
JOSEPHINE CO OR 233-C7
BOLEN RD
CLARK CO WA 192-C1
LA CENTER WA 192-C1
BOLESKINE RD
DISTRICT OF SAANICH BC 256-F5
BOLLAND RD
CLACKAMAS CO OR 199-C7
N BOLLENBAUGH HILL RD
SNOHOMISH CO WA 110-C1
BOLTON RD
LANE CO OR 133-B3
VENETA OR 133-B3
BOMBING RANGE RD
MORROW CO OR 128-C2
WEST RICHLAND WA 341-A3
BONAPARTE RD
OKANOGAN CO WA 105-A1
BONAPARTE LAKE RD
OKANOGAN CO WA 105-A2
BOND DR
COWLITZ CO WA 187-C7
COWLITZ CO WA 189-C1
BOND RD
COWLITZ CO WA 189-C1
LINN CO OR 207-D4
BOND RD NE
POULSBO WA 170-B6
BOND RD NE Rt#-307
KITSAP CO WA 170-C6
POULSBO WA 170-C6
BOND ST
ASTORIA OR 300-C4
COWLITZ CO WA 187-C7
DISTRICT OF BURNABY BC 156-C5
NW BOND ST
BEND OR 332-E6
W BOND ST
ASTORIA OR 300-B4
BOND BUTTE DR
LINN CO OR 210-B4
BOND CREEK RD
SHOSHONE CO ID 115-B2
BOND MILL RD
SAN JUAN CO WA 160-A3
BONITA RD
MALHEUR CO OR 138-B3
W BONNEVILLE ST
PASCO WA 343-E8
BONNEY MEADOWS TR
WASCO CO OR 202-C7
BONSON RD
BRITISH COLUMBIA 157-C6
PITT MEADOWS BC 157-C5
BONY RD
YAMHILL CO OR 198-B4
BOOKER RD
ADAMS CO WA 121-A1
BOOMER HILL RD
DOUGLAS CO OR 225-B1
BOON RD
ISLAND CO WA 167-B3
BOONE RD
LEWIS CO WA 187-D3
N BOONE ST Rt#-105
ABERDEEN WA 178-B7
S BOONE ST Rt#-105
ABERDEEN WA 117-A1
ABERDEEN WA 178-B7
GRAYS HARBOR CO WA 117-A1
BOONE CREEK RD
COOS CO OR 220-D3

BOONES FERRY RD
CLACKAMAS OR 320-B6
CLACKAMAS CO OR 199-B6
LAKE OSWEGO OR 199-B6
LAKE OSWEGO OR 320-B6
MARION CO OR 199-B6
MARION CO OR 205-B1
SW BOONES FERRY RD
CLACKAMAS OR 320-D3
DURHAM OR 199-B4
LAKE OSWEGO OR 320-D3
MULTNOMAH OR 320-D3
PORTLAND OR 316-E7
PORTLAND OR 317-E7
PORTLAND OR 320-D2
TUALATIN OR 199-B4
WASHINGTON CO OR 199-B4
WILSONVILLE OR 199-B4
BOONES FERRY RD NE
MARION CO OR 199-B7
MARION CO OR 205-B1
WOODBURN OR 205-B1
BOOTH LN
UNION CO OR 130-A2
BOOTH RD
DOUGLAS CO OR 214-A6
SW BOOTH BEND RD
MCMINNVILLE OR 198-A7
BOOTH HILL RD
HOOD RIVER CO OR 202-D1
N BOOTHILL RD
KOOTENAI CO ID 245-B4
BOOTH KELLY RD
SPRINGFIELD OR 331-D8
BORBA RD
TILLAMOOK CO OR 197-C5
BORDEAUX RD SW
THURSTON CO WA 184-A2
BOREN AV
SEATTLE WA 278-A5
BOREN AV S
SEATTLE WA 278-B6
BORGEN RD
LATAH CO ID 250-B1
WALLA WALLA CO WA 121-C3
SE BORGES RD
CLACKAMAS CO OR 200-B3
NE BORIN RD
CLARK CO WA 193-D6
SE BORING RD
GRESHAM OR 200-B2
SW BORLAND RD
CLACKAMAS CO OR 199-C4
TUALATIN OR 199-C4
WEST LINN OR 199-C4
SE BORNSTEDT RD
CLACKAMAS CO OR 200-C4
N BORSETH ST Rt#-9
SEDRO-WOOLLEY WA 161-C5
BOSK RD
SNOHOMISH CO WA 168-B3
BOSSBURG RD
STEVENS CO WA 106-A1
BOSTIAN RD
SNOHOMISH CO WA 171-D6
BOSTON ST
SEATTLE WA 277-H1
BOSTON HARBOR RD NE
THURSTON CO WA 180-C5
BOSTON MILL DR
LINN CO OR 210-B1
BOSWELL RD
DOUGLAS CO OR 219-B3
NE BOTHELL WY Rt#-522
BOTHELL WA 171-B6
KENMORE WA 171-B6
KING CO WA 171-B6
LAKE FOREST PARK WA 171-B6
BOTHELL WY NE Rt#-522
BOTHELL WA 171-C6
LAKE FOREST PARK WA 171-B6
SHORELINE WA 171-B7
BOTHELL WY NE Rt#-527
BOTHELL WA 171-C6
BOTHELL EVERETT HWY Rt#-527
BOTHELL WA 171-C4
MILL CREEK WA 171-C4
SNOHOMISH CO WA 171-C4
BOTTLE BAY RD
BONNER CO ID 244-A3
BOULDER CREEK RD
ADAMS CO ID 131-C3
ADAMS CO ID 251-A1
TILLAMOOK CO OR 197-C6
BOULDER LAKE RD
VALLEY CO ID 251-D6
BOULDER RIDGE RD
WASCO CO OR 202-C7
BOULEVARD PL
MERCER ISLAND WA 283-J3
BOULEVARD RD SE
OLYMPIA WA 297-C7
THURSTON CO WA 297-C10
BOUNDARY HWY Rt#-251
NORTHPORT WA 106-B1
STEVENS CO WA 106-B1
BOUNDARY RD
DISTRICT OF BURNABY BC 156-C5
DISTRICT OF BURNABY BC 255-F12
DISTRICT OF CHILLIWACK BC 102-C1
JACKSON CO OR 150-A1
PEND OREILLE CO WA 106-B1
VANCOUVER BC 156-C5
VANCOUVER BC 255-F12
W BOUNDARY RD
KLAMATH CO OR 142-C3
LANE CO OR 134-A3
BOUNDARY RD S
DISTRICT OF BURNABY BC 156-C5
VANCOUVER BC 156-C5
BOUNDARY BAY RD
DISTRICT OF DELTA BC 101-C1
WHATCOM CO WA 101-C1
BOUNDARY CREEK RD
BOUNDARY CO ID 107-A1
BOURBON RD
SHERMAN CO OR 127-C2
BOW RD
SKAGIT CO WA 161-A5

PNW
INDEX

PNW

INDEX

362 BURRARD ST STREET INDEX CASCADE HWY S Rt#-213

STREET
City State Page-Grid

BURRARD ST
VANCOUVER BC 254-F10
BURRELL AV
LEWISTON ID 250-C5
BURRES RD
CLARK CO WA 192-D1
BURRI RD
LEWIS CO WA 187-A2
BURRIS ST
DISTRICT OF BURNABY BC 156-D5
BURROUGHS RD
KITTITAS CO WA 241-C5
BURROWS RD
GRAYS HARBOR CO WA 177-C6
WALLA WALLA CO WA 121-C3
BURROWS ST
ANACORTES WA 259-C6
BURSELL RD
POLK CO OR 204-A7
BURTON LN
WASHINGTON CO ID 139-B1
NE BURTON RD
VANCOUVER WA 306-E3
VANCOUVER WA 307-F3
BURTON-FRASER RD
TILLAMOOK CO OR 197-B2
BURWELL PL Rt#-304
BREMERTON WA 270-G11
BURWELL ST Rt#-304
BREMERTON WA 270-G11
BUSBY RD
WHITMAN CO WA 249-B5
BUSBY-JOHNSON RD
WHITMAN CO WA 249-B6
BUSCH RD
WHITMAN CO WA 250-A2
BUSH ST
Walla Walla East WA 345-E7
BUSH CREEK RD
GRAYS HARBOR CO WA 179-C6
SKAMANIA CO WA 195-A4
BUSH GARDEN DR
LINN CO OR 210-B6
BUSHLACH RD
SKAMANIA CO WA 193-D7
BUSH POINT RD
Freeland WA 170-C1
ISLAND CO WA 170-C1
BUSH RANCH TO COUNTY LINE RD
GRANT CO OR 136-C3
BUSHWELL RD
GRAYS HARBOR CO WA 179-B7
NE BUTLER AV
DESCHUTES CO OR 213-A4
BUTLER BLVD
MALHEUR CO OR 139-A3
BUTLER RD
COLUMBIA CO OR 189-C6
CROOK CO OR 213-A3
SW BUTLER RD
GRESHAM OR 200-A2
BUTLER BRIDGE RD SE
LINCOLN CO OR 206-C5
TOLEDO OR 206-C4
BUTLER CREEK RD
BONNER CO ID 244-A5
DOUGLAS CO OR 218-D1
KOOTENAI CO ID 248-D4
SKAGIT CO WA 161-B3
BUTLER GRADE RD
UMATILLA CO OR 121-B3
BUTLER MARKET RD
DESCHUTES CO OR 217-D2
NE BUTLER MARKET RD
BEND OR 217-C2
BEND OR 332-G4
DESCHUTES CO OR 217-C2
BUTTE AV
JEFFERSON CO OR 208-B6
BUTTE CT
WEST RICHLAND WA 340-A12
BUTTE RD
CANYON CO ID 147-C2
CLACKAMAS CO OR 200-A7
E BUTTE ST
PASCO WA 343-H8
BUTTE CREEK RD
CLACKAMAS CO OR 205-D4
WHEELER CO OR 128-A3
BUTTE FALLS RD
BUTTE FALLS OR 150-A1
JACKSON CO OR 149-C1
JACKSON CO OR 150-A1
JACKSON CO OR 230-D4
BUTTE FALLS-FISH LAKE RD
JACKSON CO OR 150-A1
BUTTE FALLS-PROSPECT RD
BUTTE FALLS OR 150-A1
JACKSON CO OR 150-A1
JACKSON CO OR 226-C7
BUTTER CREEK RD
MORROW CO OR 128-C1
MORROW CO OR 129-A2
UMATILLA CO OR 128-C1
UMATILLA CO OR 129-A2
BUTTER CREEK RD Rt#-207
HERMISTON OR 129-A1
UMATILLA CO OR 129-A1
BUTTERMILK CANYON RD
GILLIAM CO OR 128-B3
MORROW CO OR 128-B3
BUTTEVILLE RD
CLACKAMAS CO OR 199-B6
DONALD OR 199-A7
MARION CO OR 199-A7
MARION CO OR 205-B1
BUTTEVILLE RD NE
DONALD OR 199-A7
GERVAIS OR 205-B2
MARION CO OR 205-B1
BUTTEVILLE RD NE Rt#-219
MARION CO OR 205-B1
BUTTON
PIERCE CO WA 182-B6
BUTTON BRIDGE RD U.S.-30
HOOD RIVER CO OR 195-D5
BUYSERIE RD
MARION CO OR 198-D7
BUZZARD MINE RD
JACKSON CO OR 226-B5
SE BYBEE BLVD
PORTLAND OR 317-J5
PORTLAND OR 318-A5
BYBEE CREEK RD
JACKSON CO OR 226-D3
BYBEE CREEK BRANCH RD
JACKSON CO OR 227-A3
SE BYERS AV
PENDLETON OR 129-B1
NW BYHAM RD
LEWIS CO WA 187-C3
BY-PASS HWY
RICHLAND WA 340-F11
BY-PASS HWY Rt#-240
RICHLAND WA 340-E12
RICHLAND WA 341-E3
BYRAM RD
DESCHUTES CO OR 217-D3
BYRNES RD
WALLA WALLA CO WA 121-B3
B Z CORNER-GLENWOOD RD
KLICKITAT CO WA 119-A3
KLICKITAT CO WA 195-D2
KLICKITAT CO WA 196-A1

C

C AV
LA GRANDE OR 130-A2
C RD NW Rt#-172
DOUGLAS CO WA 112-B1
C ST
CULVER OR 208-B7
NESPELEM WA 105-A3
PORT ANGELES WA 261-C4
VANCOUVER WA 305-G4
WALLA WALLA CO WA 345-H4
C ST Rt#-214
SILVERTON OR 205-C4
E C ST
RAINIER OR 189-C4
NE C ST
COLLEGE PLACE WA 344-F9
WALLA WALLA CO WA 344-F9
C ST NW
EPHRATA WA 112-C3
C ST S
PIERCE CO WA 181-D4
C ST SE
QUINCY WA 112-B3
C ST SW
AUBURN WA 182-B2
EPHRATA WA 112-C3
QUINCY WA 112-B3
CABIN LN
YAKIMA CO WA 243-B4
CABIN LAKE RD
LAKE CO OR 143-B2
CACHE CREEK RD
FERRY CO WA 105-B3
NESPELEM WA 105-B3
OKANOGAN CO WA 105-B3
CADBORO BAY RD
DISTRICT OF OAK BAY BC 257-D6
DISTRICT OF SAANICH BC 257-E5
CADLE RD
POLK CO OR 204-B5
CADY RD
JACKSON CO OR 149-B2
CAGEY RD
WHATCOM CO WA 158-C7
S CAHILL RD
SPOKANE CO WA 114-C2
CAIN RD SE
OLYMPIA WA 297-B9
CAIN LAKE RD
SKAGIT CO WA 161-B3
WHATCOM CO WA 161-B3
CALAMITY PEAK RD
SKAMANIA CO WA 190-C7
SKAMANIA CO WA 194-A1
CALAPOOIA ST
ALBANY OR 326-C8
CALAPOOYA ST Rt#-99
DOUGLAS CO OR 221-C1
SUTHERLIN OR 221-C1
CALAWAH WY
CLALLAM CO WA 169-D1
CALDWELL BLVD U.S.-30
CANYON CO ID 147-B1
NAMPA ID 147-B1
CALEB PIKE RD
BRITISH COLUMBIA 159-B5
CALHOUN RD
SKAGIT CO WA 168-A1
CALIFORNIA AV
KLAMATH FALLS OR 338-C7
CALIFORNIA AV E
Colby WA 271-G13
CALIFORNIA AV SE
Colby WA 271-G14
CALIFORNIA AV SW
SEATTLE WA 276-E7
SEATTLE WA 280-E2
SEATTLE WA 284-D2
CALIFORNIA ST Rt#-238
JACKSONVILLE OR 149-B2
E CALIFORNIA ST
JACKSONVILLE OR 149-B2
E CALIFORNIA ST Rt#-238
JACKSONVILLE OR 149-B2
W CALIFORNIA ST Rt#-238
JACKSONVILLE OR 149-B2
CALIFORNIA WY
LONGVIEW WA 303-A11
CALIFORNIA WY SW
SEATTLE WA 276-E7
SEATTLE WA 280-E1
SEATTLE WA 281-E1
N CALIMUS RD
KLAMATH CO OR 151-A1
S CALISPELL AV
NEWPORT WA 106-C3
CALISTOGA AV
ORTING WA 182-C5
PIERCE CO WA 182-C5
CALISTOGA ST W
ORTING WA 182-C5
CALISTOGA ST W
PIERCE CO WA 182-C5
CALKINS LN
YAMHILL CO OR 198-C4
NW CALKINS RD
ROSEBURG OR 334-C5
CALLAHAN RD
CLACKAMAS CO OR 126-A3
COLUMBIA CO OR 192-A4
S CALLAHAN RD
CLACKAMAS CO OR 126-A3
CALLIGAN AV
MAPLE RIDGE BC 157-C5
CALLOW AV N Rt#-304
BREMERTON WA 270-G10
CALLOW AV S Rt#-304
BREMERTON WA 270-G11
CALLOW RD
SNOHOMISH CO WA 171-D1
CALLOWAY RD
ADAMS CO WA 121-B1
CALONE RD
LANE CO OR 210-D7
CALVERT DR
DISTRICT OF DELTA BC 101-C1
DISTRICT OF DELTA BC 156-C7
CALVIN RD
LEWIS CO WA 187-C4
CAL YOUNG RD
EUGENE OR 329-J2
EUGENE OR 330-A2
CAMANO AV
ISLAND CO WA 171-A1
LANGLEY WA 171-A1
E CAMANO DR
ISLAND CO WA 167-D4
ISLAND CO WA 168-A7
N CAMANO DR
ISLAND CO WA 167-D4
S CAMANO DR
ISLAND CO WA 167-D6
ISLAND CO WA 168-A6
W CAMANO DR
ISLAND CO WA 167-D4
CAMANO ST
STANWOOD WA 168-A4
CAMANO HILL RD
ISLAND CO WA 167-D5
ISLAND CO WA 168-A4
W CAMANO HILL RD
ISLAND CO WA 167-D5
CAMANO RIDGE RD
ISLAND CO WA 167-D5
CAMAS RD
LEWIS CO ID 123-B2
LEWIS CO ID 123-B2
CAMAS ST
UKIAH OR 129-B3
WINCHESTER ID 123-B2
WINCHESTER ID 123-B2
CAMAS CREEK RD
CHELAN CO WA 238-B3
CAMAS PRAIRIE RD
MORROW CO OR 128-C3
WASCO CO OR 127-A3
CAMAS SWALE RD
CRESWELL OR 215-A5
LANE CO OR 215-A5
CAMBIE BRDG
VANCOUVER BC 254-G12
CAMBIE RD
CITY OF RICHMOND BC 156-B6
CAMBIE ST
VANCOUVER BC 156-B5
VANCOUVER BC 254-G14
CAMBRIAN AV N
BREMERTON WA 270-F11
CAMBRIAN AV S
BREMERTON WA 270-F11
CAMBRIAN AV S Rt#-304
BREMERTON WA 270-F12
E CAMERON RD
SPOKANE CO WA 247-A7
SW CAMERON RD
PORTLAND OR 316-A4
CAMERON ST
DISTRICT OF BURNABY BC 156-D5
DISTRICT OF COQUITLAM BC 156-D5
CAMERON WY
MOUNT VERNON WA 260-C11
CAMP RD
WHITMAN CO WA 122-A1
CAMP 2 RD
WHATCOM CO WA 161-B3
CAMP 10 RD
COLUMBIA CO OR 189-A7
CAMP 12
CHELAN CO WA 111-C1
CAMP ADAIR RD
BENTON CO OR 207-B3
CAMP BAY RD
BONNER CO ID 244-C3
CAMPBELL RD
ISLAND CO WA 171-A2
JACKSON CO OR 234-B2
KLAMATH CO OR 151-B1
Otis Orchards WA 351-J3
SPOKANE CO WA 351-J3
YAKIMA CO WA 120-A2
S CAMPBELL RD
SPOKANE CO WA 247-A5
SW CAMPBELL RD
WASHINGTON CO OR 198-D3
CAMPBELL ST
BAKER CITY OR 138-B1
CAMPBELL ST Rt#-7
BAKER CITY OR 138-B1
CAMPBELL WY
BREMERTON WA 270-J8
CAMPBELL LAKE RD
SKAGIT CO WA 259-G11
S CAMPBELL LAKE RD
SKAGIT CO WA 259-G13
CAMP CREEK RD
BAKER CO OR 137-C1
CROOK CO OR 136-A3
DOUGLAS CO OR 140-C1
GRAYS HARBOR CO WA 178-D7
LANE CO OR 133-C3
LANE CO OR 215-D2
CAMP CREEK RD
LANE CO OR 331-E4
E CAMP CREEK RD
BAKER CO OR 138-A2
CAMP DAVID JR RD
CLALLAM CO WA 164-A6
CAMP DISCOVERY RD
JEFFERSON CO WA 170-A5
CAMP HARMONY RD
JEFFERSON CO WA 170-A6
CAMP HAYDEN RD
CLALLAM CO WA 164-D5
CAMP KETTLE CREEK RD
MALHEUR CO OR 147-A1
CAMP MORRISON DR
LINN CO OR 134-A1
CAMP POLK RD
DESCHUTES CO OR 211-D4
DESCHUTES CO OR 212-A4
CAMP SHERMAN RD
DESCHUTES CO OR 211-C2
JEFFERSON CO OR 211-C2
CAMP TWELVE LP
LINCOLN CO OR 206-C3
CAMPUS DR
KLAMATH FALLS OR 338-D4
SW CAMPUS DR
FEDERAL WAY WA 182-A1
CAMPUS WY
BENTON CO OR 327-C9
CORVALLIS OR 327-E9
CAMUS RD
LEWIS CO WA 187-C4
CAMWELL DR
DIST OF WEST VANCOUVER BC 254-C1
CANAAN RD
COLUMBIA CO OR 189-B7
S CANAAN RD
COLUMBIA CO OR 189-B7
CANAAN RD S
COLUMBIA CO OR 189-B7
CANADA WY
DISTRICT OF BURNABY BC 156-D5
DISTRICT OF BURNABY BC 255-G14
CANADY RD
LEWIS CO WA 187-B5
CANAL BLVD
DESCHUTES CO OR 212-D6
N CANAL BLVD
DESCHUTES CO OR 212-D5
REDMOND OR 212-D5
S CANAL BLVD
DESCHUTES CO OR 212-D6
REDMOND OR 212-D6
W CANAL DR
KENNEWICK WA 342-D8
KENNEWICK WA 343-A9
CANAL RD
UMATILLA CO OR 129-A1
CANAL CREEK RD
LINCOLN CO OR 209-C2
CANAL W-20
GRANT CO WA 242-A1
CANARY RD
DUNES CITY OR 214-B4
CANARY RD S
LANE CO OR 214-B4
CANARY CREEK RD
KOOTENAI CO ID 248-D3
CANBY-MARQUAM HWY
CLACKAMAS CO OR 205-D1
SE CANBY-MARQUAM HWY
CANBY OR 199-C7
CLACKAMAS CO OR 199-C7
CLACKAMAS CO OR 205-D1
CANDIANI RD
MARION CO OR 198-C7
CANDLEWOOD DR NE
KEIZER OR 323-A8
MARION CO OR 323-A8
SALEM OR 323-A8
CANFIELD LOOP RD
KOOTENAI CO ID 245-B6
CANNA ST N
SOAP LAKE WA 112-C2
CANNA ST S
SOAP LAKE WA 112-C2
CANNIBAL MOUNTAIN RD
LINCOLN CO OR 209-C3
CANORA RD
DIST OF NORTH SAANICH BC 159-C2
TOWN OF SIDNEY BC 159-C2
CANTON CREEK RD
DOUGLAS CO OR 141-C1
S CANYON BLVD U.S.-395
JOHN DAY OR 137-B2
CANYON DR
DESCHUTES CO OR 212-C7
CANYON DR SE Rt#-516
KENT WA 175-C7
CANYON RD
ELLENSBURG WA 241-B6
GRAYS HARBOR CO WA 178-D4
KLICKITAT CO WA 196-B3
LANE CO OR 134-B3
WHITMAN CO WA 122-A1
CANYON RD Rt#-821
ELLENSBURG WA 241-B6
KITTITAS CO WA 241-B6
NE CANYON RD
CLARK CO WA 193-B3
SW CANYON RD
JEFFERSON CO OR 208-B5
SW CANYON RD Rt#-8
BEAVERTON OR 199-B2
WASHINGTON CO OR 199-B2
SW CANYON RD U.S.-26
PORTLAND OR 312-C6
CANYON RD E
PIERCE CO WA 182-A5
E CANYON ST Rt#-272
COLFAX WA 122-C1
WHITMAN CO WA 122-C1
CANYON WY
WASCO CO OR 196-B5
CANYON CITY EAST RD
CANYON CITY OR 137-B2
GRANT CO OR 137-B2
CANYON CREEK RD
CROOK CO OR 136-A2
CANYON CREEK RD
DOUGLAS CO OR 225-C3
GRANT CO OR 137-B2
JEFFERSON CO OR 211-B1
CANYON CREEK TR
SKAMANIA CO WA 193-D1
SKAMANIA CO WA 194-A1
CANYON CREST DR
DESCHUTES CO OR 212-A4
CANYONVIEW RD
YAMHILL CO OR 198-B3
CANYONVILLE-RIDDLE RD
CANYONVILLE OR 225-C3
DOUGLAS CO OR 225-C3
CAPE ARAGO HWY
Barview OR 220-C1
COOS BAY OR 333-B6
COOS CO OR 220-B2
COOS CO OR 333-A8
NORTH BEND OR 333-D6
CAPE BLANCO HWY
CURRY CO OR 224-A4
CAPE CREEK RD
LANE CO OR 209-A7
CAPE FERRELO RD
CURRY CO OR 232-C4
CAPE GEORGE RD
JEFFERSON CO WA 166-D6
JEFFERSON CO WA 263-A7
CAPE GEORGE RD W
JEFFERSON CO WA 166-D6
CAPE HORN RD
SKAMANIA CO WA 193-D7
E CAPE HORN RD
KOOTENAI CO ID 245-C1
CAPE KIWANDA DR
TILLAMOOK CO OR 197-A7
CAPE LOOKOUT RD
TILLAMOOK CO OR 197-A4
CAPE MEARES LOOP RD
TILLAMOOK CO OR 197-A2
CAPE SAINT MARY RD
SAN JUAN CO WA 160-A7
CAPE SEBASTIAN FRONTAGE RD
CURRY CO OR 228-A7
CAPILANO RD
DIST OF N VANCOUVER BC 254-G3
CAPITAL MALL DR
OLYMPIA WA 296-C5
CAPITOL BLVD
OLYMPIA WA 296-H7
THURSTON CO WA 296-H13
TUMWATER WA 296-H10
S CAPITOL BLVD
BOISE ID 253-C3
SW CAPITOL HWY
PORTLAND OR 316-B6
PORTLAND OR 320-A1
SW CAPITOL HWY I-99
PORTLAND OR 317-E4
SW CAPITOL HWY Rt#-10
PORTLAND OR 316-D4
PORTLAND OR 317-E4
CAPITOL ST NE
SALEM OR 322-J12
SALEM OR 323-A11
CAPITOL WY
OLYMPIA WA 296-H5
N CAPITOL WY
OLYMPIA WA 296-H5
CAPITOL HILL RD
MASON CO WA 180-B3
CAPLES RD
COWLITZ CO WA 192-B1
NE CAPLES RD
CLARK CO WA 193-A4
CAPLINGER RD SE
MARION CO OR 325-G2
SALEM OR 325-G2
CARAVELLE RD
KOOTENAI CO ID 245-B2
CARBERRY RD
JACKSON CO OR 149-B2
JOSEPHINE CO OR 149-B2
CARBUHN RD
NEZ PERCE CO ID 250-B2
NW CARDEN AV
PENDLETON OR 129-B1
CARDWELL RD
DESCHUTES CO OR 217-D2
CAREY RD
DISTRICT OF SAANICH BC 256-D1
CAREY ST
MANZANITA OR 191-B4
TILLAMOOK CO OR 191-B4
CARIBOO RD
DISTRICT OF BURNABY BC 156-D5
NEW WESTMINSTER BC 156-D5
N CARIBOU RD
KITTITAS CO WA 241-D5
CARICO HILLS RD
ADAMS CO WA 114-A3
CARKEEK DR S
SEATTLE WA 287-E4
CARL RD NE
MARION CO OR 205-B1
CARLIN BAY RD
KOOTENAI CO ID 248-A2
CARLIN CREEK RD
KOOTENAI CO ID 248-A3
CARLISLE AV
LEWIS CO WA 118-A2
CARLISLE GRADE
GRAYS HARBOR CO WA 177-C3
CARLOCK RD NW
DOUGLAS CO WA 236-C6
NW CARLON AV
BEND OR 332-D8
CARLON RD
LAKE CO OR 143-C3
CARLSBORG RD
CLALLAM CO WA 166-A7
CARLSON RD
KITTITAS CO WA 241-C4
LINCOLN CO WA 113-C2
S CARLSON RD
YAKIMA CO WA 243-A7
W CARLSON RD
SPOKANE CO WA 246-A1
CARLYLE HALL RD NW
SHORELINE WA 171-A6
SW CARMAN DR
CLACKAMAS OR 320-A6
CLACKAMAS CO OR 199-B3
LAKE OSWEGO OR 199-B3
LAKE OSWEGO OR 320-A6
CARMARIA CT
DIST OF N VANCOUVER BC 255-F4
CARMEL RD
COLUMBIA CO OR 189-B5
CARMICHAEL DR
KENNEWICK WA 343-C11
S CARNAHAN RD
SPOKANE CO WA 349-H10
CARNATION-DUVALL RD NE Rt#-203
DUVALL WA 110-C1
KING CO WA 110-C1
KING CO WA 176-A1
NE CARNATION FARM RD
KING CO WA 176-B1
SW CARNES RD
DOUGLAS CO OR 221-B6
DOUGLAS CO OR 334-B14
CARNEY LAKE RD SW
KITSAP CO WA 174-A6
S CARNIE RD
KOOTENAI CO ID 247-D4
W CARNIE RD
KOOTENAI CO ID 247-D4
CARNINE RD
COWLITZ CO WA 187-D7
CAROLINA ST
SKAGIT CO WA 259-J14
CAROLINA ST U.S.-20
LEBANON OR 133-C1
CAROLYN DR
DIST OF N VANCOUVER BC 254-J1
CAROTHERS RD
WHITMAN CO WA 249-A5
CARPENTER RD
KITTITAS CO WA 241-C4
CARPENTER RD NE
LACEY WA 297-J2
THURSTON CO WA 297-J2
CARPENTER RD SE
LACEY WA 297-J6
THURSTON CO WA 181-A7
THURSTON CO WA 297-J6
CARPENTER CREEK RD
WASHINGTON CO OR 198-A1
CARPENTER HILL RD
JACKSON CO OR 234-A2
CARPENTERVILLE FRONTAGE RD
CURRY CO OR 232-C2
CARPER ST SW
THURSTON CO WA 184-B4
CARR RD
ADAMS CO ID 251-A5
KING CO WA 175-C5
RENTON WA 175-C5
CARRALL ST
VANCOUVER BC 254-H10
CARRIE ST
JOSEPHINE CO OR 229-C2
CARROL RD
WASCO CO OR 196-A6
CARROLL AV
BONANZA OR 151-A2
KLAMATH CO OR 151-A2
CARROLL RD
LEWIS CO WA 187-C1
CARROLL WY
LEWIS CO WA 187-A1
CARRS INLET WOLLOCHET
PIERCE CO WA 181-B1
CARSON GULER RD
SKAMANIA CO WA 194-D1
SKAMANIA CO WA 195-A1
CARTER RD SE
MARION CO OR 205-C7
CARTNEY DR
LINN CO OR 210-A3
CARTWRIGHT RD
ADA CO ID 139-C3
ADA CO ID 253-C1
NW CARTY RD
CLARK CO WA 192-C3
S CARUS RD
CLACKAMAS CO OR 199-D6
CLACKAMAS CO OR 200-A6
SW CARUTHERS ST
PORTLAND OR 317-E1
SE CARVER HWY Rt#-212
CLACKAMAS CO OR 200-A3
CASCADE AV
LANGLEY WA 171-A1
CASCADE AV U.S.-30
HOOD RIVER OR 195-C5
HOOD RIVER CO OR 195-C5
NW CASCADE AV
DOUGLAS CO WA 239-A3
East Wenatchee Bench WA 239-A4
CASCADE DR
JOSEPHINE CO OR 233-A5
CASCADE HWY
BURLINGTON WA 260-D4
MARION CO OR 205-B6
SILVERTON OR 205-B6
CASCADE HWY Rt#-9
SEDRO-WOOLLEY WA 161-C6
CASCADE HWY Rt#-20
BURLINGTON WA 260-E4
SEDRO-WOOLLEY WA 161-C6
SEDRO-WOOLLEY WA 260-E4
SKAGIT CO WA 260-E4
CASCADE HWY Rt#-213
CLACKAMAS CO OR 126-A3
CLACKAMAS CO OR 205-C4
MARION CO OR 205-C4
SE CASCADE HWY Rt#-213
CLACKAMAS CO OR 199-D3
CASCADE HWY S Rt#-213
CLACKAMAS CO OR 126-A3
CLACKAMAS CO OR 199-D4
CLACKAMAS CO OR 205-D3
MARION CO OR 205-D3
MOLALLA OR 126-A3

PNW
INDEX

CASCADE HWY S Rt#-213 STREET INDEX NE CHKALOV DR 363

Thomas Bros. Maps ® COPYRIGHT 1999

STREET City State Page-Grid

CASCADE HWY S Rt#-213
OREGON CITY OR 199-D4
CASCADE HWY SE
MARION CO OR 133-C1
MARION CO OR 205-C7
STAYTON OR 133-C1
SUBLIMITY OR 133-C1
CASCADE RD
GEM CO ID 139-B3
SKAGIT CO WA 103-A2
CASCADE ST U.S.-20
DESCHUTES CO OR 211-D5
SISTERS OR 211-D5
CASCADE VW
EVERETT WA 265-E6
CASCADE WY
ELLENSBURG WA 241-B5
W CASCADE WY
Town and Country WA 346-J13
Town and Country WA 347-A13
CASCADE CREEK RD
LINCOLN CO OR 209-C3
CASCADE CREST TR
SKAMANIA CO WA 195-A1
CASCADE ESTATES DR
DESCHUTES CO OR 212-A6
CASCADE HEAD RD
TILLAMOOK CO OR 203-B3
CASCADE LAKES HWY
DESCHUTES CO OR 216-B3
DOUGLAS CO OR 223-C4
CASCADE LOCKS HWY U.S.-30
CASCADE LOCKS OR 194-D6
HOOD RIVER CO OR 194-D6
CASCADIAN WY
SNOHOMISH CO WA 171-C4
CASE RD
MARION CO OR 199-A7
CASE RD SW
THURSTON CO WA 184-C1
CASEY RD
COWLITZ CO WA 187-C6
WALLA WALLA CO WA 121-C2
CASEY CREEK RD
GARFIELD CO WA 122-B1
CASHMUR CT
DESCHUTES CO OR 212-C5
CASHUP NORTH RD
WHITMAN CO WA 114-C3
E CASINO RD
EVERETT WA 268-C4
W CASINO RD
EVERETT WA 267-H5
EVERETT WA 268-A4
CASON RD
TILLAMOOK CO OR 197-D5
SE CASON RD
CLACKAMAS CO OR 199-D4
GLADSTONE OR 199-D4
NE CASPER ST
ROSEBURG OR 334-H7
CASPERS ST Rt#-524
EDMONDS WA 171-A5
SE CASS AV
ROSEBURG OR 334-F8
CASSIA RD
PAYETTE CO ID 139-B3
CASSIA ST
BOISE ID 253-C3
CASTLE DR
BOISE ID 253-C2
CASTLE CREEK RD
JACKSON CO OR 226-D3
JACKSON CO OR 227-A3
OWYHEE CO ID 147-C3
CASTLEMAN RD
DISTRICT OF CHILLIWACK BC 94-C3
CASTLEROCK AV
WENATCHEE WA 238-D4
CASTLE ROCK RD
MALHEUR CO OR 138-A3
CASTLE ROCK TKTR
COWLITZ CO WA 187-A6
CASWELL ST
ADA CO ID 253-B1
CATALA AV SE
OCEAN SHORES WA 298-F4
CATALPA DR
BOISE ID 253-C2
CATCHING CREEK RD
COOS CO OR 140-B3
COOS CO OR 220-D7
E CATCHING SLOUGH RD
COOS CO OR 140-B2
COOS CO OR 220-D1
CATER RD
COLUMBIA CO OR 192-A2
CATHERINE ST
CITY OF VICTORIA BC 256-F8
CATHERINE CREEK LN
UNION CO OR 130-B3
CATLIN ST Rt#-4
KELSO WA 303-C8
CATLOW VALLEY RD
HARNEY CO OR 153-B2
CATLOW VALLEY RD Rt#-205
HARNEY CO OR 153-B1
CATRON RD
WASCO CO OR 196-A6
CATTLE POINT RD
SAN JUAN CO WA 101-C2
CAVALEROS RD
SNOHOMISH CO WA 171-D2
CAVE CREEK RD
SKAMANIA CO WA 195-B1
CAVENDISH RD
CLEARWATER CO ID 123-B2
CLEARWATER CO ID 123-B2
CAVITT CREEK RD
DOUGLAS CO OR 141-B2
CAYS RD
CLALLAM CO WA 166-A6
CAYUSE RD
Mission OR 129-C1
UMATILLA CO OR 129-C1
CC ST
WOODLAND WA 192-B1
CECIL RD
MORROW CO OR 128-B1

CEDAR AV
PIERCE CO WA 182-A6
S CEDAR AV
PASCO WA 343-J8
CEDAR DR
COLUMBIA CO OR 189-B4
COQUITLAM BC 157-B4
PORT COQUITLAM BC 157-B4
W CEDAR DR
WALDPORT OR 328-D5
N CEDAR RD
SPOKANE CO WA 114-B1
S CEDAR RD
SPOKANE WA 246-B5
CEDAR ST
BAKER CITY OR 138-B1
BAKER CO OR 138-B1
BINGEN WA 195-D5
DISTRICT OF MISSION BC 94-B3
KELSO WA 303-D9
SANDPOINT ID 244-A2
CEDAR ST Rt#-5
BENEWAH CO ID 115-A2
BENEWAH CO ID 248-A7
PLUMMER ID 115-A2
CEDAR ST Rt#-231
STEVENS CO WA 106-B3
CEDAR ST U.S.-95
SANDPOINT ID 244-A2
N CEDAR ST
COLFAX WA 122-C1
WALDPORT OR 328-D4
N CEDAR ST Rt#-99
DRAIN OR 219-A3
NE CEDAR ST
ROSEBURG OR 334-F5
S CEDAR ST
SPOKANE WA 348-H12
TACOMA WA 292-D6
TACOMA WA 294-D1
WALDPORT OR 328-D5
S CEDAR ST Rt#-99
DRAIN OR 219-A3
CEDAR WY
MAPLE RIDGE BC 157-C5
CEDAR BURN RD
WASCO CO OR 126-C3
CEDAR CREEK RD
CLARK CO WA 118-A3
LANE CO OR 219-C2
LATAH CO ID 123-B1
CEDARDALE RD
MOUNT VERNON WA 168-B2
MOUNT VERNON WA 260-C14
SKAGIT CO WA 168-B2
CEDAR FALLS RD SE
KING CO WA 176-C6
CEDAR FLAT RD
JOSEPHINE CO OR 149-A2
CEDAR FLATS RD SW
THURSTON CO WA 180-B6
CEDAR GROVE RD
COLUMBIA CO OR 189-A4
KING CO WA 175-D6
KING CO WA 176-A5
CEDAR HILL RD
DISTRICT OF SAANICH BC 159-D5
DISTRICT OF SAANICH BC 256-J6
DISTRICT OF SAANICH BC 257-A1
CEDAR HILL CROSS RD
DISTRICT OF OAK BAY BC 257-B4
DISTRICT OF SAANICH BC 256-H2
DISTRICT OF SAANICH BC 257-B4
SW CEDAR HILLS BLVD
BEAVERTON OR 199-B2
WASHINGTON CO OR 199-B2
CEDARHOME RD
SNOHOMISH CO WA 168-B3
CEDAR LINKS RD
JACKSON CO OR 336-G8
MEDFORD OR 336-G8
N CEDAR PARK RD
LANE CO OR 215-C7
CEDAR RIVER PIPELINE RD
KING CO WA 176-A7
MAPLE VALLEY WA 176-A7
CEDAR SPRINGS RD
GILLIAM CO OR 128-A1
CEDAR SWAMP RD
SKAMANIA CO WA 194-B6
N CEDARVALE LOOP RD
SNOHOMISH CO WA 168-D3
CEDARWOOD AV
BELLINGHAM WA 258-A3
WHATCOM CO WA 258-A3
CEDARWOOD RD NE
MARION CO OR 199-B7
CEDONIA-ADDY Y RD
STEVENS CO WA 105-C3
STEVENS CO WA 106-A3
E CELESTA AV
SPOKANE WA 349-C10
CELILO-WASCO HWY
SHERMAN CO OR 127-C1
CELILO-WASCO HWY Rt#-206
SHERMAN CO OR 127-C1
N CEMENT ST
SPOKANE CO WA 350-H4
CEMETERY RD
ADAMS CO ID 251-B3
ASOTIN CO WA 250-B6
CANYON CO ID 147-B1
KLICKITAT CO WA 119-A3
LANE CO OR 215-B7
SNOHOMISH CO WA 168-C5
WINLOCK WA 187-C3
CEMETERY RD Rt#-55
MARSING ID 147-B1
OWYHEE CO ID 147-B1
CEMETERY RD U.S.-95
OWYHEE CO ID 147-B1
S CEMETERY RD
CLACKAMAS CO OR 205-D4
SW CEMETERY RD
KING CO WA 174-D6
CEMETERY HILL RD
COLUMBIA CO WA 122-A2
CENTENNIAL BLVD
EUGENE OR 330-C5
SPRINGFIELD OR 330-H6

CENTENNIAL BLVD
SPRINGFIELD OR 331-B6
W CENTENNIAL BLVD
LANE CO OR 330-E6
SPRINGFIELD OR 330-E6
E CENTENNIAL ST
CALDWELL ID 147-B1
CENTENNIAL TR
SPOKANE CO WA 348-B5
CENTENNIAL WY U.S.-30
CALDWELL ID 147-B1
CENTER AV Rt#-25
NORTHPORT WA 106-A1
STEVENS CO WA 106-A1
E CENTER AV
PAYETTE ID 139-A3
CENTER DR
DUPONT WA 181-B5
N CENTER PKWY
KENNEWICK WA 342-B8
CENTER RD
JEFFERSON CO WA 109-C1
JEFFERSON CO WA 170-A2
CENTER ST
SUBLIMITY OR 133-C1
N CENTER ST
SPOKANE WA 349-C6
S CENTER ST
TACOMA WA 294-B1
TACOMA WA 295-E1
CENTER ST E
EATONVILLE WA 118-B1
CENTER ST NE
Four Corners OR 204-D6
Four Corners OR 323-F13
MARION CO OR 323-F13
SALEM OR 322-H12
SALEM OR 323-B13
CENTER ST NE Rt#-22
SALEM OR 322-H12
CENTER ST W
EATONVILLE WA 118-B1
CENTER RIDGE MARKET RD
WASCO CO OR 127-B2
CENTER SCHOOL RD
LINN CO OR 210-C3
CENTER ST BRDG Rt#-22
SALEM OR 322-H12
CENTER ST BRDG NE Rt#-22
SALEM OR 322-H12
CENTERVILLE HWY
KLICKITAT CO WA 196-D5
CENTRAL
DESCHUTES CO OR 212-A6
CENTRAL AV
COOS BAY OR 333-G10
GRANTS PASS OR 335-D10
E CENTRAL AV
DOUGLAS CO OR 221-C1
SUTHERLIN OR 221-C1
N CENTRAL AV
MEDFORD OR 336-C11
S CENTRAL AV
MEDFORD OR 336-D12
S CENTRAL AV U.S.-2
WATERVILLE WA 236-C7
SW CENTRAL AV
GRANTS PASS OR 335-E10
CENTRAL AV N
KENT WA 175-C6
CENTRAL AV N Rt#-516
KENT WA 175-C7
CENTRAL AV S
AUBURN WA 175-B7
GRANT CO WA 112-B3
KENT WA 175-B7
KING CO WA 175-B7
QUINCY WA 112-B3
CENTRAL AV S Rt#-281
GRANT CO WA 112-B3
QUINCY WA 112-B3
CENTRAL AV S Rt#-516
KENT WA 175-C7
CENTRAL AV W
OROVILLE WA 104-C1
CENTRAL BLVD U.S.-95
CAMBRIDGE ID 139-B1
WASHINGTON CO ID 139-B1
N CENTRAL BLVD Rt#-42
COQUILLE OR 220-D4
W CENTRAL BLVD Rt#-42
COQUILLE OR 220-D4
CENTRAL DR
MUKILTEO WA 266-C7
CENTRAL RD
LANE CO OR 133-B3
CENTRAL WY NE
KIRKLAND WA 175-C1
CENTRAL FERRY CANYON RD
DOUGLAS CO WA 112-B1
CENTRAL GRADE RD
NEZ PERCE CO ID 250-C3
CENTRALIA ALPHA RD
LEWIS CO WA 118-A1
LEWIS CO WA 184-C6
LEWIS CO WA 299-H8
CENTRAL OREGON HWY U.S.-20
BEND OR 217-C2
BEND OR 332-G7
BURNS OR 145-A1
DESCHUTES CO OR 135-B3
DESCHUTES CO OR 143-C1
DESCHUTES CO OR 144-A1
DESCHUTES CO OR 217-C2
DESCHUTES CO OR 332-G7
HARNEY CO OR 138-A3
HARNEY CO OR 144-B1
HARNEY CO OR 145-A1
HARNEY CO OR 146-A1
HINES OR 145-A1
LAKE CO OR 144-A1
MALHEUR CO OR 138-C3
MALHEUR CO OR 139-A3
MALHEUR CO OR 146-A1
NYSSA OR 139-A3
VALE OR 138-C3
VALE OR 139-A3
S CENTRAL POINT RD
CLACKAMAS CO OR 199-C6

CENTRAL RIDGE RD
LEWIS CO ID 123-C2
LEWIS CO ID 123-C2
NEZ PERCE CO ID 123-C2
NEZ PERCE CO ID 123-C2
PECK ID 123-C2
PECK ID 123-C2
CENTRAL SAANICH RD
DIST OF CENTRAL SAANICH BC 159-C4
CENTRAL VALE DR
HOOD RIVER CO OR 195-C7
CENTRAL VALLEY RD NE
KITSAP CO WA 174-B1
KITSAP CO WA 270-G3
Tracyton WA 270-G3
CENTRAL VALLEY RD NW
KITSAP CO WA 270-G1
CENTURY DR
ALBANY OR 326-H6
LINN CO OR 326-H6
S CENTURY DR
DESCHUTES CO OR 143-A1
DESCHUTES CO OR 216-D7
DESCHUTES CO OR 217-A6
Three Rivers OR 216-D7
Three Rivers OR 217-A7
CENTURY LN
WALLOWA CO OR 130-C2
CENTURY DRIVE HWY Rt#-372
BEND OR 332-A11
DESCHUTES CO OR 216-C4
DESCHUTES CO OR 217-B3
DESCHUTES CO OR 332-A11
CERES HILL RD
LEWIS CO WA 184-A7
LEWIS CO WA 187-A1
SE CHADWICK ST
ROSEBURG OR 334-G8
CHAIN LAKE RD
SNOHOMISH CO WA 110-C1
CHALET RD
DIST OF N SAANICH BC 159-B1
CHALK BUTTE RD
MALHEUR CO OR 139-A3
CHALK HILLS RD NE
DOUGLAS CO WA 112-C1
SW CHAMBERLAIN ST
BEND OR 332-E9
CHAMBERS LN W
UNIVERSITY PLACE WA 181-C3
CHAMBERS RD
WHITMAN CO WA 249-B7
CHAMBERS ST
EUGENE OR 329-G6
LANE CO OR 329-G9
CHAMBERS CREEK RD
PIERCE CO WA 181-C3
STEILACOOM WA 181-C3
UNIVERSITY PLACE WA 181-C3
CHAMBERS CREEK RD W
UNIVERSITY PLACE WA 181-C3
CHAMPOEG RD
MARION CO OR 198-D6
MARION CO OR 199-A7
CHANCE RD
TILLAMOOK CO OR 197-C3
CHANCELLOR BLVD
UNIV ENDOWMENT LANDS BC 156-A4
CHANDLER LN
BAKER CO OR 130-B3
CHANDLER RD
LAKE OSWEGO OR 321-E5
CHANEY RD
LATAH CO ID 249-C2
CHANNEL DR
SKAGIT CO WA 160-D7
CHANNEL VIEW DR
SKAGIT CO WA 160-C5
CHANUTE ST
GRANT CO WA 242-C2
CHAPEL DR
BENTON CO OR 133-B1
PHILOMATH OR 133-B1
CHAPMAN PL
CORVALLIS OR 327-G11
CHAPMAN RD
WASHINGTON CO OR 199-A5
S CHAPMAN RD
LATAH WA 114-C3
SPOKANE CO WA 114-C3
SPOKANE CO WA 247-A5
CHARLES RD
CLALLAM CO WA 165-A5
W CHARLES RD
SPOKANE CO WA 246-A1
CHARLES ST
PORT MOODY BC 157-A4
CHARLESTON BEACH RD W
Navy Yard City WA 270-E13
CHARLOTTE AV W
Navy Yard City WA 270-F12
CHARLTON RD
KITTITAS CO WA 241-C3
CHAROLAIS RD
WALLOWA CO OR 130-C1
E CHARRON RD
YAKIMA CO WA 243-D7
CHARTWELL DR
DIST OF WEST VANCOUVER BC 254-D1
N CHASE AV
PASCO WA 343-D4
N CHASE RD
KOOTENAI CO ID 353-G4
POST FALLS ID 353-G4
CHASE MOUNTAIN RD
KLAMATH CO OR 235-A6
CHATCOLET RD
KOOTENAI CO ID 115-A2
KOOTENAI CO ID 115-A2
CHATHAM HILL DR
Sunnyslope WA 238-D3
CHAUFTY RD
LEWIS CO WA 187-B4
CHEAM AV Rt#-9
DISTRICT OF KENT BC 94-C3
CHEESE FACTORY RD
KLAMATH CO OR 151-A2
CHEHALEM DR
NEWBERG OR 198-D5

CHEHALEM DR
YAMHILL CO OR 198-D5
CHEHALIS AV
GRAYS HARBOR CO WA 183-A2
N CHELAN AV
DOUGLAS CO WA 236-C7
WATERVILLE WA 236-C7
N CHELAN AV Rt#-285
WENATCHEE WA 238-D4
N CHELAN AV U.S.-2
WATERVILLE WA 236-C7
S CHELAN AV
WATERVILLE WA 236-C7
S CHELAN AV Rt#-285
WENATCHEE WA 238-D4
WENATCHEE WA 239-A4
S CHELAN ST
RITZVILLE WA 113-C3
CHELAN BUTTE RD
CHELAN CO WA 236-C3
CHELAN FALLS RD
CHELAN CO WA 236-D3
CHELAN FALLS RD Rt#-150
CHELAN CO WA 236-D3
CHELAN FALLS RD U.S.-97
CHELAN CO WA 236-D3
CHELAN-OKANOGAN HWY
Sunnyslope WA 238-D3
CHELAN-STEHEKIN FERRY
CHELAN WA 236-B2
CHELAN CO WA 112-A1
CHELAN CO WA 236-B2
CHEMAWA RD N
KEIZER OR 322-H5
KEIZER OR 323-A5
CHEMAWA RD NE
KEIZER OR 323-A5
MARION CO OR 204-D4
MARION CO OR 323-E4
SALEM OR 204-D4
SALEM OR 323-E4
CHEMEKETA ST NE
SALEM OR 322-H12
CHEMICAL RD Rt#-397
Finley WA 121-A3
Finley WA 343-G12
KENNEWICK WA 343-F11
CHENEY CREEK RD
JOSEPHINE CO OR 229-A7
CHENEY-PLAZA RD
SPOKANE CO WA 114-B2
S CHENEY-PLAZA RD
CHENEY WA 246-A7
SPOKANE CO WA 114-B2
SPOKANE CO WA 246-A7
W CHENEY-SPANGLE RD
CHENEY WA 246-A7
SPOKANE CO WA 114-B2
SPOKANE CO WA 246-A7
S CHENEY-SPOKANE RD
SPOKANE WA 246-A7
SPOKANE WA 348-H14
SPOKANE CO WA 246-A7
W CHENEY-SPOKANE RD
SPOKANE WA 246-B5
SPOKANE CO WA 246-B5
CHENNAULT BEACH DR
MUKILTEO WA 266-C7
CHENNAULT BEACH RD
MUKILTEO WA 266-D7
MUKILTEO WA 267-E7
CHENOWETH RD
WASCO CO OR 196-B7
CHENOWETH CREEK RD
THE DALLES OR 196-B7
WASCO CO OR 196-B7
CHEROKEE
CROOK CO OR 213-D7
CHEROKEE RD
GRANT CO WA 242-D2
CHEROKEE CREEK RD
MALHEUR CO OR 154-B2
NE CHERRY AV
KEIZER OR 322-J6
KEIZER OR 323-A6
CHERRY AV NE
KEIZER OR 323-A6
SALEM OR 323-A6
CHERRY LN
CANYON CO ID 147-B1
LINN CO OR 207-C5
MEDFORD OR 234-B1
E CHERRY LN
CANYON CO ID 147-C1
NE CHERRY LN
JEFFERSON CO OR 208-C4
W CHERRY LN
ADA CO ID 147-C1
ADA CO ID 253-A3
MERIDIAN ID 253-A3
CHERRY ST
PORT TOWNSEND WA 263-G4
WENATCHEE WA 238-D4
E CHERRY ST
SEATTLE WA 278-C6
WALLA WALLA WA 345-A7
W CHERRY ST
WALLA WALLA WA 344-J7
WALLA WALLA WA 345-A7
W CHERRY ST Rt#-507
CENTRALIA WA 299-E4
SE CHERRY BLOSSOM DR
PORTLAND OR 315-J7
CHERRY CREEK RD
BENEWAH CO ID 248-C7
WHITMAN CO WA 114-B3
CHERRY HEIGHTS RD
WASCO CO OR 196-B7
CHERRY HILL RD
GRANGER WA 120-A2
CHERRY LANE RD
NEZ PERCE CO ID 123-B2
CHESNIMNUS LN
WALLOWA CO OR 131-A1
CHESTER AV
GRAYS HARBOR CO WA 183-B3
E CHESTER RD
Colby WA 271-F13
KITSAP CO WA 271-F13

CHESTERFIELD AV
CITY OF N VANCOUVER BC 255-B5
E CHESTNUT AV
GENESEE ID 250-C1
NE CHESTNUT AV
ROSEBURG OR 334-F5
W CHESTNUT AV
GENESEE ID 250-C1
LATAH CO ID 250-C1
CHESTNUT DR
DESCHUTES CO OR 211-D5
WALLA WALLA WA 345-D9
Walla Walla East WA 345-D9
CHESTNUT ST
ASHLAND OR 337-B6
ASOTIN CO WA 250-B4
CLARKSTON WA 250-B4
KELSO WA 303-C9
E CHESTNUT ST
WALLA WALLA WA 345-C8
Walla Walla East WA 345-C8
S CHESTNUT ST
SPOKANE WA 348-G12
W CHESTNUT ST
WALLA WALLA WA 344-J9
WALLA WALLA WA 345-A9
CHETCO AV U.S.-101
BROOKINGS OR 232-C6
W CHEWACK RD
OKANOGAN CO WA 104-A2
CHEWILIKEN RD
OKANOGAN CO WA 105-A2
CHEWILIKEN VALLEY RD
OKANOGAN CO WA 104-C2
E CHEWUCH RD
OKANOGAN CO WA 104-A2
CHEYNE RD
KLAMATH CO OR 235-D7
CHIAWA LOOP RD
CHELAN CO WA 111-C1
CHICAGO ST
PASCO WA 343-H6
CHICAGO ST SE
TURNER OR 325-G12
CHICKADEE DR
JEFFERSON CO OR 212-C2
CHICKAHOMINY RD
LANE CO OR 133-A3
CHICKEN DINNER RD
CANYON CO ID 147-B1
CHICO WY NW
BREMERTON WA 270-A7
KITSAP CO WA 270-B3
Silverdale WA 270-B3
Tracyton WA 270-A7
CHIEF MARTIN RD
WHATCOM CO WA 158-C7
CHILBERG RD
LA CONNER WA 167-D1
SKAGIT CO WA 167-D1
SKAGIT CO WA 168-A1
E CHILCO AV
KOOTENAI CO ID 245-A3
SW CHILDS RD
CLACKAMAS CO OR 199-C4
CHILKO DR
COQUITLAM BC 157-A5
CHILLIWACK LAKE RD
BRITISH COLUMBIA 102-C1
BRITISH COLUMBIA 103-A1
DISTRICT OF CHILLIWACK BC 102-C1
CHILOQUIN HWY
CHILOQUIN OR 231-C3
KLAMATH CO OR 231-C3
S CHILOQUIN RD
CHILOQUIN OR 231-D4
KLAMATH CO OR 231-D4
CHILOQUIN CAMP RD
KLAMATH CO OR 142-C3
CHILOQUIN RIDGE RD
KLAMATH CO OR 231-D4
CHILVERS RD
LEWIS CO WA 184-A7
CHIMACUM RD
Hadlock-Irondale WA 170-A1
JEFFERSON CO WA 170-A1
CHIMNEY CREEK RD
MALHEUR CO OR 138-A3
MALHEUR CO OR 146-A1
CHIN RD
KLAMATH CO OR 235-D7
CHINA CREEK RD
DOUGLAS CO WA 105-A3
CHINA GARDEN RD
KALAMA WA 189-D6
CHINA GRADE RD
SISKIYOU CO CA 149-A3
CHINA HAT RD
DESCHUTES CO OR 135-B3
DESCHUTES CO OR 143-B1
DESCHUTES CO OR 217-C4
DESCHUTES CO OR 332-D14
Deschutes River Woods OR 332-D14
CHINA MOUNTAIN RD
CURRY CO OR 224-B6
E CHINDEN BLVD U.S.-20
ADA CO ID 253-B2
BOISE ID 253-B2
EAGLE ID 253-B2
GARDEN CITY ID 253-C2
W CHINDEN BLVD U.S.-20
ADA CO ID 147-C1
ADA CO ID 253-A2
CHINOOK PASS HWY Rt#-410
PIERCE CO WA 111-A3
CHINOOK VALLEY RD
PACIFIC CO WA 186-B6
CHIPMUNK
JEFFERSON CO OR 212-C2
CHIPMUNK TR
DOUGLAS CO WA 239-B1
CHIPPEWA
CROOK CO OR 213-D7
CHIWAWA LP
CHELAN CO WA 111-C1
CHIWAWA RIVER RD
CHELAN CO WA 103-C3
CHELAN CO WA 111-C1
NE CHKALOV DR
VANCOUVER WA 307-J6

PNW INDEX

PNW

INDEX

COMO LAKE AV — STREET INDEX — CROOKS RD 365

PNW
INDEX

STREET / City State / Page-Grid

COMO LAKE AV
COQUITLAM BC 157-A4
DISTRICT OF COQUITLAM BC 156-D4
COMOX RD
NANAIMO BC 93-A3
COMPTON LN
LANE CO OR 210-A6
COMPTON RD
BRITISH COLUMBIA 159-B5
SE COMPTON RD
CLACKAMAS CO OR 200-C3
COMSTOCK RD
SUTHERLIN OR 221-C1
CONCOMLY RD NE
MARION CO OR 205-A3
CONCONULLY RD
CONCONULLY WA 104-B2
OKANOGAN CO WA 104-B2
CONCRETE SAUK VALLEY RD
CONCRETE WA 102-C2
SKAGIT CO WA 102-C2
SKAGIT CO WA 103-A2
CONDON RD
CLARK CO WA 193-A1
CONDON WY W
SEATTLE WA 276-D1
CONGER CREEK RD
OKANOGAN CO WA 104-B2
CONIFER BLVD
CORVALLIS OR 207-B5
CORVALLIS OR 327-J5
CONIFER ST NE
MARION CO OR 205-A5
CONKLIN RD
DESCHUTES CO OR 217-A5
S CONKLIN RD
SPOKANE CO WA 247-A5
CONKLING PARK RD
KOOTENAI CO ID 115-A2
KOOTENAI CO ID 115-A2
KOOTENAI CO ID 248-A6
CONNARN RD
DESCHUTES CO OR 212-B7
CONNECTICUT AV
NORTH BEND OR 333-G4
CONNECTICUT AV SE
Four Corners OR 325-F2
SALEM OR 325-F2
W CONNECTICUT ST
BELLINGHAM WA 258-C4
CONNECTING RD
MAPLE RIDGE BC 157-C5
PITT MEADOWS BC 157-C5
CONNELL HILL RD
GARFIELD CO WA 122-C2
CONNELLS PRAIRIE RD
PIERCE CO WA 182-C4
CONNELLY RD
SNOHOMISH CO WA 171-D4
CONNER RD
NEZ PERCE CO ID 250-D2
CONNER RD SE
THURSTON CO WA 184-C4
CONNETT RD
CLACKAMAS CO OR 200-D3
E CONNOR RD
SPOKANE CO WA 246-D6
CONRAD RD
LEWIS CO WA 187-C2
CONRADI RD
LEWIS CO WA 187-C2
CONRAD JOHNSON
PIERCE CO WA 182-C3
CONSER DR
CORVALLIS OR 207-B5
CONSER RD
LINN CO OR 207-C3
LINN CO OR 326-E1
MILLERSBURG OR 326-E1
CONSTANCE AV
TOWN OF ESQUIMALT BC 256-C8
CONWAY RD
SKAGIT CO WA 168-B2
COOK AV
DESCHUTES CO OR 217-B1
JEFFERSON CO WA 263-B3
PORT TOWNSEND WA 263-D1
NE COOK LN
JEFFERSON CO OR 208-C2
COOK RD
BAKER CO OR 130-C3
ISLAND CO WA 167-B4
LEWIS CO WA 187-A2
SEDRO-WOOLLEY WA 161-B5
SKAGIT CO WA 161-B5
YAKIMA CO WA 120-A2
SW COOK RD
WASHINGTON CO OR 198-C1
COOK ST
CITY OF VICTORIA BC 256-J6
DISTRICT OF SAANICH BC 256-H5
COOK CREEK RD
TILLAMOOK CO OR 191-D4
COOKE RD
KLICKITAT CO WA 196-A4
COOKE CANYON RD
KITTITAS CO WA 241-D4
COOKS CREEK RD
LINCOLN CO OR 206-D3
COOKS HILL RD
CENTRALIA WA 299-A4
LEWIS CO WA 299-A4
COOK-UNDERWOOD RD
SKAMANIA CO WA 195-B4
COOLEY RD
DESCHUTES CO OR 217-C1
COOLEY RD NE
MARION CO OR 205-B2
WOODBURN OR 205-B2
W COOLIDGE AV
YAKIMA CO WA 243-A7
COOMBS RD
YAKIMA CO WA 243-D7
COOMBS CANYON RD
UMATILLA CO OR 129-B1
COON CREEK RD
BENEWAH CO ID 248-A7
COOPER RD
LEWIS CO WA 187-D4
LINN CO OR 207-C3
E COOPER RD
SPOKANE CO WA 247-A1
COOPER CREEK RD
DOUGLAS CO OR 221-C1
COOPER HOLLOW RD
POLK CO OR 204-A7
COOPER MOUNTAIN RD
CHELAN CO WA 236-C2
COOPER POINT RD NW
OLYMPIA WA 296-E2
THURSTON CO WA 180-C5
THURSTON CO WA 296-E2
COOPER POINT RD SW
OLYMPIA WA 296-E5
COOPER SPUR RD
HOOD RIVER CO OR 202-C2
COOS BAY-ROSEBURG HWY Rt#-42
COOS CO OR 140-C2
COOS CO OR 220-D4
COQUILLE OR 220-D4
DOUGLAS CO OR 140-C3
DOUGLAS CO OR 141-A2
DOUGLAS CO OR 221-A6
MYRTLE POINT OR 140-C2
WINSTON OR 221-B6
COOS BAY-ROSEBURG HWY Rt#-99
DOUGLAS CO OR 221-B6
DOUGLAS CO OR 334-D14
WINSTON OR 221-B6
COOS BAY-WAGON RD
DOUGLAS CO OR 141-A2
DOUGLAS CO OR 221-A5
COOS CITY-SUMNER RD
COOS CO OR 140-B2
COOS CO OR 220-D2
COOS RIVER HWY
COOS BAY OR 220-D1
COOS CO OR 140-B2
COOS CO OR 218-D7
COOS CO OR 220-D1
COOS RIVER RD
COOS CO OR 140-B2
S COOS RIVER RD
COOS CO OR 140-C2
COPALIS BEACH RD
GRAYS HARBOR CO WA 177-B4
COPCO RD
KLAMATH CO OR 231-C5
SISKIYOU CO CA 150-A3
COPE RD
LEWIS CO WA 187-B4
COPELAND CREEK RD
DOUGLAS CO OR 222-C4
COPLEY RD
CROOK CO OR 213-B6
COPPEI AV U.S.-12
WAITSBURG WA 122-A2
COPPER QUEEN RD
JOSEPHINE CO OR 229-B2
COQUILLE-BANDON HWY Rt#-42S
BANDON OR 220-C6
COOS CO OR 220-C6
COQUILLE OR 220-C6
COQUILLE-FAIRVIEW RD
COOS CO OR 140-C2
COOS CO OR 220-D4
COQUILLE OR 220-D4
COQUILLE-FAT ELK RD
COOS CO OR 220-D5
W CORAL SEA AV
OAK HARBOR WA 167-C3
CORBET DR
BREMERTON WA 270-F9
KITSAP CO WA 270-F9
CORBETT AV
PORTLAND OR 317-F1
CORDATA PKWY
BELLINGHAM WA 158-D7
CORDON RD
Four Corners OR 323-G14
Four Corners OR 325-G1
Hayesville OR 323-G8
MARION CO OR 323-G10
MARION CO OR 325-G1
SALEM OR 323-G10
SALEM OR 325-G3
CORDOVA ST
VANCOUVER BC 254-H10
VANCOUVER BC 255-A10
CORDOVA BAY RD
DISTRICT OF SAANICH BC 159-C5
CORDUROY RD
KELSO WA 303-G8
COREY RD
JACKSON CO OR 230-D6
CORKSCREW CANYON RD
STEVENS CO WA 114-A1
CORKSCREW CANYON RD Rt#-291
STEVENS CO WA 114-B1
STEVENS CO WA 246-A1
NW CORNELIUS PASS RD
HILLSBORO OR 199-A1
MULTNOMAH CO OR 192-A6
WASHINGTON CO OR 192-A7
WASHINGTON CO OR 199-A1
CORNELIUS-SCHEFFLIN RD
WASHINGTON CO OR 198-C1
NE CORNELL RD
HILLSBORO OR 198-D1
HILLSBORO OR 199-A1
NW CORNELL RD
BEAVERTON OR 199-A1
HILLSBORO OR 199-A1
MULTNOMAH CO OR 199-B1
PORTLAND OR 199-B1
PORTLAND OR 199-B1
PORTLAND OR 312-A5
WASHINGTON CO OR 199-B1
CORNETT RD
CROOK CO OR 213-B5
CORNWALL AV
BELLINGHAM WA 258-D5
VANCOUVER BC 254-C11
CORONA AV
MEDFORD OR 336-D9
CORRAL CREEK RD
MALHEUR CO OR 154-C2
YAMHILL CO OR 198-D5
YAMHILL CO OR 199-A6
CORSON AV S
SEATTLE WA 282-B7
CORVALLIS RD
INDEPENDENCE OR 204-B7
POLK CO OR 204-B7
POLK CO OR 207-B2
POLK CO OR 207-B3
CORVALLIS-LEBANON HWY Rt#-34
LEBANON OR 133-C1
LINN CO OR 133-C1
LINN CO OR 207-B6
TANGENT OR 207-B6
CORVALLIS-NEWPORT HWY Rt#-34
CORVALLIS OR 327-H11
LINN CO OR 207-B6
LINN CO OR 327-H11
CORVALLIS-NEWPORT HWY U.S.-20
BENTON CO OR 133-A1
CORVALLIS OR 133-A1
CORVALLIS OR 327-E11
LINCOLN CO OR 133-A1
LINCOLN CO OR 206-B4
NEWPORT OR 206-B4
PHILOMATH OR 133-A1
TOLEDO OR 206-B4
COTTAGE AV
CASHMERE WA 238-C2
CLATSOP CO OR 301-G3
GEARHART OR 301-G3
COTTAGE ST
MEDFORD OR 336-D12
E COTTAGE GROVE CONN
COTTAGE GROVE OR 215-B7
COTTAGE GRVE-LORANE RD
COTTAGE GROVE OR 215-A6
LANE CO OR 133-B3
LANE CO OR 215-A6
COTTAGE GRVE RESERVOIR RD
LANE CO OR 219-D2
COTTON RD
CITY OF N VANCOUVER BC 255-E7
DIST OF N VANCOUVER BC 255-E7
COTTONWOOD BAY
KOOTENAI CO ID 115-A2
KOOTENAI CO ID 115-A2
KOOTENAI CO ID 248-A5
COTTONWOOD DR
Birch Bay WA 158-B4
MAPLE RIDGE BC 157-D6
RICHLAND WA 341-D2
COTTONWOOD RD
ADAMS CO ID 139-C1
STEVENS CO WA 114-A1
WALLA WALLA CO WA 121-C3
WALLA WALLA CO WA 122-A3
WALLA WALLA CO WA 345-E13
COTTONWOOD ST Rt#-19
ARLINGTON OR 128-A1
SW COTTONWOOD ST
GRANTS PASS OR 335-C10
COTTONWOOD BUTTE RD
IDAHO CO ID 123-B3
COTTONWOOD CANYON RD
YAKIMA CO WA 119-C2
YAKIMA CO WA 243-A7
COTTONWOOD CREEK RD
NEZ PERCE CO ID 123-B2
STEVENS CO WA 106-B3
COUCH RD
DESCHUTES CO OR 217-A2
COUCH MARKET RD
DESCHUTES CO OR 212-B7
COUGAR RD
CROOK CO OR 135-C1
JEFFERSON CO OR 212-C3
COUGAR WY
SKAMANIA CO WA 195-B1
COUGAR BEND RD
LANE CO OR 219-D4
COUGAR CREEK RD
ASOTIN CO WA 122-C3
E COUGAR GULCH RD
KOOTENAI CO ID 247-D4
KOOTENAI CO ID 354-H14
KOOTENAI CO ID 355-A13
W COUGAR GULCH RD
KOOTENAI CO ID 247-D4
COUGAR MOUNTAIN RD
LANE CO OR 219-D3
COUGAR SMITH RD
GRAYS HARBOR CO WA 178-D3
GRAYS HARBOR CO WA 179-A3
COUGHANOUR LN
UNION CO OR 130-A3
COULEE BLVD Rt#-155
ELECTRIC CITY WA 237-C3
GRANT CO WA 237-C3
COULSON RD
LEWIS CO WA 187-D2
COUNCIL RD
ADAMS CO ID 139-C1
VALLEY CO ID 251-C7
COUNCIL ST Rt#-47
FOREST GROVE OR 198-B1
COUNTRY LN
LANE CO OR 210-B7
COUNTRY RD
LINN CO OR 207-B7
COUNTRY CLUB DR
BENTON CO OR 327-A12
CORVALLIS OR 327-A12
COUNTRY CLUB RD
CLACKAMAS CO OR 320-C5
EUGENE OR 329-J4
EUGENE OR 330-A4
HOOD RIVER CO OR 195-C6
LAKE OSWEGO OR 320-C5
WHITMAN CO WA 249-A6
SW COUNTRY CLUB RD
CLACKAMAS OR 320-D5
CLACKAMAS OR 321-E5
LAKE OSWEGO OR 320-D5
SW COUNTRY CLUB RD
LAKE OSWEGO OR 321-E5
COUNTRY CLUB RD NE
KITSAP CO WA 174-D2
N COUNTRY HOMES BLVD
Country Homes WA 346-H13
SPOKANE WA 346-H13
SPOKANE WA 347-A12
Town and Country WA 346-H13
COUNTRY QUARRY RD
SKAMANIA CO WA 194-B6
COUNTRYSIDE RD
CLACKAMAS CO OR 199-B6
COUNTY RD Rt#-27
WHITMAN CO WA 114-C3
COUNTY 1 RD
LA CENTER WA 192-C1
COUNTY 5 RD Rt#-503
CLARK CO WA 193-A2
COUNTY RD 5
CLARK CO WA 193-A1
COUNTY RD 12
CLARK CO WA 193-C2
COUNTY RD 139
MODOC CO CA 152-A3
COUNTY RD 722
UMATILLA CO OR 129-C1
COUNTY RD 725
UMATILLA CO OR 129-C1
COUNTY RD 802
UMATILLA CO OR 129-B1
COUNTY RD 821
UMATILLA CO OR 129-B1
COUNTY RD 900
Mission OR 129-B1
UMATILLA CO OR 129-B1
COUNTY RD 900 U.S.-30
PENDLETON OR 129-B1
UMATILLA CO OR 129-B1
COUNTY RD 1046
UMATILLA CO OR 129-C2
COUNTY LINE RD
BENTON CO WA 120-B3
CLATSOP CO OR 191-D2
DOUGLAS CO OR 214-A5
GEM CO ID 139-B3
SKAGIT CO WA 168-B3
WASCO CO OR 135-A1
COUNTY WELL RD
BENTON CO WA 120-C3
COUPLAND RD
CLACKAMAS CO OR 200-C6
ESTACADA OR 200-C6
NW COURT AV
PENDLETON OR 129-B1
NW COURT AV U.S.-30
PENDLETON OR 129-B1
SE COURT AV U.S.-30
PENDLETON OR 129-B1
SW COURT AV U.S.-30
PENDLETON OR 129-B1
SE COURT PL
PENDLETON OR 129-B1
SW COURT PL
PENDLETON OR 129-B1
SW COURT PL Rt#-37
PENDLETON OR 129-B1
COURT ST
DUFUR OR 127-B2
JACKSON CO OR 336-C9
MEDFORD OR 336-C10
COURT ST Rt#-74
HEPPNER OR 128-C2
E COURT ST
GOLDENDALE WA 127-C1
NE COURT ST
DUFUR OR 127-B2
W COURT ST
FRANKLIN CO WA 340-H14
FRANKLIN CO WA 341-J2
FRANKLIN CO WA 342-B4
FRANKLIN CO WA 343-B6
GOLDENDALE WA 127-C1
PASCO WA 341-J2
PASCO WA 343-B6
COURT ST NE
SALEM OR 322-H13
COURTNEY RD
WASHINGTON CO OR 198-D5
YAMHILL CO OR 198-D5
COURTNEY CREEK DR
LINN CO OR 210-D3
COURTNEY CREEK RD
LINN CO OR 210-D3
COUSE CREEK RD
ASOTIN CO WA 123-A3
ASOTIN CO WA 123-A3
COUSINS RD
LEWIS CO WA 187-B1
COVE HWY Rt#-237
COVE OR 130-A2
UNION OR 130-A2
UNION CO OR 130-A2
E COVE HWY Rt#-237
UNION OR 130-B2
COVE RD
KITTITAS CO WA 241-A6
WASHINGTON CO ID 139-B2
SW COVE RD
KING CO WA 174-D5
COVE ORCHARD RD
YAMHILL CO OR 198-B4
COVERED BRIDGE RD
WAHKIAKUM CO WA 117-A2
COVILLE RD
POLK CO OR 204-A5
COVINGTON WY SE
COVINGTON WA 175-D7
COVINGTON-SAWYER RD
KING CO WA 182-D1
COW CAMP RD
DESCHUTES CO OR 211-C5
WASHINGTON CO ID 139-A1
COW CREEK RD
DOUGLAS CO OR 141-A3
DOUGLAS CO OR 225-A3
NEZ PERCE CO ID 250-B2
RIDDLE OR 225-A3
WASHINGTON CO ID 139-B1
W COW CREEK RD
MALHEUR CO OR 146-C3
COWEN PL NE
SEATTLE WA 274-C4
COW HOLLOW RD
MALHEUR CO OR 139-A3
N COWICHE RD
YAKIMA CO WA 119-C1
W COWICHE CANYON RD
YAKIMA CO WA 243-A6
COWICHE MILL RD
YAKIMA CO WA 119-C1
COWICHE-TIETON RD
TIETON WA 119-C1
YAKIMA CO WA 119-C1
COWLITZ AV
CASTLE ROCK WA 187-C7
COWLITZ CO WA 187-C7
E COWLITZ AV
CASTLE ROCK WA 187-C7
COWLITZ ST Rt#-505
LEWIS CO WA 187-D4
TOLEDO WA 187-D4
COWLITZ WY
KELSO WA 303-D8
COWLITZ GARDEN RD
COWLITZ CO WA 303-D4
COWLITZ LOOP RD
LEWIS CO WA 187-C4
COWLITZ RIDGE RD
LEWIS CO WA 187-C4
COX RD
DOUGLAS CO OR 219-B3
COX CREEK RD
DOUGLAS CO OR 219-C3
NW COYER AV
DESCHUTES CO OR 212-C4
COYLE RD
JEFFERSON CO WA 170-A4
NW COYNER AV
DESCHUTES CO OR 212-D4
Terrebonne OR 212-D4
COYOTE
CROOK CO OR 213-D6
SW COYOTE
DESCHUTES CO OR 212-C6
COYOTE CREEK RD
JOSEPHINE CO OR 229-B1
COYOTE GRADE RD
NEZ PERCE CO ID 250-D2
E COZZA DR U.S.-2
SPOKANE WA 347-A14
CRAB CREEK RD
GRANT CO WA 120-C1
E CRAB CREEK RD
LINCOLN CO OR 209-D4
CRACKER CREEK RD
BAKER CO OR 138-A1
CRAIG LN
CROOK CO OR 213-D6
N CRAIG RD
SPOKANE CO WA 246-A4
S CRAIG RD
SPOKANE CO WA 246-A4
CRAIGFLOWER RD
BRITISH COLUMBIA 256-D6
TOWN OF ESQUIMALT BC 256-D6
TOWN OF VIEW ROYAL BC 256-D6
CRAIGFLOWER RD Rt#-1A
TOWN OF VIEW ROYAL BC 256-A5
CRAIG JUNCTION RD
LEWIS CO ID 123-B2
LEWIS CO ID 123-B2
CRAMER RD
CLARK CO WA 192-D4
CRAMER RD KPN
PIERCE CO WA 174-A7
CRANBERRY RD
GRAYS HARBOR CO WA 183-B3
PACIFIC CO WA 186-A4
N CRANE RD
WASHINGTON CO ID 139-C2
CRANE-BUCHANAN RD
HARNEY CO OR 145-C1
CRANE CREEK RD
WASHINGTON CO ID 139-B2
CRANE CREEK RESV RD
WASHINGTON CO ID 139-B2
CRANE ORCHARD
DOUGLAS CO WA 112-B1
CRANE ORCHARD RD
DOUGLAS CO WA 104-B3
CRANES RD NW
DOUGLAS CO WA 104-B3
CRANE-VENATOR RD
HARNEY CO OR 145-C2
HARNEY CO OR 146-A2
MALHEUR CO OR 146-A2
CRANLEY DR
DISTRICT OF SURREY BC 158-A2
CRATER LP
JEFFERSON CO OR 212-C2
CRATER CREEK MTWY
JACKSON CO OR 227-A2
CRATER CREEK RD
KLAMATH CO OR 227-C5
CRATER LAKE AV
JACKSON CO OR 336-F3
MEDFORD OR 336-E11
CRATER LAKE HWY Rt#-62
EAGLE POINT OR 230-D4
JACKSON CO OR 149-C1
JACKSON CO OR 150-A1
JACKSON CO OR 226-C7
JACKSON CO OR 227-D7
JACKSON CO OR 230-D4
JACKSON CO OR 336-F3
KLAMATH CO OR 227-D7
KLAMATH CO OR 231-C2
MEDFORD OR 336-D8
SHADY COVE OR 230-D4
White City OR 230-D6
CRATER LAKE RD
MALHEUR CO OR 146-C2
CRATER LAKE NORTH HWY
DOUGLAS CO OR 223-C7
DOUGLAS CO OR 227-C2
KLAMATH CO OR 227-C2
CRAW RD
ISLAND CO WA 171-A1
NE CRAWFORD DR
KITSAP CO WA 170-C5
CRAWFORD LN
YAMHILL CO OR 198-C6
CRAWFORD RD
DESCHUTES CO OR 217-A6
LINCOLN CO OR 206-C1
CRAWFORD ST
Appleyard WA 239-A5
WENATCHEE WA 238-D5
WENATCHEE WA 239-A5
E CRAWFORD ST
DEER PARK WA 114-B1
W CRAWFORD ST
DEER PARK WA 114-B1
CREASY RD
WHATCOM CO WA 158-C4
CREEK DR
LINN CO OR 210-A2
CREEK RD
HARNEY CO OR 137-B3
SISKIYOU CO CA 149-A3
E CREEK RD
TILLAMOOK CO OR 197-D5
CREEK BEND RD
LINN CO OR 210-A2
CREGO HILL RD
LEWIS CO WA 187-A1
CRESCENT AV
EUGENE OR 215-B1
KELSO WA 303-D6
CRESCENT RD
CITY OF VICTORIA BC 257-B11
DISTRICT OF OAK BAY BC 257-B11
DISTRICT OF SURREY BC 158-A1
CRESCENT RD NW
SALEM OR 322-E12
CRESCENT BEACH RD
CLALLAM CO WA 164-C5
CRESCENT BEACH RD KPN
PIERCE CO WA 181-A1
CRESCENT CUT-OFF RD
KLAMATH CO OR 142-C1
CRESCENT HARBOR RD
ISLAND CO WA 167-C2
OAK HARBOR WA 167-C2
CRESCENT LAKE HWY
KLAMATH CO OR 142-B1
CRESCENT VALLEY DR NW
PIERCE CO WA 174-C7
CRESCENT VALLEY RD SE
KITSAP CO WA 174-C6
CREST DR
EUGENE OR 329-J10
EUGENE OR 330-A10
LANE CO OR 329-H11
W CREST DR
EUGENE OR 329-H11
LANE CO OR 329-H11
CRESTLINE BLVD NW
OLYMPIA WA 296-G2
CRESTLINE DR
LINCOLN CO OR 328-D9
WALDPORT OR 328-E5
S CRESTLINE DR
WALDPORT OR 328-E5
N CRESTLINE ST
SPOKANE WA 347-D13
SPOKANE WA 349-D2
SPOKANE CO WA 347-D13
CRESTVIEW DR
MASON CO WA 180-B3
CRESTVIEW LN
SKAGIT CO WA 161-A6
CRESTVIEW RD
CROOK CO OR 213-D5
Sunnyslope WA 238-D3
CREVISTON DR NW
PIERCE CO WA 174-B7
CREVISTON RD KPS
PIERCE CO WA 181-A3
CRISP LN
LANE CO OR 215-B5
CRITCHFIELD RD
ASOTIN CO WA 250-B5
Vineland WA 250-B5
CRITES RD
SHERMAN CO OR 127-C2
CRITESER RD
DOUGLAS CO OR 221-A5
S CRITSER RD
CLACKAMAS CO OR 199-D6
CROCKER LN
ALBANY OR 326-A4
CROCKER RD
Santa Clara OR 215-A1
CROFT AV U.S.-2
GOLD BAR WA 110-C1
SNOHOMISH CO WA 110-C1
CROFT LAKE RD
COOS CO OR 224-B1
CROISAN CREEK RD S
MARION CO OR 324-D5
SALEM OR 324-D5
CROMWELL DR NW
PIERCE CO WA 181-B2
CRONIN RD
CROOK CO OR 213-A6
CROOK DR
LINN CO OR 210-A3
CROOKED CREEK RD
LANE CO OR 210-D5
MALHEUR CO OR 146-B3
MALHEUR CO OR 154-B1
CROOKED CREEK RANGE RD
MALHEUR CO OR 154-A1
CROOKED FINGER RD
MARION CO OR 205-D4
CROOKED FINGER RD NE
MARION CO OR 126-A3
CROOKED MILE RD
GRANITE FALLS WA 102-C3
SNOHOMISH CO WA 102-C3
CROOKED RIVER HWY Rt#-27
CROOK CO OR 135-C3
CROOK CO OR 213-C6
DESCHUTES CO OR 135-C3
PRINEVILLE OR 213-C6
CROOKS RD
GRANT CO WA 237-B3

366 CROOKS CREEK RD **STREET INDEX** DEVERELL RD

STREET City State Page-Grid

CROOKS CREEK RD
JOSEPHINE CO OR 233-C1
CROSBY RD
Ault Field WA 167-B2
BENTON CO WA 120-C2
ISLAND CO WA 167-B2
CROSBY RD NE
MARION CO OR 205-A1
CROSBY ST Rt#-27
TEKOA WA 114-C3
CROSS RD
KLAMATH CO OR 235-C6
CROSS CREEK RD
DIST OF WEST VANCOUVER BC 254-D1
CROSS ISLAND RD
ISLAND CO WA 167-D4
E CROSSROAD LN
LANE CO OR 210-A6
N CROSS STATE HWY Rt#-20
SEDRO-WOOLLEY WA 161-C5
SKAGIT CO WA 161-C5
CROSSWINDS
DESCHUTES CO OR 217-C1
CROW RD
JOSEPHINE CO OR 229-A4
LANE CO OR 133-B3
LANE CO OR 215-A2
CROW CREEK RD
WALLOWA CO OR 130-C2
WALLOWA CO OR 131-A1
CROWELL LN
NORTH BEND OR 333-F5
CROWFOOT RD
JACKSON CO OR 149-C1
CROWLEY RD
MALHEUR CO OR 138-B3
MALHEUR CO OR 146-B1
POLK CO OR 204-B5
CROWLEY-RIVERSIDE RD
MALHEUR CO OR 146-A1
SE CROWN RD
CLARK CO WA 193-B7
CROWN ST
VANCOUVER BC 156-A5
CROWN POINT HWY
MULTNOMAH CO OR 194-A7
MULTNOMAH CO OR 200-D1
MULTNOMAH CO OR 201-A1
E CROWN POINT HWY
MULTNOMAH CO OR 200-D1
MULTNOMAH CO OR 201-A1
CROWN POINT RD Rt#-174
DOUGLAS CO WA 237-C2
CROWN PT RD
COOS CO OR 220-C2
CROWSNEST HWY Rt#-3
BRITISH COLUMBIA 103-C1
CROWSON RD
JACKSON CO OR 234-D4
JACKSON CO OR 337-J11
W CROW VALLEY RD
SAN JUAN CO WA 101-C2
CROW-VAUGHN RD
LANE CO OR 133-A3
CRUMARINE LOOP RD
LATAH CO ID 249-D4
CRUM CANYON RD
CHELAN CO WA 236-A6
CRUSH CRES
TOWNSHIP OF LANGLEY BC 157-C7
CRUSHER CANYON RD
YAKIMA CO WA 243-B5
CRYSTAL CREEK RD
CROOK CO OR 136-A2
CURRY CO OR 224-B4
CRYSTAL LAKE DR
BENTON CO OR 327-H12
CORVALLIS OR 327-H12
CRYSTAL LAKE RD
SNOHOMISH CO WA 171-D6
CRYSTAL MOUNTAIN HWY
PIERCE CO WA 119-A1
CRYSTAL SPRINGS RD
KLAMATH CO OR 150-C2
KLAMATH CO OR 235-D5
CRYSTAL SPRINGS RD NE
KITSAP CO WA 271-F7
C-SW DODSON RD
GRANT CO WA 120-C1
ROYAL CITY WA 120-C1
CUB CREEK RD
OKANOGAN CO WA 104-A2
CULBERTSON DR
HOOD RIVER CO OR 202-C2
CULDESAC CUTOFF RD
CULDESAC ID 123-B2
CULDESAC ID 123-B2
CULLABY LAKE RD
CLATSOP CO OR 188-B3
CULLEN RD
YAMHILL CO OR 198-D5
CULLUM AV
RICHLAND WA 341-G3
NE CULLY BLVD
PORTLAND OR 310-E7
PORTLAND OR 311-E7
PORTLAND OR 314-D1
CULTUS BAY RD
ISLAND CO WA 171-A3
CULTUS LAKE RD
BRITISH COLUMBIA 102-C1
DISTRICT OF CHILLIWACK BC 102-C1
CULVER DR SE
MARION CO OR 325-H3
CULVER HWY Rt#-361
CULVER OR 208-B7
JEFFERSON CO OR 208-B6
JEFFERSON CO OR 212-D1
MADRAS OR 208-B6
METOLIUS OR 208-B6
SW CULVER HWY
JEFFERSON CO OR 212-D2
CULVER RD
LANE CO OR 210-A6
CUMBERLAND ST
NEW WESTMINSTER BC 156-D5
CUMBERLAND-KANASKAT RD
KING CO WA 110-C3
CUMMINGS LN N
KEIZER OR 322-H6
CUMMINS CREEK RD
LANE CO OR 209-A4
CUMMINS PEAK RD
LINCOLN CO OR 209-A4
CUNNINGHAM LN
YAMHILL CO OR 198-C4
CUNNINGHAM RD
ADAMS CO WA 121-C1
W CUNNINGHAM RD
ADAMS CO WA 121-B1
W CURLEW LAKE RD
FERRY CO WA 105-B2
CURLY CREEK RD
SKAMANIA CO WA 118-C3
CURRIN RD
CLACKAMAS CO OR 200-C5
CURRY RD
DOUGLAS CO OR 221-B3
CURTIN RD
DOUGLAS CO OR 219-B2
CURTIS RD
LINN CO OR 210-A6
WHATCOM CO WA 158-D7
White Swan WA 119-C2
N CURTIS RD
BOISE ID 253-C3
S CURTIS RD
ADA CO ID 253-C5
BOISE ID 253-C3
W CURTIS RD
SPOKANE CO WA 246-B7
CURTIS ST
DISTRICT OF BURNABY BC 156-D4
W CURTIS ST U.S.-101
ABERDEEN WA 178-B7
CURTIS HILL RD
LEWIS CO WA 184-A7
LEWIS CO WA 187-A1
W CUSTER DR
SPOKANE WA 348-F6
CUSTER RD SW
LAKEWOOD WA 181-C3
LAKEWOOD WA 294-A7
CUSTER RD W
LAKEWOOD WA 181-C3
CUSTER ST
TUMWATER WA 296-H9
CUSTER SCHOOL RD
WHATCOM CO WA 158-C4
CUTOFF RD
JEFFERSON CO OR 211-D2
JEFFERSON CO OR 212-A2
CUTRATE RD
JOSEPHINE CO OR 335-C8
C W HUGHES RD
WHITMAN CO WA 114-C3
C WILLIAMS RD
BENTON CO WA 121-A3
CY BINGHAM RD
HARNEY CO OR 137-C3
CYMIOTTI RD
KLICKITAT CO WA 196-B3
CYPRESS BOWL RD
DIST OF WEST VANCOUVER BC 156-A2

D

D AV
ANACORTES WA 259-F4
D ST
BAKER CITY OR 138-B1
CULVER OR 208-B7
GRANTS PASS OR 335-E8
HUBBARD OR 205-B1
SALEM OR 322-J12
SALEM OR 323-B12
SPRINGFIELD OR 330-H7
WASHOUGAL WA 193-C7
D ST Rt#-218
SHANIKO OR 127-C3
D ST Rt#-507
TENINO WA 184-D3
D ST U.S.-12
LEWISTON ID 250-B4
E D ST
GRANTS PASS OR 335-G9
MOSCOW ID 249-D5
TACOMA WA 293-H6
TACOMA WA 295-J1
SW D ST Rt#-361
MADRAS OR 208-C5
W D ST
LANE CO OR 330-F7
SPRINGFIELD OR 330-G7
DABOB RD
JEFFERSON CO WA 170-A3
DABOB POST OFFICE RD
JEFFERSON CO WA 170-A4
DAHL RD
YAKIMA CO WA 243-A6
DAHLGREN RD
COLUMBIA CO OR 192-A3
DAHLIA WY
POLK CO OR 204-C5
POLK CO OR 322-A10
DAHLKE RD SW
DOUGLAS CO WA 239-D2
DAILY LN
JOSEPHINE CO OR 229-A6
DAIRY-BONANZA HWY Rt#-70
BONANZA OR 151-A2
KLAMATH CO OR 151-A2
SW DAISY ST
KITSAP CO WA 174-A6
DAISY ST N Rt#-17
GRANT CO WA 112-C2
SOAP LAKE WA 112-C2
DAISY ST S Rt#-17
SOAP LAKE WA 112-C2
DAISY MINE RD
JACKSON CO OR 229-D2
JOSEPHINE CO OR 229-C2
STEVENS CO WA 105-C3
STEVENS CO WA 106-A3
DAKIN ST
BELLINGHAM WA 258-J5
DAKOTA AV
MEDFORD OR 336-B13
DALBY RD
MASON CO WA 173-B7
DALE DR
LINN CO OR 210-B5
DALE LN
CLACKAMAS CO OR 200-B4
DALE RD
BRITISH COLUMBIA 94-B3
DALE ST
WOODLAND WA 192-C1
DALLAS RD
BENTON CO WA 341-A4
CITY OF VICTORIA BC 256-F10
CITY OF VICTORIA BC 257-A11
RICHLAND WA 341-A4
WEST RICHLAND WA 341-A4
NE DALLAS ST Rt#-500
CAMAS WA 193-B7
DALLAS-RICKREALL HWY Rt#-223
DALLAS OR 204-A6
POLK CO OR 204-A6
DALLES MILITARY RD
COLLEGE PLACE WA 344-G11
WALLA WALLA WA 344-G11
WALLA WALLA WA 345-A10
WALLA WALLA CO WA 344-F13
DALLES MOUNTAIN RD
KLICKITAT CO WA 127-B1
KLICKITAT CO WA 196-D6
DALLESPORT RD
KLICKITAT CO WA 196-C6
DALLMAN RD
ISLAND CO WA 168-A7
E DALTON AV
COEUR D'ALENE ID 355-F4
DALTON GARDENS ID 355-F4
KOOTENAI CO ID 355-F4
W DALTON AV
COEUR D'ALENE ID 354-H5
COEUR D'ALENE ID 355-D5
KOOTENAI CO ID 354-H5
DALY CREEK RD
BAKER CO OR 139-A1
DAMMAN RD
KITTITAS CO WA 241-B6
DAMON RD
ADAMS CO WA 113-B3
ADAMS CO WA 121-B1
DAMON RD Rt#-115
GRAYS HARBOR CO WA 177-B6
OCEAN SHORES WA 177-B6
DAMSON RD
SNOHOMISH CO WA 171-C5
DANBY DR SW
THURSTON CO WA 184-C3
DANE LN
LANE CO OR 210-A6
N DANEBO AV
EUGENE OR 329-A4
S DANEBO AV
EUGENE OR 329-A6
DANEKAS RD
ADAMS CO WA 113-C3
ADAMS CO WA 114-A3
LINCOLN CO WA 114-A3
RITZVILLE WA 113-C3
DANIELS RD
MASON CO WA 180-B2
DAN KELLY RD
CLALLAM CO WA 165-A6
DANNEN RD
LINN CO OR 210-B2
DANNER LP
MALHEUR CO OR 147-A3
DANNER RD
MALHEUR CO OR 146-C3
MALHEUR CO OR 147-A3
DARBY RD
LATAH CO ID 249-D4
DARK HOLLOW RD
JACKSON CO OR 234-A2
S DARKNELL RD
SPOKANE CO WA 247-A6
E DARLAND ST
GOLDENDALE WA 127-C1
DARLEY RD
MARION CO OR 133-C1
DARRELL AV
WINSTON OR 221-B6
DARRINGTN BNTTS STR RD Rt#-530
DARRINGTON WA 103-A3
SKAGIT CO WA 103-A3
DART CREEK RD
COLUMBIA CO OR 192-A1
DARTER RD
KITSAP CO WA 170-B6
W DARTFORD DR
Fairwood WA 346-J6
Fairwood WA 347-A6
SPOKANE CO WA 346-J6
DARTMOUTH ST U.S.-95
ADAMS CO ID 139-C1
COUNCIL ID 139-C1
S DASH POINT RD Rt#-509
FEDERAL WAY WA 182-B1
SW DASH POINT RD Rt#-509
FEDERAL WAY WA 182-A1
PIERCE CO WA 182-A1
SE DATE AV
COLLEGE PLACE WA 344-F11
DAVENPORT ST
RICHLAND WA 341-G2
DAVID AV
COQUITLAM BC 157-B4
DAVID RD
WHITMAN CO WA 249-C4
DAVID HILL RD
WASHINGTON CO OR 198-B1
DAVIDSON AV
COWLITZ CO WA 192-B1
WOODLAND WA 192-B1
DAVIDSON RD
POLK CO OR 207-B1
DAVIE ST
VANCOUVER BC 254-E9
DAVIES
PIERCE CO WA 182-B7
DAVIES RD
BRITISH COLUMBIA 159-B5
N DAVIES RD
SNOHOMISH CO WA 171-D1
S DAVIES RD
SNOHOMISH CO WA 171-D2
DAVIS DR
HOOD RIVER CO OR 195-C6
DAVIS RD
ADAMS CO WA 113-B3
ASOTIN CO WA 123-A3
ASOTIN CO WA 123-A3
COWLITZ CO WA 189-D1
CROOK CO OR 213-D6
LATAH CO ID 249-D2
LINCOLN CO WA 113-B3
LINN CO OR 207-C7
SISKIYOU CO CA 150-C3
SW DAVIS RD
BEAVERTON OR 199-A2
DAVIS ST
MCCALL ID 251-D5
DAVIS WY Rt#-270
PULLMAN WA 249-A5
WHITMAN CO WA 249-A5
DAVIS CREEK LN
VALLEY CO ID 252-D2
DAVIS CREEK RD
JOSEPHINE CO OR 233-B1
DAVIS CREEK RD NE
MARION CO OR 205-D4
DAVIS PEAK RD
COWLITZ CO WA 118-A3
DAVISSON RD
LANE CO OR 215-C6
S DAVIS SPUR RD
COWLITZ CO WA 189-D1
DAWES HILL RD
COQUITLAM BC 157-A5
DAWSON RD
BENTON CO OR 133-B2
DAY RD
IDAHO CO ID 123-C3
ISLAND CO WA 167-C7
WASHINGTON CO OR 199-B5
E DAY RD
SPOKANE CO WA 246-D1
NE DAY RD E
KITSAP CO WA 174-D1
NE DAY RD W
KITSAP CO WA 174-C1
DAY HILL RD
CLACKAMAS CO OR 200-C6
DAY ISLAND RD
EUGENE OR 330-B6
DAY-MT SPOKANE RD
SPOKANE CO WA 246-D1
SPOKANE CO WA 347-J3
DAY SCHOOL RD
KLAMATH CO OR 231-D5
DAYS CREEK RD
DOUGLAS CO OR 141-B3
DAYS CREEK CUTOFF RD
DOUGLAS CO OR 225-C1
E DAYTON AV
DAYTON WA 122-A2
W DAYTON AV
DAYTON WA 122-A2
DAYTON AV N
SHORELINE WA 171-A7
DAYTON RD
DESCHUTES CO OR 212-B7
DAYTON ST
Altamont OR 338-H9
S DAYTON ST
KENNEWICK WA 343-D14
DAYTON-AIRPORT RD
MASON CO WA 179-D2
DAYTON-AIRPORT RD Rt#-102
MASON CO WA 179-D2
MASON CO WA 180-A2
SE DAYTON BYPASS RD Rt#-18
DAYTON OR 198-B7
YAMHILL CO OR 198-B7
DEAD INDIAN RD
ASHLAND OR 337-J9
JACKSON CO OR 150-A2
JACKSON CO OR 234-D4
JACKSON CO OR 337-J9
KLAMATH CO OR 150-B2
DEAD MAN RD
CHELAN CO WA 238-B2
N DEADMAN RD
GARFIELD CO WA 122-B2
DEADMAN CREEK RD
DOUGLAS CO OR 141-C3
DEADMAN GULCH RD
MALHEUR CO OR 146-C1
DEADMOND FERRY RD
LANE CO OR 330-G2
North Springfield OR 330-G2
SPRINGFIELD OR 330-G2
DEAD POINT RD
HOOD RIVER CO OR 195-B7
DEADY CROSSING RD
DOUGLAS CO OR 221-C2
DEAL RD
ADAMS CO WA 113-B3
ADAMS CO WA 121-B1
DEAN MOUNTAIN RD
COOS CO OR 218-C6
DOUGLAS CO OR 218-D2
DEAN PARK RD
DIST OF NORTH SAANICH BC 159-C3
DEARBORN AV NE
KEIZER OR 322-J5
KEIZER OR 323-A5
S DEARBORN ST
SEATTLE WA 278-A7
DE ARMOND RD
POLK CO OR 207-A3
DEBAST RD
COLUMBIA CO OR 189-B4
DE BERRY RD
LANE CO OR 215-B5
DECATUR AV
BREMERTON WA 270-G11
DECEPTION RD
SKAGIT CO WA 160-C7
SKAGIT CO WA 259-H14
DECKER RD
BENTON CO OR 133-B2
DECKERVILLE RD
MASON CO WA 179-B2
DEEGAN RD W
MASON CO WA 180-A3
DEEP CREEK RD
CLACKAMAS CO OR 200-B3
LEWIS CO WA 184-A7
DEEP LAKE BOUNDARY RD
STEVENS CO WA 106-B1
DEEP RIVER VALLEY RD
WAHKIAKUM CO WA 117-A2
DEER DR
KOOTENAI CO ID 248-A3
DEER RD
WHEELER CO OR 136-B2
N DEER ST
PRINEVILLE OR 213-D5
DEER CREEK RD
JACKSON CO OR 226-D3
JACKSON CO OR 227-A3
JOSEPHINE CO OR 233-B2
KLAMATH CO OR 227-A3
STEVENS CO WA 106-A3
S DEER CREEK RD
DOUGLAS CO OR 221-D5
DEER CREEK-BOULDER CREEK RD
FERRY CO WA 105-B1
DEER FLAT RD
ADA CO ID 253-A5
CANYON CO ID 147-B1
W DEER FLAT RD
ADA CO ID 253-A5
DEERHORN RD
LANE CO OR 133-C3
DEER LAKE AV
DISTRICT OF BURNABY BC 156-D5
DEER LAKE PL
DISTRICT OF BURNABY BC 156-D5
DEER LAKE RD
Clinton WA 171-A2
DEER LAKE LOOP RD
STEVENS CO WA 106-B3
DEER PARK DR SE
MARION CO OR 325-J5
SALEM OR 325-J5
DEER PARK RD
CLALLAM CO WA 165-C7
DEER PARK-MILAN RD
DEER PARK WA 114-B1
SPOKANE CO WA 114-B1
E DEER PARK-MILAN RD
SPOKANE CO WA 114-B1
W DEER PARK-MILAN RD
SPOKANE CO WA 114-B1
DEER RIDGE RD
DESCHUTES CO OR 211-D4
DEER TRAIL LN
JACKSON CO OR 234-B3
DEER VALLEY RD
NEWPORT WA 106-C3
PEND OREILLE CO WA 106-C3
DE FRATES RD
COLUMBIA CO OR 189-C6
DEGGLER RD
LEWIS CO WA 118-A2
SW DEHAVEN ST
MILTON-FREEWATER OR 121-C3
DEHLER RD
CROOK CO OR 213-C3
DEHLINGER LN
KLAMATH CO OR 235-D6
DEINHARD LN
MCCALL ID 251-C5
DEJONG RD
POLK CO OR 204-A3
SW DEJONG RD
YAMHILL CO OR 204-A3
DEKAY RD
GRAYS HARBOR CO WA 177-D5
DEKKER RD
YAKIMA CO WA 120-A2
DELAMETER RD
COWLITZ CO WA 187-B7
COWLITZ CO WA 189-B1
DELANEY RD
FRANKLIN CO WA 121-B2
DELANEY RD SE
MARION CO OR 133-C1
MARION CO OR 207-D1
MARION CO OR 324-J12
MARION CO OR 325-A12
TURNER OR 325-E12
DELANO RD KPS
PIERCE CO WA 181-A2
DELBROOK AV
DIST OF N VANCOUVER BC 255-A2
DELENA-MAYGER RD
COLUMBIA CO OR 189-A4
DELEZENNE RD
GRAYS HARBOR CO WA 117-B1
DELFATTI LN
KLAMATH CO OR 235-C5
DELICIOUS ST
DESCHUTES CO OR 212-A7
DELINTMENT LAKE RD
HARNEY CO OR 136-C3
DELL AV
Walla Walla West WA 344-F7
WALLA WALLA WA 344-F7
DELL RD W
WASCO CO OR 196-B6
DELL ADAMS RD
MASON CO WA 179-C3
DELLMOOR LP
CLATSOP CO OR 188-B4
DELMAR DR E
SEATTLE WA 278-B1
DELMAR RD
COOS CO OR 220-D3
DELPHI RD NW
THURSTON CO WA 296-A3
DELPHI RD SW
THURSTON CO WA 180-B7
THURSTON CO WA 184-B1
THURSTON CO WA 296-A6
DELRIDGE WY SW
KING WA 285-G3
DELRIDGE WY SW
SEATTLE WA 281-G7
SEATTLE WA 285-G2
DEL RIO RD
DOUGLAS CO WA 113-A1
DEL RIO RD E
DOUGLAS CO WA 237-A2
DEL RIO COULEE CITY RD
DOUGLAS CO WA 113-A1
DELTA AV
DISTRICT OF BURNABY BC 255-J13
DELTA HWY
EUGENE OR 329-J3
DELTA ST
KLAMATH FALLS OR 338-C6
DELTA LINE RD
WHATCOM CO WA 158-C4
DELTAPORT WY
DISTRICT OF DELTA BC 101-C1
DELTA WATERS RD
JACKSON CO OR 336-F7
MEDFORD OR 336-F7
DEMARAY DR
JOSEPHINE CO OR 229-A7
JOSEPHINE CO OR 335-A12
DEMPSEY RD
CLALLAM CO WA 164-D6
DIST OF N VANCOUVER BC 255-E1
DENBROOK RD
CLACKAMAS CO OR 199-B6
E DENISON-CHATTAROY RD
SPOKANE CO WA 114-C1
W DENISON-CHATTAROY RD
SPOKANE CO WA 114-B1
DENMAN ST
VANCOUVER BC 254-E9
DENMARK ST SW
THURSTON CO WA 184-B4
SW DENNEY RD
BEAVERTON OR 199-B2
DENNIS RD
BENTON CO WA 120-C3
DENNY WY
SEATTLE WA 277-H4
SEATTLE WA 278-A4
E DENNY WY
SEATTLE WA 278-A4
SEATTLE WA 279-E4
W DENNY WY
SEATTLE WA 277-H4
DENNY SCHOOL RD
LINN CO OR 133-C1
W DENO RD
SPOKANE CO WA 246-A4
DENT RD
FRANKLIN CO WA 340-J14
N DENVER AV
PORTLAND OR 308-E4
DENVER RD
IDAHO CO ID 123-C3
IDAHO CO ID 123-C3
S DENVER ST
ASTORIA OR 300-B6
DENVER ST SE
TURNER OR 325-G12
DEPARTURE BAY RD
NANAIMO BC 93-A3
DERRICK CAVES RD
LAKE CO OR 143-B2
DESAVADO RD
SISKIYOU CO CA 150-A3
DESCHUTES AV U.S.-197
MAUPIN OR 127-B3
DESCHUTES DR
JEFFERSON CO OR 208-B5
NW DESCHUTES DR
JEFFERSON CO OR 208-B3
DESCHUTES PKWY
OLYMPIA WA 296-G6
TUMWATER WA 296-G6
NW DESCHUTES PL U.S.-20
BEND OR 332-E6
E DESCHUTES RD
DESCHUTES CO OR 142-C1
DESCHUTES ST
WASCO OR 127-C1
DESCHUTES WY
TUMWATER WA 296-H9
DESCHUTS-PLEASNT RIDGE MRKT RD
DESCHUTES CO OR 212-C7
DESCHUTES RIVER RD
MAUPIN OR 127-B3
WASCO CO OR 127-B3
DESERT RD
GEM CO ID 139-B3
W DESKA DR
SPOKANE CO WA 348-D11
DES MOINES MEMORIAL DR S
BURIEN WA 288-A4
DES MOINES WA 290-A3
KING WA 286-B4
KING WA 288-A4
SEATAC WA 288-A4
SEATAC WA 290-A3
DES MOINES MEM DR S Rt#-509
BURIEN WA 288-A7
BURIEN WA 290-A1
SEATAC WA 290-A1
NW DESPAIN AV
PENDLETON OR 129-B1
DESPAIN RD
UMATILLA CO OR 129-A1
DESPAIN GULCH RD
UMATILLA CO OR 129-B1
DETHMAN RIDGE DR
HOOD RIVER CO OR 195-C6
DETROIT BLVD
AUBURN WA 182-B1
DETROIT BLVD S
PACIFIC WA 182-B2
DETTLING RD
SNOHOMISH CO WA 168-B3
DEVELOPMENT AV
BOISE ID 253-C3
DEVER-CONNER RD
LINN CO OR 207-C3
DEVERELL RD
MULTNOMAH CO OR 200-D2

PNW

INDEX

STREET City State Page-Grid

DEVILLE RD
SKAMANIA CO WA 194-A6
DEVILS CANYON RD
FRANKLIN CO WA 121-B2
DEVILS GAP RD
LINCOLN CO WA 114-A1
E DEVILS LAKE RD
LINCOLN CITY OR 203-B4
LINCOLN CO OR 203-B4
W DEVILS LAKE RD
LINCOLN CITY OR 203-A4
LINCOLN CO OR 203-A4
DEVILS MTN RD
SKAGIT CO WA 168-B1
DEVILS WELL RD
LINCOLN CO OR 206-D4
DEVINE RIDGE RD
HARNEY CO OR 137-B3
DE VRIES RD
ISLAND CO WA 167-C2
DEWATO RD W
KITSAP CO WA 173-C3
DEWATTO RD
KITSAP CO WA 173-D4
MASON CO WA 173-D4
MASON CO WA 174-A4
DEWATTO-HOLLY RD
MASON CO WA 173-B5
DEWDNEY TRUNK RD
DISTRICT OF MISSION BC 94-B3
MAPLE RIDGE BC 94-B3
MAPLE RIDGE BC 157-C5
PITT MEADOWS BC 157-B5
DEWEY AV Rt#-7
BAKER CITY OR 138-B1
DEWEY ST
BREMERTON WA 270-G11
DEWEY CREEK LP
LINCOLN CO OR 206-C2
DEW VALLEY RD
COOS CO OR 220-A7
S DHOOGHE RD
CLACKAMAS CO OR 126-A3
DIAGONAL ST Rt#-129
CLARKSTON WA 250-B4
DIAL LN
UNION CO OR 130-A2
DIAMOND LN
HARNEY CO OR 145-B3
DIAMOND HILL DR
LINN CO OR 210-A4
DIAMOND HILL RD
HARRISBURG OR 210-A5
LINN CO OR 210-A5
NE DIAMOND LAKE BLVD Rt#-138
ROSEBURG OR 221-C4
ROSEBURG OR 334-H7
E DIAMOND LAKE HWY Rt#-138
DOUGLAS CO OR 223-D7
KLAMATH CO OR 142-B2
KLAMATH CO OR 223-D7
W DIAMOND LAKE HWY Rt#-230
DOUGLAS CO OR 223-B7
DOUGLAS CO OR 226-D3
DOUGLAS CO OR 227-A1
JACKSON CO OR 226-D3
KLAMATH CO OR 142-C3
DIAMOND MATCH CAMP RD
CLEARWATER CO ID 123-C1
CLEARWATER CO ID 123-C1
DIAMOND POINT RD
CLALLAM CO WA 166-C7
JEFFERSON CO WA 166-C7
DICK RD
GRANT CO WA 242-C2
NW DICK RD
WASHINGTON CO OR 192-A7
DICKENSHEET RD
BONNER CO ID 107-A2
DICKENSON RD
BRITISH COLUMBIA 93-A3
NANAIMO BC 93-A3
DICKEY RD
DESCHUTES CO OR 217-D2
DICKEY RD NW
KITSAP CO WA 174-A1
DICKEY PRAIRIE RD
CLACKAMAS CO OR 126-A3
DICK GEORGE RD
JOSEPHINE CO OR 233-B5
DIETZ AV NE
KEIZER OR 322-J6
KEIZER OR 323-A6
E DIGBY RD
MOUNT VERNON WA 260-E13
DIGGER RD
WASCO CO OR 196-A6
DIKE BYPS U.S.-12
LEWISTON ID 250-B4
DIKE RD
COLUMBIA CO OR 189-D7
COLUMBIA CO OR 192-A4
COWLITZ CO WA 189-D7
COWLITZ CO WA 192-B1
SKAGIT CO WA 168-B1
SKAGIT CO WA 260-A14
SNOHOMISH CO WA 168-D5
WHATCOM CO WA 161-D1
W DIKE ST
MOUNT VERNON WA 260-A14
SKAGIT CO WA 260-A14
DIKE ACCESS RD
COWLITZ CO WA 189-D7
WOODLAND WA 189-D7
DILLARD HWY Rt#-99
DOUGLAS CO OR 221-B7
WINSTON OR 221-B7
DILLARD RD
LANE CO OR 215-B4
SW DILLEY RD
WASHINGTON CO OR 198-B1
DILLON FALLS RD
DESCHUTES CO OR 217-A4
NW DIMMICK ST
GRANTS PASS OR 335-E8
SW DIMMICK ST
GRANTS PASS OR 335-E8
DIMRILL DALE RD
SKAMANIA CO WA 194-A6
DINGO
JEFFERSON CO OR 212-C3
DINSMORE BRDG
CITY OF RICHMOND BC 156-B6
DINWITTY LN
MALHEUR CO OR 147-A3
DISASTER PEAK RD
MALHEUR CO OR 154-B2
DISCOVERY AV SE
OCEAN SHORES WA 298-F4
DISCOVERY RD
JEFFERSON CO WA 166-D7
JEFFERSON CO WA 263-A9
PORT TOWNSEND WA 263-F4
S DISHMAN RD
Dishman WA 350-D9
SPOKANE CO WA 350-D9
E DISHMAN-MICA RD
SPOKANE CO WA 246-D5
SPOKANE CO WA 247-A5
S DISHMAN-MICA RD
Dishman WA 350-E12
SPOKANE CO WA 246-D5
SPOKANE CO WA 350-E12
S DISHMAN-MICA RD Rt#-27
SPOKANE CO WA 247-A5
DISTRICT LINE RD
BENTON CO WA 120-C3
DITCH RD
DESCHUTES CO OR 212-D4
DITCH CREEK RD
JACKSON CO OR 229-D3
DIVERS RD
CLACKAMAS CO OR 200-C6
NE DIVIDE RD
JEFFERSON CO OR 135-C1
DIVISION AV
EPHRATA WA 112-C3
TACOMA WA 293-F4
S DIVISION AV Rt#-225
BENTON CITY WA 120-C3
DIVISION AV E
EPHRATA WA 112-C3
DIVISION AV NE
Suquamish WA 170-C7
DIVISION AV W
EPHRATA WA 112-C3
E DIVISION LN
TACOMA WA 295-J2
N DIVISION RD
DOUGLAS CO WA 112-B2
GRANT CO WA 242-A3
S DIVISION RD
DOUGLAS CO WA 112-B2
GRANT CO WA 242-A4
DIVISION ST
BEND OR 332-E7
CASHMERE WA 238-C2
DOUGLAS CO OR 225-C1
GRANT CO WA 242-C3
KELSO WA 303-D6
MOSES LAKE WA 242-C3
MYRTLE CREEK OR 225-C1
OLYMPIA WA 296-F2
THURSTON CO WA 296-F2
DIVISION ST Rt#-20
TWISP WA 104-A3
DIVISION ST Rt#-204
ELGIN OR 130-A1
UNION CO OR 130-A1
DIVISION ST Rt#-372
BEND OR 332-E8
DIVISION ST U.S.-20
BEND OR 332-F6
E DIVISION ST
MOUNT VERNON WA 260-D12
N DIVISION ST
CASHMERE WA 238-C2
CHELAN CO WA 238-C2
RITZVILLE WA 113-C3
SANDPOINT ID 244-A2
WALLA WALLA WA 345-C7
N DIVISION ST Rt#-21
ODESSA WA 113-B3
N DIVISION ST Rt#-27
PALOUSE WA 249-B1
N DIVISION ST U.S.-2
SPOKANE WA 346-J12
SPOKANE WA 347-A14
SPOKANE WA 349-A3
Town and Country WA 346-J12
Town and Country WA 347-A14
Town and Country WA 349-A3
N DIVISION ST U.S.-395
Country Homes WA 346-J11
Country Homes WA 347-A8
Fairwood WA 347-A8
SPOKANE WA 346-J11
Town and Country WA 346-J11
NE DIVISION ST
GRESHAM OR 200-B2
NW DIVISION ST
GRESHAM OR 200-A2
MYRTLE CREEK OR 225-C1
S DIVISION ST
ADAMS CO WA 113-C3
CASHMERE WA 238-C2
MOSES LAKE WA 242-C3
RITZVILLE WA 113-C3
SANDPOINT ID 244-A2
WALLA WALLA WA 345-C8
Walla Walla East WA 345-C8
S DIVISION ST Rt#-225
BENTON CITY WA 120-C3
S DIVISION ST U.S.-2
SPOKANE WA 349-A9
SE DIVISION ST
GRESHAM OR 200-A2
PORTLAND OR 200-A2
PORTLAND OR 313-G7
PORTLAND OR 317-G1
PORTLAND OR 318-C1
PORTLAND OR 319-H1
W DIVISION ST Rt#-536
MOUNT VERNON WA 260-B12
DIVISION ST E
QUINCY WA 112-B3
DIVISION ST N
SOAP LAKE WA 112-C2
DIVISION ST NE
SALEM OR 322-H12
DIVISION ST S
GRANT CO WA 112-C2
KELLOGG ID 115-C2
KELLOGG ID 115-C2
SOAP LAKE WA 112-C2
DIVISION FENCE RD
KLICKITAT CO WA 196-C1
DIXIE CREEK RD
BAKER CO OR 138-C2
GRANT CO OR 137-B2
WASHINGTON CO ID 139-B1
DIXIE MOUNTAIN RD
WASHINGTON CO OR 125-C1
SE DIXON DR
JEFFERSON CO OR 208-C6
DIXON LP
DESCHUTES CO OR 217-D2
DIXON RD
CROOK CO OR 213-B5
DIXON MILL RD
WASHINGTON CO OR 198-C3
DIXONVILLE RD
DOUGLAS CO OR 221-D5
D MEYER RD
WHITMAN CO WA 249-A7
DOAK RD
KLAMATH CO OR 231-D5
DOAKS FERRY RD
POLK CO OR 322-D9
SALEM OR 322-D9
DOAN RD
COLUMBIA CO OR 189-B4
E DOBBIE POINT LN
SHERMAN CO OR 127-C3
DOBBIN RD
WALLOWA CO OR 130-C2
DOBER RD
WASHINGTON CO OR 198-C2
DOCK RD
KLICKITAT CO WA 196-D7
DOCK ST Rt#-105
WESTPORT WA 298-G11
DOCKTON RD SW
KING CO WA 174-D6
E DODD RD
KOOTENAI CO ID 245-A4
DODDS RD
DESCHUTES CO OR 135-B3
DODES CREEK RD
JACKSON CO OR 226-A7
DODGE RD
JACKSON CO OR 230-C4
DODGE PARK BLVD
MULTNOMAH CO OR 200-C2
SE DODGE PARK BLVD
MULTNOMAH CO OR 200-C2
DODGE VALLEY RD
SKAGIT CO WA 167-D1
DODSON RD
EPHRATA WA 112-C3
GRANT CO WA 112-C3
DOE CREEK RD
DOUGLAS CO OR 225-A3
DOERFLER RD SE
MARION CO OR 205-C6
DOERNER CTO
DOUGLAS CO OR 221-A4
DOERNER RD
DOUGLAS CO OR 221-A4
DOETSCH RD
COLUMBIA CO OR 189-C6
DOG RD
GRANT CO OR 137-B2
DOG LAKE RD
LAKE CO OR 151-C2
LAKE CO OR 152-A2
DOG RIDGE RD
NEWBERG OR 198-D6
YAMHILL CO OR 198-D6
DOGWOOD AV
ALBANY OR 326-H7
DOGWOOD DR
EVERETT WA 264-B7
EVERETT WA 268-B1
DOGWOOD LN
JEFFERSON CO OR 208-B4
NE DOGWOOD LN
JEFFERSON CO OR 208-C4
E DOGWOOD RD
FRANKLIN CO WA 121-A2
W DOLARWAY RD
ELLENSBURG WA 241-B5
DOLE RD
DOUGLAS CO OR 221-B7
DOUGLAS CO OR 225-C1
MYRTLE CREEK OR 225-C1
NE DOLE VALLEY RD
CLARK CO WA 193-C3
DOLLARHIDE RD
WHEELER CO OR 136-B1
DOLLARTON HWY
DIST OF N VANCOUVER BC 156-D3
DIST OF N VANCOUVER BC 255-H7
DOMINIC RD NE
MARION CO OR 205-C3
DONAHUE RD
MULTNOMAH CO OR 200-D2
MULTNOMAH CO OR 201-A2
DONALD RD
MARION CO OR 199-A7
WAPATO WA 120-A2
YAKIMA CO WA 120-A2
DONALDSON RD
JOSEPHINE CO OR 335-D1
DONALD-WAPATO RD
YAKIMA CO WA 120-A2
DONELLY RD
HARNEY CO OR 136-C3
HARNEY CO OR 144-C1
HARNEY CO OR 145-A1
DONEY RD
DESCHUTES CO OR 212-D3
JEFFERSON CO OR 212-D3
DONKEY CREEK RD
GRAYS HARBOR CO WA 109-A2
GRAYS HARBOR CO WA 178-A1
DONNELLY RD
SKAGIT CO WA 161-A7
DONOVAN AV
BELLINGHAM WA 258-D11
DONRUSS DR
DOUGLAS CO OR 221-A3
DOOLEY MOUNTAIN HWY Rt#-245
BAKER CO OR 138-A1
DOPP RD
YAMHILL CO OR 198-C4
DORAN RD
WHATCOM CO WA 161-C2
SE DORION AV U.S.-30
PENDLETON OR 129-B1
SW DORION AV U.S.-30
PENDLETON OR 129-B1
DORMAIER RD
SHERMAN CO OR 127-C1
DORNING RD
LEWIS CO WA 187-C2
DORRANCE MEADOW RD
DESCHUTES CO OR 143-A1
DORRIS BROWNELL RD
SISKIYOU CO CA 150-C3
S DORSET RD
SPOKANE CO WA 246-B5
DORSEY RD
KLICKITAT CO WA 196-A3
SW DOSCH RD
PORTLAND OR 316-B2
DOSEWALLIPS RD
JEFFERSON CO WA 109-C1
DOT RD
KLICKITAT CO WA 120-A3
KLICKITAT CO WA 128-A1
DOUBLE BLUFF RD
ISLAND CO WA 170-D2
DOUBLE CREEK LN
SKAGIT CO WA 161-B4
DOUBLEDAY RD
JACKSON CO OR 150-A1
DOUBLE O RD
HARNEY CO OR 145-A2
DOUGHERTY DR
CASTLE ROCK WA 187-C7
COWLITZ CO WA 187-C7
DOUGHTY RD
BAY CITY OR 197-B1
TILLAMOOK CO OR 197-B1
DOUGLAS AV
GERVAIS OR 205-A2
MARION CO OR 205-A2
SNOHOMISH WA 265-H4
N DOUGLAS AV
PASCO WA 343-J7
NE DOUGLAS AV
DOUGLAS CO OR 221-C5
ROSEBURG OR 221-C5
ROSEBURG OR 334-J7
SE DOUGLAS AV
ROSEBURG OR 334-H7
N DOUGLAS BLVD Rt#-99
WINSTON OR 221-B6
W DOUGLAS BLVD Rt#-42
WINSTON OR 221-B6
DOUGLAS CRES
LANGLEY BC 158-C1
VANCOUVER BC 254-E13
DOUGLAS DR
PACIFIC CO WA 186-A2
DOUGLAS RD
DISTRICT OF BURNABY BC 156-D4
DISTRICT OF BURNABY BC 255-G11
FERNDALE WA 158-C6
WHATCOM CO WA 158-B6
YAKIMA CO WA 243-A7
DOUGLAS ST
LONGVIEW WA 302-J10
LONGVIEW WA 303-A10
DOUGLAS ST Rt#-1
CITY OF VICTORIA BC 256-G6
DISTRICT OF SAANICH BC 256-G6
DOUGLAS FALLS RD
STEVENS CO WA 106-A2
SE DOVER LN
JEFFERSON CO OR 208-C6
SW DOVER LN
JEFFERSON CO OR 208-B6
S DOVER RD
SPOKANE CO WA 114-B2
DOVER ST
DISTRICT OF BURNABY BC 156-C5
GRANT CO WA 242-C2
DOW RD
KLICKITAT CO WA 196-D6
DOWANS CREEK RD
JEFFERSON CO WA 169-D3
DOWD RD
COLUMBIA CO OR 192-A1
W DOWER RD
KOOTENAI CO ID 247-D4
SE DOWLING RD
CLACKAMAS CO OR 200-D5
DOWNES RD
DISTRICT OF MATSQUI BC 102-B1
DOWNEY RD
DISTRICT OF N SAANICH BC 159-B2
SKAGIT CO WA 160-D7
DOWNEY GULCH RD
CHELAN CO WA 236-C3
S DOWNING DR
SEASIDE OR 301-F10
E DOWNING RD Rt#-507
CENTRALIA WA 184-C5
LEWIS CO WA 184-C5
S DOWNING ST
SEASIDE OR 301-F9
DOWN RIVER RD Rt#-128
LEWISTON ID 250-B4
W DOWNRIVER PARK DR
SPOKANE WA 348-D6
DOWNS RD NE
MARION CO OR 205-B4
DOWTY RD
CLACKAMAS CO OR 200-B5
DOYLE RD
CLARK CO WA 192-C1
N DOYLE RD
KOOTENAI CO ID 248-D2
DRAGICH RD
COWLITZ CO WA 189-A1
DRAHAM ST NE
THURSTON CO WA 297-H3
DRAIN RD
DOUGLAS CO OR 219-A3
DRAIN 10 RD
MODOC CO CA 151-A3
DRAIN-YONCALLA HWY Rt#-99
DOUGLAS CO OR 219-A3
DRAIN OR 219-A3
YONCALLA OR 219-A3
DRAKE RD
CLACKAMAS CO OR 205-D3
NW DRAKE RD
BEND OR 332-D6
DRAKE RD NE
CLACKAMAS CO OR 205-C3
MARION CO OR 205-C3
DRAPER SPRINGS RD
KLICKITAT CO WA 119-A3
DRAPER VALLEY RD
JOSEPHINE CO OR 233-B1
W DRAVUS ST
SEATTLE WA 273-E7
DRAYTON ST
LYNDEN WA 102-B1
DRAYTON HARBOR RD
Birch Bay WA 158-A3
BLAINE WA 158-A3
WHATCOM CO WA 158-A3
DRAZIL RD
KLAMATH CO OR 151-A2
DRESSER RD Rt#-500
CLARK CO WA 193-B6
DREWS RD
KLAMATH CO OR 151-A1
DREWSEY RD
HARNEY CO OR 137-C3
HARNEY CO OR 145-C1
DREWSEY MARKET RD
HARNEY CO OR 137-C3
DREWS PRAIRIE RD
LEWIS CO WA 187-C4
D REX RD
DOUGLAS CO WA 105-A3
DRIFT CREEK RD
LINCOLN CO OR 203-A5
LINCOLN CO OR 209-B1
DRIFT CREEK RD NE
MARION CO OR 205-C5
DRIFT CREEK RD SE
MARION CO OR 205-C7
DRIFTWOOD RD NW
THURSTON CO WA 180-C5
THURSTON CO WA 296-C1
N DRISCOLL BLVD
SPOKANE WA 348-D2
DRIVER RD
LINN CO OR 207-C7
DRIVER VALLEY RD
DOUGLAS CO OR 219-B7
DRUMHELLAR RD
GRANT CO WA 242-A1
DRUMHELLER RD
SPOKANE CO WA 247-B7
E DRUMHELLER RD
SPOKANE CO WA 247-A7
DRY COULEE RD
GRANT CO WA 112-C2
DRY CREEK CTO
MALHEUR CO OR 146-B1
DRY CREEK LN
UNION CO OR 130-A2
DRY CREEK RD
CROOK CO OR 213-D3
IDAHO CO ID 131-B1
JEFFERSON CO OR 208-B2
KITTITAS CO WA 241-B5
MALHEUR CO OR 146-C1
PAYETTE CO ID 139-B2
Warm Springs OR 208-B2
WASCO CO OR 196-A6
WHITMAN CO WA 114-C3
DRY CREEK RD U.S.-97
KITTITAS CO WA 241-A4
SISKIYOU CO CA 150-B3
DRY CREEK CANYON RD
DOUGLAS CO OR 225-C3
DRY CREEK TRAIL RD
Warm Springs OR 208-A2
DRYDEN RD
JOSEPHINE CO OR 233-C2
N DRYDEN RD
CHELAN CO WA 238-B2
DRYDEN OVERLOOK RD
JOSEPHINE CO OR 233-C2
DRY HOLLOW RD
JEFFERSON CO OR 208-A4
THE DALLES OR 196-C7
WASCO CO OR 196-C7
WHEELER CO OR 136-A1
DRY LAKE RD
CHELAN CO WA 236-B1
ISLAND CO WA 167-D5
MALHEUR CO OR 146-B2
DRYLAND RD
CLACKAMAS CO OR 199-C7
S DRYLAND RD
CLACKAMAS CO OR 205-D1
DRY SLOUGH RD
SKAGIT CO WA 168-A2
DRY VALLEY HWY
HARNEY CO OR 144-B2
DRY VALLEY RD
HARNEY CO OR 144-C2
N DUBOIS RD
COWLITZ CO WA 118-A3
DUBUQUE RD
SNOHOMISH CO WA 110-C1
DUCKABUSH RD
JEFFERSON CO WA 173-C1
DUCK CREEK RD
BAKER CO OR 131-A3
DUCK LAKE DR
OCEAN SHORES WA 177-B7
DUCK LAKE DR SE
OCEAN SHORES WA 298-E1
DUCK LAKE RD
LINCOLN CO WA 113-B2
DUDLEY RD
KITTITAS CO WA 240-D3
KOOTENAI CO ID 115-B2
YAMHILL CO OR 198-C5
E DUFFIELD RD
YAKIMA CO WA 243-D7
DUFORT RD
BONNER CO ID 107-A3
E DUFORT RD
BONNER CO ID 244-A4
DUFUR BYPASS RD
WASCO CO OR 127-B2
DUFUR GAP RD
WASCO CO OR 127-B2
DUFUR VALLEY RD
WASCO CO OR 127-B2
DUGOUT LAKE RD
DESCHUTES CO OR 211-B4
DUGUALLA BAY RD
ISLAND CO WA 167-C1
DUKE LN
MARION CO OR 198-D7
W DUKE RD
DOUGLAS CO OR 221-C1
DULEY CREEK RD
CURRY CO OR 232-C5
DUMAR WY SW
SEATTLE WA 285-G1
DUMP RD
NEZ PERCE CO ID 250-D2
DUNBAR RD
SKAGIT CO WA 161-A7
DUNBAR ST
UNIV ENDOWMENT LANDS BC 156-A5
VANCOUVER BC 156-A5
VANCOUVER BC 254-A14
DUNBAR DIV
VANCOUVER BC 254-A13
DUNCAN CREEK RD
SKAMANIA CO WA 194-B6
DUNDAS ST
VANCOUVER BC 255-D10
DUNDEE RD
WASHINGTON CO OR 198-A2
DUNIVAN RD
LEWIS CO WA 187-B4
DUNIWAY RD
YAMHILL CO OR 198-B6
DUNKARD RD
KLICKITAT CO WA 196-B1
DUNLAP RD SW
THURSTON CO WA 184-C4
DUNN RD
CLARK CO WA 192-D1
S DUNN RD
SPOKANE CO WA 246-D6
SE DUNN RD
CLACKAMAS CO OR 200-C3
DUNNING RD
WHITMAN CO WA 249-A6
DUNSMUIR ST
VANCOUVER BC 254-G10
DUPONT ST
BELLINGHAM WA 258-C5
DUPONT-STEILACOOM RD SW
DUPONT WA 181-B4
PIERCE CO WA 181-B4
DUPORTAIL ST
RICHLAND WA 341-E2
DURBIN CREEK RD
BAKER CO OR 138-C2
SW DURHAM LN
YAMHILL CO OR 204-B1
SW DURHAM RD
TIGARD OR 199-B3
DURR RD
KITTITAS CO WA 241-B7
KITTITAS CO WA 243-B1
YAKIMA CO WA 243-B2
DURRWACHTER RD
CLALLAM CO WA 164-D5
DURY RD
ADAMS CO WA 113-C3
DUSTY LP
DESCHUTES CO OR 212-B6
DUTCH CANYON RD
COLUMBIA CO OR 125-C1
COLUMBIA CO OR 192-A4
DUTCH HENRY RD
DOUGLAS CO OR 141-A3
DUTCHY CREEK RD
JOSEPHINE CO OR 148-C1
DUTHIE AV
DISTRICT OF BURNABY BC 156-D4
SE DUTHIE HILL RD
KING CO WA 176-A3
SAMMAMISH WA 176-A3
DUTTON RD
UNION CO OR 130-B2
DUUS RD
CLACKAMAS CO OR 200-C5
DUVAL RD
DIST OF N VANCOUVER BC 255-G2
DUVALL AV NE
RENTON WA 175-C5
DUVALL-MONROE RD Rt#-203
KING CO WA 110-C1
SNOHOMISH CO WA 110-C1
DUVALL-MONROE RD NE Rt#-203
DUVALL WA 110-C1
KING CO WA 110-C1
DWIGHT HALSEY RD
ASOTIN CO WA 123-A3
ASOTIN CO WA 123-A3
DYKE RD
CITY OF RICHMOND BC 156-B7
PITT MEADOWS BC 157-B5

E

E RD
COTTONWOOD ID 123-C3
IDAHO CO ID 123-C3
E RD SE
DOUGLAS CO WA 112-C2
E ST
COLUMBIA CITY OR 192-B1

368 E ST
STREET INDEX
ENUMCLAW BUCKLEY RD

STREET
City State Page-Grid

E ST
CULVER OR 208-B7
ENDICOTT WA 122-B1
GRANTS PASS OR 335-E8
NESPELEM WA 105-A3
NORTH POWDER OR 130-B3
WALLA WALLA CO WA 345-H4
WASHOUGAL WA 193-C7
WHITMAN CO WA 122-B1
E ST Rt#-8
FOREST GROVE OR 198-B1
E ST Rt#-207
LEXINGTON OR 128-C2
E ST Rt#-272
PALOUSE WA 249-C1
E ST U.S.-97
SHANIKO OR 127-C3
E E ST
GRANTS PASS OR 335-G9
N E ST
TACOMA WA 293-G3
N E ST Rt#-272
PALOUSE WA 249-C1
S E ST
ABERDEEN WA 178-B7
E ST NE
GRANT CO WA 112-C2
EADEN RD
CLACKAMAS CO OR 200-B4
EADON RD
LEWIS CO WA 187-D4
NE EADS ST
NEWPORT OR 206-B4
EAGAR RD
COLUMBIA CO WA 122-A2
EAGLE DR
DESCHUTES CO OR 212-C5
JACKSON CO OR 230-C4
EAGLE LN
JEFFERSON CO OR 208-C2
E EAGLE RD
BAKER CO OR 130-C3
N EAGLE RD
ADA CO ID 253-B1
EAGLE ID 253-B1
S EAGLE RD
ADA CO ID 253-B4
S EAGLE RD Rt#-55
ADA CO ID 253-B2
EAGLE ID 253-B2
MERIDIAN ID 253-B2
EAGLE WY
YAKIMA CO WA 243-C6
EAGLE CREEK DR
BAKER CO OR 130-C3
EAGLE CREEK LN
UNION CO OR 130-B3
EAGLE CREEK RD
CHELAN CO WA 111-C2
CLACKAMAS CO OR 200-C5
EAGLE CREEK RANCH RD
CLALLAM CO WA 163-C7
EAGLE CREEK-SANDY HWY Rt#-211
CLACKAMAS CO OR 200-C4
SANDY OR 200-C4
EAGLE CREST RD
POLK CO OR 204-C5
EAGLE FERN RD
CLACKAMAS CO OR 200-C5
NE EAGLE HARBOR DR
KITSAP CO WA 174-D2
KITSAP CO WA 271-J3
EAGLE MILL RD
JACKSON CO OR 337-A4
N EAGLE MILL RD
JACKSON CO OR 337-D5
EAGLEMOUNT RD
JEFFERSON CO WA 170-A2
EAGLE PEAK RD
KOOTENAI CO ID 248-D4
SW EAGLE POINT RD
YAMHILL CO OR 204-A1
EAGLE RIDGE RD
KLAMATH CO OR 231-B7
EAGLE ROCK RD
DESCHUTES CO OR 211-D5
EAGLE VALLEY RD Rt#-99
DOUGLAS CO OR 219-A3
EARLES ST
VANCOUVER BC 156-C5
EARLWOOD RD
CLACKAMAS CO OR 199-A6
YAMHILL CO OR 199-A6
EAST BLVD NE
KITSAP CO WA 271-C3
EAST MALL
UNIV ENDOWMENT LANDS BC 156-A4
EAST RD
ANMORE BC 157-A3
KLICKITAT CO WA 120-A3
KLICKITAT CO WA 128-A1
EAST RD W
SISKIYOU CO CA 150-C3
EAST AND WEST TKTR
COWLITZ CO WA 187-A7
EAST BAY DR
COOS BAY OR 220-D1
COOS CO OR 140-B2
COOS CO OR 218-B7
COOS CO OR 220-D1
COOS CO OR 333-H1
EAST BEACH RD
CLALLAM CO WA 164-C6
EAST BEAVER CREEK RD
TILLAMOOK CO OR 197-C5
EAST COVE RD
LATAH CO ID 249-D1
EASTERDAY RD
WASHINGTON CO OR 198-B1
EASTERN BOUNDARY RD
KITSAP CO WA 170-B6
EAST FORK RD
DOUGLAS CO OR 225-B1
JOSEPHINE CO OR 149-B2
EAST FORK EVANS CRK RD
JACKSON CO OR 230-C1
EAST FORK GLENN CRK RD
COOS CO OR 140-C1
EAST FORK PINE CREEK RD
SHOSHONE CO ID 115-C2
SHOSHONE CO ID 115-C2
EAST GATE RD
PIERCE CO WA 181-C6
WASCO CO OR 126-C3
WASCO CO OR 127-A3
SE EASTGATE WY
BELLEVUE WA 175-C3
EASTLAKE AV E
SEATTLE WA 274-B7
SEATTLE WA 278-B1
EASTLAKE DR
DISTRICT OF BURNABY BC 156-D4
NW EASTMAN PKWY
GRESHAM OR 200-B2
N EASTMONT AV
DOUGLAS CO WA 239-A4
EAST WENATCHEE WA 239-A4
East Wenatchee Bench WA 239-A4
EASTON CANYON RD
WASCO CO OR 127-B2
EAST POINT RD
KOOTENAI CO ID 248-A4
EAST PORTLAND FRWY I-205
CLACKAMAS CO OR 199-D3
GLADSTONE OR 199-D4
OREGON CITY OR 199-D4
PORTLAND OR 319-G7
WEST LINN OR 199-D4
EAST RIVERSIDE RD
OKANOGAN CO WA 104-C2
EAST SAANICH RD
DISTRICT OF N SAANICH BC 159-C3
EAST SHORE RD
BONNER CO ID 107-A1
EASTSIDE DR
VALLEY CO ID 251-D4
EAST SIDE RD
UMATILLA CO OR 121-C3
EASTSIDE RD
BONNER CO ID 107-A2
HOOD RIVER CO OR 195-D6
EASTSIDE ST
OLYMPIA WA 297-A5
N EASTSIDE ST
OLYMPIA WA 296-J5
OLYMPIA WA 297-A5
EASTSIDE ACCESS RD
OKANOGAN CO WA 104-C3
EASTSIDE CHEWACK RD
OKANOGAN CO WA 104-A2
WINTHROP WA 104-A2
EASTSIDE OROVILLE RD
OKANOGAN CO WA 104-C1
EASTSIDE OSOYOOS RD
OKANOGAN CO WA 104-C1
EASTSIDE-SUMNER RD
COOS CO OR 140-B2
COOS CO OR 220-D2
EAST SOOKE RD
BRITISH COLUMBIA 164-D1
BRITISH COLUMBIA 165-A1
DISTRICT OF METCHOSIN BC 165-A1
EAST TWISP-WINTHROP RD
OKANOGAN CO WA 104-A2
TWISP WA 104-A2
EAST VALLEY HWY
AUBURN WA 182-B2
PACIFIC WA 182-B2
PIERCE CO WA 182-B2
SUMNER WA 182-B2
EAST WEST RD
SISKIYOU CO CA 151-A3
EASY ST
BROOKINGS OR 232-C6
Sunnyslope WA 238-D3
S EASY ST
ROCKAWAY BEACH OR 191-B6
EATON RD
CLARK CO WA 118-A3
CLARK CO WA 193-B1
EATONVILLE HWY
EATONVILLE WA 118-B1
PIERCE CO WA 118-B1
EATONVILLE CUT-OFF RD
PIERCE CO WA 118-B1
EATONVILLE CUT-OFF RD Rt#-161
EATONVILLE WA 118-B1
PIERCE CO WA 118-B1
EATONVILLE-LA GRANDE Rt#-161
EATONVILLE WA 118-B1
PIERCE CO WA 118-B1
EBELL CREEK RD
BAKER CO OR 138-B1
EBEY RD
ISLAND CO WA 167-B4
NE EBY AV
DESCHUTES CO OR 212-D3
Terrebonne OR 212-D3
S EBY RD
CLACKAMAS CO OR 205-D1
ECHAVE RANCH RD
MALHEUR CO OR 154-B2
ECHO LAKE CTO SE Rt#-18
KING CO WA 176-B5
ECHO LAKE RD
SNOHOMISH CO WA 171-D5
ECHO LAKE-SNOQUALMIE CTO SE
KING CO WA 176-B4
ECKENSTAM-JOHNSON RD
PIERCE CO WA 181-A4
S ECKERT RD
ADA CO ID 253-D3
ECKLER MOUNTAIN RD
COLUMBIA CO WA 122-B2
ECKMAN CREEK RD
LINCOLN CO OR 209-B3
ECKS FLAT RD
ADAMS CO ID 251-B5
EDDYVILLE RD
KOOTENAI CO ID 248-B1
EDDYVILLE BLODGETT HWY
BENTON CO OR 133-A1
LINCOLN CO OR 133-A1
EDENBOWER MILLWOOD RD
DOUGLAS CO OR 221-B2
EDENS RD
SKAGIT CO WA 160-C5
EDENVALE RD
LANE CO OR 215-D3
LANE CO OR 331-J14
EDEN VALLEY RD
CLALLAM CO WA 164-D6
CLALLAM CO WA 165-A6
EDEN VALLEY RD Rt#-403
WAHKIAKUM CO WA 117-A2
EDER RD
OKANOGAN CO WA 104-C1
EDGEMONT BLVD
DIST OF N VANCOUVER BC 254-H2
EDGEWATER ST NW Rt#-221
SALEM OR 322-F12
EDGEWOOD DR
CLALLAM CO WA 165-A6
CLALLAM CO WA 261-A5
PORT ANGELES WA 165-A6
PORT ANGELES WA 261-A5
EDGEWOOD LN
KLAMATH CO OR 235-D1
EDISON AV SW
BANDON OR 220-B6
N EDISON ST
BENTON CO WA 342-F9
KENNEWICK WA 342-F9
S EDISON ST
BENTON CO WA 342-F11
KENNEWICK WA 342-F11
EDISON ICE CAVE RD
DESCHUTES CO OR 216-C5
EDLER RD
KLAMATH CO OR 151-B1
SW EDMINSTON RD
CLACKAMAS CO OR 199-A6
EDMONDS AV NE
RENTON WA 175-C5
EDMONDS ST
DISTRICT OF BURNABY BC 156-D5
EDMONDS WY Rt#-104
EDMONDS WA 171-A6
SNOHOMISH CO WA 171-A6
WOODWAY WA 171-A6
EDMONDS-KINGSTON FERRY
EDMONDS WA 171-A5
Kingston WA 170-D5
KITSAP CO WA 170-D5
SNOHOMISH CO WA 171-A5
EDMUNDSON RD
DESCHUTES CO OR 212-A4
EDMUNSON DR SE
MARION CO OR 205-B6
W EDNA ST
BOISE ID 253-B2
EDSON CREEK RD
CURRY CO OR 228-A4
EDWARDS DR
WHATCOM CO WA 101-C1
EDWARDS RD E
PIERCE CO WA 182-C2
EDWARDS BUTTE RD
TILLAMOOK CO OR 197-D3
ED WILLIAMS RD
CROOK CO OR 213-B6
SW EDY RD
WASHINGTON CO OR 199-A4
EELLS ST
TACOMA WA 182-A2
EELS RD
CHELAN CO WA 238-C2
S EGAN AV
BURNS OR 145-B1
HARNEY CO OR 145-B1
EGAN SPRINGS RD
KLAMATH CO OR 142-C3
EGG AND I RD
JEFFERSON CO WA 170-A2
NE EGLON RD
KITSAP CO WA 170-D4
EGYPT CANYON RD
HARNEY CO OR 144-C1
EHLEN RD
MARION CO OR 199-A7
N EHORN LN
CHEWELAH WA 106-B3
EICHER RD
LINN CO OR 207-D5
EID RD
LATAH CO ID 249-D6
EIGHT DOLLAR MOUNTAIN RD
JOSEPHINE CO OR 233-A2
EILERS RD
CLACKAMAS CO OR 199-B6
SW EISCHEN DR
WASHINGTON CO OR 198-C2
S EKELMAN RD
YAKIMA CO WA 243-C7
EKROTH RD
TILLAMOOK CO OR 191-B7
ELBE DR
JEFFERSON CO OR 212-D2
NW ELBE DR
JEFFERSON CO OR 208-B4
SW ELBE DR
JEFFERSON CO OR 208-B7
ELDER RD
WHATCOM CO WA 158-C6
E ELDER RD
SPOKANE CO WA 246-D7
SPOKANE CO WA 247-A7
W ELDER RD
KOOTENAI CO ID 247-C6
W ELDER RD U.S.-95
KOOTENAI CO ID 247-D5
ELDORADO AV
KLAMATH FALLS OR 338-D5
ELDORADO BLVD
KLAMATH FALLS OR 338-D4
NW EL DORADO BLVD
KITSAP CO WA 270-A3
ELDORADO RD
CLACKAMAS CO OR 199-D7
ELDRGE-FRAZIER RD
PIERCE CO WA 182-C4
ELDRIDGE AV
BELLINGHAM WA 258-B5
ELECTRIC AV
BELLINGHAM WA 258-J6
W ELECTRIC AV
SPOKANE CO WA 246-A5
ELEPHANT MOUNTAIN RD
DOUGLAS CO OR 223-B3
ELFENDAHL PASS RD
MASON CO WA 173-C5
ELGAROSE LOOP RD
DOUGLAS CO OR 221-A3
ELGER BAY RD
ISLAND CO WA 167-D5
ELGIN AV U.S.-20
CANYON CO ID 147-B1
NOTUS ID 147-B1
ELGIN RD
DISTRICT OF SURREY BC 158-A1
PAYETTE CO ID 139-B3
ELGIN-CLIFTON Rt#-302
PIERCE CO WA 174-A7
ELIJAH RD
STEVENS CO WA 114-A1
ELISHA RD
CLACKAMAS CO OR 199-C7
CLACKAMAS CO OR 205-D1
ELIZA DR
SAN JUAN CO WA 160-A6
ELIZABETH ST Rt#-27
TEKOA WA 114-C3
NE ELIZABETH ST
MILTON-FREEWATER OR 121-C3
SW ELIZABETH ST
NEWPORT OR 206-A4
NW ELK DR
JEFFERSON CO OR 208-B5
SW ELK DR
JEFFERSON CO OR 208-B5
ELK RD
JACKSON CO OR 226-C5
ELK BUTTE RD
CLEARWATER CO ID 123-C1
CLEARWATER CO ID 123-C1
N ELK- CHATTAROY RD
SPOKANE CO WA 114-C1
ELK CITY RD
LINCOLN CO OR 206-D4
ELK CREEK RD
COLUMBIA CO OR 189-A4
JACKSON CO OR 226-B6
SISKIYOU CO CA 149-A3
ELK CREEK RIDGE RD
CLALLAM CO WA 169-D1
ELKHEAD RD
DOUGLAS CO OR 219-B4
ELKHORN CREEK RD
LINCOLN CO OR 206-B6
ELKHORN RIDGE RD
JACKSON CO OR 226-A5
ELKINS RD
CROOK CO OR 213-A4
POLK CO OR 207-A1
ELK LAKE RD
IDAHO CO ID 131-C2
ELK MOUNTAIN RD
COOS CO OR 218-D7
ELKOFF RD
TILLAMOOK CO OR 197-B3
ELK PRAIRIE RD
PACIFIC CO WA 117-A2
ELK RIDGE RD N
YAKIMA CO WA 243-A2
ELK RIVER RD
CLEARWATER CO ID 123-C1
CLEARWATER CO ID 123-C1
CURRY CO OR 140-B3
CURRY CO OR 224-B6
CURRY CO OR 228-C1
ELK RIVER RD Rt#-3
LATAH CO ID 123-B1
LATAH CO ID 123-B1
ELKTON-SUTHERLIN HWY Rt#-138
DOUGLAS CO OR 141-A1
DOUGLAS CO OR 221-C1
ELKTON OR 141-A1
SUTHERLIN OR 221-C1
E ELKTON-SUTHERLIN HWY Rt#-99
SUTHERLIN OR 221-C1
W ELKTON-SUTHERLIN HWY Rt#-138
DOUGLAS CO OR 221-C1
SUTHERLIN OR 221-C1
ELK VIEW RD
DISTRICT OF CHILLIWACK BC 102-C1
ELLA RD
MORROW CO OR 128-B2
E ELLENDALE AV Rt#-223
DALLAS OR 204-A6
W ELLENDALE AV
DALLAS OR 204-A6
ELLENDALE RD
DALLAS OR 204-A6
POLK CO OR 125-B3
POLK CO OR 204-A6
W ELLENDALE RD
POLK CO OR 125-B3
ELLENS FERRY DR
BOISE ID 253-C2
ELLIGSEN RD
WASHINGTON CO OR 199-B5
WILSONVILLE OR 199-B5
ELLINGSON RD
ALBANY OR 326-C14
ALGONA WA 182-B2
AUBURN WA 182-B2
KING CO WA 182-B2
LINN CO OR 326-C14
PACIFIC WA 182-B2
ELLIOT DR
SPOKANE WA 348-D6
ELLIOT RD
CLARK CO WA 193-B1
DESCHUTES CO OR 213-A4
MULTNOMAH CO OR 192-A6
ELLIOT ST
DISTRICT OF DELTA BC 101-C1
ELLIOTT AV
SEATTLE WA 277-H4
ELLIOTT AV W
SEATTLE WA 277-F2
ELLIOTT LN
CROOK CO OR 213-C4
ELLIOTT RD
SNOHOMISH CO WA 171-D5
ELLIOTT PRAIRIE RD NE
MARION CO OR 205-C2
ELLIS AV S
SEATTLE WA 282-B7
SEATTLE WA 286-B1
ELLIS LN
BENEWAH CO ID 248-A7
ELLIS RD
BAKER CO OR 130-A3
UNION CO OR 130-A3
ELLIS RD SW
DOUGLAS CO WA 239-C3
ELLIS ST
BELLINGHAM WA 258-E4
SE ELLSWORTH RD
VANCOUVER WA 307-H7
VANCOUVER WA 311-H1
ELLSWORTH ST U.S.-20
ALBANY OR 326-C8
ELM AV
TILLAMOOK OR 197-B2
E ELM AV
COEUR D'ALENE ID 355-G10
HERMISTON OR 129-A1
UMATILLA CO OR 129-A1
S ELM AV
PASCO WA 343-J8
W ELM AV
HERMISTON OR 129-A1
ELM LN
CANYON CO ID 147-C1
NE ELM LN
JEFFERSON CO OR 208-C4
NW ELM LN
JEFFERSON CO OR 208-B4
ELM ST
ALBANY OR 326-B8
ASOTIN CO WA 250-B4
BELLINGHAM WA 258-C5
CANNON BEACH OR 188-B7
CHENEY WA 246-A7
CLARKSTON WA 250-B4
SISTERS OR 211-D5
SUMNER WA 182-B3
WHATCOM CO WA 101-C1
ELM ST U.S.-30
BAKER CITY OR 138-B1
E ELM ST
DOUGLAS CO WA 236-C7
WATERVILLE WA 236-C7
S ELM ST Rt#-22
TOPPENISH WA 120-A2
ELMA-GATE RD
GRAYS HARBOR CO WA 117-B1
ELMA-HICKLIN RD
GRAYS HARBOR CO WA 179-C6
ELMA-MCCLEARY RD
GRAYS HARBOR CO WA 179-C6
MCCLEARY WA 179-C6
ELMORE RD
PAYETTE CO ID 139-A3
ELMWAY Rt#-20
OKANOGAN WA 104-C3
OKANOGAN CO WA 104-C3
OMAK WA 104-C3
ELO RD
VALLEY CO ID 251-D6
ELOCHOMAN MAINLINE Rt#-407
WAHKIAKUM CO WA 117-B3
EL RIO LN
LANE CO OR 210-A6
ELROD AV
COOS BAY OR 333-G10
ELSNER RD
CLACKAMAS CO OR 200-D3
SW ELSNER RD
WASHINGTON CO OR 199-A4
ELTOPIA WEST RD
FRANKLIN CO WA 121-A2
ELTOPIA WEST RD W
FRANKLIN CO WA 121-A2
SW ELWERT RD
WASHINGTON CO OR 199-A4
ELWHA RIVER RD
CLALLAM CO WA 165-A6
ELWOOD DR SW
LAKEWOOD WA 181-C4
N ELY PL
KENNEWICK WA 342-J9
KENNEWICK WA 343-A9
N ELY ST U.S.-395
KENNEWICK WA 342-J10
S ELY ST
KENNEWICK WA 342-J13
KENNEWICK WA 343-A12
S ELY ST U.S.-395
KENNEWICK WA 342-J11
EMANDER RD
EVERETT WA 268-A5
SNOHOMISH WA 268-A5
EMENS AV Rt#-530
DARRINGTON WA 103-A3
EMERALD RD
GRANGER WA 120-B2
YAKIMA CO WA 120-B2
EMERALD ST
BOISE ID 253-C3
EMERSON AV Rt#-109
HOQUIAM WA 178-A7
NE EMERSON DR
JEFFERSON CO OR 208-D3
EMERSON LN
JEFFERSON CO OR 208-D4
W EMERSON PL
SEATTLE WA 272-E6
SEATTLE WA 273-E6
EMERSON RD
DOUGLAS CO OR 222-B7
W EMERSON ST
SEATTLE WA 272-C6
SEATTLE WA 273-F6
EMERSON LOOP RD
WASCO CO OR 127-B2
WASCO CO OR 196-D7
EMERY RD
CLALLAM CO WA 165-D7
SE EMIGRANT AV Rt#-37
PENDLETON OR 129-B1
SW EMIGRANT AV Rt#-37
PENDLETON OR 129-B1
EMIGRANT CREEK RD
HARNEY CO OR 136-C3
HARNEY CO OR 137-A3
EMIGRANTS RD
UMATILLA CO OR 129-B1
EMIGRANT SPRINGS RD
SHERMAN CO OR 127-C1
W EMMA AV
COEUR D'ALENE ID 355-D9
KOOTENAI CO ID 355-D9
EMMA ST Rt#-278
ROCKFORD WA 114-C2
EMMETT HWY Rt#-16
ADA CO ID 139-C3
ADA CO ID 147-C1
EMMETT RD
ADAMS CO ID 139-C1
CANYON CO ID 147-B1
NW EMPIRE AV
East Wenatchee Bench WA 239-A4
EMPIRE BLVD
BEND OR 332-F2
DESCHUTES CO OR 332-F2
S EMPIRE BLVD
CLATSOP CO OR 188-B2
COOS BAY OR 333-A8
COOS CO OR 220-C1
COOS CO OR 333-A8
WARRENTON OR 188-B2
E EMPIRE WY
MILLWOOD WA 350-D5
SPOKANE CO WA 350-F4
EMPIRE WY S
SEATTLE WA 278-D7
SEATTLE WA 282-D1
SEATTLE WA 283-E7
SEATTLE WA 287-E1
TUKWILA WA 287-E5
EMPIRE-COOS BAY HWY
COOS BAY OR 333-D8
ENCHANTED PKWY Rt#-161
FEDERAL WAY WA 182-B1
ENCHANTED PKWY S Rt#-161
EDGEWOOD WA 182-B2
FEDERAL WAY WA 182-B2
KING CO WA 182-B2
MILTON WA 182-B2
S ENDICOTT RD
ENDICOTT WA 122-B1
WHITMAN CO WA 122-B1
ENDICOTT RD E
WHITMAN CO WA 122-B1
ENDICOTT RD SW
THURSTON CO WA 184-B2
ENDICOTT RD W
ENDICOTT WA 122-A1
WHITMAN CO WA 122-A1
ENDICOTT-SAINT JOHN RD
ENDICOTT WA 122-B1
WHITMAN CO WA 114-B3
WHITMAN CO WA 122-B1
ENDICOTT-SAINT JOHN RD Rt#-23
SAINT JOHN WA 114-B3
WHITMAN CO WA 114-B3
ENDRESEN RD
HOQUIAM WA 178-A7
ENGEL RD
LINCOLN CO WA 113-C2
LINN CO OR 207-D5
ENGLE RD
ISLAND CO WA 167-B5
ENGLEWOOD AV
YAKIMA WA 243-A6
YAKIMA CO WA 243-A6
ENGLEWOOD-SHINGLEHOUSE RD
COOS CO OR 220-D2
COOS CO OR 333-F14
ENGLISH RD
SKAGIT CO WA 168-B2
ENGLISH BLUFF RD
DISTRICT OF DELTA BC 101-C1
ENGLISH GRADE RD
SNOHOMISH CO WA 168-B3
ENGLISH PT RD
KOOTENAI CO ID 245-A5
E ENID RD
LANE CO OR 215-A1
ENMAN-KINCAID RD
WHITMAN CO WA 249-A5
ENNIS CREEK RD
WHATCOM CO WA 161-C3
W ENOCH RD
SPOKANE CO WA 114-B1
ENTERPRISE AV
MALHEUR CO OR 139-A3
ENTERPRISE RD
COLUMBIA CO OR 189-A6
FERNDALE WA 158-C5
POLK CO OR 125-B3
POLK CO OR 204-A4
WHATCOM CO WA 158-C5
E ENTERPRISE RD
LANE CO OR 215-C5
N ENTERPRISE RD
WHATCOM CO WA 158-D4
ENTERPRISE-LEWISTON HWY Rt#-3
WALLOWA CO OR 122-C3
WALLOWA CO OR 130-C1
ENTIAT RIVER RD
CHELAN CO WA 112-A1
CHELAN CO WA 236-A6
ENTRANCE MOUNTAIN RD
SAN JUAN CO WA 160-A3
ENUMCLW BLK DMND RD SE Rt#-169
BLACK DIAMOND WA 110-C3
KING CO WA 110-C3
ENUMCLAW BUCKLEY RD Rt#-410
ENUMCLAW WA 110-C3
KING CO WA 110-C3

PNW
INDEX

PNW

INDEX

FREEWAY I-90 STREET INDEX GEORGE WASHINGTON WY 371

STREET City State Page-Grid

FREEWAY I-90
KITTITAS CO WA 120-A1
KITTITAS CO WA 240-D4
KITTITAS CO WA 241-C6
KOOTENAI CO ID 115-B2
KOOTENAI CO ID 245-B7
KOOTENAI CO ID 248-B1
KOOTENAI CO ID 352-J9
KOOTENAI CO ID 353-F7
KOOTENAI CO ID 354-B7
KOOTENAI CO ID 355-A7
LINCOLN CO WA 114-B2
MERCER ISLAND WA 175-C3
MERCER ISLAND WA 283-J1
MOSES LAKE WA 242-D3
NORTH BEND WA 176-B4
OSBURN ID 115-C2
PINEHURST ID 115-C2
POST FALLS ID 352-J9
POST FALLS ID 353-G6
POST FALLS ID 354-B7
SEATTLE WA 278-B7
SEATTLE WA 282-C1
SEATTLE WA 283-J1
SHOSHONE CO ID 115-C2
SHOSHONE CO ID 115-C2
SNOQUALMIE WA 176-B4
SPOKANE WA 348-B14
SPOKANE WA 349-B10
SPOKANE CO WA 114-B2
SPOKANE CO WA 246-B5
SPOKANE CO WA 348-B14
SPOKANE CO WA 349-J8
SPOKANE CO WA 350-F6
SPOKANE CO WA 351-D7
SPOKANE CO WA 352-C12
SPRAGUE WA 114-B2
Veradale WA 351-D7
WALLACE ID 115-C2
WALLACE ID 115-C2
FREEWAY I-99
DISTRICT OF DELTA BC 101-C1
FREEWAY I-182
BENTON CO WA 121-A3
BENTON CO WA 341-E4
FRANKLIN CO WA 342-B2
FRANKLIN CO WA 343-A4
PASCO WA 342-C1
PASCO WA 343-A4
RICHLAND WA 341-J3
RICHLAND WA 342-A3
FREEWAY I-184
ADA CO ID 253-B3
BOISE ID 253-C3
FREEWAY I-205
CLARK WA 307-H2
CLARK CO WA 192-D5
MAYWOOD PARK OR 315-H4
PORTLAND OR 193-A7
PORTLAND OR 311-J2
PORTLAND OR 315-H4
PORTLAND OR 319-G1
VANCOUVER WA 192-D5
VANCOUVER WA 307-H2
VANCOUVER WA 311-J2
FREEWAY I-405
BELLEVUE WA 175-C1
BOTHELL WA 171-C6
KING CO WA 171-C7
KING CO WA 175-C4
KIRKLAND WA 171-C7
KIRKLAND WA 175-C1
NEWCASTLE WA 175-C4
PORTLAND OR 312-E3
PORTLAND OR 313-F3
PORTLAND OR 317-E1
RENTON WA 175-C4
RENTON WA 289-J4
SNOHOMISH CO WA 171-C6
TUKWILA WA 289-J4
FREEWAY I-705
TACOMA WA 293-H4
TACOMA WA 295-J2
FREEWAY Rt#-3
BREMERTON WA 174-B4
BREMERTON WA 270-C6
KITSAP CO WA 170-B6
KITSAP CO WA 174-B1
KITSAP CO WA 270-B1
Navy Yard City WA 270-E11
Silverdale WA 174-B1
Silverdale WA 270-B1
Tracyton WA 270-A4
FREEWAY Rt#-7
TACOMA WA 295-H1
FREEWAY Rt#-16
GIG HARBOR WA 174-B7
GIG HARBOR WA 181-C1
KITSAP CO WA 174-B7
PIERCE CO WA 174-B7
PIERCE CO WA 181-C1
PORT ORCHARD WA 174-B7
TACOMA WA 292-B7
TACOMA WA 294-D1
TACOMA WA 295-E1
FREEWAY Rt#-18
AUBURN WA 182-B1
FEDERAL WAY WA 182-B1
KING CO WA 182-B1
FREEWAY Rt#-26
GRANT CO WA 120-B1
FREEWAY Rt#-91
CITY OF RICHMOND BC 156-B6
FREEWAY Rt#-99
CITY OF RICHMOND BC 156-B6
DISTRICT OF DELTA BC 156-C7
DISTRICT OF SURREY BC 158-A1
KING WA 286-B4
SEATTLE WA 281-J7
SEATTLE WA 285-J1
SEATTLE WA 286-B4
TUKWILA WA 286-B4
WHATCOM CO WA 158-B3
FREEWAY Rt#-167
PACIFIC WA 182-B3
PIERCE CO WA 182-B3
PUYALLUP WA 182-B3
SUMNER WA 182-B3
FREEWAY Rt#-240
KENNEWICK WA 342-D7
FREEWAY Rt#-240
KENNEWICK WA 343-A9
RICHLAND WA 341-H4
RICHLAND WA 342-A6
FREEWAY Rt#-410
PIERCE CO WA 182-C3
FREEWAY Rt#-509
BURIEN WA 175-A5
BURIEN WA 288-A2
BURIEN WA 290-A1
KING WA 286-A5
KING WA 288-A2
SEATAC WA 288-A6
SEATAC WA 290-A1
SEATTLE WA 285-J1
SEATTLE WA 286-A5
TACOMA WA 182-A2
TACOMA WA 293-J6
FREEWAY Rt#-512
LAKEWOOD WA 181-D4
PIERCE CO WA 181-D4
PIERCE CO WA 182-A4
PUYALLUP WA 182-A4
FREEWAY Rt#-518
BURIEN WA 175-A5
BURIEN WA 288-B4
SEATAC WA 288-B4
TUKWILA WA 288-D5
TUKWILA WA 289-E4
FREEWAY Rt#-520
BELLEVUE WA 175-D1
CLYDE HILL WA 175-D1
HUNTS POINT WA 175-D1
KING CO WA 175-D1
MEDINA WA 175-D1
MEDINA WA 279-E1
REDMOND WA 175-D1
SEATTLE WA 278-D1
SEATTLE WA 279-E1
YARROW POINT WA 175-D1
FREEWAY Rt#-522
BOTHELL WA 171-C6
SNOHOMISH CO WA 171-C6
WOODINVILLE WA 171-C6
FREEWAY Rt#-526
EVERETT WA 267-F4
EVERETT WA 268-A4
MUKILTEO WA 267-F4
SNOHOMISH WA 267-F4
FREEWAY Rt#-599
TUKWILA WA 286-D7
TUKWILA WA 287-E7
TUKWILA WA 289-E1
FREEWAY U.S.-2
CASHMERE WA 238-C2
CHELAN CO WA 238-C2
DOUGLAS CO WA 239-A3
East Wenatchee Bench WA 238-C2
East Wenatchee Bench WA 239-A3
EVERETT WA 265-J4
SNOHOMISH WA 265-J4
SNOHOMISH CO WA 171-D2
Sunnyslope WA 238-C2
FREEWAY U.S.-12
PASCO WA 343-H5
FREEWAY U.S.-97
Sunnyslope WA 238-D3
FREEWAY U.S.-101
MASON CO WA 180-B5
OLYMPIA WA 296-E7
THURSTON CO WA 180-B5
THURSTON CO WA 296-B5
TUMWATER WA 296-E7
FREEWAY U.S.-395
BENTON CO WA 121-A3
Finley WA 121-A3
KENNEWICK WA 343-B9
LEWISTON OR 121-A3
PASCO WA 343-D5
UMATILLA CO OR 121-A3
FREIMUTH RD
YAKIMA CO WA 243-B4
E FREMONT AV
SELAH WA 243-B5
W FREMONT AV
SELAH WA 243-B5
FREMONT AV N
SEATTLE WA 273-H5
FREMONT HWY Rt#-31
DESCHUTES CO OR 143-A1
KLAMATH CO OR 143-A1
LAKE CO OR 143-B2
LAKE CO OR 151-C1
LAKE CO OR 152-A1
PAISLEY OR 151-C1
FREMONT HWY U.S.-395
LAKE CO OR 152-A2
LAKEVIEW OR 152-A2
MODOC CO CA 152-A3
FREMONT PL N
SEATTLE WA 273-H6
NE FREMONT ST
PORTLAND OR 313-H2
PORTLAND OR 314-C2
PORTLAND OR 315-E2
FREMONT ST E
THE DALLES OR 196-D7
FREMONT WY N
SEATTLE WA 273-H6
FRENCH RD
ISLAND CO WA 171-A2
FRENCHGLEN HWY Rt#-205
HARNEY CO OR 145-B1
FRENCHGLEN RD
LAKE CO OR 152-C1
LAKE CO OR 153-A1
E FRENCH GULCH RD
KOOTENAI CO ID 245-B7
FRENCH HILL RD
DEL NORTE CO CA 148-B3
FRENCHMAN CREEK RD
MALHEUR CO OR 154-C2
FRENCHMAN HILL RD
GRANT CO WA 112-B3
GRANT CO WA 120-B1
FRENCH MOUNTAIN RD
JOSEPHINE CO OR 233-C5
FRENCH PRAIRIE RD
MARION CO OR 198-D7
MARION CO OR 199-A6
FRENCH PRAIRIE RD Rt#-219
MARION CO OR 198-D7
MARION CO OR 205-A1
FRENCH PRAIRIE RD NE
MARION CO OR 205-A2
FRESHWATER BAY RD
CLALLAM CO WA 164-D5
N FREYA ST
SPOKANE WA 349-F8
S FREYA ST
SPOKANE WA 246-C5
SPOKANE WA 349-F11
SPOKANE CO WA 246-C5
FRIDAY CREEK RD
SKAGIT CO WA 161-B4
FRIEDA AV
Altamont OR 338-J9
Altamont OR 339-A9
FRIEND RD
WASCO CO OR 127-A2
FRIENDLY ST
EUGENE OR 329-H10
FRIENDS RD
CANYON CO ID 147-B1
FRIES RD
LEWIS CO WA 187-B3
FRITZ HOEFT RD
UMATILLA CO OR 129-B2
FRIZZELL RD
POLK CO OR 204-B4
SW FROBASE RD
WASHINGTON CO OR 199-B5
FROG CREEK RD
WASCO CO OR 202-B7
FROG HOLLOW RD
WALLA WALLA CO WA 121-C3
WALLA WALLA CO WA 344-A14
FROG LAKE BUTTE RD
WASCO CO OR 202-B7
FROGNER RD
LEWIS CO WA 187-B1
NW FRONT AV
PORTLAND OR 312-C2
S FRONT AV
PASCO WA 343-H8
SW FRONT AV U.S.-26
PORTLAND OR 317-F1
W FRONT AV Rt#-21
LINCOLN CO WA 113-B1
WILBUR WA 113-B1
FRONT ST
COOS BAY OR 333-H12
IDAHO CO ID 123-B3
IDAHO CO ID 123-B3
JOSEPHINE CO OR 229-B1
LYNDEN WA 102-B1
LYNDEN WA 158-D4
MARION CO OR 205-B1
POULSBO WA 170-B6
SHOSHONE CO ID 115-C2
SHOSHONE CO ID 115-C2
WALLACE ID 115-C2
WALLACE ID 115-C2
WOODBURN OR 205-B1
FRONT ST Rt#-23
SAINT JOHN WA 114-B3
FRONT ST Rt#-47
GASTON OR 198-B3
YAMHILL CO OR 198-B3
FRONT ST Rt#-99
YONCALLA OR 219-B4
FRONT ST Rt#-409
CATHLAMET WA 117-B3
CLATSOP CO OR 117-B3
FRONT ST Rt#-507
BUCODA WA 184-D4
THURSTON CO WA 184-D4
FRONT ST Rt#-547
SUMAS WA 102-B1
WHATCOM CO WA 102-B1
FRONT ST U.S.-20
BOISE ID 253-C2
FRONT ST U.S.-26
GRANT CO OR 137-B2
PRAIRIE CITY OR 137-B2
FRONT ST U.S.-30
HOOD RIVER OR 195-D5
E FRONT ST
ALBION WA 249-A4
E FRONT ST Rt#-39
MERRILL OR 150-C2
N FRONT ST Rt#-99
CENTRAL POINT OR 230-C7
NW FRONT ST
CHEHALIS WA 299-D11
S FRONT ST Rt#-99
CENTRAL POINT OR 230-C7
OAKLAND OR 219-A7
SE FRONT ST Rt#-202
ASTORIA OR 300-D7
CLATSOP CO OR 300-D7
W FRONT ST
ALBION WA 249-A4
W FRONT ST Rt#-39
MERRILL OR 150-C2
FRONT ST N
ISSAQUAH WA 176-A4
FRONT ST NE
SALEM OR 322-J10
FRONT ST NE Rt#-22
SALEM OR 322-H12
FRONT ST NE Rt#-99E
SALEM OR 322-H12
FRONT ST S
ISSAQUAH WA 176-A4
FRONT ST SE Rt#-22
SALEM OR 322-H13
FRONTAGE RD
CURRY CO OR 232-B1
GRANT CO WA 242-A3
MORROW CO OR 128-C1
N FRONTAGE RD
GRANT CO WA 112-C3
GRANT CO WA 242-A3
JOSEPHINE CO OR 225-B7
N FRONTAGE RD Rt#-509
TACOMA WA 182-A2
S FRONTAGE RD Rt#-509
TACOMA WA 182-A2
W FRONTAGE RD
BAKER CO OR 130-B3
FROST RD
KOOTENAI CO ID 247-C6
LEWIS CO WA 187-C3
FROSTAD RD
ISLAND CO WA 167-C2
FROSTY CREEK RD
OKANOGAN CO WA 105-A2
FROZEN CREEK RD
DOUGLAS CO OR 221-D7
FRUITDALE DR
GRANTS PASS OR 335-F11
JOSEPHINE CO OR 335-F11
FRUITDALE LN
ISLAND CITY OR 130-A2
UNION CO OR 130-A2
FRUITDALE RD
SEDRO-WOOLLEY WA 161-C6
SKAGIT CO WA 161-C5
FRUIT FARM RD
POLK CO OR 207-B1
FRUITLAND AV E
PIERCE CO WA 182-A4
PUYALLUP WA 182-A4
FRUITLAND RD NE
MARION CO OR 323-H13
FRUITVALE BLVD
YAKIMA WA 243-B6
W FRUITVALE BLVD
YAKIMA WA 243-B6
FRUITVALE RD
ADAMS CO ID 131-C3
LINCOLN CO OR 206-B4
FRUIT VALLEY RD
VANCOUVER WA 304-E3
NW FRUIT VALLEY RD
VANCOUVER WA 192-C5
VANCOUVER WA 304-E1
FRY LN
HARNEY CO OR 145-B1
FRY RD
LINN CO OR 207-D6
LINN CO OR 326-J14
MARION CO OR 199-A7
FRYER RD
YAMHILL CO OR 198-B5
FRYREAR RD
DESCHUTES CO OR 212-A5
FS RD 307
ADAMS CO ID 251-B4
FUGATE RD
WHITMAN CO WA 249-A2
FUHRMAN AV E
SEATTLE WA 274-B7
FULLER RD
LEWIS CO WA 187-A1
FULLER CANYON RD
MORROW CO OR 128-C2
FULLERTON RD
COLUMBIA CO OR 192-A3
FULTON AV
DIST OF WEST VANCOUVER BC 254-C3
FULTON RD
UMATILLA CO OR 129-B1
FUNKE RD
LANE CO OR 210-B7
LANE CO OR 215-B1

G

G ST
CLATSOP CO OR 301-H5
GEARHART OR 301-H5
LEWISTON ID 250-C4
SPRINGFIELD OR 330-H6
SPRINGFIELD OR 331-A6
WALLA WALLA CO WA 345-H4
E G ST
TACOMA WA 293-J7
N G ST
ABERDEEN WA 178-B7
S G ST
ABERDEEN WA 178-B7
TACOMA WA 295-G2
S G ST U.S.-101
ABERDEEN WA 178-B7
W G ST
GRANTS PASS OR 335-D8
JOSEPHINE CO OR 335-D8
G ST N U.S.-395
LAKEVIEW OR 152-A2
G 100 RD
GRAYS HARBOR CO WA 179-A6
G 1100 RD
GRAYS HARBOR CO WA 179-A5
SW GAARDE ST
TIGARD OR 199-B3
GABLE RD
COLUMBIA CO OR 192-A2
SAINT HELENS OR 192-A2
GAFFIN RD SE
MARION CO OR 325-G3
SALEM OR 325-G3
GAGE BLVD
KENNEWICK WA 342-A8
RICHLAND WA 341-H8
RICHLAND WA 342-A8
GAGE RD
POLK CO OR 133-A1
SW GAGE RD
CLACKAMAS CO OR 199-B5
GAGLARDI WY
DISTRICT OF BURNABY BC 156-D4
GAITHER ST Rt#-229
LINCOLN CO OR 206-C2
SILETZ OR 206-C2
GALE RD
KLAMATH CO OR 151-A2
GALENA DR
DESCHUTES CO OR 212-C3
W GALER ST
SEATTLE WA 276-D2
GALES CREEK RD Rt#-8
FOREST GROVE OR 198-B1
WASHINGTON CO OR 125-B1
WASHINGTON CO OR 198-B1
GALICE RD
JOSEPHINE CO OR 148-C1
JOSEPHINE CO OR 149-A1
GALLAGHER RD
MASON CO WA 179-D3
GALLAHER RD
DOUGLAS CO WA 112-B1
GALLOWAY DR
JEFFERSON CO OR 208-B6
GALLOWAY RD
TILLAMOOK CO OR 197-A5
YAKIMA CO WA 243-B5
GALLS CREEK RD
JACKSON CO OR 230-A6
NW GALVESTON AV
BEND OR 332-C7
GALVIN RD
CENTRALIA WA 184-B5
CENTRALIA WA 299-A1
LEWIS CO WA 184-B5
LEWIS CO WA 299-A1
GAMBLE PL NE
KITSAP CO WA 170-C5
S GAMBLE BAY RD NE
KITSAP CO WA 170-C5
GAME FARM RD
EUGENE OR 330-E1
KITTITAS CO WA 241-C5
LANE CO OR 330-E1
SPRINGFIELD OR 330-F1
N GAME FARM RD
LANE CO OR 215-B1
GAME FARM RD E
LANE CO OR 330-F2
SPRINGFIELD OR 330-F2
GAME FARM RD N
SPRINGFIELD OR 330-E1
GAME FARM RD S
North Springfield OR 330-G2
SPRINGFIELD OR 330-G2
GAME RIDGE RD
YAKIMA CO WA 243-B4
GANON ST SE
MARION CO OR 325-J5
GAP RD
BROWNSVILLE OR 210-C4
LINN CO OR 210-C4
N GAP RD
BENTON CO WA 120-B3
S GAP RD
BENTON CO WA 120-B3
PROSSER WA 120-B3
GAP RANCH-WAGONTIRE RD
HARNEY CO OR 144-B2
GARBAGE DUMP RD
CLALLAM CO WA 169-C2
GARD RD
CLACKAMAS CO OR 200-A7
GARDEN AV
BENTON CO OR 207-B5
W GARDEN AV
COEUR D'ALENE ID 355-D11
GARDEN WY
LANE CO OR 330-F7
SPRINGFIELD OR 330-F7
GARDENA RD
WALLA WALLA CO WA 121-B3
GARDENA SCHOOL RD
WALLA WALLA CO WA 121-B3
GARDEN CITY RD
CITY OF RICHMOND BC 156-B6
GARDEN SPRINGS RD
SPOKANE WA 348-C13
SPOKANE CO WA 348-C13
NE GARDEN VALLEY BLVD
ROSEBURG OR 334-F5
NW GARDEN VALLEY BLVD
DOUGLAS CO OR 334-B4
ROSEBURG OR 334-F5
GARDEN VALLEY RD
COOS CO OR 220-D4
DOUGLAS CO OR 221-B3
DOUGLAS CO OR 334-A1
GARDNER RD
POLK CO OR 125-B3
SKAGIT CO WA 260-F5
N GARDNER RD
SKAGIT CO WA 260-F2
S GARDNER RD
SPOKANE CO WA 246-B6
S GARDNER ST
BURLINGTON WA 260-F5
SKAGIT CO WA 260-F5
GARDNER RIDGE RD
CURRY CO OR 232-D4
GARFIELD AV
CORVALLIS OR 327-F7
GARFIELD AV SE
KITSAP CO WA 174-C4
N GARFIELD RD
SPOKANE CO WA 246-A3
NE GARFIELD ST Rt#-500
CAMAS WA 193-B7
S GARFIELD ST
KENNEWICK WA 343-C12
S GARFIELD ST Rt#-126
EUGENE OR 329-G6
GARFIELD BAY CTO
BONNER CO ID 244-B4
GARFIELD BAY RD
BONNER CO ID 244-B4
GARFIELD-FARMINGTON RD
FARMINGTON WA 115-A3
FARMINGTON WA 115-A3
GARFIELD WA 114-C3
WHITMAN CO WA 114-C3
WHITMAN CO WA 115-A3
WHITMAN CO WA 115-A3
GARIBALDI AV U.S.-101
GARIBALDI OR 191-B7
TILLAMOOK CO OR 191-B7
N GARL ST
BURLINGTON WA 260-C4
SKAGIT CO WA 260-C4
S GARL ST
BURLINGTON WA 260-C8
W GARLAND AV
SPOKANE WA 348-F4
SPOKANE WA 349-A4
GARLOCK RD
COWLITZ CO WA 189-B1
GARNER RD
CLARK CO WA 193-B2
GARNER RD
JOSEPHINE CO OR 233-B4
KLICKITAT CO WA 127-B1
YACOLT WA 193-B2
NE GARNER RD
CLARK CO WA 193-B1
GARRARD CREEK RD
GRAYS HARBOR CO WA 117-B1
OAKVILLE WA 117-B1
GARRETT ST
GARDEN CITY ID 253-B2
GARRISON RD Rt#-547
WHATCOM CO WA 102-B1
GARRISON ST
WALLA WALLA WA 345-F7
Walla Walla East WA 345-F7
GARRISON BUTTE RD
JEFFERSON CO OR 211-D3
GARRITY BLVD
CANYON CO ID 147-C1
GARRITY BLVD U.S.-30
CANYON CO ID 147-C1
NAMPA ID 147-C1
S GARRY RD
Liberty Lake WA 247-B4
SPOKANE CO WA 247-B4
E GARWOOD RD
KOOTENAI CO ID 245-A4
GARY LN
BOISE ID 253-C1
GASSY CREEK RD
DOUGLAS CO OR 219-C7
SW GASTON RD
GASTON OR 198-B3
WASHINGTON CO OR 198-B3
GATE CREEK RD
WASCO CO OR 202-D7
GATE MIMA RD
THURSTON CO WA 184-A3
GATENSBURY RD
COQUITLAM BC 157-A5
PORT MOODY BC 157-A5
GATENSBURY ST
COQUITLAM BC 157-A4
GATEWAY DR
COOS CO OR 220-C4
GATEWAY RD
COOS CO OR 220-C5
GATEWAY ST
SPRINGFIELD OR 330-F4
NE GATEWAY GRADE
JEFFERSON CO OR 208-C2
GATFIELD
GEM CO ID 139-C3
GAZLEY RD
DOUGLAS CO OR 225-C3
GAZLEY BRIDGE RD
DOUGLAS CO OR 225-C3
GAZLEY NORTH RD
DOUGLAS CO OR 225-C2
GAZLEY PACIFIC HWY
DOUGLAS CO OR 225-C3
GEARHART LOOP RD
CLATSOP CO OR 301-G2
GEARHART OR 301-G2
GEARY ST
ALBANY OR 326-E10
GEHRING RD
PIERCE CO WA 182-A3
S GEIGER BLVD
SPOKANE CO WA 246-B5
SPOKANE CO WA 348-B13
W GEIGER BLVD
SPOKANE CO WA 246-A5
SPOKANE CO WA 348-C11
GEIGER RD
FOREST GROVE OR 198-C1
WASHINGTON CO OR 198-C1
GEISSLER RD
GRAYS HARBOR CO WA 178-C6
W GEISSLER RD
GRAYS HARBOR CO WA 178-C7
GEKELER LN
BOISE ID 253-D3
LA GRANDE OR 130-B2
UNION CO OR 130-B2
GELLOR RD
CLALLAM CO WA 165-D7
GEM AV
MALHEUR CO OR 139-A3
SW GEM LN
JEFFERSON CO OR 208-B7
GEM HEIGHTS DR E
PIERCE CO WA 182-B5
GENE BROWN RD
JOSEPHINE CO OR 233-A6
S GENESEE ST
SEATTLE WA 282-E5
SEATTLE WA 283-F5
SW GENESEE ST
SEATTLE WA 281-F4
GENESEE-JULIAETTA RD
LATAH CO ID 250-D1
GENESEE-TROY RD
LATAH CO ID 249-D7
GENSMAN RD
COLUMBIA CO OR 192-A1
GENZER RD
WASHINGTON CO OR 125-B1
GEO CYPRUS RD
DESCHUTES CO OR 212-A5
GEORGE RD
CLACKAMAS CO OR 200-C5
GEORGE CLARK RD
GRAYS HARBOR CO WA 183-C2
GEORGE HOPPER RD
BURLINGTON WA 260-A8
SKAGIT CO WA 260-A8
GEORGE KNOTT RD
WHITMAN CO WA 114-A3
GEORGE MASSEY TUN Rt#-99
CITY OF RICHMOND BC 156-B7
DISTRICT OF DELTA BC 156-C7
GEORGE SMITH RD
MULTNOMAH CO OR 200-D1
GEORGE TAYLOR RD
COWLITZ CO WA 187-D6
GEORGE WASHINGTON WY
BENTON CO WA 340-F4
RICHLAND WA 340-G9

PNW INDEX

374 HART MOUNTAIN RD STREET INDEX HILYARD AV

COPYRIGHT 1999 Thomas Bros. Maps ®

PNW
INDEX

STREET City State Page-Grid

HART MOUNTAIN RD
LAKE CO OR 152-B1
HARTS LAKE RD S
PIERCE CO WA 118-A1
HARTS LAKE LOOP RD
PIERCE CO WA 118-A1
PIERCE CO WA 181-D7
E HARTSON AV
SPOKANE WA 349-C10
W HARTSON AV
SPOKANE WA 348-F10
HARTSTENE ISLAND NORTH RD
MASON CO WA 180-D2
HARTSTENE ISLAND SOUTH RD
MASON CO WA 180-D3
HARVARD AV E
SEATTLE WA 278-B2
SW HARVARD BLVD Rt#-138
ROSEBURG OR 334-F7
W HARVARD BLVD
ROSEBURG OR 334-B7
W HARVARD BLVD Rt#-138
ROSEBURG OR 334-E7
N HARVARD RD
Otis Orchards WA 352-B9
SPOKANE CO WA 352-B9
S HARVARD RD
SPOKANE CO WA 247-B7
HARVEST DR
LINN CO OR 207-B7
SW HARVEST LN
DESCHUTES CO OR 212-C6
HARVEY AV
ROSEBURG OR 334-C6
HARVEY RD
AUBURN WA 182-C1
CLACKAMAS CO OR 200-D6
LANE CO OR 215-C4
WHATCOM CO WA 158-B3
HARVEY SHAW RD
WALLA WALLA CO WA 121-C3
WALLA WALLA CO WA 344-F1
HARVIE RD
DISTRICT OF SURREY BC 157-B7
HARWOOD ST
PRINEVILLE OR 213-D5
HARYU RD
COWLITZ CO WA 189-A2
HASIS DR
JOSEPHINE CO OR 229-B3
HASKINS RD
KLAMATH CO OR 151-A2
SISKIYOU CO CA 151-A3
HASTIE LAKE RD
ISLAND CO WA 167-B3
HASTINGS AV W
JEFFERSON CO WA 166-D6
JEFFERSON CO WA 263-A4
PORT TOWNSEND WA 263-A4
E HASTINGS RD
Fairwood WA 346-J8
Fairwood WA 347-A8
SPOKANE CO WA 347-A8
W HASTINGS RD
Fairwood WA 346-J8
HASTINGS ST
VANCOUVER BC 254-G10
HASTINGS ST Rt#-7A
DISTRICT OF BURNABY BC 156-D4
DISTRICT OF BURNABY BC 255-G10
VANCOUVER BC 255-F10
HASTINGS ST E Rt#-7A
VANCOUVER BC 254-J10
VANCOUVER BC 255-B10
HASTINGS HILL RD
GARFIELD CO WA 122-B1
S HATCH RD
SPOKANE WA 246-C5
SPOKANE CO WA 246-C5
HATCHET SLOUGH RD
COOS CO OR 220-C5
HATFIELD HWY Rt#-39
KLAMATH CO OR 151-A2
SISKIYOU CO CA 151-A3
HATLEY RD
WHITMAN CO WA 249-A6
S HATTAN RD
CLACKAMAS CO OR 200-A4
W HATTON RD
ADAMS CO WA 121-A1
HAUGEN RD
SKAGIT CO WA 168-B3
WASHINGTON CO OR 199-A5
YAMHILL CO OR 199-A5
SE HAUGLUM RD
CLACKAMAS CO OR 200-C3
HAUSER LAKE RD
HAUSER ID 353-B1
KOOTENAI CO ID 353-B1
E HAUSER LAKE RD
HAUSER ID 247-C1
SPOKANE CO WA 247-B1
N HAVANA ST
SPOKANE WA 349-G2
SPOKANE CO WA 349-G2
S HAVANA ST
SPOKANE WA 246-C5
SPOKANE WA 349-G12
SPOKANE CO WA 246-C5
SPOKANE CO WA 349-G12
HAVANA-HELIX HWY
HELIX OR 129-B1
UMATILLA CO OR 129-B1
HAVEKOST RD
ANACORTES WA 259-D8
SKAGIT CO WA 259-D8
HAVERLAND KOONTZ RD
FRANKLIN CO WA 121-B2
HAVLINA RD Rt#-260
FRANKLIN CO WA 121-B1
HAWKINS RD
LEWIS CO WA 187-C3
HAWKINS RD S
LEWIS CO WA 187-C3
HAWKS CLIFF RD NE
DOUGLAS CO WA 113-A1
DOUGLAS CO WA 237-A5
HAWKS PRAIRIE RD NE
THURSTON CO WA 180-D5
THURSTON CO WA 181-A5
HAWLEY CREEK RD
LANE CO OR 215-A6
HAWN CREEK RD
YAMHILL CO OR 198-B6
HAWORTH AV
NEWBERG OR 198-D5
HAWTHORNE AV
MEDFORD OR 336-D12
NW HAWTHORNE AV
GRANTS PASS OR 335-F6
HAWTHORNE AV NE
SALEM OR 323-D11
SALEM OR 325-C1
SE HAWTHORNE BLVD
PORTLAND OR 313-H7
PORTLAND OR 314-A7
HAWTHORNE RD
BELLINGHAM WA 258-A12
E HAWTHORNE RD
Country Homes WA 346-J10
Country Homes WA 347-A10
SPOKANE WA 347-B10
SPOKANE CO WA 347-C10
W HAWTHORNE RD
Country Homes WA 346-J10
S HAWTHORNE ST
Finley WA 343-E12
KENNEWICK WA 343-E12
HAXTON WY
WHATCOM CO WA 158-C7
WHATCOM CO WA 160-C1
NE HAY CREEK RD
JEFFERSON CO OR 135-B1
JEFFERSON CO OR 208-D4
SE HAY CREEK RD
JEFFERSON CO OR 135-B1
JEFFERSON CO OR 213-C1
E HAYDEN AV
HAYDEN ID 245-A5
W HAYDEN AV
HAYDEN ID 245-A5
HAYDEN ID 247-D1
KOOTENAI CO ID 247-C1
HAYDEN RD
CLACKAMAS CO OR 200-B6
LINN CO OR 133-C1
HAYDEN BRIDGE RD
North Springfield OR 330-J4
North Springfield OR 331-A4
SPRINGFIELD OR 330-J4
HAYDEN BRIDGE WY
North Springfield OR 330-G4
SPRINGFIELD OR 330-G4
E HAYDEN LAKE RD
KOOTENAI CO ID 245-B6
N HAYDEN LAKE RD
KOOTENAI CO ID 245-B4
S HAYDEN LAKE RD
HAYDEN ID 355-F1
KOOTENAI CO ID 355-F1
HAYES LN
LANE CO OR 210-A6
HAYES RD
CLARK CO WA 118-A3
CLARK CO WA 192-C1
S HAYES ST
MOSCOW ID 249-D5
W HAYES ST
WOODBURN OR 205-B2
HAYES HILL RD
JOSEPHINE CO OR 233-B1
HAYESVILLE DR NE
Hayesville OR 323-E6
MARION CO OR 323-E6
SALEM OR 323-E6
S HAYFORD RD
AIRWAY HEIGHTS WA 246-A4
SPOKANE CO WA 246-A5
HAYHURST RD
DOUGLAS CO OR 219-A3
HAY-LA CROSSE RD
WHITMAN CO WA 122-A1
HAYNES WY
COOS CO OR 218-C6
HAYNIE RD
WHATCOM CO WA 158-C3
HAYSTACK DR
JEFFERSON CO OR 212-D1
HAYSTACK ROCK RD
MALHEUR CO OR 146-C1
HAYWARD RD
KITTITAS CO WA 240-D3
HAYWIRE RD
LEWIS CO WA 187-C1
N HAZARD RD
SPOKANE CO WA 346-G4
W HAZARD RD
SPOKANE CO WA 346-H5
HAZARD LAKE RD
IDAHO CO ID 131-C2
IDAHO CO ID 251-B1
HAZEL AV
BENTON CITY WA 120-C3
W HAZEL ST
MOUNT VERNON WA 260-B14
HAZEL CAMP RD
CURRY CO OR 232-D3
NE HAZEL DELL AV
CLARK WA 305-G1
CLARK CO WA 192-C5
VANCOUVER WA 305-G1
HAZEL DELL RD
COWLITZ CO WA 187-B7
COWLITZ CO WA 189-B1
HAZELGREEN RD NE
Hayesville OR 323-F4
MARION CO OR 205-B4
MARION CO OR 323-F4
SALEM OR 323-F4
HAZELNUT RIDGE RD NE
MARION CO OR 205-D4
HAZEL POINT RD
JEFFERSON CO WA 170-A7
HAZEN RD
CLARK CO WA 193-A1
COLUMBIA CO OR 192-A2
H COOKE RD
KITTITAS CO WA 241-C5
HEADQUARTERS RD
COWLITZ CO WA 189-D1
HEADQUATERS RD
COWLITZ CO WA 189-D1
HEALY RD
CLARK CO WA 190-A7
HEART LAKE RD
ANACORTES WA 259-F10
SKAGIT CO WA 259-G6
HEART OF THE HILLS
CLALLAM CO WA 109-B1
HEART OF THE HILLS PKWY
CLALLAM CO WA 261-G14
HEATER RD
CLACKAMAS CO OR 199-A6
WASHINGTON CO OR 199-A6
HEATHER OAK DR
LANE CO OR 210-A7
HEATH LAKE RD
BONNER CO ID 244-A4
HEBER RD
UNION CO OR 130-A3
HECETA BEACH RD
LANE CO OR 214-A2
HECKARD RD
PACIFIC CO WA 117-A1
E HEDGER AV Rt#-225
BENTON CITY WA 120-C3
E HEGLAR RD
SPOKANE CO WA 246-D1
HEIGHTS LN NE
THURSTON CO WA 180-D5
HEIKKLA LN
VALLEY CO ID 251-D6
HEIMER RD
SNOHOMISH CO WA 168-D3
HEIMRICH ST
DUFUR OR 127-B2
WASCO CO OR 127-B2
HEINE RD
STEVENS CO WA 106-A3
HEINEMAN RD
ADAMS CO WA 113-C3
HEINRICH RD
VALLEY CO ID 251-C6
HEINZ BLVD
MALHEUR CO OR 139-A3
S HEINZ RD
CLACKAMAS CO OR 205-D1
HEINZ RD NE
MARION CO OR 205-D4
HEIPLE RD
CLACKAMAS CO OR 200-B5
HEISSON RD
BATTLE GROUND WA 193-A3
CLARK CO WA 193-A3
HELIX-VANCYCLE RD
HELIX OR 129-B1
UMATILLA CO OR 121-B3
UMATILLA CO OR 129-B1
HELLER RD
Ault Field WA 167-B2
ISLAND CO WA 167-B2
OAK HARBOR WA 167-B2
HELLS CANYON RD
WASHINGTON CO OR 199-A5
HELLS GULCH RD
BENEWAH CO ID 248-C6
KOOTENAI CO ID 248-C6
HELM RD
JOSEPHINE CO OR 229-A6
HELMAN ST
ASHLAND OR 337-C7
HELMCKEN RD
DISTRICT OF SAANICH BC 256-C2
TOWN OF VIEW ROYAL BC 256-A4
NW HELMHOLTZ WY
DESCHUTES CO OR 212-D5
SW HELMHOLTZ WY
DESCHUTES CO OR 212-D5
HELMICK RD
POLK CO OR 207-B1
SKAGIT CO WA 161-C5
NW HELVETIA RD
WASHINGTON CO OR 125-C1
HEMENWAY RD
LEWIS CO WA 187-B4
NE HEMLOCK AV
DESCHUTES CO OR 212-D5
NW HEMLOCK AV
DESCHUTES CO OR 212-D5
HEMLOCK RD
SKAMANIA CO WA 194-C3
HEMLOCK ST
LONGVIEW WA 302-G9
VANCOUVER BC 254-E13
N HEMLOCK ST
CANNON BEACH OR 188-A7
S HEMLOCK ST
CANNON BEACH OR 188-A7
CANNON BEACH OR 191-A1
W HEMLOCK ST Rt#-34
WALDPORT OR 328-E4
HEMLOCK BUTTE RD
DOUGLAS CO OR 223-B6
HEMLOCK VALLEY RD
BRITISH COLUMBIA 94-C3
HEMMERING RD
LINCOLN CO WA 113-B2
W HEMMI RD
WHATCOM CO WA 158-D5
HENDERER RD
DOUGLAS CO OR 141-A1
HENDERSON BLVD
OLYMPIA WA 296-J7
HENDERSON BLVD SE
OLYMPIA WA 296-J7
OLYMPIA WA 297-A8
THURSTON CO WA 296-J7
THURSTON CO WA 297-A8
TUMWATER WA 297-A8
NE HENDERSON DR
JEFFERSON CO OR 208-C5
HENDERSON LN
OWYHEE CO ID 147-C2
HENDERSON RD
DISTRICT OF OAK BAY BC 257-C5
S HENDERSON ST
SEATTLE WA 287-F3
SW HENDERSON ST
SEATTLE WA 285-G3
HENDERSON CREEK RD
LANE CO OR 214-C3
HENDRICKS RD
YAMHILL CO OR 198-B5
HENDRICKSON RD
LEWIS CO WA 187-B5
HENKLE ST Rt#-6
PACIFIC CO WA 117-A1
RAYMOND WA 117-A1
HENKLE BUTTE DR
DESCHUTES CO OR 212-A4
HENLEY RD
KLAMATH CO OR 235-D5
HENLEY-HORNBROOK WY
SISKIYOU CO CA 150-A3
HENNI RD
ISLAND CO WA 167-C1
HENRICHS RD
SHERMAN CO OR 127-C2
HENRICI RD
CLACKAMAS CO OR 200-A5
S HENRICI RD
CLACKAMAS CO OR 199-D5
CLACKAMAS CO OR 200-A5
HENRIOT RD
LEWIS CO WA 187-C3
HENRY RD
DOUGLAS CO OR 221-B2
LINCOLN CO OR 133-A1
WHATCOM CO WA 158-B5
E HENRY RD
SPOKANE CO WA 247-B5
N HENRY RD
Greenacres WA 351-J8
SPOKANE CO WA 247-B4
SPOKANE CO WA 351-J8
SPOKANE CO WA 352-A14
S HENRY RD
Greenacres WA 351-J9
SPOKANE CO WA 247-B4
SPOKANE CO WA 351-J9
W HENRY ST
FRANKLIN CO WA 342-J6
PASCO WA 342-J6
PASCO WA 343-D6
HENRY CREEK RD
WHEELER CO OR 128-B3
HENRY FOSTER RD
GRAYS HARBOR CO WA 179-A7
HENSEL RD
GRAYS HARBOR CO WA 178-A3
HENSON RD
BENTON CO WA 120-C3
HEPPNER HWY Rt#-74
GILLIAM CO OR 128-B1
HEPPNER OR 128-C2
IONE OR 128-B1
LEXINGTON OR 128-C2
MORROW CO OR 128-B1
MORROW CO OR 129-A2
UMATILLA CO OR 129-A2
HEPPNER-SPRAY HWY Rt#-207
MORROW CO OR 128-C3
WHEELER CO OR 128-C3
WHEELER CO OR 136-C1
HERBERT HOOVER HWY Rt#-99W
NEWBERG OR 198-D5
YAMHILL CO OR 198-D5
HERD RD
YAMHILL CO OR 198-D5
NE HEREFORD LN
JEFFERSON CO OR 208-D4
HEREFORD RD
CURRY CO OR 224-B4
HERFERD RD
LANE CO OR 210-C7
SW HERGERT RD
WASHINGTON CO OR 198-C2
HERITAGE MOUNTAIN RD
PORT MOODY BC 157-A4
HERITAGE MOUNTAIN WY
PORT MOODY BC 157-A4
HERMAN RD
ADAMS CO WA 121-C1
LANE CO OR 210-B6
LATAH CO ID 250-C1
OLYMPIA WA 297-E9
HERMAN CREEK RD
HOOD RIVER CO OR 194-D5
HOOD RIVER CO OR 195-A5
W HERMISTON AV Rt#-207
HERMISTON OR 129-A1
HERMISTON HWY Rt#-207
HERMISTON OR 129-A1
UMATILLA CO OR 129-A1
HERMISTON-HINKLE RD
HERMISTON OR 129-A1
UMATILLA CO OR 129-A1
HERMISTON LOOP RD
HERMISTON OR 129-A1
UMATILLA CO OR 129-A1
HERON ST
BOISE ID 253-C2
E HERON ST U.S.-101
ABERDEEN WA 178-B7
W HERON ST U.S.-101
ABERDEEN WA 178-B7
HERRIN RD
SHERMAN CO OR 127-C1
HERRING LN
YAMHILL CO OR 198-C5
HERRING RD
WASHINGTON CO OR 198-A2
S HERRON RD KPN
PIERCE CO WA 181-A2
E HERSEY ST
ASHLAND OR 337-D7
W HERSEY ST
ASHLAND OR 337-C6
HERSHBERGER RD
DOUGLAS CO OR 226-C1
HESS RD
BENTON CO WA 120-C3
HESSELTINE RD
STEVENS CO WA 106-A3
HESSLER FLAT RD
YAKIMA CO WA 243-A2
HEWITT AV
EVERETT WA 264-D3
EVERETT WA 265-F3
E HEWITT AV
SNOHOMISH CO WA 171-D2
HEWITT PARK HWY
BAKER CO OR 139-A1
HEYBURN RD
CHATCOLET ID 248-A6
KOOTENAI CO ID 248-A6
HEYDON RD
DOUGLAS CO OR 221-A3
HIACK RD
TILLAMOOK CO OR 203-D2
HIAWATHA RD NE
GRANT CO WA 242-B3
HIBBARD RD NE
MARION CO OR 205-B5
HICKEY RD
BONNER CO ID 244-B1
NW HICKORY LN
JEFFERSON CO OR 208-B3
HICKOX RD
SKAGIT CO WA 168-B1
HIDDEN ACRES RD
LEWIS CO WA 187-C4
NE HIDDEN COVE LN
KITSAP CO WA 174-C1
NE HIDDEN COVE RD
KITSAP CO WA 174-C1
HIDDEN FALLS RD
CLARK CO WA 193-C7
HIDDEN SPRINGS RD
YAMHILL CO OR 198-C5
HIDDEN VALLEY RD
BONNER CO ID 244-A1
KITTITAS CO WA 240-D2
LINCOLN CO OR 206-B5
W HIDDEN VALLEY RD
KOOTENAI CO ID 247-C1
HIDDEN VALLEY RIM RD
ADA CO ID 253-B4
HIGGINS AIRPORT WY
SKAGIT CO WA 161-A7
HIGGINS LOOP RD NW
DOUGLAS CO WA 236-B5
E HIGH DR
SPOKANE WA 246-C5
S HIGH DR
SPOKANE WA 246-C5
SPOKANE WA 348-H13
SPOKANE CO WA 246-C5
W HIGH DR
SPOKANE WA 246-C5
SPOKANE WA 348-J14
SPOKANE WA 349-A14
HIGH PORT
BAY CITY OR 191-B7
BELLINGHAM WA 258-C8
PORT ORCHARD WA 174-B4
PORT ORCHARD WA 270-H14
PRIEST RIVER ID 107-A3
SW HIGH ST
GRANTS PASS OR 335-D9
HIGH ST NE
SALEM OR 322-H13
HIGH ST SE
SALEM OR 322-H14
SALEM OR 324-H1
HIGH BRIDGE RD
SNOHOMISH CO WA 110-C1
HIGHGRADE RD
MODOC CO CA 152-A3
HIGHLAND AV
ASOTIN CO WA 250-B4
CLARKSTON WA 250-B4
GRANTS PASS OR 335-D4
JOSEPHINE CO OR 335-B1
E HIGHLAND AV
HERMISTON OR 129-A1
NW HIGHLAND AV
GRANTS PASS OR 335-E7
SW HIGHLAND AV Rt#-126
DESCHUTES CO OR 212-D5
REDMOND OR 212-D5
W HIGHLAND AV
HERMISTON OR 129-A1
UMATILLA CO OR 129-A1
HIGHLAND AV NE
SALEM OR 322-J10
SALEM OR 323-A10
HIGHLAND BLVD
DIST OF N VANCOUVER BC 156-B2
DIST OF N VANCOUVER BC 254-J1
E HIGHLAND BLVD
SPOKANE WA 349-B12
HIGHLAND DR
BELLEVUE WA 175-C3
BELLINGHAM WA 258-C10
BENTON CO OR 327-H3
CORVALLIS OR 327-H3
ISLAND CO WA 168-A6
MEDFORD OR 336-F13
YAKIMA CO WA 120-A2
E HIGHLAND DR
ARLINGTON WA 168-D5
SW HIGHLAND LN
JEFFERSON CO OR 208-B7
HIGHLAND RD
BRITISH COLUMBIA 159-B6
COLUMBIA CO OR 189-C6
COLUMBIA CO WA 122-B2
MASON CO WA 179-D4
POLK CO OR 207-B1
TOWN OF VIEW ROYAL BC 159-B6
HIGHLAND RD NE
KITSAP CO WA 170-C5
HIGHLAND FLATS RD
BOUNDARY CO ID 107-B2
HIGHLAND PARK WY SW
SEATTLE WA 285-H1
HIGHLAND SCHOOL RD SE
DOUGLAS CO WA 112-C2
W HIGHLAND VIEW DR
BOISE ID 253-D2
S HIGHLINE DR
EAST WENATCHEE WA 239-A4
East Wenatchee Bench WA 239-A4
HIGHLINE RD
DESCHUTES CO OR 217-A2
HIGH PASS RD
JUNCTION CITY OR 210-A6
LANE CO OR 133-A2
LANE CO OR 210-A6
SE HIGH POINT WY
KING CO WA 176-A4
HIGH PRAIRIE RD
KLICKITAT CO WA 196-C4
LANE CO OR 134-A3
HIGH RIM RD
DOUGLAS CO WA 236-D4
HIGH SCHOOL DR
LINCOLN CITY OR 203-A5
NE HIGH SCHOOL RD
KITSAP CO WA 271-H1
Winslow WA 271-H1
HIGH VALLEY RD
UNION CO OR 130-B2
HIGHWAY ADRIAN RD
CANYON CO ID 139-A3
HILDERBRAND LN
SHERMAN CO OR 127-C1
HILL AV
MOSES LAKE WA 242-C3
E HILL AV
MOSES LAKE WA 242-C3
HILL RD
ADA CO ID 253-B1
BOISE ID 253-C2
ISLAND CO WA 167-B5
KLAMATH CO OR 235-D5
LANE CO OR 215-C1
LANE CO OR 331-F1
MODOC CO CA 151-A3
OWYHEE CO ID 147-A1
SISKIYOU CO CA 150-C3
SISKIYOU CO CA 151-A3
WASHINGTON CO ID 139-A2
WHITMAN CO WA 249-C3
YAKIMA CO WA 243-D7
N HILL RD
YAMHILL CO OR 198-A6
NW HILL RD
YAMHILL CO OR 198-A6
SW HILL RD
YAMHILL CO OR 198-A7
HILL RD NE
THURSTON CO WA 181-A5
HILL ST
ALBANY OR 326-D7
KLICKITAT CO WA 196-C7
HILL ST Rt#-162
KAMIAH ID 123-C2
KAMIAH ID 123-C2
HILLAIRE RD
WHATCOM CO WA 158-C7
HILLARY GRADE
WASCO CO OR 202-D2
E HILLCREST DR
KITSAP CO WA 271-D11
NE HILLCREST DR
GRANTS PASS OR 335-G6
JOSEPHINE CO OR 335-G6
NW HILLCREST DR
GRANTS PASS OR 335-F6
HILLCREST RD
HOOD RIVER CO OR 195-C7
JACKSON CO OR 234-C1
JACKSON CO OR 336-J11
MEDFORD OR 234-C1
MEDFORD OR 336-G11
HILLCREST LOOP RD
CLATSOP CO OR 117-A3
HILLDALE RD E
KITSAP CO WA 271-E9
S HILLHURST RD
RIDGEFIELD WA 192-C3
HILL LOOP RD
STEVENS CO WA 106-A1
HILLOCKBURN RD
CLACKAMAS CO OR 200-C7
HILL PASSAGE
PIERCE CO WA 181-B1
HILLS AV
LEWIS CO WA 187-D3
S HILLS DR
WENATCHEE WA 238-D4
West Wenatchee WA 238-D4
HILLS RD
ADAMS CO WA 113-C3
HILLSBORO HWY Rt#-219
NEWBERG OR 198-D5
WASHINGTON CO OR 198-D5
YAMHILL CO OR 198-D5
SW HILLSBORO HWY Rt#-219
HILLSBORO OR 198-D2
WASHINGTON CO OR 198-D2
HILLSBORO-SILVRTON HWY Rt#-214
MARION CO OR 205-B1
MOUNT ANGEL OR 205-C3
SILVERTON OR 205-C3
WOODBURN OR 205-B2
HILLSBRO-SLVRTN HWY NE Rt#-219
MARION CO OR 205-A1
HILLSHAVEN AV
COLUMBIA CO OR 189-C7
HILLSIDE AV
CITY OF VICTORIA BC 256-H7
CITY OF VICTORIA BC 257-A6
HILLSIDE DR
PIERCE CO WA 181-C5
YAMHILL CO OR 198-C5
HILLSIDE RD
WASHINGTON CO OR 125-B1
HILLTOP
CROOK CO OR 213-D6
HILLTOP DR
LANE CO OR 215-D4
HILLVIEW RD
GEM CO ID 139-B3
LANE CO OR 215-C5
HILYARD AV
Altamont OR 339-C11

HILYARD ST
STREET INDEX
INDIAN CHURCH RD 375

STREET City State Page-Grid

HILYARD ST
EUGENE OR 330-B9
HINCH RD
COOS CO OR 220-C3
HINCK RD
LINN CO OR 207-C6
HINES ST SE
SALEM OR 324-J1
SALEM OR 325-A1
HINES LOGGING RD
HARNEY CO OR 137-A3
HARNEY CO OR 145-A1
HINKLE CREEK RD
DOUGLAS CO OR 219-D7
NE HINNESS RD
CLARK CO WA 193-B4
HINTON RD
WASCO CO OR 127-C3
HINTZVILLE RD NW
KITSAP CO WA 173-D3
HIPKINS RD SW
LAKEWOOD WA 181-C4
HIRTZEL RD
COLUMBIA CO OR 189-B4
HISTORIC COLUMBIA RIVER HWY
TROUTDALE OR 200-B1
E HISTORIC COLUMBIA RIVER HWY
MULTNOMAH CO OR 200-C1
TROUTDALE OR 200-C1
W HISTORIC COLUMBIA RIVER HWY
TROUTDALE OR 200-B1
NW HITE CENTER RD
KITSAP CO WA 173-D2
H LAWRENCE RD
CLARK CO WA 193-A1
HOAG RD
MOUNT VERNON WA 260-D9
HOBART RD NE
MARION CO OR 205-C4
SILVERTON OR 205-C4
NW HOBBS RD
WASHINGTON CO OR 198-C1
HOBO PASS RD
SHOSHONE CO ID 115-C3
SHOSHONE CO ID 115-C3
HOBSON RD
SKAGIT CO WA 161-B5
HOBSON RD SW
THURSTON CO WA 184-B4
HOBSONVILLE POINT DR
BAY CITY OR 191-B7
TILLAMOOK CO OR 191-B7
HODGEN RD
UMATILLA CO OR 121-C3
NW HODGEN RD
MILTON-FREEWATER OR 121-C3
HOEHN RD
SKAGIT CO WA 161-D6
HOERSTER LN
JACKSON CO OR 229-D4
HOFF RD
PIERCE CO WA 181-A2
HOFFMAN RD
CLACKAMAS CO OR 199-C5
INDEPENDENCE OR 204-B7
POLK CO OR 204-B7
WASHINGTON CO OR 125-B1
HOFFMAN RD NE
KITSAP CO WA 170-D4
HOFFMAN RD NW
THURSTON CO WA 180-C5
HOFFMAN RD SE
OLYMPIA WA 297-D8
HOFFMAN ST
WOODLAND WA 192-C1
SE HOFFMEISTER RD
CLACKAMAS CO OR 200-B3
NE HOGAN DR
GRESHAM OR 200-B1
HOGAN RD
CLACKAMAS CO OR 200-B3
DOUGLAS CO OR 219-A6
GRAYS HARBOR CO WA 177-C5
SE HOGAN RD
GRESHAM OR 200-B2
HOGBACK RD
LAKE CO OR 144-B3
LAKE CO OR 152-B1
HOG CREEK RD
WASHINGTON CO ID 139-B1
HOGEN RANCH RD
COLUMBIA CO OR 192-A3
HOGG HILL RD
MULTNOMAH CO OR 200-D3
HOG RANCH RD
KITTITAS CO WA 240-B6
HOGUM BAY RD NE
LACEY WA 181-A6
HOGUM CREEK RD
DOUGLAS CO OR 225-D6
HOIER RD
WHATCOM CO WA 158-B3
HOKO OZETTE RD
CLALLAM CO WA 162-C4
CLALLAM CO WA 163-A3
HOLBROOK RD
COLUMBIA CO OR 189-C6
S HOLCOMB BLVD
CLACKAMAS CO OR 199-D4
CLACKAMAS CO OR 200-A4
HOLCOMB RD
ADA CO ID 253-D4
BOISE ID 253-D4
HOLCOMB HOMES RD
COWLITZ CO WA 303-F3
HOLCOMB SPRING RD
KLAMATH CO OR 235-D2
HOLCUM RD
LEWIS CO WA 187-C1
HOLDEN RD SW
LAKEWOOD WA 181-C4
SW HOLDEN ST
SEATTLE WA 284-E2
SEATTLE WA 285-F2
HOLDER LN SE
MARION CO OR 324-F7
SALEM OR 324-F7

HOLDMAN RD
HELIX OR 129-B1
UMATILLA CO OR 129-B1
HOLDOM AV
DISTRICT OF BURNABY BC 156-D4
SE HOLGATE BLVD
PORTLAND OR 317-J3
PORTLAND OR 318-B3
PORTLAND OR 319-H3
S HOLGATE ST
SEATTLE WA 282-A2
HOLIDAY BLVD
SKAGIT CO WA 160-C5
HOLIDAY VALLEY DR NW
THURSTON CO WA 180-B5
N HOLLADAY DR
SEASIDE OR 301-G7
S HOLLADAY DR
SEASIDE OR 301-G9
E HOLLAND AV
SPOKANE WA 346-J11
SPOKANE WA 347-A11
W HOLLAND AV
Country Homes WA 346-J11
HOLLAND LP
JOSEPHINE CO OR 233-B4
HOLLILYNN DR
ADA CO ID 253-C4
HOLLY DR
EVERETT WA 268-B5
SNOHOMISH WA 267-J7
SNOHOMISH WA 268-A6
SE HOLLY LN
JEFFERSON CO OR 208-C7
HOLLY RD
MALHEUR CO OR 139-A2
NW HOLLY RD
KITSAP CO WA 173-D2
KITSAP CO WA 174-A2
HOLLY ST
MAPLE RIDGE BC 157-C5
E HOLLY ST
BELLINGHAM WA 258-D7
N HOLLY ST
CLACKAMAS CO OR 199-C6
MEDFORD OR 336-C12
S HOLLY ST
MEDFORD OR 336-C12
W HOLLY ST
BELLINGHAM WA 258-D6
HOLLY GULCH RD
BENEWAH CO ID 248-C6
HOLLY HILL RD
WASHINGTON CO OR 198-C3
HOLLYWOOD CRES
CITY OF VICTORIA BC 257-A11
HOLLYWOOD DR NE
Hayesville OR 323-E9
SALEM OR 323-E10
HOLM RD SW
THURSTON CO WA 184-A3
HOLMAN RD NW
SEATTLE WA 171-A7
SEATTLE WA 273-F1
HOLMES RD
DESCHUTES CO OR 212-B4
HOLMES POINT DR NE
KING CO WA 171-B7
HOLST RD
CLACKAMAS CO OR 200-B4
ISLAND CO WA 171-A2
HOLTON RD
JACKSON CO OR 234-B3
HOLYOKE PL S
SEATTLE WA 287-H5
HOLYOKE WY S
SEATTLE WA 287-H5
HOME AV
WALLA WALLA WA 345-D9
Walla Walla East WA 345-D9
HOME ST
WALLA WALLA WA 345-D9
Walla Walla East WA 345-D9
HOME ACRES RD
SNOHOMISH WA 265-H4
SNOHOMISH WA 269-J2
HOME ACRES RANCH RD
KLICKITAT CO WA 196-D2
HOMEDALE RD
Altamont OR 235-D5
Altamont OR 339-A14
CANYON CO ID 147-B1
KLAMATH CO OR 235-D6
KLAMATH CO OR 339-A14
KLAMATH FALLS OR 339-A14
HOMER RD
ADA CO ID 139-C3
HOMESTEAD RD
MORROW CO OR 128-C1
SAN JUAN CO WA 160-A3
HOMESTEAD WY
DESCHUTES CO OR 212-C4
HOMESTEADER RD
CLACKAMAS CO OR 199-B5
WASHINGTON CO OR 199-B5
WHATCOM CO WA 161-C1
E HONEYMAN RD
COLUMBIA CO OR 192-B4
N HONEYMAN RD
COLUMBIA CO OR 192-A3
SCAPPOOSE OR 192-A3
HONEYMOON BAY RD
Freeland WA 170-C1
ISLAND CO WA 167-C7
HONEYSUCKLE AV
HAYDEN ID 355-A1
KOOTENAI CO ID 355-A1
N HONEYSUCKLE DR
COEUR D'ALENE ID 355-F6
W HOOD AV
KENNEWICK WA 342-H10
HOOD ST NE
SALEM OR 322-J11
HOOD CANAL DR NE
KITSAP CO WA 170-C3
HOOD RIVER HWY
HOOD RIVER CO OR 195-B7
HOOD RIVER CO OR 202-C1
HOOD RIVER RD
MOSIER OR 196-A5

HOOD RIVER RD
WASCO CO OR 196-A5
HOOGDAL RD
SKAGIT CO WA 161-C5
SW HOOK AND EYE LN
YAMHILL CO OR 204-B2
HOOKER RD
CLALLAM CO WA 166-A7
HOOPER WOOLAM RD
CLARK CO WA 193-A1
HOOT N HOLLER LN
DOUGLAS CO OR 221-D5
HOOVER CREEK LN
WHEELER CO OR 128-A3
HOOVER HILL RD
DOUGLAS CO OR 221-A7
HOP CREEK RD
JACKSON CO OR 226-B5
HOPE ST
Altamont OR 338-J11
Altamont OR 339-A12
HOPE PENINSULA RD
BONNER CO ID 244-D3
HOPEWELL RD Rt#-9
WHATCOM CO WA 102-B1
HOPEWELL RD NW
POLK CO OR 204-C3
YAMHILL CO OR 204-C3
W HOPKINS ST
PASCO WA 343-B7
HOPPER AV Rt#-71
CAMBRIDGE ID 139-B1
WASHINGTON CO ID 139-B1
E HOQUIAM RD
GRAYS HARBOR CO WA 178-A6
HOQUIAM WA 178-A6
HOQUIAM WISHKAH RD
GRAYS HARBOR CO WA 178-B4
HORLICK RD
KITTITAS CO WA 240-D3
HORN LN
EUGENE OR 329-F2
LANE CO OR 329-F2
HORN RD Rt#-225
BENTON CITY WA 120-C2
BENTON CO WA 120-C2
NW HORNECKER RD
WASHINGTON CO OR 198-C1
HORNER RD
DESCHUTES CO OR 212-D7
N HORNET CREEK RD
ADAMS CO ID 131-B3
ADAMS CO ID 139-B1
WASHINGTON CO ID 131-B3
HORNY HOLLOW TR
JEFFERSON CO OR 212-C2
HORRIGAN RD
BENTON CO WA 120-B3
HORSE CREEK RD
LINCOLN CO OR 206-C5
SISKIYOU CO CA 149-B3
WALLOWA CO OR 123-A3
WALLOWA CO OR 123-A3
HORSEFALL BEACH RD
COOS CO OR 218-A6
HORSEHEAD BAY DR
PIERCE CO WA 181-B1
HORSEMAN LN
DESCHUTES CO OR 217-B1
HORSESHOE LN
LINN CO OR 207-B5
HORSESHOE BEND RD
ADA CO ID 253-B1
EAGLE ID 253-B1
KLICKITAT CO WA 196-D3
SHERMAN CO OR 127-C3
HORSESHOE BEND RD Rt#-55
ADA CO ID 139-C3
ADA CO ID 253-B1
BOISE CO ID 139-C3
EAGLE ID 253-B1
HORSESHOE BEND ID 139-C3
HORSESHOE LAKE RD
MARION CO OR 198-C7
HORTON RD
LANE CO OR 133-A2
HORTON GRADE RD
WHITMAN CO WA 122-B1
SE HORTSMAN RD
KITSAP CO WA 271-C14
PORT ORCHARD WA 271-B14
HOSKINS RD
DIST OF N VANCOUVER BC 255-F1
HOSKINS-SUMMIT RD
BENTON CO OR 133-A1
S HOSMER ST
PIERCE CO WA 181-D4
TACOMA WA 181-D4
TACOMA WA 295-E7
HOSPITAL WY
BREWSTER WA 104-B3
HOSTETLER RD
ASOTIN CO WA 250-B7
HOSTETLER ST W
THE DALLES OR 196-C7
WASCO CO OR 196-C7
NE HOSTMARK ST
POULSBO WA 170-B7
HOTCHKISS LN
HARNEY CO OR 145-A1
HOT SPRINGS AV
CARSON WA 194-D4
CARSON WA 195-A4
HOT SPRINGS RD
ADAMS CO ID 251-A3
MALHEUR CO OR 154-B2
HOT SPRINGS RD Rt#-9
CITY OF HARRISN HT SPNGS BC 94-C3
DISTRICT OF KENT BC 94-C3
HOUSER WY S Rt#-900
RENTON WA 175-C5
NE HOUSLEY AV
DOUGLAS CO OR 334-F2
ROSEBURG OR 334-F2
HOUSTON RD
ISLAND CO WA 167-C5
JACKSON CO OR 234-B2
LEWIS CO ID 123-B3
SPOKANE CO WA 348-C6

N HOUSTON RD
SPOKANE CO WA 348-B6
W HOUSTON RD
SPOKANE CO WA 348-B7
HOUSTON LAKE RD
CROOK CO OR 213-C5
HOUTCHEN ST
PACIFIC CO WA 186-B7
HOVANDER RD
FERNDALE WA 158-C6
HOVENDEN RD NE
MARION CO OR 205-B1
HOWARD AV
EUGENE OR 329-E1
LANE CO OR 329-E1
HOWARD LN
LANE CO OR 210-A5
HOWARD RD
KITTITAS CO WA 241-A4
E HOWARD RD
KOOTENAI CO ID 245-B1
SE HOWARD RD
MULTNOMAH CO OR 200-D2
HOWARD ST
WALLA WALLA WA 345-C9
Walla Walla East WA 345-C9
S HOWARD ST
WALLA WALLA WA 345-C11
HOWARD CREEK RD
CROOK CO OR 136-A2
HOWARD FLAT RD
CHELAN CO WA 236-D2
HOWARDS MILL RD
CLACKAMAS CO OR 199-D7
CLACKAMAS CO OR 200-A7
HOWE
PIERCE CO WA 182-B6
HOWE LN
LANE CO OR 215-B5
HOWE ST
VANCOUVER BC 254-G9
HOWE ST Rt#-99
VANCOUVER BC 254-F10
W HOWE ST
SEATTLE WA 276-D1
SEATTLE WA 277-F2
HOWELL ST
SEATTLE WA 278-A5
HOWELL GRADE RD
GARFIELD CO WA 122-C2
HOWELL PRAIRIE RD
MARION CO OR 205-B4
HOWLETT RD
CLACKAMAS CO OR 200-C4
E HOXIE RD
SPOKANE CO WA 115-A2
SPOKANE CO WA 115-A2
E HOXIE RD Rt#-278
ROCKFORD WA 114-C2
SPOKANE CO WA 114-C2
HOYT RD SW
FEDERAL WAY WA 182-A1
NW HOYT ST
PORTLAND OR 313-E5
HOYT ST S
SALEM OR 324-G2
HOYT ST SE
SALEM OR 324-H2
H STREET RD
BLAINE WA 158-C3
WHATCOM CO WA 158-D3
HUBBARD RD
ADAMS CO ID 251-A4
LEWIS CO WA 187-A2
E HUBBARD RD
ADA CO ID 253-B4
W HUBBARD RD
ADA CO ID 253-A5
N HUBBARD ST
COEUR D'ALENE ID 355-D11
HUBBARD CREEK RD
DOUGLAS CO OR 221-A1
HUBBARD GULCH RD
NEZ PERCE CO ID 123-B2
HUBER LN
JEFFERSON CO OR 208-B7
HUBER RD
PACIFIC CO WA 117-B2
HUCKELBERRY LN
COOS CO OR 220-B4
HUCKLEBERRY RD
JACKSON CO OR 226-D5
JACKSON CO OR 227-A4
HUDDLESTON RD
WHEELER CO OR 128-B3
E HUDLOW RD
KOOTENAI CO ID 245-A4
HUDSON RD
SKAMANIA CO WA 193-D7
SE HUDSON RD
CLACKAMAS CO OR 200-C3
HUDSON ST
CITY OF RICHMOND BC 156-B5
LONGVIEW WA 303-A9
VANCOUVER BC 156-B5
SW HUDSON ST
SEATTLE WA 280-C5
HUETTER RD
HAYDEN ID 247-D1
HAYDEN ID 354-H2
KOOTENAI CO ID 247-D1
KOOTENAI CO ID 354-H2
N HUETTER RD
KOOTENAI CO ID 354-H6
POST FALLS ID 354-H6
NE HUFF RD
CLARK CO WA 193-A1
HUGHES AV
BLAINE WA 158-B3
WHATCOM CO WA 158-B3
HUGHES RD
CHELAN CO WA 238-C2
NE HUGHES RD
CLARK CO WA 193-C6
HUGHEY LN
TILLAMOOK CO OR 197-C2
HUGO RD
JOSEPHINE CO OR 229-A4
HUHTALA RD
LINCOLN CO OR 206-C2

HULL RD
JACKSON CO OR 234-A2
HULL ST
PORT ORCHARD WA 174-B4
HULSE RD
CLALLAM CO WA 165-D6
HULTMAN RD
POLK CO OR 207-C1
HUMBOLDT ST
CITY OF VICTORIA BC 256-H9
HUME RD
WHITMAN CO WA 114-C3
HUMMINGBIRD RD
DOUGLAS CO WA 239-B1
HUMORIST RD
Burbank WA 121-B3
WALLA WALLA CO WA 121-B3
HUMPBACK RD
BRITISH COLUMBIA 159-A6
DISTRICT OF LANGFORD BC 159-A6
HUMPERT LN NE
MARION CO OR 205-C3
SW HUMPHREY BLVD
MULTNOMAH OR 316-B1
PORTLAND OR 316-B1
HUMPHREY RD
ISLAND CO WA 171-A2
HUMPHREY HILL RD
SKAGIT CO WA 161-B4
E HUMPHREYS RD
COOS CO OR 220-B4
W HUMPHREYS RD
COOS CO OR 220-B4
E HUMPTULIPS RD
GRAYS HARBOR CO WA 178-B2
HUMPTULIPS VALLEY RD
GRAYS HARBOR CO WA 177-D3
HUMPTULIPS VALLEY DIKE RD
GRAYS HARBOR CO WA 177-C4
HUNGRY HILL RD
LANE CO OR 215-B5
HUNGRY JUNCTION RD
KITTITAS CO WA 241-B5
HUNNELL RD
DESCHUTES CO OR 217-C1
HUNT LN
JOSEPHINE CO OR 229-A6
HUNT RD
CLALLAM CO WA 165-A5
DESCHUTES CO OR 212-B4
HUNT ST NW
GIG HARBOR WA 181-B1
PIERCE CO WA 181-B1
HUNT CLUB RD
GRAYS HARBOR CO WA 183-B2
HUNTER RD
ISLAND CITY OR 130-A2
KITTITAS CO WA 241-A5
UNION CO OR 130-A2
SW HUNTER RD
KITSAP CO WA 174-B6
HUNTER RD SW
THURSTON CO WA 184-A3
HUNTER CREEK LP
CURRY CO OR 228-A6
HUNTER CREEK RD
CURRY CO OR 228-A6
HUNTER POINT RD NW
THURSTON CO WA 180-C4
HUNTINGDON RD
DISTRICT OF ABBOTSFORD BC 102-B1
DISTRICT OF MATSQUI BC 102-B1
HUNTINGTON AV
CASTLE ROCK WA 187-C7
CASTLE ROCK WA 189-C1
COWLITZ CO WA 187-C7
COWLITZ CO WA 189-C1
HUNTINGTON HWY U.S.-30
BAKER CO OR 138-C2
BAKER CO OR 139-A2
HUNTINGTON OR 138-C2
MALHEUR CO OR 139-A2
HUNTINGTON PL
LONGVIEW WA 302-J6
HUNTINGTON RD
MALHEUR CO OR 138-C2
W HUNTLEY ST
ABERDEEN WA 178-B7
COSMOPOLIS WA 178-B7
W HUNTZINGER RD
YAKIMA CO WA 243-B4
HURD RD
GRAYS HARBOR CO WA 179-B7
SE HURLBURT RD
MULTNOMAH CO OR 200-C2
HURLEY-WALDRIP RD
MASON CO WA 180-A5
HURRICANE CREEK RD
ENTERPRISE OR 130-C2
JOSEPH OR 130-C2
WALLOWA CO OR 130-C2
HURTLEY RANCH RD
DESCHUTES CO OR 212-A5
HUSKEY RD
HOOD RIVER CO OR 195-D7
WASCO CO OR 196-A6
HUSSEY ST
COLLEGE PLACE WA 344-E9
Walla Walla West WA 344-E9
WALLA WALLA WA 344-E9
WALLA WALLA CO WA 344-E9
HUTCHENS HILL RD
GARFIELD CO WA 122-B2
HUTCHINSON RD
BRITISH COLUMBIA 159-A1
COLUMBIA CO OR 189-B5
HUTSON DR
HOOD RIVER CO OR 202-C2
HYACINTH ST NE
SALEM OR 323-B7
HYANNIS DR
DIST OF N VANCOUVER BC 255-J4
HYATT RD SE
THURSTON CO WA 184-D2
HYATT PRAIRIE RD
JACKSON CO OR 150-A2
HYLINE RD
MALHEUR CO OR 139-A2

HYLO RD S
MARION CO OR 324-F11

I

I AV
ANACORTES WA 259-G4
I RD SW
DOUGLAS CO WA 239-D1
I ST
COLUMBIA CITY OR 192-B1
NEHALEM OR 191-B4
N I ST
LIND WA 121-B1
TACOMA WA 293-F3
S I ST
TACOMA WA 293-G4
SW I ST
GRANTS PASS OR 335-D9
ICE HARBOR DR
WALLA WALLA CO WA 121-B3
ICE HARBOR DR Rt#-124
WALLA WALLA CO WA 121-B3
ICICLE RD
CHELAN CO WA 238-A1
IDAHO AV U.S.-30
ONTARIO OR 139-A3
E IDAHO AV U.S.-95
HOMEDALE ID 147-A1
W IDAHO AV
ONTARIO OR 139-A3
W IDAHO AV Rt#-19
HOMEDALE ID 147-A1
W IDAHO BLVD
GEM CO ID 139-B3
N IDAHO RD
KOOTENAI CO ID 247-C1
Otis Orchards WA 352-G6
SPOKANE CO WA 352-G6
S IDAHO RD
SPOKANE CO WA 247-B4
IDAHO ST
CASCADE ID 252-D6
N IDAHO ST
KOOTENAI CO ID 353-J3
POST FALLS ID 353-J3
S IDAHO ST
KOOTENAI CO ID 247-C1
W IDAHO ST U.S.-95
WEISER ID 139-A2
IDAHO-OREGON-NEV HWY U.S.-95
HUMBOLDT CO NV 154-B3
JORDAN VALLEY OR 147-A3
MALHEUR CO OR 146-B3
MALHEUR CO OR 147-A2
MALHEUR CO OR 154-B1
OWYHEE CO ID 147-A2
IDAHO POWER RD
BAKER CO OR 131-A3
IDLERS REST RD
LATAH CO ID 249-D4
IDYLWOOD DR SE
SALEM OR 324-F5
IGO RD
GILLIAM CO OR 128-A2
IHRIG RD
WASHINGTON CO OR 198-B1
S ILER ST
MOXEE (MOXEE CITY) WA 243-D7
ILLAHEE RD NE
KITSAP CO WA 174-C1
KITSAP CO WA 271-C6
ILLINOIS AV U.S.-95
COUNCIL ID 139-C1
S ILLINOIS AV
PASCO WA 343-E8
ILLINOIS RIVER RD
JOSEPHINE CO OR 233-A1
ILLINOIS VALLEY PARK RD
CAVE JUNCTION OR 233-B4
JOSEPHINE CO OR 233-B4
ILMARI RD
COLUMBIA CO OR 189-A3
IMBLER LN
JEFFERSON CO OR 208-C7
IMBODEN RD
LEWIS CO WA 187-B5
IMHOFF RD
WHATCOM CO WA 158-C6
IMMIGRANT RD
LANE CO OR 215-D4
S IMMONEN RD
LINCOLN CO OR 203-A6
IMPERIAL ST
DISTRICT OF BURNABY BC 156-C5
INCHELIUM-KETTLE FALLS RD
FERRY CO WA 105-C2
Inchelium WA 105-C2
INDEPENDENCE HWY
BENTON CO OR 207-B4
INDEPENDENCE HWY Rt#-51
POLK CO OR 204-B6
INDEPENDENCE RD
YAKIMA CO WA 120-B2
INDEPENDENCE RD SW
LEWIS CO WA 117-B1
INDEX-GALENA RD
SNOHOMISH CO WA 111-A1
INDIAN RD
Shelter Bay WA 167-D1
SKAGIT CO WA 160-D7
SKAGIT CO WA 167-D1
INDIAN ST
BELLINGHAM WA 258-D8
E INDIANA AV
SPOKANE WA 349-A7
S INDIANA AV
CANYON CO ID 147-B1
W INDIANA AV
SPOKANE WA 348-J7
SPOKANE WA 349-A7
INDIAN CAMP RD SW
DOUGLAS CO WA 239-B2
INDIAN CEMETERY RD
KOOTENAI CO ID 248-A5
INDIAN CHURCH RD
GRANGER WA 120-A2
YAKIMA CO WA 120-A2

PNW
INDEX

PNW · INDEX

COPYRIGHT 1999 Thomas Bros. Maps ®

JORDAN ST SW — STREET INDEX — NW KNIGHTS BRIDGE RD 377

STREET City State Page-Grid

JORDAN ST SW
Rochester WA 184-A3
THURSTON CO WA 184-A4
JORDAN CRATERS RD
MALHEUR CO OR 147-A2
JORDAN CREEK RD
WASCO CO OR 202-D5
JORDAN MEADOW RD
HUMBOLDT CO NV 154-B3
JOSELYN SW
THURSTON CO WA 184-B4
JOSEPH AV U.S.-95
WINCHESTER ID 123-B2
JOSEPH ST SE
MARION CO OR 205-A7
MARION CO OR 325-J7
JOSEPH CREEK RD
ASOTIN CO WA 123-A3
NE JOSEPHINE ST
GRANTS PASS OR 335-F8
JOSEPH-WALLOWA LK HWY Rt#-82
WALLOWA CO OR 130-C2
JOSH WILSON RD
SKAGIT CO WA 160-D6
SKAGIT CO WA 161-A6
SKAGIT CO WA 260-A3
JOVITA BLVD E
EDGEWOOD WA 182-B2
PACIFIC WA 182-B2
PIERCE CO WA 182-B2
JOYCE ST
VANCOUVER BC 156-C5
SW JP WEST RD
COLUMBIA CO OR 192-A3
J SCHNEBLY RD
KITTITAS CO WA 241-C4
NE JUANITA DR
KING CO WA 171-C7
KIRKLAND WA 171-C7
JUANITA DR NE
KENMORE WA 171-B6
KING CO WA 171-B7
JUANITA-WOODINVILLE WY NE
KING CO WA 171-C7
JUBB RD
CLACKAMAS CO OR 200-B6
JUDD RD
CLACKAMAS CO OR 200-B4
E JUDKINS RD
SPOKANE CO WA 247-A2
E JUMPOFF RD
STEVENS CO WA 106-B3
JUMP-OFF JOE RD
JOSEPHINE CO OR 229-C3
JUMP-OFF JOE CREEK RD
JOSEPHINE CO OR 229-B3
JUMPOFF RIDGE RD
KITTITAS CO WA 241-D1
JUNCTION AV
EVERETT WA 265-E7
JUNCTION RD
DOUGLAS CO OR 225-B6
JUNGQUIST RD
SKAGIT CO WA 161-A7
NE JUNIPER LN
JEFFERSON CO OR 208-C2
NW JUNIPER LN
JEFFERSON CO OR 208-B2
JUNIPER RD
MORROW CO OR 128-C1
JUNIPER BEACH RD
ISLAND CO WA 168-A4
JUNIPER CANYON RD
CROOK CO OR 135-C3
CROOK CO OR 213-D6
N JUNIPER CANYON RD
UMATILLA CO OR 121-B3
S JUNIPER CANYON RD
UMATILLA CO OR 129-B1
JUNIPER MOUNTAIN RD
OWYHEE CO ID 155-A1
JUNTURA CUTOFF RD
HARNEY CO OR 138-A3
JUNTURA-RIVERSIDE RD
MALHEUR CO OR 146-A1
JUSTICE RANCH WEST RD
GRANT CO OR 137-A1

K

K AV
LA GRANDE OR 130-A2
K ST
BREMERTON WA 270-D12
Navy Yard City WA 270-D12
SW K ST
GRANTS PASS OR 335-D9
K 4-10-NE
GRANT CO WA 242-C1
KACHESS LAKE RD
KITTITAS CO WA 111-A3
NW KACHINA AV
DESCHUTES CO OR 212-C5
KACKMAN RD
SNOHOMISH CO WA 168-C4
WHITMAN CO WA 114-B3
WHITMAN CO WA 122-B1
KAGY ST SE
THURSTON CO WA 181-A7
KAHLER BASIN RD
WHEELER CO OR 128-B3
WHEELER CO OR 136-B1
KAHOUT RD
LEWIS CO WA 187-A2
KAHUT LN NE
MARION CO OR 205-B2
NW KAISER RD
MULTNOMAH CO OR 192-A7
WASHINGTON CO OR 192-A7
KAISER RD NW
OLYMPIA WA 296-C1
THURSTON CO WA 180-C5
THURSTON CO WA 296-C1
KAISER RD SW
THURSTON CO WA 296-C6
KAKELA RD
LEWIS CO WA 187-C3
KALAMA RIVER RD
COWLITZ CO WA 118-A3
COWLITZ CO WA 189-D5
KALE ST Rt#-544
EVERSON WA 102-B1
KALE ST NE
Hayesville OR 323-E5
MARION CO OR 323-E5
SALEM OR 323-E5
KALMBACH RD
COWLITZ CO WA 187-C7
COWLITZ CO WA 189-C1
KAMB RD
SKAGIT CO WA 168-A1
KAME TER
CLACKAMAS CO OR 199-B5
NE KAMIAKEN ST
PULLMAN WA 249-B5
NE KAMIAKEN ST Rt#-270
PULLMAN WA 249-B5
KAMILCHE POINT RD
MASON CO WA 180-B4
KAMMEYER RD
COLUMBIA CO OR 192-A4
KAMPH RD
LINN CO OR 207-D4
S KAMRATH RD
CLACKAMAS CO OR 200-A6
KANAKA CREEK RD
MAPLE RIDGE BC 157-D6
SKAMANIA CO WA 194-D5
KANASKAT KANGLEY RD SE
KING CO WA 110-C3
KING CO WA 176-B7
SE KANE DR
GRESHAM OR 200-B2
SE KANE ST
ROSEBURG OR 334-G8
KANE CREEK RD
JACKSON CO OR 230-B7
KANGAROO RD
DISTRICT OF METCHOSIN BC 159-A7
KANGAS RD
LEWIS CO WA 187-D4
KANNIWAI CREEK RD
GRANT CO WA 113-A2
KANSAS CITY RD
WASHINGTON CO OR 125-B1
KANTOLA LN
VALLEY CO ID 252-D3
KAPKA BUTTE RD
DESCHUTES CO OR 216-D5
KAPOWSIN HWY
PIERCE CO WA 118-B1
PIERCE CO WA 182-C7
KAPOWSIN-EATONVILLE-LA GRANDE
EATONVILLE WA 118-B1
PIERCE CO WA 118-B1
W KAPPLER RD
COLUMBIA CO OR 192-A1
KARCHER RD Rt#-55
CANYON CO ID 147-B1
NAMPA ID 147-B1
KARIN DR
YAKIMA CO WA 243-C6
KARNOWSKY CREEK RD
LANE CO OR 214-C2
KARTH RD
COLUMBIA CO OR 189-A7
N KATH RD
SPOKANE CO WA 247-B1
W KATHLEEN AV
COEUR D'ALENE ID 355-B6
KOOTENAI CO ID 355-B6
KATON RD
GRAYS HARBOR CO WA 178-D7
KATTENBACK VOLLMER RD
NEZ PERCE CO ID 250-C5
KAUFFMAN RD
CLACKAMAS CO OR 205-D2
KAUFMAN RD NE
MARION CO OR 205-B5
KAYAK POINT RD
SNOHOMISH CO WA 168-B6
KEAN ST
BREMERTON WA 270-D11
KEANE RD SW
DOUGLAS CO WA 239-C5
KEASEY RD
COLUMBIA CO OR 125-B1
NW KEASEY ST
ROSEBURG OR 334-C5
KEASLING RD
LEWIS CO WA 187-D2
KEATING RD NW
THURSTON CO WA 180-B5
KEATING CROSS RD
DIST OF CENTRAL SAANICH BC 159-C4
KEATING CUTOFF RD
BAKER CO OR 130-B3
BAKER CO OR 138-B1
KEATING GRANGE HALL RD
BAKER CO OR 130-C3
KEEFER RD
DESCHUTES CO OR 142-C1
KEENE RD
BENTON CO WA 341-A4
RICHLAND WA 341-C5
KEENE RD NE
MARION CO OR 205-A2
SW KEENEY LN
JEFFERSON CO OR 212-C2
KEENEY FORKS RD
GRANT CO OR 137-B1
LONG CREEK OR 137-B1
E KEEVEY RD
SPOKANE CO WA 114-C2
KEIL RD NE
MARION CO OR 199-B7
KEITH RD
CITY OF N VANCOUVER BC 255-B5
DIST OF N VANCOUVER BC 254-G4
DIST OF N VANCOUVER BC 255-C5
DIST OF WEST VANCOUVER BC 254-D4
KEITHLY CREEK RD
WASHINGTON CO ID 139-B1
KEITH WILSON RD
DISTRICT OF CHILLIWACK BC 102-C1
NE KEIZER RD
KEIZER OR 323-B5
KEIZER RD NE
KEIZER OR 323-B5
KELLEHER RD
SKAGIT CO WA 161-B5
KELLER RD
Altamont OR 339-C13
KELLOGG RD
DEL NORTE CO CA 148-B3
N KELLOGG ST
KENNEWICK WA 342-E9
S KELLOGG ST
BENTON CO WA 342-E11
KENNEWICK WA 342-E11
SW KELLY AV
PORTLAND OR 317-F1
KELLY RD
CHELAN CO WA 238-C3
CITY OF COLWOOD BC 159-B6
CLARK CO WA 193-A1
DISTRICT OF LANGFORD BC 159-B6
GRAYS HARBOR CO WA 179-A1
LINN CO OR 133-C1
NE KELLY RD
CLARK CO WA 193-A1
KELLY CREEK RD
LANE CO OR 215-A7
KELLY CUTOFF RD
WASCO CO OR 127-B1
KELLY HALL RD
MASON CO WA 179-B1
KELSAY MOUNTAIN RD
DOUGLAS CO OR 223-C2
KELSAY POINT RD
DOUGLAS CO OR 223-C3
N KELSO AV
COWLITZ CO WA 303-E5
KELSO WA 303-E5
S KELSO DR
KELSO WA 303-F12
SE KELSO RD
CLACKAMAS CO OR 200-C3
KEMP RD
CLACKAMAS CO OR 200-C6
KEMP LAKE RD
BRITISH COLUMBIA 101-A2
BRITISH COLUMBIA 164-C1
KENDALL RD
WALLA WALLA CO WA 345-D13
Walla Walla East WA 345-D13
KENDALL RD Rt#-547
WHATCOM CO WA 102-B1
KENNEDY LN
LANE CO OR 219-C1
KENNEDY RD
BENTON CO WA 120-C3
BENTON CO WA 121-A3
BENTON CO WA 341-A4
RICHLAND WA 341-A4
WEST RICHLAND WA 121-A3
WEST RICHLAND WA 341-A4
KENNEDY RD Rt#-224
BENTON CO WA 120-C3
KENNEL RD
LINN CO OR 207-D5
W KENNEWICK AV
KENNEWICK WA 342-H10
KENNEWICK WA 343-B10
E KENNEY RD
SPOKANE CO WA 352-A13
N KENNEY RD
SPOKANE CO WA 352-A14
KENO WORDEN RD
KLAMATH CO OR 235-A6
KENSINGTON AV
ASTORIA OR 300-C5
DISTRICT OF BURNABY BC 156-D4
W KENSINGTON AV
ASTORIA OR 300-B5
KENT AV W
KITSAP CO WA 270-D14
Navy Yard City WA 270-D14
SW KENT LN
JEFFERSON CO OR 212-C1
KENT RD
DESCHUTES CO OR 212-A5
KENT BLACK DIAMOND RD
KING CO WA 175-C7
KING CO WA 182-D1
KENT CREEK RD
DOUGLAS CO OR 221-A7
KENT-DES MOINES RD Rt#-516
DES MOINES WA 290-B7
KENT WA 175-B7
KENT WA 290-B7
KENT-DES MOINES RD S Rt#-516
KENT WA 175-B7
KENT WA 290-E7
KING WA 290-E7
KING CO WA 175-B7
KENT-GRASS VALLEY RD
SHERMAN CO OR 127-C2
KENT KANGLEY RD
KENT WA 176-A7
KING CO WA 176-A7
MAPLE VALLEY WA 176-A7
KENT KANGLEY RD Rt#-516
COVINGTON WA 175-C7
KENT WA 175-C7
KING CO WA 175-C7
KING CO WA 176-A7
MAPLE VALLEY WA 175-C7
MAPLE VALLEY WA 176-A7
KENTUCK WY
COOS CO OR 218-C7
N KENTUCKY AV
East Wenatchee Bench WA 239-A4
KENWORTHY RD
LINN CO OR 326-H4
KERBY CREEK RD
JACKSON CO OR 227-A7
KERBY MAINLINE RD
JOSEPHINE CO OR 233-B3
KERN RD SW
DOUGLAS CO WA 239-B2
KERN SWAMP RD
KLAMATH CO OR 235-B6
KERR PKWY
LAKE OSWEGO OR 320-A3
PORTLAND OR 320-A3
KERR ST
VANCOUVER BC 156-C5
KERRON AV
LEWIS CO WA 187-C2
WINLOCK WA 187-C3
KERRON AV Rt#-505
WINLOCK WA 187-C3
W KERRON AV
LEWIS CO WA 187-C2
NAPAVINE WA 187-C2
KERRY RD
COLUMBIA CO OR 117-B3
KERSEY WY
AUBURN WA 182-C2
KERSHAW RD
JACKSON CO OR 230-D6
KESSLER BLVD
LONGVIEW WA 302-J8
LONGVIEW WA 303-A10
W KETTLE RIVER RD
FERRY CO WA 105-B1
KEY RD
UMATILLA CO OR 129-C1
WESTON OR 129-C1
KEYES RD
GRAYS HARBOR CO WA 179-A7
KEY PENINSULA HWY
PIERCE CO WA 174-A7
PIERCE CO WA 181-A2
KEY PENINSULA HWY Rt#-302
PIERCE CO WA 174-B6
KEYS RD
YAKIMA CO WA 243-C6
KEYSTONE AV
DISTRICT OF MISSION BC 94-B3
ISLAND CO WA 167-C5
KEYSTONE RD
ISLAND CO WA 167-C5
OKANOGAN CO WA 104-C2
KEYSTONE RANCH RD
CROOK CO OR 135-C2
KIACUT RD
YAMHILL CO OR 198-B3
KICKERVILLE RD
Birch Bay WA 158-B4
WHATCOM CO WA 158-B4
KIDD ISLAND RD
KOOTENAI CO ID 247-D4
KOOTENAI CO ID 248-A1
S KIESLING RD
SPOKANE CO WA 246-D6
KIGER RD
MALHEUR CO OR 146-B3
KIGER ISLAND DR
BENTON CO OR 207-A7
KILCHIS FOREST RD
TILLAMOOK CO OR 197-C1
KILCHIS RIVER RD
TILLAMOOK CO OR 191-C7
TILLAMOOK CO OR 197-C1
KILLDEER RD
CLACKAMAS CO OR 200-A6
KILLEBREW DR
PAYETTE CO ID 139-A3
N KILLINGSWORTH ST
PORTLAND OR 308-E7
PORTLAND OR 309-F7
NE KILLINGSWORTH ST
PORTLAND OR 309-H7
PORTLAND OR 310-C7
PORTLAND OR 311-E7
NE KILLINGSWORTH ST U.S.-30
PORTLAND OR 311-F7
KILLMORE RD
KITTITAS CO WA 241-A5
KILMER RD
CLALLAM CO WA 169-B2
KIMBALL DR
GIG HARBOR WA 181-C1
KIMBALL RD
LANE CO OR 215-D5
KIMBERLY-LONG CREEK HWY
GRANT CO OR 136-C1
GRANT CO OR 137-A1
LONG CREEK OR 137-A1
MONUMENT OR 136-C1
KIMBLE RD
MOUNT VERNON WA 260-A14
SKAGIT CO WA 260-A14
KINCAID RD
JOSEPHINE CO OR 149-A2
YAMHILL CO OR 198-D5
KINCAID ST Rt#-536
MOUNT VERNON WA 260-C13
KINDER DR
GRANT CO WA 242-C2
KING LN
JEFFERSON CO OR 212-D1
SW KING LN
JEFFERSON CO OR 212-C1
JEFFERSON CO OR 213-A1
KING RD
CROOK CO OR 213-C4
DISTRICT OF MATSQUI BC 102-B1
DISTRICT OF SURREY BC 157-A5
LEWIS CO WA 187-B2
E KING RD
ADA CO ID 253-B5
SE KING RD
CLACKAMAS CO OR 199-D3
CLACKAMAS CO OR 200-A3
HAPPY VALLEY OR 200-A3
KITSAP CO WA 174-C4
MILWAUKIE OR 199-D3
W KING RD
ADA CO ID 253-A5
KING ST
COTTONWOOD ID 123-C3
COTTONWOOD ID 123-C3
IDAHO CO ID 123-C3
IDAHO CO ID 123-C3
YACHATS OR 209-A3
N KING ST
GOLDENDALE WA 127-C1
NE KING WY
DESCHUTES CO OR 212-D5
KING EDWARD AV E
VANCOUVER BC 156-B5
KING EDWARD AV W
VANCOUVER BC 156-B5
VANCOUVER BC 254-A14
KINGFISHER DR
BRITISH COLUMBIA 104-C1
OSOYOOS BC 104-C1
KING GEORGE HWY Rt#-99A
DISTRICT OF SURREY BC 156-D5
DISTRICT OF SURREY BC 157-A7
DISTRICT OF SURREY BC 158-A1
KING GEORGE TR
DISTRICT OF OAK BAY BC 257-C11
KING GRADE RD
COLUMBIA CO WA 122-B2
KING HEZEKIAH WY
DESCHUTES CO OR 332-J11
KING MOUNTAIN RD
JOSEPHINE CO OR 229-C2
KINGS BLVD
CORVALLIS OR 327-F8
KINGS HWY
JACKSON CO OR 234-A2
MEDFORD OR 336-C14
KINGSBURY RD
CHELAN CO WA 239-A6
KINGS CORNER RD
UMATILLA CO OR 129-B1
KINGS GRADE
YAMHILL CO OR 198-C4
KINGSLEY RD
HOOD RIVER CO OR 195-B6
PACIFIC CO WA 183-D7
KINGSLEY-FRIEND MARKET RD
WASCO CO OR 127-B2
KING SOLOMON LN
DESCHUTES CO OR 332-H12
KINGS RIVER RD
HUMBOLDT CO NV 154-A3
KINGS RIVER RD Rt#-293
HUMBOLDT CO NV 154-A3
S KINGSTON RD NE
Indianola WA 170-D6
KITSAP CO WA 170-D6
W KINGSTON RD NE
KITSAP CO WA 170-C5
KINGSTON ST
CITY OF VICTORIA BC 256-F9
KINGSTON-JORDAN DR
LINN CO OR 133-C1
KINGSTON-JORDAN RD
LINN CO OR 134-A1
KINGS VALLEY HWY Rt#-223
BENTON CO OR 133-A1
DALLAS OR 204-A5
POLK CO OR 125-B3
POLK CO OR 133-B1
POLK CO OR 204-A5
KINGS VALLEY RD
DEL NORTE CO CA 148-B3
KINGSWAY
VANCOUVER BC 254-J13
KINGSWAY Rt#-1A
VANCOUVER BC 156-C5
VANCOUVER BC 254-J13
VANCOUVER BC 255-A14
KINGSWAY Rt#-99A
DISTRICT OF BURNABY BC 156-C5
NEW WESTMINSTER BC 156-C5
KINGSWAY AV
PORT COQUITLAM BC 157-B4
KING TULL RD
BENTON CO WA 120-C3
E KING TULL RD
BENTON CO WA 120-B3
W KING TUT RD
WHATCOM CO WA 158-D5
KINGWOOD AV
MILL CITY OR 134-A1
KINGWOOD DR NW
SALEM OR 322-E12
KINNEY RD
YAMHILL CO OR 198-C5
KINNS LN NE
MARION CO OR 205-A1
KINSMAN RD
PIERCE CO WA 181-D7
KINZEL CREEK RD
CLACKAMAS CO OR 201-D7
CLACKAMAS CO OR 202-A7
KINZER RD
NEZ PERCE CO ID 250-B2
KINZUA LN
WHEELER CO OR 128-A3
KINZUA RD
MORROW CO OR 128-C3
WHEELER CO OR 128-B3
KINZY RD
CLACKAMAS CO OR 200-C7
KIPLING RD
OKANOGAN CO WA 105-A1
KIRBY MAYVIEW RD
GARFIELD CO WA 122-C2
KIRK AV
BROWNSVILLE OR 210-C2
LINN CO OR 210-C2
KIRK DR
LINN CO OR 210-D2
KIRK RD
BENTON CO WA 121-A3
KIRKENDAHL RD
WHITMAN CO WA 249-A6
KIRKHAM RD
JOSEPHINE CO OR 233-B5
KIRKLAND RD
LEWIS CO WA 187-C1
KIRKPATRICK RD
GRAYS HARBOR CO WA 177-D3
KIRKSTONE RD
DIST OF N VANCOUVER BC 255-D3
KIRKWOOD RD NW
YAMHILL CO OR 204-C3
KIRSOP RD SW
THURSTON CO WA 296-C13
KIRTLAND RD
JACKSON CO OR 230-C6
KISSLER RD
CROOK CO OR 213-B6
KITER CREEK RD
JACKSON CO OR 226-B6
KITER CREEK SPUR
JACKSON CO OR 226-C6
KITSAP CT NW
Silverdale WA 174-B1
KITSAP WY
BREMERTON WA 270-B9
KITSAP WY Rt#-310
BREMERTON WA 270-D10
W KITSAP LAKE RD NW
BREMERTON WA 270-A9
Erlands Point-Kitsap Lake WA 270-A10
KITSILANO DIV
VANCOUVER BC 254-B12
KITSON SPRINGS RD
LANE CO OR 142-A1
KITTITAS HWY
ELLENSBURG WA 241-B6
KITTITAS WA 241-C6
KITTITAS CO WA 241-B6
KITTSON PKWY
DISTRICT OF DELTA BC 156-D7
DISTRICT OF SURREY BC 156-D7
KITZMILLER RD
CLACKAMAS CO OR 200-C5
WHITMAN CO WA 249-B4
KIWANIS WY
CITY OF VICTORIA BC 256-J6
KIWA SPRING RD
DESCHUTES CO OR 217-A5
KIZER AV
LINN CO OR 326-H4
SE KLAHANIE BLVD
KING CO WA 176-A3
KLAHOWYA LN
DOUGLAS CO OR 221-B3
NW KLAHOWYA TR
KITSAP CO WA 174-A2
KLAK BUTTE RD
DESCHUTES CO OR 216-C6
KLAMATH AV Rt#-39
KLAMATH FALLS OR 338-D8
S KLAMATH FALLS HWY Rt#-140
Altamont OR 235-D5
KLAMATH CO OR 235-C5
KLAMATH CO OR 338-D12
KLAMATH FALLS OR 235-C5
KLAMATH FALLS OR 338-C12
KLAMATH FALLS-LKVW HWY Rt#-39
Altamont OR 338-F9
Altamont OR 339-C11
Altamont OR 339-C11
KLAMATH CO OR 150-C2
KLAMATH CO OR 151-A1
KLAMATH CO OR 339-E12
KLAMATH FALLS OR 338-F9
LAKE CO OR 151-C2
LAKE CO OR 152-A2
KLAMATH FALLS-MALIN HWY
KLAMATH CO OR 151-A3
KLAMATH FALLS OR 338-C4
MALIN OR 151-A3
KLAMATH FALLS-MALIN HWY Rt#-39
Altamont OR 338-C4
Altamont OR 339-A10
KLAMATH CO OR 150-C2
KLAMATH CO OR 235-D5
KLAMATH CO OR 338-C4
KLAMATH FALLS OR 338-C4
MERRILL OR 150-C2
KLAMATH FALLS-MALN HWY Rt#-140
Altamont OR 339-D14
KLAMATH CO OR 235-D5
KLAMATH CO OR 339-D14
KLAMATHON RD
SISKIYOU CO CA 150-A3
KLASKANINE AV
ASTORIA OR 300-C6
KLEIN RD
ADAMS CO WA 113-C3
KLEINSMITH RD
CLACKAMAS CO OR 200-D5
KLEMGARD RD
WHITMAN CO WA 249-A6
KLICKITAT APPLETON RD
KLICKITAT CO WA 196-C3
KLICKITAT TRAIL RD
LANE CO OR 209-B5
KLONDIKE RD
FERRY CO WA 105-B2
SHERMAN CO OR 127-C2
N KLONDIKE RD
SHERMAN CO OR 127-C1
KLOOCHMAN CREEK RD
CROOK CO OR 136-A3
KLUPENGER RD
MARION CO OR 199-B6
KLUSS RD
LATAH CO ID 249-D7
LATAH CO ID 250-C1
KNAPPA RD
CLATSOP CO OR 117-A3
KNAPPTON FERRY RD Rt#-401
PACIFIC CO WA 186-C7
NW KNICKERBOCKER AV
DESCHUTES CO OR 212-D4
KNIERIEM RD
MULTNOMAH CO OR 200-C1
KNIGHT RD
KLICKITAT CO WA 127-C1
KLICKITAT CO WA 196-C4
LANE CO OR 133-A3
KNIGHT ST
CITY OF RICHMOND BC 156-C5
VANCOUVER BC 156-C5
VANCOUVER BC 255-A14
KNIGHTS BRIDGE RD
CANBY OR 199-C6
CLACKAMAS CO OR 199-C6
NW KNIGHTS BRIDGE RD
CANBY OR 199-C6

PNW INDEX

378 KNOB HILL RD STREET INDEX LAWTON RD

STREET City State Page-Grid

KNOB HILL RD
WASCO CO OR 196-C7
KNOB HILL-TROUT CREEK RD
FERRY CO WA 105-B2
KNOBLE RD E
PIERCE CO WA 182-A6
NE KNOLL AV
DOUGLAS CO OR 334-G2
KNOTGRASS RIDGE RD
ASOTIN CO WA 122-C2
KNOTT RD
DESCHUTES CO OR 217-B4
DESCHUTES CO OR 332-G14
KNOTT CREEK RD
HUMBOLDT CO NV 153-B3
KNOWLES RD
JACKSON CO OR 234-A2
KNOWLES RD SE
THURSTON CO WA 184-D3
KNOX AV
BELLINGHAM WA 258-B10
KNOX RD
CLACKAMAS CO OR 200-B4
KNOX BUTTE RD
ALBANY OR 207-D4
ALBANY OR 326-J7
LINN CO OR 133-C1
LINN CO OR 207-D4
LINN CO OR 326-J7
KNUDSEN RD
KOOTENAI CO ID 245-A4
KOCH RD
ADAMS CO WA 113-B3
KOENIG RD
WHITMAN CO WA 249-A2
KOHFIELD RD
DESCHUTES CO OR 212-A7
KOLLOCK-KNAPP RD
SKAMANIA CO WA 195-C4
KONKOLVILLE RD
CLEARWATER CO ID 123-C2
CLEARWATER CO ID 123-C2
OROFINO ID 123-C2
OROFINO ID 123-C2
KOOL RD
COWLITZ CO WA 189-D4
KOONTZ RD
LEWIS CO WA 187-C2
KOOSBAY BLVD
COOS BAY OR 333-G8
NORTH BEND OR 333-G8
KOOTENAI CTO
PONDERAY ID 244-A1
N KOOTENAI RD
BONNER CO ID 244-A1
KOOTENAI ST
BOISE ID 253-C3
BONNERS FERRY ID 107-B2
KOPACHUCK DR NW
PIERCE CO WA 181-B1
KOPF RD
WHITMAN CO WA 249-C7
KOSKELLA RD
VALLEY CO ID 252-D2
KOSYDAR RD
LINCOLN CO OR 206-C1
KOWITZ RD
LINN CO OR 133-C1
KRAETZ RD
SNOHOMISH CO WA 168-D5
KRAIMIEN RD
YAMHILL CO OR 199-A6
KRAIN WABASH RD
KING CO WA 182-D2
KRAUSS RD
JOSEPHINE CO OR 233-A5
KRAXBERGER RD
CLACKAMAS CO OR 199-C7
KRESKY AV
CENTRALIA WA 299-F6
LEWIS CO WA 299-F6
KRIEGER RD
DESCHUTES CO OR 212-C7
KROENIG RD
POLK CO OR 204-A3
SE KROHN RD
CLARK CO WA 193-C6
KROLL RD
COWLITZ CO WA 187-C6
KRONQUIST
PIERCE CO WA 182-A7
E KRONQUIST RD
SPOKANE CO WA 246-D1
S KROPF RD
CLACKAMAS CO OR 205-D3
SW KRUGER RD
WASHINGTON CO OR 199-A4
SW KRUSE RD
CLACKAMAS CO OR 199-B5
KRUSE WY
CLACKAMAS OR 320-A6
CLACKAMAS CO OR 199-B3
LAKE OSWEGO OR 199-B3
LAKE OSWEGO OR 320-A6
KUEBLER BLVD SE
MARION CO OR 325-B6
SALEM OR 204-D7
SALEM OR 324-F6
SALEM OR 325-B6
KUEBLER RD
MARION CO OR 324-D6
SALEM OR 324-D6
KUEFFLER RD
SKAMANIA CO WA 194-B6
KUEHNE RD
YAMHILL CO OR 198-C5
KUHNHAUSEN RD
SNOHOMISH CO WA 168-C3
KUHNIS RD
COWLITZ CO WA 192-B1
KULM RD
GRANT CO WA 242-C7
KUNA RD Rt#-69
ADA CO ID 253-A5
E KUNA RD
ADA CO ID 253-B5
W KUNA RD
ADA CO ID 147-C1
ADA CO ID 253-A5
KUNA CAVE RD
ADA CO ID 253-A7
KUNA-MERIDIAN RD Rt#-69
ADA CO ID 253-A4
MERIDIAN ID 253-A4
KUNA MORA RD
ADA CO ID 253-A6
KUNZE RD
MORROW CO OR 128-B1
KUNZE RD SW
BOARDMAN OR 128-C1
MORROW CO OR 128-C1
KURTZ RD
POLK CO OR 204-A4
NW KUYKENDALL RD
YAMHILL CO OR 198-A5
KWINA RD
WHATCOM CO WA 158-C7
KWNEESUM RD
SKAMANIA CO WA 193-D5

L

L RD NE
DOUGLAS CO WA 112-C1
L RD NW
DOUGLAS CO WA 236-D5
L RD SE
DOUGLAS CO WA 112-C2
L ST U.S.-101
CRESCENT CITY CA 148-B3
E L ST
TACOMA WA 182-A3
N L ST
TOPPENISH WA 120-A2
YAKIMA CO WA 120-A2
S L ST
TOPPENISH WA 120-A2
YAKIMA CO WA 120-A2
L 1/2-SW RD
GRANT CO WA 112-B3
LABARRE RD
SKAMANIA CO WA 193-D6
LABIEUX RD
NANAIMO BC 93-A3
LABISH CENTER RD NE
MARION CO OR 205-A4
LABISKE RD
CLATSOP CO OR 188-D3
LABOR CAMP
CANYON CO ID 147-B1
NW LA CENTER RD
CLARK CO WA 192-C2
LA CENTER WA 192-C2
LACEY BLVD SE
LACEY WA 297-F6
LACKEY RD
PIERCE CO WA 181-A1
LACOMB DR
LINN CO OR 133-C1
LA CROSSE AIRPORT RD
LA CROSSE WA 122-A1
WHITMAN CO WA 122-A1
LADD CREEK RD
UNION CO OR 130-A3
SW LADD HILL RD
CLACKAMAS CO OR 199-A6
SHERWOOD OR 199-A6
WASHINGTON CO OR 199-A6
LADNER TRUNK RD
DISTRICT OF DELTA BC 101-C1
LADNER TRUNK RD Rt#-10
DISTRICT OF DELTA BC 156-D7
LAEL-FLAT CREEK RD
STEVENS CO WA 106-A1
NE LAFAYETTE AV
MCMINNVILLE OR 198-A7
LAFAYETTE HWY
YAMHILL CO OR 198-B7
YAMHILL CO OR 204-C1
SE LAFAYETTE HWY
LAFAYETTE OR 198-B7
YAMHILL CO OR 198-B7
YAMHILL CO OR 204-C1
SE LAFAYETTE HWY Rt#-233
YAMHILL CO OR 198-B7
LAFAYETTE RD
SKAGIT CO WA 260-F4
LAFAYETTE ST
STEILACOOM WA 181-C4
LAFOLETT RD
WASHINGTON CO OR 198-C1
LAGOON DR
MALHEUR CO OR 139-A3
VALE OR 139-A3
LAGOON POINT RD
ISLAND CO WA 167-C7
LA GRANDE-BAKER HWY Rt#-30
NORTH POWDER OR 130-B3
UNION CO OR 130-B3
LA GRANDE-BAKER HWY Rt#-203
UNION OR 130-A2
UNION CO OR 130-A2
LA GRANDE-BAKER HWY Rt#-237
NORTH POWDER OR 130-B3
UNION OR 130-B3
UNION CO OR 130-B3
LA GRANDE-BAKER HWY U.S.-30
BAKER CITY OR 138-B1
BAKER CO OR 130-A3
BAKER CO OR 138-B1
HAINES OR 130-A3
LA GRANDE OR 130-A3
UNION CO OR 130-A3
LA GRANGE ST
ADA CO ID 253-B4
LAIRD RD
CLALLAM CO WA 165-A6
LAITY ST
MAPLE RIDGE BC 157-C5
LAKE AV
CANYON CO ID 147-B1
LAKE AV Rt#-97
HARRISON ID 248-A4
LAKE DR
DESCHUTES CO OR 212-A4
EUGENE OR 329-F1
LANE CO OR 329-F1
WARRENTON OR 188-B1
LAKE RD
ASOTIN CO WA 122-C3
KLICKITAT CO WA 119-A3
SNOHOMISH CO WA 171-B4
YAMHILL OR 198-A5
YAMHILL CO OR 198-A5
N LAKE RD
WALLA WALLA CO WA 121-B3
S LAKE RD
Burbank WA 121-B3
WALLA WALLA CO WA 121-B3
SE LAKE RD
CLACKAMAS CO OR 199-D3
MILWAUKIE OR 199-D3
MILWAUKIE OR 321-J3
W LAKE RD
YAMHILL CO OR 198-A5
E LAKE ST Rt#-55
MCCALL ID 251-C5
LAKE ST S
KIRKLAND WA 175-C1
LAKE BALLINGER WY Rt#-104
EDMONDS WA 171-B6
MOUNTLAKE TERRACE WA 171-B6
SHORELINE WA 171-B6
LAKE CAVANAUGH RD
SKAGIT CO WA 168-C2
LAKE CITY WY NE
SEATTLE WA 274-C2
LAKE CITY WY NE Rt#-522
SEATTLE WA 171-B7
SEATTLE WA 274-C2
LAKE CREEK DR
LINN CO OR 207-C6
LINN CO OR 210-A3
TANGENT OR 207-C6
LAKE CREEK RD
DOUGLAS CO OR 223-C5
JACKSON CO OR 234-D1
LEWIS CO WA 187-A1
LAKE CUSHMAN RD Rt#-119
MASON CO WA 109-B2
MASON CO WA 173-A6
LAKE EARL DR Rt#-D3
DEL NORTE CO CA 148-B3
SW LAKE FLORA RD
KITSAP CO WA 174-A5
E LAKE FORK RD
VALLEY CO ID 251-D6
W LAKE FORK RD
VALLEY CO ID 251-C7
LAKE FRANCIS RD SE
KING CO WA 176-A6
E LAKE GOODWIN RD Rt#-531
SNOHOMISH CO WA 168-B5
W LAKE GOODWIN RD
SNOHOMISH CO WA 168-B6
LAKE GROVE ST
LAKE OSWEGO OR 320-A7
E LAKE HAZEL RD
ADA CO ID 253-B4
W LAKE HAZEL RD
ADA CO ID 253-A4
SW LAKE HELENA RD
KITSAP CO WA 174-A5
LAKE HILLS BLVD
BELLEVUE WA 175-C2
LAKE HILLS CONNECTOR
BELLEVUE WA 175-C2
SE LAKE HOLM RD
KING CO WA 182-C1
LAKEHURST DR
BREMERTON WA 270-B11
LAKE JOSEPHINE BLVD
PIERCE CO WA 181-B4
LAKE LOMA DR
SNOHOMISH CO WA 168-C6
LAKE LOUISE RD
Sudden Valley WA 161-A1
WHATCOM CO WA 161-A1
LAKEMONT BLVD SE
BELLEVUE WA 175-D3
ISSAQUAH WA 175-D3
LAKE OF THE WOODS HWY Rt#-96
SISKIYOU CO CA 149-A3
LAKE OF THE WOODS HWY Rt#-99
CENTRAL POINT OR 230-C7
JACKSON CO OR 230-C7
MEDFORD OR 230-C7
LAKE OF THE WOODS HWY Rt#-140
JACKSON CO OR 149-C1
JACKSON CO OR 150-A1
JACKSON CO OR 230-D6
KLAMATH CO OR 150-B1
KLAMATH CO OR 231-A6
KLAMATH CO OR 235-A1
KLAMATH CO OR 338-A10
KLAMATH FALLS OR 235-A1
KLAMATH FALLS OR 338-B12
White City OR 230-D6
LAKE OF THE WOODS HWY Rt#-263
SISKIYOU CO CA 149-C3
YREKA CA 149-C3
N LAKE OF THE WOODS HWY Rt#-3
SISKIYOU CO CA 149-C3
W LAKE OF THE WOODS HWY Rt#-3
SISKIYOU CO CA 149-C3
YREKA CA 149-C3
E LAKE PLEASANT RD
CLALLAM CO WA 163-A6
W LAKE PLEASANT RD
CLALLAM CO WA 163-A6
LAKERIDGE DR
OLYMPIA WA 296-G7
LAKE SAMISH DR
WHATCOM CO WA 161-A2
LAKE SAMISH RD
SKAGIT CO WA 161-B3
WHATCOM CO WA 161-B3
E LK SAMMAMISH PKWY NE
REDMOND WA 175-D2
SAMMAMISH WA 175-D2
W LK SAMMAMISH PKWY NE
BELLEVUE WA 175-D1
KING CO WA 175-D1
REDMOND WA 175-D1
E LK SAMMAMISH PKWY SE
ISSAQUAH WA 176-A4
KING CO WA 175-D3
KING CO WA 176-A3
SAMMAMISH WA 175-D3
W LK SAMMAMISH PKWY SE
BELLEVUE WA 175-D2
KING CO WA 175-D2
LAKES DIVIDE RD
KOOTENAI CO ID 248-C2
LAKE SHORE DR
CANYON CO ID 147-B1
LAKESHORE DR
BONNER CO ID 107-A3
BONNER CO ID 244-A3
CASCADE ID 252-D7
CLARK CO WA 192-C1
COOS BAY OR 333-B5
COWLITZ CO WA 192-C1
JOSEPHINE CO OR 233-B2
KLAMATH CO OR 235-B3
KLAMATH CO OR 338-A6
KLAMATH FALLS OR 338-A6
VALLEY CO ID 252-D7
WOODLAND WA 192-C1
WOODLAND WA 192-C1
E LAKESHORE DR
LAKE STEVENS WA 171-D1
N LAKESHORE DR
LAKE STEVENS WA 171-D1
SNOHOMISH CO WA 171-D1
S LAKESHORE RD
CHELAN CO WA 236-B3
LAKESIDE RD
KLICKITAT CO WA 119-A3
S LAKESIDE RD
Liberty Lake WA 247-B4
Liberty Lake WA 352-F14
SPOKANE CO WA 247-B4
SPOKANE CO WA 352-F14
E LAKE STEVENS RD
LAKE STEVENS WA 171-D2
SNOHOMISH CO WA 171-D2
S LAKE STEVENS RD
SNOHOMISH CO WA 171-D2
LAKE TERRELL RD
WHATCOM CO WA 158-B6
LAKEVIEW BLVD
LAKE OSWEGO OR 320-A7
LAKEVIEW BLVD E
SEATTLE WA 278-B3
N LAKEVIEW DR
HAYDEN LAKE ID 245-A5
LAKEVIEW-BURNS HWY U.S.-395
HARNEY CO OR 144-C2
LAKE CO OR 144-B3
LAKE CO OR 152-A1
LAKE VISTA DR
GRANT CO WA 242-B1
LAKE WASHINGTON BLVD
SEATTLE WA 279-E6
LAKE WASHINGTON BLVD E
SEATTLE WA 278-D2
SEATTLE WA 279-F4
LAKE WASHINGTON BLVD N
RENTON WA 175-C4
LAKE WASHINGTON BLVD NE
BELLEVUE WA 175-C2
KIRKLAND WA 175-C1
LAKE WASHINGTON BLVD S
SEATTLE WA 278-E7
SEATTLE WA 282-E1
SEATTLE WA 283-E3
LAKE WASHINGTON BLVD SE
BELLEVUE WA 175-C3
NEWCASTLE WA 175-C3
RENTON WA 175-C4
LAKEWAY DR
BELLINGHAM WA 258-F7
BONNEY LAKE WA 182-C4
PIERCE CO WA 182-C4
WHATCOM CO WA 161-A1
WHATCOM CO WA 258-F7
LAKE WHATCOM BLVD
Sudden Valley WA 161-A1
WHATCOM CO WA 161-A1
LAKEWOOD DR
ALBANY OR 326-B11
LAKEWOOD DR W
LAKEWOOD WA 294-A7
PIERCE WA 294-A7
TACOMA WA 294-A7
UNIVERSITY PLACE WA 294-A7
LAKEWOOD RD
SNOHOMISH CO WA 168-B5
LAKEWOOD RD Rt#-531
SNOHOMISH CO WA 168-B5
SE LAKE YOUNGS WY
KING CO WA 175-C6
LAMAR RD
WALLA WALLA CO WA 121-C2
LAMB RD
KOOTENAI CO ID 248-B4
UMATILLA CO OR 128-C1
UMATILLA CO OR 129-A1
LAMBERSON RD
GILLIAM CO OR 128-A2
SW LAMBERT LN
WASHINGTON CO OR 198-C3
LAMBERT RD
KITTITAS CO WA 240-C2
W LAMBERT RD
DESCHUTES CO OR 212-B3
LAMBERTIANA RD
DESCHUTES CO OR 217-A7
LAMERS RD
POLK CO OR 207-B1
LAMOINE RD NW
DOUGLAS CO WA 112-B1
DOUGLAS CO WA 236-C5
LA MONT RD
ADA CO ID 253-A3
LAMONT RD
WHITMAN CO WA 114-A3
LAMONTA RD
CROOK CO OR 213-C3
LAMPA VALLEY RD
COOS CO OR 220-C6
LAMPERTI LN
COLLEGE PLACE WA 344-F12
WALLA WALLA CO WA 344-F12
LAMPMAN RD
WHATCOM CO WA 158-C6
LAMPSON ST
TOWN OF ESQUIMALT BC 256-C9
LANA AV NE
SALEM OR 323-B9
LANCASTER DR
Four Corners OR 323-E12
Four Corners OR 325-D1
Hayesville OR 323-E8
SALEM OR 204-D5
SALEM OR 323-E12
SALEM OR 325-E3
LANCASTER DR Rt#-213
Hayesville OR 323-E11
SALEM OR 204-D5
SALEM OR 323-E11
LANCASTER RD
Freeland WA 170-D2
KOOTENAI CO ID 245-A5
SAINT JOHN WA 114-B3
WHITMAN CO WA 114-B3
WHITMAN CO WA 122-B1
W LANCASTER RD
HAYDEN ID 247-D1
KOOTENAI CO ID 247-D1
SW LANCEFIELD RD
YAMHILL CO OR 204-B2
S LANDER ST
SEATTLE WA 282-A2
NE LANDERHOLM RD
CLARK CO WA 192-D2
LANDES ST
PORT TOWNSEND WA 263-F5
LANDING RD
COOS CO OR 220-D6
SKAGIT CO WA 168-A1
LANDRITH RD
COOS CO OR 140-C2
LANDSBURG RD SE
KING CO WA 176-A7
LANDS END RD
DIST OF N SAANICH BC 159-B1
LANE AV
ROSEBURG OR 334-F7
LANEDA AV
MANZANITA OR 191-A4
E LANE PARK RD
SPOKANE CO WA 347-E4
LANES TURN RD
LANE CO OR 210-A6
LANEWOOD RD
ADA CO ID 253-A1
LANEY RD
LINCOLN CO WA 113-C3
LANGE RD
SKAGIT CO WA 161-C7
LANGE GATEWAY RD
TILLAMOOK CO OR 191-B4
E LANGELL VALLEY RD
BONANZA OR 151-A2
KLAMATH CO OR 151-A2
W LANGELL VALLEY RD
KLAMATH CO OR 151-A2
LANGENSAND RD
CLACKAMAS CO OR 200-D4
SANDY OR 200-D4
LANGFORD RD
FRANKLIN CO WA 121-A2
LANGLEY BYPS
LANGLEY BC 158-C1
LANGLEY BYPS Rt#-10
DISTRICT OF SURREY BC 157-C7
DISTRICT OF SURREY BC 158-B1
LANGLEY BC 157-C7
LANGLEY RD
ISLAND CO WA 171-A1
LANGLEY WA 171-A1
LANGLOIS MOUNTAIN RD
CURRY CO OR 224-B2
LANGWORTHY RD SW
THURSTON CO WA 184-A4
LANSDOWNE RD
DISTRICT OF OAK BAY BC 257-C6
DISTRICT OF SAANICH BC 257-B6
LANSKY RD
MASON CO WA 180-D3
LANTZ LN
UNION CO OR 130-B2
LA PUSH RD
CLALLAM CO WA 169-A2
LA PUSH RD Rt#-110
CLALLAM CO WA 169-C1
FORKS WA 169-C1
SE LARCH AV
COLLEGE PLACE WA 344-G12
WALLA WALLA CO WA 344-G12
W LARCH AV
YAKIMA CO WA 243-B7
LARCH DR
DESCHUTES CO OR 212-C5
LARCH ST
LONGVIEW WA 303-A9
SANDPOINT ID 244-A2
VANCOUVER BC 156-B5
LARCH WY SW
SNOHOMISH CO WA 171-B5
LARCH MOUNTAIN RD
HOOD RIVER CO OR 195-B6
MULTNOMAH CO OR 200-D1
MULTNOMAH CO OR 201-A1
LARGENT RD
FRANKLIN CO WA 121-B2
LARIMER RD
EVERETT WA 269-H7
SNOHOMISH WA 269-H7
LARKIN RD
PACIFIC CO WA 183-B4
S LARKIN RD
CLACKAMAS CO OR 200-A7
SW LARKINS MILL RD
WASHINGTON CO OR 198-C3
LARMON RD
LEWIS CO WA 187-D2
LARSON LN NW
KITSAP CO WA 173-D2
LARSON RD
CITY OF N VANCOUVER BC 254-J4
CITY OF N VANCOUVER BC 255-A4
COLUMBIA CO OR 189-B4
COLUMBIA CO OR 302-D14
DOUGLAS CO OR 221-A5
KITSAP CO WA 174-A2
SNOHOMISH CO WA 168-B4
LARSON ST Rt#-161
EATONVILLE WA 118-B1
LARSON WY
COOS CO OR 218-C6
LARSON BEACH SHORE ACC RD
STEVENS CO WA 106-B3
LARSON CREEK RD
JACKSON CO OR 226-C6
LARSON LAKE RD
JEFFERSON CO WA 170-A3
SW LA SALLE LN
JEFFERSON CO OR 212-C1
LA SALLE RD
WASHINGTON CO OR 198-B3
LA SALLE ST
HARRISBURG OR 210-A5
LASSEN LN
LANE CO OR 210-A7
LAST CHANCE CREEK RD
JACKSON CO OR 225-D7
S LATAH ST
BOISE ID 253-C3
S LATAH CREEK RD
SPOKANE CO WA 246-D7
SW LATHAM RD
YAMHILL CO OR 204-A2
LATIMER RD
TILLAMOOK CO OR 197-C2
TILLAMOOK CO OR 197-C2
LATORIA RD
CITY OF COLWOOD BC 159-B7
DISTRICT OF LANGFORD BC 159-B7
LAUCK RD
SNOHOMISH CO WA 168-D7
LAUER CROSSING RD U.S.-95
IDAHO CO ID 123-B3
IDAHO CO ID 123-B3
LAUFERS RD
LEWIS CO ID 123-B2
LEWIS CO ID 123-B2
LAUGHLIN RD
PRINEVILLE OR 213-D5
YAMHILL CO OR 198-B4
LAURA ST
North Springfield OR 330-G5
SPRINGFIELD OR 330-G5
LAURANCE LAKE DR
HOOD RIVER CO OR 202-B3
LAUREL AV
BUTTE FALLS OR 150-A1
JOSEPHINE CO OR 229-A6
LAUREL LN
JEFFERSON CO OR 213-A1
LAUREL PL
Navy Yard City WA 270-E13
LAUREL RD
CAVE JUNCTION OR 233-B4
JOSEPHINE CO OR 233-B4
LONGVIEW WA 302-J6
LONGVIEW WA 303-A6
SW LAUREL RD
WASHINGTON CO OR 198-D3
W LAUREL RD
WHATCOM CO WA 158-D6
N LAUREL ST
ASHLAND OR 337-C6
LAUREL HILLS RD
DOUGLAS CO OR 219-A2
LAURELVIEW RD
WASHINGTON CO OR 198-C3
LAURELWOOD RD
WASHINGTON CO OR 198-C3
W LAURIDSEN BLVD
CLALLAM CO WA 261-A4
PORT ANGELES WA 261-A4
SW LAVA AV
DESCHUTES CO OR 212-C5
LAVA BEDS RD
HARNEY CO OR 145-B2
LAVA BEDS NATIONAL MONUMENT RD
MODOC CO CA 151-A3
LAVA CAST FOREST RD
DESCHUTES CO OR 217-B6
LAVA LAKE RD
DESCHUTES CO OR 142-C1
DESCHUTES CO OR 216-A5
LAVA-ODELL RD
KLAMATH CO OR 142-B1
N LA VENTURE RD
MOUNT VERNON WA 260-E11
LAVERNE AV
Altamont OR 338-G12
LAVERNE PARK NORTH RD
COOS CO OR 140-C2
LAW DR
BOISE ID 253-D3
LAWEN LN
HARNEY CO OR 145-B2
LAWEN-HARNEY RD
HARNEY CO OR 145-B1
LAWRENCE RD
CHEHALIS WA 299-C9
COLUMBIA CO OR 189-C7
LANE CO OR 133-B2
LEWIS CO WA 299-C9
LAWRENCE RD Rt#-9
WHATCOM CO WA 102-B1
LAWRENCE ST
PORT TOWNSEND WA 263-G5
LAWTON RD
SPOKANE CO WA 348-C13

PNW
INDEX

LAWYERS CANYON RD STREET INDEX LONG LAKE RD SE 379

Thomas Bros. Maps ® COPYRIGHT 1999

STREET City State Page-Grid

LAWYERS CANYON RD Rt#-162
LEWIS CO ID 123-C3
LEWIS CO ID 123-C3
NEZPERCE ID 123-C3
NEZPERCE ID 123-C3
LAYALL RD
KLICKITAT CO WA 196-B2
LAYNG RD
LANE CO OR 215-C7
LAZY ALLEN OAKS RD
KLICKITAT CO WA 196-A4
L COOKE RD
KITTITAS CO WA 241-D5
NE LEADBETTER RD
CLARK CO WA 193-B6
LEAFWOOD DR
JACKSON CO OR 230-D4
LEA HILL RD SE
KING CO WA 182-C1
LEAHY RD N
DOUGLAS CO WA 112-C1
LEAHY RD S Rt#-17
DOUGLAS CO WA 112-C1
LEAHY-MANSFIELD-MAYFIELD RD NE
DOUGLAS CO WA 112-C1
LEANDER DR
YAMHILL CO OR 198-D5
LEAP LN
WALLOWA CO OR 130-C1
LEARY AV NW
SEATTLE WA 273-E4
LEARY RD NE
MARION CO OR 205-A1
LEARY WY NW
SEATTLE WA 273-G5
E LEAVENWORTH RD
CHELAN CO WA 238-A1
LEBANON ST
ARLINGTON WA 168-D5
SNOHOMISH CO WA 168-D5
SW LEBEAU RD
WASHINGTON CO OR 199-A4
LEBO BLVD
BREMERTON WA 270-H8
LE BRUN RD NE
MARION CO OR 205-A2
LE CLERC CREEK RD
PEND OREILLE CO WA 106-C3
LEDGERWOOD SPUR RD
GARFIELD CO WA 122-C2
LEE BLVD
RICHLAND WA 341-E1
LEE RD
WASHINGTON CO OR 198-A2
LEE MCKINLEY RD
COOS CO OR 140-C2
LEES CREEK RD
DOUGLAS CO OR 219-B3
LEFEUVRE RD
DISTRICT OF MATSQUI BC 102-B1
LEFEVRE ST Rt#-902
MEDICAL LAKE WA 114-B2
LEFFEL RD
UNION CO OR 130-A2
LEFT FORK FOOTS CREEK RD
JACKSON CO OR 230-A7
LEFT FORK SARDINE CREEK RD
JACKSON CO OR 230-A5
LEGALL RD
KLICKITAT CO WA 196-B2
LEGION WY
OLYMPIA WA 296-H5
OLYMPIA WA 297-A5
LEGOE BAY RD
WHATCOM CO WA 160-B1
N LEHMAN RD
SPOKANE CO WA 246-D2
LEISLE RD
ADAMS CO WA 113-B3
LEITNER ST SW
THURSTON CO WA 184-B3
LELAND RD
JOSEPHINE CO OR 229-A1
S LELAND RD
CLACKAMAS CO OR 199-D6
LE-LOU-WA PL Rt#-509
PIERCE CO WA 181-D1
S LE MAIRE ST
MOXEE (MOXEE CITY) WA 243-D7
LEMLEY RD
BENTON CO WA 120-B3
LEMMON RD NE
THURSTON CO WA 180-D5
LEMOLO RD
DOUGLAS CO OR 223-B3
E LEMOLO LAKE RD
DOUGLAS CO OR 223-C3
LEMOLO SHORE DR NE
KITSAP CO WA 170-B7
Suquamish WA 170-B7
LEMON RD
CLALLAM CO WA 165-D6
LEMONDS RD
JEFFERSON CO WA 170-A6
LENORA ST
EVERETT WA 269-F1
LENTZ RD
COLUMBIA CO OR 189-B5
LEWIS CO WA 187-B2
LENTZ RD N
LEWIS CO WA 187-B2
LENVILLE RD
LATAH CO ID 123-A1
LATAH CO ID 123-A1
LATAH CO ID 249-D5
LEON RD
WHITMAN CO WA 250-B2
LEONARD RD
JOSEPHINE CO OR 229-A6
LEWIS CO WA 118-A2
LESLIE AV
LA CROSSE WA 122-A1
WHITMAN CO WA 122-A1
LESLIE LN
BENTON CO WA 341-H12
RICHLAND WA 341-H12
LESLIE RD
BENTON CO WA 341-H11
RICHLAND WA 341-H7
YAMHILL CO OR 199-A6
LESLIE GULCH RD
MALHEUR CO OR 146-C2
MALHEUR CO OR 147-A2
NE LESSARD RD
CLARK CO WA 193-C5
LESSIG SOUTH FORK RD
STEVENS CO WA 106-A3
LESTER AV
BENTON CO OR 327-F4
LESTER CAMP RD
WHITMAN CO WA 122-B1
LEVEE
KLAMATH CO OR 231-C3
LEVEE ST U.S.-101
HOQUIAM WA 178-A7
LEWELLEN RD
CLACKAMAS CO OR 200-B7
LEWELLEN CREEK RD
KOOTENAI CO ID 245-B2
LEWIS AV
CLATSOP CO OR 188-B3
LEWIS DR
PIERCE CO WA 181-B5
LEWIS LN
CANYON CO ID 147-C1
W LEWIS LN
CANYON CO ID 147-B1
LEWIS RD
CLALLAM CO WA 165-D6
GARFIELD CO WA 122-B2
WALLOWA CO OR 131-A1
LEWIS RD W
KITSAP CO WA 173-D3
LEWIS ST Rt#-214
SILVERTON OR 205-C4
E LEWIS ST
PASCO WA 121-A3
PASCO WA 343-J7
N LEWIS ST Rt#-203
MONROE WA 110-C1
S LEWIS ST Rt#-203
MONROE WA 110-C1
SNOHOMISH CO WA 110-C1
W LEWIS ST
PASCO WA 343-D7
LEWIS AND CLARK FRWY Rt#-14
VANCOUVER WA 193-A7
LEWIS AND CLARK FRWY U.S.-14
VANCOUVER WA 305-G6
VANCOUVER WA 306-A6
VANCOUVER WA 307-E7
VANCOUVER WA 311-G1
LEWIS AND CLARK HWY Rt#-14
BINGEN WA 195-C5
CAMAS WA 193-A7
CLARK CO WA 193-A7
KLICKITAT CO WA 127-B1
KLICKITAT CO WA 195-C5
KLICKITAT CO WA 196-C6
SKAMANIA CO WA 195-C5
VANCOUVER WA 193-A7
WASHOUGAL WA 193-C7
WHITE SALMON WA 195-C5
LEWIS AND CLARK RD
CLATSOP CO OR 188-C3
CLATSOP CO OR 300-A14
CLATSOP CO OR 301-J6
SEASIDE OR 188-C5
SEASIDE OR 301-J6
LEWIS GULCH RD
COLUMBIA CO WA 122-B2
LEWIS RIVER DR Rt#-503
COWLITZ CO WA 118-A3
COWLITZ CO WA 190-A6
WOODLAND WA 118-A3
LEWIS RIVER RD Rt#-503
COWLITZ CO WA 190-A6
LEWIS ROGERS LN
YAMHILL CO OR 198-C5
LEWISTON RD
WALLA WALLA CO WA 122-A3
NE LEWISVILLE HWY Rt#-503
CLARK CO WA 193-A1
LEXINGTON AV
ASTORIA OR 300-C5
W LEXINGTON AV
ASTORIA OR 300-B5
LEXINGTON-ECHO HWY
UMATILLA CO OR 129-A1
LEXINGTON-ECHO HWY Rt#-207
LEXINGTON OR 128-C2
MORROW CO OR 128-C2
UMATILLA CO OR 128-C2
UMATILLA CO OR 129-A1
SW LEXINGTON-ECHO HWY Rt#-207
UMATILLA CO OR 128-C1
UMATILLA CO OR 129-A1
LEY RD
KITTITAS CO WA 240-D1
L GILBERT RD
KITTITAS CO WA 241-D5
LIBBEY RD
ISLAND CO WA 167-A4
LIBBY RD NE
THURSTON CO WA 180-D4
THURSTON CO WA 297-C1
LIBBY CREEK RD
OKANOGAN CO WA 104-A3
S LIBERTY DR
Liberty Lake WA 247-B4
SPOKANE CO WA 247-B4
LIBERTY RD
KITTITAS CO WA 241-A1
POLK CO OR 204-A6
SHERMAN CO OR 127-C2
LIBERTY RD S
MARION CO OR 133-C1
MARION CO OR 207-D1
MARION CO OR 324-E10
SALEM OR 324-F6
LIBERTY ST
ALBANY OR 326-B11
LIBERTY ST NE
SALEM OR 322-H12
LIBERTY ST NE Rt#-99E
SALEM OR 322-J10
LIBERTY ST SE
SALEM OR 322-H13
SALEM OR 324-H1
N LIBERTY LAKE RD
Liberty Lake WA 247-B4
Liberty Lake WA 352-B13
SPOKANE CO WA 247-B4
SPOKANE CO WA 352-B13
S LIBERTY LAKE RD
Liberty Lake WA 247-B4
LIBERTY PARK PL
SPOKANE WA 349-C9
LICK CREEK RD
MCCALL ID 251-D5
VALLEY CO ID 251-D5
LICKFORK RD
ASOTIN CO WA 122-C2
LICKMAN RD
DISTRICT OF CHILLIWACK BC 94-C3
DISTRICT OF CHILLIWACK BC 102-C1
SE LIDER RD
KITSAP CO WA 174-B5
LIDFORD
PIERCE CO WA 182-A3
LIDSTROM RD
CROOK CO OR 213-D4
LIDSTROM RD E
KITSAP CO WA 271-C14
E LIDSTROM HILL RD
KITSAP CO WA 271-B13
LIESER RD
VANCOUVER WA 307-F7
LIGHTNING CREEK RD Rt#-200
CLARK FORK ID 107-C3
LIGNITE RD
BONNER CO ID 244-A3
LILAC HILL RD
YAMHILL CO OR 198-A4
LILLENAS RD
CLATSOP CO OR 188-D3
LILLIAN ST
DOUGLAS CO OR 225-C1
MYRTLE CREEK OR 225-C1
LILLOOET AV
CITY OF HARRISON HT SPNGS BC 94-C3
LILLOOET RD
DIST OF N VANCOUVER BC 156-C2
DIST OF N VANCOUVER BC 255-G6
LILLY RD NE
OLYMPIA WA 297-E4
THURSTON CO WA 297-E4
LILLY RD SE
OLYMPIA WA 297-E5
LILLY WHEATON RD
PACIFIC CO WA 117-A1
LIMBERT RD
DISTRICT OF KENT BC 94-C3
LIME KILN RD
WALLOWA CO OR 130-C2
LIMESTONE AV
DESCHUTES CO OR 212-C7
LINCOLN AV
COQUITLAM BC 157-B4
KENT WA 175-B7
PORT COQUITLAM BC 157-B4
SNOHOMISH WA 171-D3
SNOHOMISH CO WA 171-D3
TACOMA WA 182-A2
YAMHILL CO OR 198-B4
E LINCOLN AV
SUNNYSIDE WA 120-B2
W LINCOLN AV
CHEWELAH WA 106-B3
YAKIMA WA 243-B6
LINCOLN AV SE
East Port Orchard WA 174-B4
NE LINCOLN DR
POULSBO WA 170-C6
W LINCOLN DR
PASCO WA 343-E5
LINCOLN LN
GRANTS PASS OR 335-C9
JOSEPHINE CO OR 335-C9
LINCOLN RD
BENTON CO WA 120-B3
GRANTS PASS OR 335-C9
JOSEPHINE CO OR 335-C9
LINCOLN CO WA 113-C1
E LINCOLN RD
PIERCE CO WA 181-C5
SPOKANE WA 347-C13
SPOKANE CO WA 347-C13
Town and Country WA 347-C13
LINCOLN RD NE
MARION CO OR 205-B2
LINCOLN ST
ASTORIA OR 300-B5
KLAMATH FALLS OR 338-C7
PIERCE CO WA 181-C5
LINCOLN ST U.S.-101
HOQUIAM WA 178-A7
S LINCOLN ST
SPOKANE WA 348-J13
S LINCOLN ST U.S.-101
PORT ANGELES WA 261-E5
LINCOLN WY U.S.-95
COEUR D'ALENE ID 355-D8
N LINCOLN WY
COEUR D'ALENE ID 355-D10
KOOTENAI CO ID 355-D10
LINCOLN CREEK RD
LEWIS CO WA 117-B1
LEWIS CO WA 184-B5
LINCOLN MOUNTAIN RD
UMATILLA CO OR 129-C1
LINCOLN PARK WY
SEATTLE WA 284-D1
LINCOLN-ZENA RD
POLK CO OR 204-C4
LINCTON MOUNTAIN RD
UMATILLA CO OR 130-A1
LIND AV SW
RENTON WA 175-C5
LIND RD
FRANKLIN CO WA 121-B1
LINDBECK RD
LEWIS CO WA 187-C2
LINDBERG
PIERCE CO WA 182-A7
LINDBERG RD
COLUMBIA CO OR 189-A4
LINDEN AV N
SEATTLE WA 273-J3
LINDEN LN
POLK CO OR 207-B1
LINDEN ST
MILTON-FREEWATER OR 121-C3
W LINDEN ST
BOISE ID 253-D3
W LINDEN WY Rt#-74
HEPPNER OR 128-C2
N LINDER RD
ADA CO ID 253-A1
S LINDER RD
ADA CO ID 253-A4
MERIDIAN ID 253-A2
LINDGREN RD
PACIFIC CO WA 183-B4
LIND-HATTON RD
ADAMS CO WA 121-B1
LINDHOLM RD
DISTRICT OF METCHOSIN BC 159-A7
LIND-KAHLOTUS RD Rt#-21
ADAMS CO WA 121-C1
FRANKLIN CO WA 121-C1
KAHLOTUS WA 121-C1
LINDSAY DR
LINN CO OR 207-B7
LINDSEY DR
COWLITZ CO WA 302-J5
LINDSEY RD
KOOTENAI CO ID 245-B2
LINDSEY CREEK RD
NEZ PERCE CO ID 250-C4
LINDSTROM RD
STANWOOD WA 168-B4
LIND-WARDEN RD
ADAMS CO WA 121-B1
LINE RD
MARYSVILLE WA 171-D1
SNOHOMISH CO WA 171-D1
LINGENFELTER RD
PACIFIC CO WA 186-B7
LINGER LONGER RD
JEFFERSON CO WA 109-C1
LINGO LN
LANE CO OR 210-A5
LINK LN
LANE CO OR 210-A5
S LINKE RD
SPOKANE CO WA 247-A5
SPOKANE CO WA 351-F14
W LINN RD
JACKSON CO OR 230-D5
LINN WY
BROWNSVILLE OR 210-C2
LINNEY CREEK RD
CLACKAMAS CO OR 201-D7
LINN WEST DR
LINN CO OR 210-B2
LINTON ST
COQUITLAM BC 157-A5
LINVILLE GULCH RD
GARFIELD CO WA 122-B2
LINVILLE RIDGE RD
GARFIELD CO WA 122-B2
SE LINWOOD AV
CLACKAMAS CO OR 199-D3
MILWAUKIE OR 199-D3
LINWOOD AV SW
TUMWATER WA 296-G10
SE LION LAKE RD
REDMOND OR 212-D5
LIONS GATE BRDG Rt#-99
DIST OF WEST VANCOUVER BC 254-E5
VANCOUVER BC 254-E5
LIONS GATE BRIDGE RD Rt#-99
DIST OF WEST VANCOUVER BC 254-E7
VANCOUVER BC 254-E7
LIPPMAN RD
HOOD RIVER CO OR 195-C6
LISHER CTO
LATAH CO ID 249-D1
LITHIA WY
ASHLAND OR 337-C7
LITHIA WY Rt#-99
ASHLAND OR 337-C7
LITTLE RD
WHITMAN CO WA 249-A7
LITTLE ALKALI RD
WHITMAN CO WA 122-B1
LITTLE APPLEGATE RD
JACKSON CO OR 234-A5
LITTLE BEAR CREEK RD
CROOK CO OR 135-C3
LITTLE BLACKTAIL MOUNTAIN RD
BONNER CO ID 244-A6
LITTLE BOSTON RD NE
KITSAP CO WA 170-C4
LITTLE BURMA RD
DOUGLAS CO OR 214-D6
LITTLE BUTTER CREEK RD
MORROW CO OR 129-A2
LITTLE EGYPT RD
MASON CO WA 179-D3
LITTLE FALL CREEK RD
LANE CO OR 134-A3
LITTLE FALLS RD
LINCOLN CO WA 114-A1
LITTLE FALLS CHAMOKANA RD
STEVENS CO WA 114-A1
LITTLE FALLS LONGLAKE RD
STEVENS CO WA 114-A1
LITTLE GOOSE DAM RD
COLUMBIA CO WA 122-A2
LITTLE GREYBACK RD
JOSEPHINE CO OR 233-C4
LITTLE HANAFORD RD
LEWIS CO WA 184-D6
LEWIS CO WA 299-J2
LITTLE JUNIPER RD
HARNEY CO OR 144-B3
LITTLE KALAMA RIVER RD
COWLITZ CO WA 118-A3
LITTLE MCKAY RD
CROOK CO OR 135-C2
LITTLE MOUNTAIN RD
KLICKITAT CO WA 119-A3
SKAGIT CO WA 168-B1
SKAGIT CO WA 260-F14
LITTLE MUD CREEK RD
ADAMS CO ID 251-A3
LITTLE NESTUCCA HWY
TILLAMOOK CO OR 203-D2
LITTLE NESTUCCA RIVER RD
TILLAMOOK CO OR 203-C1
LITTLE RIVER RD
CLALLAM CO WA 165-A7
DOUGLAS CO OR 141-B2
DOUGLAS CO OR 222-A5
LITTLE RIVER-POWLL RVR FERRY
BRITISH COLUMBIA 92-B1
LITTLEROCK RD SW
Rochester WA 184-A3
THURSTON CO WA 184-B1
THURSTON CO WA 296-D14
TUMWATER WA 296-D14
LITTLE SHEEP CREEK HWY
JOSEPH OR 130-C2
WALLOWA CO OR 130-C2
WALLOWA CO OR 131-A2
LITTLE SHEEP CREEK RD Rt#-25
STEVENS CO WA 106-A1
LITTLE SPOKANE DR
SPOKANE CO WA 347-C1
SW LITTLE SQUAWBACK RD
JEFFERSON CO OR 211-D2
LITTLE SQUAW BAY RD
KOOTENAI CO ID 248-A6
LITTLE VALLEY LN
LINN CO OR 210-D4
LITTLE WEISER RD
ADAMS CO ID 252-B6
LITTLE WEISER RD U.S.-95
ADAMS CO ID 139-B1
LITTLE WEISER RIVER RD
ADAMS CO ID 252-A6
LITTLE WILLOW RD
PAYETTE CO ID 139-B3
LIVERMORE RD
POLK CO OR 204-B4
LIVESAY RD
DESCHUTES CO OR 211-D7
LIVINGSTON RD
CLARK CO WA 193-C5
LIZARD CREEK RD
DESCHUTES CO OR 144-A1
L JOHNSON RD
CLARK CO WA 192-D1
LLEWELLYN RD
BENTON CO OR 133-B2
NE LLOYD BLVD
PORTLAND OR 313-H5
LLOYD DR
JOSEPHINE CO OR 229-B4
LLOYD WY
DESCHUTES CO OR 216-D7
DESCHUTES CO OR 217-A6
Three Rivers OR 217-A6
LOBSTER CREEK RD
CURRY CO OR 228-B3
LINCOLN CO OR 209-D3
LOBSTER VALLEY RD
BENTON CO OR 133-A2
BENTON CO OR 209-D3
LOCARNO CRES
UNIV ENDOWMENT LANDS BC 156-A4
LOCHNER RD
ALBANY OR 326-D14
LINN CO OR 326-D14
LOCHSIDE DR
DIST OF NORTH SAANICH BC 159-C3
TOWN OF SIDNEY BC 159-C3
LOCKART AV
COOS BAY OR 333-G12
LOCKER RD SE
KITSAP CO WA 174-C4
LOCKETT RD
MALHEUR CO OR 139-A2
LOCKHAVEN DR N
KEIZER OR 322-J4
KEIZER OR 323-A4
LOCKHAVEN DR NE
KEIZER OR 323-B4
LOCKITT BUTTE RD
DESCHUTES CO OR 217-C5
SE LOCKS RD
YAMHILL CO OR 198-B7
LOCKWOOD RD
SNOHOMISH CO WA 171-B6
NE LOCKWOOD CREEK RD
CLARK CO WA 192-D2
LOCUST AV
BROWNSVILLE OR 210-C2
E LOCUST AV
COEUR D'ALENE ID 355-E9
LOCUST LN
CANYON CO ID 147-C1
LOCUST ST
ALMIRA WA 237-D7
DESCHUTES CO OR 211-D5
OAKLAND OR 219-A7
SISTERS OR 211-D5
LOCUST ST Rt#-19
ARLINGTON OR 128-A1
N LOCUST ST Rt#-19
ARLINGTON OR 128-A1
GILLIAM CO OR 128-A1
S LOCUST ST Rt#-19
ARLINGTON OR 128-A1
LOCUST WY
SNOHOMISH CO WA 171-B6
LOCUST GROVE RD
BENTON CO WA 121-A3
NEZ PERCE CO ID 250-D7
N LOCUST GROVE RD
ADA CO ID 253-A2
S LOCUST GROVE RD
ADA CO ID 253-B4
LODGEPOLE RD
JACKSON CO OR 150-A1
LOERLAND LN
ISLAND CO WA 167-B2
LOFFS BAY RD
KOOTENAI CO ID 247-D6
KOOTENAI CO ID 248-A2
LOFTON CREEK RD
CROOK CO OR 213-D2
LOGAN RD
CLATSOP CO OR 188-C3
NE LOGAN RD
LINCOLN CO OR 203-A4
NW LOGAN RD
LINCOLN CO OR 203-A4
SW LOGANBERRY LN
SHERIDAN OR 125-B3
YAMHILL CO OR 125-B3
YAMHILL CO OR 204-A2
LOGAN HILL RD
LEWIS CO WA 184-D7
LOGAN VALLEY RD
GRANT CO OR 137-B3
SENECA OR 137-B3
LOG CABIN RD SE
OLYMPIA WA 297-B9
LOG CORRAL RD
KLICKITAT CO WA 196-B1
LOGEN RD
SNOHOMISH CO WA 168-A3
LOGGING 1600 RD
COWLITZ CO WA 118-A3
COWLITZ CO WA 189-D1
LOGIE TRAIL RD
MULTNOMAH CO OR 192-A6
LOGSDEN RD
LINCOLN CO OR 133-A1
LINCOLN CO OR 206-D2
SILETZ OR 206-D2
S LOIS DR
SPOKANE CO WA 246-B7
W LOLAH BUTTE RD
DESCHUTES CO OR 216-B7
LOLO BUTTE RD
DESCHUTES CO OR 216-C6
LOLO PASS RD
BENEWAH CO ID 115-A3
BENEWAH CO ID 115-A3
CLACKAMAS CO OR 201-D4
HOOD RIVER CO OR 202-A3
LOMBARD DR NW
PIERCE CO WA 181-B1
N LOMBARD ST
PORTLAND OR 192-B6
N LOMBARD ST U.S.-30
PORTLAND OR 192-B7
PORTLAND OR 308-B4
PORTLAND OR 309-E5
NE LOMBARD ST U.S.-30
PORTLAND OR 309-G5
PORTLAND OR 310-B6
LOMBARDY LN
KLAMATH CO OR 235-C5
LONDON DR
HOOD RIVER CO OR 202-C2
LONDON RD
LANE CO OR 219-D1
LONDON HILL RD
DOUGLAS CO OR 219-C4
S LONE ELDER RD
CLACKAMAS CO OR 199-C7
LONE FIR RD
BAKER CO OR 131-A3
LONE LAKE RD
ISLAND CO WA 167-D7
ISLAND CO WA 170-D1
LONE MOUNTAIN RD
JOSEPHINE CO OR 233-A6
LONE OAK RD
COWLITZ CO WA 302-F3
LONGVIEW WA 302-F3
LONE OAK RD SE
SALEM OR 324-G7
LONE PINE DR
LANE CO OR 210-A7
LONE PINE RD
CROOK CO OR 213-A4
JACKSON CO OR 336-G9
JEFFERSON CO OR 213-A3
MEDFORD OR 336-G9
LONE PINE-DORA RD
COOS CO OR 140-C2
LONE PINE SCHOOL RD
CROOK CO OR 213-A3
LONE ROCK RD
MORO OR 127-C2
SHERMAN CO OR 127-C2
LONEROCK RD
GILLIAM CO OR 128-B3
WHEELER CO OR 128-B3
LONE STAR RD NW
POLK CO OR 204-C3
LONE YEW RD
LEWIS CO WA 187-D5
LONG AV
KELSO WA 303-C8
LONG RD
KLICKITAT CO WA 196-D2
NW LONG RD
WASHINGTON CO OR 198-C1
S LONG RD
Greenacres WA 351-F9
LONG CREEK RD
GRANT CO OR 129-A3
GRANT CO OR 137-A1
LONG HOLLOW RD
WHITMAN CO WA 122-A1
LONG HOLLOW MARKET RD
WASCO CO OR 127-B2
LONG JOHN MORASCH RD
WHITMAN CO WA 122-B1
LONG LAKE RD
KLAMATH CO OR 235-A3
LINCOLN CO WA 114-A1
W LONG LAKE RD
SPOKANE CO WA 114-B1
LONG LAKE RD SE
KITSAP CO WA 174-C4

PNW
INDEX

380 LONGMIRE LN
STREET INDEX
MAIN ST Rt#-524

STREET / City State / Page-Grid

LONGMIRE LN
YAKIMA CO WA 243-A3
LONG PRAIRIE RD
STEVENS CO WA 106-B3
TILLAMOOK CO OR 197-C3
LONG RIDGE RD
DOUGLAS CO OR 141-A2
LONG VALLEY RD
DOUGLAS CO OR 219-C7
LONGVIEW RD
ADAMS CO ID 251-C5
LONGWOOD DR
REEDSPORT OR 218-C2
LONSDALE AV
CITY OF N VANCOUVER BC 255-B3
DIST OF N VANCOUVER BC 255-B3
LONSETH RD
WHATCOM CO WA 158-B5
LOOK RD
KITTITAS CO WA 241-B5
LOOKINGGLASS RD
DOUGLAS CO OR 221-A5
DOUGLAS CO OR 334-A8
ROSEBURG OR 334-A8
WINSTON OR 221-A5
NW LOOKINGGLASS RD
WINSTON OR 221-B6
LOOKNGGLASS-BRCKWY RD
DOUGLAS CO OR 221-A5
LOOKOUT RD
KLAMATH CO OR 151-A1
N LOOKOUT RD
DESCHUTES CO OR 216-B7
LOOKOUT MOUNTAIN RD
DESCHUTES CO OR 216-B7
MARION CO OR 134-A1
UNION CO OR 130-B1
LOOKOUT POINT RD
SELAH WA 243-B6
LOOMIS LN
VALLEY CO ID 252-D2
LOOMIS-OROVILLE RD
OKANOGAN CO WA 104-C1
LOOMIS TRAIL RD
WHATCOM CO WA 158-C4
LOON LAKE RD
DOUGLAS CO OR 140-C1
LOON LAKE-MCVAY PIT RD
STEVENS CO WA 106-B3
LOON LAKE SOUTHSIDE RD
STEVENS CO WA 106-B3
STEVENS CO WA 114-B1
LOOP RD
JACKSON CO OR 226-C5
SKAMANIA CO WA 194-D4
STEVENS CO WA 114-A1
N LOOP RD
UMATILLA CO OR 129-A1
SE LOOP RD
YAMHILL CO OR 198-B7
LOOSLEY RD
KLAMATH CO OR 231-C2
LOPER AV
PRINEVILLE OR 213-D5
LORAINE AV
DIST OF N VANCOUVER BC 254-H2
LORANE HWY
EUGENE OR 329-C14
LANE CO OR 133-B3
LANE CO OR 215-A4
LANE CO OR 329-C14
LORD ST
KELSO WA 303-D7
LORDS LAKE LOOP RD
JEFFERSON CO WA 109-C1
LORENZ RD KPS
PIERCE CO WA 181-A2
LORIMER RD
BRITISH COLUMBIA 159-B5
LOST HWY W
KITSAP CO WA 173-D4
LOST CREEK RD
COLUMBIA CO OR 189-A4
DOUGLAS CO OR 223-B4
LANE CO OR 133-C3
SKAMANIA CO WA 195-B3
LOSTINE RIVER RD
WALLOWA CO OR 130-C2
LOST LAKE RD
HOOD RIVER CO OR 195-B7
HOOD RIVER CO OR 202-A1
MASON CO WA 179-D4
MASON CO WA 180-A3
SHELTON WA 180-A3
LOST MTN RD
CLALLAM CO WA 109-C1
LOST PRAIRIE RD
WALLOWA CO OR 122-C3
LOST RIVER RD
OKANOGAN CO WA 104-A2
LOST VALLEY RD
WHEELER CO OR 128-B3
LOTZGESELL RD
CLALLAM CO WA 166-A5
CLALLAM CO WA 262-A3
NE LOUCKS RD
JEFFERSON CO OR 208-C5
LOUDEN RD
MULTNOMAH CO OR 200-D2
LOUGHEED HWY Rt#-7
BRITISH COLUMBIA 94-B3
COQUITLAM BC 157-A5
DISTRICT OF BURNABY BC 156-D4
DISTRICT OF BURNABY BC 255-G12
DISTRICT OF COQUITLAM BC 156-D4
DISTRICT OF KENT BC 94-B3
DISTRICT OF MISSION BC 94-B3
MAPLE RIDGE BC 94-B3
MAPLE RIDGE BC 157-D6
PITT MEADOWS BC 157-B4
PORT COQUITLAM BC 157-B4
LOUIE FAVE RD
WASHINGTON CO ID 139-B1
LOUISIANA ST
LONGVIEW WA 303-A8
NW LOVEJOY ST
PORTLAND OR 312-D4
PORTLAND OR 313-F4
LOVE LAKE RD
LANE CO OR 210-A5
LOVELL VALLEY RD
BENEWAH CO WA 115-A3
BENEWAH CO ID 115-A3
LOVE RESERVOIR RD
BAKER CO OR 138-C1
LOVES AV
WOODLAND WA 192-B1
NE LOVGREN RD E
KITSAP CO WA 174-D1
NE LOVGREN RD W
KITSAP CO WA 174-C1
LOWDEN GARDENA RD
WALLA WALLA CO WA 121-C3
LOW DIVIDE RD
DEL NORTE CO CA 148-B3
W LOWELL AV
SPOKANE CO WA 246-A2
SPOKANE CO WA 346-A12
LOWELL LARIMER RD
SNOHOMISH WA 269-G5
LOWELL-LARIMER RD
SNOHOMISH WA 269-H7
SNOHOMISH CO WA 171-C4
E LOWELL-LARIMER RD Rt#-96
SNOHOMISH CO WA 171-D4
LOWELL-SNOHOMISH RIVER RD
EVERETT WA 269-F1
SNOHOMISH WA 269-J4
SNOHOMISH CO WA 171-D3
LOWER ANTELOPE RD Rt#-293
ANTELOPE OR 127-C3
WASCO CO OR 127-C3
LOWER BENCH RD
GEM CO ID 139-B3
SW LOWER BEND RD
JEFFERSON CO OR 208-A5
LOWER BOONES FERRY RD
LAKE OSWEGO OR 199-B4
TUALATIN OR 199-B4
SW LOWR BOONS FERRY RD
DURHAM OR 199-B4
TUALATIN OR 199-B4
LOWER BRIDGE RD
DESCHUTES CO OR 212-B3
SW LOWER BRIDGE RD
JEFFERSON CO OR 212-B2
LOWER BURNETT RD E
PIERCE CO WA 182-D5
LOWER COVE RD
UNION CO OR 130-B2
LOWER COW CREEK RD
MALHEUR CO OR 146-C2
MALHEUR CO OR 147-A3
LOWER CRAB CREEK RD
GRANT CO WA 120-B1
LOWER DEADMAN RD
GARFIELD CO WA 122-B1
LOWER DEADWOOD CRK RD
LANE CO OR 133-A2
LOWER DIAMOND RD
WALLOWA CO OR 130-B1
LOWER DRY CREEK RD
WALLA WALLA CO WA 121-C3
LOWER EIGHTMILE RD
THE DALLES OR 196-D7
WASCO CO OR 127-B2
WASCO CO OR 196-D7
LOWER ELWHA RD
CLALLAM CO WA 165-A5
LOWER FORDS CREEK RD
CLEARWATER CO ID 123-C2
CLEARWATER CO ID 123-C2
LOWER FOURMILE RD
COOS CO OR 224-B1
LOWER FOX HOLLOW RD
LANE CO OR 215-A4
LOWER GRAVE CREEK RD
JOSEPHINE CO OR 149-A1
JOSEPHINE CO OR 229-A1
LOWER GREEN CANYON RD
KITTITAS CO WA 241-A4
LOWER HIGHLAND RD
CLACKAMAS CO OR 200-A6
LOWER HOGEYE RD
COLUMBIA CO WA 122-A2
LOWER HOH RD
JEFFERSON CO WA 169-C5
SE LOWER ISLAND RD
YAMHILL CO OR 204-D1
LOWER JOE CREEK RD
CHELAN CO WA 236-B1
LOWER KEITH RD
CITY OF N VANCOUVER BC 255-B5
LOWER KLAMATH LAKE RD
KLAMATH CO OR 150-C3
KLAMATH CO OR 235-C7
LOWER LITTLE SHASTA RD
SISKIYOU CO CA 150-A3
LOWER MONITOR RD
Sunnyslope WA 238-D3
LOWER MONUMENTAL RD
WALLA WALLA CO WA 121-C2
LOWER NEHALEM RD
CLATSOP CO OR 125-A1
LOWER NORWAY RD
COOS CO OR 220-D6
LOWER PACK RIVER RD
BONNER CO ID 244-B1
LOWER PEOH POINT RD
KITTITAS CO WA 240-C2
LOWER PLEASANT RIDGE RD
CANYON CO ID 147-B1
LOWER RIVER RD Rt#-501
CLARK WA 304-A1
CLARK CO WA 192-C5
VANCOUVER WA 192-B5
VANCOUVER WA 304-A1
NW LOWER RIVER RD
CLARK CO WA 192-B4
NW LOWER RIVER RD Rt#-501
CLARK CO WA 192-B5
VANCOUVER WA 192-B5
LOWER SMITH RIVER RD
DOUGLAS CO OR 214-B7
DOUGLAS CO OR 218-D1
LOWER SUMAS MTN RD
DISTRICT OF ABBOTSFORD BC 102-B1
LOWER SUNNYSLOPE RD
Sunnyslope WA 238-D3
LOWER TAMMANY CREEK RD
NEZ PERCE CO ID 250-D5
LOWER WAITSBURG RD
WALLA WALLA WA 345-C5
WALLA WALLA CO WA 121-C3
WALLA WALLA CO WA 345-C5
LOWER WAITSBURG RD Rt#-124
WALLA WALLA CO WA 122-A2
LOWER WHETSTONE RD
COLUMBIA CO WA 122-A2
LOWER WOLF CREEK RD
JOSEPHINE CO OR 229-A1
LOW LEVEL RD
CITY OF N VANCOUVER BC 255-C7
LOYAL AV NW
SEATTLE WA 272-D1
LOZIER LN
JACKSON CO OR 336-A13
MEDFORD OR 336-A13
L SCHULTHEIS RD
WHITMAN CO WA 250-B3
SW LUANA BEACH RD
KING CO WA 175-A6
NE LUCIA FALLS RD
CLARK CO WA 193-B2
S LUCILE ST
SEATTLE WA 281-J6
SEATTLE WA 282-A6
LUCKENBILL RD
WALLA WALLA CO WA 121-B3
LUCKIAMUTE RD
BENTON CO OR 133-A1
LUCKY SEVEN COW CAMP RD
MALHEUR CO OR 154-C2
LUCKY STRIKE RD
JOSEPHINE CO OR 233-B7
LUCY REEDER RD
MULTNOMAH CO OR 192-A5
LUDEMAN RD NW
DOUGLAS CO WA 236-D5
LUDLOW BAY RD
JEFFERSON CO WA 170-B3
LUDLOW PARADISE RD
JEFFERSON CO WA 170-B3
E LUDLOW RIDGE RD
JEFFERSON CO WA 170-B3
LUFT RD
WHITMAN CO WA 122-B1
SW LUKAS RD
WASHINGTON CO OR 198-D3
LUMMI SHORE DR
WHATCOM CO WA 158-C7
LUMMI SHORE RD
WHATCOM CO WA 158-C7
WHATCOM CO WA 160-C1
LUMMI VIEW DR
WHATCOM CO WA 160-C1
LUNBLAD
PIERCE CO WA 182-B4
E LUNCEFORD AV
COEUR D'ALENE ID 355-F6
KOOTENAI CO ID 355-F6
SE LUND AV
East Port Orchard WA 174-B4
LUND RD
SNOHOMISH CO WA 168-B3
LUNDEEN RD SW
THURSTON CO WA 184-A4
LUNDGREN MILL RD
DESCHUTES CO OR 211-D4
LUNDY RD
DESCHUTES CO OR 211-D4
NW LUOTO RD Rt#-308
KITSAP CO WA 170-B7
LUSK CREEK RD
SKAMANIA CO WA 195-B1
LUSTED RD
CLACKAMAS CO OR 200-C3
SE LUSTED RD
GRESHAM OR 200-B2
MULTNOMAH CO OR 200-B2
LUTZ LN
WASCO CO OR 196-B7
L WEST RD
WHITMAN CO WA 249-B2
N LYLE AV
East Wenatchee Bench WA 239-A4
LYLE GOLDENDALE RD
KLICKITAT CO WA 127-B1
LYLE SNOWDEN RD
KLICKITAT CO WA 196-B3
LYMAN HAMILTON RD
SKAGIT CO WA 161-D5
LYMAN LAKE-MOSES MOUNTAIN RD
OKANOGAN CO WA 105-A3
LYNCH RD
MASON CO WA 180-B4
LYNN BLVD
CROOK CO OR 213-D5
PRINEVILLE OR 213-D5
LYNN ST
BELLINGHAM WA 258-B4
E LYNN ST
SEATTLE WA 278-C1
W LYNN ST
SEATTLE WA 276-C1
LYNN VALLEY RD
CITY OF N VANCOUVER BC 255-D4
DIST OF N VANCOUVER BC 255-D4
LYNWOOD RD
CANYON CO ID 147-B1
LYNWOOD CENTER RD NE
KITSAP CO WA 271-H4
LYNX HOLLOW RD
LANE CO OR 215-B6
LYON ST U.S.-20
ALBANY OR 326-C8
E LYONS AV
SPOKANE WA 349-A1
Town and Country WA 349-A1
W LYONS AV
Town and Country WA 348-J1
Town and Country WA 349-A1
LYONS DR S
PIERCE CO WA 181-C7
LYONS RD
CLARK CO WA 118-A3
CLARK CO WA 192-C1
KITTITAS CO WA 241-C5
SISKIYOU CO CA 151-A3
S LYONS RD
AIRWAY HEIGHTS WA 246-A4
CLACKAMAS CO OR 200-A6
LYONS FERRY RD
WALLA WALLA CO WA 121-C2
LYONS-MILL CITY DR
LINN CO OR 134-A1
W LYRE RIVER RD
CLALLAM CO WA 164-B5
LYTLE BLVD
MALHEUR CO OR 139-A3

M

M AV
ANACORTES WA 259-G2
S M ST
TACOMA WA 295-F2
SE M ST
GRANTS PASS OR 335-F10
SW M ST
GRANTS PASS OR 335-E9
M ST NE
AUBURN WA 182-C1
M ST SE
AUBURN WA 182-C1
MABEE MINES RD
SKAMANIA CO WA 194-A6
MABLES CT
LEWIS CO WA 187-D2
MABTON-BICKLETON RD
MABTON WA 120-B3
YAKIMA CO WA 120-A3
MABTON-SUNNYSIDE RD
SUNNYSIDE WA 120-B2
YAKIMA CO WA 120-B2
MABTON-SUNNYSIDE RD Rt#-241
SUNNYSIDE WA 120-B3
YAKIMA CO WA 120-B3
SW MACADAM AV Rt#-43
MULTNOMAH OR 321-G1
PORTLAND OR 317-F6
PORTLAND OR 321-G1
MACARTHUR BLVD
VANCOUVER WA 306-D6
VANCOUVER WA 307-E6
MACDONALD ST
VANCOUVER BC 254-B14
N MACHIAS RD
LAKE STEVENS WA 110-C1
SNOHOMISH CO WA 110-C1
S MACHIAS RD
SNOHOMISH WA 171-D2
SNOHOMISH CO WA 110-C1
SNOHOMISH CO WA 171-D2
MACHIAS CUTOFF
SNOHOMISH CO WA 110-C1
SNOHOMISH CO WA 171-D2
MAC HOKE RD
UMATILLA CO OR 129-A1
MACK RD
ADAMS CO WA 122-A1
MACKENZIE ST
VANCOUVER BC 156-B5
VANCOUVER BC 254-B14
MACKSBURG RD
CLACKAMAS CO OR 199-C7
MACLEAY RD SE
Four Corners OR 325-E2
MARION CO OR 205-A6
MARION CO OR 325-H3
SALEM OR 325-F2
MACLURE RD
DISTRICT OF MATSQUI BC 102-B1
E MACMAHAN RD
SPOKANE CO WA 247-A2
S MADELIA ST
SPOKANE WA 349-C9
MADER RD
WHITMAN CO WA 122-B1
WHITMAN CO WA 249-B2
MADISON AV
CORVALLIS OR 327-G10
N MADISON AV NE
KITSAP CO WA 174-D1
MADISON AV S
KITSAP CO WA 174-D2
N MADISON RD
SPOKANE CO WA 246-D1
NE MADISON RD
KITSAP CO WA 174-B1
S MADISON RD
SPOKANE CO WA 246-D6
MADISON ST
Altamont OR 339-B11
EVERETT WA 268-C2
EVERETT WA 269-E3
LAFAYETTE OR 198-B7
SEATTLE WA 277-J6
SEATTLE WA 278-A6
E MADISON ST
CALDWELL ID 147-B1
SEATTLE WA 278-C5
SEATTLE WA 279-F2
N MADISON ST Rt#-82
WALLOWA CO OR 130-B1
SE MADISON ST
PORTLAND OR 313-H7
SW MADISON ST
PORTLAND OR 313-E6
MADISON ST NE
SALEM OR 322-J10
SALEM OR 323-A11
MADRAS-PRINEVILLE HWY U.S.-26
CROOK CO OR 213-C3
JEFFERSON CO OR 213-C3
PRINEVILLE OR 213-C3
SE MADRAS-PRINEVILLE HWY
JEFFERSON CO OR 213-B2
SE MADRAS-PRNEVLLE HWY U.S.-26
JEFFERSON CO OR 208-C7
JEFFERSON CO OR 213-B2
SW MADRAS-PRNEVLLE HWY U.S.-26
JEFFERSON CO OR 208-C6
MADRONA AV S
SALEM OR 324-E3
MADRONA AV SE
SALEM OR 324-H4
SALEM OR 325-A4
NE MADRONA BLVD
KITSAP CO WA 170-C3
MADRONA DR
DIST OF NORTH SAANICH BC 159-B2
SEATTLE WA 279-E5
MADRONA RD SW
KITSAP CO WA 174-B6
MADRONA WY
ISLAND CO WA 167-B4
E MADRONE AV
Colby WA 271-G12
NE MADRONE ST
GRANTS PASS OR 335-G8
MAE VALLEY RD
GRANT CO WA 242-A3
NE MAFFET RD
MULTNOMAH CO OR 200-D1
E MAGNESIUM RD
SPOKANE WA 346-J12
SPOKANE WA 347-B12
SPOKANE CO WA 347-B12
Town and Country WA 346-J12
MAGNOLIA BLVD W
SEATTLE WA 272-B7
SEATTLE WA 276-B1
MAGNOLIA BRDG
SEATTLE WA 276-E2
SEATTLE WA 277-E2
MAGNOLIA WY W
SEATTLE WA 276-E2
MAGNUS-LARSON
PIERCE CO WA 182-A4
MAGPIE GRADE
NEZ PERCE CO ID 123-B2
NEZ PERCE CO ID 123-B2
MAGUIRE GULCH RD
ASOTIN CO WA 250-A5
MAHNCKE RD KPS
PIERCE CO WA 181-A3
MAHOGANY RD
MALHEUR CO OR 146-C2
MAHOGANY GAP RD
MALHEUR CO OR 147-A2
MAHONY RD NE
MARION CO OR 205-A2
MAIDEN LN
WENATCHEE WA 238-D4
West Wenatchee WA 238-D4
MAIL ROUTE RD
ASOTIN CO WA 250-A5
MAIN AV
LA CROSSE WA 122-A1
PINEHURST ID 115-C2
SHOSHONE CO ID 115-C2
SUMNER WA 182-B3
WHITMAN CO WA 122-A1
MAIN AV Rt#-5
SAINT MARIES ID 248-C7
MAIN AV Rt#-508
MORTON WA 118-B2
MAIN AV U.S.-101
TILLAMOOK OR 197-B2
TILLAMOOK CO OR 197-B2
E MAIN AV
BREWSTER WA 104-B3
CHEWELAH WA 106-B3
PIERCE CO WA 182-B3
PUYALLUP WA 182-B3
SUMNER WA 182-B3
E MAIN AV U.S.-2
LINCOLN CO WA 113-B1
WILBUR WA 113-B1
N MAIN AV
GRESHAM OR 200-B2
KLICKITAT CO WA 195-D4
WARRENTON OR 188-B2
WHITE SALMON WA 195-D4
S MAIN AV
MORROW CO OR 128-C1
WARRENTON OR 188-B2
W MAIN AV
BREWSTER WA 104-B3
OKANOGAN CO WA 104-B3
W MAIN AV U.S.-2
WILBUR WA 113-B1
MAIN AV E
SOAP LAKE WA 112-C2
MAIN AV E U.S.-730
IRRIGON OR 128-C1
S MAIN AV E
IRRIGON OR 128-C1
MAIN AV S Rt#-515
RENTON WA 175-C5
MAIN AV W
GRANT CO WA 112-C2
SOAP LAKE WA 112-C2
S MAIN AV W
IRRIGON OR 128-C1
MORROW CO OR 128-C1
MAIN RD
BREWSTER WA 104-B3
LEBANON OR 133-C1
OKANOGAN CO WA 104-B3
W MAIN RD
COTTAGE GROVE OR 215-B7
LANE CO OR 215-B7
MAIN ST
ALBANY OR 326-D7
AUMSVILLE OR 133-C1
BAKER CITY OR 138-B1
BELLEVUE WA 175-C2
BOISE ID 253-C2
BONNERS FERRY ID 107-B2
BOTHELL WA 171-C6
BROWNSVILLE OR 210-C2
CANYON CITY OR 137-B2
CHEHALIS WA 299-D12
CHELAN CO WA 238-C3
MAIN ST
CONCONULLY WA 104-B2
COTTONWOOD ID 123-B2
COTTONWOOD ID 123-B2
CRAIGMONT ID 123-B2
Crowfoot OR 133-C1
CULDESAC ID 123-B2
DIST OF N VANCOUVER BC 255-E7
DOUGLAS CO OR 225-B3
DUFUR OR 127-B2
ECHO OR 129-A1
EDMONDS WA 171-A5
ELLENSBURG WA 241-B6
FERNDALE WA 158-C6
FOREST GROVE OR 198-B1
Freeland WA 170-D1
GRANGER WA 120-A2
HALFWAY OR 131-A3
IONE OR 128-B2
KITTITAS WA 241-C6
KLAMATH FALLS OR 338-E7
KLICKITAT CO WA 119-A3
LAKE STEVENS WA 171-A5
LAPWAI ID 123-B2
LEWISTON ID 250-B4
LINN CO OR 133-C1
LYNDEN WA 102-B1
MABTON WA 120-B3
MALIN OR 151-A3
MARION CO OR 198-D7
MILTON-FREEWATER OR 121-C3
MOUNT VERNON WA 260-C12
NEZ PERCE CO ID 123-B2
PACIFIC CO WA 117-A1
PECK ID 123-B2
PIERCE CO WA 182-B3
POLK CO OR 207-C2
RIDDLE OR 225-B2
RUFUS OR 127-C1
SAINT PAUL OR 198-D7
SCIO OR 133-C1
SODAVILLE OR 133-C2
STEVENS CO WA 106-A3
SUMNER WA 182-B3
TROY ID 123-B2
UNION GAP WA 243-C7
VANCOUVER BC 156-B5
VANCOUVER BC 254-H13
VANCOUVER WA 305-G3
WAITSBURG WA 122-A2
WARDNER ID 115-C2
WINTHROP WA 104-A2
YAKIMA CO WA 120-A2
YAMHILL OR 198-D7
MAIN ST Rt#-3
BRITISH COLUMBIA 104-C1
JULIAETTA ID 123-B1
KENDRICK ID 123-B1
OSOYOOS BC 104-C1
MAIN ST Rt#-5
SAINT MARIES ID 248-D7
MAIN ST Rt#-6
PE ELL WA 117-B2
MAIN ST Rt#-7
BAKER CITY OR 138-B1
MAIN ST Rt#-8
TROY ID 123-A1
MAIN ST Rt#-9
SKAGIT CO WA 168-C2
MAIN ST Rt#-19
CANYON CO ID 147-B1
GREENLEAF ID 147-B1
MAIN ST Rt#-31
PAISLEY OR 151-C1
MAIN ST Rt#-39
KLAMATH FALLS OR 338-D8
MAIN ST Rt#-44
CANYON CO ID 147-B1
MAIN ST Rt#-55
CASCADE ID 252-D6
MARSING ID 147-B1
OWYHEE CO ID 147-B1
MAIN ST Rt#-62
CRAIGMONT ID 123-B2
CRAIGMONT ID 123-B2
MAIN ST Rt#-74
HEPPNER OR 128-C2
LEXINGTON OR 128-C2
MAIN ST Rt#-86
RICHLAND OR 139-A1
MAIN ST Rt#-99
CANYONVILLE OR 225-C3
DOUGLAS CO OR 225-C3
PHOENIX OR 234-B2
MAIN ST Rt#-124
WAITSBURG WA 122-A2
MAIN ST Rt#-126
LANE CO OR 330-H7
SPRINGFIELD OR 215-D2
SPRINGFIELD OR 330-H7
SPRINGFIELD OR 331-A7
MAIN ST Rt#-203
DUVALL WA 110-C1
KING CO WA 110-C1
MAIN ST Rt#-206
HEPPNER OR 128-C2
MAIN ST Rt#-212
OREGON CITY OR 199-D4
MAIN ST Rt#-214
MOUNT ANGEL OR 205-C3
MAIN ST Rt#-219
SAINT PAUL OR 198-D7
MAIN ST Rt#-226
LINN CO OR 133-C1
LYONS OR 134-A1
SCIO OR 133-C1
MAIN ST Rt#-231
LINCOLN CO WA 114-A2
MAIN ST Rt#-237
COVE OR 130-B2
UNION CO OR 130-B2
MAIN ST Rt#-240
YAMHILL OR 198-B5
YAMHILL CO OR 198-B5
MAIN ST Rt#-260
WASHTUCNA WA 121-C1
MAIN ST Rt#-409
CATHLAMET WA 117-B3
MAIN ST Rt#-524
EDMONDS WA 171-A5

PNW
INDEX

382 MARVIN RD NE STREET INDEX MERRY CREEK RD

STREET City State Page-Grid

MARVIN RD NE
THURSTON CO WA 181-A5
MARVIN RD NE Rt#-510
LACEY WA 181-A6
MARVIN RD SE
THURSTON CO WA 181-A7
MARVIN RD SE Rt#-510
LACEY WA 181-A6
THURSTON CO WA 181-A6
E MARVIN ST
PASCO WA 343-H7
MARX ST U.S.-95
IDAHO CO ID 131-C2
RIGGINS ID 131-C2
MARY GATES MEMORIAL DR
SEATTLE WA 274-E5
MARY HILL BYPS
PORT COQUITLAM BC 157-B5
MARYHILL DR
EVERETT WA 171-B4
SNOHOMISH CO WA 171-B4
MARY HILL RD
PORT COQUITLAM BC 157-A5
MARYLAND AV Rt#-42
MYRTLE POINT OR 140-B2
MARY M KNIGHT RD
MASON CO WA 179-B3
MARYS PEAK RD
BENTON CO OR 133-A1
MARYS RIVER RD
BENTON CO OR 133-A1
MASCHER RD NE
MARION CO OR 205-B5
MASCHKE RD
LEWIS CO WA 187-B5
MASHELL AV S Rt#-161
EATONVILLE WA 118-B1
W MASON AV
BUCKLEY WA 110-C3
BUCKLEY WA 182-D4
MASON DR
CROOK CO OR 213-D5
PRINEVILLE OR 213-D5
MASON RD
WASCO CO OR 127-B2
MASON ANDERSON RD
TILLAMOOK CO OR 191-B3
MASON BENSON RD
MASON CO WA 173-C7
MASON CO WA 180-C1
MASON CREEK RD
KITTITAS CO WA 240-C1
NE MASON CREEK RD
CLARK CO WA 192-D2
MASON LAKE DR W
MASON CO WA 173-C7
MASON CO WA 180-C1
MASON LAKE RD W
MASON CO WA 180-B1
SW MASONVILLE RD
YAMHILL CO OR 204-A1
E MASTERSON RD
KITTITAS CO WA 240-C2
W MASTERSON RD
KITTITAS CO WA 240-C2
MATEJECK RD
TILLAMOOK CO OR 197-B2
MATHENY RD N
MARION CO OR 204-D3
MATHENY RD NE
MARION CO OR 204-D3
MATHENY CREEK RD
COOS CO OR 220-D7
MATHER MEMORIAL PKWY Rt#-410
PIERCE CO WA 119-A1
MATHERS AV
DIST OF WEST VANCOUVER BC 254-A2
MATHIAS RD E
PIERCE CO WA 182-A6
MATLOCK-BRADY RD
MASON CO WA 179-A4
MATNEY RD
KLAMATH CO OR 235-D6
MATNEY WY
KLAMATH CO OR 235-D6
MATSEN RD
KLICKITAT CO WA 120-A3
MATSON RD
LATAH CO ID 249-D2
MATTESON RD
YAMHILL CO OR 198-B3
MATTHIEU LN
MARION CO OR 199-A7
MATTOON RD
CLACKAMAS CO OR 200-B5
MATTSON RD
LEWIS CO WA 184-B5
NE MATTSON RD
CLARK CO WA 193-A4
MAUI AV
OAK HARBOR WA 167-C3
MAUPIN RD
DOUGLAS CO OR 141-A1
SKAGIT CO WA 168-A2
MAXFIELD CREEK RD
BENTON CO OR 133-B1
POLK CO OR 133-B1
POLK CO OR 207-A2
W MAXWELL AV
SPOKANE WA 348-G7
MAXWELL CRES
TOWNSHIP OF LANGLEY BC 157-C7
MAXWELL RD
COOS BAY OR 333-C4
EUGENE OR 329-E1
LANE CO OR 329-E1
NORTH BEND OR 333-C4
MAXWELTON RD
ISLAND CO WA 171-A2
MAY AV
HOOD RIVER OR 195-D5
W MAY AV Rt#-21
ODESSA WA 113-B3
MAY DR
HOOD RIVER OR 195-C5
HOOD RIVER CO OR 195-C5
MAY RD
POLK CO OR 204-A5
S MAY RD
ADAMS CO WA 242-C7
E MAY ST Rt#-74
HEPPNER OR 128-C2
MAY ST NW
Tracyton WA 270-G4
MAYFIELD RD NE
DOUGLAS CO WA 112-C1
MAYS CREEK RD
JACKSON CO OR 230-A2
MAYTOWN RD SW
THURSTON CO WA 184-B2
MAYTOWN RD SW Rt#-121
THURSTON CO WA 184-C2
SE MAY VALLEY RD
KING CO WA 175-D4
KING CO WA 176-A5
MAZAMA RD
OKANOGAN CO WA 104-A2
MCADAMS CREEK RD
SISKIYOU CO CA 149-C3
S MCALISTER RD
ISLAND CITY OR 130-A2
UNION CO OR 130-A2
E MCANDREWS RD
JACKSON CO OR 336-C10
MEDFORD OR 336-C10
W MCANDREWS RD
JACKSON CO OR 336-B11
MEDFORD OR 336-B11
MCARDLE RD
DESCHUTES CO OR 217-D3
MCBEE RD
BENTON CO WA 120-C3
MCBETH RD
LANE CO OR 215-A3
LANE CO OR 329-D14
MCBRIDE BLVD
NEW WESTMINSTER BC 156-D5
MCBRIDE BLVD Rt#-99A
NEW WESTMINSTER BC 156-D5
MCBRIDE DR
DISTRICT OF SURREY BC 157-A5
MCBRIDE RD
LATAH CO ID 249-D1
MALHEUR CO OR 147-A2
NW MCBRIDE CEM RD
YAMHILL CO OR 198-A5
MCBRYDE AV E
MONTESANO WA 178-D7
MCCABE RD
CLACKAMAS CO OR 200-D5
CROOK CO OR 213-C3
MCCAFFERY RD
CROOK CO OR 213-A6
MCCALEB RD
POLK CO OR 204-A7
MCCALL BLVD
Navy Yard City WA 270-F13
MCCALLAN RD
CITY OF RICHMOND BC 156-B6
MCCALLUM RD
DISTRICT OF ABBOTSFORD BC 102-B1
DISTRICT OF KENT BC 94-C3
DISTRICT OF MATSQUI BC 102-B1
MCCANLIES RD
HARNEY CO OR 144-C1
MCCANN RD
LEWIS CO ID 123-B3
POLK CO OR 204-A3
MCCANN GRADE
NEZ PERCE CO ID 250-D5
MCCANSE RD
UNION CO OR 130-A3
MCCARVER ST
TACOMA WA 293-E2
MCCLAINE ST Rt#-213
MARION CO OR 205-C4
SILVERTON OR 205-C4
MCCLAIN TUTHILL RD
KLICKITAT CO WA 196-B5
S MCCLELLAN ST
SPOKANE WA 349-A10
MCCLENNY RD
FRANKLIN CO WA 121-B2
MCCLOSKEY CREEK RD
SKAMANIA CO WA 194-A6
MCCLURE RD
LEWIS CO WA 187-C4
MCCOIN RD
CROOK CO OR 213-B2
MCCONIHE RD
GRANT CO WA 242-B2
SW MCCONNELL RD
CLACKAMAS CO OR 199-A5
MCCORKLE RD SE
THURSTON CO WA 184-D1
MCCORMICK LP
TILLAMOOK CO OR 197-C2
MCCORMICK HILL RD
WASHINGTON CO OR 198-D4
YAMHILL CO OR 198-D4
MCCOY RD
COLUMBIA CO OR 189-C6
POLK CO OR 204-B4
MCCRORY RD
COWLITZ CO WA 187-B5
MCCROSKEY RD
WHITMAN CO WA 114-C3
W MCCULLOCH RD
YAKIMA CO WA 243-B7
MCCULLOUGH CREEK RD
DOUGLAS CO OR 225-A6
MCCUNE RD
LEWIS CO WA 187-D2
MCCUTCHEON RD
PIERCE CO WA 182-C4
MCDANIEL RD
CROOK CO OR 213-B5
MCDERMITT RD
MALHEUR CO OR 154-B2
MCDERMOTT RD
COLUMBIA CO OR 189-C7
S MCDERMOTT RD
ADA CO ID 147-C1
CANYON CO ID 147-C1
MCDONALD DR
CROOK CO OR 213-B6
MCDONALD RD
COLUMBIA CO OR 125-B1
MCDONALD RD
PIERCE CO WA 182-B7
SKAMANIA CO WA 193-D7
TILLAMOOK CO OR 191-B3
WALLA WALLA CO WA 121-C3
WALLA WALLA CO WA 345-A13
N MCDONALD RD
SPOKANE CO WA 350-J8
S MCDONALD RD
SPOKANE CO WA 350-J10
MCDONALD RDG
SKAMANIA CO WA 119-A3
SW MCDONALD ST
TIGARD OR 199-B3
MCDOUGALL RD
YAMHILL CO OR 198-C7
MCDOWELL CREEK DR
LINN CO OR 133-C2
LINN CO OR 134-A2
MCDUFF RD SE
THURSTON CO WA 184-D3
MCELLIGOTT RD
MORROW CO OR 128-B2
MCELROY RD
SNOHOMISH CO WA 168-D6
MCEWAN RD KPN
PIERCE CO WA 181-A2
MCEWAN PRAIRIE RD
MASON CO WA 180-A2
MCEWEN RD
MALHEUR CO OR 146-A1
NE MCFARLAND LN
JEFFERSON CO OR 208-C2
MCFARLAND RD
TANGENT OR 207-C6
W MCFARLANE RD
AIRWAY HEIGHTS WA 246-A4
SPOKANE CO WA 114-B2
SPOKANE CO WA 246-A4
SW MCFEE PL
WASHINGTON CO OR 198-C4
MCFEELY RD
WALLA WALLA CO WA 121-C2
MCGARIGLE RD
SEDRO-WOOLLEY WA 161-C5
SKAGIT CO WA 161-C5
MCGEE RD
WHATCOM CO WA 158-C3
MCGILCHRIST ST SE
SALEM OR 324-J2
SALEM OR 325-A2
MCGILL ST
VANCOUVER BC 255-D9
SE MCGILLIVRAY BLVD
VANCOUVER WA 193-A7
VANCOUVER WA 307-J7
MCGINNIS LAKE RD
OKANOGAN CO WA 237-D1
MCGLAUGHLIN RD
LEWIS CO WA 187-C4
MCGONAGLE RD
YAKIMA CO WA 243-B5
MCGOWAN CREEK RD
LANE CO OR 210-D7
MCGOWEN RD
KLICKITAT CO WA 196-B4
MCGRADY RD
WHITMAN CO WA 114-C3
MCGRATH RD
DESCHUTES CO OR 217-D1
W MCGRAW ST
SEATTLE WA 276-C1
SEATTLE WA 277-G1
MCGREEVY RD
WHITMAN CO WA 249-B4
MCGREGOR RD
WHITMAN CO WA 122-A1
MCGUIRE RD
DISTRICT OF CHILLIWACK BC 94-C3
N MCGUIRE RD
KOOTENAI CO ID 353-D1
POST FALLS ID 353-E5
MCINTOSH RD
DOUGLAS CO WA 237-A2
HOOD RIVER CO OR 202-C2
WHITMAN CO WA 122-A1
MCINTOSH HILL RD
NEZ PERCE CO ID 250-D5
MCINTYRE SPRING RD
MALHEUR CO OR 147-A1
MCKAY AV
CITY OF N VANCOUVER BC 254-J4
MCKAY DR
UMATILLA CO OR 129-B1
MCKAY RD
CROOK CO OR 213-D3
MARION CO OR 199-A7
PRINEVILLE OR 213-D4
WALLA WALLA CO WA 121-B3
MCKAY CREEK RD
CROOK CO OR 135-C2
CROOK CO OR 213-D2
MCKECHNIE RD
PITT MEADOWS BC 157-C5
MCKEE RD
COWLITZ CO WA 189-B1
SW MCKEE RD
YAMHILL CO OR 204-B2
MCKEE SCHOOL RD NE
MARION CO OR 205-B2
MCKENNA TANWAX Rt#-702
PIERCE CO WA 118-A1
MCKENNA-YELM HWY Rt#-507
PIERCE CO WA 118-A1
THURSTON CO WA 118-A1
YELM WA 118-A1
MCKENZIE AV
DISTRICT OF SAANICH BC 256-G3
DISTRICT OF SAANICH BC 257-A3
MCKENZIE HWY Rt#-126
DESCHUTES CO OR 211-D5
DESCHUTES CO OR 212-A5
LANE CO OR 133-C3
LANE CO OR 134-B2
LANE CO OR 215-D2
LINN CO OR 134-B2
SPRINGFIELD OR 215-D2
MCKENZIE HWY Rt#-242
DESCHUTES CO OR 211-C4
LANE CO OR 134-C2
MCKENZIE HWY Rt#-242
LANE CO OR 211-A6
LINN CO OR 211-A6
SISTERS OR 211-C4
MCKENZIE LN
SUMMERVILLE OR 130-A2
UNION CO OR 130-A2
MCKENZIE RD
CURRY CO OR 224-A5
WHITMAN CO WA 249-C1
MCKENZIE RD SW
THURSTON CO WA 180-B6
MCKENZIE-BEND HWY U.S.-20
BEND OR 332-F1
DESCHUTES CO OR 211-D5
DESCHUTES CO OR 212-A6
DESCHUTES CO OR 217-C1
DESCHUTES CO OR 332-F1
MCKENZIE CANYON RD
DESCHUTES CO OR 212-B4
MCKENZIE VIEW DR
LANE CO OR 215-C1
LANE CO OR 330-H1
LANE CO OR 331-A1
MCKERN-SCOTT RD
STEVENS CO WA 106-A3
MCKIBBIN RD
WASHINGTON CO OR 198-C1
MCKILLOP RD NE
MARION CO OR 205-D4
MCKIMMENS RD
TILLAMOOK CO OR 191-B4
MCKINLEY AV
PIERCE CO WA 181-D4
TACOMA WA 181-D4
E MCKINLEY AV
PIERCE WA 295-J7
TACOMA WA 295-J5
MCKINLEY AV W
KELLOGG ID 115-C2
SHOSHONE CO ID 115-C2
W MCKINLEY RD
SMELTERVILLE ID 115-C2
MCKINLEY ST
COLTON WA 250-A1
E MCKINLEY WY
TACOMA WA 295-J1
MCKINLEY SPRINGS RD
BENTON CO WA 120-B3
MCKINNEY RD
ADAMS CO WA 121-A1
MCKINNON CRES
TOWNSHIP OF LANGLEY BC 157-C6
MCKNIGHT RD
GRAYS HARBOR CO WA 179-C6
MCLAGEN RD
LINN CO OR 207-C7
MCLAIN-LIBBY DR
Barview OR 220-C1
COOS CO OR 220-C1
COOS CO OR 333-B13
MCLAUGHLIN DR
JACKSON CO OR 336-H3
MCLEAN AV
PORT COQUITLAM BC 157-B5
MCLEAN RD
MOUNT VERNON WA 260-A12
SKAGIT CO WA 160-D7
SKAGIT CO WA 161-A7
SKAGIT CO WA 260-A12
UMATILLA CO OR 129-C1
MCLEOD RD
BELLINGHAM WA 258-B2
E MCLEOD RD
BELLINGHAM WA 258-J2
WHATCOM CO WA 258-J2
E MCLOUGHLIN BLVD
VANCOUVER WA 305-H4
VANCOUVER WA 306-A4
SE MCLOUGHLIN BLVD Rt#-99E
CLACKAMAS OR 321-J2
CLACKAMAS CO OR 199-D3
GLADSTONE OR 199-D3
MILWAUKIE OR 317-J6
MILWAUKIE OR 321-J2
OREGON CITY OR 199-D3
PORTLAND OR 317-J6
W MCLOUGHLIN BLVD
VANCOUVER WA 305-G4
MCLOUGHLIN BLVD E Rt#-99E
CLACKAMAS OR 199-D5
OREGON CITY OR 199-D5
E MCLOUGHLIN ST
VANCOUVER WA 305-G4
MCMANAMY RD
KITTITAS CO WA 241-A4
MCMANOMON RD
ADAMS CO WA 121-A1
ADAMS CO WA 242-C7
MCMILLAN RD
ADA CO ID 253-B2
W MCMILLAN RD
ADA CO ID 253-A2
MCMULLEN LN
LANE CO OR 210-A5
MCMULLIN CREEK RD
JOSEPHINE CO OR 233-C2
E MCMULLIN CREEK RD
JOSEPHINE CO OR 233-C3
MCMURRAY RD
TACOMA WA 182-A2
MCMURRAY ST
RICHLAND WA 340-F12
MCNABB CREEK RD
DOUGLAS CO OR 221-A7
MCNAIR DR
DIST OF N VANCOUVER BC 156-C2
NW MCNAMEE RD
MULTNOMAH CO OR 192-A6
MCNARY HWY I-82
UMATILLA OR 129-A1
UMATILLA CO OR 129-A1
MCNARY HWY U.S.-395
UMATILLA OR 129-A1
UMATILLA CO OR 129-A1
MCNAUGHT ST Rt#-507
ROY WA 181-C7
SW MCNAY RD
WASHINGTON CO OR 198-D3
MCNEALY WY
COOS CO OR 220-D6
MCNEIL RD
KITTITAS CO WA 241-A6
PITT MEADOWS BC 157-B4
MCNEIL CANYON RD NW
DOUGLAS CO WA 112-B1
DOUGLAS CO WA 236-D3
MCNEILLY RD
WHITMAN CO WA 122-B1
MCNULTY RD
LEWIS CO WA 187-D4
MCNUTT RD
GRAYS HARBOR CO WA 178-A2
MCPHILLIPS RD
TILLAMOOK CO OR 197-A7
MCQUISTON RD
KLAMATH CO OR 231-B2
MCRAE RD NE
SNOHOMISH CO WA 168-C6
MCREAVY RD
MASON CO WA 173-A7
MASON CO WA 180-A1
MCSWEEN RD
DISTRICT OF CHILLIWACK BC 94-C3
MCTAVISH RD Rt#-17A
DIST OF NORTH SAANICH BC 159-C3
MCVAY HWY Rt#-99
LANE CO OR 330-G11
MCVEY AV
LAKE OSWEGO OR 321-F7
NE MCWILLIAMS RD
KITSAP CO WA 270-H3
KITSAP CO WA 271-A3
Tracyton WA 270-H3
M DRUFFEL RD
WHITMAN CO WA 249-A7
E MEAD AV
YAKIMA WA 243-C7
W MEAD AV
YAKIMA WA 243-B7
MEAD RD
COLUMBIA CO WA 122-A2
NE MEADOW AV
DOUGLAS CO OR 334-F4
ROSEBURG OR 334-F4
MEADOW LN
COOS CO OR 218-B6
MEADOW RD
LINN CO OR 207-B5
SNOHOMISH CO WA 171-C4
W MEADOWBROOK RD
YAKIMA CO WA 243-A7
MEADOW CREEK RD
BOUNDARY CO ID 107-B1
GARFIELD CO WA 122-B2
PEND OREILLE CO WA 106-B2
SKAMANIA CO WA 118-C3
SKAMANIA CO WA 194-C1
STEVENS CO WA 106-B1
MEADOW CREEK RD U.S.-95
IDAHO CO ID 123-B3
NW MEADOW LAKE RD
YAMHILL CO OR 125-B2
YAMHILL CO OR 198-A6
MEADOWLARK DR
JEFFERSON CO OR 212-C2
MEADOWS RD
JACKSON CO OR 230-C3
MEALS RD
BENTON CO WA 121-A3
MEDA LOOP RD
TILLAMOOK CO OR 203-B1
MEDCO RD
JACKSON CO OR 336-C9
MEDFORD OR 336-C9
MEDCO HAUL RD
MEDFORD OR 336-D8
MEDICAL LAKE RD Rt#-902
MEDICAL LAKE WA 114-B2
SPOKANE CO WA 114-B2
S MEDICAL LK TYLER RD Rt#-902
MEDICAL LAKE WA 114-B2
MEDICAL SPRINGS HWY Rt#-203
BAKER CO OR 130-B3
UNION OR 130-B2
UNION CO OR 130-B2
E MEDICAL SPRINGS HWY Rt#-203
UNION OR 130-B2
MEDIMONT RD
KOOTENAI CO ID 248-C4
MEDLEYS ELKHEAD RD
DOUGLAS CO OR 219-B5
MEDOHILL RD
COOS CO OR 220-B4
MEEKER DR
COWLITZ CO WA 189-C4
N MEEKER DR
COWLITZ CO WA 189-C5
MEEKER RD
CROOK CO OR 213-B6
W MEEKER ST
KENT WA 175-B7
MEENACH DR
SPOKANE WA 348-F6
MEGAN BLVD
YAKIMA CO WA 243-C6
MEHL CREEK RD
DOUGLAS CO OR 141-A1
MEIER RD
LEWIS CO WA 187-C2
NW MEIER RD
WASHINGTON CO OR 192-A6
MEINIG AV Rt#-211
SANDY OR 200-D4
MEISS LAKE
SISKIYOU CO CA 150-B3
MEISS LAKE SAMS NECK RD
SISKIYOU CO CA 150-B3
MEISSNER RD
COLUMBIA CO OR 189-B6
MELBA RD
CANYON CO ID 147-B1
MELBOURNE ST
WESTPORT WA 183-B2
MELLEN ST
CENTRALIA WA 299-D5
MELLEN ST Rt#-507
CENTRALIA WA 299-D5
MELMONT RD
CANYON CO ID 147-B1
MELODY LN
LANE CO OR 215-B5
MELOTT RD
YAMHILL CO OR 198-C4
MELQUA RD
DOUGLAS CO OR 221-A2
MELROSE RD
DOUGLAS CO OR 221-A4
DOUGLAS CO OR 334-A3
MELROSE ST
LAKE OSWEGO OR 320-A5
WALLA WALLA WA 345-C6
WALLA WALLA CO WA 345-F5
W MELVILLE RD
SPOKANE CO WA 246-A5
MELVILLE ST
VANCOUVER BC 254-F9
MELVILLE ST SE
THURSTON CO WA 184-C3
MELVIN RD
DOUGLAS CO WA 239-B1
MEMORIAL HWY Rt#-20
SKAGIT CO WA 160-D6
SKAGIT CO WA 161-A7
MEMORIAL HWY Rt#-536
MOUNT VERNON WA 260-A11
SKAGIT CO WA 161-A7
SKAGIT CO WA 260-A11
MEMORIAL PARK DR
COWLITZ CO WA 302-D7
LONGVIEW WA 302-D7
MENLO SOUTH FORK RD
PACIFIC CO WA 117-A1
MENZEL LAKE RD
SNOHOMISH CO WA 102-C3
MENZIE RD SE
KITSAP CO WA 174-C4
W MERCER PL
SEATTLE WA 277-G3
MERCER ST
SEATTLE WA 277-H3
SEATTLE WA 278-A3
W MERCER ST
SEATTLE WA 277-G3
E MERCER WY
MERCER ISLAND WA 175-C4
W MERCER WY
MERCER ISLAND WA 175-C3
MERCER ISLAND WA 283-J3
MERCER ISLAND WA 287-J2
MERCER LAKE RD
LANE CO OR 214-B2
MERCHANTS RD
CLALLAM CO WA 169-D1
N MERIDIAN
PUYALLUP WA 182-B3
N MERIDIAN Rt#-161
PUYALLUP WA 182-B3
S MERIDIAN
PUYALLUP WA 182-B4
S MERIDIAN Rt#-161
PUYALLUP WA 182-B4
MERIDIAN E Rt#-161
EDGEWOOD WA 182-B3
MILTON WA 182-B3
PIERCE CO WA 118-B1
PIERCE CO WA 182-B6
PUYALLUP WA 182-B3
MERIDIAN AV E Rt#-161
EATONVILLE WA 118-B1
PIERCE CO WA 118-B1
PIERCE CO WA 182-B7
MERIDIAN AV N
SEATTLE WA 171-B7
SHORELINE WA 171-B7
MERIDIAN RD
ADA CO ID 253-A1
ANMORE BC 157-A4
COQUITLAM BC 157-A4
LINN CO OR 133-C1
MARION CO OR 205-C4
MERIDIAN ID 253-A2
MOSES LAKE WA 242-C3
PORT MOODY BC 157-A4
SILVERTON OR 205-C4
S MERIDIAN RD
CLACKAMAS CO OR 199-B7
CLACKAMAS CO OR 205-C2
MERIDIAN RD NE
LACEY WA 181-A6
MARION CO OR 205-C3
MERIDIAN RD SE
THURSTON CO WA 181-A7
MERIDIAN ST
BELLINGHAM WA 258-C3
MERIDIAN ST Rt#-539
BELLINGHAM WA 258-C2
E MERLENE AV
SPOKANE CO WA 347-F4
MERLIN RD
JOSEPHINE CO OR 229-A4
JOSEPHINE CO OR 335-A1
MERLIN-GALICE RD
JOSEPHINE CO OR 149-A1
JOSEPHINE CO OR 229-A4
MERRILL RD
DESCHUTES CO OR 136-A3
WALLA WALLA WA 345-F7
S MERRILL RD
KLAMATH CO OR 150-C3
SISKIYOU CO CA 150-C3
MERRILL CREEK PKWY
EVERETT WA 267-H2
EVERETT WA 268-A2
MERRILL CREEK RD
COLUMBIA CO OR 189-C7
MERRIMAN RD
CENTRAL POINT OR 336-B7
MEDFORD OR 336-B7
MERRITT LN
UNION CO OR 130-B1
MERRY CREEK RD
SHOSHONE CO ID 115-C3
SHOSHONE CO ID 115-C3

PNW
INDEX

384 MOSBY CREEK RD STREET INDEX N NEWMAN LAKE DR

PNW
INDEX

STREET
City State Page-Grid

MOSBY CREEK RD
LANE CO OR 215-B7
MOSCOW RD Rt#-27
PALOUSE WA 249-B1
MOSCOW MOUNTAIN RD
LATAH CO ID 249-D4
MOSCROP ST
DISTRICT OF BURNABY BC 156-C5
MOSE RD
SNOHOMISH CO WA 168-D4
MOSELEY RD
DEL NORTE CO CA 148-B3
MOSER RD
NEZ PERCE CO ID 250-B2
MOSES RD
OKANOGAN CO WA 105-B3
MOSES COULEE RD SE
DOUGLAS CO WA 112-C2
MOSES CREEK LN
UNION CO OR 130-A1
SE MOSHER AV
ROSEBURG OR 334-F8
MOSIER RD
CLACKAMAS CO OR 200-A6
COLUMBIA CO OR 189-A3
SKAGIT CO WA 161-C5
MOSIER CREEK RD
WASCO CO OR 196-A6
MOSIER-THE DALLES HWY U.S.-30
MOSIER OR 196-A5
THE DALLES OR 196-A5
WASCO CO OR 196-A5
MOSQUITO CREEK RD
COWLITZ CO WA 187-A7
MOSQUITO LAKE RD
WHATCOM CO WA 102-B1
WHATCOM CO WA 161-D1
MOSS ST
CITY OF VICTORIA BC 256-J11
MOSS CREEK RD
TILLAMOOK CO OR 191-B7
MOSS HILL RD
CLACKAMAS CO OR 200-C6
MOTTMAN RD SW
OLYMPIA WA 296-D7
TUMWATER WA 296-D7
MOUNT ADAMS RD
KLICKITAT CO WA 119-A3
MOUNT ADAMS ST
HARRAH WA 119-C2
YAKIMA CO WA 119-C2
MOUNT ADAMS RECREATION AREA RD
KLICKITAT CO WA 119-A3
YAKIMA CO WA 119-A3
N MOUNTAIN AV
ASHLAND OR 337-E6
JACKSON CO OR 337-E6
S MOUNTAIN AV
ASHLAND OR 337-E8
MOUNTAIN BLVD U.S.-395
MOUNT VERNON OR 137-A2
MOUNTAIN HWY
DIST OF N VANCOUVER BC 255-E2
MOUNTAIN HWY E Rt#-7
PIERCE CO WA 118-B1
PIERCE CO WA 181-D6
PIERCE CO WA 182-A7
MOUNTAIN HWY E Rt#-706
PIERCE CO WA 118-B1
MOUNTAIN RD
ASOTIN CO WA 122-C3
GARFIELD CO WA 122-B2
KLAMATH CO OR 231-C1
SW MOUNTAIN RD
CLACKAMAS CO OR 199-C5
MOUNTAIN HOME DR
LINN CO OR 210-D2
MOUNTAIN HOME RD
CHELAN CO WA 238-A1
WASHINGTON CO OR 198-D4
YAMHILL CO OR 198-D5
MOUNTAIN LOOP HWY
GRANITE FALLS WA 102-C3
SNOHOMISH CO WA 102-C3
SNOHOMISH CO WA 103-A3
SNOHOMISH CO WA 111-A1
MOUNTAIN MEADOWS RD
PIERCE CO WA 185-A2
MOUNTAIN MEADOWS RD Rt#-165
PIERCE CO WA 185-A2
MOUNTAIN TOP RD
YAMHILL CO OR 198-D4
E MOUNTAIN VIEW AV
ELLENSBURG WA 241-B6
KITTITAS CO WA 241-B6
W MOUNTAIN VIEW AV
ELLENSBURG WA 241-B6
MOUNTAIN VIEW DR
BENTON CO OR 207-A4
BENTON CO OR 327-H1
BOISE ID 253-C2
BONNER CO ID 244-A2
CLACKAMAS CO OR 201-C5
GARDEN CITY ID 253-C2
MOUNTAINVIEW DR
NEWBERG OR 198-D5
YAMHILL CO OR 198-D5
SW MOUNTAIN VIEW DR
JEFFERSON CO OR 208-A6
MOUNTAIN VIEW DR E
KITSAP CO WA 271-D12
MOUNTAIN VIEW DR S
SALEM OR 324-G2
MOUNTAIN VIEW RD
COLUMBIA CO OR 192-A3
COWLITZ CO WA 189-D5
DESCHUTES CO OR 212-A4
FERNDALE WA 158-B6
SKAGIT CO WA 260-J14
WHATCOM CO WA 158-B6
N MOUNTAIN VIEW RD
LATAH CO ID 249-D4
MOUNT ANGEL HWY NE
MARION CO OR 205-B4
MOUNT ANGELES RD
CLALLAM CO WA 261-G8
PORT ANGELES WA 261-G8
MOUNT ANGEL-GERVAIS RD NE
MARION CO OR 205-B3
MOUNT ANGEL-SCOTTS MILLS RD NE
MARION CO OR 205-C3
MOUNT ASHLAND SKI RD
JACKSON CO OR 234-D6
MOUNT BAKER HWY Rt#-542
WHATCOM CO WA 102-B1
WHATCOM CO WA 103-A1
MOUNT BRYNION RD
COWLITZ CO WA 303-H5
N MOUNT CARROL ST
DALTON GARDENS ID 355-F2
MOUNT GLEN RD
UNION CO OR 130-A2
MOUNT HOOD AV Rt#-214
MARION CO OR 205-B1
WOODBURN OR 205-B1
MOUNT HOOD HWY Rt#-35
CLACKAMAS CO OR 202-C5
HOOD RIVER CO OR 195-C7
HOOD RIVER CO OR 202-C1
MOUNT HOOD HWY U.S.-26
CLACKAMAS CO OR 200-C3
CLACKAMAS CO OR 201-B4
CLACKAMAS CO OR 202-A6
GRESHAM OR 200-C3
MULTNOMAH CO OR 200-C3
SANDY OR 200-C3
SE MOUNT HOOD HWY U.S.-26
MULTNOMAH CO OR 200-A2
PORTLAND OR 200-A2
S MOUNT HOPE RD
CLACKAMAS CO OR 205-D2
MOUNT HOREB RD SE
MARION CO OR 134-A1
MOUNT JUPITER RD
JEFFERSON CO WA 173-C1
MOUNT LEHMAN RD
DISTRICT OF MATSQUI BC 102-B1
MOUNT MATHESON RD
BRITISH COLUMBIA 165-A1
DISTRICT OF METCHOSIN BC 165-A1
MOUNT NEWTON CROSS RD
DIST OF CENTRAL SAANICH BC 159-B3
MOUNT OLYMPUS AV
OCEAN SHORES WA 298-E4
MOUNT OLYMPUS AV SE
OCEAN SHORES WA 298-D2
MOUNT PLEASANT RD
COWLITZ CO WA 189-D4
SKAMANIA CO WA 193-D7
MOUNT REUBEN RD
DOUGLAS CO OR 225-A7
NW MOUNT RICHMOND RD
YAMHILL CO OR 198-A4
SE MOUNT SCOTT BLVD
CLACKAMAS OR 319-J7
CLACKAMAS CO OR 200-A3
HAPPY VALLEY OR 200-A3
MULTNOMAH OR 319-H6
PORTLAND OR 200-A3
PORTLAND OR 319-H6
PORTLAND OR 319-J7
MOUNT SEYMOUR PKWY
DIST OF N VANCOUVER BC 156-D3
DIST OF N VANCOUVER BC 255-H6
MOUNT SEYMOUR RD
DIST OF N VANCOUVER BC 156-D3
MOUNT SHASTA DR
VANCOUVER WA 307-G7
MOUNT SOLO RD
COWLITZ CO WA 302-B5
LONGVIEW WA 302-B5
MOUNT SOLO RD Rt#-432
COWLITZ CO WA 302-C6
E MOUNT SPOKANE PK DR Rt#-206
SPOKANE CO WA 114-C1
SPOKANE CO WA 246-D1
SPOKANE CO WA 247-A1
SPOKANE CO WA 347-H5
N MOUNT SPOKANE PK DR Rt#-206
SPOKANE CO WA 114-C1
MOUNT STELLA RD
JACKSON CO OR 226-D3
MOUNT TOM DR
LINN CO OR 210-B6
MOUNT TOM RD
LANE CO OR 210-C7
MOUNT VERNON RD
LANE CO OR 331-H9
SPRINGFIELD OR 331-H9
MOUNT VERNON RD S
SKAGIT CO WA 168-B1
MOUNT VERNON-BIG LK RD
MOUNT VERNON WA 260-H12
SKAGIT CO WA 161-C7
SKAGIT CO WA 260-H12
MOUNT VIEW RD
SPOKANE CO WA 247-A1
NW MOUNT WASHINGTON DR
BEND OR 332-B3
MOWICH RD
DOUGLAS CO OR 223-A4
MOWICH SECTION Rt#-165
CARBONADO WA 182-D6
PIERCE CO WA 110-C3
PIERCE CO WA 118-C1
PIERCE CO WA 182-D6
MOWREY RD
CHELAN CO WA 236-B3
MOX-CHEHALIS RD
GRAYS HARBOR CO WA 117-B1
GRAYS HARBOR CO WA 179-C7
E MOXEE AV
MOXEE (MOXEE CITY) WA 243-D7
YAKIMA CO WA 243-D7
MOYIE RIVER RD
BOUNDARY CO ID 107-B1
MUCK-KAPOWSIN HWY
PIERCE CO WA 182-A6
MUD BAY HWY SW
OLYMPIA WA 296-A4
THURSTON CO WA 180-B6
THURSTON CO WA 296-A4
MUD BAY RD
SAN JUAN CO WA 160-A7
MUD CREEK RD
ADAMS CO ID 251-A3
MUDDY RD
WASCO CO OR 135-C1
MUDDY CREEK RD
BAKER CO OR 130-A3
SW MUDDY VALLEY RD
YAMHILL CO OR 204-A2
MUD FLAT RD
MALHEUR CO OR 146-C2
OWYHEE CO ID 147-C3
OWYHEE CO ID 155-B1
WHITMAN CO WA 122-B1
MUD LAKE RD
DESCHUTES CO OR 216-A4
SKAGIT CO WA 161-C6
MUD SPRING RD
MALHEUR CO OR 154-A2
MUD SPRINGS RD NE
DOUGLAS CO WA 112-C1
MUD SPRINGS RD NW
DOUGLAS CO WA 112-B1
MUEKE RD
CLACKAMAS CO OR 199-B6
MUELLER RD
UMATILLA CO OR 121-C3
MUFFORD AV
LANGLEY BC 157-C7
TOWNSHIP OF LANGLEY BC 157-C7
MUIR CREEK RD
DOUGLAS CO OR 223-A7
DOUGLAS CO OR 227-A1
MUKILTEO BLVD
EVERETT WA 171-B2
EVERETT WA 264-A7
MUKILTEO WA 171-B2
MUKILTEO BLVD SE
EVERETT WA 264-C6
MUKILTEO BLVD SW
EVERETT WA 264-B7
MUKILTEO SPEEDWAY Rt#-525
MUKILTEO WA 171-B2
MUKILTEO WA 266-D3
MUKILTEO WA 267-E5
SNOHOMISH WA 267-E6
SNOHOMISH CO WA 171-B4
MULEDEER RD
DOUGLAS CO WA 239-B1
MULE SPRING RD
HARNEY CO OR 144-C3
MULFORD RD
LEWIS CO WA 187-C4
NW MULHOLLAND DR
ROSEBURG OR 334-E4
MULINO RD
CLACKAMAS CO OR 199-C7
S MULINO RD
CLACKAMAS CO OR 199-C6
MULKEY RD
WHITMAN CO WA 114-B3
E MULLAN AV
KOOTENAI CO ID 353-H6
KOOTENAI CO ID 354-B6
OSBURN ID 115-C2
POST FALLS ID 353-H6
POST FALLS ID 354-B6
W MULLAN AV
KOOTENAI CO ID 354-H6
POST FALLS ID 353-G6
MULLAN RD
ADAMS CO WA 122-A1
N MULLAN RD
Dishman WA 350-D8
SPOKANE CO WA 350-D8
MULLEN RD SE
LACEY WA 297-H10
THURSTON CO WA 181-A7
THURSTON CO WA 297-J11
SE MULLENIX RD
KITSAP CO WA 174-C5
MULLER DR
LINN CO OR 207-D5
S MULLINIX RD
SPOKANE CO WA 114-B2
SW MULTNOMAH BLVD
PORTLAND OR 199-B2
PORTLAND OR 199-B2
PORTLAND OR 316-A6
MULTNOMAH DR
HOOD RIVER CO OR 195-C5
NE MULTNOMAH ST
PORTLAND OR 313-H4
PORTLAND OR 314-A4
MULTNOMAH BASIN RD
MULTNOMAH CO OR 201-A1
MUNCH RD
CLARK CO WA 193-A1
MUNDUN CANYON RD
CHELAN CO WA 238-A2
MUNDY ST
COQUITLAM BC 157-A5
MUNDY LOSS RD
PIERCE CO WA 182-D4
MUNN RD
BRITISH COLUMBIA 159-B5
DISTRICT OF SAANICH BC 256-A1
MUNSEL LAKE RD
FLORENCE OR 214-B2
LANE CO OR 214-B2
MUNSON DR SW
THURSTON CO WA 180-B6
MUNSON CREEK RD
TILLAMOOK CO OR 197-C4
MURCHIE RD
TOWNSHIP OF LANGLEY BC 158-C2
MURDER CREEK DR
LINN CO OR 326-H3
MURPHY DR NW
PIERCE CO WA 181-C1
MURPHY RD
BEND OR 332-E12
DESCHUTES CO OR 332-E12
DOUGLAS CO OR 225-C7
FRANKLIN CO WA 121-B2
LINCOLN CO OR 203-D4
S MURPHY RD
SPOKANE CO WA 246-A6
MURPHY CREEK RD
JOSEPHINE CO OR 149-A2
MURPHY-GRANDVIEW RD Rt#-78
OWYHEE CO ID 147-C2
MURPHY GULCH RD
JACKSON CO OR 230-A4
NW MURRAY BLVD
WASHINGTON CO OR 199-B1
SW MURRAY BLVD
BEAVERTON OR 199-A2
WASHINGTON CO OR 199-A2
MURRAY RD SW
LAKEWOOD WA 181-C5
PIERCE CO WA 181-C5
MURRAY ST
PORT MOODY BC 157-A4
MUSTANG RESERVOIR RD
MALHEUR CO OR 146-C3
MALHEUR CO OR 154-C1
MUTINY BAY RD
Clinton WA 171-A2
Freeland WA 170-C1
MYERS RD
POLK CO OR 204-A5
TOPPENISH WA 120-A2
YAKIMA CO WA 120-A2
MYERS RD E
BONNEY LAKE WA 182-C4
MYERS WY S
KING WA 285-J6
KING WA 286-A4
SEATTLE WA 285-J3
SEATTLE WA 286-A4
MYERS CREEK RD
CURRY CO OR 232-B1
MYRA RD
COLLEGE PLACE WA 344-G9
WALLA WALLA WA 344-G9
WALLA WALLA CO WA 344-G9
MYRNA LN
JOSEPHINE CO OR 233-A4
S MYRTLE PL
SEATTLE WA 286-D1
E MYRTLE ST U.S.-20
BOISE ID 253-C3
S MYRTLE ST
SEATTLE WA 286-D1
W MYRTLE ST U.S.-20
BOISE ID 253-C3
MYRTLE CREEK RD
COOS CO OR 140-C3
N MYRTLE CREEK RD
DOUGLAS CO OR 141-B2
DOUGLAS CO OR 221-D7
DOUGLAS CO OR 225-D1
S MYRTLE CREEK RD
DOUGLAS CO OR 225-D1
MYRTLE PARK RD
HARNEY CO OR 137-A3
MYRTLE POINT-COOPER BRIDGE RD
COOS CO OR 140-B2
MYRTLE POINT OR 140-B2
MYRTLE POINT-LAMPA RD
COOS CO OR 140-B2
COOS CO OR 220-C6
MYRTLE POINT OR 140-B2
MYRTLE POINT-SITKUM RD
COOS CO OR 140-C2

N

N ST
GRANTS PASS OR 335-G10
JOSEPHINE CO OR 335-H10
SE N ST
GRANTS PASS OR 335-G10
NACHES AV
TIETON WA 119-C1
E NACHES AV Rt#-823
SELAH WA 243-B5
S NACHES AV
YAKIMA WA 243-C6
S NACHES RD
NACHES WA 119-C1
YAKIMA CO WA 119-C1
YAKIMA CO WA 243-A5
S NACHES WY
YAKIMA CO WA 119-C1
W NACHES WY
YAKIMA CO WA 119-C1
NACHES HEIGHTS RD
YAKIMA CO WA 243-A5
NACHES-TIETON RD
TIETON WA 119-C1
YAKIMA CO WA 119-C1
NACHES WENAS RD
YAKIMA CO WA 243-A4
NAGLER RD
YAKIMA CO WA 243-B5
NAHAHUM CANYON RD
CHELAN CO WA 238-C2
NAITO PKWY
PORTLAND OR 312-E3
PORTLAND OR 313-F5
NW NAITO PKWY
PORTLAND OR 312-E4
PORTLAND OR 313-F4
SW NAITO PKWY
PORTLAND OR 313-F6
PORTLAND OR 317-F1
SW NAITO PKWY I-99
PORTLAND OR 317-F2
NAMPA BLVD Rt#-55
NAMPA ID 147-B1
NANAIMO ST
VANCOUVER BC 156-C5
VANCOUVER BC 255-C12
NANAIMO-HRSSHOE FERRY
BRITISH COLUMBIA 93-A3
NANAIMO LAKES RD
NANAIMO BC 93-A3
NANAIMO-TSAWASN FERRY
BRITISH COLUMBIA 93-A3
BRITISH COLUMBIA 101-B1
NANAIMO BC 93-A3
NANCY GREENE WY
DIST OF N VANCOUVER BC 156-B2
NANEUM RD
KITTITAS CO WA 241-C4
NANEUM RIDGE RD
KITTITAS CO WA 241-D1
NAPOLEON-BARSTOW RD
STEVENS CO WA 106-A1
NARROWS DR
TACOMA WA 181-C2
NARROWS-PRINCETON RD
HARNEY CO OR 145-B2
NASH AV
BENTON CO OR 327-C13
NASH LN
CANYON CO ID 147-B1
NASHUA LN
DESCHUTES CO OR 212-A4
NW NASHVILLE AV
BEND OR 332-D6
NASI LN
VALLEY CO ID 252-D1
NASTY FLAT RD
HARNEY CO OR 144-B3
SW NATERLIN DR
NEWPORT OR 206-B4
NATIONAL AV
CHEHALIS WA 299-E9
LEWIS CO WA 299-E9
S NATIONAL AV
Navy Yard City WA 270-E12
NATIONAL AV N
BREMERTON WA 270-E11
Navy Yard City WA 270-E11
NATIONAL PARK HWY
LEWIS CO WA 185-A5
PIERCE CO WA 185-A5
NATIONAL PARK HWY Rt#-62
KLAMATH CO OR 227-B4
NATIONAL PARK HWY U.S.-12
LEWIS CO WA 118-B2
MORTON WA 118-B2
NAVAL AV
BREMERTON WA 270-G10
NAVARRE ST
CHELAN WA 236-D3
NAVARRE COULEE RD Rt#-971
CHELAN CO WA 236-B3
NEACOXIE DR
GEARHART OR 301-G5
NEAH BAY RD
CLALLAM CO WA 100-B2
Neah Bay WA 100-B2
NEAH BAY RD Rt#-112
CLALLAM CO WA 100-B2
Neah Bay WA 100-B2
NEAL LN
DOUGLAS CO OR 225-C1
NEAL CREEK RD
HOOD RIVER CO OR 195-C7
NEALEY RD
OKANOGAN CO WA 105-A1
NEATHAMMER GULCH RD
JACKSON CO OR 230-A3
NEAVES RD
PITT MEADOWS BC 157-C5
NEBRASKA ST
SKAGIT CO WA 259-J14
NECANICUM DR
SEASIDE OR 301-G8
NECANICUM HWY Rt#-53
CLATSOP CO OR 188-D7
CLATSOP CO OR 191-C3
TILLAMOOK CO OR 191-C3
NECK RD
YAMHILL CO OR 198-C7
NEEDLE CREEK RD
JACKSON CO OR 226-C5
NEEDLE RIDGE RD
JACKSON CO OR 226-C5
NEEDLE ROCK RD
JACKSON CO OR 226-B5
S NEEDY RD
CLACKAMAS CO OR 205-D1
NEER CITY RD
COLUMBIA CO OR 189-C4
NEER CITY CEMETERY RD
COLUMBIA CO OR 189-C5
NEERGAARD RD
ADAMS CO WA 113-B3
NEFF RD
BEND OR 217-C2
DESCHUTES CO OR 217-C2
JEFFERSON CO OR 208-C3
NE NEFF RD
BEND OR 217-C2
BEND OR 332-H6
NEGUS WY
DESCHUTES CO OR 212-D5
NEHALEM DR
CLATSOP CO OR 191-D1
NEHALEM HWY Rt#-47
COLUMBIA CO OR 117-B3
COLUMBIA CO OR 125-B1
WASHINGTON CO OR 125-B1
NEHALEM HWY Rt#-202
CLATSOP CO OR 117-B3
CLATSOP CO OR 188-D3
CLATSOP CO OR 300-F8
COLUMBIA CO OR 117-B3
NEHALEM RD
TILLAMOOK CO OR 191-A4
NEHALEM ST
CLATSKANIE OR 117-B3
NEHALEM QUARRY RD
TILLAMOOK CO OR 191-B3
E NEIDER AV
COEUR D'ALENE ID 355-E7
NEILL RD
WASHINGTON CO OR 198-D5
NEILSEN RD
WHATCOM CO WA 158-C6
E NELSON RD
KOOTENAI CO ID 245-B5
NELLITA RD NW
KITSAP CO WA 173-C2
NELS NELSON RD NW
DOUGLAS CO WA 236-B6
KITSAP CO WA 174-B1
KITSAP CO WA 270-F1
NELS NELSON RD NW
Silverdale WA 174-B1
NELSON AV
DISTRICT OF BURNABY BC 156-C5
NELSON LP
KOOTENAI CO ID 247-C1
NELSON RD
DESCHUTES CO OR 217-D2
DOUGLAS CO OR 219-B1
LEWIS CO WA 187-B2
WALLA WALLA CO WA 121-B3
WASHINGTON CO OR 198-A1
E NELSON RD
GRANT CO WA 242-D3
SE NELSON RD
KITSAP CO WA 174-C6
NELSON ST
TOWN OF ESQUIMALT BC 256-B8
VANCOUVER BC 254-E9
NELSON SIDING RD
KITTITAS CO WA 111-B3
NEPPEL RD
GRANT CO WA 242-B1
NESIKA RD
CURRY CO OR 228-A4
NESS RD
KOOTENAI CO ID 247-C7
NESS RD Rt#-116
Hadlock-Irondale WA 170-A1
JEFFERSON CO WA 170-A1
NESS CORNER RD Rt#-116
Hadlock-Irondale WA 170-A1
NESTUCCA RIVER RD
TILLAMOOK CO OR 125-B2
YAMHILL CO OR 125-B2
NW NESTUCCA RIVER RD
YAMHILL CO OR 125-B2
NETARTS HWY
TILLAMOOK OR 197-B2
TILLAMOOK CO OR 197-A2
NETARTS BAY DR
TILLAMOOK CO OR 197-A2
N NETTLETON ST
SPOKANE WA 348-F5
NEUGERBAUER RD
WASHINGTON CO OR 198-D4
NEVADA AV
KLAMATH FALLS OR 338-B5
W NEVADA AV Rt#-903
ROSLYN WA 240-A1
N NEVADA DR
COWLITZ CO WA 302-J5
COWLITZ CO WA 303-A5
E NEVADA ST
ASHLAND OR 337-D5
N NEVADA ST
SPOKANE WA 347-B11
SPOKANE WA 349-B4
SPOKANE CO WA 347-B12
W NEVADA ST
ASHLAND OR 337-C5
NEVADA STATE ROUTE Rt#-140
HARNEY CO OR 153-A3
HUMBOLDT CO NV 153-C3
NEVADA STATE ROUTE Rt#-292
HUMBOLDT CO NV 153-C3
NEVIL RD
LEWIS CO WA 187-C3
NEVILLE LN
JACKSON CO OR 234-A2
NEVIN RD
DISTRICT OF CHILLIWACK BC 94-C3
E NEWARK AV
SPOKANE WA 349-C10
NEWBERG HWY Rt#-214
WOODBURN OR 205-B1
NEWBERG HWY Rt#-219
MARION CO OR 205-B1
WASHINGTON CO OR 198-D2
WOODBURN OR 205-B1
NEWBERG RD
TILLAMOOK CO OR 197-B5
NW NEWBERRY RD
MULTNOMAH CO OR 192-B6
PORTLAND OR 192-B6
NEWBERRY CRATER RD
DESCHUTES CO OR 143-A1
NW NEWBERRY HILL RD
KITSAP CO WA 174-A2
Silverdale WA 270-A1
NEW BRIDGE RD
BAKER CO OR 139-A1
NE NEW BROOKLYN RD
KITSAP CO WA 174-C1
NEWBURY RD
GRAYS HARBOR CO WA 178-A2
SE NEWCASTLE COAL CREEK RD
NEWCASTLE WA 175-C3
NEWCOMB RD
DESCHUTES CO OR 212-C6
NEW CREEK RD
MALHEUR CO OR 146-B1
S NEW ERA RD
CLACKAMAS CO OR 199-C6
NEW HOPE RD
JOSEPHINE CO OR 149-A2
JOSEPHINE CO OR 229-B7
JOSEPHINE CO OR 335-C14
NEW JONES RD
JACKSON CO OR 230-C4
S NEW KIRCHNER RD
CLACKAMAS CO OR 199-D7
NEW LAKE RD
COOS CO OR 224-B2
NEWLAND RD
CLACKAMAS CO OR 199-C5
JACKSON CO OR 230-C6
NEWMAN RD
ISLAND CO WA 170-D1
S NEWMAN RD
CLACKAMAS CO OR 205-C2
NEWMAN CREEK RD
GRAYS HARBOR CO WA 179-B7
N NEWMAN LAKE DR
SPOKANE CO WA 247-B1
SPOKANE CO WA 352-E1

W NEWMAN LAKE DR STREET INDEX NFD RD 2066 385

Thomas Bros. Maps® COPYRIGHT 1999

STREET City State Page-Grid

W NEWMAN LAKE DR
SPOKANE CO WA 247-B1
SPOKANE CO WA 352-D1
NEWMARK AV
COOS BAY OR 333-B6
NORTH BEND OR 333-D7
NEWMARK ST
NORTH BEND OR 333-F6
NEW OMAK LAKE RD
OKANOGAN CO WA 104-C3
NEW PINE RD
MODOC CO CA 152-A3
NEWPORT AV
COOS CO OR 220-D1
COOS CO OR 333-J12
DISTRICT OF OAK BAY BC 257-D9
NEWPORT AV U.S.-101
COOS BAY OR 333-J12
COOS CO OR 333-J12
NW NEWPORT AV
BEND OR 332-D6
N NEWPORT HWY U.S.-2
Fairwood WA 347-B9
SPOKANE CO WA 347-E5
SE NEWPORT WY
BELLEVUE WA 175-D3
NEWPORT WY NW
ISSAQUAH WA 175-D4
ISSAQUAH WA 176-A4
NEWSKAH RD
GRAYS HARBOR CO WA 183-D1
NEWSOME CREEK RD
CROOK CO OR 136-A3
NEWTON RD
STEVENS CO WA 106-B3
NEWTON ST
CITY OF VICTORIA BC 257-B7
DISTRICT OF SAANICH BC 257-B7
NE NEWTON CREEK RD
DOUGLAS CO OR 334-H2
ROSEBURG OR 334-G3
NEWTON HILL RD
LINCOLN CO OR 206-B3
NEZ PERCE AV
WINCHESTER ID 123-B2
WINCHESTER ID 123-B2
W NEZ PERCE RD
COEUR D'ALENE ID 354-J6
COEUR D'ALENE ID 355-A6
NEZPERCE-CRAIGMONT RD
LEWIS CO ID 123-B2
LEWIS CO ID 123-B2
NFD RD 2
ADAMS CO ID 131-B3
NFD RD 9
SHOSHONE CO ID 115-C1
SHOSHONE CO ID 115-C1
WASHINGTON CO ID 139-A1
NFD RD 10
CLACKAMAS CO OR 201-A3
GRANT CO OR 129-B3
GRANT CO OR 137-B1
MULTNOMAH CO OR 201-B2
NFD RD 11
JOSEPHINE CO OR 233-A5
NFD RD 12
CLACKAMAS CO OR 201-A3
JEFFERSON CO OR 134-C1
JEFFERSON CO OR 211-B2
LEWIS CO WA 185-A6
MULTNOMAH CO OR 201-B2
TILLAMOOK CO OR 203-C3
NFD RD 13
BAKER CO OR 137-C2
GRANT CO OR 137-C2
HOOD RIVER CO OR 201-D2
HOOD RIVER CO OR 202-A1
NFD RD 14
CLACKAMAS CO OR 201-A3
GRANT CO OR 137-C3
LEWIS CO WA 185-A7
TILLAMOOK CO OR 197-C6
YAMHILL CO OR 197-D7
NFD RD 15
GRANT CO OR 137-B3
JOSEPHINE CO OR 233-B7
TILLAMOOK CO OR 203-C2
NFD RD 16
BAKER CO OR 138-A2
GRANT CO OR 137-C2
GRANT CO OR 138-A2
HOOD RIVER CO OR 202-A2
JOSEPHINE CO OR 233-A1
NFD RD 17
HOOD RIVER CO OR 202-C3
JOSEPHINE CO OR 233-C7
LINCOLN CO OR 203-C4
NFD RD 18
LAKE CO OR 143-B1
NFD RD 19
LINCOLN CO OR 203-B6
NFD RD 20
CURRY CO OR 224-B7
MULTNOMAH CO OR 201-A1
NFD RD 21
GRANT CO OR 137-A2
LANE CO OR 142-A1
MORROW CO OR 128-C3
UMATILLA CO OR 129-C3
UNION CO OR 129-C2
NFD RD 22
BONNER CO ID 244-A7
KLAMATH CO OR 143-A1
LAKE CO OR 143-A1
LANE CO OR 142-A1
NFD RD 23
CURRY CO OR 148-C1
DOUGLAS CO OR 214-C6
LANE CO OR 142-B1
LEWIS CO WA 118-C2
MASON CO WA 109-B2
SKAMANIA CO WA 119-A3
NFD RD 24
GRANT CO OR 136-C2
GRANT CO OR 137-A2
LAKE CO OR 143-A1
LANE CO OR 142-B1
MASON CO WA 109-B2
MASON CO WA 173-A4
NFD RD 25
LANE CO OR 209-C6
LEWIS CO WA 118-C2
MASON CO WA 173-A2
SKAMANIA CO WA 118-C2
SKAMANIA CO WA 190-D3
WASHINGTON CO ID 139-A1
WHEELER CO OR 128-B3
NFD RD 28
GRANT CO OR 137-B3
NFD RD 29
CLALLAM CO WA 163-C7
NFD RD 30
CLALLAM CO WA 163-C6
CLALLAM CO WA 164-A5
COWLITZ CO WA 190-A3
DESCHUTES CO OR 217-C5
NFD RD 31
GRANT CO OR 137-A3
UMATILLA CO OR 130-A1
WASHINGTON CO ID 139-B1
NFD RD 32
LANE CO OR 209-D6
OKANOGAN CO WA 105-A1
UMATILLA CO OR 130-A1
NFD RD 33
CURRY CO OR 148-B1
KLAMATH CO OR 231-B1
NFD RD 34
DOUGLAS CO OR 222-D2
DOUGLAS CO OR 223-A2
NFD RD 35
DOUGLAS CO OR 222-D4
KITTITAS CO WA 238-B7
NFD RD 36
GRANT CO OR 137-B1
NFD RD 37
GRANT CO OR 137-A3
NFD RD 38
LANE CO OR 142-A1
OKANOGAN CO WA 104-B2
NFD RD 40
GARFIELD CO WA 122-B2
NFD RD 41
JOSEPHINE CO OR 233-D7
NFD RD 42
JOSEPHINE CO OR 233-C5
SKAMANIA CO WA 194-A2
NFD RD 43
KLAMATH CO OR 142-C3
SKAMANIA CO WA 194-B3
NFD RD 44
HOOD RIVER CO OR 202-C4
LEWIS CO WA 185-D6
NFD RD 46
KLAMATH CO OR 151-A1
LEWIS CO WA 185-D7
MARION CO OR 126-C3
MARION CO OR 134-C1
NFD RD 48
HOOD RIVER CO OR 202-B6
LANE CO OR 214-D4
WASCO CO OR 127-A3
WASCO CO OR 202-C7
NFD RD 48N
KLAMATH CO OR 151-B3
LAKE CO OR 151-B3
MODOC CO CA 151-B3
NFD RD 49
KLAMATH CO OR 143-A3
NFD RD 50
KING CO WA 176-D7
LINCOLN CO OR 206-C7
SHOSHONE CO ID 115-B2
SHOSHONE CO ID 115-B2
NFD RD 51
GRANT CO OR 129-C3
UNION CO OR 129-C3
NFD RD 52
GRANT CO OR 129-C3
JEFFERSON CO OR 211-C2
LANE CO OR 209-A7
LINCOLN CO OR 206-D7
UMATILLA CO OR 129-B3
NFD RD 53
MORROW CO OR 129-A3
SKAMANIA CO WA 193-D2
UMATILLA CO OR 129-A3
NFD RD 54
LANE CO OR 209-C4
SKAMANIA CO WA 190-B7
SKAMANIA CO WA 193-D1
SKAMANIA CO WA 194-A1
NFD RD 55
WASHINGTON CO ID 131-B3
NFD RD 58
CROOK CO OR 136-C2
GRANT CO OR 136-C2
LANE CO OR 209-C5
SKAMANIA CO WA 194-A1
NFD RD 59
DOUGLAS CO OR 214-B6
NFD RD 60
DOUGLAS CO OR 223-D2
KLAMATH CO OR 142-B1
NFD RD 62
UNION CO OR 130-B1
NFD RD 63
UNION CO OR 130-A1
NFD RD 64
SKAMANIA CO WA 190-D6
UNION CO OR 130-A1
NFD RD 65
CHELAN CO WA 111-B1
SKAMANIA CO WA 194-D1
NFD RD 67
JOSEPHINE CO OR 233-A1
NFD RD 68
SKAMANIA CO WA 195-A3
NFD RD 70
CURRY CO OR 232-C1
NFD RD 73
GRANT CO OR 129-C3
GRANT CO OR 130-A3
GRANITE OR 137-C1
GRANT CO OR 137-C1
UNION CO OR 130-A3
NFD RD 75
DOUGLAS CO OR 222-D4
NFD RD 77
BAKER CO OR 130-C3
NFD RD 80
GRAYS HARBOR CO WA 109-A2
JOSEPHINE CO OR 233-D6
NFD RD 81
COWLITZ CO WA 190-A3
SKAMANIA CO WA 190-B3
NFD RD 83
HUMBOLDT CO NV 154-C3
HUMBOLDT CO NV 155-A3
SKAMANIA CO WA 190-D2
NFD RD 84
HUMBOLDT CO NV 154-C3
LEWIS CO WA 185-A6
LINCOLN CO OR 203-C7
NFD RD 85
JOSEPHINE CO OR 233-C7
TILLAMOOK CO OR 197-D6
TILLAMOOK CO OR 125-A2
NFD RD 87
HUMBOLDT CO NV 154-C3
NFD RD 89
ADAMS CO ID 131-C3
NFD RD 90
SKAMANIA CO WA 118-C3
SKAMANIA CO WA 190-D5
NFD RD 92 Rt#-508
LINCOLN CO MT 107-C1
NFD RD 94
SKAMANIA CO WA 190-D1
NFD RD 96
HUMBOLDT CO NV 154-C3
HUMBOLDT CO NV 155-A3
NFD RD 98
JOSEPHINE CO OR 233-D7
NFD RD 99
SKAMANIA CO WA 190-C1
NFD RD 100
DESCHUTES CO OR 211-D6
DOUGLAS CO OR 222-B1
OKANOGAN CO WA 105-B2
NFD RD 105
ADAMS CO ID 131-B3
NFD RD 110
CURRY CO OR 228-D1
KLAMATH CO OR 231-A2
NFD RD 111
KITTITAS CO WA 241-B1
NFD RD 112
CHELAN CO WA 111-C2
KITTITAS CO WA 241-A2
TILLAMOOK CO OR 125-A2
NFD RD 113
KITTITAS CO WA 241-B1
NFD RD 114
KITTITAS CO WA 241-A1
NFD RD 115
KITTITAS CO WA 238-A7
KITTITAS CO WA 241-B2
NFD RD 116
KITTITAS CO WA 238-A6
KITTITAS CO WA 241-B2
VALLEY CO ID 252-C4
NFD RD 118
KITTITAS CO WA 238-A7
NFD RD 128
ADAMS CO ID 131-B3
NFD RD 129
LINCOLN CO OR 203-B4
NFD RD 130
CURRY CO OR 232-D2
JEFFERSON CO OR 211-C2
NFD RD 134
LEWIS CO WA 185-A7
NFD RD 150
CURRY CO OR 228-B1
GRANT CO OR 129-A3
LANE CO OR 211-A6
NFD RD 151
SHOSHONE CO ID 115-C1
SHOSHONE CO ID 115-C1
NFD RD 160
DESCHUTES CO OR 211-C4
DESCHUTES CO OR 216-D6
NFD RD 165
ADAMS CO ID 139-C1
ADAMS CO ID 252-A1
NFD RD 172
ADAMS CO ID 251-A7
NFD RD 181
ADAMS CO ID 251-A7
NFD RD 183
ADAMS CO ID 251-A7
ADAMS CO ID 252-A1
NFD RD 186
ADAMS CO ID 252-B2
VALLEY CO ID 252-C1
NFD RD 199
ADAMS CO ID 252-A2
NFD RD 200
ADAMS CO ID 252-A2
CHELAN CO WA 238-B3
DESCHUTES CO OR 217-A5
DOUGLAS CO OR 222-B2
JEFFERSON CO OR 211-B1
OKANOGAN CO WA 105-B2
NFD RD 201
CLACKAMAS CO OR 201-A3
NFD RD 203
SKAMANIA CO WA 190-D7
NFD RD 206
ADAMS CO ID 252-B4
KOOTENAI CO ID 245-C4
NFD RD 207
SKAMANIA CO WA 190-D6
NFD RD 208
SHOSHONE CO ID 115-C1
SHOSHONE CO ID 115-C1
NFD RD 209
KOOTENAI CO ID 245-C2
NFD RD 213
KITTITAS CO WA 241-B1
NFD RD 214
ADAMS CO ID 252-A4
NFD RD 217
ADAMS CO ID 252-A4
NFD RD 218
ADAMS CO ID 252-C2
NFD RD 230
CURRY CO OR 232-D1
DESCHUTES CO OR 217-D5
KLAMATH CO OR 231-A2
NFD RD 231
BOUNDARY CO ID 107-A2
NFD RD 243
ADAMS CO ID 252-B5
NFD RD 250
DESCHUTES CO OR 217-D7
NFD RD 255
CLACKAMAS CO OR 201-A6
NFD RD 258
KOOTENAI CO ID 245-D3
NFD RD 268
KOOTENAI CO ID 245-B6
NFD RD 270
SKAMANIA CO WA 190-D2
NFD RD 278
BONNER CO ID 244-D5
BONNER CO ID 245-D1
KOOTENAI CO ID 245-D2
NFD RD 280
JEFFERSON CO OR 211-B1
NFD RD 281
DOUGLAS CO OR 223-A7
NFD RD 288
KLAMATH CO OR 143-B3
KLAMATH CO OR 151-B1
LAKE CO OR 143-B3
NFD RD 291
BOUNDARY CO ID 107-B2
NFD RD 294
BOUNDARY CO ID 107-B2
NFD RD 300
DESCHUTES CO OR 217-A3
NFD RD 301
SHOSHONE CO ID 115-C3
SHOSHONE CO ID 115-C3
NFD RD 302
BONNER CO ID 106-C2
NFD RD 306
SHOSHONE CO ID 244-D7
NFD RD 317
SKAMANIA CO WA 190-D7
NFD RD 320
SKAMANIA CO WA 190-C7
NFD RD 331
KLAMATH CO OR 151-B1
NFD RD 332
BONNER CO ID 244-C7
BONNER CO ID 245-D2
SHOSHONE CO ID 244-D6
NFD RD 348
KLAMATH CO OR 151-B1
LAKE CO OR 151-C1
NFD RD 350
KLAMATH CO OR 231-A4
NFD RD 360
KLAMATH CO OR 231-A4
NFD RD 370
DESCHUTES CO OR 216-C1
NFD RD 375
KLAMATH CO OR 151-B2
NFD RD 380
SKAMANIA CO WA 190-D2
NFD RD 381
KLAMATH CO OR 151-B2
NFD RD 382
CLACKAMAS CO OR 201-D4
NFD RD 392
KOOTENAI CO ID 245-C4
NFD RD 400
CHELAN CO WA 238-A2
DESCHUTES CO OR 211-C5
DESCHUTES CO OR 216-D5
JEFFERSON CO OR 211-B1
SHOSHONE CO ID 115-C1
SHOSHONE CO ID 115-C1
NFD RD 406
KOOTENAI CO ID 245-C3
NFD RD 410
CLACKAMAS CO OR 201-A3
NFD RD 411
KOOTENAI CO ID 245-D5
NFD RD 413
KOOTENAI CO ID 245-D7
SKAMANIA CO WA 194-B2
NFD RD 422
VALLEY CO ID 252-D7
NFD RD 434
KOOTENAI CO ID 245-D6
NFD RD 435
VALLEY CO ID 252-C5
NFD RD 437
KOOTENAI CO ID 245-C4
NFD RD 438
KOOTENAI CO ID 248-C2
NFD RD 450
DESCHUTES CO OR 216-A3
NFD RD 454
ADAMS CO ID 131-A3
NFD RD 456
SHOSHONE CO ID 115-C2
SHOSHONE CO ID 115-C2
NFD RD 471
HUMBOLDT CO NV 154-C3
NFD RD 472
JOSEPHINE CO OR 233-D6
NFD RD 480
LANE CO OR 142-A1
NFD RD 487
ADAMS CO ID 251-B7
ADAMS CO ID 252-B1
NFD RD 489
BONNER CO ID 244-D2
NFD RD 500
DOUGLAS CO OR 222-B2
NFD RD 503
SHOSHONE CO ID 115-C1
SHOSHONE CO ID 115-C1
NFD RD 508 Rt#-508
LINCOLN CO MT 107-C2
NFD RD 510
CHELAN CO WA 238-A2
NFD RD 527
SKAMANIA CO WA 194-A1
NFD RD 529
HUMBOLDT CO NV 154-C3
NFD RD 531
HUMBOLDT CO NV 154-C3
NFD RD 587
ADAMS CO ID 251-A5
NFD RD 600
DESCHUTES CO OR 211-C7
DESCHUTES CO OR 217-C4
JEFFERSON CO OR 211-B2
NFD RD 610
KOOTENAI CO ID 245-D5
NFD RD 612
KOOTENAI CO ID 245-C5
NFD RD 616
KOOTENAI CO ID 245-D5
NFD RD 618
GEM CO ID 252-B7
NFD RD 625
GEM CO ID 252-B7
KOOTENAI CO ID 245-B4
NFD RD 700
DOUGLAS CO OR 223-C2
LINN CO OR 134-A2
SKAMANIA CO WA 190-D3
NFD RD 719
LANE CO OR 214-C2
NFD RD 760
DOUGLAS CO OR 223-C7
NFD RD 794
KOOTENAI CO ID 245-D3
NFD RD 800
DESCHUTES CO OR 211-B3
NFD RD 808
KOOTENAI CO ID 248-B3
NFD RD 810
KOOTENAI CO ID 248-C2
SKAMANIA CO WA 190-D3
NFD RD 831
LANE CO OR 214-D3
NFD RD 835
ADAMS CO ID 252-B5
NFD RD 855
KLAMATH CO OR 142-C1
NFD RD 950
DOUGLAS CO OR 222-C6
DOUGLAS CO OR 226-B3
NFD RD 953
LANE CO OR 214-B4
NFD RD 958
LANE CO OR 214-D4
NFD RD 980
KLAMATH CO OR 231-A4
NFD RD 1000
LINCOLN CO OR 206-D7
NFD RD 1008
MULTNOMAH CO OR 201-A2
NFD RD 1010
MULTNOMAH CO OR 201-A2
NFD RD 1012
DESCHUTES CO OR 211-C4
NFD RD 1013
BOUNDARY CO ID 106-C1
NFD RD 1014
LINCOLN CO OR 206-D7
NFD RD 1017
BONNER CO ID 245-D2
NFD RD 1018
DESCHUTES CO OR 211-B6
NFD RD 1024
DESCHUTES CO OR 211-B6
NFD RD 1026
DESCHUTES CO OR 211-B6
NFD RD 1027
CLACKAMAS CO OR 201-C3
NFD RD 1028
DESCHUTES CO OR 211-B4
NFD RD 1030
LINCOLN CO OR 206-D7
NFD RD 1031
TILLAMOOK CO OR 203-B1
NFD RD 1050
BONNER CO ID 244-B7
NFD RD 1066
BONNER CO ID 244-D6
NFD RD 1080
BONNER CO ID 245-D2
NFD RD 1088
BONNER CO ID 244-C6
NFD RD 1101
CURRY CO OR 232-D7
NFD RD 1110
JEFFERSON CO OR 211-C2
NFD RD 1176
JEFFERSON CO OR 208-C5
NFD RD 1179
JEFFERSON CO OR 212-A2
NFD RD 1207
YAKIMA CO WA 119-A2
NFD RD 1210
CLACKAMAS CO OR 201-B3
NFD RD 1217
CLACKAMAS CO OR 201-C2
MULTNOMAH CO OR 201-C2
NFD RD 1228
CLACKAMAS CO OR 201-C4
NFD RD 1268
TILLAMOOK CO OR 203-B2
NFD RD 1270
LEWIS CO WA 185-D7
NFD RD 1280
TILLAMOOK CO OR 203-C2
NFD RD 1310
HOOD RIVER CO OR 202-A1
NFD RD 1340
HOOD RIVER CO OR 202-A2
NFD RD 1341
BONNER CO ID 107-A1
NFD RD 1376
CURRY CO OR 148-B2
NFD RD 1393
JEFFERSON CO OR 212-B3
NFD RD 1394
JEFFERSON CO OR 213-A2
NFD RD 1395
JEFFERSON CO OR 213-A2
NFD RD 1399
JEFFERSON CO OR 212-B1
NFD RD 1414
CLACKAMAS CO OR 201-B3
NFD RD 1425
JEFFERSON CO OR 211-C1
NFD RD 1432
TILLAMOOK CO OR 197-C7
NFD RD 1441
CHELAN CO WA 103-C3
NFD RD 1491
TILLAMOOK CO OR 197-C7
NFD RD 1509
MULTNOMAH CO OR 201-A2
NFD RD 1510
DESCHUTES CO OR 211-C5
NFD RD 1514
DESCHUTES CO OR 211-C6
NFD RD 1516
DESCHUTES CO OR 211-C7
NFD RD 1520
DESCHUTES CO OR 211-C5
NFD RD 1522
DESCHUTES CO OR 211-C6
NFD RD 1526
DESCHUTES CO OR 211-C7
NFD RD 1587
KOOTENAI CO ID 245-C4
NFD RD 1590
TILLAMOOK CO OR 197-B7
NFD RD 1594
KOOTENAI CO ID 245-D4
NFD RD 1608
DESCHUTES CO OR 211-D6
NFD RD 1610
DESCHUTES CO OR 211-D7
HOOD RIVER CO OR 202-B2
NFD RD 1611
HOOD RIVER CO OR 202-B2
NFD RD 1614
IDAHO CO ID 131-C2
NFD RD 1620
DESCHUTES CO OR 211-C7
NFD RD 1628
DESCHUTES CO OR 211-C7
DESCHUTES CO OR 216-C1
NFD RD 1631
HOOD RIVER CO OR 202-B3
NFD RD 1633
TILLAMOOK CO OR 203-C2
NFD RD 1640
HOOD RIVER CO OR 202-A2
NFD RD 1650
HOOD RIVER CO OR 202-A3
TILLAMOOK CO OR 203-C2
NFD RD 1660
HOOD RIVER CO OR 202-A3
NFD RD 1670
HOOD RIVER CO OR 202-A3
NFD RD 1686
TILLAMOOK CO OR 203-D2
NFD RD 1700
MASON CO WA 179-B2
NFD RD 1701
LINCOLN CO OR 203-C5
YAKIMA CO WA 240-B7
NFD RD 1703
KITTITAS CO WA 240-A7
NFD RD 1708
KITTITAS CO WA 240-A6
NFD RD 1710
HOOD RIVER CO OR 202-D1
NFD RD 1711
HOOD RIVER CO OR 202-D1
NFD RD 1720
HOOD RIVER CO OR 202-D3
KITTITAS CO WA 240-B7
NFD RD 1721
KITTITAS CO WA 240-A7
NFD RD 1726
LINCOLN CO OR 203-B4
NFD RD 1770
LINCOLN CO OR 203-C6
NFD RD 1783
LINCOLN CO OR 203-B5
NFD RD 1800
YAKIMA CO WA 119-B1
NFD RD 1810
DESCHUTES CO OR 217-C7
HOOD RIVER CO OR 202-A3
NFD RD 1814
DESCHUTES CO OR 217-C5
NFD RD 1815
DESCHUTES CO OR 217-C4
NFD RD 1818
DESCHUTES CO OR 217-D7
NFD RD 1819
DESCHUTES CO OR 217-D5
NFD RD 1820
DESCHUTES CO OR 217-D6
NFD RD 1825
CLACKAMAS CO OR 201-D4
DESCHUTES CO OR 217-D6
NFD RD 1828
CLACKAMAS CO OR 201-D4
NFD RD 1846
CURRY CO OR 232-D2
NFD RD 1888
LINCOLN CO OR 203-C3
Rose Lodge OR 203-C3
NFD RD 1928
LINCOLN CO OR 203-B6
NFD RD 1929
LINCOLN CO OR 203-B6
NFD RD 1956
LINCOLN CO OR 203-B6
NFD RD 1980
LINCOLN CO OR 203-C6
NFD RD 2022
LINN CO OR 134-A2
NFD RD 2025
JACKSON CO OR 234-A7
NFD RD 2026
LINN CO OR 134-A2
NFD RD 2040
JACKSON CO OR 234-B5
NFD RD 2050
JEFFERSON CO OR 212-A3
NFD RD 2060
DESCHUTES CO OR 211-B4
JACKSON CO OR 234-C5
NFD RD 2061
DESCHUTES CO OR 211-B3
NFD RD 2066
JEFFERSON CO OR 211-B2

PNW
INDEX

386 NFD RD 2068 STREET INDEX NORTH PRAIRIE RD

STREET City State Page-Grid

NFD RD 2068
JEFFERSON CO OR 211-B3
NFD RD 2076
JEFFERSON CO OR 211-A3
NFD RD 2134
DOUGLAS CO OR 223-A1
LANE CO OR 142-A1
NFD RD 2153
DOUGLAS CO OR 223-C1
GRAYS HARBOR CO WA 179-A1
NFD RD 2160
LANE CO OR 209-D6
NFD RD 2199
MASON CO WA 179-C1
NFD RD 2207
MARION CO OR 134-A1
NFD RD 2210
YAMHILL CO OR 197-D7
NFD RD 2233
BONNER CO ID 244-B4
NFD RD 2234
YAMHILL CO OR 203-D2
NFD RD 2255
MASON CO WA 179-B1
NFD RD 2260
GRAYS HARBOR CO WA 109-B2
NFD RD 2282
YAMHILL CO OR 203-D1
NFD RD 2283
YAMHILL CO OR 197-D7
NFD RD 2302
GRAYS HARBOR CO WA 109-A2
KOOTENAI CO ID 245-C3
NFD RD 2308
CURRY CO OR 148-C1
NFD RD 2312
GRAYS HARBOR CO WA 109-B2
NFD RD 2320
KOOTENAI CO ID 245-D6
NFD RD 2341
MASON CO WA 179-B1
NFD RD 2399
MASON CO WA 179-B1
NFD RD 2401
MASON CO WA 173-A3
NFD RD 2403
JEFFERSON CO WA 173-B2
NFD RD 2420
MASON CO WA 173-A3
NFD RD 2421
MASON CO WA 173-A2
NFD RD 2464
MASON CO WA 173-A4
NFD RD 2469
MASON CO WA 173-A3
NFD RD 2470
MASON CO WA 173-A3
NFD RD 2472
MASON CO WA 173-B2
NFD RD 2480
LANE CO OR 214-D4
MASON CO WA 173-B3
NFD RD 2510
JEFFERSON CO WA 109-C1
JEFFERSON CO WA 173-B1
NFD RD 2512
BONNER CO ID 107-A2
NFD RD 2515
JEFFERSON CO WA 173-C1
NFD RD 2516
KLAMATH CO OR 143-A2
LAKE CO OR 143-A2
NFD RD 2524
JEFFERSON CO WA 173-B2
NFD RD 2530
JEFFERSON CO WA 173-B1
NFD RD 2540
JEFFERSON CO WA 173-B1
NFD RD 2546
JEFFERSON CO WA 173-B1
NFD RD 2550
BONNER CO ID 107-A3
NFD RD 2560
SKAMANIA CO WA 190-D1
NFD RD 2586
SKAMANIA CO WA 190-D3
NFD RD 2588
SKAMANIA CO WA 190-D3
NFD RD 2605
BOUNDARY CO ID 107-A2
NFD RD 2610
LANE CO OR 214-C2
NFD RD 2612
CLACKAMAS CO OR 201-C6
NFD RD 2618
CLACKAMAS CO OR 201-C6
NFD RD 2652
BONNER CO ID 245-A1
NFD RD 2654
LINN CO OR 134-B2
NFD RD 2720
WASCO CO OR 202-D5
NFD RD 2820
HOOD RIVER CO OR 195-A6
NFD RD 2823
LAKE CO OR 143-B3
LAKE CO OR 151-C1
NFD RD 2840
HOOD RIVER CO OR 202-B3
NFD RD 2902
CLALLAM CO WA 163-B7
CLALLAM CO WA 169-D1
NFD RD 2903
CLALLAM CO WA 163-B7
NFD RD 2918
CLALLAM CO WA 109-A1
NFD RD 2922
CLALLAM CO WA 163-C7
NFD RD 2923
CLALLAM CO WA 163-C7
NFD RD 2924
CLALLAM CO WA 169-D1
NFD RD 2929
CLALLAM CO WA 163-D7
NFD RD 2933
CLALLAM CO WA 163-A7
NFD RD 2937
CLALLAM CO WA 163-B7
NFD RD 2938
CLALLAM CO WA 163-B7
NFD RD 2946
CLALLAM CO WA 164-A7
NFD RD 2978
CLALLAM CO WA 163-D7
NFD RD 3006
CLALLAM CO WA 163-B5
NFD RD 3007
CLALLAM CO WA 163-B6
NFD RD 3010
OKANOGAN CO WA 105-A2
NFD RD 3027
KOOTENAI CO ID 245-D5
NFD RD 3028
CLALLAM CO WA 163-D5
NFD RD 3029
CLALLAM CO WA 163-D5
NFD RD 3030
CLALLAM CO WA 165-A7
NFD RD 3031
CLALLAM CO WA 163-C5
NFD RD 3040
CLALLAM CO WA 163-C6
CLALLAM CO WA 164-A6
NFD RD 3041
CLALLAM CO WA 163-C6
NFD RD 3062
SKAMANIA CO WA 194-C1
NFD RD 3067
CLALLAM CO WA 163-D6
NFD RD 3068
CLALLAM CO WA 164-A6
NFD RD 3069
CLALLAM CO WA 163-D6
NFD RD 3080
SKAMANIA CO WA 194-C2
NFD RD 3105
SKAMANIA CO WA 190-D6
NFD RD 3116
CLALLAM CO WA 163-B5
NFD RD 3117
CLALLAM CO WA 163-B5
NFD RD 3120
LINCOLN CO OR 206-D6
NFD RD 3142
LAKE CO OR 143-B3
NFD RD 3230
DOUGLAS CO OR 141-C3
NFD RD 3310
CURRY CO OR 228-D1
NFD RD 3312
KLAMATH CO OR 151-B1
NFD RD 3313
CURRY CO OR 228-C5
NFD RD 3334
KLAMATH CO OR 231-A1
NFD RD 3340
CURRY CO OR 228-D3
NFD RD 3348
COOS CO OR 140-C3
NFD RD 3384
KLAMATH CO OR 231-A1
NFD RD 3402
CURRY CO OR 228-B1
NFD RD 3413
KLAMATH CO OR 231-A2
NFD RD 3414
KLAMATH CO OR 231-A2
NFD RD 3419
KLAMATH CO OR 231-A4
NFD RD 3449
KLAMATH CO OR 231-A2
NFD RD 3450
KLAMATH CO OR 231-A3
NFD RD 3454
KLAMATH CO OR 231-A6
NFD RD 3455
KLAMATH CO OR 231-A5
NFD RD 3484
KLAMATH CO OR 231-A3
NFD RD 3506
KITTITAS CO WA 241-A2
NFD RD 3507
KITTITAS CO WA 241-A1
NFD RD 3512
HOOD RIVER CO OR 202-B3
NFD RD 3517
KITTITAS CO WA 241-B2
NFD RD 3521
KITTITAS CO WA 241-B1
NFD RD 3530
KITTITAS CO WA 238-B7
NFD RD 3533
CURRY CO OR 228-C4
NFD RD 3540
HOOD RIVER CO OR 202-C6
NFD RD 3550
HOOD RIVER CO OR 202-C6
NFD RD 3610
KLAMATH CO OR 231-A7
NFD RD 3640
GRANT CO OR 137-B1
NFD RD 3660
GRANT CO OR 137-B1
NFD RD 3670
GRANT CO OR 137-B1
NFD RD 3680
CURRY CO OR 228-B6
NFD RD 3817
DOUGLAS CO OR 222-B1
NFD RD 4000
DESCHUTES CO OR 217-A6
NFD RD 4017
LAKE CO OR 151-C3
NFD RD 4050
JACKSON CO OR 234-C7
NFD RD 4104
SKAMANIA CO WA 193-D3
NFD RD 4105
JOSEPHINE CO OR 233-A1
NFD RD 4109
SKAMANIA CO WA 193-D3
NFD RD 4130
DESCHUTES CO OR 217-A4
NFD RD 4180
DESCHUTES CO OR 216-D5
NFD RD 4201
JOSEPHINE CO OR 233-A2
NFD RD 4211
SKAMANIA CO WA 193-D2
NFD RD 4220
DESCHUTES CO OR 216-D6
NFD RD 4235
CROOK CO OR 136-A2
NFD RD 4240
WALLOWA CO OR 131-B2
NFD RD 4260
WALLOWA CO OR 131-B1
NFD RD 4273
DESCHUTES CO OR 142-C1
NFD RD 4305
UNION CO OR 129-C3
NFD RD 4306
SKAMANIA CO WA 194-B2
NFD RD 4410
HOOD RIVER CO OR 202-C4
NFD RD 4420
HOOD RIVER CO OR 202-D5
NFD RD 4430
WASCO CO OR 202-D3
NFD RD 4450
WASCO CO OR 202-D4
NFD RD 4510
LEWIS CO WA 185-D6
NFD RD 4601
DESCHUTES CO OR 216-D3
NFD RD 4609
JOSEPHINE CO OR 233-D4
NFD RD 4610
DESCHUTES CO OR 217-A3
NFD RD 4612
DESCHUTES CO OR 216-D3
JOSEPHINE CO OR 233-D6
LEWIS CO WA 185-D7
NFD RD 4613
CLACKAMAS CO OR 201-A7
DESCHUTES CO OR 216-D4
JOSEPHINE CO OR 233-D5
NFD RD 4614
CLACKAMAS CO OR 200-D7
NFD RD 4615
CLACKAMAS CO OR 201-A7
DESCHUTES CO OR 216-D3
NFD RD 4630
DESCHUTES CO OR 216-A7
NFD RD 4635
DESCHUTES CO OR 216-A7
NFD RD 4650
DESCHUTES CO OR 142-C1
NFD RD 4703
JOSEPHINE CO OR 233-C7
NFD RD 4720
LEWIS CO WA 185-B7
NFD RD 4803
JOSEPHINE CO OR 233-A7
NFD RD 4808
JOSEPHINE CO OR 233-B7
NFD RD 4811
DOUGLAS CO OR 214-D5
HOOD RIVER CO OR 202-C6
WASCO CO OR 202-D7
NFD RD 4814
WASCO CO OR 202-D7
NFD RD 4820
DOUGLAS CO OR 214-D5
WASCO CO OR 202-D7
NFD RD 4830
LANE CO OR 214-C4
NFD RD 4860
HOOD RIVER CO OR 202-C6
NFD RD 4870
WASCO CO OR 202-C7
NFD RD 4880
HOOD RIVER CO OR 202-C6
WASCO CO OR 202-C7
NFD RD 5087
LINCOLN CO OR 206-C7
NFD RD 5125
UNION CO OR 129-C3
UNION CO OR 130-A3
NFD RD 5130
OKANOGAN CO WA 104-A2
NFD RD 5185
BAKER CO OR 130-A3
GRANT CO OR 130-A3
UNION CO OR 130-A3
NFD RD 5210
LEWIS CO WA 185-A6
NFD RD 5215
CHELAN CO WA 238-D1
NFD RD 5260
LEWIS CO WA 185-B7
NFD RD 5270
LEWIS CO WA 185-C6
NFD RD 5300
CHELAN CO WA 236-A4
NFD RD 5400
CURRY CO OR 224-B7
OKANOGAN CO WA 103-C2
NFD RD 5701
SKAMANIA CO WA 190-B7
NFD RD 5842
LANE CO OR 209-A7
LANE CO OR 214-B1
NFD RD 5850
LANE CO OR 142-A1
NFD RD 5875
LANE CO OR 142-A1
NFD RD 5900
CHELAN CO WA 112-A1
NFD RD 6020
KLAMATH CO OR 142-C2
NFD RD 6052
SKAMANIA CO WA 194-D1
NFD RD 6210
KLAMATH CO OR 231-C2
NFD RD 6214
KLAMATH CO OR 231-C1
NFD RD 6231
UNION CO OR 130-B1
NFD RD 6401
SKAMANIA CO WA 190-D7
NFD RD 6403
SKAMANIA CO WA 190-D6
NFD RD 6406
SKAMANIA CO WA 190-D7
NFD RD 6500
CHELAN CO WA 111-B1
NFD RD 6517
SKAMANIA CO WA 194-D3
NFD RD 6728
KOOTENAI CO ID 245-D3
NFD RD 6750
CHELAN CO WA 111-C1
NFD RD 7100
CHELAN CO WA 238-C5
NFD RD 7184 Rt#-410
PIERCE CO WA 111-A3
NFD RD 7200
CHELAN CO WA 238-B3
NFD RD 7202
CHELAN CO WA 238-B3
NFD RD 7300
CHELAN CO WA 238-A2
NFD RD 7320
CHELAN CO WA 238-A5
NFD RD 7324
CHELAN CO WA 238-A5
NFD RD 7400
CHELAN CO WA 238-B1
NFD RD 7412
CHELAN CO WA 238-C1
NFD RD 7413
CHELAN CO WA 238-D1
NFD RD 7600
CHELAN CO WA 111-B2
NFD RD 7601
CHELAN CO WA 111-C2
NFD RD 7755
BAKER CO OR 130-C3
NFD RD 8020
CHELAN CO WA 236-C1
NFD RD 8123
COWLITZ CO WA 190-B3
NFD RD 8170
TILLAMOOK CO OR 197-C5
NFD RD 8171
TILLAMOOK CO OR 197-C4
NFD RD 8172
TILLAMOOK CO OR 197-C5
NFD RD 8208
TILLAMOOK CO OR 197-A5
NFD RD 8303
SKAMANIA CO WA 190-B4
NFD RD 8320
SKAMANIA CO WA 190-D3
NFD RD 8376
TILLAMOOK CO OR 197-D6
NFD RD 8410
CHELAN CO WA 236-A1
LEWIS CO WA 185-A6
NFD RD 8415
LEWIS CO WA 185-A6
NFD RD 8420
LEWIS CO WA 185-A6
NFD RD 8425
LEWIS CO WA 185-A6
NFD RD 8430
LEWIS CO WA 185-A6
NFD RD 8440
LEWIS CO WA 185-A7
NFD RD 8500
CHELAN CO WA 236-A3
NFD RD 8550
CHELAN CO WA 236-B3
NFD RD 8594
TILLAMOOK CO OR 197-D6
NFD RD 9015
SKAMANIA CO WA 190-C4
NFD RD 9403
SKAMANIA CO WA 190-D1
NFD RD 9701
DESCHUTES CO OR 217-C5
NFD RD 9705
KITTITAS CO WA 238-A6
NFD RD 9711
KITTITAS CO WA 238-A6
NFD RD 9712
KITTITAS CO WA 238-A7
NFD RD 9713
KLAMATH CO OR 231-D5
NFD RD 9714
KITTITAS CO WA 238-A6
NFD RD 9715
KITTITAS CO WA 238-A6
KLAMATH CO OR 231-D5
NFD RD 9716
KITTITAS CO WA 238-A6
NFD RD 9717
KLAMATH CO OR 231-D5
NFD RD 9718
KITTITAS CO WA 238-A7
NFD RD 9720
DESCHUTES CO OR 217-A6
NFD RD 9723
DESCHUTES CO OR 217-B6
NFD RD 9724
DESCHUTES CO OR 217-B7
NFD RD 9726
KITTITAS CO WA 241-A1
NFD RD 9730
KLAMATH CO OR 231-D2
NFD RD 9734
KLAMATH CO OR 231-D1
NFD RD 9938
JOSEPHINE CO OR 233-A7
NFD RD 91013
SKAMANIA CO WA 190-C4
NFH 50
BENEWAH CO ID 115-B2
BENEWAH CO ID 115-B2
NF HWY 50
SHOSHONE CO ID 115-C3
SHOSHONE CO ID 115-C3
NHS 11 Rt#-60
BENEWAH CO ID 115-A3
BENEWAH CO ID 115-A3
W NIAGARA AV
ASTORIA OR 300-D6
NICE RD
UNION CO OR 130-A3
NICEWOOD DR
LINN CO OR 210-A2
NICEWOOD LN
LINN CO OR 210-A3
NW NICHOLS AV
Tracyton WA 270-G4
NW NICHOLS BLVD
LONGVIEW WA 302-J9
LONGVIEW WA 303-A10
NICHOLS LN
FOREST GROVE OR 198-B1
LANE CO OR 219-D1
WASHINGTON CO OR 198-B1
SE NICHOLS RD
YAMHILL CO OR 204-D1
NICHOLSON RD
KLAMATH CO OR 231-B1
LEWIS CO WA 187-D3
NICKEL MINE RD
DOUGLAS CO OR 225-B3
NICKERSON ST
SEATTLE WA 273-H7
W NICKERSON ST
SEATTLE WA 273-G6
NICK THOMAS RD
COLUMBIA CO OR 189-C5
NICK YOUNG RD
EAGLE POINT OR 230-D5
JACKSON CO OR 230-D5
NICOLAI RD
COLUMBIA CO OR 189-C6
NW NICOLAI ST
PORTLAND OR 312-C3
NICOLAI CUTOFF RD
COLUMBIA CO OR 189-C6
NIEHENKE RD
WHITMAN CO WA 249-C7
NIELSON RD
TILLAMOOK CO OR 197-C2
NIKULA RD
LEWIS CO WA 187-C3
N NILE AV
DOUGLAS CO WA 239-A4
S NILE AV
DOUGLAS CO WA 239-A4
NILLES RD
DOUGLAS CO WA 112-C1
NINE CANYON RD
BENTON CO WA 121-A3
NINEMILE RD
HUMBOLDT CO NV 154-A3
N NINE MILE RD Rt#-291
SPOKANE WA 246-A2
SPOKANE WA 346-A14
SPOKANE WA 348-B1
SPOKANE CO WA 246-A2
SPOKANE CO WA 346-A13
NINTH ST
WENATCHEE WA 238-D4
NISQUALLY RD SW
PIERCE CO WA 181-B6
NISULA RD
VALLEY CO ID 251-C6
VALLEY CO ID 252-C1
NIXON DR
LINN CO OR 210-A3
W NIXON ST
PASCO WA 343-E7
NO 1 RD
CITY OF RICHMOND BC 156-A7
DISTRICT OF ABBOTSFORD BC 94-B3
NO 2 RD
CITY OF RICHMOND BC 156-B7
NO 3 RD
CITY OF RICHMOND BC 156-B7
DISTRICT OF ABBOTSFORD BC 102-B1
NO 4 RD
CITY OF RICHMOND BC 156-B7
NO 5 RD
CITY OF RICHMOND BC 156-B6
NO 6 RD
CITY OF RICHMOND BC 156-C6
NO 7 RD
CITY OF RICHMOND BC 156-C6
E NOB HILL BLVD
YAKIMA WA 243-C7
YAKIMA CO WA 243-C7
W NOB HILL BLVD
YAKIMA WA 243-B7
NOBLE CREEK RD
COOS CO OR 218-D4
NOLL RD NE
KITSAP CO WA 170-C7
NONPAREIL RD
DOUGLAS CO OR 219-C7
NOOKSACK AV Rt#-9
NOOKSACK WA 102-B1
NOOKSACK RD Rt#-9
NOOKSACK WA 102-B1
WHATCOM CO WA 102-B1
NORATEN RD
LANE CO OR 210-A5
NORDEL WY
DISTRICT OF DELTA BC 156-D6
NORKENZIE RD
EUGENE OR 330-A2
NORMA BEACH RD
SNOHOMISH CO WA 171-B4
NORMAN RD
SNOHOMISH CO WA 168-B4
E NORMAN RD
YAKIMA CO WA 243-C7
S NORMANDY RD
BURIEN WA 288-A7
NORPOINT WY NE
TACOMA WA 182-A2
NORRIS AV Rt#-55
NEW MEADOWS ID 251-A4
NORRIS AV U.S.-95
ADAMS CO ID 251-A4
NEW MEADOWS ID 251-A4
NORRIS LN
JEFFERSON CO OR 212-D2
NORTH AV
JEFFERSON OR 207-D3
NORTH RD
CHELAN CO WA 238-B2
DISTRICT OF COQUITLAM BC 156-D5
FRANKLIN CO WA 340-H3
KOOTENAI CO ID 245-C1
NEW WESTMINSTER BC 156-D5
SNOHOMISH CO WA 171-C5
NORTH RD NW
DOUGLAS CO WA 236-C6
NORTH SPUR
JACKSON CO OR 227-A5
NORTH ST Rt#-26
WASHTUCNA WA 121-C1
E NORTH ST
ENTERPRISE OR 130-C2
W NORTH ST Rt#-82
ENTERPRISE OR 130-C2
NORTH ST SE
OLYMPIA WA 296-J9
OLYMPIA WA 297-A9
TUMWATER WA 296-J9
TUMWATER WA 297-A9
NORTH WY
COOS CO OR 218-B5
NORTH ALBANY RD
ALBANY OR 326-B5
NORTH BANK RD
DOUGLAS CO OR 141-B2
DOUGLAS CO OR 221-C2
LINCOLN CO OR 203-B4
Rose Lodge OR 203-B4
NORTH BANK RD U.S.-197
DEL NORTE CO CA 148-B3
NORTH BANK CHETCO RIVER RD
CURRY CO OR 232-D5
NORTH BANK PISTOL RIVER RD
CURRY CO OR 232-C1
NORTH BANK ROGUE RIVER RD
CURRY CO OR 228-B4
NORTH BAY DR
COOS CO OR 218-B6
NORTH BEND BLVD N Rt#-202
NORTH BEND WA 176-C4
NORTH BEND BLVD S Rt#-202
NORTH BEND WA 176-C5
E NORTH BEND WY
KING CO WA 176-C5
NORTH BEND WA 176-C5
SE NORTH BEND WY
KING CO WA 176-C4
SNOQUALMIE WA 176-C4
W NORTH BEND WY
NORTH BEND WA 176-C4
NORTH BLUFF RD
ISLAND CO WA 167-C6
NORTH CASCADES HWY Rt#-20
CHELAN CO WA 103-C2
OKANOGAN CO WA 103-C2
SKAGIT CO WA 103-A2
WHATCOM CO WA 103-A2
N NORTHCLIFF RD
SHELTON WA 180-A2
NORTHCRAFT RD SE
THURSTON CO WA 184-D3
NORTHCREST DR Rt#-D3
CRESCENT CITY CA 148-B3
DEL NORTE CO CA 148-B3
NORTH DAIRY RD
CITY OF VICTORIA BC 257-A6
DISTRICT OF SAANICH BC 257-A6
NORTH END OMAK LAKE RD
OKANOGAN CO WA 104-C3
NORTHERN DR
LINN CO OR 210-C2
NORTHERNWOOD DR
LINN CO OR 210-C4
NORTH FORK RD
CLACKAMAS CO OR 200-D7
DOUGLAS CO OR 214-C6
LANE CO OR 134-A3
LANE CO OR 142-A1
LEWIS CO WA 184-D7
LEWIS CO WA 187-D1
MARION CO OR 134-A1
NEHALEM OR 191-B4
SKAMANIA CO WA 193-D6
TILLAMOOK CO OR 191-B4
TILLAMOOK CO OR 197-D2
WESTFIR OR 142-A1
NORTH FORK BURNT RIVER RD
BAKER CO OR 138-A1
NORTH FORK COUNTY RD
KING CO WA 176-D3
NORTH FORK SIUSLAW RD
FLORENCE OR 214-B3
LANE CO OR 214-B3
NORTH FORK YACHATS RD
LINCOLN CO OR 209-B3
NORTH FOURMILE RD
COOS CO OR 224-C1
NORTH GATE RD
PIERCE CO WA 181-C4
N NORTHGATE WY
SEATTLE WA 171-B7
NE NORTHGATE WY
SEATTLE WA 171-B7
NORTH HEAD RD
ILWACO WA 186-A6
PACIFIC CO WA 186-A6
NORTH HEAD LIGHTHSE RD
PACIFIC CO WA 186-A6
NORTH LAKE RD
COOS CO OR 218-C4
NORTHLAKE WY NW
BREMERTON WA 270-A8
Tracyton WA 270-A8
NORTH MISSION RD W
KITSAP CO WA 173-D3
NORTH MOUNTAIN RD
CLACKAMAS CO OR 201-C4
NORTH PINE CREEK RD
BAKER CO OR 131-A3
NORTHPORT-FLAT CREEK RD
STEVENS CO WA 106-A1
NORTH POWDER-LADD CANYON RD
NORTH POWDER OR 130-B3
UNION CO OR 130-A3
NORTH POWDER RIVER LN
UNION CO OR 130-A3
NORTH POWDER RIVER RD
NORTH POWDER OR 130-A3
UNION CO OR 130-A3
NORTH PRAIRIE RD
LEWIS CO WA 187-D2

PNW INDEX

Thomas Bros. Maps®
COPYRIGHT 1999

PNW

INDEX

PNW

INDEX

390 PETERSVILLE RD NE
STREET INDEX
S PRAIRIE VIEW RD

STREET
City State Page-Grid

PETERSVILLE RD NE
KITSAP CO WA 271-A6
PETES MOUNTAIN RD
CLACKAMAS CO OR 199-C5
PETROVITSKY RD
KING CO WA 175-D6
N PETTET DR
SPOKANE WA 348-F6
PETTIBONE DR
BENTON CO OR 207-B4
PETTIGREW RD
BEND OR 332-J9
DESCHUTES CO OR 332-J9
PETTYJOHN RD
WALLA WALLA CO WA 121-C3
PETZOLD RD
LANE CO OR 133-B3
PFEIFER RD
LINCOLN CO WA 113-A2
PH 15
FRANKLIN CO WA 121-B2
PHARR RD
OKANOGAN CO WA 104-C2
PHEASANT LN
LANE CO OR 215-D4
PHELPS RD
CLACKAMAS CO OR 200-D3
PHELPS RD NE
KITSAP CO WA 174-C1
N PHILADELPHIA AV U.S.-30
PORTLAND OR 192-B7
PHILLIPS RD
YAMHILL CO OR 198-B3
NW PHILLIPS RD
WASHINGTON CO OR 192-A7
W PHILLIPS RD
ADAMS CO WA 242-C7
PHILLIPS RD SE
KITSAP CO WA 174-C5
PHILOMATH BLVD U.S.-20
BENTON CO OR 133-B1
BENTON CO OR 327-A12
CORVALLIS OR 133-B1
CORVALLIS OR 327-A12
PHILOMATH RD
BENTON CO OR 133-B1
PHINNEY AV N
SEATTLE WA 273-H4
N PHINNEY WY
SEATTLE WA 273-H5
NW PHINNEY BAY DR
BREMERTON WA 270-E8
KITSAP CO WA 270-E8
PH NO 10
CASTLE ROCK WA 187-C7
COWLITZ CO WA 187-C7
N PHOENIX RD
JACKSON CO OR 234-B2
JACKSON CO OR 336-J14
MEDFORD OR 234-B2
MEDFORD OR 336-J14
PHYS POINT RD
UNION CO OR 130-B2
PICARD RD
SISKIYOU CO CA 150-B3
PICKERING RD
MASON CO WA 180-C2
PICKETT RD
KLAMATH CO OR 151-A2
PICNIC POINT RD
SNOHOMISH CO WA 171-B4
PICTURE LN
LAKE CO OR 143-B2
PIEDMONT RD
CLALLAM CO WA 164-C6
PIEDMONT RD Rt#-112
CLALLAM CO WA 164-C5
CLALLAM CO WA 165-A6
PIERCE RD
MEDFORD OR 336-H11
UNION CO OR 130-A2
PIERCE RD NW
DOUGLAS CO WA 236-D5
PIERCE PARK LN
BOISE ID 253-C1
PIERCE PARK RD
ADA CO ID 253-C1
PIERSON RD
WHITMAN CO WA 114-B3
PIKE RD
YAMHILL OR 198-B4
YAMHILL CO OR 198-A4
NW PIKE RD
YAMHILL CO OR 198-A4
SW PIKE RD
JEFFERSON CO OR 212-C1
PILLER PL
JOSEPHINE CO OR 233-A4
PILOT ROCK RD
KOOTENAI CO ID 247-D6
KOOTENAI CO ID 248-A3
PINCUS
PIERCE CO WA 181-D7
N PINE
LA GRANDE OR 130-A2
PINE AV
SNOHOMISH WA 171-D3
E PINE AV
MERIDIAN ID 253-A3
W PINE AV
MERIDIAN ID 253-A3
PINE AV NE
OLYMPIA WA 297-A4
THURSTON CO WA 297-A4
PINE LN
COOS CO OR 220-B4
SE PINE RD
KITSAP CO WA 174-B6
SW PINE RD
KITSAP CO WA 174-B6
PINE RD NE
BREMERTON WA 270-H7
KITSAP CO WA 270-H5
Tracyton WA 270-H5
PINE ST
CHELAN CO WA 238-A1
LEAVENWORTH WA 238-A1
MARION CO OR 205-C4
NORTHPORT WA 106-A1
PINE ST
ROGUE RIVER OR 229-D6
SANDPOINT ID 244-A2
SILVERTON OR 205-C4
PINE ST Rt#-524
EDMONDS WA 171-A5
PINE ST U.S.-2
SANDPOINT ID 244-A2
PINE ST U.S.-12
OAKVILLE WA 117-B1
PINE ST U.S.-95
SANDPOINT ID 244-A2
E PINE ST
CENTRAL POINT OR 230-C7
JACKSON CO OR 230-C7
JACKSON CO OR 336-A5
E PINE ST Rt#-3
MASON CO WA 180-A3
SHELTON WA 180-A3
N PINE ST
CANBY OR 199-C6
S PINE ST
TACOMA WA 294-D1
SE PINE ST Rt#-99
ROSEBURG OR 334-F8
SE PINE ST Rt#-138
ROSEBURG OR 334-G7
W PINE ST
CENTRAL POINT OR 230-C7
Walla Walla West WA 344-H7
WALLA WALLA WA 344-H7
W PINE ST Rt#-125
WALLA WALLA WA 344-J7
PINE ST NE
MARION CO OR 205-B4
SALEM OR 322-J10
SALEM OR 323-A10
SILVERTON OR 205-B4
W PINE BLUFF RD
SPOKANE CO WA 114-B1
SPOKANE CO WA 246-A1
N PINE BLUFF WYE RD
SPOKANE CO WA 114-B1
PINE CITY RD
MALDEN WA 114-B3
WHITMAN CO WA 114-B3
PINECONE DR
JOSEPHINE CO OR 233-B5
PINE CREEK HWY
BAKER CO OR 131-A3
HALFWAY OR 131-A3
PINE CREEK RD
GRANT CO OR 137-B2
HARNEY CO OR 137-C3
HARNEY CO OR 145-C1
OKANOGAN CO WA 104-C2
SHOSHONE CO ID 115-C2
UMATILLA CO OR 129-C1
WALLOWA CO OR 131-A1
E PINE CREEK RD
BAKER CO OR 131-A3
N PINE CREEK RD
OKANOGAN CO WA 104-C2
PINECREST DR
JOSEPHINE CO OR 229-B5
JOSEPHINE CO OR 335-A7
LA GRANDE OR 130-A2
PINE CREST RD
LATAH CO ID 249-D5
PINE GROVE RD
LANE CO OR 133-B3
PINEHURST RD
DESCHUTES CO OR 217-B1
PINE MOUNT DR
HOOD RIVER CO OR 195-C7
HOOD RIVER CO OR 202-C1
N PINES RD Rt#-27
SPOKANE CO WA 350-H5
S PINES RD Rt#-27
SPOKANE CO WA 350-H10
S PINE SPRING RD
SPOKANE CO WA 114-B2
S PINE SPRINGS RD
SPOKANE CO WA 114-B2
PINE TOWN RD
BAKER CO OR 131-A3
PINE TREE RD
LEWIS CO WA 187-D3
PINETREE WY
COQUITLAM BC 157-A4
N PINEWOOD WY
KOOTENAI CO ID 245-A4
PING GULCH RD
GARFIELD CO WA 122-B1
PINKNEY RD
COLUMBIA CO OR 189-B7
PINTO RIDGE RD
GRANT CO WA 113-A2
PIOCH LN
LANE CO OR 210-D7
PIONEER AV
CASHMERE WA 238-C2
E PIONEER AV
PUYALLUP WA 182-B3
W PIONEER AV
PUYALLUP WA 182-B3
PIONEER AV E
GRAYS HARBOR CO WA 178-D7
MONTESANO WA 178-D7
PIONEER AV W
GRAYS HARBOR CO WA 178-D7
MONTESANO WA 178-D7
PIONEER BLVD U.S.-26
SANDY OR 200-C4
PIONEER DR
CASHMERE WA 238-B2
CHELAN CO WA 238-B2
PIONEER HWY
SKAGIT CO WA 168-B2
SNOHOMISH CO WA 168-B4
STANWOOD WA 168-B2
PIONEER HWY Rt#-530
SKAGIT CO WA 168-B2
PIONEER HWY E
SNOHOMISH CO WA 168-C5
PIONEER HWY E Rt#-530
SNOHOMISH CO WA 168-C4
PIONEER LP
DESCHUTES CO OR 217-C1
PIONEER PKWY
SKAGIT CO WA 160-D7
Swinomish Village WA 167-D1
PIONEER PKWY E
North Springfield OR 330-G4
SPRINGFIELD OR 330-G4
PIONEER PKWY W
North Springfield OR 330-G4
SPRINGFIELD OR 330-G4
PIONEER RD
JACKSON CO OR 234-A2
LONG BEACH WA 186-A5
OWYHEE CO ID 147-A1
PACIFIC CO WA 186-A5
S PIONEER RD
PIERCE CO WA 182-C5
PIONEER RD NW
KITSAP CO WA 174-A1
PIONEER ST
LANE CO OR 133-C3
LOWELL OR 133-C3
PIONEER ST Rt#-501
RIDGEFIELD WA 192-C2
PIONEER WY
CHELAN CO WA 238-C3
GIG HARBOR WA 181-C1
MOSES LAKE WA 242-C3
PIONEER WY Rt#-20
OAK HARBOR WA 167-B3
PIONEER WY Rt#-162
ORTING WA 182-B5
PIERCE CO WA 182-B5
SOUTH PRAIRIE WA 182-B5
SUMNER WA 182-B5
E PIONEER WY
TACOMA WA 182-A2
N PIONEER WY
YAKIMA CO WA 243-A5
S PIONEER WY
SHELTON WA 180-A3
S PIONEER WY Rt#-162
PIERCE CO WA 182-C6
W PIONEER WY Rt#-162
PIERCE CO WA 182-D5
PIONEER WY E
PIERCE CO WA 182-A3
PUYALLUP WA 182-B4
TACOMA WA 182-A3
PIONEER WY NW
KITSAP CO WA 170-B6
NW PIONEER HILL RD
KITSAP CO WA 170-B6
PIONEER MEMORIAL BRDG U.S.-395
KENNEWICK WA 343-B8
PASCO WA 343-B8
PIONEER PARKWAY RD
LA CONNER WA 167-D1
Shelter Bay WA 167-D1
SKAGIT CO WA 167-D1
Swinomish Village WA 167-D1
PIPELINE RD
COQUITLAM BC 157-B4
DOUGLAS CO OR 221-B2
WHATCOM CO WA 158-B3
SE PIPE LINE RD
MULTNOMAH CO OR 200-C2
PIPER RD
WHATCOM CO WA 158-D5
E PIPER RD
SPOKANE CO WA 246-D2
PIPER CANYON RD
WALLA WALLA CO WA 121-C2
PISCALE LOOKOUT RD
CROOK CO OR 136-A2
PISTOL BUTTE RD
DESCHUTES CO OR 216-D7
PISTOL RIVER LP
CURRY CO OR 232-B1
PITCHER CANYON RD
CHELAN CO WA 238-D5
PITNEY LN
LANE CO OR 210-A6
PITSUA BUTTE RD
DESCHUTES CO OR 216-D5
PITT AV
BREMERTON WA 271-A10
PITT RIVER RD
COQUITLAM BC 157-A5
PORT COQUITLAM BC 157-A5
PITTSBURG RD
COLUMBIA CO OR 192-A1
PLACE RD
CLALLAM CO WA 165-A5
LANE CO OR 133-C3
PLACER RD
JOSEPHINE CO OR 229-B2
PLAINVIEW DR
LINN CO OR 210-C1
PLANETZ RD NW
DOUGLAS CO WA 236-C7
PLANK RD
YAKIMA CO WA 120-A3
PLATEAU BLVD
COQUITLAM BC 157-B4
PLAT I RD
DOUGLAS CO OR 221-D1
PLAT K RD
DOUGLAS CO OR 221-D1
PLAT M RD
DOUGLAS CO OR 221-C1
PLATT RD
KLICKITAT CO WA 196-A4
PLAZA WY
WALLA WALLA WA 345-A10
WALLA WALLA CO WA 345-A11
PLEASANT DR
BREMERTON WA 270-D10
E PLEASANT ST
WALLA WALLA WA 345-E8
Walla Walla East WA 345-E8
PLEASANT BEACH DR NE
KITSAP CO WA 271-H6
PLEASANT CREEK RD
JACKSON CO OR 229-D2
PLEASANT HILL RD
COWLITZ CO WA 189-C2
COWLITZ CO WA 303-E1
GRANT CO OR 137-A2
POLK CO OR 204-A3
PLEASANT HILL RD
YAKIMA CO WA 243-B5
E PLEASANT PRAIRIE RD
SPOKANE CO WA 246-D2
PLEASANT RIDGE RD
WASCO CO OR 127-B2
PLEASANT VALLEY RD
ADA CO ID 253-C6
COOS CO OR 220-D7
DOUGLAS CO OR 219-B5
JOSEPHINE CO OR 229-A4
LEWIS CO WA 187-B1
LINN CO OR 133-C2
OWYHEE CO ID 155-C2
YAKIMA CO WA 243-A5
SW PLEASANT VALLEY RD
WASHINGTON CO OR 199-A3
PLEASANT VIEW RD
KOOTENAI CO ID 353-B1
POST FALLS ID 353-C8
E PLEASANT VIEW RD
SPOKANE CO WA 352-H10
W PLEASANT VIEW RD
KOOTENAI CO ID 352-H10
PLOMONDON RD
LEWIS CO WA 187-D4
PLUG MILL RD
MASON CO WA 179-B5
PLUM ST
OLYMPIA WA 296-J5
PLUMLEE RD
WASHINGTON CO OR 198-B1
PLUMTREE LN
JOSEPHINE CO OR 335-A2
PLUSH CUTOFF RD
LAKE CO OR 152-B2
PLYMOUTH AV U.S.-30
NEW PLYMOUTH ID 139-B3
PLYMOUTH RD
BENTON CO OR 327-B13
BENTON CO WA 121-A3
PLYMPTON CREEK Rt#-409
CLATSOP CO OR 117-B3
POCAHONTAS RD
BAKER CITY OR 138-A1
BAKER CO OR 130-A3
BAKER CO OR 138-A1
POE RD
WHITMAN CO WA 249-C3
POEN RD
ADA CO ID 253-A7
POETSCH RD
LEWIS CO WA 187-D4
N POE VALLEY RD
KLAMATH CO OR 151-A2
S POE VALLEY RD
KLAMATH CO OR 150-C2
KLAMATH CO OR 151-A2
S POINT RD
JEFFERSON CO WA 170-B4
W POINT RD
DOUGLAS CO OR 223-A4
POINT BROWN AV
OCEAN SHORES WA 177-B6
OCEAN SHORES WA 298-D3
POINT DEFIANCE TAHLEQUAH FERRY
KING CO WA 181-D1
PIERCE CO WA 181-D1
TACOMA WA 181-D1
POINT FOSDICK DR NW
PIERCE CO WA 181-C2
POINT GREY RD
VANCOUVER BC 254-B11
POINT ROBERTS RD
DISTRICT OF DELTA BC 101-C1
SW POINT ROBINSON RD
KING CO WA 175-A6
POINT WHITE DR NE
KITSAP CO WA 271-E6
POINT WHITEHORN RD
Birch Bay WA 158-B5
POINT WILSON RD
MASON CO WA 180-D3
POISON CREEK CTO
OWYHEE CO ID 147-C3
POKORNY RD
MARION CO OR 199-A7
E POLE RD Rt#-544
EVERSON WA 102-B1
WHATCOM CO WA 102-B1
WHATCOM CO WA 158-D5
W POLE RD
WHATCOM CO WA 158-D5
POLE CREEK RD
DESCHUTES CO OR 211-C6
MALHEUR CO OR 138-B3
MALHEUR CO OR 154-B2
MALHEUR CO OR 155-A1
POLEHN RD SW
THURSTON CO WA 184-B3
E POLE LINE AV
KOOTENAI CO ID 353-H4
KOOTENAI CO ID 354-A4
POST FALLS ID 353-H4
W POLE LINE AV
COEUR D'ALENE ID 355-A4
KOOTENAI CO ID 353-D4
KOOTENAI CO ID 354-H4
KOOTENAI CO ID 355-A4
POST FALLS ID 353-F5
POLE LINE RD
BAKER CO OR 130-A3
MORROW CO OR 128-C1
POLK RD
LATAH CO ID 249-C4
POLK ST
EUGENE OR 329-H6
INDEPENDENCE OR 204-B7
POLLMAN RD
LEWIS CO WA 184-D7
POLNELL RD
ISLAND CO WA 167-D3
POLSON RD
SKAGIT CO WA 168-A1
POMEROY RD
JACKSON CO OR 230-C2
PONDEROSA AV
CORVALLIS OR 327-C5
E PONDEROSA BLVD
POST FALLS ID 354-B8
PONDEROSA DR
DOUGLAS CO OR 221-A3
PONDEROSA RD
BONNER CO ID 244-B5
PONY BUTTE RD
JEFFERSON CO OR 135-B1
PONY CREEK RD
NORTH BEND OR 333-F5
POODLE CREEK RD
LANE CO OR 133-A3
POPLAR AV
DISTRICT OF SAANICH BC 257-B4
POPLAR DR
DESCHUTES CO OR 212-C5
MEDFORD OR 336-D9
POPLAR LN
POLK CO OR 204-B6
POPLAR ST
POWERS OR 140-B3
E POPLAR ST U.S.-2
DOUGLAS CO WA 236-C7
WATERVILLE WA 236-C7
NW POPLAR ST
MILTON-FREEWATER OR 121-C3
W POPLAR ST
WALLA WALLA WA 344-H9
WALLA WALLA WA 345-A8
POPULAR ST Rt#-27
TEKOA WA 114-C3
POPULAR ST Rt#-274
TEKOA WA 114-C3
PORCUPINE BAY RD
LINCOLN CO WA 114-A1
PORCUPINE RIDGE RD
MORROW CO OR 129-A3
PORTAL WY
FERNDALE WA 158-C5
WHATCOM CO WA 158-C4
PORTER RD
CLACKAMAS CO OR 200-C6
NEZ PERCE CO ID 250-D2
WASHINGTON CO OR 198-C1
PORTER RD NW
DOUGLAS CO WA 236-B6
PORTER ST Rt#-169
ENUMCLAW WA 110-C3
KING CO WA 110-C3
PORTER WY
MILTON WA 182-A2
PORTER CREEK RD
DOUGLAS CO OR 221-A6
GRAYS HARBOR CO WA 117-B1
GRAYS HARBOR CO WA 179-C7
PORT GAMBLE RD NE
KITSAP CO WA 170-C5
PORT INDUSTRIAL RD
ABERDEEN WA 178-B7
PORTLAND AV
FAIRFIELD WA 114-C2
SPOKANE CO WA 114-C2
E PORTLAND AV
TACOMA WA 182-A3
TACOMA WA 293-J5
NW PORTLAND AV
BEND OR 332-D6
PORTLAND AV E
PIERCE CO WA 182-A4
TACOMA WA 182-A4
N PORTLAND BLVD
PORTLAND OR 308-D6
PORTLAND OR 309-G6
NE PORTLAND BLVD
PORTLAND OR 309-G6
PORTLAND DR
HOOD RIVER CO OR 195-C6
E PORTLAND FRWY I-205
CLACKAMAS OR 319-G7
CLACKAMAS CO OR 199-D4
PORTLAND OR 319-G7
TUALATIN OR 199-D4
WASHINGTON CO OR 199-D4
NE PORTLAND HWY U.S.-30
PORTLAND OR 310-D6
PORTLAND OR 311-E7
PORTLAND RD Rt#-99W
NEWBERG OR 198-D5
YAMHILL CO OR 198-D5
YAMHILL CO OR 199-A5
N PORTLAND RD
PORTLAND OR 304-C7
PORTLAND OR 308-B2
PORTLAND RD NE
SALEM OR 323-B9
N PORTLAND ST
WILBUR WA 113-B1
PORTLAND HUBBARD HWY
CLACKAMAS CO OR 199-B6
W PORT MADISON RD
KITSAP CO WA 170-C7
PORT OF TACOMA RD
FIFE WA 182-A2
TACOMA WA 182-A2
SE PORTOLA DR
GRANTS PASS OR 335-H11
JOSEPHINE CO OR 335-H11
PORT ORCHARD BLVD
PORT ORCHARD WA 174-B4
PORT ORCHARD WA 270-H14
PORT ORFORD HWY
CURRY CO OR 224-A6
PORT ORFORD OR 224-A6
PORT TOWNSEND-KEYSTONE FERRY
ISLAND CO WA 167-B6
POSSESSION RD
ISLAND CO WA 171-A3
N POST ST
SPOKANE WA 348-J5
POST CANYON DR
HOOD RIVER CO OR 195-C5
POSTGREN RD
KLICKITAT CO WA 195-D2
POSTMA RD
YAKIMA CO WA 243-D7
E POSTMA RD
YAKIMA CO WA 243-C7
POTATO HILL RD
GRANT CO WA 242-C4
POTOMAC RANCH RD
MALHEUR CO OR 154-C1
POTTER LN
VALLEY CO ID 251-D6
POTTER RD
LATAH CO ID 249-C2
LINN CO OR 210-A2
POTTERY AV
PORT ORCHARD WA 174-B4
POTTS RD
WHITMAN CO WA 114-A3
POVERTY BEND RD
YAMHILL CO OR 198-A6
POWDER CREEK RD
TILLAMOOK CO OR 197-D6
E POWELL BLVD U.S.-26
GRESHAM OR 200-B2
SE POWELL BLVD U.S.-26
GRESHAM OR 200-A2
PORTLAND OR 200-A2
PORTLAND OR 317-H1
PORTLAND OR 318-B2
PORTLAND OR 319-H2
W POWELL BLVD U.S.-26
GRESHAM OR 200-A2
POWELL RD
COWLITZ CO WA 187-C7
GRAYS HARBOR CO WA 177-C5
NEZ PERCE CO ID 250-D6
NE POWELL RD
CLARK CO WA 193-B4
POWELL ST
VANCOUVER BC 254-J10
VANCOUVER BC 255-B10
POWELL BUTTE HWY
CROOK CO OR 213-A7
DESCHUTES CO OR 135-B3
DESCHUTES CO OR 213-A7
DESCHUTES CO OR 217-D1
POWELL BUTTE CEM RD
CROOK CO OR 213-B6
SE POWELL VALLEY RD
GRESHAM OR 200-B2
POWER RD
MALHEUR CO OR 139-A2
POWER CREEK RD
GRAYS HARBOR CO WA 179-C6
POWERHOUSE RD
KLICKITAT CO WA 195-C4
YAKIMA WA 243-B6
YAKIMA CO WA 243-B6
POWER LINE RD
UMATILLA CO OR 121-C3
WALLA WALLA CO WA 345-C12
POWERLINE RD
IDAHO CO ID 123-C3
LANE CO OR 210-B6
LEWIS CO ID 123-C2
LINN CO OR 210-B3
E POWER LINE RD
ADA CO ID 253-A4
CANYON CO ID 147-C1
POWERLINE RD SW
THURSTON CO WA 180-A7
POWER LINE EASEMENT RD
JOSEPHINE CO OR 233-B5
POWERS AV
NEZ PERCE CO ID 250-D5
POWERS HWY
COOS CO OR 140-B3
POWERS RD
COLUMBIA CO WA 122-A2
E POWERS RD
NEZ PERCE CO ID 250-D5
POWERS CREEK LP NE
MARION CO OR 205-D5
POWERS SOUTH RD
COOS CO OR 140-B3
CURRY CO OR 140-B3
POWERS OR 140-B3
POW WAH KEE RD
GARFIELD CO WA 122-C2
PRAIRIE AV
PORT COQUITLAM BC 157-B4
PRAIRIE AV U.S.-95
CRAIGMONT ID 123-B2
CRAIGMONT ID 123-B2
E PRAIRIE AV
DALTON GARDENS ID 355-E2
KOOTENAI CO ID 353-H2
KOOTENAI CO ID 354-B2
KOOTENAI CO ID 355-E2
W PRAIRIE AV
COEUR D'ALENE ID 354-J3
COEUR D'ALENE ID 355-B2
DALTON GARDENS ID 355-B2
HAYDEN ID 354-G2
HAYDEN ID 355-B2
KOOTENAI CO ID 353-D2
KOOTENAI CO ID 354-J3
KOOTENAI CO ID 355-B2
PRAIRIE RD
JUNCTION CITY OR 210-A6
LANE CO OR 210-A7
LANE CO OR 215-A1
SKAGIT CO WA 161-B4
S PRAIRIE RD
LEWIS CO WA 187-D2
SKAMANIA CO WA 195-A1
PRAIRIE CITY S SIDE OF RIV RD
GRANT CO OR 137-C2
PRAIRIE CITY OR 137-C2
PRAIRIE CREEK RD
DOUGLAS CO OR 226-D2
S PRAIRIE CREEK RD
PIERCE CO WA 182-C5
PRAIRIE FARM CTO
JEFFERSON CO OR 135-A1
JEFFERSON CO OR 211-D1
PRAIRIE PKWY LN SW
THURSTON CO WA 184-B2
PRAIRIE RIDGE DR E
PIERCE CO WA 182-C5
PRAIRIE ROAD CONN
LANE CO OR 210-A6
PRAIRIE ROAD CONN Rt#-36
LANE CO OR 210-A6
S PRAIRIE VIEW RD
SPOKANE CO WA 114-C2

PNW
INDEX

STREET
City State Page-Grid

PRATER RD
DESCHUTES CO OR 216-C6
PRATHER RD
POLK CO OR 207-B2
PRATHER RD SW
THURSTON CO WA 184-A4
PRATT RD
WALLOWA CO OR 130-C2
PREACHER CREEK RD
LANE CO OR 133-A2
PREBLE ST
BREMERTON WA 270-E12
Navy Yard City WA 270-E12
NE PRESCOTT ST
MAYWOOD PARK OR 315-H1
PORTLAND OR 313-H1
PORTLAND OR 314-B1
PORTLAND OR 315-E1
PRESLEY
PIERCE CO WA 182-B6
W PRESLEY RD
KOOTENAI CO ID 247-D4
KOOTENAI CO ID 248-A1
PRESTON AV
LEWISTON ID 250-C5
PRESTON AV U.S.-12
WAITSBURG WA 122-A2
PRESTON-FALL CITY RD SE
KING CO WA 176-B4
W PREWETT RD
SPOKANE CO WA 114-B1
W PRICE AV
Town and Country WA 346-J12
PRICE RD
ALBANY OR 326-H7
BREMERTON WA 270-C10
KITSAP CO WA 270-C10
LINN CO OR 326-H7
YAKIMA CO WA 120-B2
N PRICE RD
YAKIMA CO WA 120-B2
PRICEBORO DR
LINN CO OR 210-A5
PRICE-TWELVEMILE RD
CROOK CO OR 136-B3
PRIEST RAPIDS RD
BENTON CO WA 120-B2
YAKIMA CO WA 120-B2
PRINCESS AV
DIST OF N VANCOUVER BC 255-C2
PRINCETON AV NE
SEATTLE WA 275-F4
NE PRINCETON WY
SEATTLE WA 275-F3
PRINGLE PKWY SE Rt#-22
SALEM OR 322-J13
PRINGLE RD
WASHINGTON CO ID 139-A2
PRINGLE RD SE
SALEM OR 324-J5
PRINGLE FALLS LP
DESCHUTES CO OR 142-C1
DESCHUTES CO OR 143-A1
PRINGLE FLAT RD
CROOK CO OR 136-A3
PRIOR ST
VANCOUVER BC 254-J11
VANCOUVER BC 255-A11
PRIVATE RD
CLARK CO WA 190-A7
PROCTOR BLVD U.S.-26
SANDY OR 200-C4
N PROCTOR ST
TACOMA WA 292-C4
S PROCTOR ST
TACOMA WA 292-C6
PROFFITT RD
LEWIS CO WA 184-D6
N PROGRESS RD
SPOKANE CO WA 351-B2
Trentwood WA 351-B2
W PROGRESS RD
UMATILLA CO OR 129-A1
PROGRESSIVE RD
White Swan WA 119-C2
N PROM
SEASIDE OR 301-F8
S PROM
SEASIDE OR 301-F9
PROMISE RD
WALLOWA CO OR 130-B1
PROMONTORY RD
DISTRICT OF CHILLIWACK BC 102-C1
PROSPECT AV
Irondale WA 263-D13
WALLA WALLA WA 345-B11
WALLA WALLA CO WA 345-B11
PROSPECT DR
BENTON CITY WA 120-C3
PROSPECT RD
DIST OF N VANCOUVER BC 255-B1
PROSPECT ST
BELLINGHAM WA 258-D6
PROSPECT LAKE RD
DISTRICT OF SAANICH BC 159-B5
DISTRICT OF SAANICH BC 256-A1
PROTEST RD
BOISE ID 253-C3
PROVIDENCE RD
ADAMS CO WA 121-C1
PROVIDENCE RD Rt#-261
ADAMS CO WA 121-C1
PROVOST RD NW
KITSAP CO WA 270-A2
Silverdale WA 270-A2
PROWELL ST
CHELAN CO WA 238-A1
PRUNEDALE RD
UMATILLA CO OR 121-C3
PRUNER RD
DOUGLAS CO OR 225-B2
RIDDLE OR 225-B2
P S OGDEN RD
DESCHUTES CO OR 212-D3
SW PUCKER HUDDLE RD Rt#-141
KLICKITAT CO WA 195-D4
PUCKETT RD
CROOK CO OR 213-C3

STREET
City State Page-Grid

PUDDING RIVER RD NE
MARION CO OR 205-C1
NW PUDDY GULCH RD
YAMHILL CO OR 198-A5
PUGET DR
VANCOUVER BC 254-B14
PUGET DR Rt#-524
EDMONDS WA 171-A5
PUGET DR E
Colby WA 271-G14
PUGET DR SE
Colby WA 271-G14
RENTON WA 175-C5
PUGET RD NE
THURSTON CO WA 180-D5
N PUGET ST
OLYMPIA WA 297-A4
PUGET BEACH RD NE
THURSTON CO WA 181-A4
PUGH RD NE
KITSAP CO WA 170-C6
PUITT RD
CROOK CO OR 136-B2
PULLEN LN
JOSEPHINE CO OR 233-B5
PULLMAN ALBION RD
ALBION WA 249-A4
WHITMAN CO WA 249-A4
PULVER RD
SKAGIT CO WA 260-A2
SW PUMA DR
WASHINGTON CO OR 198-B2
PUMP RD
CANYON CO ID 147-B1
NW PUMPKIN RIDGE RD
WASHINGTON CO OR 125-C1
PUNCH BOWL RD
HOOD RIVER CO OR 195-B7
PUNKIN CENTER RD
UMATILLA CO OR 129-A1
NW PURDIN RD
WASHINGTON CO OR 198-B1
PURDY DR Rt#-302
KITSAP CO WA 174-B6
PIERCE CO WA 174-B6
PURDY CRESCENT
PIERCE CO WA 174-C6
PURDY CUTOFF RD
MASON CO WA 180-A1
PURDY KITSAP RD
KITSAP CO WA 174-C6
PIERCE CO WA 174-C6
PURTTEMAN GULCH RD
CHELAN CO WA 236-C2
PUYALLUP AV
TACOMA WA 182-A2
TACOMA WA 293-J7
S PUYALLUP AV
TACOMA WA 293-H7
PUYALLUP ST
STEILACOOM WA 181-C4
N PUYALLUP MOTOR NATURE TR
PIERCE CO WA 185-A3
PYLE RD
KLICKITAT CO WA 196-B3

Q

Q RD NW
DOUGLAS CO WA 236-C7
Q ST
PORT TOWNSEND WA 263-H3
SPRINGFIELD OR 330-G5
SPRINGFIELD OR 331-A5
NE QUAALE RD
JEFFERSON CO OR 208-D3
QUADRA ST
CITY OF VICTORIA BC 256-H6
DISTRICT OF SAANICH BC 159-C5
DISTRICT OF SAANICH BC 256-F1
VANCOUVER BC 254-A13
S QUADRANT ST
ROCKAWAY BEACH OR 191-B6
QUARRY RD
ALBANY OR 326-C5
COQUITLAM BC 157-B3
YAMHILL CO OR 198-D5
QUARTZ CREEK RD
DOUGLAS CO OR 222-B7
JOSEPHINE CO OR 229-A3
QUARTZ MOUNTAIN RD
DOUGLAS CO OR 222-A5
KITTITAS CO WA 240-C4
QUARTZVILLE DR
LINN CO OR 134-A1
QUEBEC ST
CITY OF VICTORIA BC 256-F9
VANCOUVER BC 254-H11
QUEEN AV
ALBANY OR 326-B9
LINN CO OR 326-B9
S QUEEN ANN BLVD
YAKIMA WA 243-B7
QUEEN ANNE AV N
SEATTLE WA 273-H7
SEATTLE WA 277-H1
QUEEN ANNE DR
SEATTLE WA 277-H1
W QUEEN ANNE DR WY
SEATTLE WA 277-H3
QUEEN MARY BLVD
DISTRICT OF SURREY BC 157-A6
QUEENS AV
DIST OF WEST VANCOUVER BC 254-A1
QUEENS RD
DIST OF N VANCOUVER BC 254-J2
DIST OF N VANCOUVER BC 255-B3
QUEENSBOROUGH BRDG Rt#-91A
CITY OF RICHMOND BC 156-D6
NEW WESTMINSTER BC 156-D6
QUEENS BRANCH RD
JACKSON CO OR 229-D4
QUEENSBURY AV
CITY OF N VANCOUVER BC 255-C7
QUEENSGATE DR
BENTON CO WA 341-D5
RICHLAND WA 341-D5

STREET
City State Page-Grid

QUEETS RIVER RD
JEFFERSON CO WA 172-D2
QUESNEL DR
VANCOUVER BC 254-B14
QUICK RD
COWLITZ CO WA 187-C7
QUILCEDA RD
SNOHOMISH CO WA 168-C7
E QUILCENE RD
JEFFERSON CO WA 109-C1
QUILLAYUTE RD
CLALLAM CO WA 169-B2
QUINABY RD NE
MARION CO OR 204-D4
MARION CO OR 205-A4
W QUINAULT AV
KENNEWICK WA 342-C9
QUINCE AV
DESCHUTES CO OR 212-C5
N QUINCY AV
DOUGLAS CO WA 239-A4
QUINCY ST
PORT TOWNSEND WA 263-H4
QUINCY-MAYGER RD
COLUMBIA CO OR 117-B3
COLUMBIA CO OR 189-A2
QUINES CREEK RD
DOUGLAS CO OR 225-C6
QUINN RD
GILLIAM CO OR 128-A3

R

R AV
ANACORTES WA 259-H2
R RD NE Rt#-17
DOUGLAS CO WA 112-C1
R RD SW
DOUGLAS CO WA 239-B3
S R ST
COTTAGE GROVE OR 215-B7
R ST SE
AUBURN WA 182-C2
KING CO WA 182-C2
NW RABAUL DR
KITSAP CO WA 170-B7
RABBIT CAMP RD
LINN CO OR 134-B2
RABY LN
PAYETTE CO ID 139-A3
RACCOON DR
DOUGLAS CO OR 219-A5
RACE RD
EPHRATA WA 112-C3
GRANT CO WA 112-C3
ISLAND CO WA 167-C5
RACE ST
PORT ANGELES WA 261-G5
RADAR RD
HARNEY CO OR 145-A1
RADAR HILL RD
ADAMS CO WA 121-A1
FRANKLIN CO WA 121-A1
RADER RD
KITTITAS CO WA 241-C4
RAFT AV
OLYMPIA WA 296-G2
RAGER RD
CROOK CO OR 136-B2
RAGLAND RD
COWLITZ CO WA 189-B1
RAIL HOLLOW RD
HOOD RIVER CO OR 202-D4
WASCO CO OR 127-B2
WASCO CO OR 202-D4
RAILROAD AV
JOSEPHINE CO OR 225-B7
JOSEPHINE CO OR 229-B1
KITTITAS WA 241-C6
LEWISTON ID 250-C4
MOUNT ANGEL OR 205-C3
POWERS OR 140-B3
RAILROAD AV Rt#-200
KOOTENAI ID 244-A1
E RAILROAD AV
Otis Orchards WA 352-D9
SPOKANE CO WA 349-J7
N RAILROAD AV
COOS CO OR 140-B3
KOOTENAI CO ID 353-C7
POST FALLS ID 353-C7
POWERS OR 140-B3
SAINT HELENS OR 192-B2
NE RAILROAD AV
CLARK CO WA 193-B2
W RAILROAD AV
MASON CO WA 180-A3
SHELTON WA 180-A3
RAILROAD AV SE Rt#-202
KING CO WA 176-C4
NORTH BEND WA 176-C4
SNOQUALMIE WA 176-C4
RAILROAD BLVD
EUGENE OR 329-H4
RAILROAD ST Rt#-27
ROCKFORD WA 114-C2
SPOKANE CO WA 114-C2
RAILROAD ST U.S.-95
MIDVALE ID 139-B1
SW RAILROAD ST
SHERIDAN OR 125-B3
SHERWOOD OR 199-A4
RAILWAY AV
CITY OF RICHMOND BC 156-B7
RAINBOW DR
JEFFERSON CO OR 212-C2
NW RAINBOW DR
DESCHUTES CO OR 212-C3
RAINBOW RD
WHATCOM CO WA 158-B5
RAINBOW ROCK RD
CURRY CO OR 232-C5
RAINEY RD
DOUGLAS CO WA 239-A2
RAINIER AV N
KING CO WA 175-C5
RENTON WA 175-C5
RAINIER AV S
KING WA 287-F4
KING CO WA 175-C4

STREET
City State Page-Grid

RAINIER AV S
RENTON WA 175-C4
SEATTLE WA 278-C7
SEATTLE WA 282-D2
SEATTLE WA 283-E6
SEATTLE WA 287-F1
RAINIER AV S Rt#-167
RENTON WA 175-C5
RAINIER DR
PIERCE CO WA 181-C5
RAINIER RD SE
RAINIER WA 118-A1
THURSTON CO WA 118-A1
RAINIER ST
STEILACOOM WA 181-C4
RAINIER DIKE RD
RAINIER OR 302-G14
W RAINIER DIKE RD
COLUMBIA CO OR 302-C12
RAINIER OR 302-C12
RAINIER-YELM HWY Rt#-507
THURSTON CO WA 118-A1
YELM WA 118-A1
RAISOR RD
LANE CO OR 219-D3
RALSTON-BENGE RD
ADAMS CO WA 121-C1
ADAMS CO WA 122-A1
RAMBLER DR NE
MARION CO OR 205-B4
N RAMBO RD
SPOKANE CO WA 114-B2
RAMMS RD
JEFFERSON CO OR 213-A1
S RAMSBY RD
CLACKAMAS CO OR 126-A3
RAMSEY LN
KLICKITAT CO WA 195-D5
RAMSEY RD
COEUR D'ALENE ID 355-C3
HAYDEN ID 245-A5
HAYDEN ID 355-C3
JACKSON CO OR 230-B4
KOOTENAI CO ID 245-A5
KOOTENAI CO ID 355-C3
N RAMSEY RD
COEUR D'ALENE ID 355-C6
KOOTENAI CO ID 245-A2
S RAMSEY ST Rt#-27
TEKOA WA 114-C3
RAMSEY-CANYON RD
JACKSON CO OR 230-B3
RANCH RD
DESCHUTES CO OR 144-B1
DOUGLAS CO OR 218-C1
KOOTENAI CO ID 245-A2
RANCHERO RD
DOUGLAS CO OR 225-C6
RAND RD
HOOD RIVER OR 195-C5
RANDAL RD
COOS CO OR 220-B6
RANDALL RD SW
THURSTON CO WA 180-B6
RANDOLPH RD
GRANT CO WA 242-C2
RANEY LN
ADAMS CO ID 251-B4
W RANGE DR
LINCOLN CO OR 328-D6
WALDPORT OR 328-D6
RANGER RD
CLALLAM CO WA 165-A5
RANIER RD
LACEY WA 297-G13
THURSTON CO WA 297-G13
RANIER RD SE
THURSTON CO WA 184-D1
THURSTON CO WA 297-G14
RANKIN RD
JEFFERSON CO OR 211-C1
RANKIN HILL RD
Vineland WA 250-B5
RAT CREEK RD
LANE CO OR 215-D7
RATHERT RD
KLICKITAT CO WA 196-C1
RATTLESNAKE RD
HARNEY CO OR 145-B1
KLICKITAT CO WA 195-D3
KLICKITAT CO WA 196-A2
RATTLESNAKE CREEK RD
MALHEUR CO OR 154-B1
RAUBUCK RD
LEWIS CO WA 187-B2
RAVENA DR N
MARION CO OR 204-D3
RAVENNA AV NE
SEATTLE WA 274-D1
NE RAVENNA BLVD
SEATTLE WA 274-B3
RAWLINS RD
SKAGIT CO WA 168-A1
RAWLISON CRES
TOWNSHIP OF LANGLEY BC 157-D7
RAWLISON CRES Rt#-10
TOWNSHIP OF LANGLEY BC 157-C7
NE RAWSON RD
CLARK CO WA 193-B4
RAY RD
LEWIS CO WA 187-D4
S RAY ST
SPOKANE WA 349-F12
RAY BELL RD
MARION CO OR 198-D6
RAYE ST
SEATTLE WA 277-H1
RAYMOND CREEK RD
COLUMBIA CO OR 192-A4
RAY NASH DR NW
PIERCE CO WA 181-B1
RAZOR CLAM DR
OCEAN SHORES WA 298-C3
R DRUFFEL RD
WHITMAN CO WA 249-B7
REASON CT
DESCHUTES CO OR 212-C5
REATA RD
BENTON CO WA 341-D12

STREET
City State Page-Grid

REAVIS LN
WALLOWA CO OR 130-C2
SE REBMAN RD
CLACKAMAS CO OR 200-B4
RECORD ST
BAKER CO OR 131-A3
HALFWAY OR 131-A3
RECREATIONAL CORR
GRANT CO WA 121-A1
RED APPLE RD
WENATCHEE WA 238-D4
REDBERG RD
TILLAMOOK CO OR 203-B1
RED BLANKET RD
JACKSON CO OR 226-C7
S RED BLANKET RD
JACKSON CO OR 226-D7
RED BLANKET MOUNTAIN RD
JACKSON CO OR 226-D6
JACKSON CO OR 227-A6
RED BRIDGE RD
LINN CO OR 207-D6
RED CLOUD LN
CROOK CO OR 213-B6
RED CLOUD RD
CROOK CO OR 213-B6
REDDING RD
MORROW CO OR 128-B2
REDFIELD RD
DOUGLAS CO WA 239-B1
RED FIR RD
BONNER CO ID 244-D3
KLAMATH CO OR 151-B1
RED HILL RD
DOUGLAS CO OR 219-B5
HOOD RIVER CO OR 202-B2
WALLOWA CO OR 131-A1
RED HILLS RD
YAMHILL CO OR 198-C6
RED HOUSE RD
LAKE CO OR 152-A1
S REDLAND RD
CLACKAMAS CO OR 199-D4
CLACKAMAS CO OR 200-A5
OREGON CITY OR 199-D4
RED MARBLE RD
STEVENS CO WA 106-A3
SW REDMOND RD
MCMINNVILLE OR 198-A7
YAMHILL CO OR 198-A7
NE REDMOND WY Rt#-202
REDMOND WA 175-D1
NE REDMOND WY Rt#-908
REDMOND WA 175-C1
REDMOND-BEND HWY
DESCHUTES CO OR 212-C7
DESCHUTES CO OR 217-C1
REDMOND FALL CITY RD Rt#-202
KING CO WA 175-D1
KING CO WA 176-A1
REDMOND WA 175-D1
SAMMAMISH WA 175-D1
SE REDMND FALL CITY RD Rt#-202
KING CO WA 176-B3
REDMND FALL CITY RD NE Rt#-202
KING CO WA 176-A2
REDMND FALL CITY RD SE Rt#-202
KING CO WA 176-A2
REDMOND GRADE RD
WALLOWA CO OR 122-C3
REDMOND-POWELL BUTE RD
DESCHUTES CO OR 212-D5
REDONDO WY S
DES MOINES WA 175-B7
FEDERAL WAY WA 175-B7
RED RIDGE RD
ADAMS CO ID 251-C5
VALLEY CO ID 251-C7
N RED RIVER RD
WHATCOM CO WA 158-C6
RED ROCK RD
SISKIYOU CO CA 150-B3
REDWOOD AV
GRANTS PASS OR 335-A11
JOSEPHINE CO OR 229-B6
JOSEPHINE CO OR 335-A11
REDWOOD HWY
GRANTS PASS OR 335-F9
REDWOOD HWY U.S.-101
CRESCENT CITY CA 148-B3
DEL NORTE CO CA 148-B3
DEL NORTE CO CA 232-D7
REDWOOD HWY U.S.-199
CAVE JUNCTION OR 233-B3
DEL NORTE CO CA 148-B3
DEL NORTE CO CA 233-A6
GRANTS PASS OR 335-F6
JOSEPHINE CO OR 149-A1
JOSEPHINE CO OR 229-A7
JOSEPHINE CO OR 233-B3
JOSEPHINE CO OR 335-A12
NE REDWOOD HWY U.S.-199
GRANTS PASS OR 335-F7
REECER CREEK RD
KITTITAS CO WA 241-B2
REED RD
BEND OR 332-E10
HOOD RIVER CO OR 195-C6
LEWIS CO WA 187-C4
N REED RD
COEUR D'ALENE ID 355-D2
HAYDEN ID 245-A5
HAYDEN ID 355-D1
REED RD SE
SALEM OR 325-A6
REEDER RD
COLUMBIA CO OR 192-B3
KLAMATH CO OR 235-D5
MULTNOMAH CO OR 192-B5
REEDER RD SW
THURSTON CO WA 184-C2
SE REED MARKET RD
BEND OR 332-G10
DESCHUTES CO OR 217-C3
DESCHUTES CO OR 332-G10

STREET
City State Page-Grid

REESE RD
LAKE OSWEGO OR 320-A7
REESE CREEK RD
JACKSON CO OR 230-D5
REESE HILL RD Rt#-547
WHATCOM CO WA 102-B1
REEVES RD KPS
PIERCE CO WA 181-A3
REEVES CREEK RD
JOSEPHINE CO OR 233-B3
S REGAL RD
SPOKANE CO WA 246-C5
S REGAL ST
SPOKANE WA 349-E14
REGENTS BLVD
FIRCREST WA 181-C2
FIRCREST WA 292-A7
FIRCREST WA 294-A1
E REGINA AV
Fairwood WA 346-J8
Fairwood WA 347-A8
W REGINA AV
Fairwood WA 346-J9
SE REGNER RD
GRESHAM OR 200-B2
REHKLAU RD SE
THURSTON CO WA 181-A7
REHN RD
ADAMS CO WA 113-C3
REICHENBACK RD
PITT MEADOWS BC 157-B5
REID DR NW
GIG HARBOR WA 181-C1
PIERCE CO WA 181-C1
REID RD
CLARK CO WA 193-A1
WHITMAN CO WA 249-A4
REIMANN ST NE
Hayesville OR 323-E6
SE REINIG RD
KING CO WA 176-C4
REITER RD
SNOHOMISH CO WA 111-A1
REITH RD
KENT WA 175-B7
REKDAL RD
ISLAND CO WA 168-A4
W REMINGTON RD
KOOTENAI CO ID 245-A2
REMY LN
LEWIS CO WA 187-D1
RENFREW ST
VANCOUVER BC 255-D12
RENFRO CREEK RD
BENEWAH CO ID 115-B3
RENNE RD
YAMHILL CO OR 198-D6
RENTON AV S
KING WA 287-G5
KING WA 289-J1
SEATTLE WA 287-F3
SE RENTON ISSAQUAH RD Rt#-900
KING CO WA 175-D4
RENTON WA 175-D4
RENTON ISSAQUAH RD SE Rt#-900
ISSAQUAH WA 175-D4
KING CO WA 175-D4
RENTON MAPLE VALLEY RD Rt#-169
KING CO WA 175-D5
KING CO WA 176-A6
MAPLE VALLEY WA 175-D5
RENTON WA 175-D5
RESEARCH WY
CORVALLIS OR 327-C11
RESERVATION RD
ISLAND CO WA 167-C2
OAK HARBOR WA 167-C2
SKAGIT CO WA 160-D7
WASCO CO OR 127-A3
RESERVATION RD Rt#-241
YAKIMA CO WA 120-B3
W RESERVATION RD Rt#-241
YAKIMA CO WA 120-B3
RESERVATION RD SE
THURSTON CO WA 181-A6
RESERVATION LINE RD
IDAHO CO ID 123-C3
NEZ PERCE CO ID 250-D4
RESERVE ST
BOISE ID 253-D3
RESERVOIR RD
BENTON CO OR 327-A10
CORVALLIS OR 327-A10
CROOK CO OR 135-B3
MALHEUR CO OR 138-C3
MALHEUR CO OR 146-A1
RESERVOIR LOOP RD
YAKIMA CO WA 243-B5
RESOR RD
WALLA WALLA CO WA 345-H11
Walla Walla East WA 345-C11
RESORT DR
TILLAMOOK CO OR 197-A7
RESTHAVEN DR
TOWN OF SIDNEY BC 159-C2
RESTON RD
DOUGLAS CO OR 141-A2
RETREAT KANASKAT RD
KING CO WA 110-C3
RETSIL RD SE
East Port Orchard WA 271-A14
PORT ORCHARD WA 271-A14
REUBEN RD
DOUGLAS CO OR 225-A7
N REUBEN RD
DOUGLAS CO OR 225-A6
REUBENS RD
LEWIS CO ID 123-B2
LEWIS CO ID 123-B2
REUBENS GRADE
NEZ PERCE CO ID 123-B2
NEZ PERCE CO ID 123-B2
SE REVENUE RD
CLACKAMAS CO OR 200-C3
NE REVERE AV U.S.-20
BEND OR 332-E6

PNW INDEX

392 REVETMENT DR — STREET INDEX — ROAD Q-SW

PNW

INDEX

STREET / City State / Page-Grid

REVETMENT DR
WESTPORT WA 298-G10
REX RD
DOUGLAS CO WA 237-B1
REYNOLD RD
CLALLAM CO WA 164-B5
W REYNOLDS AV
CENTRALIA WA 299-C1
LEWIS CO WA 299-E1
REYNOLDS RD
FRANKLIN CO WA 121-B2
REYNOLDS CREEK RD
DOUGLAS CO OR 222-B1
REYNOLDS CREEK STAGE RD
OWYHEE CO ID 147-B2
REYNOLDS RIDGE RD
DOUGLAS CO OR 222-B3
RHEA RD
GILLIAM CO OR 128-A1
RHEA CREEK RD
MORROW CO OR 128-B2
RHINEHART RD
UNION CO OR 130-A2
RHODES RD
LEWIS CO WA 187-C3
RHODESIA BEACH RD
PACIFIC CO WA 183-C7
RHODESIDE RD
DESCHUTES CO OR 213-A4
RHODES LAKE RD E
PIERCE CO WA 182-C4
RHODODENDRON DR
FLORENCE OR 214-A2
LANE CO OR 214-A2
RHODODENDRON LN NW
KITSAP CO WA 170-B6
RHODODENDRON RD
DOUGLAS CO OR 222-C5
RHODY DR Rt#-19
Hadlock-Irondale WA 170-A1
Irondale WA 263-E14
JEFFERSON CO WA 170-A1
JEFFERSON CO WA 263-E14
RIBBON RIDGE RD
YAMHILL CO OR 198-C4
SE RICE AV
ROSEBURG OR 334-F9
RICE RD
BAKER CO OR 138-A1
RICE ST
MYRTLE CREEK OR 225-C1
RICE CREEK RD
DOUGLAS CO OR 221-B7
DOUGLAS CO OR 225-A1
RICE KANDLE
PIERCE CO WA 181-D7
RICE-ORIN RD
STEVENS CO WA 105-C2
STEVENS CO WA 106-A2
RICE VALLEY RD
DOUGLAS CO OR 219-A5
RICH RD SE
THURSTON CO WA 184-D1
THURSTON CO WA 297-C12
RICHARDS RD
BELLEVUE WA 175-C2
KITTITAS CO WA 241-A6
RICHARDSON RD
DOUGLAS CO OR 221-C7
LINCOLN CO WA 113-C2
PITT MEADOWS BC 157-C4
SISKIYOU CO CA 150-B3
RICHARDSON RD NE
MARION CO OR 205-D5
RICHARDSONS GAP RD
LINN CO OR 133-C1
RICHART RD
FRANKLIN CO WA 121-A2
RICHES RD SE
MARION CO OR 205-C6
RICHMOND AV
CITY OF VICTORIA BC 257-B8
DISTRICT OF SAANICH BC 257-B8
N RICHMOND AV
PORTLAND OR 192-B7
RICHMOND FRWY Rt#-91
CITY OF RICHMOND BC 156-C6
RICHMOND RD
DISTRICT OF SAANICH BC 257-B4
GILLIAM CO OR 128-A2
N RICHMOND BEACH RD
SHORELINE WA 171-A6
NW RICHMOND BEACH RD
SHORELINE WA 171-A6
RICHMOND SIXSHOOTER RD
WHEELER CO OR 136-B1
RICKARD RD
BENTON CO OR 210-A4
DESCHUTES CO OR 217-C3
RICKEY ST SE
SALEM OR 325-E2
RICKREALL RD
POLK CO OR 204-B6
RIDDELL RD
POLK CO OR 204-B7
NE RIDDELL RD
BREMERTON WA 270-G5
KITSAP CO WA 270-G5
KITSAP CO WA 271-A5
Tracyton WA 270-G5
NW RIDDELL RD
KITSAP CO WA 270-G5
RIDDLE BYPS
DOUGLAS CO OR 225-B2
RIDDLE OR 225-B2
Tri-City OR 225-B2
RIDGE DR
ASTORIA OR 300-C6
HOOD RIVER CO OR 195-C6
LINN CO OR 207-C7
OROVILLE WA 104-C1
RIDGE DR NE
KEIZER OR 323-C4
RIDGE RD
ADAMS CO ID 252-A6
CLACKAMAS CO OR 200-B5
COOS CO OR 218-B6
GILLIAM CO OR 128-B2
HARNEY CO OR 137-B3
MORROW CO OR 128-B2

RIDGE RD
WARRENTON OR 188-B2
YAMHILL CO OR 198-B4
RIDGE TR
SKAMANIA CO WA 194-B1
SE RIDGECREST RD
CLACKAMAS CO OR 200-A3
HAPPY VALLEY OR 200-A3
RIDGELINE TR
EUGENE OR 329-J14
EUGENE OR 330-B14
LANE CO OR 215-B3
LANE CO OR 329-J14
RIDGETOP BLVD
Silverdale WA 174-B1
RIDGEVIEW DR NE
KITSAP CO WA 271-C7
RIDGEWAY DR
REEDSPORT OR 218-C1
RIDGEWAY DR SE
MARION CO OR 207-D1
SW RIEDWEG RD
WASHINGTON CO OR 198-C2
RIETH RD
UMATILLA CO OR 129-A1
RIFE RD
CLALLAM CO WA 165-A6
RIFLE RANGE RD
BENTON CO OR 207-B3
NE RIFLE RANGE RD
ROSEBURG OR 334-J7
RIGDON RD
LANE CO OR 142-A1
SW RIGERT RD
WASHINGTON CO OR 199-A2
RIGGS RD
CROOK CO OR 213-B6
WALLA WALLA CO WA 121-B3
RIGHT FORK RD
DOUGLAS CO OR 221-D6
RIGHT FORK FOOTS CREEK RD
JACKSON CO OR 229-D7
RIGHT FORK SARDINE CREEK RD
JACKSON CO OR 230-B4
RIM DR
KLAMATH CO OR 227-C2
RIM RD
CANYON CO ID 147-B1
JEFFERSON CO OR 212-C2
RIMROCK RD
COLTON WA 250-A1
WHITMAN CO WA 250-A1
N RIMROCK RD
KOOTENAI CO ID 245-A4
NW RIMROCK RD
JEFFERSON CO OR 208-B3
RIMROCK ACRES RD
CROOK CO OR 213-C4
RIM VIEW RD
KLICKITAT CO WA 196-A5
RINEHART RD
MALHEUR CO OR 146-C2
RINEHART RANCH RD
MALHEUR CO OR 146-B2
RINGO RD
CLACKAMAS CO OR 199-D7
WHITMAN CO WA 249-C2
RINGOLD RD
FRANKLIN CO WA 121-A2
RINK CREEK RD
COOS CO OR 220-D5
RIO NES LN
DOUGLAS CO OR 221-C3
RIORDAN HILL DR
HOOD RIVER CO OR 195-B6
RIO VISTA AV
BURLINGTON WA 260-E5
SKAGIT CO WA 260-E5
RIO VISTA AV Rt#-20
BURLINGTON WA 260-C5
RIO VISTA BLVD
VALLEY CO ID 251-C5
RIPON AV
LEWISTON ID 250-C5
RIPPEE LN
YAKIMA CO WA 243-A6
RIPPINGTON RD
PITT MEADOWS BC 157-B5
RISLEY CREEK RD
LINCOLN CO OR 209-C1
NE RISTO RD
CLARK CO WA 193-A3
RITCHEY RD
WASHINGTON CO OR 198-B1
RITTER RD
WHATCOM CO WA 158-D5
RITTER SPRINGS RD
GRANT CO OR 129-A3
S RIVARD RD
YAKIMA CO WA 243-D7
RIVER AV
EUGENE OR 215-B1
TILLAMOOK CO OR 197-A7
RIVER DR
LANE CO OR 215-C5
RIVER DR Rt#-155
COULEE DAM WA 237-C2
OKANOGAN CO WA 237-C2
N RIVER DR
LINN CO OR 133-C2
RIVER RD
CITY OF RICHMOND BC 156-B6
DISTRICT OF DELTA BC 156-C7
DISTRICT OF SURREY BC 156-D6
EUGENE OR 215-A1
EUGENE OR 329-G1
JACKSON CO OR 150-A1
JACKSON CO OR 226-C6
JACKSON CO OR 230-B3
JUNCTION CITY OR 210-A6
KOOTENAI CO ID 115-B2
KOOTENAI CO ID 115-B2
LAKE CO OR 151-C1
LANE CO OR 210-A6
LANE CO OR 215-A1
LANE CO OR 329-G1
LINN CO OR 134-B2
MARION CO OR 198-D7

RIVER RD
MARION CO OR 205-A1
Santa Clara OR 210-A7
Santa Clara OR 215-A1
SKAGIT CO WA 161-C6
TOWNSHIP OF LANGLEY BC 157-D6
UMATILLA OR 129-A1
UMATILLA CO OR 129-A1
WASCO CO OR 196-C6
WHITMAN CO WA 249-A4
YAKIMA WA 243-B6
RIVER RD Rt#-155
ELMER CITY WA 237-C1
OKANOGAN CO WA 237-C1
RIVER RD Rt#-167
PIERCE CO WA 182-A3
PUYALLUP WA 182-A3
TACOMA WA 182-A3
E RIVER RD
PUYALLUP WA 182-B3
N RIVER RD
JACKSON CO OR 229-D6
JACKSON CO OR 230-A6
LATAH CO ID 249-C1
ROGUE RIVER OR 229-D6
WHITMAN CO WA 249-C1
S RIVER RD
COTTAGE GROVE OR 215-B7
WHITMAN CO WA 249-C1
SE RIVER RD
CLACKAMAS OR 321-J4
CLACKAMAS CO OR 199-C4
GLADSTONE OR 199-D4
HILLSBORO OR 198-D2
MILWAUKIE OR 321-J4
WASHINGTON CO OR 198-D2
SW RIVER RD
HILLSBORO OR 198-D2
WASHINGTON CO OR 198-D2
RIVER RD N
KEIZER OR 322-J7
KEIZER OR 323-A4
SALEM OR 322-J7
RIVER RD NE
KEIZER OR 323-A2
MARION CO OR 204-D1
MARION CO OR 205-A1
MARION CO OR 323-A2
RIVER RD S
MARION CO OR 204-B7
MARION CO OR 324-D3
SALEM OR 322-G14
SALEM OR 324-D3
S RIVER RD S
INDEPENDENCE OR 204-B7
RIVER RD W
DISTRICT OF DELTA BC 101-C1
RIVER ST
CAVE JUNCTION OR 233-B4
JOSEPHINE CO OR 233-B4
LEBANON OR 133-C1
N RIVER ST Rt#-82
ENTERPRISE OR 130-C2
N RIVER ST Rt#-99W
NEWBERG OR 198-D5
S RIVER ST Rt#-82
ENTERPRISE OR 130-C2
W RIVER ST
CAVE JUNCTION OR 233-A4
RIVER BEND RD
SALEM OR 322-F9
RIVERBEND RD
MOUNT VERNON WA 260-A9
SKAGIT CO WA 161-A7
SKAGIT CO WA 260-A9
SW RIVER BEND RD
YAMHILL CO OR 204-B1
RIVER BOTTOM RD
KITTITAS CO WA 241-B6
RIVERCREST DR N
KEIZER OR 322-J6
NW RIVERFRONT BLVD
BEND OR 332-D7
RIVERFRONT RD
COLUMBIA CO OR 117-B3
RIVERGREEN AV
BENTON CO OR 327-H14
CORVALLIS OR 327-H14
RIVERHAVEN ST
PASCO WA 343-A7
RIVERIA RD
COLUMBIA CO WA 122-A2
RIVERSHORE RD
SNOHOMISH WA 269-H2
RIVERSIDE AV Rt#-7
OROFINO ID 123-C2
RIVERSIDE AV Rt#-20
OKANOGAN CO WA 104-A2
WINTHROP WA 104-A2
RIVERSIDE AV U.S.-101
HOQUIAM WA 178-A7
N RIVERSIDE AV Rt#-99
MEDFORD OR 336-C10
S RIVERSIDE AV Rt#-99
MEDFORD OR 336-D13
W RIVERSIDE AV
SPOKANE WA 348-H9
NW RIVERSIDE BLVD
BEND OR 332-D7
RIVERSIDE DR
BANDON OR 220-B5
COOS CO OR 220-B5
DIST OF N VANCOUVER BC 255-J3
DOUGLAS CO OR 225-C1
DOUGLAS CO WA 239-B5
LINN CO OR 207-C5
LINN CO OR 326-A10
MARION CO OR 198-D6
MOUNT VERNON WA 260-C10
MYRTLE CREEK OR 225-C1
PIERCE CO WA 182-C3
RIVERSIDE DR Rt#-20
OKANOGAN CO WA 104-C2
OMAK WA 104-C2
RIVERSIDE DR Rt#-129
ASOTIN CO WA 250-B5
Vineland WA 250-B5
RIVERSIDE DR U.S.-101
NEHALEM OR 191-B4

NE RIVERSIDE DR
MCMINNVILLE OR 198-B7
SE RIVERSIDE DR
VANCOUVER WA 306-C7
SW RIVERSIDE DR Rt#-43
CLACKAMAS OR 321-G5
LAKE OSWEGO OR 321-G5
MULTNOMAH OR 321-G5
RIVERSIDE DR NE
BANDON OR 220-B6
S RIVERSIDE RD
YAKIMA CO WA 243-C7
RIVERSIDE RD S
MARION CO OR 207-C1
MARION CO OR 324-A14
RIVERSIDE ST
BONNERS FERRY ID 107-B2
BOUNDARY CO ID 107-B2
RIVERSIDE CUTOFF RD
OKANOGAN CO WA 104-C2
RIVERSIDE WA 104-C2
RIVERSIDE PARK DR
SPOKANE CO WA 348-A1
RIVERVIEW BLVD
CLARKSTON WA 250-B4
RIVERVIEW DR
DESCHUTES CO OR 143-A1
LANE CO OR 210-A7
ROSEBURG OR 334-C5
W RIVERVIEW DR
KOOTENAI CO ID 353-E9
RIVERVIEW RD
JEFFERSON CO OR 208-A6
SNOHOMISH WA 171-D3
SNOHOMISH WA 269-H4
SNOHOMISH CO WA 171-D3
RIVERWOOD RD
YAMHILL CO OR 198-C7
RIXIE DR SE
THURSTON CO WA 184-D1
RIXON RD
PACIFIC CO WA 183-D7
ROAD 1-NE
GRANT CO WA 242-D3
ROAD 1-NW
GRANT CO WA 112-B3
ROAD 1-SW
GRANT CO WA 112-B3
GRANT CO WA 242-A4
ROAD 2-NE
GRANT CO WA 242-A3
ROAD 2-NW
GRANT CO WA 112-B3
GRANT CO WA 242-A3
ROAD 3-NE
GRANT CO WA 113-A2
GRANT CO WA 242-A3
MOSES LAKE WA 242-D3
ROAD 3-NW
GRANT CO WA 242-A3
ROAD 3-SE
GRANT CO WA 113-A3
GRANT CO WA 242-D4
ROAD 3-SW
GRANT CO WA 112-B3
ROAD 4-NE
GRANT CO WA 242-B2
ROAD 4-NW
GRANT CO WA 112-C3
GRANT CO WA 242-A2
ROAD 4-SE
GRANT CO WA 242-D5
ROAD 4-SW
GRANT CO WA 112-C3
ROAD 4-10-NE
GRANT CO WA 113-A2
GRANT CO WA 113-A2
ROAD 5-NE
GRANT CO WA 242-A2
ROAD 5-NW
GRANT CO WA 112-C3
GRANT CO WA 242-A2
ROAD 5-SE
GRANT CO WA 242-C5
ROAD 5-SW
GRANT CO WA 112-B3
ROAD 6-NE
GRANT CO WA 242-D2
ROAD 6-NW
GRANT CO WA 112-B3
ROAD 6-SW
GRANT CO WA 112-B3
ROAD 7-NE
GRANT CO WA 113-A3
GRANT CO WA 242-A2
ROAD 7-NW
GRANT CO WA 112-C3
GRANT CO WA 242-A2
ROAD 7-SW
GRANT CO WA 120-B1
GRANT CO WA 242-A6
ROAD 7-10-NE
GRANT CO WA 113-A2
W ROAD 7-10-NE
GRANT CO WA 113-A2
ROAD 8-NE
GRANT CO WA 242-D1
ROAD 8-NW
GRANT CO WA 242-A1
ROAD 8-SE Rt#-170
GRANT CO WA 121-A1
WARDEN WA 121-A1
ROAD 9-NE
GRANT CO WA 113-A3
GRANT CO WA 242-D1
ROAD 9-NW
GRANT CO WA 112-C3
GRANT CO WA 242-A1
ROAD 10-NE
GRANT CO WA 242-C1
ROAD 10-NW Rt#-28
GRANT CO WA 121-B3
ROAD 10-NW Rt#-281
GRANT CO WA 121-B3
ROAD 11-NW Rt#-28
GRANT CO WA 112-C3
ROAD 11-SW
GRANT CO WA 120-B1
GRANT CO WA 242-A7

ROAD 12-NE
GRANT CO WA 113-A3
GRANT CO WA 113-A3
ROAD 12-NW
GRANT CO WA 112-C3
ROAD 12 SE
ADAMS CO WA 242-C7
GRANT CO WA 242-C7
ROAD 12-SE
GRANT CO WA 242-B7
ROAD 13-SE
GRANT CO WA 242-B7
ROAD 13-SW
GRANT CO WA 242-A7
ROAD 13-SW Rt#-26
GRANT CO WA 120-B1
ROAD 15-NE
GRANT CO WA 113-A3
ROAD 15-1-31
LANE CO OR 210-D5
LINN CO OR 210-D5
ROAD 15-2-25
LANE CO OR 210-D5
ROAD 15-2-25-1
LANE CO OR 210-D6
ROAD 15-2-26-1
LINN CO OR 210-D5
ROAD 16-2-10
LANE CO OR 210-D6
ROAD 16-2-10-2
LANE CO OR 210-D6
ROAD 16-2-17-1
LANE CO OR 210-C6
ROAD 16-2-18
LANE CO OR 210-D7
ROAD 16-2-18-1
LANE CO OR 210-C6
ROAD 16-2-27
LANE CO OR 210-C7
ROAD 16-2-28
LANE CO OR 210-D7
ROAD 16-2-29
LANE CO OR 210-C7
ROAD 16-2-7-1
LANE CO OR 210-C6
ROAD 16-3-13-2
LANE CO OR 210-C7
ROAD 16-NE
GRANT CO WA 113-A3
ROAD 19-NE
GRANT CO WA 112-C2
ROAD 19-NW
GRANT CO WA 112-C2
ROAD 20-NE
GRANT CO WA 112-C2
GRANT CO WA 113-A2
ROAD 20-NW
GRANT CO WA 112-C2
ROAD 21 1/2-NE
GRANT CO WA 113-A2
ROAD 22-NE
GRANT CO WA 113-A2
ROAD 23-NE
GRANT CO WA 112-C2
GRANT CO WA 113-A2
ROAD 23 SW
GRANT CO WA 120-B1
ROAD 24-NW
GRANT CO WA 112-B2
ROAD 24-SW
GRANT CO WA 120-B1
MATTAWA WA 120-B1
ROAD 25-NE
GRANT CO WA 112-C2
ROAD 27-SW
GRANT CO WA 120-B1
ROAD 28
PASCO WA 343-C5
ROAD 29-NE
GRANT CO WA 112-C2
ROAD 31-NE
GRANT CO WA 113-A2
ROAD 36
FRANKLIN CO WA 343-B6
PASCO WA 343-B6
ROAD 36-NE
GRANT CO WA 113-A2
ROAD 42-NE
GRANT CO WA 113-A2
ROAD 43-NE
GRANT CO WA 237-B7
ROAD 44
FRANKLIN CO WA 343-A4
PASCO WA 343-A4
ROAD 44-NE
GRANT CO WA 237-A7
ROAD 45-NE
GRANT CO WA 237-B7
ROAD 46-NE
GRANT CO WA 237-B6
ROAD 47-NE
GRANT CO WA 237-B6
ROAD 48
FRANKLIN CO WA 343-A5
PASCO WA 343-A5
ROAD 48-NE
GRANT CO WA 237-B6
ROAD 49-NE
GRANT CO WA 237-C5
ROAD 50-NE
GRANT CO WA 237-C5
ROAD 51-NE
GRANT CO WA 237-C5
ROAD 52-NE
GRANT CO WA 237-C5
ROAD 60
FRANKLIN CO WA 342-H5
ROAD 68
FRANKLIN CO WA 342-G6
PASCO WA 342-G6
ROAD 68 N
FRANKLIN CO WA 121-A2
FRANKLIN CO WA 340-J5
PASCO WA 121-A2
PASCO WA 342-G1
ROAD 76
FRANKLIN CO WA 342-F5
PASCO WA 342-F5
ROAD 84
FRANKLIN CO WA 342-E4

ROAD 92
FRANKLIN CO WA 342-D4
ROAD 100
FRANKLIN CO WA 342-C2
PASCO WA 342-C2
ROAD 170
FRANKLIN CO WA 121-A2
ROAD 4370
LINCOLN CO WA 113-B1
WILBUR WA 113-B1
ROAD 7009
GRAYS HARBOR CO WA 177-D1
ROAD 8002
GRAYS HARBOR CO WA 178-A1
ROAD A-NE
GRANT CO WA 112-C2
GRANT CO WA 242-A2
ROAD A-NW
GRANT CO WA 242-A1
ROAD A-SE
GRANT CO WA 120-C1
GRANT CO WA 242-A4
ROAD A-SE Rt#-262
GRANT CO WA 120-C1
GRANT CO WA 242-A7
ROAD A-LINE
GRAYS HARBOR CO WA 117-B1
GRAYS HARBOR CO WA 178-D4
GRAYS HARBOR CO WA 179-A4
ROAD B-210
WASCO CO OR 135-A1
ROAD B-1000
GRAYS HARBOR CO WA 179-D7
ROAD B-NE
GRANT CO WA 112-C2
ROAD B-NW
GRANT CO WA 112-C2
GRANT CO WA 242-A2
ROAD B-SE
GRANT CO WA 120-C1
GRANT CO WA 242-B7
ROAD B-LINE
GRAYS HARBOR CO WA 179-A4
ROAD C-NW
EPHRATA WA 112-C3
GRANT CO WA 112-C3
ROAD CS30
MASON CO WA 179-B4
ROAD C-LINE RD
GRAYS HARBOR CO WA 179-D7
ROAD C-SE
GRANT CO WA 242-B4
ROAD D-NE
GRANT CO WA 112-C2
GRANT CO WA 242-B3
ROAD D-SE
GRANT CO WA 120-C1
ROAD D-LINE
GRAYS HARBOR CO WA 178-D4
ROAD E-NE
GRANT CO WA 242-B3
ROAD E-NW
GRANT CO WA 112-C3
ROAD E-SW
GRANT CO WA 120-C1
ROAD F-NE
GRANT CO WA 112-C2
GRANT CO WA 242-B2
ROAD H SE
GRANT CO WA 242-C7
ROAD I-NE
GRANT CO WA 242-C2
ROAD J-NE
GRANT CO WA 113-A2
ROAD K-NE
GRANT CO WA 113-A3
GRANT CO WA 242-D2
ROAD K-NW
GRANT CO WA 112-C3
ROAD K-SE
GRANT CO WA 242-D4
ROAD K-SW
GRANT CO WA 112-C3
ROAD L-5-SW
GRANT CO WA 112-B3
GRANT CO WA 120-B1
ROAD L 7-NE
GRANT CO WA 237-A7
ROAD L-NE
GRANT CO WA 113-A2
GRANT CO WA 242-D1
ROAD L-SE
GRANT CO WA 242-D5
ROAD L-SW
GRANT CO WA 120-B1
ROAD M-110
JEFFERSON CO OR 208-A6
ROAD M-NW
GRANT CO WA 112-B3
ROAD M-SE
GRANT CO WA 242-D5
ROAD M-SW
GRANT CO WA 112-B3
GRANT CO WA 120-B1
ROAD N-NE
GRANT CO WA 237-A7
GRANT CO WA 242-D1
ROAD N-SE
GRANT CO WA 242-D4
ROAD O-NE
GRANT CO WA 237-A6
GRANT CO WA 242-D1
ROAD O-SE
GRANT CO WA 242-D4
ROAD O-SW
GRANT CO WA 120-B1
ROAD P-110
JEFFERSON CO OR 208-A4
ROAD P-NE
GRANT CO WA 113-A3
GRANT CO WA 237-B6
ROAD P-NW
GRANT CO WA 112-B3
ROAD Q-NE
GRANT CO WA 113-A3
GRANT CO WA 237-B6
ROAD Q-SE
GRANT CO WA 113-A3
ROAD Q-SW
GEORGE WA 112-B3

STREET
City State Page-Grid

ROAD Q-SW
GRANT CO WA 112-B3
GRANT CO WA 120-B1
ROAD R-NE
GRANT CO WA 113-A2
GRANT CO WA 237-B6
HARTLINE WA 113-A2
ROAD R-NW
GRANT CO WA 112-B3
ROAD R-SW
GRANT CO WA 112-B3
GRANT CO WA 120-B1
ROAD S-322
WASCO CO OR 127-B3
ROAD S-NE
GRANT CO WA 113-A3
GRANT CO WA 237-B6
ROAD S-NW
GRANT CO WA 112-B3
ROAD T-2 NE
GRANT CO WA 237-B5
ROAD T-NE
GRANT CO WA 237-B6
ROAD U-NE
GRANT CO WA 113-A3
GRANT CO WA 237-C5
ROAD U-NW
GRANT CO WA 112-B3
ROAD U-SE
GRANT CO WA 113-A3
GRANT CO WA 121-A1
WARDEN WA 121-A1
ROAD U-SW
GRANT CO WA 112-B3
GRANT CO WA 120-B1
ROAD V-NE
GRANT CO WA 237-C5
ROAD W-NE
GRANT CO WA 113-A2
GRANT CO WA 237-C4
LINCOLN CO WA 113-A2
MARLIN WA 113-A2
ROAD W-SE
GRANT CO WA 121-A1
ROANOKE DR NE
MARION CO OR 205-A3
E ROANOKE ST
SEATTLE WA 278-B1
ROARING CREEK RD
WASHINGTON CO OR 198-A3
ROBBINS RD
KITTITAS CO WA 241-B4
ROBERTA AV
LAKE CO OR 152-A2
ROBERT BUSH DR U.S.-101
PACIFIC CO WA 183-D6
SOUTH BEND WA 117-A1
SOUTH BEND WA 183-D6
ROBERT CREEK RD
COOS CO OR 218-D4
ROBERT GRAY DR
PACIFIC CO WA 186-A6
SE ROBERTS AV
GRESHAM OR 200-B2
ROBERTS DR
BLACK DIAMOND WA 110-C3
ROBERTS RD
CROOK CO OR 135-C3
CROOK CO OR 136-A3
GRAYS HARBOR CO WA 183-B2
LEWIS CO WA 187-D1
LINN CO OR 210-B1
MEDFORD OR 336-E9
YAKIMA CO WA 243-A5
ROBERTS RD KPN
PIERCE CO WA 181-A1
ROBERTS BANK SUPERPORT CSWY
DISTRICT OF DELTA BC 101-C1
ROBERTS BUTTE RD
WALLOWA CO OR 130-C1
ROBERTS CREEK RD
DOUGLAS CO OR 221-B6
ROBERTS MOUNTAIN RD
DOUGLAS CO OR 221-B6
ROBERTSON CRES
TOWNSHIP OF LANGLEY BC 158-D1
ROBERTSON ST
CITY OF VICTORIA BC 257-A11
ROBERTSON BRIDGE RD
JOSEPHINE CO OR 229-A4
ROBIN DR
JEFFERSON CO OR 212-C2
ROBINETTE RD
COLUMBIA CO OR 192-A1
ROBINSON RD
JOSEPHINE CO OR 233-C4
SNOHOMISH CO WA 168-C7
ROBINSON ST
COQUITLAM BC 157-A4
ROBINSON CANYON RD
KITTITAS CO WA 241-A5
ROBINSON LAKE RD
LATAH CO ID 249-D4
ROBINSON PARK RD
LATAH CO ID 249-D4
ROBISON RD
BENTON CO OR 207-A3
POLK CO OR 207-A3
ROBSON RD
COQUITLAM BC 157-B4
ROBSON ST
VANCOUVER BC 254-F9
ROCHAT RD
KOOTENAI CO ID 115-B2
KOOTENAI CO ID 115-B2
ROCHAT DIVIDE RD
BENEWAH CO ID 115-B2
BENEWAH CO ID 115-B2
ROCHE HARBOR RD
FRIDAY HARBOR WA 101-C2
SAN JUAN CO WA 101-C2
ROCK RD Rt#-547
WHATCOM CO WA 102-B1
ROCK RD NW
DOUGLAS CO WA 236-C6
ROCKAWAY BEACH RD
KITSAP CO WA 174-D2
ROCK CANDY MOUNTAIN RD SW
THURSTON CO WA 180-A7
ROCK CANYON RD
MALHEUR CO OR 146-C1
ROCK CREEK RD
COLUMBIA CO OR 125-B1
COOS CO OR 140-C3
DOUGLAS CO OR 141-C2
DOUGLAS CO OR 219-B2
HARNEY CO OR 145-A3
HARNEY CO OR 153-A1
JACKSON CO OR 227-A3
JACKSON CO OR 230-B1
KLICKITAT CO WA 128-A1
LINCOLN CO OR 133-A1
MALHEUR CO OR 146-C3
WASHINGTON CO ID 139-A2
NW ROCK CREEK RD
MULTNOMAH CO OR 192-A6
S ROCK CREEK RD
BAKER CO OR 130-A3
ROCK CREEK DAM RD
WASCO CO OR 127-A3
ROCKCREST ST
COLUMBIA CO OR 189-B4
RAINIER OR 189-B4
RAINIER OR 302-G14
ROCK CUT RD
STEVENS CO WA 105-C1
ROCKFORD BAY RD
KOOTENAI CO ID 247-D6
ROCK HILL DR
Crowfoot OR 133-C1
LANE CO OR 215-B4
LINN CO OR 133-C1
LINN CO OR 210-C1
ROCK ISLAND AV
DOUGLAS CO WA 239-B5
ROCK ISLAND WA 239-B5
ROCK ISLAND RD
DOUGLAS CO WA 239-A5
East Wenatchee Bench WA 239-A5
ROCK ISLAND GRADE SW
DOUGLAS CO WA 239-C5
ROCK LAKE RD
WHITMAN CO WA 114-B3
S ROCK LAKE RD
SPOKANE CO WA 114-B3
ROCKLAND AV
CITY OF VICTORIA BC 256-J10
CITY OF VICTORIA BC 257-A10
W ROCKLAND RD
DIST OF N VANCOUVER BC 255-B1
ROCKLYN RD
LINCOLN CO WA 113-C2
ROCKPORT CASCADE RD
SKAGIT CO WA 103-A2
ROCK SPRINGS RD
JEFFERSON CO OR 211-D3
WHITMAN CO WA 122-A1
ROCKWELL DR
CITY OF HARRISN HT SPNGS BC 94-C3
DISTRICT OF KENT BC 94-C3
E ROCKWOOD BLVD
SPOKANE WA 349-A11
S ROCKWOOD BLVD
SPOKANE WA 349-B12
ROCKY RD
DOUGLAS CO WA 236-D4
ROCKY BAY PT Rt#-302
MASON CO WA 173-D7
ROCKY BAY POINT DR Rt#-302
MASON CO WA 174-A7
ROCKY BAY POINT DR KPN Rt#-302
MASON CO WA 174-A7
PIERCE CO WA 174-A7
ROCKY BUTTE RD
WASCO CO OR 202-D7
ROCKY CANYON RD
IDAHO CO ID 123-B3
IDAHO CO ID 131-C1
ROCKY CREEK RD KPN
PIERCE CO WA 174-A6
ROCKYDALE RD
JOSEPHINE CO OR 233-B6
ROCKY FORD RD
LINCOLN CO WA 113-C2
YAKIMA CO WA 120-A2
NW ROCKYFORD RD
YAMHILL CO OR 198-A4
ROCKY POINT RD
BREMERTON WA 270-E8
DISTRICT OF METCHOSIN BC 159-A7
DISTRICT OF METCHOSIN BC 165-A1
KITSAP CO WA 270-E8
MULTNOMAH CO OR 125-C1
MULTNOMAH CO OR 192-A5
ROCKY TOP RD
YAKIMA CO WA 243-A6
RODGERS RD
LANE CO OR 215-C5
RODMAN RD
YAKIMA CO WA 243-B4
ROE RD
LEWIS CO WA 187-B4
ROE RD E
LEWIS CO WA 187-B3
ROE ST
STEILACOOM WA 181-C4
ROGERS RD
COWLITZ CO WA 189-D5
DOUGLAS CO OR 221-C2
LEWIS CO WA 187-C5
POLK CO OR 204-B7
ROGERS AND HOBSON RD
CHELAN CO WA 236-D2
ROGERSON RD
LEWIS CO WA 184-D7
SE ROGUE DR
GRANTS PASS OR 335-G11
ROGUE RIVER DR
JACKSON CO OR 230-D4
SHADY COVE OR 230-D4
ROGUE RIVER HWY Rt#-99
GRANTS PASS OR 335-F11
JACKSON CO OR 229-C6
JACKSON CO OR 230-A6
ROGUE RIVER HWY Rt#-99
JOSEPHINE CO OR 229-C6
JOSEPHINE CO OR 335-J11
ROGUE RIVER OR 229-C6
ROGUE RIVER HWY U.S.-199
GRANTS PASS OR 335-G11
ROGUE RIVER LOOP HWY
GRANTS PASS OR 335-A9
JOSEPHINE CO OR 149-A1
JOSEPHINE CO OR 229-A5
JOSEPHINE CO OR 335-A9
ROGUE VALLEY HWY
MEDFORD OR 336-C9
ROGUE VALLEY HWY Rt#-99
ASHLAND OR 337-A4
CENTRAL POINT OR 230-C7
JACKSON CO OR 230-C7
JACKSON CO OR 234-B2
JACKSON CO OR 336-A7
JACKSON CO OR 337-A4
MEDFORD OR 230-C7
MEDFORD OR 234-B2
MEDFORD OR 336-A7
PHOENIX OR 234-B2
TALENT OR 234-B2
ROITZ RD
STEVENS CO WA 106-B3
ROLLING HILLS RD
POLK CO OR 207-B2
ROLOFF RD
ADAMS CO WA 113-C3
ROME RD
MALHEUR CO OR 146-C3
ROMIE HOWARD RD
DOUGLAS CO OR 219-C5
ROMINE CREEK RD
JACKSON CO OR 230-C1
ROMMERMAN RD
LEWIS CO WA 187-C1
RONDO RD
PIERCE CO WA 181-C7
SW ROOD BRIDGE RD
WASHINGTON CO OR 198-D2
ROOSEVELT AV Rt#-410
ENUMCLAW WA 110-C3
SW ROOSEVELT AV
BEND OR 332-E9
W ROOSEVELT AV
CANYON CO ID 147-B1
ROOSEVELT AV E Rt#-410
ENUMCLAW WA 110-C3
KING CO WA 110-C3
ROOSEVELT DR U.S.-101
SEASIDE OR 301-G6
ROOSEVELT ST
ABERDEEN WA 178-B7
N ROOSEVELT ST
BOISE ID 253-C3
WALLA WALLA WA 345-D6
S ROOSEVELT ST
BOISE ID 253-C3
WALLA WALLA WA 345-D8
ROOSEVELT WY
WHATCOM CO WA 101-C1
ROOSEVELT WY NE
SEATTLE WA 171-B7
SEATTLE WA 274-B2
ROOSEVELT GRADE RD
KLICKITAT CO WA 128-A1
ROPPERT RD
LEWIS CO WA 187-C3
ROSA RD
COOS CO OR 220-B7
ROSALYNN SUMNERS BLVD
EDMONDS WA 171-A5
ROSARIO RD
SKAGIT CO WA 160-C7
SKAGIT CO WA 259-D10
ROSARIO BEACH RD
SKAGIT CO WA 259-C14
ROSE AV Rt#-47
COLUMBIA CO OR 125-B1
VERNONIA OR 125-B1
ROSE RD
LANE CO OR 210-D6
SISKIYOU CO CA 151-A3
SNOHOMISH CO WA 168-C4
ROSE ST
PHOENIX OR 234-B2
N ROSE ST
WALLA WALLA WA 345-B6
W ROSE ST
COLLEGE PLACE WA 344-F9
WALLA WALLA WA 344-H9
ROSEBERG ST SW
THURSTON CO WA 184-A4
E ROSEBERRY RD
DONNELLY ID 252-D1
VALLEY CO ID 252-D1
W ROSEBERRY RD
VALLEY CO ID 252-D1
ROSEBROOK RD
LEWIS CO WA 187-D1
ROSE CREEK RD
MALHEUR CO OR 138-A2
WHITMAN CO WA 249-B3
ROSEDALE RD
CATHLAMET WA 117-B3
WAHKIAKUM CO WA 117-B3
SW ROSEDALE RD
WASHINGTON CO OR 198-D2
WASHINGTON CO OR 199-A2
ROSEDALE ST NW
GIG HARBOR WA 181-B1
PIERCE CO WA 181-B1
ROSEDALE BAY
PIERCE CO WA 181-B1
ROSEDALE PURDY
PIERCE CO WA 174-B7
ROSE HILL ST
BOISE ID 253-C3
ROSEMONT AV NW
SALEM OR 322-F12
SW ROSEMONT RD
CLACKAMAS CO OR 199-C4
ROSENAU RD
LATAH CO ID 250-D1
ROSENKRANTZ RD
NEZ PERCE CO ID 250-C5
ROSENOFF RD
ADAMS CO WA 113-B3
RITZVILLE WA 113-B3
ROSENOFF RD Rt#-21
ADAMS CO WA 113-B3
ROSE VALLEY RD
COWLITZ CO WA 118-A3
COWLITZ CO WA 189-C4
ROSS LN
JACKSON CO OR 234-A1
JACKSON CO OR 336-A12
LANE CO OR 215-C7
MEDFORD OR 336-A12
ROSS LN Rt#-238
JACKSON CO OR 336-A12
ROSS RD
DISTRICT OF MATSQUI BC 102-B1
DIST OF N VANCOUVER BC 255-F3
ROSSANLEY DR
JACKSON CO OR 234-A1
JACKSON CO OR 336-A10
MEDFORD OR 336-A10
ROSS INLET RD
COOS CO OR 220-D2
S ROSS POINT RD
KOOTENAI CO ID 354-D7
POST FALLS ID 354-D7
ROSS POINT-RATHDRUM HWY Rt#-41
KOOTENAI CO ID 247-D1
KOOTENAI CO ID 354-D2
POST FALLS ID 354-D2
ROSWELL RD
MALHEUR CO OR 147-A1
ROTH RD
LEWIS CO WA 187-C3
ROTHFORK RD
LATAH CO ID 249-C3
ROTHROCK RD
BENTON CO WA 120-C2
NE ROTSCHY RD
CLARK CO WA 193-B1
ROUGH & RUGGED RD
JACKSON CO OR 230-B7
SW ROUND BUTTE DR
JEFFERSON CO OR 208-A6
ROUND BUTTE LOOP RD
KLAMATH CO OR 142-C3
ROUND LAKE RD
JEFFERSON CO OR 211-B1
KLAMATH CO OR 235-A2
ROUNDS AV
JOSEPHINE CO OR 229-A6
ROUND TOP RD
JACKSON CO OR 230-B1
ROUNDTREE RD
LEWIS CO WA 187-A2
ROUND VALLEY RD
ADAMS CO ID 131-C3
ADAMS CO ID 251-A1
ROUPE RD
ASOTIN CO WA 122-C2
ROUSE RD KPS
PIERCE CO WA 181-A3
ROUTE 16 FRWY Rt#-16
PIERCE CO WA 181-C2
TACOMA WA 181-C2
TACOMA WA 292-A6
NE ROVA RD
KITSAP CO WA 170-C6
ROWDY CREEK RD
DEL NORTE CO CA 148-B3
ROWE CREEK RD
WHEELER CO OR 128-A3
WHEELER CO OR 136-A1
ROWLAND RD
LINN CO OR 210-B4
YAMHILL CO OR 198-B5
ROW RIVER RD
COTTAGE GROVE OR 215-C7
LANE CO OR 141-C1
LANE CO OR 215-C7
ROW RIVER CUTOFF RD
COTTAGE GROVE OR 215-B7
SW ROXBURY ST
KING WA 285-F4
SEATTLE WA 285-F4
ROXY ANN RD
JACKSON CO OR 234-C1
ROY RD
WHATCOM CO WA 161-A2
NW ROY RD
WASHINGTON CO OR 125-C1
ROY ST
SEATTLE WA 277-H3
E ROY ST
SEATTLE WA 278-B3
ROYAL AV
EUGENE OR 215-A2
EUGENE OR 329-A3
LANE CO OR 215-A2
MEDFORD OR 336-D11
NEW WESTMINSTER BC 156-D5
ROYAL AV N
EAGLE POINT OR 230-D5
JACKSON CO OR 230-D5
ROYAL AV S
EAGLE POINT OR 230-D5
S ROYAL BROUGHAM WY Rt#-519
SEATTLE WA 281-J1
SEATTLE WA 282-A1
ROYAL OAK AV
DISTRICT OF BURNABY BC 156-C5
ROYAL OAK DR
DISTRICT OF SAANICH BC 159-C5
ROY CHRISTIE
PIERCE CO WA 118-B1
SE ROYER RD
CLACKAMAS CO OR 200-B4
ROY JONES RD
SISKIYOU CO CA 150-A3
ROY PAYNE RD
LANE CO OR 219-D1
ROY PETTIT
PIERCE CO WA 181-D7
ROZA HILL DR
YAKIMA CO WA 243-D6
E ROZA HILL DR
YAKIMA CO WA 243-C6
N RUBY ST U.S.-2
SPOKANE WA 349-A6
RUCKEL RD
UNION CO OR 130-A1
RUCKER AV
EVERETT WA 264-D3
RUCKMAN AV Rt#-82
IMBLER OR 130-A2
RUDDELL RD SE
LACEY WA 297-H11
THURSTON CO WA 297-H11
NW RUDE RD
KITSAP CO WA 170-B6
SE RUDE RD
CLACKAMAS CO OR 200-C5
RUDI RD
DESCHUTES CO OR 212-B7
RUE CREEK RD
PACIFIC CO WA 117-A1
RUEPPELL ST
TILLAMOOK CO OR 197-A7
RUMBLE ST
DISTRICT OF BURNABY BC 156-C5
SE RUPERT DR
CLACKAMAS OR 321-J6
RUPERT RD
COLUMBIA CO OR 189-A7
RUPERT ST
VANCOUVER BC 156-C5
VANCOUVER BC 255-E14
RUPP RD
LEWIS CO WA 187-C5
RUPPERT RD
BENTON CO WA 120-C2
RURAL AV
WHATCOM CO WA 158-C7
RURAL AV SE
SALEM OR 324-H1
RURAL RD SW
THURSTON CO WA 296-F11
TUMWATER WA 296-F11
RURAL S ST
HARNEY CO OR 145-B2
RUSH AV
KLAMATH CO OR 151-A3
MALIN OR 151-A3
RUSH RD
ADA CO ID 253-A1
LEWIS CO WA 187-C1
RUSH CREEK RD
WASHINGTON CO ID 139-B1
RUSS BAKER WY
CITY OF RICHMOND BC 156-B6
RUSSEL RD
JOSEPHINE CO OR 229-B3
RUSSELL LN
JOSEPH OR 130-C2
WALLOWA CO OR 130-C2
RUSSELL RD
KENT WA 291-F4
LEWIS CO WA 187-B3
MALHEUR CO OR 138-C3
RUSSELL ST
WENATCHEE WA 238-D4
RUSSELL CREEK RD
WALLA WALLA CO WA 345-F9
Walla Walla East WA 345-E9
RUSSELL RIDGE RD
LEWIS CO ID 123-C2
RUSSELL RIDGE RD Rt#-7
CLEARWATER CO ID 123-C2
RUSTEMEYER RD
GRAYS HARBOR CO WA 183-C1
RUSTIC LN
LANE CO OR 214-B1
S RUSTLE ST
SPOKANE WA 348-D12
RUSTON WY
TACOMA WA 292-D1
TACOMA WA 293-E2
RUTLEDGE LN
SHERMAN CO OR 127-C2
RUTLEDGE RD
SHERMAN CO OR 127-C2
E RUTTER AV
SPOKANE WA 349-J6
SPOKANE WA 350-A5
SPOKANE CO WA 349-J6
SPOKANE CO WA 350-A5
N RUTTER PKWY
SPOKANE CO WA 346-B6
RUTTER PKWY
Fairwood WA 346-A7
SPOKANE CO WA 246-A1
SPOKANE CO WA 346-A7
RYALS AV
BENTON CO OR 207-B4
RYAN RD
DESCHUTES CO OR 213-A4
RYAN-ALLEN RD
SKAMANIA CO WA 194-C5
RYAN-TAVELLI RD
SKAMANIA CO WA 194-A7
RYE GRASS LN
HARNEY CO OR 145-B1
RYEGRASS RD
CROOK CO OR 213-B3
RYE VALLEY-MORMON BASIN RD
BAKER CO OR 138-C2

S

SAANICH RD
DISTRICT OF SAANICH BC 256-G5
SAARI RD
LEWIS CO WA 187-C4
SACHS RD SW
DOUGLAS CO WA 239-C3
SADDLE DR
KOOTENAI CO ID 245-B7
SADDLE BUTTE RD
HARNEY CO OR 145-C2
SADDLE MOUNTAIN RD
CLATSOP CO OR 188-D4
SADDLE RIDGE RD
LATAH CO ID 249-C3
SAGE RD
GRANT CO WA 242-C3
JACKSON CO OR 336-B10
SAGE RD
MALHEUR CO OR 139-A3
OWYHEE CO ID 147-A1
SAGEBRUSH FLAT RD
EPHRATA WA 112-C2
GRANT CO WA 112-C2
SAGEHILL RD
FRANKLIN CO WA 121-A1
W SAGEMOOR RD
FRANKLIN CO WA 121-A2
FRANKLIN CO WA 340-J2
SAGINAW EAST RD
LANE CO OR 215-B6
SAGINAW WEST RD
LANE CO OR 215-B6
S SAGLE RD
BONNER CO ID 244-A4
SAHALEE WY NE
KING CO WA 175-D1
SAMMAMISH WA 175-D1
SAMMAMISH WA 176-A2
SAINT ST
RICHLAND WA 340-F11
SAINT ANDREWS AV
CITY OF N VANCOUVER BC 255-C5
SAINT ANDREWS RD E
DOUGLAS CO WA 112-C2
SAINT ANDREWS RD S
DOUGLAS CO WA 112-C2
SAINT ANDREWS RD W
DOUGLAS CO WA 112-C2
SAINT CHARLES ST
CITY OF VICTORIA BC 257-A9
SAINT CLAIR RD
DESCHUTES CO OR 135-B3
DESCHUTES CO OR 217-D3
SAINT GEORGES AV
CITY OF N VANCOUVER BC 255-B5
SAINT HELENS AV
CHEHALIS WA 299-C10
SAINT HELENS AV
VANCOUVER WA 307-F7
S SAINT HELENS AV
TACOMA WA 293-G4
SAINT HELENS RD
PORTLAND OR 312-A2
NW SAINT HELENS RD
PORTLAND OR 199-B1
NW SAINT HELENS RD U.S.-30
MULTNOMAH CO OR 192-A5
PORTLAND OR 192-A5
PORTLAND OR 199-B1
SAINT HELENS ST
SAINT HELENS OR 192-B1
SAINT HILAIRE RD
YAKIMA CO WA 243-D7
NE SAINT JAMES RD
VANCOUVER WA 192-D5
VANCOUVER WA 306-A2
E SAINT JOE DR
KOOTENAI CO ID 245-A1
SAINT JOE RD
BENEWAH CO ID 248-D7
SAINT JOHN RD
WHITMAN CO WA 114-C3
SAINT JOHNS BLVD
CLARK WA 306-A2
VANCOUVER WA 305-H3
VANCOUVER WA 306-A2
NE SAINT JOHNS RD
CLARK WA 306-A2
CLARK CO WA 192-D5
VANCOUVER WA 192-D5
VANCOUVER WA 306-A2
SAINT JOHNS ST Rt#-7A
CITY OF PORT MOODY BC 156-D4
DISTRICT OF BURNABY BC 156-D4
PORT MOODY BC 157-A4
SAINT LAWRENCE ST
CITY OF VICTORIA BC 256-F9
SAINT LOUIS RD NE
MARION CO OR 205-A2
SAINT PAUL AV
TACOMA WA 182-A2
TACOMA WA 293-J5
SAINT PAUL HWY
MARION CO OR 198-D7
MARION CO OR 199-A7
SAINT PAUL HWY Rt#-219
MARION CO OR 198-D7
NEWBERG OR 198-D7
SAINT PAUL OR 198-D7
YAMHILL CO OR 198-D7
SALAL LN
COOS CO OR 220-C2
SALEM AV
ALBANY OR 326-F7
LINN CO OR 326-F7
MILLERSBURG OR 326-F7
SALEM EXWY Rt#-99E
KEIZER OR 323-C6
SALEM OR 323-C6
SALEM HWY Rt#-22
SALEM OR 322-J14
SALEM PKWY
KEIZER OR 323-C5
SALEM PKWY Rt#-99E
KEIZER OR 323-A8
MARION CO OR 323-A8
SALEM OR 322-J8
SALEM OR 323-A8
SE SALEM-DAYTON HWY Rt#-221
POLK CO OR 204-D2
POLK CO OR 322-E6
YAMHILL CO OR 204-D2
SALEM-DAYTON HWY NW Rt#-221
SALEM OR 322-E13
SALMI RD
LEWIS CO WA 187-B2
SW SALMON AV
REDMOND OR 212-D6
SE SALMONBERRY RD
East Port Orchard WA 174-B4
SALMON BUTTE RD
CLACKAMAS CO OR 201-C7
NE SALMON CREEK AV
CLARK CO WA 192-D4

PNW

INDEX

COPYRIGHT 1999 *Thomas Bros. Maps* ®

STREET / City State	Page-Grid

396 SNOWDEN WHITE SALMN RD — STREET INDEX — SE STEPHENS ST Rt#-99

STREET / City State / Page-Grid

SNOWDEN WHITE SALMN RD
- KLICKITAT CO WA 195-D4

SNUFFIN RD
- CLACKAMAS CO OR 200-C6

SOAP CREEK RD
- BENTON CO OR 207-A4

SOAP HILL RD
- UMATILLA CO OR 129-B3

SODA PEAK TR
- SKAMANIA CO WA 194-B1

SODA SPRINGS RD
- KLICKITAT CO WA 196-D1

SODAVILLE RD
- LINN CO OR 133-C1
- SODAVILLE OR 133-C1

SODAVILLE-WATERLOO DR
- LINN CO OR 133-C1
- SODAVILLE OR 133-C2

SOLAR LN
- YAKIMA CO WA 243-D6

SOLDIER CREEK RD
- JOSEPHINE CO OR 229-B4
- MALHEUR CO OR 147-A3

SOLDIERS CANYON RD
- NEZ PERCE CO ID 250-D4

SOLDIERS MEADOW RD
- NEZ PERCE CO ID 123-A3

SOL DUC VALLEY RD
- CLALLAM CO WA 163-B7

SOLE RD
- YAKIMA CO WA 243-B5

SOLKI RD
- Central Park WA 178-C7

SOMMER CAMP RD
- OWYHEE CO ID 147-B1

SOMMERS RD
- WHITMAN CO WA 122-B1

SOMMERVILLE RD
- LEWIS CO WA 187-C1

SOOKE RD
- CITY OF COLWOOD BC 159-A7
- DISTRICT OF LANGFORD BC 159-A7

SOOKE RD Rt#-14
- BRITISH COLUMBIA 101-A2
- BRITISH COLUMBIA 159-A7
- DISTRICT OF LANGFORD BC 159-A7
- DISTRICT OF METCHOSIN BC 159-A7

SOPER HILL RD
- SNOHOMISH CO WA 171-D1

SORENSON RD
- CLARK CO WA 192-D1

SOUNDVIEW DR
- GIG HARBOR WA 181-C1
- PIERCE CO WA 181-C1

W SOUTH AV
- CHEWELAH WA 106-B3
- STEVENS CO WA 106-B3

SOUTH DR
- PIERCE CO WA 181-A4

SOUTH RD
- KOOTENAI CO ID 245-C1
- WASHINGTON CO OR 198-A3
- YAMHILL CO OR 198-A3

SOUTH ST Rt#-293
- ANTELOPE OR 127-C3

SOUTH BANK RD
- DOUGLAS CO OR 221-D3
- GRAYS HARBOR CO WA 178-D7
- GRAYS HARBOR CO WA 179-B7

SOUTH BANK RD Rt#-107
- GRAYS HARBOR CO WA 178-D7

W SOUTH BANK RD
- SPOKANE CO WA 114-B1

SOUTH BANK CHETCO RIVER RD
- CURRY CO OR 232-D6

SOUTH BANK MAPLETON WEST RD
- LANE CO OR 214-D2

SOUTH BAY DR
- WHATCOM CO WA 161-B2

SOUTHBAY RD
- LINCOLN CO OR 206-C5

SOUTH BEND PALIX RD
- PACIFIC CO WA 183-D7

SOUTHBOROUGH DR
- DIST OF WEST VANCOUVER BC 156-B2
- DIST OF WEST VANCOUVER BC 254-F1

SOUTHCENTER BLVD
- TUKWILA WA 289-G5

SOUTHCENTER PKWY
- TUKWILA WA 289-G6
- TUKWILA WA 291-G1

SOUTH CRANE CREEK RD
- WASHINGTON CO ID 139-B2

SOUTHEAST AV U.S.-30
- NEW PLYMOUTH ID 139-B3
- PAYETTE CO ID 139-B3

SOUTHEAST BLVD
- EPHRATA WA 112-C3

E SOUTHEAST BLVD
- SPOKANE WA 349-D12

S SOUTHEAST BLVD
- SPOKANE WA 349-B11

SOUTH END RD
- ADAMS CO ID 251-A4
- CLACKAMAS CO OR 199-C5

SOUTHERN RD
- DESCHUTES CO OR 217-A1

SOUTH FORK RD
- BENTON CO OR 133-A2
- DEL NORTE CO CA 148-B3
- GRANT CO OR 136-C2
- LANE CO OR 134-B3
- TILLAMOOK CO OR 125-A2

SOUTH FORK BURNT RIVER RD
- BAKER CO OR 138-A2

SOUTH FORK JOHN DAY RD
- GRANT CO OR 136-C2

SOUTH FORK LITTLE BUTTE RD
- JACKSON CO OR 150-A1

SOUTH FORK MILL CREEK RD
- STEVENS CO WA 106-B2

SOUTH FRASER WY
- DISTRICT OF ABBOTSFORD BC 102-B1
- DISTRICT OF MATSQUI BC 102-B1

SOUTHGATE PL
- PENDLETON OR 129-B1
- UMATILLA CO OR 129-B1

SW SOUTHGATE PL
- UMATILLA CO OR 129-B1

SOUTHGATE ST
- CITY OF VICTORIA BC 256-G10

SOUTH HILL ST
- ALBANY OR 326-E11

SOUTH JUNCTION RD
- WASCO CO OR 208-C1

SOUTH PASS RD
- WHATCOM CO WA 102-B1

SOUTH POST RD
- CLATSOP CO OR 188-B3

SOUTH PRAIRIE RD
- TILLAMOOK CO OR 197-C3

SOUTH PRAIRIE RD E
- BONNEY LAKE WA 182-C4
- PIERCE CO WA 182-C4
- SOUTH PRAIRIE WA 182-C4

SOUTH PRAIRIE CARBON RIVER RD
- PIERCE CO WA 182-C5

SOUTH PRAIRIE-CONNELL
- PIERCE CO WA 182-D4

SOUTH ROCK CREEK RD
- BAKER CO OR 130-A3

SOUTH SHORE BLVD
- LAKE OSWEGO OR 199-C4
- LAKE OSWEGO OR 320-A7
- LAKE OSWEGO OR 321-E7

SOUTH SHORE RD
- CLALLAM CO WA 164-C6
- GRAYS HARBOR CO WA 109-A2
- JEFFERSON CO WA 109-A2

SOUTHSIDE BLVD
- CANYON CO ID 147-C1

SOUTH SIDE RD
- DOUGLAS CO OR 218-D1
- DOUGLAS CO OR 221-C1
- JOSEPHINE CO OR 149-A2
- JOSEPHINE CO OR 229-B7

SOUTH SLOUGH RD
- LANE CO OR 214-B4

SOUTH SUMAS RD
- DISTRICT OF CHILLIWACK BC 94-C3

SOUTH TOUTLE RD
- COWLITZ CO WA 118-A2

SOUTH UNION RD
- GRAYS HARBOR CO WA 179-C7

SOUTH VALLEY RD
- WASCO CO OR 127-A2

SOUTHWEST AV
- NEW PLYMOUTH ID 139-B3

SOUTHWEST BLVD
- COOS BAY OR 333-F13
- COOS CO OR 333-F13

SOUTHWOOD LN
- EUGENE OR 330-B5

SOVERN LN
- LANE CO OR 210-A6

SPADES RD
- BONNER CO ID 244-A3

SPANAWAY LOOP RD S
- PIERCE CO WA 181-D4

SPANAWAY-MCKENNA HWY Rt#-507
- PIERCE CO WA 118-A1
- PIERCE CO WA 181-C7
- ROY WA 181-C7

W SPANGLE RD
- CHENEY WA 246-A7
- SPOKANE CO WA 246-A7

S SPANGLE CREEK RD
- SPOKANE CO WA 246-C7

S SPANGLER RD
- CLACKAMAS CO OR 199-D6

E SPANGLE WAVERLY RD
- SPOKANE CO WA 114-C2

SPARROW DR
- JEFFERSON CO OR 212-C2

SE SPARROW ST
- MILWAUKIE OR 321-J4

SPARROW PARK RD
- DOUGLAS CO OR 214-A7

SPARTA RD
- BAKER CO OR 130-C3
- BAKER CO OR 138-C1
- BAKER CO OR 139-A1

SPAULDING AV
- GRANTS PASS OR 335-H9
- JOSEPHINE CO OR 335-H9

SPEAKER RD
- JOSEPHINE CO OR 225-C7

SPEARE CANYON RD
- UMATILLA CO OR 129-A1

SPENCER RD
- LEWIS CO WA 187-D3

SPENCER CREEK RD
- COWLITZ CO WA 189-D5
- DOUGLAS CO OR 214-D6
- LANE CO OR 133-B3
- LANE CO OR 215-A3
- LANE CO OR 329-A14

SPENCER LAKE RD
- MASON CO WA 180-B2

SPENCER WELLS RD
- DESCHUTES CO OR 135-B3

SPEOS RD
- PAYETTE CO ID 139-A3

SPERLING AV
- DISTRICT OF BURNABY BC 156-D4

SPERRY RD
- SAN JUAN CO WA 160-A6

SPEYERS RD
- SELAH WA 243-B5
- YAKIMA CO WA 243-B5

SPICER DR
- ALBANY OR 326-H9
- LINN CO OR 133-C1
- LINN CO OR 207-D5
- LINN CO OR 326-H9

SPINK LN
- VALLEY CO ID 251-D7

SPIRIT LAKE HWY Rt#-504
- CASTLE ROCK WA 187-C7
- COWLITZ CO WA 118-A2
- COWLITZ CO WA 187-C7

SPIRIT LAKE RD
- BONNER CO ID 107-A3
- KOOTENAI CO ID 115-A1
- KOOTENAI CO ID 115-A1

SPOFFORD RD
- UMATILLA CO OR 121-C3

N SPOKANE ST
- KOOTENAI CO ID 353-H5
- POST FALLS ID 353-H5

S SPOKANE ST
- KOOTENAI CO ID 353-H9
- POST FALLS ID 353-H8
- SEATTLE WA 281-J3
- SEATTLE WA 282-A3

SW SPOKANE ST
- SEATTLE WA 281-G3

SPOKANE WY
- GRAND COULEE WA 237-C3
- GRANT CO WA 237-C3

N SPOKANE BRIDGE RD
- SPOKANE CO WA 352-H10

W SPOKANE FALLS BLVD
- SPOKANE WA 348-J9
- SPOKANE WA 349-A9

W SPOKANE FALLS BLVD U.S.-2
- SPOKANE WA 349-A9

SPOONER RD
- LEWIS CO WA 184-A7

SPORTMENS WY
- OCEAN SHORES WA 298-B6

SPORTSMAN CLUB RD NE
- KITSAP CO WA 174-D1
- KITSAP CO WA 271-J2

S SPOTTED RD
- SPOKANE CO WA 246-A5
- SPOKANE CO WA 348-A13

SPOUT CREEK RD
- LINCOLN CO OR 133-A1

SPRAGUE AV
- WESTPORT WA 298-G13

E SPRAGUE AV
- Dishman WA 350-B9
- Greenacres WA 351-G8
- SPOKANE WA 349-B9
- SPOKANE CO WA 349-H9
- SPOKANE CO WA 350-H8
- SPOKANE CO WA 351-A8
- Veradale WA 351-A8

S SPRAGUE AV
- TACOMA WA 293-E6

W SPRAGUE AV
- SPOKANE WA 348-J9
- SPOKANE WA 349-A9

S SPRAGUE RD
- CLACKAMAS CO OR 200-A5

SPRAGUE ST
- WILSON CREEK WA 113-A2

E SPRAGUE AVE ACCESS 1
- SPOKANE WA 349-C9

E SPRAGUE AVE ACCESS 3
- SPOKANE WA 349-B9

SPRAGUE RIVER RD
- KLAMATH CO OR 150-C1
- KLAMATH CO OR 151-A1
- KLAMATH CO OR 231-D3

SPRAUER RD NW
- DOUGLAS CO WA 112-B1

SPRENGER RD
- LATAH CO ID 250-B1

SPRING ST
- IONE OR 128-B2
- KLAMATH FALLS OR 338-E7
- KLICKITAT CO WA 195-D4
- MAUPIN OR 127-B3
- MEDFORD OR 336-E10
- WHITE SALMON WA 195-D4

N SPRING ST
- KLAMATH FALLS OR 338-E7

SE SPRING ST
- PULLMAN WA 249-B5

W SPRING ST
- WALDPORT OR 328-D4

SPRING BROOK RD
- DOUGLAS CO OR 225-C1

SPRINGBROOK RD
- MEDFORD OR 336-F7
- YAMHILL CO OR 198-D5

SPRINGBROOK ST
- NEWBERG OR 198-D6
- YAMHILL CO OR 198-D6

SPRING COULEE RD
- OKANOGAN CO WA 104-C3

SPRING CREEK RD
- UNION CO OR 129-C2

SPRING CREEK RD Rt#-231
- LINCOLN CO WA 114-A1

N SPRING CREEK RD
- BONNER CO ID 244-D3

SPRINGDALE-HUNTERS RD
- SPRINGDALE WA 106-A3
- STEVENS CO WA 105-C3
- STEVENS CO WA 106-A3
- STEVENS CO WA 114-A1

SPRINGER RD
- JEFFERSON CO OR 213-A1

SPRING HILL DR
- ALBANY OR 326-C6
- BENTON CO OR 207-B3
- BENTON CO OR 326-C6

SPRING HILL RD
- WASHINGTON CO OR 198-B3

SPRING HOLLOW RD
- UMATILLA CO OR 129-C1

SPRING LAKE RD
- KLAMATH CO OR 235-C5

SPRINGRIDGE RD NE
- KITSAP CO WA 271-F2

SPRING RIVER RD
- DESCHUTES CO OR 217-A5

SPRINGS RD
- JEFFERSON CO OR 211-D2

SPRINGSTON RD
- KOOTENAI CO ID 248-B4

SPRING VALLEY RD
- WHITMAN CO WA 114-C3

E SPRING VALLEY RD
- SPOKANE CO WA 114-C3

SPRING VALLEY RD NW
- POLK CO OR 204-C4

NW SPRINGVILLE RD
- WASHINGTON CO OR 192-A7

SPRINGWATER AV
- WENATCHEE WA 238-D4
- West Wenatchee WA 238-D4

SPRINGWATER RD
- CLACKAMAS CO OR 200-B6

S SPRINGWATER RD
- CLACKAMAS CO OR 200-A4

SPROTT ST
- DISTRICT OF BURNABY BC 156-D5

SPROUT RD
- RICHLAND WA 340-G8

NW SPRUCE
- DESCHUTES CO OR 212-D5

NW SPRUCE AV
- DESCHUTES CO OR 212-C5

SW SPRUCE RD
- KITSAP CO WA 174-B6

SPRUCE ST
- CANNON BEACH OR 188-B7
- MYRTLE POINT OR 140-B2
- PACIFIC CO WA 186-A5
- PORT TOWNSEND WA 263-G2

N SPRUCE ST
- BURLINGTON WA 260-D4
- LA GRANDE OR 130-A2

S SPRUCE ST
- BURLINGTON WA 260-D5

SE SPRUCE ST
- ROSEBURG OR 334-F7

SPRUCE ST E U.S.-101
- ILWACO WA 186-A6

SPRUCE ST W
- ILWACO WA 186-A6

SPRUCE TRAIL RD
- CLALLAM CO WA 164-B6

SPURAWAY DR
- COQUITLAM BC 157-A4

SQUAW RD
- WHITMAN CO WA 114-B3

SQUAWBACK RIDGE RD
- JEFFERSON CO OR 135-A1
- JEFFERSON CO OR 211-D1

SQUAW BUTTE RD
- HARNEY CO OR 144-C1

SQUAW CREEK DR
- DESCHUTES CO OR 212-A4

SQUAW CREEK RD
- ADAMS CO ID 252-B7
- DOUGLAS CO OR 221-A7
- TILLAMOOK CO OR 203-C2

S SQUAW CREEK RD
- SPOKANE CO WA 114-B3

SW SQUAW CREEK RD
- JEFFERSON CO OR 212-A2

SQUAW FLAT RD
- KLAMATH CO OR 151-A2

SW SQUAW FLAT RD
- JEFFERSON CO OR 212-B1

SW SQUAW GULCH RD
- JEFFERSON CO OR 212-A2

SQUAW MOUNTAIN RD
- CLACKAMAS CO OR 200-C6
- CLACKAMAS CO OR 201-A7

SE SQUAW MOUNTAIN RD
- CLACKAMAS CO OR 200-D7

SQUAW VALLEY RD
- CURRY CO OR 228-B3

SQUEEDUNK RD
- TILLAMOOK CO OR 197-B1

SQUILCHUCK RD
- CHELAN CO WA 238-D5

STACKPOLE RD
- PACIFIC CO WA 186-A1

NE STADIUM WY
- PULLMAN WA 249-B5

NW STADIUM WY
- PULLMAN WA 249-B5

S STADIUM WY
- TACOMA WA 293-G3

SE STADIUM WY
- PULLMAN WA 249-B5

STADSVOLD RD
- WHATCOM CO WA 158-B3

NE STAFFER RD
- CLARK CO WA 193-C6

STAFFORD AV Rt#-903
- CLE ELUM WA 240-B2

STAFFORD RD
- CLACKAMAS CO OR 199-B5

SW STAFFORD RD
- CLACKAMAS CO OR 199-C4
- LAKE OSWEGO OR 199-C4
- LAKE OSWEGO OR 321-E7

STAGE RD
- COOS CO OR 218-B5

S STAGE RD
- JACKSON CO OR 234-A2
- JACKSONVILLE OR 234-A2

STAGE RD S
- JACKSONVILLE OR 149-B2
- JACKSONVILLE OR 234-A1

STAGECOACH RD
- LANE CO OR 133-A3

STAG HOLLOW RD
- YAMHILL CO OR 198-B5

STAHANCYK LN
- CROOK CO OR 213-C4

STAINWOOD ST
- BENTON CO OR 327-H4
- CORVALLIS OR 327-H6

STALEY RD
- WHITMAN CO WA 249-B6

W STALEY RD
- SPOKANE CO WA 114-B1

STAMPEDE BLVD NW
- KITSAP CO WA 270-F3

STAMPER RD
- ELMA WA 179-B7
- GRAYS HARBOR CO WA 179-B7

N STANDARD ST
- SPOKANE WA 347-A13

STANDLEY LN
- UNION CO OR 130-A2

STANFIELD MEADOWS RD
- UMATILLA CO OR 129-A1

STANKEY RD
- COWLITZ CO WA 187-D7

STANLEY AV S
- SEATTLE WA 282-B7

E STANLEY ST Rt#-92
- GRANITE FALLS WA 102-C3

W STANLEY ST Rt#-92
- GRANITE FALLS WA 102-C3

STANTON BLVD
- MALHEUR CO OR 139-A3

STANTON PARK RD Rt#-99
- DOUGLAS CO OR 225-C3

STANWOOD-BRYANT RD
- SNOHOMISH CO WA 168-C4

STAPLETON RD
- POLK CO OR 207-B1

STAR BLVD Rt#-44
- CANYON CO ID 147-B1
- MIDDLETON ID 147-B1

STARBIRD RD
- SKAGIT CO WA 168-B2
- SNOHOMISH CO WA 168-B3

N STARK AV
- DOUGLAS CO WA 239-A4

SE STARK ST
- GRESHAM OR 200-A1
- MULTNOMAH CO OR 200-B1
- PORTLAND OR 200-A1
- PORTLAND OR 313-H6
- PORTLAND OR 314-B6
- PORTLAND OR 315-H6
- TROUTDALE OR 200-B1

SW STARK ST
- PORTLAND OR 313-E5

STAR LAKE RD
- MASON CO WA 179-C4

STARR RD
- POLK CO OR 204-A4

N STARR RD
- Otis Orchards WA 352-E6
- SPOKANE CO WA 352-E5

S STARR RD
- SPOKANE CO WA 247-B6

STARR ST
- MARION CO OR 133-C1
- SUBLIMITY OR 133-C1

STAR RANCH RD
- MALHEUR CO OR 146-A2

STARR CREEK RD
- LINCOLN CO OR 209-A3

SE STARR QUARRY RD
- YAMHILL CO OR 204-C1

STARVEOUT CREEK RD
- DOUGLAS CO OR 225-D6

STATE AV
- COLUMBIA CO OR 125-B1
- MARYSVILLE WA 168-C7
- MARYSVILLE WA 171-C1
- OLYMPIA WA 296-J5
- OLYMPIA WA 297-A5
- SNOHOMISH CO WA 168-C7
- VERNONIA OR 125-B1

STATE AV Rt#-529
- MARYSVILLE WA 171-C1

STATE AV U.S.-30
- HOOD RIVER OR 195-D5
- HOOD RIVER CO OR 195-D5

N STATE AV Rt#-41
- NEWPORT ID 106-C3

NW STATE AV
- CHEHALIS WA 299-D11

S STATE AV Rt#-41
- NEWPORT ID 106-C3
- NEWPORT WA 106-C3

STATE RD
- WASCO CO OR 127-B2
- WASCO CO OR 196-A5

STATE ST
- Four Corners OR 204-D6
- Four Corners OR 323-B14
- Four Corners OR 325-E1
- MARION CO OR 205-A6
- MARION CO OR 325-H1
- OAKVILLE WA 117-B1
- SALEM OR 322-H13
- SALEM OR 323-B14
- SALEM OR 325-E1
- SEDRO-WOOLLEY WA 161-C6
- SKAGIT CO WA 161-C6
- VANCOUVER WA 306-D7

STATE ST Rt#-82
- LOSTINE OR 130-C2

STATE ST U.S.-95
- WEISER ID 139-A2

E STATE ST
- SEDRO-WOOLLEY WA 161-C6

N STATE ST
- BELLINGHAM WA 258-E6

N STATE ST Rt#-43
- CLACKAMAS OR 321-G6
- LAKE OSWEGO OR 321-G6

NE STATE ST Rt#-99
- DOUGLAS CO OR 221-C1
- SUTHERLIN OR 221-C1

NW STATE ST
- PULLMAN WA 249-B5

S STATE ST
- BELLINGHAM WA 258-B8
- TACOMA WA 293-E7

S STATE ST Rt#-43
- LAKE OSWEGO OR 321-G6

W STATE ST
- ADA CO ID 253-C2
- BOISE ID 253-C2
- GARDEN CITY ID 253-C2
- SEDRO-WOOLLEY WA 161-C6

W STATE ST Rt#-44
- ADA CO ID 147-C1
- ADA CO ID 253-A1
- BOISE ID 253-B1
- EAGLE ID 253-B1

STATE FARM RD
- POLK CO OR 204-C6

STATE FOREST RD
- CLALLAM CO WA 165-A6

STATE LINE RD
- CANYON CO ID 147-A1
- MALHEUR CO OR 147-A1
- MODOC CO CA 151-A3
- OWYHEE CO ID 155-C2

STATE LINE RD Rt#-161
- SISKIYOU CO CA 150-C3
- SISKIYOU CO CA 151-A3

STATE PARK ST
- MCCALL ID 251-D4
- VALLEY CO ID 251-D4

STATE TOLL FERRY
- SAN JUAN CO WA 160-B5
- SKAGIT CO WA 160-B5

STAUCH RD
- KLICKITAT CO WA 196-A2

STAUFFER RD NE
- MARION CO OR 205-C1

STAVE LAKE RD
- BRITISH COLUMBIA 94-B3

STAVE LAKE ST
- DISTRICT OF MISSION BC 94-B3

NW STAVIS BAY RD
- KITSAP CO WA 173-D2

STAYMAN RD
- CHELAN CO WA 236-B4

STAYTE RD
- CITY OF WHITE ROCK BC 158-B2
- DISTRICT OF SURREY BC 158-B2

W STAYTON
- MARION CO OR 133-C1

STAYTON RD
- MARION CO OR 133-C1
- STAYTON OR 133-C1

W STAYTON RD
- AUMSVILLE OR 133-C1
- MARION CO OR 133-C1

STAYTON RD SE
- MARION CO OR 133-C1

STAYTON-SCIO RD
- LINN CO OR 133-C1
- MARION CO OR 133-C1
- STAYTON OR 133-C1

STEAMBOAT CREEK RD
- DOUGLAS CO OR 142-A1
- DOUGLAS CO OR 222-A2

STEAMBOAT ISLAND RD NW
- THURSTON CO WA 180-B5

STEARNS LN
- DOUGLAS CO OR 219-A7
- DOUGLAS CO OR 221-C1

STEARNS RD
- CROOK CO OR 135-B3

STECKLEY RD
- LINN CO OR 207-D7

STEDMAN RD SE
- THURSTON CO WA 184-D1

STEELE RD
- WASCO CO OR 127-B2
- WASCO CO OR 196-C7

S STEELE ST
- PIERCE CO WA 181-D4
- TACOMA WA 181-D4
- TACOMA WA 294-E2

STEELE ST S
- LAKEWOOD WA 181-D4
- PIERCE CO WA 181-D4

STEELE SWAMP RD
- MODOC CO CA 151-B3

STEELHEAD RD
- JEFFERSON CO OR 212-C2

SW STEELHEAD FALLS DR
- DESCHUTES CO OR 212-C3
- JEFFERSON CO OR 212-C3

STEELMAN RD
- COLUMBIA CO OR 192-A4

STEENS HWY Rt#-78
- HARNEY CO OR 145-B1
- HARNEY CO OR 146-A2
- MALHEUR CO OR 146-B3

STEENS MOUNTAIN LOOP RD
- HARNEY CO OR 153-B1

STEFFENSEN RD
- PIERCE CO WA 181-A4

STEFFY LN
- CROOK CO OR 213-C6

STEGEMAN RD
- KLICKITAT CO WA 120-A3

STEHEKIN VALLEY RD
- CHELAN CO WA 103-B2

STEILACOOM BLVD
- STEILACOOM WA 181-C4

STEILACOOM BLVD SW
- LAKEWOOD WA 181-C4
- STEILACOOM WA 181-C4

STEILACOOM RD SE
- THURSTON CO WA 181-A6

STEILACOOM-ANDERSON ISLAND FER
- STEILACOOM WA 181-B4

STEILACOOM-DUPONT RD SW
- PIERCE CO WA 181-C4

STEILACOOM-KETRON ISLAND FERRY
- PIERCE CO WA 181-B4
- STEILACOOM WA 181-B4

STEIN RD
- WHATCOM CO WA 158-C4

S STEIN RD
- YAKIMA CO WA 243-A7

STEINER RD
- TILLAMOOK CO OR 197-C3
- WHITMAN CO WA 249-A3

S STEINER RD
- CLACKAMAS CO OR 200-A6

STEIWER RD SE
- MARION CO OR 207-D2

STELLA RD
- COWLITZ CO WA 189-A2

STELLYS CROSS RD
- DIST OF CENTRAL SAANICH BC 159-B4

STEMILT CREEK RD
- CHELAN CO WA 239-A5

STEMILT LOOP RD
- CHELAN CO WA 238-D6
- CHELAN CO WA 239-A7

STENKAMP RD
- DESCHUTES CO OR 217-D2

S STENTZ RD
- SPOKANE CO WA 246-C7

STEPHEN RD
- GRAYS HARBOR CO WA 179-A6

NE STEPHENS ST Rt#-99
- ROSEBURG OR 334-F5

SE STEPHENS ST Rt#-99
- ROSEBURG OR 334-G7

PNW

INDEX

ThomasBros.Maps® COPYRIGHT 1999 PNW INDEX

398 STREET INDEX N TOWER AV Rt#-507

STREET / City State Page-Grid

T

T AV
ANACORTES WA 259-H4
T RD NW
DOUGLAS CO WA 236-B5
T 1-2-SW ST
GRANT CO WA 120-B1
TABLE ROCK RD
JACKSON CO OR 230-C6
JACKSON CO OR 336-C3
MEDFORD OR 336-B8
TABLE ROCK TRAIL RD
JACKSON CO OR 230-C5
N TACOMA AV
PASCO WA 343-G7
TACOMA WA 293-F3
S TACOMA AV
TACOMA WA 293-G5
TACOMA WA 295-H3
SE TACOMA ST
PORTLAND OR 317-H6
PORTLAND OR 318-A7
S TACOMA WY
LAKEWOOD WA 181-D4
TACOMA WA 181-D4
TACOMA WA 293-H7
TACOMA WA 294-D2
TACOMA WA 295-H1
TACOMA MALL
TACOMA WA 295-E5
TACOMA MALL BLVD
TACOMA WA 295-E7
S TACOMA MALL BLVD
TACOMA WA 294-E3
TACOMA WA 295-E4
TACOMA-ORTING-PRAIRIE
PIERCE CO WA 182-A6
TAFT ST
BOISE ID 253-C2
TAFT ST Rt#-8
ELK RIVER ID 123-C1
ELK RIVER ID 123-C1
TAHUYA BLACKSMITH RD
MASON CO WA 173-B5
TAHUYA LAKE RD NW
KITSAP CO WA 173-D2
TAHUYA RIVER DR
MASON CO WA 173-C6
TAHUYA RIVER RD
MASON CO WA 173-B6
TALACHE RD
BONNER CO ID 244-A4
TALAPUS RIDGE RD
MULTNOMAH CO OR 194-C7
MULTNOMAH CO OR 201-C1
TALA SHORE DR
JEFFERSON CO WA 170-B3
TALBOT RD
MARION CO OR 207-D2
TALBOT RD S
KING CO WA 175-C6
MARION CO OR 207-D2
RENTON WA 175-C6
TALBOT RD SE
MARION CO OR 207-C2
TALBOTT LN
LANE CO OR 210-A5
TALLEY AV
KELSO WA 303-E11
TALLEY WY
KELSO WA 303-E11
TALLMAN RD
LINN CO OR 207-D6
PIERCE CO WA 182-B7
TALL PINES RD
KOOTENAI CO ID 247-D4
TALMAGE RD
POLK CO OR 204-B7
TALMAKS RD
LEWIS CO ID 123-B3
LEWIS CO ID 123-B3
TAMARACK LN
MAPLE RIDGE BC 157-D6
TAMARACK FALLS RD
VALLEY CO ID 252-C2
TAMPICO RD
BENTON CO OR 207-A3
TANDY LN
LINN CO OR 210-A4
TANEUM RD
KITTITAS CO WA 240-D4
TANGELWOOD LN
DOUGLAS CO OR 221-A4
TANGEN RD
YAMHILL CO OR 198-C5
TANGENT DR
LINN CO OR 207-B6
TANGENT OR 207-C6
TANGENT LP
LINN CO OR 207-C7
TANGENT ST Rt#-34
LEBANON OR 133-C1
TANKE RD
LINCOLN CO WA 113-C2
TANNER RD
DIST OF CENTRAL SAANICH BC 159-C4
TANNER CREEK RD
MULTNOMAH CO OR 194-C7
WASHINGTON CO OR 198-A1
S TAPPS DR E
PIERCE CO WA 182-C3
W TAPPS DR E
PIERCE CO WA 182-C3
W TAPPS HWY
BONNEY LAKE WA 182-C3
TARBOO LAKE RD
JEFFERSON CO WA 109-C1
TARGEE ST
ADA CO ID 253-B3
TARLATT RD
PACIFIC CO WA 186-A5
TARTAR GULCH RD
JOSEPHINE CO OR 233-C5
TATLOW RD
DIST OF NORTH SAANICH BC 159-C1
TATTERSALL DR
DISTRICT OF SAANICH BC 256-G4
TAUFFEN RD
WHITMAN CO WA 250-A2
TAUMARSON RD
COLLEGE PLACE WA 344-G12
WALLA WALLA WA 344-H12
WALLA WALLA CO WA 344-H12
WALLA WALLA CO WA 345-A12
TAURUS ST
OCEAN SHORES WA 298-B1
TAUSCHER RD
LEWIS CO WA 187-D1
TAUSICK WY
WALLA WALLA WA 345-G6
WALLA WALLA CO WA 345-G6
TAYLOR AV
ASTORIA OR 300-A5
BELLINGHAM WA 258-C10
TAYLOR AV N
SEATTLE WA 277-J2
TAYLOR RD
JACKSON CO OR 230-C7
LEWIS CO WA 187-D1
WALLA WALLA CO WA 344-E12
YAKIMA CO WA 243-B5
E TAYLOR RD
SPOKANE CO WA 246-B6
N TAYLOR RD
ISLAND CO WA 167-C2
TAYLOR ST E
MILTON WA 182-B2
TAYLOR WY
DIST OF WEST VANCOUVER BC 254-F2
TACOMA WA 182-A2
TAYLOR WY Rt#-99
DIST OF WEST VANCOUVER BC 254-E4
TAYLOR FLATS RD
FRANKLIN CO WA 121-A2
TAYLOR RICE
PIERCE CO WA 181-D7
SW TAYLORS FERRY RD
PORTLAND OR 316-B7
PORTLAND OR 317-F6
PORTLAND OR 320-A1
TAYLOR VALLEY RD
CLARK CO WA 192-D1
T CARRY RD
CLARK CO WA 193-A1
TEAGUE RD
LEWIS CO WA 184-A5
TEAL RD
DESCHUTES CO OR 217-D3
TEAL LAKE RD
JEFFERSON CO WA 170-B4
TEANAWAY RD
KITTITAS CO WA 240-C1
TEANAWAY WILSN STOCK TR
KITTITAS CO WA 241-B1
TEATERS RD
CROOK CO OR 136-A3
TECHNOLOGY LP
CORVALLIS OR 327-B12
TECHNOR ROBISON RD
SISKIYOU CO CA 150-B3
TEITZEL RD
LEWIS CO WA 184-C5
TEKOA-FARMINGTON RD
TEKOA WA 114-C3
WHITMAN CO WA 115-A3
TEKOA OAKSDALE RD Rt#-27
OAKESDALE WA 114-C3
WHITMAN CO WA 114-C3
TELEGRAPH RD
BRITISH COLUMBIA 159-A1
LEWIS CO WA 187-C4
TELEGRAPH TR
TOWNSHIP OF LANGLEY BC 157-C7
TELEPHONE RD
DESCHUTES CO OR 216-D5
TELEPHONE POLE RD
UMATILLA CO OR 121-C3
SE TELFORD RD
CLACKAMAS CO OR 200-B3
MULTNOMAH CO OR 200-B2
TELOCASET LN
UNION CO OR 130-B3
E TEMPLE RD
SPOKANE CO WA 247-A1
TEMPLETON RD
COOS CO OR 218-C4
TEN BAR RD
DESCHUTES CO OR 217-D3
TEN EYCK RD
CLACKAMAS CO OR 200-D3
NW TENINO RD
JEFFERSON CO OR 135-A1
Warm Springs OR 208-A3
TEN MILE RD
ADA CO ID 253-A2
TENMILE RD
MALHEUR CO OR 154-B2
N TEN MILE RD
ADA CO ID 253-A5
S TEN MILE RD
ADA CO ID 253-A4
TEN MILE CREEK RD
ADA CO ID 253-B5
TENMILE CREEK RD
LANE CO OR 209-A5
TENNANT WY
LONGVIEW WA 303-A10
TENNANT WY Rt#-432
COWLITZ CO WA 303-C12
LONGVIEW WA 303-C12
TENNESSEE RD
LEWIS CO WA 187-C3
LINN CO OR 133-C1
TENT CREEK RD
MALHEUR CO OR 155-A2
TENTH ST
KETTLE FALLS WA 106-A2
NESPELEM WA 105-A3
TERMINAL AV
VANCOUVER BC 254-J11
VANCOUVER BC 255-B12
SW TERRA DR
JEFFERSON CO OR 212-C1
TERRACE HEIGHTS DR
YAKIMA WA 243-C6
YAKIMA CO WA 243-C6
TERRA FERN DR
CLACKAMAS CO OR 201-A4
TERREBONNE-LWR BRDG WY
DESCHUTES CO OR 212-C3
Terrebonne OR 212-C3
NE TERRE VIEW DR
PULLMAN WA 249-B4
TERRI DR
JACKSON CO OR 234-C2
TERRITORIAL HWY
BENTON CO OR 133-B2
DOUGLAS CO OR 133-B3
LANE CO OR 133-B2
VENETA OR 133-B3
TERRITORIAL RD
COLUMBIA CO WA 122-A2
DOUGLAS CO OR 219-B1
NE TERRITORIAL RD
CANBY OR 199-C6
CLACKAMAS CO OR 199-C6
TERRITORIAL ST
HARRISBURG OR 210-A5
LINN CO OR 210-A5
TERRY RD
COUPEVILLE WA 167-B4
ISLAND CO WA 167-B4
SW TERWILLIGER BLVD
CLACKAMAS OR 321-F3
LAKE OSWEGO OR 321-F3
MULTNOMAH OR 321-F3
PORTLAND OR 316-E3
PORTLAND OR 317-E1
PORTLAND OR 320-E1
PORTLAND OR 321-E2
TETHEROW RD
DESCHUTES CO OR 212-C5
N TEXAS RD
SKAGIT CO WA 160-C6
TEXAS LAKE RD
WHITMAN CO WA 114-A3
TEXMAR ST SW
OCEAN SHORES WA 298-C3
THAIN RD
LEWISTON ID 250-C4
THATCHER RD
FOREST GROVE OR 198-B1
WASHINGTON CO OR 125-B1
WASHINGTON CO OR 198-B1
THATCHER PASS RD
SAN JUAN CO WA 160-A5
THAYER DR
RICHLAND WA 340-F13
RICHLAND WA 341-F1
THAYER RD
LEWIS CO WA 187-D3
S THAYER RD
CLACKAMAS CO OR 199-D5
NW THEATER AV
DESCHUTES CO OR 212-C4
THE CRESCENT
INDEX WA 111-A1
THE DALLES-CALIF HWY U.S.-97
BEND OR 332-D14
BEND OR 332-F3
CHILOQUIN OR 231-D3
DESCHUTES CO OR 143-A1
DESCHUTES CO OR 212-C7
DESCHUTES CO OR 217-C1
DESCHUTES CO OR 332-D14
DESCHUTES CO OR 332-F3
Deschutes River Woods OR 217-C1
Deschutes River Woods OR 332-D14
DUFUR OR 127-B2
JEFFERSON CO OR 135-B1
JEFFERSON CO OR 208-C4
JEFFERSON CO OR 208-C6
JEFFERSON CO OR 212-D3
KLAMATH CO OR 142-C2
KLAMATH CO OR 143-A1
KLAMATH CO OR 150-C1
KLAMATH CO OR 231-D3
KLAMATH CO OR 235-C1
KLAMATH CO OR 338-A1
KLAMATH FALLS OR 338-A1
MADRAS OR 208-C4
MADRAS OR 208-C5
MAUPIN OR 127-B3
REDMOND OR 212-D3
Terrebonne OR 212-D3
THE DALLES OR 196-D7
WASCO CO OR 127-B2
WASCO CO OR 127-B3
WASCO CO OR 135-B1
WASCO CO OR 196-D7
THE EVERGREEN COLLEGE PKWY
THURSTON CO WA 296-A2
THERMAL DR
COQUITLAM BC 157-A4
THIEF CREEK RD
DOUGLAS CO OR 219-B3
THIELSON ST
ECHO OR 129-A1
UMATILLA CO OR 129-A1
N THIERMAN RD
SPOKANE CO WA 350-A1
S THIERMAN ST
SPOKANE CO WA 350-A10
THIESEN RD
NEZ PERCE CO ID 250-C5
SE THIESSEN RD
CLACKAMAS CO OR 199-D3
THILLBERG RD
SKAGIT CO WA 260-G7
THIRD
DESCHUTES CO OR 212-A6
THIRD AV
FERNDALE WA 158-C6
E THIRD AV
East Port Orchard WA 271-A14
THIRD AV NW
OKANOGAN WA 104-C3
THIRD AV SW
OKANOGAN WA 104-C3
THIRD ST
FARMINGTON WA 115-A3
LINCOLN CO WA 114-A2
WHITMAN CO WA 115-A3
THIRD ST Rt#-507
TENINO WA 184-D3
THIRD FORK RD
GEM CO ID 139-C2
SW THIRTEENTH ST
CHEHALIS WA 299-E13
THOMAS
CROOK CO OR 213-D6
THOMAS RD
CLACKAMAS CO OR 126-A3
CLACKAMAS CO OR 205-D2
KING CO WA 182-D1
KITTITAS CO WA 241-C4
SKAGIT CO WA 161-A5
STEVENS CO WA 105-C3
STEVENS CO WA 106-A3
SE THOMAS RD
CLACKAMAS CO OR 200-D3
THOMAS RD KPN
PIERCE CO WA 174-A7
E THOMAS ST
SEATTLE WA 278-C4
THOMAS CREEK DR
LINN CO OR 134-A1
THOMAS CREEK RD
LAKE CO OR 152-A2
S THOMAS-MALLEN RD
SPOKANE CO WA 246-A5
THOMLE RD
SNOHOMISH CO WA 168-A4
THOMPSON AV
DOUGLAS CO OR 221-B6
WINSTON OR 221-B6
S THOMPSON AV
TACOMA WA 295-G1
THOMPSON LN
YAMHILL CO OR 198-C7
THOMPSON RD
CLALLAM CO WA 166-C7
COOS BAY OR 333-F7
YAKIMA CO WA 243-A5
W THOMPSON RD
KOOTENAI CO ID 247-D4
THOMPSON ST
SUMNER WA 182-B3
THOMPSON CREEK RD
JACKSON CO OR 149-B2
JOSEPHINE CO OR 149-B2
JOSEPHINE CO OR 233-C2
LANE CO OR 209-C7
LANE CO OR 214-D1
THOMPSON LAKE RD
KOOTENAI CO ID 248-B4
THOMPSON MILL RD
MULTNOMAH CO OR 200-D1
THOMSEN RD
HOOD RIVER CO OR 195-D7
S THOR ST
SPOKANE WA 349-F10
SE THORBURN ST
PORTLAND OR 314-E6
PORTLAND OR 315-E6
THORMAN AV NE
KEIZER OR 323-A6
THORN CREEK RD
WHITMAN CO WA 114-B3
THORNDYKE AV W
SEATTLE WA 273-E7
SEATTLE WA 276-E1
SEATTLE WA 277-E1
THORNDYKE RD
JEFFERSON CO WA 170-B5
N THORNE LN SW
LAKEWOOD WA 181-C5
THORN HOLLOW RD
COLUMBIA CO WA 122-A2
THORN PRAIRIE RD
DOUGLAS CO OR 223-A3
THORN SPRING RD
JEFFERSON CO OR 211-D1
THORNTON RD
WHATCOM CO WA 158-C5
THORNTON CREEK RD
LINCOLN CO OR 206-D3
W THORNTON LAKE DR
ALBANY OR 326-A6
THORP HWY
KITTITAS CO WA 241-A4
S THORPE RD
SPOKANE WA 348-G12
W THORPE RD
SPOKANE WA 348-E14
SPOKANE CO WA 114-B2
SPOKANE CO WA 246-A5
SPOKANE CO WA 348-E14
THORP PRAIRIE RD
KITTITAS CO WA 240-C2
THOUSAND SPRINGS RD
JACKSON CO OR 227-A4
THRALL RD
KITTITAS CO WA 241-C7
THRALL RD Rt#-821
KITTITAS CO WA 241-B7
THREE CREEKS LAKE RD
DESCHUTES CO OR 211-D5
DESCHUTES CO OR 216-C1
SISTERS OR 211-D5
THREE DEVILS GRADE RD SW
DOUGLAS CO WA 112-B2
THREE FORKS RD
MALHEUR CO OR 146-C3
MALHEUR CO OR 147-A3
MALHEUR CO OR 155-A1
N THREE FORKS RD
KOOTENAI CO ID 247-C1
THREE FORKS RESVR RD
MALHEUR CO OR 146-A3
THREE LAKES RD
ALBANY OR 326-H11
LINN CO OR 326-H11
SNOHOMISH CO WA 110-C1
SNOHOMISH CO WA 171-D3
THREE MILE LN
MCMINNVILLE OR 198-B7
YAMHILL CO OR 198-B7
NE THREE MILE LN
MCMINNVILLE OR 198-A7
YAMHILL CO OR 198-A7
SE THREE MILE LN
MCMINNVILLE OR 198-A7
YAMHILL CO OR 198-A7
THREEMILE RD
WASCO CO OR 127-A2
WASCO CO OR 196-C7
THREE MILE LN HWY Rt#-18
MCMINNVILLE OR 198-B7
YAMHILL CO OR 198-B7
THREE PINES RD
JOSEPHINE CO OR 229-B3
THREE RIVERS HWY Rt#-22
POLK CO OR 125-A3
TILLAMOOK CO OR 197-B6
TILLAMOOK CO OR 197-B6
TILLAMOOK CO OR 203-D1
YAMHILL CO OR 125-A3
YAMHILL CO OR 203-D1
THREE ROCKS RD
LINCOLN CO OR 203-B3
THREE TRAPPER RD
DESCHUTES CO OR 216-C7
THRESHER AV
Olympic View WA 170-B7
THRIFT
PIERCE CO WA 182-B6
THUMPER RD
DESCHUTES CO OR 211-C5
NW THURMAN ST
PORTLAND OR 312-E4
THURSTON RD
LANE CO OR 215-D2
SPRINGFIELD OR 215-D2
SPRINGFIELD OR 331-J6
THURSTON ST E
PIERCE CO WA 182-B4
PUYALLUP WA 182-B4
NE THURSTON WY
VANCOUVER WA 307-F1
TIBBETS MOUNTAIN RD
CHELAN CO WA 238-C1
TIBBLING RD
YAKIMA CO WA 243-B4
TICKLE CREEK RD
CLACKAMAS CO OR 200-B3
TICKNER RD
SISKIYOU CO CA 151-A3
TIDE AV
TILLAMOOK CO OR 191-A3
TIDE CREEK RD
COLUMBIA CO OR 189-C6
TIDELAND RD
TILLAMOOK CO OR 191-B4
TIDEWATER RD
LINCOLN CO OR 209-D2
TIEDMAN RD KPS
PIERCE CO WA 180-D2
E TIETAN ST
WALLA WALLA WA 345-C10
W TIETAN ST
WALLA WALLA WA 345-A10
WALLA WALLA CO WA 345-A10
W TIETON AV
Country Homes WA 346-J12
TIETON DR
YAKIMA WA 243-A6
YAKIMA CO WA 243-A7
TIETON RESERVOIR RD
YAKIMA CO WA 119-B2
SE TIGER MOUNTAIN RD
KING CO WA 176-A5
TIGNER RD
CHELAN CO WA 238-C2
W TILDEN ST
SEATTLE WA 272-D6
TILE FLAT RD
WASHINGTON CO OR 198-D3
WASHINGTON CO OR 199-A3
TILLAMOOK
CROOK CO OR 213-D7
TILLAMOOK AV
BAY CITY OR 197-B1
NE TILLAMOOK ST
PORTLAND OR 314-B3
TILLAMOOK HEAD COVE RD
CLATSOP CO OR 301-C11
SEASIDE OR 301-C11
TILLAMOOK RIVER RD
TILLAMOOK OR 197-B3
TILLAMOOK CO OR 197-B3
TILLAMOOK CO OR 197-B3
TILLER-SOUTH UMPQUA CAMP RD
DOUGLAS CO OR 141-C3
DOUGLAS CO OR 222-A7
DOUGLAS CO OR 226-A1
TILLER-TRAIL HWY Rt#-227
CANYONVILLE OR 225-D3
DOUGLAS CO OR 141-B3
DOUGLAS CO OR 225-D3
JACKSON CO OR 141-C3
JACKSON CO OR 230-D1
TILLEY RD SW
THURSTON CO WA 184-C3
TILLEY RD SW Rt#-121
THURSTON CO WA 184-C2
TILLICUM RD
DISTRICT OF SAANICH BC 256-D5
TOWN OF ESQUIMALT BC 256-D7
SE TILLSTROM RD
CLACKAMAS CO OR 200-B3
TIMBER RD
COLUMBIA CO OR 125-B1
LINN CO OR 210-D3
WASHINGTON CO OR 125-B1
TIMBER ST
ALBANY OR 326-H7
TIMBER TR NE
MARION CO OR 205-D5
TIMBER WY
COOS CO OR 220-D3
TIMBER CREEK RD
JACKSON CO OR 226-A6
TIMBERLINE HWY
CLACKAMAS CO OR 202-A6
TIMBERLINE EAST LEG
CLACKAMAS CO OR 202-A6
TIMBERLINE WEST LEG
CLACKAMAS CO OR 202-A6
NE TIMMEN RD
CLARK CO WA 192-C2
NW TIMMEN RD
CLARK CO WA 192-C2
TIMOTHY LAKE RD
CLACKAMAS CO OR 126-C3
TINGLE RD
LEWIS CO WA 187-C2
TINGLEY LN
KLAMATH CO OR 235-C5
TIPTON RD
KITTITAS CO WA 241-B4
TISCH
PIERCE CO WA 118-A1
TITCHENAL CANYON RD SW
DOUGLAS CO WA 239-C2
TITUS LN
VALLEY CO ID 252-D1
TOAD RD
JACKSON CO OR 229-D3
TOANDOS RD
JEFFERSON CO WA 170-A5
TODEY RD
LEWIS CO WA 187-D5
TOE JAM HILL RD NE
KITSAP CO WA 174-D3
TOFTDAHL RD N
LANE CO OR 210-A5
TOKELAND RD
PACIFIC CO WA 183-C5
TOKIO RD
ADAMS CO WA 113-B3
HARRINGTON WA 113-C3
LINCOLN CO WA 113-C3
TOLEDO SALMON CREEK RD
LEWIS CO WA 187-D5
TOLEDO SALMON HANKIN RD
LEWIS CO WA 187-D4
TOLEDO VADER RD
LEWIS CO WA 187-C4
TOLEDO WA 187-C4
TOLER RD NW
DOUGLAS CO WA 236-D7
TOLIVER RD
CLACKAMAS CO OR 205-D1
TOLL RD
MULTNOMAH CO OR 200-D1
S TOLL RD
SPOKANE CO WA 247-B7
TOLL STATION RD
DESCHUTES CO OR 211-B3
JEFFERSON CO OR 211-B2
TOLMAN RD
LANE CO OR 215-A4
SE TOLMAN ST
PORTLAND OR 318-A5
TOLMAN CREEK RD
JACKSON CO OR 234-D5
N TOLMAN CREEK RD
ASHLAND OR 337-H9
JACKSON CO OR 337-H9
S TOLMAN CREEK RD
ASHLAND OR 337-H11
TOLMIE RD
DISTRICT OF ABBOTSFORD BC 102-B1
TOLO RD
JACKSON CO OR 230-B7
TOLT AV Rt#-203
CARNATION WA 176-B2
KING CO WA 176-B2
NE TOLT HILL RD
KING CO WA 176-A2
TOMLINSON RD
TILLAMOOK CO OR 197-B2
TOM SMITH RD
COOS CO OR 220-B5
TOM WRIGHT
PIERCE CO WA 182-A6
TONASKET-HAVILLAH RD
OKANOGAN CO WA 104-C2
OKANOGAN CO WA 105-A1
TONASKET WA 104-C2
TONE RD
TILLAMOOK CO OR 197-B2
TONGUE LN
WASHINGTON CO OR 198-C2
TONO RD SE
THURSTON CO WA 184-D4
SW TONQUIN RD
WASHINGTON CO OR 199-B5
TONY CREEK RD
HOOD RIVER CO OR 202-B1
TOONERVILLE DR
MASON CO WA 173-D4
SW TOOZE RD
CLACKAMAS CO OR 199-A5
TOPE RD
WALLOWA CO OR 130-C1
E TOPPENISH AV
TOPPENISH WA 120-A2
S TOPPENISH AV
TOPPENISH WA 120-A2
TOPPENISH-ZILLAH RD
YAKIMA CO WA 120-A2
ZILLAH WA 120-A2
TOQUA RD
KLAMATH CO OR 231-C5
TORNQUIST RD
GRAYS HARBOR CO WA 179-D5
TORODA BRDG CUSTOMS RD
FERRY CO WA 105-B1
TORODA CREEK RD
FERRY CO WA 105-B1
OKANOGAN CO WA 105-A2
TORPEDO RD
ISLAND CO WA 167-C2
OAK HARBOR WA 167-C2
TORVEND RD NE
MARION CO OR 205-B4
TOTTEN RD NE
Suquamish WA 170-C7
TOUCHET RD
WALLA WALLA CO WA 121-B3
S TOUCHET RD
COLUMBIA CO WA 122-A3
TOUCHET-GARDENA RD
WALLA WALLA CO WA 121-B3
TOUVELLE RD
JACKSON CO OR 230-C5
N TOWER AV Rt#-507
CENTRALIA WA 299-F3

PNW

INDEX

Thomas Bros. Maps ®
COPYRIGHT 1999

PNW

INDEX

PNW

INDEX

N WASHINGTON AV — STREET INDEX — WHITNEY HWY Rt#-7 401

STREET City State Page-Grid

N WASHINGTON AV
CENTRALIA WA 299-E3
N WASHINGTON AV Rt#-52
GEM CO ID 139-C3
N WASHINGTON AV U.S.-2
NEWPORT WA 106-C3
S WASHINGTON AV
CENTRALIA WA 299-E4
S WASHINGTON AV Rt#-52
EMMETT ID 139-C3
GEM CO ID 139-C3
S WASHINGTON AV U.S.-2
NEWPORT WA 106-C3
SE WASHINGTON AV
ROSEBURG OR 334-G8
SW WASHINGTON AV Rt#-138
ROSEBURG OR 334-F7
W WASHINGTON AV
YAKIMA WA 243-B7
WASHINGTON AV N Rt#-161
EATONVILLE WA 118-B1
PIERCE CO WA 118-B1
WASHINGTON AV N Rt#-162
ORTING WA 182-C5
WASHINGTON AV S
LONG BEACH WA 186-A5
WASHINGTON AV S Rt#-161
EATONVILLE WA 118-B1
WASHINGTON AV S Rt#-162
ORTING WA 182-C5
WASHINGTON BLVD
LAKEWOOD WA 181-C4
NW WASHINGTON BLVD
GRANTS PASS OR 335-F7
E WASHINGTON RD
SPOKANE CO WA 246-D6
SPOKANE CO WA 247-A6
WASHINGTON ST
ASTORIA OR 300-B4
CHELAN CO WA 236-B1
CHENEY WA 246-A7
EUGENE OR 329-J7
FERNDALE WA 158-C6
LEWIS CO WA 187-C1
MABTON WA 120-B3
MORROW CO OR 128-C1
NAPAVINE WA 187-C1
OREGON CITY OR 199-D4
PORT TOWNSEND WA 263-G5
SEDRO-WOOLLEY WA 161-C5
SKAGIT CO WA 259-H14
SODAVILLE OR 133-C2
SPOKANE CO WA 246-A7
VANCOUVER WA 305-F5
WENATCHEE WA 238-D4
WOODLAND WA 192-C1
WASHINGTON ST Rt#-26
ADAMS CO WA 121-A1
OTHELLO WA 121-A1
WASHINGTON ST Rt#-129
ASOTIN WA 250-B5
WASHINGTON ST Rt#-218
FOSSIL OR 128-A3
E WASHINGTON ST
STAYTON OR 133-C1
E WASHINGTON ST U.S.-101
CLALLAM CO WA 166-B7
CLALLAM CO WA 262-F12
SEQUIM WA 262-F12
N WASHINGTON ST
KENNEWICK WA 343-D10
SPOKANE WA 348-J6
N WASHINGTON ST Rt#-19
CONDON OR 128-A2
S WASHINGTON ST
Finley WA 343-D13
KENNEWICK WA 343-D13
SPOKANE WA 348-J10
S WASHINGTON ST Rt#-19
CONDON OR 128-A2
S WASHINGTON ST U.S.-95
MOSCOW ID 249-C5
SE WASHINGTON ST
PORTLAND OR 315-G6
SE WASHINGTON ST Rt#-223
DALLAS OR 204-A6
SW WASHINGTON ST
PORTLAND OR 313-F6
SW WASHINGTON ST Rt#-223
DALLAS OR 204-A6
W WASHINGTON ST
STAYTON OR 133-C1
W WASHINGTON ST U.S.-101
CLALLAM CO WA 165-D6
CLALLAM CO WA 166-A6
CLALLAM CO WA 262-A12
SEQUIM WA 262-B12
WASHINGTON ST E
HUNTINGTON OR 138-C2
WASHINGTON ST E U.S.-20
VALE OR 139-A3
WASHINGTON ST E U.S.-30
HUNTINGTON OR 138-C2
WASHINGTON ST W U.S.-20
VALE OR 139-A3
WASHINGTON ST W U.S.-30
HUNTINGTON OR 138-C2
WASHINGTON WY
COLUMBIA CO OR 189-B4
GEORGE WA 112-B3
GRANT CO WA 112-B3
LONGVIEW WA 302-J9
LONGVIEW WA 303-B8
RAINIER OR 189-B4
WASHOUGAL RIVER RD
CLARK CO WA 193-D7
SKAMANIA CO WA 193-D7
SKAMANIA CO WA 194-A6
SE WASHOUGAL RIVER RD
CLARK CO WA 193-C7
WASHOUGAL WA 193-C7
WASHUM RD
ADA CO ID 253-A1
WASSER RD
COLUMBIA CO OR 189-C6
WATER ST
PORT MOODY BC 157-A4
PORT TOWNSEND WA 263-J4
VANCOUVER BC 254-H10
WATER ST Rt#-20
PORT TOWNSEND WA 263-H5
WATER ST Rt#-27
TEKOA WA 114-C3
WHITMAN CO WA 114-C3
WATER ST Rt#-82
LOSTINE OR 130-C2
N WATER ST
OLYMPIA WA 296-H5
SILVERTON OR 205-C4
WESTON OR 129-C1
N WATER ST Rt#-214
SILVERTON OR 205-C4
S WATER ST
WESTON OR 129-C1
S WATER ST Rt#-214
SILVERTON OR 205-C4
WATERFRONT ST
YAMHILL CO OR 198-D6
WATER GAP RD
JOSEPHINE CO OR 149-B2
WATER GULCH RD
BAKER CO OR 138-A1
WATERLOO RD
LINN CO OR 133-C1
WATERLOO OR 133-C1
WATERMAN RD
WHITMAN CO WA 114-C3
WATERS AV S
SEATTLE WA 287-H5
WATERS RD
COWLITZ CO WA 189-C1
WATER TANK RD
SKAGIT CO WA 161-A6
WATER WHEEL RD
GEM CO ID 139-C3
WATERWORKS RD
CLACKAMAS CO OR 200-D3
SNOHOMISH CO WA 168-B7
SW WATSON AV
BEAVERTON OR 199-B2
WATSON RD
JEFFERSON CO WA 170-B3
KITTITAS CO WA 241-C5
WALLA WALLA CO WA 121-B3
YAKIMA CO WA 243-A5
S WATSON RD
KOOTENAI CO ID 247-D6
WATSON ST U.S.-2
CRESTON WA 113-C1
WATT CANYON RD
KITTITAS CO WA 240-D4
WAUGH RD
DESCHUTES CO OR 217-D2
LINCOLN CO OR 206-C2
N WAUGH RD
MOUNT VERNON WA 260-G11
WAUKON RD
LINCOLN CO WA 114-A2
WAUNA VISTA DR
WALLA WALLA WA 345-C9
WAUNCHER GULCH RD
LATAH CO ID 123-B1
LATAH CO ID 123-B1
NEZ PERCE CO ID 123-B1
NEZ PERCE CO ID 123-B1
SW WAVA LN
KITSAP CO WA 174-A6
WAVERLY DR
ALBANY OR 326-F9
E WAVERLY RD
SPOKANE CO WA 114-C2
WAVERLY WA 114-C2
WAWAWAI RD
WHITMAN CO WA 249-A7
WHITMAN CO WA 250-A1
WAWAWAI GRADE RD
WHITMAN CO WA 122-C1
WAWAWAI-PULLMAN RD
PULLMAN WA 249-A6
WHITMAN CO WA 249-A6
WAWAWAI-PULLMAN RD Rt#-194
WHITMAN CO WA 249-A5
WAWAWAI RIVER RD
WHITMAN CO WA 122-C2
WHITMAN CO WA 250-B4
WAWAWAI RIVER RD Rt#-193
WHITMAN CO WA 122-C2
WHITMAN CO WA 250-A4
SE WAX RD
COVINGTON WA 175-D7
KING CO WA 175-D7
MAPLE VALLEY WA 175-D7
WAX ORCHARD RD SW
KING CO WA 174-D7
WAYNE DR N
KEIZER OR 322-J6
WAYNITA WY NE
BOTHELL WA 171-C7
WAYPARK DR NE
MARION CO OR 205-B3
WEATHERFORD RD
LINN CO OR 210-B5
WEAVER RD
DOUGLAS CO OR 225-C2
KITTITAS CO WA 241-A5
WEAVER RD N
KITSAP CO WA 271-J2
S WEBB AV
DOUGLAS CO WA 239-B5
WEBB CANAL RD
NEZ PERCE CO ID 250-D5
WEBB CUTOFF RD
NEZ PERCE CO ID 250-D6
WEBB DISTRICT RD
COLUMBIA CO OR 117-B3
WEBBER CANYON RD
BENTON CO WA 120-C3
WEBBER CANYON RD Rt#-224
BENTON CO WA 120-C3
WEBBER CANYON RD Rt#-225
BENTON CO WA 120-C3
WEBB HILL RD
MASON CO WA 180-A1
WEBB RIDGE RD
NEZ PERCE CO ID 250-D6
WEBER RD
ADAMS CO WA 113-C3
CLACKAMAS CO OR 201-A5
LINCOLN CO WA 113-C3
LINN CO OR 210-C3
WHITMAN CO WA 249-B6
S WEBER COULEE RD
ADAMS CO WA 113-B3
WEBERG RD
CROOK CO OR 136-C3
WEBFOOT RD
DAYTON OR 198-C7
YAMHILL CO OR 198-C7
SE WEBFOOT RD
YAMHILL CO OR 204-C2
WEBSTER AV
CHELAN WA 236-D3
W WEBSTER AV
CHEWELAH WA 106-B3
WEBSTER EXT
PIERCE CO WA 182-A6
WEBSTER RD
GLADSTONE OR 199-D4
PIERCE CO WA 118-B1
SE WEBSTER RD
CLACKAMAS CO OR 199-D3
GLADSTONE OR 199-D3
WEBSTER RD E
PIERCE CO WA 182-A7
WEBSTER FLAT RD
JEFFERSON CO OR 208-B1
W WEDGEWOOD AV
Town and Country WA 346-H14
Town and Country WA 347-A14
WEED RD
KLAMATH CO OR 231-C2
S WEGER RD
SPOKANE CO WA 246-D6
N WEHE AV
PASCO WA 343-H7
S WEHE AV
PASCO WA 343-H8
WEHRLI CANYON RD
GILLIAM CO OR 128-A3
WEIDKAMP RD
WHATCOM CO WA 158-D3
NE WEIDLER ST
PORTLAND OR 313-H4
PORTLAND OR 315-J4
WEIGAND RD
CROOK CO OR 213-B6
WEIKEL RD
YAKIMA CO WA 243-A6
N WEIPERT DR
Country Homes WA 346-J12
Town and Country WA 346-J12
SW WEIR RD
BEAVERTON OR 199-A3
WEISER SPUR U.S.-95
MALHEUR CO OR 139-A2
WEISER RIVER RD
WASHINGTON CO ID 139-A2
WEISER ID 139-A2
WEISS RD
LANE CO OR 215-A5
WEISSENFELS RIDGE RD
ASOTIN CO WA 123-A3
ASOTIN CO WA 123-A3
ASOTIN CO WA 250-C7
WEITZ LN
CLACKAMAS CO OR 200-B5
WEITZ RD
CANYON CO ID 147-B1
WELCH ST
DIST OF N VANCOUVER BC 254-G5
WELCHER RD
ISLAND CO WA 167-C5
WELCHES RD
CLACKAMAS CO OR 201-C5
WELLER RD
KOOTENAI CO ID 247-C6
E WELLESLEY AV
Otis Orchards WA 351-H2
Otis Orchards WA 352-C9
SPOKANE WA 349-C3
SPOKANE CO WA 350-D3
SPOKANE CO WA 351-H2
Trentwood WA 350-H2
Trentwood WA 351-B2
W WELLESLEY AV
SPOKANE WA 348-F3
SPOKANE WA 349-A3
WELLESLEY RD
LATAH CO ID 249-C1
WELLINGTON AV
WALLA WALLA WA 345-D6
E WELLINGTON RD
NANAIMO BC 93-A3
WELLPINIT-LITTLE FALLS RD
STEVENS CO WA 114-A1
WELLPINIT-MCCOY LAKE RD
STEVENS CO WA 113-C1
STEVENS CO WA 114-A1
WELLS RD
DOUGLAS CO OR 141-A1
S WELLS RD
SPOKANE CO WA 114-B2
WELLSANDT RD
ADAMS CO WA 113-C3
ADAMS CO WA 114-A3
RITZVILLE WA 113-C3
WELLS BENCH RD
CLEARWATER CO ID 123-C2
CLEARWATER CO ID 123-C2
WELLSIAN WY
RICHLAND WA 341-F3
WELLS LANDING RD
POLK CO OR 207-C2
WELLS LINE
DISTRICT OF ABBOTSFORD BC 102-B1
WELLS STATION RD
UMATILLA CO OR 129-A1
WEMBLEY DR
DIST OF N VANCOUVER BC 255-G3
WENAS AV Rt#-823
SELAH WA 243-B5
YAKIMA CO WA 243-B5
WENAS RD
YAKIMA CO WA 119-C1
YAKIMA CO WA 240-D7
YAKIMA CO WA 241-A7
YAKIMA CO WA 243-A3
S WENAS RD
YAKIMA CO WA 243-B4
WENATCHEE AV
WENATCHEE WA 238-D4
WENATCHEE WA 239-A4
WENATCHEE AV Rt#-285
WENATCHEE WA 239-A4
N WENATCHEE AV Rt#-285
WENATCHEE WA 238-D4
West Wenatchee WA 238-D4
S WENATCHEE AV
Appleyard WA 239-A5
WENATCHEE WA 239-A4
S WENATCHEE AV Rt#-285
WENATCHEE WA 239-A4
WENATCHEE HEIGHTS RD
CHELAN CO WA 238-D6
WENIGER HILL RD
KOOTENAI CO ID 248-A1
WENTWORTH RD
CLALLAM CO WA 169-B1
WENTWORTH ST
NANAIMO BC 93-A3
WENZEL SLOUGH RD
GRAYS HARBOR CO WA 179-A7
SW WERNER RD
BREMERTON WA 270-D12
KITSAP CO WA 270-D12
W WERNETT ST
FRANKLIN CO WA 342-F5
FRANKLIN CO WA 343-A5
PASCO WA 343-A5
WERRON RD
PIERCE CO WA 182-D4
WESGATE PL
PENDLETON OR 129-B1
UMATILLA CO OR 129-B1
WESLEY RD
White Swan WA 119-C2
WEST AV
ARLINGTON WA 168-D5
WEST BLVD
VANCOUVER BC 156-B5
S WEST BLVD U.S.-101
ABERDEEN WA 178-B7
COSMOPOLIS WA 178-B7
WEST LN
COLUMBIA CO OR 192-A3
WEST MALL
UNIV ENDOWMENT LANDS BC 156-A4
WEST RD
PIERCE CO WA 181-D4
WEST SPUR
JACKSON CO OR 226-C4
WEST ST
DESCHUTES CO OR 212-A6
LINCOLN CO WA 114-A2
SAINT HELENS OR 192-B1
NW WEST ST
CHEHALIS WA 299-C11
S WEST ST Rt#-21
WILBUR WA 113-B1
WEST BEACH RD
Ault Field WA 167-A4
ISLAND CO WA 167-A4
WEST BOUNDARY DR
LANE CO OR 133-C3
WESTBROOK DR SW
KITSAP CO WA 174-B6
WESTBROOK MALL
UNIV ENDOWMENT LANDS BC 156-A4
WEST COAST RD Rt#-14
BRITISH COLUMBIA 101-A2
BRITISH COLUMBIA 164-C1
WEST COVE RD
LATAH CO ID 249-C1
NE WESTERHOLM RD
CLARK CO WA 193-B4
WESTERMAN RD SW
DOUGLAS CO WA 239-D1
WESTERN AV
SEATTLE WA 277-G4
N WESTERN AV
WENATCHEE WA 238-D4
West Wenatchee WA 238-D4
S WESTERN AV
WENATCHEE WA 238-D4
West Wenatchee WA 238-D4
SW WESTERN AV
GRANTS PASS OR 335-D9
WESTERN BLVD
BENTON CO OR 327-D11
CORVALLIS OR 327-D11
WESTERN ST
Altamont OR 339-D11
WESTERN ROUTE RD
MORROW CO OR 128-C3
SW WESTFALL RD
CLACKAMAS CO OR 199-A5
WESTFIR RD
LANE CO OR 142-A1
WESTFIR OR 142-A1
WEST FORK RD
OKANOGAN CO WA 104-B2
WEST FORK EVANS CRK RD
JACKSON CO OR 230-A1
WEST FORK INDIAN CRK RD
LANE CO OR 209-C7
WEST FORK-MILLICOMA RD
COOS CO OR 218-D6
WESTGATE AV U.S.-30
PENDLETON OR 129-B1
WESTHAVEN DR
WESTPORT WA 298-G10
WEST HILLS RD
BENTON CO OR 133-B1
BENTON CO OR 327-A11
CORVALLIS OR 327-A11
WESTLAKE AV
SEATTLE WA 273-J7
SEATTLE WA 277-J1
WESTLAKE AV N
SEATTLE WA 277-J5
WESTLAKE RD
LEWIS CO ID 123-B2
LEWIS CO ID 123-B2
WESTLAND RD
UMATILLA CO OR 129-A1
WESTMINSTER HWY
CITY OF RICHMOND BC 156-A6
WESTMINSTER HWY S
CITY OF RICHMOND BC 156-C6
WESTMINSTER WY N
SHORELINE WA 171-A7
WESTMOND RD
BONNER CO ID 244-A5
WEST MOUNTAIN RD
VALLEY CO ID 251-C5
VALLEY CO ID 252-C1
WESTON-ELGIN HWY Rt#-204
UMATILLA CO OR 129-C1
UMATILLA CO OR 130-A1
UNION CO OR 130-A1
WESTPORT RD Rt#-105
GRAYS HARBOR CO WA 117-A1
WESTPORT DOCK RD Rt#-409
CLATSOP CO OR 117-B3
WEST SAANICH RD
DIST OF NORTH SAANICH BC 159-B2
WEST SAANICH RD Rt#-17A
DIST OF CENTRAL SAANICH BC 159-B3
DIST OF NORTH SAANICH BC 159-B3
DIST OF SAANICH BC 159-C5
WEST SHORE DR
WASHINGTON CO OR 198-A2
WESTSHORE DR
GRANT CO WA 242-C2
MOSES LAKE WA 242-C3
WEST SIDE HWY Rt#-411
COWLITZ CO WA 187-C6
COWLITZ CO WA 189-C1
COWLITZ CO WA 303-C7
KELSO WA 303-C7
LEWIS CO WA 187-C6
LONGVIEW WA 303-C7
VADER WA 187-C6
WESTSIDE HWY SW
KING CO WA 174-D5
WEST SIDE RD
COOS CO OR 140-B3
COOS CO OR 220-D7
JOSEPHINE CO OR 233-A4
KLAMATH CO OR 231-B2
LAKE CO OR 151-C3
LAKE CO OR 152-A2
MODOC CO CA 151-C3
MODOC CO CA 152-A3
MYRTLE POINT OR 140-B3
WESTSIDE RD
PIERCE CO WA 185-A5
YAMHILL CO OR 198-A5
NE WESTSIDE RD
MCMINNVILLE OR 198-A7
YAMHILL CO OR 198-A7
NW WESTSIDE RD
YAMHILL CO OR 198-A6
WEST SIDE WOLLOCHET BAY
PIERCE CO WA 181-C2
WEST TWIN RD
LATAH CO ID 249-D4
NW WEST UNION RD
WASHINGTON CO OR 125-C1
WASHINGTON CO OR 192-A7
WASHINGTON CO OR 199-A1
WEST VALLEY HWY
AUBURN WA 175-B7
AUBURN WA 182-B1
EDGEWOOD WA 182-B1
KENT WA 175-B7
KING CO WA 175-B7
PACIFIC WA 182-B1
PIERCE CO WA 182-B1
SUMNER WA 182-B3
WEST VALLEY HWY Rt#-181
KENT WA 175-B7
KENT WA 291-H3
TUKWILA WA 289-J5
TUKWILA WA 291-H3
WEST VALLEY HWY N
ALGONA WA 182-B1
WEST VALLEY HWY S
ALGONA WA 182-B1
KING CO WA 182-B2
PACIFIC WA 182-B2
WEST VALLEY RD
JEFFERSON CO WA 170-A2
WESTVIEW DR
CITY OF N VANCOUVER BC 254-J4
CITY OF N VANCOUVER BC 255-A4
DISTRICT OF DELTA BC 156-D7
DIST OF N VANCOUVER BC 255-A4
DOUGLAS CO OR 221-B2
WESTWARD HO
LINCOLN CO OR 328-C3
WESTWOOD DR NE
KITSAP CO WA 271-E5
WESTWOOD ST
PORT COQUITLAM BC 157-A4
WETHERBEE RD
JOSEPHINE CO OR 229-A7
WEXLER RD
WHITMAN CO WA 249-B4
WEYERHAEUSER RD
SPRINGFIELD OR 331-G8
WEYERHAUSER RD
LANE CO OR 219-D1
WHALEN RD
COWLITZ CO WA 192-B1
WHARF ST
CITY OF VICTORIA BC 256-G9
WHATCOM RD
DISTRICT OF ABBOTSFORD BC 102-B1
SE WHEATLAND RD
YAMHILL CO OR 204-D2
WHEATLAND RD N
KEIZER OR 204-D3
KEIZER OR 323-A2
MARION CO OR 204-D3
WHEATON WY
BREMERTON WA 270-J8
BREMERTON WA 271-A9
WHEATON WY Rt#-303
BREMERTON WA 270-J6
KITSAP CO WA 270-J6
WHEELER RD
CLALLAM CO WA 163-A7
GRANT CO WA 242-D3
JACKSON CO OR 230-C5
LANE CO OR 215-D4
MOSES LAKE WA 242-D3
E WHEELER RD
MOSES LAKE WA 242-C3
S WHEELER RD
SPOKANE CO WA 114-C3
WHELAN RD
WHITMAN CO WA 249-B4
WHERRY RD
YAKIMA CO WA 243-A5
WHETSTONE RD
COLUMBIA CO WA 122-A2
WHIFFIN SPIT RD
BRITISH COLUMBIA 164-C1
WHISKEY CREEK DR
HOOD RIVER CO OR 195-D5
WHISKEY CREEK RD
COLUMBIA CO WA 122-A3
JACKSON CO OR 226-D3
MALHEUR CO OR 146-A1
TILLAMOOK CO OR 197-A3
WALLOWA OR 130-C1
WALLOWA CO OR 130-C1
E WHISKEY CREEK RD
WALLOWA OR 130-C1
S WHISKEY HILL RD
CLACKAMAS CO OR 205-C1
WHISKEY HILL RD NE
HUBBARD OR 205-C1
MARION CO OR 205-C1
WHISKEY JACK RD
BONNER CO ID 244-A1
JEFFERSON CO OR 211-B1
WHISKEY RUN RD
COOS CO OR 220-B4
WHISKEY SPRING CREEK RD
CROOK CO OR 135-C2
WHISKEY SPRINGS RD
JEFFERSON CO OR 211-D2
WHISTLE CREEK RD
HARNEY CO OR 136-C3
WHISTLERS LN
DOUGLAS CO OR 221-D3
WHISTLERS BEND PARK RD
DOUGLAS CO OR 221-D3
WHITAKER RD
POLK CO OR 204-A7
WHITCOMB AV U.S.-97
OKANOGAN CO WA 104-C2
TONASKET WA 104-C2
WHITE RD
WALLA WALLA CO WA 121-B3
W WHITE RD
SPOKANE CO WA 246-B5
E WHITEAKER AV
COTTAGE GROVE OR 215-B7
WHITE CREEK RD
JOSEPHINE CO OR 233-D3
E WHITE CREEK RD
JOSEPHINE CO OR 233-D3
WHITEHALL RD SE
DOUGLAS CO WA 112-C2
WHITEHORSE CTO
MALHEUR CO OR 154-B1
WHITEHORSE RD
MALHEUR CO OR 154-A1
WHITEHORSE CREEK RD
DOUGLAS CO OR 225-D6
WHITEHORSE RANCH RD
HARNEY CO OR 153-C2
HARNEY CO OR 154-A2
WHITELINE RD
KLAMATH CO OR 235-D1
WHITEMAN RD KPS
PIERCE CO WA 181-A3
WHITE OAK RD
LINN CO OR 207-B6
WHITE PINE DR Rt#-6
BENEWAH CO ID 115-B3
LATAH CO ID 115-B3
WHITE RIVER RD
CHELAN CO WA 111-B1
WASCO CO OR 127-A3
WHITE ROCK LOOP RD
DESCHUTES CO OR 212-B7
WHITE SCHOOL HOUSE RD
JOSEPHINE CO OR 233-B4
WHITES CREEK RD
LANE CO OR 219-D1
SE WHITESON RD
YAMHILL CO OR 204-B1
N WHITE SWAN RD
White Swan WA 119-C2
W WHITE SWAN RD Rt#-220
White Swan WA 119-C2
WHITHAM RD NE
THURSTON CO WA 180-D4
WHITING WY
DISTRICT OF COQUITLAM BC 156-D5
WHITLEY DR U.S.-95
FRUITLAND ID 139-A3
N WHITLEY DR U.S.-95
FRUITLAND ID 139-A3
PAYETTE CO ID 139-A3
E WHITMAN DR
COLLEGE PLACE WA 344-F10
W WHITMAN DR
COLLEGE PLACE WA 344-E10
WALLA WALLA CO WA 344-D10
WHITMAN RD
WHITMAN CO WA 249-C6
E WHITMAN RD
SPOKANE CO WA 114-C3
WHITMAN ST
WALLA WALLA WA 345-C8
S WHITMAN ST
MONMOUTH OR 204-B7
ROSALIA WA 114-C3
WHITMAN CO WA 114-C3
W WHITMAN ST
ROSALIA WA 114-C3
WHITMORE DR NW
PIERCE CO WA 181-B1
WHITMORE RD
WASHINGTON CO OR 198-C3
WHITNEY HWY Rt#-7
BAKER CITY OR 138-B1
BAKER CO OR 137-C1
BAKER CO OR 138-A1

PNW
INDEX

PNW

INDEX

Thomas Bros. Maps ®   COPYRIGHT 1999   PNW   INDEX

10TH ST NE — STREET INDEX — 27TH ST 405

PNW

INDEX

STREET — City State — Page-Grid

10TH ST NE
- DOUGLAS CO WA 239-A4
- EAST WENATCHEE WA 239-A4
- East Wenatchee Bench WA 239-A4

10TH ST SE
- DOUGLAS CO WA 239-B5

10 5 SE RD
- GRANT CO WA 242-C7

11TH AV
- BREMERTON WA 270-F10
- LEWISTON ID 250-B4
- NAMPA ID 147-B1

11TH AV Rt#-11
- DISTRICT OF MISSION BC 94-B3

11TH AV U.S.-30
- NAMPA ID 147-B1

E 11TH AV
- EUGENE OR 330-A7

NE 11TH AV
- PORTLAND OR 313-H4

NW 11TH AV
- CLARK CO WA 192-C2
- PORTLAND OR 313-E5
- RIDGEFIELD WA 192-C2

SE 11TH AV
- PORTLAND OR 313-H6
- PORTLAND OR 317-H1

SW 11TH AV
- PORTLAND OR 312-E6
- PORTLAND OR 313-E6

W 11TH AV
- EUGENE OR 329-H7
- EUGENE OR 330-A7

W 11TH AV Rt#-126
- EUGENE OR 215-A2
- EUGENE OR 329-B6
- LANE CO OR 215-A2

11TH AV N U.S.-30
- NAMPA ID 147-C1

11TH AV NE
- SEATTLE WA 274-B5
- SNOHOMISH CO WA 168-C6
- THURSTON CO WA 297-B4

11TH AV NW
- OLYMPIA WA 296-B3
- THURSTON CO WA 296-A3

11TH ST
- BELLINGHAM WA 258-B10
- BREMERTON WA 270-G10
- CORVALLIS OR 327-F10
- DIST OF WEST VANCOUVER BC 254-D4
- WALLA WALLA CO WA 345-J4

E 11TH ST
- BREMERTON WA 271-A10
- TACOMA WA 182-A2
- TACOMA WA 293-J5

N 11TH ST
- AUMSVILLE OR 133-C1
- COEUR D'ALENE ID 355-G11

NE 11TH ST
- DESCHUTES CO OR 212-D4

S 11TH ST
- COEUR D'ALENE ID 355-G12
- TACOMA WA 293-F5

SW 11TH ST Rt#-207
- HERMISTON OR 129-A1
- UMATILLA CO OR 129-A1

W 11TH ST
- KETTLE FALLS WA 106-A2
- STEVENS CO WA 106-A2
- WARDEN WA 121-A1

11TH ST NE
- EAST WENATCHEE WA 239-A4

12 AV
- DISTRICT OF DELTA BC 101-C1

12TH AV
- ALBANY OR 326-B9
- CLATSOP CO OR 301-G7
- SEASIDE OR 301-G7
- SEATTLE WA 278-B6
- TOWNSHIP OF LANGLEY BC 158-D2
- VANCOUVER BC 254-J13
- VANCOUVER BC 255-A13

E 12TH AV
- SPOKANE WA 349-F11

NE 12TH AV
- PORTLAND OR 313-H5

SE 12TH AV
- PORTLAND OR 313-H6
- PORTLAND OR 317-H1

SW 12TH AV
- PORTLAND OR 312-E6

W 12TH AV
- AIRWAY HEIGHTS WA 246-A4

12TH AV E
- SEATTLE WA 278-B4
- VANCOUVER BC 254-H13

12TH AV NE
- SEATTLE WA 274-C4
- THURSTON CO WA 297-B4

12TH AV S
- SEATAC WA 288-B6
- SEATTLE WA 278-B7
- WALLA WALLA WA 344-J8

12TH AV S Rt#-45
- NAMPA ID 147-B1

12TH AV W
- VANCOUVER BC 254-C13

12 RD NE
- DOUGLAS CO WA 112-C2

12 RD NE U.S.-2
- DOUGLAS CO WA 112-C2

12 RD SW
- DOUGLAS CO WA 239-C4

12TH ST
- BELLINGHAM WA 258-B10
- HOOD RIVER OR 195-D5
- LEBANON OR 133-C1
- LINN CO OR 133-C1
- NEW WESTMINSTER BC 156-D5
- TILLAMOOK OR 197-C2
- TILLAMOOK CO OR 197-C2

12TH ST Rt#-11
- BELLINGHAM WA 258-B11

12TH ST Rt#-20
- ANACORTES WA 259-F2

E 12TH ST
- MEDFORD OR 336-D12

NE 12TH ST
- BELLEVUE WA 175-C2

NE 12TH ST
- BEND OR 332-G6
- CLYDE HILL WA 175-C2
- MEDINA WA 175-C2
- NEWPORT OR 206-B4
- RENTON WA 175-C4

NW 12TH ST
- LINCOLN CITY OR 203-A4
- NEWPORT OR 206-A4

S 12TH ST
- TACOMA WA 292-A6
- TACOMA WA 293-F5

SE 12TH ST
- PENDLETON OR 129-B1

12TH ST E
- PIERCE CO WA 182-C2

12TH ST N U.S.-26
- MALHEUR CO OR 139-A3
- VALE OR 139-A3

12TH ST NE
- SALEM OR 322-J12

12TH ST SE
- DOUGLAS CO WA 239-B5
- SALEM OR 322-J14
- SALEM OR 324-H5

12TH ST SE Rt#-22
- SALEM OR 322-J14

12TH AVENUE RD Rt#-45
- CANYON CO ID 147-B1
- NAMPA ID 147-B1
- OWYHEE CO ID 147-B1

13TH AV
- TOWNSHIP OF LANGLEY BC 158-D2

E 13TH AV
- EUGENE OR 330-B7
- SPOKANE WA 349-F11

NE 13TH AV
- PORTLAND OR 313-H4

SE 13TH AV
- PORTLAND OR 317-H6

SW 13TH AV
- PORTLAND OR 312-E6

W 13TH AV
- EUGENE OR 329-G7
- EUGENE OR 330-A7

13TH AV N Rt#-125
- WALLA WALLA WA 344-J5

13TH AV S
- SEATTLE WA 282-B7

13TH AV W
- SNOHOMISH CO WA 171-B5

13 RD NE
- DOUGLAS CO WA 113-A1

13TH ST
- ANACORTES WA 259-H2
- ASOTIN CO WA 250-B4
- CITY OF N VANCOUVER BC 254-J5
- CITY OF N VANCOUVER BC 255-B5
- CLARKSTON WA 250-B4
- DESCHUTES CO OR 212-D3
- HOOD RIVER OR 195-D5
- SNOHOMISH WA 171-D3
- Vineland WA 250-B5

E 13TH ST
- WASCO CO OR 196-D7

N 13TH ST
- BOISE ID 253-C2

NE 13TH ST
- DESCHUTES CO OR 212-D5

S 13TH ST
- MOUNT VERNON WA 260-D13
- SKAGIT CO WA 260-D13
- TACOMA WA 293-H5

SW 13TH ST
- PENDLETON OR 129-B1

W 13TH ST
- THE DALLES OR 196-C7
- WASCO CO OR 196-C7

13TH ST NE
- SALEM OR 322-J13
- SALEM OR 323-A13

14TH AV
- OLYMPIA WA 296-H6
- SEATTLE WA 278-C6
- TOWNSHIP OF LANGLEY BC 158-D2

E 14TH AV
- ELLENSBURG WA 241-B5
- SPOKANE WA 349-D11

N 14TH AV
- PASCO WA 343-E6

NE 14TH AV Rt#-500
- CAMAS WA 193-B7

NW 14TH AV
- PORTLAND OR 312-E4

W 14TH AV
- SPOKANE WA 348-H11
- SPOKANE WA 349-A11

W 14TH AV U.S.-2
- AIRWAY HEIGHTS WA 246-A4
- SPOKANE CO WA 246-A4

14TH AV NW
- OLYMPIA WA 296-C3
- PIERCE CO WA 174-C7
- PIERCE CO WA 181-C1
- THURSTON CO WA 296-C3

14TH AV S
- KING WA 286-B3
- SEATTLE WA 278-C7
- SEATTLE WA 286-B3

14 RD NE
- DOUGLAS CO WA 112-C1

14 RD NE Rt#-172
- DOUGLAS CO WA 112-C1

14 RD NW Rt#-172
- DOUGLAS CO WA 112-B1

14TH ST
- LEWISTON ID 250-C4
- PORT TOWNSEND WA 263-D5
- REEDSPORT OR 218-C1

E 14TH ST
- BREMERTON WA 271-A10

N 14TH ST
- SPRINGFIELD OR 330-J7

NE 14TH ST
- CLARK CO WA 193-B6

NW 14TH ST
- BEND OR 332-C7
- PENDLETON OR 129-B1

SE 14TH ST
- CLARK CO WA 193-C7

SW 14TH ST
- BEND OR 332-C8
- DESCHUTES CO OR 332-C8

14TH ST NE
- SALEM OR 322-J13
- SALEM OR 323-A13

14TH ST SE
- SALEM OR 322-J14
- SALEM OR 324-J1

15TH AV
- LONGVIEW WA 303-A8

E 15TH AV
- POST FALLS ID 353-H5

N 15TH AV
- BOISE ID 253-C2

NE 15TH AV
- PORTLAND OR 309-H7
- PORTLAND OR 313-H1

W 15TH AV
- ELLENSBURG WA 241-B5
- KITTITAS CO WA 241-B5
- POST FALLS ID 353-E5

15TH AV E
- SEATTLE WA 278-C4

15TH AV NE
- LACEY WA 297-F3
- LAKE FOREST PARK WA 171-B7
- SEATTLE WA 171-B7
- SEATTLE WA 274-C2
- SHORELINE WA 171-B7
- SNOHOMISH CO WA 168-C4
- THURSTON CO WA 297-F3

15TH AV NW
- SEATTLE WA 273-F2
- SHORELINE WA 171-A6

15TH AV S
- SEATTLE WA 282-B3

15TH AV SW
- EPHRATA WA 112-C3

15TH AV W
- SEATTLE WA 273-F7
- SEATTLE WA 277-F2

15 RD NE
- DOUGLAS CO WA 112-C1

15TH ST
- BREMERTON WA 270-G9
- DIST OF WEST VANCOUVER BC 254-D3
- OROVILLE WA 104-C1
- WALLA WALLA CO WA 345-J3
- WASHOUGAL WA 193-C7

15TH ST Rt#-128
- ASOTIN CO WA 250-B4
- CLARKSTON WA 250-B4

E 15TH ST
- TACOMA WA 293-J6
- VANCOUVER WA 305-G4

N 15TH ST
- COEUR D'ALENE ID 355-G8
- DALTON GARDENS ID 355-G2
- KOOTENAI CO ID 355-G2

S 15TH ST Rt#-128
- POMEROY WA 122-B2

SE 15TH ST
- BEND OR 332-H10
- CLARK CO WA 193-B7
- DESCHUTES CO OR 332-H12

SW 15TH ST
- PENDLETON OR 129-B1

15TH ST NE
- AUBURN WA 182-C1

15TH ST NW
- AUBURN WA 182-B1
- East Wenatchee Bench WA 239-A4

15TH ST NW U.S.-2
- East Wenatchee Bench WA 239-A4

15TH ST SW
- AUBURN WA 182-B1

16TH AV
- ASOTIN CO WA 250-B4
- CITY OF WHITE ROCK BC 158-A2
- DISTRICT OF SURREY BC 158-A2
- LEWISTON ID 250-B4
- LONGVIEW WA 303-A9
- TOWNSHIP OF LANGLEY BC 102-B1
- TOWNSHIP OF LANGLEY BC 158-C2

E 16TH AV
- Dishman WA 350-F11
- SPOKANE CO WA 349-H11
- SPOKANE CO WA 350-H10
- SPOKANE CO WA 351-A10
- Veradale WA 351-A10

N 16TH AV
- YAKIMA WA 243-B6

NE 16TH AV
- PORTLAND OR 313-H4

S 16TH AV
- YAKIMA WA 243-B7
- YAKIMA CO WA 243-B7

16TH AV NW
- SNOHOMISH CO WA 168-C6

16TH AV S
- DES MOINES WA 175-B7
- DES MOINES WA 290-B7
- KING WA 286-B2
- KING CO WA 175-B7
- SEATTLE WA 286-B3
- TUKWILA WA 286-B2

16TH AV S Rt#-99
- FEDERAL WAY WA 182-B1

16TH AV S Rt#-161
- FEDERAL WAY WA 182-B1

16TH AV SW
- KING WA 285-G6
- SEATTLE WA 285-G6

16TH AV W
- UNIV ENDOWMENT LANDS BC 156-A4
- VANCOUVER BC 254-A13

NE 16TH DR
- PORTLAND OR 313-H4

16 RD NE
- DOUGLAS CO WA 112-C1

16TH ST
- ASTORIA OR 300-D6
- EVERETT WA 264-E1
- EVERETT WA 265-F1
- HOQUIAM WA 178-A7
- LEWISTON ID 250-C5
- NORTH BEND OR 333-E5

E 16TH ST
- KOOTENAI CO ID 353-J5

E 16TH ST
- KOOTENAI CO ID 354-B5
- POST FALLS ID 353-J5
- POST FALLS ID 354-B5

N 16TH ST U.S.-95
- PAYETTE ID 139-A3

NE 16TH ST
- FRUITLAND ID 139-A3
- PAYETTE CO ID 139-A3

NE 16TH ST Rt#-30
- FRUITLAND ID 139-A3
- PAYETTE CO ID 139-A3

S 16TH ST
- MOUNT VERNON WA 260-D13
- SUNNYSIDE WA 120-B2

S 16TH ST U.S.-95
- PAYETTE ID 139-A3

SE 16TH ST
- BELLEVUE WA 175-D3

SW 16TH ST
- RENTON WA 175-C5

16TH ST E
- PIERCE CO WA 182-C2

16TH ST W
- CITY OF N VANCOUVER BC 254-J4

17TH AV
- LONGVIEW WA 303-A9

SE 17TH AV
- CLACKAMAS OR 321-H1
- MILWAUKIE OR 317-H7
- MILWAUKIE OR 321-H1
- PORTLAND OR 317-H2
- PORTLAND OR 317-H7
- PORTLAND OR 321-H1

17TH AV NW
- THURSTON CO WA 296-A3

17TH AV NW Rt#-900
- ISSAQUAH WA 175-D3

17TH ST
- ASOTIN CO WA 250-C4
- BAKER CITY OR 138-B1
- LEWISTON ID 250-C4
- NORTH BEND OR 333-E6
- WASHOUGAL WA 193-C7

17TH ST Rt#-173
- BRIDGEPORT WA 112-C1

NE 17TH ST
- DESCHUTES CO OR 212-D4

SE 17TH ST
- PENDLETON OR 129-B1

SW 17TH ST Rt#-37
- PENDLETON OR 129-B1

17TH ST NE
- SALEM OR 323-A12

17TH ST SE
- SALEM OR 323-A14

18TH AV
- LONGVIEW WA 302-J10
- LONGVIEW WA 303-A9
- TOWNSHIP OF LANGLEY BC 158-C2

E 18TH AV
- EUGENE OR 330-A8
- SPOKANE WA 349-B12

N 18 AV
- PASCO WA 343-E6

N 18TH AV
- PASCO WA 343-E6

NW 18TH AV
- PORTLAND OR 312-E5

SW 18TH AV
- MALHEUR CO OR 139-A3

W 18TH AV
- EUGENE OR 329-D7
- EUGENE OR 330-A8
- JUNCTION CITY OR 210-A5
- LANE CO OR 210-A5

18TH AV N
- KELSO WA 303-E7

18TH ST
- LEWISTON ID 250-C4

18TH ST U.S.-12
- LEWISTON ID 250-C4

E 18TH ST
- THE DALLES OR 196-C7
- VANCOUVER WA 305-G4
- VANCOUVER WA 306-B4
- WASCO CO OR 196-C7

N 18TH ST
- MOUNT VERNON WA 260-E11
- SPRINGFIELD OR 331-A6

NE 18TH ST
- VANCOUVER WA 193-A6
- VANCOUVER WA 306-E4
- VANCOUVER WA 307-J4

S 18TH ST
- MOUNT VERNON WA 260-E13
- POMEROY WA 122-B2
- SKAGIT CO WA 260-E13
- YAKIMA WA 243-C7

S 18TH ST Rt#-52
- PAYETTE ID 139-A3

W 18TH ST
- VANCOUVER WA 305-G4

19TH AV
- TOWNSHIP OF LANGLEY BC 158-D2

19TH AV Rt#-8
- FOREST GROVE OR 198-B1

E 19TH AV
- Finley WA 343-E13
- KENNEWICK WA 343-E13

NW 19TH AV
- PORTLAND OR 312-D5

W 19TH AV
- BENTON CO WA 343-C13
- KENNEWICK WA 342-H13
- KENNEWICK WA 343-C13

19TH AV NE
- SNOHOMISH CO WA 168-C4

19TH AV SE
- BOTHELL WA 171-C6

19TH AV SE Rt#-527
- EVERETT WA 171-C4
- EVERETT WA 268-D6
- SNOHOMISH CO WA 171-C4

19TH ST
- BENTON CO OR 133-B1
- CITY OF N VANCOUVER BC 254-H4
- CITY OF N VANCOUVER BC 255-C4
- DISTRICT OF BURNABY BC 156-D5
- DIST OF N VANCOUVER BC 254-H4

19TH ST
- EVERETT WA 264-E2
- EVERETT WA 265-E2
- North Springfield OR 331-A5
- PHILOMATH OR 133-B1
- PORT TOWNSEND WA 263-F5
- SPRINGFIELD OR 331-A5

E 19TH ST
- THE DALLES OR 196-C7

NE 19TH ST
- CLARK CO WA 193-B6

NW 19TH ST
- DESCHUTES CO OR 212-D4
- REDMOND OR 212-D5
- Terrebonne OR 212-D4

S 19TH ST
- FIRCREST WA 181-C2
- FIRCREST WA 292-A6
- TACOMA WA 181-C2
- TACOMA WA 292-A6
- TACOMA WA 293-F6
- UNIVERSITY PLACE WA 181-C2

SW 19TH ST
- DESCHUTES CO OR 212-D5
- REDMOND OR 212-D5

W 19TH ST
- KENNEWICK WA 342-J13

19TH ST NE
- East Wenatchee Bench WA 239-A4

19TH ST NW
- East Wenatchee Bench WA 239-A4

19TH WY Rt#-8
- FOREST GROVE OR 198-C1

19-20 ST DIV
- DISTRICT OF BURNABY BC 156-D5

20TH AV
- DISTRICT OF SURREY BC 158-A2
- TOWNSHIP OF LANGLEY BC 158-D2

N 20TH AV
- PASCO WA 343-D7

NE 20TH AV
- CLARK CO WA 192-C4
- PORTLAND OR 313-J5

NW 20TH AV
- MALHEUR CO OR 139-A3

S 20TH AV
- PASCO WA 343-D8

SE 20TH AV
- PORTLAND OR 313-J7
- PORTLAND OR 317-J1

SW 20TH AV
- BATTLE GROUND WA 192-D3
- CLARK CO WA 192-D3

20TH AV NW
- OLYMPIA WA 296-F2

20TH AV W
- EVERETT WA 267-H4
- SEATTLE WA 273-E7

20 RD NE
- DOUGLAS CO WA 112-C1
- DOUGLAS CO WA 113-A1

20TH ST
- BELLINGHAM WA 258-C10
- DIST OF N VANCOUVER BC 255-E4
- LA GRANDE OR 130-A2
- NEW WESTMINSTER BC 156-D5

NE 20TH ST
- BELLEVUE WA 175-D2

SE 20TH ST
- CLARK CO WA 193-C7
- SAMMAMISH WA 175-D3

SW 20TH ST
- PENDLETON OR 129-B1

20TH ST E
- FIFE WA 182-A3

20TH ST KPN
- PIERCE CO WA 181-A2

20TH ST SE
- SNOHOMISH WA 265-J4
- SNOHOMISH CO WA 171-D2

21ST AV
- LONGVIEW WA 302-J8
- LONGVIEW WA 303-A8
- TOWNSHIP OF LANGLEY BC 158-D2

E 21ST AV
- SPOKANE WA 349-B12

NE 21ST AV
- PORTLAND OR 313-J4

NW 21ST AV
- CLARK CO WA 192-C5

SE 21ST AV
- PORTLAND OR 317-J1

W 21ST AV
- SPOKANE WA 348-J12

21ST AV SW
- FEDERAL WAY WA 182-A1

21ST ST
- BELLINGHAM WA 258-C10
- DIST OF WEST VANCOUVER BC 254-C3
- LEWISTON ID 250-C4

N 21ST ST
- TACOMA WA 292-B3
- TACOMA WA 293-E3

NW 21ST ST
- LINCOLN CITY OR 203-A4

21ST ST NE
- SALEM OR 323-B12

21ST ST SE
- AUBURN WA 182-C2

22ND AV
- GRANT CO WA 242-C2
- OLYMPIA WA 297-A7
- VANCOUVER BC 255-C14

N 22ND AV
- PASCO WA 343-D6

NE 22ND AV
- CLARK CO WA 192-C3

SE 22ND AV
- MILWAUKIE OR 321-J3

22ND AV E
- PIERCE CO WA 182-A6

22ND ST
- ANACORTES WA 259-H3
- DIST OF N VANCOUVER BC 254-H3
- EVERETT WA 264-D2
- HOOD RIVER OR 195-C5
- HOOD RIVER CO OR 195-C5
- HOQUIAM WA 178-A7
- LEWISTON ID 250-D5
- NEZ PERCE CO ID 250-D5

NE 22ND ST
- LINCOLN CITY OR 203-A4

S 22ND ST
- REEDSPORT OR 218-C1

22ND ST SE
- SALEM OR 325-A2

23RD AV
- LONGVIEW WA 302-J8
- SEATTLE WA 278-D6

NW 23RD AV
- PORTLAND OR 312-D4

23RD AV E
- SEATTLE WA 278-D4

23RD AV NE
- SNOHOMISH CO WA 168-C5

23RD AV S
- SEATTLE WA 278-D7
- SEATTLE WA 282-D1

23RD AV SE
- PUYALLUP WA 182-B4

23RD ST
- CITY OF N VANCOUVER BC 255-A3

S 23RD ST
- COEUR D'ALENE ID 355-H12
- KOOTENAI CO ID 355-H12

SE 23RD ST
- CLARK CO WA 193-B7

SW 23RD ST
- DESCHUTES CO OR 212-D5

23RD ST NE
- SALEM OR 323-B13

24TH AV
- ALBANY OR 326-B10
- ASOTIN CO WA 250-B5
- DISTRICT OF SURREY BC 158-A2
- FOREST GROVE OR 198-C1
- LONGVIEW WA 302-J8
- SEASIDE OR 301-G6
- TOWNSHIP OF LANGLEY BC 158-C2

E 24TH AV
- EUGENE OR 330-A9
- SPOKANE CO WA 350-J11
- SPOKANE CO WA 351-G11
- Veradale WA 351-B11

N 24TH AV
- PASCO WA 343-D6

NE 24TH AV
- PORTLAND OR 313-J4

S 24TH AV
- YAKIMA WA 243-B7

24TH AV E
- SEATTLE WA 278-D2

24TH AV NE
- SEATTLE WA 274-D2
- SHORELINE WA 171-B6

24TH AV NW
- SEATTLE WA 272-E2

24TH AV S
- DES MOINES WA 290-C4
- KING WA 286-C7
- KING WA 288-C3
- NAMPA ID 147-C1
- SEATAC WA 288-C3
- SEATAC WA 290-C4

24TH PL S
- DES MOINES WA 290-C6

24 RD NW
- DOUGLAS CO WA 112-B2
- GRANT CO WA 112-B2

N 24TH ST
- TACOMA WA 292-D3

NE 24TH ST
- CLYDE HILL WA 175-C2
- REDMOND WA 175-D2

SE 24TH ST
- BELLEVUE WA 175-D3

24TH ST E
- EDGEWOOD WA 182-B3

24TH ST NE
- SALEM OR 323-B14

E 25TH AV
- SPOKANE CO WA 350-J12

25TH AV NE
- SEATTLE WA 274-D3
- SHORELINE WA 171-B7

25TH AV SW
- TUMWATER WA 296-E7

25TH ST
- DESCHUTES CO OR 213-A4

E 25TH ST
- TACOMA WA 293-J7

S 25TH ST
- TACOMA WA 293-G7

25TH ST SE
- SALEM OR 323-B14
- SALEM OR 325-B1

26TH AV
- LONGVIEW WA 302-H10
- TOWNSHIP OF LANGLEY BC 158-D2

N 26TH AV
- PASCO WA 343-C7

26TH AV NE
- OLYMPIA WA 297-A2
- THURSTON CO WA 297-D1

W 26TH PL
- KENNEWICK WA 343-D14

26TH ST
- CORVALLIS OR 327-F10

E 26TH ST
- TACOMA WA 293-J7

N 26TH ST
- TACOMA WA 181-C2
- TACOMA WA 292-B3

S 26TH ST
- TACOMA WA 293-H7

27TH AV
- ALBANY OR 326-A10
- LINN CO OR 326-A10

E 27TH AV
- Finley WA 343-F14
- KENNEWICK WA 343-F14

W 27TH AV
- BENTON CO WA 343-B14
- Finley WA 343-B14
- KENNEWICK WA 342-H14
- KENNEWICK WA 343-B14

27TH AV NE
- SNOHOMISH CO WA 168-C4

27TH ST
- DIST OF WEST VANCOUVER BC 254-A2

406 N 27TH ST
STREET INDEX
60 ST

STREET City State Page-Grid

N 27TH ST
BOISE ID 253-C2
NE 27TH ST
BEND OR 217-C2
DESCHUTES CO OR 217-C2
NW 27TH ST
DESCHUTES CO OR 212-D3
S 27TH ST
BOISE ID 253-C2
SE 27TH ST
BEND OR 217-C3
CLARK CO WA 193-C7
DESCHUTES CO OR 217-C3
SW 27TH ST
DESCHUTES CO OR 212-D6
REDMOND OR 212-D6
27TH ST W
UNIVERSITY PLACE WA 181-C2
27B AV
DISTRICT OF DELTA BC 101-C1
28 AV
DISTRICT OF DELTA BC 101-C1
28TH AV
TOWNSHIP OF LANGLEY BC 158-C2
N 28TH AV
PASCO WA 343-C7
SE 28TH AV
PORTLAND OR 317-J4
PORTLAND OR 318-A4
W 28TH AV
EUGENE OR 329-H9
28TH AV NW
SEATTLE WA 272-D1
SNOHOMISH CO WA 168-B4
THURSTON CO WA 296-E1
28TH AV S
KING CO WA 182-B2
28TH AV W
EVERETT WA 267-G4
SEATTLE WA 272-D6
SNOHOMISH WA 267-G5
SNOHOMISH CO WA 171-B5
NE 28TH CT
DESCHUTES CO OR 213-A4
N 28TH ST
BOISE ID 253-C2
SPRINGFIELD OR 331-B6
NE 28TH ST
CLARK CO WA 193-B6
VANCOUVER WA 193-A6
VANCOUVER WA 307-J3
28TH ST NE
LAKE STEVENS WA 110-C1
SNOHOMISH CO WA 110-C1
29TH AV
VANCOUVER BC 156-B5
E 29TH AV
EUGENE OR 330-A10
SPOKANE WA 349-H13
SPOKANE CO WA 349-H13
NE 29TH AV
CLARK CO WA 192-D3
W 29TH AV
EUGENE OR 329-J10
EUGENE OR 330-A10
SPOKANE WA 348-J13
SPOKANE WA 349-C13
29TH AV W
SEATTLE WA 272-D6
SEATTLE WA 276-D2
29TH ST
ANACORTES WA 259-G4
CORVALLIS OR 327-E5
LEWISTON ID 250-C4
MANZANITA OR 191-B4
NE 29TH ST
DESCHUTES CO OR 213-A4
29TH ST E
DIST OF N VANCOUVER BC 255-C3
29TH ST NE
FEDERAL WAY WA 182-A2
TACOMA WA 182-A2
29TH ST SE
AUBURN WA 182-C2
30TH AV
LINN CO OR 207-B5
LONGVIEW WA 302-H8
TOWNSHIP OF LANGLEY BC 158-D2
E 30TH AV
EUGENE OR 330-C10
LANE CO OR 330-G12
30TH AV NE
SEATTLE WA 274-E5
30TH ST
BELLINGHAM WA 258-D12
CORVALLIS OR 327-E10
E 30TH ST
KITSAP CO WA 271-B7
N 30TH ST
RENTON WA 175-C4
TACOMA WA 181-C2
TACOMA WA 292-B2
TACOMA WA 293-E2
NE 30TH ST
KITSAP CO WA 271-C7
SE 30TH ST
CLARK CO WA 193-C7
SW 30TH ST
PENDLETON OR 129-B1
NW 31ST AV
CLARK CO WA 192-C2
RIDGEFIELD WA 192-C2
31ST AV NE
LACEY WA 181-A6
31ST AV SW Rt#-161
PUYALLUP WA 182-B4
N 31ST ST
North Springfield OR 331-C3
SPRINGFIELD OR 331-C4
NW 31ST ST
DESCHUTES CO OR 212-D4
31ST ST NE
TACOMA WA 182-A2
32ND AV
DISTRICT OF SURREY BC 158-B1
LONGVIEW WA 302-G9
TOWNSHIP OF LANGLEY BC 158-C1
E 32ND AV
Dishman WA 350-H12
SPOKANE CO WA 350-H12

E 32ND AV
SPOKANE CO WA 351-E12
Veradale WA 351-A12
NE 32ND AV
PORTLAND OR 314-A2
SE 32ND AV
HILLSBORO OR 198-D1
MILWAUKIE OR 199-D3
MILWAUKIE OR 318-A7
PORTLAND OR 318-A7
32ND AV NW
SEATTLE WA 272-D2
32ND AV S
FEDERAL WAY WA 175-B7
KENT WA 175-B7
KING CO WA 175-B7
KING CO WA 182-B2
32ND AV W
SEATTLE WA 272-D5
32ND ST
ANACORTES WA 259-F4
BELLINGHAM WA 258-D11
WASHOUGAL WA 193-C7
S 32ND ST
LANE CO OR 331-C8
SPRINGFIELD OR 331-C8
SE 32ND ST
KING CO WA 176-A3
SAMMAMISH WA 176-A3
32ND ST KPN
PIERCE CO WA 181-A1
32ND ST NW
PIERCE CO WA 181-B1
32ND ST SE
SNOHOMISH CO WA 171-D2
32ND DIVISION DR
PIERCE CO WA 181-B5
33RD AV
VANCOUVER BC 156-B5
E 33RD AV
EUGENE OR 330-A10
NE 33RD AV
PORTLAND OR 310-A7
PORTLAND OR 314-A1
NE 33RD DR
PORTLAND OR 310-A4
33RD ST
ASTORIA OR 300-F5
E 33RD ST
VANCOUVER WA 305-H3
VANCOUVER WA 306-A3
33RD ST NE
TACOMA WA 182-A2
33A AV
DISTRICT OF DELTA BC 101-C1
34TH AV
ALBANY OR 326-B11
SEATTLE WA 278-E5
SEATTLE WA 279-E4
TOWNSHIP OF LANGLEY BC 158-D1
34TH AV E
PIERCE CO WA 182-A4
34TH AV W
SEATTLE WA 272-C7
SEATTLE WA 276-C1
34TH ST
ANACORTES WA 259-H4
CLARK CO WA 193-C7
MOUNT VERNON WA 260-G13
WASHOUGAL WA 193-C7
E 34TH ST
TACOMA WA 295-J1
N 34TH ST
SEATTLE WA 273-H7
SEATTLE WA 274-A7
S 34TH ST
TACOMA WA 295-H1
SW 35TH AV
PORTLAND OR 316-B7
PORTLAND OR 320-B1
35TH AV NE
SEATTLE WA 274-E2
35TH AV SE
BOTHELL WA 171-C6
SNOHOMISH WA 269-F7
SNOHOMISH CO WA 171-C4
35TH AV SW
SEATTLE WA 281-E7
SEATTLE WA 285-E3
35TH AV W
SNOHOMISH CO WA 171-B4
SW 35TH DR
CLACKAMAS CO OR 199-C5
35TH ST
ASTORIA OR 300-F5
BENTON CO OR 327-E11
CORVALLIS OR 327-E11
FLORENCE OR 214-B2
SPRINGFIELD OR 331-C6
NW 35TH ST
DESCHUTES CO OR 212-D5
S 35TH ST
TACOMA WA 294-C2
SW 35TH ST
DESCHUTES CO OR 212-D5
REDMOND OR 212-D5
35TH ST NE
DOUGLAS CO WA 239-A3
35TH ST W
UNIVERSITY PLACE WA 181-C3
36 AV
DISTRICT OF DELTA BC 101-C1
36TH AV
BELLINGHAM WA 258-E9
TOWNSHIP OF LANGLEY BC 158-C1
NW 36TH AV
CLARK CO WA 192-C4
S 36TH AV
YAKIMA WA 243-B7
YAKIMA CO WA 243-B7
36TH AV NE
THURSTON CO WA 180-D5
36TH AV NW
SNOHOMISH CO WA 168-B4
THURSTON CO WA 180-C5
36TH AV NW Rt#-531
SNOHOMISH CO WA 168-B6
36TH AV S
KENT WA 175-B7
KING CO WA 175-B7

36TH AV W
LYNNWOOD WA 171-B5
SNOHOMISH CO WA 171-B5
NE 36TH DR
LINCOLN CITY OR 203-A4
36TH ST
CORVALLIS OR 327-E8
E 36TH ST
GARDEN CITY ID 253-C2
N 36TH ST
BOISE ID 253-C2
SEATTLE WA 273-H6
NW 36TH ST
SEATTLE WA 273-H6
S 36TH ST
TACOMA WA 294-C2
W 36TH ST
BOISE ID 253-C2
GARDEN CITY ID 253-C2
37TH AV
LACEY WA 297-F9
TOWNSHIP OF LANGLEY BC 158-C1
E 37TH AV
SPOKANE WA 349-H14
SPOKANE CO WA 349-H14
W 37TH AV
SPOKANE WA 348-J14
SPOKANE WA 349-A14
37TH ST
ANACORTES WA 259-F5
N 37TH ST
TACOMA WA 292-A1
NE 37TH ST
DESCHUTES CO OR 213-A4
SW 37TH ST
PENDLETON OR 129-B1
UMATILLA CO OR 129-B1
37TH ST NE
AUBURN WA 182-C1
37TH ST NW
AUBURN WA 182-B1
38TH AV
COWLITZ CO WA 302-F6
LONGVIEW WA 302-F6
TOWNSHIP OF LANGLEY BC 158-C1
S 38TH AV
WEST RICHLAND WA 340-A13
38TH AV E
PIERCE CO WA 182-A5
38TH AV NW
GIG HARBOR WA 181-C1
PIERCE CO WA 181-C1
NE 38TH PL
KIRKLAND WA 175-C1
38TH ST
EVERETT WA 265-E5
E 38TH ST
TACOMA WA 182-A3
TACOMA WA 295-J2
E 38TH ST Rt#-7
TACOMA WA 295-J2
NE 38TH ST
CLARK CO WA 193-B6
S 38TH ST
TACOMA WA 294-D2
TACOMA WA 295-G2
39TH AV
SKAMANIA CO WA 193-D6
NE 39TH AV
PORTLAND OR 314-B5
SE 39TH AV
PORTLAND OR 314-B7
PORTLAND OR 318-B1
39TH AV S
SEATTLE WA 287-E3
39TH AV SE
PUYALLUP WA 182-B4
SNOHOMISH CO WA 171-C6
39TH AV SW
PUYALLUP WA 182-B4
39TH ST
WASHOUGAL WA 193-C7
E 39TH ST
VANCOUVER WA 305-G2
N 39TH ST
SEATTLE WA 273-H6
NE 39TH ST
CLARK CO WA 193-D6
NW 39TH ST
SEATTLE WA 273-H6
W 39TH ST
VANCOUVER WA 304-E2
VANCOUVER WA 305-F2
40TH AV
DISTRICT OF SURREY BC 158-B1
TOWNSHIP OF LANGLEY BC 158-C1
N 40TH AV
YAKIMA WA 243-B6
S 40TH AV
YAKIMA WA 243-B7
40TH AV NW
POLK CO OR 322-A10
SNOHOMISH CO WA 168-B3
40TH AV S
PIERCE CO WA 118-A1
PIERCE CO WA 181-D7
NE 40TH CIR
CLARK CO WA 193-C6
N 40TH ST
SEATTLE WA 273-J6
SEATTLE WA 274-A6
NE 40TH ST
REDMOND WA 175-D2
SEATTLE WA 274-B6
NW 40TH ST
LINCOLN CITY OR 203-A4
SE 40TH ST
MERCER ISLAND WA 175-C3
MERCER ISLAND WA 283-J3
40TH ST E
PIERCE CO WA 182-C3
40TH ST NW
PIERCE CO WA 181-B1
40TH ST W
FIRCREST WA 294-A3
UNIVERSITY PLACE WA 181-C3
UNIVERSITY PLACE WA 294-A3
41ST AV
UNIV ENDOWMENT LANDS BC 156-B5
VANCOUVER BC 156-B5

NE 41ST AV
PORTLAND OR 314-B2
NW 41ST AV
CLARK CO WA 192-C4
41ST AV NE
THURSTON CO WA 180-D5
41 PL
PACIFIC CO WA 186-A6
41ST ST
ANACORTES WA 259-F5
CLARK CO WA 192-D1
N 41ST ST
YAKIMA CO WA 243-C6
NE 41ST ST
SEATTLE WA 274-E6
SEATTLE WA 275-E6
41ST ST SE
AUBURN WA 182-B2
EVERETT WA 264-D6
EVERETT WA 265-E5
41B ST
DISTRICT OF DELTA BC 101-C1
41ST DIVISION DR
PIERCE CO WA 181-C5
NE 42ND AV
PORTLAND OR 310-B7
PORTLAND OR 314-B1
S 42ND AV
YAKIMA CO WA 243-B7
42ND AV E
PIERCE CO WA 182-A5
42ND AV NE
Hayesville OR 323-E7
SEATTLE WA 275-F6
42ND AV NW
THURSTON CO WA 180-B5
42ND ST
SPRINGFIELD OR 331-D5
S 42ND ST
LANE CO OR 331-E8
SPRINGFIELD OR 331-E8
E 43RD AV
SPOKANE WA 246-C5
43RD AV NE
SEATTLE WA 275-F6
43RD AV NW
THURSTON CO WA 180-C5
43RD AV SE
PIERCE CO WA 182-B4
PUYALLUP WA 182-B4
SNOHOMISH WA 265-G7
SNOHOMISH WA 269-H1
NW 43RD ST
DESCHUTES CO OR 212-D3
S 43RD ST
RENTON WA 175-C6
SW 43RD ST
KENT WA 175-C6
KENT WA 291-J1
RENTON WA 175-C6
RENTON WA 291-J1
TUKWILA WA 291-J1
SE 43RD WY
KING CO WA 175-D3
KING CO WA 176-A3
SAMMAMISH WA 175-D3
SAMMAMISH WA 176-A3
44TH AV
TOWNSHIP OF LANGLEY BC 158-D1
E 44TH AV
SPOKANE WA 246-C5
44TH AV E
PIERCE CO WA 182-A3
44TH AV NW
SNOHOMISH CO WA 168-B3
44TH AV W
LYNNWOOD WA 171-B5
MOUNTLAKE TERRACE WA 171-B6
SNOHOMISH CO WA 171-B4
NFD 44 RD
OKANOGAN CO WA 104-A3
E 44TH ST
GARDEN CITY ID 253-C2
NE 44TH ST
RENTON WA 175-C4
NE 44TH ST Rt#-500
CLARK CO WA 193-B6
44TH ST NE
MARYSVILLE WA 171-D1
SNOHOMISH CO WA 171-D1
45TH AV
VANCOUVER BC 156-C5
E 45TH AV
Finley WA 121-A3
SW 45TH AV
PORTLAND OR 316-A5
W 45TH AV
Finley WA 121-A3
KENNEWICK WA 121-A3
45TH AV NE
Four Corners OR 323-E13
SALEM OR 323-F12
45TH AV SE
SNOHOMISH CO WA 171-C6
45TH AV SW
SEATTLE WA 284-D4
THURSTON CO WA 296-F10
TUMWATER WA 296-F10
SW 45TH DR
PORTLAND OR 316-A7
NE 45TH PL
SEATTLE WA 274-E5
N 45TH ST
SEATTLE WA 273-J5
SEATTLE WA 274-A5
NE 45TH ST
DESCHUTES CO OR 213-A4
SEATTLE WA 274-B5
SEATTLE WA 275-E5
NE 45TH ST Rt#-513
SEATTLE WA 274-D5
SEATTLE WA 275-E5
46TH AV
LONGVIEW WA 302-D5
46TH AV E
PIERCE CO WA 182-A6
46TH AV NE
THURSTON CO WA 180-D5
THURSTON CO WA 181-A5

46TH AV NW
THURSTON CO WA 180-C5
N 46TH ST
SEATTLE WA 273-H5
TACOMA WA 181-D1
47TH AV
TOWNSHIP OF LANGLEY BC 158-D1
47TH AV NE
MARYSVILLE WA 168-C7
47TH AV SW
FEDERAL WAY WA 182-A1
S 47TH ST
TACOMA WA 294-D3
TACOMA WA 295-E4
47A AV
DISTRICT OF DELTA BC 101-C1
48TH AV
COWLITZ CO WA 302-D4
LANGLEY BC 158-C1
TOWNSHIP OF LANGLEY BC 158-C1
S 48TH AV
YAKIMA WA 243-B7
SW 48TH AV
PORTLAND OR 316-A7
PORTLAND OR 320-A1
48TH AV NW
SNOHOMISH CO WA 168-B5
48TH AV S
PIERCE CO WA 181-D7
48TH AV SW
SEATTLE WA 280-D7
SEATTLE WA 284-D1
48 ST
DISTRICT OF DELTA BC 101-C1
E 48TH ST
TACOMA WA 295-J4
NE 48TH ST
CLARK CO WA 193-D6
S 48TH ST
TACOMA WA 295-F4
48TH ST E
EDGEWOOD WA 182-B3
PIERCE CO WA 182-A3
SW 49TH AV
LAKE OSWEGO OR 320-A2
PORTLAND OR 320-A2
49TH AV E
VANCOUVER BC 156-B5
49TH AV NE
TACOMA WA 182-A1
49TH AV SW
SEATTLE WA 280-D5
THURSTON CO WA 296-B10
49TH AV W
VANCOUVER BC 156-B5
49TH ST
CLARK CO WA 193-C7
PORT TOWNSEND WA 263-E2
WASHOUGAL WA 193-C7
50TH AV
TOWNSHIP OF LANGLEY BC 158-D1
NE 50TH AV
CLARK CO WA 192-D3
50TH AV E
PIERCE CO WA 182-A5
50TH AV NE
MARION CO OR 205-A3
50TH AV NW
PIERCE CO WA 181-C2
SNOHOMISH CO WA 168-B5
50TH AV S
SEATTLE WA 283-F6
N 50TH ST
SEATTLE WA 273-J5
SEATTLE WA 274-A5
NE 50TH ST
LINCOLN CO OR 203-B4
SEATTLE WA 274-C5
NW 50TH ST
SEATTLE WA 273-G5
NW 51ST AV
CLARK CO WA 192-C2
RIDGEFIELD WA 192-C2
51ST AV NE
MARYSVILLE WA 168-C7
SNOHOMISH CO WA 168-C7
51ST AV S
KING CO WA 182-B1
51ST AV SE
SNOHOMISH WA 265-H4
SNOHOMISH CO WA 171-C5
51ST AV SW
LAKEWOOD WA 181-D4
N 51ST ST
RUSTON WA 181-D1
NE 51ST ST
REDMOND WA 175-D1
SE 51ST ST
LINCOLN CITY OR 203-A5
SW 51ST ST
DESCHUTES CO OR 212-C6
51ST ST W
FIRCREST WA 292-A7
FIRCREST WA 294-A2
TACOMA WA 292-A7
TACOMA WA 294-A2
UNIVERSITY PLACE WA 294-A2
52ND AV
TOWNSHIP OF LANGLEY BC 158-C1
S 52ND AV
YAKIMA CO WA 243-B7
SE 52ND AV
PORTLAND OR 318-C3
52ND AV NW
SNOHOMISH CO WA 168-B5
52ND AV W
LYNNWOOD WA 171-B5
SNOHOMISH CO WA 171-B4
52ND ST NE
AUBURN WA 175-C7
KING CO WA 175-B7
52ND ST SE
EVERETT WA 268-D1
EVERETT WA 269-H1
SNOHOMISH WA 269-H1
W 53RD AV
SPOKANE CO WA 246-B5
53RD AV NE
TACOMA WA 182-A2

53RD AV NW
POLK CO OR 204-C6
53RD ST
BENTON CO OR 207-A7
BENTON CO OR 327-B11
CORVALLIS OR 327-B11
NE 53RD ST
CLARK CO WA 193-B6
53RD ST KPN
PIERCE CO WA 181-A1
54TH AV
TOWNSHIP OF LANGLEY BC 158-D1
VANCOUVER BC 156-C5
54TH AV E
FIFE WA 182-A2
PIERCE CO WA 182-A5
TACOMA WA 182-A2
54TH AV E Rt#-99
FIFE WA 182-A2
54TH AV NW
PIERCE CO WA 174-C7
THURSTON CO WA 180-B5
54TH AV SW
THURSTON CO WA 296-C11
TUMWATER WA 296-C11
NE 54TH ST Rt#-500
CLARK CO WA 193-B6
NW 54TH ST
SEATTLE WA 272-D4
55TH AV NE
MARION CO OR 323-H5
SEATTLE WA 275-G3
SNOHOMISH CO WA 168-D4
55TH AV NW
POLK CO OR 204-C6
55TH AV S
KING CO WA 175-B7
SW 55TH PL
DESCHUTES CO OR 212-C5
55 ST
PACIFIC CO WA 186-A5
NE 55TH ST
SEATTLE WA 274-D4
SEATTLE WA 275-F4
SW 55TH ST
DESCHUTES CO OR 212-C5
56TH AV
DISTRICT OF SURREY BC 158-C1
LANGLEY BC 158-C1
TOWNSHIP OF LANGLEY BC 102-B1
TOWNSHIP OF LANGLEY BC 158-D1
56TH AV Rt#-10
DISTRICT OF SURREY BC 157-A7
DISTRICT OF SURREY BC 158-B1
N 56TH AV
YAKIMA WA 243-B6
56TH AV NW
SNOHOMISH CO WA 168-B4
56 ST
DISTRICT OF DELTA BC 101-C1
E 56TH ST
TACOMA WA 295-J5
S 56TH ST
TACOMA WA 294-D5
TACOMA WA 295-G5
56TH ST NW
GIG HARBOR WA 181-C1
PIERCE CO WA 181-C1
56TH ST SE
SNOHOMISH CO WA 171-D3
57TH AV
VANCOUVER BC 156-B5
E 57TH AV
SPOKANE WA 246-C5
SPOKANE CO WA 246-C5
NE 57TH AV
PORTLAND OR 314-D2
57TH AV SE
SNOHOMISH CO WA 171-C6
N 57TH ST
YAKIMA CO WA 243-C6
S 57TH ST
LANE CO OR 331-H9
SPRINGFIELD OR 331-H9
57TH ST KPN
PIERCE CO WA 181-A1
57TH ST NE
TACOMA WA 182-A1
57TH WY NW
THURSTON CO WA 180-C5
58TH AV Rt#-10
DISTRICT OF DELTA BC 156-D7
DISTRICT OF SURREY BC 156-D7
DISTRICT OF SURREY BC 157-A7
58TH AV E
PIERCE CO WA 182-A5
58TH AV SE
THURSTON CO WA 181-A7
N 58TH ST
SPRINGFIELD OR 331-H7
NE 58TH ST
CLARK CO WA 192-D5
NE 58TH ST Rt#-500
CLARK CO WA 193-B5
S 58TH ST
SPRINGFIELD OR 331-H8
SW 58TH ST
DESCHUTES CO OR 212-C6
59TH AV NE
ARLINGTON WA 168-D5
MARION CO OR 205-A3
SNOHOMISH CO WA 168-D4
59TH AV SW
SEATTLE WA 280-C3
NW 59TH ST
DESCHUTES CO OR 212-C5
60TH AV
DISTRICT OF SURREY BC 157-B7
TOWNSHIP OF LANGLEY BC 157-D7
NE 60TH AV
PORTLAND OR 314-D5
SE 60TH AV
PORTLAND OR 314-D6
PORTLAND OR 318-D1
60TH AV E
PIERCE CO WA 182-A7
60TH AV W
LYNNWOOD WA 171-B5
60 ST
DISTRICT OF DELTA BC 101-C1

PNW
INDEX

408 NE 117TH AV Rt#-500 STREET INDEX SW 204TH ST

PNW

INDEX

STREET City State Page-Grid

NE 117TH AV Rt#-500
CLARK CO WA 192-D5
NE 117TH AV Rt#-503
CLARK CO WA 192-D5
CLARK CO WA 193-A4
117TH AV NE
MARION CO OR 205-B6
118TH AV
MAPLE RIDGE BC 157-D5
118TH AV NW
KITSAP CO WA 174-B7
PIERCE CO WA 174-B7
118TH AV SE
BELLEVUE WA 175-C3
NE 118TH ST
CLARK CO WA 193-B5
S 118TH ST
KING WA 286-B7
118TH ST KPN
PIERCE CO WA 174-A7
118TH ST NE
SNOHOMISH CO WA 168-C7
119TH AV
CLARK CO WA 193-A1
PITT MEADOWS BC 157-B5
119TH AV SE
BELLEVUE WA 175-C3
NE 119TH ST
CLARK CO WA 192-D5
CLARK CO WA 193-A5
NW 119TH ST
CLARK CO WA 192-C5
120TH AV NE
KIRKLAND WA 171-C7
NE 120TH PL
KIRKLAND WA 171-C7
120 ST
DISTRICT OF DELTA BC 156-D7
DISTRICT OF SURREY BC 156-D7
120TH ST E
PIERCE CO WA 182-C4
SW 121ST AV
WASHINGTON CO OR 199-B3
121ST ST E
PIERCE CO WA 182-A4
122ND AV
MAPLE RIDGE BC 157-C5
NE 122ND AV
PORTLAND OR 200-A1
NE 122ND AV Rt#-503
BATTLE GROUND WA 193-A3
CLARK CO WA 193-A3
SE 122ND AV
CLACKAMAS CO OR 200-A3
PORTLAND OR 200-A2
122ND AV E
EDGEWOOD WA 182-B3
PIERCE CO WA 182-B5
NE 122ND BLVD
PORTLAND OR 193-A7
PORTLAND OR 200-A1
NE 122ND ST
CLARK CO WA 193-B5
122ND ST E
PIERCE CO WA 182-B4
123RD AV
MAPLE RIDGE BC 157-C5
123RD AV NE
SNOHOMISH CO WA 168-D5
123RD AV SE
SNOHOMISH CO WA 171-D2
124TH AV
MAPLE RIDGE BC 157-C5
124TH AV NE
KING CO WA 171-C7
KIRKLAND WA 175-C1
WOODINVILLE WA 171-C7
124TH AV SE
KING CO WA 175-C6
NE 124TH ST
KING CO WA 171-C7
KIRKLAND WA 171-C7
REDMOND WA 171-C7
NE 124TH WY
KING CO WA 171-D7
125TH AV
MAPLE RIDGE BC 157-D5
NE 125TH ST
SEATTLE WA 171-B7
126TH AV E
PIERCE CO WA 182-B6
126TH AV KPN
PIERCE CO WA 174-B7
126TH ST NW
SNOHOMISH CO WA 168-B6
127TH AV
MAPLE RIDGE BC 157-D5
127TH AV SE
SNOHOMISH CO WA 171-D4
127TH PL SE
BELLEVUE WA 175-C2
NW 127TH ST
CLARK CO WA 192-C4
128TH AV
MAPLE RIDGE BC 157-C5
128TH AV SE
BELLEVUE WA 175-C5
KING CO WA 175-C5
128TH ST
DISTRICT OF SURREY BC 157-A7
DISTRICT OF SURREY BC 158-A2
NE 128TH ST
KING CO WA 171-D7
S 128TH ST
BURIEN WA 288-B1
KING WA 288-B1
KING WA 289-J1
SEATAC WA 288-B1
SE 128TH ST
KING CO WA 175-D5
128TH ST E
PIERCE CO WA 182-A4
128TH ST KPN
PIERCE CO WA 174-A7
128TH ST NE
SNOHOMISH CO WA 168-C6
128TH ST SE Rt#-96
SNOHOMISH CO WA 171-C4
128TH ST SW
SNOHOMISH CO WA 171-C4

128TH ST SW Rt#-96
SNOHOMISH CO WA 171-C4
SE 128TH WY
KING CO WA 175-D5
129TH AV
MAPLE RIDGE BC 157-C5
PITT MEADOWS BC 157-B5
SE 129TH AV
HAPPY VALLEY OR 200-A3
129TH PL SE
BELLEVUE WA 175-C3
NE 130TH AV
CLARK CO WA 193-A5
130TH AV NE
BELLEVUE WA 175-C2
BOTHELL WA 171-C6
KING CO WA 171-C6
WOODINVILLE WA 171-C6
N 130TH ST
SEATTLE WA 171-A7
NE 130TH ST
KING CO WA 171-D7
NE 131ST AV
CLARK CO WA 193-A5
131ST AV NE Rt#-202
BOTHELL WA 171-C6
WOODINVILLE WA 171-C6
131ST AV NE Rt#-92
SNOHOMISH CO WA 110-C1
131ST AV SE
THURSTON CO WA 184-C2
131ST ST E
PIERCE CO WA 181-D4
131ST ST NW
SNOHOMISH CO WA 168-C6
132ND AV
MAPLE RIDGE BC 157-C5
PITT MEADOWS BC 157-C5
NE 132ND AV
CLARK CO WA 193-A2
132ND AV E
PIERCE CO WA 182-B7
132ND AV NE
BOTHELL WA 171-C6
KING CO WA 171-C7
KIRKLAND WA 175-C1
REDMOND WA 175-C1
WOODINVILLE WA 171-C6
132ND AV SE
BELLEVUE WA 175-C7
KENT WA 175-C7
KING CO WA 175-C7
KING CO WA 182-C1
132ND ST
DISTRICT OF SURREY BC 157-A7
NE 132ND ST
KING CO WA 171-C7
KIRKLAND WA 171-C7
132ND ST NE
SNOHOMISH CO WA 168-D6
132ND ST SE
SNOHOMISH CO WA 171-C4
132ND ST SE Rt#-96
MILL CREEK WA 171-C4
SNOHOMISH CO WA 171-C4
133RD AV SE
NEWCASTLE WA 175-C4
133RD AV SW
THURSTON CO WA 184-B2
NE 133RD ST
KING CO WA 171-D7
134TH AV E
PIERCE CO WA 182-B5
134TH AV NE
BELLEVUE WA 175-C2
NE 134TH ST
CLARK CO WA 192-C4
135 RD
NEZ PERCE CO ID 250-C2
SE 136TH AV
PORTLAND OR 200-A2
136 RD
NEZ PERCE CO ID 250-C2
S 136TH ST
BURIEN WA 288-A2
SEATAC WA 288-B2
136TH ST E
PIERCE CO WA 182-B5
136TH ST NE
MARYSVILLE WA 168-C6
SNOHOMISH CO WA 168-C6
NE 137TH AV
CLARK CO WA 193-A5
138TH AV SE
KING CO WA 175-C5
RENTON WA 175-C5
138TH ST S
PIERCE CO WA 181-D5
NE 139TH ST
CLARK CO WA 192-D4
CLARK CO WA 193-A4
NW 139TH ST
CLARK CO WA 192-C4
140TH AV NE
BELLEVUE WA 175-C2
WOODINVILLE WA 171-C6
140TH AV SE
BELLEVUE WA 175-C2
KING CO WA 175-C6
140TH AV SW
THURSTON CO WA 184-B2
140TH PL NE
KING CO WA 171-C6
WOODINVILLE WA 171-C6
140 RD
NEZ PERCE CO ID 250-C2
140TH ST
CITY OF WHITE ROCK BC 158-A2
DISTRICT OF SURREY BC 157-A6
DISTRICT OF SURREY BC 158-A2
140TH ST NE
SNOHOMISH CO WA 168-C6
140TH ST NW
SNOHOMISH CO WA 168-B6
140TH WY SE
KING CO WA 175-C5
NE 142ND AV
CLARK CO WA 193-A4
SE 142ND AV
CLACKAMAS CO OR 200-A3

NW 143RD AV
WASHINGTON CO OR 199-A1
143RD AV SE
THURSTON CO WA 184-C2
143RD AV SW
THURSTON CO WA 184-C2
144TH AV SE
KENT WA 175-C7
144TH ST
DISTRICT OF SURREY BC 158-A1
NE 144TH ST
CLARK CO WA 193-A4
S 144TH ST
SEATAC WA 288-D3
TUKWILA WA 288-D3
TUKWILA WA 289-E3
144TH ST E
PIERCE CO WA 182-A5
144TH ST KPN
PIERCE CO WA 174-A6
144TH ST NW
PIERCE CO WA 174-C6
SE 145TH AV
CLACKAMAS CO OR 200-A3
HAPPY VALLEY OR 200-A3
145TH PL SE
BELLEVUE WA 175-C2
N 145TH ST
SEATTLE WA 171-A7
SHORELINE WA 171-A7
N 145TH ST Rt#-523
SEATTLE WA 171-A7
SHORELINE WA 171-A7
NE 145TH ST
KING CO WA 171-C7
NE 145TH ST Rt#-202
KING CO WA 171-D7
WOODINVILLE WA 171-C7
NE 145TH ST Rt#-523
SEATTLE WA 171-B7
SHORELINE WA 171-B7
146TH AV E
PIERCE CO WA 182-B6
NE 147TH AV
CLARK CO WA 193-A2
NE 148TH AV
PORTLAND OR 200-A1
148TH AV NE
BELLEVUE WA 175-C2
REDMOND WA 175-C2
148TH AV SE
BELLEVUE WA 175-C3
COVINGTON WA 175-C7
KENT WA 175-C7
KING CO WA 175-D4
KING CO WA 182-C1
148TH ST
DISTRICT OF SURREY BC 157-A6
SW 148TH ST
BURIEN WA 175-A5
148TH ST SW
SNOHOMISH CO WA 171-B4
NW 149TH ST
CLARK CO WA 192-C4
150TH AV
PITT MEADOWS BC 157-C4
SW 150TH AV
WASHINGTON CO OR 199-A3
150TH AV E
PIERCE CO WA 182-B7
150TH AV SE
BELLEVUE WA 175-D3
KING CO WA 175-D3
150TH ST SW
LAKEWOOD WA 181-C5
PIERCE CO WA 181-C5
150 NW ST
OAK HARBOR WA 167-B2
NE 152ND AV
CLARK CO WA 193-A2
152ND AV SE
COVINGTON WA 175-C7
KENT WA 175-C7
KING CO WA 175-C7
152ND AV SW
THURSTON CO WA 184-B3
152ND ST
DISTRICT OF SURREY BC 157-A6
DISTRICT OF SURREY BC 158-A1
SW 152ND ST
BURIEN WA 175-A5
152ND ST E
PIERCE CO WA 182-A5
152ND ST NE
MARYSVILLE WA 168-C6
SNOHOMISH CO WA 168-C6
154TH AV E
PIERCE CO WA 182-B7
154TH AV SE
KING CO WA 182-C1
154TH PL SE
KING CO WA 175-D5
154TH ST
DISTRICT OF SURREY BC 157-A6
S 154TH ST
SEATAC WA 288-C4
TUKWILA WA 288-D4
TUKWILA WA 289-E4
N 155TH ST
SHORELINE WA 171-B7
155TH ST SW
LAKEWOOD WA 181-C5
PIERCE CO WA 181-C5
156TH AV NE
BELLEVUE WA 175-D2
REDMOND WA 175-D2
WOODINVILLE WA 171-D6
156TH AV NE Rt#-202
KING CO WA 171-D7
REDMOND WA 171-D7
WOODINVILLE WA 171-D7
156TH AV SE
BELLEVUE WA 175-D3
KING CO WA 175-D5
156TH ST
DISTRICT OF SURREY BC 157-A6
NE 156TH ST
CLARK CO WA 192-D4
S 156TH ST
BURIEN WA 175-A5

S 156TH ST
BURIEN WA 288-A4
SE 156TH ST
KING CO WA 176-A5
SW 156TH ST
BURIEN WA 175-A5
156TH ST NE
SNOHOMISH CO WA 168-C6
156TH ST SE
SNOHOMISH CO WA 171-D4
S 156TH WY
SEATAC WA 288-B4
157TH ST
DISTRICT OF SURREY BC 158-A2
NW 158TH AV
BEAVERTON OR 199-A1
SW 158TH AV
BEAVERTON OR 199-A1
WASHINGTON CO OR 199-A1
158TH AV E
PIERCE CO WA 182-B7
158TH AV KPS
PIERCE CO WA 181-A3
159TH AV NE
SNOHOMISH CO WA 102-C3
NE 159TH ST
CLARK CO WA 192-D4
CLARK CO WA 193-A4
159TH ST E
PIERCE CO WA 181-D5
160TH AV E
SUMNER WA 182-C3
160TH PL SE
KING CO WA 182-D2
160TH ST
DISTRICT OF SURREY BC 157-B6
NE 160TH ST
KING CO WA 171-D7
S 160TH ST
BURIEN WA 288-A5
SEATAC WA 288-A5
TUKWILA WA 288-A5
160TH ST E
PIERCE CO WA 181-D5
PIERCE CO WA 182-A5
NE 162ND AV
CLARK CO WA 193-A5
GRESHAM OR 200-A1
PORTLAND OR 200-A1
VANCOUVER WA 193-A6
SE 162ND AV
MULTNOMAH CO OR 200-A2
PORTLAND OR 200-A2
162ND AV KPS
PIERCE CO WA 181-A3
162ND ST E
PIERCE CO WA 182-D5
162ND ST SE
MONROE WA 110-C1
163RD AV NE
SNOHOMISH CO WA 102-C3
163RD AV SW
THURSTON CO WA 184-C3
SE 164TH AV
VANCOUVER WA 193-A7
164TH AV NE
BELLEVUE WA 175-D2
164TH AV NE Rt#-202
REDMOND WA 175-D1
164TH AV SE
BELLEVUE WA 175-D2
COVINGTON WA 175-D7
KING CO WA 175-D5
NE 164TH ST
CLARK CO WA 193-A4
NW 164TH ST
CLARK CO WA 192-C4
164TH ST NE
SNOHOMISH CO WA 168-D6
164TH ST SE
MILL CREEK WA 171-C4
MONROE WA 110-C1
SNOHOMISH CO WA 110-C1
SNOHOMISH CO WA 171-C4
164TH ST SW
LYNNWOOD WA 171-B4
SNOHOMISH CO WA 171-B4
NE 165TH ST
KING CO WA 171-D7
166TH AV E
PIERCE CO WA 182-C3
166TH AV NE
REDMOND WA 175-D1
NE 167TH AV
CLARK CO WA 193-A4
168TH AV NE
KING CO WA 171-D7
168TH ST
DISTRICT OF SURREY BC 157-B6
DISTRICT OF SURREY BC 158-B2
168TH ST SW
LYNNWOOD WA 171-B5
169TH AV SW
THURSTON CO WA 184-B3
NE 169TH ST
CLARK CO WA 193-B4
NW 169TH ST
CLARK CO WA 192-C4
169TH ST SE
SNOHOMISH CO WA 171-C5
SW 170TH AV
WASHINGTON CO OR 199-A2
S 170TH ST
SEATAC WA 288-C6
170TH ST E
PIERCE CO WA 182-A5
171ST AV SE
SNOHOMISH CO WA 110-C1
THURSTON CO WA 184-C3
171ST PL NE
KING CO WA 171-D7
NE 172ND AV
CLARK CO WA 193-A5
SE 172ND AV
CLACKAMAS CO OR 200-A3
NE 172ND ST
KING CO WA 171-D6
SW 172ND ST
BURIEN WA 175-A5

172ND ST NE Rt#-531
ARLINGTON WA 168-C6
SNOHOMISH CO WA 168-C6
173RD AV SW
Rochester WA 184-A3
THURSTON CO WA 184-A3
174TH AV KPS
PIERCE CO WA 181-A3
NE 174TH ST
CLARK CO WA 193-A4
S 174TH ST Rt#-509
BURIEN WA 175-A5
174TH ST S
PIERCE CO WA 181-D5
SW 175TH AV
WASHINGTON CO OR 199-A3
175TH AV SW
THURSTON CO WA 184-A3
NE 175TH ST
KING CO WA 171-D6
SHORELINE WA 171-B6
WOODINVILLE WA 171-B6
NE 176TH AV
CLARK CO WA 193-A3
176TH AV SW
THURSTON CO WA 184-A3
176TH ST
DISTRICT OF SURREY BC 157-B6
176TH ST Rt#-15
BRITISH COLUMBIA 158-B2
DISTRICT OF SURREY BC 157-B7
DISTRICT OF SURREY BC 158-B2
WHATCOM CO WA 158-B2
S 176TH ST
BURIEN WA 288-A7
SEATAC WA 288-A7
SEATAC WA 289-F7
SE 176TH ST
KING CO WA 175-C5
176TH ST E
PIERCE CO WA 181-D5
PIERCE CO WA 182-A5
176TH ST S
PIERCE CO WA 181-D5
176TH ST SW
LYNNWOOD WA 171-B5
177TH ST
PACIFIC CO WA 186-A4
177TH ST E
PIERCE CO WA 182-C5
178TH AV E
BONNEY LAKE WA 182-C3
S 178TH ST
SEATAC WA 289-F7
TUKWILA WA 289-F7
TUKWILA WA 291-G1
NE 179TH ST
CLARK CO WA 192-D4
NW 179TH ST
CLARK CO WA 192-C4
SE 179TH ST
KING CO WA 175-C5
RENTON WA 175-C5
180TH AV SE
COVINGTON WA 175-D7
KING CO WA 175-D7
KING CO WA 182-D2
S 180TH ST
TUKWILA WA 291-G1
SE 180TH ST
KENT WA 175-C6
KENT WA 291-J1
RENTON WA 175-C6
RENTON WA 291-J1
TUKWILA WA 291-H1
180TH ST E
PIERCE CO WA 182-A5
180TH WY SW
THURSTON CO WA 184-B3
NE 181ST AV
GRESHAM OR 200-A1
NE 182ND AV
CLARK CO WA 193-A3
SE 182ND AV
GRESHAM OR 200-A2
182ND AV E
PIERCE CO WA 182-C2
182ND ST
DISTRICT OF SURREY BC 157-B6
183RD AV SW
THURSTON CO WA 184-A3
183RD AV SW U.S.-12
Rochester WA 184-A3
THURSTON CO WA 184-A3
184TH AV SE
KING CO WA 175-D6
184 RD
NEZ PERCE CO ID 250-D2
184TH ST
DISTRICT OF SURREY BC 157-B7
DISTRICT OF SURREY BC 158-B1
NW 184TH ST
CLARK CO WA 192-C4
184TH ST E
PIERCE CO WA 182-A5
NW 185TH AV
HILLSBORO OR 199-A1
WASHINGTON CO OR 192-A7
SW 185TH AV
WASHINGTON CO OR 199-A2
N 185TH ST
SHORELINE WA 171-B6
NE 185TH ST
KING CO WA 171-D6
186TH AV E
PIERCE CO WA 182-C5
186TH AV KPN
PIERCE CO WA 174-A7
PIERCE CO WA 181-A2
186TH ST NE
SNOHOMISH CO WA 168-D5
187TH AV SE
KING CO WA 175-D7
187TH AV SW
THURSTON CO WA 184-B4
188TH AV SW
THURSTON CO WA 184-A4
188TH ST
PITT MEADOWS BC 157-B5

S 188TH ST
SEATAC WA 290-C1
SEATAC WA 291-E2
188TH ST NE
ARLINGTON WA 168-C5
SNOHOMISH CO WA 168-C5
188TH ST NW
SNOHOMISH CO WA 168-B5
188TH ST SW
LYNNWOOD WA 171-B5
S 188TH WY
SEATAC WA 290-B1
NE 189TH ST
CLARK CO WA 193-B4
NW 189TH ST
CLARK CO WA 192-C4
190TH AV E
PIERCE CO WA 182-C4
190TH AV KPS
PIERCE CO WA 181-A2
SE 190TH DR
MULTNOMAH CO OR 200-A2
191ST AV SW
THURSTON CO WA 184-B4
NE 192ND AV
CLARK CO WA 193-A5
SW 192ND AV
WASHINGTON CO OR 199-A4
192ND AV SE
KING CO WA 182-D1
192ND PL SE
KING CO WA 182-D3
192ND ST
DISTRICT OF SURREY BC 157-B6
DISTRICT OF SURREY BC 158-B1
SE 192ND ST
KING CO WA 175-C6
192ND ST E
PIERCE CO WA 182-A6
NW 194TH ST
CLARK CO WA 192-C3
195TH AV SW
THURSTON CO WA 184-B4
NW 195TH ST
SHORELINE WA 171-A6
196TH AV SE
KING CO WA 175-D6
KING CO WA 182-D3
196TH AV SW
Grand Mound WA 184-B4
196TH ST
DISTRICT OF SURREY BC 158-C2
S 196TH ST
KENT WA 291-G3
SE 196TH ST
KING CO WA 176-A6
196TH ST NW
SNOHOMISH CO WA 168-B5
196TH ST SE
SNOHOMISH CO WA 171-C5
196TH ST SW Rt#-524
EDMONDS WA 171-B5
LYNNWOOD WA 171-B5
SNOHOMISH CO WA 171-B5
196C ST
PITT MEADOWS BC 157-C4
197TH ST
TOWNSHIP OF LANGLEY BC 157-C7
SW 198TH AV
WASHINGTON CO OR 199-A2
198TH AV E
PIERCE CO WA 182-C5
198 PL
PACIFIC CO WA 186-A3
198TH ST
TOWNSHIP OF LANGLEY BC 157-C6
TOWNSHIP OF LANGLEY BC 158-C2
NE 199TH AV
CLARK CO WA 193-A6
NE 199TH ST
CLARK CO WA 192-D3
CLARK CO WA 193-A3
NW 199TH ST
CLARK CO WA 192-C3
S 199TH ST
DES MOINES WA 175-A6
DES MOINES WA 290-A3
199A ST
TOWNSHIP OF LANGLEY BC 157-C6
200TH AV SE
KING CO WA 182-D2
200TH ST
LANGLEY BC 157-C7
LANGLEY BC 158-C1
TOWNSHIP OF LANGLEY BC 157-C7
TOWNSHIP OF LANGLEY BC 158-C1
N 200TH ST
SHORELINE WA 171-A6
S 200TH ST
DES MOINES WA 290-B3
SEATAC WA 290-B3
SE 200TH ST
KING CO WA 176-A6
200TH ST E
PIERCE CO WA 182-A6
200TH ST NE
SNOHOMISH CO WA 168-C5
NE 202ND AV
CLARK CO WA 193-A4
202ND ST
TOWNSHIP OF LANGLEY BC 158-C2
202A ST
TOWNSHIP OF LANGLEY BC 157-C7
202B ST
TOWNSHIP OF LANGLEY BC 157-C7
203RD ST
MAPLE RIDGE BC 157-C5
PITT MEADOWS BC 157-C5
204TH AV NE
KING CO WA 171-D6
204TH PL NE
KING CO WA 175-D1
204TH ST
TOWNSHIP OF LANGLEY BC 157-C7
TOWNSHIP OF LANGLEY BC 158-C1
NE 204TH ST
CLARK CO WA 193-B3
SW 204TH ST
KING CO WA 174-D6

Thomas Bros. Maps®   COPYRIGHT 1999   PNW   INDEX

STREET — City   State   Page-Grid

410 I-5 PACIFIC HWY — STREET INDEX — Rt#-11 HIGHWAY

PNW
INDEX

STREET City State Page-Grid

I-5 PACIFIC HWY
TUALATIN OR 199-B4
VANCOUVER WA 192-C5
WASHINGTON CO OR 199-B4
WILSONVILLE OR 199-B5
WOODBURN OR 205-A2
WOODLAND WA 192-B1
I-18 HIGHWAY
BRITISH COLUMBIA 101-A1
I-82 FRWY
BENTON CO WA 120-B2
BENTON CO WA 121-A3
BENTON CO WA 341-A9
BENTON CO WA 342-A13
GRANDVIEW WA 120-B2
GRANGER WA 120-A2
KENNEWICK WA 341-H13
KITTITAS CO WA 241-B6
KITTITAS CO WA 243-C1
PROSSER WA 120-B2
SUNNYSIDE WA 120-B2
UNION GAP WA 120-A2
UNION GAP WA 243-C7
YAKIMA WA 243-C7
YAKIMA CO WA 120-A2
YAKIMA CO WA 243-C4
ZILLAH WA 120-A2
I-82 MCNARY HWY
UMATILLA OR 129-A1
UMATILLA CO OR 129-A1
I-84 BANFIELD FRWY
PORTLAND OR 313-H4
PORTLAND OR 314-D5
PORTLAND OR 315-J2
I-84 COLUMBIA RIVER HWY
ARLINGTON OR 128-A1
BOARDMAN OR 128-B1
CASCADE LOCKS OR 194-C6
FAIRVIEW OR 200-A1
GILLIAM CO OR 127-C1
GILLIAM CO OR 128-A1
GRESHAM OR 200-A1
HOOD RIVER OR 195-A5
HOOD RIVER CO OR 194-C6
HOOD RIVER CO OR 195-A5
MORROW CO OR 128-B1
MOSIER OR 196-D7
MULTNOMAH CO OR 194-B7
MULTNOMAH CO OR 200-C1
MULTNOMAH CO OR 201-A1
PORTLAND OR 200-A1
PORTLAND OR 315-J2
RUFUS OR 127-C1
SHERMAN CO OR 127-C1
THE DALLES OR 196-D7
TROUTDALE OR 200-A1
WASCO CO OR 127-B1
WASCO CO OR 195-A5
WASCO CO OR 196-D7
WOOD VILLAGE OR 200-A1
I-84 FRWY
ADA CO ID 147-C1
ADA CO ID 253-B3
BOISE ID 253-B3
CALDWELL ID 147-B1
CANYON CO ID 139-B3
CANYON CO ID 147-B1
MERIDIAN ID 253-B3
NAMPA ID 147-B1
PAYETTE CO ID 139-A3
I-84 OLD OREGON TRAIL HWY
BAKER CITY OR 138-B1
BAKER CO OR 130-A3
BAKER CO OR 138-B1
LA GRANDE OR 130-A2
MALHEUR CO OR 138-B1
MALHEUR CO OR 139-A2
MORROW CO OR 128-C1
NORTH POWDER OR 130-A3
ONTARIO OR 139-A2
PAYETTE CO ID 139-A2
PENDLETON OR 129-A1
UMATILLA CO OR 128-C1
UMATILLA CO OR 129-A1
UNION CO OR 129-C2
UNION CO OR 130-A2
I-90 COLUMBIA BASIN HWY
ADAMS CO WA 113-C3
I-90 FRWY
ADAMS CO WA 113-C3
ADAMS CO WA 114-B2
BELLEVUE WA 175-C3
CLE ELUM WA 240-D4
COEUR D'ALENE ID 354-H7
COEUR D'ALENE ID 355-A7
Dishman WA 350-F6
ELLENSBURG WA 241-C6
FERNAN LAKE VILLAGE ID 355-H11
GRANT CO WA 112-C3
GRANT CO WA 113-C3
GRANT CO WA 120-B1
GRANT CO WA 242-D3
Greenacres WA 351-D7
ISSAQUAH WA 175-C3
ISSAQUAH WA 176-B4
KELLOGG ID 115-C2
KING CO WA 111-A2
KING CO WA 175-C3
KING CO WA 176-B4
KITTITAS CO WA 111-A2
KITTITAS CO WA 120-A1
KITTITAS CO WA 240-D4
KITTITAS CO WA 241-C6
KOOTENAI CO ID 115-B2
KOOTENAI CO ID 245-B7
KOOTENAI CO ID 248-B1
KOOTENAI CO ID 352-J9
KOOTENAI CO ID 353-F7
KOOTENAI CO ID 354-B7
KOOTENAI CO ID 355-A7
LINCOLN CO WA 114-B2
MERCER ISLAND WA 175-C3
MERCER ISLAND WA 283-J1
MOSES LAKE WA 242-D3
NORTH BEND WA 176-B4
OSBURN ID 115-C2
PINEHURST ID 115-C2
POST FALLS ID 352-J9
POST FALLS ID 353-G6

STREET City State Page-Grid

I-90 FRWY
POST FALLS ID 354-B7
SEATTLE WA 278-B7
SEATTLE WA 282-C1
SEATTLE WA 283-J1
SHOSHONE CO ID 115-C2
SNOQUALMIE WA 176-B4
SPOKANE WA 348-B14
SPOKANE WA 349-B10
SPOKANE CO WA 114-B2
SPOKANE CO WA 246-B5
SPOKANE CO WA 348-B14
SPOKANE CO WA 349-J8
SPOKANE CO WA 350-F6
SPOKANE CO WA 351-D7
SPOKANE CO WA 352-C12
SPRAGUE WA 114-B2
Veradale WA 351-D7
WALLACE ID 115-C2
I-99 SW BARBUR BLVD
PORTLAND OR 316-E3
PORTLAND OR 317-E2
I-99 SW CAPITOL HWY
PORTLAND OR 317-E4
I-99 FRWY
DISTRICT OF DELTA BC 101-C1
DISTRICT OF SURREY BC 101-C1
I-99 HIGHWAY
PORTLAND OR 317-F1
I-99 SW NAITO PKWY
PORTLAND OR 317-F2
I-105
EUGENE-SPRINGFIELD HWY
EUGENE OR 329-J4
EUGENE OR 330-A5
SPRINGFIELD OR 330-A5
I-182 FRWY
BENTON CO WA 121-A3
BENTON CO WA 341-E4
FRANKLIN CO WA 342-B2
FRANKLIN CO WA 343-A4
PASCO WA 342-C1
PASCO WA 343-A4
RICHLAND WA 341-J3
RICHLAND WA 342-A3
I-184 FRWY
ADA CO ID 253-B3
BOISE ID 253-C3
I-205 EAST PORTLAND FRWY
CLACKAMAS CO OR 199-D3
GLADSTONE OR 199-D4
OREGON CITY OR 199-D4
OREGON CITY OR 319-G7
WEST LINN OR 199-D4
I-205 FRWY
CLARK WA 307-H2
CLARK CO WA 192-D5
MAYWOOD PARK OR 315-H4
PORTLAND OR 193-A7
PORTLAND OR 311-J2
PORTLAND OR 315-H4
PORTLAND OR 319-G1
VANCOUVER WA 192-D5
VANCOUVER WA 307-H2
VANCOUVER WA 311-J2
I-205 E PORTLAND FRWY
CLACKAMAS OR 319-G7
CLACKAMAS CO OR 199-D4
PORTLAND OR 319-G7
TUALATIN OR 199-D4
WASHINGTON CO OR 199-D4
I-405 FRWY
BELLEVUE WA 175-C1
BOTHELL WA 171-C6
KING CO WA 171-C7
KING CO WA 175-C4
KIRKLAND WA 171-C7
KIRKLAND WA 175-C1
NEWCASTLE WA 175-C4
PORTLAND OR 312-E3
PORTLAND OR 313-F3
PORTLAND OR 317-E1
RENTON WA 175-C4
RENTON WA 289-J4
SNOHOMISH CO WA 171-C6
TUKWILA WA 289-J4
I-705 FRWY
TACOMA WA 293-H4
TACOMA WA 295-J2
Rt#-D2 VALLEY RD
DEL NORTE CO CA 148-B3
Rt#-D3 LAKE EARL DR
DEL NORTE CO CA 148-B3
Rt#-D3 NORTHCREST DR
CRESCENT CITY CA 148-B3
DEL NORTE CO CA 148-B3
Rt#-D5 OCEAN VIEW DR
DEL NORTE CO CA 232-D7
Rt#-1 DOUGLAS ST
CITY OF VICTORIA BC 256-G6
DISTRICT OF SAANICH BC 256-G6
Rt#-1 HIGHWAY
BOUNDARY CO ID 107-B1
Rt#-1 ISLAND HWY
BRITISH COLUMBIA 101-A1
BRITISH COLUMBIA 159-A2
DISTRICT OF LANGFORD BC 159-A2
DISTRICT OF SAANICH BC 256-D4
DUNCAN BC 101-A1
TOWN OF VIEW ROYAL BC 159-A2
TOWN OF VIEW ROYAL BC 256-D4
Rt#-1 SEA TO SKY HWY
DIST OF WEST VANCOUVER BC 156-A2
Rt#-1 SECOND NARROWS BRDG
DIST OF N VANCOUVER BC 255-F9
VANCOUVER BC 255-F9
Rt#-1 TRANS CANADA HWY
BRITISH COLUMBIA 93-C1
BRITISH COLUMBIA 94-C3
BRITISH COLUMBIA 95-A1
BRITISH COLUMBIA 101-A1
BRITISH COLUMBIA 102-B1
BRITISH COLUMBIA 156-A2
BRITISH COLUMBIA 159-A1
CITY OF N VANCOUVER BC 255-A3
CITY OF VICTORIA BC 256-G11
COQUITLAM BC 157-B6
CITY OF ABBOTSFORD BC 94-C3
DISTRICT OF ABBOTSFORD BC 102-B1

STREET City State Page-Grid

Rt#-1 TRANS CANADA HWY
DISTRICT OF BURNABY BC 156-D4
DISTRICT OF BURNABY BC 255-F12
DISTRICT OF CHILLIWACK BC 94-C3
DISTRICT OF COQUITLAM BC 156-D4
DISTRICT OF LANGFORD BC 159-A6
DISTRICT OF MATSQUI BC 102-B1
DIST OF N VANCOUVER BC 254-F2
DIST OF N VANCOUVER BC 255-A3
DISTRICT OF SAANICH BC 256-G5
DISTRICT OF SURREY BC 157-B6
DIST OF WEST VANCOUVER BC 156-A2
DIST OF WEST VANCOUVER BC 254-F2
DUNCAN BC 101-A1
HOPE BC 95-A3
NANAIMO BC 93-A3
SQUAMISH BC 93-C1
TOWN OF VIEW ROYAL BC 159-A6
TOWN OF VIEW ROYAL BC 256-B3
TOWNSHIP OF LANGLEY BC 102-B1
TOWNSHIP OF LANGLEY BC 157-B6
TOWNSHIP OF LANGLEY BC 158-D1
VANCOUVER BC 255-F12
WHISTLER BC 93-C1
Rt#-1 UPPER LEVELS HWY
CITY OF N VANCOUVER BC 255-D4
DIST OF N VANCOUVER BC 254-H3
DIST OF N VANCOUVER BC 255-D4
DIST OF WEST VANCOUVER BC 156-A2
DIST OF WEST VANCOUVER BC 254-A1
Rt#-1A CRAIGFLOWER RD
TOWN OF VIEW ROYAL BC 256-A5
Rt#-1A FRASER HWY
DISTRICT OF MATSQUI BC 102-B1
DISTRICT OF SURREY BC 157-A6
LANGLEY BC 157-B7
LANGLEY BC 158-D1
TOWNSHIP OF LANGLEY BC 102-B1
TOWNSHIP OF LANGLEY BC 158-D1
Rt#-1A GOLDSTREAM AV
CITY OF COLWOOD BC 159-B6
DISTRICT OF LANGFORD BC 159-B6
Rt#-1A GORGE RD E
CITY OF VICTORIA BC 256-F6
Rt#-1A GORGE RD W
CITY OF VICTORIA BC 256-C5
DISTRICT OF SAANICH BC 256-C5
Rt#-1A HIGHWAY
CITY OF VICTORIA BC 256-F6
DISTRICT OF SAANICH BC 256-B5
LANGLEY BC 158-C1
Rt#-1A KINGSWAY
VANCOUVER BC 156-C5
VANCOUVER BC 254-J13
VANCOUVER BC 255-A14
Rt#-1A OLD ISLAND HWY
CITY OF COLWOOD BC 159-B6
DISTRICT OF SAANICH BC 256-B5
TOWN OF ESQUIMALT BC 256-B5
TOWN OF VIEW ROYAL BC 159-B6
TOWN OF VIEW ROYAL BC 256-A4
Rt#-1A VEDDER RD
DISTRICT OF CHILLIWACK BC 94-C3
Rt#-1A YALE RD E
BRITISH COLUMBIA 94-C3
DISTRICT OF CHILLIWACK BC 94-C3
Rt#-1A YALE RD W
DISTRICT OF CHILLIWACK BC 94-C3
Rt#-2 HIGHWAY
CHELAN CO WA 111-C1
Rt#-2 NE STEVENS PASS HWY
KING CO WA 111-A1
Rt#-3 1ST AV
BOVILL ID 123-B1
Rt#-3 NW 1ST ST
ENTERPRISE OR 130-C2
WALLOWA CO OR 130-C2
Rt#-3 CROWSNEST HWY
BRITISH COLUMBIA 103-C1
Rt#-3 ELK RIVER RD
LATAH CO ID 123-B1
LATAH CO ID 123-B1
Rt#-3
ENTERPRISE-LEWISTON HWY
WALLOWA CO OR 122-C3
WALLOWA CO OR 130-C1
Rt#-3 FORT JONES RD
YREKA CA 149-C3
Rt#-3 FRWY
BREMERTON WA 174-B4
BREMERTON WA 270-C6
KITSAP CO WA 170-B6
KITSAP CO WA 174-B1
KITSAP CO WA 270-B1
Navy Yard City WA 270-E11
Silverdale WA 174-B1
Silverdale WA 270-B1
Tracyton WA 270-A4
Rt#-3 HIGHWAY
BENEWAH CO ID 115-B3
BENEWAH CO ID 248-B6
BREMERTON WA 174-B4
BRITISH COLUMBIA 95-C3
BRITISH COLUMBIA 104-B1
BRITISH COLUMBIA 105-C1
BRITISH COLUMBIA 106-C1
GRAND FORKS BC 105-C1
GREENWOOD BC 105-B1
HOPE BC 95-A3
JULIAETTA ID 123-B2
KENDRICK ID 123-B1
KITSAP CO WA 170-C4
KITSAP CO WA 174-B4
KITSAP CO WA 270-D14
KOOTENAI CO ID 115-B2
KOOTENAI CO ID 248-D2
LATAH CO ID 115-B3
LATAH CO ID 123-B1
MASON CO WA 173-D5
MASON CO WA 174-A5
MASON CO WA 180-D1
Navy Yard City WA 270-E14
NEZ PERCE CO ID 123-A2
PRINCETON BC 95-C3
SAINT MARIES ID 248-D7
SHOSHONE CO ID 115-B3
Rt#-3 N LAKE OF THE WOODS HWY
SISKIYOU CO CA 149-C3

STREET City State Page-Grid

Rt#-3 W LAKE OF THE WOODS HWY
SISKIYOU CO CA 149-C3
YREKA CA 149-C3
Rt#-3 MAIN ST
BRITISH COLUMBIA 104-C1
JULIAETTA ID 123-B1
JULIAETTA ID 123-B1
KENDRICK ID 123-B1
OSOYOOS BC 104-C1
Rt#-3 N MAIN ST
YREKA CA 149-C3
Rt#-3 S MAIN ST
YREKA CA 149-C3
Rt#-3 MONTAGUE RD
YREKA CA 149-C3
Rt#-3 MONTAGUE-YREKA RD
MONTAGUE CA 150-A3
SISKIYOU CO CA 149-C3
SISKIYOU CO CA 150-A3
YREKA CA 149-C3
Rt#-3 OLD OLYMPIC HWY
MASON CO WA 180-A3
SHELTON WA 180-A3
Rt#-3 PARK AV
BOVILL ID 123-B1
LATAH CO ID 123-B1
LATAH CO ID 123-B1
Rt#-3 E PINE ST
MASON CO WA 180-A3
SHELTON WA 180-A3
Rt#-3 SECOND AV
DEARY ID 123-B1
LATAH CO ID 123-B1
Rt#-3 WYOMING ST
DEARY ID 123-B1
LATAH CO ID 123-B1
Rt#-3B HIGHWAY
BRITISH COLUMBIA 106-A1
MONTROSE BC 106-B1
ROSSLAND BC 106-A1
Rt#-4 1ST ST
SHOSHONE CO ID 115-C2
Rt#-4 ALLEN ST
KELSO WA 303-D8
Rt#-4 BURKE-CANYON CREEK RD
SHOSHONE CO ID 115-C2
Rt#-4 BURKE RD
SHOSHONE CO ID 115-C2
WALLACE ID 115-C2
Rt#-4 CATLIN ST
KELSO WA 303-C8
Rt#-4 HIGHWAY
BRITISH COLUMBIA 92-A3
CATHLAMET WA 117-B3
PACIFIC CO WA 186-C4
PORT ALBERNI BC 92-B3
SHOSHONE CO ID 115-C2
WAHKIAKUM CO WA 117-A2
WAHKIAKUM CO WA 186-D5
WALLACE ID 115-C2
Rt#-4 OCEAN BEACH HWY
CATHLAMET WA 117-B3
COWLITZ CO WA 117-B3
COWLITZ CO WA 189-A2
COWLITZ CO WA 302-B3
LONGVIEW WA 302-F7
LONGVIEW WA 303-A8
WAHKIAKUM CO WA 117-B3
Rt#-5 4TH ST
SAINT MARIES ID 248-D7
Rt#-5 CEDAR ST
BENEWAH CO ID 115-A2
BENEWAH CO ID 115-A2
BENEWAH CO ID 248-A7
PLUMMER ID 115-A2
PLUMMER ID 115-A2
Rt#-5 COLLEGE AV
SAINT MARIES ID 248-D7
Rt#-5 HIGHWAY
BENEWAH CO ID 248-A7
BRITISH COLUMBIA 95-C1
CHATCOLET ID 248-B6
HOPE BC 95-A3
SAINT MARIES ID 248-C7
Rt#-5 MAIN AV
SAINT MARIES ID 248-C7
Rt#-5 MAIN ST
SAINT MARIES ID 248-D7
Rt#-5A HIGHWAY
BRITISH COLUMBIA 95-C1
PRINCETON BC 95-C3
Rt#-6 1ST ST
TILLAMOOK OR 197-B2
TILLAMOOK OR 197-C2
Rt#-6 3RD ST
TILLAMOOK OR 197-B2
TILLAMOOK OR 197-C2
Rt#-6 W FOURTH AV
PE ELL WA 117-B2
Rt#-6 HENKLE ST
PACIFIC CO WA 117-A1
RAYMOND WA 117-A1
Rt#-6 HIGHWAY
BRITISH COLUMBIA 106-C1
LATAH CO ID 123-B1
LATAH CO ID 249-D1
LEWIS CO WA 117-B2
PACIFIC CO WA 117-A1
PE ELL WA 117-B2
POTLATCH ID 249-D1
Rt#-6 MAIN ST
PE ELL WA 117-B2
Rt#-6 OCEAN BEACH HWY
CHEHALIS WA 299-A13
LEWIS CO WA 117-B1
LEWIS CO WA 184-B7
LEWIS CO WA 187-A1
LEWIS CO WA 299-A13
PE ELL WA 117-B2
Rt#-6 SIXTH ST
POTLATCH ID 249-D1
Rt#-6 WHITE PINE DR
BENEWAH CO ID 115-B3
LATAH CO ID 115-B3
Rt#-6 WILSON RIVER HWY
BANKS OR 125-B1
TILLAMOOK OR 197-C2
TILLAMOOK CO OR 125-B1

STREET City State Page-Grid

Rt#-6 WILSON RIVER HWY
TILLAMOOK CO OR 197-C2
WASHINGTON CO OR 125-B1
Rt#-7 1ST AV
DISTRICT OF MISSION BC 94-B3
Rt#-7 2ND AV
MORTON WA 118-B2
Rt#-7 E 38TH ST
TACOMA WA 295-J2
Rt#-7 AHSAHKA RD
OROFINO ID 123-C2
Rt#-7 BROADWAY E
VANCOUVER BC 254-H13
VANCOUVER BC 255-A13
Rt#-7 BROADWAY W
VANCOUVER BC 254-E12
Rt#-7 CAMPBELL ST
BAKER CITY OR 138-B1
Rt#-7 DEWEY AV
BAKER CITY OR 138-B1
Rt#-7 FRWY
TACOMA WA 295-H1
Rt#-7 GILBERT GRADE
CLEARWATER CO ID 123-C2
CLEARWATER CO ID 123-C2
Rt#-7 HIGHWAY
BRITISH COLUMBIA 95-A3
CLEARWATER CO ID 123-C2
LEWIS CO WA 118-B1
OROFINO ID 123-C2
PIERCE CO WA 118-B1
Rt#-7 LOUGHEED HWY
BRITISH COLUMBIA 94-B3
COQUITLAM BC 157-A5
DISTRICT OF BURNABY BC 156-D4
DISTRICT OF BURNABY BC 255-G12
DISTRICT OF COQUITLAM BC 156-D4
DISTRICT OF KENT BC 94-B3
DISTRICT OF MISSION BC 94-B3
MAPLE RIDGE BC 94-B3
MAPLE RIDGE BC 157-D6
PITT MEADOWS BC 157-B4
PORT COQUITLAM BC 157-B4
Rt#-7 MAIN ST
BAKER CITY OR 138-B1
Rt#-7 MORTON RD
LEWIS CO WA 118-B2
MORTON WA 118-B2
Rt#-7 MOUNTAIN HWY E
PIERCE CO WA 118-B1
PIERCE CO WA 181-D6
PIERCE CO WA 182-A7
Rt#-7 NORTH RAILWAY AV
DISTRICT OF MISSION BC 94-B3
Rt#-7 PACIFIC AV
PIERCE CO WA 181-D4
TACOMA WA 181-D4
TACOMA WA 295-H3
Rt#-7 PACIFIC AV S
PIERCE CO WA 181-D5
Rt#-7 RIVERSIDE AV
OROFINO ID 123-C2
Rt#-7 RUSSELL RIDGE RD
CLEARWATER CO ID 123-C2
Rt#-7 WHITNEY HWY
BAKER CITY OR 138-B1
BAKER CO OR 137-C1
BAKER CO OR 138-A1
GRANT CO OR 137-C1
Rt#-7A BARNET HWY
COQUITLAM BC 157-A4
DISTRICT OF BURNABY BC 156-D4
PORT MOODY BC 157-A4
Rt#-7A HASTINGS ST
DISTRICT OF BURNABY BC 156-D4
DISTRICT OF BURNABY BC 255-G10
VANCOUVER BC 255-F10
Rt#-7A HASTINGS ST E
VANCOUVER BC 254-J10
VANCOUVER BC 255-B10
Rt#-7A HIGHWAY
DISTRICT OF BURNABY BC 156-D4
Rt#-7A INLET DR
DISTRICT OF BURNABY BC 156-D4
Rt#-7A SAINT JOHNS ST
CITY OF PORT MOODY BC 156-D4
DISTRICT OF BURNABY BC 156-D4
PORT MOODY BC 157-A4
Rt#-8 19TH AV
FOREST GROVE OR 198-B1
Rt#-8 19TH WY
FOREST GROVE OR 198-C1
Rt#-8 E 3RD ST
MOSCOW ID 249-C5
Rt#-8 W 3RD ST
MOSCOW ID 249-C5
Rt#-8 N ADAIR ST
CORNELIUS OR 198-C1
FOREST GROVE OR 198-C1
Rt#-8 E BASELINE ST
CORNELIUS OR 198-C1
Rt#-8 SE BASELINE ST
HILLSBORO OR 198-D1
Rt#-8 SW BASELINE ST
HILLSBORO OR 198-D1
Rt#-8 W BASELINE ST
CORNELIUS OR 198-C1
Rt#-8 SW CANYON RD
BEAVERTON OR 199-B2
WASHINGTON CO OR 199-B2
Rt#-8 FIRST ST
ELK RIVER ID 123-C1
Rt#-8 GALES CREEK RD
FOREST GROVE OR 198-B1
WASHINGTON CO OR 125-B1
WASHINGTON CO OR 198-B1
Rt#-8 HIGHWAY
BOVILL ID 123-B1
BRITISH COLUMBIA 95-C1
CLEARWATER CO ID 123-B1
ELK RIVER ID 123-C1
ELMA WA 179-B7
GRAYS HARBOR CO WA 179-C6
LATAH CO ID 123-B1
LATAH CO ID 249-D5
MCCLEARY WA 179-C6
MOSCOW ID 249-C5
THURSTON CO WA 179-D6
THURSTON CO WA 180-B6
TROY ID 123-A1

STREET City State Page-Grid

Rt#-8 HIGHWAY
WASHINGTON CO OR 199-B1
Rt#-8 MAIN ST
TROY ID 123-A1
Rt#-8 SE OAK ST
HILLSBORO OR 198-D1
Rt#-8 SW OAK ST
HILLSBORO OR 198-D1
Rt#-8 PACIFIC AV
CORNELIUS OR 198-C1
FOREST GROVE OR 198-C1
Rt#-8 SECOND AV
DEARY ID 123-B1
LATAH CO ID 123-B1
Rt#-8 E ST
FOREST GROVE OR 198-B1
Rt#-8 TAFT ST
ELK RIVER ID 123-C1
Rt#-8 TUALATIN VALLEY HWY
CORNELIUS OR 198-D1
HILLSBORO OR 198-D1
HILLSBORO OR 199-A2
WASHINGTON CO OR 198-D1
WASHINGTON CO OR 199-A2
Rt#-8 SW TUALATIN VALLEY HWY
BEAVERTON OR 199-B2
WASHINGTON CO OR 199-B2
Rt#-9 N BORSETH ST
SEDRO-WOOLLEY WA 161-C5
Rt#-9 CASCADE HWY
SEDRO-WOOLLEY WA 161-C6
Rt#-9 CHEAM AV
DISTRICT OF KENT BC 94-C3
Rt#-9 EVERGREEN DR
DISTRICT OF KENT BC 94-C3
Rt#-9 HAIG HWY
DISTRICT OF KENT BC 94-C3
Rt#-9 HIGHWAY
ARLINGTON WA 168-D5
BRITISH COLUMBIA 94-C3
DISTRICT OF KENT BC 94-C3
LATAH CO ID 123-A1
SEDRO-WOOLLEY WA 161-C6
SKAGIT CO WA 161-C3
SKAGIT CO WA 168-C1
SKAGIT CO WA 260-J11
SNOHOMISH WA 171-D3
SNOHOMISH CO WA 168-C3
SNOHOMISH CO WA 171-D1
Rt#-9 HOPEWELL RD
WHATCOM CO WA 102-B1
Rt#-9 HOT SPRINGS RD
CITY OF HARRISON HT SPNGS BC 94-C3
DISTRICT OF KENT BC 94-C3
Rt#-9 LAWRENCE RD
WHATCOM CO WA 102-B1
Rt#-9 MAIN ST
SKAGIT CO WA 168-C2
Rt#-9 MOORE ST
SEDRO-WOOLLEY WA 161-C5
Rt#-9 NOOKSACK RD
NOOKSACK WA 102-B1
WHATCOM CO WA 102-B1
Rt#-9 TOWNSHIP RD
SEDRO-WOOLLEY WA 161-C5
SKAGIT CO WA 161-C5
Rt#-9 VALLEY HWY
WHATCOM CO WA 102-B1
WHATCOM CO WA 161-C2
Rt#-9 WOODINVLLE SNHOMISH RD
SNOHOMISH CO WA 171-D6
Rt#-10 232ND ST
TOWNSHIP OF LANGLEY BC 157-D7
Rt#-10 56TH AV
DISTRICT OF SURREY BC 157-A7
DISTRICT OF SURREY BC 158-B1
Rt#-10 58TH AV
DISTRICT OF DELTA BC 156-D7
DISTRICT OF SURREY BC 156-D7
DISTRICT OF SURREY BC 157-A7
Rt#-10 SW
BEAVERTN-HLLSDL HWY
BEAVERTON OR 199-B2
PORTLAND OR 199-B2
PORTLAND OR 199-B2
PORTLAND OR 316-A3
WASHINGTON CO OR 199-B2
Rt#-10 SW CAPITOL HWY
PORTLAND OR 316-D4
PORTLAND OR 317-E4
Rt#-10 SW FARMINGTON RD
BEAVERTON OR 199-A2
WASHINGTON CO OR 198-D3
WASHINGTON CO OR 199-A2
Rt#-10 GLOVER RD
LANGLEY BC 157-C7
TOWNSHIP OF LANGLEY BC 157-C7
Rt#-10 HIGHWAY
KITTITAS CO WA 240-C2
KITTITAS CO WA 241-A3
TOWNSHIP OF LANGLEY BC 157-D7
Rt#-10 LADNER TRUNK RD
DISTRICT OF DELTA BC 156-D7
Rt#-10 LANGLEY BYPS
DISTRICT OF SURREY BC 157-C7
DISTRICT OF SURREY BC 158-B1
LANGLEY BC 157-C7
Rt#-10 RAWLISON CRES
TOWNSHIP OF LANGLEY BC 157-C7
Rt#-11 11TH AV
DISTRICT OF MISSION BC 94-B3
Rt#-11 12TH ST
BELLINGHAM WA 258-B11
Rt#-11
ABBOTSFORD-MISSION HWY
DISTRICT OF MATSQUI BC 94-B3
DISTRICT OF MATSQUI BC 102-B1
Rt#-11 CHUCKANUT DR
BELLINGHAM WA 258-B12
SKAGIT CO WA 160-D2
SKAGIT CO WA 161-A3
SKAGIT CO WA 260-B1
WHATCOM CO WA 160-D2
WHATCOM CO WA 258-B14
Rt#-11 HIGHWAY
CLEARWATER CO ID 123-C2
CLEARWATER CO ID 123-C2

Rt#-11 HIGHWAY STREET INDEX Rt#-36 MAPLETON-JCT 411

STREET City State Page-Grid

Rt#-11 HIGHWAY
SKAGIT CO WA 161-A5
SKAGIT CO WA 260-A1
Rt#-11 S MAIN ST
MILTON-FREEWATER OR 121-C3
Rt#-11 OLD FAIRHAVEN PKWY
BELLINGHAM WA 258-B11
Rt#-11 OREGON-WASHINGTON HWY
ADAMS OR 129-B1
ATHENA OR 129-B1
MILTON-FREEWATER OR 121-C3
PENDLETON OR 129-B1
UMATILLA CO OR 121-C3
UMATILLA CO OR 129-B1
WALLA WALLA CO WA 121-C3
Rt#-11 PACIFIC AV
TACOMA WA 295-H1
Rt#-11 VALLEY PKWY
BELLINGHAM WA 258-C11
Rt#-12 HIGHWAY
CLEARWATER CO ID 123-C2
CLEARWATER CO ID 123-C2
Rt#-13 264TH ST
TOWNSHIP OF LANGLEY BC 158-D2
Rt#-13 HARPSTER GRADE RD
IDAHO CO ID 123-C3
IDAHO CO ID 123-C3
Rt#-13 HIGHWAY
TOWNSHIP OF LANGLEY BC 158-D2
Rt#-13 E MAIN ST
GRANGEVILLE ID 123-C3
IDAHO CO ID 123-C3
Rt#-13 W MAIN ST
GRANGEVILLE ID 123-C3
IDAHO CO ID 123-C3
Rt#-14 EVERGREEN HWY
CARSON WA 194-C6
CARSON WA 195-B5
CLARK CO WA 193-D7
CLARK CO WA 200-C1
NORTH BONNEVILLE WA 194-C6
SKAMANIA CO WA 193-D7
SKAMANIA CO WA 194-A7
SKAMANIA CO WA 195-B5
SKAMANIA CO WA 200-D1
STEVENSON WA 194-C6
Rt#-14 HIGHWAY
BENTON CO WA 120-C3
BENTON CO WA 121-A3
BENTON CO WA 128-C1
BRITISH COLUMBIA 100-C2
IDAHO CO ID 123-C3
KLICKITAT CO WA 128-B1
Rt#-14 LEWIS AND CLARK FRWY
VANCOUVER WA 193-A7
Rt#-14 LEWIS AND CLARK HWY
BINGEN WA 195-C5
CAMAS WA 193-A7
CLARK CO WA 193-A7
KLICKITAT CO WA 127-B1
KLICKITAT CO WA 195-C5
KLICKITAT CO WA 196-C6
SKAMANIA CO WA 195-C5
VANCOUVER WA 193-A7
WASHOUGAL WA 193-C7
WHITE SALMON WA 195-C5
Rt#-14 SOOKE RD
BRITISH COLUMBIA 101-A2
BRITISH COLUMBIA 159-A7
DISTRICT OF LANGFORD BC 159-A7
DISTRICT OF METCHOSIN BC 159-A7
Rt#-14 STEUBEN ST
BINGEN WA 195-D5
Rt#-14 WEST COAST RD
BRITISH COLUMBIA 101-A2
BRITISH COLUMBIA 164-C1
Rt#-15 176TH ST
BRITISH COLUMBIA 158-B2
DISTRICT OF SURREY BC 157-B7
DISTRICT OF SURREY BC 158-B2
WHATCOM CO WA 158-B2
Rt#-15 CLOVERDALE BYPS
DISTRICT OF SURREY BC 157-B7
Rt#-15 PACIFIC HWY
DISTRICT OF SURREY BC 158-B1
Rt#-16 EMMETT HWY
ADA CO ID 139-C3
ADA CO ID 147-C1
Rt#-16 FRWY
GIG HARBOR WA 174-B7
GIG HARBOR WA 181-C1
KITSAP CO WA 174-B7
KITSAP CO WA 174-B7
PIERCE CO WA 174-B7
PIERCE CO WA 181-C1
PORT ORCHARD WA 174-B7
TACOMA WA 292-B7
TACOMA WA 294-D1
TACOMA WA 295-E1
Rt#-16 HIGHWAY
ADA CO ID 139-C3
BREMERTON WA 174-B4
GEM CO ID 139-C3
KITSAP CO WA 174-B4
Rt#-16 ROUTE 16 FRWY
PIERCE CO WA 181-C2
TACOMA WA 181-C2
TACOMA WA 292-A6
Rt#-17 60TH ST
DISTRICT OF DELTA BC 156-C7
Rt#-17 BLANSHARD ST
CITY OF VICTORIA BC 256-G6
DISTRICT OF SAANICH BC 256-G5
Rt#-17 DAISY ST N
GRANT CO WA 112-C2
SOAP LAKE WA 112-C2
Rt#-17 DAISY ST S
SOAP LAKE WA 112-C2
Rt#-17 HIGHWAY
ADAMS CO WA 121-A1
BRIDGEPORT WA 112-C1
DOUGLAS CO WA 112-C1
DOUGLAS CO WA 113-A2
FRANKLIN CO WA 121-A1
GRANT CO WA 112-C2
GRANT CO WA 113-A2

Rt#-17 HIGHWAY
GRANT CO WA 121-A1
GRANT CO WA 242-B1
MESA WA 121-A2
MOSES LAKE WA 242-C2
OKANOGAN CO WA 104-C3
OKANOGAN CO WA 112-C1
SOAP LAKE WA 112-C2
Rt#-17 LEAHY RD S
DOUGLAS CO WA 112-C1
Rt#-17 PATRICIA BAY HWY
DIST OF CENTRAL SAANICH BC 159-C2
DIST OF NORTH SAANICH BC 159-C2
DISTRICT OF SAANICH BC 159-C2
DISTRICT OF SAANICH BC 256-F2
TOWN OF SIDNEY BC 159-C2
Rt#-17A HIGHWAY
DISTRICT OF SAANICH BC 159-C5
Rt#-17A MCTAVISH RD
DIST OF NORTH SAANICH BC 159-C3
Rt#-17A WEST SAANICH RD
DIST OF CENTRAL SAANICH BC 159-B3
DIST OF NORTH SAANICH BC 159-B3
DIST OF SAANICH BC 159-C5
Rt#-17 R RD NE
DOUGLAS CO WA 112-C1
Rt#-18 AUBURN-ECHO LAKE CTO
KING CO WA 175-D6
KING CO WA 176-A6
KING CO WA 182-C1
AUBURN WA 182-C1
COVINGTON WA 175-D7
KENT WA 175-D7
KING CO WA 175-D7
KING CO WA 176-A6
KING CO WA 182-C1
MAPLE VALLEY WA 175-D7
KING CO WA 176-A6
Rt#-18 SE DAYTON BYPASS RD
DAYTON OR 198-B7
YAMHILL CO OR 198-B7
Rt#-18 ECHO LAKE CTO SE
KING CO WA 176-B5
Rt#-18 FRWY
AUBURN WA 182-B1
FEDERAL WAY WA 182-B1
KING CO WA 182-B1
Rt#-18 HIGHWAY
BRITISH COLUMBIA 100-C1
Lake Cowichan BC 100-C1
Rt#-18 HIGHWAY 99 S
YAMHILL CO OR 204-B1
Rt#-18 E MAIN ST
SHERIDAN OR 125-B3
WILLAMINA OR 125-A3
Rt#-18 S MAIN ST
WILLAMINA OR 125-A3
Rt#-18 W MAIN ST
SHERIDAN OR 125-B3
Rt#-18 SALMON RIVER HWY
LINCOLN CO OR 203-B4
MCMINNVILLE OR 198-A7
MCMINNVILLE OR 204-A2
POLK CO OR 125-A3
Rose Lodge OR 203-D3
SHERIDAN OR 125-B3
TILLAMOOK CO OR 125-A3
TILLAMOOK CO OR 203-D3
YAMHILL CO OR 125-B3
YAMHILL CO OR 198-A7
YAMHILL CO OR 204-A2
Rt#-18 NE SALMON RIVER HWY
YAMHILL CO OR 198-B7
Rt#-18 SE SALMON RIVER HWY
MCMINNVILLE OR 198-A7
YAMHILL CO OR 198-B7
Rt#-18 THREE MILE LN HWY
MCMINNVILLE OR 198-B7
YAMHILL CO OR 198-B7
Rt#-18 W VALLEY HWY
SHERIDAN OR 125-B3
WILLAMINA OR 125-B3
YAMHILL CO OR 125-B3
Rt#-18 WILLAMINA-SHERIDAN HWY
POLK CO OR 125-A3
WILLAMINA OR 125-A3
Rt#-19 E 7TH ST
FOSSIL OR 128-A3
Rt#-19 AIRPORT CUTOFF RD
Irondale WA 263-B11
JEFFERSON CO WA 263-B11
Rt#-19 BEAVER VALLEY RD
JEFFERSON CO WA 170-A1
Rt#-19 COTTONWOOD ST
ARLINGTON OR 128-A1
Rt#-19 HIGHWAY
BRITISH COLUMBIA 92-A1
CAMPBELL RIVER BC 92-A1
COURTENAY BC 92-A2
PARKSVILLE BC 92-C3
Rt#-19 W IDAHO AV
HOMEDALE ID 147-A1
Rt#-19 ISLAND HWY N
BRITISH COLUMBIA 93-A3
NANAIMO BC 93-A3
Rt#-19 JOHN DAY HWY
ARLINGTON OR 128-A2
CONDON OR 128-A2
FOSSIL OR 128-A3
GILLIAM CO OR 128-A2
GRANT CO OR 136-B1
SPRAY OR 136-B1
WHEELER CO OR 128-A3
WHEELER CO OR 136-B1
Rt#-19 LOCUST ST
ARLINGTON OR 128-A1
Rt#-19 N LOCUST ST
ARLINGTON OR 128-A1
GILLIAM CO OR 128-A1
Rt#-19 S LOCUST ST
ARLINGTON OR 128-A1
Rt#-19 MAIN ST
CANYON CO ID 147-B1
GREENLEAF ID 147-B1

Rt#-19 S MAIN ST
CONDON OR 128-A2
Rt#-19 OWYHEE BLVD
OWYHEE CO ID 147-A1
Rt#-19 RHODY DR
Hadlock-Irondale WA 170-A1
Irondale WA 263-E14
JEFFERSON CO WA 170-A1
JEFFERSON CO WA 263-E14
Rt#-19 SIMPLOT BLVD
CALDWELL ID 147-B1
CANYON CO ID 147-B1
WILDER ID 147-B1
Rt#-19 E WALNUT ST
CONDON OR 128-A2
Rt#-19 N WASHINGTON ST
CONDON OR 128-A2
Rt#-19 S WASHINGTON ST
CONDON OR 128-A2
Rt#-20 12TH ST
ANACORTES WA 259-F2
Rt#-20 E 3RD AV
COLVILLE WA 106-A2
STEVENS CO WA 106-A2
Rt#-20 W 6TH ST
REPUBLIC WA 105-B2
Rt#-20 AVON AV
BURLINGTON WA 260-C4
Rt#-20 AVON CTO
SKAGIT CO WA 161-A6
SKAGIT CO WA 260-A6
Rt#-20 AVON CUT-OFF
SKAGIT CO WA 161-A7
Rt#-20 BURLINGTON BLVD
BURLINGTON WA 260-C5
Rt#-20 S BURLINGTON BLVD
BURLINGTON WA 260-C7
Rt#-20 CASCADE HWY
BURLINGTON WA 260-E4
SEDRO-WOOLLEY WA 161-C6
SEDRO-WOOLLEY WA 260-E4
SKAGIT CO WA 260-E4
Rt#-20 S CLARK AV
REPUBLIC WA 105-B2
Rt#-20 COLVILLE-TIGER RD
STEVENS CO WA 106-A2
Rt#-20 COMMERCIAL AV
ANACORTES WA 259-H4
Rt#-20 N CROSS STATE HWY
SEDRO-WOOLLEY WA 161-C5
SKAGIT CO WA 161-C5
Rt#-20 DIVISION ST
TWISP WA 104-A3
Rt#-20 ELMWAY
OKANOGAN WA 104-C3
OKANOGAN CO WA 104-C3
OMAK WA 104-C3
Rt#-20 FOURTH AV W
OMAK WA 104-C3
Rt#-20 HIGHWAY
ANACORTES WA 259-H5
Ault Field WA 167-C2
BURLINGTON WA 260-C5
CONCRETE WA 102-C2
COUPEVILLE WA 167-B4
CUSICK WA 106-C3
FERRY CO WA 105-B2
FERRY CO WA 106-A2
HAMILTON WA 102-C2
ISLAND CO WA 160-C7
ISLAND CO WA 167-C1
JEFFERSON CO WA 109-C1
JEFFERSON CO WA 170-A1
JEFFERSON CO WA 263-C6
LYMAN WA 102-C2
NEWPORT WA 106-C3
OAK HARBOR WA 167-C2
OKANOGAN WA 104-C3
OKANOGAN CO WA 104-C2
OKANOGAN CO WA 105-A2
PEND OREILLE CO WA 106-B2
PORT TOWNSEND WA 263-C6
REPUBLIC WA 105-B2
SKAGIT CO WA 102-C2
SKAGIT CO WA 160-C6
SKAGIT CO WA 161-D5
SKAGIT CO WA 259-J6
SKAGIT CO WA 260-B6
WINTHROP WA 104-A2
Rt#-20 MAIN ST S
OMAK WA 104-C3
Rt#-20 MEMORIAL HWY
SKAGIT CO WA 160-D6
SKAGIT CO WA 161-A7
Rt#-20 E METHOW VALLEY HWY
OKANOGAN CO WA 104-B3
TWISP WA 104-A3
Rt#-20 NORTH CASCADES HWY
CHELAN CO WA 103-C2
OKANOGAN CO WA 103-C2
SKAGIT CO WA 103-A2
WHATCOM CO WA 103-A2
Rt#-20 OAKES AV
ANACORTES WA 259-B3
Rt#-20 OKOMA DR
OKANOGAN CO WA 104-C3
OMAK WA 104-C3
Rt#-20 PIONEER WY
OAK HARBOR WA 167-B3
Rt#-20 RIO VISTA AV
BURLINGTON WA 260-C5
Rt#-20 RIVERSIDE AV
OKANOGAN CO WA 104-A2
WINTHROP WA 104-A2
Rt#-20 RIVERSIDE DR
OKANOGAN CO WA 104-C2
OMAK WA 104-C2
Rt#-20 SANTIAM HWY
Crowfoot OR 133-C1
LEBANON OR 133-C1
LINN CO OR 133-C1
Rt#-20 SECOND AV N
OKANOGAN WA 104-C3
Rt#-20 SECOND AV NW
OKANOGAN WA 104-C3
Rt#-20 SECOND AV SW
OKANOGAN WA 104-C3

Rt#-20 SIMS WY
PORT TOWNSEND WA 263-C6
Rt#-20 SIXTH ST
OKANOGAN CO WA 104-C2
TONASKET WA 104-C2
Rt#-20 WANAMAKER RD
ISLAND CO WA 167-C5
Rt#-20 WATER ST
PORT TOWNSEND WA 263-H5
Rt#-21 W 1ST AV
ODESSA WA 113-B3
Rt#-21 N 1ST ST
ODESSA WA 113-B3
Rt#-21 E 6TH AV
ODESSA WA 113-B3
Rt#-21 S ALDER ST
ODESSA WA 113-B3
Rt#-21 N DIVISION ST
ODESSA WA 113-B3
Rt#-21 W FIRST ST
LIND WA 121-B1
Rt#-21 W FRONT AV
LINCOLN CO WA 113-B1
WILBUR WA 113-B1
Rt#-21 E GOWEN RD
ADA CO ID 253-D4
BOISE ID 253-D4
Rt#-21 HIGHWAY
ADAMS CO WA 113-B3
ADAMS CO WA 121-B1
BOUNDARY CO ID 107-B1
BRITISH COLUMBIA 105-C1
BRITISH COLUMBIA 107-B1
FERRY CO WA 105-C1
FERRY CO WA 113-B1
GRAND FORKS BC 105-C1
LINCOLN CO WA 113-B1
LIND WA 121-B1
ODESSA WA 113-B3
REPUBLIC WA 105-B2
Rt#-21 LIND-KAHLOTUS RD
ADAMS CO WA 121-C1
FRANKLIN CO WA 121-C1
KAHLOTUS WA 121-C1
Rt#-21 W MAY AV
ODESSA WA 113-B3
Rt#-21 MONSOR RD
LINCOLN CO WA 113-B2
Rt#-21 ROSENOFF RD
ADAMS CO WA 113-B3
Rt#-21 E SECOND ST
LIND WA 121-B1
Rt#-21 VIOLET AV
KAHLOTUS WA 121-C1
Rt#-21 S WEST ST
WILBUR WA 113-B1
Rt#-22 12TH ST SE
SALEM OR 322-J14
Rt#-22A HIGHWAY
BRITISH COLUMBIA 106-B1
Rt#-22 BUENA RD
YAKIMA CO WA 120-A2
Rt#-22 BUENA WY
TOPPENISH WA 120-A2
Rt#-22 CENTER ST NE
SALEM OR 322-H12
Rt#-22 CENTER ST BRDG
SALEM OR 322-H12
Rt#-22 CENTER ST BRDG NE
SALEM OR 322-H12
Rt#-22 S ELM ST
TOPPENISH WA 120-A2
Rt#-22 EVERGREEN HWY
TOPPENISH WA 120-A2
YAKIMA CO WA 120-A2
Rt#-22 FERRY ST SE
SALEM OR 322-H13
Rt#-22 FRONT ST NE
SALEM OR 322-H12
Rt#-22 FRONT ST SE
SALEM OR 322-H13
Rt#-22 HIGHWAY
BENTON CO WA 120-B3
BRITISH COLUMBIA 106-A1
MABTON WA 120-B3
PROSSER WA 120-C3
TOPPENISH WA 120-A2
YAKIMA CO WA 120-A2
Rt#-22 MARION ST
SALEM OR 322-H12
Rt#-22 MARION ST BRDG
SALEM OR 322-H12
Rt#-22 MISSION ST SE
SALEM OR 322-J14
SALEM OR 323-A14
SALEM OR 325-B1
Rt#-22 PRINGLE PKWY SE
SALEM OR 322-J13
Rt#-22 SALEM HWY
SALEM OR 322-J14
Rt#-22 N SANTIAM HWY
AUMSVILLE OR 205-A7
DETROIT OR 134-A1
GATES OR 134-A1
IDANHA OR 134-A1
LINN CO OR 134-C1
MARION CO OR 133-C1
MARION CO OR 134-A1
MARION CO OR 205-A7
MARION CO OR 325-G3
MILL CITY OR 134-A1
SALEM OR 204-D6
SALEM OR 325-G3
STAYTON OR 133-C1
SUBLIMITY OR 133-C1
Rt#-22 THREE RIVERS HWY
POLK CO OR 125-A3
TILLAMOOK CO OR 197-B6
TILLAMOOK CO OR 197-B6
TILLAMOOK CO OR 203-D1
YAMHILL CO OR 125-A3
YAMHILL CO OR 203-D1
Rt#-22 TRADE ST SE
SALEM OR 322-H13
Rt#-22 WAPENISH RD
YAKIMA CO WA 120-A2
Rt#-22 WILLAMINA-SALEM HWY
POLK CO OR 125-B3
POLK CO OR 204-A5

Rt#-22 WILLAMINA-SALEM HWY
POLK CO OR 322-G12
SALEM OR 322-G12
Rt#-22 WILLAMINA-SALEM HWY NW
POLK CO OR 204-B6
POLK CO OR 322-B14
SALEM OR 322-B14
Rt#-23 S 3RD ST
HARRINGTON WA 113-C2
Rt#-23 ENDICOTT-ST JOHN RD
SAINT JOHN WA 114-B3
WHITMAN CO WA 114-B3
Rt#-23 FRONT ST
SAINT JOHN WA 114-B3
Rt#-23 HIGHWAY
HARRINGTON WA 113-C2
LINCOLN CO WA 113-C2
LINCOLN CO WA 114-A2
SAINT JOHN WA 114-B3
SPRAGUE WA 114-A3
WHITMAN CO WA 114-A3
Rt#-23 E MAIN ST
HARRINGTON WA 113-C2
Rt#-23 E SHERLOCK ST
HARRINGTON WA 113-C2
Rt#-24 S BROADWAY AV
ADAMS CO WA 121-A1
OTHELLO WA 121-A1
Rt#-24 HANFORD RD
YAKIMA CO WA 120-A2
Rt#-24 HIGHWAY
ADAMS CO WA 120-C1
ADAMS CO WA 121-A1
BENTON CO WA 120-C1
GRANT CO WA 120-C1
MOXEE WA 243-D7
YAKIMA WA 243-C7
YAKIMA CO WA 120-A2
YAKIMA CO WA 243-C7
Rt#-25 CENTER AV
NORTHPORT WA 106-A1
STEVENS CO WA 106-A1
Rt#-25 HIGHWAY
DAVENPORT WA 114-A2
LINCOLN CO WA 113-C1
LINCOLN CO WA 114-A1
MARCUS WA 106-A2
NORTHPORT WA 106-A1
STEVENS CO WA 105-C2
STEVENS CO WA 106-A1
STEVENS CO WA 113-C1
Rt#-25 LITTLE SHEEP CREEK RD
STEVENS CO WA 106-A1
Rt#-26 FRWY
GRANT CO WA 120-B1
Rt#-26 HIGHWAY
ADAMS CO WA 120-C1
ADAMS CO WA 121-A1
ADAMS CO WA 122-A1
COLFAX WA 122-C1
GRANT CO WA 120-B1
OTHELLO WA 121-A1
ROYAL CITY WA 120-C1
WASHTUCNA WA 121-C1
WHITMAN CO WA 122-C1
Rt#-26 NORTH ST
WASHTUCNA WA 121-C1
Rt#-26 ROAD 13-SW
GRANT CO WA 120-B1
Rt#-26 T W WALTERS RD
COLFAX WA 122-C1
Rt#-26 WASHINGTON ST
ADAMS CO WA 121-A1
OTHELLO WA 121-A1
Rt#-27 1ST ST
OAKESDALE WA 114-C3
Rt#-27 4TH ST
GARFIELD WA 114-C3
Rt#-27 ALMOTA ST
PALOUSE WA 249-B1
Rt#-27 BLAKE RD
SPOKANE CO WA 350-H10
SPOKANE CO WA 351-A12
Rt#-27 N BRIDGE ST
PALOUSE WA 249-B1
Rt#-27 S BRIDGE ST
PALOUSE WA 249-C1
Rt#-27 COUNTY RD
WHITMAN CO WA 114-C3
Rt#-27 CROOKED RIVER HWY
CROOK CO OR 135-C3
CROOK CO OR 213-C6
DESCHUTES CO OR 135-C3
PRINEVILLE OR 213-C6
Rt#-27 CROSBY ST
TEKOA WA 114-C3
Rt#-27 S DISHMAN-MICA RD
SPOKANE CO WA 247-A5
Rt#-27 N DIVISION ST
PALOUSE WA 249-B1
Rt#-27 ELIZABETH ST
TEKOA WA 114-C3
Rt#-27 FIRST ST
FAIRFIELD WA 114-C2
Rt#-27 N GRAND AV
PULLMAN WA 249-B5
Rt#-27 S GRAND AV
PULLMAN WA 249-B5
Rt#-27 HIGHWAY
FAIRFIELD WA 114-C2
GARFIELD WA 114-C3
LATAH WA 114-C3
OAKESDALE WA 114-C3
PALOUSE WA 249-B1
PULLMAN WA 249-B4
SPOKANE CO WA 114-C2
SPOKANE CO WA 247-A5
SPOKANE CO WA 351-A14
TEKOA WA 114-C3
WHITMAN CO WA 114-C3
WHITMAN CO WA 249-B1
Rt#-27 E MAIN ST
GARFIELD WA 114-C3
Rt#-27 W MAIN ST
GARFIELD WA 114-C3

Rt#-27 MARKET ST
LATAH WA 114-C3
Rt#-27 MOSCOW RD
PALOUSE WA 249-B1
Rt#-27 W PARK ST
TEKOA WA 114-C3
Rt#-27 N PINES RD
SPOKANE CO WA 350-H5
Rt#-27 S PINES RD
SPOKANE CO WA 350-H10
Rt#-27 POPULAR ST
TEKOA WA 114-C3
Rt#-27 RAILROAD ST
ROCKFORD WA 114-C2
SPOKANE CO WA 114-C2
Rt#-27 S RAMSEY ST
TEKOA WA 114-C3
Rt#-27 STEPTOE AV
OAKESDALE WA 114-C3
Rt#-27 TEKOA OAKSDALE RD
OAKESDALE WA 114-C3
WHITMAN CO WA 114-C3
Rt#-27 WATER ST
TEKOA WA 114-C3
WHITMAN CO WA 114-C3
Rt#-28 E 1ST AV
ODESSA WA 113-B3
Rt#-28 W 1ST AV
ODESSA WA 113-B3
Rt#-28 BASIN ST N
EPHRATA WA 112-C3
GRANT CO WA 112-C3
Rt#-28 BASIN ST NW
EPHRATA WA 112-C3
GRANT CO WA 112-C3
Rt#-28 BASIN ST S
EPHRATA WA 112-C3
GRANT CO WA 112-C3
Rt#-28 F ST SE
GRANT CO WA 112-B3
QUINCY WA 112-B3
Rt#-28 F ST SW
GRANT CO WA 112-B3
QUINCY WA 112-B3
Rt#-28 HIGHWAY
DAVENPORT WA 114-A2
DOUGLAS CO WA 112-B3
DOUGLAS CO WA 239-A5
EAST WENATCHEE WA 239-A4
East Wenatchee Bench WA 239-A3
GRANT CO WA 112-C2
GRANT CO WA 113-A2
HARRINGTON WA 113-C2
LINCOLN CO WA 113-C2
LINCOLN CO WA 114-A2
ODESSA WA 113-B3
ROCK ISLAND WA 239-B5
SOAP LAKE WA 112-C2
Rt#-28 ROAD 10-NW
GRANT CO WA 112-B3
Rt#-28 ROAD 11-NW
GRANT CO WA 112-C3
Rt#-28 TWELFTH ST
DAVENPORT WA 114-A2
Rt#-30 NE 16TH ST
FRUITLAND ID 139-A3
PAYETTE CO ID 139-A3
Rt#-30 2ND ST
NORTH POWDER OR 130-B3
Rt#-30 LA GRANDE-BAKER HWY
NORTH POWDER OR 130-B3
UNION CO OR 130-B3
Rt#-31 FREMONT HWY
DESCHUTES CO OR 143-A1
KLAMATH CO OR 143-A1
LAKE CO OR 143-B2
LAKE CO OR 151-C1
LAKE CO OR 152-A1
PAISLEY OR 151-C1
Rt#-31 HIGHWAY
IONE WA 106-B1
METALINE WA 106-B1
METALINE FALLS WA 106-B1
PEND OREILLE CO WA 106-C1
Rt#-31 MAIN ST
PAISLEY OR 151-C1
Rt#-31 S SECOND AV
IONE WA 106-B1
Rt#-33 HIGHWAY
BRITISH COLUMBIA 105-A1
Rt#-34 2ND ST
LEBANON OR 133-C1
Rt#-34 ALSEA HWY
BENTON CO OR 133-A1
LINCOLN CO OR 133-A2
LINCOLN CO OR 209-D2
LINCOLN CO OR 328-F6
WALDPORT OR 328-F6
Rt#-34 CORVALLIS-LEBANON HWY
LEBANON OR 133-C1
LINN CO OR 133-C1
LINN CO OR 207-B6
TANGENT OR 207-B6
Rt#-34 CORVALLIS-NEWPORT HWY
CORVALLIS OR 327-H11
LINN CO OR 207-B6
LINN CO OR 327-H11
Rt#-34 HARRISON BLVD
CORVALLIS OR 327-G9
LINN CO OR 327-G9
Rt#-34 W HEMLOCK ST
WALDPORT OR 328-E4
Rt#-34 MORTON ST
LEBANON OR 133-C1
Rt#-34 TANGENT ST
LEBANON OR 133-C1
Rt#-34 VAN BUREN AV
CORVALLIS OR 327-F9
LINN CO OR 327-F9
Rt#-35 MOUNT HOOD HWY
CLACKAMAS CO OR 202-C5
HOOD RIVER CO OR 195-C7
HOOD RIVER CO OR 202-C1
Rt#-36 MAPLETON-JCT CITY HWY
LANE CO OR 132-C3
LANE CO OR 133-B2

PNW

INDEX

COPYRIGHT 1999 Thomas Bros. Maps®

PNW · INDEX · Thomas Bros. Maps® · COPYRIGHT 1999

Rt#-99 MAIN ST
STREET INDEX
Rt#-160 HIGHWAY 413

STREET
City State Page-Grid

Rt#-99 MAIN ST
DOUGLAS CO OR 225-C3
PHOENIX OR 234-B2
Rt#-99 N MAIN ST
ASHLAND OR 337-C6
CANYONVILLE OR 225-C3
JACKSON CO OR 337-C6
PHOENIX OR 234-B2
Rt#-99 S MAIN ST
CANYONVILLE OR 225-C3
Rt#-99 W MAIN ST
CANYONVILLE OR 225-C3
Rt#-99 E MARGINAL WY S
SEATTLE WA 281-J5
Rt#-99 MARINE DR
DIST OF WEST VANCOUVER BC 254-E4
Rt#-99 MCVAY HWY
LANE CO OR 330-G11
Rt#-99 OAKLAND-SHADY HWY
DOUGLAS CO OR 219-A7
DOUGLAS CO OR 221-C3
DOUGLAS CO OR 334-F2
OAKLAND OR 219-A7
ROSEBURG OR 334-F2
SUTHERLIN OR 221-C3
Rt#-99 OAK ST
CITY OF RICHMOND BC 156-B5
VANCOUVER BC 156-B5
Rt#-99 OLD PACIFIC HWY
DOUGLAS CO OR 225-C2
MYRTLE CREEK OR 225-C2
Tri-City OR 225-C2
Rt#-99 OLD STAGE RD
JACKSON CO OR 230-B6
Rt#-99 PACIFIC HWY
FEDERAL WAY WA 182-A2
Rt#-99 PACIFIC HWY E
FEDERAL WAY WA 182-A2
FIFE WA 182-A2
MILTON WA 182-A2
PIERCE CO WA 182-A2
Rt#-99 PACIFIC HWY S
DES MOINES WA 175-B7
DES MOINES WA 290-C6
FEDERAL WAY WA 175-B7
FEDERAL WAY WA 182-B1
KENT WA 175-B7
KENT WA 290-C6
KING WA 286-D6
KING CO WA 175-B7
SEATAC WA 288-D1
TUKWILA WA 286-D6
TUKWILA WA 288-D1
Rt#-99 PACIFIC HWY W
EUGENE OR 215-A1
EUGENE OR 329-D2
JUNCTION CITY OR 210-A7
LANE CO OR 210-A7
LANE CO OR 215-A1
Rt#-99 SE PINE ST
ROSEBURG OR 334-F8
Rt#-99 N RIVERSIDE AV
MEDFORD OR 336-C10
Rt#-99 S RIVERSIDE AV
MEDFORD OR 336-D13
Rt#-99 ROGUE RIVER HWY
GRANTS PASS OR 335-F11
JACKSON CO OR 229-C6
JACKSON CO OR 230-A6
JOSEPHINE CO OR 229-C6
JOSEPHINE CO OR 335-J11
ROGUE RIVER OR 229-C6
Rt#-99 ROGUE VALLEY HWY
ASHLAND OR 337-A4
CENTRAL POINT OR 230-C7
JACKSON CO OR 230-C7
JACKSON CO OR 234-B2
JACKSON CO OR 336-A7
JACKSON CO OR 337-A4
MEDFORD OR 230-C7
MEDFORD OR 234-B2
MEDFORD OR 336-A7
PHOENIX OR 234-B2
TALENT OR 234-B2
Rt#-99 SAMS VALLEY HWY
GOLD HILL OR 230-A6
JACKSON CO OR 230-A6
Rt#-99 SEYMOUR ST
VANCOUVER BC 254-F11
Rt#-99 SISKIYOU BLVD
ASHLAND OR 337-D8
JACKSON CO OR 337-H10
Rt#-99 STANTON PARK RD
DOUGLAS CO OR 225-C3
Rt#-99 NE STATE ST
DOUGLAS CO OR 221-C1
SUTHERLIN OR 221-C1
Rt#-99 NE STEPHENS ST
ROSEBURG OR 334-F5
Rt#-99 SE STEPHENS ST
ROSEBURG OR 334-G7
Rt#-99 TAYLOR WY
DIST OF WEST VANCOUVER BC 254-E4
Rt#-99 UMPQUA HWY
DOUGLAS CO OR 219-A2
DRAIN OR 219-A2
Rt#-99A 10TH AV
DISTRICT OF BURNABY BC 156-D5
NEW WESTMINSTER BC 156-D5
Rt#-99A HIGHWAY
DISTRICT OF SURREY BC 156-D5
NEW WESTMINSTER BC 156-D5
Rt#-99A KING GEORGE HWY
DISTRICT OF SURREY BC 156-D5
DISTRICT OF SURREY BC 157-A7
DISTRICT OF SURREY BC 158-A1
Rt#-99A KINGSWAY
DISTRICT OF BURNABY BC 156-C5
NEW WESTMINSTER BC 156-C5
Rt#-99A MCBRIDE BLVD
NEW WESTMINSTER BC 156-D5
Rt#-99A PATTULLO BRDG
DISTRICT OF SURREY BC 156-D5
Rt#-99E SE 1ST AV
CANBY OR 199-C6
Rt#-99E SW 1ST AV
CANBY OR 199-C6
Rt#-99E COMMERCIAL ST NE
SALEM OR 322-J10
Rt#-99E FRONT ST NE
SALEM OR 322-H12
Rt#-99E NE GRAND AV
PORTLAND OR 313-G4
Rt#-99E SE GRAND AV
PORTLAND OR 313-G7
PORTLAND OR 317-G2
Rt#-99E HIGHWAY
MILWAUKIE OR 321-J2
SALEM OR 322-H12
Rt#-99E S HIGHWAY 99E
MARION CO OR 199-B7
MARION CO OR 205-C1
Rt#-99E HIGHWAY 99E NE
AURORA OR 199-B7
Rt#-99E LIBERTY ST NE
SALEM OR 322-J10
Rt#-99 E
ELKTON-SUTHERLIN HWY
SUTHERLIN OR 221-C1
Rt#-99E N MARINE DR
PORTLAND OR 309-F1
Rt#-99E NE MARTIN
LUTHER KING
PORTLAND OR 309-G3
PORTLAND OR 313-G4
Rt#-99E SE MARTIN
LUTHER KING
PORTLAND OR 313-G7
PORTLAND OR 317-G1
Rt#-99E SE MCLOUGHLIN
BLVD
CLACKAMAS OR 321-J2
CLACKAMAS CO OR 199-D3
GLADSTONE OR 199-D3
MILWAUKIE OR 317-J6
MILWAUKIE OR 321-J2
OREGON CITY OR 199-D3
PORTLAND OR 317-J6
Rt#-99E MCLOUGHLIN BLVD
E
CLACKAMAS CO OR 199-D5
OREGON CITY OR 199-D5
Rt#-99E PACIFIC HWY
MARION CO OR 205-B2
WOODBURN OR 205-B1
Rt#-99E PACIFIC HWY E
BARLOW OR 199-C6
CANBY OR 199-C6
CLACKAMAS CO OR 199-D4
GERVAIS OR 205-B1
GLADSTONE OR 199-D4
Hayesville OR 204-D5
Hayesville OR 323-E5
HUBBARD OR 205-B1
MARION CO OR 199-C6
MARION CO OR 205-A3
MARION CO OR 323-E5
OREGON CITY OR 199-D4
SALEM OR 323-E5
WOODBURN OR 205-B1
Rt#-99E PACIFIC HWY S
MARION CO OR 205-C1
Rt#-99E SALEM EXWY
KEIZER OR 323-C6
SALEM OR 323-C6
Rt#-99E SALEM PKWY
KEIZER OR 323-A8
MARION CO OR 323-A8
SALEM OR 322-J8
SALEM OR 323-A8
Rt#-99W 1ST ST
NEWBERG OR 198-D5
Rt#-99W 3RD ST
LAFAYETTE OR 198-B6
YAMHILL CO OR 198-B6
Rt#-99W 3RD ST W
CORVALLIS OR 207-A7
CORVALLIS OR 327-G14
Rt#-99W 4TH ST W
CORVALLIS OR 327-H9
Rt#-99W 5TH AV
MONROE OR 133-B2
Rt#-99W NW ADAMS ST
MCMINNVILLE OR 198-A7
Rt#-99W SW ADAMS ST
MCMINNVILLE OR 198-A7
Rt#-99W NE BAKER ST
MCMINNVILLE OR 198-A7
Rt#-99W SE BAKER ST
MCMINNVILLE OR 198-A7
Rt#-99W SW BARBUR BLVD
PORTLAND OR 199-B3
TIGARD OR 199-B3
Rt#-99W E HANCOCK ST
NEWBERG OR 198-D5
Rt#-99W W HANCOCK ST
NEWBERG OR 198-D5
Rt#-99W HERBERT HOOVER
HWY
NEWBERG OR 198-D5
YAMHILL CO OR 198-D5
Rt#-99W HIGHWAY
AMITY OR 204-B2
YAMHILL CO OR 204-B1
Rt#-99W HIGHWAY 99 S
MCMINNVILLE OR 198-A7
MCMINNVILLE OR 204-B1
YAMHILL CO OR 198-A7
YAMHILL CO OR 204-B1
Rt#-99W HIGHWAY 99 W
DUNDEE OR 198-C6
MCMINNVILLE OR 198-B7
YAMHILL CO OR 198-C6
Rt#-99W NE HIGHWAY 99 W
MCMINNVILLE OR 198-B7
YAMHILL CO OR 198-B7
Rt#-99W SW HIGHWAY 99 W
MCMINNVILLE OR 198-A7
YAMHILL CO OR 198-A7
YAMHILL CO OR 204-B1
Rt#-99W N PACIFIC AV
MONMOUTH OR 204-B7
POLK CO OR 204-B7
Rt#-99W S PACIFIC AV
MONMOUTH OR 204-B7
Rt#-99W PACIFIC HWY
YAMHILL CO OR 204-B1
Rt#-99W PACIFIC HWY W
ADAIR VILLAGE OR 207-B3
Rt#-99W PACIFIC HWY W
BENTON CO OR 133-B2
BENTON CO OR 207-A7
BENTON CO OR 327-H7
CORVALLIS OR 207-A7
CORVALLIS OR 327-H7
JUNCTION CITY OR 210-A5
KING CITY OR 199-B3
LANE CO OR 133-B2
LANE CO OR 210-A5
MONMOUTH OR 204-B5
MONROE OR 133-B2
NEWBERG OR 198-C6
POLK CO OR 204-B5
POLK CO OR 207-B3
SHERWOOD OR 199-A4
TIGARD OR 199-B3
TUALATIN OR 199-B3
WASHINGTON CO OR 199-B3
YAMHILL CO OR 198-C6
YAMHILL CO OR 204-B5
Rt#-99W PORTLAND RD
NEWBERG OR 198-D5
YAMHILL CO OR 198-D5
YAMHILL CO OR 199-A5
Rt#-99W N RIVER ST
NEWBERG OR 198-D5
Rt#-99W TRADE ST
AMITY OR 204-B2
Rt#-99W S TRADE ST
AMITY OR 204-B2
Rt#-101 HIGHWAY
BRITISH COLUMBIA 92-B1
BRITISH COLUMBIA 93-A1
Gibson BC 93-B3
PACIFIC CO WA 186-C4
POWELL RIVER BC 92-C1
Sechelt BC 93-A2
Rt#-102 DAYTON-AIRPORT
RD
MASON CO WA 179-D2
MASON CO WA 180-A2
Rt#-103 BAY AV
Ocean Park WA 186-A2
Rt#-103 OCEAN BEACH HWY
LONG BEACH WA 186-A5
PACIFIC CO WA 186-A5
Rt#-103 PACIFIC HWY
Ocean Park WA 186-A2
PACIFIC CO WA 186-A3
Rt#-103 PACIFIC HWY S
LONG BEACH WA 186-A5
Rt#-103 PACIFIC HWY W
LONG BEACH WA 186-A5
Rt#-104 NE 205TH ST
EDMONDS WA 171-B6
MOUNTLAKE TERRACE WA 171-B6
SHORELINE WA 171-B6
Rt#-104 244TH ST SW
MOUNTLAKE TERRACE WA 171-B6
SHORELINE WA 171-B6
Rt#-104 BALLINGER WY NE
LAKE FOREST PARK WA 171-B6
SHORELINE WA 171-B6
Rt#-104 EDMONDS WY
EDMONDS WA 171-A6
SNOHOMISH CO WA 171-A6
WOODWAY WA 171-A6
Rt#-104 HIGHWAY
JEFFERSON CO WA 109-C1
JEFFERSON CO WA 170-A3
Kingston WA 170-D5
KITSAP CO WA 170-C4
Rt#-104 LAKE BALLINGER
WY
EDMONDS WA 171-B6
MOUNTLAKE TERRACE WA 171-B6
SHORELINE WA 171-B6
Rt#-105 N BOONE ST
ABERDEEN WA 178-B7
Rt#-105 S BOONE ST
ABERDEEN WA 117-A1
ABERDEEN WA 178-B7
GRAYS HARBOR CO WA 117-A1
Rt#-105 DOCK ST
WESTPORT WA 298-G11
Rt#-105 S FORREST AV
WESTPORT WA 298-G14
Rt#-105 HIGHWAY
ABERDEEN WA 117-A1
GRAYS HARBOR CO WA 117-A1
GRAYS HARBOR CO WA 183-D1
PACIFIC CO WA 117-A1
PACIFIC CO WA 183-B3
RAYMOND WA 117-A1
WESTPORT WA 183-B2
WESTPORT WA 298-G11
Rt#-105 MONTESANO ST
WESTPORT WA 298-H11
Rt#-105 OCEAN AV
WESTPORT WA 298-F13
Rt#-105 PARK AV
RAYMOND WA 117-A1
Rt#-105 WESTPORT RD
GRAYS HARBOR CO WA 117-A1
Rt#-106 HIGHWAY
MASON CO WA 173-D5
MASON CO WA 180-A1
Rt#-107 S BANK RD
GRAYS HARBOR CO WA 117-A1
Rt#-107 HIGHWAY
GRAYS HARBOR CO WA 178-D7
MONTESANO WA 178-D7
Rt#-107 SOUTH BANK RD
GRAYS HARBOR CO WA 178-D7
Rt#-108 3RD ST
MCCLEARY WA 179-D6
Rt#-108 HIGHWAY
GRAYS HARBOR CO WA 179-D5
MASON CO WA 179-D5
MASON CO WA 180-A4
Rt#-108 SINE RD
GRAYS HARBOR CO WA 179-D6
MCCLEARY WA 179-D6
Rt#-108 SUMMIT RD
GRAYS HARBOR CO WA 179-D6
MCCLEARY WA 179-D6
Rt#-109 5TH AV
Taholah WA 172-B6
Rt#-109 EMERSON AV
HOQUIAM WA 178-A7
Rt#-109 FIR LP
Taholah WA 172-B6
Rt#-109 HIGHWAY
GRAYS HARBOR CO WA 172-B7
GRAYS HARBOR CO WA 177-B1
GRAYS HARBOR CO WA 178-A7
HOQUIAM WA 178-A7
Taholah WA 172-B7
Rt#-110 LA PUSH RD
CLALLAM CO WA 169-C1
FORKS WA 169-C1
Rt#-110 MORA RD
CLALLAM CO WA 169-B2
Rt#-112 3RD ST
Neah Bay WA 100-B2
Rt#-112 HIGHWAY
CLALLAM CO WA 100-B2
CLALLAM CO WA 162-C1
CLALLAM CO WA 163-A2
CLALLAM CO WA 164-A4
CLALLAM CO WA 165-A6
Neah Bay WA 100-B2
Rt#-112 NEAH BAY RD
CLALLAM CO WA 100-B2
Neah Bay WA 100-B2
Rt#-112 PIEDMONT RD
CLALLAM CO WA 164-C5
CLALLAM CO WA 165-A6
Rt#-113 BURNT MOUNTAIN
RD
CLALLAM CO WA 163-B6
Rt#-115 DAMON RD
GRAYS HARBOR CO WA 177-B6
OCEAN SHORES WA 177-B6
Rt#-115 N JETTY RD
GRAYS HARBOR CO WA 177-B6
Rt#-116 FLAGLER RD
Hadlock-Irondale WA 170-B1
JEFFERSON CO WA 167-B7
JEFFERSON CO WA 170-B1
Rt#-116 NESS CORNER RD
Hadlock-Irondale WA 170-A1
Rt#-116 NESS RD
Hadlock-Irondale WA 170-A1
JEFFERSON CO WA 170-A1
Rt#-116 OAK BAY RD
Hadlock-Irondale WA 170-A1
JEFFERSON CO WA 170-A1
Rt#-117 E 1ST ST
PORT ANGELES WA 261-F4
Rt#-117 W 1ST ST
PORT ANGELES WA 261-E4
Rt#-117 MARINE DR
PORT ANGELES WA 261-E3
Rt#-117 TUNWATER ACCESS
RD
CLALLAM CO WA 261-C5
PORT ANGELES WA 261-C5
Rt#-119 HIGHWAY
MASON CO WA 109-B2
MASON CO WA 173-A6
Rt#-119 LAKE CUSHMAN RD
MASON CO WA 109-B2
MASON CO WA 173-A6
Rt#-121 93RD AV SW
THURSTON CO WA 184-C1
Rt#-121 MAYTOWN RD SW
THURSTON CO WA 184-C2
Rt#-121 TILLEY RD SW
THURSTON CO WA 184-C2
Rt#-122 HARMONY RD
LEWIS CO WA 118-A2
MOSSYROCK WA 118-A2
Rt#-122 SILVERCREEK RD
LEWIS CO WA 118-A2
Rt#-123 HIGHWAY
LEWIS CO WA 185-D5
PIERCE CO WA 119-A1
PIERCE CO WA 185-D4
Rt#-124 W 2ND ST
WAITSBURG WA 122-A2
WALLA WALLA CO WA 122-A2
Rt#-124 HIGHWAY
PRESCOTT WA 121-C2
WALLA WALLA CO WA 121-C2
WALLA WALLA CO WA 122-A2
Rt#-124 ICE HARBOR DR
WALLA WALLA CO WA 121-B3
Rt#-124 LOWER WAITSBURG
RD
WALLA WALLA CO WA 122-A2
Rt#-124 MAIN ST
WAITSBURG WA 122-A2
Rt#-124 SECOND ST
PRESCOTT WA 121-C2
WALLA WALLA CO WA 121-C2
Rt#-125 13TH AV N
WALLA WALLA WA 344-J5
Rt#-125 8TH AV N
WALLA WALLA WA 344-J8
Rt#-125 9TH AV S
WALLA WALLA WA 344-J8
WALLA WALLA WA 345-A9
Rt#-125 HIGHWAY
COLLEGE PLACE WA 344-G12
WALLA WALLA WA 344-J5
WALLA WALLA WA 345-A10
WALLA WALLA CO WA 121-C2
WALLA WALLA CO WA 344-G1
Rt#-125 W PINE ST
WALLA WALLA WA 344-J7
Rt#-126 W 11TH AV
EUGENE OR 215-A2
EUGENE OR 329-B6
LANE CO OR 215-A2
Rt#-126 W 3RD ST
CROOK CO OR 213-D5
PRINEVILLE OR 213-D5
Rt#-126 BELKNAP SPRINGS
HWY
LANE CO OR 134-B2
LINN CO OR 134-B2
Rt#-126
EUGENE-SPRINGFLD HWY
EUGENE OR 330-E5
LANE CO OR 331-G6
SPRINGFIELD OR 330-E5
SPRINGFIELD OR 331-C5
Rt#-126 SE EVERGREEN AV
REDMOND OR 212-D5
Rt#-126 FLORENCE-EUGENE
HWY
FLORENCE OR 214-C2
LANE CO OR 132-C3
LANE CO OR 133-A3
LANE CO OR 214-C2
LANE CO OR 215-A2
VENETA OR 133-B3
Rt#-126 S GARFIELD ST
EUGENE OR 329-G6
Rt#-126 SW HIGHLAND AV
DESCHUTES CO OR 212-D5
REDMOND OR 212-D5
Rt#-126 HIGHWAY
COLUMBIA CO WA 122-B2
Rt#-126 MAIN ST
LANE CO OR 330-H7
SPRINGFIELD OR 215-D2
SPRINGFIELD OR 330-H7
SPRINGFIELD OR 331-A7
Rt#-126 MCKENZIE HWY
DESCHUTES CO OR 211-D5
DESCHUTES CO OR 212-A5
LANE CO OR 133-C3
LANE CO OR 134-B2
LANE CO OR 215-D2
LINN CO OR 134-B2
SPRINGFIELD OR 215-D2
Rt#-126 OCHOCO HWY
CROOK CO OR 213-A5
DESCHUTES CO OR 212-D5
DESCHUTES CO OR 213-A5
PRINEVILLE OR 213-B6
REDMOND OR 212-D5
REDMOND OR 213-A5
Rt#-126 E OLIPHANT RD
COLUMBIA CO WA 122-B2
GARFIELD CO WA 122-B2
Rt#-126 OWSLEY GRADE RD
GARFIELD CO WA 122-B2
Rt#-127 HIGHWAY
GARFIELD CO WA 122-B1
WHITMAN CO WA 122-B1
Rt#-128 15TH ST
ASOTIN CO WA 250-B4
CLARKSTON WA 250-B4
Rt#-128 S 15TH ST
POMEROY WA 122-B2
Rt#-128 6TH AV
ASOTIN CO WA 250-B5
Vineland WA 250-B5
Rt#-128 APPLESIDE BLVD
ASOTIN CO WA 250-B5
Vineland WA 250-B5
Rt#-128 DOWN RIVER RD
LEWISTON ID 250-B4
Rt#-128 HIGHWAY
ASOTIN CO WA 122-C2
ASOTIN CO WA 250-A5
GARFIELD CO WA 122-B2
LEWISTON ID 250-B4
POMEROY WA 122-B2
Rt#-128 OLD SPIRAL HWY
LEWISTON ID 250-B4
Rt#-128 PATAHA CREEK RD
GARFIELD CO WA 122-B2
Rt#-128 SCENIC WY
ASOTIN CO WA 250-B4
Vineland WA 250-B4
Rt#-129 1ST ST
ASOTIN WA 250-B5
Rt#-129 5TH ST
ASOTIN CO WA 250-B4
CLARKSTON WA 250-B4
Rt#-129 6TH ST
CLARKSTON WA 250-B4
Rt#-129 DIAGONAL ST
CLARKSTON WA 250-B4
Rt#-129 HIGHWAY
ASOTIN WA 250-B5
ASOTIN CO WA 122-C3
ASOTIN CO WA 123-A3
ASOTIN CO WA 250-B5
CLARKSTON WA 250-B4
Vineland WA 250-B5
Rt#-129 RIVERSIDE DR
ASOTIN CO WA 250-B5
Vineland WA 250-B5
Rt#-129 WASHINGTON ST
ASOTIN WA 250-B5
Rt#-131 CISPUS RD
LEWIS CO WA 118-C2
Rt#-131 WOODS CREEK RD
LEWIS CO WA 118-C2
Rt#-138 NE DIAMOND LAKE
BLVD
ROSEBURG OR 221-C4
ROSEBURG OR 334-H7
Rt#-138 E DIAMOND LAKE
HWY
DOUGLAS CO OR 223-D7
KLAMATH CO OR 142-B2
KLAMATH CO OR 223-D7
Rt#-138
ELKTON-SUTHERLIN HWY
DOUGLAS CO OR 141-A1
DOUGLAS CO OR 221-C1
ELKTON OR 141-A1
SUTHERLIN OR 221-C1
Rt#-138 W
ELKTON-SUTHERLN HWY
DOUGLAS CO OR 221-C1
SUTHERLIN OR 221-C1
Rt#-138 SW HARVARD BLVD
ROSEBURG OR 334-F7
Rt#-138 W HARVARD BLVD
ROSEBURG OR 334-E7
Rt#-138 NORTH UMPQUA HWY
DOUGLAS CO OR 141-C2
DOUGLAS CO OR 221-D4
DOUGLAS CO OR 222-B3
DOUGLAS CO OR 223-A4
ROSEBURG OR 221-D4
Rt#-138 SE OAK AV
ROSEBURG OR 334-F7
Rt#-138 SW OAK AV
ROSEBURG OR 334-F7
Rt#-138 SE PINE ST
ROSEBURG OR 334-G7
Rt#-138 SE STEPHENS ST
ROSEBURG OR 334-F8
Rt#-138 SW WASHINGTON AV
ROSEBURG OR 334-F7
Rt#-139 HIGHWAY
MODOC CO CA 151-A3
SISKIYOU CO CA 151-A3
Rt#-140 4TH ST N
LAKE CO OR 152-A2
LAKEVIEW OR 152-A2
Rt#-140 GREEN SPRINGS
HWY
KLAMATH CO OR 338-B12
Rt#-140 S KLAMATH FALLS
HWY
Altamont OR 235-D5
KLAMATH CO OR 235-C5
KLAMATH CO OR 338-D12
KLAMATH FALLS OR 235-C5
KLAMATH FALLS OR 338-C12
Rt#-140 KLAMATH
FALS-LKVW HWY
Altamont OR 339-C11
KLAMATH CO OR 150-C2
KLAMATH CO OR 151-A1
KLAMATH CO OR 339-E12
LAKE CO OR 151-C2
LAKE CO OR 152-A2
Rt#-140 KLAMATH
FALS-MALN HWY
Altamont OR 339-D14
KLAMATH CO OR 235-D5
KLAMATH CO OR 339-D14
Rt#-140 LAKE OF THE
WOODS HWY
JACKSON CO OR 149-C1
JACKSON CO OR 150-A1
JACKSON CO OR 230-D6
KLAMATH CO OR 150-B1
KLAMATH CO OR 231-A6
KLAMATH CO OR 235-A1
KLAMATH CO OR 338-A10
KLAMATH FALLS OR 235-A1
KLAMATH FALLS OR 338-B12
White City OR 230-D6
Rt#-140 NEVADA STATE
ROUTE
HARNEY CO OR 153-A3
HUMBOLDT CO NV 153-C3
Rt#-140 WARNER HWY
HARNEY CO OR 153-A3
LAKE CO OR 152-A2
LAKE CO OR 153-A3
Rt#-141 HIGHWAY
BINGEN WA 195-D5
KLICKITAT CO WA 119-A3
KLICKITAT CO WA 195-D1
WHITE SALMON WA 195-D4
Rt#-141 E JEWETT BLVD
WHITE SALMON WA 195-D4
Rt#-141 W JEWETT BLVD
KLICKITAT CO WA 195-D4
WHITE SALMON WA 195-D4
Rt#-141 OAK ST
BINGEN WA 195-D5
Rt#-141 SW PUCKER
HUDDLE RD
KLICKITAT CO WA 195-D4
Rt#-142 E BROADWAY
GOLDENDALE WA 127-C1
KLICKITAT CO WA 127-C1
Rt#-142 W BROADWAY
GOLDENDALE WA 127-C1
KLICKITAT CO WA 127-C1
Rt#-142 HIGHWAY
KLICKITAT CO WA 127-B1
KLICKITAT CO WA 196-D2
Rt#-150 CHELAN FALLS RD
CHELAN CO WA 236-D3
Rt#-150 COLUMBIA ST
CHELAN WA 236-D3
Rt#-150 HIGHWAY
CHELAN WA 236-C3
CHELAN CO WA 236-C3
Rt#-150 NORTHSHORE RD
CHELAN CO WA 236-C2
Rt#-150 PARK RD
CHELAN WA 236-C3
Rt#-150 WAPATO WY
CHELAN CO WA 236-B2
Rt#-150 WOODIN AV
CHELAN WA 236-D3
Rt#-153 HIGHWAY
OKANOGAN CO WA 104-B3
OKANOGAN CO WA 112-B1
Rt#-155 COLUMBIA AV
COULEE DAM WA 237-C2
Rt#-155 COULEE BLVD
ELECTRIC CITY WA 237-C3
GRANT CO WA 237-C3
Rt#-155 GRAND COULEE AV
ELECTRIC CITY WA 237-C3
GRAND COULEE WA 237-C3
GRANT CO WA 237-C3
Rt#-155 GRAND COULEE HWY
GRAND COULEE WA 237-C3
Rt#-155 HIGHWAY
COULEE DAM WA 237-C2
COULEE DAM WA 237-C2
GRAND COULEE WA 237-C3
GRANT CO WA 113-A1
GRANT CO WA 237-C2
NESPELEM WA 105-A3
OKANOGAN CO WA 104-C3
OKANOGAN CO WA 105-A3
OMAK WA 104-C3
Rt#-155 OMAK AV E
OKANOGAN CO WA 104-C3
OMAK WA 104-C3
Rt#-155 RIVER DR
COULEE DAM WA 237-C2
OKANOGAN CO WA 237-C2
Rt#-155 RIVER RD
ELMER CITY WA 237-C1
OKANOGAN CO WA 237-C1
Rt#-160 HIGHWAY
KITSAP CO WA 174-D4

PNW
INDEX

414 Rt#-160 SE SEDGWICK RD — STREET INDEX — Rt#-224 KENNEDY RD

STREET
City State Page-Grid

Rt#-160 SE SEDGWICK RD
KITSAP CO WA 174-C4
PORT ORCHARD WA 174-B4
Rt#-161 16TH AV S
FEDERAL WAY WA 182-B1
Rt#-161 31ST AV SW
PUYALLUP WA 182-B4
Rt#-161 EATONVILLE CUT-OFF RD
EATONVILLE WA 118-B1
PIERCE CO WA 118-B1
Rt#-161 EATONVILLE-LA GRANDE
EATONVILLE WA 118-B1
PIERCE CO WA 118-B1
Rt#-161 ENCHANTED PKWY
FEDERAL WAY WA 182-B1
Rt#-161 ENCHANTED PKWY S
EDGEWOOD WA 182-B2
FEDERAL WAY WA 182-B2
KING CO WA 182-B2
MILTON WA 182-B2
Rt#-161 HIGHWAY
SISKIYOU CO CA 150-C3
Rt#-161 LARSON ST
EATONVILLE WA 118-B1
Rt#-161 MASHELL AV S
EATONVILLE WA 118-B1
Rt#-161 N MERIDIAN
PUYALLUP WA 182-B3
Rt#-161 S MERIDIAN
PUYALLUP WA 182-B4
Rt#-161 MERIDIAN E
EDGEWOOD WA 182-B3
MILTON WA 182-B3
PIERCE CO WA 118-B1
PIERCE CO WA 182-B6
PUYALLUP WA 182-B3
Rt#-161 MERIDIAN AV E
EATONVILLE WA 118-B1
PIERCE CO WA 118-B1
PIERCE CO WA 182-B7
Rt#-161 STATE LINE RD
SISKIYOU CO CA 150-C3
SISKIYOU CO CA 151-A3
Rt#-161 WASHINGTON AV N
EATONVILLE WA 118-B1
PIERCE CO WA 118-B1
Rt#-161 WASHINGTON AV S
EATONVILLE WA 118-B1
Rt#-162 5TH ST
KAMIAH ID 123-C2
KAMIAH ID 123-C2
Rt#-162 8TH AV
NEZPERCE ID 123-C2
NEZPERCE ID 123-C2
Rt#-162 BRIDGE ST SW
ORTING WA 182-C5
Rt#-162 HARMAN WY S
ORTING WA 182-C5
PIERCE CO WA 182-C5
Rt#-162 HIGHWAY 162ND E
SOUTH PRAIRIE WA 182-D4
Rt#-162 HIGHWAY 162ND W
SOUTH PRAIRIE WA 182-D5
Rt#-162 HILL ST
KAMIAH ID 123-C2
Rt#-162 LAWYERS CANYON RD
LEWIS CO ID 123-C3
NEZPERCE ID 123-C3
Rt#-162 OAK ST
NEZPERCE ID 123-C2
Rt#-162 PIONEER WY
ORTING WA 182-B5
PIERCE CO WA 182-B5
SOUTH PRAIRIE WA 182-B5
SUMNER WA 182-B5
Rt#-162 S PIONEER WY
PIERCE CO WA 182-C6
Rt#-162 W PIONEER WY
PIERCE CO WA 182-D5
Rt#-162 SEVEN MILE RD
KAMIAH ID 123-C2
LEWIS CO ID 123-C2
Rt#-162 VALLEY AV
PIERCE CO WA 182-B3
SUMNER WA 182-B3
Rt#-162 WASHINGTON AV N
ORTING WA 182-C5
Rt#-162 WASHINGTON AV S
ORTING WA 182-C5
Rt#-163 PEARL ST
RUSTON WA 181-C2
TACOMA WA 181-C2
Rt#-164 SE 436TH ST
KING CO WA 110-C3
KING CO WA 182-D3
Rt#-164 SE 436TH WY
ENUMCLAW WA 110-C3
KING CO WA 110-C3
Rt#-164 AUBURN ENUMCLAW RD
AUBURN WA 182-C2
KING CO WA 182-C2
Rt#-164 AUBURN WY N
AUBURN WA 182-C1
Rt#-164 AUBURN WY S
AUBURN WA 182-C1
Rt#-164 GRIFFIN AV
ENUMCLAW WA 110-C3
KING CO WA 110-C3
Rt#-165 BURNETT-FAIRFAX
BUCKLEY WA 182-D5
CARBONADO WA 182-D5
PIERCE CO WA 182-D5
WILKESON WA 182-D5
Rt#-165 CHURCH ST
WILKESON WA 182-D5
Rt#-165 HIGHWAY
PIERCE CO WA 118-C1
PIERCE CO WA 185-A2
Rt#-165 MOUNTAIN MEADOWS RD
PIERCE CO WA 185-A2
Rt#-165 MOWICH SECTION
CARBONADO WA 182-D6
PIERCE CO WA 110-C3
PIERCE CO WA 118-C1
PIERCE CO WA 182-D6

STREET
City State Page-Grid

Rt#-166 BAY ST
PORT ORCHARD WA 174-B4
PORT ORCHARD WA 270-H14
Rt#-166 BETHEL RD
PORT ORCHARD WA 174-B4
PORT ORCHARD WA 270-J14
Rt#-166 HIGHWAY
KITSAP CO WA 174-B4
PORT ORCHARD WA 174-B4
PORT ORCHARD WA 270-F14
Rt#-166 MILE HILL DR SE
East Port Orchard WA 174-C4
KITSAP CO WA 174-C4
PORT ORCHARD WA 174-B4
Rt#-167 BAY ST
TACOMA WA 182-A2
Rt#-167 FRWY
PACIFIC WA 182-B3
PIERCE CO WA 182-B3
PUYALLUP WA 182-B3
SUMNER WA 182-B3
Rt#-167 RAINIER AV S
RENTON WA 175-C5
Rt#-167 RIVER RD
PIERCE CO WA 182-A3
PUYALLUP WA 182-A3
TACOMA WA 182-A3
Rt#-167 VALLEY FRWY
ALGONA WA 182-B2
AUBURN WA 175-B7
AUBURN WA 182-B2
KENT WA 175-B7
KENT WA 291-J7
KING CO WA 175-B7
PACIFIC WA 182-B2
PACIFIC WA 182-B2
RENTON WA 175-B7
Rt#-169 264TH AV SE
KING CO WA 110-C3
Rt#-169 3RD AV
BLACK DIAMOND WA 110-C3
Rt#-169 ENUMCLAW BLK DMND RD
BLACK DIAMOND WA 110-C3
KING CO WA 110-C3
Rt#-169 MAPLE VLY-BLK DMND RD
BLACK DIAMOND WA 110-C3
KING CO WA 110-C3
MAPLE VALLEY WA 110-C3
MAPLE VALLEY WA 175-D7
MAPLE VALLEY WA 176-A7
Rt#-169 MAPLE VALLEY RD
RENTON WA 175-C5
Rt#-169 PORTER ST
ENUMCLAW WA 110-C3
KING CO WA 110-C3
Rt#-169 RENTON MAPLE VLY RD
KING CO WA 175-D5
KING CO WA 176-A6
MAPLE VALLEY WA 175-D5
RENTON WA 175-D5
Rt#-169 WASHINGTON AV
ENUMCLAW WA 110-C3
Rt#-170 E 1ST ST
GRANT CO WA 121-A1
WARDEN WA 121-A1
Rt#-170 W 1ST ST
WARDEN WA 121-A1
Rt#-170 ROAD 8-SE
GRANT CO WA 121-A1
WARDEN WA 121-A1
Rt#-171 BROADWAY AV
GRANT CO WA 242-C3
MOSES LAKE WA 242-C3
Rt#-172 14 RD NE
DOUGLAS CO WA 112-C1
Rt#-172 14 RD NW
DOUGLAS CO WA 112-B1
Rt#-172 C RD NW
DOUGLAS CO WA 112-B1
Rt#-172 FIFTH AV
DOUGLAS CO WA 112-C1
MANSFIELD WA 112-C1
Rt#-173 10TH ST
BRIDGEPORT WA 112-C1
Rt#-173 17TH ST
BRIDGEPORT WA 112-C1
Rt#-173 BRIDGE ST N
BREWSTER WA 104-B3
Rt#-173 BRIDGE ST S
BREWSTER WA 104-B3
Rt#-173 COLUMBIA AV
BRIDGEPORT WA 112-C1
Rt#-173 FOSTER CREEK AV
BRIDGEPORT WA 112-C1
Rt#-173 HIGHWAY
BREWSTER WA 104-B3
BRIDGEPORT WA 112-C1
DOUGLAS CO WA 104-B3
DOUGLAS CO WA 112-C1
OKANOGAN CO WA 104-B3
Rt#-173 MAPLE ST
BRIDGEPORT WA 112-C1
DOUGLAS CO WA 112-C1
Rt#-174 BRIDGEPORT HWY
GRAND COULEE WA 237-C3
Rt#-174 CROWN POINT RD
DOUGLAS CO WA 237-C2
Rt#-174 GRAND COULEE AV E
GRAND COULEE WA 237-C3
GRANT CO WA 237-C3
Rt#-174 GRAND COULEE AV W
GRAND COULEE WA 237-C3
Rt#-174 HIGHWAY
DOUGLAS CO WA 112-C1
DOUGLAS CO WA 113-A1
DOUGLAS CO WA 237-C2
GRAND COULEE WA 237-C3
GRANT CO WA 237-C2
LINCOLN CO WA 113-B1
LINCOLN CO WA 237-C3
Rt#-181 68TH AV S
KENT WA 175-B7
KENT WA 291-H5
Rt#-181 WASHINGTON AV
KENT WA 175-B7

STREET
City State Page-Grid

Rt#-181 WEST VALLEY HWY
KENT WA 175-B7
KENT WA 291-H3
TUKWILA WA 289-J5
TUKWILA WA 291-H3
Rt#-193 WAWAWAI RIVER RD
WHITMAN CO WA 122-C2
WHITMAN CO WA 250-A4
Rt#-194 ALMOTA RD
WHITMAN CO WA 122-B1
Rt#-194 GOOSE CREEK RD
WHITMAN CO WA 122-C1
Rt#-194 WAWAWAI-PULLMAN RD
WHITMAN CO WA 249-A5
Rt#-194 WILBUR GULCH RD
WHITMAN CO WA 122-C1
WHITMAN CO WA 249-A5
Rt#-200 HIGHWAY
BONNER CO ID 107-C3
BONNER CO ID 244-B1
CLARK FORK ID 107-C3
EAST HOPE ID 244-D2
HOPE ID 244-C2
KOOTENAI ID 244-A1
PONDERAY ID 244-A1
SANDERS CO MT 107-C3
Rt#-200 LIGHTNING CREEK RD
CLARK FORK ID 107-C3
Rt#-200 RAILROAD AV
KOOTENAI ID 244-A1
Rt#-201 SW 4TH AV
ONTARIO OR 139-A3
Rt#-201 ADRIAN BLVD
NYSSA OR 139-A3
Rt#-201 ADRIAN BLVD W
NYSSA OR 139-A3
Rt#-201 OLDS FRRY-ONTARIO HWY
MALHEUR CO OR 139-A2
ONTARIO OR 139-A2
Rt#-201 SUCCOR CREEK HWY
ADRIAN OR 147-A1
MALHEUR CO OR 139-A3
MALHEUR CO OR 147-A1
NYSSA OR 139-A3
Rt#-202 131ST AV NE
BOTHELL WA 171-C6
WOODINVILLE WA 171-C6
Rt#-202 NE 145TH ST
KING CO WA 171-D7
WOODINVILLE WA 171-C7
Rt#-202 156TH AV NE
KING CO WA 171-D7
REDMOND WA 171-D7
WOODINVILLE WA 171-D7
Rt#-202 164TH AV NE
REDMOND WA 175-D1
Rt#-202 NE 77TH ST
REDMOND WA 175-D1
Rt#-202 CLEVELAND ST
REDMOND WA 175-D1
Rt#-202 FALL CTY-SNQUALMIE RD
KING CO WA 176-B3
SNOQUALMIE WA 176-B3
Rt#-202 SE FRONT ST
ASTORIA OR 300-D7
CLATSOP CO OR 300-D7
Rt#-202 W MARINE DR
ASTORIA OR 300-A6
Rt#-202 NEHALEM HWY
CLATSOP CO OR 117-B3
CLATSOP CO OR 188-D3
CLATSOP CO OR 300-F8
COLUMBIA CO OR 117-B3
Rt#-202 NORTH BEND BLVD N
NORTH BEND WA 176-C4
Rt#-202 NORTH BEND BLVD S
NORTH BEND WA 176-C5
Rt#-202 OLNEY AV
ASTORIA OR 300-C7
Rt#-202 RAILROAD AV SE
KING CO WA 176-C4
NORTH BEND WA 176-C4
SNOQUALMIE WA 176-C4
Rt#-202 SE REDMOND FALL CITY
KING CO WA 176-B3
Rt#-202 REDMOND FALL CITY RD
KING CO WA 175-D1
KING CO WA 176-A1
REDMOND WA 175-D1
SAMMAMISH WA 175-D1
KING CO WA 176-A2
KING CO WA 176-A2
Rt#-202 NE REDMOND WY
REDMOND WA 175-D1
Rt#-202 WOODINVLLE REDMOND RD
KING CO WA 171-D7
REDMOND WA 171-D7
REDMOND WA 175-D1
WOODINVILLE WA 171-D7
Rt#-202 WOODNVLLE SNHOMISH RD
WOODINVILLE WA 171-C6
Rt#-203 E BEAKMAN ST
UNION OR 130-B2
Rt#-203 CARNATION-DUVALL RD
DUVALL WA 110-C1
KING CO WA 110-C1
KING CO WA 176-A1
Rt#-203 DUVALL-MONROE RD
KING CO WA 110-C1
SNOHOMISH CO WA 110-C1
Rt#-203 DUVALL-MONROE RD NE
DUVALL WA 110-C1
KING CO WA 110-C1
Rt#-203 FALL CITY-CRNTN RD
CARNATION WA 176-B2
KING CO WA 176-B2
KING CO WA 176-B3

STREET
City State Page-Grid

Rt#-203 LA GRANDE-BAKER HWY
UNION OR 130-A2
UNION CO OR 130-A2
Rt#-203 N LEWIS ST
MONROE WA 110-C1
Rt#-203 S LEWIS ST
MONROE WA 110-C1
SNOHOMISH CO WA 110-C1
Rt#-203 MAIN ST
DUVALL WA 110-C1
KING CO WA 110-C1
Rt#-203 N MAIN ST
UNION OR 130-B2
Rt#-203 MEDICAL SPRINGS HWY
BAKER CO OR 130-B3
UNION OR 130-B2
UNION CO OR 130-B2
Rt#-203 E MEDICAL SPRINGS HWY
UNION OR 130-B2
Rt#-203 TOLT AV
CARNATION WA 176-B2
KING CO WA 176-B2
Rt#-204 DIVISION ST
ELGIN OR 130-A1
UNION CO OR 130-A1
Rt#-204 HIGHWAY
SNOHOMISH CO WA 171-D1
Rt#-204 WESTON-ELGIN HWY
UMATILLA CO OR 129-C1
UMATILLA CO OR 130-A1
UNION CO OR 130-A1
Rt#-205 CATLOW VALLEY RD
HARNEY CO OR 153-B1
Rt#-205 FRENCHGLEN HWY
HARNEY CO OR 145-B1
Rt#-206 ARMSWORTHY ST
WASCO OR 127-C1
Rt#-206 BAYARD ST
CONDON OR 128-A2
Rt#-206 E BAYARD ST
CONDON OR 128-A2
Rt#-206 CELILO-WASCO HWY
SHERMAN CO OR 127-C1
Rt#-206 HIGHWAY
SPOKANE CO WA 114-C1
Rt#-206 MAIN ST
HEPPNER OR 128-C2
Rt#-206 E MOUNT SPOKANE PK DR
SPOKANE CO WA 114-C1
SPOKANE CO WA 246-D1
SPOKANE CO WA 247-A1
SPOKANE CO WA 347-H5
Rt#-206 N MOUNT SPOKANE PK DR
SPOKANE CO WA 114-C1
Rt#-206 W WALNUT ST
CONDON OR 128-A2
GILLIAM CO OR 128-A2
Rt#-206 WASCO-HEPPNER HWY
GILLIAM CO OR 128-A2
Rt#-206 WASCO-HEPPNER HWY
CONDON OR 128-A2
GILLIAM CO OR 128-A2
HEPPNER OR 128-B2
MORROW CO OR 128-B2
SHERMAN CO OR 127-C2
SHERMAN CO OR 128-A2
WASCO OR 127-C2
Rt#-207 SW 11TH ST
HERMISTON OR 129-A1
UMATILLA CO OR 129-A1
Rt#-207 BUTTER CREEK RD
HERMISTON OR 129-A1
UMATILLA CO OR 129-A1
Rt#-207 HEPPNER-SPRAY HWY
MORROW CO OR 128-C3
WHEELER CO OR 128-C3
WHEELER CO OR 136-C1
Rt#-207 W HERMISTON AV
HERMISTON OR 129-A1
Rt#-207 HERMISTON HWY
HERMISTON OR 129-A1
UMATILLA CO OR 129-A1
Rt#-207 HIGHWAY
CHELAN CO WA 111-C1
Rt#-207 LEXINGTON-ECHO HWY
LEXINGTON OR 128-C2
MORROW CO OR 128-C2
UMATILLA CO OR 128-C2
UMATILLA CO OR 129-A1
Rt#-207 SW LEXINGTON-ECHO HWY
UMATILLA CO OR 128-C1
UMATILLA CO OR 129-A1
Rt#-207 SERVCE CRK-MTCHLL HWY
Mitchell OR 136-A1
WHEELER CO OR 136-A1
Rt#-207 E ST
LEXINGTON OR 128-C2
Rt#-210 SW SCHOLLS FERRY RD
BEAVERTON OR 199-B2
TIGARD OR 199-B2
WASHINGTON CO OR 198-D3
WASHINGTON CO OR 199-B2
Rt#-211 CLACKAMAS HWY
CLACKAMAS CO OR 200-B4
ESTACADA OR 200-C6
Rt#-211 EAGLE CREEK-SANDY HWY
CLACKAMAS CO OR 200-C4
SANDY OR 200-C4
Rt#-211 HIGHWAY
PEND OREILLE CO WA 106-C3
Rt#-211 E MAIN ST
MOLALLA OR 126-A3
Rt#-211 W MAIN ST
CLACKAMAS CO OR 126-A3
MOLALLA OR 126-A3
Rt#-211 MEINIG AV
SANDY OR 200-D4

STREET
City State Page-Grid

Rt#-211 S WOODBRN-ESTACADA HW
CLACKAMAS CO OR 126-A3
Rt#-211 WOODBURN-ESTACADA HWY
CLACKAMAS CO OR 126-A3
CLACKAMAS CO OR 200-C6
CLACKAMAS CO OR 205-D2
ESTACADA OR 200-C6
MARION CO OR 205-B1
MOLALLA OR 126-A3
WOODBURN OR 205-B1
Rt#-212 SE CARVER HWY
CLACKAMAS CO OR 200-A3
Rt#-212 CLACKAMAS-BORING RD
CLACKAMAS CO OR 200-B3
Rt#-212 CLACKAMAS HWY
CLACKAMAS CO OR 199-D3
CLACKAMAS CO OR 200-A4
Rt#-212 MAIN ST
OREGON CITY OR 199-D4
Rt#-213 NE 82ND AV
PORTLAND OR 311-G6
PORTLAND OR 315-F2
Rt#-213 SE 82ND AV
CLACKAMAS OR 319-F6
CLACKAMAS CO OR 199-D3
MULTNOMAH OR 319-F6
PORTLAND OR 315-F7
PORTLAND OR 319-F3
Rt#-213 CASCADE HWY
CLACKAMAS CO OR 126-A3
CLACKAMAS CO OR 205-C4
MARION CO OR 205-C4
Rt#-213 SE CASCADE HWY
CLACKAMAS CO OR 199-D3
Rt#-213 CASCADE HWY S
CLACKAMAS CO OR 126-A3
CLACKAMAS CO OR 199-D4
CLACKAMAS CO OR 205-D3
MARION CO OR 205-D3
MOLALLA OR 126-A3
OREGON CITY OR 199-D4
Rt#-213 LANCASTER DR
Hayesville OR 323-E11
SALEM OR 204-D5
SALEM OR 323-E11
Rt#-213 W MAIN ST
SILVERTON OR 205-C4
Rt#-213 MARKET ST NE
SALEM OR 323-D11
Rt#-213 MCCLAINE ST
MARION CO OR 205-C4
SILVERTON OR 205-C4
Rt#-213 OAK ST
MARION CO OR 205-C4
SILVERTON OR 205-C4
Rt#-213 NE SILVERTON HWY
MARION CO OR 205-B4
Rt#-213 SILVERTON RD NE
Hayesville OR 323-E9
MARION CO OR 205-A5
MARION CO OR 323-E9
Rt#-214 1ST ST
SILVERTON OR 205-C4
Rt#-214 N 1ST ST
SILVERTON OR 205-C4
Rt#-214 ANDERSON RD SE
MARION CO OR 205-B7
Rt#-214 C ST
SILVERTON OR 205-C4
Rt#-214 HILLSBORO-SILVRTN HWY
MARION CO OR 205-B2
MOUNT ANGEL OR 205-C3
SILVERTON OR 205-C3
WOODBURN OR 205-B2
Rt#-214 LEWIS ST
SILVERTON OR 205-C4
Rt#-214 MAIN ST
MOUNT ANGEL OR 205-C3
Rt#-214 N MAIN ST
MOUNT ANGEL OR 205-C3
Rt#-214 MOUNT HOOD AV
MARION CO OR 205-B1
WOODBURN OR 205-B1
Rt#-214 NEWBERG HWY
WOODBURN OR 205-B1
Rt#-214 SILVER FALLS HWY
MARION CO OR 205-A7
Rt#-214 SILVER FALLS HWY NE
MARION CO OR 205-C5
SILVERTON OR 205-C5
Rt#-214 SILVER FALLS HWY NW
MARION CO OR 205-B7
Rt#-214 SILVER FALLS HWY SE
MARION CO OR 205-D6
Rt#-214 SILVERTON AV
MARION CO OR 205-B2
WOODBURN OR 205-B2
Rt#-214 SILVERTON HWY
WOODBURN OR 205-B2
Rt#-214 N WATER ST
SILVERTON OR 205-C4
Rt#-214 S WATER ST
SILVERTON OR 205-C4
Rt#-216 CHURCH ST
GRASS VALLEY OR 127-C2
Rt#-216 SHEARERS BRIDGE HWY
WASCO CO OR 127-B2
Rt#-216 SHERARS BRIDGE HWY
GRASS VALLEY OR 127-B2
SHERMAN CO OR 127-B2
Rt#-216 WAPINITIA HWY
WASCO CO OR 127-A3
Rt#-217 BEAVERTON-TIGARD FRWY
BEAVERTON OR 199-B3
LAKE OSWEGO OR 199-B3
TIGARD OR 199-B3
WASHINGTON CO OR 199-B3
Rt#-218 D ST
SHANIKO OR 127-C3

STREET
City State Page-Grid

Rt#-218 FOSSIL ST
ANTELOPE OR 127-C3
Rt#-218 SHANIKO-FOSSIL HWY
ANTELOPE OR 127-C3
FOSSIL OR 128-A3
SHANIKO OR 127-C3
WASCO CO OR 127-C3
WASCO CO OR 128-A3
WHEELER CO OR 128-A3
Rt#-218 WASHINGTON ST
FOSSIL OR 128-A3
Rt#-219 E 1ST ST
NEWBERG OR 198-D5
YAMHILL CO OR 198-D5
Rt#-219 W 1ST ST
NEWBERG OR 198-D5
Rt#-219 BARR-ALEX RD
WASHINGTON CO OR 198-D3
Rt#-219 BUTTEVILLE RD NE
MARION CO OR 205-B1
Rt#-219 CHURCH AV
MARION CO OR 198-D7
SAINT PAUL OR 198-D7
Rt#-219 COLLEGE ST
NEWBERG OR 198-D5
YAMHILL CO OR 198-D5
Rt#-219 N COLLEGE ST
NEWBERG OR 198-D5
Rt#-219 FRENCH PRAIRIE RD
MARION CO OR 198-D7
MARION CO OR 205-A1
Rt#-219 HILLSBORO HWY
NEWBERG OR 198-D5
WASHINGTON CO OR 198-D5
YAMHILL CO OR 198-D5
Rt#-219 SW HILLSBORO HWY
HILLSBORO OR 198-D2
WASHINGTON CO OR 198-D2
Rt#-219 HILLSBORO-SILVRTN HWY
MARION CO OR 205-A1
MARION CO OR 205-B1
Rt#-219 MAIN ST
SAINT PAUL OR 198-D7
Rt#-219 NEWBERG HWY
MARION CO OR 205-B1
WASHINGTON CO OR 198-D2
WOODBURN OR 205-B1
Rt#-219 SAINT PAUL HWY
MARION CO OR 198-D7
NEWBERG OR 198-D7
SAINT PAUL OR 198-D7
YAMHILL CO OR 198-D7
Rt#-220 FORT RD
White Swan WA 119-C2
YAKIMA CO WA 119-C2
YAKIMA CO WA 120-A2
Rt#-220 SIGNAL PEAK RD
White Swan WA 119-C2
Rt#-220 W WHITE SWAN RD
White Swan WA 119-C2
Rt#-221 3RD ST
DAYTON OR 198-C7
YAMHILL CO OR 198-C7
Rt#-221 EDGEWATER ST NW
SALEM OR 322-F12
Rt#-221 HIGHWAY
BENTON CO WA 120-C3
DAYTON OR 198-C7
PROSSER WA 120-C3
YAMHILL CO OR 198-C7
Rt#-221 SE SALEM-DAYTON HWY
POLK CO OR 204-D2
POLK CO OR 322-E6
YAMHILL CO OR 204-D2
Rt#-221 SALEM-DAYTON HWY NW
SALEM OR 322-E13
Rt#-221 WALLACE RD
DAYTON OR 198-C7
YAMHILL CO OR 198-C7
YAMHILL CO OR 204-D1
Rt#-221 SE WALLACE RD
YAMHILL CO OR 204-D1
Rt#-221 WALLACE RD NW
POLK CO OR 322-E8
SALEM OR 322-E8
Rt#-223 ALFALFA-GRANGER RD
YAKIMA CO WA 120-A2
Rt#-223 DALLAS-RICKREALL HWY
DALLAS OR 204-A6
POLK CO OR 204-A6
Rt#-223 E ELLENDALE AV
DALLAS OR 204-A6
Rt#-223 SW FAIRVIEW AV
DALLAS OR 204-A6
Rt#-223 HIGHWAY
GRANGER WA 120-A2
YAKIMA CO WA 120-A2
Rt#-223 SE JEFFERSON ST
DALLAS OR 204-A6
Rt#-223 KINGS VALLEY HWY
BENTON CO OR 133-A1
DALLAS OR 204-A5
POLK CO OR 125-B3
POLK CO OR 133-B1
POLK CO OR 204-A5
Rt#-223 S MAIN ST
DALLAS OR 204-A6
Rt#-223 VAN BELLE RD
GRANGER WA 120-A2
YAKIMA CO WA 120-A2
Rt#-223 SE WASHINGTON ST
DALLAS OR 204-A6
Rt#-223 SW WASHINGTON ST
DALLAS OR 204-A6
Rt#-224 CLACKAMAS HWY
CLACKAMAS CO OR 126-B3
CLACKAMAS CO OR 200-B4
ESTACADA OR 200-C7
Rt#-224 HIGHWAY
BENTON CO WA 120-C2
WEST RICHLAND WA 120-C2
Rt#-224 KENNEDY RD
BENTON CO WA 120-C3

PNW
INDEX

STREET
City State Page-Grid

Rt#-224 MILWAUKIE EXWY
CLACKAMAS CO OR 199-D3
MILWAUKIE OR 199-D3
MILWAUKIE OR 321-J2
Rt#-224 VAN GIESEN ST
RICHLAND WA 340-B12
WEST RICHLAND WA 120-C2
Rt#-224 W VAN GIESEN ST
BENTON CO WA 340-A12
RICHLAND WA 340-A12
WEST RICHLAND WA 121-A2
WEST RICHLAND WA 340-A12
Rt#-224 WEBBER CANYON RD
BENTON CO WA 120-C3
Rt#-225 9TH ST
BENTON CITY WA 120-C3
BENTON CO WA 120-C3
Rt#-225 S DIVISION AV
BENTON CITY WA 120-C3
Rt#-225 S DIVISION ST
BENTON CITY WA 120-C3
Rt#-225 E HEDGER AV
BENTON CITY WA 120-C3
Rt#-225 HORN RD
BENTON CITY WA 120-C2
BENTON CO WA 120-C2
Rt#-225 US RESERVATION RD
BENTON CO WA 120-C2
Rt#-225 WEBBER CANYON RD
BENTON CO WA 120-C3
Rt#-226 1ST AV
SCIO OR 133-C1
Rt#-226 5TH ST
LYONS OR 134-A1
MARION CO OR 134-A1
Rt#-226 6TH ST
LINN CO OR 134-A1
LYONS OR 134-A1
Rt#-226 ALBANY-LYONS HWY
LINN CO OR 133-C1
LINN CO OR 134-A1
SCIO OR 133-C1
Rt#-226 MAIN ST
LINN CO OR 133-C1
LYONS OR 134-A1
SCIO OR 133-C1
Rt#-227 TILLER-TRAIL HWY
CANYONVILLE OR 225-D3
DOUGLAS CO OR 141-B3
DOUGLAS CO OR 225-D3
JACKSON CO OR 141-C3
JACKSON CO OR 230-D1
Rt#-228 HALSEY-SWEET HOME HWY
BROWNSVILLE OR 210-B2
HALSEY OR 210-B2
LINN CO OR 133-C2
LINN CO OR 210-B2
SWEET HOME OR 133-C2
Rt#-229 GAITHER ST
LINCOLN CO OR 206-C2
SILETZ OR 206-C2
Rt#-229 SILETZ HWY
LINCOLN CO OR 203-A6
LINCOLN CO OR 206-C1
SILETZ OR 206-C1
TOLEDO OR 206-C4
Rt#-230 W DIAMOND LAKE HWY
DOUGLAS CO OR 223-B7
DOUGLAS CO OR 226-D3
DOUGLAS CO OR 227-A1
JACKSON CO OR 226-D3
KLAMATH CO OR 142-C3
Rt#-231 N ASPEN ST
LINCOLN CO WA 114-A2
REARDAN WA 114-A2
Rt#-231 CEDAR ST
STEVENS CO WA 106-B3
Rt#-231 FOURTH AV
STEVENS CO WA 106-B3
Rt#-231 HIGHWAY
LINCOLN CO WA 114-A1
SPRINGDALE WA 106-B3
STEVENS CO WA 106-B3
STEVENS CO WA 114-B1
Rt#-231 MAIN ST
LINCOLN CO WA 114-A2
Rt#-231 N MAIN ST
SPRINGDALE WA 106-B3
Rt#-231 OREGON ST
LINCOLN CO WA 114-A2
Rt#-231 N SECOND ST
SPRINGDALE WA 106-B3
Rt#-231 S SECOND ST
SPRINGDALE WA 106-B3
Rt#-231 W SHAFFER AV
SPRINGDALE WA 106-B3
Rt#-231 SPRING CREEK RD
LINCOLN CO WA 114-A1
Rt#-232 HIGHWAY
STEVENS CO WA 106-B3
Rt#-233 AMITY DAYTON HWY
YAMHILL CO OR 198-B7
YAMHILL CO OR 204-C1
Rt#-233 SE AMITY-DAYTON HWY
YAMHILL CO OR 204-C1
Rt#-233 SE LAFAYETTE HWY
YAMHILL CO OR 198-B7
Rt#-234 4TH AV
GOLD HILL OR 230-B6
Rt#-234 4TH ST
GOLD HILL OR 230-B6
Rt#-234 SAMS VALLEY AV
GOLD HILL OR 230-B6
JACKSON CO OR 230-B6
Rt#-234 SAMS VALLEY HWY
JACKSON CO OR 230-B6
Rt#-237 1ST ST
ISLAND CITY OR 130-A2
UNION CO OR 130-A2
Rt#-237 2ND ST
NORTH POWDER OR 130-B3
Rt#-237 COVE HWY
COVE OR 130-A2
UNION OR 130-A2
UNION CO OR 130-A2

STREET
City State Page-Grid

Rt#-237 E COVE HWY
UNION OR 130-B2
Rt#-237 LA GRANDE-BAKER HWY
NORTH POWDER OR 130-B3
UNION OR 130-B3
UNION CO OR 130-B3
Rt#-237 MAIN ST
COVE OR 130-B2
UNION CO OR 130-B2
Rt#-237 S MAIN ST
UNION OR 130-B2
Rt#-238 N 5TH ST
JACKSONVILLE OR 149-B2
Rt#-238 E 8TH ST
MEDFORD OR 336-D12
Rt#-238 W 8TH ST
MEDFORD OR 336-B12
Rt#-238 CALIFORNIA ST
JACKSONVILLE OR 149-B2
Rt#-238 E CALIFORNIA ST
JACKSONVILLE OR 149-B2
Rt#-238 W CALIFORNIA ST
JACKSONVILLE OR 149-B2
Rt#-238 S COLUMBUS AV
MEDFORD OR 336-B12
Rt#-238 JACKSONVILLE HWY
GRANTS PASS OR 335-C14
JACKSON CO OR 149-B2
JACKSON CO OR 234-A1
JACKSONVILLE OR 149-B2
JACKSONVILLE OR 234-A1
JOSEPHINE CO OR 149-B2
JOSEPHINE CO OR 229-B7
JOSEPHINE CO OR 335-C14
Rt#-238 E MAIN ST
MEDFORD OR 336-D12
Rt#-238 W MAIN ST
JACKSON CO OR 234-A1
JACKSON CO OR 336-A12
MEDFORD OR 336-C12
Rt#-238 ROSS LN
JACKSON CO OR 336-A12
Rt#-240 BY-PASS HWY
RICHLAND WA 340-E12
RICHLAND WA 341-E3
Rt#-240 FRWY
KENNEWICK WA 342-D7
KENNEWICK WA 343-A9
RICHLAND WA 341-H4
RICHLAND WA 342-A6
Rt#-240 HIGHWAY
BENTON CO WA 120-C2
RICHLAND WA 120-C2
RICHLAND WA 121-A2
RICHLAND WA 340-A7
Rt#-240 MAIN ST
YAMHILL OR 198-B5
YAMHILL CO OR 198-B5
Rt#-240 N MAIN ST
NEWBERG OR 198-D5
Rt#-240 YAMHILL HWY
NEWBERG OR 198-B5
YAMHILL CO OR 198-B5
Rt#-241 1ST AV
MABTON WA 120-B3
YAKIMA CO WA 120-B3
Rt#-241 ALEXANDER RD
SUNNYSIDE WA 120-B2
YAKIMA CO WA 120-B2
Rt#-241 HIGHWAY
BENTON CO WA 120-B2
SUNNYSIDE WA 120-B2
YAKIMA CO WA 120-B2
Rt#-241 MABTON-SUNNYSIDE RD
SUNNYSIDE WA 120-B3
YAKIMA CO WA 120-B3
Rt#-241 RESERVATION RD
YAKIMA CO WA 120-B3
Rt#-241 W RESERVATION RD
YAKIMA CO WA 120-B3
Rt#-241 WANETA RD
SUNNYSIDE WA 120-B2
YAKIMA CO WA 120-B2
Rt#-242 MCKENZIE HWY
DESCHUTES CO OR 211-C4
LANE CO OR 134-C2
LANE CO OR 211-A6
LINN CO OR 211-A6
SISTERS OR 211-C4
Rt#-243 HIGHWAY
GRANT CO WA 120-B1
Rt#-244 UKIAH-HILGARD HWY
UKIAH OR 129-B3
UMATILLA CO OR 129-B3
UNION CO OR 129-C3
UNION CO OR 130-A2
Rt#-245 DOOLEY MOUNTAIN HWY
BAKER CO OR 138-A1
Rt#-251 BOUNDARY HWY
NORTHPORT WA 106-B1
STEVENS CO WA 106-B1
Rt#-251 HIGHWAY
STEVENS CO WA 106-A1
Rt#-260 BLANTON RD
FRANKLIN CO WA 121-B1
Rt#-260 HAVLINA RD
FRANKLIN CO WA 121-B1
Rt#-260 HIGHWAY
ADAMS CO WA 121-C1
CONNELL WA 121-B1
FRANKLIN CO WA 121-C1
KAHLOTUS WA 121-C1
Rt#-260 MAIN ST
WASHTUCNA WA 121-C1
Rt#-261 HIGHWAY
ADAMS CO WA 113-C3
ADAMS CO WA 121-C1
COLUMBIA CO WA 122-A2
FRANKLIN CO WA 121-C1
FRANKLIN CO WA 122-A2
STARBUCK WA 122-A2
Rt#-261 MAIN ST
WASHTUCNA WA 121-C1
Rt#-261 PROVIDENCE RD
ADAMS CO WA 121-C1

STREET
City State Page-Grid

Rt#-262 OSULLIVAN DAM RD
GRANT CO WA 121-A1
GRANT CO WA 242-B6
Rt#-262 ROAD A-SE
GRANT CO WA 120-C1
GRANT CO WA 242-A7
Rt#-263 HIGHWAY
SISKIYOU CO CA 150-A3
Rt#-263 LAKE OF THE WOODS HWY
SISKIYOU CO CA 149-C3
YREKA CA 149-C3
Rt#-263 N MAIN ST
YREKA CA 149-C3
Rt#-270 DAVIS WY
PULLMAN WA 249-A5
WHITMAN CO WA 249-A5
Rt#-270 HIGHWAY
MOSCOW ID 249-C5
PULLMAN WA 249-B5
WHITMAN CO WA 249-C5
Rt#-270 NE KAMIAKEN ST
PULLMAN WA 249-B5
Rt#-270 E MAIN ST
PULLMAN WA 249-B5
Rt#-270 SE OLSEN ST
PULLMAN WA 249-B5
Rt#-271 HIGHWAY
OAKESDALE WA 114-C3
WHITMAN CO WA 114-C3
Rt#-272 E CANYON ST
COLFAX WA 122-C1
WHITMAN CO WA 122-C1
Rt#-272 W CHURCH ST
PALOUSE WA 249-B1
WHITMAN CO WA 249-B1
Rt#-272 N E ST
PALOUSE WA 249-C1
Rt#-272 HIGHWAY
COLFAX WA 122-C1
LATAH CO ID 249-C1
PALOUSE WA 249-C1
WHITMAN CO WA 122-C1
WHITMAN CO WA 249-B1
Rt#-272 E MAIN ST
PALOUSE WA 249-C1
Rt#-272 E ST
PALOUSE WA 249-C1
Rt#-274 HIGHWAY
BENEWAH CO ID 115-A3
TEKOA WA 114-C3
WHITMAN CO WA 114-C3
WHITMAN CO WA 115-A3
Rt#-274 POPULAR ST
TEKOA WA 114-C3
Rt#-278 EMMA ST
ROCKFORD WA 114-C2
Rt#-278 E HOXIE RD
ROCKFORD WA 114-C2
SPOKANE CO WA 114-C2
Rt#-281 CENTRAL AV S
GRANT CO WA 112-B3
QUINCY WA 112-B3
Rt#-281 HIGHWAY
GRANT CO WA 112-B3
Rt#-281 ROAD 10-NW
GRANT CO WA 112-B3
Rt#-282 HIGHWAY
EPHRATA WA 112-C3
GRANT CO WA 112-C3
Rt#-283 HIGHWAY
GRANT CO WA 112-C3
Rt#-285 N CHELAN AV
WENATCHEE WA 238-D4
Rt#-285 S CHELAN AV
WENATCHEE WA 238-D4
WENATCHEE WA 239-A4
Rt#-285 HIGHWAY
EAST WENATCHEE WA 239-A4
Sunnyslope WA 238-D3
WENATCHEE WA 238-D3
WENATCHEE WA 239-A4
West Wenatchee WA 238-D3
Rt#-285 N MILLER ST
WENATCHEE WA 238-D4
Rt#-285 N MISSION ST
WENATCHEE WA 238-D4
Rt#-285 S MISSION ST
WENATCHEE WA 238-D4
WENATCHEE WA 239-A4
Rt#-285 PEACHEY ST
WENATCHEE WA 239-A4
Rt#-285 STEVENS ST
WENATCHEE WA 239-A4
Rt#-285 WENATCHEE AV
WENATCHEE WA 239-A4
Rt#-285 N WENATCHEE AV
WENATCHEE WA 238-D4
West Wenatchee WA 238-D4
Rt#-285 S WENATCHEE AV
WENATCHEE WA 239-A4
Rt#-290 E TRENT AV
MILLWOOD WA 350-C5
SPOKANE WA 349-F7
SPOKANE CO WA 349-F7
SPOKANE CO WA 350-C6
Rt#-290 E TRENT RD
MILLWOOD WA 350-E5
Otis Orchards WA 351-C3
Otis Orchards WA 352-C7
SPOKANE CO WA 350-E5
SPOKANE CO WA 351-C3
SPOKANE CO WA 352-C7
Trentwood WA 350-E5
Trentwood WA 351-C3
Rt#-291 CORKSCREW CANYON RD
STEVENS CO WA 114-B1
STEVENS CO WA 246-A1
Rt#-291 W FRANCIS AV
SPOKANE WA 348-D1
SPOKANE WA 349-A1
Town and Country WA 348-D1
Town and Country WA 349-A1
Rt#-291 N NINE MILE RD
SPOKANE WA 246-A2
SPOKANE WA 346-A14
SPOKANE WA 348-B1
SPOKANE CO WA 246-A2
SPOKANE CO WA 346-A13

STREET
City State Page-Grid

Rt#-292 HIGHWAY
SPRINGDALE WA 106-B3
STEVENS CO WA 106-B3
Rt#-292 NEVADA STATE ROUTE
HUMBOLDT CO NV 153-C3
Rt#-293 ANTELOPE HWY
JEFFERSON CO OR 135-C1
WASCO CO OR 127-C3
WASCO CO OR 135-C1
Rt#-293 KINGS RIVER RD
HUMBOLDT CO NV 154-A3
Rt#-293 LOWER ANTELOPE RD
ANTELOPE OR 127-C3
WASCO CO OR 127-C3
Rt#-293 SOUTH ST
ANTELOPE OR 127-C3
Rt#-300 HIGHWAY
MASON CO WA 173-D5
Rt#-300 NORTH SHORE RD
MASON CO WA 173-D6
Rt#-300 OLD BELFAIR HWY
MASON CO WA 173-D5
Rt#-302 ELGIN-CLIFTON
PIERCE CO WA 174-A7
Rt#-302 HIGHWAY
MASON CO WA 173-D6
Rt#-302 KEY PENINSULA HWY
PIERCE CO WA 174-B6
Rt#-302 PURDY DR
KITSAP CO WA 174-B6
PIERCE CO WA 174-B6
Rt#-302 ROCKY BAY POINT DR
MASON CO WA 174-A7
MASON CO WA 174-A7
PIERCE CO WA 174-A7
Rt#-302 ROCKY BAY PT
MASON CO WA 173-D7
Rt#-302 VICTOR CUT-OFF RD
MASON CO WA 173-D6
Rt#-303 NE BUCKLIN HILL RD
KITSAP CO WA 174-B1
Rt#-303 NW BUCKLIN HILL RD
KITSAP CO WA 174-B1
Silverdale WA 174-B1
Rt#-303 HIGHWAY
KITSAP CO WA 174-B1
KITSAP CO WA 270-J1
Rt#-303 WAAGA WY
KITSAP CO WA 174-B1
Silverdale WA 174-B1
Rt#-303 WARREN AV
BREMERTON WA 270-J10
Rt#-303 WHEATON WY
BREMERTON WA 270-J6
KITSAP CO WA 270-J6
Rt#-304 1ST ST
BREMERTON WA 270-J11
Rt#-304 4TH ST
BREMERTON WA 270-H11
Rt#-304 BURWELL PL
BREMERTON WA 270-G11
Rt#-304 BURWELL ST
BREMERTON WA 270-G11
Rt#-304 CALLOW AV N
BREMERTON WA 270-G10
Rt#-304 CALLOW AV S
BREMERTON WA 270-G11
Rt#-304 CAMBRIAN AV S
BREMERTON WA 270-F12
Rt#-304 FARRAGUT ST
BREMERTON WA 270-F12
Rt#-304 HIGHWAY
BREMERTON WA 270-F12
Navy Yard City WA 270-F12
Rt#-304 WASHINGTON AV
BREMERTON WA 270-J11
Rt#-305 HIGHWAY
KITSAP CO WA 170-B6
KITSAP CO WA 174-C1
POULSBO WA 170-B6
Suquamish WA 170-C7
Winslow WA 174-D1
Rt#-305 OLYMPIC WY SE
Winslow WA 174-D2
Rt#-307 BOND RD NE
KITSAP CO WA 170-C6
POULSBO WA 170-C6
Rt#-308 HIGHWAY
KITSAP CO WA 170-B7
Rt#-308 NW LUOTO RD
KITSAP CO WA 170-B7
Rt#-310 6TH ST
BREMERTON WA 270-G10
Rt#-310 KITSAP WY
BREMERTON WA 270-D10
Rt#-361 1ST AV
CULVER OR 208-B7
Rt#-361 CULVER HWY
CULVER OR 208-B7
JEFFERSON CO OR 208-B6
JEFFERSON CO OR 212-D1
MADRAS OR 208-B6
METOLIUS OR 208-B6
Rt#-361 SW D ST
MADRAS OR 208-C5
Rt#-361 JEFFERSON AV
JEFFERSON CO OR 208-B6
METOLIUS OR 208-B6
Rt#-372 CENTURY DRIVE HWY
BEND OR 332-A11
DESCHUTES CO OR 216-C4
DESCHUTES CO OR 217-B3
DESCHUTES CO OR 332-A11
Rt#-372 NW COLORADO AV
BEND OR 332-E8
Rt#-372 SW COLORADO AV
BEND OR 332-D9
Rt#-372 DIVISION ST
BEND OR 332-E8
Rt#-372 SE WILSON AV
BEND OR 332-F9

STREET
City State Page-Grid

Rt#-380 HARDING RD
CROOK CO OR 213-D5
Rt#-380 PAULINA HWY
CROOK CO OR 135-C2
CROOK CO OR 136-A3
CROOK CO OR 213-D5
PRINEVILLE OR 213-D5
Rt#-395 HIGHWAY
BRITISH COLUMBIA 105-C1
Rt#-397 S 10TH AV
PASCO WA 343-F9
Rt#-397 E AINSWORTH AV
PASCO WA 343-G9
Rt#-397 W AINSWORTH AV
PASCO WA 343-F8
Rt#-397 BENTON-FRANKLIN BRDG
KENNEWICK WA 343-E10
PASCO WA 343-F9
Rt#-397 CHEMICAL RD
Finley WA 121-A3
Finley WA 343-G12
KENNEWICK WA 343-F11
Rt#-397 N GUM ST
KENNEWICK WA 343-E10
Rt#-397 HIGHWAY
Finley WA 121-A3
Rt#-397 N OREGON AV
PASCO WA 343-G6
Rt#-397 S OREGON AV
PASCO WA 343-H8
Rt#-401 HIGHWAY
PACIFIC CO WA 186-C5
Rt#-401 KNAPPTON FERRY RD
PACIFIC CO WA 186-C7
Rt#-403 EDEN VALLEY RD
WAHKIAKUM CO WA 117-A2
Rt#-403 HIGHWAY
WAHKIAKUM CO WA 117-A2
Rt#-407 ELOCHOMAN MAINLINE
WAHKIAKUM CO WA 117-B3
Rt#-407 HIGHWAY
WAHKIAKUM CO WA 117-B2
Rt#-407 SCHOONOVER RD
WAHKIAKUM CO WA 117-B2
Rt#-409 FRONT ST
CATHLAMET WA 117-B3
CLATSOP CO OR 117-B3
Rt#-409 HIGHWAY
CATHLAMET WA 117-B3
WAHKIAKUM CO WA 117-B3
Rt#-409 MAIN ST
CATHLAMET WA 117-B3
Rt#-409 PLYMPTON CREEK
CLATSOP CO OR 117-B3
Rt#-409 WESTPORT DOCK RD
CLATSOP CO OR 117-B3
Rt#-410 CHINOOK PASS HWY
PIERCE CO WA 111-A3
Rt#-410 ENUMCLAW BUCKLEY RD
ENUMCLAW WA 110-C3
KING CO WA 110-C3
Rt#-410 SE ENMCLW CHNK PASS R
KING CO WA 110-C3
PIERCE CO WA 110-C3
PIERCE CO WA 111-A3
Rt#-410 ENUMCLAW CHINOOK PASS
ENUMCLAW WA 110-C3
KING CO WA 110-C3
Rt#-410 FRWY
PIERCE CO WA 182-C3
Rt#-410 HIGHWAY
BONNEY LAKE WA 182-C4
BUCKLEY WA 110-C3
BUCKLEY WA 182-D4
KING CO WA 110-C3
PIERCE CO WA 111-A3
PIERCE CO WA 119-A1
PIERCE CO WA 182-C3
SUMNER WA 182-C3
YAKIMA CO WA 119-B1
YAKIMA CO WA 240-A6
Rt#-410 MATHER MEMORIAL PKWY
PIERCE CO WA 119-A1
Rt#-410 NFD RD 7184
PIERCE CO WA 111-A3
Rt#-410 ROOSEVELT AV
ENUMCLAW WA 110-C3
Rt#-410 ROOSEVELT AV E
ENUMCLAW WA 110-C3
KING CO WA 110-C3
Rt#-410 SUMNER-BUCKLEY HWY
PIERCE CO WA 182-B3
SUMNER WA 182-B3
Rt#-411 1ST AV
KELSO WA 303-C9
LONGVIEW WA 303-C9
Rt#-411 1ST AV NW
KELSO WA 303-C7
Rt#-411 3RD AV
LONGVIEW WA 303-C9
Rt#-411 PEARDALE LN
LONGVIEW WA 303-C9
Rt#-411 WEST SIDE HWY
COWLITZ CO WA 187-C6
COWLITZ CO WA 189-C1
COWLITZ CO WA 303-C7
KELSO WA 303-C7
LEWIS CO WA 187-C6
LONGVIEW WA 303-C7
VADER WA 187-C6
Rt#-431 PACIFIC AV N
KELSO WA 303-D7
Rt#-431 PACIFIC HWY N
KELSO WA 303-E6
Rt#-432 3RD AV
LONGVIEW WA 303-B11
Rt#-432 HIGHWAY
COWLITZ CO WA 303-C12
KELSO WA 303-E13
LONGVIEW WA 303-C12
Rt#-432 INDUSTRIAL WY
COWLITZ CO WA 302-D8

STREET
City State Page-Grid

Rt#-432 INDUSTRIAL WY
LONGVIEW WA 302-D8
LONGVIEW WA 303-A12
Rt#-432 MOUNT SOLO RD
COWLITZ CO WA 302-C6
Rt#-432 OLD PACIFIC HWY
KELSO WA 303-F13
Rt#-432 TENNANT WY
COWLITZ CO WA 303-C12
LONGVIEW WA 303-C12
Rt#-432 WILLOW GROVE CONN RD
COWLITZ CO WA 302-A5
LONGVIEW WA 302-A5
Rt#-432 WILLOW GROVE RD
COWLITZ CO WA 302-A5
LONGVIEW WA 302-A5
Rt#-433 OREGON WY
COLUMBIA CO OR 189-B4
COWLITZ CO WA 302-H13
LONGVIEW WA 302-J12
RAINIER OR 189-B4
RAINIER OR 302-H13
Rt#-500 NE 3RD AV
CAMAS WA 193-B7
Rt#-500 NE 3RD ST
CLARK CO WA 193-B6
Rt#-500 SE 6TH AV
CAMAS WA 193-B7
Rt#-500 NE 14TH AV
CAMAS WA 193-B7
Rt#-500 NE 44TH ST
CLARK CO WA 193-B6
Rt#-500 NE 54TH ST
CLARK CO WA 193-B6
Rt#-500 NE 58TH ST
CLARK CO WA 193-B5
Rt#-500 NE 117TH AV
CLARK CO WA 192-D5
Rt#-500 NE 232ND AV
CLARK CO WA 193-B5
Rt#-500 NE 237TH AV
CLARK CO WA 193-B6
Rt#-500 NE 238TH AV
CLARK CO WA 193-B6
Rt#-500 NE 242ND AV
CLARK CO WA 193-B6
Rt#-500 NE 267TH AV
CLARK CO WA 193-B6
Rt#-500 BRUNNER RD
CLARK CO WA 193-B6
Rt#-500 NE DALLAS ST
CAMAS WA 193-B7
Rt#-500 DRESSER RD
CLARK CO WA 193-B6
Rt#-500 SE EVERETT RD
CLARK CO WA 193-B6
Rt#-500 NE EVERETT ST
CAMAS WA 193-B7
CLARK CO WA 193-B7
Rt#-500 NE FOURTH PLAIN RD
CLARK CO WA 192-D5
CLARK CO WA 193-A5
VANCOUVER WA 192-D5
VANCOUVER WA 193-A5
Rt#-500 NE GARFIELD ST
CAMAS WA 193-B7
Rt#-500 HIGHWAY
CLARK WA 306-C2
CLARK WA 307-J1
CLARK CO WA 192-D5
VANCOUVER WA 192-D5
VANCOUVER WA 305-H2
VANCOUVER WA 306-E2
VANCOUVER WA 307-H1
Rt#-500 SE UNION ST
CAMAS WA 193-B7
Rt#-501 E FOURTH PLAIN BLVD
VANCOUVER WA 305-G3
Rt#-501 W FOURTH PLAIN BLVD
VANCOUVER WA 304-E3
VANCOUVER WA 305-F3
Rt#-501 J ST
VANCOUVER WA 305-G3
Rt#-501 LOWER RIVER RD
CLARK WA 304-A1
CLARK CO WA 192-C5
VANCOUVER WA 192-B5
VANCOUVER WA 304-A1
Rt#-501 NW LOWER RIVER RD
CLARK CO WA 192-B5
VANCOUVER WA 192-B5
Rt#-501 PIONEER ST
RIDGEFIELD WA 192-C2
Rt#-502 NE 10TH AV
CLARK CO WA 192-C3
Rt#-502 NE 219TH ST
BATTLE GROUND WA 192-D3
CLARK CO WA 192-D3
Rt#-502 W MAIN ST
BATTLE GROUND WA 192-D3
BATTLE GROUND WA 193-A3
Rt#-503 SW 10TH AV
BATTLE GROUND WA 193-A3
CLARK CO WA 193-A3
Rt#-503 NE 117TH AV
CLARK CO WA 192-D5
CLARK CO WA 193-A4
Rt#-503 NE 122ND AV
BATTLE GROUND WA 193-A3
CLARK CO WA 193-A3
Rt#-503 AMBOY
CLARK CO WA 193-B1
Rt#-503 COUNTY 5 RD
CLARK CO WA 193-A2
Rt#-503 GOERIG ST
WOODLAND WA 118-A3
WOODLAND WA 192-C1
Rt#-503 HIGHWAY
CLARK CO WA 118-A3
CLARK CO WA 190-A7
CLARK CO WA 193-A1
COWLITZ CO WA 118-A3
COWLITZ CO WA 190-A6
WOODLAND WA 192-C1

PNW

INDEX

416 Rt#-503 LEWIS RIVER DR — STREET INDEX — U.S.-2 HIGHWAY

STREET / City State Page-Grid

Rt#-503 LEWIS RIVER DR
COWLITZ CO WA 118-A3
COWLITZ CO WA 190-A6
WOODLAND WA 118-A3
Rt#-503 LEWIS RIVER RD
COWLITZ CO WA 190-A6
Rt#-503 NE LEWISVILLE HWY
CLARK CO WA 193-A1
Rt#-504 HIGHWAY
COWLITZ CO WA 118-A2
SKAMANIA CO WA 118-B2
SKAMANIA CO WA 190-B1
Rt#-504 SPIRIT LAKE HWY
CASTLE ROCK WA 187-C7
COWLITZ CO WA 118-A2
COWLITZ CO WA 187-C7
Rt#-505 N 5TH ST
LEWIS CO WA 187-D4
TOLEDO WA 187-D4
Rt#-505 COWLITZ ST
LEWIS CO WA 187-D4
TOLEDO WA 187-D4
Rt#-505 HIGHWAY
COWLITZ CO WA 118-A2
LEWIS CO WA 118-A2
LEWIS CO WA 187-C3
TOLEDO WA 187-D4
WINLOCK WA 187-C3
Rt#-505 KERRON AV
WINLOCK WA 187-C3
Rt#-505 E WALNUT ST
WINLOCK WA 187-C3
Rt#-505 WINLOCK-TOLEDO RD
LEWIS CO WA 187-C3
Rt#-506 7TH ST
VADER WA 187-B5
Rt#-506 HIGHWAY
COWLITZ CO WA 187-B5
LEWIS CO WA 187-C4
VADER WA 187-C5
Rt#-507 ALDER ST
CENTRALIA WA 299-E4
Rt#-507 BINGHAMPTON ST
RAINIER WA 118-A1
THURSTON CO WA 118-A1
Rt#-507 BUCODA HWY
LEWIS CO WA 184-C5
Rt#-507 W CHERRY ST
CENTRALIA WA 299-E4
Rt#-507 E DOWNING RD
CENTRALIA WA 184-C5
LEWIS CO WA 184-C5
Rt#-507 D ST
TENINO WA 184-D3
Rt#-507 FRONT ST
BUCODA WA 184-D4
THURSTON CO WA 184-D4
Rt#-507 HIGHWAY
LEWIS CO WA 184-C5
THURSTON CO WA 118-A1
THURSTON CO WA 184-D3
Rt#-507 MCKENNA-YELM HWY
PIERCE CO WA 118-A1
THURSTON CO WA 118-A1
YELM WA 118-A1
Rt#-507 MCNAUGHT ST
ROY WA 181-C7
Rt#-507 MELLEN ST
CENTRALIA WA 299-D5
Rt#-507 N PEARL ST
CENTRALIA WA 184-C5
CENTRALIA WA 299-F1
LEWIS CO WA 184-C5
Rt#-507 S PEARL ST
CENTRALIA WA 299-F4
Rt#-507 RAINIER-YELM HWY
THURSTON CO WA 118-A1
YELM WA 118-A1
Rt#-507 SIXTH ST
TENINO WA 184-D3
Rt#-507 E SIXTH ST
CENTRALIA WA 299-F2
Rt#-507 SPANAWAY-MCKENNA HWY
PIERCE CO WA 118-A1
PIERCE CO WA 181-C7
ROY WA 181-C7
Rt#-507 SUMNER ST
BUCODA WA 184-D4
TENINO WA 184-D4
THURSTON CO WA 184-D4
Rt#-507 SUSSEX ST
TENINO WA 184-D3
THURSTON CO WA 184-D3
Rt#-507 THIRD ST
TENINO WA 184-D3
Rt#-507 N TOWER AV
CENTRALIA WA 299-F3
Rt#-507 S TOWER AV
CENTRALIA WA 299-F4
Rt#-507 YELM AV
YELM WA 118-A1
Rt#-508 HIGHWAY
LEWIS CO WA 118-A2
LEWIS CO WA 187-C1
MORTON WA 118-B2
Rt#-508 MAIN AV
MORTON WA 118-B2
Rt#-508 MORTON-BEAR CANYON RD
LEWIS CO WA 118-B2
MORTON WA 118-B2
Rt#-508 NFD RD 508
LINCOLN CO MT 107-C2
Rt#-508 NFD RD 92
LINCOLN CO MT 107-C1
Rt#-509 S 174TH ST
BURIEN WA 175-A5
Rt#-509 1ST AV S
BURIEN WA 175-A6
DES MOINES WA 175-A6
NORMANDY PARK WA 175-A6
Rt#-509 S 216TH ST
DES MOINES WA 175-A6
DES MOINES WA 290-A5
NORMANDY PARK WA 175-A6
NORMANDY PARK WA 290-A5
Rt#-509 AMBAUM BLVD S
BURIEN WA 175-A5
BURIEN WA 288-A7
Rt#-509 S DASH POINT RD
FEDERAL WAY WA 182-B1
Rt#-509 SW DASH POINT RD
FEDERAL WAY WA 182-A1
PIERCE CO WA 182-A1
Rt#-509 DES MOINES MEM DR
BURIEN WA 288-A7
BURIEN WA 290-A1
SEATAC WA 290-A1
Rt#-509 N FRONTAGE RD
TACOMA WA 182-A2
Rt#-509 S FRONTAGE RD
TACOMA WA 182-A2
Rt#-509 FRWY
BURIEN WA 175-A5
BURIEN WA 288-A2
BURIEN WA 290-A1
KING WA 286-A5
KING WA 288-A2
SEATAC WA 288-A6
SEATAC WA 290-A1
SEATTLE WA 285-J1
SEATTLE WA 286-A5
TACOMA WA 182-A2
TACOMA WA 293-J6
Rt#-509 LE-LOU-WA PL
PIERCE CO WA 181-D1
Rt#-509 MARINE VIEW DR
DES MOINES WA 290-A7
PIERCE CO WA 182-A1
TACOMA WA 181-D1
TACOMA WA 182-A1
Rt#-509 E SIDE DR NE
PIERCE CO WA 181-D1
PIERCE CO WA 182-A1
Rt#-510 CLAIR CUT-OFF RD
THURSTON CO WA 181-A7
Rt#-510 HIGHWAY
THURSTON CO WA 181-A6
Rt#-510 MARVIN RD NE
LACEY WA 181-A6
Rt#-510 MARVIN RD SE
LACEY WA 181-A6
THURSTON CO WA 181-A6
Rt#-510 OLYMPIA-YELM HWY
THURSTON CO WA 118-A1
THURSTON CO WA 181-B7
YELM WA 118-A1
Rt#-510 PACIFIC AV SE
THURSTON CO WA 181-A6
Rt#-510 PACIFIC HWY SE
THURSTON CO WA 181-A6
Rt#-510 YELM AV
YELM WA 118-A1
Rt#-512 FRWY
LAKEWOOD WA 181-D4
PIERCE CO WA 181-D4
PIERCE CO WA 182-A4
PUYALLUP WA 182-A4
Rt#-513 NE 45TH ST
SEATTLE WA 274-D5
SEATTLE WA 275-E5
Rt#-513 MONTLAKE BLVD NE
SEATTLE WA 274-D6
SEATTLE WA 278-D1
Rt#-513 SAND POINT WY NE
SEATTLE WA 171-B7
SEATTLE WA 275-G1
Rt#-515 104TH AV SE
KENT WA 175-C7
Rt#-515 108TH AV SE
KENT WA 175-C6
KING CO WA 175-C6
Rt#-515 BENSON RD
KENT WA 175-C6
KING CO WA 175-C6
Rt#-515 BENSON RD SE
KING CO WA 175-C6
Rt#-515 S GRADY WY
RENTON WA 175-C5
Rt#-515 HIGHWAY
KING CO WA 175-C5
RENTON WA 175-C5
Rt#-515 MAIN AV S
RENTON WA 175-C5
Rt#-516 SE 256TH ST
KENT WA 175-C7
Rt#-516 SE 272ND ST
COVINGTON WA 175-D7
KENT WA 175-C7
KING CO WA 175-D7
MAPLE VALLEY WA 175-D7
Rt#-516 CANYON DR SE
KENT WA 175-C7
Rt#-516 CENTRAL AV N
KENT WA 175-C7
Rt#-516 CENTRAL AV S
KENT WA 175-C7
Rt#-516 KENT-DES MOINES RD
DES MOINES WA 290-B7
KENT WA 175-B7
KENT WA 290-B7
Rt#-516 KENT-DES MOINES RD S
KENT WA 175-B7
KENT WA 290-E7
KING WA 290-E7
KING CO WA 175-B7
Rt#-516 KENT KANGLEY RD
COVINGTON WA 175-C7
KENT WA 175-C7
KING CO WA 175-C7
KING CO WA 176-A7
MAPLE VALLEY WA 175-C7
MAPLE VALLEY WA 176-A7
Rt#-516 E SMITH ST
KENT WA 175-C7
Rt#-516 W WILLIS ST
KENT WA 175-C7
Rt#-518 FRWY
BURIEN WA 175-A5
BURIEN WA 288-B4
SEATAC WA 288-B4
TUKWILA WA 288-D5
TUKWILA WA 289-E4
Rt#-519 4TH AV S
SEATTLE WA 278-A7
SEATTLE WA 282-A1
Rt#-519 ALASKAN WY S
SEATTLE WA 277-J7
SEATTLE WA 278-A7
SEATTLE WA 281-J1
Rt#-519 S ROYAL BROUGHAM WY
SEATTLE WA 281-J1
SEATTLE WA 282-A1
Rt#-520 FRWY
BELLEVUE WA 175-D1
CLYDE HILL WA 175-D1
HUNTS POINT WA 175-D1
KING CO WA 175-D1
MEDINA WA 175-D1
MEDINA WA 279-E1
REDMOND WA 175-D1
SEATTLE WA 278-D1
SEATTLE WA 279-E1
YARROW POINT WA 175-D1
Rt#-522 NE BOTHELL WY
BOTHELL WA 171-B6
KENMORE WA 171-B6
KING CO WA 171-B6
LAKE FOREST PARK WA 171-B6
Rt#-522 BOTHELL WY NE
BOTHELL WA 171-C6
LAKE FOREST PARK WA 171-B6
SHORELINE WA 171-B7
Rt#-522 FISCHER PL NE
SEATTLE WA 171-B7
Rt#-522 FRWY
BOTHELL WA 171-C6
SNOHOMISH CO WA 171-C6
WOODINVILLE WA 171-C6
Rt#-522 HIGHWAY
MONROE WA 110-C1
SNOHOMISH CO WA 110-C1
SNOHOMISH CO WA 171-D5
Rt#-522 HIGHWAY ROUTE 522
SNOHOMISH CO WA 171-D5
Rt#-522 LAKE CITY WY NE
SEATTLE WA 171-B7
SEATTLE WA 274-C2
Rt#-522 WOODINVILLE DR
BOTHELL WA 171-C6
Rt#-523 N 145TH ST
SEATTLE WA 171-A7
SHORELINE WA 171-A7
Rt#-523 NE 145TH ST
SEATTLE WA 171-B7
SHORELINE WA 171-B7
Rt#-524 196TH ST SW
EDMONDS WA 171-B5
LYNNWOOD WA 171-B5
SNOHOMISH CO WA 171-B5
Rt#-524 208TH ST SE
BOTHELL WA 171-C5
SNOHOMISH CO WA 171-C5
Rt#-524 3RD AV N
EDMONDS WA 171-A5
Rt#-524 3RD AV S
EDMONDS WA 171-A5
Rt#-524 9TH AV N
EDMONDS WA 171-A5
Rt#-524 CASPERS ST
EDMONDS WA 171-A5
Rt#-524 FILBERT RD
BOTHELL WA 171-C5
LYNNWOOD WA 171-B5
SNOHOMISH CO WA 171-C5
Rt#-524 MAIN ST
EDMONDS WA 171-A5
Rt#-524 MALTBY RD
BOTHELL WA 171-C5
SNOHOMISH CO WA 171-C5
Rt#-524 PARADISE LAKE RD
SNOHOMISH CO WA 171-D5
Rt#-524 PINE ST
EDMONDS WA 171-A5
Rt#-524 PUGET DR
EDMONDS WA 171-A5
Rt#-524 YEW WY
SNOHOMISH CO WA 171-D5
Rt#-525 HIGHWAY
Clinton WA 171-A2
Freeland WA 170-C1
ISLAND CO WA 167-C5
ISLAND CO WA 170-C1
ISLAND CO WA 171-A1
SNOHOMISH CO WA 171-B4
Rt#-525 MUKILTEO SPEEDWAY
MUKILTEO WA 171-B2
MUKILTEO WA 266-D3
MUKILTEO WA 267-E5
SNOHOMISH WA 267-E6
SNOHOMISH CO WA 171-B4
Rt#-526 84TH ST SW
MUKILTEO WA 266-E4
MUKILTEO WA 267-F4
Rt#-526 FRWY
EVERETT WA 267-F4
EVERETT WA 268-A4
MUKILTEO WA 267-F4
SNOHOMISH WA 267-F4
Rt#-526 PAINE FIELD BLVD
MUKILTEO WA 267-E6
SNOHOMISH WA 267-E6
Rt#-527 19TH AV SE
EVERETT WA 171-C4
EVERETT WA 268-D6
SNOHOMISH CO WA 171-C4
Rt#-527 BOTHELL EVERETT HWY
BOTHELL WA 171-C4
MILL CREEK WA 171-C4
SNOHOMISH CO WA 171-C4
Rt#-527 BOTHELL WY NE
BOTHELL WA 171-C6
BOTHELL WA 171-C6
Rt#-528 4TH ST
MARYSVILLE WA 171-C1
SNOHOMISH CO WA 171-C1
Rt#-528 64TH ST NE
MARYSVILLE WA 168-D7
MARYSVILLE WA 171-C1
Rt#-528 64TH ST NE
SNOHOMISH CO WA 168-D7
SNOHOMISH CO WA 171-D1
Rt#-529 BROADWAY
EVERETT WA 171-C1
Rt#-529 EVERETT AV
EVERETT WA 264-D3
EVERETT WA 265-E3
Rt#-529 HIGHWAY
MARYSVILLE WA 171-C1
SNOHOMISH CO WA 171-C1
Rt#-529 MAPLE ST
EVERETT WA 265-F4
Rt#-529 E MARINE VIEW DR
EVERETT WA 171-C1
Rt#-529 W MARINE VIEW DR
EVERETT WA 171-C1
EVERETT WA 264-D3
Rt#-529 PACIFIC AV
EVERETT WA 265-F4
Rt#-529 PACIFIC HWY
EVERETT WA 171-C1
MARYSVILLE WA 171-C1
SNOHOMISH CO WA 171-C1
Rt#-529 STATE AV
MARYSVILLE WA 171-C1
Rt#-530 DARINGTN BNTTS STR RD
DARRINGTON WA 103-A3
SKAGIT CO WA 103-A3
SNOHOMISH CO WA 103-A3
Rt#-530 EMENS AV
DARRINGTON WA 103-A3
Rt#-530 HIGHWAY
ARLINGTON WA 168-D5
DARRINGTON WA 103-A3
MARYSVILLE WA 168-C5
SNOHOMISH CO WA 102-C3
SNOHOMISH CO WA 103-A3
SNOHOMISH CO WA 168-D4
Rt#-530 PIONEER HWY
SKAGIT CO WA 168-B2
Rt#-530 PIONEER HWY E
SNOHOMISH CO WA 168-C4
Rt#-530 SAUK VALLEY RD
SKAGIT CO WA 103-A2
Rt#-530 SEEMANN ST
DARRINGTON WA 103-A3
Rt#-531 172ND ST NE
ARLINGTON WA 168-C6
SNOHOMISH CO WA 168-C6
Rt#-531 36TH AV NW
SNOHOMISH CO WA 168-B6
Rt#-531 E LAKE GOODWIN RD
SNOHOMISH CO WA 168-B5
Rt#-531 LAKEWOOD RD
SNOHOMISH CO WA 168-B5
Rt#-531 SISCO HEIGHTS RD
ARLINGTON WA 168-D6
SNOHOMISH CO WA 168-D6
Rt#-532 268TH ST NW
SNOHOMISH CO WA 168-A4
STANWOOD WA 168-A4
Rt#-532 HIGHWAY
ISLAND CO WA 167-D4
ISLAND CO WA 168-A4
SNOHOMISH CO WA 168-A4
STANWOOD WA 168-B4
Rt#-534 HIGHWAY
SKAGIT CO WA 168-B2
Rt#-536 S 3RD ST
MOUNT VERNON WA 260-C12
Rt#-536 W DIVISION ST
MOUNT VERNON WA 260-B12
Rt#-536 KINCAID ST
MOUNT VERNON WA 260-C13
Rt#-536 MEMORIAL HWY
MOUNT VERNON WA 260-A11
SKAGIT CO WA 161-A7
SKAGIT CO WA 260-A11
Rt#-538 COLLEGE WY
MOUNT VERNON WA 260-D10
SKAGIT CO WA 161-C7
SKAGIT CO WA 260-H10
Rt#-539 GUIDE MERIDIAN RD
BELLINGHAM WA 158-D6
BELLINGHAM WA 258-C1
LYNDEN WA 158-D6
WHATCOM CO WA 158-D6
Rt#-539 MERIDIAN ST
BELLINGHAM WA 258-C2
Rt#-540 SLATER RD
FERNDALE WA 158-C6
WHATCOM CO WA 158-C6
Rt#-542 MOUNT BAKER HWY
WHATCOM CO WA 102-B1
WHATCOM CO WA 103-A1
Rt#-542 E SUNSET DR
BELLINGHAM WA 258-G3
WHATCOM CO WA 102-B1
WHATCOM CO WA 258-G3
Rt#-543 HIGHWAY
BLAINE WA 158-B3
WHATCOM CO WA 158-B3
Rt#-544 COLUMBIA ST
NOOKSACK WA 102-B1
Rt#-544 EVERSON AV
EVERSON WA 102-B1
NOOKSACK WA 102-B1
Rt#-544 EVERSON GOSHEN RD
EVERSON WA 102-B1
WHATCOM CO WA 102-B1
Rt#-544 KALE ST
EVERSON WA 102-B1
Rt#-544 MAIN ST
NOOKSACK WA 102-B1
Rt#-544 E POLE RD
EVERSON WA 102-B1
WHATCOM CO WA 102-B1
WHATCOM CO WA 158-D5
Rt#-546 E BADGER RD
WHATCOM CO WA 102-B1
WHATCOM CO WA 158-D3
Rt#-547 E BADGER RD
WHATCOM CO WA 102-B1
Rt#-547 FRONT ST
SUMAS WA 102-B1
Rt#-547 FRONT ST
WHATCOM CO WA 102-B1
Rt#-547 GARRISON RD
WHATCOM CO WA 102-B1
Rt#-547 HALVERSTICK RD
SUMAS WA 102-B1
WHATCOM CO WA 102-B1
Rt#-547 KENDALL RD
WHATCOM CO WA 102-B1
Rt#-547 REESE HILL RD
WHATCOM CO WA 102-B1
Rt#-547 ROCK RD
WHATCOM CO WA 102-B1
Rt#-547 SUMAS RD
WHATCOM CO WA 102-B1
Rt#-548 BLAINE RD
Birch Bay WA 158-B4
BLAINE WA 158-B3
WHATCOM CO WA 158-B3
Rt#-548 GRANDVIEW RD
Birch Bay WA 158-B5
WHATCOM CO WA 158-B5
Rt#-599 FRWY
TUKWILA WA 286-D7
TUKWILA WA 287-E7
TUKWILA WA 289-E1
Rt#-702 MCKENNA TANWAX
PIERCE CO WA 118-A1
Rt#-706 HIGHWAY
PIERCE CO WA 118-C1
PIERCE CO WA 185-A5
Rt#-706 MOUNTAIN HWY E
PIERCE CO WA 118-B1
Rt#-730 COLUMBIA RIVER HWY
UMATILLA CO OR 121-A3
WALLA WALLA CO WA 121-A3
Rt#-730 HIGHWAY
WALLA WALLA CO WA 121-B3
Rt#-821 CANYON RD
ELLENSBURG WA 241-B6
KITTITAS CO WA 241-B6
Rt#-821 HIGHWAY
KITTITAS CO WA 241-B7
KITTITAS CO WA 243-B1
YAKIMA CO WA 243-C4
Rt#-821 THRALL RD
KITTITAS CO WA 241-B7
Rt#-823 S 1ST ST
SELAH WA 243-B5
YAKIMA CO WA 243-B5
Rt#-823 HARRISON RD
YAKIMA CO WA 243-B5
Rt#-823 HIGHWAY
YAKIMA CO WA 243-B6
Rt#-823 E NACHES AV
SELAH WA 243-B5
Rt#-823 SELAH RD
YAKIMA CO WA 243-B6
Rt#-823 WENAS AV
SELAH WA 243-B5
YAKIMA CO WA 243-B5
Rt#-900 17TH AV NW
ISSAQUAH WA 175-D3
Rt#-900 S 2ND ST
RENTON WA 175-C5
Rt#-900 S 3RD ST
RENTON WA 175-C5
Rt#-900 BRONSON WY N
RENTON WA 175-C5
Rt#-900 HOUSER WY S
RENTON WA 175-C5
Rt#-900 MLK JR WY
KING WA 287-E6
KING WA 289-G1
KING CO WA 175-C5
SEATTLE WA 287-E6
TUKWILA WA 287-E6
TUKWILA WA 289-G1
Rt#-900 MILL AV S
RENTON WA 175-C5
Rt#-900 N PARK DR
RENTON WA 175-C4
Rt#-900 NE PARK DR
RENTON WA 175-C4
Rt#-900 SE RENTON ISSAQUAH RD
KING CO WA 175-D4
RENTON WA 175-C4
Rt#-900 RENTON ISSAQUAH RD SE
ISSAQUAH WA 175-D4
KING CO WA 175-D4
Rt#-900 NE SUNSET BLVD
RENTON WA 175-C4
Rt#-900 SW SUNSET BLVD
KING CO WA 175-C5
RENTON WA 175-C5
Rt#-900 SUNSET BLVD N
RENTON WA 175-C5
Rt#-902 W HALLETT RD
SPOKANE CO WA 246-A5
Rt#-902 HIGHWAY
MEDICAL LAKE WA 114-B2
SPOKANE CO WA 114-B2
SPOKANE CO WA 246-A5
Rt#-902 LEFEVRE ST
MEDICAL LAKE WA 114-B2
Rt#-902 MEDICAL LAKE RD
MEDICAL LAKE WA 114-B2
SPOKANE CO WA 114-B2
Rt#-902 S MEDICAL LAKE TYLER
MEDICAL LAKE WA 114-B2
Rt#-902 W SALNAVE RD
MEDICAL LAKE WA 114-B2
SPOKANE CO WA 114-B2
Rt#-903 2ND AV
KITTITAS CO WA 240-A1
Rt#-903 E FIRST ST
CLE ELUM WA 240-B2
Rt#-903 N FIRST ST
ROSLYN WA 240-A1
Rt#-903 S FIRST ST
ROSLYN WA 240-A1
Rt#-903 W FIRST ST
CLE ELUM WA 240-B2
Rt#-903 HIGHWAY
CLE ELUM WA 240-B2
KITTITAS CO WA 240-A1
Rt#-903 HIGHWAY
ROSLYN WA 240-A1
Rt#-903 W NEVADA AV
ROSLYN WA 240-A1
Rt#-903 SALMON LA SAC RD
KITTITAS CO WA 111-B3
KITTITAS CO WA 240-A1
Rt#-903 W SECOND ST
CLE ELUM WA 240-B2
Rt#-903 SECOND ST W
CLE ELUM WA 240-B2
Rt#-903 N SEVENTH ST
ROSLYN WA 240-A1
Rt#-903 STAFFORD AV
CLE ELUM WA 240-B2
Rt#-904 COLUMBIA BASIN HWY
CHENEY WA 246-A7
SPOKANE CO WA 246-A7
Rt#-904 FIRST ST
CHENEY WA 246-A7
Rt#-904 W FIRST ST
CHENEY WA 246-A7
Rt#-904 HIGHWAY
CHENEY WA 246-A7
SPOKANE CO WA 114-B2
SPOKANE CO WA 246-A6
Rt#-906 HIGHWAY
KING CO WA 111-A2
KITTITAS CO WA 111-A2
Rt#-908 NE 85TH ST
KIRKLAND WA 175-C1
Rt#-908 NE REDMOND WY
REDMOND WA 175-C1
Rt#-970 HIGHWAY
KITTITAS CO WA 240-D1
Rt#-970 SUNSET HWY
KITTITAS CO WA 240-B2
Rt#-971 NAVARRE COULEE RD
CHELAN CO WA 236-B3
U.S.-2 1 RD SE
DOUGLAS CO WA 112-C2
U.S.-2 2 1/2 RD NW
DOUGLAS CO WA 236-C7
WATERVILLE WA 236-C7
U.S.-2 6TH ST
NEWPORT WA 106-C3
U.S.-2 12 RD NE
DOUGLAS CO WA 112-C2
U.S.-2 W 14TH AV
AIRWAY HEIGHTS WA 246-A4
SPOKANE CO WA 246-A4
U.S.-2 15TH ST NW
East Wenatchee Bench WA 239-A4
U.S.-2 ALBANY RD
BONNER CO ID 107-A3
PRIEST RIVER ID 107-A3
U.S.-2 E BROADWAY ST
REARDAN WA 114-A2
U.S.-2 W BROADWAY ST
REARDAN WA 114-A2
U.S.-2 N BROWNE ST
SPOKANE WA 349-A9
U.S.-2 S BROWNE ST
SPOKANE WA 349-A10
U.S.-2 S CENTRAL AV
WATERVILLE WA 236-C7
U.S.-2 N CHELAN AV
WATERVILLE WA 236-C7
U.S.-2 E COZZA DR
SPOKANE WA 347-A14
U.S.-2 CROFT AV
GOLD BAR WA 110-C1
SNOHOMISH CO WA 110-C1
U.S.-2 N DIVISION ST
SPOKANE WA 346-J12
SPOKANE WA 347-A14
SPOKANE WA 349-A3
Town and Country WA 346-J12
Town and Country WA 347-A14
Town and Country WA 349-A3
U.S.-2 S DIVISION ST
SPOKANE WA 349-A9
U.S.-2 FRWY
CASHMERE WA 238-C2
CHELAN CO WA 238-C2
DOUGLAS CO WA 239-A3
East Wenatchee Bench WA 238-C2
East Wenatchee Bench WA 239-A3
EVERETT WA 265-J4
SNOHOMISH WA 265-J4
SNOHOMISH CO WA 171-D2
Sunnyslope WA 238-C2
U.S.-2 HIGHWAY
ALMIRA WA 237-D7
BONNER CO ID 106-C3
BONNER CO ID 107-A3
BONNER CO ID 244-A2
BOUNDARY CO ID 107-B1
CHELAN CO WA 111-B1
CHELAN CO WA 238-A1
COULEE CITY WA 113-A2
Country Homes WA 347-B10
CRESTON WA 113-C1
DAVENPORT WA 114-A2
DOUGLAS CO WA 112-C2
DOUGLAS CO WA 113-A2
DOUGLAS CO WA 236-B6
DOUGLAS CO WA 239-A1
DOVER ID 107-A3
DOVER ID 244-A2
Fairchild AFB WA 114-B2
Fairwood WA 347-C7
GRANT CO WA 113-A2
LEAVENWORTH WA 238-A1
LINCOLN CO MT 107-C2
LINCOLN CO WA 113-C1
LINCOLN CO WA 114-A2
LINCOLN CO WA 237-D7
MOYIE SPRINGS ID 107-B1
NEWPORT ID 106-C3
PEND OREILLE CO WA 106-C3
SANDPOINT ID 244-A2
SPOKANE WA 346-J12
SPOKANE WA 347-A11
SPOKANE CO WA 106-C3
SPOKANE CO WA 114-C1
SPOKANE CO WA 246-A4
SPOKANE CO WA 347-F1

PNW
INDEX

U.S.-2 HIGHWAY STREET INDEX U.S.-95 MEADOW CREEK RD 417

STREET
City State Page-Grid

U.S.-2 HIGHWAY
SPOKANE CO WA 348-A11
TROY MT 107-C2
WATERVILLE WA 236-C7
WILBUR WA 113-B1
U.S.-2 E MAIN AV
LINCOLN CO WA 113-B1
WILBUR WA 113-B1
U.S.-2 W MAIN AV
WILBUR WA 113-B1
U.S.-2 MISSOULA AV
LINCOLN CO MT 107-C2
TROY MT 107-C2
U.S.-2 E MISSOULA AV
TROY MT 107-C2
U.S.-2 MORGAN ST
DAVENPORT WA 114-A2
LINCOLN CO WA 114-A2
U.S.-2 N NEWPORT HWY
Fairwood WA 347-B9
SPOKANE CO WA 347-E5
U.S.-2 PINE ST
SANDPOINT ID 244-A2
U.S.-2 E POPLAR ST
DOUGLAS CO WA 236-C7
WATERVILLE WA 236-C7
U.S.-2 N RUBY ST
SPOKANE WA 349-A6
U.S.-2 SAND HILL RD
BOUNDARY CO ID 107-B1
U.S.-2 W SPOKANE FALLS BLVD
SPOKANE WA 349-A9
U.S.-2 STEVENS PASS HWY
GOLD BAR WA 110-C1
KING CO WA 111-A1
MONROE WA 110-C1
SNOHOMISH WA 171-D3
SNOHOMISH CO WA 110-C1
SNOHOMISH CO WA 111-A1
SNOHOMISH CO WA 171-D3
SULTAN WA 110-C1
U.S.-2 NE STEVENS PASS HWY
KING CO WA 111-A1
SKYKOMISH WA 111-A1
U.S.-2 STEVENS PASS RD
SNOHOMISH CO WA 171-D2
U.S.-2 SUNSET FRWY
DOUGLAS CO WA 238-D3
East Wenatchee Bench WA 238-D3
Sunnyslope WA 238-D3
U.S.-2 W SUNSET HWY
AIRWAY HEIGHTS WA 246-A4
SPOKANE CO WA 246-A4
SPOKANE CO WA 348-A12
U.S.-2 WALNUT ST
NEWPORT ID 106-C3
NEWPORT WA 106-C3
U.S.-2 N WASHINGTON AV
NEWPORT WA 106-C3
U.S.-2 S WASHINGTON AV
NEWPORT WA 106-C3
U.S.-2 WATSON ST
CRESTON WA 113-C1
U.S.-11 HIGHWAY
CLEARWATER CO ID 123-C2
LEWIS CO ID 123-C2
U.S.-12 1ST ST
LEWISTON ID 250-B4
U.S.-12 5TH ST
LEWISTON ID 250-B4
U.S.-12 18TH ST
LEWISTON ID 250-C4
U.S.-12 183RD AV SW
Rochester WA 184-A3
THURSTON CO WA 184-A3
U.S.-12 ARROW AV
NEZ PERCE CO ID 123-A2
U.S.-12 BRIDGE ST
CLARKSTON WA 250-B4
LEWISTON ID 250-B4
U.S.-12 COPPEI AV
WAITSBURG WA 122-A2
U.S.-12 DIKE BYPS
LEWISTON ID 250-B4
U.S.-12 D ST
LEWISTON ID 250-B4
U.S.-12 FRWY
PASCO WA 343-H5
U.S.-12 HIGHWAY
ASOTIN CO WA 122-C2
ASOTIN CO WA 250-A4
Burbank WA 121-A3
Central Park WA 178-C7
CLEARWATER CO ID 123-B2
COLUMBIA CO WA 122-A2
DAYTON WA 122-A2
ELMA WA 179-B7
FRANKLIN CO WA 121-A3
GARFIELD CO WA 122-A2
Walla Walla West WA 344-H7
Grand Mound WA 184-B4
GRAYS HARBOR CO WA 117-B1
GRAYS HARBOR CO WA 178-B7
GRAYS HARBOR CO WA 184-A3
IDAHO CO ID 123-C2
KAMIAH ID 123-C2
LEWIS CO ID 123-C2
LEWIS CO WA 118-C2
LEWIS CO WA 119-A1
LEWIS CO WA 185-D6
LEWIS CO WA 187-C2
LEWISTON ID 250-C4
MONTESANO WA 178-D7
MORTON WA 118-B2
MOSSYROCK WA 118-A2
NACHES WA 119-C1
NACHES WA 243-A4
NEZ PERCE CO ID 123-B2
NEZ PERCE CO ID 250-D3
OAKVILLE WA 117-B1
OROFINO ID 123-C2
PASCO WA 121-A3
PASCO WA 343-H5
POMEROY WA 122-B2
Rochester WA 184-A3
THURSTON CO WA 184-A3
WAITSBURG WA 122-A2
WALLA WALLA WA 344-J7
U.S.-12 HIGHWAY
WALLA WALLA WA 345-J4
WALLA WALLA CO WA 121-A3
WALLA WALLA CO WA 122-A2
WALLA WALLA CO WA 344-A9
WALLA WALLA CO WA 345-J3
YAKIMA WA 243-B6
YAKIMA CO WA 119-C1
YAKIMA CO WA 243-A4
U.S.-12 INLAND EMPIRE HWY
ASOTIN CO WA 250-B4
Walla Walla West WA 344-D7
WALLA WALLA CO WA 344-D7
U.S.-12 MAIN ST
DAYTON WA 122-B2
LEWISTON ID 250-C4
POMEROY WA 122-B2
U.S.-12 E MAIN ST
COLUMBIA CO WA 122-A2
DAYTON WA 122-A2
LEWISTON ID 250-C4
U.S.-12 W MAIN ST
DAYTON WA 122-A2
U.S.-12 NATIONAL PARK HWY
LEWIS CO WA 118-B2
MORTON WA 118-B2
U.S.-12 PINE ST
OAKVILLE WA 117-B1
U.S.-12 PRESTON AV
WAITSBURG WA 122-A2
U.S.-12 WISHKAH ST
ABERDEEN WA 178-B7
GRAYS HARBOR CO WA 178-B7
U.S.-14 LEWIS AND CLARK FRWY
VANCOUVER WA 305-G6
VANCOUVER WA 306-A6
VANCOUVER WA 307-E7
VANCOUVER WA 311-G1
U.S.-20 2ND ST
BENTON CO OR 327-H9
CORVALLIS OR 327-H9
U.S.-20 3RD ST W
CORVALLIS OR 327-G10
U.S.-20 NE 3RD ST
BEND OR 332-F4
U.S.-20 4TH ST W
CORVALLIS OR 327-H9
U.S.-20 ALBANY-CORVALLIS HWY
ALBANY OR 207-B5
ALBANY OR 326-A7
BENTON CO OR 207-B5
BENTON CO OR 326-A7
BENTON CO OR 327-J8
CORVALLIS OR 207-B5
CORVALLIS OR 327-J8
U.S.-20 A ST E
VALE OR 139-A3
U.S.-20 A ST W
VALE OR 139-A3
U.S.-20 BROADWAY AV
ADA CO ID 253-D3
BOISE ID 253-D3
U.S.-20 N BROADWAY AV
BURNS OR 145-B1
U.S.-20 CAROLINA ST
LEBANON OR 133-C1
U.S.-20 CASCADE ST
DESCHUTES CO OR 211-D5
SISTERS OR 211-D5
U.S.-20 CENTRAL OREGON HWY
BEND OR 217-C2
BEND OR 332-G7
BURNS OR 145-A1
DESCHUTES CO OR 135-B3
DESCHUTES CO OR 143-C1
DESCHUTES CO OR 144-A1
DESCHUTES CO OR 217-C2
DESCHUTES CO OR 332-G7
HARNEY CO OR 138-A3
HARNEY CO OR 144-B1
HARNEY CO OR 145-A1
HARNEY CO OR 146-A1
HINES OR 145-A1
LAKE CO OR 144-A1
MALHEUR CO OR 138-C3
MALHEUR CO OR 139-A3
MALHEUR CO OR 146-A1
NYSSA OR 139-A3
VALE OR 138-C3
VALE OR 139-A3
U.S.-20 E CHINDEN BLVD
ADA CO ID 253-B2
BOISE ID 253-B2
EAGLE ID 253-B2
GARDEN CITY ID 253-C2
U.S.-20 W CHINDEN BLVD
ADA CO ID 147-C1
ADA CO ID 253-A2
U.S.-20 CORVALLIS-NEWPORT HWY
BENTON CO OR 133-A1
CORVALLIS OR 133-A1
CORVALLIS OR 327-E11
LINCOLN CO OR 133-A1
LINCOLN CO OR 206-B4
NEWPORT OR 206-B4
PHILOMATH OR 133-A1
TOLEDO OR 206-B4
U.S.-20 NW DESCHUTES PL
BEND OR 332-E6
U.S.-20 DIVISION ST
BEND OR 332-F6
U.S.-20 ELGIN AV
CANYON CO ID 147-B1
NOTUS ID 147-B1
U.S.-20 ELLSWORTH ST
ALBANY OR 326-C8
U.S.-20 FRANKLIN RD
CALDWELL ID 147-B1
CANYON CO ID 147-B1
U.S.-20 FRONT ST
BOISE ID 253-C2
U.S.-20 NE GREENWOOD AV
BEND OR 332-F7
U.S.-20 NW GREENWOOD AV
BEND OR 332-E7
U.S.-20 HIGHWAY
CANYON CO ID 139-A3
CANYON CO ID 147-B1
LINCOLN CO OR 206-C4
MALHEUR CO OR 139-A3
TOLEDO OR 206-C4
VALE OR 139-A3
U.S.-20 LYON ST
ALBANY OR 326-C8
U.S.-20 MAIN ST
BENTON CO OR 133-B1
LEBANON OR 133-C1
LINN CO OR 133-C1
MALHEUR CO OR 139-A3
NYSSA OR 139-A3
PHILOMATH OR 133-B1
SWEET HOME OR 133-C2
U.S.-20 MCKENZIE-BEND HWY
BEND OR 332-F1
DESCHUTES CO OR 211-D5
DESCHUTES CO OR 212-A6
DESCHUTES CO OR 217-C1
DESCHUTES CO OR 332-F1
U.S.-20 W MONROE ST
BURNS OR 145-B1
U.S.-20 E MYRTLE ST
BOISE ID 253-C3
U.S.-20 W MYRTLE ST
BOISE ID 253-C3
U.S.-20 OLIVE ST
NEWPORT OR 206-B4
U.S.-20 E OLIVE ST
NEWPORT OR 206-B4
U.S.-20 OREGON CENTRAL HWY
CANYON CO ID 139-A3
U.S.-20 PARK ST
LEBANON OR 133-C1
U.S.-20 PHILOMATH BLVD
BENTON CO OR 133-B1
BENTON CO OR 327-A12
CORVALLIS OR 133-B1
CORVALLIS OR 327-A12
U.S.-20 NE REVERE AV
BEND OR 332-E6
U.S.-20 SANTIAM HWY
ALBANY OR 326-F8
DESCHUTES CO OR 211-C3
JEFFERSON CO OR 211-A2
LINN CO OR 133-C1
LINN CO OR 134-A2
LINN CO OR 207-D5
LINN CO OR 211-A2
LINN CO OR 326-F8
SISTERS OR 211-C3
SWEET HOME OR 133-C2
SWEET HOME OR 134-A2
U.S.-20 THE DALLES-CALIF HWY
BEND OR 332-F3
DESCHUTES CO OR 332-F3
U.S.-20 VALE-WEST HWY
VALE OR 139-A3
U.S.-20 NW WALL ST
BEND OR 332-E6
U.S.-20 WASHINGTON ST E
VALE OR 139-A3
U.S.-20 WASHINGTON ST W
VALE OR 139-A3
U.S.-26 NW 4TH ST
MADRAS OR 208-C5
U.S.-26 SW 4TH ST
MADRAS OR 208-C5
U.S.-26 5TH ST
MADRAS OR 208-C5
U.S.-26 12TH ST N
MALHEUR CO OR 139-A3
VALE OR 139-A3
U.S.-26 SW CANYON RD
PORTLAND OR 312-C6
U.S.-26 FRANKLIN AV
DAYVILLE OR 136-C2
GRANT CO OR 136-C2
U.S.-26 SW FRONT AV
PORTLAND OR 317-F1
U.S.-26 FRONT ST
GRANT CO OR 137-B2
PRAIRIE CITY OR 137-B2
U.S.-26 HIGHWAY
PORTLAND OR 317-F1
U.S.-26 JOHN DAY HWY
BAKER CO OR 137-C2
BAKER CO OR 138-A2
DAYVILLE OR 136-C1
GRANT CO OR 136-C1
GRANT CO OR 137-C2
JOHN DAY OR 137-C2
MALHEUR CO OR 138-B2
MALHEUR CO OR 139-A3
MOUNT VERNON OR 137-C2
UNITY OR 138-A2
VALE OR 139-A3
U.S.-26 SE MADRAS-PRINVLL HWY
JEFFERSON CO OR 208-C7
JEFFERSON CO OR 213-B2
U.S.-26 SW MADRAS-PRINVLL HWY
JEFFERSON CO OR 208-C6
U.S.-26 MADRAS-PRINEVILLE HWY
CROOK CO OR 213-C3
JEFFERSON CO OR 213-C3
PRINEVILLE OR 213-C3
U.S.-26 E MAIN ST
GRANT CO OR 137-B2
JOHN DAY OR 137-B2
U.S.-26 W MAIN ST
MOUNT VERNON OR 137-A2
U.S.-26 MOUNT HOOD HWY
CLACKAMAS CO OR 200-C3
CLACKAMAS CO OR 201-B4
CLACKAMAS CO OR 202-A6
GRESHAM OR 200-C3
MULTNOMAH CO OR 200-C3
SANDY OR 200-C3
U.S.-26 SE MOUNT HOOD HWY
MULTNOMAH CO OR 200-A2
PORTLAND OR 200-A2
U.S.-26 OCHOCO HWY
CROOK CO OR 135-C2
CROOK CO OR 136-A2
CROOK CO OR 213-D5
GRANT CO OR 136-B1
Mitchell OR 136-B1
PRINEVILLE OR 213-D5
WHEELER CO OR 136-B1
U.S.-26 PIONEER BLVD
SANDY OR 200-C4
U.S.-26 E POWELL BLVD
GRESHAM OR 200-B2
U.S.-26 SE POWELL BLVD
GRESHAM OR 200-A2
PORTLAND OR 200-A2
PORTLAND OR 317-H1
PORTLAND OR 318-B2
PORTLAND OR 319-H2
U.S.-26 W POWELL BLVD
GRESHAM OR 200-A2
U.S.-26 PROCTOR BLVD
SANDY OR 200-C4
U.S.-26 SUNSET HWY
BEAVERTON OR 199-A1
CLATSOP CO OR 117-A3
CLATSOP CO OR 125-A1
CLATSOP CO OR 188-C7
COLUMBIA CO OR 125-A1
HILLSBORO OR 125-C1
HILLSBORO OR 192-A7
HILLSBORO OR 199-A1
MULTNOMAH OR 312-B7
MULTNOMAH CO OR 199-A1
NORTH PLAINS OR 125-C1
PORTLAND OR 199-A1
PORTLAND OR 312-B7
PORTLAND OR 316-B1
TILLAMOOK CO OR 125-A1
WASHINGTON CO OR 125-C1
WASHINGTON CO OR 192-A7
WASHINGTON CO OR 199-A1
U.S.-26 THE DALLES-CALIF HWY
JEFFERSON CO OR 208-C6
MADRAS OR 208-C5
U.S.-26 WARM SPRINGS HWY
CLACKAMAS CO OR 202-A7
JEFFERSON CO OR 135-A1
JEFFERSON CO OR 208-B3
MADRAS OR 208-B3
Warm Springs OR 135-A1
Warm Springs OR 208-A2
WASCO CO OR 126-C3
WASCO CO OR 127-A3
WASCO CO OR 135-A1
WASCO CO OR 202-A7
U.S.-30 2ND ST S
NAMPA ID 147-B1
U.S.-30 3RD ST S
NAMPA ID 147-B1
U.S.-30 8TH ST
ASTORIA OR 300-C5
U.S.-30 10TH ST
BAKER CITY OR 138-B1
U.S.-30 11TH AV
NAMPA ID 147-B1
U.S.-30 11TH AV N
NAMPA ID 147-C1
U.S.-30 ADAMS AV
LA GRANDE OR 130-A2
U.S.-30 AUBURN AV
BAKER CITY OR 138-B1
U.S.-30 BLAINE ST
CALDWELL ID 147-B1
U.S.-30 NW BRIDGE AV
PORTLAND OR 192-B7
U.S.-30 BRIDGE ST
BAKER CITY OR 138-B1
U.S.-30 BROADWAY ST
BAKER CITY OR 138-B1
U.S.-30 E B ST
RAINIER OR 189-C4
U.S.-30 W B ST
RAINIER OR 189-C4
U.S.-30 BUTTON BRIDGE RD
HOOD RIVER CO OR 195-D5
U.S.-30 CALDWELL BLVD
CANYON CO ID 147-B1
NAMPA ID 147-B1
U.S.-30 CASCADE AV
HOOD RIVER OR 195-C5
HOOD RIVER CO OR 195-C5
U.S.-30 CASCADE LOCKS HWY
CASCADE LOCKS OR 194-D6
HOOD RIVER CO OR 194-D6
U.S.-30 CENTENNIAL WY
CALDWELL ID 147-B1
U.S.-30 CLEVELAND BLVD
CALDWELL ID 147-B1
CANYON CO ID 147-B1
U.S.-30 NE COLUMBIA BLVD
PORTLAND OR 315-H1
U.S.-30 COLUMBIA RIVER HWY
ASTORIA OR 188-D1
ASTORIA OR 300-E5
CLATSKANIE OR 117-B3
CLATSOP CO OR 188-D1
COLUMBIA CITY OR 192-A3
COLUMBIA CO OR 117-B3
COLUMBIA CO OR 189-A4
COLUMBIA CO OR 192-A3
COLUMBIA CO OR 302-A14
RAINIER OR 189-A4
SAINT HELENS OR 192-A3
SCAPPOOSE OR 192-A3
U.S.-30 COMMERCIAL ST
ASTORIA OR 300-C5
U.S.-30 CO RD 900
PENDLETON OR 129-B1
UMATILLA CO OR 129-B1
U.S.-30 NW COURT AV
PENDLETON OR 129-B1
U.S.-30 SE COURT AV
PENDLETON OR 129-B1
U.S.-30 SW COURT AV
PENDLETON OR 129-B1
U.S.-30 SE DORION AV
PENDLETON OR 129-B1
U.S.-30 SW DORION AV
PENDLETON OR 129-B1
U.S.-30 ELM ST
BAKER CITY OR 138-B1
U.S.-30 FRONT ST
HOOD RIVER OR 195-D5
U.S.-30 GARRITY BLVD
CANYON CO ID 147-C1
NAMPA ID 147-C1
U.S.-30 E H AV
LA GRANDE OR 130-A2
U.S.-30 HIGHWAY
HOOD RIVER OR 195-D5
HOOD RIVER CO OR 195-C5
MALHEUR CO OR 139-A3
NEW PLYMOUTH ID 139-B3
PAYETTE CO ID 139-B3
U.S.-30 HUNTINGTON HWY
BAKER CO OR 138-C2
BAKER CO OR 139-A2
HUNTINGTON OR 138-C2
MALHEUR CO OR 139-A2
U.S.-30 IDAHO AV
ONTARIO OR 139-A3
U.S.-30 NE KILLINGSWORTH ST
PORTLAND OR 311-F7
U.S.-30 LA GRANDE-BAKER HWY
BAKER CITY OR 138-B1
BAKER CO OR 130-A3
BAKER CO OR 138-B1
HAINES OR 130-A3
LA GRANDE OR 130-A3
UNION CO OR 130-A3
U.S.-30 N LOMBARD ST
PORTLAND OR 192-B7
PORTLAND OR 308-B4
PORTLAND OR 309-E5
U.S.-30 NE LOMBARD ST
PORTLAND OR 309-G5
PORTLAND OR 310-B6
U.S.-30 MAIN ST
BAKER CITY OR 138-B1
U.S.-30 MARINE DR
ASTORIA OR 300-C5
U.S.-30 W MARINE DR
ASTORIA OR 300-B4
U.S.-30 MOSIER-THE DALLES HWY
MOSIER OR 196-A5
THE DALLES OR 196-A5
WASCO CO OR 196-A5
U.S.-30 OAK ST
HOOD RIVER OR 195-C5
U.S.-30 OLDS FRRY-ONTARIO HWY
MALHEUR CO OR 139-A3
ONTARIO OR 139-A3
U.S.-30 OREGON ST
MALHEUR CO OR 139-A3
ONTARIO OR 139-A3
U.S.-30 N OREGON ST
ONTARIO OR 139-A3
U.S.-30 PENDLETON HWY
UMATILLA CO OR 129-B1
U.S.-30 NW PENDLETON HWY
PENDLETON OR 129-B1
UMATILLA CO OR 129-B1
U.S.-30 N PHILADELPHIA AV
PORTLAND OR 192-B7
U.S.-30 PLYMOUTH AV
NEW PLYMOUTH ID 139-B3
U.S.-30 NE PORTLAND HWY
PORTLAND OR 310-D6
PORTLAND OR 311-E7
U.S.-30 NW SAINT HELENS RD
MULTNOMAH CO OR 192-A5
PORTLAND OR 192-A5
PORTLAND OR 199-B1
U.S.-30 NE SANDY BLVD
FAIRVIEW OR 200-A1
GRESHAM OR 200-A1
PORTLAND OR 200-A1
PORTLAND OR 315-J1
WOOD VILLAGE OR 200-A1
U.S.-30 SOUTHEAST AV
NEW PLYMOUTH ID 139-B3
PAYETTE CO ID 139-B3
U.S.-30 STATE AV
HOOD RIVER OR 195-D5
HOOD RIVER CO OR 195-D5
U.S.-30 WASHINGTON ST E
HUNTINGTON OR 138-C2
U.S.-30 WASHINGTON ST W
HUNTINGTON OR 138-C2
U.S.-30 WESTGATE AV
PENDLETON OR 129-B1
U.S.-30 NW YEON AV
PORTLAND OR 199-B1
PORTLAND OR 312-A1
U.S.-95 N 1ST AV
SANDPOINT ID 244-A2
U.S.-95 S 1ST AV
SANDPOINT ID 244-A2
U.S.-95 S 3RD ST
FRUITLAND ID 139-A3
U.S.-95 5TH AV
SANDPOINT ID 244-A2
U.S.-95 N 5TH AV
SANDPOINT ID 244-A2
U.S.-95 5TH ST
CANYON CO ID 147-A1
WILDER ID 147-A1
U.S.-95 7TH ST
WEISER ID 139-A2
U.S.-95 E 7TH ST
WEISER ID 139-A2
U.S.-95 S 7TH ST
PAYETTE ID 139-A3
U.S.-95 N 16TH ST
PAYETTE ID 139-A3
U.S.-95 S 16TH ST
PAYETTE ID 139-A3
U.S.-95 A
COTTONWOOD ID 123-C3
GRANGEVILLE ID 123-C3
IDAHO CO ID 123-B3
U.S.-95 CEDAR ST
SANDPOINT ID 244-A2
U.S.-95 CEMETERY RD
OWYHEE CO ID 147-B1
U.S.-95 CENTRAL BLVD
CAMBRIDGE ID 139-B1
WASHINGTON CO ID 139-B1
U.S.-95 CLARK ST
LEWIS CO ID 123-B2
WINCHESTER ID 123-B2
U.S.-95 E COEUR D'ALENE AV
BENEWAH CO ID 115-A3
TENSED ID 115-A3
U.S.-95 DARTMOUTH ST
ADAMS CO ID 139-C1
COUNCIL ID 139-C1
U.S.-95 W ELDER RD
KOOTENAI CO ID 247-D5
U.S.-95 F ST
WORLEY ID 115-A2
U.S.-95 E GROVE ST
CANYON CO ID 139-A3
PARMA ID 139-A3
U.S.-95 W GROVE ST
PARMA ID 139-A3
U.S.-95 HIGHWAY
ADAMS CO ID 131-C2
ADAMS CO ID 139-C1
ADAMS CO ID 251-A1
ATHOL ID 245-B2
BENEWAH CO ID 115-A2
BONNER CO ID 107-B2
BONNER CO ID 244-A1
BONNER CO ID 245-B1
BONNERS FERRY ID 107-B1
CANYON CO ID 139-A3
CANYON CO ID 147-A1
COEUR D'ALENE ID 355-D2
COUNCIL ID 139-C1
CRAIGMONT ID 123-B2
CULDESAC ID 123-B2
FRUITLAND ID 139-A3
GRANGEVILLE ID 123-C3
HAYDEN ID 245-A5
HAYDEN ID 355-D1
HOMEDALE ID 147-A1
IDAHO CO ID 123-B3
IDAHO CO ID 131-C1
IDAHO CO ID 251-A1
KOOTENAI CO ID 115-A2
KOOTENAI CO ID 245-B1
KOOTENAI CO ID 247-D4
KOOTENAI CO ID 354-J13
KOOTENAI CO ID 355-D2
LAPWAI ID 123-A2
LATAH CO ID 115-A3
LATAH CO ID 249-D1
LATAH CO ID 250-C1
LEWIS CO ID 123-B2
LEWISTON ID 250-C4
MALHEUR CO OR 139-A2
MIDVALE ID 139-B1
MOSCOW ID 249-C5
NEZ PERCE CO ID 123-A2
NEZ PERCE CO ID 250-C1
OWYHEE CO ID 147-A1
PAYETTE ID 139-A3
PAYETTE CO ID 139-A2
PLUMMER ID 115-A2
PONDERAY ID 244-A1
RIGGINS ID 131-C2
SANDPOINT ID 244-A2
WASHINGTON CO ID 139-B1
WEISER ID 139-A2
WILDER ID 147-A1
WINCHESTER ID 123-B2
WORLEY ID 115-A2
U.S.-95 E IDAHO AV
HOMEDALE ID 147-A1
U.S.-95 IDAHO-OREGN-NVADA HWY
HUMBOLDT CO NV 154-B3
JORDAN VALLEY OR 147-A3
MALHEUR CO OR 146-B3
MALHEUR CO OR 147-A2
MALHEUR CO OR 154-B1
OWYHEE CO ID 147-A2
U.S.-95 W IDAHO ST
WEISER ID 139-A2
U.S.-95 ILLINOIS AV
COUNCIL ID 139-C1
U.S.-95 N JACKSON ST
MOSCOW ID 249-C5
U.S.-95 S JACKSON ST
MOSCOW ID 249-C5
U.S.-95 JOSEPH AV
WINCHESTER ID 123-B2
U.S.-95 LAUER CROSSING RD
IDAHO CO ID 123-B3
U.S.-95 LINCOLN WY
COEUR D'ALENE ID 355-D8
U.S.-95 LITTLE WEISER RD
ADAMS CO ID 139-B1
U.S.-95 MAIN ST
BONNERS FERRY ID 107-B2
FERDINAND ID 123-B3
HOMEDALE ID 147-A1
IDAHO CO ID 123-B3
U.S.-95 E MAIN ST
WEISER ID 139-A2
U.S.-95 N MAIN ST
LATAH CO ID 249-C4
MOSCOW ID 249-C5
U.S.-95 S MAIN ST
BONNERS FERRY ID 107-B2
MOSCOW ID 249-C5
U.S.-95 W MAIN ST
WEISER ID 139-A2
U.S.-95 MARX ST
IDAHO CO ID 131-C2
RIGGINS ID 131-C2
U.S.-95 MEADOW CREEK RD
IDAHO CO ID 123-B3

PNW
INDEX

POINTS OF INTEREST

PNW

INDEX

PNW

INDEX

424 CAMPGROUNDS POINTS OF INTEREST CAMPGROUNDS

FEATURE NAME	City State	Page-Grid
KOA PORT ANGELES/SEQUIM	OBRIEN RD, CLALLAM CO WA	165 - D6
KOA SEATTLE/TACOMA	5801 S 212TH ST, KENT WA	291 - G5
KOA SISTERS/BEND	67667 MCKENZIE-BEND HWY, DESCHUTES CO OR	212 - A5
KOA SPOKANE	3025 N BARKER RD, SPOKANE CO WA	351 - E5
KOA SWEET HOME/FOSTER LAKE	6191 SANTIAM HWY, LINN CO OR	134 - A2
KOA VANCOUVER	40TH AV & HWY 99A, DISTRICT OF SURREY BC	158 - A1
KOA VANTAGE	VANTAGE HWY, KITTITAS CO WA	120 - B1
KOA VICTORIA WEST	TRANS CANADA HWY, BC	159 - A5
KOA WALDPORT/ALSEA BAY	OREGON COAST HWY, LINCOLN CO OR	328 - D3
KOA YAKIMA	1500 KEYS RD, YAKIMA CO WA	243 - C7
KULSHAN CAMPGROUND	WELKER PEAK, WHATCOM CO WA	102 - C2
KUM BACK SHELTER	BURNT PEAK, SKAMANIA CO WA	118 - C3
LADD CREEK CAMPGROUND	BULL RUN LAKE, HOOD RIVER CO OR	202 - A3
LAFFERTY CAMPGROUND	NFD RD 2, ADAMS CO ID	131 - B3
LAGOON CAMPGROUND	OFF OREGON COAST HWY, LANE CO OR	214 - A5
LAKE CREEK CAMPGROUND	POE MOUNTAIN, CHELAN CO WA	111 - B1
LAKE CREEK CAMPGROUND	SILVER FALLS, CHELAN CO WA	111 - C1
LAKE ELLEN CAMPGROUND	BANGS MOUNTAIN, FERRY CO WA	105 - C2
LAKE FORK CAMPGROUND	NORTH PINE CREEK RD, BAKER CO OR	131 - A3
LAKE IN THE WOODS CAMPGROUND	QUARTZ MOUNTAIN, DOUGLAS CO OR	141 - C2
LAKE LEO CAMPGROUND	IONE, PEND OREILLE CO WA	106 - B2
LAKE LOVELY WATER REC AREA CAMPGROUND	LK LOVELY WATER REC AREA, BC	93 - C2
LAKE MARIE CAMPGROUND	WINCHESTER BAY, DOUGLAS CO OR	218 - C2
LAKE SELMAC CAMPGROUND	LAKESHORE DR, JOSEPHINE CO OR	233 - B2
LAKE THOMAS CAMPGROUND	LAKE GILLETTE, STEVENS CO WA	106 - B2
LAKEVIEW PARK CAMPGROUND	HIGHWAY 18, BC	100 - C1
LAKE WENATCHEE CAMPGROUND	LAKE WENATCHEE, CHELAN CO WA	111 - C1
LANE CREEK CAMPGROUND	UKIAH-HILGARD HWY, UMATILLA CO OR	129 - B3
LARCH LAKE CAMPGROUND	SASKA PEAK, CHELAN CO WA	103 - C3
LAST CHANCE CAMPGROUND	GOOSE CREEK PARK RD, ADAMS CO ID	251 - B3
LATGOWE COVE CAMPGROUND	SQUAW LAKES, JACKSON CO OR	149 - B2
LAVA CAMPGROUND	HAMNER BUTTE, KLAMATH CO OR	142 - C1
LAVA CAST FOREST CAMPGROUND	LAVA CAST FOREST, DESCHUTES CO OR	217 - C7
LAVA FLOW CAMPGROUND	HAMNER BUTTE, DESCHUTES CO OR	142 - C1
LAVA ISLAND CAMPGROUND	BENHAM FALLS, DESCHUTES CO OR	217 - B4
LAVA ISLAND SHELTER	BENHAM FALLS, DESCHUTES CO OR	217 - A4
LAVA ISLAND SHELTER (PREHISTORIC)	BENHAM FALLS, DESCHUTES CO OR	217 - B4
LAVA LAKE CAMPGROUND	LAVA LAKE RD, DESCHUTES CO OR	216 - B5
LA WIS WIS CAMPGROUND	OHANAPECOSH HOT SPRINGS, LEWIS CO WA	185 - D7
LEADER LAKE CAMPGROUND	MALOTT, OKANOGAN CO WA	104 - C3
LEE THOMAS CAMPGROUND	LEE THOMAS CROSSING, LAKE CO OR	151 - C1
LELAND LAKE CAMPGROUND	CENTER, JEFFERSON CO WA	109 - C1
LEMITI CAMPGROUND	PINHEAD BUTTES, CLACKAMAS CO OR	126 - C3
LEMOLO FALLS CAMPGROUND	LEMOLO LAKE, DOUGLAS CO OR	223 - B2
LEMOLO TWO FOREBAY CAMPGROUND	TOKETEE FALLS, DOUGLAS CO OR	222 - D3
LENA CREEK CAMPGROUND	NFD RD 25, MASON CO WA	173 - A2
LENA LAKE CAMPGROUND	MOUNT WASHINGTON, JEFFERSON CO WA	173 - A2
LEWIS CAMP	FISH MOUNTAIN, DOUGLAS CO OR	226 - D1
LEWIS RIVER CAMPGROUND	QUARTZ CREEK BUTTE, SKAMANIA CO WA	118 - C3
LICK CREEK CAMPGROUND	WALLOWA MOUNTAIN RD, WALLOWA CO OR	131 - A3
LIGHTING CREEK CAMPGROUND	HOZOMEEN MOUNTAIN, WHATCOM CO WA	103 - B1
LILLIAN SHELTER	HURRICANE HILL, CLALLAM CO WA	109 - B1
LILLIWAUP CREEK CAMPGROUND	NFD RD 24, MASON CO WA	173 - A4
LINDSAY CAMPGROUND	OLD SCAB MOUNTAIN, YAKIMA CO WA	119 - B1
LINNEY CREEK CAMPGROUND	WOLF PEAK, CLACKAMAS CO OR	201 - D7
LION ROCK SPRING CAMPGROUND	BLEWETT PASS, KITTITAS CO WA	241 - B1
LITTLE BADGER CAMPGROUND	FRIEND, WASCO CO OR	127 - A2
LITTLE BEAVER CAMPGROUND	HOZOMEEN MOUNTAIN, WHATCOM CO WA	103 - B1
LITTLE BLANKET SHELTER	OFF WINBERRY CREEK RD, LANE CO OR	134 - A3
LITTLE BOULDER CAMPGROUND	BOVILL, LATAH CO ID	123 - B1
LITTLE CHILLIWACK SHELTER	COPPER MOUNTAIN, WHATCOM CO WA	103 - A1
LITTLE CRANE CAMPGROUND	NFD RD 16, GRANT CO OR	137 - C2
LITTLE CRATER CAMPGROUND	NEWBERRY CRATER RD, DESCHUTES CO OR	143 - B1
LITTLE CRATER LAKE CAMPGROUND	WAPINITIA PASS, CLACKAMAS CO OR	126 - C3
LITTLE CULTUS CAMPGROUND	OFF LAVA LAKE RD, DESCHUTES CO OR	134 - C3
LITTLE DESCHUTES CAMPGROUND	ODELL BUTTE, KLAMATH CO OR	142 - C2
LITTLE FAN CREEK CAMPGROUND	BULL OF THE WOODS, CLACKAMAS CO OR	126 - B3
LITTLE FAWN CAMPGROUND	OFF CASCADE LAKES HWY, DESCHUTES CO OR	216 - A4
LITTLE FISH SHELTER	SKAGIT PEAK, WHATCOM CO WA	103 - B1
LITTLE GOOSE CAMPGROUND	SLEEPING BEAUTY, SKAMANIA CO WA	118 - C3
LITTLE LAVA LAKE CAMPGROUND	OFF LAVA LAKE RD, DESCHUTES CO OR	216 - B5
LITTLE NACHES CAMPGROUND	CLIFFDELL, YAKIMA CO WA	119 - B1
LITTLE QUALICUM FALL CAMPGROUND	HWY 4, BC	92 - B3
LITTLE REDWOOD CAMPGROUND	BOSLEY BUTTE, CURRY CO OR	148 - B2
LITTLE SODA SPRINGS CAMPGROUND	STABLER, SKAMANIA CO WA	194 - C2
LITTLE SUMMIT CAMPGROUND	OFF DEER RD, WHEELER CO OR	136 - B2
LOBSTER CREEK CAMPGROUND	QUOSATANA BUTTE, CURRY CO OR	228 - B4
LOCKABY CAMPGROUND	BEDFORD POINT, CLACKAMAS CO OR	126 - B3
LODGEPOLE CAMPGROUND	NORSE PEAK, YAKIMA CO WA	119 - A1
LODGEPOLE CAMPGROUND	OREGON COAST HWY, LANE CO OR	214 - A5
LOFTON RESERVOIR CAMPGROUND	QUARTZ VALLEY, LAKE CO OR	151 - C2
LONE FIR CAMPGROUND	WASHINGTON PASS, OKANOGAN CO WA	103 - C2
LONE PEAK CAMPGROUND	OFF NFD RD 5900, CHELAN CO WA	112 - A1
LONESOME COVE CAMPGROUND	RIMROCK LAKE, YAKIMA CO WA	119 - B2
LONESOME SPRING CAMPGROUND	OFF PETERSON CREEK RD, CROOK CO OR	136 - B2
LONE WOLF SHELTER	WESTFIR WEST, LANE CO OR	142 - A1
LONG CREEK CAMPGROUND	OFF NFD RD 16, BAKER CO OR	138 - A2
LONG LAKE CAMPGROUND	BALD KNOB, FERRY CO WA	105 - B2
LONGMILE MEADOWS CAMPGROUND	MOUNT CLIFTY, KITTITAS CO WA	111 - B3
LONGMIRE CAMPGROUND	WAHPENAYO PEAK, LEWIS CO WA	185 - B5
LONG RIDGE CAMPGROUND	QUAIL PRAIRIE MOUNTAIN, CURRY CO OR	148 - B2
LONG SWAMP CAMPGROUND	CORRAL BUTTE, OKANOGAN CO WA	104 - B1
LOOKOUT SPRINGS CAMPGROUND	THREE LYNX, CLACKAMAS CO OR	126 - B3
LOONEY SPRING CAMPGROUND	OFF JOHN DAY HWY, GRANT CO OR	137 - C2
LOST LAKE CAMPGROUND	BULL RUN LAKE, HOOD RIVER CO OR	201 - D2
LOST LAKE CAMPGROUND	MOUNT BONAPARTE, OKANOGAN CO WA	105 - A1
LOST LAKE CAMPGROUND	OREGON COAST HWY, DOUGLAS CO OR	214 - A6
LOST LAKE CAMPGROUND	SANTIAM HWY, LINN CO OR	134 - C2
LOST LAKE CAMPGROUND	TIETON BASIN, YAKIMA CO WA	119 - B1
LOST SPRINGS CAMPGROUND	POLAND BUTTE, YAKIMA CO WA	119 - B3
LOUP LOUP CAMPGROUND	LOUP LOUP SUMMIT, OKANOGAN CO WA	104 - B3
LOWER BOWMAN CAMPSITE	WHITE PINE BUTTES, KLICKITAT CO WA	119 - B3
LOWER BRIDGE CAMPGROUND	OFF METOLIUS RIVER RD, JEFFERSON CO OR	134 - C1
LOWER EIGHTMILE CAMPGROUND	FIVEMILE BUTTE, WASCO CO OR	202 - D3
LOWER FALLS CAMPGROUND	SPENCER BUTTE, SKAMANIA CO WA	118 - C3
LOWER TWIN CAMPGROUND	WAPINITIA PASS, WASCO CO OR	202 - B7
LUBY BAY CAMPGROUND	PRIEST LAKE SW, BONNER CO ID	107 - A2
LUCERNE CAMPGROUND	LUCERNE, CHELAN CO WA	103 - C3
LYNCH CREEK CAMPGROUND	OFF NFD RD 454, WALLOWA CO OR	131 - B2
LYRE RIVER CAMPGROUND	LYRE RIVER RD, CLALLAM CO WA	164 - B5
MACMILLAN CAMPGROUND	HWY 4, BC	92 - B3
MAGONE LAKE CAMPGROUND	OFF KEENEY FORKS RD, GRANT CO OR	137 - B1
MAIN EAGLE BRIDGE CAMPGROUND	NFD RD 77, BAKER CO OR	130 - C3
MAITLEN	METALINE FALLS, PEND OREILLE CO WA	106 - C1
MALLARD MARSH CAMPGROUND	OFF MUD LAKE RD, DESCHUTES CO OR	216 - A4
MAMMOTH SPRING CAMPGROUND	SOUTH FORK BURNT RIVER RD, BAKER CO OR	137 - C2
MANLY WHAM CAMPGROUND	STEHEKIN, CHELAN CO WA	103 - C3
MANSON LANDING CAMPGROUND	BC	92 - A1
MAPLE CREEK CAMPGROUND	TRINITY, CHELAN CO WA	111 - C1
MAPLE GROVE CAMPGROUND	WELKER PEAK, WHATCOM CO WA	103 - A2
MAPLE LEAF CAMPGROUND	PURCELL MOUNTAIN, LEWIS CO WA	118 - C2
MAPLE MOUNTAIN CENTENNIAL CAMPGROUND	TRANS CANADA HWY, BC	101 - B1
MAPLE RIDGE CAMPSITE	132ND AV & 236TH ST, MAPLE RIDGE BC	157 - D5
MARBLE CREEK CAMPGROUND	BIG DEVIL PEAK, SKAGIT CO WA	103 - B2
MARBLE CREEK CAMPGROUND	MARBLE MOUNTAIN, SHOSHONE CO ID	115 - C3
MARCUS ISLAND CAMPGROUND	MARCUS, STEVENS CO WA	106 - A2
MARGARET MCKENNY CAMPGROUND	LITTLEROCK, THURSTON CO WA	184 - A1
MARIEN CREEK CAMPGROUND	SILVERTON, SNOHOMISH CO WA	103 - A3
MARINE PARK AND CAMPGROUND	BONNEVILLE DAM, CASCADE LOCKS OR	194 - D6
MARION FORKS CAMPGROUND	N SANTIAM HWY, LINN CO OR	134 - C1
MARMES ROCK SHELTER	HWY 261, FRANKLIN CO WA	121 - C2
MARMES ROCK SHELTER	STARBUCK WEST, FRANKLIN CO WA	122 - A2
MARSTERS SPRING CAMPGROUND	MORGAN BUTTE, LAKE CO OR	151 - C1
MARYS PEAK CAMPGROUND	MARYS PEAK, BENTON CO OR	133 - A1
MASON DAM CAMPGROUND	WHITNEY HWY, BAKER CO OR	138 - A1
MAZAMA CAMPGROUND	UNION PEAK, KLAMATH CO OR	227 - C5
MAZAMA CREEK CAMPGROUND	OFF N SANTIAM HWY, LINN CO OR	134 - C1
MCBRIDE CAMPGROUND	EAGLE CREEK DR, BAKER CO OR	130 - C3
MCCORNICK CAMPGROUND	OFF HWY 71, ADAMS CO ID	131 - A3
MCCUBBINS GULCH CAMPGROUND	FOREMAN POINT, WASCO CO OR	127 - A3
MCCULLY FORKS CAMPGROUND	GRANITE HILL RD, BAKER CO OR	138 - A1
MCCURDY CAMPGROUND	OPHIR MOUNTAIN, CURRY CO OR	228 - D1
MCGRIBBLE CAMPGROUND	PORT ORFORD, CURRY CO OR	224 - B7
MCKENZIE BRIDGE CAMPGROUND	MCKENZIE HWY, LANE CO OR	134 - B2
MCNAUGHTON SPRING CAMPGROUND	STRAWBERRY RD, GRANT CO OR	137 - B2
MCQUDE CREEK SHELTER	OFF QUARTZVILLE DR, LINN CO OR	134 - B1
MEADOW CAMPGROUND	BENHAM FALLS, DESCHUTES CO OR	217 - B4
MEADOW CAMPGROUND	OFF NFD RD 9712, CHELAN CO WA	238 - C6
MEADOW CREEK CAMPGROUND	GOLDEN, JOSEPHINE CO OR	148 - C2
MEADOW CREEK CAMPGROUND	MEADOW CREEK, BOUNDARY CO ID	107 - C1
MEADOW CREEK CAMPGROUND	PLAIN, CHELAN CO WA	111 - C1
MEADOW CREEK SHELTER	LUCERNE, CHELAN CO WA	103 - C3
MEADOWS CAMPGROUND	SLATE PEAK, OKANOGAN CO WA	103 - C2
MEDITATION POINT CAMPGROUND	WOLF PEAK, CLACKAMAS CO OR	126 - C3
MEMORIAL CAMPGROUND	LEWIS BUTTE, OKANOGAN CO WA	104 - A2
MENEARS BEND CAMPGROUND	SANTIAM HWY, LINN CO OR	134 - A2
MERRILL LAKE CAMPGROUND	COUGAR, COWLITZ CO WA	190 - A4
MERRYS BAY CAMPGROUND	AHSAHKA, CLEARWATER CO ID	123 - C2
MIDDLE EEL CAMPGROUND	LAKESIDE, COOS CO OR	218 - B4
MIDDLE FORK CAMPGROUND	UPPER MIDDLE FORK RD, GRANT CO OR	137 - B1
MIDDLE WADDEL CAMPGROUND	LITTLEROCK, THURSTON CO WA	184 - A1
MILE CAMPGROUND	CASCADE LAKES HWY, DESCHUTES CO OR	216 - B6
MILL CREEK CAMPGROUND	PROSPECT NORTH, JACKSON CO OR	226 - C6
MILLER RIVER CAMPGROUND	GROTTO, KING CO WA	111 - A2
MILL POND CAMPGROUND	METALINE FALLS, PEND OREILLE CO WA	106 - C1
MILLPOND CAMPGROUND	OFF GRANT RD, JACKSON CO OR	230 - C7
MINA FALLS TRAILHEAD CAMPGROUND	LITTLEROCK, THURSTON CO WA	184 - B2
MINERAL CAMPGROUND	FAIRVIEW PEAK, LANE CO OR	141 - C1
MINERAL PARK CAMPGROUND	SONNY BOY LAKES, SKAGIT CO WA	103 - B2
MINERAL SPRINGS CAMPGROUND	LIBERTY, KITTITAS CO WA	111 - C3
MINERS CREEK SHELTER	GAMMA PEAK, SNOHOMISH CO WA	103 - B3
MINK LAKE SHELTER	THREE SISTERS WILDERNESS AREA, LANE CO OR	134 - C3
MINNIE PETERSON CAMPGROUND	WINFIELD CREEK, JEFFERSON CO WA	108 - C1
MISERY SPRING CAMPGROUND	SADDLE BUTTE, GARFIELD CO WA	122 - B3
MITCHELL CREEK CAMPGROUND	LAKE CHELAN, CHELAN CO WA	112 - A1
MOKINS BAY CAMPGROUND	HAYDEN LAKE, KOOTENAI CO ID	245 - B5
MONA CAMPGROUND	OFF RABBIT CAMP RD, LANE CO OR	134 - B2
MONCK CAMPGROUND	HWY 5A, BC	95 - C1
MONEY CREEK CAMPGROUND	NE STEVENS PASS HWY, KING CO WA	111 - A1
MONTAGUE HARBOUR CAMPGROUND	BC	101 - B1
MONTE CRISTO CAMPGROUND	MONTE CRISTO, SNOHOMISH CO WA	111 - A1
MONTY CAMPGROUND	METOLIUS BENCH, JEFFERSON CO OR	135 - A1
MOON LAKE SHELTER	WARNER MOUNTAIN, LANE CO OR	142 - A1
MOORE POINT CAMPGROUND	LUCERNE, CHELAN CO WA	103 - C3
MORA CAMPGROUND	QUILLAYUTE PRAIRIE, CLALLAM CO WA	169 - A2
MORGAN CREEK CAMPGROUND	CLE ELUM LAKE, KITTITAS CO WA	111 - B3
MORRISON CREEK CAMPGROUND	MOUNT ADAMS WEST, YAKIMA CO WA	119 - A3
MORSE CREEK CAMPGROUND	NORSE PEAK, YAKIMA CO WA	119 - A1
MOSS CREEK CAMPGROUND	OKLAHOMA RD, SKAMANIA CO WA	195 - B3
MOSS SPRING CAMPGROUND	MILL CREEK RD, UNION CO OR	130 - B2
MOTTET CAMPGROUND	NORTH OF NFD RD 63, WALLOWA CO OR	130 - A1
MOUNT HEBO CAMPGROUND	NIAGARA CREEK, TILLAMOOK CO OR	197 - D7
MOUNT MOLLY CAMPGROUND	LITTLEROCK, THURSTON CO WA	184 - A1
MOUNT TOM SHELTER	OWL MOUNTAIN, JEFFERSON CO WA	109 - A1
MOWITCH CAMPGROUND	WHITNEY HWY, BAKER CO OR	138 - A1
MUD CREEK CAMPGROUND	OFF NFD RD 3615, LAKE CO OR	152 - A2
MUD LAKE CAMPGROUND	ANTHONY LAKES RD, BAKER CO OR	130 - A3
MUD SPRING CAMPGROUND	OFF RAGER RD, CROOK CO OR	136 - C2
MULE DEER CAMPGROUND	HWY 3, BC	103 - C1
MULKEY SHELTER	LAKE QUINAULT EAST, GRAYS HARBOR CO WA	109 - A2
MULLIGAN BAY CAMPGROUND	SQUAW LAKES, JACKSON CO OR	149 - B2

PNW

INDEX

PNW

INDEX

Thomas Bros. Maps®   COPYRIGHT 1999

PNW

INDEX

PNW

INDEX

PNW
INDEX

OPEN SPACE PRESERVES

COPYRIGHT 1999 *Thomas Bros. Maps* ®

PNW

INDEX

Thomas Bros. Maps ® COPYRIGHT 1999

PNW INDEX

440 PARKS & RECREATION
POINTS OF INTEREST
PARKS & RECREATION

FEATURE NAME / City State	Page-Grid
PARK S HOLLY ST, SEATTLE WA	286 - E1
PARK SHOSHONE ST & 14TH AVE, PASCO WA	343 - E7
PARK S JACKSON ST & 3RD AV S, SEATTLE WA	278 - A7
PARK S LANE ST & 7TH AV S, SEATTLE WA	278 - B7
PARK S MAIN ST & OCCIDENTAL AV S, SEATTLE WA	278 - C6
PARK S NORMAN ST, SEATTLE WA	282 - C1
PARK STEVENS DR & SAINT ST, RICHLAND WA	340 - F11
PARK STURGUS AV S, SEATTLE WA	282 - C1
PARK SW ATWATER & SW ATWATER, LAKE OSWEGO OR	320 - D5
PARK SW RIVERSIDE DR, MULTNOMAH OR	321 - H3
PARK TANDY TURN, EUGENE OR	330 - C3
PARK TANEY ST, EUGENE OR	329 - C2
PARK TAURUS ST, OCEAN SHORES WA	298 - C1
PARK VICTORIA DR S, VANCOUVER BC	255 - B12
PARK W 16TH AV, EUGENE OR	329 - J7
PARK W 18TH AV, EUGENE OR	329 - G8
PARK W 27TH AV, EUGENE OR	329 - F9
PARK WAGNER ST, EUGENE OR	329 - C1
PARK WASHINGTON ST & 17TH AVE, PASCO WA	343 - E8
PARK WASHINGTON ST & RAILROAD AVE, PASCO WA	343 - G9
PARK W D ST, LANE CO OR	330 - F7
PARK WEHE AVE & ALTON ST, PASCO WA	343 - H7
PARK WILLAKENZIE RD, EUGENE OR	330 - C2
PARK WILLAMETTE ST, LANE CO OR	329 - H13
PARK W IRWIN WY, EUGENE OR	329 - A1
PARK W OLYMPIC PL & 1ST AV W, SEATTLE WA	277 - H3
PARK WORTHINGTON DR, VANCOUVER BC	255 - F14
PARK WRIGLEY DR & ROBERT WAYNE DR, PASCO WA	342 - H1
PARK YESLER WY & 4TH AV, SEATTLE WA	278 - A6
PARROTT CREEK PARK BOOTH AV & SE STARMER ST, ROSEBURG OR	334 - F9
PARSONS GARDENS 8TH PL W & W HIGHLAND DR, SEATTLE WA	277 - G3
PATTON SQUARE PARK N INTERSTATE AV & N EMERSON ST, PORTLAND	309 - E7
PAUL DUNN STATE FOREST TAMPICO RD, BENTON CO OR	207 - A3
PAYETTE NATIONAL FOREST ADAMS CO ID	251 - B2
PECK ATHLETIC FIELD S SPRAGUE AV & S 15TH ST, TACOMA WA	293 - E6
PEMBERTON PARK FOUL BAY RD, CITY OF VICTORIA BC	257 - B10
PENINSULA GOLF COURSE GOLF COURSE RD, PORT ANGELES WA	261 - H6
PENINSULA PARK N ALBINA AV & N AINSWORTH ST, PORTLAND OR	309 - F6
PENROSE POINT STATE PARK 158TH AV KPS, PIERCE CO WA	181 - A2
PEOPLES COMMUNITY CENTER M L KING JR WY & S 17TH ST, TACOMA WA	293 - G6
PEOPLES PARK S L ST & S 10TH ST, TACOMA WA	293 - F5
PERCIVAL LANDING PARK OLYMPIA WA	296 - H4
PERIWINKLE PARK ERMINE ST, ALBANY OR	326 - F10
PETER KERR PARK ELK ROCK ISLAND, MILWAUKIE OR	321 - H3
PETTUS, TERRY PARK E NEWTON ST & FAIRVIEW AV E, SEATTLE WA	278 - A2
PETTYGROVE PARK SW HARRISON ST, PORTLAND OR	313 - F7
PICCOLO PARK SE 27TH AV & SE DIVISION ST, PORTLAND OR	317 - J1
PIER PARK N SAINT JOHNS AV, PORTLAND OR	192 - B7
PILOT BUTTE STATE PARK CENTRAL OREGON HWY, DESCHUTES CO OR	332 - H7
PINEWAY PARK RAMONA WY, ALBANY OR	326 - E12
PIONEER PARK CORVALLIS-NEWPORT HWY, CORVALLIS OR	327 - G11
PIONEER PARK NW WALL ST & NW PORTLAND AV, BEND OR	332 - E6
PIONEER PARK WHITMAN ST, WALLA WALLA WA	345 - C8
PIONEER SQUARE PARK SW YAMHILL ST, PORTLAND OR	313 - E6
PIONEER SQUARE PARK YESLER WY & 1ST AV, SEATTLE WA	278 - A6
PISTOL RIVER STATE PARK OREGON COAST HWY, CURRY CO OR	232 - B1
PITTOCK ACRES PARK NW PITTOCK DR, PORTLAND OR	312 - B5
PLAYFAIR PARK QUADRA ST, DISTRICT OF SAANICH BC	256 - H4
PLAYGROUND 12TH AV NE & NE 71ST ST, SEATTLE WA	274 - C3
PLAYGROUND 13TH AV S & S LUCILE ST, SEATTLE WA	282 - B6
PLAYGROUND 19TH AV E & E HARRISON ST, SEATTLE WA	278 - C4
PLAYGROUND 23RD AV & E JEFFERSON ST, SEATTLE WA	278 - D6
PLAYGROUND 2ND AV N & GALER ST, SEATTLE WA	277 - H2
PLAYGROUND 3RD AV N, SEATTLE WA	277 - H2
PLAYGROUND 50TH AV S & S FERDINAND ST, SEATTLE WA	283 - F5
PLAYGROUND 51ST AV S & S GRAHAM ST, SEATTLE WA	283 - F7
PLAYGROUND 8TH AV S & S SULLIVAN ST, SEATTLE WA	286 - A3

FEATURE NAME / City State	Page-Grid
PLAYGROUND BLAINE ST & 3RD AV W, SEATTLE WA	277 - G2
PLAYGROUND E ALDER ST & 29TH AV, SEATTLE WA	278 - D6
PLAYGROUND EASTLAKE AV & ROANOKE ST, SEATTLE WA	278 - B1
PLAYGROUND E DENNY WY & MADRONA PL E, SEATTLE WA	279 - E4
PLAYGROUND E PINE ST & 11TH AV E, SEATTLE WA	278 - B5
PLAYGROUND E ROY ST & E FEDERAL AV, SEATTLE WA	278 - B3
PLAYGROUND HOWE ST & 2ND AV N, SEATTLE WA	277 - H2
PLAYGROUND MARION ST & 34TH AV, SEATTLE WA	278 - E5
PLAYGROUND N 41ST ST & FREMONT AV N, SEATTLE WA	273 - H6
PLAYGROUND NE 50TH ST & 9TH AV NE, SEATTLE WA	274 - B5
PLAYGROUND NW 43RD ST & BAKER AV NW, SEATTLE WA	273 - G5
PLAYGROUND NW 60TH ST & 28TH AV NW, SEATTLE WA	272 - D3
PLAYGROUND RAINIER AV S & S ALASKA ST, SEATTLE WA	282 - E5
PLAYGROUND RANIER AV S & S WINTHROP ST, SEATTLE WA	282 - D3
PLAYGROUND ROOSEVELT WY NE & NE 82ND ST, SEATTLE WA	274 - C1
PLAYGROUND S GRAND ST & 14TH AV S, SEATTLE WA	282 - B1
PLAYGROUND S GRAND ST & 23RD AV S, SEATTLE WA	282 - D1
PLAYGROUND S HOMER ST & CORSON AV S, SEATTLE WA	282 - B6
PLAYGROUND S NORFOLK ST & 59TH AV S, SEATTLE WA	287 - G5
PLAYGROUND SW CLOVERDALE ST & SW 11TH AV, SEATTLE WA	285 - H3
PLAYGROUND WALLINGFORD AV & N 43RD ST, SEATTLE WA	273 - J6
PLAYGROUND WARREN PL & 1ST AV N, SEATTLE WA	277 - H2
POINT DEFIANCE PARK N PARK AV & PEARL ST, TACOMA WA	181 - C1
PONDEROSA PARK SE 15TH ST & SE WILSON AV, BEND OR	332 - G9
PONDEROSA STATE PARK VALLEY CO ID	251 - D3
PONDER PARK 80TH AV, TOWNSHIP OF LANGLEY BC	157 - D7
PORTAGE REGIONAL PARK OLD ISLAND HIGHWAY, TOWN OF VIEW ROYAL BC	256 - A5
PORT COQUITLAM NATURE PARK LINCOLN & COAST MERIDN, PORT COQUITLAM BC	157 - B4
PORTER PARK CORVALLIS OR	327 - F7
PORTLAND HEIGHTS PARK SW PATTON RD, PORTLAND OR	316 - C1
PORT OF BELLINGHAM MARINE PARK HARRIS AV, BELLINGHAM WA	258 - A11
PORTSMOUTH PARK N STANFORD AV & N DEPAUW ST, PORTLAND OR	308 - A4
POTHOLES STATE PARK OSULLIVAN DAM RD, GRANT CO WA	242 - C6
POWELL BUTTE NATURE PARK SE 162ND AV & SE POWELL BL, PORTLAND OR	200 - A2
POWELL PARK SE POWELL BLVD & SE 22ND AV, PORTLAND OR	317 - J2
POWERS MARINE PARK SW MACADAM AV, PORTLAND OR	317 - F7
PRATT PARK 18TH AV S & S MAIN ST, SEATTLE WA	278 - C7
PRIDE PARK S 34TH ST, SPRINGFIELD OR	331 - C7
PRIEST POINT PARK E BAY DR, OLYMPIA WA	296 - J1
PRINCESS MARGARET MARINE PARK PORTLAND ISLAND, BC	159 - D1
PRINCESS PARK PRINCESS AV, DIST OF N VANCOUVER BC	255 - D2
PRINGLE FALLS EXPRMTL FOREST ADDITION DESCHUTES CO OR	216 - B7
PRINGLE PARK SALEM OR	322 - H13
PUGET GARDENS PARK N 36TH ST & N ALDER ST, TACOMA WA	292 - D2
PUGET PARK 18TH AV SW, SEATTLE WA	281 - G5
PUGET PARK PROCTOR ST & N 31ST ST, TACOMA WA	292 - C2
PUGNETTI PARK S 21ST ST & PACIFIC AV, TACOMA WA	293 - H7
QEMILIN PARK POST FALLS ID	353 - G8
QUARNBERG PARK E MILL PLAIN BL & U ST, VANCOUVER WA	305 - J5
QUINTUS PARK SW CENTER ST, ROSEBURG OR	334 - B6
RAILROAD HISTORICAL PARK MEDCO RD, MEDFORD OR	336 - C8
RAINBOW PARK MCKENZIE AVE, DISTRICT OF SAANICH BC	256 - F3
RAPID RIVER RECREATION AREA ADAMS CO ID	131 - B2
RATTLESNAKE MOUNTAIN SCENIC AREA KING CO WA	176 - C5
RAVENNA PARK NE 62ND ST & 15TH AV NE, SEATTLE WA	274 - D4
RED BRIDGE STATE PARK UKIAH-HILGARD HWY, UNION CO OR	129 - C2
RED FOX HILLS PARK #1 TIMBERLINE DR & FOX RUN, LAKE OSWEGO OR	320 - E4
RED FOX HILLS PARK #3 HIDEAWAY LN, LAKE OSWEGO OR	321 - E4
REDWOOD NATIONAL PARK DEL NORTE CO CA	148 - B3
REGRADE PARK 3RD AV & BELL ST, SEATTLE WA	277 - J5
RENFREW PARK 22ND AV, VANCOUVER BC	255 - D14
REYNOLDS PARK CEDAR HILL CROSS RD, DIST OF SAANICH BC	256 - J3
RISLEY PARK SE SWAIN AV & SE RUBY DR, CLACKAMAS OR	321 - J7
RIVERFRONT PARK MONROE ST AND BRIDGE AV, SPOKANE WA	348 - J8
RIVER FRONT PARK STEWART PARK DR, ROSEBURG OR	334 - E6
RIVER ROAD PARK SALEM OR	322 - J9
RIVERSIDE PARK 7TH ST & PARK ST, GRANTS PASS OR	335 - E10

FEATURE NAME / City State	Page-Grid
RIVERSIDE PARK HARRISON AV & LOWE ST, CENTRALIA WA	299 - D2
RIVERSIDE PARK SE GRAND AV, PORTLAND OR	317 - G2
RIVERSIDE PARK SW OAK ST, ROSEBURG OR	334 - F7
RIVERSIDE STATE PARK N AUBREY L WHITE PKWY, SPOKANE CO WA	348 - B2
RIVERVIEW HEIGHTS PARK ALBANY OR	326 - A4
RIVERVIEW PLAYFIELD 12TH AV SW & SW WEBSTER ST, SEATTLE WA	285 - H1
RIVER VILLA PARK SE BLUFF RD, CLACKAMAS OR	321 - H5
ROANOKE PARK ROANOKE ST & 10TH AV N, SEATTLE WA	278 - B1
ROANOKE PARK W MERCER & ROANOKE WY, MERCER ISLAND WA	283 - J1
ROBERDEAU PLAYGROUND ROBERDEAU ST & PERKINS AVE, RICHLAND WA	340 - E14
ROBERT J. PORTER PARK FAIRFIELD RD, CITY OF VICTORIA BC	256 - J10
ROBERT W SAWYER STATE PARK O B RILEY RD & HWY 97, BEND OR	332 - E3
ROBSON PARK 100TH AV, DISTRICT OF SURREY BC	157 - A6
ROCHE COVE REGIONAL PARK MOUNT MATHESON RD, BC	165 - A1
ROCK CREEK PROVINCIAL PARK HWY 3, BC	105 - A1
ROCK ISLAND STATE PARK HWY 28 & ROCK ISLAND GRADE, DOUGLAS CO WA	239 - C5
ROCKY BUTTE STATE PARK NE ROCKY BUTTE RD, PORTLAND OR	315 - H3
RODGERS PARK 3RD AV W & RAYE ST, SEATTLE WA	273 - G7
ROEHR WATERFRONT PARK OSWEGO POINTE DR, LAKE OSWEGO OR	321 - G6
ROGUE RIVER NATIONAL FOREST JACKSON CO OR	337 - F13
ROLLEY LAKE PROVINCIAL PARK BELL RD, DISTRICT OF MISSION BC	94 - B3
ROOSEVELT FIELD CAROLINA ST, BELLINGHAM WA	258 - F5
ROSE CITY PARK NE 62ND AV & NE TILLAMOOK ST, PORTLAND OR	314 - D3
ROSS LAKE NATIONAL RECREATION AREA SKAGIT CO WA	103 - A2
ROSSMAN PARK 4TH ST & C AV, LAKE OSWEGO OR	321 - F5
ROTARY PARK LOWELL-SNO RIVER RD, EVERETT WA	269 - F1
ROXHILL PARK SW ROXBURY ST & 28TH AV SW, SEATTLE WA	285 - F4
ROYAL ATHLETIC PARK COOK ST, CITY OF VICTORIA BC	256 - H8
ROYAL OAKS PARK SALEM OR	323 - G12
ROY MORSE PARK MORSE PARK WY, LONGVIEW WA	302 - C5
RUDD PARK BOLESKINE RD, DISTRICT OF SAANICH BC	256 - F5
RUPERT PARK 1ST AV, VANCOUVER BC	255 - F12
RUSSELL WOODS PARK RUSSEL RD & S 228TH ST, KENT WA	291 - F7
SACAJAWEA PARK NE 76TH AV & NE ALBERTA ST, PORTLAND OR	315 - F1
SADDLEBAG ISLAND STATE PARK SADDLEBAG ISLAND, SKAGIT CO WA	160 - D5
SADDLE MOUNTAIN STATE PARK CLATSOP CO OR	188 - D6
SAINT CLAIR PARK SAINT CLAIR ST, BELLINGHAM WA	258 - H6
SAINT FRANCIS PARK SE STARK ST, PORTLAND OR	313 - H6
SAINT HELENS PARK E 13TH ST, VANCOUVER WA	306 - B5
SAINT JOE NATIONAL FOREST SHOSHONE CO ID	115 - C3
SALMON BAY PARK NW CANOE PL & 19TH AV NW, SEATTLE WA	273 - E2
SALMON CREEK PARK 8TH AV SW & SW 118TH ST, KING WA	285 - H7
SALT CREEK RECREATION AREA OFF CAMP HAYDEN RD, CLALLAM CO WA	164 - D5
SALTWATER STATE PARK MARINE VIEW DR S & S 257TH, DES MOINES WA	175 - A7
SAM BROWN PARK E DEVINE RD & IDAHO ST, VANCOUVER WA	306 - C5
SAM JACKSON PARK SW TERWILLIGER BL, PORTLAND OR	317 - E1
SAMUEL H BOARDMAN STATE PARK OREGON COAST HWY, CURRY CO OR	232 - B3
SANDEL PLAYGROUND 92ND ST N & 1ST AV NW, SEATTLE WA	273 - H1
SANDY ISLAND PARK BC	92 - B2
SANTANA COUNTY PARK Four Corners OR	325 - F2
SANTIAM STATE FOREST LINN CO OR	134 - A1
SANTIAM STATE FOREST S SAWTELL RD, MARION CO OR	126 - A3
SASQUATCH PROVINCIAL PARK ROCKWELL DR, DISTRICT OF KENT BC	94 - C3
SATHER PARK FOSTER ST, PORT TOWNSEND WA	263 - G3
SAWYER PARK SAWYER ST, TACOMA WA	295 - F2
SAXE POINT PARK FRASER ST, TOWN OF ESQUIMALT BC	256 - B9
SAYRES, STAN MEMORIAL PARK 46TH AV S & LK WASHINGTON BL, SEATTLE WA	283 - F3
SCENIC PARK PENZANCE DR, DIST OF BURNABY BC	255 - J9
SCHAFER STATE PARK MASON CO WA	179 - B5
SCHMITZ, EMMA MEMORIAL OVERLOOK PARK SW BEACH DR & SW OREGON ST, SEATTLE WA	280 - B5
SCHMITZ PARK SCHMITZ BLVD & ADMIRAL WY SW, SEATTLE WA	280 - C3
SCHROEDER PARK SCHROEDER LN, JOSEPHINE CO OR	335 - A9
SCOGGINS VALLEY PARK SCOGGINS VALLEY RD, WASHINGTON CO OR	198 - A2
SCOTT PARK SE HARRISON ST & SE 23RD AV, MILWAUKIE OR	321 - J2
SEACREST MARINA PARK HARBOR AV SW, SEATTLE WA	281 - F1
SEALAND OF THE PUBLIC BEACH DR, DIST OF OAK BAY BC	257 - D9
SEAQUEST STATE PARK SPIRIT LAKE HWY, COWLITZ CO WA	187 - D7

PNW
INDEX

PNW

INDEX

PNW

INDEX

Thomas Bros. Maps® COPYRIGHT 1999

PNW / INDEX

PNW

INDEX

COPYRIGHT 1999 *Thomas Bros. Maps* ®

Thomas Bros. Maps ®
COPYRIGHT 1999

PNW

INDEX

PRODUCT INFORMATION LIST

THOMAS GUIDES®
NOW INCLUDING ZIP CODE BOUNDARIES

CALIFORNIA

Alameda County
Alameda / Contra Costa Counties
Alameda / Santa Clara Counties
Central Valley Cities
   (Coverage includes all urban areas from Stockton to Bakersfield)
Contra Costa County
Fresno County *(NEW - available 4/2000)*
Golden Gate
   (Marin, San Francisco, San Mateo, and Santa Clara Counties)
Kern County *(NEW - available 4/2000)*
Los Angeles County
Los Angeles County Spanish Edition
Los Angeles / Orange Counties
Los Angeles / Ventura Counties
Marin County
Metropolitan Monterey Bay *(NEW)*
Napa / Sonoma Counties *(NEW)*
Orange County
Orange County Spanish Edition
Orange / Los Angeles Counties
Riverside County
Riverside / Orange Counties
Riverside / San Diego Counties
Sacramento County
   (Coverage includes portions of Placer & El Dorado Counties)
Sacramento / Solano Counties
San Bernardino County
San Bernardino / Riverside Counties
San Diego County including Imperial County
San Diego / Orange Counties
San Francisco County
San Francisco / Alameda / Contra Costa Counties
San Francisco / San Mateo Counties
San Mateo County
Santa Barbara and San Luis Obispo Counties
Santa Barbara and San Luis Obispo / Ventura Counties
Santa Clara County
Santa Clara / San Mateo Counties
Solano County including portions of Napa & Yolo Counties
Ventura County

ARIZONA - NEVADA - OREGON - WASHINGTON

Clark County, NV
Phoenix Metro Area, AZ *(NEW - available 7/2000)*
Tucson Metropolitan Area, AZ *(NEW - available 9/2000)*
Portland Metro Area, OR
   (Coverage includes Clackamas, Columbia, Multnomah, Washington &
   Yamhill Counties and Greater Vancouver Area)
King County, WA
King / Pierce Counties, WA
King / Snohomish Counties, WA
Pierce County, WA
Snohomish County, WA

WASHINGTON, D.C. & VICINITY

Anne Arundel County, MD
Frederick County, MD
Howard County, MD
Loudoun County, VA
Montgomery County, VA
Northern Virginia & the Beltway
Prince George's County, VA
Prince William County, VA

ROAD ATLAS & DRIVER'S GUIDES

California Road Atlas & Driver's Guide
Pacific Northwest Road Atlas & Driver's Guide

METROPOLITAN THOMAS GUIDES®

CALIFORNIA

Metropolitan Bay Area
   (Coverage includes the metropolitan areas of Alameda, Contra Costa,
   Marin, San Francisco, San Mateo, and Santa Clara Counties)
Metropolitan Inland Empire
   (Coverage includes Metro areas of San Bernardino, Riverside, Eastern
   Los Angeles, and Northeastern Orange Counties)

WASHINGTON

Metropolitan Puget Sound
   (Coverage includes Metro areas of King, Pierce, and Snohomish
   Counties)

METROPOLITAN BALTIMORE & METROPOLITAN WASHINGTON, D.C.

Metropolitan Baltimore, MD
Metropolitan Washington DC includes Montgomery & Prince George's
   Counties, MD, and Northern Virginia

THOMAS GUIDE DIGITALEDITION™ (CD-ROM)

Tool Box *(NEW)* - Tool Box is a companion to any Thomas Guide Digital
Edition CD-ROM. It allows you to customize your maps with a full set of
drawing tools and e-mail them to others , address locator, GPS interface,
and query tools.

CALIFORNIA

California *(NEW)*

SOUTHERN CALIFORNIA

Los Angeles / Orange Counties
Los Angeles / Ventura Counties
Metropolitan Inland Empire
   (Coverage includes all of San Bernardino and Riverside,
   Eastern Los Angeles and Northeastern Orange Counties)
Santa Barbara / Ventura Counties

NORTHERN CALIFORNIA

Bay Area
   (Coverage includes Alameda, Contra Costa, Marin, San Francisco,
   San Mateo, and Santa Clara Counties)
Sacramento / Solano Counties

ARIZONA

Phoenix / Tucson *(NEW - available 9/2000)*

OREGON - WASHINGTON

Portland Metro Area, OR
Metropolitan Puget Sound, WA
   (Coverage includes all of King, Pierce, and Snohomish Counties)

NEVADA

Clark County

THOMAS GUIDE & DIGITALEDITION™ COMBO PACKS

Our Thomas Guide and DigitalEdition sold together in one convenient
package. Now available for major Metro geographical areas. Call for more
information.

EXPRESS MAPS & EXPRESS WALL MAPS™

Affordable, high quality custom maps designed to your specifications. You
select the coverage, choose black & white or full-color, optional ZIP &
Census overlays. Lamination & mounting additional. Call for more
information.

**For more information, or to order, please contact Customer Service at 1-800-899-6277 or
e-mail us at cust-serv@thomas.com or visit our web site at www.thomas.com**
Our Secure On-line Store is Now Open!

Information subject to change without notice